**$89.50**

D0907251

# 2015
# NATIONAL RENOVATION & INSURANCE REPAIR ESTIMATOR

## edited by Jonathan Russell

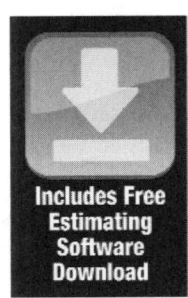

**Includes Free Estimating Software Download**

### Includes inside the back cover:

Inside the back cover of this book you'll find a software download certificate. To access the download, follow the instructions printed there. The download includes the *National Estimator*, an easy-to-use estimating program with all the cost estimates in this book. The software will run on PCs using Windows XP, Vista, 7 or 8 operating systems.

**Quarterly price updates on the Web are free** and automatic all during 2015. You'll be prompted when it's time to collect the next update. A connection to the Web is required.

Download all of Craftsman's most popular costbooks for one low price with the Craftsman Site License. http://www.craftsmansitelicense.com

- Turn your estimate into a bid.
- Turn your bid into a contract.
- ConstructionContractWriter.com

**Craftsman Book Company**
6058 Corte del Cedro, Carlsbad, CA 92011

Cover design by: Jennifer Johnson
© 2014 Craftsman Book Company    ISBN 978-1-57218-311-7    Published December 2014 for the year 2015.

# contents

# about this book

## WHAT'S NEW IN 2015

Since 2008, overhead and profit margins for many restoration and repair contractors have been slipping. Material cost increases - primarily pushed higher by rising fuel costs - have often been partially absorbed by contractors working to remain competitive. Contractors have also offered small labor increases to keep skilled workers and many have absorbed some of those costs as well. Last year, as the economy and the construction landscape improved, this trend began to change, and in the second half of 2014 contractors started to recover some of the costs they absorbed in the previous seven years. We expect this trend to continue in 2015, and to see larger wage increases offered to key employees.

## A TOOL

This book is a tool, and like all tools it can be misused. It is an excellent tool for the renovation and repair professional. It is not a substitute for experience, skill, and knowledge.

Prices in this book are based on research of actual jobs and successful estimates. They represent an average of the typical conditions. Estimators should compare the conditions described in this book with actual conditions on site and adjust the price accordingly.

## UNIQUE TO RENOVATION AND REPAIR WORK

This book is compiled specifically for the unique problems and conditions found in renovation and repair work. It is not a new construction cost book.

Renovation and repair work involve completely different circumstances than those found in new construction.

For example, the renovation or repair professional must work around existing conditions including home contents, access problems, out-of-plumb or out-of-square buildings, outdated materials, existing conditions that violate current building codes.

New-construction professionals have the luxury of placing items in a logical order, but renovation, remodel, or repair professionals must deal with conditions as they find them.

This means that joists have to be replaced in an existing floor system, paint has to be applied in a room where stain-grade base and carpeting are already installed, structures may have to be braced, contents have to be moved or worked around and materials and installation techniques must be matched.

## DETERMINING COSTS

All costs in this book are based on typical conditions and typical problems found when remodeling or repairing a structure.

This means a door takes 10 to 15 minutes longer to install than it would in the ideal circumstances found in new construction.

Stairs are more difficult to install around pre-existing walls, wall framing takes longer when walls are typically splicing into existing work, and so on.

Some prices in this book will very closely match prices used in new construction. Other prices will reflect the complex conditions found in renovation and repair and will be dramatically different.

For example, using this book's stair building prices to estimate stair work in a series of 150 tract homes will result in an estimate that is far too high.

## THE ART OF ESTIMATING

Estimating is part art, part science. Estimators must consider many factors, including access, crew productivity, special techniques, special abilities, temperament of the owner, and how busy the company is.

A contractor who is desperate for work will estimate much lower than a contractor who is swamped with work.

All of these factors — and many other similar ones — cannot be included in this or any other price book. They are part of the art of estimating.

The science of estimating, which includes prices, typical techniques, and materials, is included in this book.

This book is designed to make the science of estimating easier, which allows you to spend much more time focusing on the art of estimating, where your skill is crucial to the success of your company.

## GENERAL VS. SPECIFIC

It is important to note that the more specific the estimator is, the more accurate the final estimate will be.

For example, when an estimator calculates all electrical costs for a typical home using a square foot cost, it may not be as accurate as if the estimator priced each fixture, outlet, and appliance hook-up.

Since the square foot price is based on a typical installation, it will not be exact for a home that is atypical in any way — for example, one with special outdoor lighting or with an expensive crystal fixture in the entry.

The more specific the item, the more exact the prices. The more general an item, the more assumptions must be made.

To help ensure the accuracy of your estimates, we describe any assumptions made when determining general items.

For example, the Rough Carpentry chapter contains a square foot price for estimating 2" by 4" wall framing. To help you make sure that this price will work for you, we describe our assumptions: the stud centers, the number of openings, headers, corners, plates and so forth, that would typically be found in a wall.

## rounding

This book rounds hourly wage rates and the material, labor, and equipment components of a unit price.

These prices are rounded to "three significant digits." This means that prices under three digits (including two to the right of the decimal) are not rounded. Prices four digits and larger are rounded to the third digit from the left.

For example:

.23 is not rounded

2.33 is not rounded

23.33 is rounded to 23.30

233.33 is rounded to 233.00

2,333.33 is rounded to 2,330.00

23,333.33 is rounded to 23,300.00

In most cases, the square foot price will apply, but you will always want to carefully consider items that are more general, and if needed, adjust them to fit the conditions.

In the case above, the estimator may want to use the square foot price for average fixtures, then add an allowance for the crystal fixture and the outdoor lighting.

## TIME AND MATERIAL CHARTS

Almost all chapters include time and material charts at the end. These time and material charts are designed to show you the materials used, waste, labor rates, labor burden costs, and labor productivity.

When materials with a range of sizes appear, only the small and large size are usually listed.

When materials with a range of qualities appear, only the low and high prices are usually listed.

These charts are designed to give you accurate detail on the exact prices used. When prices change, this book does not become obsolete. Compare current prices with those used and factor accordingly.

## MATERIAL COSTS

National average material costs are compiled from surveys of suppliers throughout the country.

Costs for some materials, such as clay tile, building stone and hardwood, will vary a great deal from region to region.

For example, clay tile plants are located near naturally occurring clay sources. Because clay tiles are heavy, the further the tiles have to be shipped, the more expensive the tiles will be. The user of this book must be aware of local price variations.

Materials commonly found in every city are priced based on local delivery. In most cases this will be delivery no greater than 20 miles away from a local source. However, many rural areas have lumber yards that will deliver to a wider area at no additional charge.

Materials that are not commonly available locally, like hand-carved moldings or historical wallpaper, include shipping costs anywhere in North America. Estimators in Hawaii, Alaska and remote areas of Canada should add for additional shipping costs when applicable.

Material waste is often indicated with the items, but it's always a good idea to check the time and material charts for the exact waste calculated for all the components of an item.

Waste indicates material that is discarded during installation. It does not include waste that occurs when materials are taken to storage and ruined, run over at the job site, spilled, improperly cut, or damaged due to mishandling.

These types of occurrences are kept to a minimum by every good contractor, but will still occur on any job site.

Another common waste issue in renovation and repair is when a contractor must buy a minimum quantity for a small repair. For example, to replace a six-inch section of base, it is necessary to buy a piece of base that is eight-feet long or longer. In these cases, use the minimum price.

Material prices may not be listed with the time and material charts in some chapters. In these chapters, little new information would be provided by the materials chart so the space is saved for other information.

For example, a materials chart in the Appliance chapter will not provide an estimator with any new information.

The materials component of the unit price for an oven as listed in the main body of the chapter will tell the estimator how much the oven and connections cost.

Relisting these appliances in a materials chart wastes valuable space.

## LABOR COSTS

Labor costs are national average rates that usually are consistent with union labor wages.

See the time and material charts for specific benefit costs and labor rates.

Crew labor rates are an average hourly rate for each member of the crew. For example, a masonry crew might consist of a mason, a mason's helper, and a hod carrier.

The hourly rate for this crew is the average cost of all three. In other words, the hourly rate is for 20 minutes work by the mason, 20 minutes work by the mason's helper, and 20 minutes work by the hod carrier.

Separation of labor in renovation and insurance repair work is much more difficult than is separation of labor on large commercial construction projects.

On a typical repair or renovation job a carpenter may participate in demolition, frame walls, set doors, set toilets, install electrical outlets and fixtures, and do a little painting.

In the jobs analyzed for this cost book, well over 40 percent of the demolition work was done by skilled workers. This is because demolition is often selective, requiring a skilled worker to ensure that additional damage does not occur.

Many renovation and repair companies are relatively small, so skilled workers participate in all phases of construction.

These realities are reflected in the labor costs used in this book. This means that a demolition laborer's hourly rate may seem higher than is normal for an unskilled worker.

The time and material charts show all items that are built into each labor rate.

Some contractors may not provide health insurance or retirement plans to some or all of their workers. Estimators can "back-out" these expenses from the labor costs.

It is critical that estimators examine the Workers' Compensation costs calculated in the wage rates. Some states have Workers' Compensation rates that are double, triple, or even quadruple the national average rates used in this book.

Workers' Compensation rates should be adjusted to match local conditions.

Labor productivity is based on observation of work performed in renovation and repair conditions.

These conditions differ from new construction in many ways, but a few of the most common are: ❶ difficulty matching existing work, ❷ access problems, ❸ materials that must be more carefully shaped and attached than is typical in new construction, ❹ out-of-plumb or out-of-square structures, ❺ reinforcing, ❻ more trips and effort are required to find materials, ❼ much more travel time is required because most jobs will have a relatively small amount of work in some trades, ❽ more vehicles are required by the renovation or repair contractor because many tradespeople are often traveling between jobs, compared to new construction where crews may spend weeks or months on one job, and because crews tend to be smaller and each crew may need a vehicle, ❾ more unexpected problems, ❿ more restrictions in established neighborhoods.

Labor productivity is based on a clean job site where tools are put away and secured at the end of each day.

Depending on the trade, 20 to 30 minutes per eight hours is allowed for clean-up and putting away tools. Normally, skilled workers spend half as much time cleaning up as do unskilled workers.

As is typical in new construction, labor includes unpacking materials, in some cases unloading materials from a truck on site, some travel to pick up minor materials (e.g. a forgotten tube of caulk, or a forgotten tool), typical breaks, lay-out, planning, discussion, coordination, mobilization (many companies meet at a central location each morning to receive instructions), recording hours (including specific information needed for job costing), occasional correction of mistakes in installation, and so forth.

Supervision is not included in these costs but should not generally be required. This is because each crew includes a skilled tradesperson who normally would not require supervision beyond the normal dispatch and mobilization discussed previously.

## EQUIPMENT COSTS

Equipment costs are included only when equipment will be used that is not typically a part of the tools used by the majority of renovation or repair contractors.

For example, each carpenter should have a worm-drive saw, miter box, compressor, nail guns, and so forth. These types of tools are not included in the equipment costs.

However, equipment like cranes, backhoes, concrete saws, and jack hammers are not assumed to be part of the equipment and tools owned by a typical renovation or repair contractor. When these are needed, equipment rates are included in the unit price.

Equipment costs include the typical cost to rent the equipment from a local equipment rental shop. When applicable, they also include fuel or blade costs.

Check each item to determine if it includes delivery to the job site or operator labor. Also be careful to note minimum costs for work where rented equipment is needed.

## MARKUP

Prices in this book do not include markup. Insurance repair markup is almost always 20 percent: 10 percent for overhead and 10 percent for profit.

In renovation work on historical structures, markup may be as high as 30 percent, although markup over 20 percent may be "hidden" inside the unit cost. Typical remodeling work markup varies from 15 percent to 25 percent. The most common markup for all types of work is 20 percent.

## THE COST LINES

The cost tables in each section of this manual consist of individual tasks or items followed by a description.

Beneath the description is a list of the items to be replaced or removed. For instance, under Appliances on page 17, you'll see Electric range, followed by a list of different ranges. Looking across, you'll see five columns of numbers and symbols. Let me explain how to read the numbers and symbols in those columns.

First let's look at the column headed Craft@Hrs. The Craft@Hrs column shows the recommended crew and manhours per unit for installation. For example, 2A in the Craft@Hrs column means that we recommend a crew of one appliance installer. The crew composition, with the cost per hour, is listed on page 12.

The manhours (following the @ symbol) is our estimate of the crew time required for installation (or demolition) of each unit. Manhours are listed in hundredths of an hour rather than minutes because it's easier to add, subtract, multiply and divide hundredths of a unit. For example, if the Craft@Hrs column shows 2A@.250, the Labor Cost column will show $12.88. That's the labor cost per unit for a crew of one appliance installer at $51.50 per hour multiplied by .250 manhours, rounded to the nearest penny. The unit is listed right after the Craft@Hrs, and may be the cost per square foot (sf), linear foot (lf), each (ea), or another unit of measurement.

The crew costs include the basic wage, taxable fringe benefits (vacation pay), Workers' Compensation insurance, liability insurance, taxes (state and federal unemployment, Social Security and Medicare), and typical nontaxable fringe benefits such as medical insurance and retirement. A breakdown of these expenses is included as a percentage in the footnote beneath the Labor table at the end of each section.

If your hourly crew cost is much lower or much higher, you can adjust your totals. For example, if your hourly labor cost is 25 percent less, reduce the labor figures in the cost tables by 25 percent to find your local cost.

The Material column shows your material cost for the item described under the heading.

The Total column is the sum of the Material and Labor cost columns.

## CHARTS

Material charts show the material description, the material cost priced per typical unit purchased, the gross coverage, the typical waste, the net coverage after waste has been subtracted, and the resulting materials price including waste and often converted to a different unit of measure.

Equipment charts show the cost to rent equipment, the amount of work that can be done with the equipment per a period of time, and the resulting unit price.

Labor charts show the base wage, then add all additional costs that are based on wage. More information is always listed below this chart. It's important to note the "True" wage before adding labor related expenses. The true wage is the wage rate plus an allowance for vacation time. Since all the other costs must be paid even when an employee is on vacation, it is important that they become a component in the cost calculations when estimating work.

Labor productivity charts show the description of the work, the laborer or crew who will do the work, the average cost per man hour, the productivity and the resulting cost per unit.

## REGIONAL DIFFERENCES

Construction techniques vary from region to region. Different cli-

mates and different local customs provide a variety of unique regional methods.

For example, in southern Florida it is common to build the first floor of a home from concrete block capped with a grade beam. This method won't be found in Colorado.

Similarly, coral stone walls won't be commonly found in Denver, although they are widely used in Miami.

Slate roofs are common on historical homes and newer custom homes in Philadelphia but are virtually nonexistent in Rapid City.

Homes in the south often include screened porches which aren't nearly so common in the west.

A Georgia home is much more likely to include a series of architecturally-correct columns with Corinthian capitals than is a home in Minnesota.

A Hawaii home may be built entirely from treated wood, when an Arizona home only uses treated lumber when it contacts dirt or concrete.

Many regional materials and techniques are priced in this book. Keep in mind that you should not use these prices if the item is not common to your area.

## NATIONAL ESTIMATOR '15

The software download in the back of this book has all the information that appears in the printed book, but with one advantage. The National Estimator program makes it easy to copy and paste these costs into an estimate, or bid, and then add whatever markup you select. Quarterly price updates on the Web are free and automatic all during 2015. You'll be

prompted when it's time to collect the next update. A connection to the Web is required.

To access the software download, follow the instructions printed on the certificate in the back of the book. The software will run on PCs using Windows XP, Vista, 7 or 8 operating systems.

When you've installed the National Estimator program, click Help on the menu bar to see a list of topics that will get you up and running. Or, go online to www.costbook.com and click the ShowMe tutorial link to view an interactive tutorial for National Estimator. ShowMe is designed to speed your mastery of National Estimator.

If you have any problems using National Estimator, we'll be glad to help. Free telephone assistance is available from 8 a.m. until 5 p.m. Pacific time, Monday through Friday (except holidays). Call 760-438-7828.

### WE WANT TO HEAR FROM YOU

If you have questions or concerns about this cost book, let us hear from you. Send letters to:

Craftsman Book Company
NRI Editor
6058 Corte del Cedro
Carlsbad, CA 92011

# abbreviations

| | | |
|---|---|---|
| ABS . .Acrylonitrile butadiene styrene | lf . . . . . . . . . . . . . . . . .lineal foot | SBS . . . . . . . . .styrene butyl styrene |
| ac . . . . . . . . . .alternating current | li . . . . . . . . . . . . . . . . .lineal inch | sf . . . . . . . . . . . . . . .square foot |
| bf . . . . . . . . . . . . . . . . .board foot | m . . . . . . . . . . . .one thousand | sh . . . . . . . . . . . . . . . . . . . . .sheet |
| Btu . . . . . . . . .British thermal units | mbf . . . . . . . . . . .1,000 board feet | si . . . . . . . . . . . . . . . .square inch |
| CEC . .California Earthquake Code | mBtu . . .1,000 British thermal units | sq . . . . . . . . . . . .100 square feet |
| . . . . . . . . . . . .(also see page 56) | mh . . . . . . . . . . . . . . . .man hour | st . . . . . . . . . . . . . . . . . . . . . .step |
| cf . . . . . . . . . . . . . . . . . .cubic foot | mi . . . . . . . . . . . . . . . . . . . .mile | sy . . . . . . . . . . . . . . .square yard |
| cfm . . . . . . .cubic foot per minute | mlf . . . . . . . . . .1,000 linear feet | t&g . . . . . .tongue-&-groove edge |
| ci . . . . . . . . . . . . . . . . . .cubic inch | mm . . . . . . . . . . . . .millimeter(s) | TV . . . . . . . . . . . . . . . .television |
| cy . . . . . . . . . . . . . . . . .cubic yard | mo . . . . . . . . . . . . . . . . .month | UBC . . . . . .Uniform Building Code |
| ea . . . . . . . . . . . . . . . . . . . .each | mph . . . . . . . . . . .miles per hour | UL . . . . . . .Underwriters' Laboratory |
| FUTA . . . . . .Federal Unemployment | msf . . . . . . . . . .1,000 square feet | vlf . . . . . . . . . . .vertical linear foot |
| . . . . . . . . . . Compensation Act tax | no. . . . . . . . . . . . . . . . .number | wk . . . . . . . . . . . . . . . . . . . . .week |
| gal . . . . . . . . . . . . . . . . . . .gallon | oc . . . . . . . . . . . . .on center | w/ . . . . . . . . . . . . . . . . . . . . . .with |
| GFCI .ground fault circuit interrupter | oz . . . . . . . . . . . . . . . . . . .ounce | x . . . . . . . . . . . . . . .by or times |
| gph . . . . . . . . . .gallon(s) per hour | pr . . . . . . . . . . . . . . . . . . . .pair | |
| gpm . . . . . . . .gallon(s) per minute | psi . . . . . .pounds per square inch | **SYMBOLS** |
| hp . . . . . . . . . . . . . . .horsepower | PVC . . . . . . . . . . .polyvinyl chloride | / . . . . . . . . . . . . . . . . . . . . . .per |
| hr(s) . . . . . . . . . . . . . . .hour(s) | qt . . . . . . . . . . . . . . . . . .quart | - . . . . . . . . . . . . .through or to |
| IMC . . . .intermediate metal conduit | R/L . . . . . . . . . .random length(s) | @ . . . . . . . . . . . . . . . . . . . . . .at |
| kd . . . . . . . . . . . . . . . .kiln dried | R/W/L . .random widths and lengths | % . . . . . . . . . . . . . . . . . .percent |
| kv . . . . . . . . . . . . . . . .kilovolt(s) | RSC . . . . . . . . . .rigid steel conduit | $ . . . . . . . . . . . . . . .U.S. dollars |
| kva . . . . . . . . . .1,000 volt amps | S1S2E . . . .surfaced 1 side, 2 edges | ' . . . . . . . . . . . . . . . . . . . . . .feet |
| kw . . . . . . . . . . . . . . .kilowatt(s) | S2S . . . . . . . . . . .surfaced 2 sides | " . . . . . . . . . . . . . . . . . . .inches |
| lb(s) . . . . . . . . . . . . . . .pound(s) | S4S . . . . . . . . . . .surfaced 4 sides | # . . . . . . . . . . .pound or number |

# acknowledgements

The editor wishes to gratefully acknowledge the contribution of the following:  18th Century Hardware Co., Inc. - A-Ball Plumbing Supply - A&Y Lumber - American Building Restoration Chemicals, Inc. - American Custom Millwork, Inc. - American Society for Testing and Materials (ASTM) - Anderson Windows - Anthony Lombardo Architectural Paneling Inc. - Anthony Wood Products Incorporated - The Antique Hardware Store - Architectural Components, Inc. - Architectural Woodwork Institute - The Balmer Architectural Art Studios - Bathroom Hardware, Inc. - Bathroom Machineries - Bendix Mouldings, Inc. - Brass Reproductions - Brick Institute of America - C & H Roofing, Inc. - C. G. Girolami & Sons - Caradco - Cataumet Sawmills - CertainTeed - Chadsworth Incorporated - Chelsea Decorative Metal Company - Classic Accents, Inc. - Classic Ceilings - CMW, Inc. - Conant Custom Brass - Conklin Metal Industries - Craftsman Lumber Company - Crown City Hardware Co. - Cumberland General Stores - Cumberland Woodcraft Co. Inc. - Designs in Tile - Dimension Hardwood - Donnell's Clapboard Mill - Driwood Moulding - Eisenhart Wallcoverings - Empire Wood Works - Raymond Enkeboll Designs - James Facenelli, CGR #28 - Focal Point Architectural Products - Four Seasons Sun Rooms - Futurbilt - Garland - Gates Moore - General Electric Company - George Taylor Specialties Co. - Goodwin Heart Pine Company - Gougeon Brothers, Inc. - Grand Era, Inc. - Granville Manufacturing Company - Groff & Hearne Lumber - Hampton Decor - Harris-Tarkett, Inc. - Heatway - Heritage Vinyl Products - Michael Higuera - Italian Tile Center - J. G. Braun Company - Jeffries Wood Works, Inc. - Jennifer's Glass Works - JGR Enterprises - Johnson Paint Company, Inc. - Joseph Biunno Ltd - Kenmore Industries - King's Chandelier Company - Kraftmaid Cabinetry, Inc. - David Lawrence, illustrator - Lasting Impression Doors - Lehman's - Linoleum City, Inc. - Ludowici-Celadon, Inc. - MCA, Inc. - Millwork Specialties - The Millworks, Inc. - Mountain Lumber Co. - National Oak Flooring Manufacturers Association (NOFMA) - National Wood Flooring Association - Northwest Energy, Inc. - Oak Flooring Institute - The Old Fashioned Milk Paint Company, Inc. - Ole Fashion Things - Omega Too - Pagliacco Turning & Milling - Pella Corporation - Permaglaze - Piedmont Home Products, Inc. - Piedmont Mantel & Millwork Ltd - Pinecrest - Radiantec - The Readybuilt Products Company - Rejuvenation Lamp & Fixture, Co. - Runtal Radiators - The Saltbox - Salvage One Architectural Artifacts - Silverton Victorian Millworks - Stairways Inc. - Steptoe and Wife Antiques Ltd - Stromberg's Architectural Stone - The Structural Slate Co. - Sunbilt - Supradur Manufacturing Corporation - Taylor Door - Brian Thaut - Touchstone Woodworks - Turncraft - USG Company - Vande Hey's Roofing Tile Co., Inc. - Velux-America Inc. - Vixen Hill Manufacturing Co. - W. F. Norman Corporation - Watercolors, Inc. - WELco - Western Wood Products Association - Williamsburg Blacksmiths - Windy Hill Forge - Wolverine Technologies - The Wood Factory - Worthington Group Ltd

# area modification factors

Construction costs are higher in some cities than in other cities. Use the factors on this and the following page to adapt the costs listed in this book to your job site. Increase or decrease your estimated total project cost by the percentage listed for the appropriate city in this table to find your estimated building cost.

These factors were compiled by comparing the actual construction cost of residential, institutional and commercial buildings in communities throughout the United States. Because these factors are based on completed project costs, they consider all construction cost variables, including labor, equipment and material cost, labor productivity, climate, job conditions and markup.

Use the factor for the nearest or most comparable city. If the city you need is not listed in the table, use the factor for the appropriate state. Note that these location factors are composites of many costs and will not necessarily be accurate when estimating the cost of any particular part of a building. But when used to modify all estimated costs on a job, they should improve the accuracy of your estimates.

**ALABAMA .........-6%**
Anniston .............-9%
Auburn ...............-6%
Bellamy ..............-3%
Birmingham ...........3%
Dothan ...............-6%
Evergreen ...........-12%
Gadsden .............-13%
Huntsville ...........-3%
Jasper ..............-11%
Mobile ...............-3%
Montgomery ..........-2%
Scottsboro ...........-6%
Selma ................-6%
Sheffield ............-1%
Tuscaloosa ...........-5%

**ALASKA .........21%**
Anchorage ...........27%
Fairbanks ...........24%
Juneau ..............22%
Ketchikan ...........11%
King Salmon .........24%

**ARIZONA .........-4%**
Chambers .............-4%
Douglas ..............-3%
Flagstaff ............-9%
Kingman ..............-5%
Mesa .................1%
Phoenix ..............1%
Prescott .............-7%
Show Low .............-9%
Tucson ...............-6%
Yuma .................0%

**ARKANSAS .......-7%**
Batesville ..........-10%
Camden ...............-5%
Fayetteville .........-5%
Fort Smith ...........-7%
Harrison ............-14%
Hope .................-1%
Hot Springs .........-13%
Jonesboro ............-8%
Little Rock ..........-3%

Pine Bluff ...........-2%
Russellville .........-6%
West Memphis .........-6%

**CALIFORNIA .....8%**
Alhambra .............9%
Bakersfield ..........3%
El Centro ............-1%
Eureka ...............-4%
Fresno ...............-1%
Herlong ..............-1%
Inglewood ............9%
Irvine ...............13%
Lompoc ...............6%
Long Beach ...........10%
Los Angeles ..........8%
Marysville ...........-1%
Modesto ..............-1%
Mojave ...............6%
Novato ...............13%
Oakland ..............19%
Orange ...............12%
Oxnard ...............4%
Pasadena .............9%
Rancho Cordova .......6%
Redding ..............-3%
Richmond .............19%
Riverside ............3%
Sacramento ...........6%
Salinas ..............3%
San Bernardino .......4%
San Diego ............7%
San Francisco ........28%
San Jose .............18%
San Mateo ............20%
Santa Barbara ........6%
Santa Rosa ...........6%
Stockton .............1%
Sunnyvale ............20%
Van Nuys .............8%
Whittier .............8%

**COLORADO .......1%**
Aurora ...............6%
Boulder ..............3%
Colorado Springs .....-1%
Denver ...............6%

Durango ..............0%
Fort Morgan ..........-3%
Glenwood Springs .....4%
Grand Junction .......-1%
Greeley ..............4%
Longmont .............2%
Pagosa Springs .......-6%
Pueblo ...............2%
Salida ...............-5%

**CONNECTICUT ....12%**
Bridgeport ...........12%
Bristol ..............12%
Fairfield ............14%
Hartford .............14%
New Haven ............12%
Norwich ..............8%
Stamford .............16%
Waterbury ............12%
West Hartford ........9%

**DELAWARE .......2%**
Dover ................-5%
Newark ...............7%
Wilmington ...........5%

**DISTRICT OF COLUMBIA ......12%**
Washington ...........12%

**FLORIDA .........-7%**
Altamonte Springs ....-6%
Bradenton ............-8%
Brooksville ..........-9%
Daytona Beach .......-12%
Fort Lauderdale ......-1%
Fort Myers ...........-9%
Fort Pierce .........-13%
Gainesville ..........-9%
Jacksonville .........-4%
Lakeland .............-8%
Melbourne ...........-10%
Miami ................-2%
Naples ...............-5%
Ocala ...............-13%
Orlando ..............-2%
Panama City .........-12%
Pensacola ............-9%

Saint Augustine ......-7%
Saint Cloud ..........-5%
St Petersburg ........-7%
Tallahassee ..........-9%
Tampa ................-3%
West Palm Beach ......-3%

**GEORGIA .........-4%**
Albany ...............-9%
Athens ...............-6%
Atlanta ..............13%
Augusta ..............-4%
Buford ...............-4%
Calhoun .............-11%
Columbus .............-6%
Dublin/Fort Valley ...-9%
Hinesville ...........-6%
Kings Bay ............-4%
Macon ................-3%
Marietta .............4%
Savannah .............-5%
Statesboro ..........-11%
Valdosta .............-3%

**HAWAII .........24%**
Aliamanu .............25%
Ewa ..................23%
Halawa Heights .......23%
Hilo .................23%
Honolulu .............25%
Kailua ...............25%
Lualualei ............23%
Mililani Town ........23%
Pearl City ...........23%
Wahiawa ..............23%
Waianae ..............23%
Wailuku (Maui) .......23%

**IDAHO ...........-9%**
Boise ................-2%
Coeur d'Alene .......-11%
Idaho Falls ..........-8%
Lewiston ............-12%
Meridian .............-9%
Pocatello ...........-10%
Sun Valley ..........-10%

**ILLINOIS .........5%**
Arlington Heights ....16%
Aurora ...............15%
Belleville ...........0%
Bloomington ..........1%
Carbondale ...........-5%
Carol Stream .........15%
Centralia ............-3%
Champaign ............0%
Chicago ..............17%
Decatur ..............-8%
Galesburg ............-6%
Granite City .........3%
Green River ..........4%
Joliet ...............16%
Kankakee .............1%
Lawrenceville ........-6%
Oak Park .............19%
Peoria ...............7%
Peru .................3%
Quincy ...............17%
Rockford .............4%
Springfield ..........0%
Urbana ...............-3%

**INDIANA ..........-2%**
Aurora ...............-4%
Bloomington ..........-1%
Columbus .............-4%
Elkhart ..............-4%
Evansville ...........4%
Fort Wayne ...........-3%
Gary .................20%
Indianapolis .........7%
Jasper ...............-8%
Jeffersonville .......-4%
Kokomo ...............-8%
Lafayette ............-6%
Muncie ...............-9%
South Bend ...........-3%
Terre Haute ..........-3%

**IOWA ............-4%**
Burlington ...........-3%
Carroll .............-11%
Cedar Falls ..........-4%

| | | | | |
|---|---|---|---|---|
| Cedar Rapids .3% | **MAINE** -7% | Mankato -3% | North Platte -10% | Ithaca -3% |
| Cherokee -1% | Auburn -5% | Minneapolis 12% | Omaha -1% | Jamaica 22% |
| Council Bluffs -1% | Augusta -8% | Rochester -2% | Valentine -15% | Jamestown -5% |
| Creston -8% | Bangor -8% | St Cloud 5% | | Kingston -3% |
| Davenport .3% | Bath -7% | St Paul 11% | **NEW HAMPSHIRE** 0% | Long Island 36% |
| Decorah -7% | Brunswick -2% | Thief River Falls -1% | Charlestown -4% | Montauk 13% |
| Des Moines .4% | Camden -11% | Willmar -3% | Concord -1% | New York (Manhattan) 37% |
| Dubuque -3% | Cutler -10% | | Dover 3% | New York City 37% |
| Fort Dodge -3% | Dexter -8% | **MISSISSIPPI** -8% | Lebanon -2% | Newcomb 1% |
| Mason City -3% | Northern Area -10% | Clarksdale -9% | Littleton -3% | Niagara Falls -6% |
| Ottumwa -6% | Portland 0% | Columbus -1% | Manchester 3% | Plattsburgh -1% |
| Sheldon -8% | | Greenville -15% | New Boston 5% | Poughkeepsie 2% |
| Shenandoah -13% | **MARYLAND** 2% | Greenwood -11% | | Queens 25% |
| Sioux City .3% | Annapolis 8% | Gulfport -2% | **NEW JERSEY** 14% | Rochester 2% |
| Spencer -8% | Baltimore 8% | Jackson -5% | Atlantic City 10% | Rockaway 18% |
| Waterloo -5% | Bethesda 13% | Laurel -8% | Brick 6% | Rome -4% |
| | Church Hill -4% | McComb -11% | Dover 15% | Staten Island 15% |
| **KANSAS** -7% | Cumberland -10% | Meridian -4% | Edison 17% | Stewart -3% |
| Colby -7% | Elkton -2% | Tupelo -9% | Hackensack 15% | Syracuse 2% |
| Concordia -13% | Frederick 5% | | Monmouth 16% | Tonawanda -1% |
| Dodge City -6% | Laurel 9% | **MISSOURI** -4% | Newark 16% | Utica -6% |
| Emporia -5% | Salisbury -6% | Cape Girardeau -4% | Passaic 16% | Watertown 2% |
| Fort Scott -8% | | Caruthersville -9% | Paterson 13% | West Point 9% |
| Hays -13% | **MASSACHUSETTS** 13% | Chillicothe -8% | Princeton 15% | White Plains 19% |
| Hutchinson -7% | Ayer 8% | Columbia -5% | Summit 21% | |
| Independence 0% | Bedford 18% | East Lynne -6% | Trenton 13% | **NORTH CAROLINA** -5% |
| Liberal -7% | Boston 34% | Farmington -9% | | Asheville -8% |
| Salina -8% | Brockton 21% | Hannibal -2% | **NEW MEXICO** -10% | Charlotte 6% |
| Wichita -5% | Cape Cod 4% | Independence 5% | Alamogordo -13% | Durham 1% |
| | Chicopee 8% | Jefferson City -5% | Albuquerque -4% | Elizabeth City -8% |
| **KENTUCKY** -4% | Dedham 17% | Joplin -8% | Clovis -12% | Fayetteville -7% |
| Ashland -6% | Fitchburg 13% | Kansas City 7% | Farmington -1% | Goldsboro -1% |
| Bowling Green -5% | Hingham 20% | Kirksville -13% | Fort Sumner -3% | Greensboro -4% |
| Campton -10% | Lawrence 16% | Knob Noster -7% | Gallup -8% | Hickory -10% |
| Covington 1% | Nantucket 11% | Lebanon -13% | Holman -11% | Kinston -10% |
| Elizabethtown -9% | New Bedford 10% | Poplar Bluff -7% | Las Cruces -13% | Raleigh 2% |
| Frankfort -1% | Northfield 1% | Saint Charles 2% | Santa Fe -9% | Rocky Mount -7% |
| Hazard -6% | Pittsfield 1% | Saint Joseph 2% | Socorro -17% | Wilmington -8% |
| Hopkinsville -7% | Springfield 9% | Springfield -9% | Truth or Consequences -13% | Winston-Salem -6% |
| Lexington 2% | | St Louis 7% | Tucumcari -11% | |
| London -7% | **MICHIGAN** 1% | | | **NORTH DAKOTA** 5% |
| Louisville 1% | Battle Creek -1% | **MONTANA** -4% | **NEVADA** 4% | Bismarck 4% |
| Owensboro -3% | Detroit 8% | Billings 0% | Carson City -6% | Dickinson 10% |
| Paducah -2% | Flint -5% | Butte -5% | Elko 21% | Fargo 3% |
| Pikeville -4% | Grand Rapids 1% | Fairview 3% | Ely 1% | Grand Forks 1% |
| Somerset -10% | Grayling -8% | Great Falls -4% | Fallon 2% | Jamestown -3% |
| White Plains -5% | Jackson -2% | Havre -10% | Las Vegas 3% | Minot 11% |
| | Lansing 2% | Helena -3% | Reno 1% | Nekoma -8% |
| **LOUISIANA** 0% | Marquette 1% | Kalispell -7% | | Williston 21% |
| Alexandria -4% | Pontiac 10% | Miles City -7% | **NEW YORK** 9% | |
| Baton Rouge 10% | Royal Oak 8% | Missoula -7% | Albany 9% | **OHIO** 0% |
| Houma 6% | Saginaw -6% | | Amityville 15% | Akron 1% |
| Lafayette 2% | Traverse City -1% | **NEBRASKA** -9% | Batavia 1% | Canton -1% |
| Lake Charles 0% | | Alliance -10% | Binghamton 0% | Chillicothe -4% |
| Mandeville -1% | **MINNESOTA** 0% | Columbus -6% | Bronx 16% | Cincinnati 4% |
| Minden -6% | Bemidji -5% | Grand Island -7% | Brooklyn 14% | Cleveland 3% |
| Monroe -9% | Brainerd -1% | Hastings -9% | Buffalo 2% | Columbus 6% |
| New Orleans 2% | Duluth 1% | Lincoln -5% | Elmira -1% | Dayton -1% |
| Shreveport -4% | Fergus Falls -8% | McCook -11% | Flushing 23% | Lima -6% |
| | Magnolia -9% | Norfolk -9% | Garden City 21% | Marietta -4% |
| | | | Hicksville 20% | Marion -3% |

| | |
|---|---|
| Newark | .4% |
| Sandusky | -1% |
| Steubenville | .1% |
| Toledo | .6% |
| Warren | -3% |
| Youngstown | .0% |
| Zanesville | -1% |

**OKLAHOMA .....-6%**

| | |
|---|---|
| Adams | -9% |
| Ardmore | -6% |
| Clinton | -3% |
| Durant | -13% |
| Enid | -4% |
| Lawton | -12% |
| McAlester | -9% |
| Muskogee | -8% |
| Norman | -4% |
| Oklahoma City | -3% |
| Ponca City | -1% |
| Poteau | -9% |
| Pryor | -8% |
| Shawnee | -10% |
| Tulsa | -1% |
| Woodward | .2% |

**OREGON ......-5%**

| | |
|---|---|
| Adrian | -14% |
| Bend | -8% |
| Eugene | -3% |
| Grants Pass | -6% |
| Klamath Falls | -10% |
| Pendleton | -4% |
| Portland | .10% |
| Salem | -3% |

**PENNSYLVANIA ....-1%**

| | |
|---|---|
| Allentown | .4% |
| Altoona | -8% |
| Beaver Springs | -5% |
| Bethlehem | .6% |
| Bradford | -8% |
| Butler | -2% |
| Chambersburg | -8% |
| Clearfield | -2% |
| DuBois | -10% |
| East Stroudsburg | -4% |
| Erie | -7% |
| Genesee | -7% |
| Greensburg | -2% |
| Harrisburg | .3% |
| Hazleton | -5% |
| Johnstown | -9% |
| Kittanning | -6% |
| Lancaster | .1% |
| Meadville | -11% |
| Montrose | .2% |
| New Castle | -3% |
| Philadelphia | .13% |
| Pittsburgh | .5% |
| Pottsville | -8% |

| | |
|---|---|
| Punxsutawney | -2% |
| Reading | .2% |
| Scranton | -1% |
| Somerset | -9% |
| Southeastern | .10% |
| Uniontown | -5% |
| Valley Forge | .13% |
| Warminster | .11% |
| Warrendale | .6% |
| Washington | .8% |
| Wilkes Barre | -3% |
| Williamsport | -2% |
| York | .2% |

**RHODE ISLAND ....6%**

| | |
|---|---|
| Bristol | .7% |
| Coventry | .7% |
| Cranston | .6% |
| Davisville | .7% |
| Narragansett | .7% |
| Newport | .7% |
| Providence | .6% |
| Warwick | .7% |

**SOUTH CAROLINA ..-4%**

| | |
|---|---|
| Aiken | .2% |
| Beaufort | -6% |
| Charleston | -1% |
| Columbia | -5% |
| Greenville | -4% |
| Myrtle Beach | -9% |
| Rock Hill | -8% |
| Spartanburg | -4% |

**SOUTH DAKOTA ....-8%**

| | |
|---|---|
| Aberdeen | -7% |
| Mitchell | -8% |
| Mobridge | -11% |
| Pierre | -13% |
| Rapid City | -8% |
| Sioux Falls | -2% |
| Watertown | -8% |

**TENNESSEE ......-3%**

| | |
|---|---|
| Chattanooga | .0% |
| Clarksville | .1% |
| Cleveland | -2% |
| Columbia | -7% |
| Cookeville | -10% |
| Jackson | -4% |
| Kingsport | -5% |
| Knoxville | -1% |
| McKenzie | -8% |
| Memphis | .2% |
| Nashville | .5% |

**TEXAS .........-1%**

| | |
|---|---|
| Abilene | -3% |
| Amarillo | -2% |
| Arlington | .1% |

| | |
|---|---|
| Austin | .4% |
| Bay City | .23% |
| Beaumont | .8% |
| Brownwood | -9% |
| Bryan | -5% |
| Childress | -14% |
| Corpus Christi | .5% |
| Dallas | .5% |
| Del Rio | -8% |
| El Paso | -12% |
| Fort Worth | .1% |
| Galveston | .10% |
| Giddings | -1% |
| Greenville | .4% |
| Houston | .12% |
| Huntsville | .11% |
| Longview | -1% |
| Lubbock | -7% |
| Lufkin | -6% |
| McAllen | -13% |
| Midland | .9% |
| Palestine | -6% |
| Plano | .6% |
| San Angelo | -8% |
| San Antonio | -1% |
| Texarkana | -9% |
| Tyler | -7% |
| Victoria | .0% |
| Waco | -6% |
| Wichita Falls | -10% |
| Woodson | -6% |

**UTAH ..........-4%**

| | |
|---|---|
| Clearfield | -1% |
| Green River | -2% |
| Ogden | -10% |
| Provo | -9% |
| Salt Lake City | .1% |

**VERMONT ........-5%**

| | |
|---|---|
| Albany | -7% |
| Battleboro | -4% |
| Beecher Falls | -8% |
| Bennington | -8% |
| Burlington | .3% |
| Montpelier | -4% |
| Rutland | -8% |
| Springfield | -7% |
| White River Junction | -6% |

**VIRGINIA ........-5%**

| | |
|---|---|
| Abingdon | -9% |
| Alexandria | .11% |
| Charlottesville | -6% |
| Chesapeake | -3% |
| Culpeper | -5% |
| Farmville | -13% |
| Fredericksburg | -5% |
| Galax | -12% |
| Harrisonburg | -8% |

| | |
|---|---|
| Lynchburg | -9% |
| Norfolk | -2% |
| Petersburg | -4% |
| Radford | -10% |
| Reston | .8% |
| Richmond | .2% |
| Roanoke | -10% |
| Staunton | -9% |
| Tazewell | -6% |
| Virginia Beach | -5% |
| Williamsburg | -4% |
| Winchester | -5% |

**WASHINGTON ......0%**

| | |
|---|---|
| Clarkston | -6% |
| Everett | .3% |
| Olympia | -1% |
| Pasco | .2% |
| Seattle | .12% |
| Spokane | -3% |
| Tacoma | .3% |
| Vancouver | .2% |
| Wenatchee | -5% |
| Yakima | -4% |

**WEST VIRGINIA ....-5%**

| | |
|---|---|
| Beckley | -6% |
| Bluefield | .0% |
| Charleston | .6% |
| Clarksburg | -4% |
| Fairmont | -11% |
| Huntington | -1% |
| Lewisburg | -15% |
| Martinsburg | -6% |
| Morgantown | -5% |
| New Martinsville | -10% |
| Parkersburg | .2% |
| Romney | -8% |
| Sugar Grove | -8% |
| Wheeling | -1% |

**WISCONSIN ........1%**

| | |
|---|---|
| Amery | .0% |
| Beloit | .6% |
| Clam Lake | -6% |
| Eau Claire | -3% |
| Green Bay | .2% |
| La Crosse | -1% |
| Ladysmith | .1% |
| Madison | .8% |
| Milwaukee | .7% |
| Oshkosh | .3% |
| Portage | .4% |
| Prairie du Chien | -6% |
| Wausau | -2% |

**WYOMING ........-2%**

| | |
|---|---|
| Casper | .2% |
| Cheyenne/Laramie | -3% |
| Gillette | .2% |

| | |
|---|---|
| Powell | -8% |
| Rawlins | .2% |
| Riverton | -7% |
| Rock Springs | .2% |
| Sheridan | -5% |
| Wheatland | -7% |

**CANADIAN AREA MODIFIERS**

These figures assume an exchange rate of $1.00 Canadian to $0.93 U.S. ..........

**ALBERTA AVERAGE ..13%**

| | |
|---|---|
| Calgary | .14% |
| Edmonton | .14% |
| Fort McMurray | .11% |

**BRITISH COLUMBIA AVERAGE .........7%**

| | |
|---|---|
| Fraser Valley | .6% |
| Okanagan | .6% |
| Vancouver | .9% |

**MANITOBA AVERAGE ..0%**

| | |
|---|---|
| North Manitoba | .0% |
| South Manitoba | .0% |
| Selkirk | .0% |
| Winnipeg | .0% |

**NEW BRUNSWICK AVERAGE ........-13%**

| | |
|---|---|
| Moncton | -13% |

**NOVA SCOTIA AVERAGE .........-8%**

| | |
|---|---|
| Amherst | -8% |
| Nova Scotia | -7% |
| Sydney | -8% |

**NEWFOUNDLAND/ LABRADOR AVERAGE .-3%**

**ONTARIO AVERAGE ...7%**

| | |
|---|---|
| London | .7% |
| Thunder Bay | .6% |
| Toronto | .7% |

**QUEBEC AVERAGE ...-1%**

| | |
|---|---|
| Montreal | -1% |
| Quebec City | -1% |

**SASKATCHEWAN AVERAGE .........3%**

| | |
|---|---|
| La Ronge | .3% |
| Prince Albert | .2% |
| Saskatoon | .5% |

# crews

| CRAFT CODE | AVG. COST /HR | CREW COMPOSITION |
|---|---|---|
| 1A | $45.50 | acoustic ceiling installer |
| 2A | $51.50 | appliance installer |
| 3A | $61.50 | appliance refinisher |
| 4A | $53.70 | awning installer |
| 5A | $40.50 | awning installer's helper |
| 6A | $47.10 | awning installer<br>awning installer's helper |
| 1B | $33.30 | cleaning laborer |
| 2B | $72.00 | post & beam carpenter |
| 3B | $51.20 | post & beam carpenter's helper |
| 4B | $61.60 | post & beam carpenter<br>post & beam carpenter's helper |
| 1C | $56.90 | carpenter |
| 5C | $42.40 | carpenter's helper |
| 6C | $49.70 | carpenter<br>carpenter's helper |
| 1D | $38.90 | demolition laborer |
| 2D | $45.20 | drywall hanger<br>drywall hanger's helper |
| 3D | $51.50 | drywall hanger |
| 4D | $38.80 | drywall hanger's helper |
| 5D | $52.00 | drywall taper |
| 6D | $47.40 | drywall hanger<br>drywall hanger's helper<br>drywall taper |
| 5E | $37.20 | excavation laborer |
| 6E | $56.00 | excavation laborer<br>equipment operator |
| 7E | $61.30 | electrician |
| 8E | $45.60 | electrician's helper |
| 9E | $53.50 | electrician<br>electrician's helper |
| 1F | $54.60 | concrete form installer |
| 2F | $39.60 | concrete laborer |
| 3F | $47.10 | concrete form installer<br>concrete laborer |
| 4F | $49.70 | carpenter (fence installer)<br>carpenter's helper |
| 5F | $55.10 | painter |
| 6F | $54.40 | concrete finisher |
| 7F | $45.10 | concrete finisher's helper |
| 8F | $49.80 | concrete finisher<br>concrete finisher's helper |
| 9F | $48.50 | concrete form installer<br>concrete laborer<br>concrete finisher<br>concrete finisher's helper |
| 1G | $76.30 | compaction grouting specialist |
| 2G | $58.00 | compaction grouting specialist<br>concrete laborer |
| 1H | $48.90 | hazardous materials laborer |
| 2H | $61.50 | HVAC installer |
| 3H | $44.90 | wallpaper hanger |

| CRAFT CODE | AVG. COST /HR | CREW COMPOSITION |
|---|---|---|
| 1I | $42.10 | insulation installer |
| 2I | $47.30 | cabinet installer<br>laborer |
| 3I | $54.70 | flooring installer |
| 4I | $40.90 | flooring installer's helper |
| 5I | $47.80 | flooring installer<br>flooring installer's helper |
| 6I | $56.90 | paneling installer |
| 7I | $42.40 | paneling installer's helper |
| 2L | $37.70 | cabinet installer's helper |
| 3L | $35.50 | masking & moving laborer |
| 1M | $59.40 | mason |
| 2M | $54.50 | mason's helper |
| 3M | $42.00 | hod carrier |
| 4M | $52.00 | mason<br>mason's helper<br>hod carrier / laborer |
| 5M | $57.00 | mason<br>mason's helper |
| 6M | $96.00 | stone carver |
| 7M | $41.80 | mobile home repair specialist |
| 1O | $74.70 | equipment operator |
| 2O | $53.80 | concrete saw operator |
| 4P | $53.50 | plasterer |
| 5P | $46.00 | plasterer's helper |
| 6P | $49.80 | plasterer<br>plasterer's helper |
| 7P | $66.80 | plumber |
| 8P | $49.70 | paneling installer<br>paneling installer's helper |
| 9P | $53.30 | plumber's helper |
| 3R | $56.10 | retaining wall installer |
| 4R | $65.50 | roofer |
| 5R | $55.50 | roofer's helper |
| 6R | $60.50 | roofer<br>roofer's helper |
| 1S | $46.40 | susp. ceiling installer<br>susp. ceiling installer's helper |
| 2S | $53.00 | susp. ceiling installer |
| 3S | $39.80 | susp. ceiling installer's helper |
| 4S | $56.00 | siding installer |
| 5S | $41.90 | siding installer's helper |
| 6S | $49.00 | siding installer<br>siding installer's helper |
| 7S | $50.80 | security system installer |
| 8S | $64.70 | swimming pool installer |
| 9S | $48.70 | water extractor |
| 1T | $54.00 | tile layer |
| 7Z | $38.80 | mildew remediation specialist |
| 8Z | $24.00 | mildew remediation assistant |
| 9Z | $31.40 | mildew remediation specialist<br>mildew remediation assistant |

| | Craft@Hrs | Unit | Material | Labor | Total |
|---|---|---|---|---|---|

## Acoustic Ceilings

### Minimum charge.

| | Craft@Hrs | Unit | Material | Labor | Total |
|---|---|---|---|---|---|
| for acoustic ceiling tile work | 1A@1.25 | ea | 21.50 | 56.90 | 78.40 |

**1/2" on strips.** 12" x 12" tiles stapled in place. Includes 12" x 12" ceiling tiles, staples, and installation labor. Does not include furring strips. Includes 3% waste.

| 1/2" ceiling tiles on furring strips | Craft@Hrs | Unit | Material | Labor | Total |
|---|---|---|---|---|---|
| replace, smooth face | 1A@.025 | sf | 1.31 | 1.14 | 2.45 |
| replace, fissured face | 1A@.025 | sf | 1.68 | 1.14 | 2.82 |
| replace, textured face | 1A@.025 | sf | 1.94 | 1.14 | 3.08 |
| replace, patterned face | 1A@.025 | sf | 2.05 | 1.14 | 3.19 |
| remove only | 1D@.012 | sf | — | .47 | .47 |

**1/2" on flat ceiling.** 12" x 12" tiles glued in place. Includes 12" x 12" ceiling tiles, glue, and installation labor. Includes 3% waste.

| 1/2" ceiling tiles on flat ceiling | Craft@Hrs | Unit | Material | Labor | Total |
|---|---|---|---|---|---|
| replace, smooth face | 1A@.029 | sf | 1.31 | 1.32 | 2.63 |
| replace, fissured face | 1A@.029 | sf | 1.68 | 1.32 | 3.00 |
| replace, textured face | 1A@.029 | sf | 1.94 | 1.32 | 3.26 |
| replace, patterned face | 1A@.029 | sf | 2.05 | 1.32 | 3.37 |
| remove only | 1D@.016 | sf | — | .62 | .62 |

**5/8" on strips.** 12" x 12" tiles stapled in place. Includes 12" x 12" ceiling tiles, staples, and installation labor. Does not include furring strips. Includes 3% waste.

| 5/8" ceiling tiles on furring strips | Craft@Hrs | Unit | Material | Labor | Total |
|---|---|---|---|---|---|
| replace, smooth face | 1A@.025 | sf | 1.68 | 1.14 | 2.82 |
| replace, fissured face | 1A@.025 | sf | 1.94 | 1.14 | 3.08 |
| replace, textured face | 1A@.025 | sf | 2.16 | 1.14 | 3.30 |
| replace, patterned face | 1A@.025 | sf | 2.31 | 1.14 | 3.45 |
| remove only | 1D@.012 | sf | — | .47 | .47 |

**5/8" on flat ceiling.** 12" x 12" tiles glued in place. Includes 12" x 12" ceiling tiles, glue, and installation labor. Includes 3% waste.

| 5/8" ceiling tiles on flat ceiling | Craft@Hrs | Unit | Material | Labor | Total |
|---|---|---|---|---|---|
| replace, smooth face | 1A@.029 | sf | 1.68 | 1.32 | 3.00 |
| replace, fissured face | 1A@.029 | sf | 1.94 | 1.32 | 3.26 |
| replace, textured face | 1A@.029 | sf | 2.16 | 1.32 | 3.48 |
| replace, patterned face | 1A@.029 | sf | 2.31 | 1.32 | 3.63 |
| remove only | 1D@.016 | sf | — | .62 | .62 |

**3/4" on strips.** 12" x 12" tiles stapled in place. Includes 12" x 12" ceiling tiles, staples, and installation labor. Does not include furring strips. Includes 3% waste.

| 3/4" ceiling tiles on furring strips | Craft@Hrs | Unit | Material | Labor | Total |
|---|---|---|---|---|---|
| replace, smooth face | 1A@.025 | sf | 1.94 | 1.14 | 3.08 |
| replace, fissured face | 1A@.025 | sf | 2.16 | 1.14 | 3.30 |
| replace, textured face | 1A@.025 | sf | 2.25 | 1.14 | 3.39 |
| replace, patterned face | 1A@.025 | sf | 2.49 | 1.14 | 3.63 |
| remove | 1D@.012 | sf | — | .47 | .47 |

|  | Craft@Hrs | Unit | Material | Labor | Total |
|---|---|---|---|---|---|

**3/4" on flat ceiling.** 12" x 12" tiles glued in place. Includes 12" x 12" ceiling tiles, glue, and installation labor. Includes 3% waste.

| 3/4" ceiling tiles on flat ceiling | | | | | |
|---|---|---|---|---|---|
| replace, smooth face | 1A@.029 | sf | 1.94 | 1.32 | 3.26 |
| replace, fissured face | 1A@.029 | sf | 2.16 | 1.32 | 3.48 |
| replace, textured face | 1A@.029 | sf | 2.25 | 1.32 | 3.57 |
| replace, patterned face | 1A@.029 | sf | 2.49 | 1.32 | 3.81 |
| remove | 1D@.016 | sf | — | .62 | .62 |

**Additional costs for acoustical ceiling tile.**

| add for 3/4" tiles with fire rating | — | sf | .36 | — | .36 |
|---|---|---|---|---|---|
| add for aluminum-coated tiles | — | sf | .54 | — | .54 |

**Furring strips.** Includes 1" x 2" furring strips, nails, construction adhesive as needed, and installation labor. Furring strips placed as fireblocking is included. Includes 4% waste.

| replace 1" x 2" furring strips 12" on center | 1A@.007 | sf | .31 | .32 | .63 |
|---|---|---|---|---|---|
| remove | 1D@.009 | sf | — | .35 | .35 |

**Repair loose ceiling tile.**

| repair loose acoustic tile | 1A@.253 | ea | .15 | 11.50 | 11.65 |
|---|---|---|---|---|---|

**Angled install for ceiling tile.**

add 24% for diagonal install
add 31% for chevron install
add 40% for herringbone install

| **Time & Material Charts** (selected items) | | | | | |
|---|---|---|---|---|---|
| **Acoustic Ceiling Materials** | | | | | |

| 1/2" thick acoustic tile (per 12" x 12" tile) | | | | | |
|---|---|---|---|---|---|
| smooth face, ($1.09 each, 1 sf, 3% waste) | — | sf | 1.14 | — | 1.14 |
| fissured face, ($1.47 each, 1 sf, 3% waste) | — | sf | 1.54 | — | 1.54 |
| textured face, ($1.70 each, 1 sf, 3% waste) | — | sf | 1.79 | — | 1.79 |
| patterned face, ($1.82 each, 1 sf, 3% waste) | — | sf | 1.91 | — | 1.91 |
| 5/8" thick acoustic tile (per 12" x 12" tile) | | | | | |
| smooth face, ($1.47 each, 1 sf, 3% waste) | — | sf | 1.54 | — | 1.54 |
| fissured face, ($1.70 each, 1 sf, 3% waste) | — | sf | 1.79 | — | 1.79 |
| textured face, ($1.95 each, 1 sf, 3% waste) | — | sf | 2.05 | — | 2.05 |
| patterned face, ($2.05 each, 1 sf, 3% waste) | — | sf | 2.15 | — | 2.15 |
| 3/4" thick acoustic tile (per 12" x 12" tile) | | | | | |
| smooth face, ($1.70 each, 1 sf, 3% waste) | — | sf | 1.79 | — | 1.79 |
| fissured face, ($1.95 each, 1 sf, 3% waste) | — | sf | 2.05 | — | 2.05 |
| textured face, ($2.02 each, 1 sf, 3% waste) | — | sf | 2.12 | — | 2.12 |
| patterned face, ($2.22 each, 1 sf, 3% waste) | — | sf | 2.34 | — | 2.34 |

## Acoustic Ceiling Labor

| Laborer | base wage | paid leave | true wage | taxes & ins. | total |
|---|---|---|---|---|---|
| Acoustic ceiling installer | $25.00 | 1.95 | $26.95 | 18.55 | $45.50 |
| Demolition laborer | $20.70 | 1.61 | $22.30 | 16.59 | $38.90 |

**Paid Leave** is calculated based on two weeks paid vacation, one week sick leave, and seven paid holidays. Employer's matching portion of **FICA** is 7.65 percent. **FUTA** (Federal Unemployment) is .8 percent. **Worker's compensation** for the acoustic ceiling trade was calculated using a national average of 12.30 percent. **Unemployment insurance** was calculated using a national average of 8 percent. **Health insurance** was calculated based on a projected national average for 2015 of $1,025 per employee (and family when applicable) per month. Employer pays 80 percent for a per month cost of $820 per employee. **Retirement** is based on a 401(k) retirement program with employer matching of 50 percent. Employee contributions to the 401(k) plan are an average of 6 percent of the true wage. **Liability insurance** is based on a national average of 10.0 percent.

| | Craft@Hrs | Unit | Material | Labor | Total |
|---|---|---|---|---|---|
| **Acoustic Ceiling Labor Productivity** | | | | | |
| Repair of ceiling tile | | | | | |
|    repair loose tile | 1A@.253 | ea | — | 11.50 | 11.50 |
| Installation of ceiling tile | | | | | |
|    tiles on furring strips | 1A@.025 | sf | — | 1.14 | 1.14 |
|    tiles on flat ceiling | 1A@.029 | sf | — | 1.32 | 1.32 |
|    furring strips | 1A@.007 | sf | — | .32 | .32 |

# Appliances

| | Craft@Hrs | Unit | Material | Labor | Total |
|---|---|---|---|---|---|
| **Minimum charge for appliances.** | | | | | |
|    for appliance work | 2A@1.05 | ea | 16.60 | 54.10 | 70.70 |
| **Gas cook top.** | | | | | |
|    replace, standard grade | 7P@1.99 | ea | 605.00 | 133.00 | 738.00 |
|    replace, high grade | 7P@1.99 | ea | 797.00 | 133.00 | 930.00 |
|    replace, with grill / griddle | 7P@1.99 | ea | 1,070.00 | 133.00 | 1,203.00 |
|    remove | 1D@.615 | ea | — | 23.90 | 23.90 |
|    remove for work, then reinstall | 7P@2.20 | ea | 4.78 | 147.00 | 151.78 |
| **Gas range, free standing.** | | | | | |
|    replace, economy grade | 7P@2.05 | ea | 635.00 | 137.00 | 772.00 |
|    replace, standard grade | 7P@2.05 | ea | 851.00 | 137.00 | 988.00 |
|    replace, high grade | 7P@2.05 | ea | 1,160.00 | 137.00 | 1,297.00 |
|    replace, with grill / griddle | 7P@2.10 | ea | 1,560.00 | 140.00 | 1,700.00 |
|    remove | 1D@.618 | ea | — | 24.00 | 24.00 |
|    remove for work, then reinstall | 7P@2.80 | ea | 5.08 | 187.00 | 192.08 |
| **Space-saver gas range, free-standing.** | | | | | |
|    replace, standard grade | 7P@1.99 | ea | 827.00 | 133.00 | 960.00 |
|    replace, high grade | 7P@1.99 | ea | 1,070.00 | 133.00 | 1,203.00 |
|    remove | 1D@.618 | ea | — | 24.00 | 24.00 |
|    remove for work, then reinstall | 7P@2.80 | ea | 5.08 | 187.00 | 192.08 |

| | Craft@Hrs | Unit | Material | Labor | Total |
|---|---|---|---|---|---|

## Gas range, free-standing with double oven.

Gas range, free-standing with double oven

| | Craft@Hrs | Unit | Material | Labor | Total |
|---|---|---|---|---|---|
| replace, standard grade | 7P@2.05 | ea | 1,350.00 | 137.00 | 1,487.00 |
| replace, high grade | 7P@2.05 | ea | 1,600.00 | 137.00 | 1,737.00 |
| replace, deluxe grade | 7P@2.05 | ea | 1,910.00 | 137.00 | 2,047.00 |
| remove | 1D@.618 | ea | — | 24.00 | 24.00 |
| remove for work, then reinstall | 7P@2.80 | ea | 5.08 | 187.00 | 192.08 |

## Restaurant-style gas range. Some common manufacturers are Viking, Thermador and Garland. Also, be aware of "mimicked" restaurant styles from prominent manufacturers of home kitchen ranges that sell from $1,000 to $2,500.

| | Craft@Hrs | Unit | Material | Labor | Total |
|---|---|---|---|---|---|
| replace, standard grade | 7P@2.88 | ea | 3,460.00 | 192.00 | 3,652.00 |
| replace, high grade | 7P@2.88 | ea | 7,560.00 | 192.00 | 7,752.00 |
| replace, deluxe grade | 7P@2.88 | ea | 12,000.00 | 192.00 | 12,192.00 |
| remove | 1D@1.58 | ea | — | 61.50 | 61.50 |
| remove for work, then reinstall | 7P@3.55 | ea | 7.20 | 237.00 | 244.20 |

## Gas wall oven.

| | Craft@Hrs | Unit | Material | Labor | Total |
|---|---|---|---|---|---|
| replace, economy grade | 7P@1.79 | ea | 621.00 | 120.00 | 741.00 |
| replace, standard grade | 7P@1.79 | ea | 811.00 | 120.00 | 931.00 |
| replace, high grade | 7P@1.79 | ea | 1,030.00 | 120.00 | 1,150.00 |
| replace, deluxe grade | 7P@1.79 | ea | 1,280.00 | 120.00 | 1,400.00 |
| remove | 1D@.630 | ea | — | 24.50 | 24.50 |
| remove for work, then reinstall | 7P@2.48 | ea | 6.00 | 166.00 | 172.00 |

## Gas double wall oven.

| | Craft@Hrs | Unit | Material | Labor | Total |
|---|---|---|---|---|---|
| replace, economy grade | 7P@2.22 | ea | 1,360.00 | 148.00 | 1,508.00 |
| replace, standard grade | 7P@2.22 | ea | 1,590.00 | 148.00 | 1,738.00 |
| replace, high grade | 7P@2.22 | ea | 2,010.00 | 148.00 | 2,158.00 |
| replace, deluxe grade | 7P@2.22 | ea | 2,490.00 | 148.00 | 2,638.00 |
| remove | 1D@.782 | ea | — | 30.40 | 30.40 |
| remove for work, then reinstall | 7P@2.70 | ea | 7.20 | 180.00 | 187.20 |

## Electric cook top.

| | Craft@Hrs | Unit | Material | Labor | Total |
|---|---|---|---|---|---|
| replace, economy grade | 7E@1.32 | ea | 327.00 | 80.90 | 407.90 |
| replace, standard grade | 7E@1.32 | ea | 478.00 | 80.90 | 558.90 |
| replace, high grade | 7E@1.32 | ea | 600.00 | 80.90 | 680.90 |
| replace, cook top with grill / griddle | 7E@1.32 | ea | 720.00 | 80.90 | 800.90 |
| remove | 1D@.612 | ea | — | 23.80 | 23.80 |
| remove for work, then reinstall | 7E@2.21 | ea | 2.39 | 135.00 | 137.39 |

## Solid-disk electric cook top.

| | Craft@Hrs | Unit | Material | Labor | Total |
|---|---|---|---|---|---|
| replace, standard grade | 7E@1.32 | ea | 754.00 | 80.90 | 834.90 |
| replace, high grade | 7E@1.32 | ea | 851.00 | 80.90 | 931.90 |
| replace, with grill / griddle | 7E@1.32 | ea | 921.00 | 80.90 | 1,001.90 |
| remove | 1D@.612 | ea | — | 23.80 | 23.80 |
| remove for work, then reinstall | 7E@2.21 | ea | 2.39 | 135.00 | 137.39 |

| | Craft@Hrs | Unit | Material | Labor | Total |
|---|---|---|---|---|---|
| **Flat-surface radiant electric cook top.** | | | | | |
| replace, standard grade | 7E@1.32 | ea | 911.00 | 80.90 | 991.90 |
| replace, high grade | 7E@1.32 | ea | 1,030.00 | 80.90 | 1,110.90 |
| replace, cook top with grill / griddle | 7E@1.32 | ea | 1,100.00 | 80.90 | 1,180.90 |
| remove | 1D@.612 | ea | — | 23.80 | 23.80 |
| remove for work, then reinstall | 7E@2.21 | ea | 2.39 | 135.00 | 137.39 |
| **Modular electric cook top.** | | | | | |
| replace, two coil (Calrod) burners | 7E@.287 | ea | 371.00 | 17.60 | 388.60 |
| replace, two solid disk burners | 7E@.287 | ea | 444.00 | 17.60 | 461.60 |
| replace, two flat-surface radiant burners | 7E@.287 | ea | 503.00 | 17.60 | 520.60 |
| replace, griddle | 7E@.287 | ea | 528.00 | 17.60 | 545.60 |
| replace, grill | 7E@.287 | ea | 563.00 | 17.60 | 580.60 |
| replace, downdraft unit | 7E@.287 | ea | 276.00 | 17.60 | 293.60 |
| add for telescopic downdraft unit | | ea | 181.00 | — | 181.00 |
| remove | 1D@.215 | ea | — | 8.36 | 8.36 |
| **Remove for work and reinstall.** | | | | | |
| Modular cooking unit | 7E@.344 | ea | — | 21.10 | 21.10 |
| Modular downdraft unit | 7E@.394 | ea | 2.39 | 24.20 | 26.59 |
| **Electric range, free-standing.** | | | | | |
| replace, economy grade | 2A@1.05 | ea | 456.00 | 54.10 | 510.10 |
| replace, standard grade | 2A@1.05 | ea | 656.00 | 54.10 | 710.10 |
| replace, high grade | 2A@1.05 | ea | 930.00 | 54.10 | 984.10 |
| replace, deluxe grade | 2A@1.05 | ea | 1,210.00 | 54.10 | 1,264.10 |
| replace, cook top with grill / griddle | 2A@1.05 | ea | 1,370.00 | 54.10 | 1,424.10 |
| remove | 1D@.505 | ea | — | 19.60 | 19.60 |
| remove for work, then reinstall | 2A@1.72 | ea | 4.78 | 88.60 | 93.38 |
| **Solid-disk electric range, free-standing.** | | | | | |
| replace, standard grade | 2A@1.05 | ea | 874.00 | 54.10 | 928.10 |
| replace, high grade | 2A@1.05 | ea | 972.00 | 54.10 | 1,026.10 |
| replace, deluxe grade | 2A@1.05 | ea | 1,150.00 | 54.10 | 1,204.10 |
| replace, cook top with grill / griddle | 2A@1.05 | ea | 1,420.00 | 54.10 | 1,474.10 |
| remove | 1D@.505 | ea | — | 19.60 | 19.60 |
| remove for work, then reinstall | 2A@1.72 | ea | 4.78 | 88.60 | 93.38 |
| **Flat-surface radiant electric range, free-standing.** | | | | | |
| replace, standard grade | 2A@1.05 | ea | 1,040.00 | 54.10 | 1,094.10 |
| replace, high grade | 2A@1.05 | ea | 1,150.00 | 54.10 | 1,204.10 |
| replace, deluxe grade | 2A@1.05 | ea | 1,420.00 | 54.10 | 1,474.10 |
| replace, cook top with grill / griddle | 2A@1.05 | ea | 2,160.00 | 54.10 | 2,214.10 |
| remove | 1D@.505 | ea | — | 19.60 | 19.60 |
| remove for work, then reinstall | 2A@1.72 | ea | 4.78 | 88.60 | 93.38 |

| | Craft@Hrs | Unit | Material | Labor | Total |
|---|---|---|---|---|---|
| **Drop-in or slide-in electric range.** | | | | | |
| replace, standard grade | 2A@1.05 | ea | 911.00 | 54.10 | 965.10 |
| replace, high grade | 2A@1.05 | ea | 1,210.00 | 54.10 | 1,264.10 |
| replace, deluxe grade | 2A@1.05 | ea | 1,390.00 | 54.10 | 1,444.10 |
| replace, cook top with grill / griddle | 2A@1.05 | ea | 1,750.00 | 54.10 | 1,804.10 |
| remove | 1D@.505 | ea | — | 19.60 | 19.60 |
| remove for work, then reinstall | 2A@1.72 | ea | 6.00 | 88.60 | 94.60 |
| **Space-saver electric range, free-standing.** | | | | | |
| replace, standard grade | 2A@.980 | ea | 1,220.00 | 50.50 | 1,270.50 |
| replace, high grade | 2A@.980 | ea | 1,280.00 | 50.50 | 1,330.50 |
| remove | 1D@.505 | ea | — | 19.60 | 19.60 |
| remove for work, then reinstall | 2A@1.72 | ea | 4.78 | 88.60 | 93.38 |
| **High-low electric range with microwave high.** | | | | | |
| replace, standard grade | 2A@1.90 | ea | 389.00 | 97.90 | 486.90 |
| replace, high grade | 2A@1.90 | ea | 521.00 | 97.90 | 618.90 |
| replace, deluxe grade | 2A@1.90 | ea | 805.00 | 97.90 | 902.90 |
| remove | 1D@.883 | ea | — | 34.30 | 34.30 |
| remove for work, then reinstall | 2A@2.11 | ea | 6.00 | 109.00 | 115.00 |
| **Electric range, free-standing with double oven.** | | | | | |
| replace, standard grade | 2A@.980 | ea | 1,140.00 | 50.50 | 1,190.50 |
| replace, high grade | 2A@.980 | ea | 1,390.00 | 50.50 | 1,440.50 |
| replace, deluxe grade | 2A@.980 | ea | 1,870.00 | 50.50 | 1,920.50 |
| remove | 1D@.505 | ea | — | 19.60 | 19.60 |
| remove for work, then reinstall | 2A@1.72 | ea | 2.39 | 88.60 | 90.99 |
| **Electric wall oven.** | | | | | |
| replace, economy grade | 7E@1.55 | ea | 670.00 | 95.00 | 765.00 |
| replace, standard grade | 7E@1.55 | ea | 775.00 | 95.00 | 870.00 |
| replace, high grade | 7E@1.55 | ea | 983.00 | 95.00 | 1,078.00 |
| replace, deluxe grade | 7E@1.55 | ea | 1,230.00 | 95.00 | 1,325.00 |
| remove | 1D@.652 | ea | — | 25.40 | 25.40 |
| remove for work, then reinstall | 7E@2.50 | ea | 2.39 | 153.00 | 155.39 |
| **Electric double wall oven.** | | | | | |
| replace, economy grade | 7E@2.72 | ea | 979.00 | 167.00 | 1,146.00 |
| replace, standard grade | 7E@2.72 | ea | 1,240.00 | 167.00 | 1,407.00 |
| replace, high grade | 7E@2.72 | ea | 1,780.00 | 167.00 | 1,947.00 |
| replace, deluxe grade | 7E@2.72 | ea | 2,370.00 | 167.00 | 2,537.00 |
| remove | 1D@.774 | ea | — | 30.10 | 30.10 |
| remove for work, then reinstall | 7E@2.78 | ea | 3.61 | 170.00 | 173.61 |

|  | Craft@Hrs | Unit | Material | Labor | Total |
|---|---|---|---|---|---|
| **Warming drawer.** | | | | | |
| replace, standard grade | 7E@.977 | ea | 801.00 | 59.90 | 860.90 |
| replace, high grade | 7E@.977 | ea | 961.00 | 59.90 | 1,020.90 |
| replace, deluxe grade | 7E@.977 | ea | 1,360.00 | 59.90 | 1,419.90 |
| remove | 1D@.444 | ea | — | 17.30 | 17.30 |
| remove for work, then reinstall | 7E@1.66 | ea | 9.61 | 102.00 | 111.61 |

**Range hood.** Under-cabinet range hoods. Economy and standard grades may be non-vented. Stainless steel hoods usually range from high to custom grade. Designer hoods are usually deluxe or custom grade.

|  | Craft@Hrs | Unit | Material | Labor | Total |
|---|---|---|---|---|---|
| replace, economy grade | 2A@1.33 | ea | 78.00 | 68.50 | 146.50 |
| replace, standard grade | 2A@1.33 | ea | 130.00 | 68.50 | 198.50 |
| replace, high grade | 2A@1.33 | ea | 158.00 | 68.50 | 226.50 |
| replace, deluxe grade | 2A@1.33 | ea | 192.00 | 68.50 | 260.50 |
| replace, custom grade | 2A@1.33 | ea | 252.00 | 68.50 | 320.50 |
| remove | 1D@.422 | ea | — | 16.40 | 16.40 |
| remove for work, then reinstall | 2A@1.58 | ea | 2.39 | 81.40 | 83.79 |

**Range hood, oversized.** Under-cabinet range hoods. Economy and standard grades may be non-vented. Stainless steel hoods usually range from high to custom grade. Designer hoods are usually deluxe or custom grade.

|  | Craft@Hrs | Unit | Material | Labor | Total |
|---|---|---|---|---|---|
| replace, standard grade | 2A@1.46 | ea | 419.00 | 75.20 | 494.20 |
| replace, high grade | 2A@1.46 | ea | 504.00 | 75.20 | 579.20 |
| replace, deluxe grade | 2A@1.46 | ea | 616.00 | 75.20 | 691.20 |
| replace, custom grade | 2A@1.46 | ea | 810.00 | 75.20 | 885.20 |
| remove | 1D@.422 | ea | — | 16.40 | 16.40 |
| remove for work, then reinstall | 2A@2.04 | ea | 2.39 | 105.00 | 107.39 |

**Range hood, slide-out.** Under-cabinet slide-out range hoods.

|  | Craft@Hrs | Unit | Material | Labor | Total |
|---|---|---|---|---|---|
| replace, standard grade | 2A@1.58 | ea | 570.00 | 81.40 | 651.40 |
| replace, high grade | 2A@1.58 | ea | 688.00 | 81.40 | 769.40 |
| replace, deluxe grade | 2A@1.58 | ea | 790.00 | 81.40 | 871.40 |
| remove | 1D@.492 | ea | — | 19.10 | 19.10 |
| remove for work, then reinstall | 2A@2.84 | ea | 2.39 | 146.00 | 148.39 |

**Chimney range hood.** Island-mount or wall-mount vented chimney hood. The most common finish (and the most popular) is stainless steel, but a wide range of finishes are available. Copper chimney hoods usually fall in the deluxe to custom deluxe grades.

|  | Craft@Hrs | Unit | Material | Labor | Total |
|---|---|---|---|---|---|
| replace, economy grade | 2A@2.62 | ea | 998.00 | 135.00 | 1,133.00 |
| replace, standard grade | 2A@2.62 | ea | 1,360.00 | 135.00 | 1,495.00 |
| replace, high grade | 2A@2.62 | ea | 1,760.00 | 135.00 | 1,895.00 |
| replace, deluxe grade | 2A@2.88 | ea | 2,230.00 | 148.00 | 2,378.00 |
| replace, custom grade | 2A@2.88 | ea | 3,040.00 | 148.00 | 3,188.00 |
| replace, custom deluxe grade | 2A@3.04 | ea | 4,280.00 | 157.00 | 4,437.00 |
| remove | 1D@.787 | ea | — | 30.60 | 30.60 |
| remove for work, then reinstall | 2A@4.00 | ea | 2.39 | 206.00 | 208.39 |

**Downdraft ventilation system.** Stand-alone downdraft ventilation systems used with cook tops and ranges. These units are often telescopic and retract when not in use. Do not use these prices for cook tops and ranges that have integrated downdraft systems.

|  | Craft@Hrs | Unit | Material | Labor | Total |
|---|---|---|---|---|---|
| replace, standard grade | 2A@1.87 | ea | 592.00 | 96.30 | 688.30 |
| replace, high grade | 2A@1.87 | ea | 712.00 | 96.30 | 808.30 |
| replace, deluxe grade | 2A@1.87 | ea | 1,000.00 | 96.30 | 1,096.30 |
| remove | 1D@.576 | ea | — | 22.40 | 22.40 |
| remove for work, then reinstall | 2A@3.04 | ea | 2.39 | 157.00 | 159.39 |

| | Craft@Hrs | Unit | Material | Labor | Total |
|---|---|---|---|---|---|
| **Microwave oven.** Countertop microwave. | | | | | |
| replace, economy grade | 2A@.290 | ea | 119.00 | 14.90 | 133.90 |
| replace, standard grade | 2A@.290 | ea | 321.00 | 14.90 | 335.90 |
| replace, high grade | 2A@.290 | ea | 464.00 | 14.90 | 478.90 |
| replace, deluxe grade | 2A@.290 | ea | 660.00 | 14.90 | 674.90 |
| replace, custom grade | 2A@.290 | ea | 796.00 | 14.90 | 810.90 |
| remove | 1D@.182 | ea | — | 7.08 | 7.08 |
| remove for work, then reinstall | 2A@.345 | ea | — | 17.80 | 17.80 |
| **Microwave, under cabinet.** Microwave oven mounted to wall and/or cabinets. Also called an "over-the-range" microwave. | | | | | |
| replace, standard grade | 2A@.950 | ea | 428.00 | 48.90 | 476.90 |
| replace, high grade | 2A@.950 | ea | 665.00 | 48.90 | 713.90 |
| replace, deluxe grade | 2A@.950 | ea | 789.00 | 48.90 | 837.90 |
| remove | 1D@.346 | ea | — | 13.50 | 13.50 |
| remove for work, then reinstall | 2A@.677 | ea | — | 34.90 | 34.90 |
| **Dishwasher.** | | | | | |
| replace, economy grade | 2A@1.85 | ea | 269.00 | 95.30 | 364.30 |
| replace, standard grade | 2A@1.85 | ea | 412.00 | 95.30 | 507.30 |
| replace, high grade | 2A@1.85 | ea | 665.00 | 95.30 | 760.30 |
| replace, deluxe grade | 2A@1.85 | ea | 971.00 | 95.30 | 1,066.30 |
| replace, custom deluxe grade | 2A@1.85 | ea | 1,570.00 | 95.30 | 1,665.30 |
| remove | 1D@.649 | ea | — | 25.20 | 25.20 |
| remove for work, then reinstall | 2A@2.32 | ea | — | 119.00 | 119.00 |
| **Dishwasher, convertible (portable).** | | | | | |
| replace, standard grade | 2A@1.18 | ea | 484.00 | 60.80 | 544.80 |
| replace, high grade | 2A@1.18 | ea | 613.00 | 60.80 | 673.80 |
| replace, deluxe grade | 2A@1.18 | ea | 778.00 | 60.80 | 838.80 |
| remove | 1D@.388 | ea | — | 15.10 | 15.10 |
| remove for work, then reinstall | 2A@1.56 | ea | — | 80.30 | 80.30 |
| **Dishwasher, space-saver under-sink .** | | | | | |
| replace, standard grade | 2A@2.63 | ea | 717.00 | 135.00 | 852.00 |
| replace, high grade | 2A@2.63 | ea | 842.00 | 135.00 | 977.00 |
| remove | 1D@.732 | ea | — | 28.50 | 28.50 |
| remove for work, then reinstall | 2A@3.22 | ea | 6.00 | 166.00 | 172.00 |
| **Garbage disposal.** | | | | | |
| replace, 1/3 hp | 7P@1.51 | ea | 124.00 | 101.00 | 225.00 |
| replace, 1/2 hp, standard grade | 7P@1.51 | ea | 152.00 | 101.00 | 253.00 |
| replace, 1/2 hp, high grade | 7P@1.51 | ea | 238.00 | 101.00 | 339.00 |
| replace, 3/4 hp, standard grade | 7P@1.51 | ea | 242.00 | 101.00 | 343.00 |
| replace, 3/4 hp, high grade | 7P@1.51 | ea | 360.00 | 101.00 | 461.00 |
| replace, 1 hp, standard grade | 7P@1.51 | ea | 331.00 | 101.00 | 432.00 |
| replace, 1 hp, high grade | 7P@1.51 | ea | 364.00 | 101.00 | 465.00 |
| remove | 1D@.628 | ea | — | 24.40 | 24.40 |
| remove for work, then reinstall | 7P@2.51 | ea | 6.00 | 168.00 | 174.00 |

| | Craft@Hrs | Unit | Material | Labor | Total |
|---|---|---|---|---|---|

## Refrigerator / freezer, side-by-side.

**24 to 29 cf capacity refrigerator / freezer**

| | Craft@Hrs | Unit | Material | Labor | Total |
|---|---|---|---|---|---|
| replace, economy grade | 2A@.813 | ea | 1,120.00 | 41.90 | 1,161.90 |
| replace, standard grade | 2A@.813 | ea | 1,420.00 | 41.90 | 1,461.90 |
| replace, high grade | 2A@.813 | ea | 2,090.00 | 41.90 | 2,131.90 |
| replace, deluxe grade | 2A@.813 | ea | 2,420.00 | 41.90 | 2,461.90 |
| replace, custom deluxe grade | 2A@.813 | ea | 3,750.00 | 41.90 | 3,791.90 |
| remove | 1D@.794 | ea | — | 30.90 | 30.90 |
| remove for work, then reinstall | 2A@1.77 | ea | 6.00 | 91.20 | 97.20 |

**19 to 23 cf capacity refrigerator / freezer**

| | Craft@Hrs | Unit | Material | Labor | Total |
|---|---|---|---|---|---|
| replace, economy grade | 2A@.813 | ea | 1,320.00 | 41.90 | 1,361.90 |
| replace, standard grade | 2A@.813 | ea | 1,450.00 | 41.90 | 1,491.90 |
| replace, high grade | 2A@.813 | ea | 2,120.00 | 41.90 | 2,161.90 |
| replace, deluxe grade | 2A@.813 | ea | 2,490.00 | 41.90 | 2,531.90 |
| replace, custom deluxe grade | 2A@.813 | ea | 4,360.00 | 41.90 | 4,401.90 |
| remove | 1D@.976 | ea | — | 38.00 | 38.00 |
| remove for work, then reinstall | 2A@1.77 | ea | 6.00 | 91.20 | 97.20 |

## Refrigerator with top freezer.

**21 to 25 cf capacity**

| | Craft@Hrs | Unit | Material | Labor | Total |
|---|---|---|---|---|---|
| replace, economy grade | 2A@.700 | ea | 780.00 | 36.10 | 816.10 |
| replace, standard grade | 2A@.700 | ea | 1,130.00 | 36.10 | 1,166.10 |
| replace, high grade | 2A@.700 | ea | 1,370.00 | 36.10 | 1,406.10 |
| replace, deluxe grade | 2A@.700 | ea | 2,670.00 | 36.10 | 2,706.10 |
| replace, custom deluxe grade | 2A@.700 | ea | 4,480.00 | 36.10 | 4,516.10 |
| remove | 1D@.365 | ea | — | 14.20 | 14.20 |
| remove for work, then reinstall | 2A@1.42 | ea | 6.00 | 73.10 | 79.10 |

**17 to 20 cf capacity**

| | Craft@Hrs | Unit | Material | Labor | Total |
|---|---|---|---|---|---|
| replace, economy grade | 2A@.700 | ea | 562.00 | 36.10 | 598.10 |
| replace, standard grade | 2A@.700 | ea | 1,000.00 | 36.10 | 1,036.10 |
| replace, high grade | 2A@.700 | ea | 1,230.00 | 36.10 | 1,266.10 |
| replace, deluxe grade | 2A@.700 | ea | 1,680.00 | 36.10 | 1,716.10 |
| replace, custom deluxe grade | 2A@.700 | ea | 4,200.00 | 36.10 | 4,236.10 |
| remove | 1D@.365 | ea | — | 14.20 | 14.20 |
| remove for work, then reinstall | 2A@1.42 | ea | 6.11 | 73.10 | 79.21 |

## Refrigerator with bottom freezer. Higher grades sometimes have French-style refrigerator doors. Deluxe and custom deluxe grades may have French-style refrigerator doors and/or armoire-style freezer drawers.

**21 to 25 cf capacity**

| | Craft@Hrs | Unit | Material | Labor | Total |
|---|---|---|---|---|---|
| replace, economy grade | 2A@.700 | ea | 822.00 | 36.10 | 858.10 |
| replace, standard grade | 2A@.700 | ea | 1,200.00 | 36.10 | 1,236.10 |
| replace, high grade | 2A@.700 | ea | 1,450.00 | 36.10 | 1,486.10 |
| replace, deluxe grade | 2A@.700 | ea | 2,850.00 | 36.10 | 2,886.10 |
| replace, custom deluxe grade | 2A@.700 | ea | 4,730.00 | 36.10 | 4,766.10 |
| remove | 1D@.365 | ea | — | 14.20 | 14.20 |
| remove for work, then reinstall | 2A@1.42 | ea | 6.00 | 73.10 | 79.10 |

**17 to 20 cf capacity**

| | Craft@Hrs | Unit | Material | Labor | Total |
|---|---|---|---|---|---|
| replace, economy grade | 2A@.700 | ea | 594.00 | 36.10 | 630.10 |
| replace, standard grade | 2A@.700 | ea | 1,060.00 | 36.10 | 1,096.10 |
| replace, high grade | 2A@.700 | ea | 1,290.00 | 36.10 | 1,326.10 |
| replace, deluxe grade | 2A@.700 | ea | 1,770.00 | 36.10 | 1,806.10 |
| replace, custom deluxe grade | 2A@.700 | ea | 4,440.00 | 36.10 | 4,476.10 |
| remove | 1D@.365 | ea | — | 14.20 | 14.20 |
| remove for work, then reinstall | 2A@1.42 | ea | 6.00 | 73.10 | 79.10 |

|  | Craft@Hrs | Unit | Material | Labor | Total |
|---|---|---|---|---|---|

**Refrigerator / freezer, counter-depth.** Also called cabinet-depth refrigerators.

| 23 to 26 cf capacity | | | | | |
|---|---|---|---|---|---|
| replace, standard grade | 2A@.733 | ea | 2,610.00 | 37.70 | 2,647.70 |
| replace, high grade | 2A@.733 | ea | 3,310.00 | 37.70 | 3,347.70 |
| replace, deluxe grade | 2A@.733 | ea | 4,020.00 | 37.70 | 4,057.70 |
| replace, custom deluxe grade | 2A@.733 | ea | 4,650.00 | 37.70 | 4,687.70 |
| remove | 1D@.548 | ea | — | 21.30 | 21.30 |
| remove for work, then reinstall | 2A@1.67 | ea | — | 86.00 | 86.00 |
| 19 to 22 cf capacity | | | | | |
| replace, standard grade | 2A@.733 | ea | 2,370.00 | 37.70 | 2,407.70 |
| replace, high grade | 2A@.733 | ea | 3,220.00 | 37.70 | 3,257.70 |
| replace, deluxe grade | 2A@.733 | ea | 3,660.00 | 37.70 | 3,697.70 |
| replace, custom deluxe grade | 2A@.733 | ea | 4,360.00 | 37.70 | 4,397.70 |
| remove | 1D@.548 | ea | — | 21.30 | 21.30 |
| remove for work, then reinstall | 2A@1.67 | ea | — | 86.00 | 86.00 |

**Refrigerator / freezer, cabinet-match.** Refrigerator and freezer doors made to match kitchen cabinetry.

| Add for refrigerator / freezer doors made to match cabinets | | | | | |
|---|---|---|---|---|---|
| replace | — | ea | 528.00 | — | 528.00 |

**Refrigerator drawer.** Cabinet-match or stainless steel drawer face. Per unit installed in lower cabinets, with two to three drawers per unit.

| replace, standard grade | 2A@1.49 | ea | 2,610.00 | 76.70 | 2,686.70 |
|---|---|---|---|---|---|
| replace, high grade | 2A@1.49 | ea | 3,240.00 | 76.70 | 3,316.70 |
| remove | 1D@.599 | ea | — | 23.30 | 23.30 |
| remove for work, then reinstall | 2A@2.11 | ea | — | 109.00 | 109.00 |

**Refrigerator / freezer refreshment center.**

| Add for refreshment center in refrigerator / freezer | | | | | |
|---|---|---|---|---|---|
| replace | 2A@1.88 | ea | 269.00 | 96.80 | 365.80 |

**Refreshment center plumbing.** With supply lines and hook-up to appliances. For installation of supply lines only, see Plumbing on page 320.

| Disconnect water supply line for work, then reinstall | | | | | |
|---|---|---|---|---|---|
| replace | 7P@.283 | ea | .83 | 18.90 | 19.73 |
| Refreshment center plumbing hook-up | | | | | |
| replace, in existing building | 7P@2.22 | ea | 33.40 | 148.00 | 181.40 |
| replace, in new construction | 7P@1.37 | ea | 31.10 | 91.50 | 122.60 |

**Refinish refrigerator.**

| replace, typical | 3A@2.21 | ea | 38.20 | 136.00 | 174.20 |
|---|---|---|---|---|---|
| replace, refinish and recondition (replace gaskets) | 3A@2.69 | ea | 88.20 | 165.00 | 253.20 |

**Washing machine, top loading.**

| replace, economy grade | 2A@1.49 | ea | 415.00 | 76.70 | 491.70 |
|---|---|---|---|---|---|
| replace, standard grade | 2A@1.49 | ea | 551.00 | 76.70 | 627.70 |
| replace, high grade | 2A@1.49 | ea | 775.00 | 76.70 | 851.70 |
| replace, deluxe grade | 2A@1.49 | ea | 1,110.00 | 76.70 | 1,186.70 |
| replace, custom deluxe grade | 2A@1.49 | ea | 1,520.00 | 76.70 | 1,596.70 |
| remove | 1D@.421 | ea | — | 16.40 | 16.40 |
| remove for work, then reinstall | 2A@2.04 | ea | — | 105.00 | 105.00 |

| | Craft@Hrs | Unit | Material | Labor | Total |
|---|---|---|---|---|---|
| **Washing machine, front loading.** | | | | | |
| replace, economy grade | 2A@1.49 | ea | 690.00 | 76.70 | 766.70 |
| replace, standard grade | 2A@1.49 | ea | 1,020.00 | 76.70 | 1,096.70 |
| replace, high grade | 2A@1.49 | ea | 1,290.00 | 76.70 | 1,366.70 |
| replace, deluxe grade | 2A@1.49 | ea | 1,860.00 | 76.70 | 1,936.70 |
| replace, custom deluxe grade | 2A@1.49 | ea | 2,420.00 | 76.70 | 2,496.70 |
| remove | 1D@.421 | ea | — | 16.40 | 16.40 |
| remove for work, then reinstall | 2A@2.04 | ea | — | 105.00 | 105.00 |
| **Washing machine, steam.** | | | | | |
| replace, standard grade | 2A@1.49 | ea | 1,520.00 | 76.70 | 1,596.70 |
| replace, high grade | 2A@1.49 | ea | 1,680.00 | 76.70 | 1,756.70 |
| replace, deluxe grade | 2A@1.49 | ea | 2,070.00 | 76.70 | 2,146.70 |
| remove | 1D@.421 | ea | — | 16.40 | 16.40 |
| remove for work, then reinstall | 2A@2.04 | ea | — | 105.00 | 105.00 |

**Washing machine and dryer, stacked.** Also called unitized, Spacemaker by GE, and sometimes referred to as combo units, but most manufacturers refer to these space-saver styles as stacked or stackable units.

| | Craft@Hrs | Unit | Material | Labor | Total |
|---|---|---|---|---|---|
| with electric dryer | | | | | |
| replace, standard grade | 2A@2.04 | ea | 1,000.00 | 105.00 | 1,105.00 |
| replace, high grade | 2A@2.04 | ea | 1,390.00 | 105.00 | 1,495.00 |
| replace, deluxe grade | 2A@2.04 | ea | 1,570.00 | 105.00 | 1,675.00 |
| remove | 1D@.542 | ea | — | 21.10 | 21.10 |
| remove for work, then reinstall | 2A@2.88 | ea | — | 148.00 | 148.00 |
| with gas dryer | | | | | |
| replace, standard grade | 2A@2.54 | ea | 1,070.00 | 131.00 | 1,201.00 |
| replace, high grade | 2A@2.54 | ea | 1,520.00 | 131.00 | 1,651.00 |
| replace, deluxe grade | 2A@2.54 | ea | 1,660.00 | 131.00 | 1,791.00 |
| remove | 1D@.533 | ea | — | 20.70 | 20.70 |
| remove for work, then reinstall | 2A@3.22 | ea | — | 166.00 | 166.00 |

**Clothes dryer, electric.** Electric dryer with up to 20' of vent pipe. Deluxe and custom deluxe grades include steam dryers.

| | Craft@Hrs | Unit | Material | Labor | Total |
|---|---|---|---|---|---|
| replace, economy grade | 2A@.932 | ea | 434.00 | 48.00 | 482.00 |
| replace, standard grade | 2A@.932 | ea | 619.00 | 48.00 | 667.00 |
| replace, high grade | 2A@.932 | ea | 961.00 | 48.00 | 1,009.00 |
| replace, deluxe grade | 2A@.932 | ea | 1,160.00 | 48.00 | 1,208.00 |
| replace, custom deluxe grade | 2A@.932 | ea | 1,520.00 | 48.00 | 1,568.00 |
| remove | 1D@.400 | ea | — | 15.60 | 15.60 |
| remove for work, then reinstall | 2A@1.46 | ea | — | 75.20 | 75.20 |

**Clothes dryer, gas.** Gas dryer with up to 20' of vent pipe. Deluxe and custom deluxe grades include steam dryers.

| | Craft@Hrs | Unit | Material | Labor | Total |
|---|---|---|---|---|---|
| replace, economy grade | 2A@1.94 | ea | 502.00 | 99.90 | 601.90 |
| replace, standard grade | 2A@1.94 | ea | 687.00 | 99.90 | 786.90 |
| replace, high grade | 2A@1.94 | ea | 1,030.00 | 99.90 | 1,129.90 |
| replace, deluxe grade | 2A@1.94 | ea | 1,240.00 | 99.90 | 1,339.90 |
| replace, custom deluxe grade | 2A@1.94 | ea | 1,610.00 | 99.90 | 1,709.90 |
| remove | 1D@.488 | ea | — | 19.00 | 19.00 |
| remove for work, then reinstall | 2A@2.59 | ea | — | 133.00 | 133.00 |

| | Craft@Hrs | Unit | Material | Labor | Total |
|---|---|---|---|---|---|

**Trash compactor.** Use high grade for compactor with cabinet-match door.

| | Craft@Hrs | Unit | Material | Labor | Total |
|---|---|---|---|---|---|
| replace, economy grade | 2A@1.09 | ea | 557.00 | 56.10 | 613.10 |
| replace, standard grade | 2A@1.09 | ea | 661.00 | 56.10 | 717.10 |
| replace, high grade | 2A@1.09 | ea | 961.00 | 56.10 | 1,017.10 |
| remove | 1D@.288 | ea | — | 11.20 | 11.20 |
| remove for work, then reinstall | 2A@1.39 | ea | .83 | 71.60 | 72.43 |

## Time & Material Charts (selected items)
## Appliance Materials

See Appliance material prices above.

## Appliance Labor

| Laborer | base wage | paid leave | true wage | taxes & ins. | total |
|---|---|---|---|---|---|
| Appliance installer | $29.70 | 2.32 | $32.02 | 19.48 | $51.50 |
| Appliance refinisher | $34.40 | 2.68 | $37.08 | 24.52 | $61.60 |
| Electrician | $36.10 | 2.82 | $38.92 | 22.48 | $61.40 |
| Plumber | $38.30 | 2.99 | $41.29 | 25.21 | $66.50 |
| Demolition laborer | $20.70 | 1.61 | $22.31 | 16.59 | $38.90 |

**Paid leave** is calculated based on two weeks paid vacation, one week sick leave, and seven paid holidays. Employer's matching portion of **FICA** is 7.65 percent. **FUTA** (Federal Unemployment) is .8 percent. **Worker's compensation** was calculated using a national average of 7.20 percent for the appliance installer; 14.70 percent for the appliance refinisher; 6.93 percent for the electrician; 11.00 percent for the plumber; and 13.96 percent for the demolition laborer. **Unemployment insurance** was calculated using a national average of 8 percent. **Health insurance** was calculated based on a projected national average for 2015 of $1,025 per employee (and family when applicable) per month. Employer pays 80 percent for a per month cost of $820 per employee. **Retirement** is based on a 401(k) retirement program with employer matching of 50 percent. Employee contributions to the 401(k) plan are an average of 6 percent of the true wage. **Liability insurance** is based on a national average of 10.0 percent.

## Appliances Labor Productivity

Install appliances

| | Craft@Hrs | Unit | Material | Labor | Total |
|---|---|---|---|---|---|
| gas cook top | 7P@1.99 | ea | — | 133.00 | 133.00 |
| gas range | 7P@2.05 | ea | — | 137.00 | 137.00 |
| space-saver gas range | 7P@1.99 | ea | — | 133.00 | 133.00 |
| gas range with double oven | 7P@2.05 | ea | — | 137.00 | 137.00 |
| restaurant-style gas range | 7P@2.88 | ea | — | 192.00 | 192.00 |
| gas wall oven | 7P@1.79 | ea | — | 120.00 | 120.00 |
| gas double wall oven | 7P@2.22 | ea | — | 148.00 | 148.00 |
| electric cook top | 7E@1.32 | ea | — | 80.90 | 80.90 |
| modular cooking unit | 7E@.287 | ea | — | 17.60 | 17.60 |
| modular electric cook top downdraft unit | 7E@.287 | ea | — | 17.60 | 17.60 |
| electric range | 2A@1.05 | ea | — | 54.10 | 54.10 |
| drop-in or slide-in electric range | 2A@1.05 | ea | — | 54.10 | 54.10 |
| space-saver electric range | 2A@.980 | ea | — | 50.50 | 50.50 |
| electric wall oven | 7E@1.55 | ea | — | 95.00 | 95.00 |
| electric double wall-oven | 7E@2.72 | ea | — | 167.00 | 167.00 |
| range hood | 2A@1.33 | ea | — | 68.50 | 68.50 |
| oversized range hood | 2A@1.46 | ea | — | 75.20 | 75.20 |
| dishwasher | 2A@1.85 | ea | — | 95.30 | 95.30 |
| convertible (portable) dishwasher | 2A@1.18 | ea | — | 60.80 | 60.80 |
| space-saver under-sink dishwasher | 2A@2.63 | ea | — | 135.00 | 135.00 |

| | Craft@Hrs | Unit | Material | Labor | Total |
|---|---|---|---|---|---|
| garbage disposal | 7P@1.51 | ea | — | 101.00 | 101.00 |
| microwave oven | 2A@.290 | ea | — | 14.90 | 14.90 |
| microwave oven under cabinet | 2A@.950 | ea | — | 48.90 | 48.90 |
| side-by-side refrigerator / freezer | 2A@.813 | ea | — | 41.90 | 41.90 |
| refrigerator with freezer top or bottom | 2A@.700 | ea | — | 36.10 | 36.10 |
| disconnect refrig. water lines for work, reinstall | 2A@.283 | ea | — | 14.60 | 14.60 |
| refreshment center plumbing hook-up in existing building | 7P@2.22 | ea | — | 148.00 | 148.00 |
| refreshment center plumbing hook-up in new construction | 7P@1.37 | ea | — | 91.50 | 91.50 |
| trash compactor | 2A@1.09 | ea | — | 56.10 | 56.10 |
| clothes washing machine | 2A@1.49 | ea | — | 76.70 | 76.70 |
| clothes dryer, electric | 2A@.932 | ea | — | 48.00 | 48.00 |

# Awnings

**Free-standing carport.** 40 psf. Aluminum with baked enamel finish. Includes 4 posts for carports under 200 sf, 6 to 8 posts for carports over 200 sf.

| Free-standing aluminum carport | | | | | |
|---|---|---|---|---|---|
| replace, 150 sf or less | 6A@.077 | sf | 18.40 | 3.63 | 22.03 |
| replace, 151 to 250 sf | 6A@.077 | sf | 17.20 | 3.63 | 20.83 |
| replace, 251 to 480 sf | 6A@.077 | sf | 15.60 | 3.63 | 19.23 |
| add for heavy gauge aluminum | — | sf | 2.14 | — | 2.14 |
| remove | 1D@.050 | sf | — | 1.95 | 1.95 |
| remove for work, then reinstall | 6A@.161 | sf | .60 | 7.58 | 8.18 |

**Attached carport.** 40 psf. Aluminum with baked enamel finish. Includes 3 posts for carports and patio covers under 200 sf, 4 to 5 posts for carports and patio covers over 200 sf.

| Attached aluminum carport or patio cover | | | | | |
|---|---|---|---|---|---|
| replace, 150 sf or less | 6A@.071 | sf | 17.80 | 3.34 | 21.14 |
| replace, 151 to 250 sf | 6A@.071 | sf | 16.90 | 3.34 | 20.24 |
| replace, 251 to 480 sf | 6A@.071 | sf | 15.20 | 3.34 | 18.54 |
| add for heavy gauge aluminum | — | sf | 2.24 | — | 2.24 |
| remove | 1D@.054 | sf | — | 2.10 | 2.10 |
| remove for work, then reinstall | 6A@.150 | sf | .60 | 7.07 | 7.67 |

**Minimum charge.**

| for carport or patio cover work | 6A@1.85 | ea | 60.50 | 87.10 | 147.60 |
|---|---|---|---|---|---|

**Carport or patio cover parts.**

| Post | | | | | |
|---|---|---|---|---|---|
| replace | 6A@.687 | ea | 28.80 | 32.40 | 61.20 |
| remove | 1D@.280 | ea | — | 10.90 | 10.90 |
| remove, for work, then reinstall | 6A@.925 | ea | 2.60 | 43.60 | 46.20 |
| Scroll post | | | | | |
| replace, cover post scroll | 6A@.722 | ea | 52.80 | 34.00 | 86.80 |
| remove | 1D@.280 | ea | — | 10.90 | 10.90 |
| remove, for work, then reinstall | 6A@.994 | ea | 1.19 | 46.80 | 47.99 |

| | Craft@Hrs | Unit | Material | Labor | Total |
|---|---|---|---|---|---|
| **Fascia, aluminum** | | | | | |
| replace | 6A@.080 | lf | 8.58 | 3.77 | 12.35 |
| remove | 1D@.028 | lf | — | 1.09 | 1.09 |
| remove, for work, then reinstall | 6A@.110 | lf | — | 5.18 | 5.18 |
| **Roof panel** | | | | | |
| replace | 6A@.622 | ea | 59.10 | 29.30 | 88.40 |
| remove | 1D@.488 | ea | — | 19.00 | 19.00 |
| remove, for work, then reinstall | 6A@1.14 | ea | 4.74 | 53.70 | 58.44 |
| **Downspout** | | | | | |
| replace | 6A@.082 | ea | 24.80 | 3.86 | 28.66 |
| remove | 1D@.075 | ea | — | 2.92 | 2.92 |
| remove for work, then reinstall | 6A@.145 | ea | — | 6.83 | 6.83 |

**Door awning.** 25 to 40 psf.  Aluminum with baked enamel finish.  Includes all hardware and adjustable supports.

| | Craft@Hrs | Unit | Material | Labor | Total |
|---|---|---|---|---|---|
| **42" projection door awning** | | | | | |
| replace, 2 to 4 lf | 6A@.464 | lf | 74.70 | 21.90 | 96.60 |
| replace, 5 to 8 lf | 6A@.464 | lf | 79.80 | 21.90 | 101.70 |
| replace, 9 to 12 lf | 6A@.464 | lf | 86.80 | 21.90 | 108.70 |
| remove | 1D@.248 | lf | — | 9.65 | 9.65 |
| remove for work, then reinstall | 6A@.873 | lf | 7.70 | 41.10 | 48.80 |
| **54" projection door awning** | | | | | |
| replace, 2 to 4 lf | 6A@.484 | lf | 84.00 | 22.80 | 106.80 |
| replace, 5 to 8 lf | 6A@.484 | lf | 89.90 | 22.80 | 112.70 |
| replace, 9 to 12 lf | 6A@.484 | lf | 98.90 | 22.80 | 121.70 |
| remove | 1D@.250 | lf | — | 9.73 | 9.73 |
| remove for work, then reinstall | 6A@.878 | lf | 7.70 | 41.40 | 49.10 |
| **Minimum charge** | | | | | |
| for door awning work | 6A@1.85 | ea | 60.50 | 87.10 | 147.60 |

**Window awning.** 25 to 40 psf.  Aluminum with baked enamel finish.  Includes all hardware and adjustable supports.

| | Craft@Hrs | Unit | Material | Labor | Total |
|---|---|---|---|---|---|
| **3' high window awning** | | | | | |
| replace, 2 to 4 lf | 6A@.424 | lf | 68.50 | 20.00 | 88.50 |
| replace, 5 to 8 lf | 6A@.424 | lf | 53.60 | 20.00 | 73.60 |
| replace, 9 to 12 lf | 6A@.424 | lf | 50.40 | 20.00 | 70.40 |
| remove | 1D@.024 | lf | — | .93 | .93 |
| remove for work, then reinstall | 6A@.550 | lf | 7.70 | 25.90 | 33.60 |
| **4' high window awning** | | | | | |
| replace, 2 to 4 lf | 6A@.454 | lf | 80.10 | 21.40 | 101.50 |
| replace, 5 to 8 lf | 6A@.454 | lf | 66.20 | 21.40 | 87.60 |
| replace, 9 to 12 lf | 6A@.454 | lf | 61.90 | 21.40 | 83.30 |
| remove | 1D@.028 | lf | — | 1.09 | 1.09 |
| remove for work, then reinstall | 6A@.589 | lf | 7.70 | 27.70 | 35.40 |
| **5' high window awning** | | | | | |
| replace, 2 to 4 lf | 6A@.470 | lf | 107.00 | 22.10 | 129.10 |
| replace, 5 to 8 lf | 6A@.470 | lf | 96.70 | 22.10 | 118.80 |
| replace, 9 to 12 lf | 6A@.470 | lf | 76.60 | 22.10 | 98.70 |
| remove | 1D@.030 | lf | — | 1.17 | 1.17 |
| remove for work, then reinstall | 6A@.595 | lf | 7.70 | 28.00 | 35.70 |
| **6' high window awning** | | | | | |
| replace, 2 to 4 lf | 6A@.479 | lf | 123.00 | 22.60 | 145.60 |
| replace, 5 to 8 lf | 6A@.479 | lf | 118.00 | 22.60 | 140.60 |

| | Craft@Hrs | Unit | Material | Labor | Total |
|---|---|---|---|---|---|
| replace, 9 to 12 lf | 6A@.479 | lf | 90.00 | 22.60 | 112.60 |
| remove | 1D@.038 | lf | — | 1.48 | 1.48 |
| remove for work, then reinstall | 6A@.631 | lf | 7.70 | 29.70 | 37.40 |
| Minimum charge | | | | | |
| for window awning work | 6A@1.85 | ea | 60.50 | 87.10 | 147.60 |

**Door or window awning slat.** Includes prefinished standard length single slat up to 8' long in slat-style aluminum awning. Can be horizontal- or vertical-slat style. Includes replacement slat and hardware. Does not include painting or finishing slat to match.

| | Craft@Hrs | Unit | Material | Labor | Total |
|---|---|---|---|---|---|
| replace | 6A@.381 | ea | 20.90 | 17.90 | 38.80 |
| remove | 1D@.232 | ea | — | 9.02 | 9.02 |

**Roll-up awning.** Security awning that covers window. Aluminum with baked enamel finish. Includes all hardware and adjustable supports.

| | Craft@Hrs | Unit | Material | Labor | Total |
|---|---|---|---|---|---|
| replace, 2 to 5 lf | 6A@.274 | lf | 76.90 | 12.90 | 89.80 |
| replace, 6 to 12 lf | 6A@.274 | lf | 58.70 | 12.90 | 71.60 |
| remove | 1D@.409 | lf | — | 15.90 | 15.90 |
| remove for work, then reinstall | 6A@.599 | lf | 5.92 | 28.20 | 34.12 |

**Canvas awning.** Waterproof acrylic duck colorfast fabric with retractable metal frame and hardware.

| | Craft@Hrs | Unit | Material | Labor | Total |
|---|---|---|---|---|---|
| 24" drop canvas awning | | | | | |
| replace, 2 to 3 lf | 6A@.484 | lf | 105.00 | 22.80 | 127.80 |
| replace, 4 to 5 lf | 6A@.493 | lf | 98.50 | 23.20 | 121.70 |
| 30" drop canvas awning | | | | | |
| replace, 2 to 3 lf | 6A@.526 | lf | 123.00 | 24.80 | 147.80 |
| replace, 4 to 5 lf | 6A@.526 | lf | 108.00 | 24.80 | 132.80 |
| replace, 5 to 6 lf | 6A@.526 | lf | 97.60 | 24.80 | 122.40 |
| replace, 7 to 8 lf | 6A@.526 | lf | 86.90 | 24.80 | 111.70 |
| replace, 9 to 10 lf | 6A@.526 | lf | 71.40 | 24.80 | 96.20 |
| replace, 11 to 12 lf | 6A@.526 | lf | 66.00 | 24.80 | 90.80 |
| remove | 1D@.324 | lf | — | 12.60 | 12.60 |
| remove canvas awning for work, then reinstall | 6A@1.15 | lf | 6.05 | 54.20 | 60.25 |
| Minimum charge | | | | | |
| for canvas awning work | 6A@1.65 | ea | 51.00 | 77.70 | 128.70 |

**Vinyl awning.** Vinyl awning with acrylic coating. Includes metal frame and all hardware.

| | Craft@Hrs | Unit | Material | Labor | Total |
|---|---|---|---|---|---|
| 24" drop vinyl awning | | | | | |
| replace, 2 to 3 lf | 6A@.491 | lf | 62.60 | 23.10 | 85.70 |
| replace, 4 to 5 lf | 6A@.491 | lf | 57.20 | 23.10 | 80.30 |
| 30" drop vinyl awning | | | | | |
| replace, 2 to 3 lf | 6A@.520 | lf | 73.30 | 24.50 | 97.80 |
| replace, 4 to 5 lf | 6A@.520 | lf | 64.10 | 24.50 | 88.60 |
| replace, 5 to 6 lf | 6A@.520 | lf | 58.40 | 24.50 | 82.90 |
| replace, 7 to 8 lf | 6A@.520 | lf | 46.70 | 24.50 | 71.20 |
| replace, 9 to 10 lf | 6A@.520 | lf | 42.70 | 24.50 | 67.20 |
| replace, 11 to 12 lf | 6A@.520 | lf | 41.60 | 24.50 | 66.10 |
| remove | 1D@.324 | lf | — | 12.60 | 12.60 |
| remove awning for work then reinstall | 6A@1.13 | lf | 6.05 | 53.20 | 59.25 |
| Minimum charge | | | | | |
| for vinyl awning work | 6A@1.47 | ea | 34.40 | 69.20 | 103.60 |

|  | Craft@Hrs | Unit | Material | Labor | Total |
|---|---|---|---|---|---|

| **Time & Material Charts** (selected items) | | | | | |
|---|---|---|---|---|---|
| **Awning Materials** | | | | | |
| Aluminum carport | | | | | |
| free-standing, 151 to 250 sf | — | sf | 17.40 | — | 17.40 |
| attached, 151 to 250 sf | — | sf | 17.10 | — | 17.10 |
| Aluminum door awning | | | | | |
| with 42" projection, 5 to 8 lf | — | lf | 80.90 | — | 80.90 |
| with 54" projection, 5 to 8 lf | — | lf | 91.10 | — | 91.10 |
| Aluminum window awning | | | | | |
| 3' high, 5 to 8 lf | — | lf | 54.30 | — | 54.30 |
| 6' high, 5 to 8 lf | — | lf | 119.00 | — | 119.00 |
| Roll-up aluminum awning | | | | | |
| 2 to 5 lf | — | lf | 78.10 | — | 78.10 |
| 6 to 12 lf | — | lf | 59.50 | — | 59.50 |
| Canvas awning | | | | | |
| 24" drop, 2 to 3 lf | — | lf | 106.00 | — | 106.00 |
| 24" drop, 4 to 5 lf | — | lf | 99.70 | — | 99.70 |
| 30" drop, 2 to 3 lf | — | lf | 124.00 | — | 124.00 |
| 30" drop, 7 to 8 lf | — | lf | 88.20 | — | 88.20 |
| 30" drop, 11 to 12 lf | — | lf | 66.80 | — | 66.80 |
| Vinyl awning | | | | | |
| 24" drop, 2 to 3 lf | — | lf | 63.40 | — | 63.40 |
| 24" drop, 4 to 5 lf | — | lf | 58.20 | — | 58.20 |
| 30" drop, 2 to 3 lf | — | lf | 74.20 | — | 74.20 |
| 30" drop, 7 to 8 lf | — | lf | 47.30 | — | 47.30 |
| 30" drop, 11 to 12 lf | — | lf | 42.20 | — | 42.20 |

**Awning Labor**

| Laborer | base wage | paid leave | true wage | taxes & ins. | total |
|---|---|---|---|---|---|
| Awning installer | $29.20 | 2.28 | $31.48 | 22.22 | $53.70 |
| Awning installer's helper | $21.30 | 1.66 | $22.96 | 17.54 | $40.50 |
| Demolition laborer | $20.70 | 1.61 | $22.31 | 16.59 | $38.90 |

**Paid leave** is calculated based on two weeks paid vacation, one week sick leave, and seven paid holidays. Employer's matching portion of **FICA** is 7.65 percent. **FUTA** (Federal Unemployment) is .8 percent. **Worker's compensation** for the awning trade was calculated using a national average of 16.80 percent. **Unemployment insurance** was calculated using a national average of 8 percent. **Health insurance** was calculated based on a projected national average for 2015 of $1,025 per employee (and family when applicable) per month. Employer pays 80 percent for a per month cost of $820 per employee. **Retirement** is based on a 401(k) retirement program with employer matching of 50 percent. Employee contributions to the 401(k) plan are an average of 6 percent of the true wage. **Liability insurance** is based on a national average of 10.0 percent.

**Awning Installation Crew**

| install, awnings and patio covers | awning installer | $53.70 |
|---|---|---|
| install, awnings and patio covers | awning installer's helper | $40.50 |
| awning installation crew | awning installation crew | $47.10 |

| | Craft@Hrs | Unit | Material | Labor | Total |
|---|---|---|---|---|---|
| **Awning Labor Productivity** | | | | | |
| Install aluminum carport or patio cover | | | | | |
|     free-standing carport | 6A@.077 | sf | — | 3.63 | 3.63 |
|     attached carport or patio | 6A@.071 | sf | — | 3.34 | 3.34 |
| Install aluminum door awning | | | | | |
|     42" projection | 6A@.464 | lf | — | 21.90 | 21.90 |
|     54" projection | 6A@.484 | lf | — | 22.80 | 22.80 |
| Install aluminum window awning | | | | | |
|     3' high | 6A@.424 | lf | — | 20.00 | 20.00 |
|     4' high | 6A@.454 | lf | — | 21.40 | 21.40 |
|     5' high | 6A@.470 | lf | — | 22.10 | 22.10 |
|     6' high | 6A@.479 | lf | — | 22.60 | 22.60 |
| Install roll-up aluminum awning | | | | | |
|     per lf | 6A@.274 | lf | — | 12.90 | 12.90 |
| Install canvas awning | | | | | |
|     24" drop | 6A@.493 | lf | — | 23.20 | 23.20 |
|     30" drop | 6A@.526 | lf | — | 24.80 | 24.80 |
| Install vinyl awning | | | | | |
|     24" drop | 6A@.491 | lf | — | 23.10 | 23.10 |
|     30" drop | 6A@.520 | lf | — | 24.50 | 24.50 |

## Bathroom Hardware

**Hardware Quality.** Here are some "rules of thumb" for determining bathroom hardware quality. Economy: Light-gauge metal, chrome plated. May have some plastic components. Little or no pattern. Standard: Heavier gauge metal, chrome or brass plated with little or no pattern, or wood hardware made of ash or oak. High: Brass, chrome over brass, or nickel over brass with minimal detail, or plated hardware with ornate detail, or European-style curved plastic, or hardware with porcelain components, or wood hardware made of walnut, cherry or similar wood. Deluxe: Brass, chrome over brass, or nickel over brass with ornate detail. Antique Reproduction / Custom: Brass, chrome over brass, or nickel over brass with ornate antique-style detail.

### Minimum charge.

| | Craft@Hrs | Unit | Material | Labor | Total |
|---|---|---|---|---|---|
| for bathroom hardware work | 1C@.563 | ea | 27.50 | 32.00 | 59.50 |

**Complete bath hardware.** Bathroom with toilet, sink, and bathtub / shower. Includes towel bar, wash cloth bar, door-mount robe hook, toilet paper dispenser, and cup / toothbrush holder.

| | Craft@Hrs | Unit | Material | Labor | Total |
|---|---|---|---|---|---|
| replace, economy grade | 1C@4.02 | ea | 138.00 | 229.00 | 367.00 |
| replace, standard grade | 1C@4.02 | ea | 259.00 | 229.00 | 488.00 |
| replace, high grade | 1C@4.02 | ea | 379.00 | 229.00 | 608.00 |
| replace, deluxe grade | 1C@4.02 | ea | 511.00 | 229.00 | 740.00 |
| replace, custom grade | 1C@4.02 | ea | 582.00 | 229.00 | 811.00 |
| replace, antique reproduction | 1C@4.02 | ea | 955.00 | 229.00 | 1,184.00 |
| remove | 1D@2.22 | ea | — | 86.40 | 86.40 |

|  | Craft@Hrs | Unit | Material | Labor | Total |
|---|---|---|---|---|---|

**1/2 bath hardware.** Bathroom with toilet and sink. Includes wash cloth bar, towel ring, and toilet paper dispenser.

|  | Craft@Hrs | Unit | Material | Labor | Total |
|---|---|---|---|---|---|
| replace, economy grade | 1C@2.17 | ea | 45.30 | 123.00 | 168.30 |
| replace, standard grade | 1C@2.17 | ea | 88.20 | 123.00 | 211.20 |
| replace, high grade | 1C@2.17 | ea | 128.00 | 123.00 | 251.00 |
| replace, deluxe grade | 1C@2.17 | ea | 174.00 | 123.00 | 297.00 |
| replace, custom grade | 1C@2.17 | ea | 198.00 | 123.00 | 321.00 |
| replace, antique reproduction | 1C@2.17 | ea | 335.00 | 123.00 | 458.00 |
| remove | 1D@1.60 | ea | — | 62.20 | 62.20 |

**Glass bathroom shelf.** 21" x 5-1/2".

|  | Craft@Hrs | Unit | Material | Labor | Total |
|---|---|---|---|---|---|
| replace, glass | 1C@.283 | ea | 48.10 | 16.10 | 64.20 |
| replace, glass & brass | 1C@.283 | ea | 67.90 | 16.10 | 84.00 |
| remove | 1D@.205 | ea | — | 7.97 | 7.97 |
| remove for work, then reinstall | 1C@.300 | ea | — | 17.10 | 17.10 |

**Cup & toothbrush holder.**

|  | Craft@Hrs | Unit | Material | Labor | Total |
|---|---|---|---|---|---|
| replace, standard grade | 1C@.169 | ea | 13.20 | 9.62 | 22.82 |
| replace, high grade | 1C@.169 | ea | 21.70 | 9.62 | 31.32 |
| remove | 1D@.163 | ea | — | 6.34 | 6.34 |
| remove for work, then reinstall | 1C@.217 | ea | — | 12.30 | 12.30 |

**Door-mounted clothes hanger.**

|  | Craft@Hrs | Unit | Material | Labor | Total |
|---|---|---|---|---|---|
| replace, standard grade | 1C@.141 | ea | 11.80 | 8.02 | 19.82 |
| replace, high grade | 1C@.141 | ea | 19.60 | 8.02 | 27.62 |
| remove | 1D@.139 | ea | — | 5.41 | 5.41 |
| remove for work, then reinstall | 1C@.175 | ea | — | 9.96 | 9.96 |

**Robe hook.**

|  | Craft@Hrs | Unit | Material | Labor | Total |
|---|---|---|---|---|---|
| replace, standard grade | 1C@.141 | ea | 13.20 | 8.02 | 21.22 |
| replace, high grade | 1C@.141 | ea | 22.50 | 8.02 | 30.52 |
| remove | 1D@.139 | ea | — | 5.41 | 5.41 |
| remove for work, then reinstall | 1C@.175 | ea | — | 9.96 | 9.96 |

**Soap holder.**

|  | Craft@Hrs | Unit | Material | Labor | Total |
|---|---|---|---|---|---|
| replace, standard grade | 1C@.169 | ea | 25.10 | 9.62 | 34.72 |
| replace, high grade | 1C@.169 | ea | 42.60 | 9.62 | 52.22 |
| remove | 1D@.163 | ea | — | 6.34 | 6.34 |
| remove for work, then reinstall | 1C@.217 | ea | — | 12.30 | 12.30 |

**Recessed soap holder.**

|  | Craft@Hrs | Unit | Material | Labor | Total |
|---|---|---|---|---|---|
| replace, standard grade | 1C@.201 | ea | 26.10 | 11.40 | 37.50 |
| replace, high grade | 1C@.201 | ea | 54.10 | 11.40 | 65.50 |
| remove | 1D@.163 | ea | — | 6.34 | 6.34 |
| remove for work, then reinstall | 1C@.267 | ea | — | 15.20 | 15.20 |

| | Craft@Hrs | Unit | Material | Labor | Total |
|---|---|---|---|---|---|
| **Soap dispenser.** | | | | | |
| replace, standard grade | 1C@.182 | ea | 22.50 | 10.40 | 32.90 |
| replace, high grade | 1C@.182 | ea | 50.10 | 10.40 | 60.50 |
| remove | 1D@.163 | ea | — | 6.34 | 6.34 |
| remove for work, then reinstall | 1C@.224 | ea | — | 12.70 | 12.70 |
| **Recessed tissue holder.** | | | | | |
| replace, standard grade | 1C@.171 | ea | 33.80 | 9.73 | 43.53 |
| replace, high grade | 1C@.171 | ea | 53.90 | 9.73 | 63.63 |
| remove | 1D@.139 | ea | — | 5.41 | 5.41 |
| remove for work, then reinstall | 1C@.248 | ea | — | 14.10 | 14.10 |
| **Toilet paper dispenser.** | | | | | |
| replace, economy grade | 1C@.188 | ea | 15.60 | 10.70 | 26.30 |
| replace, standard grade | 1C@.188 | ea | 36.60 | 10.70 | 47.30 |
| replace, high grade | 1C@.188 | ea | 54.40 | 10.70 | 65.10 |
| replace, deluxe grade | 1C@.188 | ea | 66.20 | 10.70 | 76.90 |
| remove | 1D@.325 | ea | — | 12.60 | 12.60 |
| remove for work, then reinstall | 1C@.244 | ea | — | 13.90 | 13.90 |
| **Towel bar.** | | | | | |
| replace, economy grade | 1C@.393 | ea | 20.30 | 22.40 | 42.70 |
| replace, standard grade | 1C@.393 | ea | 29.80 | 22.40 | 52.20 |
| replace, high grade | 1C@.393 | ea | 47.70 | 22.40 | 70.10 |
| replace, deluxe grade | 1C@.393 | ea | 71.50 | 22.40 | 93.90 |
| remove | 1D@.325 | ea | — | 12.60 | 12.60 |
| remove for work, then reinstall | 1C@.563 | ea | — | 32.00 | 32.00 |
| **Towel ring.** | | | | | |
| replace, economy grade | 1C@.238 | ea | 15.70 | 13.50 | 29.20 |
| replace, standard grade | 1C@.238 | ea | 26.10 | 13.50 | 39.60 |
| replace, high grade | 1C@.238 | ea | 29.80 | 13.50 | 43.30 |
| replace, deluxe grade | 1C@.238 | ea | 33.20 | 13.50 | 46.70 |
| remove | 1D@.325 | ea | — | 12.60 | 12.60 |
| remove for work, then reinstall | 1C@.299 | ea | — | 17.00 | 17.00 |
| **Wash cloth bar.** | | | | | |
| replace, economy grade | 1C@.393 | ea | 14.40 | 22.40 | 36.80 |
| replace, standard grade | 1C@.393 | ea | 22.50 | 22.40 | 44.90 |
| replace, high grade | 1C@.393 | ea | 29.80 | 22.40 | 52.20 |
| replace, deluxe grade | 1C@.393 | ea | 40.50 | 22.40 | 62.90 |
| remove | 1D@.325 | ea | — | 12.60 | 12.60 |
| remove for work, then reinstall | 1C@.563 | ea | — | 32.00 | 32.00 |
| **Shower curtain rod.** | | | | | |
| replace, stainless steel rod | 1C@.113 | ea | 32.30 | 6.43 | 38.73 |
| remove | 1D@.089 | ea | — | 3.46 | 3.46 |
| remove for work, then reinstall | 1C@.130 | ea | — | 7.40 | 7.40 |

| | Craft@Hrs | Unit | Material | Labor | Total |
|---|---|---|---|---|---|

**Recessed medicine cabinet.** Economy and standard grades have a plastic or polystyrene box with two to three shelves, box measures up to 16" wide and 25" tall with mirror doors. Higher grades have a steel box with adjustable shelves, box measures up to 20" wide and 32" tall with chrome-plated, brass or wood trim, bevel-edged mirrors and top-arched or oval doors.

| | Craft@Hrs | Unit | Material | Labor | Total |
|---|---|---|---|---|---|
| replace, economy grade | 1C@1.31 | ea | 65.50 | 74.50 | 140.00 |
| replace, standard grade | 1C@1.31 | ea | 79.80 | 74.50 | 154.30 |
| replace, high grade | 1C@1.31 | ea | 114.00 | 74.50 | 188.50 |
| replace, deluxe grade | 1C@1.31 | ea | 136.00 | 74.50 | 210.50 |
| replace, custom grade | 1C@1.31 | ea | 169.00 | 74.50 | 243.50 |
| remove | 1D@.609 | ea | — | 23.70 | 23.70 |
| remove for work, then reinstall | 1C@1.88 | ea | — | 107.00 | 107.00 |

*high grade*

**Surface-mounted medicine cabinet.** All grades have two to three adjustable shelves. Box size and material vary with grade. Highest grades have three doors, are larger and have oak trim.

| | Craft@Hrs | Unit | Material | Labor | Total |
|---|---|---|---|---|---|
| replace, economy grade | 1C@1.51 | ea | 81.10 | 85.90 | 167.00 |
| replace, standard grade | 1C@1.51 | ea | 115.00 | 85.90 | 200.90 |
| replace, high grade | 1C@1.51 | ea | 196.00 | 85.90 | 281.90 |
| replace, deluxe grade | 1C@1.51 | ea | 332.00 | 85.90 | 417.90 |
| replace, custom grade | 1C@1.51 | ea | 476.00 | 85.90 | 561.90 |
| remove | 1D@.650 | ea | — | 25.30 | 25.30 |
| remove for work, then reinstall | 1C@1.97 | ea | — | 112.00 | 112.00 |

**Bathroom mirror.**

| | Craft@Hrs | Unit | Material | Labor | Total |
|---|---|---|---|---|---|
| replace, with stainless steel trim | 1C@.106 | sf | 22.50 | 6.03 | 28.53 |
| replace, with brass-finished trim | 1C@.106 | sf | 23.80 | 6.03 | 29.83 |
| replace, with wood frame | 1C@.106 | sf | 23.80 | 6.03 | 29.83 |
| replace, beveled glass | 1C@.106 | sf | 25.00 | 6.03 | 31.03 |
| remove bathroom mirror attached with glue | 1D@.041 | ea | — | 1.59 | 1.59 |
| remove for work, then reinstall | 1C@.169 | sf | — | 9.62 | 9.62 |

**Time & Material Charts** (selected items)
**Bathroom Hardware Materials**

See Bathroom Hardware material prices above.

**Bathroom Hardware Labor**

| Laborer | base wage | paid leave | true wage | taxes & ins. | total |
|---|---|---|---|---|---|
| Carpenter (installer) | $31.10 | 2.43 | $33.53 | 23.37 | $56.90 |
| Demolition laborer | $20.70 | 1.61 | $22.31 | 16.59 | $38.90 |

**Paid leave** is calculated based on two weeks paid vacation, one week sick leave, and seven paid holidays. Employer's matching portion of **FICA** is 7.65 percent. **FUTA** (Federal Unemployment) is .8 percent. **Worker's compensation** for the bathroom hardware trade was calculated using a national average of 16.85 percent. **Unemployment insurance** was calculated using a national average of 8 percent. **Health insurance** was calculated based on a projected national average for 2015 of $1,025 per employee (and family when applicable) per month. Employer pays 80 percent for a per month cost of $820 per employee. **Retirement** is based on a 401(k) retirement program with employer matching of 50 percent. Employee contributions to the 401(k) plan are an average of 6 percent of the true wage. **Liability insurance** is based on a national average of 10.0 percent.

| | Craft@Hrs | Unit | Material | Labor | Total |
|---|---|---|---|---|---|
| **Bathroom Hardware Labor Productivity** | | | | | |
| Install complete bathroom hardware | | | | | |
| full bathroom | 1C@4.02 | ea | — | 229.00 | 229.00 |
| 1/2 bathroom | 1C@2.17 | ea | — | 123.00 | 123.00 |
| Install hardware | | | | | |
| soap holder | 1C@.169 | ea | — | 9.62 | 9.62 |
| recessed tissue holder | 1C@.171 | ea | — | 9.73 | 9.73 |
| towel bar | 1C@.393 | ea | — | 22.40 | 22.40 |
| toilet paper dispenser | 1C@.188 | ea | — | 10.70 | 10.70 |
| towel ring | 1C@.238 | ea | — | 13.50 | 13.50 |
| wash cloth bar | 1C@.393 | ea | — | 22.40 | 22.40 |
| recessed medicine cabinet | 1C@1.31 | ea | — | 74.50 | 74.50 |
| surface-mounted medicine cabinet | 1C@1.51 | ea | — | 85.90 | 85.90 |
| bathroom mirror | 1C@.106 | sf | — | 6.03 | 6.03 |

# Cabinets

**Cabinet Construction.** Stock-grade cabinets are manufactured in standard sizes and warehoused until sold. Semi-custom grade cabinets are available in a wide variety of styles and shapes. Within limits, the manufacturer builds the cabinets to match the kitchen. Custom-grade cabinets are built specifically for the kitchen and include specialty doors, interior features, woods, and construction.

**Cabinet Grades.** Economy grade: Stock-grade cabinets with flush-face doors. Doors made from veneered particleboard. Standard grade: Stock-grade cabinets with raised panel or cathedral doors. Interior panel may be plywood. Lower grade plastic-laminate face cabinets. Semi-custom cabinets: Semi-custom grade cabinets are available in a wide variety of styles and shapes. Within limits, the manufacturer builds the cabinets to match the kitchen. High grade: Semi-custom cabinets with raised panel or cathedral doors. Higher grade plastic-laminate face and foil-face cabinets. Deluxe grade: Semi-custom cabinets with raised panel or cathedral doors. Door corners may be miter cut. May include special slide-out drawers, pull-out baskets, glass doors, or foil-face cabinets. Materials include cherry, pecan, and Shaker-style maple or pine. Custom grade: Custom cabinets with raised panel or cathedral doors. May include special slide-out drawers, pull-out baskets, mullion or leaded glass doors. Materials include cherry, pecan, and Shaker-style maple or pine. Custom deluxe grade: Same as Custom Grade, may have some curved wood cabinets and more custom features.

**Foil-Face Cabinets.** Foil-faced cabinets (also called thermo foil) are coated with rigid polyvinyl chloride (PVC) that has been heated and pressed. The interior core is usually medium density particleboard. Currently, there is no good way to repair scratched or dented foil-face cabinets. Although colors do not fade from foil-faces, it is almost impossible to replace doors or other parts with colors that will match. Foil-face cabinets are high to custom deluxe quality depending on the selection of interior features and the complexity of the design.

| | Craft@Hrs | Unit | Material | Labor | Total |
|---|---|---|---|---|---|
| **Minimum charge.** | | | | | |
| for cabinet work | 2I@2.67 | ea | 57.00 | 126.00 | 183.00 |

**Lower kitchen cabinet.** Includes prefabricated, prefinished lower cabinets assembled in shop or on site. Includes shims, backing, screws, attachment hardware, and installation labor. Installation includes cutting the cabinet to fit site conditions. This price is an overall allowance when replacing all or most cabinets in a kitchen and is based on a typical mixture of drawer units, door units, and corner units.

| | Craft@Hrs | Unit | Material | Labor | Total |
|---|---|---|---|---|---|
| replace, economy grade | 2I@.360 | lf | 88.60 | 17.00 | 105.60 |
| replace, standard grade | 2I@.360 | lf | 111.00 | 17.00 | 128.00 |
| replace, high grade | 2I@.360 | lf | 143.00 | 17.00 | 160.00 |
| replace, deluxe grade | 2I@.360 | lf | 203.00 | 17.00 | 220.00 |
| replace, custom grade | 2I@.360 | lf | 291.00 | 17.00 | 308.00 |
| replace, custom deluxe grade | 2I@.360 | lf | 374.00 | 17.00 | 391.00 |
| remove | 1D@.262 | lf | — | 10.20 | 10.20 |
| remove for work, then reinstall | 2I@.636 | lf | — | 30.10 | 30.10 |

| | Craft@Hrs | Unit | Material | Labor | Total |
|---|---|---|---|---|---|

**Upper kitchen cabinet.** Includes prefabricated, prefinished upper cabinets assembled in shop or on site. Includes shims, screws, backing, attachment hardware, and installation labor. Installation includes cutting the cabinet to fit site conditions. This price is an overall allowance when replacing all or most cabinets in a kitchen and is based on a typical mixture of door units, corner units, and over refrigerator units.

| | Craft@Hrs | Unit | Material | Labor | Total |
|---|---|---|---|---|---|
| replace, economy grade | 2I@.349 | lf | 77.70 | 16.50 | 94.20 |
| replace, standard grade | 2I@.349 | lf | 104.00 | 16.50 | 120.50 |
| replace, high grade | 2I@.349 | lf | 127.00 | 16.50 | 143.50 |
| replace, deluxe grade | 2I@.349 | lf | 187.00 | 16.50 | 203.50 |
| replace, custom grade | 2I@.349 | lf | 269.00 | 16.50 | 285.50 |
| replace, custom deluxe grade | 2I@.349 | lf | 343.00 | 16.50 | 359.50 |
| remove | 1D@.236 | lf | — | 9.18 | 9.18 |
| remove for work, then reinstall | 2I@.611 | lf | — | 28.90 | 28.90 |

**Lower kitchen island cabinet.** Includes prefabricated, prefinished lower island cabinets assembled in shop or on site. Includes shims, backing, screws, attachment hardware, and installation labor. Installation includes cutting the cabinet to fit site conditions. This price is an overall allowance when replacing all or most cabinets in a kitchen.

| | Craft@Hrs | Unit | Material | Labor | Total |
|---|---|---|---|---|---|
| replace, economy grade | 2I@.371 | lf | 92.10 | 17.50 | 109.60 |
| replace, standard grade | 2I@.371 | lf | 116.00 | 17.50 | 133.50 |
| replace, high grade | 2I@.371 | lf | 150.00 | 17.50 | 167.50 |
| replace, deluxe grade | 2I@.371 | lf | 211.00 | 17.50 | 228.50 |
| replace, custom grade | 2I@.371 | lf | 302.00 | 17.50 | 319.50 |
| replace, custom deluxe grade | 2I@.371 | lf | 389.00 | 17.50 | 406.50 |
| remove | 1D@.253 | lf | — | 9.84 | 9.84 |
| remove for work, then reinstall | 2I@.653 | lf | — | 30.90 | 30.90 |

**Upper kitchen island cabinet.** Includes prefabricated, prefinished upper island cabinets assembled in shop or on site. Includes shims, backing, screws, attachment hardware, and installation labor. Installation includes cutting the cabinet to fit site conditions. This price is an overall allowance when replacing all or most cabinets in a kitchen.

| | Craft@Hrs | Unit | Material | Labor | Total |
|---|---|---|---|---|---|
| replace, economy grade | 2I@.359 | lf | 81.10 | 17.00 | 98.10 |
| replace, standard grade | 2I@.359 | lf | 108.00 | 17.00 | 125.00 |
| replace, high grade | 2I@.359 | lf | 133.00 | 17.00 | 150.00 |
| replace, deluxe grade | 2I@.359 | lf | 195.00 | 17.00 | 212.00 |
| replace, custom grade | 2I@.359 | lf | 281.00 | 17.00 | 298.00 |
| replace, custom deluxe grade | 2I@.359 | lf | 356.00 | 17.00 | 373.00 |
| remove | 1D@.238 | lf | — | 9.26 | 9.26 |
| remove for work, then reinstall | 2I@.633 | lf | — | 29.90 | 29.90 |

**Full-height utility cabinet.** Includes prefabricated, prefinished full-height cabinet assembled in shop or on site, shims, screws, and installation labor. Any cabinet that is 5'6" or taller is considered a full-height cabinet. Includes shims, backing, attachment hardware and cutting the cabinet to fit site conditions.

| | Craft@Hrs | Unit | Material | Labor | Total |
|---|---|---|---|---|---|
| replace, economy grade | 2I@.593 | lf | 214.00 | 28.00 | 242.00 |
| replace, standard grade | 2I@.593 | lf | 268.00 | 28.00 | 296.00 |
| replace, high grade | 2I@.593 | lf | 329.00 | 28.00 | 357.00 |
| replace, deluxe grade | 2I@.593 | lf | 418.00 | 28.00 | 446.00 |
| replace, custom grade | 2I@.593 | lf | 458.00 | 28.00 | 486.00 |
| replace, custom deluxe grade | 2I@.593 | lf | 514.00 | 28.00 | 542.00 |
| remove | 1D@.331 | lf | — | 12.90 | 12.90 |
| remove for work, then reinstall | 2I@.706 | lf | — | 33.40 | 33.40 |

|  | Craft@Hrs | Unit | Material | Labor | Total |
|---|---|---|---|---|---|

**Full-height built-in oven cabinet.** Includes prefabricated, prefinished full-height cabinet assembled in shop or on site, shims, screws, and installation labor. Any cabinet that is 5'6" or taller is considered a full-height cabinet. Includes shims, backing, attachment hardware and cutting the cabinet to fit site conditions.

|  | Craft@Hrs | Unit | Material | Labor | Total |
|---|---|---|---|---|---|
| replace, economy grade | 2I@.592 | lf | 203.00 | 28.00 | 231.00 |
| replace, standard grade | 2I@.592 | lf | 255.00 | 28.00 | 283.00 |
| replace, high grade | 2I@.592 | lf | 311.00 | 28.00 | 339.00 |
| replace, deluxe grade | 2I@.592 | lf | 399.00 | 28.00 | 427.00 |
| replace, custom grade | 2I@.592 | lf | 435.00 | 28.00 | 463.00 |
| replace, custom deluxe grade | 2I@.592 | lf | 488.00 | 28.00 | 516.00 |
| remove | 1D@.331 | lf | — | 12.90 | 12.90 |
| remove for work, then reinstall | 2I@.706 | lf | — | 33.40 | 33.40 |

**Full-height built-in double oven cabinet.** Includes prefabricated, pre-finished full-height cabinet assembled in shop or on site, shims, screws, and installation labor. Any cabinet that is 5'6" or taller is considered a full-height cabinet. Includes shims, backing, attachment hardware and cutting the cabinet to fit site conditions.

|  | Craft@Hrs | Unit | Material | Labor | Total |
|---|---|---|---|---|---|
| replace, economy grade | 2I@.592 | lf | 196.00 | 28.00 | 224.00 |
| replace, standard grade | 2I@.592 | lf | 246.00 | 28.00 | 274.00 |
| replace, high grade | 2I@.592 | lf | 300.00 | 28.00 | 328.00 |
| replace, deluxe grade | 2I@.592 | lf | 384.00 | 28.00 | 412.00 |
| replace, custom grade | 2I@.592 | lf | 421.00 | 28.00 | 449.00 |
| replace, custom deluxe grade | 2I@.592 | lf | 471.00 | 28.00 | 499.00 |
| remove | 1D@.331 | lf | — | 12.90 | 12.90 |
| remove for work, then reinstall | 2I@.706 | lf | — | 33.40 | 33.40 |

**Cabinet drawer fronts.** Includes drawer front and attachment screws only. Front is attached to existing drawer frame. Does not include staining, painting, or finishing to match.

|  | Craft@Hrs | Unit | Material | Labor | Total |
|---|---|---|---|---|---|
| replace, drawer front | 2I@.118 | ea | 17.20 | 5.58 | 22.78 |
| remove | 1D@.144 | ea | — | 5.60 | 5.60 |

*flat panel*

*raised panel*

*raised panel cathedral*

*with leaded glass*

**Cabinet doors.** Includes cabinet door only, milled to attach to existing hardware. Does not include staining, painting, or finishing to match.

|  | Craft@Hrs | Unit | Material | Labor | Total |
|---|---|---|---|---|---|
| replace, flush-face | 2I@.252 | ea | 21.00 | 11.90 | 32.90 |
| replace, flat panel | 2I@.252 | ea | 29.30 | 11.90 | 41.20 |
| replace, raised panel | 2I@.252 | ea | 43.50 | 11.90 | 55.40 |
| replace, raised panel cathedral | 2I@.252 | ea | 55.20 | 11.90 | 67.10 |
| replace, with glass | 2I@.252 | ea | 66.80 | 11.90 | 78.70 |
| replace, with leaded glass | 2I@.252 | ea | 134.00 | 11.90 | 145.90 |
| remove | 1D@.267 | ea | — | 10.40 | 10.40 |

|  | Craft@Hrs | Unit | Material | Labor | Total |
|---|---|---|---|---|---|

**Refinish cabinets.** Cabinets are stripped and restained. Edge surfaces that are finished with 1/4" hardwood plywood are replaced.

| Replace only | | | | | |
|---|---|---|---|---|---|
| cabinet drawer front | 5F@.219 | ea | 1.88 | 12.10 | 13.98 |
| cabinet door | 5F@.513 | ea | 4.24 | 28.30 | 32.54 |
| cabinet door with glass | 5F@.516 | ea | 1.99 | 28.40 | 30.39 |
| cabinets & doors, reface plywood ends | 5F@1.13 | lf | 16.60 | 62.30 | 78.90 |
| island cabinets and doors, | | | | | |
|     reface plywood ends and faces | 5F@1.47 | lf | 17.60 | 81.00 | 98.60 |

**Cabinet repair.** Gouge or hole is filled, then "grained" by the painter to look like natural wood grain, matched to the finish of the cabinets.

| Replace only | | | | | |
|---|---|---|---|---|---|
| repair gouge or hole in cabinet, | | | | | |
|     grain patch to match | 5F@1.19 | ea | 8.21 | 65.60 | 73.81 |

**Plastic laminate countertop.** Includes plastic laminate, medium-density fiberboard core, glue, and installation labor. Flat-laid countertops can be fabricated on site. Post-formed countertops are formed in shop. Flat-laid tops include a plastic-laminate backsplash up to 6" tall glued to the wall with the top and side edges finished with aluminum trim. Post-formed backsplashes are built in. Most commonly known by the trade name "Formica". Add **6%** for installation on bathroom vanity. Post-formed countertops have integrated backsplash with a rounded cove transition. Flat-laid countertops butt into wall with a flat edge.

| replace, post-formed | 2I@.286 | sf | 4.69 | 13.50 | 18.19 |
|---|---|---|---|---|---|
| replace, flat-laid | 2I@.309 | sf | 4.58 | 14.60 | 19.18 |
| remove | 1D@.132 | sf | — | 5.13 | 5.13 |

**Cultured marble countertop.** Includes prefabricated cultured marble countertop and installation labor. Poured to custom size in shop and transported to site. Sometimes large pieces are joined on site. Includes built-in or separate backsplash up to four inches tall. Add **6%** for installation on bathroom vanity.

| replace | 2I@.314 | sf | 21.00 | 14.90 | 35.90 |
|---|---|---|---|---|---|
| remove | 1D@.132 | sf | — | 5.13 | 5.13 |
| add for integrated sink | — | ea | 184.00 | — | 184.00 |

**Cultured granite countertop.** Includes prefabricated cultured granite countertop and installation labor. Poured to custom size in shop and transported to site. Sometimes large pieces are joined on site. Includes built-in or separate backsplash up to four inches tall. Add **6%** for installation on bathroom vanity.

| replace | 2I@.314 | sf | 28.30 | 14.90 | 43.20 |
|---|---|---|---|---|---|
| remove | 1D@.132 | sf | — | 5.13 | 5.13 |
| add for integrated sink | — | ea | 234.00 | — | 234.00 |

**Cultured onyx countertop.** Includes prefabricated cultured onyx countertop and installation labor. Poured to custom size in shop and transported to site. Sometimes large pieces are joined on site. Includes built-in or separate backsplash up to four inches tall. Add **6%** for installation on bathroom vanity.

| replace | 2I@.314 | sf | 28.30 | 14.90 | 43.20 |
|---|---|---|---|---|---|
| remove | 1D@.132 | sf | — | 5.13 | 5.13 |
| add for integrated sink | — | ea | 227.00 | — | 227.00 |

**Solid-surface countertop.** Includes custom-poured solid-surface countertop and installation labor. Some assembly of the custom-built sections on site is often necessary. Includes solid-surface backsplash. Commonly known by the trade name Corian. Other trade names include Avonite, Surell, Gibraltar, and Fountainhead. Add **9%** for installation on bathroom vanity. The following features vary with the countertop's grade: color options, alternating color layering, use of wood strip / pattern inlays and complexity of edge detail.

| replace, economy grade | 2I@.331 | sf | 129.00 | 15.70 | 144.70 |
|---|---|---|---|---|---|
| replace, standard grade | 2I@.331 | sf | 186.00 | 15.70 | 201.70 |
| replace, high grade | 2I@.331 | sf | 258.00 | 15.70 | 273.70 |

|  | Craft@Hrs | Unit | Material | Labor | Total |
|---|---|---|---|---|---|
| replace, deluxe grade | 2I@.331 | sf | 314.00 | 15.70 | 329.70 |
| replace, custom grade | 2I@.331 | sf | 349.00 | 15.70 | 364.70 |
| remove countertop | 1D@.132 | sf | — | 5.13 | 5.13 |

**Granite countertop.** Includes polished, filled and sealed natural granite countertop cut to fit site conditions, and installation labor. Heavy sections are joined on site. Add **6%** for installation on bathroom vanity.

|  | Craft@Hrs | Unit | Material | Labor | Total |
|---|---|---|---|---|---|
| replace | 2I@.414 | sf | 200.00 | 19.60 | 219.60 |
| remove | 1D@.132 | sf | — | 5.13 | 5.13 |

**Stainless steel countertop.** Includes custom-formed stainless steel countertop with integrated backsplash and installation labor.

|  | Craft@Hrs | Unit | Material | Labor | Total |
|---|---|---|---|---|---|
| replace | 2I@.378 | sf | 31.80 | 17.90 | 49.70 |
| remove | 1D@.132 | sf | — | 5.13 | 5.13 |

**Butcher-block countertop.** Includes prefabricated and prefinished butcher-block countertop with hardware, glue, caulk, screws, and installation labor. Assembly on site or in shop. Some onsite cutting to fit is included. Includes prefinished hardwood or similar backsplash, typically 1/2" to 5/8" thick and up to 6" tall. Add **6%** for installation on bathroom vanity.

|  | Craft@Hrs | Unit | Material | Labor | Total |
|---|---|---|---|---|---|
| replace | 2I@.314 | sf | 28.30 | 14.90 | 43.20 |
| remove | 1D@.132 | sf | — | 5.13 | 5.13 |

**Solid wood maple or oak countertop.** Includes prefabricated and prefinished solid-wood countertop with hardware, glue, caulk, screws, and installation labor. Assembly on site or in shop. Some onsite cutting to fit is included. Includes prefinished hardwood or similar backsplash, typically 1/2" to 5/8" thick and up to 6" tall. Add **6%** for installation on bathroom vanity.

|  | Craft@Hrs | Unit | Material | Labor | Total |
|---|---|---|---|---|---|
| replace | 2I@.292 | sf | 9.73 | 13.80 | 23.53 |
| remove | 1D@.132 | sf | — | 5.13 | 5.13 |
| remove for work, then reinstall | 2I@.447 | sf | — | 21.10 | 21.10 |

**Tile countertop.** Includes tile, mortar, grout, sealer, and installation labor. Tile is thinset over cement backerboard except for deluxe grade which is set over a full mortar bed. Also includes edge tile and tile backsplash. Add **6%** for installation on bathroom vanity. For all grades except deluxe the tile is set in a thinset mortar bed over cement backerboard.

|  | Craft@Hrs | Unit | Material | Labor | Total |
|---|---|---|---|---|---|
| replace, economy grade tile | 1T@.222 | sf | 15.20 | 12.00 | 27.20 |
| replace, standard grade tile | 1T@.222 | sf | 22.30 | 12.00 | 34.30 |
| replace, high grade tile | 1T@.222 | sf | 28.30 | 12.00 | 40.30 |
| replace, deluxe grade tile | 1T@.222 | sf | 44.60 | 12.00 | 56.60 |
| remove | 1D@.229 | sf | — | 8.91 | 8.91 |

**Repair tile countertop.** Includes selective hand removal of a single tile without damaging surrounding tiles, scraping and removal of old mortar, placement of a new tile, mortar, and grout. Matching tile color is usually not possible unless an original tile is available.

|  | Craft@Hrs | Unit | Material | Labor | Total |
|---|---|---|---|---|---|
| replace tile to match | 1T@.813 | ea | 37.50 | 43.90 | 81.40 |
| reaffix loose tile | 1T@.553 | ea | 23.50 | 29.90 | 53.40 |
| minimum charge for tile countertop work | 1T@1.96 | ea | 25.80 | 106.00 | 131.80 |

**Bathroom vanity cabinet.** Includes prefabricated, prefinished bathroom vanity assembled in shop or on site, shims, screws, backing, attachment hardware, and installation labor. Installation includes cutting the cabinet to match plumbing, wall shape, and other site conditions.

|  | Craft@Hrs | Unit | Material | Labor | Total |
|---|---|---|---|---|---|
| replace, economy grade | 2I@.371 | lf | 88.00 | 17.50 | 105.50 |
| replace, standard grade | 2I@.371 | lf | 111.00 | 17.50 | 128.50 |
| replace, high grade | 2I@.371 | lf | 144.00 | 17.50 | 161.50 |
| replace, deluxe grade | 2I@.371 | lf | 202.00 | 17.50 | 219.50 |
| replace, custom grade | 2I@.371 | lf | 288.00 | 17.50 | 305.50 |
| replace, deluxe grade | 2I@.371 | lf | 373.00 | 17.50 | 390.50 |
| remove | 1D@.270 | lf | — | 10.50 | 10.50 |
| remove for work, then reinstall | 2I@.653 | lf | — | 30.90 | 30.90 |

## Time & Material Charts (selected items)
## Cabinet Materials

See Cabinet material prices above.

### Cabinet Labor

| Laborer | base wage | paid leave | true wage | taxes & ins. | total |
|---|---|---|---|---|---|
| Cabinet installer | $31.10 | 2.43 | $33.53 | 23.37 | $56.90 |
| Painter | $30.60 | 2.39 | $32.99 | 22.11 | $55.10 |
| Tile layer | $29.00 | 2.26 | $31.26 | 22.74 | $54.00 |
| Laborer | $19.60 | 1.53 | $21.13 | 16.57 | $37.70 |
| Demolition laborer | $20.70 | 1.61 | $22.31 | 16.59 | $38.90 |

**Paid leave** is calculated based on two weeks paid vacation, one week sick leave, and seven paid holidays. Employer's matching portion of **FICA** is 7.65 percent. **FUTA** (Federal Unemployment) is .8 percent. **Worker's compensation** was calculated using a national average of 16.96 percent for the cabinet installer and helper; 14.20 percent for the painter; and 19.00 percent for the tile layer. **Unemployment insurance** was calculated using a national average of 8 percent. **Health insurance** was calculated based on a projected national average for 2015 of $1,025 per employee (and family when applicable) per month. Employer pays 80 percent for a per month cost of $820 per employee. **Retirement** is based on a 401(k) retirement program with employer matching of 50 percent. Employee contributions to the 401(k) plan are an average of 6 percent of the true wage. **Liability insurance** is based on a national average of 10.0 percent.

### Cabinet crew

| | | |
|---|---|---|
| install cabinets & countertop | cabinet installer | $56.90 |
| install cabinets & countertop | laborer | $37.70 |
| cabinet installation | crew | $47.30 |

| | Craft@Hrs | Unit | Material | Labor | Total |
|---|---|---|---|---|---|
| **Cabinet Labor Productivity** | | | | | |
| Install kitchen cabinets | | | | | |
| lower kitchen cabinets | 2I@.360 | lf | — | 17.00 | 17.00 |
| upper kitchen cabinets | 2I@.349 | lf | — | 16.50 | 16.50 |
| lower kitchen island cabinets | 2I@.371 | lf | — | 17.50 | 17.50 |
| upper kitchen island cabinets | 2I@.359 | lf | — | 17.00 | 17.00 |
| full-height cabinet | 2I@.593 | lf | — | 28.00 | 28.00 |
| Install cabinet drawer fronts & doors | | | | | |
| drawer front | 2I@.118 | ea | — | 5.58 | 5.58 |
| door | 2I@.252 | ea | — | 11.90 | 11.90 |
| Refinish cabinets | | | | | |
| cabinet drawer front | 5F@.219 | ea | — | 12.10 | 12.10 |
| cabinet door | 5F@.513 | ea | — | 28.30 | 28.30 |
| cabinet door with glass | 5F@.516 | ea | — | 28.40 | 28.40 |
| cabinets & doors, reface plywood ends | 5F@1.13 | lf | — | 62.30 | 62.30 |
| island cabinets & doors, reface plywood ends & faces | 5F@1.47 | lf | — | 81.00 | 81.00 |
| Cabinet repair | | | | | |
| repair gouge or hole in cabinet, grain to match | 5F@1.19 | ea | — | 65.60 | 65.60 |

| | Craft@Hrs | Unit | Material | Labor | Total |
|---|---|---|---|---|---|
| Install countertop | | | | | |
| post-formed plastic laminate | 2I@.286 | sf | — | 13.50 | 13.50 |
| flat-laid plastic laminate | 2I@.309 | sf | — | 14.60 | 14.60 |
| cultured material | 2I@.314 | sf | — | 14.90 | 14.90 |
| solid-surface | 2I@.331 | sf | — | 15.70 | 15.70 |
| granite | 2I@.414 | sf | — | 19.60 | 19.60 |
| stainless-steel | 2I@.378 | sf | — | 17.90 | 17.90 |
| butcher block | 2I@.314 | sf | — | 14.90 | 14.90 |
| solid wood | 2I@.292 | sf | — | 13.80 | 13.80 |
| tile (ceramic) | 1T@.222 | sf | — | 12.00 | 12.00 |
| Install bathroom vanity cabinet | | | | | |
| bathroom vanity cabinet | 2I@.371 | lf | — | 17.50 | 17.50 |

# Cleaning

Unless otherwise noted, all cleaning prices are for items typically smoke-stained. For lightly stained items deduct **10%**. For heavily stained items add 15%.

### Minimum charge.

| | Craft@Hrs | Unit | Material | Labor | Total |
|---|---|---|---|---|---|
| for cleaning work | 1B@1.80 | ea | 2.31 | 59.90 | 62.21 |

### Acoustic tile.

| | Craft@Hrs | Unit | Material | Labor | Total |
|---|---|---|---|---|---|
| clean acoustic ceiling tiles | 1B@.014 | sf | .02 | .47 | .49 |

### Appliances.

| | Craft@Hrs | Unit | Material | Labor | Total |
|---|---|---|---|---|---|
| clean cook top | 1B@.876 | ea | 1.04 | 29.20 | 30.24 |
| clean range | 1B@1.54 | ea | 1.85 | 51.30 | 53.15 |
| clean space-saver range | 1B@1.45 | ea | 1.74 | 48.30 | 50.04 |
| clean high-low range | 1B@2.02 | ea | 2.42 | 67.30 | 69.72 |
| clean restaurant-style gas range | 1B@2.11 | ea | 2.55 | 70.30 | 72.85 |
| clean wall oven | 1B@1.27 | ea | 1.50 | 42.30 | 43.80 |
| clean double wall oven | 1B@2.11 | ea | 2.55 | 70.30 | 72.85 |
| clean modular electric cook top unit | 1B@.440 | ea | .60 | 14.70 | 15.30 |
| clean drop-in or slide-in range | 1B@1.40 | ea | 1.74 | 46.60 | 48.34 |
| clean range hood | 1B@.428 | ea | .46 | 14.30 | 14.76 |
| clean oversize range hood | 1B@.455 | ea | .60 | 15.20 | 15.80 |
| clean dishwasher | 1B@1.00 | ea | 1.14 | 33.30 | 34.44 |
| clean microwave | 1B@.486 | ea | .60 | 16.20 | 16.80 |
| clean side-by-side refrigerator | 1B@1.80 | ea | 2.19 | 59.90 | 62.09 |
| clean over-under refrigerator | 1B@1.62 | ea | 1.96 | 53.90 | 55.86 |
| clean trash compactor | 1B@.561 | ea | .71 | 18.70 | 19.41 |
| clean clothes washing machine | 1B@.642 | ea | .82 | 21.40 | 22.22 |
| clean clothes dryer | 1B@.475 | ea | .60 | 15.80 | 16.40 |

### Awnings.

| | Craft@Hrs | Unit | Material | Labor | Total |
|---|---|---|---|---|---|
| clean aluminum or steel carport or patio cover | 1B@.019 | sf | .02 | .63 | .65 |
| clean aluminum or steel door or window awning | 1B@.193 | lf | .22 | 6.43 | 6.65 |

|  | Craft@Hrs | Unit | Material | Labor | Total |
|---|---|---|---|---|---|
| **Bathroom hardware.** | | | | | |
| clean complete bathroom, fixtures and hardware | 1B@4.01 | ea | 4.84 | 134.00 | 138.84 |
| clean complete 1/2 bath, fixtures and hardware | 1B@2.57 | ea | 3.12 | 85.60 | 88.72 |
| clean bathroom hardware (per piece) | 1B@.246 | ea | .28 | 8.19 | 8.47 |
| clean medicine cabinet | 1B@.570 | ea | .70 | 19.00 | 19.70 |
| clean bathroom mirror | 1B@.026 | sf | .03 | .87 | .90 |
| **Cabinets.** | | | | | |
| clean lower cabinets | 1B@.446 | lf | .56 | 14.90 | 15.46 |
| clean upper cabinets | 1B@.418 | lf | .53 | 13.90 | 14.43 |
| clean lower island cabinets | 1B@.455 | lf | .57 | 15.20 | 15.77 |
| clean upper island cabinets | 1B@.514 | lf | .64 | 17.10 | 17.74 |
| clean full-height cabinets | 1B@.747 | lf | .90 | 24.90 | 25.80 |
| **Countertops.** | | | | | |
| clean plastic laminate countertop | 1B@.035 | sf | .04 | 1.17 | 1.21 |
| clean cultured stone countertop | 1B@.038 | sf | .04 | 1.27 | 1.31 |
| clean solid-surface countertop | 1B@.039 | sf | .04 | 1.30 | 1.34 |
| clean granite countertop | 1B@.043 | sf | .04 | 1.43 | 1.47 |
| clean stainless steel countertop | 1B@.040 | sf | .04 | 1.33 | 1.37 |
| clean wood countertop (butcher block or solid) | 1B@.045 | sf | .05 | 1.50 | 1.55 |
| clean tile countertop | 1B@.062 | sf | .06 | 2.06 | 2.12 |
| clean bathroom vanity cabinet | 1B@.346 | lf | .38 | 11.50 | 11.88 |
| **Columns.** | | | | | |
| clean column | 1B@.158 | lf | .17 | 5.26 | 5.43 |
| clean pilaster | 1B@.087 | lf | .09 | 2.90 | 2.99 |
| clean capital | 1B@1.38 | ea | 1.68 | 46.00 | 47.68 |
| clean ornate capital (Corinthian) | 1B@2.46 | ea | 2.96 | 81.90 | 84.86 |
| clean column base | 1B@.856 | ea | 1.03 | 28.50 | 29.53 |
| clean pilaster base | 1B@.459 | ea | .58 | 15.30 | 15.88 |
| **Concrete.** | | | | | |
| clean wall | 1B@.014 | sf | .02 | .47 | .49 |
| clean floor | 1B@.012 | sf | .02 | .40 | .42 |
| clean step (per step) | 1B@.222 | lf | .25 | 7.39 | 7.64 |
| **Doors.** | | | | | |
| clean jamb and casing (per lf) | 1B@.020 | lf | .02 | .67 | .69 |
| clean jamb and casing (per door) | 1B@.349 | ea | .38 | 11.60 | 11.98 |
| clean folding door | 1B@.260 | ea | .29 | 8.66 | 8.95 |
| clean louvered folding door | 1B@.438 | ea | .56 | 14.60 | 15.16 |
| clean bypassing door | 1B@.462 | ea | .58 | 15.40 | 15.98 |
| clean louvered bypassing door | 1B@.623 | ea | .77 | 20.70 | 21.47 |
| clean French door | 1B@.817 | ea | .97 | 27.20 | 28.17 |
| clean standard flush door | 1B@.438 | ea | .56 | 14.60 | 15.16 |
| clean pocket door | 1B@.447 | ea | .57 | 14.90 | 15.47 |
| clean panel door | 1B@.459 | ea | .58 | 15.30 | 15.88 |
| clean transom | 1B@.230 | ea | .26 | 7.66 | 7.92 |
| clean batten door | 1B@.479 | ea | .60 | 16.00 | 16.60 |
| clean storm door | 1B@.454 | ea | .57 | 15.10 | 15.67 |

|  | Craft@Hrs | Unit | Material | Labor | Total |
|---|---|---|---|---|---|
| clean exterior door side lite | 1B@.370 | ea | .43 | 12.30 | 12.73 |
| clean Dutch door | 1B@.462 | ea | .58 | 15.40 | 15.98 |
| clean fan lite | 1B@.339 | ea | .37 | 11.30 | 11.67 |
| clean cafe doors | 1B@.352 | ea | .39 | 11.70 | 12.09 |

## Sliding patio doors.

|  | Craft@Hrs | Unit | Material | Labor | Total |
|---|---|---|---|---|---|
| clean 6' wide sliding patio door | 1B@1.06 | ea | 1.24 | 35.30 | 36.54 |
| clean 8' wide sliding patio door | 1B@1.20 | ea | 1.39 | 40.00 | 41.39 |
| clean 12' wide sliding patio door | 1B@1.38 | ea | 1.63 | 46.00 | 47.63 |

## Garage doors.

|  | Craft@Hrs | Unit | Material | Labor | Total |
|---|---|---|---|---|---|
| clean 8' wide garage door | 1B@1.56 | ea | 1.85 | 51.90 | 53.75 |
| clean 9' wide garage door | 1B@1.65 | ea | 1.96 | 54.90 | 56.86 |
| clean 10' wide garage door | 1B@1.74 | ea | 2.06 | 57.90 | 59.96 |
| clean 12' wide garage door | 1B@1.83 | ea | 2.19 | 60.90 | 63.09 |
| clean 14' wide garage door | 1B@1.93 | ea | 2.31 | 64.30 | 66.61 |
| clean 16' wide garage door | 1B@2.04 | ea | 2.42 | 67.90 | 70.32 |
| clean 18' wide garage door | 1B@2.16 | ea | 2.55 | 71.90 | 74.45 |
| clean garage door opener | 1B@.965 | ea | 1.14 | 32.10 | 33.24 |

## Drywall or plaster.

|  | Craft@Hrs | Unit | Material | Labor | Total |
|---|---|---|---|---|---|
| clean wall | 1B@.013 | sf | .02 | .43 | .45 |
| clean ceiling | 1B@.014 | sf | .01 | .47 | .48 |
| clean ceiling acoustic texture | 1B@.017 | sf | .01 | .57 | .58 |

## Electrical.

|  | Craft@Hrs | Unit | Material | Labor | Total |
|---|---|---|---|---|---|
| clean outlet or switch | 1B@.084 | ea | .09 | 2.80 | 2.89 |
| clean breaker panel | 1B@.693 | ea | .84 | 23.10 | 23.94 |
| clean circuit breaker | 1B@.227 | ea | .26 | 7.56 | 7.82 |
| clean door bell or chime button | 1B@.034 | ea | .04 | 1.13 | 1.17 |
| clean bathroom exhaust fan | 1B@.290 | ea | .32 | 9.66 | 9.98 |
| clean bathroom exhaust fan with heat lamp | 1B@.321 | ea | .35 | 10.70 | 11.05 |
| clean kitchen exhaust fan | 1B@.299 | ea | .33 | 9.96 | 10.29 |
| clean whole-house exhaust fan | 1B@.352 | ea | .39 | 11.70 | 12.09 |
| clean intercom system station | 1B@.193 | ea | .22 | 6.43 | 6.65 |
| clean detector | 1B@.185 | ea | .21 | 6.16 | 6.37 |
| clean thermostat | 1B@.211 | ea | .24 | 7.03 | 7.27 |

## Light fixtures.

|  | Craft@Hrs | Unit | Material | Labor | Total |
|---|---|---|---|---|---|
| clean light fixture | 1B@.447 | ea | .57 | 14.90 | 15.47 |
| clean bathroom light bar (per light) | 1B@.160 | ea | .19 | 5.33 | 5.52 |
| clean chandelier, typical detail | 1B@1.28 | ea | 1.57 | 42.60 | 44.17 |
| clean chandelier, ornate detail | 1B@2.00 | ea | 2.42 | 66.60 | 69.02 |
| clean chandelier, very ornate detail | 1B@2.99 | ea | 3.57 | 99.60 | 103.17 |
| clean crystal chandelier, typical detail | 1B@4.47 | ea | 5.42 | 149.00 | 154.42 |
| clean crystal chandelier, ornate detail | 1B@5.80 | ea | 6.98 | 193.00 | 199.98 |
| clean crystal chandelier, very ornate detail | 1B@7.82 | ea | 9.35 | 260.00 | 269.35 |
| clean fluorescent light fixture | 1B@.518 | ea | .66 | 17.20 | 17.86 |
| clean ceiling fan | 1B@.580 | ea | .71 | 19.30 | 20.01 |
| clean ceiling fan with light | 1B@.686 | ea | .82 | 22.80 | 23.62 |
| clean recessed spot light fixture | 1B@.392 | ea | .46 | 13.10 | 13.56 |

| | Craft@Hrs | Unit | Material | Labor | Total |
|---|---|---|---|---|---|
| clean strip light (per spot) | 1B@.195 | ea | .22 | 6.49 | 6.71 |
| clean exterior flood light fixture (per spot) | 1B@.207 | ea | .24 | 6.89 | 7.13 |
| clean exterior light fixture | 1B@.486 | ea | .60 | 16.20 | 16.80 |
| clean exterior post light fixture | 1B@.580 | ea | .71 | 19.30 | 20.01 |

**Fencing.**

| | Craft@Hrs | Unit | Material | Labor | Total |
|---|---|---|---|---|---|
| clean 4' high wood fence | 1B@.064 | lf | .07 | 2.13 | 2.20 |
| clean 6' high wood fence | 1B@.078 | lf | .08 | 2.60 | 2.68 |
| clean 8' high wood fence | 1B@.100 | lf | .10 | 3.33 | 3.43 |
| clean 4' high chain-link fence | 1B@.044 | lf | .05 | 1.47 | 1.52 |
| clean 6' high chain-link fence | 1B@.050 | lf | .05 | 1.67 | 1.72 |
| clean 8' high chain-link fence | 1B@.058 | lf | .06 | 1.93 | 1.99 |
| clean 4' high vinyl fence | 1B@.056 | lf | .06 | 1.86 | 1.92 |
| clean 6' high vinyl fence | 1B@.067 | lf | .07 | 2.23 | 2.30 |
| clean 8' high vinyl fence | 1B@.082 | lf | .09 | 2.73 | 2.82 |
| clean 60" high ornamental iron fence | 1B@.078 | lf | .08 | 2.60 | 2.68 |
| clean 72" high ornamental iron fence | 1B@.069 | lf | .07 | 2.30 | 2.37 |

**Finish carpentry.**

| | Craft@Hrs | Unit | Material | Labor | Total |
|---|---|---|---|---|---|
| clean molding | 1B@.015 | lf | .02 | .50 | .52 |
| clean interior wood architrave | 1B@.037 | lf | .04 | 1.23 | 1.27 |
| clean exterior wood architrave | 1B@.042 | lf | .04 | 1.40 | 1.44 |
| clean exterior door surround | 1B@.082 | lf | .09 | 2.73 | 2.82 |
| clean exterior window surround | 1B@.072 | lf | .07 | 2.40 | 2.47 |
| clean closet shelf and brackets | 1B@.038 | lf | .04 | 1.27 | 1.31 |
| clean closet organizer | 1B@.030 | sf | .03 | 1.00 | 1.03 |
| clean linen closet shelves | 1B@.036 | sf | .04 | 1.20 | 1.24 |
| clean closet rod | 1B@.020 | lf | .02 | .67 | .69 |
| clean bookcase | 1B@.029 | sf | .03 | .97 | 1.00 |
| clean fireplace mantel | 1B@.977 | ea | 1.16 | 32.50 | 33.66 |
| clean ceiling with exposed beams | 1B@.028 | sf | .03 | .93 | .96 |
| clean coffered ceiling | 1B@.037 | sf | .04 | 1.23 | 1.27 |
| clean wall niche | 1B@.227 | ea | .26 | 7.56 | 7.82 |
| clean gingerbread trim | 1B@.025 | lf | .03 | .83 | .86 |
| clean gingerbread bracket | 1B@.193 | ea | .22 | 6.43 | 6.65 |
| clean gingerbread corbel | 1B@.214 | ea | .24 | 7.13 | 7.37 |
| clean gingerbread spandrel | 1B@.193 | lf | .22 | 6.43 | 6.65 |
| clean gingerbread cornice | 1B@.171 | lf | .20 | 5.69 | 5.89 |
| clean gingerbread gable ornament | 1B@.440 | ea | .56 | 14.70 | 15.26 |
| clean gingerbread finial | 1B@.359 | ea | .39 | 12.00 | 12.39 |
| clean porch post | 1B@.042 | lf | .04 | 1.40 | 1.44 |

**Fireplaces.**

| | Craft@Hrs | Unit | Material | Labor | Total |
|---|---|---|---|---|---|
| clean screen | 1B@1.12 | ea | 1.32 | 37.30 | 38.62 |
| clean door | 1B@1.06 | ea | 1.24 | 35.30 | 36.54 |
| clean marble face | 1B@.047 | sf | .05 | 1.57 | 1.62 |
| clean brick face | 1B@.054 | sf | .06 | 1.80 | 1.86 |
| clean stone face | 1B@.058 | sf | .06 | 1.93 | 1.99 |
| clean tile face | 1B@.056 | sf | .06 | 1.86 | 1.92 |
| clean marble hearth | 1B@.095 | lf | .10 | 3.16 | 3.26 |
| clean brick hearth | 1B@.106 | lf | .11 | 3.53 | 3.64 |
| clean stone hearth | 1B@.112 | lf | .12 | 3.73 | 3.85 |
| clean tile hearth | 1B@.106 | lf | .11 | 3.53 | 3.64 |

| | Craft@Hrs | Unit | Material | Labor | Total |
|---|---|---|---|---|---|
| **Flooring.** | | | | | |
| clean carpet | 1B@.008 | sf | .01 | .27 | .28 |
| clean wool carpet | 1B@.013 | sf | .01 | .43 | .44 |
| clean carpet cove | 1B@.018 | lf | .02 | .60 | .62 |
| add per step for carpet cleaning | 1B@.155 | ea | .17 | 5.16 | 5.33 |
| clean stone floor | 1B@.009 | sf | .01 | .30 | .31 |
| clean tile floor | 1B@.008 | sf | .01 | .27 | .28 |
| clean tile base | 1B@.010 | lf | .01 | .33 | .34 |
| clean and wax vinyl floor | 1B@.009 | sf | .01 | .30 | .31 |
| clean vinyl cove | 1B@.010 | lf | .01 | .33 | .34 |
| clean and wax wood floor | 1B@.011 | sf | .01 | .37 | .38 |
| **HVAC.** | | | | | |
| clean and deodorize ducts (per lf of duct) | 1B@.156 | lf | .17 | 5.19 | 5.36 |
| clean furnace | 1B@2.95 | ea | 3.51 | 98.20 | 101.71 |
| clean heat pump | 1B@1.28 | ea | 1.57 | 42.60 | 44.17 |
| clean humidifier | 1B@.946 | ea | 1.14 | 31.50 | 32.64 |
| clean through-wall AC unit | 1B@1.12 | ea | 1.32 | 37.30 | 38.62 |
| clean evaporative cooler | 1B@1.38 | ea | 1.69 | 46.00 | 47.69 |
| clean evaporative cooler grille | 1B@.250 | ea | .28 | 8.33 | 8.61 |
| clean heat register | 1B@.240 | ea | .27 | 7.99 | 8.26 |
| clean cold-air return cover | 1B@.243 | ea | .27 | 8.09 | 8.36 |
| **Masonry.** | | | | | |
| clean brick wall | 1B@.025 | sf | .03 | .83 | .86 |
| clean block wall | 1B@.023 | sf | .02 | .77 | .79 |
| clean slump block wall | 1B@.025 | sf | .03 | .83 | .86 |
| clean fluted block wall | 1B@.029 | sf | .03 | .97 | 1.00 |
| clean glazed block wall | 1B@.028 | sf | .03 | .93 | .96 |
| clean split-face block wall | 1B@.032 | sf | .03 | 1.07 | 1.10 |
| clean split-rib block wall | 1B@.030 | sf | .03 | 1.00 | 1.03 |
| clean stone wall | 1B@.033 | sf | .03 | 1.10 | 1.13 |
| clean glazed structural tile wall | 1B@.024 | sf | .02 | .80 | .82 |
| clean glass block wall | 1B@.024 | sf | .02 | .80 | .82 |
| clean pavers | 1B@.025 | sf | .03 | .83 | .86 |
| clean stone veneer panels | 1B@.025 | sf | .03 | .83 | .86 |
| clean cultured stone veneer panels | 1B@.025 | sf | .03 | .83 | .86 |
| clean stone architrave | 1B@.045 | lf | .05 | 1.50 | 1.55 |
| clean stone trim stones | 1B@.040 | lf | .04 | 1.33 | 1.37 |
| **Paneling.** | | | | | |
| clean wood paneling | 1B@.017 | sf | .02 | .57 | .59 |
| clean wood paneling with moldings or onlays | 1B@.021 | sf | .02 | .70 | .72 |
| clean panel wall | 1B@.035 | sf | .04 | 1.17 | 1.21 |
| clean pegboard | 1B@.018 | sf | .02 | .60 | .62 |
| clean rough-sawn wood paneling | 1B@.023 | sf | .02 | .77 | .79 |
| **Stucco.** | | | | | |
| clean stucco | 1B@.024 | sf | .02 | .80 | .82 |
| clean stucco architrave | 1B@.046 | lf | .05 | 1.53 | 1.58 |
| clean tongue-and-groove paneling | 1B@.020 | sf | .02 | .67 | .69 |

| | Craft@Hrs | Unit | Material | Labor | Total |
|---|---|---|---|---|---|

**Plaster.**  (See Drywall heading in this section for costs to clean interior plaster walls.)

| | Craft@Hrs | Unit | Material | Labor | Total |
|---|---|---|---|---|---|
| clean plaster molding | 1B@.035 | lf | .04 | 1.17 | 1.21 |
| clean plaster architrave | 1B@.042 | lf | .04 | 1.40 | 1.44 |
| clean ceiling medallion | 1B@.556 | ea | .69 | 18.50 | 19.19 |
| clean ceiling rose | 1B@.946 | ea | 1.12 | 31.50 | 32.62 |

**Plumbing.**

| | Craft@Hrs | Unit | Material | Labor | Total |
|---|---|---|---|---|---|
| clean sink faucet | 1B@.475 | ea | .59 | 15.80 | 16.39 |
| clean shower faucet and head | 1B@.580 | ea | .71 | 19.30 | 20.01 |
| clean tub faucet | 1B@.499 | ea | .63 | 16.60 | 17.23 |
| clean tub faucet and shower head | 1B@.620 | ea | .76 | 20.60 | 21.36 |
| clean wet bar sink | 1B@.391 | ea | .48 | 13.00 | 13.48 |
| clean bathroom sink | 1B@.418 | ea | .53 | 13.90 | 14.43 |
| clean kitchen sink, per bowl | 1B@.428 | ea | .53 | 14.30 | 14.83 |
| clean laundry sink, per bowl | 1B@.447 | ea | .57 | 14.90 | 15.47 |
| clean visible sink supply lines | 1B@.257 | ea | .29 | 8.56 | 8.85 |
| clean toilet | 1B@.665 | ea | .81 | 22.10 | 22.91 |
| clean bidet | 1B@.693 | ea | .84 | 23.10 | 23.94 |
| clean toilet seat | 1B@.180 | ea | .21 | 5.99 | 6.20 |
| clean porcelain enamel finish tub | 1B@1.00 | ea | 1.18 | 33.30 | 34.48 |
| clean porcelain enamel finish tub with whirlpool jets | 1B@1.28 | ea | 1.57 | 42.60 | 44.17 |
| clean fiberglass finish tub | 1B@1.20 | ea | 1.45 | 40.00 | 41.45 |
| clean fiberglass finish tub with whirlpool jets | 1B@1.63 | ea | 1.96 | 54.30 | 56.26 |
| clean tub and shower combination | 1B@1.63 | ea | 1.96 | 54.30 | 56.26 |
| clean fiberglass or metal shower stall | 1B@1.17 | ea | 1.39 | 39.00 | 40.39 |
| clean glass shower stall | 1B@1.47 | ea | 1.80 | 49.00 | 50.80 |
| clean tub surround | 1B@.545 | ea | .66 | 18.10 | 18.76 |
| clean shower door | 1B@.879 | ea | 1.04 | 29.30 | 30.34 |
| clean sliding glass tub door | 1B@1.18 | ea | 1.45 | 39.30 | 40.75 |
| clean folding plastic bathtub door | 1B@1.20 | ea | 1.45 | 40.00 | 41.45 |
| clean water heater | 1B@.946 | ea | 1.14 | 31.50 | 32.64 |
| clean claw-foot tub faucet | 1B@.498 | ea | .60 | 16.60 | 17.20 |
| clean claw-foot tub faucet and shower conversion | 1B@.681 | ea | .82 | 22.70 | 23.52 |
| clean free-standing water feeds | 1B@.284 | ea | .32 | 9.46 | 9.78 |
| clean pedestal sink | 1B@.513 | ea | .66 | 17.10 | 17.76 |
| clean pill-box toilet | 1B@.817 | ea | .97 | 27.20 | 28.17 |
| clean low-tank toilet | 1B@1.06 | ea | 1.24 | 35.30 | 36.54 |
| clean high-tank toilet | 1B@1.38 | ea | 1.69 | 46.00 | 47.69 |
| clean antique tub | 1B@1.17 | ea | 1.39 | 39.00 | 40.39 |

**Siding.**

| | Craft@Hrs | Unit | Material | Labor | Total |
|---|---|---|---|---|---|
| clean fiberglass corrugated siding | 1B@.014 | sf | .02 | .47 | .49 |
| clean aluminum or vinyl siding | 1B@.015 | sf | .02 | .50 | .52 |
| clean wood lap siding | 1B@.015 | sf | .02 | .50 | .52 |
| clean vertical wood siding (board-on-board, etc.) | 1B@.015 | sf | .02 | .50 | .52 |
| clean cement fiber shingle siding | 1B@.017 | sf | .02 | .57 | .59 |
| clean shake or wood shingle siding | 1B@.019 | sf | .02 | .63 | .65 |
| clean hardboard or plywood siding | 1B@.015 | sf | .02 | .50 | .52 |

| | Craft@Hrs | Unit | Material | Labor | Total |
|---|---|---|---|---|---|
| clean tongue-and-groove siding | 1B@.016 | sf | .02 | .53 | .55 |
| clean metal or vinyl fascia | 1B@.016 | sf | .02 | .53 | .55 |
| clean wood fascia | 1B@.016 | sf | .02 | .53 | .55 |
| clean metal or vinyl soffit | 1B@.014 | sf | .01 | .47 | .48 |
| clean wood soffit | 1B@.015 | sf | .02 | .50 | .52 |
| clean rough-sawn wood soffit | 1B@.018 | sf | .02 | .60 | .62 |
| clean shutter | 1B@.359 | ea | .39 | 12.00 | 12.39 |

## Stairs.

| | Craft@Hrs | Unit | Material | Labor | Total |
|---|---|---|---|---|---|
| clean wood stair tread | 1B@.163 | ea | .19 | 5.43 | 5.62 |
| clean spiral stair balustrade | 1B@.113 | lf | .12 | 3.76 | 3.88 |
| clean stair balustrade | 1B@.114 | lf | .12 | 3.80 | 3.92 |
| clean disappearing attic stair | 1B@2.40 | ea | 2.88 | 79.90 | 82.78 |
| clean stair bracket | 1B@.310 | ea | .34 | 10.30 | 10.64 |

## Suspended ceiling.

| | Craft@Hrs | Unit | Material | Labor | Total |
|---|---|---|---|---|---|
| clean suspended ceiling grid | 1B@.010 | sf | .02 | .33 | .35 |

## Tile. (See Cabinet heading in this section for costs to clean tile countertops. See Flooring heading for costs to clean tile floors and base.)

| | Craft@Hrs | Unit | Material | Labor | Total |
|---|---|---|---|---|---|
| clean tile shower | 1B@1.38 | ea | 1.69 | 46.00 | 47.69 |
| clean tile tub surround | 1B@1.80 | ea | 2.12 | 59.90 | 62.02 |

## Wallpaper.

| | Craft@Hrs | Unit | Material | Labor | Total |
|---|---|---|---|---|---|
| clean vinyl wallpaper | 1B@.015 | sf | .02 | .50 | .52 |
| clean paper wallpaper | 1B@.017 | sf | .02 | .57 | .59 |
| clean grass or rice cloth wallpaper | 1B@.025 | sf | .03 | .83 | .86 |

## Windows.

| | Craft@Hrs | Unit | Material | Labor | Total |
|---|---|---|---|---|---|
| clean window to 8 sf | 1B@.408 | ea | .49 | 13.60 | 14.09 |
| clean window 9 to 14 sf | 1B@.475 | ea | .59 | 15.80 | 16.39 |
| clean window 15 to 20 sf | 1B@.580 | ea | .71 | 19.30 | 20.01 |
| clean window 21 to 30 sf | 1B@.856 | ea | 1.03 | 28.50 | 29.53 |
| clean window, per sf | 1B@.030 | sf | .03 | 1.00 | 1.03 |
| clean skylight to 8 sf | 1B@.428 | ea | .53 | 14.30 | 14.83 |
| clean skylight 9 to 14 sf | 1B@.498 | ea | .63 | 16.60 | 17.23 |
| clean skylight 15 to 20 sf | 1B@.619 | ea | .76 | 20.60 | 21.36 |
| clean skylight 21 to 30 sf | 1B@.899 | ea | 1.07 | 29.90 | 30.97 |
| clean skylight per sf | 1B@.032 | sf | .03 | 1.07 | 1.10 |
| add to clean multiple, small panes | — | % | — | 15.0 | — |

## Mirrors. (Also see Bathroom Hardware heading in this section for costs to clean other bathroom mirrors.)

| | Craft@Hrs | Unit | Material | Labor | Total |
|---|---|---|---|---|---|
| clean wall mirror | 1B@.027 | sf | .03 | .90 | .93 |

## Final construction clean-up.

| | Craft@Hrs | Unit | Material | Labor | Total |
|---|---|---|---|---|---|
| broom clean | 1B@.002 | sf | .02 | .07 | .09 |

## Time & Material Charts (selected items)
## Cleaning Materials

See Cleaning material prices above.

### Cleaning Labor

| Laborer | base wage | paid leave | true wage | taxes & ins. | total |
|---|---|---|---|---|---|
| Cleaning laborer | $17.80 | 1.39 | $19.19 | 14.11 | $33.30 |

**Paid leave** is calculated based on two weeks paid vacation, one week sick leave, and seven paid holidays. Employer's matching portion of **FICA** is 7.65 percent. **FUTA** (Federal Unemployment) is .8 percent. **Worker's compensation** for the cleaning trade was calculated using a national average of 9.04 percent. **Unemployment insurance** was calculated using a national average of 8 percent. **Health insurance** was calculated based on a projected national average for 2015 of $1,025 per employee (and family when applicable) per month. Employer pays 80 percent for a per month cost of $820 per employee. **Retirement** is based on a 401(k) retirement program with employer matching of 50 percent. Employee contributions to the 401(k) plan are an average of 6 percent of the true wage. **Liability insurance** is based on a national average of 10.0 percent.

### Cleaning Labor Productivity

| | Craft@Hrs | Unit | Material | Labor | Total |
|---|---|---|---|---|---|
| Clean appliances | | | | | |
| cook top | 1B@.876 | ea | — | 29.20 | 29.20 |
| range | 1B@1.54 | ea | — | 51.30 | 51.30 |
| wall oven | 1B@1.27 | ea | — | 42.30 | 42.30 |
| range hood | 1B@.428 | ea | — | 14.30 | 14.30 |
| dishwasher | 1B@1.00 | ea | — | 33.30 | 33.30 |
| microwave | 1B@.486 | ea | — | 16.20 | 16.20 |
| side-by-side refrigerator | 1B@1.80 | ea | — | 59.90 | 59.90 |
| over-under refrigerator | 1B@1.62 | ea | — | 53.90 | 53.90 |
| trash compactor | 1B@.561 | ea | — | 18.70 | 18.70 |
| Clean awnings | | | | | |
| aluminum or steel carport or patio | 1B@.019 | sf | — | .63 | .63 |
| aluminum or steel door or window awning | 1B@.193 | lf | — | 6.43 | 6.43 |
| Clean bathroom hardware | | | | | |
| bathroom hardware (per piece) | 1B@.246 | ea | — | 8.19 | 8.19 |
| medicine cabinet | 1B@.570 | ea | — | 19.00 | 19.00 |
| Clean cabinets | | | | | |
| lower cabinets | 1B@.446 | lf | — | 14.90 | 14.90 |
| upper cabinets | 1B@.418 | lf | — | 13.90 | 13.90 |
| full-height cabinets | 1B@.747 | lf | — | 24.90 | 24.90 |
| plastic laminate countertop | 1B@.035 | sf | — | 1.17 | 1.17 |
| tile countertop | 1B@.062 | sf | — | 2.06 | 2.06 |
| Clean concrete | | | | | |
| wall | 1B@.014 | sf | — | .47 | .47 |
| floor | 1B@.012 | sf | — | .40 | .40 |

| | Craft@Hrs | Unit | Material | Labor | Total |
|---|---|---|---|---|---|
| **Clean door** | | | | | |
| folding door (per section) | 1B@.260 | ea | — | 8.66 | 8.66 |
| bypassing door | 1B@.462 | ea | — | 15.40 | 15.40 |
| door | 1B@.438 | ea | — | 14.60 | 14.60 |
| storm door | 1B@.454 | ea | — | 15.10 | 15.10 |
| **Clean drywall or plaster** | | | | | |
| wall | 1B@.013 | sf | — | .43 | .43 |
| ceiling | 1B@.014 | sf | — | .47 | .47 |
| ceiling acoustic texture | 1B@.017 | sf | — | .57 | .57 |
| **Clean electrical** | | | | | |
| light fixture | 1B@.447 | ea | — | 14.90 | 14.90 |
| bathroom light bar (per light) | 1B@.160 | ea | — | 5.33 | 5.33 |
| chandelier, typical detail | 1B@1.28 | ea | — | 42.60 | 42.60 |
| fluorescent light fixture | 1B@.518 | ea | — | 17.20 | 17.20 |
| ceiling fan | 1B@.580 | ea | — | 19.30 | 19.30 |
| ceiling fan with light | 1B@.686 | ea | — | 22.80 | 22.80 |
| **Clean fence** | | | | | |
| 4' high wood | 1B@.064 | lf | — | 2.13 | 2.13 |
| 4' high chain-link | 1B@.044 | lf | — | 1.47 | 1.47 |
| 4' high vinyl | 1B@.056 | lf | — | 1.86 | 1.86 |
| 60" high ornamental iron | 1B@.078 | lf | — | 2.60 | 2.60 |
| **Clean finish carpentry** | | | | | |
| molding | 1B@.015 | lf | — | .50 | .50 |
| **Clean fireplace** | | | | | |
| screen | 1B@1.12 | ea | — | 37.30 | 37.30 |
| door | 1B@1.06 | ea | — | 35.30 | 35.30 |
| **Clean flooring** | | | | | |
| carpet | 1B@.008 | sf | — | .27 | .27 |
| stone floor | 1B@.009 | sf | — | .30 | .30 |
| tile floor | 1B@.008 | sf | — | .27 | .27 |
| vinyl floor and wax | 1B@.009 | sf | — | .30 | .30 |
| wood floor and wax | 1B@.011 | sf | — | .37 | .37 |
| **Clean HVAC** | | | | | |
| furnace | 1B@2.95 | ea | — | 98.20 | 98.20 |
| through-wall AC unit | 1B@1.12 | ea | — | 37.30 | 37.30 |
| evaporative cooler | 1B@1.38 | ea | — | 46.00 | 46.00 |
| **Clean masonry** | | | | | |
| brick wall | 1B@.025 | sf | — | .83 | .83 |
| block wall | 1B@.023 | sf | — | .77 | .77 |
| stone wall | 1B@.033 | sf | — | 1.10 | 1.10 |
| glass block wall | 1B@.024 | sf | — | .80 | .80 |
| stone veneer panels | 1B@.025 | sf | — | .83 | .83 |
| **Clean paneling** | | | | | |
| wood paneling | 1B@.017 | sf | — | .57 | .57 |
| wood paneling with moldings or onlays | 1B@.021 | sf | — | .70 | .70 |
| panel wall | 1B@.035 | sf | — | 1.17 | 1.17 |
| rough-sawn wood paneling | 1B@.023 | sf | — | .77 | .77 |
| tongue-and-groove paneling | 1B@.020 | sf | — | .67 | .67 |

| | Craft@Hrs | Unit | Material | Labor | Total |
|---|---|---|---|---|---|
| **Clean plaster** (also see Drywall heading in this section) | | | | | |
| stucco | 1B@.024 | sf | — | .80 | .80 |
| **Clean plumbing** | | | | | |
| sink faucet | 1B@.475 | ea | — | 15.80 | 15.80 |
| tub faucet | 1B@.499 | ea | — | 16.60 | 16.60 |
| tub faucet and shower head | 1B@.620 | ea | — | 20.60 | 20.60 |
| bathroom sink | 1B@.418 | ea | — | 13.90 | 13.90 |
| kitchen sink, per bowl | 1B@.428 | ea | — | 14.30 | 14.30 |
| laundry sink, per bowl | 1B@.447 | ea | — | 14.90 | 14.90 |
| toilet | 1B@.665 | ea | — | 22.10 | 22.10 |
| bidet | 1B@.693 | ea | — | 23.10 | 23.10 |
| porcelain-enamel finish bathtub | 1B@1.00 | ea | — | 33.30 | 33.30 |
| fiberglass finish bathtub | 1B@1.20 | ea | — | 40.00 | 40.00 |
| tub and shower combination | 1B@1.63 | ea | — | 54.30 | 54.30 |
| fiberglass or metal shower stall | 1B@1.17 | ea | — | 39.00 | 39.00 |
| glass shower stall | 1B@1.47 | ea | — | 49.00 | 49.00 |
| tub surround | 1B@.545 | ea | — | 18.10 | 18.10 |
| shower door | 1B@.879 | ea | — | 29.30 | 29.30 |
| sliding glass bathtub door | 1B@1.18 | ea | — | 39.30 | 39.30 |
| pedestal sink | 1B@.513 | ea | — | 17.10 | 17.10 |
| pill-box toilet | 1B@.817 | ea | — | 27.20 | 27.20 |
| **Clean siding** | | | | | |
| fiberglass corrugated | 1B@.014 | sf | — | .47 | .47 |
| metal or vinyl siding | 1B@.015 | sf | — | .50 | .50 |
| wood lap siding | 1B@.015 | sf | — | .50 | .50 |
| vertical wood siding (board-on-board, etc.) | 1B@.015 | sf | — | .50 | .50 |
| cement fiber shingle siding | 1B@.017 | sf | — | .57 | .57 |
| shake or wood shingle siding | 1B@.019 | sf | — | .63 | .63 |
| plywood siding | 1B@.015 | sf | — | .50 | .50 |
| tongue-and-groove siding | 1B@.016 | sf | — | .53 | .53 |
| **Clean stairs** | | | | | |
| wood stair tread | 1B@.163 | ea | — | 5.43 | 5.43 |
| stair balustrade | 1B@.114 | lf | — | 3.80 | 3.80 |
| disappearing attic stair | 1B@2.40 | ea | — | 79.90 | 79.90 |
| **Clean tile** | | | | | |
| tile shower | 1B@1.38 | ea | — | 46.00 | 46.00 |
| tile bathtub surround | 1B@1.80 | ea | — | 59.90 | 59.90 |
| **Clean wallpaper** | | | | | |
| vinyl wallpaper | 1B@.015 | sf | — | .50 | .50 |
| paper wallpaper | 1B@.017 | sf | — | .57 | .57 |
| grass or rice cloth wallpaper | 1B@.025 | sf | — | .83 | .83 |
| **Clean window** | | | | | |
| window up to 8 sf | 1B@.408 | ea | — | 13.60 | 13.60 |
| window 21 to 30 sf | 1B@.856 | ea | — | 28.50 | 28.50 |
| window, per sf | 1B@.030 | ea | — | 1.00 | 1.00 |
| skylight up to 8 sf | 1B@.428 | ea | — | 14.30 | 14.30 |
| skylight 21 to 30 sf | 1B@.899 | ea | — | 29.90 | 29.90 |
| skylight per sf | 1B@.032 | ea | — | 1.07 | 1.07 |

|  | Craft@Hrs | Unit | Material | Labor | Total |
|---|---|---|---|---|---|

# Columns

**Column Materials.** Composite materials: A combination of marble (or similar material) polymers, and fiberglass or columns made from high-density polyurethane. Pine: Made from laminated staves of Douglas fir or Ponderosa pine. Redwood: Made from laminated staves of redwood. Oak: Made from laminated staves of red oak. Stone: Crushed and reconstructed limestone reinforced with glass fibers. Synthetic stone: Light-weight simulated stone which are either cement or gypsum-based fiberglass. Aluminum: Cast aluminum. Plaster: Made from fibrous plaster and gypsum products reinforced with fiberglass or jute, or steel or sisal for use on interior of structure. Stucco: Made from fibrous plaster products reinforced with fiberglass or jute or steel or sisal for use on exterior of structure.

## Minimum charge for columns.

|  | Craft@Hrs | Unit | Material | Labor | Total |
|---|---|---|---|---|---|
| for column or pilaster work | 1C@1.25 | ea | 47.30 | 71.10 | 118.40 |

## 12" round columns. See Additional costs for columns and pilasters below to add for taper, fluting, and architecturally correct taper.

|  | Craft@Hrs | Unit | Material | Labor | Total |
|---|---|---|---|---|---|
| replace, composite materials | 1C@.333 | lf | 50.90 | 18.90 | 69.80 |
| replace, pine | 1C@.333 | lf | 53.50 | 18.90 | 72.40 |
| replace, redwood | 1C@.333 | lf | 63.80 | 18.90 | 82.70 |
| replace, oak | 1C@.333 | lf | 117.00 | 18.90 | 135.90 |
| replace, stone | 1C@.333 | lf | 94.50 | 18.90 | 113.40 |
| replace, synthetic stone | 1C@.333 | lf | 88.30 | 18.90 | 107.20 |
| replace, aluminum | 1C@.333 | lf | 55.30 | 18.90 | 74.20 |
| replace, interior plaster | 1C@.333 | lf | 51.40 | 18.90 | 70.30 |
| replace, exterior stucco | 1C@.333 | lf | 49.80 | 18.90 | 68.70 |
| remove, all material types | 1D@.212 | lf | — | 8.25 | 8.25 |

## 12" round pilasters. Half-round with no taper. See Additional costs for columns and pilasters below to add for taper, fluting, and architecturally correct taper.

|  | Craft@Hrs | Unit | Material | Labor | Total |
|---|---|---|---|---|---|
| replace, composite materials | 1C@.292 | lf | 32.30 | 16.60 | 48.90 |
| replace, pine | 1C@.292 | lf | 34.10 | 16.60 | 50.70 |
| replace, redwood | 1C@.292 | lf | 40.80 | 16.60 | 57.40 |
| replace, oak | 1C@.292 | lf | 75.50 | 16.60 | 92.10 |
| replace, stone | 1C@.292 | lf | 60.20 | 16.60 | 76.80 |
| replace, synthetic stone | 1C@.292 | lf | 56.40 | 16.60 | 73.00 |
| replace, aluminum | 1C@.292 | lf | 35.50 | 16.60 | 52.10 |
| replace, interior plaster | 1C@.292 | lf | 32.60 | 16.60 | 49.20 |
| replace, exterior stucco | 1C@.292 | lf | 31.80 | 16.60 | 48.40 |
| remove, all material types | 1D@.134 | lf | — | 5.21 | 5.21 |

## Additional column and pilaster costs.

|  | Craft@Hrs | Unit | Material | Labor | Total |
|---|---|---|---|---|---|
| add for round fluted column or pilaster | — | % | 18.0 | — | — |
| add for tapered column or pilaster consistent taper from bottom to top | — | % | 13.0 | — | — |
| add for architecturally correct tapered column or pilaster | — | % | 65.0 | — | — |

|  | Craft@Hrs | Unit | Material | Labor | Total |
|---|---|---|---|---|---|
| **12" square column.** | | | | | |
| replace, composite materials | 1C@.308 | lf | 67.00 | 17.50 | 84.50 |
| replace, pine | 1C@.308 | lf | 70.30 | 17.50 | 87.80 |
| replace, redwood | 1C@.308 | lf | 84.10 | 17.50 | 101.60 |
| replace, oak | 1C@.308 | lf | 158.00 | 17.50 | 175.50 |
| replace, stone | 1C@.308 | lf | 125.00 | 17.50 | 142.50 |
| replace, synthetic stone | 1C@.308 | lf | 116.00 | 17.50 | 133.50 |
| replace, aluminum | 1C@.308 | lf | 73.10 | 17.50 | 90.60 |
| replace, interior plaster | 1C@.308 | lf | 68.00 | 17.50 | 85.50 |
| exterior stucco | 1C@.308 | lf | 65.90 | 17.50 | 83.40 |
| remove, all material types | 1D@.212 | lf | — | 8.25 | 8.25 |
| **12" square pilaster.** | | | | | |
| replace, composite materials | 1C@.269 | lf | 42.50 | 15.30 | 57.80 |
| replace, pine | 1C@.269 | lf | 45.20 | 15.30 | 60.50 |
| replace, redwood | 1C@.269 | lf | 53.90 | 15.30 | 69.20 |
| replace, oak | 1C@.269 | lf | 99.60 | 15.30 | 114.90 |
| replace, stone | 1C@.269 | lf | 79.40 | 15.30 | 94.70 |
| replace, synthetic stone | 1C@.269 | lf | 74.70 | 15.30 | 90.00 |
| replace, aluminum | 1C@.269 | lf | 46.80 | 15.30 | 62.10 |
| replace, interior plaster | 1C@.269 | lf | 43.20 | 15.30 | 58.50 |
| replace, exterior stucco | 1C@.269 | lf | 41.90 | 15.30 | 57.20 |
| remove, all material types | 1D@.134 | lf | — | 5.21 | 5.21 |
| **Column and pilaster repair.** | | | | | |
| repair, wood column with wood patch | 1C@.706 | ea | 4.39 | 40.20 | 44.59 |
| repair, fluted wood column with wood patch | 1C@.863 | ea | 4.39 | 49.10 | 53.49 |
| repair, wood column by replacing section | 1C@1.94 | ea | 7.83 | 110.00 | 117.83 |
| repair, fluted wood column by replacing section | 1C@2.59 | ea | 9.73 | 147.00 | 156.73 |
| repair, dry rot in wood column with epoxy | 1C@2.74 | ea | 7.83 | 156.00 | 163.83 |
| repair, dry rot in fluted wood column with epoxy | 1C@3.24 | ea | 7.83 | 184.00 | 191.83 |
| add for column repair if column is removed from structure, includes temporary brace wall and column removal | 1C@9.31 | ea | 78.30 | 530.00 | 608.30 |
| repair, minimum charge | 1C@2.33 | ea | 21.40 | 133.00 | 154.40 |
| **Contemporary capital.** Capital up to 4" high.  Includes load-bearing plug. | | | | | |
| replace, composite materials | 1C@.566 | ea | 195.00 | 32.20 | 227.20 |
| replace, pine | 1C@.566 | ea | 222.00 | 32.20 | 254.20 |
| replace, redwood | 1C@.566 | ea | 257.00 | 32.20 | 289.20 |
| replace, oak | 1C@.566 | ea | 493.00 | 32.20 | 525.20 |
| replace, stone | 1C@.566 | ea | 392.00 | 32.20 | 424.20 |
| replace, synthetic stone | 1C@.566 | ea | 364.00 | 32.20 | 396.20 |
| replace, aluminum | 1C@.566 | ea | 227.00 | 32.20 | 259.20 |
| replace, interior plaster | 1C@.566 | ea | 210.00 | 32.20 | 242.20 |
| replace, exterior stucco | 1C@.566 | ea | 206.00 | 32.20 | 238.20 |
| remove, all material types | 1D@.850 | ea | — | 33.10 | 33.10 |

| | Craft@Hrs | Unit | Material | Labor | Total |
|---|---|---|---|---|---|

**Corinthian capital.** Capital up to 14" high. Includes load-bearing plug.

| | Craft@Hrs | Unit | Material | Labor | Total |
|---|---|---|---|---|---|
| replace, composite materials | 1C@.566 | ea | 593.00 | 32.20 | 625.20 |
| replace, pine | 1C@.566 | ea | 1,050.00 | 32.20 | 1,082.20 |
| replace, redwood | 1C@.566 | ea | 1,190.00 | 32.20 | 1,222.20 |
| replace, oak | 1C@.566 | ea | 2,340.00 | 32.20 | 2,372.20 |
| replace, stone | 1C@.566 | ea | 790.00 | 32.20 | 822.20 |
| replace, synthetic stone | 1C@.566 | ea | 734.00 | 32.20 | 766.20 |
| replace, aluminum | 1C@.566 | ea | 459.00 | 32.20 | 491.20 |
| replace, interior plaster | 1C@.566 | ea | 426.00 | 32.20 | 458.20 |
| replace, exterior stucco | 1C@.566 | ea | 415.00 | 32.20 | 447.20 |
| remove, all material types | 1D@.850 | ea | — | 33.10 | 33.10 |

**Doric or Tuscan capital.** Capital up to 4" high. Includes load-bearing plug.

| | Craft@Hrs | Unit | Material | Labor | Total |
|---|---|---|---|---|---|
| replace, composite materials | 1C@.566 | ea | 202.00 | 32.20 | 234.20 |
| replace, pine | 1C@.566 | ea | 230.00 | 32.20 | 262.20 |
| replace, redwood | 1C@.566 | ea | 266.00 | 32.20 | 298.20 |
| replace, oak | 1C@.566 | ea | 512.00 | 32.20 | 544.20 |
| replace, stone | 1C@.566 | ea | 408.00 | 32.20 | 440.20 |
| replace, synthetic stone | 1C@.566 | ea | 377.00 | 32.20 | 409.20 |
| replace, aluminum | 1C@.566 | ea | 235.00 | 32.20 | 267.20 |
| replace, interior plaster | 1C@.566 | ea | 218.00 | 32.20 | 250.20 |
| replace, exterior stucco | 1C@.566 | ea | 210.00 | 32.20 | 242.20 |
| remove, all material types | 1D@.850 | ea | — | 33.10 | 33.10 |

**Empire capital.** Capital up to 7" high. Includes load-bearing plug.

| | Craft@Hrs | Unit | Material | Labor | Total |
|---|---|---|---|---|---|
| replace, composite materials | 1C@.566 | ea | 377.00 | 32.20 | 409.20 |
| replace, pine | 1C@.566 | ea | 671.00 | 32.20 | 703.20 |
| replace, redwood | 1C@.566 | ea | 774.00 | 32.20 | 806.20 |
| replace, oak | 1C@.566 | ea | 1,470.00 | 32.20 | 1,502.20 |
| replace, stone | 1C@.566 | ea | 505.00 | 32.20 | 537.20 |
| replace, synthetic stone | 1C@.566 | ea | 468.00 | 32.20 | 500.20 |
| replace, aluminum | 1C@.566 | ea | 292.00 | 32.20 | 324.20 |
| replace, interior plaster | 1C@.566 | ea | 269.00 | 32.20 | 301.20 |
| replace, exterior stucco | 1C@.566 | ea | 264.00 | 32.20 | 296.20 |
| remove, all material types | 1D@.850 | ea | — | 33.10 | 33.10 |

**Erechtheum capital.** Capital up to 7" high. Add **50%** for necking. Includes load-bearing plug.

| | Craft@Hrs | Unit | Material | Labor | Total |
|---|---|---|---|---|---|
| replace, composite materials | 1C@.566 | ea | 367.00 | 32.20 | 399.20 |
| replace, pine | 1C@.566 | ea | 653.00 | 32.20 | 685.20 |
| replace, redwood | 1C@.566 | ea | 749.00 | 32.20 | 781.20 |
| replace, oak | 1C@.566 | ea | 1,410.00 | 32.20 | 1,442.20 |
| replace, stone | 1C@.566 | ea | 487.00 | 32.20 | 519.20 |
| replace, synthetic stone | 1C@.566 | ea | 455.00 | 32.20 | 487.20 |
| replace, aluminum | 1C@.566 | ea | 284.00 | 32.20 | 316.20 |
| replace, interior plaster | 1C@.566 | ea | 264.00 | 32.20 | 296.20 |
| replace, exterior stucco | 1C@.566 | ea | 256.00 | 32.20 | 288.20 |
| remove, all material types | 1D@.850 | ea | — | 33.10 | 33.10 |

| | Craft@Hrs | Unit | Material | Labor | Total |
|---|---|---|---|---|---|

**Roman Ionic capital.** Capital up to 5" high. Includes load-bearing plug.

| | Craft@Hrs | Unit | Material | Labor | Total |
|---|---|---|---|---|---|
| replace, composite materials | 1C@.566 | ea | 381.00 | 32.20 | 413.20 |
| replace, pine | 1C@.566 | ea | 679.00 | 32.20 | 711.20 |
| replace, redwood | 1C@.566 | ea | 782.00 | 32.20 | 814.20 |
| replace, oak | 1C@.566 | ea | 1,510.00 | 32.20 | 1,542.20 |
| replace, stone | 1C@.566 | ea | 510.00 | 32.20 | 542.20 |
| replace, synthetic stone | 1C@.566 | ea | 472.00 | 32.20 | 504.20 |
| replace, aluminum | 1C@.566 | ea | 296.00 | 32.20 | 328.20 |
| replace, interior plaster | 1C@.566 | ea | 273.00 | 32.20 | 305.20 |
| replace, exterior stucco | 1C@.566 | ea | 266.00 | 32.20 | 298.20 |
| remove, all material types | 1D@.850 | ea | — | 33.10 | 33.10 |

**Scamozzi capital.** Capital up to 5" high. Includes load-bearing plug.

| | Craft@Hrs | Unit | Material | Labor | Total |
|---|---|---|---|---|---|
| replace, composite materials | 1C@.566 | ea | 403.00 | 32.20 | 435.20 |
| replace, pine | 1C@.566 | ea | 712.00 | 32.20 | 744.20 |
| replace, redwood | 1C@.566 | ea | 820.00 | 32.20 | 852.20 |
| replace, oak | 1C@.566 | ea | 1,580.00 | 32.20 | 1,612.20 |
| replace, stone | 1C@.566 | ea | 536.00 | 32.20 | 568.20 |
| replace, synthetic stone | 1C@.566 | ea | 495.00 | 32.20 | 527.20 |
| replace, aluminum | 1C@.566 | ea | 308.00 | 32.20 | 340.20 |
| replace, interior plaster | 1C@.566 | ea | 289.00 | 32.20 | 321.20 |
| replace, exterior stucco | 1C@.566 | ea | 282.00 | 32.20 | 314.20 |
| remove, all material types | 1D@.850 | ea | — | 33.10 | 33.10 |

**Temple-of-the-Winds capital.** Capital up to 12" high. Includes load-bearing plug.

| | Craft@Hrs | Unit | Material | Labor | Total |
|---|---|---|---|---|---|
| replace, composite materials | 1C@.566 | ea | 461.00 | 32.20 | 493.20 |
| replace, pine | 1C@.566 | ea | 814.00 | 32.20 | 846.20 |
| replace, redwood | 1C@.566 | ea | 937.00 | 32.20 | 969.20 |
| replace, oak | 1C@.566 | ea | 1,810.00 | 32.20 | 1,842.20 |
| replace, stone | 1C@.566 | ea | 611.00 | 32.20 | 643.20 |
| replace, synthetic stone | 1C@.566 | ea | 569.00 | 32.20 | 601.20 |
| replace, aluminum | 1C@.566 | ea | 354.00 | 32.20 | 386.20 |
| replace, interior plaster | 1C@.566 | ea | 329.00 | 32.20 | 361.20 |
| replace, exterior stucco | 1C@.566 | ea | 319.00 | 32.20 | 351.20 |
| remove, all material types | 1D@.850 | ea | — | 33.10 | 33.10 |

**Capital repair.**

| | Craft@Hrs | Unit | Material | Labor | Total |
|---|---|---|---|---|---|
| repair, wood capital with wood patch | 1C@1.06 | ea | 3.45 | 60.30 | 63.75 |
| repair, wood capital by replacing section | 1C@3.89 | ea | 30.80 | 221.00 | 251.80 |
| repair, dry rot in wood capital with epoxy | 1C@2.08 | ea | 3.45 | 118.00 | 121.45 |
| minimum charge, all material types | 1C@2.91 | ea | 37.80 | 166.00 | 203.80 |

**Additional column and pilaster sizes.** Add or deduct from the costs for 12" columns, pilasters, capitals and bases. (Bases are built to hold columns of the size indicated.)

| | Craft@Hrs | Unit | Material | Labor | Total |
|---|---|---|---|---|---|
| add for spiral column or pilaster | — | % | 78.0 | — | — |
| column, pilaster, capital, or base | | | | | |
| deduct for 6" diameter | — | % | - 45.0 | — | — |
| deduct for 8" diameter | — | % | - 35.0 | — | — |
| deduct for 10" diameter | — | % | - 17.0 | — | — |

| | Craft@Hrs | Unit | Material | Labor | Total |
|---|---|---|---|---|---|
| add for 14" diameter | — | % | 59.0 | — | — |
| add for 16" diameter | — | % | 81.0 | — | — |
| add for 18" diameter | — | % | 115.0 | — | — |
| add for 20" diameter | — | % | 185.0 | — | — |

## Column base.

| | Craft@Hrs | Unit | Material | Labor | Total |
|---|---|---|---|---|---|
| replace, composite materials | 1C@.566 | ea | 59.20 | 32.20 | 91.40 |
| replace, pine | 1C@.566 | ea | 62.80 | 32.20 | 95.00 |
| replace, redwood | 1C@.566 | ea | 74.70 | 32.20 | 106.90 |
| replace, oak | 1C@.566 | ea | 136.00 | 32.20 | 168.20 |
| replace, stone | 1C@.566 | ea | 110.00 | 32.20 | 142.20 |
| replace, synthetic stone | 1C@.566 | ea | 103.00 | 32.20 | 135.20 |
| replace, aluminum | 1C@.566 | ea | 65.30 | 32.20 | 97.50 |
| replace, interior plaster | 1C@.566 | ea | 60.40 | 32.20 | 92.60 |
| replace, exterior stucco | 1C@.566 | ea | 58.00 | 32.20 | 90.20 |
| remove column or pilaster base | 1D@.785 | ea | — | 30.50 | 30.50 |

*standard*          *high*          *deluxe*          *custom*

## Column pedestal. Pedestal framed with 2" x 4" up to 3' high. Outside trimmed with paint-grade pine or poplar. Moldings around top of pedestal and bottom. Grades above standard have panel moldings of increasingly complex design on all four sides.

| | Craft@Hrs | Unit | Material | Labor | Total |
|---|---|---|---|---|---|
| replace, standard grade | 1C@8.48 | ea | 222.00 | 483.00 | 705.00 |
| replace, high grade | 1C@9.40 | ea | 295.00 | 535.00 | 830.00 |
| replace, deluxe grade | 1C@10.6 | ea | 436.00 | 603.00 | 1,039.00 |
| replace, custom grade | 1C@11.7 | ea | 513.00 | 666.00 | 1,179.00 |
| remove column pedestal | 1D@.410 | ea | — | 15.90 | 15.90 |

## Pilaster pedestal. Pedestal framed with 2" x 4" up to 3' high. Outside trimmed with paint-grade pine or poplar. Moldings around top of pedestal and bottom. Grades above standard have panel moldings of increasingly complex design on all four sides.

| | Craft@Hrs | Unit | Material | Labor | Total |
|---|---|---|---|---|---|
| replace, standard grade | 1C@6.00 | ea | 136.00 | 341.00 | 477.00 |
| replace, high grade | 1C@6.67 | ea | 179.00 | 380.00 | 559.00 |
| replace, deluxe grade | 1C@7.47 | ea | 264.00 | 425.00 | 689.00 |
| replace, custom grade | 1C@8.33 | ea | 309.00 | 474.00 | 783.00 |
| remove pilaster pedestal | 1D@.334 | ea | — | 13.00 | 13.00 |

## Add for other wood species.

| | Craft@Hrs | Unit | Material | Labor | Total |
|---|---|---|---|---|---|
| add for stain-grade redwood materials | — | % | 12.0 | — | — |
| add for mahogany materials | — | % | 16.0 | — | — |

| | Craft@Hrs | Unit | Material | Labor | Total |
|---|---|---|---|---|---|

**Time & Material Charts** (selected items)
**Columns Materials**

| | Craft@Hrs | Unit | Material | Labor | Total |
|---|---|---|---|---|---|
| Minimum materials charge for 8' column or pilaster work | — | ea | 48.40 | — | 48.40 |
| 12" round column | | | | | |
|     composite materials | — | ea | 416.00 | — | 416.00 |
|     pine | — | ea | 437.00 | — | 437.00 |
| 12" round pilaster | | | | | |
|     composite materials | — | ea | 264.00 | — | 264.00 |
|     pine | — | ea | 276.00 | — | 276.00 |
| 12" square column | | | | | |
|     composite materials | — | ea | 549.00 | — | 549.00 |
|     pine | — | ea | 576.00 | — | 576.00 |
| 12" square pilaster | | | | | |
|     composite materials | — | ea | 349.00 | — | 349.00 |
|     pine pilaster | — | ea | 370.00 | — | 370.00 |
| Contemporary capital | | | | | |
|     composite materials | — | ea | 199.00 | — | 199.00 |
|     pine | — | ea | 227.00 | — | 227.00 |
| Corinthian capital | | | | | |
|     composite materials | — | ea | 606.00 | — | 606.00 |
|     pine | — | ea | 1,080.00 | — | 1,080.00 |
| Doric or Tuscan capital | | | | | |
|     composite materials | — | ea | 206.00 | — | 206.00 |
|     pine | — | ea | 236.00 | — | 236.00 |
| Empire capital | | | | | |
|     composite materials | — | ea | 385.00 | — | 385.00 |
|     pine | — | ea | 687.00 | — | 687.00 |
| Erechtheum capital | | | | | |
|     composite materials | — | ea | 374.00 | — | 374.00 |
|     pine | — | ea | 667.00 | — | 667.00 |
| Roman Ionic capital | | | | | |
|     composite materials | — | ea | 390.00 | — | 390.00 |
|     pine | — | ea | 693.00 | — | 693.00 |
| Scamozzi capital | | | | | |
|     composite materials | — | ea | 412.00 | — | 412.00 |
|     pine | — | ea | 727.00 | — | 727.00 |
| Temple-of-the-Winds capital | | | | | |
|     composite materials | — | ea | 471.00 | — | 471.00 |
|     pine | — | ea | 830.00 | — | 830.00 |
| Column base | | | | | |
|     composite materials | — | ea | 60.50 | — | 60.50 |
|     pine | — | ea | 64.30 | — | 64.30 |
| Column pedestal | | | | | |
|     standard grade | — | ea | 227.00 | — | 227.00 |
|     custom grade | — | ea | 524.00 | — | 524.00 |
| Pilaster pedestal | | | | | |
|     standard grade | — | ea | 139.00 | — | 139.00 |
|     custom grade | — | ea | 315.00 | — | 315.00 |

## Columns Labor

| Laborer | base wage | paid leave | true wage | taxes & ins. | total |
|---|---|---|---|---|---|
| Carpenter | $31.10 | 2.43 | $33.58 | 23.37 | $56.90 |
| Demolition laborer | $20.70 | 1.61 | $22.31 | 16.59 | $38.90 |

**Paid leave** is calculated based on two weeks paid vacation, one week sick leave, and seven paid holidays. Employer's matching portion of **FICA** is 7.65 percent. **FUTA** (Federal Unemployment) is .8 percent. **Worker's compensation** for columns was calculated using a national average of 16.85 percent. **Unemployment insurance** was calculated using a national average of 8 percent. **Health insurance** was calculated based on a projected national average for 2015 of $1,025 per employee (and family when applicable) per month. Employer pays 80 percent for a per month cost of $820 per employee. **Retirement** is based on a 401(k) retirement program with employer matching of 50 percent. Employee contributions to the 401(k) plan are an average of 6 percent of the true wage. **Liability insurance** is based on a national average of 10.0 percent.

| | Craft@Hrs | Unit | Material | Labor | Total |
|---|---|---|---|---|---|
| **Columns Labor Productivity** | | | | | |
| Demolition | | | | | |
|     remove column | 1D@.212 | lf | — | 8.25 | 8.25 |
|     remove pilaster | 1D@.134 | lf | — | 5.21 | 5.21 |
|     remove column or pilaster capital | 1D@.850 | ea | — | 33.10 | 33.10 |
|     remove column or pilaster base | 1D@.785 | ea | — | 30.50 | 30.50 |
|     remove column pedestal | 1D@.410 | ea | — | 15.90 | 15.90 |
|     remove pilaster pedestal | 1D@.334 | ea | — | 13.00 | 13.00 |
| Install column | | | | | |
|     round | 1C@.333 | lf | — | 18.90 | 18.90 |
|     square | 1C@.308 | lf | — | 17.50 | 17.50 |
| Install pilaster | | | | | |
|     round | 1C@.292 | lf | — | 16.60 | 16.60 |
|     square | 1C@.269 | lf | — | 15.30 | 15.30 |
| Install capital | | | | | |
|     column or pilaster capital | 1C@.566 | ea | — | 32.20 | 32.20 |
| Install column or pilaster base | | | | | |
|     column or pilaster base | 1C@.566 | ea | — | 32.20 | 32.20 |
| Repair column or pilaster | | | | | |
|     round with wood patch | 1C@.706 | ea | — | 40.20 | 40.20 |
|     fluted with wood patch | 1C@.863 | ea | — | 49.10 | 49.10 |
|     round by replacing section | 1C@1.94 | ea | — | 110.00 | 110.00 |
|     fluted by replacing section | 1C@2.59 | ea | — | 147.00 | 147.00 |
|     round dry rot with epoxy | 1C@2.74 | ea | — | 156.00 | 156.00 |
|     fluted dry rot with epoxy | 1C@3.24 | ea | — | 184.00 | 184.00 |
|     minimum charge | 1C@2.33 | ea | — | 133.00 | 133.00 |
| Repair wood capital | | | | | |
|     with wood patch | 1C@1.06 | ea | — | 60.30 | 60.30 |
|     by replacing section | 1C@3.89 | ea | — | 221.00 | 221.00 |
|     dry rot with epoxy | 1C@2.08 | ea | — | 118.00 | 118.00 |
|     minimum charge | 1C@2.91 | ea | — | 166.00 | 166.00 |
| Build and install column pedestal | | | | | |
|     standard grade | 1C@8.48 | ea | — | 483.00 | 483.00 |
|     custom grade | 1C@11.7 | ea | — | 666.00 | 666.00 |
| Build and install pilaster pedestal | | | | | |
|     standard grade | 1C@6.00 | ea | — | 341.00 | 341.00 |
|     custom grade | 1C@8.33 | ea | — | 474.00 | 474.00 |

|  | Craft@Hrs | Unit | Material | Labor | Equip. | Total |
|---|---|---|---|---|---|---|

## Concrete

**CEC.** Items that include CEC in the description are priced according to California earthquake code requirements. Although these Uniform Building Code or similar standards are also required in other areas of the country, they are most commonly associated with efforts initiated in the State of California to improve the construction and engineering of structures in quake zones.

### Minimum charge.

| | Craft@Hrs | Unit | Material | Labor | Equip. | Total |
|---|---|---|---|---|---|---|
| for concrete repair work | 9F@2.47 | ea | 83.50 | 120.00 | — | 203.50 |

**Epoxy repair.** Includes epoxy, equipment, and installation. A pressure pot or similar device is used to inject epoxy into the crack. In structural settings the type of epoxy used must often be determined by an engineer and for long cracks core samples may be necessary to test the effectiveness of the repairs.

| | Craft@Hrs | Unit | Material | Labor | Equip. | Total |
|---|---|---|---|---|---|---|
| Concrete crack repair with pressurized epoxy injection, per linear foot | | | | | | |
| replace | 6F@.111 | lf | .92 | 6.04 | 2.05 | 9.01 |
| Minimum charge for pressurized epoxy injection concrete crack repair | | | | | | |
| replace | 6F@2.00 | ea | 87.20 | 109.00 | 127.00 | 323.20 |
| Concrete hole repair with epoxy system, per cubic inch of hole | | | | | | |
| replace | 6F@.053 | ci | .03 | 2.88 | — | 2.91 |
| Minimum charge for concrete hole repair with epoxy system | | | | | | |
| replace | 6F@.501 | ea | 78.60 | 27.30 | — | 105.90 |
| Concrete crack repair with caulking gun epoxy injection, per linear foot | | | | | | |
| replace | 6F@.025 | lf | .55 | 1.36 | — | 1.91 |
| Minimum charge for concrete crack repair with epoxy injection | | | | | | |
| replace | 6F@.501 | ea | 87.20 | 27.30 | — | 114.50 |
| Repair spalled concrete with concrete resurfacer, per square foot | | | | | | |
| replace | 6F@.009 | sf | 1.08 | .49 | — | 1.57 |
| Minimum charge to repair spalled concrete | | | | | | |
| replace | 6F@1.00 | ea | 52.30 | 54.40 | — | 106.70 |

**Footings.** Standard 16", 20", and 24" footings include three horizontal lengths of #4 rebar. Standard 32" footing includes four horizontal lengths of #4 rebar. CEC 16" and 20" footings include three horizontal lengths of #5 rebar. CEC 24" and 32" footings include four horizontal lengths of #5 rebar. Tie-in rebar from foundation wall bent continuously into footing is included in the foundation wall prices. Does not include excavation or grading. Includes covering to protect concrete from the weather as needed.

| | Craft@Hrs | Unit | Material | Labor | Equip. | Total |
|---|---|---|---|---|---|---|
| Concrete footings including rebar package and forming, per cubic yard | | | | | | |
| replace | 9F@2.44 | cy | 158.00 | 118.00 | — | 276.00 |
| remove | 1D@1.64 | cy | — | 63.80 | 79.10 | 142.90 |
| Concrete footings including CEC rebar package and forming, per cubic yard | | | | | | |
| replace | 9F@2.94 | cy | 191.00 | 143.00 | — | 334.00 |
| remove | 1D@1.96 | cy | — | 76.20 | 131.00 | 207.20 |

| | Craft@Hrs | Unit | Material | Labor | Equip. | Total |
|---|---|---|---|---|---|---|
| 16" wide by 10" deep concrete footings with rebar, per linear foot | | | | | | |
| replace | 9F@.150 | lf | 6.86 | 7.28 | — | 14.14 |
| remove | 1D@.121 | lf | — | 4.71 | 4.08 | 8.79 |
| 16" wide by 10" deep concrete footings with CEC rebar, per linear foot | | | | | | |
| replace | 9F@.180 | lf | 8.78 | 8.73 | — | 17.51 |
| remove | 1D@.147 | lf | — | 5.72 | 4.95 | 10.67 |
| 20" wide by 10" deep concrete footings with rebar, per linear foot | | | | | | |
| replace | 9F@.159 | lf | 8.24 | 7.71 | — | 15.95 |
| remove | 1D@.121 | lf | — | 4.71 | 4.08 | 8.79 |
| 20" wide by 10" deep concrete footings with CEC rebar, per linear foot | | | | | | |
| replace | 9F@.190 | lf | 10.30 | 9.22 | — | 19.52 |
| remove | 1D@.147 | lf | — | 5.72 | 4.95 | 10.67 |
| 24" wide by 12" deep concrete footings with rebar, per linear foot | | | | | | |
| replace | 9F@.167 | lf | 11.70 | 8.10 | — | 19.80 |
| remove | 1D@.121 | lf | — | 4.71 | 4.08 | 8.79 |
| 24" wide by 12" deep concrete footings with CEC rebar, per linear foot | | | | | | |
| replace | 9F@.197 | lf | 14.00 | 9.55 | — | 23.55 |
| remove | 1D@.147 | lf | — | 5.72 | 4.95 | 10.67 |
| 32" wide by 14" deep concrete footings with rebar, per linear foot | | | | | | |
| replace | 9F@.177 | lf | 17.40 | 8.58 | — | 25.98 |
| remove | 1D@.121 | lf | — | 4.71 | 4.08 | 8.79 |
| 32" wide by 14" deep concrete footings with CEC rebar, per linear foot | | | | | | |
| replace | 9F@.207 | lf | 19.60 | 10.00 | — | 29.60 |
| remove | 1D@.147 | lf | — | 5.72 | 4.95 | 10.67 |
| Minimum charge for concrete footing work | | | | | | |
| replace | 9F@1.03 | ea | 62.10 | 50.00 | — | 112.10 |

**Foundation.** Includes concrete, forms, and installation. Installation is on top of footings with appropriate tie-in rebar, forming, pouring, and finishing concrete with J-bolts and straps. Includes covering to protect concrete from the weather as needed. Standard foundation walls include horizontal and vertical lengths of #4 rebar 24" on center. Vertical rebar is bent continuously into footing. Foundations that follow California earthquake standards include horizontal and vertical lengths of #5 rebar 12" on center.

| | Craft@Hrs | Unit | Material | Labor | Equip. | Total |
|---|---|---|---|---|---|---|
| Concrete foundation wall including rebar package and forming, per cubic yard | | | | | | |
| replace | 9F@2.70 | cy | 149.00 | 131.00 | 41.50 | 321.50 |
| remove | 1D@2.44 | cy | — | 94.90 | 99.10 | 194.00 |
| Concrete foundation wall including CEC rebar package & forming, per cubic yard | | | | | | |
| replace | 9F@3.13 | cy | 177.00 | 152.00 | 41.50 | 370.50 |
| remove | 1D@2.94 | cy | — | 114.00 | 131.00 | 245.00 |

| | Craft@Hrs | Unit | Material | Labor | Equip. | Total |
|---|---|---|---|---|---|---|
| **Concrete foundation wall, per square foot** | | | | | | |
| replace, 5" wide | 9F@.059 | sf | 2.08 | 2.86 | 1.02 | 5.96 |
| replace, 6" wide | 9F@.064 | sf | 2.52 | 3.10 | 1.02 | 6.64 |
| remove 5" or 6" wide | 1D@.073 | sf | — | 2.84 | 2.43 | 5.27 |
| replace, 8" wide | 9F@.074 | sf | 3.36 | 3.59 | 1.02 | 7.97 |
| replace, 10" wide | 9F@.084 | sf | 4.21 | 4.07 | 1.02 | 9.30 |
| remove 8" or 10" wide | 1D@.076 | sf | — | 2.96 | 2.82 | 5.78 |
| **Rebar package for 5", 6", 8", or 10" wide concrete foundation wall, per square foot** | | | | | | |
| replace | 3F@.037 | sf | .29 | 1.74 | — | 2.03 |
| **CEC rebar package for 5", 6", 8", or 10" wide concrete foundation wall, per square foot** | | | | | | |
| replace | 3F@.067 | sf | .96 | 3.16 | — | 4.12 |
| **Add for insulating foam stay-in-place foundation wall forms, per square foot** | | | | | | |
| replace | 3F@.045 | sf | 1.84 | 2.12 | — | 3.96 |
| **Minimum charge for concrete foundation wall work** | | | | | | |
| replace | 9F@3.00 | ea | 78.60 | 146.00 | 140.00 | 364.60 |

**Single-pour footing & foundation.** Includes concrete, forms, rebar and installation. Installation includes minor finish excavation but not general excavation, forming, pouring, and finishing concrete. Includes covering to protect concrete from the weather as needed.

| | Craft@Hrs | Unit | Material | Labor | Equip. | Total |
|---|---|---|---|---|---|---|
| **Single-pour footing and foundation wall with rebar package, per cubic yard** | | | | | | |
| replace | 9F@.589 | cy | 140.00 | 28.60 | 51.20 | 219.80 |
| remove | 1D@1.96 | cy | — | 76.20 | 89.10 | 165.30 |
| **Single-pour footing and foundation wall with CEC rebar package, per cubic yard** | | | | | | |
| replace | 9F@.713 | cy | 142.00 | 34.60 | 51.20 | 227.80 |
| remove | 1D@2.33 | cy | — | 90.60 | 95.90 | 186.50 |
| **Single-pour footing, per linear foot** | | | | | | |
| with 6" wide by 3' stem wall, replace | 9F@.346 | lf | 14.50 | 16.80 | 6.15 | 37.45 |
| with 8" wide by 3' stem wall, replace | 9F@.346 | lf | 17.30 | 16.80 | 6.15 | 40.25 |
| with 10" wide by 3' stem wall, replace | 9F@.346 | lf | 17.70 | 16.80 | 6.15 | 40.65 |
| **Single-pour footing and 3' stem wall, per linear foot, remove** | 1D@.346 | lf | — | 13.50 | 12.60 | 26.10 |
| **Rebar package for single-pour footing 6", 8" or 10" wide and 3' stem wall, per linear foot, replace** | 3F@.139 | lf | 2.19 | 6.55 | — | 8.74 |
| **CEC rebar package for single-pour footing 6", 8" or 10" wide and 3' stem wall, per linear foot, replace** | 3F@.243 | lf | 5.23 | 11.40 | — | 16.63 |

| | Craft@Hrs | Unit | Material | Labor | Equip. | Total |
|---|---|---|---|---|---|---|
| **Single-pour footing, per linear foot** | | | | | | |
| with 6" wide by 4' stem wall, replace | 9F@.437 | lf | 17.30 | 21.20 | 8.19 | 46.69 |
| with 8" wide by 4' stem wall, replace | 9F@.437 | lf | 20.50 | 21.20 | 8.19 | 49.89 |
| with 10" wide by 4' stem wall, replace | 9F@.437 | lf | 24.00 | 21.20 | 8.19 | 53.39 |
| **Single-pour footing and 4' stem wall** | | | | | | |
| per linear foot, remove | 1D@.422 | lf | — | 16.40 | 12.60 | 29.00 |
| **Rebar package for single-pour footing** | | | | | | |
| **6", 8" or 10" wide and 4' stem wall,** | | | | | | |
| per linear foot, replace | 3F@.152 | lf | 2.51 | 7.16 | — | 9.67 |
| **CEC rebar package for single-pour footing** | | | | | | |
| **6", 8" or 10" wide and 4' stem wall,** | | | | | | |
| per linear foot, replace | 3F@.255 | lf | 5.85 | 12.00 | — | 17.85 |
| **Minimum charge for single-pour footing** | | | | | | |
| and stem wall work, replace | 9F@3.00 | ea | 31.90 | 146.00 | 140.00 | 317.90 |

**Drill pier hole.**  Pier hole from 12" to 24" in diameter.  (Most common sizes are 16" and 18".)

| | Craft@Hrs | Unit | Material | Labor | Equip. | Total |
|---|---|---|---|---|---|---|
| **Tractor-mounted auger,** | | | | | | |
| mobilization | 10@6.25 | ea | — | 467.00 | 610.00 | 1,077.00 |
| **Drill concrete pier hole,** | | | | | | |
| hillside residential construction | 10@.083 | lf | — | 6.20 | 3.11 | 9.31 |
| minimum charge | 10@3.50 | ea | — | 261.00 | 345.00 | 606.00 |

**Pier.**  Includes concrete, rebar cage, equipment, and installation. Does not include drilling the pier hole or pump truck fees. Rebar cage includes rebar, wire, welding, assembly (usually off-site), hauling to site, and installation in hole. Includes equipment to lift unit from truck and place in hole. The rebar cage is engineered to match California earthquake standards for a pier that is from 12" to 24" in diameter with 16" and 18" being the most common sizes. Rebar includes vertical members the length of the pier and round horizontal members. In practice, rebar cages for piers are often engineered.

| | Craft@Hrs | Unit | Material | Labor | Equip. | Total |
|---|---|---|---|---|---|---|
| **Concrete pier including rebar cage** | | | | | | |
| replace | 9F@14.9 | cy | 567.00 | 723.00 | — | 1,290.00 |
| remove | 1D@.699 | cy | — | 27.20 | 73.30 | 100.50 |
| **Concrete pier with up to 36" fiber** | | | | | | |
| **tube wrapped cap** | | | | | | |
| replace | 9F@1.75 | lf | 21.40 | 84.90 | — | 106.30 |
| remove | 1D@.082 | lf | — | 3.19 | 8.55 | 11.74 |
| **Above grade concrete pier** | | | | | | |
| **with fiber tube wrap** | | | | | | |
| replace | 9F@1.81 | lf | 52.90 | 87.80 | — | 140.70 |
| remove | 1D@.082 | lf | — | 3.19 | 8.55 | 11.74 |
| **Rebar cage for concrete pier** | | | | | | |
| **(meets CEC requirements)** | | | | | | |
| replace | 3F@.091 | lf | 50.40 | 4.29 | — | 54.69 |
| **Concrete piers** | | | | | | |
| minimum charge | 9F@7.25 | ea | 413.00 | 352.00 | — | 765.00 |

| | Craft@Hrs | Unit | Material | Labor | Equip. | Total |
|---|---|---|---|---|---|---|

**Jacket pier.** Includes forming, rebar, epoxy, concrete, equipment and installation. The existing pier top is jackhammered. The new rebar is secured to rebar in the pier exposed by jackhammering and with epoxy in holes drilled in the concrete. The pier top is formed and a concrete jacket is poured.

| | Craft@Hrs | Unit | Material | Labor | Equip. | Total |
|---|---|---|---|---|---|---|
| replace, new concrete and rebar ties | 9F@4.92 | ea | 49.60 | 239.00 | 48.20 | 336.80 |
| minimum charge | 9F@4.00 | ea | 125.00 | 194.00 | 168.00 | 487.00 |

**Shallow pier.** Includes concrete, stirrup or similar fastener, and installation. Installation includes hand digging a hole up to three feet deep, pouring concrete, finish the top and placing the stirrup. Pre-cast pier includes pre-cast pier, hand excavation, and installation.

Shallow concrete pier (less than 3' deep)

| | Craft@Hrs | Unit | Material | Labor | Equip. | Total |
|---|---|---|---|---|---|---|
| for deck or light structure | | | | | | |
| replace | 9F@2.94 | ea | 25.60 | 143.00 | — | 168.60 |
| remove | 1D@1.14 | ea | — | 44.30 | — | 44.30 |
| Pre-cast concrete pier | | | | | | |
| for deck or light structure | | | | | | |
| replace | 2F@.322 | ea | 29.50 | 12.80 | — | 42.30 |
| remove | 1D@.233 | ea | — | 9.06 | — | 9.06 |

**Grade beam with rebar cage.** Prefabricated rebar cage included. All rebar cages are to CEC standards. When removed, grade beams are detached from piers with a jackhammer or concrete saw. The beams are broken into manageable chunks and loaded by crane or backhoe into a truck. (Does not include hauling or dump fees.)

| | Craft@Hrs | Unit | Material | Labor | Equip. | Total |
|---|---|---|---|---|---|---|
| Grade beam, per cubic yard | | | | | | |
| replace | 9F@4.01 | cy | 808.00 | 194.00 | — | 1,002.00 |
| remove | 1D@2.33 | cy | — | 90.60 | 54.80 | 145.40 |
| Grade beam, per linear foot | | | | | | |
| replace, 12" wide by 18" deep | 9F@.264 | lf | 56.80 | 12.80 | 4.10 | 73.70 |
| replace, 12" wide by 20" deep | 9F@.289 | lf | 57.60 | 14.00 | 4.10 | 75.70 |
| remove, 12" wide by 18" or 20" deep | 1D@.174 | lf | — | 6.77 | 5.86 | 12.63 |
| replace, 12" wide by 22" deep | 9F@.339 | lf | 58.50 | 16.40 | 4.10 | 79.00 |
| remove, 12" wide by 22" deep | 1D@.195 | lf | — | 7.59 | 7.08 | 14.67 |
| replace, 12" wide by 24" deep | 9F@.279 | lf | 59.40 | 13.50 | 4.10 | 77.00 |
| remove, 12" wide by 24" deep | 1D@.195 | lf | — | 7.59 | 7.08 | 14.67 |
| replace, 14" wide by 18" deep | 9F@.310 | lf | 58.00 | 15.00 | 4.10 | 77.10 |
| replace, 14" wide by 20" deep | 9F@.370 | lf | 58.90 | 17.90 | 4.10 | 80.90 |
| remove, 14" wide by 18" or 20" deep | 1D@.174 | lf | — | 6.77 | 5.86 | 12.63 |
| replace, 14" wide by 22" deep | 9F@.370 | lf | 60.20 | 17.90 | 4.10 | 82.20 |
| replace, 14" wide by 24" deep | 9F@.429 | lf | 61.00 | 20.80 | 4.10 | 85.90 |
| remove, 14" wide by 22" or 24" deep | 1D@.199 | lf | — | 7.74 | 7.22 | 14.96 |
| replace, 16" wide by 18" deep | 9F@.550 | lf | 59.40 | 26.70 | 4.10 | 90.20 |
| replace, 16" wide by 20" deep | 9F@.672 | lf | 60.50 | 32.60 | 4.10 | 97.20 |
| remove, 16" wide by 18" or 20" deep | 1D@.216 | lf | — | 8.40 | 7.84 | 16.24 |
| replace, 16" wide by 22" deep | 9F@.550 | lf | 61.50 | 26.70 | 4.10 | 92.30 |
| replace, 16" wide by 24" deep | 9F@.672 | lf | 62.50 | 32.60 | 4.10 | 99.20 |
| remove 16" wide by 22" or 24" deep | 1D@.223 | lf | — | 8.67 | 8.10 | 16.77 |
| replace, 18" wide by 18" deep | 9F@.310 | lf | 60.60 | 15.00 | 4.10 | 79.70 |
| replace, 18" wide by 20" deep | 9F@.370 | lf | 61.70 | 17.90 | 4.10 | 83.70 |
| remove 18" wide by 18" or 20" deep | 1D@.216 | lf | — | 8.40 | 7.82 | 16.22 |
| replace, 18" wide by 22" deep | 9F@.370 | lf | 63.10 | 17.90 | 4.10 | 85.10 |
| replace, 18" wide by 24" deep | 9F@.430 | lf | 64.30 | 20.90 | 4.10 | 89.30 |
| remove 18" wide by 22" or 24" deep | 1D@.223 | lf | — | 8.67 | 8.10 | 16.77 |
| Concrete grade beams, minimum charge | 9F@1.03 | ea | 430.00 | 50.00 | 140.00 | 620.00 |

| | Craft@Hrs | Unit | Material | Labor | Equip. | Total |
|---|---|---|---|---|---|---|

**Jacket grade beam with new concrete and rebar ties.** Includes forming, rebar, epoxy, concrete, equipment and installation. The existing grade beam is jackhammered and holes are drilled for rebar. The rebar is secured with epoxy. The grade beam is formed and a concrete jacket is poured.

| | Craft@Hrs | Unit | Material | Labor | Equip. | Total |
|---|---|---|---|---|---|---|
| Jacket concrete grade beam | | | | | | |
| replace | 9F@.537 | lf | 14.70 | 26.00 | 6.39 | 47.09 |
| minimum charge | 9F@4.00 | ea | 70.00 | 194.00 | 168.00 | 432.00 |

**Lightweight flatwork.** Includes concrete, forms, and installation. Installation includes minor finish excavation but not general excavation, forming, pouring, and finishing concrete with control joints. Includes covering to protect concrete from the weather as needed.

| | Craft@Hrs | Unit | Material | Labor | Equip. | Total |
|---|---|---|---|---|---|---|
| Lightweight concrete flatwork (no rebar), | | | | | | |
| per cubic yard | | | | | | |
| replace | 9F@2.04 | cy | 170.00 | 98.90 | — | 268.90 |
| remove | 1D@2.35 | cy | — | 91.40 | 71.10 | 162.50 |
| 2" slab, per square foot | | | | | | |
| replace | 9F@.023 | sf | 1.06 | 1.12 | — | 2.18 |
| remove | 1D@.026 | sf | — | 1.01 | .91 | 1.92 |
| 4" slab, per square foot | | | | | | |
| replace | 9F@.024 | sf | 2.07 | 1.16 | — | 3.23 |
| remove | 1D@.026 | sf | — | 1.01 | .91 | 1.92 |
| 6" slab, per square foot | | | | | | |
| replace | 9F@.026 | sf | 3.19 | 1.26 | — | 4.45 |
| remove | 1D@.026 | sf | — | 1.01 | .91 | 1.92 |
| Minimum charge | 9F@3.00 | ea | 79.80 | 146.00 | — | 225.80 |

**Flatwork.** Includes concrete, forms, and installation. Installation includes minor finish excavation but not general excavation, forming, pouring, and finishing concrete with control joints. Includes covering to protect concrete from the weather as needed.

| | Craft@Hrs | Unit | Material | Labor | Equip. | Total |
|---|---|---|---|---|---|---|
| Concrete flatwork (no rebar), per cubic yard | | | | | | |
| replace | 9F@2.04 | cy | 137.00 | 98.90 | — | 235.90 |
| remove | 1D@2.39 | cy | — | 93.00 | 71.70 | 164.70 |
| 4" slab, per square foot | | | | | | |
| replace | 9F@.035 | sf | 1.70 | 1.70 | — | 3.40 |
| remove | 1D@.027 | sf | — | 1.05 | .91 | 1.96 |
| 6" slab, per square foot | | | | | | |
| replace | 9F@.048 | sf | 2.53 | 2.33 | — | 4.86 |
| remove | 1D@.027 | sf | — | 1.05 | .91 | 1.96 |
| 8" slab, per square foot | | | | | | |
| replace | 9F@.048 | sf | 3.37 | 2.33 | — | 5.70 |
| remove | 1D@.027 | sf | — | 1.05 | .91 | 1.96 |
| Minimum charge | 9F@3.00 | ea | 64.90 | 146.00 | — | 210.90 |

**Utility flatwork.** Includes concrete, forms, and installation. Installation includes minor finish excavation but not general excavation, forming, pouring, and finishing concrete with control joints. Includes covering to protect concrete from the weather as needed.

| | Craft@Hrs | Unit | Material | Labor | Equip. | Total |
|---|---|---|---|---|---|---|
| Concrete footing for chimney | | | | | | |
| replace | 9F@.044 | sf | 3.70 | 2.13 | — | 5.83 |
| remove | 1D@.030 | sf | — | 1.17 | 1.02 | 2.19 |
| Concrete slab for exterior heat pump, | | | | | | |
| condenser, or other equipment | | | | | | |
| replace | 9F@.044 | sf | 2.00 | 2.13 | — | 4.13 |
| remove | 1D@.027 | sf | — | 1.05 | .91 | 1.96 |

| | Craft@Hrs | Unit | Material | Labor | Equip. | Total |
|---|---|---|---|---|---|---|

**Rebar for flatwork.** Includes rebar, wire, and installation. For placement of rebar only does not include forming or grading. Wire mesh includes 6" x 6" #10 wire mesh, wire, and installation.

| Concrete slab | | | | | | |
|---|---|---|---|---|---|---|
| replace, #4 24" on center | 3F@.036 | sf | .67 | 1.70 | — | 2.37 |
| replace, #4 12" on center | 3F@.080 | sf | 1.40 | 3.77 | — | 5.17 |
| Wire mesh for concrete slab, 6" x 6" #10 | | | | | | |
| replace | 3F@.015 | sf | .22 | .71 | — | .93 |

**Flatwork base.** Includes slab base, hauling and finish grading of base. Does not include tearout of existing slab, or rough grading.

| Slab base | | | | | | |
|---|---|---|---|---|---|---|
| replace, 2" aggregate | 2F@.017 | sf | .05 | .67 | .16 | .88 |
| replace, 4" aggregate | 2F@.018 | sf | .11 | .71 | .16 | .98 |
| replace, 2" sand | 2F@.014 | sf | .05 | .55 | .16 | .76 |
| replace, 4" sand | 2F@.016 | sf | .11 | .63 | .16 | .90 |

**Flatwork vapor barrier.** Includes membrane and installation.

| Slab membrane | | | | | | |
|---|---|---|---|---|---|---|
| replace, 6 mil | 2F@.002 | sf | .04 | .08 | — | .12 |
| replace, 5 mil | 2F@.002 | sf | .04 | .08 | — | .12 |

**Sidewalk.** Sidewalk to 3' wide. Includes concrete, forms, and installation. Installation includes minor finish excavation but not general excavation, forming, pouring, and finishing concrete with control joints. Includes covering to protect concrete from the weather as needed.

| Concrete sidewalk, per cubic yard, 3" to 6" thick | | | | | | |
|---|---|---|---|---|---|---|
| replace | 9F@4.17 | cy | 151.00 | 202.00 | — | 353.00 |
| remove | 1D@2.39 | cy | — | 93.00 | 71.70 | 164.70 |
| Concrete sidewalk, per square foot 3" thick | | | | | | |
| replace | 9F@.042 | sf | 1.26 | 2.04 | — | 3.30 |
| remove | 1D@.034 | sf | — | 1.32 | .91 | 2.23 |
| 4" thick | | | | | | |
| replace | 9F@.049 | sf | 1.70 | 2.38 | — | 4.08 |
| remove | 1D@.034 | sf | — | 1.32 | .91 | 2.23 |
| 6" thick | | | | | | |
| replace | 9F@.062 | sf | 2.53 | 3.01 | — | 5.54 |
| remove | 1D@.034 | sf | — | 1.32 | .91 | 2.23 |
| Concrete sidewalk work, all thicknesses | | | | | | |
| minimum charge | 9F@3.00 | ea | 160.00 | 146.00 | — | 306.00 |

**Exposed aggregate.** Where required, add for disposal of slurry.

| Exposed aggregate finish, slab or sidewalk | | | | | | |
|---|---|---|---|---|---|---|
| add | 8F@.019 | sf | .21 | .95 | — | 1.16 |

| | Craft@Hrs | Unit | Material | Labor | Equip. | Total |
|---|---|---|---|---|---|---|

### Stamping concrete.

| | | | | | | |
|---|---|---|---|---|---|---|
| Concrete slab or sidewalk stamping | | | | | | |
|    add | 8F@.053 | sf | — | 2.64 | — | 2.64 |
|    add for paver-pattern | 8F@.045 | sf | — | 2.24 | — | 2.24 |
|    add for paver w/ grouted joints | 8F@.068 | sf | .44 | 3.39 | — | 3.83 |

### Concrete dye. For concrete quantities under 350 sf add $35 per truck for wash-out. This charge does not apply to troweled-in dyes.

| | | | | | | |
|---|---|---|---|---|---|---|
| For troweled-in concrete dye | | | | | | |
|    add | 8F@.009 | sf | 1.90 | .45 | — | 2.35 |
| For concrete dye in flatwork, | | | | | | |
|   Add per 1" deep layer | | | | | | |
|    blacks and grays | — | sf | .08 | — | — | .08 |
|    blues | — | sf | .41 | — | — | .41 |
|    browns & terra cotta reds | — | sf | .40 | — | — | .40 |
|    bright reds | — | sf | .41 | — | — | .41 |
|    greens | — | sf | .82 | — | — | .82 |

### Curb & gutter. Includes concrete, forms, and installation. Installation includes minor finish excavation but not general excavation, forming, pouring, and finishing concrete with control joints. Includes barriers and covering to protect concrete from passersby and the weather.

| | | | | | | |
|---|---|---|---|---|---|---|
| Concrete curb & gutter | | | | | | |
|    replace | 9F@.274 | lf | 7.01 | 13.30 | 1.23 | 21.54 |
|    remove | 1D@.145 | lf | — | 5.64 | 1.86 | 7.50 |
| Minimum charge for curb & gutter work | 9F@3.67 | ea | 51.60 | 178.00 | 111.00 | 340.60 |

### Concrete step. Includes concrete, forms, rebar, and installation. Rebar reinforcement includes two horizontal pieces per step with vertical tie-ins. Installation includes minor finish excavation but not general excavation, forming, pouring, and finishing concrete with control joints. Includes covering to protect concrete from the weather as needed.

| | | | | | | |
|---|---|---|---|---|---|---|
| Concrete step per cubic yard | | | | | | |
|    replace | 9F@7.70 | cy | 379.00 | 373.00 | — | 752.00 |
|    remove | 1D@3.12 | cy | — | 121.00 | 79.20 | 200.20 |
| Concrete step per linear foot | | | | | | |
|    replace | 9F@.232 | lf | 4.18 | 11.30 | — | 15.48 |
|    remove | 1D@.047 | lf | — | 1.83 | .98 | 2.81 |
| Concrete step per square foot of landing | | | | | | |
|    replace | 9F@.068 | sf | 10.50 | 3.30 | — | 13.80 |
|    remove | 1D@.046 | sf | — | 1.79 | 1.22 | 3.01 |
| Minimum charge for a concrete step | | | | | | |
|    replace | 9F@5.00 | ea | 100.00 | 243.00 | — | 343.00 |

### Pargeting. Includes plaster and installation. Installation prepwork includes breaking of foundation ties as needed.

| | | | | | | |
|---|---|---|---|---|---|---|
| Foundation wall pargeting, | | | | | | |
|   per square foot, replace | 4P@.022 | sf | .46 | 1.18 | — | 1.64 |
| Foundation wall pargeting work | | | | | | |
|   minimum charge | 4P@1.00 | ea | 33.00 | 53.50 | — | 86.50 |

| | Craft@Hrs | Unit | Material | Labor | Equip. | Total |
|---|---|---|---|---|---|---|
| **Concrete sawing.** Includes blade wear. | | | | | | |
| Saw concrete wall, per lf of cut, 1" deep | | | | | | |
| with standard rebar package | 20@.111 | lf | — | 5.97 | 2.28 | 8.25 |
| with CEC rebar package | 20@.125 | lf | — | 6.73 | 3.32 | 10.05 |
| Saw concrete floor, per lf of cut, 1" deep | | | | | | |
| no rebar | 20@.050 | lf | — | 2.69 | .89 | 3.58 |
| with rebar package | 20@.054 | lf | — | 2.91 | 1.03 | 3.94 |
| with wire mesh reinforcement | 20@.052 | lf | — | 2.80 | 1.23 | 4.03 |
| Saw expansion joint in "green" pad | 20@.189 | lf | — | 10.20 | 3.54 | 13.74 |
| Minimum charge for wall sawing | 20@3.00 | ea | — | 161.00 | 146.00 | 307.00 |
| Minimum charge for slab sawing | 20@2.25 | ea | — | 121.00 | 128.00 | 249.00 |
| **Core drilling.** Includes drill bit wear. | | | | | | |
| Core drilling in concrete wall, | | | | | | |
| per inch of depth | | | | | | |
| 2" thick wall | 20@.066 | li | — | 3.55 | 1.00 | 4.55 |
| 4" thick wall | 20@.073 | li | — | 3.93 | 1.16 | 5.09 |
| Core drilling in concrete floor, | | | | | | |
| per inch of depth | | | | | | |
| 2" thick floor | 20@.064 | li | — | 3.44 | .93 | 4.37 |
| 4" thick floor | 20@.067 | li | — | 3.60 | 1.07 | 4.67 |
| **Pump truck.** When pumping concrete 50 feet or less and no more than three stories high. | | | | | | |
| add for pumping footing concrete | — | lf | — | — | 1.57 | 1.57 |
| add for pumping found. wall concrete | — | sf | — | — | .40 | .40 |
| add for pumping pier concrete | — | lf | — | — | 2.26 | 2.26 |
| add for pumping grade-beam concrete | — | lf | — | — | 1.23 | 1.23 |
| add for pumping slab, sidewalk conc. | — | sf | — | — | .37 | .37 |
| minimum charge for pump truck | — | ea | 6.59 | — | 537.00 | 543.59 |
| **Rebar.** Tied and bent into place. Includes rebar, wire, and installation. Installation includes tying and bending rebar for typical concrete work such as slabs, footings, foundations, and so on. | | | | | | |
| #3 rebar (3/8") | 3F@.014 | lf | .24 | .66 | — | .90 |
| #4 rebar (1/2") | 3F@.014 | lf | .32 | .66 | — | .98 |
| #5 rebar (5/8") | 3F@.014 | lf | .47 | .66 | — | 1.13 |
| #6 rebar (3/4") | 3F@.014 | lf | .74 | .66 | — | 1.40 |
| #7 rebar (7/8") | 3F@.015 | lf | .99 | .71 | — | 1.70 |
| #8 rebar (1") | 3F@.015 | lf | 1.28 | .71 | — | 1.99 |
| **Foundation coating.** | | | | | | |
| Foundation coating per sf | 2F@.017 | sf | .05 | .67 | — | .72 |
| **Buttress foundation.** Excavation, forming, pouring, and finishing of concrete buttress over existing foundation. Does not include shoring. | | | | | | |
| Excavate exterior of foundation | 10@.121 | sf | — | 9.04 | 2.02 | 11.06 |
| Hand excavate interior of foundation | | | | | | |
| in crawl space | 2F@.457 | sf | — | 18.10 | — | 18.10 |
| Hand excavate interior of footing | | | | | | |
| in basement | 2F@.204 | sf | — | 8.08 | — | 8.08 |

| | Craft@Hrs | Unit | Material | Labor | Equip. | Total |
|---|---|---|---|---|---|---|
| Backfill foundation | | | | | | |
| when work is complete | 1O@.028 | sf | — | 2.09 | .15 | 2.24 |
| Buttress exterior of existing foundation | 9F@.065 | sf | 5.31 | 3.15 | — | 8.46 |
| Buttress interior of existing foundation | | | | | | |
| with crawl space | 9F@.091 | sf | 5.31 | 4.41 | — | 9.72 |
| with basement | 9F@.208 | sf | 5.31 | 10.10 | — | 15.41 |
| Buttress existing foundation | | | | | | |
| with concrete, minimum charge | 9F@7.00 | ea | 257.00 | 340.00 | — | 597.00 |

**Compaction grouting.** Does not include excavation. (See excavation under concrete buttress above.) This process can form a "pier" for the foundation and compacts the destabilized soil. An engineer is required to supervise and dictate specifications.

| | Craft@Hrs | Unit | Material | Labor | Equip. | Total |
|---|---|---|---|---|---|---|
| 2" core drill footings for compaction | | | | | | |
| grouting | 2G@.379 | ea | — | 22.00 | 11.90 | 33.90 |
| Insert 2" compaction grouting pipes | | | | | | |
| into ground | 2G@.143 | lf | — | 8.29 | — | 8.29 |
| Pump pressurized concrete grout | | | | | | |
| through pipes | 2G@.251 | lf | 5.77 | 14.60 | 44.20 | 64.57 |

**Asphalt graded base.** Includes grading of driveway, hauling and placement of graded base. Does not include tear-out of existing driveway. Driveway is assumed to have already been rough-graded or to have had a previous driveway of concrete or asphalt over it.

| | Craft@Hrs | Unit | Material | Labor | Equip. | Total |
|---|---|---|---|---|---|---|
| Graded base for asphalt | | | | | | |
| replace 4" | 2G@.001 | sf | .04 | .06 | .15 | .25 |
| replace 6" | 2G@.001 | sf | .06 | .06 | .17 | .29 |
| Minimum grading charge | | | | | | |
| replace | 2G@1.66 | ea | 77.20 | 96.30 | 358.00 | 531.50 |

**Asphalt driveway.** Includes asphalt, equipment, hauling, and installation. Installed over a graded base. Does not include graded base.

| | Craft@Hrs | Unit | Material | Labor | Equip. | Total |
|---|---|---|---|---|---|---|
| 2" asphalt | | | | | | |
| replace | 2G@.010 | sf | .74 | .58 | .68 | 2.00 |
| remove | 2G@.005 | sf | — | .29 | — | .29 |
| 3" asphalt | | | | | | |
| replace | 2G@.012 | sf | 1.09 | .70 | .76 | 2.55 |
| remove | 2G@.006 | sf | — | .35 | — | .35 |
| 4" asphalt | | | | | | |
| replace | 2G@.013 | sf | 1.45 | .75 | .85 | 3.05 |
| remove | 2G@.006 | sf | — | .35 | — | .35 |

**Asphalt overlay.**

| | Craft@Hrs | Unit | Material | Labor | Equip. | Total |
|---|---|---|---|---|---|---|
| 1" asphalt | | | | | | |
| replace | 2G@.012 | sf | .38 | .70 | .72 | 1.80 |
| remove | 2G@.006 | sf | — | .35 | — | .35 |
| 2" asphalt | | | | | | |
| replace | 2G@.014 | sf | .74 | .81 | .79 | 2.34 |
| remove | 2G@.006 | sf | — | .35 | — | .35 |
| 3" asphalt | | | | | | |
| replace | 2G@.016 | sf | 1.09 | .93 | .87 | 2.89 |
| remove | 2G@.006 | sf | — | .35 | — | .35 |

| | Craft@Hrs | Unit | Material | Labor | Equip. | Total |
|---|---|---|---|---|---|---|
| Fill pothole in driveway | | | | | | |
| replace | 2G@.379 | ea | 6.02 | 22.00 | — | 28.02 |
| Seal crack in driveway | | | | | | |
| replace | 2G@.013 | lf | .37 | .75 | — | 1.12 |
| Minimum charge for asphalt paving work | | | | | | |
| replace | 2G@4.00 | ea | 184.00 | 232.00 | 1,050.00 | 1,466.00 |
| Seal asphalt | | | | | | |
| replace | 2G@.002 | sf | .06 | .12 | — | .18 |
| Seal and sand asphalt | | | | | | |
| replace | 2G@.003 | sf | .11 | .17 | — | .28 |

| | Craft@Hrs | Unit | Material | Labor | Total |
|---|---|---|---|---|---|
| **Time & Material Charts** (selected items) **Concrete Materials** | | | | | |
| Ready mix concrete delivered | | | | | |
| 5 bag mix 2,500 psi, per cy, ($125.00), 6% waste | — | cy | 133.00 | — | 133.00 |
| 5.5 bag mix 3,000 psi, per cy, ($125.00), 6% waste | — | cy | 133.00 | — | 133.00 |
| 6 bag mix, 3,500 psi, per cy, ($127.00), 6% waste | — | cy | 135.00 | — | 135.00 |
| 6.5 bag mix, 4,000 psi, per cy, ($128.00), 6% waste | — | cy | 136.00 | — | 136.00 |
| 7 bag mix, 4,500 psi, per cy, ($131.00), 6% waste | — | cy | 139.00 | — | 139.00 |
| 7.5 bag mix, 5,000 psi, per cy, ($133.00), 6% waste | — | cy | 141.00 | — | 141.00 |
| add for synthetic fiber reinforcing, 0% waste | — | cy | 15.10 | — | 15.10 |
| add for high early strength, 0% waste | — | cy | 16.20 | — | 16.20 |
| Concrete form materials | | | | | |
| form ties, box of 400 ($63.40), 5% waste | — | box | 66.60 | — | 66.60 |
| footing forms (forms 6 uses, key 3 uses) 0% waste | — | lf | .48 | — | .48 |
| Concrete footings | | | | | |
| with rebar per cy | | | | | |
| ($146.00 cy, 1 cy), 6% waste | — | cy | 155.00 | — | 155.00 |
| with CEC rebar per cy | | | | | |
| ($179.00 cy, 1 cy), 6% waste | — | cy | 190.00 | — | 190.00 |
| 16" wide by 10" deep | | | | | |
| ($128.00 lf, 24.3 lf), 6% waste | — | lf | 5.59 | — | 5.59 |
| rebar package for 16" by 10" | | | | | |
| ($.50 pound, .7 lf), 6% waste | — | lf | .75 | — | .75 |
| CEC rebar package for 16" by 10" | | | | | |
| ($.50 pound, .2 lf), 6% waste | — | lf | 2.65 | — | 2.65 |
| 20" wide by 10" deep | | | | | |
| ($128.00 lf, 19.44 lf), 6% waste | — | lf | 6.97 | — | 6.97 |
| rebar package for 20" by 10" | | | | | |
| ($.50 pound, .74 lf), 2% waste | — | lf | .69 | — | .69 |
| CEC rebar package for 20" by 10" | | | | | |
| ($.50 pound, .19 lf), 4% waste | — | lf | 2.74 | — | 2.74 |

| | Craft@Hrs | Unit | Material | Labor | Total |
|---|---|---|---|---|---|
| 24" wide by 12" deep | | | | | |
| ($128.00 lf, 13.5 lf), 6% waste | — | lf | 10.00 | — | 10.00 |
| rebar package for 24" by 12" | | | | | |
| ($.50 pound, .5 lf), 2% waste | — | lf | 1.02 | — | 1.02 |
| CEC rebar package for 24" by 10" | | | | | |
| ($.50 pound, .16 lf), 4% waste | — | lf | 3.26 | — | 3.26 |
| 32" wide by 14" deep | | | | | |
| ($128.00 lf, 8.68 lf), 6% waste | — | lf | 15.60 | — | 15.60 |
| rebar package for 32" by 14" | | | | | |
| ($.50 pound, .5 lf), 2% waste | — | lf | 1.02 | — | 1.02 |
| CEC rebar package for 32" by 14" | | | | | |
| ($.50 pound, .16 lf), 4% waste | — | lf | 3.26 | — | 3.26 |
| Foundation wall concrete | | | | | |
| including rebar package per cy | | | | | |
| ($140.00 cy, 1 cy), 6% waste | — | cy | 148.00 | — | 148.00 |
| including CEC rebar package per cy | | | | | |
| ($167.00 cy, 1 cy), 6% waste | — | cy | 177.00 | — | 177.00 |
| 5" wide wall | | | | | |
| ($128.00 cy, 65.06 ea), 6% waste | — | ea | 2.09 | — | 2.09 |
| rebar package for 5" wide | | | | | |
| ($.50 pound, 1.71 sf), 2% waste | — | sf | .30 | — | .30 |
| CEC rebar package for 5" wide | | | | | |
| ($.50 pound, .55 sf), 4% waste | — | sf | .95 | — | .95 |
| 6" wide wall | | | | | |
| ($128.00 cy, 54 ea), 6% waste | — | ea | 2.51 | — | 2.51 |
| rebar package for 6" wide wall | | | | | |
| ($.50 pound, 1.71 sf), 2% waste | — | sf | .30 | — | .30 |
| CEC rebar package for 6" wide wall | | | | | |
| ($.50 pound, .55 sf), 4% waste | — | sf | .95 | — | .95 |
| 8" wide wall | | | | | |
| ($128.00 cy, 40.5 ea), 6% waste | — | ea | 3.35 | — | 3.35 |
| rebar package for 8" wide wall | | | | | |
| ($.50 sf, 1.71 sf), 2% waste | — | sf | .30 | — | .30 |
| CEC rebar package for 8" wide wall | | | | | |
| ($.50 sf, .55 sf), 4% waste | — | sf | .95 | — | .95 |
| 10" wide wall | | | | | |
| ($128.00 cy, 32.4 ea), 6% waste | — | ea | 4.19 | — | 4.19 |
| rebar package for 10" wide wall | | | | | |
| ($.50 sf, 1.71 sf), 2% waste | — | sf | .30 | — | .30 |
| CEC rebar package for 10" wide wall | | | | | |
| ($.50 sf, .55 sf), 4% waste | — | sf | .95 | — | .95 |
| insulating foam stay-in-place foundation wall forms | | | | | |
| ($1.84 sf, 1 sf), 0% waste | — | sf | 1.84 | — | 1.84 |
| Pier concrete | | | | | |
| concrete ($128.00 cy, 8.6 lf), 6% waste | — | lf | 15.80 | — | 15.80 |
| fiber tube with bracing | | | | | |
| ($123.00 10' tube, 3.33 ea), 2% waste | — | ea | 37.60 | — | 37.60 |
| prefabricated rebar cage | | | | | |
| ($.50 pound, .01 lf), 0% waste | — | lf | 50.00 | — | 50.00 |

| | Craft@Hrs | Unit | Material | Labor | Total |
|---|---|---|---|---|---|
| Grade beam concrete | | | | | |
| concrete for 12" by 18" | | | | | |
| ($128.00 cy, 18 lf), 6% waste | — | lf | 7.54 | — | 7.54 |
| concrete for 12" by 24" | | | | | |
| ($128.000 cy, 13.5 lf), 6% waste | — | lf | 10.00 | — | 10.00 |
| concrete for 14" by 18" | | | | | |
| ($128.00 cy, 15.43 lf), 6% waste | — | lf | 8.80 | — | 8.80 |
| concrete for 14" by 24" | | | | | |
| ($128.00 cy, 11.57 lf), 6% waste | — | lf | 11.80 | — | 11.80 |
| concrete for 16" by 18" | | | | | |
| ($128.00 cy, 13.5 lf), 6% waste | — | lf | 10.00 | — | 10.00 |
| concrete for 16" by 24" | | | | | |
| ($128.00 cy, 10.13 lf), 6% waste | — | lf | 13.40 | — | 13.40 |
| concrete for 18" by 18" | | | | | |
| ($128.00 cy, 12 lf), 6% waste | — | lf | 11.30 | — | 11.30 |
| concrete for 18" by 24" | | | | | |
| ($128.00 cy, 9 lf), 6% waste | — | lf | 15.10 | — | 15.10 |
| rebar cage ($.47 pound, .01 lf), 0% waste | — | lf | 47.00 | — | 47.00 |
| | | | | | |
| Lightweight concrete flatwork | | | | | |
| per cy ($162.00 cy, 1 cy), 6% waste | — | cy | 172.00 | — | 172.00 |
| 2" slab ($162.00 cy, 162 sf), 6% waste | — | sf | 1.06 | — | 1.06 |
| 4" slab ($162.00 cy, 81 sf), 6% waste | — | sf | 2.12 | — | 2.12 |
| 6" slab ($162.00 cy, 54 sf), 6% waste | — | sf | 3.18 | — | 3.18 |
| | | | | | |
| Concrete flatwork | | | | | |
| per cy ($128.00 cy, 1 cy), 6% waste | — | cy | 136.00 | — | 136.00 |
| 4" slab ($128.00 cy, 81 sf), 6% waste | — | sf | 1.67 | — | 1.67 |
| 6" slab ($128.00 cy, 54 sf), 6% waste | — | sf | 2.51 | — | 2.51 |
| 8" slab ($128.00 cy, 40.5 sf), 6% waste | — | sf | 3.35 | — | 3.35 |
| rebar #4, 24" on center | | | | | |
| ($.50 pound, .75 sf), 2% waste | — | sf | .68 | — | .68 |
| rebar #4, 12" on center | | | | | |
| ($.50 pound, .37 sf), 2% waste | — | sf | 1.38 | — | 1.38 |
| wire mesh (6" x 6" #10) | | | | | |
| ($160.00 roll, 750 sf), 2% waste | — | sf | .21 | — | .21 |
| aggregate for 2" slab base | | | | | |
| ($9.31 cy, 162 sf), 0% waste | — | sf | .06 | — | .06 |
| aggregate for 4" slab base | | | | | |
| ($9.31 cy, 81 sf), 0% waste | — | sf | .11 | — | .11 |
| sand for 2" slab base | | | | | |
| ($9.31 cy, 162 sf), 0% waste | — | sf | .06 | — | .06 |
| sand for 4" slab base | | | | | |
| ($9.31 cy, 81 sf), 0% waste | — | sf | .11 | — | .11 |
| | | | | | |
| Sidewalk | | | | | |
| 3" sidewalk ($128.00 cy, 108 sf), 6% waste | — | sf | 1.26 | — | 1.26 |
| 4" sidewalk ($128.00 cy, 81 sf), 6% waste | — | sf | 1.67 | — | 1.67 |
| 6" sidewalk ($128.00 cy, 54 sf), 6% waste | — | sf | 2.51 | — | 2.51 |

| | Craft@Hrs | Unit | Material | Labor | Total |
|---|---|---|---|---|---|
| **Rebar** | | | | | |
| #3 (3/8" .376 pound per lf) | | | | | |
| ($4.63 20' bar, 20 lf), 4% waste | — | lf | .24 | — | .24 |
| #4 (1/2" .668 pounds per lf) | | | | | |
| ($5.89 20' bar, 20 lf), 4% waste | — | lf | .30 | — | .30 |
| #5 (5/8" 1.043 pounds per lf) | | | | | |
| ($9.18 20' bar, 20 lf), 4% waste | — | lf | .48 | — | .48 |
| #6 (3/4" 1.502 pounds per lf) | | | | | |
| ($13.90 20' bar, 20 lf), 4% waste | — | lf | .73 | — | .73 |
| #7 (7/8" 2.044 pounds per lf) | | | | | |
| ($18.90 20' bar, 20 lf), 4% waste | — | lf | .99 | — | .99 |
| #8 (1" 2.670 pounds per lf) | | | | | |
| ($24.70 20' bar, 20 lf), 4% waste | — | lf | 1.29 | — | 1.29 |

| | Craft@Hrs | Unit | Material | Labor | Equip. | Total |
|---|---|---|---|---|---|---|
| **Concrete Rental Equipment** | | | | | | |
| **Forms** | | | | | | |
| plywood wall forms (per sf of form) | | | | | | |
| ($.27 per day, .25 sf) | — | sf | — | — | 1.08 | 1.08 |
| steel curb & gutter forms | | | | | | |
| ($1.32 per day, 1 lf) | — | lf | — | — | 1.32 | 1.32 |
| **Tractor-mounted auger rental** | | | | | | |
| hourly charge ($305.00 per hour, 90 lf) | — | lf | — | — | 3.39 | 3.39 |
| delivery and take-home charge | — | ea | — | — | 659.00 | 659.00 |
| **Concrete pump truck rental** | | | | | | |
| foundation wall | | | | | | |
| ($193.00 hour, 450 sf of wall) | — | sf | — | — | .43 | .43 |
| footings ($193.00 hour, 112 lf) | — | lf | — | — | 1.72 | 1.72 |
| flatwork ($193.00 hour, 475 sf of flat) | — | sf | — | — | .41 | .41 |
| piers ($193.00 hour, 78 lf of pier) | — | lf | — | — | 2.47 | 2.47 |
| grade beam | | | | | | |
| ($193.00 hour, 146 lf of beam) | — | lf | — | — | 1.32 | 1.32 |
| pressure grout | | | | | | |
| ($193.00 hour, 4 lf 2" pipe) | — | sf | — | — | 48.30 | 48.30 |
| **Dump truck rental** | | | | | | |
| 5 cy, average aggregate base haul | | | | | | |
| ($93.90 day, 540 sf) | — | sf | — | — | .17 | .17 |
| **Jackhammer with compressor rental** | | | | | | |
| foundation wall demo | | | | | | |
| ($292.00 day, 110 sf) | — | sf | — | — | 2.65 | 2.65 |
| footing demo ($292.00 day, 66 lf) | — | lf | — | — | 4.42 | 4.42 |
| flatwork demo ($292.00 day, 295 sf) | — | sf | — | — | .99 | .99 |
| grade beam demo ($292.00 day, 46 lf) | — | lf | — | — | 6.35 | 6.35 |
| jacket grade beam ($292.00 day, 42 lf) | — | lf | — | — | 6.95 | 6.95 |
| jacket pier ($292.00 day, 5.6 each) | — | ea | — | — | 52.10 | 52.10 |
| curb & gutter ($292.00 day, 145 lf) | — | lf | — | — | 2.01 | 2.01 |

| | Craft@Hrs | Unit | Material | Labor | Equip. | Total |
|---|---|---|---|---|---|---|
| Portable concrete saw rental | | | | | | |
| wall sawing ($195.00 day, 78 1" x 1') | — | lf | — | — | 2.50 | 2.50 |
| floor sawing ($152.00 day, 160 1" x 1') | — | lf | — | — | .95 | .95 |
| Concrete core drill rental | | | | | | |
| per day ($136.00 day, 125 1" x 1') | — | lf | — | — | 1.09 | 1.09 |
| Crane rental | | | | | | |
| concrete pier removal | | | | | | |
| ($904.00 day, 98 day) | — | lf | — | — | 9.22 | 9.22 |
| Pressure pot rental | | | | | | |
| for pressurized epoxy injection | | | | | | |
| ($264.00 day, 120 day) | — | lf | — | — | 2.20 | 2.20 |
| Backhoe rental | | | | | | |
| per day ($704.00 day, 322 day) | — | cy | — | — | 2.19 | 2.19 |

## Concrete Labor

| Laborer | base wage | paid leave | true wage | taxes & ins. | total |
|---|---|---|---|---|---|
| Concrete form installer | $29.60 | 2.31 | $31.91 | 22.69 | $54.60 |
| Concrete finisher | $29.50 | 2.30 | $31.80 | 22.60 | $54.40 |
| Concrete finisher's helper | $23.90 | 1.86 | $25.76 | 19.34 | $45.10 |
| Equipment operator | $42.30 | 3.30 | $45.60 | 29.10 | $74.70 |
| Plasterer | $29.70 | 2.32 | $32.02 | 21.28 | $53.30 |
| Concrete saw operator | $29.60 | 2.31 | $31.91 | 21.89 | $53.80 |
| Compaction grouter | $42.60 | 3.32 | $45.92 | 30.38 | $76.30 |
| Laborer | $20.60 | 1.61 | $22.21 | 17.39 | $39.60 |
| Demolition laborer | $20.70 | 1.61 | $22.31 | 16.59 | $38.90 |

**Paid leave** is calculated based on two weeks paid vacation, one week sick leave, and seven paid holidays. Employer's matching portion of **FICA** is 7.65 percent. **FUTA** (Federal Unemployment) is .8 percent. **Worker's compensation** was calculated using a national average of 17.70 percent for the concrete trade; 15.00 percent for the equipment operator, 15.00 percent for the concrete saw operator; 13.00 percent for the plastering trade; 17.70 percent for the compaction grouting specialist; and 13.96 percent for the demolition laborer. **Unemployment insurance** was calculated using a national average of 8 percent. **Health insurance** was calculated based on a projected national average for 2015 of $1,025 per employee (and family when applicable) per month. Employer pays 80 percent for a per month cost of $820 per employee. **Retirement** is based on a 401(k) retirement program with employer matching of 50 percent. Employee contributions to the 401(k) plan are an average of 6 percent of the true wage. **Liability insurance** is based on a national average of 10.0 percent.

| | Craft@Hrs | Unit | Material | Labor | Total |
|---|---|---|---|---|---|
| **Concrete Labor Productivity** | | | | | |
| Demolition | | | | | |
| remove footings including rebar | 1D@1.64 | cy | — | 63.80 | 63.80 |
| remove footings including CEC rebar | 1D@1.96 | cy | — | 76.20 | 76.20 |
| remove footings with rebar | 1D@.121 | lf | — | 4.71 | 4.71 |
| remove footings with CEC rebar | 1D@.147 | lf | — | 5.72 | 5.72 |
| remove foundation including rebar | 1D@2.44 | cy | — | 94.90 | 94.90 |
| remove foundation including CEC rebar | 1D@2.94 | cy | — | 114.00 | 114.00 |
| remove 5" or 6" foundation with rebar | 1D@.073 | sf | — | 2.84 | 2.84 |
| remove 5" or 6" foundation with CEC rebar | 1D@.088 | sf | — | 3.42 | 3.42 |

| | Craft@Hrs | Unit | Material | Labor | Total |
|---|---|---|---|---|---|
| remove 8" or 10" foundation with rebar | 1D@.076 | sf | — | 2.96 | 2.96 |
| remove 8" or 10" foundation with CEC rebar | 1D@.092 | sf | — | 3.58 | 3.58 |
| remove footing & foundation with rebar | 1D@1.96 | cy | — | 76.20 | 76.20 |
| remove footing & foundation with CEC rebar | 1D@2.33 | cy | — | 90.60 | 90.60 |
| remove footing & 3' foundation | 1D@.346 | lf | — | 13.50 | 13.50 |
| remove footing & 3' foundation with CEC rebar | 1D@.418 | lf | — | 16.30 | 16.30 |
| remove footing & 4' foundation | 1D@.422 | lf | — | 16.40 | 16.40 |
| remove footing & 4' foundation with CEC rebar | 1D@.510 | lf | — | 19.80 | 19.80 |
| remove pier per cy | 1D@.699 | cy | — | 27.20 | 27.20 |
| remove pier | 1D@.082 | lf | — | 3.19 | 3.19 |
| remove grade beam per cy | 1D@2.33 | cy | — | 90.60 | 90.60 |
| remove grade beam | 1D@.174 | lf | — | 6.77 | 6.77 |
| remove lightweight slab | 1D@.026 | sf | — | 1.01 | 1.01 |
| remove lightweight slab with rebar | 1D@.029 | sf | — | 1.13 | 1.13 |
| remove lightweight slab with wire mesh | 1D@.031 | sf | — | 1.21 | 1.21 |
| remove slab | 1D@.027 | sf | — | 1.05 | 1.05 |
| remove slab with rebar | 1D@.030 | sf | — | 1.17 | 1.17 |
| remove slab with wire mesh | 1D@.033 | sf | — | 1.28 | 1.28 |
| remove sidewalk | 1D@.034 | sf | — | 1.32 | 1.32 |
| remove curb & gutter | 1D@.145 | lf | — | 5.64 | 5.64 |
| remove step | 1D@.047 | lf | — | 1.83 | 1.83 |
| remove step landing | 1D@.046 | sf | — | 1.79 | 1.79 |

## Forming and rebar setting crew

| | | |
|---|---|---|
| form and set rebar | conc. form installer | $54.60 |
| form and set rebar | laborer | $39.60 |
| form and set rebar | forming crew | $47.10 |

## Pouring and finishing crew

| | | |
|---|---|---|
| pour and finish concrete | conc. finisher | $54.40 |
| pour and finish concrete | conc. finisher's helper | $45.10 |
| pour and finish concrete | finishing crew | $49.80 |

Concrete footings

| | Craft@Hrs | Unit | Material | Labor | Total |
|---|---|---|---|---|---|
| form, set rebar, pour, & finish per cy | 9F@2.44 | cy | — | 118.00 | 118.00 |
| form, set CEC rebar, pour, & finish per cy | 9F@2.94 | cy | — | 143.00 | 143.00 |
| set forms for concrete footings | 3F@.041 | lf | — | 1.93 | 1.93 |
| strip forms from concrete footings & clean | 3F@.009 | lf | — | .42 | .42 |
| set rebar in forms for concrete footings | 3F@.036 | lf | — | 1.70 | 1.70 |
| set CEC rebar in forms for concrete footings | 3F@.067 | lf | — | 3.16 | 3.16 |
| pour and finish 16" by 10" footings | 8F@.065 | lf | — | 3.24 | 3.24 |
| pour and finish 20" by 10" footings | 8F@.074 | lf | — | 3.69 | 3.69 |
| pour and finish 24" by 12" footings | 8F@.081 | lf | — | 4.03 | 4.03 |
| pour and finish 32" by 14" footings | 8F@.091 | lf | — | 4.53 | 4.53 |

| | Craft@Hrs | Unit | Material | Labor | Total |
|---|---|---|---|---|---|
| **Concrete foundation wall** | | | | | |
| form, set rebar, pour, & finish per cy | 9F@2.70 | cy | — | 131.00 | 131.00 |
| form, set CEC rebar, pour, & finish per cy | 9F@3.13 | cy | — | 152.00 | 152.00 |
| set forms | 3F@.029 | sf | — | 1.37 | 1.37 |
| strip forms & clean | 3F@.006 | sf | — | .28 | .28 |
| set rebar package | 3F@.037 | sf | — | 1.74 | 1.74 |
| set CEC rebar package | 3F@.067 | sf | — | 3.16 | 3.16 |
| pour and finish 5" wide wall | 8F@.024 | sf | — | 1.20 | 1.20 |
| pour and finish 6" wide wall | 8F@.029 | sf | — | 1.44 | 1.44 |
| pour and finish 8" wide wall | 8F@.039 | sf | — | 1.94 | 1.94 |
| pour and finish 10" wide wall | 8F@.049 | sf | — | 2.44 | 2.44 |
| **Tractor-mounted auger (hole drilling for pier)** | | | | | |
| delivery and take home charges (mobilization) | 10@6.25 | ea | — | 467.00 | 467.00 |
| drill pier hole | 10@.083 | lf | — | 6.20 | 6.20 |
| **Concrete pier** | | | | | |
| form, set rebar cage, pour and finish per cy | 9F@14.9 | cy | — | 723.00 | 723.00 |
| set and brace fiber tube cap | 3F@.125 | lf | — | 5.89 | 5.89 |
| pour concrete pier | 8F@1.54 | lf | — | 76.70 | 76.70 |
| set and brace fiber tube for above-grade pier | 3F@.183 | lf | — | 8.62 | 8.62 |
| strip fiber tube | 3F@.056 | lf | — | 2.64 | 2.64 |
| pour above-grade concrete pier | 8F@.185 | lf | — | 9.21 | 9.21 |
| set rebar cage for concrete pier | 3F@.091 | lf | — | 4.29 | 4.29 |
| **Jacket pier** | | | | | |
| jackhammer for jacket, drill for new rebar | 1D@2.32 | ea | — | 90.20 | 90.20 |
| set forms | 3F@1.09 | ea | — | 51.30 | 51.30 |
| set rebar, secure with epoxy | 3F@.833 | ea | — | 39.20 | 39.20 |
| pour concrete jacket | 8F@1.30 | ea | — | 64.70 | 64.70 |
| **Grade beam** | | | | | |
| form, set rebar cage, pour, and finish per cy | 9F@4.00 | cy | — | 194.00 | 194.00 |
| set forms | 3F@.127 | lf | — | 5.98 | 5.98 |
| set rebar cage | 3F@.067 | lf | — | 3.16 | 3.16 |
| pour and finish 12" by 18" | 8F@.073 | lf | — | 3.64 | 3.64 |
| pour and finish 12" by 24" | 8F@.088 | lf | — | 4.38 | 4.38 |
| pour and finish 14" by 18" | 8F@.118 | lf | — | 5.88 | 5.88 |
| pour and finish 14" by 24" | 8F@.235 | lf | — | 11.70 | 11.70 |
| pour and finish 16" by 18" | 8F@.353 | lf | — | 17.60 | 17.60 |
| pour and finish 16" by 24" | 8F@.470 | lf | — | 23.40 | 23.40 |
| pour and finish 18" by 18" | 8F@.118 | lf | — | 5.88 | 5.88 |
| pour and finish 18" by 24" | 8F@.235 | lf | — | 11.70 | 11.70 |
| **Jacket grade beam** | | | | | |
| jackhammer for jacket | 1D@.088 | lf | — | 3.42 | 3.42 |
| set forms | 3F@.150 | lf | — | 7.07 | 7.07 |
| set rebar, secure with epoxy | 3F@.083 | lf | — | 3.91 | 3.91 |
| pour concrete | 8F@.240 | lf | — | 12.00 | 12.00 |

|  | Craft@Hrs | Unit | Material | Labor | Total |
|---|---|---|---|---|---|
| **Lightweight concrete flatwork** | | | | | |
| form, pour, and finish per cy | 9F@2.04 | cy | — | 98.90 | 98.90 |
| pour and finish 2" slab | 8F@.012 | sf | — | .60 | .60 |
| pour and finish 4" slab | 8F@.013 | sf | — | .65 | .65 |
| pour and finish 6" slab | 8F@.015 | sf | — | .75 | .75 |
| **Concrete flatwork** | | | | | |
| form, pour, and finish per cy | 9F@2.04 | cy | — | 98.90 | 98.90 |
| set forms for concrete slab | 3F@.011 | sf | — | .52 | .52 |
| set rebar 24" on center | 3F@.036 | sf | — | 1.70 | 1.70 |
| set rebar 12" on center | 3F@.080 | sf | — | 3.77 | 3.77 |
| set wire mesh | 3F@.015 | sf | — | .71 | .71 |
| pour and finish 4" slab | 8F@.024 | sf | — | 1.20 | 1.20 |
| pour and finish 6" slab | 8F@.036 | sf | — | 1.79 | 1.79 |
| pour and finish 8" slab | 8F@.036 | sf | — | 1.79 | 1.79 |
| haul aggregate for slab base to job site | 10@.002 | sf | — | .15 | .15 |
| spread 2" aggregate slab base | 2F@.013 | sf | — | .51 | .51 |
| spread 4" aggregate slab base | 2F@.015 | sf | — | .59 | .59 |
| haul sand for slab base to job site | 10@.001 | sf | — | .07 | .07 |
| spread 2" sand slab base | 2F@.012 | sf | — | .48 | .48 |
| spread 4" sand slab base | 2F@.014 | sf | — | .55 | .55 |
| **Sidewalk flatwork** | | | | | |
| form, pour, and finish per cy | 9F@4.17 | cy | — | 202.00 | 202.00 |
| set forms | 3F@.023 | sf | — | 1.08 | 1.08 |
| pour and finish 3" sidewalk | 8F@.019 | sf | — | .95 | .95 |
| pour and finish 4" sidewalk | 8F@.026 | sf | — | 1.29 | 1.29 |
| pour and finish 6" sidewalk | 8F@.039 | sf | — | 1.94 | 1.94 |
| **Concrete dye** | | | | | |
| trowel into wet concrete | 8F@.009 | sf | — | .45 | .45 |
| **Stamp concrete** | | | | | |
| slab or sidewalk | 8F@.053 | sf | — | 2.64 | 2.64 |
| with paver pattern | 8F@.045 | sf | — | 2.24 | 2.24 |
| grout stamped paver pattern joints | 8F@.023 | sf | — | 1.15 | 1.15 |
| **Exposed aggregate** | | | | | |
| Finish with exposed aggregate finish | 8F@.019 | sf | — | .95 | .95 |
| **Curb & gutter work** | | | | | |
| set forms | 3F@.123 | lf | — | 5.79 | 5.79 |
| pour and finish | 8F@.150 | lf | — | 7.47 | 7.47 |
| **Concrete step** | | | | | |
| form, set rebar, pour, and finish per cy | 9F@7.69 | cy | — | 373.00 | 373.00 |
| set forms and rebar per lf of step | 3F@.133 | lf | — | 6.26 | 6.26 |
| pour and finish per lf of step | 8F@.100 | lf | — | 4.98 | 4.98 |
| set forms and rebar for landing per cubic foot | 3F@.011 | sf | — | .52 | .52 |
| pour and finish landing per cubic foot | 8F@.056 | sf | — | 2.79 | 2.79 |

| | Craft@Hrs | Unit | Material | Labor | Total |
|---|---|---|---|---|---|
| **Saw concrete** | | | | | |
| wall with rebar per lf, 1" deep | 20@.111 | lf | — | 5.97 | 5.97 |
| wall with CEC rebar per lf, 1" deep | 20@.125 | lf | — | 6.73 | 6.73 |
| floor per lf, 1" deep | 20@.050 | lf | — | 2.69 | 2.69 |
| floor with rebar per lf, 1" deep | 20@.054 | lf | — | 2.91 | 2.91 |
| floor with wire mesh per lf, 1" deep | 20@.052 | lf | — | 2.80 | 2.80 |
| expansion joint in "green" slab | 20@.189 | lf | — | 10.20 | 10.20 |
| **Core drill concrete** | | | | | |
| 2" wall, per inch of depth | 20@.066 | li | — | 3.55 | 3.55 |
| 4" wall, per inch of depth | 20@.073 | li | — | 3.93 | 3.93 |
| 2" floor, per inch of depth | 20@.064 | li | — | 3.44 | 3.44 |
| 4" floor, per inch of depth | 20@.067 | li | — | 3.60 | 3.60 |
| **Set rebar** | | | | | |
| #3 (3/8") | 3F@.014 | lf | — | .66 | .66 |
| #4 (1/2") | 3F@.014 | lf | — | .66 | .66 |
| #5 (5/8") | 3F@.014 | lf | — | .66 | .66 |
| #6 (3/4") | 3F@.014 | lf | — | .66 | .66 |
| #7 (7/8") | 3F@.015 | lf | — | .71 | .71 |
| #8 (1") | 3F@.015 | lf | — | .71 | .71 |
| **Buttress foundation** | | | | | |
| machine excavate to 12" to 24" of ext. foundation | 10@.027 | sf | — | 2.02 | 2.02 |
| hand excavate exterior of foundation | 2F@.161 | sf | — | 6.38 | 6.38 |
| backfill buttressed foundation | 2F@.048 | sf | — | 1.90 | 1.90 |
| set forms for exterior buttress | 3F@.021 | sf | — | .99 | .99 |
| set rebar for exterior buttress | 3F@.017 | sf | — | .80 | .80 |
| pour and finish exterior buttress | 8F@.027 | sf | — | 1.34 | 1.34 |
| hand excavate interior crawl space for buttress | 2F@.457 | sf | — | 18.10 | 18.10 |
| set forms for interior buttress in crawl space | 3F@.032 | sf | — | 1.51 | 1.51 |
| set rebar for interior buttress in crawl space | 3F@.023 | sf | — | 1.08 | 1.08 |
| pour and finish interior buttress in crawl space | 8F@.037 | sf | — | 1.84 | 1.84 |
| hand excavate interior foundation in basement | 2F@.204 | sf | — | 8.08 | 8.08 |
| set forms for interior buttress in basement | 3F@.025 | sf | — | 1.18 | 1.18 |
| set rebar for interior buttress in basement | 3F@.019 | sf | — | .89 | .89 |
| pour and finish interior buttress in basement | 8F@.032 | sf | — | 1.59 | 1.59 |

**Compaction grouting crew**

| | | |
|---|---|---|
| core drill, insert pipes, pump grout | compaction grouting specialist | $76.30 |
| core drill, insert pipes, pump grout | laborer | $39.60 |
| compaction grouting crew | compaction grouting crew | $58.00 |

**Foundation & footing stabilization with pressurized grout**

| | Craft@Hrs | Unit | Material | Labor | Total |
|---|---|---|---|---|---|
| 2" core drill through footings | 2G@.379 | ea | — | 22.00 | 22.00 |
| insert 2" pipes into ground beneath footings | 2G@.143 | lf | — | 8.29 | 8.29 |
| pump pressurized grout through pipes | 2G@.250 | lf | — | 14.50 | 14.50 |

|                          | Craft@Hrs | Unit | Material | Labor | Equip. | Total |
|--------------------------|-----------|------|----------|-------|--------|-------|

## Demolition & Hauling

### Minimum charge.

| | Craft@Hrs | Unit | Material | Labor | Equip. | Total |
|---|---|---|---|---|---|---|
| Demolition work | 1D@2.00 | ea | — | 77.80 | 128.00 | 205.80 |

### Dump fee. Typical metro area landfill fees. Will be up to 60% higher in major metro areas and 30% to 60% lower in rural areas.

| | Craft@Hrs | Unit | Material | Labor | Equip. | Total |
|---|---|---|---|---|---|---|
| Charge per cubic yard | — | cy | 54.50 | — | — | 54.50 |
| Charge per ton | — | tn | 103.00 | — | — | 103.00 |

### Dumpster. Includes up to two dumps per week.

| | Craft@Hrs | Unit | Material | Labor | Equip. | Total |
|---|---|---|---|---|---|---|
| 3 cy, rental per week | — | ea | — | — | 140.00 | 140.00 |
| 5 cy, rental per week | — | ea | — | — | 242.00 | 242.00 |
| 10 cy, rental per week | — | ea | — | — | 307.00 | 307.00 |
| 30 cy, rental per week | — | ea | — | — | 448.00 | 448.00 |
| Minimum dumpster charge | — | ea | — | — | 193.00 | 193.00 |

### Refuse chute.

| | Craft@Hrs | Unit | Material | Labor | Equip. | Total |
|---|---|---|---|---|---|---|
| Plywood | 1D@1.63 | lf | 15.40 | 63.40 | — | 78.80 |
| Minimum charge for plywood refuse chute | 1D@3.67 | ea | 82.60 | 143.00 | — | 225.60 |
| 18" prefabricated circular steel | 1D@1.18 | lf | 17.80 | 45.90 | — | 63.70 |
| 36" prefabricated circular steel | 1D@1.60 | lf | 32.10 | 62.20 | — | 94.30 |
| Minimum charge for circular steel refuse chute | 1D@3.30 | ea | 93.30 | 128.00 | — | 221.30 |

### Debris hauling.

| | Craft@Hrs | Unit | Material | Labor | Equip. | Total |
|---|---|---|---|---|---|---|
| By trailer or dump truck | | | | | | |
| per cubic yard | — | cy | — | — | 27.80 | 27.80 |
| per ton | — | tn | — | — | 75.40 | 75.40 |
| By pick-up truck | | | | | | |
| per pick-up truck load | — | ea | — | — | 28.40 | 28.40 |

### Strip room. Remove all wall and floor coverings, doors, other trim, and underlayment. Stud walls and plywood subfloor remain. For rooms with contents add 4%.

| | Craft@Hrs | Unit | Material | Labor | Equip. | Total |
|---|---|---|---|---|---|---|
| Stripped to bare walls and subfloor, per square foot | | | | | | |
| typical room | 1D@.074 | sf | — | 2.88 | — | 2.88 |
| bathroom | 1D@.150 | sf | — | 5.84 | — | 5.84 |
| kitchen | 1D@.115 | sf | — | 4.47 | — | 4.47 |
| utility room | 1D@.086 | sf | — | 3.35 | — | 3.35 |
| laundry room | 1D@.095 | sf | — | 3.70 | — | 3.70 |

|  | Craft@Hrs | Unit | Material | Labor | Equip. | Total |
|---|---|---|---|---|---|---|

**Time & Material Charts** (selected items)
**Demolition & Hauling Materials**

| | Craft@Hrs | Unit | Material | Labor | Equip. | Total |
|---|---|---|---|---|---|---|
| Refuse chute | | | | | | |
| plywood | — | lf | 15.60 | — | — | 15.60 |
| 18" prefabricated circular steel | — | lf | 18.00 | — | — | 18.00 |
| 36" prefabricated circular steel | — | lf | 32.50 | — | — | 32.50 |

**Demolition & Hauling Rental Equipment**

| | Craft@Hrs | Unit | Material | Labor | Equip. | Total |
|---|---|---|---|---|---|---|
| Dumpster rental per week | | | | | | |
| 3 cy ($138.00 week) | — | ea | — | — | 138.00 | 138.00 |
| 5 cy ($261.00 week) | — | ea | — | — | 261.00 | 261.00 |
| 10 cy ($331.00 week) | — | ea | — | — | 331.00 | 331.00 |
| 30 cy ($484.00 week) | — | ea | — | — | 484.00 | 484.00 |
| Truck rental with driver | | | | | | |
| 3 cy dump truck | | | | | | |
| ($659.00 day, 22 cy) | — | cy | — | — | 30.00 | 30.00 |
| ($659.00 day, 8.08 ton) | — | ton | — | — | 81.60 | 81.60 |
| pick-up truck ($277.00 day, 9 load) | — | ea | — | — | 30.80 | 30.80 |

**Demolition & Hauling Labor**

| Laborer | base wage | paid leave | true wage | taxes & ins. | total |
|---|---|---|---|---|---|
| Demolition laborer | $20.70 | 1.62 | $22.32 | 16.58 | $38.90 |

**Paid leave** is calculated based on two weeks paid vacation, one week sick leave, and seven paid holidays. Employer's matching portion of **FICA** is 7.65 percent. **FUTA** (Federal Unemployment) is .8 percent. **Worker's compensation** for Demolition was calculated using a national average of 13.96 percent. **Unemployment insurance** was calculated using a national average of 8 percent. **Health insurance** was calculated based on a projected national average for 2015 of $1,025 per employee (and family when applicable) per month. Employer pays 80 percent for a per month cost of $820 per employee. **Retirement** is based on a 401(k) retirement program with employer matching of 50 percent. Employee contributions to the 401(k) plan are an average of 6 percent of the true wage. **Liability insurance** is based on a national average of 10.0 percent.

| | Craft@Hrs | Unit | Material | Labor | Equip. | Total |
|---|---|---|---|---|---|---|

**Demolition & Hauling Labor Productivity**

| | Craft@Hrs | Unit | Material | Labor | Equip. | Total |
|---|---|---|---|---|---|---|
| Build / install refuse chute | | | | | | |
| plywood | 1D@1.63 | lf | — | 63.40 | — | 63.40 |
| 18" prefabricated circular steel | 1D@1.18 | lf | — | 45.90 | — | 45.90 |
| 36" prefabricated circular steel | 1D@1.60 | lf | — | 62.20 | — | 62.20 |
| Strip room to bare walls and subfloor | | | | | | |
| typical room | 1D@.074 | sf | — | 2.88 | — | 2.88 |
| bathroom | 1D@.150 | sf | — | 5.84 | — | 5.84 |
| kitchen | 1D@.115 | sf | — | 4.47 | — | 4.47 |
| utility | 1D@.086 | sf | — | 3.35 | — | 3.35 |
| laundry | 1D@.095 | sf | — | 3.70 | — | 3.70 |

# Doors

| | Craft@Hrs | Unit | Material | Labor | Total |
|---|---|---|---|---|---|

**Using Door Items.** When replacing a door, select the door type, then the jamb type, and add the two together. Door prices are for the door slab only and include routing and drilling for standard hardware and hinges. Door tear-out is for the door slab only. Use this tear-out price when removing the slab and leaving the jamb and casing intact. Jamb and casing prices include the cost to prehang the door in the jamb and the cost of hinges (but not the door lockset). Tear-out includes removal of the entire door. Use this tear-out price when removing the door, jamb and casing.

### Minimum charge.

| | Craft@Hrs | Unit | Material | Labor | Total |
|---|---|---|---|---|---|
| for door work | 1C@2.50 | ea | 42.50 | 142.00 | 184.50 |

**Folding Door.** Folding doors usually used in closets. Includes folding door section with hardware (including track, pins, hinges and a basic pull as needed). Priced per section of folding door. Does not include jamb or casing. Folding doors are often called bi-fold doors.

Folding door (per section)

| | Craft@Hrs | Unit | Material | Labor | Total |
|---|---|---|---|---|---|
| replace, hardboard smooth or wood-textured | 1C@.394 | ea | 35.30 | 22.40 | 57.70 |
| replace, hardboard wood-textured and embossed | 1C@.394 | ea | 40.30 | 22.40 | 62.70 |
| replace, mahogany (lauan) or birch veneer | 1C@.394 | ea | 37.70 | 22.40 | 60.10 |
| replace, ash or oak veneer | 1C@.394 | ea | 41.10 | 22.40 | 63.50 |
| replace, walnut or cherry veneer | 1C@.394 | ea | 47.10 | 22.40 | 69.50 |
| replace, paint-grade pine panel | 1C@.394 | ea | 61.40 | 22.40 | 83.80 |
| replace, stain-grade pine panel | 1C@.394 | ea | 75.60 | 22.40 | 98.00 |
| replace, paint-grade pine full-louvered | 1C@.394 | ea | 72.40 | 22.40 | 94.80 |
| replace, stain-grade pine full-louvered | 1C@.394 | ea | 84.00 | 22.40 | 106.40 |
| replace, paint-grade pine half-louvered | 1C@.394 | ea | 68.80 | 22.40 | 91.20 |
| replace, stain-grade pine half-louvered | 1C@.394 | ea | 79.80 | 22.40 | 102.20 |
| replace, red oak folding panel | 1C@.394 | ea | 92.30 | 22.40 | 114.70 |
| replace, folding mirrored | 1C@.394 | ea | 106.00 | 22.40 | 128.40 |
| remove, folding door | 1D@.114 | ea | — | 4.43 | 4.43 |
| remove, folding doors for work, reinstall | 1C@.148 | ea | — | 8.42 | 8.42 |

*standard* *panel* *full-louver* *half-louver*

**Bypassing Door.** Usually used in closets. Priced per door section. Includes track and hardware. For jamb & casing see below.

Bypassing door (per section)

| | Craft@Hrs | Unit | Material | Labor | Total |
|---|---|---|---|---|---|
| replace, hardboard smooth or wood textured | 1C@.755 | ea | 69.40 | 43.00 | 112.40 |
| replace, hardboard wood-textured and embossed | 1C@.755 | ea | 78.00 | 43.00 | 121.00 |
| replace, mahogany (lauan) or birch veneer | 1C@.755 | ea | 75.60 | 43.00 | 118.60 |
| replace, ash or oak veneer | 1C@.755 | ea | 78.80 | 43.00 | 121.80 |
| replace, walnut or cherry veneer | 1C@.755 | ea | 98.10 | 43.00 | 141.10 |
| replace, paint-grade pine panel | 1C@.755 | ea | 119.00 | 43.00 | 162.00 |
| replace, stain-grade pine panel | 1C@.755 | ea | 146.00 | 43.00 | 189.00 |
| replace, red oak panel door | 1C@.755 | ea | 186.00 | 43.00 | 229.00 |
| replace, paint-grade pine full-louvered | 1C@.755 | ea | 139.00 | 43.00 | 182.00 |
| replace, stain-grade pine full-louvered | 1C@.755 | ea | 166.00 | 43.00 | 209.00 |

*standard* *panel* *full-louver*

|  | Craft@Hrs | Unit | Material | Labor | Total |
|---|---|---|---|---|---|
| replace, paint-grade pine half-louvered | 1C@.755 | ea | 134.00 | 43.00 | 177.00 |
| replace, stain-grade pine half-louvered | 1C@.755 | ea | 158.00 | 43.00 | 201.00 |
| replace, mirrored | 1C@.755 | ea | 205.00 | 43.00 | 248.00 |
| remove, bypassing door | 1D@.139 | ea | — | 5.41 | 5.41 |
| remove, bypassing sliding doors for work, then reinstall | 1C@.220 | ea | — | 12.50 | 12.50 |

*half-louver*

**Jamb & casing for closet door.** Includes jamb, casing, finish nails, and installation in opening for a folding or bypassing door set. Includes casing strip to cover door track. Does not include door hardware including the track. Per lf around opening.

| Jamb & casing for folding or bypassing door opening |  |  |  |  |  |
|---|---|---|---|---|---|
| replace, paint grade | 1C@.109 | lf | 1.23 | 6.20 | 7.43 |
| replace, stain grade | 1C@.109 | lf | 1.37 | 6.20 | 7.57 |
| replace, birch | 1C@.109 | lf | 1.34 | 6.20 | 7.54 |
| replace, mahogany | 1C@.109 | lf | 1.92 | 6.20 | 8.12 |
| replace, ash or oak | 1C@.109 | lf | 2.07 | 6.20 | 8.27 |
| replace, walnut or cherry | 1C@.109 | lf | 2.79 | 6.20 | 8.99 |
| remove, jamb & casing for closet door | 1D@.026 | lf | — | 1.01 | 1.01 |

**Interior door.** Price per door. Includes hollow-core interior door with hinges and installation in an existing jamb. Pre-drilled and routed for hardware and hinges. Does not include jamb, casing, or door hardware.

| Interior doors |  |  |  |  |  |
|---|---|---|---|---|---|
| replace, hardboard smooth or wood-textured | 1C@.215 | ea | 94.00 | 12.20 | 106.20 |
| replace, hardboard wood-textured and embossed | 1C@.215 | ea | 131.00 | 12.20 | 143.20 |
| replace, mahogany or birch veneer | 1C@.215 | ea | 104.00 | 12.20 | 116.20 |
| replace, ash or oak veneer | 1C@.215 | ea | 112.00 | 12.20 | 124.20 |
| replace, walnut or cherry veneer | 1C@.215 | ea | 149.00 | 12.20 | 161.20 |
| replace, mirrored | 1C@.215 | ea | 244.00 | 12.20 | 256.20 |
| replace, plastic laminate face | 1C@.215 | ea | 377.00 | 12.20 | 389.20 |
| remove, interior door | 1D@.217 | ea | — | 8.44 | 8.44 |
| add for solid-core, 1 hr. fire-rated door | — | ea | 134.00 | — | 134.00 |

**French door.** Includes interior French door with hinges and installation in an existing jamb. Pre-drilled and routed for hardware and hinges. Does not include jamb, casing, or door hardware.

| French doors |  |  |  |  |  |
|---|---|---|---|---|---|
| replace, paint-grade wood | 1C@.215 | ea | 244.00 | 12.20 | 256.20 |
| replace, stain-grade fir | 1C@.215 | ea | 292.00 | 12.20 | 304.20 |
| replace, metal | 1C@.215 | ea | 251.00 | 12.20 | 263.20 |
| replace, full-lite door with simulated French grid | 1C@.215 | ea | 218.00 | 12.20 | 230.20 |
| remove, French door | 1D@.217 | ea | — | 8.44 | 8.44 |
| add for double-glazed insulated glass | — | ea | 95.00 | — | 95.00 |
| add for fire-rated glass | — | ea | 109.00 | — | 109.00 |

**Full-louvered door.** Includes full-louvered door with hinges and installation in an existing jamb. Pre-drilled and routed for hardware and hinges. Does not include jamb, casing, or door hardware.

| replace, paint-grade pine | 1C@.215 | ea | 205.00 | 12.20 | 217.20 |
|---|---|---|---|---|---|
| replace, stain-grade pine | 1C@.215 | ea | 251.00 | 12.20 | 263.20 |
| remove | 1D@.217 | ea | — | 8.44 | 8.44 |

|  | Craft@Hrs | Unit | Material | Labor | Total |
|---|---|---|---|---|---|

**Half-louvered door.** Includes half-louvered door with hinges and installation in an existing jamb. Pre-drilled and routed for hardware and hinges. Does not include jamb, casing, or door hardware.

|  | Craft@Hrs | Unit | Material | Labor | Total |
|---|---|---|---|---|---|
| replace, paint-grade pine | 1C@.215 | ea | 184.00 | 12.20 | 196.20 |
| replace, stain-grade pine | 1C@.215 | ea | 243.00 | 12.20 | 255.20 |
| remove | 1D@.217 | ea | — | 8.44 | 8.44 |

**Remove interior door for work and reinstall.**

|  | Craft@Hrs | Unit | Material | Labor | Total |
|---|---|---|---|---|---|
| door slab | 1C@.151 | ea | — | 8.59 | 8.59 |
| door, jamb & casing | 1C@1.63 | ea | — | 92.70 | 92.70 |
| double door slabs | 1C@.293 | ea | — | 16.70 | 16.70 |
| double doors, jamb & casing for work | 1C@2.67 | ea | — | 152.00 | 152.00 |

**Jamb & casing for interior door.** Price per door. Includes jamb and casing for interior door, shims, finish nails, and installation. Includes hanging door in jamb, installing jamb in rough opening, and casing jamb. Does not include door, hinges, or door hardware.

| Jamb & casing for interior door | Craft@Hrs | Unit | Material | Labor | Total |
|---|---|---|---|---|---|
| replace, paint-grade pine | 1C@1.43 | ea | 22.10 | 81.40 | 103.50 |
| replace, paint-grade pine for double door | 1C@1.43 | ea | 41.40 | 81.40 | 122.80 |
| replace, stain-grade pine | 1C@1.43 | ea | 24.80 | 81.40 | 106.20 |
| replace, stain-grade pine for double door | 1C@1.43 | ea | 46.40 | 81.40 | 127.80 |
| replace, birch | 1C@1.43 | ea | 27.30 | 81.40 | 108.70 |
| replace, birch for double door | 1C@1.43 | ea | 50.30 | 81.40 | 131.70 |
| replace, mahogany | 1C@1.43 | ea | 32.60 | 81.40 | 114.00 |
| replace, mahogany veneer | 1C@1.43 | ea | 30.60 | 81.40 | 112.00 |
| replace, mahogany for double door | 1C@1.43 | ea | 63.00 | 81.40 | 144.40 |
| replace, mahogany veneer for double door | 1C@1.43 | ea | 62.20 | 81.40 | 143.60 |
| replace, ash or oak | 1C@1.43 | ea | 39.50 | 81.40 | 120.90 |
| replace, ash or oak veneer | 1C@1.43 | ea | 35.60 | 81.40 | 117.00 |
| replace, ash or oak for double door | 1C@1.43 | ea | 70.40 | 81.40 | 151.80 |
| replace, ash or oak veneer for double door | 1C@1.43 | ea | 67.40 | 81.40 | 148.80 |
| replace, walnut or cherry | 1C@1.43 | ea | 57.20 | 81.40 | 138.60 |
| replace, walnut or cherry veneer | 1C@1.43 | ea | 54.20 | 81.40 | 135.60 |
| replace, walnut or cherry for double door | 1C@1.43 | ea | 106.00 | 81.40 | 187.40 |
| replace, walnut or cherry veneer for double door | 1C@1.43 | ea | 101.00 | 81.40 | 182.40 |
| replace, steel | 1C@1.43 | ea | 152.00 | 81.40 | 233.40 |
| replace, steel for double door | 1C@1.43 | ea | 292.00 | 81.40 | 373.40 |
| remove, jamb & casing for interior door | 1D@.388 | ea | — | 15.10 | 15.10 |
| remove, jamb & casing for steel double interior door | 1D@.484 | ea | — | 18.80 | 18.80 |
| add for installation for pocket door | 1C@.322 | ea | 19.00 | 18.30 | 37.30 |
| add for installation for double pocket door | 1C@.871 | ea | 31.80 | 49.60 | 81.40 |

**Rough framing for pocket door.** Includes track, hardware, and side framing kit. Antique systems include framing for walls on each side of the pocket door.

|  | Craft@Hrs | Unit | Material | Labor | Total |
|---|---|---|---|---|---|
| replace, in 2" x 4" wall | 1C@1.50 | ea | 31.00 | 85.40 | 116.40 |
| replace, for double doors in 2" x 4" wall | 1C@2.88 | ea | 49.80 | 164.00 | 213.80 |
| replace, in 2" x 6" wall | 1C@1.52 | ea | 33.60 | 86.50 | 120.10 |
| replace, for double doors in 2" x 6" wall | 1C@2.95 | ea | 59.70 | 168.00 | 227.70 |
| replace, in 2" x 8" wall | 1C@1.54 | ea | 36.10 | 87.60 | 123.70 |
| replace, for double doors in 2" x 8" wall | 1C@3.03 | ea | 63.80 | 172.00 | 235.80 |

| | Craft@Hrs | Unit | Material | Labor | Total |
|---|---|---|---|---|---|
| replace, for antique pocket door (2" x 4" walls on both sides) | 1C@2.45 | ea | 109.00 | 139.00 | 248.00 |
| replace, for antique double pocket doors (2" x 4" walls on both sides) | 1C@5.12 | ea | 195.00 | 291.00 | 486.00 |

## Pocket door track.

| | Craft@Hrs | Unit | Material | Labor | Total |
|---|---|---|---|---|---|
| replace, overhead for antique door system | 1C@1.30 | ea | 63.80 | 74.00 | 137.80 |
| replace, overhead for antique double door system | 1C@2.34 | ea | 87.30 | 133.00 | 220.30 |
| replace, clean & realign overhead double door track | 1C@1.96 | ea | — | 112.00 | 112.00 |
| replace, floor for antique door system | 1C@1.21 | ea | 70.40 | 68.80 | 139.20 |
| replace, floor for antique double door system | 1C@2.20 | ea | 95.00 | 125.00 | 220.00 |
| clean and realign floor double door track | 1C@2.64 | ea | — | 150.00 | 150.00 |
| remove, pocket door track | 1D@.751 | ea | — | 29.20 | 29.20 |
| remove, double pocket door system | 1D@1.28 | ea | — | 49.80 | 49.80 |

## Remove pocket door for work and reinstall.

| | Craft@Hrs | Unit | Material | Labor | Total |
|---|---|---|---|---|---|
| door and trim | 1C@1.15 | ea | — | 65.40 | 65.40 |
| door, jamb & casing | 1C@3.23 | ea | — | 184.00 | 184.00 |
| double doors & trim | 1C@1.58 | ea | — | 89.90 | 89.90 |
| double doors, jamb & casing | 1C@3.39 | ea | — | 193.00 | 193.00 |

**Panel doors.** Includes paint-grade panel door with hinges and installation in an existing jamb. Pre-drilled and routed for hardware and hinges. Does not include jamb, casing, or door hardware. Door contains from 6 to 9 panels. Each wood species includes line items for a new door, a reconditioned door, and a door that is custom milled to match a specific pattern. Reconditioned Door: Reconditioned panel doors have been removed from a historical structure and reconditioned by an architectural salvage company. These doors will have some scratches, dents, patching and may have been stripped of paint. "Graining" is a method of painting wood to make it look like the grain of another wood. This process was used extensively in the 19th century, most often to paint pine to appear like quartersawn oak. Custom-Milled Door: Custom-milled doors include the additional costs for panel doors that are milled to match an existing door pattern. For these doors it is necessary to cut custom shaper knives for the panels and custom molder (or shaper) knives for the stiles and rails. Add **60%** if milling two or fewer doors.

| | Craft@Hrs | Unit | Material | Labor | Total |
|---|---|---|---|---|---|
| **Paint grade doors** | | | | | |
| replace | 1C@.178 | ea | 623.00 | 10.10 | 633.10 |
| add for panel door custom milled to match | — | % | 67.0 | — | — |
| replace, reconditioned antique | 1C@.178 | ea | 520.00 | 10.10 | 530.10 |
| replace, reconditioned grained antique | 1C@.178 | ea | 756.00 | 10.10 | 766.10 |
| **Stain-grade fir doors** | | | | | |
| replace | 1C@.178 | ea | 856.00 | 10.10 | 866.10 |
| add for panel door custom milled to match | — | % | 35.0 | — | — |
| replace, reconditioned antique | 1C@.178 | ea | 783.00 | 10.10 | 793.10 |
| **Redwood doors** | | | | | |
| replace | 1C@.178 | ea | 923.00 | 10.10 | 933.10 |
| add for panel door custom milled to match | — | % | 26.0 | — | — |
| replace, reconditioned antique | 1C@.178 | ea | 889.00 | 10.10 | 899.10 |
| **Cypress doors** | | | | | |
| replace | 1C@.178 | ea | 874.00 | 10.10 | 884.10 |
| add for panel door custom milled to match | — | % | 17.0 | — | — |
| replace, reconditioned antique | 1C@.178 | ea | 815.00 | 10.10 | 825.10 |

| | Craft@Hrs | Unit | Material | Labor | Total |
|---|---|---|---|---|---|
| **Oak doors** | | | | | |
| replace | 1C@.178 | ea | 780.00 | 10.10 | 790.10 |
| add for panel door custom milled to match | — | % | 35.0 | — | — |
| replace, reconditioned painted antique | 1C@.178 | ea | 580.00 | 10.10 | 590.10 |
| replace, reconditioned stained antique | 1C@.178 | ea | 671.00 | 10.10 | 681.10 |
| **Mahogany doors** | | | | | |
| replace | 1C@.178 | ea | 900.00 | 10.10 | 910.10 |
| add for panel door custom milled to match | — | % | 29.0 | — | — |
| replace, reconditioned antique door | 1C@.178 | ea | 831.00 | 10.10 | 841.10 |
| **Walnut doors** | | | | | |
| replace | 1C@.178 | ea | 1,350.00 | 10.10 | 1,360.10 |
| add for panel door custom milled to match | — | % | 17.0 | — | — |
| replace, reconditioned antique | 1C@.178 | ea | 1,180.00 | 10.10 | 1,190.10 |
| Remove panel door | 1D@.217 | ea | — | 8.44 | 8.44 |

**Additional panel door costs.**

| | Craft@Hrs | Unit | Material | Labor | Total |
|---|---|---|---|---|---|
| add for tempered glass lite | — | ea | 318.00 | — | 318.00 |
| add for beveled or edged glass lite | — | ea | 596.00 | — | 596.00 |
| add for leaded or colored glass lite | — | ea | 691.00 | — | 691.00 |
| add for panel door with round or elliptical top | 1C@4.55 | ea | 780.00 | 259.00 | 1,039.00 |

**Remove panel door for work and reinstall.**

| | Craft@Hrs | Unit | Material | Labor | Total |
|---|---|---|---|---|---|
| slab only | 1C@.152 | ea | — | 8.65 | 8.65 |
| door, jamb, & casing | 1C@1.63 | ea | — | 92.70 | 92.70 |

**Panel door repair.**  Not including custom knife charges.

| | Craft@Hrs | Unit | Material | Labor | Total |
|---|---|---|---|---|---|
| **Antique panel door repair** | | | | | |
| replace door panel | 1C@2.74 | ea | 131.00 | 156.00 | 287.00 |
| replace door stile | 1C@2.49 | ea | 95.70 | 142.00 | 237.70 |
| **Panel door minimum charges** | | | | | |
| repair door with no custom milling | 1C@1.50 | ea | 152.00 | 85.40 | 237.40 |
| repair door when custom milling is required | 1C@2.50 | ea | 520.00 | 142.00 | 662.00 |
| **Custom milling** | | | | | |
| shaper or molder knife charge | — | ea | 411.00 | — | 411.00 |
| shaper or molder setup charge | — | ea | 194.00 | — | 194.00 |
| minimum shaper or molder charge | — | ea | 861.00 | — | 861.00 |
| **Antique door repair** | | | | | |
| repair cracks & dry rot in door with epoxy, tighten stiles | 1C@4.49 | ea | 187.00 | 255.00 | 442.00 |
| repair cracks & dry rot in jamb with epoxy | 1C@3.40 | ea | 109.00 | 193.00 | 302.00 |
| repair cracks & dry rot in casing with epoxy | 1C@3.40 | ea | 84.00 | 193.00 | 277.00 |
| remove casing, re-plumb door, & reinstall casing | 1C@2.95 | ea | — | 168.00 | 168.00 |
| add for antique panel door transom | — | % | 38.0 | — | — |

|  | Craft@Hrs | Unit | Material | Labor | Total |
|---|---|---|---|---|---|

**Batten door.** Built from vertical boards, usually tongue-and-groove, held in place by horizontal battens and diagonal braces. Standard grade, sometimes called ledged-and-braced doors, have boards held in place by diagonally braced horizontal battens. High grade have tongue-and-groove boards held in place by a stile frame and a single horizontal batten. The frame is joined with mortise and tenon joints, and diagonal braces. These are sometimes called framed ledged-and-braced doors.

*standard*     *high*

**Batten door.** Includes batten style door with hinges and installation in an existing jamb. Pre-drilled and routed for hardware and hinges. Does not include jamb, casing, or door hardware.

|  | Craft@Hrs | Unit | Material | Labor | Total |
|---|---|---|---|---|---|
| replace, paint-grade, standard grade | 1C@.178 | ea | 486.00 | 10.10 | 496.10 |
| replace, paint grade, high grade | 1C@.178 | ea | 704.00 | 10.10 | 714.10 |
| replace, stain-grade, standard grade | 1C@.178 | ea | 889.00 | 10.10 | 899.10 |
| replace, stain-grade, high grade | 1C@.178 | ea | 1,230.00 | 10.10 | 1,240.10 |
| remove | 1D@.217 | ea | — | 8.44 | 8.44 |

**Storm/screen door.** Price per door. Includes storm/screen door set including jamb and hinges with fasteners. Complete unit is installed in jamb of existing door. Does not include furring or other modification to existing jamb.

|  | Craft@Hrs | Unit | Material | Labor | Total |
|---|---|---|---|---|---|
| replace, metal, economy grade | 1C@1.21 | ea | 163.00 | 68.80 | 231.80 |
| replace, metal, standard grade | 1C@1.21 | ea | 243.00 | 68.80 | 311.80 |
| replace, metal, high grade | 1C@1.21 | ea | 351.00 | 68.80 | 419.80 |
| replace, metal, deluxe grade | 1C@1.21 | ea | 445.00 | 68.80 | 513.80 |
| replace, wood, economy grade | 1C@1.21 | ea | 186.00 | 68.80 | 254.80 |
| replace, wood, standard grade | 1C@1.21 | ea | 303.00 | 68.80 | 371.80 |
| replace, wood, high grade | 1C@1.21 | ea | 358.00 | 68.80 | 426.80 |
| replace, wood, deluxe grade | 1C@1.21 | ea | 445.00 | 68.80 | 513.80 |
| replace, Victorian style wood, standard grade | 1C@1.21 | ea | 486.00 | 68.80 | 554.80 |
| replace, Victorian style wood, high grade | 1C@1.21 | ea | 580.00 | 68.80 | 648.80 |
| replace, Victorian style wood, deluxe grade | 1C@1.21 | ea | 815.00 | 68.80 | 883.80 |
| remove, storm door | 1D@.227 | ea | — | 8.83 | 8.83 |
| remove for work, then reinstall | 1C@1.70 | ea | — | 96.70 | 96.70 |

*economy*   *metal*

*high*   *deluxe*

*standard*   *standard*

*high*   *deluxe*

| | Craft@Hrs | Unit | Material | Labor | Total |
|---|---|---|---|---|---|

**Exterior French door.** Includes exterior French door with hinges and installation in an existing jamb. Pre-drilled and routed for hardware and hinges. Does not include jamb, casing, or door hardware.

| | Craft@Hrs | Unit | Material | Labor | Total |
|---|---|---|---|---|---|
| replace, paint-grade pine | 1C@.212 | ea | 486.00 | 12.10 | 498.10 |
| replace, stain-grade fir | 1C@.212 | ea | 555.00 | 12.10 | 567.10 |
| replace, metal | 1C@.212 | ea | 540.00 | 12.10 | 552.10 |
| replace, full-lite insulated with simulated grid | 1C@.212 | ea | 464.00 | 12.10 | 476.10 |
| remove, exterior French door | 1D@.283 | ea | — | 11.00 | 11.00 |

**Exterior veneer door.** Price per door. Includes exterior veneer door with hinges and installation in an existing jamb. Pre-drilled and routed for hardware and hinges. Does not include jamb, casing, or door hardware.

| | Craft@Hrs | Unit | Material | Labor | Total |
|---|---|---|---|---|---|
| replace, mahogany (lauan) or birch veneer | 1C@.212 | ea | 230.00 | 12.10 | 242.10 |
| replace, ash or red oak veneer | 1C@.212 | ea | 251.00 | 12.10 | 263.10 |
| replace, walnut or cherry veneer | 1C@.212 | ea | 279.00 | 12.10 | 291.10 |
| replace, insulated steel | 1C@.212 | ea | 230.00 | 12.10 | 242.10 |
| remove, exterior veneer door | 1D@.283 | ea | — | 11.00 | 11.00 |

**Additional exterior door costs.**

| | Craft@Hrs | Unit | Material | Labor | Total |
|---|---|---|---|---|---|
| add for full-lite | — | ea | 310.00 | — | 310.00 |
| add for leaded or colored glass full-lite | — | ea | 691.00 | — | 691.00 |
| add for half-lite | — | ea | 134.00 | — | 134.00 |
| add for leaded or colored glass half-lite | — | ea | 386.00 | — | 386.00 |
| add for 1' by 1' lite | — | ea | 41.10 | — | 41.10 |

*Bottom*

flush　　　raised panel　　　crossbuck　　　shelf

*Top*

full lite　　　four lite　　　six lite　　　nine lite

**Dutch door.** Includes Dutch-style door with hinges and installation in an existing jamb. Pre-drilled and routed for hardware and hinges. Includes only one of the two door segments. Does not include jamb, casing, or door hardware.

| | Craft@Hrs | Unit | Material | Labor | Total |
|---|---|---|---|---|---|
| replace, bottom section, flush | 1C@.325 | ea | 229.00 | 18.50 | 247.50 |
| replace, bottom section, raised panel | 1C@.325 | ea | 341.00 | 18.50 | 359.50 |
| replace, bottom section, cross buck | 1C@.325 | ea | 442.00 | 18.50 | 460.50 |
| replace, add for shelf on bottom section | — | ea | 71.70 | — | 71.70 |
| replace, top section with full-lite | 1C@.325 | ea | 303.00 | 18.50 | 321.50 |
| replace, top section with four lites | 1C@.325 | ea | 363.00 | 18.50 | 381.50 |
| replace, top section with six lites | 1C@.325 | ea | 386.00 | 18.50 | 404.50 |
| replace, top section with nine lites | 1C@.325 | ea | 417.00 | 18.50 | 435.50 |
| remove door, jamb, & casing for work, then reinstall | 1C@2.74 | ea | — | 156.00 | 156.00 |
| remove door slabs for work, then reinstall | 1C@.393 | ea | — | 22.40 | 22.40 |
| remove, Dutch door | 1D@.321 | ea | — | 12.50 | 12.50 |

| | Craft@Hrs | Unit | Material | Labor | Total |
|---|---|---|---|---|---|

**Entry doors.** All entry doors are solid wood with occasional veneered wood components in the lower grades. Entry door prices do not include jamb and casing. See below for exterior jambs and quality indicators.

**Entry door grades.** Standard grade includes multiple panel doors (nine and more) with some embossed components. May have lites in place of panels. High grade is the same as Standard grade with some embossed and carved components. May also may have carved onlays. Deluxe grade includes door components that have moderate carvings. May have exotic wood components. Custom grade includes door components that have extensive carvings. May have exotic wood components, leaded glass, or beveled glass. Custom Deluxe grade is the same as Custom grade with oval or elliptical top windows.

**Steel entry door.** Price per door. Standard grade is flush face and high grade is embossed. Does not include jamb or casing.

| | Craft@Hrs | Unit | Material | Labor | Total |
|---|---|---|---|---|---|
| replace, standard grade | 1C@.212 | ea | 279.00 | 12.10 | 291.10 |
| replace, high grade | 1C@.212 | ea | 371.00 | 12.10 | 383.10 |
| remove, steel entry door | 1D@.283 | ea | — | 11.00 | 11.00 |

**Steel entry door side-lite.** Includes door side-lite, fasteners, and installation. Does not include wall framing, caulking, or finishing.

| | Craft@Hrs | Unit | Material | Labor | Total |
|---|---|---|---|---|---|
| replace, standard grade | 1C@1.14 | ea | 143.00 | 64.90 | 207.90 |
| replace, high grade | 1C@1.14 | ea | 184.00 | 64.90 | 248.90 |
| remove, steel entry door side-lite | 1D@.508 | ea | — | 19.80 | 19.80 |

**Paint-grade wood entry door.** Price per door. Includes paint-grade wood entry door with hinges and installation in an existing jamb. Pre-drilled and routed for hardware and hinges. Does not include jamb, casing, or door hardware.

| | Craft@Hrs | Unit | Material | Labor | Total |
|---|---|---|---|---|---|
| replace, standard grade | 1C@.212 | ea | 299.00 | 12.10 | 311.10 |
| replace, high grade | 1C@.212 | ea | 426.00 | 12.10 | 438.10 |
| replace, deluxe grade | 1C@.212 | ea | 576.00 | 12.10 | 588.10 |
| replace, custom grade | 1C@.212 | ea | 831.00 | 12.10 | 843.10 |
| replace, custom deluxe grade | 1C@.212 | ea | 964.00 | 12.10 | 976.10 |
| remove, wood entry door | 1D@.283 | ea | — | 11.00 | 11.00 |

**Paint-grade wood entry door side-lite.** Includes door side-lite, fasteners, and installation. Does not include wall framing, caulking, or finishing.

| | Craft@Hrs | Unit | Material | Labor | Total |
|---|---|---|---|---|---|
| replace, standard grade | 1C@1.14 | ea | 203.00 | 64.90 | 267.90 |
| replace, high grade | 1C@1.14 | ea | 280.00 | 64.90 | 344.90 |
| replace, deluxe grade | 1C@1.14 | ea | 405.00 | 64.90 | 469.90 |
| replace, custom grade | 1C@1.14 | ea | 560.00 | 64.90 | 624.90 |
| replace, custom deluxe grade | 1C@1.14 | ea | 675.00 | 64.90 | 739.90 |
| remove, entry door side lite | 1D@.508 | ea | — | 19.80 | 19.80 |

**Fir entry door.** Stain grade. Price per door. Does not include jamb or casing.

| | Craft@Hrs | Unit | Material | Labor | Total |
|---|---|---|---|---|---|
| replace, standard grade | 1C@.212 | ea | 663.00 | 12.10 | 675.10 |
| replace, high grade | 1C@.212 | ea | 806.00 | 12.10 | 818.10 |
| replace, deluxe grade | 1C@.212 | ea | 1,030.00 | 12.10 | 1,042.10 |
| replace, custom grade | 1C@.212 | ea | 1,530.00 | 12.10 | 1,542.10 |
| replace, custom deluxe grade | 1C@.212 | ea | 2,020.00 | 12.10 | 2,032.10 |
| remove, entry door slab only | 1D@.283 | ea | — | 11.00 | 11.00 |

| | Craft@Hrs | Unit | Material | Labor | Total |
|---|---|---|---|---|---|

**Fir entry door side-lite.** Stain grade. Includes door side-lite, fasteners, and installation. Does not include wall framing, caulking, or finishing.

| | Craft@Hrs | Unit | Material | Labor | Total |
|---|---|---|---|---|---|
| replace, standard grade | 1C@1.14 | ea | 429.00 | 64.90 | 493.90 |
| replace, high grade | 1C@1.14 | ea | 555.00 | 64.90 | 619.90 |
| replace, deluxe grade | 1C@1.14 | ea | 688.00 | 64.90 | 752.90 |
| replace, custom grade | 1C@1.14 | ea | 1,050.00 | 64.90 | 1,114.90 |
| replace, custom deluxe grade | 1C@1.14 | ea | 1,390.00 | 64.90 | 1,454.90 |
| remove, entry door side lite | 1D@.508 | ea | — | 19.80 | 19.80 |

**Mahogany entry door.** Price per door. Does not include jamb or casing.

| | Craft@Hrs | Unit | Material | Labor | Total |
|---|---|---|---|---|---|
| replace, standard grade | 1C@.411 | ea | 561.00 | 23.40 | 584.40 |
| replace, high grade | 1C@.411 | ea | 856.00 | 23.40 | 879.40 |
| replace, deluxe grade | 1C@.411 | ea | 1,330.00 | 23.40 | 1,353.40 |
| replace, custom grade | 1C@.411 | ea | 1,770.00 | 23.40 | 1,793.40 |
| replace, custom deluxe grade | 1C@.411 | ea | 2,220.00 | 23.40 | 2,243.40 |
| remove, entry door | 1D@.283 | ea | — | 11.00 | 11.00 |

**Mahogany entry door side-lite.** Includes door side-lite, fasteners, and installation. Does not include wall framing, caulking, or finishing.

| | Craft@Hrs | Unit | Material | Labor | Total |
|---|---|---|---|---|---|
| replace, standard grade | 1C@1.14 | ea | 389.00 | 64.90 | 453.90 |
| replace, high grade | 1C@1.14 | ea | 584.00 | 64.90 | 648.90 |
| replace, deluxe grade | 1C@1.14 | ea | 926.00 | 64.90 | 990.90 |
| replace, custom grade | 1C@1.14 | ea | 1,230.00 | 64.90 | 1,294.90 |
| replace, custom deluxe grade | 1C@1.14 | ea | 1,590.00 | 64.90 | 1,654.90 |
| remove, entry door side lite | 1D@.508 | ea | — | 19.80 | 19.80 |

**Wood embossing.** Wood is often embossed to appear like it has been carved. Embossing stamps a pattern onto the wood. Embossing is far less expensive than carving and can only be used for relatively shallow patterns.

**Wood onlays.** Wood onlays are mass-produced carved wood components that are nailed and glued on doors to give a hand-carved look.

**Ash or oak entry door.** Price per door. Does not include jamb or casing.

| | Craft@Hrs | Unit | Material | Labor | Total |
|---|---|---|---|---|---|
| replace, standard grade | 1C@.411 | ea | 537.00 | 23.40 | 560.40 |
| replace, high grade | 1C@.411 | ea | 831.00 | 23.40 | 854.40 |
| replace, deluxe grade | 1C@.411 | ea | 1,100.00 | 23.40 | 1,123.40 |
| replace, custom grade | 1C@.411 | ea | 1,860.00 | 23.40 | 1,883.40 |
| replace, custom deluxe grade | 1C@.411 | ea | 2,370.00 | 23.40 | 2,393.40 |
| remove, entry door slab only | 1D@.283 | ea | — | 11.00 | 11.00 |

**Ash or oak entry door side-lite.** Includes door side-lite, fasteners, and installation. Does not include wall framing, caulking, or finishing.

| | Craft@Hrs | Unit | Material | Labor | Total |
|---|---|---|---|---|---|
| replace, standard grade | 1C@1.14 | ea | 363.00 | 64.90 | 427.90 |
| replace, high grade | 1C@1.14 | ea | 587.00 | 64.90 | 651.90 |
| replace, deluxe grade | 1C@1.14 | ea | 726.00 | 64.90 | 790.90 |
| replace, custom grade | 1C@1.14 | ea | 1,320.00 | 64.90 | 1,384.90 |
| replace, custom deluxe grade | 1C@1.14 | ea | 1,680.00 | 64.90 | 1,744.90 |
| remove, entry door side lite | 1D@.508 | ea | — | 19.80 | 19.80 |

| | Craft@Hrs | Unit | Material | Labor | Total |
|---|---|---|---|---|---|

**Redwood entry door.** Price per door.  Does not include jamb or casing.

| | Craft@Hrs | Unit | Material | Labor | Total |
|---|---|---|---|---|---|
| replace, standard grade | 1C@.411 | ea | 688.00 | 23.40 | 711.40 |
| replace, high grade | 1C@.411 | ea | 1,110.00 | 23.40 | 1,133.40 |
| replace, deluxe grade | 1C@.411 | ea | 1,430.00 | 23.40 | 1,453.40 |
| replace, custom grade | 1C@.411 | ea | 1,940.00 | 23.40 | 1,963.40 |
| replace, custom deluxe grade | 1C@.411 | ea | 2,210.00 | 23.40 | 2,233.40 |
| remove, entry door slab only | 1D@.283 | ea | — | 11.00 | 11.00 |

**Redwood entry door side-lite.** Includes door side-lite, fasteners, and installation. Does not include wall framing, caulking, or finishing.

| | Craft@Hrs | Unit | Material | Labor | Total |
|---|---|---|---|---|---|
| replace, standard grade | 1C@1.14 | ea | 453.00 | 64.90 | 517.90 |
| replace, high grade | 1C@1.14 | ea | 780.00 | 64.90 | 844.90 |
| replace, deluxe grade | 1C@1.14 | ea | 1,010.00 | 64.90 | 1,074.90 |
| replace, custom grade | 1C@1.14 | ea | 1,360.00 | 64.90 | 1,424.90 |
| replace, custom deluxe grade | 1C@1.14 | ea | 1,580.00 | 64.90 | 1,644.90 |
| remove, entry door side lite | 1D@.508 | ea | — | 19.80 | 19.80 |

**Cypress entry door.** Price per door.  Does not include jamb or casing.

| | Craft@Hrs | Unit | Material | Labor | Total |
|---|---|---|---|---|---|
| replace, standard grade | 1C@.411 | ea | 627.00 | 23.40 | 650.40 |
| replace, high grade | 1C@.411 | ea | 840.00 | 23.40 | 863.40 |
| replace, deluxe grade | 1C@.411 | ea | 1,060.00 | 23.40 | 1,083.40 |
| replace, custom grade | 1C@.411 | ea | 1,540.00 | 23.40 | 1,563.40 |
| replace, custom deluxe grade | 1C@.411 | ea | 1,990.00 | 23.40 | 2,013.40 |
| remove, entry door slab only | 1D@.283 | ea | — | 11.00 | 11.00 |

**Cypress entry door side-lite.** Includes door side-lite, fasteners, and installation. Does not include wall framing, caulking, or finishing.

| | Craft@Hrs | Unit | Material | Labor | Total |
|---|---|---|---|---|---|
| replace, standard grade | 1C@1.14 | ea | 428.00 | 64.90 | 492.90 |
| replace, high grade | 1C@1.14 | ea | 574.00 | 64.90 | 638.90 |
| replace, deluxe grade | 1C@1.14 | ea | 740.00 | 64.90 | 804.90 |
| replace, custom grade | 1C@1.14 | ea | 1,080.00 | 64.90 | 1,144.90 |
| replace, custom deluxe grade | 1C@1.14 | ea | 1,420.00 | 64.90 | 1,484.90 |
| remove, entry door side lite | 1D@.508 | ea | — | 19.80 | 19.80 |

**Walnut or cherry entry door.** Price per door.  Does not include jamb or casing.

| | Craft@Hrs | Unit | Material | Labor | Total |
|---|---|---|---|---|---|
| replace, standard grade | 1C@.411 | ea | 881.00 | 23.40 | 904.40 |
| replace, high grade | 1C@.411 | ea | 1,320.00 | 23.40 | 1,343.40 |
| replace, deluxe grade | 1C@.411 | ea | 1,660.00 | 23.40 | 1,683.40 |
| replace, custom grade | 1C@.411 | ea | 2,480.00 | 23.40 | 2,503.40 |
| replace, custom deluxe grade | 1C@.411 | ea | 3,200.00 | 23.40 | 3,223.40 |
| remove, entry door slab only | 1D@.283 | ea | — | 11.00 | 11.00 |

**Walnut or cherry entry door side-lite.** Includes door side-lite, fasteners, and installation. Does not include wall framing, caulking, or finishing.

| | Craft@Hrs | Unit | Material | Labor | Total |
|---|---|---|---|---|---|
| replace, standard grade | 1C@1.14 | ea | 573.00 | 64.90 | 637.90 |
| replace, high grade | 1C@1.14 | ea | 906.00 | 64.90 | 970.90 |
| replace, deluxe grade | 1C@1.14 | ea | 1,130.00 | 64.90 | 1,194.90 |
| replace, custom grade | 1C@1.14 | ea | 1,770.00 | 64.90 | 1,834.90 |
| replace, custom deluxe grade | 1C@1.14 | ea | 2,290.00 | 64.90 | 2,354.90 |
| remove, entry door side lite | 1D@.508 | ea | — | 19.80 | 19.80 |

| | Craft@Hrs | Unit | Material | Labor | Total |
|---|---|---|---|---|---|
| **Remove exterior door for work and reinstall.** | | | | | |
| door, jamb, & casing | 1C@2.20 | ea | — | 125.00 | 125.00 |
| door slab | 1C@.292 | ea | — | 16.60 | 16.60 |
| double door, jamb & casing | 1C@3.12 | ea | — | 178.00 | 178.00 |
| double door slab | 1C@.366 | ea | — | 20.80 | 20.80 |

**Exterior door jamb & casing.** Price per door. Includes jamb and casing for exterior door, shims, finish nails, and installation. Includes hanging door in jamb, installing jamb in rough opening, and casing jamb. Does not include door, hinges, or door hardware.

| | Craft@Hrs | Unit | Material | Labor | Total |
|---|---|---|---|---|---|
| replace, paint-grade pine | 1C@1.75 | ea | 57.20 | 99.60 | 156.80 |
| replace, paint-grade pine for double door | 1C@3.11 | ea | 102.00 | 177.00 | 279.00 |
| replace, stain-grade pine | 1C@1.75 | ea | 67.10 | 99.60 | 166.70 |
| replace, stain-grade pine for double door | 1C@3.11 | ea | 120.00 | 177.00 | 297.00 |
| replace, birch | 1C@1.75 | ea | 63.80 | 99.60 | 163.40 |
| replace, birch for double door | 1C@3.11 | ea | 112.00 | 177.00 | 289.00 |
| replace, mahogany | 1C@1.75 | ea | 75.60 | 99.60 | 175.20 |
| replace, mahogany veneered jamb & solid casing | 1C@1.75 | ea | 68.50 | 99.60 | 168.10 |
| replace, mahogany for double door | 1C@3.11 | ea | 135.00 | 177.00 | 312.00 |
| replace, mahogany veneered jamb & solid casing for double door | 1C@3.11 | ea | 124.00 | 177.00 | 301.00 |
| replace, ash or oak | 1C@1.75 | ea | 79.80 | 99.60 | 179.40 |
| replace, ash or oak veneered jamb & solid casing | 1C@1.75 | ea | 73.50 | 99.60 | 173.10 |
| replace, ash or oak for double door | 1C@3.11 | ea | 143.00 | 177.00 | 320.00 |
| replace, ash or oak veneered jamb & solid casing for double door | 1C@3.11 | ea | 134.00 | 177.00 | 311.00 |
| replace, redwood | 1C@1.75 | ea | 71.40 | 99.60 | 171.00 |
| replace, redwood for double door | 1C@3.11 | ea | 126.00 | 177.00 | 303.00 |
| replace, cypress | 1C@1.75 | ea | 66.30 | 99.60 | 165.90 |
| replace, cypress double door | 1C@3.11 | ea | 119.00 | 177.00 | 296.00 |
| replace, walnut or cherry | 1C@1.75 | ea | 94.00 | 99.60 | 193.60 |
| replace, walnut or cherry veneered jamb & solid casing | 1C@1.75 | ea | 86.90 | 99.60 | 186.50 |
| replace, walnut or cherry for double door | 1C@3.11 | ea | 161.00 | 177.00 | 338.00 |
| replace, walnut or cherry veneered jamb & solid casing for double door | 1C@3.11 | ea | 154.00 | 177.00 | 331.00 |
| replace, steel | 1C@1.75 | ea | 92.30 | 99.60 | 191.90 |
| replace, steel for double door | 1C@3.11 | ea | 134.00 | 177.00 | 311.00 |
| remove, exterior door, jamb & casing | 1D@.496 | ea | — | 19.30 | 19.30 |

**Additional exterior jamb & casing costs.**

| | Craft@Hrs | Unit | Material | Labor | Total |
|---|---|---|---|---|---|
| add for hanging Dutch door | 1C@1.75 | ea | — | 99.60 | 99.60 |
| add for round- or elliptical-top door | — | ea | 196.00 | — | 196.00 |

| | Craft@Hrs | Unit | Material | Labor | Total |
|---|---|---|---|---|---|

**Entry door fanlite.** Includes fanlite, fasteners, and installation. Fanlites are semi-circular or half-elliptical windows that appear above doors. True fanlites have mullions that fan out from the bottom center of the lite. Lower grades will have a simulated fan grid. All fanlites include jamb and casing. Does not include wall framing, caulking, or finishing.

| | Craft@Hrs | Unit | Material | Labor | Total |
|---|---|---|---|---|---|
| replace, single entry door, standard grade | 1C@1.85 | ea | 240.00 | 105.00 | 345.00 |
| replace, single entry door, high grade | 1C@1.85 | ea | 403.00 | 105.00 | 508.00 |
| replace, single entry door, deluxe grade | 1C@1.85 | ea | 560.00 | 105.00 | 665.00 |
| replace, single entry door, custom grade | 1C@1.85 | ea | 774.00 | 105.00 | 879.00 |
| replace, single entry door, custom deluxe grade | 1C@1.85 | ea | 1,020.00 | 105.00 | 1,125.00 |
| remove entry door fanlite | 1D@.747 | ea | — | 29.10 | 29.10 |
| remove fanlite & casing for work, reinstall | 1C@3.13 | ea | — | 178.00 | 178.00 |

**Additional fanlite sizes.** Includes jamb and casing.

add 34% for fanlite for single door with side-lite

add 85% for fanlite for single door with two side-lites

add 99% for fanlite for double doors

add 147% for fanlite for double doors with two side-lites

**Entry door fixed transom.** Includes transom with jamb and casing, fasteners, and installation. Does not include wall framing. Transoms may have circular, semi-circular, or elliptical components, but the unit fits in a rectangular jamb.

| | Craft@Hrs | Unit | Material | Labor | Total |
|---|---|---|---|---|---|
| replace, single entry door, standard grade | 1C@1.00 | ea | 159.00 | 56.90 | 215.90 |
| replace, high grade | 1C@1.00 | ea | 269.00 | 56.90 | 325.90 |
| replace, deluxe grade | 1C@1.00 | ea | 448.00 | 56.90 | 504.90 |
| replace, custom grade | 1C@1.00 | ea | 652.00 | 56.90 | 708.90 |
| replace, custom deluxe grade | 1C@1.00 | ea | 926.00 | 56.90 | 982.90 |
| remove fixed transom | 1D@.924 | ea | — | 35.90 | 35.90 |
| remove fixed transom for work, reinstall | 1C@2.74 | ea | — | 156.00 | 156.00 |

**Additional transom sizes.** Includes jamb and casing.

replace, add 42% for fixed transom for single door with side lite

replace, add 65% for fixed transom for single door with two side lites

replace, add 89% for fixed transom for double doors

replace, add 106% for fixed transom for double doors with two side lites

**Café (bar) doors.** Includes hardware.

| | Craft@Hrs | Unit | Material | Labor | Total |
|---|---|---|---|---|---|
| replace, louvered paint-grade | 1C@.681 | ea | 115.00 | 38.70 | 153.70 |
| replace, louvered stain-grade | 1C@.681 | ea | 149.00 | 38.70 | 187.70 |
| replace, Victorian spindle & raised-panel paint-grade *louvered* | 1C@.681 | ea | 152.00 | 38.70 | 190.70 |
| replace, Victorian spindle & raised-panel stain-grade | 1C@.681 | ea | 187.00 | 38.70 | 225.70 |
| remove café door | 1D@.254 | ea | — | 9.88 | 9.88 |
| remove café doors for work, reinstall | 1C@1.02 | ea | — | 58.00 | 58.00 |

*Victorian spindle & raised-panel*

|  | Craft@Hrs | Unit | Material | Labor | Total |
|---|---|---|---|---|---|

**Sliding patio door.** *Includes sliding patio door set with integrated jamb, roller assembly, hardware, and installation. Does not include caulking.*

| | Craft@Hrs | Unit | Material | Labor | Total |
|---|---|---|---|---|---|
| replace, 6' by 6'8" bronze finish single-glazed | 1C@4.39 | ea | 572.00 | 250.00 | 822.00 |
| replace, 6' by 6'8" mill finish double-glazed | 1C@4.39 | ea | 772.00 | 250.00 | 1,022.00 |
| replace, 8' by 6'8" bronze finish single-glazed | 1C@4.39 | ea | 691.00 | 250.00 | 941.00 |
| replace, 8' by 6'8" mill finish double-glazed | 1C@4.39 | ea | 907.00 | 250.00 | 1,157.00 |
| replace, 12' by 6'8" bronze finish single-glazed (3 lites) | 1C@5.75 | ea | 1,030.00 | 327.00 | 1,357.00 |
| replace, 12' by 6'8" mill finish double-glazed (3 lites) | 1C@5.75 | ea | 1,460.00 | 327.00 | 1,787.00 |
| replace, 6' by 6'8" wood single-glazed | 1C@4.39 | ea | 1,200.00 | 250.00 | 1,450.00 |
| replace, 6' by 6'8" wood double-glazed | 1C@4.39 | ea | 1,360.00 | 250.00 | 1,610.00 |
| replace, 8' by 6'8" wood single-glazed | 1C@4.39 | ea | 1,470.00 | 250.00 | 1,720.00 |
| replace, 8' by 6'8" wood double-glazed | 1C@4.39 | ea | 1,630.00 | 250.00 | 1,880.00 |
| replace, 12' by 6'8" wood single-glazed (3 lites) | 1C@5.75 | ea | 2,210.00 | 327.00 | 2,537.00 |
| replace, 12' by 6'8" wood double-glazed (3 lites) | 1C@5.75 | ea | 2,440.00 | 327.00 | 2,767.00 |
| replace, 6' by 6'8" wood single-glazed clad exterior | 1C@4.39 | ea | 1,230.00 | 250.00 | 1,480.00 |
| replace, 6' by 6'8" wood double-glazed clad exterior | 1C@4.39 | ea | 1,520.00 | 250.00 | 1,770.00 |
| replace, 8' by 6'8" wood single-glazed clad exterior | 1C@5.75 | ea | 1,460.00 | 327.00 | 1,787.00 |
| replace, 8' by 6'8" wood double-glazed clad exterior | 1C@5.75 | ea | 1,780.00 | 327.00 | 2,107.00 |
| replace, 12' by 6'8" wood single-glazed clad exterior (3 lites) | 1C@5.75 | ea | 2,250.00 | 327.00 | 2,577.00 |
| replace, 12' by 6'8" wood double-glazed clad exterior (3 lites) | 1C@5.75 | ea | 2,940.00 | 327.00 | 3,267.00 |
| remove, 6' or 8' wide sliding patio door | 1D@1.87 | ea | — | 72.70 | 72.70 |
| remove, 12' wide sliding patio door | 1D@2.81 | ea | — | 109.00 | 109.00 |

*two lite patio door*

*three lite patio door*

**Additional sliding patio door costs.**

| | Craft@Hrs | Unit | Material | Labor | Total |
|---|---|---|---|---|---|
| add for tinted glass (per lite) | — | ea | 282.00 | — | 282.00 |
| remove door, jamb, & casing for work, then reinstall | 1C@5.55 | ea | — | 316.00 | 316.00 |
| remove door lite for work, then reinstall | 1C@1.65 | ea | — | 93.90 | 93.90 |
| replace, minimum charge | 1C@2.50 | ea | 33.20 | 142.00 | 175.20 |
| recondition door, replace hardware | 1C@2.33 | ea | 75.60 | 133.00 | 208.60 |

**Sliding patio door screen.** *Includes screen door set to match existing sliding patio door and installation. Includes screen assembly with hardware and rollers.*

| | Craft@Hrs | Unit | Material | Labor | Total |
|---|---|---|---|---|---|
| replace, 36" door screen | 1C@.125 | ea | 75.60 | 7.11 | 82.71 |
| replace, 48" door screen | 1C@.125 | ea | 94.00 | 7.11 | 101.11 |
| remove, door screen | 1D@.125 | ea | — | 4.86 | 4.86 |

**Pet door.** *Includes lock, aluminum frame, and PVC door.*

| | Craft@Hrs | Unit | Material | Labor | Total |
|---|---|---|---|---|---|
| replace, for small dogs, cats | 1C@.840 | ea | 67.10 | 47.80 | 114.90 |
| replace, for average size dogs | 1C@.840 | ea | 115.00 | 47.80 | 162.80 |
| replace, for large dogs | 1C@.844 | ea | 184.00 | 48.00 | 232.00 |
| remove, pet door | 1D@.291 | ea | — | 11.30 | 11.30 |
| remove for work, then reinstall | 1C@1.29 | ea | 8.39 | 73.40 | 81.79 |

| | Craft@Hrs | Unit | Material | Labor | Total |
|---|---|---|---|---|---|

**Garage door with hardware.** Includes garage door, track, hardware, fasteners, and installation. Does not include garage door opener, framing, or finishing. Economy grade includes overhead doors that are plastic-faced polystyrene or flush steel or uninsulated fiberglass. Single piece doors with flush surface or tongue-and-groove boards in herringbone or chevron patterns. Standard grade includes overhead doors that are textured or embossed steel, aluminum or fiberglass, usually insulated. Single-piece doors same as economy grade with lites, and paneled patterns. High grade overhead doors are same as standard grade with lites. Single-piece stain-grade wood doors with lites and carvings. Deluxe grade overhead doors are stain-grade wood doors, specialty patterns, designed carvings or embossing, fan-tops, and so forth.

| | Craft@Hrs | Unit | Material | Labor | Total |
|---|---|---|---|---|---|
| 8' garage door with hardware | | | | | |
| replace, economy grade | 1C@6.25 | ea | 478.00 | 356.00 | 834.00 |
| replace, standard grade | 1C@6.25 | ea | 555.00 | 356.00 | 911.00 |
| replace, high grade | 1C@6.25 | ea | 763.00 | 356.00 | 1,119.00 |
| replace, deluxe grade | 1C@6.25 | ea | 856.00 | 356.00 | 1,212.00 |
| remove, garage door | 1D@3.63 | ea | — | 141.00 | 141.00 |
| 9' garage door with hardware | | | | | |
| replace, economy grade | 1C@6.25 | ea | 520.00 | 356.00 | 876.00 |
| replace, standard grade | 1C@6.25 | ea | 708.00 | 356.00 | 1,064.00 |
| replace, high grade | 1C@6.25 | ea | 831.00 | 356.00 | 1,187.00 |
| replace, deluxe grade | 1C@6.25 | ea | 940.00 | 356.00 | 1,296.00 |
| remove, garage door | 1D@3.63 | ea | — | 141.00 | 141.00 |
| 10' garage door with hardware | | | | | |
| replace, economy grade | 1C@6.25 | ea | 595.00 | 356.00 | 951.00 |
| replace, standard grade | 1C@6.25 | ea | 740.00 | 356.00 | 1,096.00 |
| replace, high grade | 1C@6.25 | ea | 915.00 | 356.00 | 1,271.00 |
| replace, deluxe grade | 1C@6.25 | ea | 1,040.00 | 356.00 | 1,396.00 |
| remove, garage door | 1D@3.63 | ea | — | 141.00 | 141.00 |
| 12' garage door with hardware | | | | | |
| replace, economy grade | 1C@6.25 | ea | 671.00 | 356.00 | 1,027.00 |
| replace, standard grade | 1C@6.25 | ea | 831.00 | 356.00 | 1,187.00 |
| high grade | 1C@6.25 | ea | 1,050.00 | 356.00 | 1,406.00 |
| replace, deluxe grade | 1C@6.25 | ea | 1,180.00 | 356.00 | 1,536.00 |
| remove, garage door | 1D@3.63 | ea | — | 141.00 | 141.00 |
| 14' garage door with hardware | | | | | |
| replace, economy grade | 1C@6.25 | ea | 719.00 | 356.00 | 1,075.00 |
| replace, standard grade | 1C@6.25 | ea | 856.00 | 356.00 | 1,212.00 |
| replace, high grade | 1C@6.25 | ea | 1,050.00 | 356.00 | 1,406.00 |
| replace, deluxe grade | 1C@6.25 | ea | 1,260.00 | 356.00 | 1,616.00 |
| remove, garage door | 1D@3.63 | ea | — | 141.00 | 141.00 |
| 16' garage door with hardware | | | | | |
| replace, economy grade | 1C@6.25 | ea | 780.00 | 356.00 | 1,136.00 |
| replace, standard grade | 1C@6.25 | ea | 992.00 | 356.00 | 1,348.00 |
| replace, high grade | 1C@6.25 | ea | 1,150.00 | 356.00 | 1,506.00 |
| replace, deluxe grade | 1C@6.25 | ea | 1,350.00 | 356.00 | 1,706.00 |
| remove, garage door | 1D@3.63 | ea | — | 141.00 | 141.00 |
| 18' garage door with hardware | | | | | |
| replace, economy grade | 1C@6.25 | ea | 856.00 | 356.00 | 1,212.00 |
| replace, standard grade | 1C@6.25 | ea | 1,050.00 | 356.00 | 1,406.00 |
| replace, high grade | 1C@6.25 | ea | 1,200.00 | 356.00 | 1,556.00 |
| replace, deluxe grade | 1C@6.25 | ea | 1,450.00 | 356.00 | 1,806.00 |
| remove, garage door | 1D@3.63 | ea | — | 141.00 | 141.00 |
| Replace, garage door spring | 1C@2.00 | ea | 69.40 | 114.00 | 183.40 |
| Remove single-car door for work, then reinstall | 1C@7.70 | ea | — | 438.00 | 438.00 |
| Remove two-car door for work, then reinstall | 1C@9.25 | ea | — | 526.00 | 526.00 |

*economy*

*standard*

*high*

*deluxe*

*deluxe (fanlite)*

| | Craft@Hrs | Unit | Material | Labor | Total |
|---|---|---|---|---|---|

**Add for tall door.**  All door types.

Add 14% for 7' tall doors
Add 22% for 8' tall doors

**Garage door opener.**  Includes garage door opener, hardware, fasteners, and installation. Does not include garage door, electrical wiring for the opener, or framing.

| | Craft@Hrs | Unit | Material | Labor | Total |
|---|---|---|---|---|---|
| replace, standard grade | 1C@2.45 | ea | 386.00 | 139.00 | 525.00 |
| replace, high grade | 1C@2.45 | ea | 419.00 | 139.00 | 558.00 |
| replace, deluxe grade | 1C@2.45 | ea | 462.00 | 139.00 | 601.00 |
| remove, garage door opener | 1D@.765 | ea | — | 29.80 | 29.80 |
| replace, remote radio transmitter for opener | — | ea | 48.30 | — | 48.30 |
| remove garage door opener for work, then reinstall | 1C@3.50 | ea | — | 199.00 | 199.00 |

**Minimum charge.**

| | Craft@Hrs | Unit | Material | Labor | Total |
|---|---|---|---|---|---|
| for garage door work | 1C@2.50 | ea | 42.50 | 142.00 | 184.50 |

## Time & Material Charts (selected items)
## Doors Materials

See Doors material prices with the line items above.

### Doors Labor

| Laborer | base wage | paid leave | true wage | taxes & ins. | total |
|---|---|---|---|---|---|
| Finish carpenter | $31.10 | 2.43 | $33.53 | 23.37 | $56.90 |
| Demolition laborer | $20.70 | 1.61 | $22.31 | 16.59 | $38.90 |

**Paid leave** is calculated based on two weeks paid vacation, one week sick leave, and seven paid holidays.  Employer's matching portion of **FICA** is 7.65 percent.  **FUTA** (Federal Unemployment) is .8 percent.  **Worker's compensation** for the doors trade was calculated using a national average of 16.85 percent.  **Unemployment insurance** was calculated using a national average of 8 percent.  **Health insurance** was calculated based on a projected national average for 2015 of $1,025 per employee (and family when applicable) per month.  Employer pays 80 percent for a per month cost of $820 per employee.  **Retirement** is based on a 401(k) retirement program with employer matching of 50 percent.  Employee contributions to the 401(k) plan are an average of 6 percent of the true wage.  **Liability insurance** is based on a national average of 10.0 percent.

| | Craft@Hrs | Unit | Material | Labor | Total |
|---|---|---|---|---|---|

### Doors Labor Productivity

Demolition of doors

| | Craft@Hrs | Unit | Material | Labor | Total |
|---|---|---|---|---|---|
| remove, folding door | 1D@.114 | ea | — | 4.43 | 4.43 |
| remove, bypassing door | 1D@.139 | ea | — | 5.41 | 5.41 |
| remove, bypassing or folding door jamb & casing | 1D@.026 | lf | — | 1.01 | 1.01 |
| remove, pre-hung interior door, jamb, & casing | 1D@.388 | ea | — | 15.10 | 15.10 |
| remove, pre-hung interior door slab only | 1D@.217 | ea | — | 8.44 | 8.44 |
| remove, double pre-hung int. door, jamb, & casing | 1D@.585 | ea | — | 22.80 | 22.80 |
| remove, double pre-hung interior door slabs only | 1D@.321 | ea | — | 12.50 | 12.50 |
| remove, gar. door, overhead tracks, jamb, & casing | 1D@3.65 | ea | — | 142.00 | 142.00 |
| remove, garage door, hardware, jamb, & casing | 1D@2.90 | ea | — | 113.00 | 113.00 |
| remove, garage door only | 1D@1.82 | ea | — | 70.80 | 70.80 |

| | Craft@Hrs | Unit | Material | Labor | Total |
|---|---|---|---|---|---|
| remove, transom | 1D@.451 | ea | — | 17.50 | 17.50 |
| remove, entry door fan lite & casing | 1D@.749 | ea | — | 29.10 | 29.10 |
| remove, double entry door fan lite & casing | 1D@1.71 | ea | — | 66.50 | 66.50 |
| remove, storm door | 1D@.227 | ea | — | 8.83 | 8.83 |
| remove, entry door, jamb & casing | 1D@.496 | ea | — | 19.30 | 19.30 |
| remove, entry door slab only | 1D@.283 | ea | — | 11.00 | 11.00 |
| remove, double entry door, jamb, cas., & threshold | 1D@.842 | ea | — | 32.80 | 32.80 |
| remove, double entry door slabs only | 1D@.492 | ea | — | 19.10 | 19.10 |
| remove, entry door side lite | 1D@.508 | ea | — | 19.80 | 19.80 |
| remove, Dutch door slabs, jamb, & casing | 1D@.883 | ea | — | 34.30 | 34.30 |
| remove, Dutch door slabs only | 1D@.321 | ea | — | 12.50 | 12.50 |
| remove, cafe door | 1D@.254 | ea | — | 9.88 | 9.88 |
| remove, sliding glass patio door, per lite | 1D@.427 | ea | — | 16.60 | 16.60 |
| remove, pet door | 1D@.290 | ea | — | 11.30 | 11.30 |
| **Install interior doors** | | | | | |
| folding door per section | 1C@.394 | ea | — | 22.40 | 22.40 |
| bypassing door per section | 1C@.755 | ea | — | 43.00 | 43.00 |
| bypassing or folding door jamb & casing | 1C@.109 | lf | — | 6.20 | 6.20 |
| pre-hung interior door & casing | 1C@1.43 | ea | — | 81.40 | 81.40 |
| pre-hung interior door slab only | 1C@.215 | ea | — | 12.20 | 12.20 |
| double pre-hung interior door & casing | 1C@2.45 | ea | — | 139.00 | 139.00 |
| double pre-hung interior door slabs only | 1C@.412 | ea | — | 23.40 | 23.40 |
| **Install garage door** | | | | | |
| with overhead tracks, jamb, & casing | 1C@6.25 | ea | — | 356.00 | 356.00 |
| with hardware, jamb, & casing | 1C@5.21 | ea | — | 296.00 | 296.00 |
| door only | 1C@3.15 | ea | — | 179.00 | 179.00 |
| opener | 1C@2.45 | ea | — | 139.00 | 139.00 |
| **Install pocket door** | | | | | |
| door slabs | 1C@.855 | ea | — | 48.60 | 48.60 |
| door, jamb, trim, & casing | 1C@1.35 | ea | — | 76.80 | 76.80 |
| double doors | 1C@2.34 | ea | — | 133.00 | 133.00 |
| double door, jamb, trim, & casing | 1C@3.12 | ea | — | 178.00 | 178.00 |
| **Install pocket door rough framing package** | | | | | |
| **Including track and hardware** | | | | | |
| single door in 2" x 4" wall | 1C@1.50 | ea | — | 85.40 | 85.40 |
| double doors in 2" x 4" wall | 1C@2.88 | ea | — | 164.00 | 164.00 |
| single door in 2" x 6" wall | 1C@1.52 | ea | — | 86.50 | 86.50 |
| double doors in 2" x 6" wall | 1C@2.95 | ea | — | 168.00 | 168.00 |
| single door in 2" x 8" wall | 1C@1.54 | ea | — | 87.60 | 87.60 |
| double doors in 2" x 8" wall | 1C@3.03 | ea | — | 172.00 | 172.00 |
| rough framing for antique door | 1C@2.45 | ea | — | 139.00 | 139.00 |
| rough framing for antique double doors | 1C@5.12 | ea | — | 291.00 | 291.00 |
| **Install pocket door track** | | | | | |
| overhead track for antique door | 1C@1.30 | ea | — | 74.00 | 74.00 |
| overhead track for antique double door | 1C@2.34 | ea | — | 133.00 | 133.00 |
| clean & realign overhead ant. door track | 1C@1.96 | ea | — | 112.00 | 112.00 |
| floor track for antique door | 1C@1.21 | ea | — | 68.80 | 68.80 |
| floor track for antique double door | 1C@2.20 | ea | — | 125.00 | 125.00 |
| clean and realign floor antique doors | 1C@2.64 | ea | — | 150.00 | 150.00 |

| | Craft@Hrs | Unit | Material | Labor | Total |
|---|---|---|---|---|---|
| **Install panel door** | | | | | |
| hang door & install casing | 1C@1.23 | ea | — | 70.00 | 70.00 |
| slab only | 1C@.178 | ea | — | 10.10 | 10.10 |
| **Install entry door, fanlite, transom** | | | | | |
| fanlite & casing | 1C@1.85 | ea | — | 105.00 | 105.00 |
| transom & casing | 1C@1.00 | ea | — | 56.90 | 56.90 |
| hang entry door & install casing | 1C@1.75 | ea | — | 99.60 | 99.60 |
| slab only | 1C@.212 | ea | — | 12.10 | 12.10 |
| hang double-entry door & casing | 1C@3.11 | ea | — | 177.00 | 177.00 |
| double door slabs only | 1C@.330 | ea | — | 18.80 | 18.80 |
| side-lite | 1C@1.14 | ea | — | 64.90 | 64.90 |
| **Install Dutch door** | | | | | |
| hang door & install casing | 1C@1.70 | ea | — | 96.70 | 96.70 |
| slabs only | 1C@.325 | ea | — | 18.50 | 18.50 |
| **Install door lite** | | | | | |
| cut hole in door and install | 1C@1.12 | ea | — | 63.70 | 63.70 |
| **Install cafe door** | | | | | |
| per set | 1C@.681 | ea | — | 38.70 | 38.70 |
| **Install sliding glass patio doors** | | | | | |
| per lite | 1C@4.39 | ea | — | 250.00 | 250.00 |
| **Install pet door** | | | | | |
| per door | 1C@.844 | ea | — | 48.00 | 48.00 |
| **Assemble & install storm door** | | | | | |
| per door | 1C@1.21 | ea | — | 68.80 | 68.80 |
| | | | | | |
| **Remove for work, then reinstall** | | | | | |
| folding doors per section | 1C@.148 | ea | — | 8.42 | 8.42 |
| bypass sliding doors per section | 1C@.220 | ea | — | 12.50 | 12.50 |
| door slab | 1C@.151 | ea | — | 8.59 | 8.59 |
| door slab, jamb & casing | 1C@1.63 | ea | — | 92.70 | 92.70 |
| double door slabs | 1C@.293 | ea | — | 16.70 | 16.70 |
| double door slabs, jamb & casing | 1C@2.67 | ea | — | 152.00 | 152.00 |
| pocket door & casing | 1C@1.15 | ea | — | 65.40 | 65.40 |
| pocket door, jamb & casing | 1C@3.23 | ea | — | 184.00 | 184.00 |
| double pocket doors & casing | 1C@1.58 | ea | — | 89.90 | 89.90 |
| double pocket doors, jamb & casing | 1C@3.39 | ea | — | 193.00 | 193.00 |
| panel door slab | 1C@.152 | ea | — | 8.65 | 8.65 |
| panel door, jamb, & casing | 1C@1.63 | ea | — | 92.70 | 92.70 |
| antique door casing & re-plumb door | 1C@2.95 | ea | — | 168.00 | 168.00 |
| transom | 1C@1.12 | ea | — | 63.70 | 63.70 |
| storm door | 1C@1.70 | ea | — | 96.70 | 96.70 |
| Dutch door, jamb, & casing | 1C@2.74 | ea | — | 156.00 | 156.00 |
| Dutch door slabs | 1C@.394 | ea | — | 22.40 | 22.40 |
| exterior door, jamb, & casing | 1C@2.20 | ea | — | 125.00 | 125.00 |
| exterior door slab | 1C@.292 | ea | — | 16.60 | 16.60 |
| exterior double door, jamb, & casing | 1C@3.12 | ea | — | 178.00 | 178.00 |
| exterior double door slabs | 1C@.366 | ea | — | 20.80 | 20.80 |
| entry door fanlite & casing | 1C@3.12 | ea | — | 178.00 | 178.00 |
| entry door fixed transom & casing | 1C@2.74 | ea | — | 156.00 | 156.00 |
| cafe door | 1C@1.02 | ea | — | 58.00 | 58.00 |
| sliding patio door, jamb, & casing | 1C@5.55 | ea | — | 316.00 | 316.00 |
| sliding patio door lites | 1C@1.65 | ea | — | 93.90 | 93.90 |

| | Craft@Hrs | Unit | Material | Labor | Total |
|---|---|---|---|---|---|
| pet door | 1C@1.29 | ea | — | 73.40 | 73.40 |
| garage door opener | 1C@3.50 | ea | — | 199.00 | 199.00 |
| single-car garage door | 1C@7.70 | ea | — | 438.00 | 438.00 |
| two-car garage door | 1C@9.25 | ea | — | 526.00 | 526.00 |
| **Door repair** | | | | | |
| replace antique panel door panel (not including custom knife charges) | 1C@2.74 | ea | — | 156.00 | 156.00 |
| replace antique panel door stile (not including custom knife charges) | 1C@2.49 | ea | — | 142.00 | 142.00 |
| repair cracks & dry rot in antique door with epoxy, tighten stiles | 1C@4.49 | ea | — | 255.00 | 255.00 |
| repair cracks & dry rot in antique door jamb with epoxy | 1C@3.40 | ea | — | 193.00 | 193.00 |
| repair cracks & dry rot in antique door casing with epoxy | 1C@3.40 | ea | — | 193.00 | 193.00 |
| **Additional door labor charges** | | | | | |
| add for install. of full-lite in ext. door | 1C@1.39 | ea | — | 79.10 | 79.10 |
| add for install. of half-lite in ext. door | 1C@1.07 | ea | — | 60.90 | 60.90 |
| add for install. of 1' by 1' lite in ext. door | 1C@.594 | ea | — | 33.80 | 33.80 |
| recondition sliding door, replace hardware | 1C@2.33 | ea | — | 133.00 | 133.00 |

## Door Hardware

**Hardware Quality.** Some rules of thumb — Standard: Light gauge metal, chrome or brass plated with little or no pattern. High: Brass, chrome over brass, or nickel over brass with minimal detail, or plated with ornate detail. Deluxe: Brass, chrome over brass, or nickel over brass with moderate detail. Custom: Brass, chrome over brass, or nickel over brass with ornate detail.

### Deadbolt.

| | Craft@Hrs | Unit | Material | Labor | Total |
|---|---|---|---|---|---|
| replace, standard grade | 1C@.678 | ea | 30.60 | 38.60 | 69.20 |
| replace, high grade | 1C@.678 | ea | 45.20 | 38.60 | 83.80 |
| replace, deluxe grade | 1C@.678 | ea | 56.20 | 38.60 | 94.80 |
| remove, deadbolt | 1D@.276 | ea | — | 10.70 | 10.70 |
| remove for work, then reinstall | 1C@1.10 | ea | — | 62.60 | 62.60 |

### Exterior lockset.

| | Craft@Hrs | Unit | Material | Labor | Total |
|---|---|---|---|---|---|
| replace, standard grade | 1C@.461 | ea | 31.40 | 26.20 | 57.60 |
| replace, high grade | 1C@.461 | ea | 50.20 | 26.20 | 76.40 |
| replace, deluxe grade | 1C@.461 | ea | 67.70 | 26.20 | 93.90 |
| remove, exterior lockset | 1D@.314 | ea | — | 12.20 | 12.20 |
| remove for work, then reinstall | 1C@1.03 | ea | — | 58.60 | 58.60 |

| | Craft@Hrs | Unit | Material | Labor | Total |
|---|---|---|---|---|---|
| **Entry lockset.** | | | | | |
| replace, standard grade | 1C@1.45 | ea | 110.00 | 82.50 | 192.50 |
| replace, high grade | 1C@1.45 | ea | 293.00 | 82.50 | 375.50 |
| replace, deluxe grade | 1C@1.45 | ea | 491.00 | 82.50 | 573.50 |
| replace, custom grade | 1C@1.45 | ea | 681.00 | 82.50 | 763.50 |
| remove, entry door lockset | 1D@.696 | ea | — | 27.10 | 27.10 |
| remove for work, then reinstall | 1C@2.73 | ea | — | 155.00 | 155.00 |
| **Thumb latch.** | | | | | |
| Antique style | | | | | |
| replace, standard grade | 1C@1.73 | ea | 301.00 | 98.40 | 399.40 |
| replace, high grade | 1C@1.73 | ea | 366.00 | 98.40 | 464.40 |
| remove, thumb latch | 1D@.516 | ea | — | 20.10 | 20.10 |
| **Interior door lockset.** | | | | | |
| replace, standard grade | 1C@.405 | ea | 23.20 | 23.00 | 46.20 |
| replace, high grade | 1C@.405 | ea | 58.50 | 23.00 | 81.50 |
| replace, deluxe grade | 1C@.405 | ea | 93.00 | 23.00 | 116.00 |
| remove, interior door lockset | 1D@.281 | ea | — | 10.90 | 10.90 |
| remove for work, then reinstall | 1C@.710 | ea | — | 40.40 | 40.40 |
| **Door closer.** | | | | | |
| replace, spring hinge style | 1C@.257 | ea | 23.20 | 14.60 | 37.80 |
| replace, standard grade | 1C@.431 | ea | 57.40 | 24.50 | 81.90 |
| replace, high grade | 1C@.431 | ea | 101.00 | 24.50 | 125.50 |
| remove, door closer | 1D@.291 | ea | — | 11.30 | 11.30 |
| remove for work, then reinstall | 1C@.742 | ea | — | 42.20 | 42.20 |
| **Security chain.** | | | | | |
| replace, typical | 1C@.262 | ea | 17.10 | 14.90 | 32.00 |
| remove, security chain | 1D@.258 | ea | — | 10.00 | 10.00 |
| remove for work, then reinstall | 1C@.445 | ea | — | 25.30 | 25.30 |
| **Door hinges.** Deluxe grade hinges include embossed antique patterns. | | | | | |
| replace, standard grade | 1C@.438 | ea | 15.80 | 24.90 | 40.70 |
| replace, high grade | 1C@.438 | ea | 32.90 | 24.90 | 57.80 |
| replace, deluxe grade | 1C@.438 | ea | 51.20 | 24.90 | 76.10 |
| replace, for batten door | 1C@.495 | ea | 76.90 | 28.20 | 105.10 |
| remove, door hinges | 1D@.485 | ea | — | 18.90 | 18.90 |
| remove for work, then reinstall | 1C@.786 | ea | — | 44.70 | 44.70 |

*deluxe grade*

|  | Craft@Hrs | Unit | Material | Labor | Total |
|---|---|---|---|---|---|
| **Door knocker.** | | | | | |
| replace, standard grade | 1C@.351 | ea | 23.20 | 20.00 | 43.20 |
| replace, high grade | 1C@.351 | ea | 52.60 | 20.00 | 72.60 |
| replace, deluxe grade | 1C@.351 | ea | 103.00 | 20.00 | 123.00 |
| remove, door knocker | 1D@.250 | ea | — | 9.73 | 9.73 |
| remove for work, then reinstall | 1C@.636 | ea | — | 36.20 | 36.20 |
| **Storm door hinges.** | | | | | |
| replace, typical | 1C@.342 | ea | 25.60 | 19.50 | 45.10 |
| remove, screen door hinges | 1D@.457 | ea | — | 17.80 | 17.80 |
| remove for work, then reinstall | 1C@.607 | ea | — | 34.50 | 34.50 |
| **Storm door lockset.** | | | | | |
| replace, standard grade | 1C@.387 | ea | 32.90 | 22.00 | 54.90 |
| replace, high grade | 1C@.387 | ea | 49.00 | 22.00 | 71.00 |
| remove, screen door lockset | 1D@.327 | ea | — | 12.70 | 12.70 |
| remove for work, then reinstall | 1C@.685 | ea | — | 39.00 | 39.00 |
| **Door stop.** | | | | | |
| replace, hinge type | 1C@.128 | ea | 6.11 | 7.28 | 13.39 |
| replace, flexible spring baseboard | 1C@.138 | ea | 7.94 | 7.85 | 15.79 |
| replace, rigid baseboard | 1C@.138 | ea | 9.18 | 7.85 | 17.03 |
| remove, door stop | 1D@.084 | ea | — | 3.27 | 3.27 |
| remove for work, then reinstall | 1C@.252 | ea | — | 14.30 | 14.30 |

*rigid*    *flexible spring*

| **Door push plate.** | | | | | |
|---|---|---|---|---|---|
| replace, standard grade | 1C@.417 | ea | 26.60 | 23.70 | 50.30 |
| replace, high grade | 1C@.417 | ea | 50.10 | 23.70 | 73.80 |
| remove, door push plate | 1D@.160 | ea | — | 6.22 | 6.22 |
| remove for work, then reinstall | 1C@.742 | ea | — | 42.20 | 42.20 |

*high grade*

| **Door kick plate.** | | | | | |
|---|---|---|---|---|---|
| replace, standard grade | 1C@.445 | ea | 46.30 | 25.30 | 71.60 |
| replace, high grade | 1C@.445 | ea | 67.30 | 25.30 | 92.60 |
| remove, door kick plate | 1D@.213 | ea | — | 8.29 | 8.29 |
| remove for work, then reinstall | 1C@.809 | ea | — | 46.00 | 46.00 |

| **Letter plate.** | | | | | |
|---|---|---|---|---|---|
| replace, standard grade | 1C@.500 | ea | 38.10 | 28.50 | 66.60 |
| replace, high grade | 1C@.500 | ea | 74.70 | 28.50 | 103.20 |
| remove, door letter plate | 1D@.216 | ea | — | 8.40 | 8.40 |
| remove for work, then reinstall | 1C@.902 | ea | — | 51.30 | 51.30 |

| | Craft@Hrs | Unit | Material | Labor | Total |
|---|---|---|---|---|---|
| **Door peep hole.** | | | | | |
| replace, typical | 1C@.504 | ea | 24.40 | 28.70 | 53.10 |
| remove, door peep hole | 1D@.205 | ea | — | 7.97 | 7.97 |
| remove for work, then reinstall | 1C@.879 | ea | — | 50.00 | 50.00 |
| **Door sweep.** | | | | | |
| replace, typical | 1C@.431 | ea | 38.10 | 24.50 | 62.60 |
| remove, door sweep | 1D@.239 | ea | — | 9.30 | 9.30 |
| remove for work, then reinstall | 1C@.763 | ea | — | 43.40 | 43.40 |
| **Door threshold.** | | | | | |
| replace, standard grade | 1C@.477 | ea | 20.90 | 27.10 | 48.00 |
| replace, high grade | 1C@.477 | ea | 39.20 | 27.10 | 66.30 |
| remove, door threshold | 1D@.262 | ea | — | 10.20 | 10.20 |
| remove for work, then reinstall | 1C@.862 | ea | — | 49.00 | 49.00 |
| **Door weatherstripping.** | | | | | |
| replace, typical | 1C@.417 | ea | 25.60 | 23.70 | 49.30 |
| remove door weatherstripping | 1D@.195 | ea | — | 7.59 | 7.59 |
| **Garage door hardware.** | | | | | |
| replace, standard grade | 1C@2.30 | ea | 101.00 | 131.00 | 232.00 |
| replace, high grade | 1C@2.30 | ea | 138.00 | 131.00 | 269.00 |
| remove, garage door hardware | 1D@.762 | ea | — | 29.60 | 29.60 |
| remove for work, then reinstall | 1C@4.05 | ea | — | 230.00 | 230.00 |

## Time & Material Charts (selected items)
## Door Hardware Materials

See Door Hardware material prices with the line items above.

## Doors Hardware Labor

| Laborer | base wage | paid leave | true wage | taxes & ins. | total |
|---|---|---|---|---|---|
| Finish carpenter | $31.10 | 2.43 | $33.53 | 23.37 | $56.90 |
| Demolition laborer | $20.70 | 1.61 | $22.31 | 16.59 | $38.90 |

**Paid leave** is calculated based on two weeks paid vacation, one week sick leave, and seven paid holidays. Employer's matching portion of **FICA** is 7.65 percent. **FUTA** (Federal Unemployment) is .8 percent. **Worker's compensation** for the door hardware trade was calculated using a national average of 16.85 percent. **Unemployment insurance** was calculated using a national average of 8 percent. **Health insurance** was calculated based on a projected national average for 2015 of $1,025 per employee (and family when applicable) per month. Employer pays 80 percent for a per month cost of $820 per employee. **Retirement** is based on a 401(k) retirement program with employer matching of 50 percent. Employee contributions to the 401(k) plan are an average of 6 percent of the true wage. **Liability insurance** is based on a national average of 10.0 percent.

| | Craft@Hrs | Unit | Material | Labor | Total |
|---|---|---|---|---|---|

## Door Hardware Labor Productivity

Demolition of door hardware

| | Craft@Hrs | Unit | Material | Labor | Total |
|---|---|---|---|---|---|
| deadbolt | 1D@.276 | ea | — | 10.70 | 10.70 |
| exterior door keyed lockset | 1D@.314 | ea | — | 12.20 | 12.20 |
| entry door keyed lockset | 1D@.696 | ea | — | 27.10 | 27.10 |
| antique-style door thumb latch | 1D@.516 | ea | — | 20.10 | 20.10 |
| interior door lockset | 1D@.281 | ea | — | 10.90 | 10.90 |
| door closer | 1D@.291 | ea | — | 11.30 | 11.30 |
| security chain | 1D@.258 | ea | — | 10.00 | 10.00 |
| hinges | 1D@.485 | ea | — | 18.90 | 18.90 |
| door knocker | 1D@.250 | ea | — | 9.73 | 9.73 |
| storm/screen door hinges | 1D@.457 | ea | — | 17.80 | 17.80 |
| storm/screen door lockset | 1D@.327 | ea | — | 12.70 | 12.70 |
| door stop | 1D@.084 | ea | — | 3.27 | 3.27 |
| door push plate | 1D@.160 | ea | — | 6.22 | 6.22 |
| door kick plate | 1D@.213 | ea | — | 8.29 | 8.29 |
| door letter plate | 1D@.216 | ea | — | 8.40 | 8.40 |
| door peep hole | 1D@.205 | ea | — | 7.97 | 7.97 |
| door sweep | 1D@.239 | ea | — | 9.30 | 9.30 |
| door threshold | 1D@.262 | ea | — | 10.20 | 10.20 |
| door weatherstripping | 1D@.195 | ea | — | 7.59 | 7.59 |
| garage door hardware | 1D@.762 | ea | — | 29.60 | 29.60 |

Install deadbolt

| | Craft@Hrs | Unit | Material | Labor | Total |
|---|---|---|---|---|---|
| install | 1C@.678 | ea | — | 38.60 | 38.60 |
| remove for work, then reinstall | 1C@1.10 | ea | — | 62.60 | 62.60 |

Install exterior door keyed lockset

| | Craft@Hrs | Unit | Material | Labor | Total |
|---|---|---|---|---|---|
| install | 1C@.461 | ea | — | 26.20 | 26.20 |
| remove for work, then reinstall | 1C@1.03 | ea | — | 58.60 | 58.60 |

Install entry door keyed lockset

| | Craft@Hrs | Unit | Material | Labor | Total |
|---|---|---|---|---|---|
| install | 1C@1.45 | ea | — | 82.50 | 82.50 |
| remove for work, then reinstall | 1C@2.73 | ea | — | 155.00 | 155.00 |

Install antique-style door thumb latch

| | Craft@Hrs | Unit | Material | Labor | Total |
|---|---|---|---|---|---|
| install | 1C@1.73 | ea | — | 98.40 | 98.40 |

Install interior door lockset

| | Craft@Hrs | Unit | Material | Labor | Total |
|---|---|---|---|---|---|
| install | 1C@.405 | ea | — | 23.00 | 23.00 |
| remove for work, then reinstall | 1C@.710 | ea | — | 40.40 | 40.40 |

Install door closer

| | Craft@Hrs | Unit | Material | Labor | Total |
|---|---|---|---|---|---|
| spring hinge | 1C@.257 | ea | — | 14.60 | 14.60 |
| typical | 1C@.431 | ea | — | 24.50 | 24.50 |
| remove for work, then reinstall | 1C@.742 | ea | — | 42.20 | 42.20 |

Install security chain

| | Craft@Hrs | Unit | Material | Labor | Total |
|---|---|---|---|---|---|
| install | 1C@.262 | ea | — | 14.90 | 14.90 |
| remove for work, then reinstall | 1C@.445 | ea | — | 25.30 | 25.30 |

Install door hinges

| | Craft@Hrs | Unit | Material | Labor | Total |
|---|---|---|---|---|---|
| typical | 1C@.438 | ea | — | 24.90 | 24.90 |
| for batten door | 1C@.495 | ea | — | 28.20 | 28.20 |
| remove for work, then reinstall | 1C@.786 | ea | — | 44.70 | 44.70 |

| | Craft@Hrs | Unit | Material | Labor | Total |
|---|---|---|---|---|---|
| Install door knocker | | | | | |
| install | 1C@.351 | ea | — | 20.00 | 20.00 |
| remove for work, then reinstall | 1C@.636 | ea | — | 36.20 | 36.20 |
| Install screen door hinges | | | | | |
| install | 1C@.342 | ea | — | 19.50 | 19.50 |
| remove for work, then reinstall | 1C@.607 | ea | — | 34.50 | 34.50 |
| Install screen door lockset | | | | | |
| install | 1C@.387 | ea | — | 22.00 | 22.00 |
| remove for work, then reinstall | 1C@.685 | ea | — | 39.00 | 39.00 |
| Install door stop | | | | | |
| hinge | 1C@.128 | ea | — | 7.28 | 7.28 |
| baseboard | 1C@.138 | ea | — | 7.85 | 7.85 |
| remove for work, then reinstall | 1C@.252 | ea | — | 14.30 | 14.30 |
| Install door push plate | | | | | |
| install | 1C@.417 | ea | — | 23.70 | 23.70 |
| remove for work, then reinstall | 1C@.742 | ea | — | 42.20 | 42.20 |
| Install door kick plate | | | | | |
| install | 1C@.445 | ea | — | 25.30 | 25.30 |
| remove for work, then reinstall | 1C@.809 | ea | — | 46.00 | 46.00 |
| Install letter plate | | | | | |
| install | 1C@.500 | ea | — | 28.50 | 28.50 |
| remove for work, then reinstall | 1C@.902 | ea | — | 51.30 | 51.30 |
| Install door peep hole | | | | | |
| install | 1C@.504 | ea | — | 28.70 | 28.70 |
| remove for work, then reinstall | 1C@.879 | ea | — | 50.00 | 50.00 |
| Install door sweep | | | | | |
| install | 1C@.431 | ea | — | 24.50 | 24.50 |
| remove for work, then reinstall | 1C@.763 | ea | — | 43.40 | 43.40 |
| Install door threshold | | | | | |
| install | 1C@.477 | ea | — | 27.10 | 27.10 |
| remove for work, then reinstall | 1C@.862 | ea | — | 49.00 | 49.00 |
| Install door weatherstripping | | | | | |
| install | 1C@.417 | ea | — | 23.70 | 23.70 |
| Install garage door hardware | | | | | |
| install | 1C@2.30 | ea | — | 131.00 | 131.00 |
| remove for work, then reinstall | 1C@4.05 | ea | — | 230.00 | 230.00 |

| | Craft@Hrs | Unit | Material | Labor | Total |
|---|---|---|---|---|---|

# Drywall

**Drywall Installation.** Drywall is hung and taped according to industry standards. Drywall is attached with nails when hung, then permanently affixed with screws. Perfatape and three coats of mud are applied plus texture. One lf of corner bead is calculated for every 24 sf of installed drywall. Productivity is based on repair installations.

**Remove drywall.** Tear-out and debris removal to a truck or dumpster on site. Does not include hauling, dumpster, or dump fees. No salvage value is assumed.

| | Craft@Hrs | Unit | Material | Labor | Total |
|---|---|---|---|---|---|
| remove, drywall & prep walls | 1D@.008 | sf | — | .31 | .31 |
| scrape (remove) acoustic ceiling texture | 1D@.011 | sf | — | .43 | .43 |
| scrape (remove) painted acoustic ceiling texture | 1D@.019 | sf | — | .74 | .74 |
| remove, furring strips on wood, 16" oc | 1D@.010 | sf | — | .39 | .39 |
| remove, furring strips on concrete / masonry, 16" oc | 1D@.011 | sf | — | .43 | .43 |
| remove, furring strips on wood, 24" oc | 1D@.009 | sf | — | .35 | .35 |
| remove, furring strips on concrete / masonry, 24" oc | 1D@.010 | sf | — | .39 | .39 |

**3/8" drywall installed.** Includes drywall board, drywall mud, drywall nails and/or screws, drywall tape, and corner bead.

| | Craft@Hrs | Unit | Material | Labor | Total |
|---|---|---|---|---|---|
| replace, with machine texture | 6D@.031 | sf | .78 | 1.47 | 2.25 |
| replace, with knock-down machine texture | 6D@.033 | sf | .78 | 1.56 | 2.34 |
| replace, with light texture | 6D@.034 | sf | .78 | 1.61 | 2.39 |
| replace, with medium texture | 6D@.035 | sf | .88 | 1.66 | 2.54 |
| replace, with heavy texture | 6D@.036 | sf | .95 | 1.71 | 2.66 |
| replace, with smooth-wall finish | 6D@.041 | sf | .83 | 1.94 | 2.77 |
| replace, all coats, no texture | 6D@.028 | sf | .64 | 1.33 | 1.97 |
| replace, hung & fire taped only | 6D@.021 | sf | .61 | 1.00 | 1.61 |
| hung only (no tape, coating or texture) | 6D@.011 | sf | .58 | .52 | 1.10 |
| remove, drywall | 1D@.008 | sf | — | .31 | .31 |
| add for installation over existing plaster wall | 6D@.003 | sf | — | .14 | .14 |
| add for 3/8" foil-backed drywall | — | sf | .16 | — | .16 |

**1/2" drywall installed.** Includes drywall board, drywall mud, drywall nails and/or screws, drywall tape, and corner bead.

| | Craft@Hrs | Unit | Material | Labor | Total |
|---|---|---|---|---|---|
| replace, with machine texture | 6D@.031 | sf | .76 | 1.47 | 2.23 |
| replace, with knock-down machine texture | 6D@.033 | sf | .76 | 1.56 | 2.32 |
| replace, with light texture | 6D@.034 | sf | .77 | 1.61 | 2.38 |
| replace, with medium texture | 6D@.035 | sf | .83 | 1.66 | 2.49 |
| replace, with heavy texture | 6D@.036 | sf | .92 | 1.71 | 2.63 |
| replace, with smooth-wall finish | 6D@.041 | sf | .79 | 1.94 | 2.73 |
| replace, all coats, no texture | 6D@.028 | sf | .61 | 1.33 | 1.94 |
| replace, hung & fire taped only | 6D@.021 | sf | .57 | 1.00 | 1.57 |
| replace, hung only (no tape, coating or texture) | 6D@.011 | sf | .54 | .52 | 1.06 |
| remove, drywall | 1D@.008 | sf | — | .31 | .31 |
| add for installation over existing plaster wall | 6D@.003 | sf | — | .14 | .14 |
| add for 1/2" moisture-resistant drywall | — | sf | .20 | — | .20 |
| add for 1/2" type X fire-rated drywall | — | sf | .14 | — | .14 |
| add for 1/2" foil-backed drywall | — | sf | .23 | — | .23 |
| add for 1/2" type X fire-rated, foil-backed drywall | — | sf | .38 | — | .38 |

| | Craft@Hrs | Unit | Material | Labor | Total |
|---|---|---|---|---|---|

**5/8" drywall installed.** Includes drywall board, drywall mud, drywall nails and/or screws, drywall tape, and corner bead.

| | Craft@Hrs | Unit | Material | Labor | Total |
|---|---|---|---|---|---|
| replace, with machine texture | 6D@.031 | sf | .88 | 1.47 | 2.35 |
| replace, with knock-down machine texture | 6D@.033 | sf | .88 | 1.56 | 2.44 |
| replace, with light texture | 6D@.034 | sf | .89 | 1.61 | 2.50 |
| replace, with medium texture | 6D@.035 | sf | .97 | 1.66 | 2.63 |
| replace, with heavy texture | 6D@.036 | sf | 1.02 | 1.71 | 2.73 |
| replace, with smooth-wall finish | 6D@.041 | sf | .94 | 1.94 | 2.88 |
| replace, all coats, no texture | 6D@.028 | sf | .72 | 1.33 | 2.05 |
| replace, hung & fire taped only | 6D@.021 | sf | .69 | 1.00 | 1.69 |
| replace, hung only (no tape, coating or texture) | 6D@.011 | sf | .67 | .52 | 1.19 |
| remove, drywall | 1D@.008 | sf | — | .31 | .31 |
| add for installation over existing plaster wall | 6D@.003 | sf | — | .14 | .14 |
| add for 5/8" moisture-resistant drywall | — | sf | .17 | — | .17 |
| add for 5/8" foil-backed drywall | — | sf | .31 | — | .31 |

**Acoustic ceiling texture (cottage cheese).** Includes acoustic ceiling texture mix, optional glitter, and installation.

| | Craft@Hrs | Unit | Material | Labor | Total |
|---|---|---|---|---|---|
| replace, light coverage | 5D@.008 | sf | .24 | .42 | .66 |
| replace, medium coverage | 5D@.011 | sf | .31 | .57 | .88 |
| replace, heavy coverage | 5D@.016 | sf | .33 | .83 | 1.16 |
| remove, acoustic ceiling | 1D@.011 | sf | — | .43 | .43 |
| glitter application to acoustic ceiling texture | 5D@.002 | sf | .01 | .10 | .11 |
| minimum charge for acoustic ceiling texture | 5D@1.25 | ea | 168.00 | 65.00 | 233.00 |

**Drywall patch.**

| | Craft@Hrs | Unit | Material | Labor | Total |
|---|---|---|---|---|---|
| drywall patch (match existing texture or finish) | 5D@1.42 | ea | 44.60 | 73.80 | 118.40 |
| minimum charge for drywall repair | 6D@6.50 | ea | 55.70 | 308.00 | 363.70 |

**Texture drywall.**

| | Craft@Hrs | Unit | Material | Labor | Total |
|---|---|---|---|---|---|
| with light hand texture | 5D@.005 | sf | .14 | .26 | .40 |
| with medium hand texture | 5D@.006 | sf | .24 | .31 | .55 |
| with heavy hand texture | 5D@.006 | sf | .31 | .31 | .62 |
| with thin-coat smooth-wall | 5D@.012 | sf | .21 | .62 | .83 |
| machine applied | 5D@.004 | sf | .14 | .21 | .35 |
| machine applied and knocked down with trowel | 5D@.005 | sf | .14 | .26 | .40 |

**Metal furring channel installed on wood.** Includes metal channel, nails and installation.

Metal hat-shaped furring channel

| | Craft@Hrs | Unit | Material | Labor | Total |
|---|---|---|---|---|---|
| replace, 16" on center | 2D@.011 | sf | .22 | .50 | .72 |
| replace, 24" on center | 2D@.008 | sf | .14 | .36 | .50 |

*hat-shaped channel*

Metal sound-resistant furring channel

| | Craft@Hrs | Unit | Material | Labor | Total |
|---|---|---|---|---|---|
| replace, 16" on center | 2D@.011 | sf | .24 | .50 | .74 |
| replace, 24" on center | 2D@.008 | sf | .19 | .36 | .55 |

Remove

| | Craft@Hrs | Unit | Material | Labor | Total |
|---|---|---|---|---|---|
| furring strips on wood, 16" oc | 1D@.010 | sf | — | .39 | .39 |
| furring strips on wood, 24" oc | 1D@.009 | sf | — | .35 | .35 |

| | Craft@Hrs | Unit | Material | Labor | Total |
|---|---|---|---|---|---|

**Metal furring channel installed on concrete or masonry.** Includes metal channel, case hardened or powder-actuated nails and installation.

| | Craft@Hrs | Unit | Material | Labor | Total |
|---|---|---|---|---|---|
| Metal hat-shaped furring channel | | | | | |
| replace, 16" on center | 2D@.012 | sf | .22 | .54 | .76 |
| replace, 24" on center | 2D@.008 | sf | .14 | .36 | .50 |
| Metal sound-resistant furring channel | | | | | |
| replace, 16" on center | 2D@.012 | sf | .24 | .54 | .78 |
| replace, 24" on center | 2D@.008 | sf | .19 | .36 | .55 |
| Remove | | | | | |
| furring strips on concrete or masonry, 16" oc | 1D@.011 | sf | — | .43 | .43 |
| furring strips on concrete or masonry, 24" oc | 1D@.010 | sf | — | .39 | .39 |

*sound-resistant channel*

**Metal Z channel.** Includes metal Z channel, case hardened or powder-actuated nails, and installation on interior of masonry walls.

| | Craft@Hrs | Unit | Material | Labor | Total |
|---|---|---|---|---|---|
| Use with rigid foam insulation | | | | | |
| replace, 16" on center | 2D@.012 | sf | .14 | .54 | .68 |
| replace, 24" on center | 2D@.008 | sf | .10 | .36 | .46 |

*Z channel*

## Time & Material Charts (selected items)
## Drywall Materials

| | Craft@Hrs | Unit | Material | Labor | Total |
|---|---|---|---|---|---|
| 3/8" drywall board | | | | | |
| standard ($513.00, 1,000 sf), 8% waste | — | sf | .55 | — | .55 |
| foil-backed ($667.00, 1,000 sf), 8% waste | — | sf | .72 | — | .72 |
| 1/2" drywall board | | | | | |
| standard ($477.00, 1,000 sf), 7% waste | — | sf | .51 | — | .51 |
| moisture-resistant ($665.00, 1,000 sf), 7% waste | — | sf | .72 | — | .72 |
| foil-backed ($695.00, 1,000 sf), 7% waste | — | sf | .75 | — | .75 |
| fire-rated type-X ($596.00, 1,000 sf), 7% waste | — | sf | .64 | — | .64 |
| fire-rated type-X foil-backed | | | | | |
| ($843.00, 1,000 sf), 7% waste | — | sf | .90 | — | .90 |
| 5/8" drywall board | | | | | |
| type X ($596.00, 1,000 sf), 7% waste | — | sf | .64 | — | .64 |
| moisture-resistant ($755.00, 1,000 sf), 7% waste | — | sf | .81 | — | .81 |
| Fasteners | | | | | |
| drywall nails, used to secure when hanging | | | | | |
| ($58.80 per box, 32,000 sf), 4% waste | — | sf | .01 | — | .01 |
| drywall screws, used to attach after hung | | | | | |
| ($122.00 per box, 8,534 sf), 3% waste | — | sf | .01 | — | .01 |
| Drywall taping materials | | | | | |
| perfatape (per 500' roll) | | | | | |
| ($7.91 per roll, 1,111 sf), 6% waste | — | sf | .01 | — | .01 |
| corner bead ($1.22 per stick, 204 sf), 4% waste | — | sf | .01 | — | .01 |
| joint compound | | | | | |
| ($23.20 per 50 lb box, 965 sf), 16% waste | — | sf | .03 | — | .03 |

|  | Craft@Hrs | Unit | Material | Labor | Total |
|---|---|---|---|---|---|
| Drywall texture compound |  |  |  |  |  |
| machine-sprayed |  |  |  |  |  |
| ($25.20 per 50 lb box, 190 sf), 13% waste | — | sf | .15 | — | .15 |
| light hand texture |  |  |  |  |  |
| ($25.20 per 50 lb box, 175 sf), 13% waste | — | sf | .16 | — | .16 |
| medium hand texture |  |  |  |  |  |
| ($25.20 per 50 lb box, 120 sf), 13% waste | — | sf | .24 | — | .24 |
| heavy hand texture |  |  |  |  |  |
| ($25.20 per 50 lb box, 93 sf), 14% waste | — | sf | .31 | — | .31 |
| heavy trowel texture |  |  |  |  |  |
| ($25.20 per 50 lb box, 77 sf), 15% waste | — | sf | .38 | — | .38 |
| smooth wall |  |  |  |  |  |
| ($25.20 per 50 lb box, 142 sf), 14% waste | — | sf | .21 | — | .21 |
| Acoustic ceiling (cottage cheese) texture compound |  |  |  |  |  |
| light texture |  |  |  |  |  |
| ($44.00 per 50 lb bag, 220 sf), 17% waste | — | sf | .23 | — | .23 |
| medium texture |  |  |  |  |  |
| ($44.00 per 50 lb box, 170 sf), 17% waste | — | sf | .30 | — | .30 |
| heavy texture |  |  |  |  |  |
| ($44.00 per 50 lb box, 153 sf), 17% waste | — | sf | .34 | — | .34 |
| Acoustic ceiling glitter (cottage cheese) texture |  |  |  |  |  |
| compound (per pound), light to heavy application |  |  |  |  |  |
| ($4.12 per pound, 2,350 sf), 22% waste | — | sf | .01 | — | .01 |
| Metal furring strips |  |  |  |  |  |
| hat-shaped channel installed 24" oc |  |  |  |  |  |
| ($3.23 per 12' stick, 21.34 sf), 3% waste | — | sf | .15 | — | .15 |
| sound-resistant channel installed 24" oc |  |  |  |  |  |
| ($3.55 per 12' stick, 21.34 sf), 3% waste | — | sf | .18 | — | .18 |
| Z channel installed 24" on center |  |  |  |  |  |
| ($1.68 per 8' stick, 15.11 sf), 3% waste | — | sf | .11 | — | .11 |

|  | Craft@Hrs | Unit | Material | Labor | Equip. | Total |
|---|---|---|---|---|---|---|
| **Drywall Rental Equipment** |  |  |  |  |  |  |
| Ames taping tools |  |  |  |  |  |  |
| ($13.80 per day, 416 sf per day) | — | sf | — | — | .03 | .03 |
| texture equipment (gun, hopper & compressor) |  |  |  |  |  |  |
| ($97.00 per day, 1,536 sf per day) | — | sf | — | — | .06 | .06 |
| glitter blower for acoustic ceilings |  |  |  |  |  |  |
| ($6.90 per day, 5,000 sf per day) | — | csf | — | — | .01 | .01 |
| drywall lifter (for one-person hanging) |  |  |  |  |  |  |
| ($27.80 per day, 102 sf per day) | — | sf | — | — | .27 | .27 |
| minimum charge | — | ea | — | — | 69.10 | 69.10 |

## Drywall Labor

| Laborer | base wage | paid leave | true wage | taxes & ins. | total |
|---|---|---|---|---|---|
| Drywall hanger | $28.90 | 2.25 | $31.15 | 20.35 | $51.50 |
| Drywall hanger's helper | $21.00 | 1.64 | $22.64 | 16.16 | $38.80 |
| Drywall taper | $29.20 | 2.28 | $31.48 | 20.52 | $52.00 |
| Demolition laborer | $20.70 | 1.61 | $22.31 | 16.59 | $38.90 |

**Paid leave** is calculated based on two weeks paid vacation, one week sick leave, and seven paid holidays. Employer's matching portion of **FICA** is 7.65 percent. **FUTA** (Federal Unemployment) is .8 percent. **Worker's compensation** for the drywall trade was calculated using a national average of 11.32 percent. **Unemployment insurance** was calculated using a national average of 8 percent. **Health insurance** was calculated based on a projected national average for 2015 of $1,025 per employee (and family when applicable) per month. Employer pays 80 percent for a per month cost of $820 per employee. **Retirement** is based on a 401(k) retirement program with employer matching of 50 percent. Employee contributions to the 401(k) plan are an average of 6 percent of the true wage. **Liability insurance** is based on a national average of 10.0 percent.

| | Craft@Hrs | Unit | Material | Labor | Total |
|---|---|---|---|---|---|
| **Drywall Labor Productivity** | | | | | |
| Demolition of drywall | | | | | |
| remove, drywall and prep walls | 1D@.008 | sf | — | .31 | .31 |
| scrape and prep acoustical ceiling | 1D@.011 | sf | — | .43 | .43 |
| scrape and prep painted acoustical ceiling | 1D@.019 | sf | — | .74 | .74 |
| remove, furring strips on wood, 16" oc | 1D@.010 | sf | — | .39 | .39 |
| remove, furring strips on conc. / masonry, 16" oc | 1D@.011 | sf | — | .43 | .43 |
| remove, furring strips on wood, 24" oc | 1D@.009 | sf | — | .35 | .35 |
| remove, furring strips on conc. / masonry, 24" oc | 1D@.010 | sf | — | .39 | .39 |

| **Hang drywall** | | | | | |
|---|---|---|---|---|---|
| hang drywall | drywall hanger | $51.50 | | | |
| hang drywall | hanger's helper | $38.80 | | | |
| hang drywall | hanging crew | $45.20 | | | |

| | Craft@Hrs | Unit | Material | Labor | Total |
|---|---|---|---|---|---|
| Tape and coat drywall | | | | | |
| to finish (no texture) | 5D@.017 | sf | — | .88 | .88 |
| tape coat only | 5D@.010 | sf | — | .52 | .52 |
| tape coat and one additional coat only | 5D@.012 | sf | — | .62 | .62 |
| to finish, apply machine-sprayed texture | 5D@.020 | sf | — | 1.04 | 1.04 |
| to finish, apply machine-sprayed, knock-down | 5D@.021 | sf | — | 1.09 | 1.09 |
| to finish, apply light hand texture | 5D@.022 | sf | — | 1.14 | 1.14 |
| to finish, apply heavy hand texture | 5D@.024 | sf | — | 1.25 | 1.25 |
| to finish, apply smooth-wall texture | 5D@.029 | sf | — | 1.51 | 1.51 |
| Apply texture on drywall | | | | | |
| with compressor and spray gun | 5D@.004 | sf | — | .21 | .21 |
| with spray gun, then knock down with trowel | 5D@.005 | sf | — | .26 | .26 |
| light hand texture | 5D@.005 | sf | — | .26 | .26 |
| heavy hand texture | 5D@.006 | sf | — | .31 | .31 |
| thin coat smooth-wall finish | 5D@.012 | sf | — | .62 | .62 |
| Apply acoustical ceiling texture | | | | | |
| Light | 5D@.008 | sf | — | .42 | .42 |
| Heavy | 5D@.016 | sf | — | .83 | .83 |
| apply glitter to freshly sprayed ceiling | 5D@.002 | sf | — | .10 | .10 |

| | Craft@Hrs | Unit | Material | Labor | Total |
|---|---|---|---|---|---|

# Electrical

## Minimum charge.

| | Craft@Hrs | Unit | Material | Labor | Total |
|---|---|---|---|---|---|
| for electrical work | 9E@3.25 | ea | 27.20 | 174.00 | 201.20 |

## Complete house electrical wiring, outlets, switches & light fixtures. Complete house wiring, boxes, switches, outlets and fixtures to code for a house that is not electrically heated. (Electrical hookups for furnace, AC unit, and/or heat pump included.) Does not include breaker panel, main disconnect, or service drop. Grades refer to quality of light fixtures.

| | Craft@Hrs | Unit | Material | Labor | Total |
|---|---|---|---|---|---|
| replace, economy grade | 9E@.053 | sf | 2.34 | 2.84 | 5.18 |
| replace, standard grade | 9E@.090 | sf | 2.66 | 4.82 | 7.48 |
| replace, high grade | 9E@.104 | sf | 3.07 | 5.56 | 8.63 |
| replace, deluxe grade | 9E@.109 | sf | 3.27 | 5.83 | 9.10 |
| replace, low-voltage system | 9E@.100 | sf | 2.95 | 5.35 | 8.30 |
| add complete house wiring in conduit | 9E@.055 | sf | 2.98 | 2.94 | 5.92 |

## Complete house rough electrical (no light fixtures). Same as above but does not include fixtures.

| | Craft@Hrs | Unit | Material | Labor | Total |
|---|---|---|---|---|---|
| replace, standard | 9E@.070 | sf | 1.48 | 3.75 | 5.23 |
| replace, in conduit | 9E@.154 | sf | 3.28 | 8.24 | 11.52 |
| replace, low-voltage system | 9E@.075 | sf | 1.62 | 4.01 | 5.63 |

## Complete house light fixtures. Fixtures only.

| | Craft@Hrs | Unit | Material | Labor | Total |
|---|---|---|---|---|---|
| replace, economy grade | 9E@.015 | sf | 1.53 | .80 | 2.33 |
| replace, standard grade | 9E@.016 | sf | 1.96 | .86 | 2.82 |
| replace, high grade | 9E@.016 | sf | 2.73 | .86 | 3.59 |
| replace, deluxe grade | 9E@.017 | sf | 3.61 | .91 | 4.52 |
| replace, low-voltage system | 9E@.013 | sf | 2.61 | .70 | 3.31 |

## Electrical outlets and switches with wiring. Unless otherwise indicated, includes outlet or switch, box, and up to 26 lf wire. Voltage listed as "120 volt" applies to 110, 115, 120 and 125 volt applications. Voltage listed as "240 volt" applies to 220, 240 or 250 volt applications.

| | Craft@Hrs | Unit | Material | Labor | Total |
|---|---|---|---|---|---|
| 120 volt outlet with wiring for general-purpose use, average of 6 outlets per single-pole breaker (breaker not included) replace, up to 15 lf of #12/2 wire | 9E@.977 | ea | 20.70 | 52.30 | 73.00 |
| 120 volt GFCI outlet with wiring for general-purpose use, average of 3 outlets per single-pole breaker replace, up to 26 lf of #12/2 wire | 9E@.977 | ea | 68.10 | 52.30 | 120.40 |
| 120 volt exterior waterproof outlet with wiring for general-purpose use, average of 3 outlets per single-pole breaker (breaker not included) replace, up to 26 lf of #12/2 wire | 9E@.977 | ea | 27.20 | 52.30 | 79.50 |
| 120 volt switch with wiring replace, up to 15 lf of #12/2 wire | 9E@.977 | ea | 27.20 | 52.30 | 79.50 |
| 120 volt 3-way switch with wiring replace, up to 20 lf of #12/2 wire | 9E@1.95 | ea | 47.80 | 104.00 | 151.80 |

| | Craft@Hrs | Unit | Material | Labor | Total |
|---|---|---|---|---|---|
| **120 volt exterior waterproof switch with wiring** | | | | | |
| replace, up to 26 lf of #12/2 wire | 9E@.977 | ea | 27.20 | 52.30 | 79.50 |
| **240 volt outlet with wiring** | | | | | |
| replace, 30 amp, with up to 30 lf #10/3 wire and 30 amp double-pole breaker | 9E@1.34 | ea | 95.70 | 71.70 | 167.40 |
| replace, 40 amp, with up to 30 lf #8/3 wire and 40 amp double-pole breaker | 9E@1.34 | ea | 110.00 | 71.70 | 181.70 |
| replace, 50 amp, with up to 30 lf #6/3 wire and 50 amp double-pole breaker | 9E@1.34 | ea | 128.00 | 71.70 | 199.70 |
| **240 volt switch with wiring** | | | | | |
| replace, with up to 15 lf of #10/2 wire | 9E@1.34 | ea | 110.00 | 71.70 | 181.70 |
| Low-voltage switch wiring with up to 18 lf of #18/2 wire | 9E@.977 | ea | 34.10 | 52.30 | 86.40 |

## Electrical outlets & switches. Includes outlet or switch and cover only (no wire or box).

| | Craft@Hrs | Unit | Material | Labor | Total |
|---|---|---|---|---|---|
| **120 volt outlet with cover** | | | | | |
| replace, outlet | 9E@.226 | ea | 13.60 | 12.10 | 25.70 |
| replace, GFCI outlet | 9E@.226 | ea | 43.70 | 12.10 | 55.80 |
| replace, exterior waterproof outlet | 9E@.226 | ea | 21.80 | 12.10 | 33.90 |
| remove | 1D@.150 | ea | — | 5.84 | 5.84 |
| **120 volt switch with cover** | | | | | |
| replace, switch | 9E@.226 | ea | 8.87 | 12.10 | 20.97 |
| replace, lighted switch | 9E@.226 | ea | 12.80 | 12.10 | 24.90 |
| replace, push-button switch | 9E@.226 | ea | 27.20 | 12.10 | 39.30 |
| replace, rotary dimmer switch | 9E@.226 | ea | 35.60 | 12.10 | 47.70 |
| replace, touch dimmer switch | 9E@.226 | ea | 42.90 | 12.10 | 55.00 |
| replace, exterior waterproof | 9E@.226 | ea | 22.40 | 12.10 | 34.50 |
| remove | 1D@.150 | ea | — | 5.84 | 5.84 |
| **240 volt outlet or switch with cover** | | | | | |
| replace, outlet | 9E@.292 | ea | 20.70 | 15.60 | 36.30 |
| replace, switch | 9E@.292 | ea | 22.40 | 15.60 | 38.00 |
| remove | 1D@.200 | ea | — | 7.78 | 7.78 |
| **Low-voltage outlet or switch with cover** | | | | | |
| replace, computer network outlet | 9E@.335 | ea | 42.90 | 17.90 | 60.80 |
| replace, sound system speaker outlet | 9E@.256 | ea | 12.80 | 13.70 | 26.50 |
| replace, TV outlet | 9E@.256 | ea | 11.60 | 13.70 | 25.30 |
| replace, phone outlet | 9E@.256 | ea | 8.19 | 13.70 | 21.89 |
| replace, switch | 9E@.226 | ea | 15.90 | 12.10 | 28.00 |
| remove | 1D@.150 | ea | — | 5.84 | 5.84 |
| add for high grade outlet or switch cover | — | ea | 1.36 | — | 1.36 |
| add for deluxe grade outlet or switch cover | — | ea | 4.10 | — | 4.10 |

*push-button switch*

## Outlet or switch covers.

| | Craft@Hrs | Unit | Material | Labor | Total |
|---|---|---|---|---|---|
| replace, standard grade | 9E@.020 | ea | 1.39 | 1.07 | 2.46 |
| replace, high grade | 9E@.020 | ea | 5.63 | 1.07 | 6.70 |
| replace, deluxe grade | 9E@.021 | ea | 9.83 | 1.12 | 10.95 |
| remove | 1D@.035 | ea | — | 1.36 | 1.36 |

| | Craft@Hrs | Unit | Material | Labor | Total |
|---|---|---|---|---|---|

**120 volt wiring runs.** Does not include breaker or finish electrical. Replace only.

| | Craft@Hrs | Unit | Material | Labor | Total |
|---|---|---|---|---|---|
| 120 volt dedicated appliance circuit with up to 26 lf #12/2 wire | 9E@1.02 | ea | 61.60 | 54.60 | 116.20 |
| 120 volt wiring for through-wall AC and/or heater with up to 26 lf of #12/2 wire and box | 9E@1.25 | ea | 47.20 | 66.90 | 114.10 |
| 120 volt wiring for bathroom fan with up to 20 lf of #12/2 wire | 9E@.779 | ea | 24.50 | 41.70 | 66.20 |
| 120 volt wiring with GFCI for bathroom ceiling heater with up to 24 lf of #12/2 wire | 9E@.820 | ea | 67.00 | 43.90 | 110.90 |
| 120 volt wiring for clothes washer, includes 1 to 2 outlets per circuit and up to 20 lf of #12/2 wire | 9E@.779 | ea | 42.90 | 41.70 | 84.60 |
| 120 volt wiring for dishwasher on direct-wired run with up to 26 lf of #13/2 wire | 9E@.779 | ea | 27.20 | 41.70 | 68.90 |
| 120 volt wiring for door bell or chime with up to 15 lf of #12/2 wire and up to 30 lf of #18 low-voltage wiring, and box | 9E@.779 | ea | 42.30 | 41.70 | 84.00 |
| 120 volt wiring for electric baseboard heater 1 direct-wired run per 9 lf of baseboard heater or per location, with up to 30 lf of #12/2 wire | 9E@.820 | ea | 29.30 | 43.90 | 73.20 |
| 120 volt wiring for electrical-resistance heating direct-wired run with a single-pole breaker, does not include electrical resistance wiring, includes up to 30 lf of #12/2 wire | 9E@.896 | ea | 41.00 | 47.90 | 88.90 |
| 120 volt wiring for furnace, direct-wired run with up to 30 lf of #12/2 wire | 9E@.779 | ea | 16.40 | 41.70 | 58.10 |
| 120 volt wiring for garage door opener with up to 30 lf of #12/2 wire | 9E@.820 | ea | 23.30 | 43.90 | 67.20 |
| 120 volt wiring for garbage disposal, direct-wired run with outlet, switch and up to 30 lf of #12/2 wire | 9E@1.00 | ea | 37.50 | 53.50 | 91.00 |
| 120 volt wiring for gas oven or range, light appliance circuit, 2 to 3 outlets per circuit with up to 20 lf of #12/2 wire | 9E@.779 | ea | 24.50 | 41.70 | 66.20 |
| 120 volt wiring for humidifier, no more than 1 to 3 fixtures or outlets per run, with up to 30 lf of #12/2 wire | 9E@.779 | ea | 23.30 | 41.70 | 65.00 |
| 120 volt wiring for in-sink hot water dispenser, direct-wired run with up to 30 lf of #12/2 wire | 9E@.779 | ea | 23.30 | 41.70 | 65.00 |
| 120 volt wiring for intercom master station with up to 20 lf of #12/2 wire | 9E@.896 | ea | 39.60 | 47.90 | 87.50 |
| 120 volt wiring for kitchen fan with up to 20 lf of #12/2 wire | 9E@.779 | ea | 26.50 | 41.70 | 68.20 |
| 120 volt light fixture circuit, general-purpose, average of 6 outlets or lights per single-pole breaker with up to15 lf #12/2 wire and box | 9E@.779 | ea | 38.90 | 41.70 | 80.60 |

| | Craft@Hrs | Unit | Material | Labor | Total |
|---|---|---|---|---|---|
| 120 volt wiring for range hood fan and light general-purpose circuit with up to 20 lf of #12/2 wire | 9E@.779 | ea | 25.40 | 41.70 | 67.10 |
| 120 volt wiring for security system, general-purpose circuit with up to 15 lf of #12/2 wire and box | 9E@.779 | ea | 42.90 | 41.70 | 84.60 |
| 120 volt wiring for smoke or carbon monoxide detector (or for direct-wired radon and carbon monoxide detectors), general-purpose circuit, with up to 15 lf of #12/2 wire and box | 9E@.779 | ea | 35.60 | 41.70 | 77.30 |
| 120 volt wiring for sump / water pump, direct-wired run, includes up to 13 lf liquid-tight flexible conduit, remote switch with box, single-pole breaker, and up to 50 lf of #12/2 wire | 9E@5.38 | ea | 27.20 | 288.00 | 315.20 |
| 120 volt wiring for trash compactor on garbage disposal run, and up to 15 lf of #12/2 wire | 9E@.977 | ea | 35.60 | 52.30 | 87.90 |
| 120 volt wiring for built-in vacuum system with up to 30 lf of #12/2 wire | 9E@.820 | ea | 23.30 | 43.90 | 67.20 |
| 120 volt wiring for typical outlet, general-purpose circuit with up to 15 lf #12/2 wire | 9E@.802 | ea | 47.80 | 42.90 | 90.70 |
| 120 volt wiring for water heater, direct-wired run, single-pole breaker, and up to 30 lf of #12/2 wire | 9E@2.11 | ea | 27.20 | 113.00 | 140.20 |
| 120 volt wiring for whole-house fan with remote switch with box, and up to 36 lf of #12/2 wire | 9E@.820 | ea | 31.30 | 43.90 | 75.20 |

**240 volt wiring runs.** Unless indicated, does not include breaker or finish electrical. Replace only.

| | Craft@Hrs | Unit | Material | Labor | Total |
|---|---|---|---|---|---|
| 240 volt wiring for air conditioner, includes up to 36 lf of #6/3 wire, up to 32 lf of #3/2 wire, box, 60 amp disconnect switch, 40 amp 2 pole breaker, and up to 6 lf of liquid-tight flexible conduit | 9E@2.99 | ea | 218.00 | 160.00 | 378.00 |
| 240 volt wiring, box & outlet for clothes dryer with a 30 amp double-pole breaker and up to 30 lf of #8/3 wire | 9E@1.34 | ea | 98.40 | 71.70 | 170.10 |
| 240 volt wiring, box & outlet for clothes dryer with a 40 amp double-pole breaker and up to 30 lf of #8/3 wire | 9E@1.34 | ea | 110.00 | 71.70 | 181.70 |
| 240 volt wiring for electric cook top, includes a 40 amp double-pole breaker and up to 38 lf of #8/3 wire | 9E@1.34 | ea | 118.00 | 71.70 | 189.70 |
| 240 volt wiring for electric baseboard heater, direct-wired run per 9 lf of baseboard heater or per location, with up to 30 lf of #10/2 wire | 9E@1.34 | ea | 35.60 | 71.70 | 107.30 |
| 240 volt wiring for electrical-resistance heating, direct-wired run and double-pole breaker, does not include electrical resistance wiring, includes up to 30 lf of #8/2 wire | 9E@1.22 | ea | 547.00 | 65.30 | 612.30 |

|  | Craft@Hrs | Unit | Material | Labor | Total |
|---|---|---|---|---|---|
| 240 volt wiring, box & outlet for electric oven or range, 40 amp double-pole breaker and up to 30 lf of #8/3 wire | 9E@1.34 | ea | 98.40 | 71.70 | 170.10 |
| 240 volt wiring, box & outlet for electric oven or range, 50 amp double-pole breaker and up to 30 lf of #6/3 wire | 9E@1.34 | ea | 125.00 | 71.70 | 196.70 |
| 240 volt wiring for heat pump, includes up to 42 lf of #6/3 wire, up to 36 lf of #3/2 wire, box, 60 amp disconnect switch, 100 amp 2 pole breaker, 40 amp 2 pole breaker, up to 6 lf of liquid-tight flexible conduit | 9E@7.69 | ea | 478.00 | 411.00 | 889.00 |
| 240 volt wiring for water heater, direct-wired run with double-pole breaker and up to 30 lf of #10/2 wire | 9E@1.34 | ea | 106.00 | 71.70 | 177.70 |

**Low-voltage wiring runs.** Does not include breaker or finish electrical. Replace only.

|  | Craft@Hrs | Unit | Material | Labor | Total |
|---|---|---|---|---|---|
| Low voltage computer network wiring (per outlet) with up to 28 lf computer network cable | 9E@.358 | ea | 39.60 | 19.20 | 58.80 |
| Low-voltage wiring for door bell or chime (per button) with up to 32 lf of #18/2 low-voltage wire | 9E@.563 | ea | 4.90 | 30.10 | 35.00 |
| Low-voltage wiring for door or gate latch release with up to 40 lf of #18/2 low-voltage wire | 9E@.716 | ea | 20.70 | 38.30 | 59.00 |
| Low-voltage wiring for intercom (per station) with up to 32 lf of #18/2 low-voltage wire | 9E@.619 | ea | 19.70 | 33.10 | 52.80 |
| Low voltage wiring for light fixture, average of 6 lights per circuit, with up to 18 lf #18/2 wire and box | 9E@.779 | ea | 42.90 | 41.70 | 84.60 |
| Low voltage wiring for phone wiring (per outlet) with up to 30 lf 4 or 8 bell wire | 9E@.358 | ea | 7.50 | 19.20 | 26.70 |
| Low voltage wiring for sound system speaker (per speaker) with up to 30 lf #20/2 wire | 9E@.358 | ea | 11.00 | 19.20 | 30.20 |
| Low-voltage wiring for thermostat with up to 28 lf of #18/2 low-voltage wire | 9E@.538 | ea | 17.70 | 28.80 | 46.50 |
| Low-voltage wiring for TV outlet (per outlet) with up to 30 lf of shielded coaxial television cable | 9E@.358 | ea | 10.30 | 19.20 | 29.50 |

**Conduit, average installation.** Based on typical home or light commercial installation. Per sf of floor. Replace only.

|  | Craft@Hrs | Unit | Material | Labor | Total |
|---|---|---|---|---|---|
| Electric metallic tubing (EMT) of various diameters: 94% 1/2"; 3% 3/4"; 2% misc. flexible and larger IMC and RMC conduit | 9E@.077 | sf | 1.11 | 4.12 | 5.23 |
| Flexible metal conduit of various diameters: 72% 1/2"; 13% 3/4"; 15% misc. EMT, IMC and RMC conduit | 9E@.041 | sf | 2.59 | 2.19 | 4.78 |
| PVC conduit of various diameters: 94% 1/2"; 3% 3/4"; 2% misc. larger sizes. | 9E@.045 | sf | .70 | 2.41 | 3.11 |
| Intermediate conduit (IMC) of various diameters: 44% 1/2"; 35% 3/4" or 1"; 22% misc. larger sizes | 9E@.113 | sf | 2.45 | 6.05 | 8.50 |
| Rigid metal conduit (RMC) of various diameters: 44% 1/2"; 35% 3/4" or 1"; 22% misc. larger sizes | 9E@.067 | sf | 7.77 | 3.58 | 11.35 |

| | Craft@Hrs | Unit | Material | Labor | Total |
|---|---|---|---|---|---|

**Wire.** With ground non-metallic sheathed cable (Romex). Average installation and conditions for single family housing and light commercial construction. Per lf of installed wire. Replace only.

| | Craft@Hrs | Unit | Material | Labor | Total |
|---|---|---|---|---|---|
| #10 2 | 9E@.051 | lf | .89 | 2.73 | 3.62 |
| #12 2 | 9E@.047 | lf | .53 | 2.51 | 3.04 |
| #14 2 | 9E@.040 | lf | .42 | 2.14 | 2.56 |

**Breaker panel.** Does not include main disconnect breaker.

| | Craft@Hrs | Unit | Material | Labor | Total |
|---|---|---|---|---|---|
| replace, 100 amp exterior panel 20 breaker capacity, 5 breakers installed | 7E@4.89 | ea | 505.00 | 300.00 | 805.00 |
| replace, 100 amp interior panel 20 breaker capacity, 5 breakers installed | 7E@4.30 | ea | 478.00 | 264.00 | 742.00 |
| replace, 150 amp exterior panel 20 breaker capacity, 10 breakers installed | 7E@7.68 | ea | 649.00 | 471.00 | 1,120.00 |
| replace, 150 amp interior panel 20 breaker capacity, 10 breakers installed | 7E@7.17 | ea | 616.00 | 440.00 | 1,056.00 |
| replace, 200 amp exterior panel 40 breaker capacity, 15 breakers installed | 7E@10.8 | ea | 834.00 | 662.00 | 1,496.00 |
| replace, 200 amp interior panel 40 breaker capacity, 15 breakers installed | 7E@9.77 | ea | 785.00 | 599.00 | 1,384.00 |
| replace, 300 amp exterior panel 42 breaker capacity, 30 breakers installed | 7E@14.3 | ea | 854.00 | 877.00 | 1,731.00 |
| replace, 300 amp interior panel 42 breaker capacity, 30 breakers installed | 7E@13.4 | ea | 799.00 | 821.00 | 1,620.00 |
| replace, 40 amp interior sub-panel 10 breaker capacity, 2 breakers installed | 7E@2.99 | ea | 218.00 | 183.00 | 401.00 |
| replace, 50 amp interior sub-panel 10 breaker capacity, 3 breakers installed. | 7E@3.16 | ea | 288.00 | 194.00 | 482.00 |
| replace, 70 amp interior sub-panel 10 breaker capacity, 4 breakers installed. | 7E@3.47 | ea | 341.00 | 213.00 | 554.00 |
| remove | 1D@6.09 | ea | — | 237.00 | 237.00 |
| remove panel for work, then reinstall | 7E@8.28 | ea | — | 508.00 | 508.00 |

*breaker panel*

*sub-panel*

**Electrical service.** Overhead installation. Add **13%** for underground supply — includes excavation, trench shaping, sand bed, backfill, up to 38 lf USE cable, and underground materials. Does not include breaker panel, see above.

**100 amp cable service** with up to 7 lf service entrance cable type SE, insulator, weather head, meter base, main disconnect breaker, up to 6 lf copper ground wire, grounding rod, clamps, fasteners, and waterproof connectors.

| | Craft@Hrs | Unit | Material | Labor | Total |
|---|---|---|---|---|---|
| replace | 7E@11.9 | ea | 887.00 | 729.00 | 1,616.00 |
| remove | 1D@10.5 | ea | — | 408.00 | 408.00 |

*cable service*

| | Craft@Hrs | Unit | Material | Labor | Total |
|---|---|---|---|---|---|

**150 amp cable service** with up to 7 lf service entrance cable type SE, insulator, weather head, meter base, main disconnect breaker, up to 6 lf copper ground wire, grounding rod, clamps, fasteners, and waterproof connectors.

| | | Craft@Hrs | Unit | Material | Labor | Total |
|---|---|---|---|---|---|---|
| replace | | 7E@14.3 | ea | 1,190.00 | 877.00 | 2,067.00 |
| remove | | 1D@10.5 | ea | — | 408.00 | 408.00 |

*cable service*

**150 amp conduit service** with up to 7 lf service entrance cable type SE, insulator, weather head for conduit, EMT conduit with liquid-tight couplings, conduit straps, conduit entrance ell, meter base, main disconnect breaker, up to 6 lf copper ground wire, grounding rod, clamps, fasteners, and waterproof connectors. Do not use this item if conduit extends through roof. See rigid steel mast installations.

| | | Craft@Hrs | Unit | Material | Labor | Total |
|---|---|---|---|---|---|---|
| replace | | 7E@15.4 | ea | 1,250.00 | 944.00 | 2,194.00 |
| remove | | 1D@13.1 | ea | — | 510.00 | 510.00 |

*conduit service*

**150 amp rigid steel mast service.** Rigid steel conduit extends through roof. Up to 10 lf service entrance cable type SE, insulator (clamps to mast), weather head for conduit, 2" galvanized rigid steel conduit with liquid-tight connections, roof flashing, conduit supports, conduit offset fittings, conduit entrance ell, meter base, main disconnect breaker, up to 6 lf copper ground wire, grounding rod, clamps, fasteners, and waterproof connectors. Add $130 if guy wire is needed to support mast.

| | | Craft@Hrs | Unit | Material | Labor | Total |
|---|---|---|---|---|---|---|
| replace | | 7E@15.4 | ea | 1,330.00 | 944.00 | 2,274.00 |
| remove | | 1D@15.4 | ea | — | 599.00 | 599.00 |

*rigid steel mast service*

**200 amp cable service** with up to 7 lf service entrance cable type SE, insulator, weather head, meter base, main disconnect breaker, up to 6 lf copper ground wire, grounding rod, clamps, fasteners, and waterproof connectors.

| | | Craft@Hrs | Unit | Material | Labor | Total |
|---|---|---|---|---|---|---|
| replace | | 7E@18.5 | ea | 1,590.00 | 1,130.00 | 2,720.00 |
| remove | | 1D@10.5 | ea | — | 408.00 | 408.00 |

**200 amp conduit service** with up to 7 lf service entrance cable type SE, insulator, weather head for conduit, EMT conduit with liquid-tight couplings, conduit straps, conduit entrance ell, meter base, main disconnect breaker, up to 6 lf copper ground wire, grounding rod, clamps, fasteners, and waterproof connectors. Do not use this item if conduit extends through roof. See rigid steel mast installations.

| | | Craft@Hrs | Unit | Material | Labor | Total |
|---|---|---|---|---|---|---|
| replace | | 7E@19.9 | ea | 1,640.00 | 1,220.00 | 2,860.00 |
| remove | | 1D@13.1 | ea | — | 510.00 | 510.00 |

**200 amp rigid steel mast service.** Rigid steel conduit extends through roof. Up to 10 lf service entrance cable type SE, insulator (clamps to mast), weather head for conduit, 2" galvanized rigid steel conduit with liquid-tight connections, roof flashing, conduit supports, conduit offset fittings, conduit entrance ell, meter base, main disconnect breaker, up to 6 lf copper ground wire, grounding rod, clamps, fasteners, and waterproof connectors. Add $130 if guy wire is needed to support mast.

| | | Craft@Hrs | Unit | Material | Labor | Total |
|---|---|---|---|---|---|---|
| replace | | 7E@19.9 | ea | 1,710.00 | 1,220.00 | 2,930.00 |
| remove | | 1D@15.4 | ea | — | 599.00 | 599.00 |

|  | **Craft@Hrs** | **Unit** | **Material** | **Labor** | **Total** |
|---|---|---|---|---|---|
| **Circuit breaker.** | | | | | |
| replace, single pole (120 volt) circuit breaker | 7E@.636 | ea | 27.20 | 39.00 | 66.20 |
| replace, double pole (240 volt) circuit breaker *single pole* | 7E@.649 | ea | 53.10 | 39.80 | 92.90 |
| replace, ground fault circuit interrupter breaker | 7E@.689 | ea | 87.40 | 42.20 | 129.60 |
| replace, main disconnect circuit breaker | 7E@3.47 | ea | 505.00 | 213.00 | 718.00 |
| remove | 1D@.200 | ea | — | 7.78 | 7.78 |
| remove breaker for work, then reinstall *double pole* | 7E@1.08 | ea | — | 66.20 | 66.20 |

**Door bell or chime.** Includes door bell or chime, fasteners, and installation. Door bell or chime unit includes interior unit and up to three buttons. Does not include door bell button wiring or electrical wiring for the main unit.

|  | **Craft@Hrs** | **Unit** | **Material** | **Labor** | **Total** |
|---|---|---|---|---|---|
| replace, economy grade, single tone, entry door only | 9E@1.24 | ea | 79.20 | 66.30 | 145.50 |
| replace, standard grade, separate tones for entry and secondary doors | 9E@1.24 | ea | 141.00 | 66.30 | 207.30 |
| replace, high grade, select from multiple tones | 9E@1.24 | ea | 197.00 | 66.30 | 263.30 |
| replace, deluxe grade, programmable, multiple tones | 9E@1.24 | ea | 368.00 | 66.30 | 434.30 |
| remove, door bell or chime | 1D@.209 | ea | — | 8.13 | 8.13 |
| replace, button only (no wire) | 9E@.137 | ea | 9.01 | 7.33 | 16.34 |
| remove, button only (no wire) | 1D@.100 | ea | — | 3.89 | 3.89 |
| remove chime for work, then reinstall | 9E@1.90 | ea | — | 102.00 | 102.00 |

**Bathroom exhaust fan.** Includes up to 10 lf of 4" flexible vent duct and wall outlet.

|  | **Craft@Hrs** | **Unit** | **Material** | **Labor** | **Total** |
|---|---|---|---|---|---|
| replace, economy grade, 50 cfm | 9E@.685 | ea | 49.00 | 36.60 | 85.60 |
| replace, standard grade, 65 cfm, low noise | 9E@.685 | ea | 81.90 | 36.60 | 118.50 |
| replace, high grade, 110 cfm, low noise | 9E@.685 | ea | 116.00 | 36.60 | 152.60 |
| replace, deluxe grade, 110 cfm, low noise, variable speeds | 9E@.685 | ea | 184.00 | 36.60 | 220.60 |
| remove | 1D@.506 | ea | — | 19.70 | 19.70 |
| remove fan for work, then reinstall | 9E@1.12 | ea | — | 59.90 | 59.90 |

**Bathroom exhaust fan with heat lamp.** Includes up to 10 lf of 4" flexible vent duct and wall outlet.

|  | **Craft@Hrs** | **Unit** | **Material** | **Labor** | **Total** |
|---|---|---|---|---|---|
| replace, standard grade, 75 cfm, single heat lamp in center, single switch | 9E@.883 | ea | 103.00 | 47.20 | 150.20 |
| replace, high grade, 110 cfm, double heat lamp in center, separate timer switch for heat lamp and wall outlet | 9E@.883 | ea | 152.00 | 47.20 | 199.20 |
| remove | 1D@.726 | ea | — | 28.20 | 28.20 |

|  | Craft@Hrs | Unit | Material | Labor | Total |
|---|---|---|---|---|---|

**Bathroom exhaust fan with heater.** Includes up to 10 lf of 4" flexible vent duct and wall outlet.

| | | | | | |
|---|---|---|---|---|---|
| replace, standard grade, 110 cfm, 200 watt heater, separate timer switch for heater | 9E@.952 | ea | 177.00 | 50.90 | 227.90 |
| replace, high grade, 110 cfm, 450 watt heater, separate timer switch for heater | 9E@.952 | ea | 259.00 | 50.90 | 309.90 |
| remove | 1D@.726 | ea | — | 28.20 | 28.20 |
| remove fan for work, then reinstall | 9E@1.44 | ea | — | 77.00 | 77.00 |

**Kitchen exhaust fan.** Standard and high grade include up to 10 lf of 4" flexible vent duct and wall outlet.

| | | | | | |
|---|---|---|---|---|---|
| replace, economy grade, 110 cfm, no outside vent, charcoal filtration system | 9E@1.12 | ea | 103.00 | 59.90 | 162.90 |
| replace, standard grade, 200 cfm | 9E@1.12 | ea | 177.00 | 59.90 | 236.90 |
| replace, high grade, 300 cfm | 9E@1.12 | ea | 336.00 | 59.90 | 395.90 |
| remove | 1D@.539 | ea | — | 21.00 | 21.00 |
| remove fan for work, then reinstall | 9E@1.61 | ea | — | 86.10 | 86.10 |

**Whole-house exhaust fan.** Includes whole house exhaust fan, fasteners, control switch, and installation, usually in attic. Does not include electrical wiring.

| | | | | | |
|---|---|---|---|---|---|
| replace, standard grade, 4,500 cfm, two-speed with automatic shutters | 9E@3.10 | ea | 841.00 | 166.00 | 1,007.00 |
| replace, high grade, 6,500 cfm, variable speed with automatic shutters | 9E@3.10 | ea | 978.00 | 166.00 | 1,144.00 |
| remove | 1D@1.52 | ea | — | 59.10 | 59.10 |
| remove fan for work, then reinstall | 9E@4.11 | ea | — | 220.00 | 220.00 |

**Intercom system master station.** Standard grade and higher have AM/FM radio, room monitor, hands-free answer, and privacy features.

| | | | | | |
|---|---|---|---|---|---|
| replace, economy grade, push to talk, release to listen | 9E@2.47 | ea | 382.00 | 132.00 | 514.00 |
| replace, standard grade | 9E@2.47 | ea | 772.00 | 132.00 | 904.00 |
| replace, high grade, includes cassette player | 9E@2.47 | ea | 994.00 | 132.00 | 1,126.00 |
| replace, deluxe grade, includes cassette player, built-in telephone, telephone answering machine, gate or door latch release | 9E@2.47 | ea | 1,590.00 | 132.00 | 1,722.00 |
| replace, custom grade, includes cassette player, built-in telephone, telephone answering machine, gate or door latch release, door video monitor | 9E@2.47 | ea | 2,390.00 | 132.00 | 2,522.00 |
| remove | 1D@.749 | ea | — | 29.10 | 29.10 |
| remove master station for work, then reinstall | 9E@3.25 | ea | — | 174.00 | 174.00 |

**Intercom system remote station.** Standard grade and higher have hands-free answer, and privacy features.

| | | | | | |
|---|---|---|---|---|---|
| replace, economy grade, push to talk, release to listen | 9E@.685 | ea | 95.70 | 36.60 | 132.30 |
| replace, standard grade | 9E@.685 | ea | 197.00 | 36.60 | 233.60 |
| replace, high grade, with built-in telephone | 9E@.685 | ea | 368.00 | 36.60 | 404.60 |
| remove | 1D@.300 | ea | — | 11.70 | 11.70 |
| remove, remote station for work, then reinstall | 9E@1.03 | ea | — | 55.10 | 55.10 |

| | Craft@Hrs | Unit | Material | Labor | Total |
|---|---|---|---|---|---|
| **Sound system speakers with grille.** | | | | | |
| replace, economy grade, 3" to 5" diameter speaker, plastic grille | 9E@.244 | ea | 27.20 | 13.10 | 40.30 |
| replace, standard grade, 5" to 8" diameter elliptical speaker, wood-grain plastic grille | 9E@.244 | ea | 41.00 | 13.10 | 54.10 |
| replace, high grade, 5" to 8" diameter elliptical speaker with 1" to 2" "tweeter" speaker, wood-grain plastic grille | 9E@.244 | ea | 54.70 | 13.10 | 67.80 |
| replace, deluxe grade, two 5" to 8" diameter speakers with two or three 1" to 2" "tweeter" speakers, wood-grain plastic grille | 9E@.244 | ea | 88.70 | 13.10 | 101.80 |
| remove sound system speaker | 1D@.235 | ea | — | 9.14 | 9.14 |
| **Check electrical circuits with megameter.** | | | | | |
| in small home | 7E@3.91 | ea | — | 240.00 | 240.00 |
| in average size home | 7E@5.66 | ea | — | 347.00 | 347.00 |
| in large home | 7E@7.79 | ea | — | 478.00 | 478.00 |
| **Smoke detector.** | | | | | |
| replace, battery operated | 9E@.355 | ea | 47.80 | 19.00 | 66.80 |
| replace, direct wired | 9E@.398 | ea | 61.60 | 21.30 | 82.90 |
| remove | 1D@.200 | ea | — | 7.78 | 7.78 |
| remove for work, then reinstall | 9E@.553 | ea | — | 29.60 | 29.60 |
| **Carbon monoxide detector.** | | | | | |
| replace, battery operated | 9E@.355 | ea | 54.70 | 19.00 | 73.70 |
| replace, direct wired | 9E@.398 | ea | 68.10 | 21.30 | 89.40 |
| remove | 1D@.200 | ea | — | 7.78 | 7.78 |
| remove for work, then reinstall | 9E@.553 | ea | — | 29.60 | 29.60 |
| **Radon detector.** | | | | | |
| replace, battery operated | 9E@.355 | ea | 61.60 | 19.00 | 80.60 |
| replace, direct wired | 9E@.398 | ea | 75.00 | 21.30 | 96.30 |
| remove | 1D@.200 | ea | — | 7.78 | 7.78 |
| remove for work, then reinstall | 9E@.553 | ea | — | 29.60 | 29.60 |
| **Thermostat.** See HVAC for additional thermostats. | | | | | |
| replace, for electric-resistance heating system | 9E@.183 | ea | 11.60 | 9.79 | 21.39 |
| replace, for electric heating system | 9E@.326 | ea | 24.50 | 17.40 | 41.90 |
| remove | 1D@.200 | ea | — | 7.78 | 7.78 |
| **Television antenna.** Includes up to 50 lf coaxial cable. Add **$205** for ground wire and grounding rod driven 8' into ground. (Required by many local codes.) | | | | | |
| replace, economy grade, 55" boom | 9E@1.24 | ea | 152.00 | 66.30 | 218.30 |
| replace, standard grade, 100" boom | 9E@1.24 | ea | 259.00 | 66.30 | 325.30 |
| replace, high grade, 150" boom | 9E@1.24 | ea | 389.00 | 66.30 | 455.30 |
| replace, deluxe grade, 200" boom | 9E@1.24 | ea | 558.00 | 66.30 | 624.30 |
| remove | 1D@.835 | ea | — | 32.50 | 32.50 |
| remove for work, then reinstall | 9E@1.82 | ea | — | 97.40 | 97.40 |

|  | Craft@Hrs | Unit | Material | Labor | Total |
|---|---|---|---|---|---|

**Electric space heater recessed in wall.** Includes recessed space heater, fasteners, and installation. Heater includes a built-in thermostat. Does not include wall framing, electrical wiring, thermostat wiring, or a wall-mounted thermostat. Heater should fit between standard wall framing spacing (e.g. 16" on center).

| | Craft@Hrs | Unit | Material | Labor | Total |
|---|---|---|---|---|---|
| replace, economy grade, 120 or 240 volt, 1,500 watt | 9E@2.47 | ea | 298.00 | 132.00 | 430.00 |
| replace, standard grade, 240 volt, 2,250 watt | 9E@2.47 | ea | 341.00 | 132.00 | 473.00 |
| replace, high grade 240 volt, 4,000 watt | 9E@2.47 | ea | 410.00 | 132.00 | 542.00 |
| remove | 1D@.506 | ea | — | 19.70 | 19.70 |
| remove heater for work, then reinstall | 9E@4.11 | ea | — | 220.00 | 220.00 |

**Electric-resistance heating cable.** Ceiling installation: Copper inner resistance wire embedded in gypsum. Floor installation: Wire contains copper inner resistance core and is sheathed with aluminum and a cross-linked polyethylene outer layer. Per sf of exposed floor space. Do not measure floor space underneath bathtubs, cabinets or appliances. When resistance heating system installed in floor is not the only heat source in the house, floor sensors determine when floor is below desired temperature.

| | Craft@Hrs | Unit | Material | Labor | Total |
|---|---|---|---|---|---|
| replace, ceiling installation | 9E@.036 | sf | 3.96 | 1.93 | 5.89 |
| replace, floor installation per sf of exposed floor space | 9E@.060 | sf | 7.24 | 3.21 | 10.45 |
| replace, floor sensor for electrical resistance heating system | 9E@.632 | ea | 123.00 | 33.80 | 156.80 |

**Electric baseboard heater.** Includes electric baseboard heater, fasteners, and installation. Heater includes a built-in thermostat but is often connected to a wall-mounted thermostat. Does not include electrical wiring, thermostat wiring, or a wall-mounted thermostat. 3 LF minimum.

| | Craft@Hrs | Unit | Material | Labor | Total |
|---|---|---|---|---|---|
| replace, economy grade, 3 lf minimum, 165 watts per lf, thermostat on heater | 9E@.512 | lf | 24.50 | 27.40 | 51.90 |
| replace, standard grade, 3 lf minimum, 188 watts per lf, includes up to 18 lf #18/2 thermostat wire, box and line thermostat | 9E@.512 | lf | 25.90 | 27.40 | 53.30 |
| remove | 1D@.165 | lf | — | 6.42 | 6.42 |
| remove heater for work, then reinstall | 9E@.717 | lf | — | 38.40 | 38.40 |

**Underground wiring for exterior post light fixture.** Includes sand bed in trench for wire and up to 10 lf of galvanized conduit. Does not include excavation.

| | Craft@Hrs | Unit | Material | Labor | Total |
|---|---|---|---|---|---|
| Up to 30 lf with up to 36 lf #12/2 UF wire | 9E@1.22 | ea | 298.00 | 65.30 | 363.30 |
| Up to 50 lf with up to 56 lf #12/2 UF wire | 9E@1.30 | ea | 464.00 | 69.60 | 533.60 |

**Lighting.** The price of a light fixture can vary a great deal, often without any visible explanation. For example, a light fixture that is designed by a prominent designer may be far more expensive than a similar light fixture with similar materials and design.

**Light fixture quality.** Economy: Very light-gauge plated metal components, simple, thin glass shades. Chandeliers may contain 4 to 8 arms with turned wood center. Standard: Light-gauge plated metal components, simple glass shades. Chandeliers may contain 4 to 8 arms. High: Heavy-gauge plated metal components, glass shades with some intricate pattern or design, may have antique finish. Chandeliers may contain 4 to 8 arms. Deluxe: Heavy-gauge metal components, solid brass components, intricate glass shades, may have antique finish. Chandeliers may contain 6 to 12 arms. Custom: Heavy-gauge metal components, solid brass components, intricate glass shades, specialty antique finishes, polished brass, antiqued brass, polished nickel (or chrome) over brass. Chandeliers may contain 6 to 14 arms. Custom deluxe: Designed by prominent designer. Heavy-gauge metal components, solid brass components, intricate glass shades, specialty antique finishes, polished brass, antiqued brass, polished nickel (or chrome) over brass. Chandeliers usually contain 6 to 20 arms, often in two tiers.

| | Craft@Hrs | Unit | Material | Labor | Total |
|---|---|---|---|---|---|
| **Light fixture allowance.** Contractor's allowance per light fixture in complete home. | | | | | |
| replace, economy grade | 9E@.574 | ea | 20.70 | 30.70 | 51.40 |
| replace, standard grade | 9E@.574 | ea | 54.70 | 30.70 | 85.40 |
| replace, high grade | 9E@.574 | ea | 95.70 | 30.70 | 126.40 |
| replace, deluxe grade | 9E@.574 | ea | 171.00 | 30.70 | 201.70 |
| remove | 1D@.300 | ea | — | 11.70 | 11.70 |
| remove light fixture for work, then reinstall | 9E@1.02 | ea | — | 54.60 | 54.60 |
| **Bathroom light bar.** Standard grade light bars contain decorative light bulbs, high grade light bars contain decorative globe covers. | | | | | |
| with 2 lights, replace, standard grade | 9E@.612 | ea | 68.10 | 32.70 | 100.80 |
| with 3 lights, replace, high grade | 9E@.612 | ea | 88.70 | 32.70 | 121.40 |
| with 3 to 4 lights, replace, standard grade | 9E@.612 | ea | 95.70 | 32.70 | 128.40 |
| with 3 to 4 lights, replace, high grade | 9E@.612 | ea | 103.00 | 32.70 | 135.70 |
| with 5 to 6 lights, replace, standard grade | 9E@.612 | ea | 128.00 | 32.70 | 160.70 |
| with 5 to 6 lights, replace, high grade | 9E@.612 | ea | 159.00 | 32.70 | 191.70 |
| with 7 to 8 lights, replace, standard grade | 9E@.612 | ea | 184.00 | 32.70 | 216.70 |
| with 7 to 8 lights, replace, high grade | 9E@.612 | ea | 224.00 | 32.70 | 256.70 |
| remove | 1D@.315 | ea | — | 12.30 | 12.30 |
| remove light bar for work, then reinstall | 9E@1.08 | ea | — | 57.80 | 57.80 |
| **Chandelier.** To 28" in diameter. Suitable for installations on 8' and taller ceilings. | | | | | |
| replace, economy grade | 9E@1.67 | ea | 184.00 | 89.30 | 273.30 |
| replace, standard grade | 9E@1.67 | ea | 288.00 | 89.30 | 377.30 |
| replace, high grade | 9E@1.67 | ea | 410.00 | 89.30 | 499.30 |
| replace, deluxe grade | 9E@1.67 | ea | 587.00 | 89.30 | 676.30 |
| replace, custom grade | 9E@1.67 | ea | 757.00 | 89.30 | 846.30 |
| replace, custom deluxe grade | 9E@1.67 | ea | 963.00 | 89.30 | 1,052.30 |
| remove | 1D@.557 | ea | — | 21.70 | 21.70 |
| **Entrance chandelier.** To 40" in diameter. Suitable for installations on 12' and taller ceilings. | | | | | |
| replace, economy grade | 9E@3.35 | ea | 410.00 | 179.00 | 589.00 |
| replace, standard grade | 9E@3.35 | ea | 587.00 | 179.00 | 766.00 |
| replace, high grade | 9E@3.35 | ea | 772.00 | 179.00 | 951.00 |
| replace, deluxe grade | 9E@3.35 | ea | 984.00 | 179.00 | 1,163.00 |
| replace, custom grade | 9E@3.35 | ea | 1,260.00 | 179.00 | 1,439.00 |
| replace, custom deluxe grade | 9E@3.35 | ea | 1,590.00 | 179.00 | 1,769.00 |
| remove | 1D@.557 | ea | — | 21.70 | 21.70 |
| **Grand entrance chandelier.** To 60" in diameter. Suitable for installations on 18' and taller ceilings. | | | | | |
| replace, economy grade | 9E@4.59 | ea | 792.00 | 246.00 | 1,038.00 |
| replace, standard grade | 9E@4.59 | ea | 1,300.00 | 246.00 | 1,546.00 |
| replace, high grade | 9E@4.59 | ea | 1,770.00 | 246.00 | 2,016.00 |
| replace, deluxe grade | 9E@4.59 | ea | 2,240.00 | 246.00 | 2,486.00 |
| replace, custom grade | 9E@4.59 | ea | 2,830.00 | 246.00 | 3,076.00 |
| replace, custom deluxe grade | 9E@4.59 | ea | 4,580.00 | 246.00 | 4,826.00 |
| remove | 1D@.557 | ea | — | 21.70 | 21.70 |

|  | Craft@Hrs | Unit | Material | Labor | Total |
|---|---|---|---|---|---|

### Early American reproduction chandelier.
Early American candle chandeliers converted to electrical. These fixtures are antique reproductions and are hand tooled from tin, distressed tin, pewter, brass, or copper. Joints are hand soldered. The electric "candles" may be coated with bees wax. Although many modern fixtures use a candle style, they should not be confused with early American reproduction fixtures. Look for hand tooling inconsistencies and hand-soldered joints.

|  | Craft@Hrs | Unit | Material | Labor | Total |
|---|---|---|---|---|---|
| replace, economy grade | 9E@1.67 | ea | 410.00 | 89.30 | 499.30 |
| replace, standard grade | 9E@1.67 | ea | 558.00 | 89.30 | 647.30 |
| replace, high grade | 9E@1.67 | ea | 772.00 | 89.30 | 861.30 |
| replace, deluxe grade | 9E@1.67 | ea | 1,110.00 | 89.30 | 1,199.30 |
| replace, custom grade | 9E@1.67 | ea | 1,330.00 | 89.30 | 1,419.30 |
| replace, custom deluxe grade | 9E@1.67 | ea | 1,770.00 | 89.30 | 1,859.30 |

### Early electric reproduction chandelier.
Reproductions of chandeliers that were made when electricity was first introduced. Use these prices for true design reproductions.

|  | Craft@Hrs | Unit | Material | Labor | Total |
|---|---|---|---|---|---|
| replace, economy grade | 9E@1.67 | ea | 478.00 | 89.30 | 567.30 |
| replace, standard grade | 9E@1.67 | ea | 616.00 | 89.30 | 705.30 |
| replace, high grade | 9E@1.67 | ea | 825.00 | 89.30 | 914.30 |
| replace, deluxe grade | 9E@1.67 | ea | 1,180.00 | 89.30 | 1,269.30 |
| replace, custom grade | 9E@1.67 | ea | 1,360.00 | 89.30 | 1,449.30 |
| replace, custom deluxe grade | 9E@1.67 | ea | 1,840.00 | 89.30 | 1,929.30 |
| remove | 1D@.557 | ea | — | 21.70 | 21.70 |

*Courtesy of: Rejuvenation Lamp & Fixture Co.*

### Early gas reproduction chandelier.
Electrified reproductions of chandeliers that were originally designed to burn coal gas. Can usually be identified by a fake gas valve on the chandelier arm. Because a flame burns upward, gas reproduction fixture shades always face upward. Also use these prices for electric reproductions of lantern style chandeliers. Modern designs which use a gas or lantern style usually fall in the economy and standard grades.

|  | Craft@Hrs | Unit | Material | Labor | Total |
|---|---|---|---|---|---|
| replace, economy grade | 9E@1.67 | ea | 499.00 | 89.30 | 588.30 |
| replace, standard grade | 9E@1.67 | ea | 606.00 | 89.30 | 695.30 |
| replace, high grade | 9E@1.67 | ea | 854.00 | 89.30 | 943.30 |
| replace, deluxe grade | 9E@1.67 | ea | 1,150.00 | 89.30 | 1,239.30 |
| replace, custom grade | 9E@1.67 | ea | 1,360.00 | 89.30 | 1,449.30 |
| replace, custom deluxe grade | 9E@1.67 | ea | 1,900.00 | 89.30 | 1,989.30 |
| remove | 1D@.557 | ea | — | 21.70 | 21.70 |

### Early electric / gas combination reproduction chandelier.
When electricity was first introduced, builders were unsure whether it or gas was the wave of the future. Many builders played it safe by installing fixtures that used both. The original gas components can be identified by the fake valve on the arm. Gas components always face up. Electrical components often have a pull switch and usually, but not always, face down.

|  | Craft@Hrs | Unit | Material | Labor | Total |
|---|---|---|---|---|---|
| replace, economy grade | 9E@1.67 | ea | 526.00 | 89.30 | 615.30 |
| replace, standard grade | 9E@1.67 | ea | 628.00 | 89.30 | 717.30 |
| replace, high grade | 9E@1.67 | ea | 860.00 | 89.30 | 949.30 |
| replace, deluxe grade | 9E@1.67 | ea | 1,180.00 | 89.30 | 1,269.30 |
| replace, custom grade | 9E@1.67 | ea | 1,380.00 | 89.30 | 1,469.30 |
| replace, custom deluxe grade | 9E@1.67 | ea | 1,840.00 | 89.30 | 1,929.30 |
| remove | 1D@.557 | ea | — | 21.70 | 21.70 |

### Imitation crystal chandelier.
Cut glass components.

|  | Craft@Hrs | Unit | Material | Labor | Total |
|---|---|---|---|---|---|
| replace, economy grade | 9E@1.67 | ea | 307.00 | 89.30 | 396.30 |
| replace, standard grade | 9E@1.67 | ea | 416.00 | 89.30 | 505.30 |
| remove | 1D@.557 | ea | — | 21.70 | 21.70 |

| | Craft@Hrs | Unit | Material | Labor | Total |
|---|---|---|---|---|---|

**Crystal chandelier.** High-quality crystal components. Deduct **15%** for lower quality crystal. To 25" diameter. Suitable for installation on 8' or taller ceilings.

| | Craft@Hrs | Unit | Material | Labor | Total |
|---|---|---|---|---|---|
| replace, standard grade | 9E@1.67 | ea | 1,000.00 | 89.30 | 1,089.30 |
| replace, high grade | 9E@1.67 | ea | 1,270.00 | 89.30 | 1,359.30 |
| replace, deluxe grade | 9E@1.67 | ea | 1,520.00 | 89.30 | 1,609.30 |
| replace, custom grade | 9E@1.67 | ea | 1,710.00 | 89.30 | 1,799.30 |
| replace, custom deluxe grade | 9E@1.67 | ea | 1,840.00 | 89.30 | 1,929.30 |
| remove | 1D@.557 | ea | — | 21.70 | 21.70 |

**Entrance crystal chandelier.** High-quality crystal components. Deduct **15%** for lower quality crystal. To 32" diameter. Suitable for installation on 14' or taller ceilings.

| | Craft@Hrs | Unit | Material | Labor | Total |
|---|---|---|---|---|---|
| replace, standard grade | 9E@3.35 | ea | 1,520.00 | 179.00 | 1,699.00 |
| replace, high grade | 9E@3.35 | ea | 1,770.00 | 179.00 | 1,949.00 |
| replace, deluxe grade | 9E@3.35 | ea | 1,970.00 | 179.00 | 2,149.00 |
| replace, custom grade | 9E@3.35 | ea | 2,590.00 | 179.00 | 2,769.00 |
| replace, custom deluxe grade | 9E@3.35 | ea | 3,680.00 | 179.00 | 3,859.00 |
| remove | 1D@.557 | ea | — | 21.70 | 21.70 |

**Grand entrance crystal chandelier.** High-quality crystal components. Deduct **15%** for lower quality crystal. To 52" diameter. Suitable for installation on 20' or taller ceilings.

| | Craft@Hrs | Unit | Material | Labor | Total |
|---|---|---|---|---|---|
| replace, standard grade | 9E@4.59 | ea | 2,180.00 | 246.00 | 2,426.00 |
| replace, high grade | 9E@4.59 | ea | 4,780.00 | 246.00 | 5,026.00 |
| replace, deluxe grade | 9E@4.59 | ea | 6,490.00 | 246.00 | 6,736.00 |
| replace, custom grade | 9E@4.59 | ea | 8,820.00 | 246.00 | 9,066.00 |
| replace, custom deluxe grade | 9E@4.59 | ea | 10,300.00 | 246.00 | 10,546.00 |
| remove | 1D@.557 | ea | — | 21.70 | 21.70 |

**Crystal tier chandelier.** High-quality crystal components. Deduct **15%** for lower quality crystal. Crystal tier chandeliers resemble an upside down wedding cake. They are usually 1.5 to 2 times taller than they are wide, so normally are installed on taller ceilings.

| | Craft@Hrs | Unit | Material | Labor | Total |
|---|---|---|---|---|---|
| replace, standard grade | 9E@1.67 | ea | 1,180.00 | 89.30 | 1,269.30 |
| replace, high grade | 9E@4.59 | ea | 1,270.00 | 246.00 | 1,516.00 |
| replace, deluxe grade | 9E@4.59 | ea | 1,590.00 | 246.00 | 1,836.00 |
| replace, custom grade | 9E@4.59 | ea | 1,710.00 | 246.00 | 1,956.00 |
| replace, custom deluxe grade | 9E@4.59 | ea | 2,330.00 | 246.00 | 2,576.00 |
| remove | 1D@.557 | ea | — | 21.70 | 21.70 |

**Crystal wall fixture.** High-quality crystal components. Deduct **15%** for lower quality crystal.

| | Craft@Hrs | Unit | Material | Labor | Total |
|---|---|---|---|---|---|
| replace, standard grade | 9E@.556 | ea | 356.00 | 29.70 | 385.70 |
| replace, high grade | 9E@.556 | ea | 547.00 | 29.70 | 576.70 |
| replace, deluxe grade | 9E@.556 | ea | 805.00 | 29.70 | 834.70 |
| replace, custom grade | 9E@.556 | ea | 1,180.00 | 29.70 | 1,209.70 |
| remove | 1D@.300 | ea | — | 11.70 | 11.70 |
| remove fixture for work, then reinstall | 9E@1.02 | ea | — | 54.60 | 54.60 |

**Repair crystal chandelier.**

| | Craft@Hrs | Unit | Material | Labor | Total |
|---|---|---|---|---|---|
| Minor repairs,<br>replace 2 to 4 components | 9E@1.84 | ea | 88.70 | 98.40 | 187.10 |

| | Craft@Hrs | Unit | Material | Labor | Total |
|---|---|---|---|---|---|
| Significant repairs, replace 5 to 10 components | 9E@3.68 | ea | 177.00 | 197.00 | 374.00 |
| Major repairs, replace 11 to 16 components | 9E@7.34 | ea | 298.00 | 393.00 | 691.00 |
| Rebuild, dismantle all or most of fixture, replace 25% to 35% of components | 9E@15.3 | ea | 581.00 | 819.00 | 1,400.00 |

### Additional chandelier costs.

| | Craft@Hrs | Unit | Material | Labor | Total |
|---|---|---|---|---|---|
| remove for work, then reinstall | 9E@2.82 | ea | — | 151.00 | 151.00 |
| remove vaulted ceiling chandelier for work, then reinstall | 9E@6.12 | ea | — | 327.00 | 327.00 |
| remove high vaulted-ceiling chandelier for work, then reinstall | 9E@8.35 | ea | — | 447.00 | 447.00 |
| add for hanging on vaulted ceiling | | | | | |
| 12' to 14' tall | 9E@.919 | ea | — | 49.20 | 49.20 |
| 14' to 16' tall | 9E@1.67 | ea | — | 89.30 | 89.30 |
| 17' to 22' tall | 9E@2.55 | ea | — | 136.00 | 136.00 |

### Single pendant light fixture. Pendant fixtures hang from a chain or rod and connect directly to an electrical box in the ceiling.

| | Craft@Hrs | Unit | Material | Labor | Total |
|---|---|---|---|---|---|
| replace, economy grade | 9E@.574 | ea | 88.70 | 30.70 | 119.40 |
| replace, standard grade | 9E@.574 | ea | 110.00 | 30.70 | 140.70 |
| replace, high grade | 9E@.574 | ea | 136.00 | 30.70 | 166.70 |
| replace, deluxe grade | 9E@.574 | ea | 164.00 | 30.70 | 194.70 |
| replace, custom grade | 9E@.574 | ea | 190.00 | 30.70 | 220.70 |
| replace, custom deluxe grade | 9E@.574 | ea | 218.00 | 30.70 | 248.70 |
| remove | 1D@.300 | ea | — | 11.70 | 11.70 |

### Double pendant light fixture. Pendant fixtures hang from a chain or rod and connect directly to an electrical box in the ceiling.

| | Craft@Hrs | Unit | Material | Labor | Total |
|---|---|---|---|---|---|
| replace, economy grade | 9E@.574 | ea | 152.00 | 30.70 | 182.70 |
| replace, standard grade | 9E@.574 | ea | 190.00 | 30.70 | 220.70 |
| replace, high grade | 9E@.574 | ea | 218.00 | 30.70 | 248.70 |
| replace, deluxe grade | 9E@.574 | ea | 254.00 | 30.70 | 284.70 |
| replace, custom grade | 9E@.574 | ea | 288.00 | 30.70 | 318.70 |
| replace, custom deluxe grade | 9E@.574 | ea | 336.00 | 30.70 | 366.70 |
| remove | 1D@.300 | ea | — | 11.70 | 11.70 |

### "Shower" style light fixture. Shower style fixtures have a large base. Two to four (sometimes more) small lights with shades hang from the base on chains or rods.

| | Craft@Hrs | Unit | Material | Labor | Total |
|---|---|---|---|---|---|
| replace, economy grade | 9E@1.67 | ea | 218.00 | 89.30 | 307.30 |
| replace, standard grade | 9E@1.67 | ea | 283.00 | 89.30 | 372.30 |
| replace, high grade | 9E@1.67 | ea | 375.00 | 89.30 | 464.30 |
| replace, deluxe grade | 9E@1.67 | ea | 437.00 | 89.30 | 526.30 |
| replace, custom grade | 9E@1.67 | ea | 566.00 | 89.30 | 655.30 |
| replace, custom deluxe grade | 9E@1.67 | ea | 616.00 | 89.30 | 705.30 |
| remove | 1D@.557 | ea | — | 21.70 | 21.70 |

| | Craft@Hrs | Unit | Material | Labor | Total |
|---|---|---|---|---|---|

**Small bowl-shade light fixture.** Fixture with a globe or bowl shade. Small sizes are typically found in halls.

| | Craft@Hrs | Unit | Material | Labor | Total |
|---|---|---|---|---|---|
| replace, economy grade | 9E@.574 | ea | 47.80 | 30.70 | 78.50 |
| replace, standard grade | 9E@.574 | ea | 61.60 | 30.70 | 92.30 |
| replace, high grade | 9E@.574 | ea | 81.90 | 30.70 | 112.60 |
| replace, deluxe grade | 9E@.574 | ea | 116.00 | 30.70 | 146.70 |
| replace, custom grade | 9E@.574 | ea | 128.00 | 30.70 | 158.70 |
| replace, custom deluxe grade | 9E@.574 | ea | 159.00 | 30.70 | 189.70 |
| remove | 1D@.300 | ea | — | 11.70 | 11.70 |

**Bowl-shade light fixture.** Fixture with a globe or bowl shade.

| | Craft@Hrs | Unit | Material | Labor | Total |
|---|---|---|---|---|---|
| replace, economy grade | 9E@.574 | ea | 68.10 | 30.70 | 98.80 |
| replace, standard grade | 9E@.574 | ea | 123.00 | 30.70 | 153.70 |
| replace, high grade | 9E@.574 | ea | 152.00 | 30.70 | 182.70 |
| replace, deluxe grade | 9E@.574 | ea | 197.00 | 30.70 | 227.70 |
| replace, custom grade | 9E@.574 | ea | 239.00 | 30.70 | 269.70 |
| replace, custom deluxe grade | 9E@.574 | ea | 272.00 | 30.70 | 302.70 |
| remove | 1D@.300 | ea | — | 11.70 | 11.70 |

**Suspended bowl-shade light fixture.** Bowl-shade suspended on three rods or chains.

| | Craft@Hrs | Unit | Material | Labor | Total |
|---|---|---|---|---|---|
| replace, economy grade | 9E@1.67 | ea | 259.00 | 89.30 | 348.30 |
| replace, standard grade | 9E@1.67 | ea | 307.00 | 89.30 | 396.30 |
| replace, high grade | 9E@1.67 | ea | 437.00 | 89.30 | 526.30 |
| replace, deluxe grade | 9E@1.67 | ea | 547.00 | 89.30 | 636.30 |
| replace, custom grade | 9E@1.67 | ea | 601.00 | 89.30 | 690.30 |
| replace, custom deluxe grade | 9E@1.67 | ea | 765.00 | 89.30 | 854.30 |
| remove | 1D@.557 | ea | — | 21.70 | 21.70 |

Courtesy of:
Rejuvenation Lamp & Fixture Co.

**Billiard-table style light fixture.**

| | Craft@Hrs | Unit | Material | Labor | Total |
|---|---|---|---|---|---|
| replace, economy grade | 9E@1.53 | ea | 288.00 | 81.90 | 369.90 |
| replace, standard grade | 9E@1.53 | ea | 628.00 | 81.90 | 709.90 |
| replace, high grade | 9E@1.53 | ea | 963.00 | 81.90 | 1,044.90 |
| replace, deluxe grade | 9E@1.53 | ea | 1,360.00 | 81.90 | 1,441.90 |
| replace, custom grade | 9E@1.53 | ea | 1,770.00 | 81.90 | 1,851.90 |
| replace, custom deluxe grade | 9E@1.53 | ea | 2,720.00 | 81.90 | 2,801.90 |
| remove | 1D@.561 | ea | — | 21.80 | 21.80 |
| remove fixture for work, then reinstall | 9E@2.61 | ea | — | 140.00 | 140.00 |

**Wall-mount light fixture.**

| | Craft@Hrs | Unit | Material | Labor | Total |
|---|---|---|---|---|---|
| replace, economy grade | 9E@.556 | ea | 27.20 | 29.70 | 56.90 |
| replace, standard grade | 9E@.556 | ea | 54.70 | 29.70 | 84.40 |
| replace, high grade | 9E@.556 | ea | 136.00 | 29.70 | 165.70 |
| replace, deluxe grade | 9E@.556 | ea | 233.00 | 29.70 | 262.70 |
| replace, custom grade | 9E@.556 | ea | 259.00 | 29.70 | 288.70 |
| replace, custom deluxe grade | 9E@.556 | ea | 382.00 | 29.70 | 411.70 |
| remove | 1D@.300 | ea | — | 11.70 | 11.70 |
| remove fixture for work, then reinstall | 9E@1.02 | ea | — | 54.60 | 54.60 |

| | Craft@Hrs | Unit | Material | Labor | Total |
|---|---|---|---|---|---|
| **Surface-mounted one-tube fluorescent strip light.** | | | | | |
| replace, 1' | 9E@1.05 | ea | 27.20 | 56.20 | 83.40 |
| replace, 1-1/2' | 9E@1.05 | ea | 27.20 | 56.20 | 83.40 |
| replace, 2' | 9E@1.05 | ea | 34.10 | 56.20 | 90.30 |
| replace, 4' | 9E@1.05 | ea | 41.00 | 56.20 | 97.20 |
| replace, 6' | 9E@1.05 | ea | 61.60 | 56.20 | 117.80 |
| replace, 8' | 9E@1.05 | ea | 88.70 | 56.20 | 144.90 |
| remove | 1D@.500 | ea | — | 19.50 | 19.50 |
| **Surface-mounted one-tube fluorescent strip light with diffuser.** | | | | | |
| replace, 2' | 9E@1.05 | ea | 41.00 | 56.20 | 97.20 |
| replace, 4' | 9E@1.05 | ea | 47.80 | 56.20 | 104.00 |
| replace, 6' | 9E@1.05 | ea | 61.60 | 56.20 | 117.80 |
| replace, 8' | 9E@1.05 | ea | 95.70 | 56.20 | 151.90 |
| remove | 1D@.500 | ea | — | 19.50 | 19.50 |
| **2' two-tube surface-mounted fluorescent strip light.** | | | | | |
| replace, exposed lights | 9E@1.05 | ea | 47.80 | 56.20 | 104.00 |
| replace, with diffuser | 9E@1.05 | ea | 75.00 | 56.20 | 131.20 |
| replace, with vinyl trim & diffuser | 9E@1.05 | ea | 81.90 | 56.20 | 138.10 |
| replace, with solid wood trim & diffuser | 9E@1.05 | ea | 103.00 | 56.20 | 159.20 |
| remove | 1D@.500 | ea | — | 19.50 | 19.50 |
| **4' two-tube surface-mounted fluorescent strip light.** | | | | | |
| replace, exposed lights | 9E@1.05 | ea | 68.10 | 56.20 | 124.30 |
| replace, with diffuser | 9E@1.05 | ea | 88.70 | 56.20 | 144.90 |
| replace, with vinyl trim & diffuser | 9E@1.05 | ea | 95.70 | 56.20 | 151.90 |
| replace, with solid wood trim & diffuser | 9E@1.05 | ea | 128.00 | 56.20 | 184.20 |
| remove | 1D@.500 | ea | — | 19.50 | 19.50 |
| **6' two-tube surface-mounted fluorescent strip light.** | | | | | |
| replace, exposed lights | 9E@1.05 | ea | 75.00 | 56.20 | 131.20 |
| replace, with diffuser | 9E@1.05 | ea | 103.00 | 56.20 | 159.20 |
| replace, with vinyl trim & diffuser | 9E@1.05 | ea | 128.00 | 56.20 | 184.20 |
| replace, with solid wood trim & diffuser | 9E@1.05 | ea | 141.00 | 56.20 | 197.20 |
| remove | 1D@.500 | ea | — | 19.50 | 19.50 |
| **8' two-tube surface-mounted fluorescent strip light.** | | | | | |
| replace, exposed lights | 9E@1.05 | ea | 103.00 | 56.20 | 159.20 |
| replace, with diffuser | 9E@1.05 | ea | 123.00 | 56.20 | 179.20 |
| replace, with vinyl trim & diffuser | 9E@1.05 | ea | 159.00 | 56.20 | 215.20 |
| replace, with solid wood trim & diffuser | 9E@1.05 | ea | 184.00 | 56.20 | 240.20 |
| remove | 1D@.500 | ea | — | 19.50 | 19.50 |
| **4' four-tube surface-mounted fluorescent strip light.** | | | | | |
| replace, exposed lights | 9E@1.05 | ea | 110.00 | 56.20 | 166.20 |
| replace, with diffuser | 9E@1.05 | ea | 164.00 | 56.20 | 220.20 |
| replace, with vinyl trim & diffuser | 9E@1.05 | ea | 190.00 | 56.20 | 246.20 |
| replace, with solid wood trim & diffuser | 9E@1.05 | ea | 239.00 | 56.20 | 295.20 |
| remove | 1D@.500 | ea | — | 19.50 | 19.50 |

|  | Craft@Hrs | Unit | Material | Labor | Total |
|---|---|---|---|---|---|

**Fluorescent fixture for suspended ceiling.** Add $15 for boxed-in fixture for fire-rated ceiling.

| | Craft@Hrs | Unit | Material | Labor | Total |
|---|---|---|---|---|---|
| replace, 2' by 2' drop-in two-tube | 9E@2.12 | ea | 110.00 | 113.00 | 223.00 |
| replace, 2' by 4' drop-in two-tube | 9E@2.12 | ea | 136.00 | 113.00 | 249.00 |
| replace, 2' by 4' drop-in four-tube | 9E@2.12 | ea | 171.00 | 113.00 | 284.00 |
| remove | 1D@.500 | ea | — | 19.50 | 19.50 |

**Additional fluorescent fixture costs.**

| | Craft@Hrs | Unit | Material | Labor | Total |
|---|---|---|---|---|---|
| remove fixture for work, then reinstall | 9E@1.84 | ea | — | 98.40 | 98.40 |
| remove and replace fluorescent fixture ballast | 9E@1.41 | ea | 88.70 | 75.40 | 164.10 |

**Fluorescent circline fixture.**

| | Craft@Hrs | Unit | Material | Labor | Total |
|---|---|---|---|---|---|
| replace, economy grade | 9E@.967 | ea | 47.80 | 51.70 | 99.50 |
| replace, standard grade | 9E@.967 | ea | 75.00 | 51.70 | 126.70 |
| replace, high grade | 9E@.967 | ea | 123.00 | 51.70 | 174.70 |
| replace, deluxe grade | 9E@.967 | ea | 239.00 | 51.70 | 290.70 |
| remove circline fixture | 1D@.371 | ea | — | 14.40 | 14.40 |
| remove circline fixture for work, then reinstall | 9E@1.67 | ea | — | 89.30 | 89.30 |
| remove and replace circline fixture ballast | 9E@1.41 | ea | 81.90 | 75.40 | 157.30 |

**Ceiling fan.** Fan only, no light.

| | Craft@Hrs | Unit | Material | Labor | Total |
|---|---|---|---|---|---|
| replace, economy grade | 9E@2.45 | ea | 88.70 | 131.00 | 219.70 |
| replace, standard grade | 9E@2.45 | ea | 141.00 | 131.00 | 272.00 |
| replace, high grade | 9E@2.45 | ea | 233.00 | 131.00 | 364.00 |
| replace, deluxe grade | 9E@2.45 | ea | 363.00 | 131.00 | 494.00 |
| remove | 1D@.500 | ea | — | 19.50 | 19.50 |
| remove fan for work, then reinstall | 9E@2.74 | ea | — | 147.00 | 147.00 |

**Ceiling fan with light.**

| | Craft@Hrs | Unit | Material | Labor | Total |
|---|---|---|---|---|---|
| replace, economy grade | 9E@3.68 | ea | 233.00 | 197.00 | 430.00 |
| replace, standard grade | 9E@3.68 | ea | 443.00 | 197.00 | 640.00 |
| replace, high grade | 9E@3.68 | ea | 389.00 | 197.00 | 586.00 |
| replace, deluxe grade | 9E@3.68 | ea | 558.00 | 197.00 | 755.00 |
| replace, custom grade | 9E@3.68 | ea | 670.00 | 197.00 | 867.00 |
| remove | 1D@.500 | ea | — | 19.50 | 19.50 |
| remove fan with light for work, then reinstall | 9E@2.82 | ea | — | 151.00 | 151.00 |

**Light for ceiling fan.**

| | Craft@Hrs | Unit | Material | Labor | Total |
|---|---|---|---|---|---|
| replace, economy grade | 9E@.525 | ea | 47.80 | 28.10 | 75.90 |
| replace, standard grade | 9E@.525 | ea | 95.70 | 28.10 | 123.80 |
| replace, high grade | 9E@.525 | ea | 136.00 | 28.10 | 164.10 |
| replace, deluxe grade | 9E@.525 | ea | 233.00 | 28.10 | 261.10 |
| replace, custom grade | 9E@.525 | ea | 363.00 | 28.10 | 391.10 |
| remove | 1D@.300 | ea | — | 11.70 | 11.70 |
| remove light from fan for work, then reinstall | 9E@.919 | ea | — | 49.20 | 49.20 |

**Hanging light fixture.** Hanging light fixtures usually hang from ceiling hooks and plug into a switched outlet.

| | Craft@Hrs | Unit | Material | Labor | Total |
|---|---|---|---|---|---|
| replace, economy grade | 9E@.305 | ea | 54.70 | 16.30 | 71.00 |
| replace, standard grade | 9E@.305 | ea | 68.10 | 16.30 | 84.40 |
| replace, high grade | 9E@.305 | ea | 81.90 | 16.30 | 98.20 |
| replace, deluxe grade | 9E@.305 | ea | 128.00 | 16.30 | 144.30 |
| remove | 1D@.100 | ea | — | 3.89 | 3.89 |

| | Craft@Hrs | Unit | Material | Labor | Total |
|---|---|---|---|---|---|
| **Double hanging light fixture.** | | | | | |
| replace, economy grade | 9E@.305 | ea | 81.90 | 16.30 | 98.20 |
| replace, standard grade | 9E@.305 | ea | 116.00 | 16.30 | 132.30 |
| replace, high grade | 9E@.305 | ea | 159.00 | 16.30 | 175.30 |
| replace, deluxe grade | 9E@.305 | ea | 213.00 | 16.30 | 229.30 |
| remove | 1D@.100 | ea | — | 3.89 | 3.89 |
| **Minimum charge.** | | | | | |
| for light fixture work | 9E@1.90 | ea | 27.20 | 102.00 | 129.20 |
| **Porcelain light fixture.** | | | | | |
| replace, standard | 9E@.230 | ea | 6.16 | 12.30 | 18.46 |
| replace, with pull chain | 9E@.230 | ea | 8.19 | 12.30 | 20.49 |
| remove | 1D@.100 | ea | — | 3.89 | 3.89 |
| remove porcelain fixture for work, then reinstall | 9E@.368 | ea | — | 19.70 | 19.70 |
| **Recessed spot light fixture.** | | | | | |
| replace, economy grade | 9E@.835 | ea | 68.10 | 44.70 | 112.80 |
| replace, standard grade | 9E@.835 | ea | 95.70 | 44.70 | 140.40 |
| replace, high grade | 9E@.835 | ea | 123.00 | 44.70 | 167.70 |
| replace, deluxe grade | 9E@.835 | ea | 164.00 | 44.70 | 208.70 |
| replace, custom grade | 9E@.835 | ea | 218.00 | 44.70 | 262.70 |
| remove | 1D@.400 | ea | — | 15.60 | 15.60 |
| remove spot fixture for work, then reinstall | 9E@.766 | ea | — | 41.00 | 41.00 |
| remove spot fixture & can for work, then reinstall | 9E@1.41 | ea | — | 75.40 | 75.40 |
| **Electric strip for strip lighting.** Surface-mounted electric strip channel. Does not include strip-mounted spot lights. 3 lf minimum. | | | | | |
| replace, electric strip for strip lights | 9E@.261 | lf | 15.20 | 14.00 | 29.20 |
| remove | 1D@.110 | lf | — | 4.28 | 4.28 |
| remove electric strip for work, then reinstall | 9E@.459 | lf | — | 24.60 | 24.60 |
| **Strip light.** Spot light for surface mounted electric strip channel. | | | | | |
| replace, economy grade | 9E@.368 | ea | 34.10 | 19.70 | 53.80 |
| replace, standard grade | 9E@.368 | ea | 47.80 | 19.70 | 67.50 |
| replace, high grade | 9E@.368 | ea | 95.70 | 19.70 | 115.40 |
| remove | 1D@.150 | ea | — | 5.84 | 5.84 |
| remove light for work, then reinstall *strip spot light* | 9E@.645 | ea | — | 34.50 | 34.50 |
| **Exterior single flood light fixture.** | | | | | |
| replace, standard grade | 9E@.591 | ea | 61.60 | 31.60 | 93.20 |
| replace, high grade | 9E@.591 | ea | 81.90 | 31.60 | 113.50 |
| remove | 1D@.300 | ea | — | 11.70 | 11.70 |
| remove fixture for work, then reinstall | 9E@1.08 | ea | — | 57.80 | 57.80 |

|  | Craft@Hrs | Unit | Material | Labor | Total |
|---|---|---|---|---|---|
| **Exterior double flood light fixture.** | | | | | |
| replace, standard grade | 9E@.591 | ea | 75.00 | 31.60 | 106.60 |
| replace, high grade | 9E@.591 | ea | 103.00 | 31.60 | 134.60 |
| remove | 1D@.300 | ea | — | 11.70 | 11.70 |
| remove fixture for work, then reinstall | 9E@1.08 | ea | — | 57.80 | 57.80 |
| **Exterior triple flood light fixture.** | | | | | |
| replace, standard grade | 9E@.591 | ea | 95.70 | 31.60 | 127.30 |
| replace, high grade | 9E@.591 | ea | 116.00 | 31.60 | 147.60 |
| remove | 1D@.300 | ea | — | 11.70 | 11.70 |
| remove fixture for work, then reinstall | 9E@1.08 | ea | — | 57.80 | 57.80 |
| **Exterior wall-mount light fixture.** | | | | | |
| replace, economy grade | 9E@.574 | ea | 47.80 | 30.70 | 78.50 |
| replace, standard grade | 9E@.574 | ea | 75.00 | 30.70 | 105.70 |
| replace, high grade | 9E@.574 | ea | 190.00 | 30.70 | 220.70 |
| replace, deluxe grade | 9E@.574 | ea | 363.00 | 30.70 | 393.70 |
| remove | 1D@.250 | ea | — | 9.73 | 9.73 |
| remove fixture for work, then reinstall | 9E@1.08 | ea | — | 57.80 | 57.80 |
| **Exterior recessed light fixture.** | | | | | |
| replace, economy grade | 9E@.835 | ea | 81.90 | 44.70 | 126.60 |
| replace, standard grade | 9E@.835 | ea | 116.00 | 44.70 | 160.70 |
| replace, high grade | 9E@.835 | ea | 207.00 | 44.70 | 251.70 |
| replace, deluxe grade | 9E@.835 | ea | 288.00 | 44.70 | 332.70 |
| remove | 1D@.500 | ea | — | 19.50 | 19.50 |
| remove fixture for work, then reinstall | 9E@1.67 | ea | — | 89.30 | 89.30 |
| **Exterior light fixture allowance.** Contractor's allowance per light fixture in complete home. | | | | | |
| replace, economy grade | 9E@.591 | ea | 34.10 | 31.60 | 65.70 |
| replace, standard grade | 9E@.591 | ea | 68.10 | 31.60 | 99.70 |
| replace, high grade | 9E@.591 | ea | 128.00 | 31.60 | 159.60 |
| replace, deluxe grade | 9E@.591 | ea | 245.00 | 31.60 | 276.60 |
| remove | 1D@.315 | ea | — | 12.30 | 12.30 |
| remove fixture for work, then reinstall | 9E@1.08 | ea | — | 57.80 | 57.80 |

Courtesy of: Rejuvenation Lamp & Fixture Co.

**Exterior post with light fixture.** Post up to 7 feet tall. Includes post hole, concrete base and hole backfill. Does not include wiring. Economy: Redwood post with beveled corners or light turnings, or straight metal post. Plastic or light metal fixture, usually one light with polystyrene lens. Standard: Turned redwood post. Black metal fixture, usually one light with polystyrene lens. High: Turned redwood post. Metal fixture, one to two lights, clear plastic or glass lens. Deluxe: Aluminum post with J bolts. Metal fixture, one to two lights, clear plastic or glass lens. Custom: Cast-iron post with J bolts. Cast-iron, brass, copper or pewter fixture, often simulated gas light with one to four lights, clear plastic or glass lens.

|  | Craft@Hrs | Unit | Material | Labor | Total |
|---|---|---|---|---|---|
| replace, economy grade | 9E@5.41 | ea | 239.00 | 289.00 | 528.00 |
| replace, standard grade | 9E@5.41 | ea | 346.00 | 289.00 | 635.00 |
| replace, high grade | 9E@5.41 | ea | 443.00 | 289.00 | 732.00 |
| replace, deluxe grade | 9E@5.41 | ea | 649.00 | 289.00 | 938.00 |
| replace, custom grade | 9E@5.41 | ea | 1,150.00 | 289.00 | 1,439.00 |
| remove | 1D@1.20 | ea | — | 46.70 | 46.70 |
| remove for work, then reinstall | 9E@10.2 | ea | — | 546.00 | 546.00 |

| | Craft@Hrs | Unit | Material | Labor | Total |
|---|---|---|---|---|---|

**Exterior post light fixture (no post).** Economy: Plastic or light metal fixture, one interior light with polystyrene lens. Standard: Metal fixture, two interior lights with clear polystyrene lens. High: Metal fixture, two to four interior lights with clear polystyrene lens. Deluxe: Copper, pewter or antique finish, two to four interior lights with clear glass lens. Custom: Ornate copper, pewter, brass or antique finish, two to four interior lights with clear glass lens

| | Craft@Hrs | Unit | Material | Labor | Total |
|---|---|---|---|---|---|
| replace, economy grade | 9E@1.15 | ea | 77.50 | 61.50 | 139.00 |
| replace, standard grade | 9E@1.15 | ea | 128.00 | 61.50 | 189.50 |
| replace, high grade | 9E@1.15 | ea | 184.00 | 61.50 | 245.50 |
| replace, deluxe grade | 9E@1.15 | ea | 288.00 | 61.50 | 349.50 |
| replace, custom grade | 9E@1.15 | ea | 416.00 | 61.50 | 477.50 |
| remove | 1D@.500 | ea | — | 19.50 | 19.50 |
| remove for work, then reinstall | 9E@1.93 | ea | — | 103.00 | 103.00 |

**Redwood post for exterior post light fixture.** To 7' tall. Diameter to 4".

| | Craft@Hrs | Unit | Material | Labor | Total |
|---|---|---|---|---|---|
| replace, standard grade, beveled edges or light turnings | 9E@4.29 | ea | 341.00 | 230.00 | 571.00 |
| replace, high grade, turned post | 9E@4.29 | ea | 478.00 | 230.00 | 708.00 |
| remove | 1D@1.20 | ea | — | 46.70 | 46.70 |

**Metal post for exterior post light fixture.**

| | Craft@Hrs | Unit | Material | Labor | Total |
|---|---|---|---|---|---|
| replace, standard grade | 9E@4.09 | ea | 218.00 | 219.00 | 437.00 |
| replace, high grade | 9E@4.09 | ea | 341.00 | 219.00 | 560.00 |
| replace, deluxe grade | 9E@4.09 | ea | 478.00 | 219.00 | 697.00 |
| replace, custom grade | 9E@4.09 | ea | 606.00 | 219.00 | 825.00 |
| replace, custom deluxe grade | 9E@4.09 | ea | 948.00 | 219.00 | 1,167.00 |
| remove | 1D@1.20 | ea | — | 46.70 | 46.70 |

**Additional exterior fixture costs.**

| | Craft@Hrs | Unit | Material | Labor | Total |
|---|---|---|---|---|---|
| add for exterior light motion sensor | — | ea | 95.70 | — | 95.70 |
| add for exterior light infrared detector | — | ea | 95.70 | — | 95.70 |

**Light fixture repair.**

| | Craft@Hrs | Unit | Material | Labor | Total |
|---|---|---|---|---|---|
| replace, light fixture socket and wiring | 9E@.482 | ea | 8.87 | 25.80 | 34.67 |
| replace, chandelier socket and wiring, per arm | 9E@.510 | ea | 11.60 | 27.30 | 38.90 |

**Bowl shade or globe for light fixture.**

| | Craft@Hrs | Unit | Material | Labor | Total |
|---|---|---|---|---|---|
| replace, economy grade | 9E@.062 | ea | 16.40 | 3.32 | 19.72 |
| replace, standard grade | 9E@.062 | ea | 27.20 | 3.32 | 30.52 |
| replace, high grade | 9E@.062 | ea | 47.20 | 3.32 | 50.52 |
| replace, deluxe grade | 9E@.062 | ea | 68.10 | 3.32 | 71.42 |
| replace, custom grade | 9E@.062 | ea | 83.40 | 3.32 | 86.72 |

## Time & Material Charts (selected items)
## Electrical Materials

See Electrical material prices with the line items above.

## Electrical Labor

| Laborer | base wage | paid leave | true wage | taxes & ins. | total |
|---|---|---|---|---|---|
| Electrician | $36.10 | 2.82 | $38.92 | 22.38 | $61.30 |
| Electrician's helper | $26.00 | 2.03 | $28.03 | 17.57 | $45.60 |
| Demolition laborer | $20.70 | 1.61 | $22.31 | 16.59 | $38.90 |

**Paid leave** is calculated based on two weeks paid vacation, one week sick leave, and seven paid holidays. Employer's matching portion of **FICA** is 7.65 percent. **FUTA** (Federal Unemployment) is .8 percent. **Worker's compensation** for the electrical trade was calculated using a national average of 6.93 percent. **Unemployment insurance** was calculated using a national average of 8 percent. **Health insurance** was calculated based on a projected national average for 2015 of $1,025 per employee (and family when applicable) per month. Employer pays 80 percent for a per month cost of $820 per employee. **Retirement** is based on a 401(k) retirement program with employer matching of 50 percent. Employee contributions to the 401(k) plan are an average of 6 percent of the true wage. **Liability insurance** is based on a national average of 10.0 percent.

|  | Craft@Hrs | Unit | Material | Labor | Total |
|---|---|---|---|---|---|
| **Electrical Labor Productivity** | | | | | |
| Demolition of electrical work | | | | | |
| remove 120 volt switch or outlet | 1D@.150 | ea | — | 5.84 | 5.84 |
| remove 240 volt switch or outlet | 1D@.200 | ea | — | 7.78 | 7.78 |
| remove bathroom fan | 1D@.506 | ea | — | 19.70 | 19.70 |
| remove bathroom fan / light with heater | 1D@.726 | ea | — | 28.20 | 28.20 |
| remove breaker panel | 1D@6.09 | ea | — | 237.00 | 237.00 |
| remove cable service drop | 1D@10.5 | ea | — | 408.00 | 408.00 |
| remove conduit service drop | 1D@13.1 | ea | — | 510.00 | 510.00 |
| remove rigid steel mast service drop | 1D@15.4 | ea | — | 599.00 | 599.00 |
| remove circuit breaker | 1D@.200 | ea | — | 7.78 | 7.78 |
| remove door bell or chime | 1D@.100 | ea | — | 3.89 | 3.89 |
| remove kitchen exhaust fan | 1D@.539 | ea | — | 21.00 | 21.00 |
| remove whole-house exhaust fan | 1D@1.52 | ea | — | 59.10 | 59.10 |
| remove intercom system master station | 1D@.749 | ea | — | 29.10 | 29.10 |
| remove intercom system remote station | 1D@.300 | ea | — | 11.70 | 11.70 |
| remove low-voltage outlet | 1D@.150 | ea | — | 5.84 | 5.84 |
| remove detector | 1D@.200 | ea | — | 7.78 | 7.78 |
| remove thermostat | 1D@.200 | ea | — | 7.78 | 7.78 |
| remove television antenna | 1D@.835 | ea | — | 32.50 | 32.50 |
| remove recessed electric space heater | 1D@.506 | ea | — | 19.70 | 19.70 |
| remove electric baseboard heater | 1D@.165 | lf | — | 6.42 | 6.42 |
| remove light fixture | 1D@.300 | ea | — | 11.70 | 11.70 |
| remove bathroom light bar | 1D@.315 | ea | — | 12.30 | 12.30 |
| remove chandelier | 1D@.557 | ea | — | 21.70 | 21.70 |
| remove florescent light fixture | 1D@.500 | ea | — | 19.50 | 19.50 |
| remove florescent circline light fixture | 1D@.371 | ea | — | 14.40 | 14.40 |
| remove ceiling fan | 1D@.500 | ea | — | 19.50 | 19.50 |
| remove hanging light fixture | 1D@.100 | ea | — | 3.89 | 3.89 |

| | Craft@Hrs | Unit | Material | Labor | Total |
|---|---|---|---|---|---|
| remove porcelain light fixture | 1D@.100 | ea | — | 3.89 | 3.89 |
| remove recessed spot light fixture | 1D@.400 | ea | — | 15.60 | 15.60 |
| remove electric strip for electric strip lights | 1D@.110 | lf | — | 4.28 | 4.28 |
| remove electric strip light | 1D@.150 | ea | — | 5.84 | 5.84 |
| remove exterior flood light | 1D@.300 | ea | — | 11.70 | 11.70 |
| remove exterior post with light fixture | 1D@1.20 | ea | — | 46.70 | 46.70 |
| remove exterior post light fixture | 1D@.500 | ea | — | 19.50 | 19.50 |

## Electrical crew

| | | Craft@Hrs | | | | |
|---|---|---|---|---|---|---|
| install wiring, boxes, and fixtures | electrician | $61.30 | | | | |
| install wiring, boxes, and fixtures | electrician's helper | $45.60 | | | | |
| install wiring, boxes, and fixtures | electrical crew | $53.50 | | | | |

| | Craft@Hrs | Unit | Material | Labor | Total |
|---|---|---|---|---|---|
| **Install complete house electrical wiring, outlets, switches & light fixtures** | | | | | |
| economy grade | 9E@.053 | sf | — | 2.84 | 2.84 |
| deluxe grade | 9E@.109 | sf | — | 5.83 | 5.83 |
| low-voltage system | 9E@.100 | sf | — | 5.35 | 5.35 |
| add for wiring installation in conduit | 9E@.055 | sf | — | 2.94 | 2.94 |
| **Install complete house rough electrical (no light fixtures)** | | | | | |
| standard | 9E@.070 | sf | — | 3.75 | 3.75 |
| in conduit | 9E@.154 | sf | — | 8.24 | 8.24 |
| low-voltage system | 9E@.075 | sf | — | 4.01 | 4.01 |
| **Install complete house light fixtures** | | | | | |
| economy grade | 9E@.015 | sf | — | .80 | .80 |
| deluxe grade | 9E@.017 | sf | — | .91 | .91 |
| for low-voltage system | 9E@.013 | sf | — | .70 | .70 |
| **240 volt system** | | | | | |
| install outlet or switch with wiring run & box | 9E@1.34 | ea | — | 71.70 | 71.70 |
| **120 volt system** | | | | | |
| install switch or outlet with wiring run & box | 9E@.977 | ea | — | 52.30 | 52.30 |
| install 3-way switch with wiring run & box | 9E@1.95 | ea | — | 104.00 | 104.00 |
| **Electric wiring run** | | | | | |
| for typical 120 volt outlet or light | 9E@.802 | ea | — | 42.90 | 42.90 |
| for 120 volt appliance | 9E@1.02 | ea | — | 54.60 | 54.60 |
| **Install conduit** | | | | | |
| electric metallic tubing (EMT), average installation | 9E@.077 | sf | — | 4.12 | 4.12 |
| flexible metal, average installation | 9E@.041 | sf | — | 2.19 | 2.19 |
| PVC, average installation | 9E@.045 | sf | — | 2.41 | 2.41 |
| intermediate (IMC), average installation | 9E@.113 | sf | — | 6.05 | 6.05 |
| rigid metal (RMC), average installation | 9E@.067 | sf | — | 3.58 | 3.58 |
| **Install wiring** | | | | | |
| #10 2 wire with ground Romex | 9E@.051 | lf | — | 2.73 | 2.73 |
| #12 2 wire with ground Romex | 9E@.047 | lf | — | 2.51 | 2.51 |
| #14 2 wire with ground Romex | 9E@.040 | lf | — | 2.14 | 2.14 |
| **Install breaker panel** | | | | | |
| 100 amp ext. breaker panel (5 breakers) | 7E@4.89 | ea | — | 300.00 | 300.00 |
| 100 amp int. breaker panel (5 breakers) | 7E@4.30 | ea | — | 264.00 | 264.00 |
| 150 amp ext. breaker panel (10 breakers) | 7E@7.68 | ea | — | 471.00 | 471.00 |
| 150 amp int. breaker panel (10 breakers) | 7E@7.17 | ea | — | 440.00 | 440.00 |

| | Craft@Hrs | Unit | Material | Labor | Total |
|---|---|---|---|---|---|
| 200 amp ext. breaker panel (15 breakers) | 7E@10.8 | ea | — | 662.00 | 662.00 |
| 200 amp int. breaker panel (15 breakers) | 7E@9.77 | ea | — | 599.00 | 599.00 |
| 300 amp ext. breaker panel (30 breakers) | 7E@14.3 | ea | — | 877.00 | 877.00 |
| 300 amp int. breaker panel (30 breakers) | 7E@13.4 | ea | — | 821.00 | 821.00 |
| 40 amp int. breaker sub-panel (5 breakers) | 7E@2.99 | ea | — | 183.00 | 183.00 |
| 50 amp int. breaker sub-panel | 7E@3.16 | ea | — | 194.00 | 194.00 |
| 70 amp int. breaker sub-panel | 7E@3.47 | ea | — | 213.00 | 213.00 |
| **Install electrical service** | | | | | |
| 100 amp cable service | 7E@11.9 | ea | — | 729.00 | 729.00 |
| 150 amp cable service | 7E@14.3 | ea | — | 877.00 | 877.00 |
| 150 amp conduit service | 7E@15.4 | ea | — | 944.00 | 944.00 |
| 150 amp rigid steel mast service | 7E@15.4 | ea | — | 944.00 | 944.00 |
| 200 amp cable service | 7E@18.5 | ea | — | 1,130.00 | 1,130.00 |
| 200 amp conduit service | 7E@19.9 | ea | — | 1,220.00 | 1,220.00 |
| 200 amp rigid steel mast service | 7E@19.9 | ea | — | 1,220.00 | 1,220.00 |
| **Install breaker** | | | | | |
| single-pole (120 volt) circuit breaker | 7E@.636 | ea | — | 39.00 | 39.00 |
| double-pole (240 volt) circuit breaker | 7E@.649 | ea | — | 39.80 | 39.80 |
| ground fault circuit interrupter breaker | 7E@.689 | ea | — | 42.20 | 42.20 |
| main disconnect circuit breaker | 7E@3.47 | ea | — | 213.00 | 213.00 |
| **Install door bell or chime** | | | | | |
| door bell or chime button | 9E@.137 | ea | — | 7.33 | 7.33 |
| door bell or chime | 9E@1.24 | ea | — | 66.30 | 66.30 |
| low-voltage wiring (per button) | 9E@.563 | ea | — | 30.10 | 30.10 |
| **Install exhaust fan** | | | | | |
| bathroom exhaust fan | 9E@.685 | ea | — | 36.60 | 36.60 |
| bathroom exhaust fan with heat lamp | 9E@.883 | ea | — | 47.20 | 47.20 |
| bathroom exhaust fan with heater | 9E@.952 | ea | — | 50.90 | 50.90 |
| kitchen exhaust fan | 9E@1.12 | ea | — | 59.90 | 59.90 |
| whole-house exhaust fan | 9E@3.10 | ea | — | 166.00 | 166.00 |
| **Install intercom** | | | | | |
| intercom system master station | 9E@2.47 | ea | — | 132.00 | 132.00 |
| intercom system remote station | 9E@.685 | ea | — | 36.60 | 36.60 |
| 120 volt wiring for intercom master station | 9E@.896 | ea | — | 47.90 | 47.90 |
| intercom wiring (per station) | 9E@.619 | ea | — | 33.10 | 33.10 |
| **Install low-voltage outlet** | | | | | |
| install outlet | 9E@.256 | ea | — | 13.70 | 13.70 |
| wiring (per outlet) | 9E@.358 | ea | — | 19.20 | 19.20 |
| **Install sound system** | | | | | |
| speaker with grill | 9E@.244 | ea | — | 13.10 | 13.10 |
| **Install detector** | | | | | |
| battery operated | 9E@.355 | ea | — | 19.00 | 19.00 |
| direct-wired | 9E@.398 | ea | — | 21.30 | 21.30 |
| **Check electrical circuits** | | | | | |
| megameter test small home | 7E@3.91 | ea | — | 240.00 | 240.00 |
| megameter test average size home | 7E@5.66 | ea | — | 347.00 | 347.00 |
| megameter test large home | 7E@7.79 | ea | — | 478.00 | 478.00 |
| **Install thermostat** | | | | | |
| for electric resistance heating system | 9E@.183 | ea | — | 9.79 | 9.79 |

| | Craft@Hrs | Unit | Material | Labor | Total |
|---|---|---|---|---|---|
| electric heating system | 9E@.326 | ea | — | 17.40 | 17.40 |
| wiring (per thermostat) | 9E@.538 | ea | — | 28.80 | 28.80 |
| Install TV antenna | | | | | |
| television antenna | 9E@1.24 | ea | — | 66.30 | 66.30 |
| Install recessed electric space heater | | | | | |
| electric space heater recessed in wall | 9E@2.47 | ea | — | 132.00 | 132.00 |
| Install electric-resistance heating | | | | | |
| cable, ceiling installation | 9E@.036 | sf | — | 1.93 | 1.93 |
| cable, floor installation | 9E@.060 | sf | — | 3.21 | 3.21 |
| electric-resistance heating floor sensor | 9E@.632 | ea | — | 33.80 | 33.80 |
| Install electric baseboard heater | | | | | |
| electric baseboard heater | 9E@.512 | lf | — | 27.40 | 27.40 |
| remove for work, then reinstall | 9E@.717 | lf | — | 38.40 | 38.40 |
| Install underground wiring for exterior post light fixture | | | | | |
| up to 30 feet | 9E@1.22 | ea | — | 65.30 | 65.30 |
| up to 50 feet | 9E@1.30 | ea | — | 69.60 | 69.60 |

Lighting

Install interior light fixture
| interior incandescent light fixture | 9E@.574 | ea | — | 30.70 | 30.70 |

Install bathroom bar light
| bathroom bar light | 9E@.612 | ea | — | 32.70 | 32.70 |

Install chandelier
| chandelier | 9E@1.67 | ea | — | 89.30 | 89.30 |
| entrance chandelier | 9E@3.35 | ea | — | 179.00 | 179.00 |
| grand entrance chandelier | 9E@4.59 | ea | — | 246.00 | 246.00 |

Install wall-mount fixture
| wall-mount light fixture | 9E@.556 | ea | — | 29.70 | 29.70 |

Install fluorescent light fixture
| surface-mounted fluorescent light fixture | 9E@1.05 | ea | — | 56.20 | 56.20 |
| drop-in fluorescent fixture in suspended ceiling | 9E@2.12 | ea | — | 113.00 | 113.00 |
| fluorescent circline fixture | 9E@.967 | ea | — | 51.70 | 51.70 |

Install ceiling fan
| assemble and install ceiling fan | 9E@2.45 | ea | — | 131.00 | 131.00 |
| remove ceiling fan for work, then reinstall | 9E@2.74 | ea | — | 147.00 | 147.00 |
| assemble and install ceiling fan with light | 9E@3.68 | ea | — | 197.00 | 197.00 |
| light for ceiling fan | 9E@.525 | ea | — | 28.10 | 28.10 |

Install hanging light fixture
| hanging light fixture | 9E@.305 | ea | — | 16.30 | 16.30 |

Install recessed spot fixture
| recessed spot light fixture | 9E@.835 | ea | — | 44.70 | 44.70 |

Install exterior flood light
| exterior flood light fixture | 9E@.591 | ea | — | 31.60 | 31.60 |

Install exterior post light fixture
| exterior post with light fixture | 9E@5.41 | ea | — | 289.00 | 289.00 |
| exterior post light fixture (no post) | 9E@1.15 | ea | — | 61.50 | 61.50 |
| wood post for exterior post light fixture | 9E@4.29 | ea | — | 230.00 | 230.00 |
| metal post for exterior post light fixture | 9E@4.09 | ea | — | 219.00 | 219.00 |

# Excavation

| | Craft@Hrs | Unit | Material | Labor | Total |
|---|---|---|---|---|---|

## Mobilization charge.

| | Craft@Hrs | Unit | Material | Labor | Total |
|---|---|---|---|---|---|
| Delivery and take-home charge | 6E@4.00 | ea | — | 224.00 | 224.00 |

| | Craft@Hrs | Unit | Material | Labor | Equip. | Total |
|---|---|---|---|---|---|---|

**Excavate for slab-on-grade structure,** per sf of floor. Under-slab excavation up to 1-1/2' deep. Footing excavation up to 3' deep. Does not include mobilization.

| | Craft@Hrs | Unit | Material | Labor | Equip. | Total |
|---|---|---|---|---|---|---|
| Typical soil | 6E@.002 | sf | — | .11 | .11 | .22 |
| Medium rocky or clay soil | 6E@.003 | sf | — | .17 | .12 | .29 |
| Rocky or hardpan soil | 6E@.004 | sf | — | .22 | .15 | .37 |
| Backfill | 6E@.002 | sf | — | .11 | .05 | .16 |

**Excavate for structure with crawl space,** per sf of floor. Crawl space excavation up to 3' deep. Footing excavation up to 4' deep. Does not include mobilization.

| | Craft@Hrs | Unit | Material | Labor | Equip. | Total |
|---|---|---|---|---|---|---|
| Typical soil | 6E@.004 | sf | — | .22 | .18 | .40 |
| Medium rocky or clay soil | 6E@.005 | sf | — | .28 | .22 | .50 |
| Rocky or hardpan soil | 6E@.005 | sf | — | .28 | .26 | .54 |
| Backfill | 6E@.002 | sf | — | .11 | .10 | .21 |

**Excavate for structure with basement,** per sf of floor. Basement excavation up to 7' deep. Footing excavation up to 8' deep. Does not include mobilization.

| | Craft@Hrs | Unit | Material | Labor | Equip. | Total |
|---|---|---|---|---|---|---|
| Typical soil | 6E@.011 | sf | — | .62 | .50 | 1.12 |
| Medium rocky or clay soil | 6E@.013 | sf | — | .73 | .60 | 1.33 |
| Rocky or hardpan soil | 6E@.015 | sf | — | .84 | .68 | 1.52 |
| Backfill | 6E@.006 | sf | — | .34 | .22 | .56 |

**Excavate footings.** Excavation slopes to 3' width at bottom of footing trench. Does not include mobilization.

| | Craft@Hrs | Unit | Material | Labor | Equip. | Total |
|---|---|---|---|---|---|---|
| 3' to 4' deep, typical soil | 6E@.011 | lf | — | .62 | .49 | 1.11 |
| 3' to 4' deep, medium rocky or clay soil | 6E@.013 | lf | — | .73 | .59 | 1.32 |
| 3' to 4' deep, rocky or hardpan soil | 6E@.015 | lf | — | .84 | .67 | 1.51 |
| 5' to 6' deep, typical soil | 6E@.013 | lf | — | .73 | .64 | 1.37 |
| 5' to 6' deep, medium rocky or clay soil | 6E@.015 | lf | — | .84 | .73 | 1.57 |
| 5' to 6' deep, rocky or hardpan soil | 6E@.019 | lf | — | 1.06 | .85 | 1.91 |
| 7' to 8' deep, typical soil | 6E@.016 | lf | — | .90 | .81 | 1.71 |
| 7' to 8' deep, medium rocky or clay soil | 6E@.020 | lf | — | 1.12 | .92 | 2.04 |
| 7' to 8' deep, rocky or hardpan soil | 6E@.023 | lf | — | 1.29 | 1.06 | 2.35 |
| 9' to 10' deep, typical soil | 6E@.020 | lf | — | 1.12 | .94 | 2.06 |
| 9' to 10' deep, medium rocky or clay soil | 6E@.024 | lf | — | 1.34 | 1.09 | 2.43 |
| 9' to 10' deep, rocky or hardpan soil | 6E@.026 | lf | — | 1.46 | 1.26 | 2.72 |

**Backfill against foundation wall.** Typical backfill on flat lot or mild slope per sf of foundation wall. Does not include mobilization.

| | Craft@Hrs | Unit | Material | Labor | Equip. | Total |
|---|---|---|---|---|---|---|
| Per sf of wall | 6E@.007 | lf | — | .39 | .29 | .68 |

**Excavate utility trench,** per lf of trench. Square trench, 2' wide. Does not include mobilization.

| | Craft@Hrs | Unit | Material | Labor | Equip. | Total |
|---|---|---|---|---|---|---|
| 1' to 2' deep, sandy loam soil | 6E@.004 | lf | — | .22 | .13 | .35 |
| 1' to 2' deep, typical soil | 6E@.004 | lf | — | .22 | .16 | .38 |
| 1' to 2' deep, medium rocky or clay soil | 6E@.004 | lf | — | .22 | .18 | .40 |
| 1' to 2' deep, rocky or hardpan soil | 6E@.005 | lf | — | .28 | .22 | .50 |
| 1' to 2' deep, backfill | 6E@.004 | lf | — | .22 | .12 | .34 |

|  | Craft@Hrs | Unit | Material | Labor | Equip. | Total |
|---|---|---|---|---|---|---|
| 3' to 4' deep, sandy loam soil | 6E@.005 | lf | — | .28 | .22 | .50 |
| 3' to 4' deep, typical soil | 6E@.005 | lf | — | .28 | .26 | .54 |
| 3' to 4' deep, rocky or clay soil | 6E@.007 | lf | — | .39 | .29 | .68 |
| 3' to 4' deep, rocky or hardpan soil | 6E@.007 | lf | — | .39 | .36 | .75 |
| 3' to 4' deep, backfill | 6E@.005 | lf | — | .28 | .26 | .54 |
| 5' to 6' deep, sandy loam soil | 6E@.007 | lf | — | .39 | .30 | .69 |
| 5' to 6' deep, typical soil | 6E@.006 | lf | — | .34 | .39 | .73 |
| 5' to 6' deep, medium rocky or clay soil | 6E@.008 | lf | — | .45 | .42 | .87 |
| 5' to 6' deep, rocky or hardpan soil | 6E@.009 | lf | — | .50 | .49 | .99 |
| 5' to 6' deep, backfill | 6E@.008 | lf | — | .45 | .39 | .84 |

**Excavate water-line trench**, per lf of trench.  Trench slopes to 2' width at bottom for 2' to 3' depth, 3' width at bottom for all other depths.  Does not include mobilization.

|  | Craft@Hrs | Unit | Material | Labor | Equip. | Total |
|---|---|---|---|---|---|---|
| 2' to 3' deep, sandy loam soil | 6E@.009 | lf | — | .50 | .30 | .80 |
| 2' to 3' deep, typical soil | 6E@.009 | lf | — | .50 | .36 | .86 |
| 2' to 3' deep, medium rocky or clay soil | 6E@.010 | lf | — | .56 | .43 | .99 |
| 2' to 3' deep, rocky or hardpan soil | 6E@.011 | lf | — | .62 | .50 | 1.12 |
| 2' to 3' deep, backfill | 6E@.007 | lf | — | .39 | .28 | .67 |
| 4' to 5' deep, sandy loam soil | 6E@.011 | lf | — | .62 | .52 | 1.14 |
| 4' to 5' deep, typical soil | 6E@.013 | lf | — | .73 | .62 | 1.35 |
| 4' to 5' deep, medium rocky or clay soil | 6E@.014 | lf | — | .78 | .72 | 1.50 |
| 4' to 5' deep, rocky or hardpan soil | 6E@.015 | lf | — | .84 | .84 | 1.68 |
| 4' to 5' deep, backfill | 6E@.011 | lf | — | .62 | .49 | 1.11 |
| 6' to 7' deep, sandy loam soil | 6E@.015 | lf | — | .84 | .74 | 1.58 |
| 6' to 7' deep, typical soil | 6E@.016 | lf | — | .90 | .87 | 1.77 |
| 6' to 7' deep, medium rocky or clay soil | 6E@.018 | lf | — | 1.01 | 1.00 | 2.01 |
| 6' to 7' deep, rocky or hardpan soil | 6E@.020 | lf | — | 1.12 | 1.13 | 2.25 |
| 6' to 7' deep, backfill | 6E@.013 | lf | — | .73 | .71 | 1.44 |
| 8' to 9' deep, sandy loam soil | 6E@.018 | lf | — | 1.01 | .94 | 1.95 |
| 8' to 9' deep, typical soil | 6E@.020 | lf | — | 1.12 | 1.10 | 2.22 |
| 8' to 9' deep, medium rocky or clay soil | 6E@.023 | lf | — | 1.29 | 1.30 | 2.59 |
| 8' to 9' deep, rocky or hardpan soil | 6E@.025 | lf | — | 1.40 | 1.52 | 2.92 |
| 8' to 9' deep, backfill | 6E@.016 | lf | — | .90 | .89 | 1.79 |

**Excavate sewer-line trench**, per lf of trench.  Trench slopes to 3-1/2' width at bottom.  Does not include mobilization.

|  | Craft@Hrs | Unit | Material | Labor | Equip. | Total |
|---|---|---|---|---|---|---|
| 3' to 4' deep, sandy loam soil | 6E@.011 | lf | — | .62 | .50 | 1.12 |
| 3' to 4' deep, typical soil | 6E@.013 | lf | — | .73 | .59 | 1.32 |
| 3' to 4' deep, medium rocky soil | 6E@.014 | lf | — | .78 | .67 | 1.45 |
| 3' to 4' deep, rocky or hardpan soil | 6E@.015 | lf | — | .84 | .80 | 1.64 |
| 3' to 4' deep, backfill | 6E@.010 | lf | — | .56 | .46 | 1.02 |
| 5' to 6' deep, sandy loam soil | 6E@.015 | lf | — | .84 | .74 | 1.58 |
| 5' to 6' deep, typical soil | 6E@.016 | lf | — | .90 | .87 | 1.77 |
| 5' to 6' deep, medium rocky soil | 6E@.018 | lf | — | 1.01 | 1.00 | 2.01 |
| 5' to 6' deep, rocky or hardpan soil | 6E@.020 | lf | — | 1.12 | 1.15 | 2.27 |
| 5' to 6' deep, backfill | 6E@.013 | lf | — | .73 | .71 | 1.44 |
| 7' to 8' deep, sandy loam soil | 6E@.018 | lf | — | 1.01 | .98 | 1.99 |
| 7' to 8' deep, typical soil | 6E@.020 | lf | — | 1.12 | 1.13 | 2.25 |
| 7' to 8' deep, medium rocky soil | 6E@.023 | lf | — | 1.29 | 1.32 | 2.61 |
| 7' to 8' deep, rocky or hardpan soil | 6E@.025 | lf | — | 1.40 | 1.52 | 2.92 |
| 7' to 8' deep, backfill | 6E@.011 | lf | — | .62 | .93 | 1.55 |

| | Craft@Hrs | Unit | Material | Labor | Equip. | Total |
|---|---|---|---|---|---|---|
| **Additional excavation costs.** | | | | | | |
| Excavate hole for repairs to water, sewer, or utility lines, per lf of depth | 6E@.044 | lf | — | 2.46 | 2.05 | 4.51 |
| General foundation, slab, & footing excavation, per cubic yard | 6E@.046 | cy | — | 2.58 | 2.17 | 4.75 |
| Minimum charge for excavation work | 6E@5.00 | ea | — | 280.00 | 446.00 | 726.00 |

**Time & Material Charts** (selected items)
**Excavation Rental Equipment**

Backhoe / loader

| | Craft@Hrs | Unit | Material | Labor | Equip. | Total |
|---|---|---|---|---|---|---|
| Excavate slab-on-grade structure | | | | | | |
| typical soil ($690.00 per day, 5,740 sf per day) | — | sf | — | — | .12 | .12 |
| rocky or hardpan soil ($690.00 per day, 4,250 sf per day) | — | sf | — | — | .16 | .16 |
| backfill ($690.00 per day, 9,420 sf per day) | — | sf | — | — | .07 | .07 |
| Excavate for structure with crawl space | | | | | | |
| typical soil ($690.00 per day, 3,530 sf per day) | — | sf | — | — | .20 | .20 |
| rocky or hardpan soil ($690.00 per day, 2,610 sf per day) | — | sf | — | — | .26 | .26 |
| backfill ($690.00 per day, 6,123 sf per day) | — | sf | — | — | .11 | .11 |
| Excavate for structure with basement | | | | | | |
| typical soil ($690.00 per day, 1,400 sf per day) | — | sf | — | — | .49 | .49 |
| rocky or hardpan soil ($690.00 per day, 1,030 sf per day) | — | sf | — | — | .67 | .67 |
| backfill ($690.00 per day, 3,140 sf per day) | — | sf | — | — | .22 | .22 |
| Excavate for 3' to 4' deep footing | | | | | | |
| typical soil ($690.00 per day, 1,420 lf per day) | — | lf | — | — | .49 | .49 |
| rocky or hardpan soil ($690.00 per day, 1,050 lf per day) | — | lf | — | — | .66 | .66 |
| Excavate for 5' to 6' deep footing | | | | | | |
| typical soil ($690.00 per day, 1,108 lf per day) | — | lf | — | — | .62 | .62 |
| rocky or hardpan soil ($690.00 per day, 830 lf per day) | — | lf | — | — | .83 | .83 |
| Excavate for 7' to 8' deep footing | | | | | | |
| typical soil ($690.00 per day, 880 lf per day) | — | lf | — | — | .78 | .78 |
| rocky or hardpan soil ($690.00 per day, 660 lf per day) | — | lf | — | — | 1.05 | 1.05 |

| | Craft@Hrs | Unit | Material | Labor | Equip. | Total |
|---|---|---|---|---|---|---|
| Excavate for 9' to 10' deep footing | | | | | | |
| typical soil | | | | | | |
| ($690.00 per day, 738 lf per day) | — | lf | — | — | .93 | .93 |
| rocky or hardpan soil | | | | | | |
| ($690.00 per day, 560 lf per day) | — | lf | — | — | 1.23 | 1.23 |
| Backfill foundation wall | | | | | | |
| backfill | | | | | | |
| ($690.00 per day, 2,230 lf per day) | — | lf | — | — | .31 | .31 |
| Excavate for 1' to 2' deep utility trench | | | | | | |
| sandy loam soil | | | | | | |
| ($690.00 per day, 4,930 lf per day) | — | lf | — | — | .14 | .14 |
| rocky or hardpan soil | | | | | | |
| ($690.00 per day, 3,150 lf per day) | — | lf | — | — | .22 | .22 |
| backfill | | | | | | |
| ($690.00 per day, 5,300 lf per day) | — | lf | — | — | .13 | .13 |
| Excavate for 3' to 4' deep utility trench | | | | | | |
| sandy loam soil | | | | | | |
| ($690.00 per day, 3,057 lf per day) | — | lf | — | — | .23 | .23 |
| rocky or hardpan soil | | | | | | |
| ($690.00 per day, 1,960 lf per day) | — | lf | — | — | .35 | .35 |
| backfill | | | | | | |
| ($690.00 per day, 2,650 lf per day) | — | lf | — | — | .26 | .26 |
| Excavate for 5' to 6' deep utility trench | | | | | | |
| sandy loam soil | | | | | | |
| ($690.00 per day, 2,219 lf per day) | — | lf | — | — | .31 | .31 |
| rocky or hardpan soil | | | | | | |
| ($690.00 per day, 1,410 lf per day) | — | lf | — | — | .49 | .49 |
| backfill | | | | | | |
| ($690.00 per day, 1,760 lf per day) | — | lf | — | — | .39 | .39 |
| Excavate for 2' to 3' deep water-line trench | | | | | | |
| sandy loam soil | | | | | | |
| ($690.00 per day, 2,200 lf per day) | — | lf | — | — | .31 | .31 |
| rocky or hardpan soil | | | | | | |
| ($690.00 per day, 1,400 lf per day) | — | lf | — | — | .49 | .49 |
| backfill | | | | | | |
| ($690.00 per day, 2,350 lf per day) | — | lf | — | — | .29 | .29 |
| Excavate for 4' to 5' deep water-line trench | | | | | | |
| sandy loam soil | | | | | | |
| ($690.00 per day, 1,330 lf per day) | — | lf | — | — | .52 | .52 |
| typical soil | | | | | | |
| ($690.00 per day, 1,140 lf per day) | — | lf | — | — | .61 | .61 |
| medium rocky or clay soil | | | | | | |
| ($690.00 per day, 980 lf per day) | — | lf | — | — | .70 | .70 |
| rocky or hardpan soil | | | | | | |
| ($690.00 per day, 850 lf per day) | — | lf | — | — | .81 | .81 |
| backfill | | | | | | |
| ($690.00 per day, 1,410 lf per day) | — | lf | — | — | .49 | .49 |

| | Craft@Hrs | Unit | Material | Labor | Equip. | Total |
|---|---|---|---|---|---|---|
| Excavate for 6' to 7' deep water-line trench | | | | | | |
| sandy loam soil | | | | | | |
| ($690.00 per day, 940 lf per day) | — | lf | — | — | .73 | .73 |
| typical soil | | | | | | |
| ($690.00 per day, 810 lf per day) | — | lf | — | — | .85 | .85 |
| medium rocky or clay soil | | | | | | |
| ($690.00 per day, 700 lf per day) | — | lf | — | — | .99 | .99 |
| rocky or hardpan soil | | | | | | |
| ($690.00 per day, 610 lf per day) | — | lf | — | — | 1.13 | 1.13 |
| backfill | | | | | | |
| ($690.00 per day, 1,010 lf per day) | — | lf | — | — | .68 | .68 |
| Excavate for 8' to 9' deep water-line trench | | | | | | |
| sandy loam soil | | | | | | |
| ($690.00 per day, 730 lf per day) | — | lf | — | — | .95 | .95 |
| typical soil | | | | | | |
| ($690.00 per day, 630 lf per day) | — | lf | — | — | 1.10 | 1.10 |
| medium rocky or clay soil | | | | | | |
| ($690.00 per day, 540 lf per day) | — | lf | — | — | 1.28 | 1.28 |
| rocky or hardpan soil | | | | | | |
| ($690.00 per day, 460 lf per day) | — | lf | — | — | 1.50 | 1.50 |
| backfill | | | | | | |
| ($690.00 per day, 780 lf per day) | — | lf | — | — | .88 | .88 |
| Excavate for 3' to 4' deep sewer-line trench | | | | | | |
| sandy loam soil | | | | | | |
| ($690.00 per day, 1,420 lf per day) | — | lf | — | — | .49 | .49 |
| typical soil | | | | | | |
| ($690.00 per day, 1,220 lf per day) | — | lf | — | — | .57 | .57 |
| medium rocky or clay soil | | | | | | |
| ($690.00 per day, 1,050 lf per day) | — | lf | — | — | .66 | .66 |
| rocky or hardpan soil | | | | | | |
| ($690.00 per day, 900 lf per day) | — | lf | — | — | .77 | .77 |
| backfill | | | | | | |
| ($690.00 per day, 1,520 lf per day) | — | lf | — | — | .45 | .45 |
| Excavate for 5' to 6' deep sewer-line trench | | | | | | |
| sandy loam soil | | | | | | |
| ($690.00 per day, 940 lf per day) | — | lf | — | — | .73 | .73 |
| typical soil | | | | | | |
| ($690.00 per day, 810 lf per day) | — | lf | — | — | .85 | .85 |
| medium rocky or clay soil | | | | | | |
| ($690.00 per day, 700 lf per day) | — | lf | — | — | .99 | .99 |
| backfill | | | | | | |
| ($690.00 per day, 1,010 lf per day) | — | lf | — | — | .68 | .68 |

| | Craft@Hrs | Unit | Material | Labor | Equip. | Total |
|---|---|---|---|---|---|---|
| Excavate for 7' to 8' deep sewer-line trench | | | | | | |
| sandy loam soil | | | | | | |
| ($690.00 per day, 710 lf per day) | — | lf | — | — | .97 | .97 |
| typical soil | | | | | | |
| ($690.00 per day, 610 lf per day) | — | lf | — | — | 1.13 | 1.13 |
| medium rocky or clay soil | | | | | | |
| ($690.00 per day, 530 lf per day) | — | lf | — | — | 1.30 | 1.30 |
| rocky or hardpan soil | | | | | | |
| ($690.00 per day, 460 lf per day) | — | lf | — | — | 1.50 | 1.50 |
| backfill | | | | | | |
| ($690.00 per day, 750 lf per day) | — | lf | — | — | .92 | .92 |
| Excavate for repairs | | | | | | |
| excavate hole | | | | | | |
| ($690.00 per day, 340 lf per day) | — | lf | — | — | 2.03 | 2.03 |
| General excavation | | | | | | |
| excavation | | | | | | |
| ($690.00 per day, 322 cy per day) | — | cy | — | — | 2.14 | 2.14 |
| minimum charge | | | | | | |
| ($442.00 per day, 1 per day) | — | ea | — | — | 442.00 | 442.00 |
| Trenching | | | | | | |
| Trenching machine | | | | | | |
| ($498.00 per day, 1 per day) | — | day | — | — | 498.00 | 498.00 |
| minimum charge for trenching machine | | | | | | |
| ($305.00 per day, 1 per day) | — | ea | — | — | 305.00 | 305.00 |
| Compacting | | | | | | |
| "Jumping jack" compactor | | | | | | |
| ($157.00 per day, 1 per day) | — | day | — | — | 157.00 | 157.00 |
| minimum charge for compactor | | | | | | |
| ($125.00 per day, 1 per day) | — | ea | — | — | 125.00 | 125.00 |

## Excavation Labor

| Laborer | wage | base leave | paid wage | true & ins. | taxes total |
|---|---|---|---|---|---|
| Equipment operator | $42.30 | 3.30 | $45.60 | 29.10 | $74.70 |
| Excavation laborer | $19.50 | 1.52 | $21.02 | 16.18 | $37.20 |

**Paid leave** is calculated based on two weeks paid vacation, one week sick leave, and seven paid holidays. Employer's matching portion of **FICA** is 7.65 percent. **FUTA** (Federal Unemployment) is .8 percent. **Worker's compensation** for the excavation trade was calculated using a national average of 15.00 percent for the equipment operator and 15.05 percent for the excavation laborer. **Unemployment insurance** was calculated using a national average of 8 percent. **Health insurance** was calculated based on a projected national average for 2015 of $1,025 per employee (and family when applicable) per month. Employer pays 80 percent for a per month cost of $820 per employee. **Retirement** is based on a 401(k) retirement program with employer matching of 50 percent. Employee contributions to the 401(k) plan are an average of 6 percent of the true wage. **Liability insurance** is based on a national average of 10.0 percent.

| | Craft@Hrs | Unit | Material | Labor | Total |
|---|---|---|---|---|---|

## Excavation Labor Productivity

| | Craft@Hrs | Unit | Material | Labor | Total |
|---|---|---|---|---|---|
| Excavation equipment delivery and return labor charges | | | | | |
| backhoe mobilization | 10@4.00 | ea | — | 299.00 | 299.00 |
| Excavate slab-on-grade structure (per sf of floor) | | | | | |
| typical soil, machine | 10@.001 | sf | — | .07 | .07 |
| typical soil, hand finish | 5E@.001 | sf | — | .04 | .04 |
| rocky or hardpan soil, machine | 10@.002 | sf | — | .15 | .15 |
| rocky or hardpan soil, hand finish | 5E@.002 | sf | — | .07 | .07 |
| Backfill slab-on-grade structure (per sf of floor) | | | | | |
| all soil types, machine | 10@.001 | sf | — | .07 | .07 |
| all soil types, hand labor | 5E@.001 | sf | — | .04 | .04 |
| Excavate for structure with crawl space (per sf of floor) | | | | | |
| typical soil, machine | 10@.002 | sf | — | .15 | .15 |
| typical soil, hand finish | 5E@.002 | sf | — | .07 | .07 |
| rocky or hardpan soil, machine | 10@.003 | sf | — | .22 | .22 |
| rocky or hardpan soil, hand finish | 5E@.002 | sf | — | .07 | .07 |
| Backfill structure with crawl space (per sf of floor) | | | | | |
| all soil types, machine | 10@.001 | sf | — | .07 | .07 |
| all soil types, hand labor | 5E@.001 | sf | — | .04 | .04 |
| Excavate for structure with basement (per sf of floor) | | | | | |
| typical soil, machine | 10@.006 | sf | — | .45 | .45 |
| typical soil, hand finish | 5E@.005 | sf | — | .19 | .19 |
| rocky or hardpan soil, machine | 10@.008 | sf | — | .60 | .60 |
| rocky or hardpan soil, hand finish | 5E@.006 | sf | — | .22 | .22 |
| Backfill structure with basement (per sf of floor) | | | | | |
| all soil types, machine | 10@.003 | sf | — | .22 | .22 |
| all soil types, hand labor | 5E@.003 | sf | — | .11 | .11 |
| Excavate for 3' to 4' deep footings | | | | | |
| typical soil, machine | 10@.006 | lf | — | .45 | .45 |
| typical soil, hand finish | 5E@.005 | lf | — | .19 | .19 |
| rocky or hardpan soil, machine | 10@.008 | lf | — | .60 | .60 |
| rocky or hardpan soil, hand finish | 5E@.006 | lf | — | .22 | .22 |
| Excavate for 5' to 6' deep footings | | | | | |
| typical soil, machine | 10@.007 | lf | — | .52 | .52 |
| typical soil, hand finish | 5E@.006 | lf | — | .22 | .22 |
| rocky or hardpan soil, machine | 10@.010 | lf | — | .75 | .75 |
| rocky or hardpan soil, hand finish | 5E@.008 | lf | — | .30 | .30 |
| Excavate for 7' to 8' deep footing | | | | | |
| typical soil, machine | 10@.009 | lf | — | .67 | .67 |
| typical soil, hand finish | 5E@.007 | lf | — | .26 | .26 |
| hardpan or rocky soil, machine | 10@.012 | lf | — | .90 | .90 |
| hardpan or rocky soil, hand finish | 5E@.010 | lf | — | .37 | .37 |
| Excavate for 9' to 10' deep footing | | | | | |
| typical soil, machine | 10@.011 | lf | — | .82 | .82 |
| typical soil, hand finish | 5E@.009 | lf | — | .33 | .33 |
| hardpan or rocky soil, machine | 10@.014 | lf | — | 1.05 | 1.05 |
| hardpan or rocky soil, hand finish | 5E@.011 | lf | — | .41 | .41 |
| Backfill foundation wall (per sf of wall) | | | | | |
| machine | 10@.004 | sf | — | .30 | .30 |
| hand labor | 5E@.003 | sf | — | .11 | .11 |

| | Craft@Hrs | Unit | Material | Labor | Total |
|---|---|---|---|---|---|
| Machine excavate for 1' to 2' deep utility trench | | | | | |
| sandy loam soil | 10@.002 | lf | — | .15 | .15 |
| rocky or hardpan soil | 10@.003 | lf | — | .22 | .22 |
| backfill | 10@.002 | lf | — | .15 | .15 |
| Machine excavate for 3' to 4' deep utility trench | | | | | |
| sandy loam soil | 10@.003 | lf | — | .22 | .22 |
| rocky or hardpan soil | 10@.004 | lf | — | .30 | .30 |
| backfill | 10@.003 | lf | — | .22 | .22 |
| Machine excavate for 5' to 6' deep utility trench | | | | | |
| sandy loam soil | 10@.004 | lf | — | .30 | .30 |
| rocky or hardpan soil | 10@.006 | lf | — | .45 | .45 |
| backfill | 10@.005 | lf | — | .37 | .37 |
| Hand finish excavation for utility trench | | | | | |
| all soil types | 5E@.002 | lf | — | .07 | .07 |
| Excavate for 2' to 3' deep water-line trench | | | | | |
| sandy loam soil | 10@.004 | lf | — | .30 | .30 |
| rocky or hardpan soil | 10@.006 | lf | — | .45 | .45 |
| backfill | 10@.003 | lf | — | .22 | .22 |
| Excavate for 4' to 5' deep water-line trench | | | | | |
| sandy loam soil | 10@.006 | lf | — | .45 | .45 |
| rocky or hardpan soil | 10@.009 | lf | — | .67 | .67 |
| backfill | 10@.006 | lf | — | .45 | .45 |
| Excavate for 6' to 7' deep water-line trench | | | | | |
| sandy loam soil | 10@.009 | lf | — | .67 | .67 |
| rocky or hardpan soil | 10@.013 | lf | — | .97 | .97 |
| backfill | 10@.008 | lf | — | .60 | .60 |
| Excavate for 8' to 9' deep water-line trench | | | | | |
| sandy loam soil | 10@.011 | lf | — | .82 | .82 |
| rocky or hardpan soil | 10@.017 | lf | — | 1.27 | 1.27 |
| backfill | 10@.010 | lf | — | .75 | .75 |
| Hand finish excavation for water-line trench | | | | | |
| all soil types | 5E@.005 | lf | — | .19 | .19 |
| Excavate for 3' to 4' deep sewer-line trench | | | | | |
| sandy loam soil | 10@.006 | lf | — | .45 | .45 |
| rocky or hardpan soil | 10@.009 | lf | — | .67 | .67 |
| backfill | 10@.005 | lf | — | .37 | .37 |
| Excavate for 5' to 6' deep sewer-line trench | | | | | |
| sandy loam soil | 10@.009 | lf | — | .67 | .67 |
| rocky or hardpan soil | 10@.013 | lf | — | .97 | .97 |
| backfill | 10@.008 | lf | — | .60 | .60 |
| Excavate for 7' to 8' deep sewer-line trench | | | | | |
| sandy loam soil | 10@.011 | lf | — | .82 | .82 |
| rocky or hardpan soil | 10@.017 | lf | — | 1.27 | 1.27 |
| backfill | 10@.006 | lf | — | .45 | .45 |
| Hand finish excavation for sewer-line trench | | | | | |
| all soil types | 5E@.005 | lf | — | .19 | .19 |
| Machine excavate hole for repairs to water, sewer, or utility lines | | | | | |
| machine excavate per lf of depth | 10@.024 | lf | — | 1.79 | 1.79 |
| hand finish per lf of depth | 5E@.019 | lf | — | .71 | .71 |
| General foundation, slab, & footing machine excavation | | | | | |
| machine excavate per cy | 10@.025 | cy | — | 1.87 | 1.87 |
| hand finish per cy | 5E@.020 | cy | — | .74 | .74 |

|  | Craft@Hrs | Unit | Material | Labor | Total |
|---|---|---|---|---|---|

## Fees

**Building permit.** Permit fees vary widely. These fees are rules of thumb for most areas of the country. Rural areas will be less and high-density areas will be more. Includes plan-check fees.

|  | Craft@Hrs | Unit | Material | Labor | Total |
|---|---|---|---|---|---|
| Minimum | — | ea | — | — | 123.00 |
| For job $2,001 to $5,000 | — | ea | — | — | 132.00 |
| For job $5,001 to $10,000 | — | ea | — | — | 394.00 |
| For job $10,001 to $20,000 | — | ea | — | — | 722.00 |
| For job $20,001 to $30,000 | — | ea | — | — | 918.00 |
| For job $30,001 to $40,000 | — | ea | — | — | 1,040.00 |
| For job $40,001 to $50,000 | — | ea | — | — | 1,180.00 |
| For job $50,001 to $60,000 | — | ea | — | — | 1,510.00 |
| For job $60,001 to $70,000 | — | ea | — | — | 1,700.00 |
| For job $70,001 to $80,000 | — | ea | — | — | 1,840.00 |
| For job $80,001 to $90,000 | — | ea | — | — | 2,040.00 |
| For job $90,001 to $100,000 | — | ea | — | — | 2,180.00 |
| For job $100,001 to $150,000 | — | ea | — | — | 2,760.00 |
| For job $150,001 to $200,000 | — | ea | — | — | 3,280.00 |
| For job $200,001 to $250,000 | — | ea | — | — | 3,940.00 |
| For job $250,001 to $300,000 | — | ea | — | — | 4,450.00 |
| For job $300,001 to $400,000 | — | ea | — | — | 5,630.00 |
| For job $400,001 to $500,000 | — | ea | — | — | 6,830.00 |

**Sewer connection fee.** Typical charges for labor and materials installed by government entity. Does not include any development upcharges added to the fee. Includes connect to a city sewer line up to 50 lf from the structure, mobilization, excavation, pipe and fittings, backfill, repair to street, curb and gutter, and temporary signs.

|  | Craft@Hrs | Unit | Material | Labor | Total |
|---|---|---|---|---|---|
| Typical charge | — | ea | — | — | 3,010.00 |

**Water connection fee.** Typical charges for labor and materials installed by government entity. Does not include any development upcharges added to the fee. Includes connect to a city water line up to 50 lf from the structure, mobilization, excavation, pipe and fittings, water meter, backfill, repair to street, curb and gutter, and temporary signs.

|  | Craft@Hrs | Unit | Material | Labor | Total |
|---|---|---|---|---|---|
| Typical charge | — | ea | — | — | 2,880.00 |

**Estimating fees.** Typical rates charged to estimate insurance repair damages. Rule of thumb for estimating insurance repair damages on losses under $200,000. Percentage rate drops to as low as .75% on large losses or multiple unit losses. This percentage is used across the country. Do not adjust with Area Modification Factor.

|  | Craft@Hrs | Unit | Material | Labor | Total |
|---|---|---|---|---|---|
| Per hour | — | hr | — | — | 62.30 |
| Per day | — | dy | — | — | 589.00 |
| As percentage of estimate | — | % | — | — | 1.5 |
| Minimum | — | ea | — | — | 248.00 |

**Soils engineer fee.**

|  | Craft@Hrs | Unit | Material | Labor | Total |
|---|---|---|---|---|---|
| Per hour | — | hr | — | — | 132.00 |

**Structural engineer fee.**

|  | Craft@Hrs | Unit | Material | Labor | Total |
|---|---|---|---|---|---|
| Per hour | — | hr | — | — | 144.00 |

**Plan drawing fee**, per sf of floor.

|  | Craft@Hrs | Unit | Material | Labor | Total |
|---|---|---|---|---|---|
| Simple structure | — | sf | — | — | .27 |
| Typical structure | — | sf | — | — | .33 |
| Complex structure | — | sf | — | — | .47 |
| Ornate structure | — | sf | — | — | .66 |
| Minimum | — | ea | — | — | 269.00 |

|  | Craft@Hrs | Unit | Material | Labor | Total |
|---|---|---|---|---|---|

# Fences

**Wood fence post.** All wood fence posts include digging of 2' deep hole and setting in concrete.  Post height is above ground.  For example, a 4' high post is made from a 6' length with 2' underground and 4' above ground.

| | Craft@Hrs | Unit | Material | Labor | Total |
|---|---|---|---|---|---|
| Cedar fence post | | | | | |
|     4' high cedar | 4F@.907 | ea | 27.10 | 45.10 | 72.20 |
|     6' high cedar | 4F@.907 | ea | 31.40 | 45.10 | 76.50 |
|     8' high cedar | 4F@.907 | ea | 35.40 | 45.10 | 80.50 |
| Redwood fence post | | | | | |
|     4' high | 4F@.907 | ea | 30.50 | 45.10 | 75.60 |
|     6' high | 4F@.907 | ea | 34.80 | 45.10 | 79.90 |
|     8' high | 4F@.907 | ea | 39.40 | 45.10 | 84.50 |
| Treated pine fence post | | | | | |
|     4' high | 4F@.907 | ea | 28.30 | 45.10 | 73.40 |
|     6' high | 4F@.907 | ea | 32.70 | 45.10 | 77.80 |
|     8' high | 4F@.907 | ea | 36.80 | 45.10 | 81.90 |
| Remove wood fence post | 1D@.367 | ea | — | 14.30 | 14.30 |

**Basketweave fence.** Posts are set in concrete and spaced up to 8' on center with an average spacing of 7.2' apart.  Fence boards are 1" x 6" to 1" x 10".  Gates are 3' wide with a frame made from 2" x 4" lumber, cross braced with turn buckle and cable.  Includes heavy-duty hinges, latch, and spring closer.

| | Craft@Hrs | Unit | Material | Labor | Total |
|---|---|---|---|---|---|
| Cedar basketweave fence | | | | | |
|     4' high | 4F@.317 | lf | 16.00 | 15.80 | 31.80 |
|     6' high | 4F@.336 | lf | 21.60 | 16.70 | 38.30 |
|     8' high | 4F@.360 | lf | 28.20 | 17.90 | 46.10 |
| Redwood basketweave fence | | | | | |
|     4' high | 4F@.317 | lf | 17.60 | 15.80 | 33.40 |
|     6' high | 4F@.336 | lf | 23.80 | 16.70 | 40.50 |
|     8' high | 4F@.360 | lf | 31.40 | 17.90 | 49.30 |
| Treated pine basketweave fence | | | | | |
|     4' high | 4F@.317 | lf | 16.60 | 15.80 | 32.40 |
|     6' high | 4F@.336 | lf | 22.30 | 16.70 | 39.00 |
|     8' high | 4F@.360 | lf | 29.50 | 17.90 | 47.40 |
| Cedar gate with hardware | | | | | |
|     4' high | 4F@2.70 | ea | 91.40 | 134.00 | 225.40 |
|     6' high | 4F@2.86 | ea | 112.00 | 142.00 | 254.00 |
|     8' high | 4F@3.04 | ea | 132.00 | 151.00 | 283.00 |
| Redwood gate with hardware | | | | | |
|     4' high | 4F@2.70 | ea | 101.00 | 134.00 | 235.00 |
|     6' high | 4F@2.86 | ea | 124.00 | 142.00 | 266.00 |
|     8' high | 4F@3.04 | ea | 145.00 | 151.00 | 296.00 |
| Treated pine gate with hardware | | | | | |
|     4' high | 4F@2.70 | ea | 95.10 | 134.00 | 229.10 |
|     6' high | 4F@2.86 | ea | 116.00 | 142.00 | 258.00 |
|     8' high | 4F@3.04 | ea | 137.00 | 151.00 | 288.00 |
| Remove wood fence | | | | | |
|     4' high wood fence | 1D@.161 | lf | — | 6.26 | 6.26 |
|     6' high wood fence | 1D@.165 | lf | — | 6.42 | 6.42 |
|     8' high wood fence | 1D@.170 | lf | — | 6.61 | 6.61 |
|     4' high fence gate | 1D@.324 | ea | — | 12.60 | 12.60 |
|     6' high fence gate | 1D@.336 | ea | — | 13.10 | 13.10 |
|     8' high fence gate | 1D@.346 | ea | — | 13.50 | 13.50 |

|  | Craft@Hrs | Unit | Material | Labor | Total |
|---|---|---|---|---|---|

**Board fence.** Fence with boards installed vertically or horizontally. Posts are set in concrete and spaced up to 8' on center with an average spacing of 7.2' apart. Fence boards are 1" x 4" to 1" x 8". 8' tall fence contains three supporting rails. All other heights contain two. Gates are 3' wide with horizontal and diagonal rails, heavy-duty hinges, latch, and spring closer.

| | Craft@Hrs | Unit | Material | Labor | Total |
|---|---|---|---|---|---|
| Cedar, replace fence | | | | | |
| 4' high | 4F@.267 | lf | 16.00 | 13.30 | 29.30 |
| 6' high | 4F@.286 | lf | 21.60 | 14.20 | 35.80 |
| 8' high | 4F@.307 | lf | 28.20 | 15.30 | 43.50 |
| Redwood, replace fence | | | | | |
| 4' high | 4F@.267 | lf | 17.60 | 13.30 | 30.90 |
| 6' high | 4F@.286 | lf | 23.80 | 14.20 | 38.00 |
| 8' high | 4F@.307 | lf | 31.40 | 15.30 | 46.70 |
| Treated pine, replace fence | | | | | |
| 4' high | 4F@.267 | lf | 16.60 | 13.30 | 29.90 |
| 6' high | 4F@.286 | lf | 22.30 | 14.20 | 36.50 |
| 8' high | 4F@.307 | lf | 29.50 | 15.30 | 44.80 |
| Cedar gate with hardware | | | | | |
| 4' high | 4F@2.17 | ea | 91.40 | 108.00 | 199.40 |
| 6' high | 4F@2.33 | ea | 112.00 | 116.00 | 228.00 |
| 8' high | 4F@2.44 | ea | 132.00 | 121.00 | 253.00 |
| Redwood gate with hardware | | | | | |
| 4' high | 4F@2.17 | ea | 101.00 | 108.00 | 209.00 |
| 6' high | 4F@2.33 | ea | 124.00 | 116.00 | 240.00 |
| 8' high | 4F@2.44 | ea | 145.00 | 121.00 | 266.00 |
| Treated pine gate with hardware | | | | | |
| 4' high | 4F@2.17 | ea | 95.10 | 108.00 | 203.10 |
| 6' high | 4F@2.33 | ea | 116.00 | 116.00 | 232.00 |
| 8' high | 4F@2.44 | ea | 137.00 | 121.00 | 258.00 |
| Remove wood fence | | | | | |
| 4' high wood fence | 1D@.161 | lf | — | 6.26 | 6.26 |
| 6' high wood fence | 1D@.165 | lf | — | 6.42 | 6.42 |
| 8' high wood fence | 1D@.170 | lf | — | 6.61 | 6.61 |
| 4' high wood gate | 1D@.324 | ea | — | 12.60 | 12.60 |
| 6' high wood gate | 1D@.336 | ea | — | 13.10 | 13.10 |
| 8' high wood gate | 1D@.346 | ea | — | 13.50 | 13.50 |

**Board fence with lattice cap.** Fence with boards installed vertically or horizontally capped with 12" of lattice on top. Lattice is trimmed with 2" x 4" lattice rail on top, bottom and sides. Posts are set in concrete and spaced up to 8' on center with an average spacing of 7.2' apart. Fence boards are 1" x 4" to 1" x 8". Gates are 3' wide with a frame made from 2" x 4" lumber, cross braced with turn buckle and cable. Includes heavy-duty hinges, latch, and spring closer.

| | Craft@Hrs | Unit | Material | Labor | Total |
|---|---|---|---|---|---|
| Cedar board fence with lattice cap | | | | | |
| 6' high | 4F@.331 | lf | 28.40 | 16.50 | 44.90 |
| 8' high | 4F@.360 | lf | 35.20 | 17.90 | 53.10 |
| Redwood board fence with lattice cap | | | | | |
| 6' high | 4F@.331 | lf | 31.60 | 16.50 | 48.10 |
| 8' high | 4F@.360 | lf | 39.10 | 17.90 | 57.00 |
| Treated pine board fence with lattice cap | | | | | |
| 6' high | 4F@.331 | lf | 29.80 | 16.50 | 46.30 |
| 8' high | 4F@.360 | lf | 36.70 | 17.90 | 54.60 |

| | Craft@Hrs | Unit | Material | Labor | Total |
|---|---|---|---|---|---|
| **Cedar gate with hardware** | | | | | |
| 6' high | 4F@2.94 | ea | 123.00 | 146.00 | 269.00 |
| 8' high | 4F@3.44 | ea | 143.00 | 171.00 | 314.00 |
| **Redwood gate with hardware** | | | | | |
| 6' high | 4F@2.94 | ea | 138.00 | 146.00 | 284.00 |
| 8' high | 4F@3.44 | ea | 160.00 | 171.00 | 331.00 |
| **Treated pine gate with hardware** | | | | | |
| 6' high | 4F@2.94 | ea | 128.00 | 146.00 | 274.00 |
| 8' high | 4F@3.44 | ea | 149.00 | 171.00 | 320.00 |
| **Remove fence** | | | | | |
| 6' high wood fence | 1D@.165 | lf | — | 6.42 | 6.42 |
| 8' high wood fence | 1D@.170 | lf | — | 6.61 | 6.61 |
| 6' high wood gate | 1D@.335 | ea | — | 13.00 | 13.00 |
| 8' high wood gate | 1D@.344 | ea | — | 13.40 | 13.40 |

**Board-on-board fence.** Fence with overlapping boards installed vertically. Posts are set in concrete and spaced up to 8' on center with an average spacing of 7.2' apart. Fence boards are 1" x 4" to 1" x 8". 8' tall fence contains three supporting rails. All other heights contain two. Gates are 3' wide with horizontal and diagonal rails. Includes heavy-duty hinges, latch, and spring closer.

| | Craft@Hrs | Unit | Material | Labor | Total |
|---|---|---|---|---|---|
| **Cedar board-on-board fence** | | | | | |
| 4' high | 4F@.296 | lf | 23.80 | 14.70 | 38.50 |
| 6' high | 4F@.312 | lf | 33.50 | 15.50 | 49.00 |
| 8' high | 4F@.331 | lf | 44.40 | 16.50 | 60.90 |
| **Redwood board-on-board fence** | | | | | |
| 4' high | 4F@.296 | lf | 26.50 | 14.70 | 41.20 |
| 6' high | 4F@.312 | lf | 37.30 | 15.50 | 52.80 |
| 8' high | 4F@.331 | lf | 49.10 | 16.50 | 65.60 |
| **Treated pine board-on-board fence** | | | | | |
| 4' high | 4F@.296 | lf | 24.90 | 14.70 | 39.60 |
| 6' high | 4F@.312 | lf | 34.90 | 15.50 | 50.40 |
| 8' high | 4F@.331 | lf | 46.30 | 16.50 | 62.80 |
| **Cedar gate with hardware** | | | | | |
| 4' high | 4F@2.56 | ea | 114.00 | 127.00 | 241.00 |
| 6' high | 4F@2.70 | ea | 149.00 | 134.00 | 283.00 |
| 8' high | 4F@2.86 | ea | 179.00 | 142.00 | 321.00 |
| **Redwood gate with hardware** | | | | | |
| 4' high | 4F@2.56 | ea | 127.00 | 127.00 | 254.00 |
| 6' high | 4F@2.70 | ea | 166.00 | 134.00 | 300.00 |
| 8' high | 4F@2.86 | ea | 199.00 | 142.00 | 341.00 |
| **Treated pine gate with hardware** | | | | | |
| 4' high | 4F@2.56 | ea | 120.00 | 127.00 | 247.00 |
| 6' high | 4F@2.70 | ea | 156.00 | 134.00 | 290.00 |
| 8' high | 4F@2.86 | ea | 185.00 | 142.00 | 327.00 |
| **Remove fence** | | | | | |
| 4' high wood fence | 1D@.161 | lf | — | 6.26 | 6.26 |
| 6' high wood fence | 1D@.165 | lf | — | 6.42 | 6.42 |
| 8' high wood fence | 1D@.170 | lf | — | 6.61 | 6.61 |
| 4' high wood gate | 1D@.324 | ea | — | 12.60 | 12.60 |
| 6' high wood gate | 1D@.336 | ea | — | 13.10 | 13.10 |
| 8' high wood gate | 1D@.346 | ea | — | 13.50 | 13.50 |

| | Craft@Hrs | Unit | Material | Labor | Total |
|---|---|---|---|---|---|

**Board-and-batten fence.** Vertically installed 1" x 8" to 1" x 12" boards with 1" x 2" to 1" x 4" battens overlapping joints. Posts are set in concrete and spaced up to 8' on center with an average spacing of 7.2' apart. Gates are 3' wide with horizontal and diagonal rails. Includes heavy-duty hinges, latch, and spring closer.

| | Craft@Hrs | Unit | Material | Labor | Total |
|---|---|---|---|---|---|
| Cedar board-and-batten fence | | | | | |
| 4' high | 4F@.302 | lf | 20.50 | 15.00 | 35.50 |
| 6' high | 4F@.307 | lf | 28.20 | 15.30 | 43.50 |
| 8' high | 4F@.323 | lf | 37.10 | 16.10 | 53.20 |
| Redwood board-and-batten fence | | | | | |
| 4' high | 4F@.302 | lf | 22.60 | 15.00 | 37.60 |
| 6' high | 4F@.307 | lf | 31.40 | 15.30 | 46.70 |
| 8' high | 4F@.323 | lf | 41.40 | 16.10 | 57.50 |
| Treated pine board-and-batten fence | | | | | |
| 4' high | 4F@.302 | lf | 21.30 | 15.00 | 36.30 |
| 6' high | 4F@.307 | lf | 29.50 | 15.30 | 44.80 |
| 8' high | 4F@.323 | lf | 38.70 | 16.10 | 54.80 |
| Cedar gate with hardware | | | | | |
| 4' high | 4F@2.63 | ea | 105.00 | 131.00 | 236.00 |
| 6' high | 4F@2.78 | ea | 132.00 | 138.00 | 270.00 |
| 8' high | 4F@2.94 | ea | 159.00 | 146.00 | 305.00 |
| Redwood gate with hardware | | | | | |
| 4' high | 4F@2.63 | ea | 115.00 | 131.00 | 246.00 |
| 6' high | 4F@2.78 | ea | 147.00 | 138.00 | 285.00 |
| 8' high | 4F@2.94 | ea | 175.00 | 146.00 | 321.00 |
| Treated pine gate with hardware | | | | | |
| 4' high | 4F@2.63 | ea | 109.00 | 131.00 | 240.00 |
| 6' high | 4F@2.78 | ea | 138.00 | 138.00 | 276.00 |
| 8' high | 4F@2.94 | ea | 166.00 | 146.00 | 312.00 |
| Remove fence | | | | | |
| 4' high wood fence | 1D@.161 | lf | — | 6.26 | 6.26 |
| 6' high wood fence | 1D@.165 | lf | — | 6.42 | 6.42 |
| 8' high wood fence | 1D@.170 | lf | — | 6.61 | 6.61 |
| 4' high wood gate | 1D@.324 | ea | — | 12.60 | 12.60 |
| 6' high wood gate | 1D@.336 | ea | — | 13.10 | 13.10 |
| 8' high wood gate | 1D@.346 | ea | — | 13.50 | 13.50 |

**Picket fence.** Posts are set in concrete and spaced up to 8' on center with an average spacing of 7.2' apart. Pickets are factory pre-cut. Gates are 3' wide with horizontal and diagonal rails. Includes heavy-duty hinges, latch, and spring closer.

| | Craft@Hrs | Unit | Material | Labor | Total |
|---|---|---|---|---|---|
| Cedar picket fence | | | | | |
| 3' high | 4F@.222 | lf | 9.36 | 11.00 | 20.36 |
| 5' high | 4F@.238 | lf | 15.90 | 11.80 | 27.70 |
| Redwood picket fence | | | | | |
| 3' high | 4F@.222 | lf | 10.40 | 11.00 | 21.40 |
| 5' high | 4F@.238 | lf | 17.40 | 11.80 | 29.20 |
| Treated pine picket fence | | | | | |
| 3' high | 4F@.222 | lf | 9.73 | 11.00 | 20.73 |
| 5' high | 4F@.238 | lf | 16.40 | 11.80 | 28.20 |

| | Craft@Hrs | Unit | Material | Labor | Total |
|---|---|---|---|---|---|
| Cedar gate with hardware | | | | | |
| 3' high | 4F@2.00 | ea | 70.90 | 99.40 | 170.30 |
| 5' high | 4F@2.38 | ea | 93.40 | 118.00 | 211.40 |
| Redwood gate with hardware | | | | | |
| 3' high | 4F@2.00 | ea | 78.70 | 99.40 | 178.10 |
| 5' high | 4F@2.38 | ea | 103.00 | 118.00 | 221.00 |
| Treated pine gate with hardware | | | | | |
| 3' high | 4F@2.00 | ea | 73.80 | 99.40 | 173.20 |
| 5' high | 4F@2.38 | ea | 97.00 | 118.00 | 215.00 |
| Remove fence | | | | | |
| 3' high wood fence | 1D@.161 | lf | — | 6.26 | 6.26 |
| 5' high wood fence | 1D@.165 | lf | — | 6.42 | 6.42 |
| 3' high wood gate | 1D@.324 | ea | — | 12.60 | 12.60 |
| 5' high wood gate | 1D@.336 | ea | — | 13.10 | 13.10 |

## Additional wood fence costs.

| | Craft@Hrs | Unit | Material | Labor | Total |
|---|---|---|---|---|---|
| minimum charge | 4F@1.75 | ea | 41.00 | 87.00 | 128.00 |
| remove and reinstall wood fence gate | 4F@.804 | ea | — | 40.00 | 40.00 |

## Wood gate hardware.

| | Craft@Hrs | Unit | Material | Labor | Total |
|---|---|---|---|---|---|
| replace, with self-closing hinges | 4F@.754 | ea | 43.50 | 37.50 | 81.00 |
| remove | 1D@.197 | ea | — | 7.66 | 7.66 |
| replace, heavy gauge with self-closing hinges | 4F@.754 | ea | 74.60 | 37.50 | 112.10 |
| remove | 1D@.197 | ea | — | 7.66 | 7.66 |
| replace, closing spring | 4F@.331 | ea | 26.60 | 16.50 | 43.10 |
| remove | 1D@.100 | ea | — | 3.89 | 3.89 |

## Chain-link fence.
11 gauge chain link. Line posts and terminal posts are set 2' deep in concrete and spaced up to 10' on center with an average spacing of 9.2' apart. Includes all post caps, tie wire, tension bands, nuts, bolts, and tension rods.

| | Craft@Hrs | Unit | Material | Labor | Total |
|---|---|---|---|---|---|
| replace, 3' high, 1-5/8" line posts, 2" terminal posts | 4F@.114 | lf | 9.50 | 5.67 | 15.17 |
| remove | 1D@.116 | lf | — | 4.51 | 4.51 |
| replace, 4' high, 1-7/8" line posts, 2" terminal posts | 4F@.145 | lf | 12.60 | 7.21 | 19.81 |
| remove | 1D@.121 | lf | — | 4.71 | 4.71 |
| replace, 5' high, 1-7/8" line posts, 2" terminal posts | 4F@.183 | lf | 15.80 | 9.10 | 24.90 |
| remove | 1D@.125 | lf | — | 4.86 | 4.86 |
| replace, 6' high, 1-7/8" line posts, 2" terminal posts | 4F@.233 | lf | 18.60 | 11.60 | 30.20 |
| remove | 1D@.131 | lf | — | 5.10 | 5.10 |
| replace, 7' high, 1-7/8" line posts, 2" terminal posts | 4F@.296 | lf | 21.80 | 14.70 | 36.50 |
| remove | 1D@.136 | lf | — | 5.29 | 5.29 |
| replace, 8' high, 2" line posts, 3" terminal posts | 4F@.376 | lf | 25.00 | 18.70 | 43.70 |
| remove | 1D@.143 | lf | — | 5.56 | 5.56 |
| replace, 10' high, 2" line posts, 3" terminal posts | 4F@.476 | lf | 31.10 | 23.70 | 54.80 |
| remove | 1D@.152 | lf | — | 5.91 | 5.91 |

| | Craft@Hrs | Unit | Material | Labor | Total |
|---|---|---|---|---|---|
| **Chain-link gate with hardware.** 3' wide. | | | | | |
| replace, 3' high | 4F@2.56 | ea | 52.00 | 127.00 | 179.00 |
| replace, 4' high | 4F@2.56 | ea | 67.10 | 127.00 | 194.10 |
| replace, 5' high | 4F@2.56 | ea | 80.90 | 127.00 | 207.90 |
| replace, 6' high | 4F@2.63 | ea | 93.40 | 131.00 | 224.40 |
| replace, 7' high | 4F@2.63 | ea | 105.00 | 131.00 | 236.00 |
| replace, 8' high | 4F@2.63 | ea | 114.00 | 131.00 | 245.00 |
| replace, 10' high | 4F@2.63 | ea | 139.00 | 131.00 | 270.00 |
| remove gate | 1D@.203 | ea | — | 7.90 | 7.90 |
| **Chain-link driveway gate with hardware.** Prices per lf. Includes all hardware. Minimum of 6 lf. | | | | | |
| replace, 3' high | 4F@.640 | lf | 15.50 | 31.80 | 47.30 |
| replace, 4' high | 4F@.640 | lf | 28.20 | 31.80 | 60.00 |
| replace, 5' high | 4F@.640 | lf | 45.50 | 31.80 | 77.30 |
| replace, 6' high | 4F@.659 | lf | 52.70 | 32.80 | 85.50 |
| replace, 7' high | 4F@.659 | lf | 59.60 | 32.80 | 92.40 |
| replace, 8' high | 4F@.659 | lf | 65.80 | 32.80 | 98.60 |
| remove gate | 1D@.043 | lf | — | 1.67 | 1.67 |

**Additional chain-link fence costs.** The chain-link fence prices in the previous tables allow for an average of 1 corner or terminal post for every 15 lf of fence. Use the additional corner price only when estimating a fence that contains more corner or terminal posts.

| | Craft@Hrs | Unit | Material | Labor | Total |
|---|---|---|---|---|---|
| add for additional corner in chain-link fence | 4F@1.93 | ea | 64.10 | 95.90 | 160.00 |
| add for vinyl privacy slats | 4F@.006 | sf | .77 | .30 | 1.07 |
| add for aluminum privacy slats | 4F@.006 | sf | .83 | .30 | 1.13 |
| add 3% for chain-link fence with top rail | | | | | |
| add 28% for 9 gauge galvanized chain-link | | | | | |
| add 25% for 9 gauge vinyl coated chain-link and posts | | | | | |
| add 41% for 6 gauge chain-link | | | | | |
| remove chain-link fence gate for work, then reinstall | 4F@.291 | ea | — | 14.50 | 14.50 |
| remove chain-link fence for work, then reinstall | 4F@.013 | sf | — | .65 | .65 |
| minimum charge | 4F@2.50 | ea | 72.10 | 124.00 | 196.10 |

**Galvanized chain-link post.** All chain-link fence posts include digging of 2' deep hole and setting in concrete. Post height is above ground. For example, a 4' high post is made from a 6' length with 2' underground and 4' above ground.

| | Craft@Hrs | Unit | Material | Labor | Total |
|---|---|---|---|---|---|
| Galvanized chain-link line posts | | | | | |
| replace, 3' high, 1-7/8" diameter post | 4F@.918 | ea | 19.50 | 45.60 | 65.10 |
| replace, 4' high, 1-7/8" diameter post | 4F@.918 | ea | 21.10 | 45.60 | 66.70 |
| replace, 5' high, 1-7/8" diameter post | 4F@.918 | ea | 22.40 | 45.60 | 68.00 |
| replace, 6' high, 1-7/8" diameter post | 4F@.918 | ea | 23.80 | 45.60 | 69.40 |
| replace, 7' high, 1-7/8" diameter post | 4F@.918 | ea | 25.30 | 45.60 | 70.90 |
| replace, 8' high, 2" diameter post | 4F@.918 | ea | 27.00 | 45.60 | 72.60 |
| replace, 10' high, 2" diameter post | 4F@.918 | ea | 30.40 | 45.60 | 76.00 |
| remove post | 1D@.401 | ea | — | 15.60 | 15.60 |
| Galvanized gate or corner post | | | | | |
| replace, 3' high, 2" diameter post | 4F@.918 | ea | 18.60 | 45.60 | 64.20 |
| replace, 4' high, 2" diameter post | 4F@.918 | ea | 20.00 | 45.60 | 65.60 |
| replace, 5' high, 2" diameter post | 4F@.918 | ea | 21.20 | 45.60 | 66.80 |
| replace, 6' high, 2-1/2" diameter post | 4F@.918 | ea | 24.10 | 45.60 | 69.70 |
| replace, 7' high, 2-1/2" diameter post | 4F@.918 | ea | 25.80 | 45.60 | 71.40 |

| | Craft@Hrs | Unit | Material | Labor | Total |
|---|---|---|---|---|---|
| replace, 8' high, 3" diameter post | 4F@.918 | ea | 41.70 | 45.60 | 87.30 |
| replace, 10' high, 3" diameter post | 4F@.918 | ea | 48.30 | 45.60 | 93.90 |
| remove post | 1D@.401 | ea | — | 15.60 | 15.60 |
| add 22% for aluminized steel post | | | | | |

**Vinyl picket fence.** 36" and 48" fences are 2 rail fences, 60" and 72" have three. Pickets are 7/8" x 1-1/2" spaced 3-7/8" apart. Top and bottom rails are 1-1/2" x 3-1/2". Bottom rail includes galvanized steel channel. Posts are 4" x 4" and spaced up to 8' on center with an average spacing of 7.2 feet apart. Includes picket and post caps. Gates are priced per lf with a 3 lf minimum and a 5 lf maximum and include all hardware. For wider gates, measure the gate lf, round up to the next even number, multiply by the fence lf price, then add **$193.**

| | Craft@Hrs | Unit | Material | Labor | Total |
|---|---|---|---|---|---|
| replace, 36" high | 4F@.352 | lf | 17.50 | 17.50 | 35.00 |
| replace, 48" high | 4F@.357 | lf | 21.50 | 17.70 | 39.20 |
| replace, 60" high | 4F@.362 | lf | 25.40 | 18.00 | 43.40 |
| replace, 72" high | 4F@.365 | lf | 29.40 | 18.10 | 47.50 |
| remove fence | 1D@.139 | lf | — | 5.41 | 5.41 |
| remove fence panels, then reinstall | 4F@.540 | lf | — | 26.80 | 26.80 |
| **Vinyl picket fence gate** | | | | | |
| replace, 36" high | 4F@.646 | lf | 51.80 | 32.10 | 83.90 |
| replace, 48" high | 4F@.661 | lf | 54.60 | 32.90 | 87.50 |
| replace, 60" high | 4F@.680 | lf | 57.20 | 33.80 | 91.00 |
| replace, 72" high | 4F@.696 | lf | 59.80 | 34.60 | 94.40 |
| remove gate | 1D@.152 | lf | — | 5.91 | 5.91 |
| remove gate, then reinstall | 4F@.680 | lf | — | 33.80 | 33.80 |

**Vinyl picket fence with large pickets.** Same as picket fence, with large 7/8" x 3-1/2" pickets spaced 3-7/8" apart.

| | Craft@Hrs | Unit | Material | Labor | Total |
|---|---|---|---|---|---|
| replace, 36" high | 4F@.352 | lf | 20.40 | 17.50 | 37.90 |
| replace, 48" high | 4F@.357 | lf | 25.20 | 17.70 | 42.90 |
| replace, 60" high | 4F@.362 | lf | 29.70 | 18.00 | 47.70 |
| remove fence | 1D@.139 | lf | — | 5.41 | 5.41 |
| remove fence panels, then reinstall | 4F@.540 | lf | — | 26.80 | 26.80 |
| **Gate for vinyl picket fence with large pickets** | | | | | |
| replace, 36" high | 4F@.646 | lf | 53.90 | 32.10 | 86.00 |
| replace, 48" high | 4F@.661 | lf | 57.20 | 32.90 | 90.10 |
| replace, 60" high | 4F@.680 | lf | 60.60 | 33.80 | 94.40 |
| remove gate | 1D@.152 | lf | — | 5.91 | 5.91 |
| remove gate, then reinstall | 4F@.680 | lf | — | 33.80 | 33.80 |

**Vinyl picket fence with scalloped pickets.** Same as picket fence, with decorative scalloped pickets.

| | Craft@Hrs | Unit | Material | Labor | Total |
|---|---|---|---|---|---|
| replace, 36" high | 4F@.352 | lf | 19.00 | 17.50 | 36.50 |
| replace, 48" high | 4F@.357 | lf | 23.10 | 17.70 | 40.80 |
| replace, 60" high | 4F@.362 | lf | 27.00 | 18.00 | 45.00 |
| remove fence, 36" or 48" high | 1D@.139 | lf | — | 5.41 | 5.41 |
| remove fence, 60" high | 1D@.139 | lf | — | 5.41 | 5.41 |
| remove fence panels, then reinstall | 4F@.540 | lf | — | 26.80 | 26.80 |
| **Gate for vinyl picket fence with scalloped pickets** | | | | | |
| replace, 36" high | 4F@.646 | lf | 52.60 | 32.10 | 84.70 |
| replace, 48" high | 4F@.661 | lf | 55.60 | 32.90 | 88.50 |
| replace, 60" high | 4F@.680 | lf | 58.40 | 33.80 | 92.20 |
| remove gate | 1D@.152 | lf | — | 5.91 | 5.91 |
| remove gate, then reinstall | 4F@.680 | lf | — | 33.80 | 33.80 |

| | Craft@Hrs | Unit | Material | Labor | Total |
|---|---|---|---|---|---|

**Vinyl three-rail fence.** Rails are 1-1/2" x 5-1/2". Posts are 5" x 5" and spaced up to 8' apart with an average spacing of 7.2'. Gates priced per lf: 3 lf minimum, 5 lf maximum. For gates larger than 5 lf, use lf fence price, round to even number and add **$115.**

| | Craft@Hrs | Unit | Material | Labor | Total |
|---|---|---|---|---|---|
| replace, 52" high | 4F@.211 | lf | 11.60 | 10.50 | 22.10 |
| remove fence | 1D@.104 | lf | — | 4.05 | 4.05 |
| remove for work, then reinstall (rails only) | 4F@.373 | lf | — | 18.50 | 18.50 |
| Gate for vinyl three-rail fence | | | | | |
| replace, 52" high | 4F@.299 | lf | 45.20 | 14.90 | 60.10 |
| remove gate | 1D@.104 | lf | — | 4.05 | 4.05 |
| remove for work, then reinstall | 4F@.540 | lf | — | 26.80 | 26.80 |

**Vinyl spaced slat fence.** Contains two widths of slats. The narrow slat is 7/8" x 1-1/2" and the wide slat is 7/8" x 3-1/2". Slats are spaced 2-1/2" apart. Top and bottom rails are 1-1/2" x 3-1/2". Bottom rail includes galvanized steel channel. Posts are 4" x 4" and spaced up to 8' on center with an average spacing of 7.2 feet apart. Includes post caps. Gates are priced per lf with a 3 lf minimum and a 5 lf maximum and include all hardware. For wider gates, measure the gate lf, round up to the next even number, multiply by the fence lf price, then add **$193.**

| | Craft@Hrs | Unit | Material | Labor | Total |
|---|---|---|---|---|---|
| replace, 48" high | 4F@.357 | lf | 17.90 | 17.70 | 35.60 |
| replace, 60" high | 4F@.362 | lf | 22.00 | 18.00 | 40.00 |
| replace, 72" high | 4F@.365 | lf | 25.90 | 18.10 | 44.00 |
| remove fence | 1D@.139 | lf | — | 5.41 | 5.41 |
| Gate for vinyl spaced slat fence | | | | | |
| replace, 48" high | 4F@.661 | lf | 52.10 | 32.90 | 85.00 |
| replace, 60" high | 4F@.680 | lf | 54.90 | 33.80 | 88.70 |
| replace, 72" high | 4F@.696 | lf | 57.50 | 34.60 | 92.10 |
| remove gate | 1D@.152 | lf | — | 5.91 | 5.91 |

**Vinyl solid slat fence.** Slat is 7/8" x 5-1/2" with no space between slats. Top and bottom rails are 1-1/2" x 3-1/2". Bottom rail includes galvanized steel channel. Posts are 5" x 5" and spaced up to 8' on center with an average spacing of 7.2 feet apart. Includes post caps. Gates are priced per lf with a 3 lf minimum and a 5 lf maximum and include all hardware. For wider gates, measure the gate lf, round up to the next even number, multiply by the fence lf price, then add **$193.**

| | Craft@Hrs | Unit | Material | Labor | Total |
|---|---|---|---|---|---|
| replace, 48" high | 4F@.357 | lf | 18.60 | 17.70 | 36.30 |
| replace, 60" high | 4F@.362 | lf | 38.30 | 18.00 | 56.30 |
| replace, 72" high | 4F@.365 | lf | 27.00 | 18.10 | 45.10 |
| remove fence | 1D@.139 | lf | — | 5.41 | 5.41 |
| Gate for vinyl solid slat fence | | | | | |
| replace, 48" high | 4F@.661 | lf | 52.50 | 32.90 | 85.40 |
| replace, 60" high | 4F@.680 | lf | 55.60 | 33.80 | 89.40 |
| replace, 72" high | 4F@.696 | lf | 58.30 | 34.60 | 92.90 |
| remove gate | 1D@.152 | lf | — | 5.91 | 5.91 |

**Vinyl solid slat fence with lattice top.**

| | Craft@Hrs | Unit | Material | Labor | Total |
|---|---|---|---|---|---|
| replace, 60" high | 4F@.373 | lf | 31.30 | 18.50 | 49.80 |
| replace, 72" high | 4F@.378 | lf | 35.20 | 18.80 | 54.00 |
| remove fence | 1D@.139 | lf | — | 5.41 | 5.41 |
| Gate for vinyl solid slat fence with lattice top | | | | | |
| replace, 60" high | 4F@.725 | lf | 61.20 | 36.00 | 97.20 |
| replace, 72" high | 4F@.757 | lf | 63.90 | 37.60 | 101.50 |
| remove gate | 1D@.152 | lf | — | 5.91 | 5.91 |

| | Craft@Hrs | Unit | Material | Labor | Total |
|---|---|---|---|---|---|

**Ornamental iron fence.** On all grades, except fences with ornamental casting, steel pickets are 5/8" square and 3-7/8" apart with 1" x 1" top and bottom rails. Posts are 93-1/2" apart. Pickets with decorative scrolls are straight pickets with the decorative scrollwork riveted or screwed to the pickets. Ornamental iron fences with ornamental casting have pickets that are cast in decorative scroll and plant-like patterns. Gates are priced per lf with a 3 lf minimum and a 5 lf maximum. For wider gates, measure the gate lf, round up to the next even number, multiply by the fence lf price, then add $247.

| | Craft@Hrs | Unit | Material | Labor | Total |
|---|---|---|---|---|---|
| Ornamental iron fence with straight pickets | | | | | |
| replace, 60" high | 4F@.373 | lf | 16.60 | 18.50 | 35.10 |
| replace, 72" high | 4F@.378 | lf | 19.10 | 18.80 | 37.90 |
| remove fence | 1D@.194 | lf | — | 7.55 | 7.55 |
| Ornamental iron gate with straight pickets | | | | | |
| replace, 60" high | 4F@.725 | lf | 66.20 | 36.00 | 102.20 |
| replace, 72" high | 4F@.757 | lf | 70.40 | 37.60 | 108.00 |
| remove gate | 1D@.202 | lf | — | 7.86 | 7.86 |
| Ornamental iron fence with twisted pickets | | | | | |
| replace, 60" high | 4F@.373 | lf | 17.80 | 18.50 | 36.30 |
| replace, 72" high | 4F@.378 | lf | 20.90 | 18.80 | 39.70 |
| remove fence | 1D@.194 | lf | — | 7.55 | 7.55 |
| Ornamental iron gate with twisted pickets | | | | | |
| replace, 60" high | 4F@.725 | lf | 70.90 | 36.00 | 106.90 |
| replace, 72" high | 4F@.757 | lf | 75.50 | 37.60 | 113.10 |
| remove gate | 1D@.202 | lf | — | 7.86 | 7.86 |
| Ornamental iron fence with decorative scrolls | | | | | |
| replace, 60" high | 4F@.373 | lf | 25.30 | 18.50 | 43.80 |
| replace, 72" high | 4F@.378 | lf | 29.30 | 18.80 | 48.10 |
| remove fence | 1D@.194 | lf | — | 7.55 | 7.55 |
| Ornamental iron gate with decorative scrolls | | | | | |
| replace, 60" high | 4F@.725 | lf | 100.00 | 36.00 | 136.00 |
| replace, 72" high | 4F@.757 | lf | 106.00 | 37.60 | 143.60 |
| remove gate | 1D@.202 | lf | — | 7.86 | 7.86 |
| Ornamental iron fence with ornamental casting | | | | | |
| replace, 60" high | 4F@.373 | lf | 44.80 | 18.50 | 63.30 |
| replace, 72" high | 4F@.378 | lf | 51.80 | 18.80 | 70.60 |
| remove fence | 1D@.194 | lf | — | 7.55 | 7.55 |
| Ornamental iron gate with ornamental casting | | | | | |
| replace, 60" high | 4F@.725 | lf | 178.00 | 36.00 | 214.00 |
| replace, 72" high | 4F@.757 | lf | 187.00 | 37.60 | 224.60 |
| remove gate | 1D@.202 | lf | — | 7.86 | 7.86 |
| Remove ornamental iron fence for work, then reinstall | | | | | |
| panels only | 4F@.558 | lf | — | 27.70 | 27.70 |
| gate | 4F@.976 | lf | — | 48.50 | 48.50 |

**Electric gate opener.** For swinging or roll-type gates. Includes two remote transmitters, keypad on post by gate, all hardware and electrical wiring up to 45 lf.

| | Craft@Hrs | Unit | Material | Labor | Total |
|---|---|---|---|---|---|
| replace, 1/2 horsepower | 7E@3.29 | ea | 3,380.00 | 202.00 | 3,582.00 |
| replace, 3/4 horsepower | 7E@3.29 | ea | 4,320.00 | 202.00 | 4,522.00 |
| replace, 1 horsepower | 7E@3.29 | ea | 4,910.00 | 202.00 | 5,112.00 |
| replace, 2 horsepower | 7E@3.29 | ea | 5,800.00 | 202.00 | 6,002.00 |
| replace, 5 horsepower | 7E@3.29 | ea | 6,610.00 | 202.00 | 6,812.00 |
| remove gate opener | 1D@.765 | ea | — | 29.80 | 29.80 |
| remove gate opener for work, then reinstall | 7E@5.30 | ea | — | 325.00 | 325.00 |

| | Craft@Hrs | Unit | Material | Labor | Total |
|---|---|---|---|---|---|
| **Time & Material Charts** (selected items) | | | | | |
| **Fences Materials** (Also see material prices with the line items above.) | | | | | |
| 4" x 4" fence posts | | | | | |
| 8' cedar, ($15.60 ea, 1 ea), 4% waste | — | ea | 16.20 | — | 16.20 |
| 10' cedar, ($19.30 ea, 1 ea), 4% waste | — | ea | 20.10 | — | 20.10 |
| 12' cedar, ($23.20 ea, 2 ea), 4% waste | — | ea | 12.10 | — | 12.10 |
| 1" x 2" x 8' fence boards | | | | | |
| #2 cedar, ($4.80 ea, 8 lf), 4% waste | — | lf | .62 | — | .62 |
| B grade redwood, | | | | | |
| ($10.80 ea, 8 lf), 4% waste | — | lf | 1.40 | — | 1.40 |
| treated-pine, ($3.06 ea, 8 lf), 4% waste | — | lf | .40 | — | .40 |
| 1" x 4" x 8' fence boards | | | | | |
| #2 cedar, ($5.98 ea, 8 lf), 4% waste | — | lf | .78 | — | .78 |
| B grade redwood, | | | | | |
| ($13.40 ea, 8 lf), 4% waste | — | lf | 1.75 | — | 1.75 |
| treated-pine, ($6.10 ea, 8 lf), 4% waste | — | lf | .79 | — | .79 |
| 1" x 6" x 8' fence boards | | | | | |
| #2 cedar, ($9.02 ea, 8 lf), 4% waste | — | lf | 1.18 | — | 1.18 |
| B grade redwood, | | | | | |
| ($20.40 ea, 8 lf), 4% waste | — | lf | 2.65 | — | 2.65 |
| treated-pine, ($5.85 ea, 8 lf), 4% waste | — | lf | .76 | — | .76 |
| 1" x 8" x 8' fence boards | | | | | |
| #2 cedar, ($19.00 ea, 8 lf), 4% waste | — | lf | 2.48 | — | 2.48 |
| B grade redwood, | | | | | |
| ($42.50 ea, 8 lf), 4% waste | — | lf | 5.52 | — | 5.52 |
| treated-pine, | | | | | |
| ($12.10 ea, 8 lf), 4% waste | — | lf | 1.57 | — | 1.57 |
| 1" x 10" x 8' fence boards | | | | | |
| #2 cedar, ($23.40 ea, 8 lf), 4% waste | — | lf | 3.05 | — | 3.05 |
| B grade redwood, | | | | | |
| ($52.60 ea, 8 lf), 4% waste | — | lf | 6.84 | — | 6.84 |
| treated-pine, | | | | | |
| ($15.10 ea, 8 lf), 4% waste | — | lf | 1.97 | — | 1.97 |
| 2" x 4" x 8' fence boards | | | | | |
| #2 cedar, ($7.31 ea, 8 lf), 4% waste | — | lf | .95 | — | .95 |
| B grade redwood, | | | | | |
| ($11.40 ea, 8 lf), 4% waste | — | lf | 1.49 | — | 1.49 |
| treated-pine, ($10.80 ea, 8 lf), 4% waste | — | lf | 1.40 | — | 1.40 |
| 1" x 3" mill-cut fence picket | | | | | |
| 3' cedar, ($1.75 ea, 1 ea), 4% waste | — | ea | 1.82 | — | 1.82 |
| 5' cedar, ($4.56 ea, 1 ea), 4% waste | — | ea | 4.74 | — | 4.74 |
| Lattice | | | | | |
| cedar lattice, | | | | | |
| ($24.50 sh, 32 sf), 4% waste | — | sf | .80 | — | .80 |
| cedar cap mold, | | | | | |
| ($9.39 ea, 8 lf), 4% waste | — | lf | 1.22 | — | 1.22 |
| Chain-link fence materials | | | | | |
| 11 gauge chain-link, | | | | | |
| ($2.30 sf, 1 sf), 3% waste | — | sf | 2.37 | — | 2.37 |

## Fences Labor

| Laborer | wage | base leave | paid wage | true & ins. | taxes total |
|---|---|---|---|---|---|
| Carpenter | $31.10 | 2.43 | $33.53 | 23.37 | $56.90 |
| Carpenter's helper | $22.40 | 1.75 | $24.15 | 18.25 | $42.40 |
| Electrician | $36.10 | 2.82 | $38.92 | 22.38 | $61.30 |
| Demolition laborer | $20.70 | 1.61 | $22.31 | 16.59 | $38.90 |

**Paid leave** is calculated based on two weeks paid vacation, one week sick leave, and seven paid holidays. Employer's matching portion of **FICA** is 7.65 percent. **FUTA** (Federal Unemployment) is .8 percent. **Worker's compensation** for the fences trade was calculated using a national average of 15.40 percent. **Unemployment insurance** was calculated using a national average of 8 percent. **Health insurance** was calculated based on a projected national average for 2015 of $1,025 per employee (and family when applicable) per month. Employer pays 80 percent for a per month cost of $820 per employee. **Retirement** is based on a 401(k) retirement program with employer matching of 50 percent. Employee contributions to the 401(k) plan are an average of 6 percent of the true wage. **Liability insurance** is based on a national average of 10.0 percent.

## Fences Labor Productivity

| | Craft@Hrs | Unit | Material | Labor | Total |
|---|---|---|---|---|---|
| Demolition of fence | | | | | |
| remove 4' high wood fence | 1D@.161 | lf | — | 6.26 | 6.26 |
| remove 6' high wood fence | 1D@.165 | lf | — | 6.42 | 6.42 |
| remove 8' high wood fence | 1D@.170 | lf | — | 6.61 | 6.61 |
| remove wood fence post | 1D@.367 | ea | — | 14.30 | 14.30 |
| remove 3' high chain-link fence | 1D@.116 | lf | — | 4.51 | 4.51 |
| remove 4' high chain-link fence | 1D@.121 | lf | — | 4.71 | 4.71 |
| remove 5' high chain-link fence | 1D@.125 | lf | — | 4.86 | 4.86 |
| remove 6' high chain-link fence | 1D@.131 | lf | — | 5.10 | 5.10 |
| remove 7' high chain-link fence | 1D@.136 | lf | — | 5.29 | 5.29 |
| remove 8' high chain-link fence | 1D@.143 | lf | — | 5.56 | 5.56 |
| remove 10' high chain-link fence | 1D@.152 | lf | — | 5.91 | 5.91 |
| remove chain-link fence gate | 1D@.203 | ea | — | 7.90 | 7.90 |
| remove chain-link fence driveway gate | 1D@.043 | lf | — | 1.67 | 1.67 |
| remove chain-link fence post | 1D@.401 | ea | — | 15.60 | 15.60 |
| remove vinyl fence | 1D@.139 | lf | — | 5.41 | 5.41 |
| remove vinyl rail fence | 1D@.104 | lf | — | 4.05 | 4.05 |
| remove vinyl fence gate | 1D@.152 | lf | — | 5.91 | 5.91 |
| remove ornamental iron fence | 1D@.194 | lf | — | 7.55 | 7.55 |
| remove ornamental iron fence gate | 1D@.202 | lf | — | 7.86 | 7.86 |
| remove electric gate opener | 1D@.765 | ea | — | 29.80 | 29.80 |

## Fencing crew

| | | |
|---|---|---|
| fencing installation | carpenter | $56.90 |
| fencing installation | carpenter's helper | $42.40 |
| fencing installation | fencing crew | $49.70 |

| | Craft@Hrs | Unit | Material | Labor | Total |
|---|---|---|---|---|---|
| **Build basketweave fence** | | | | | |
| 4' high | 6C@.317 | lf | — | 15.80 | 15.80 |
| 8' high | 6C@.360 | lf | — | 17.90 | 17.90 |
| 4' high gate | 6C@2.70 | ea | — | 134.00 | 134.00 |
| 8' high gate | 6C@3.04 | ea | — | 151.00 | 151.00 |
| **Build board fence** | | | | | |
| 4' high | 6C@.267 | lf | — | 13.30 | 13.30 |
| 8' high | 6C@.307 | lf | — | 15.30 | 15.30 |
| 4' high gate | 6C@2.17 | ea | — | 108.00 | 108.00 |
| 8' high gate | 6C@2.44 | ea | — | 121.00 | 121.00 |
| **Build board fence with lattice cap** | | | | | |
| 6' high | 6C@.331 | lf | — | 16.50 | 16.50 |
| 8' high | 6C@.360 | lf | — | 17.90 | 17.90 |
| 6' high gate | 6C@2.94 | ea | — | 146.00 | 146.00 |
| 8' high gate | 6C@3.44 | ea | — | 171.00 | 171.00 |
| **Build board-on-board fence** | | | | | |
| 4' high | 6C@.296 | lf | — | 14.70 | 14.70 |
| 8' high | 6C@.331 | lf | — | 16.50 | 16.50 |
| 4' high gate | 6C@2.56 | ea | — | 127.00 | 127.00 |
| 8' high gate | 6C@2.86 | ea | — | 142.00 | 142.00 |
| **Build board-and-batten fence** | | | | | |
| 4' high | 6C@.302 | lf | — | 15.00 | 15.00 |
| 8' high | 6C@.323 | lf | — | 16.10 | 16.10 |
| 4' high gate | 6C@2.63 | ea | — | 131.00 | 131.00 |
| 8' high gate | 6C@2.94 | ea | — | 146.00 | 146.00 |
| **Build picket fence** | | | | | |
| 3' high | 6C@.222 | lf | — | 11.00 | 11.00 |
| 5' high | 6C@.238 | lf | — | 11.80 | 11.80 |
| 3' high gate | 6C@2.00 | ea | — | 99.40 | 99.40 |
| 5' high gate | 6C@2.38 | ea | — | 118.00 | 118.00 |
| **Install chain-link fence** | | | | | |
| 3' high | 6C@.114 | lf | — | 5.67 | 5.67 |
| 5' high | 6C@.183 | lf | — | 9.10 | 9.10 |
| 7' high | 6C@.296 | lf | — | 14.70 | 14.70 |
| 10' high | 6C@.476 | lf | — | 23.70 | 23.70 |

|  | Craft@Hrs | Unit | Material | Labor | Total |
|---|---|---|---|---|---|

# Finish Carpentry

## Minimum charge.

| | Craft@Hrs | Unit | Material | Labor | Total |
|---|---|---|---|---|---|
| for finish carpentry work | 1C@3.00 | ea | 29.20 | 171.00 | 200.20 |

**Other wood species.** For moldings made from these species of wood, factor the cost of stain-grade pine by the percentage listed. All grades are kiln-dried select or better.

| | Craft@Hrs | Unit | Material | Labor | Total |
|---|---|---|---|---|---|
| add for walnut | — | % | 70.0 | — | — |
| add for teak | — | % | 563.0 | — | — |
| add for cherry | — | % | 73.0 | — | — |
| add for hard maple | — | % | 31.0 | — | — |
| add for cypress | — | % | 24.0 | — | — |
| add for redwood | — | % | 17.0 | — | — |
| add for cedar | — | % | 0.0 | — | — |

**Wood embossing.** Wood moldings are often embossed to appear like they have been carved. Embossing stamps a pattern onto the wood. Embossing is far less expensive than carving and is most successful on softer woods, such as pine.

**Clamshell base.** Includes clamshell base, finish nails, and installation labor. Outside joints are mitered; inside joints are coped. Includes 7% waste.

| | Craft@Hrs | Unit | Material | Labor | Total |
|---|---|---|---|---|---|
| **Replace 1-1/2" clamshell base** | | | | | |
| finger-joint pine | 1C@.038 | lf | 1.10 | 2.16 | 3.26 |
| stain-grade pine | 1C@.038 | lf | 1.28 | 2.16 | 3.44 |
| poplar | 1C@.038 | lf | 1.36 | 2.16 | 3.52 |
| mahogany | 1C@.038 | lf | 1.61 | 2.16 | 3.77 |
| red oak | 1C@.038 | lf | 2.08 | 2.16 | 4.24 |
| **Replace 2-1/2" clamshell base** | | | | | |
| finger-joint pine | 1C@.038 | lf | 1.27 | 2.16 | 3.43 |
| stain-grade pine | 1C@.038 | lf | 1.45 | 2.16 | 3.61 |
| poplar | 1C@.038 | lf | 1.56 | 2.16 | 3.72 |
| mahogany | 1C@.038 | lf | 1.87 | 2.16 | 4.03 |
| red oak | 1C@.038 | lf | 2.39 | 2.16 | 4.55 |
| **Replace 3-1/2" clamshell base** | | | | | |
| finger-joint pine | 1C@.038 | lf | 1.81 | 2.16 | 3.97 |
| stain-grade pine | 1C@.038 | lf | 2.05 | 2.16 | 4.21 |
| poplar | 1C@.038 | lf | 2.23 | 2.16 | 4.39 |
| mahogany | 1C@.038 | lf | 2.62 | 2.16 | 4.78 |
| red oak | 1C@.038 | lf | 3.37 | 2.16 | 5.53 |
| **Replace 4-1/2" clamshell base** | | | | | |
| add 22% to the cost of 3-1/2" clamshell base | | | | | |
| **All sizes and wood species** | | | | | |
| remove | 1D@.026 | lf | — | 1.01 | 1.01 |
| remove for work, then reinstall | 6C@.065 | lf | — | 3.23 | 3.23 |

|  | Craft@Hrs | Unit | Material | Labor | Total |
|---|---|---|---|---|---|

**Pattern base.** Includes pattern base, finish nails, and installation labor. Outside joints are mitered; inside joints are coped. Includes 4% waste. Pattern base is a generic term for a variety of standard base styles that are commonly available at home improvement centers throughout North America. In many regions this style of base is referred to as "Colonial" base.

| Replace 1-1/2" pattern base | | | | | |
|---|---|---|---|---|---|
| finger-joint pine | 1C@.038 | lf | 1.33 | 2.16 | 3.49 |
| stain-grade pine | 1C@.038 | lf | 1.55 | 2.16 | 3.71 |
| poplar | 1C@.038 | lf | 1.69 | 2.16 | 3.85 |
| mahogany | 1C@.038 | lf | 1.98 | 2.16 | 4.14 |
| red oak | 1C@.038 | lf | 2.52 | 2.16 | 4.68 |
| Replace 2-1/2" pattern base | | | | | |
| finger-joint pine | 1C@.038 | lf | 2.17 | 2.16 | 4.33 |
| stain-grade pine | 1C@.038 | lf | 2.49 | 2.16 | 4.65 |
| poplar | 1C@.038 | lf | 2.68 | 2.16 | 4.84 |
| mahogany | 1C@.038 | lf | 3.19 | 2.16 | 5.35 |
| red oak | 1C@.038 | lf | 4.12 | 2.16 | 6.28 |
| Replace 3-1/2" pattern base | | | | | |
| finger-joint pine | 1C@.038 | lf | 2.87 | 2.16 | 5.03 |
| stain-grade pine | 1C@.038 | lf | 3.30 | 2.16 | 5.46 |
| poplar | 1C@.038 | lf | 3.56 | 2.16 | 5.72 |
| mahogany | 1C@.038 | lf | 4.21 | 2.16 | 6.37 |
| red oak | 1C@.038 | lf | 5.39 | 2.16 | 7.55 |

*1-1/2" pattern base*

Replace 5" pattern base
    add 10% to the cost of 3-1/2" pattern base
Replace 8" pattern base
    add 31% to the cost of the 3-1/2" pattern base

| All sizes and wood species | | | | | |
|---|---|---|---|---|---|
| remove | 1D@.026 | lf | — | 1.01 | 1.01 |
| remove for work, then reinstall | 6C@.065 | lf | — | 3.23 | 3.23 |

**Base shoe.** Includes 3/4" base shoe, finish nails, and installation labor. Outside joints are mitered; inside joints are coped. Includes 7% waste.

| Replace 3/4" base shoe | | | | | |
|---|---|---|---|---|---|
| finger-joint pine | 1C@.038 | lf | .68 | 2.16 | 2.84 |
| stain-grade pine | 1C@.038 | lf | .78 | 2.16 | 2.94 |
| poplar | 1C@.038 | lf | .85 | 2.16 | 3.01 |
| mahogany | 1C@.038 | lf | .99 | 2.16 | 3.15 |
| red oak | 1C@.038 | lf | 1.28 | 2.16 | 3.44 |
| All wood species | | | | | |
| remove | 1D@.026 | lf | — | 1.01 | 1.01 |
| remove for work, then reinstall | 6C@.065 | lf | — | 3.23 | 3.23 |

**Clamshell casing.** Includes clamshell casing, finish nails, and installation labor. Outside corners are 45-degree miter joints; inside corners are cope joints.

| Replace 1-1/2" clamshell casing | | | | | |
|---|---|---|---|---|---|
| paint-grade pine | 1C@.041 | lf | 1.12 | 2.33 | 3.45 |
| stain-grade pine | 1C@.041 | lf | 1.29 | 2.33 | 3.62 |
| poplar | 1C@.041 | lf | 1.38 | 2.33 | 3.71 |
| mahogany | 1C@.041 | lf | 1.67 | 2.33 | 4.00 |
| red oak | 1C@.041 | lf | 2.14 | 2.33 | 4.47 |

*1-1/2" clamshell casing*

| | Craft@Hrs | Unit | Material | Labor | Total |
|---|---|---|---|---|---|
| Replace 2-1/2" clamshell casing | | | | | |
| finger-joint pine | 1C@.041 | lf | 1.29 | 2.33 | 3.62 |
| stain-grade pine | 1C@.041 | lf | 1.49 | 2.33 | 3.82 |
| poplar | 1C@.041 | lf | 1.58 | 2.33 | 3.91 |
| mahogany | 1C@.041 | lf | 1.90 | 2.33 | 4.23 |
| red oak | 1C@.041 | lf | 2.43 | 2.33 | 4.76 |
| Replace 3-1/2" clamshell casing | | | | | |
| finger-joint pine | 1C@.041 | lf | 1.84 | 2.33 | 4.17 |
| stain-grade pine | 1C@.041 | lf | 2.09 | 2.33 | 4.42 |
| poplar | 1C@.041 | lf | 2.27 | 2.33 | 4.60 |
| mahogany | 1C@.041 | lf | 2.65 | 2.33 | 4.98 |
| red oak | 1C@.041 | lf | 3.46 | 2.33 | 5.79 |
| All sizes and wood species | | | | | |
| remove | 1D@.032 | lf | — | 1.24 | 1.24 |
| remove for work, then reinstall | 6C@.083 | lf | — | 4.13 | 4.13 |

**Pattern casing.** Includes 2-1/2" pattern casing, finish nails, and installation labor. Outside corners are 45-degree miter joints; inside corners are cope joints. Laminated back, factory fabricated molding. Half-round and elliptical are priced per linear foot of casing. Casing for round windows is priced per linear foot of window diameter.

| | Craft@Hrs | Unit | Material | Labor | Total |
|---|---|---|---|---|---|
| Replace 1-1/2" pattern casing | | | | | |
| paint-grade pine | 1C@.041 | lf | 1.35 | 2.33 | 3.68 |
| stain-grade pine | 1C@.041 | lf | 1.57 | 2.33 | 3.90 |
| poplar | 1C@.041 | lf | 1.71 | 2.33 | 4.04 |
| mahogany | 1C@.041 | lf | 2.01 | 2.33 | 4.34 |
| red oak | 1C@.041 | lf | 2.57 | 2.33 | 4.90 |
| Replace 1-1/2" curved casing | | | | | |
| for half-round top window or door | 1C@.144 | lf | 9.56 | 8.19 | 17.75 |
| for elliptical-top window or door | 1C@.144 | lf | 10.00 | 8.19 | 18.19 |
| for round window, per lf of window diameter | 1C@.294 | lf | 22.50 | 16.70 | 39.20 |
| Replace 2-1/2" pattern casing | | | | | |
| finger-joint pine | 1C@.041 | lf | 2.20 | 2.33 | 4.53 |
| stain-grade pine | 1C@.041 | lf | 2.52 | 2.33 | 4.85 |
| poplar | 1C@.041 | lf | 2.73 | 2.33 | 5.06 |
| mahogany | 1C@.041 | lf | 3.25 | 2.33 | 5.58 |
| red oak | 1C@.041 | lf | 4.17 | 2.33 | 6.50 |
| Replace 2-1/2" curved casing | | | | | |
| for half-round top window or door | 1C@.144 | lf | 10.30 | 8.19 | 18.49 |
| for elliptical-top window or door | 1C@.144 | lf | 10.70 | 8.19 | 18.89 |
| for round window, per lf of window diameter | 1C@.294 | lf | 23.90 | 16.70 | 40.60 |
| Replace 3-1/2" pattern casing | | | | | |
| finger-joint pine | 1C@.041 | lf | 2.93 | 2.33 | 5.26 |
| stain-grade pine | 1C@.041 | lf | 3.35 | 2.33 | 5.68 |
| poplar | 1C@.041 | lf | 3.61 | 2.33 | 5.94 |
| mahogany | 1C@.041 | lf | 4.27 | 2.33 | 6.60 |
| red oak | 1C@.041 | lf | 5.51 | 2.33 | 7.84 |
| Replace 3-1/2" curved casing | | | | | |
| for half-round top window or door | 1C@.144 | lf | 10.40 | 8.19 | 18.59 |
| for elliptical-top window or door | 1C@.144 | lf | 11.00 | 8.19 | 19.19 |
| for round window, per lf of window diameter | 1C@.294 | lf | 24.30 | 16.70 | 41.00 |

| | Craft@Hrs | Unit | Material | Labor | Total |
|---|---|---|---|---|---|
| Replace 5" pattern casing | | | | | |
|    add 10% to the cost of 3-1/2" pattern casing | | | | | |
| Replace 5" curved casing | | | | | |
|    add 10% to the cost of 3-1/2" curved casing | | | | | |
| All sizes, species, shapes and styles of pattern casing | | | | | |
|    remove | 1D@.032 | lf | — | 1.24 | 1.24 |
|    remove for work, then reinstall | 6C@.083 | lf | — | 4.13 | 4.13 |

**Wood key.** Includes wood key, finish nails, and installation labor. Designed to be installed at the apex of curved casing. Does not include installation of casing to sides of the key.

| | Craft@Hrs | Unit | Material | Labor | Total |
|---|---|---|---|---|---|
| Replace wood key | | | | | |
|    standard wood key | 1C@.251 | ea | 26.20 | 14.30 | 40.50 |
|    with light carvings | 1C@.251 | ea | 41.70 | 14.30 | 56.00 |
|    with medium carvings | 1C@.251 | ea | 51.50 | 14.30 | 65.80 |
|    with heavy carvings | 1C@.251 | ea | 67.20 | 14.30 | 81.50 |
| All types of wood key | | | | | |
|    remove | 1D@.036 | ea | — | 1.40 | 1.40 |
|    remove for work, then reinstall | 6C@.323 | ea | — | 16.10 | 16.10 |

*with rosette*

*with carvings*

**Base block.**

| | Craft@Hrs | Unit | Material | Labor | Total |
|---|---|---|---|---|---|
| Pine | 1C@.063 | ea | 16.20 | 3.58 | 19.78 |
| poplar | 1C@.063 | ea | 17.30 | 3.58 | 20.88 |
| mahogany | 1C@.063 | ea | 19.00 | 3.58 | 22.58 |
| red oak | 1C@.063 | ea | 21.40 | 3.58 | 24.98 |
| All types and wood species of base block | | | | | |
|    remove | 1D@.036 | ea | — | 1.40 | 1.40 |
|    remove for work, then reinstall | 6C@.080 | ea | — | 3.98 | 3.98 |

*with rosette*

**Corner block.**

| | Craft@Hrs | Unit | Material | Labor | Total |
|---|---|---|---|---|---|
| Replace corner block with rosette | | | | | |
|    pine | 1C@.063 | ea | 12.90 | 3.58 | 16.48 |
|    poplar | 1C@.063 | ea | 14.90 | 3.58 | 18.48 |
|    mahogany | 1C@.063 | ea | 17.00 | 3.58 | 20.58 |
|    red oak | 1C@.063 | ea | 18.60 | 3.58 | 22.18 |
| All types and wood species of corner block | | | | | |
|    remove | 1D@.036 | ea | — | 1.40 | 1.40 |
|    remove for work, then reinstall | 6C@.080 | ea | — | 3.98 | 3.98 |

*with rosette*

Add 30% for corner blocks with carvings

| | Craft@Hrs | Unit | Material | Labor | Total |
|---|---|---|---|---|---|

**Head block.** Most commonly found on historical structures, head block is used in corners at the top of door casing and other cased openings. In addition to providing a decorative element, it is designed to provide a flat bottom edge and flat side edges that are wide enough for casing to tie into. This often allows designers to use more decorative molding as casing. Trimwork that uses head block often uses base blocks at the base of openings. Includes manufactured head block, fasteners, glue as needed, and installation labor. Does not include paint prep, painting, or caulking.

| | Craft@Hrs | Unit | Material | Labor | Total |
|---|---|---|---|---|---|
| Replace head block with rosette | | | | | |
| pine | 1C@.063 | ea | 16.20 | 3.58 | 19.78 |
| poplar | 1C@.063 | ea | 19.00 | 3.58 | 22.58 |
| mahogany | 1C@.063 | ea | 21.40 | 3.58 | 24.98 |
| red oak | 1C@.063 | ea | 23.40 | 3.58 | 26.98 |
| All types and wood species of head block | | | | | |
| remove | 1D@.037 | ea | — | 1.44 | 1.44 |
| remove for work, then reinstall | 6C@.080 | ea | — | 3.98 | 3.98 |

*with rosette*

*with carvings*

Add 31% for head block with carvings

*standard*

*with vertical milling*

*with hand carvings*

*with heavy hand carvings*

**Overdoor molding.** Includes overdoor moldings, finish board(s) as needed, finish nails, glue as needed, and installation labor. Does not include materials and labor to install side casing. Overdoor moldings can be manufactured to fit typical door sizes and installed on site or built on site. Site-built overdoor moldings are more common in the lower grades. Wherever they are built, overdoor moldings are usually a combination of trimwork such as crown, cove, half round, dentil molding, and rope molding which are often attached to a finish board. Moldings typically feature miter joints on each end that return the moldings into the wall.

| | Craft@Hrs | Unit | Material | Labor | Total |
|---|---|---|---|---|---|
| Replace overdoor horizontal molding | | | | | |
| Pine | 1C@.041 | lf | 15.40 | 2.33 | 17.73 |
| poplar | 1C@.041 | lf | 17.70 | 2.33 | 20.03 |
| mahogany | 1C@.041 | lf | 19.60 | 2.33 | 21.93 |
| red oak | 1C@.041 | lf | 22.50 | 2.33 | 24.83 |
| All types and wood species of overdoor molding | | | | | |
| remove | 1D@.028 | lf | — | 1.09 | 1.09 |
| remove for work, then reinstall | 6C@.057 | lf | — | 2.83 | 2.83 |

Add 72% for vertical milling in overdoor molding
Add 227% for hand carving in overdoor molding
Add 411% for heavy hand carving in overdoor molding

| | Craft@Hrs | Unit | Material | Labor | Total |
|---|---|---|---|---|---|

**Interior architrave.** Includes moldings, trim blocks, finish nails, glue as needed, and installation labor. The architrave is the complete set of moldings that surround and finish the opening. In this price list architrave refers primarily to the style of trimwork found on many historical structures where the complete set of moldings includes base blocks, corner blocks, or head blocks at joints in the casing. Each of these components can also be estimated separately. Standard grade: paint-grade pine or poplar, or stain-grade pine with rosettes in head and base blocks. High grade: stain-grade pine or red oak with rosettes or light embossing in base blocks and overdoor with horizontal moldings at top and bottom. Deluxe grade: red oak, birch or similar hardwood with carving in base blocks and angled overdoor with horizontal moldings at top and bottom or with light carvings. Custom grade: red oak, birch or similar hardwood with carvings in base blocks and angled or curved overdoor with horizontal moldings at top and bottom or with heavy carvings.

*standard*    *high*

| | Craft@Hrs | Unit | Material | Labor | Total |
|---|---|---|---|---|---|
| Replace interior architrave | | | | | |
| standard grade | 1C@.062 | lf | 6.51 | 3.53 | 10.04 |
| high grade | 1C@.062 | lf | 8.48 | 3.53 | 12.01 |
| deluxe grade | 1C@.062 | lf | 11.90 | 3.53 | 15.43 |
| custom grade | 1C@.062 | lf | 16.80 | 3.53 | 20.33 |
| All grades of interior architrave | | | | | |
| remove | 1D@.032 | lf | — | 1.24 | 1.24 |
| remove for work, then reinstall | 6C@.103 | lf | — | 5.12 | 5.12 |

**Exterior architrave.** Includes moldings, trim blocks, finish nails, glue as needed, and installation labor. The architrave is the complete set of moldings that surround and finish the opening. In this book, architrave refers primarily to the style of trimwork found on many historical structures where the complete set of moldings includes base blocks, corner blocks, or head blocks at joints in the casing. Each of these components can also be estimated separately. All materials are back-primed. Economy grade: a standard width casing of paint- or stain-grade pine or poplar with rosettes in head and base blocks. Standard grade: wide casing (may be made from two moldings) of paint- or stain-grade pine or poplar. High grade: wide casing (may be made from two moldings) of stain-grade pine or red oak with rosettes or light embossing in base blocks, with horizontal moldings at top and bottom of overdoor. Deluxe and higher grades: wide casing (may be made from two moldings) of red oak, birch or similar hardwood, increasingly ornate embellishment of base blocks and overdoor.

| | Craft@Hrs | Unit | Material | Labor | Total |
|---|---|---|---|---|---|
| Replace exterior architrave | | | | | |
| economy grade | 1C@.080 | lf | 6.51 | 4.55 | 11.06 |
| standard grade | 1C@.080 | lf | 9.16 | 4.55 | 13.71 |
| high grade | 1C@.080 | lf | 13.00 | 4.55 | 17.55 |
| deluxe grade | 1C@.080 | lf | 18.60 | 4.55 | 23.15 |
| custom grade | 1C@.080 | lf | 23.60 | 4.55 | 28.15 |
| custom deluxe grade | 1C@.080 | lf | 32.90 | 4.55 | 37.45 |
| All grades of exterior architrave | | | | | |
| remove | 1D@.032 | lf | — | 1.24 | 1.24 |
| remove for work, then reinstall | 6C@.127 | lf | — | 6.31 | 6.31 |

| | Craft@Hrs | Unit | Material | Labor | Total |
|---|---|---|---|---|---|

| economy | standard | high | deluxe | custom | custom deluxe |

**Exterior door surround.** Includes manufactured door surround to match door size, fasteners, and installation labor. Although door surrounds can be built on site from standard moldings, all labor productivities are based on installation of manufactured units. Material prices are based on classical door surrounds inspired by Greek and Roman designs. All grades standard are made from wood with increasingly intricate carved detail. Economy and standard grades are made of plastic or other synthetic materials. Illustrations show typical complexity for each grade, actual door styling varies widely.

| | Craft@Hrs | Unit | Material | Labor | Total |
|---|---|---|---|---|---|
| Replace exterior door surround | | | | | |
| economy grade | 1C@.234 | lf | 40.70 | 13.30 | 54.00 |
| standard grade | 1C@.257 | lf | 66.30 | 14.60 | 80.90 |
| high grade | 1C@.274 | lf | 117.00 | 15.60 | 132.60 |
| deluxe grade | 1C@.317 | lf | 227.00 | 18.00 | 245.00 |
| custom grade | 1C@.372 | lf | 352.00 | 21.20 | 373.20 |
| custom deluxe grade | 1C@.431 | lf | 587.00 | 24.50 | 611.50 |
| All grades of exterior door | | | | | |
| remove | 1D@.034 | lf | — | 1.32 | 1.32 |
| remove for work, then reinstall | 6C@.775 | lf | — | 38.50 | 38.50 |

| economy | standard | high | deluxe | custom | custom deluxe |

**Exterior window surround.** Includes manufactured window surround to match window size, fasteners, and installation labor. Although window surrounds can be built on site from standard moldings, all labor productivities are based on installation of manufactured units. Material prices are based on classical window surrounds inspired by Greek and Roman designs.

| | Craft@Hrs | Unit | Material | Labor | Total |
|---|---|---|---|---|---|
| Replace exterior window surround | | | | | |
| economy grade | 1C@.207 | lf | 33.00 | 11.80 | 44.80 |
| standard grade | 1C@.227 | lf | 53.80 | 12.90 | 66.70 |
| high grade | 1C@.239 | lf | 95.30 | 13.60 | 108.90 |
| deluxe grade | 1C@.280 | lf | 186.00 | 15.90 | 201.90 |
| custom grade | 1C@.326 | lf | 287.00 | 18.50 | 305.50 |
| custom deluxe grade | 1C@.322 | lf | 477.00 | 18.30 | 495.30 |
| All grades of exterior window surround | | | | | |
| remove | 1D@.034 | lf | — | 1.32 | 1.32 |
| remove for work, then reinstall | 6C@.690 | lf | — | 34.30 | 34.30 |

| | Craft@Hrs | Unit | Material | Labor | Total |
|---|---|---|---|---|---|

**Window stool.** Includes 2-1/2" window stool, finish nails, silicone caulking as needed, and installation labor.

| | | | | | |
|---|---|---|---|---|---|
| **Replace window stool** | | | | | |
| paint-grade pine | 1C@.058 | lf | 2.42 | 3.30 | 5.72 |
| stain-grade pine | 1C@.058 | lf | 2.84 | 3.30 | 6.14 |
| poplar | 1C@.058 | lf | 3.02 | 3.30 | 6.32 |
| mahogany | 1C@.058 | lf | 3.58 | 3.30 | 6.88 |
| red oak | 1C@.058 | lf | 3.87 | 3.30 | 7.17 |
| **All wood species of window stool** | | | | | |
| remove | 1D@.026 | lf | — | 1.01 | 1.01 |
| remove for work, then reinstall | 6C@.108 | lf | — | 5.37 | 5.37 |

**Window apron.** Includes 3-1/2" window apron, finish nails, silicone caulking as needed, and installation labor.

| | | | | | |
|---|---|---|---|---|---|
| **Replace window apron** | | | | | |
| paint-grade pine | 1C@.049 | lf | 1.56 | 2.79 | 4.35 |
| stain-grade pine | 1C@.049 | lf | 1.86 | 2.79 | 4.65 |
| poplar | 1C@.049 | lf | 1.98 | 2.79 | 4.77 |
| mahogany | 1C@.049 | lf | 2.35 | 2.79 | 5.14 |
| red oak | 1C@.049 | lf | 2.51 | 2.79 | 5.30 |
| **All wood species of window apron** | | | | | |
| remove | 1D@.028 | lf | — | 1.09 | 1.09 |
| remove for work, then reinstall | 6C@.080 | lf | — | 3.98 | 3.98 |

**Chair rail.** Includes chair rail, finish nails, and installation labor. Outside joints are mitered; inside joints are coped. Includes 4% waste.

| | | | | | |
|---|---|---|---|---|---|
| **Replace 2-1/2" chair rail** | | | | | |
| paint-grade pine | 1C@.038 | lf | 2.09 | 2.16 | 4.25 |
| stain-grade pine | 1C@.038 | lf | 2.43 | 2.16 | 4.59 |
| poplar | 1C@.038 | lf | 2.64 | 2.16 | 4.80 |
| mahogany | 1C@.038 | lf | 3.13 | 2.16 | 5.29 |
| red oak | 1C@.038 | lf | 3.34 | 2.16 | 5.50 |
| **Replace 3-1/2" chair rail** | | | | | |
| paint-grade pine | 1C@.038 | lf | 2.64 | 2.16 | 4.80 |
| stain-grade pine | 1C@.038 | lf | 3.06 | 2.16 | 5.22 |
| poplar | 1C@.038 | lf | 3.31 | 2.16 | 5.47 |
| mahogany | 1C@.038 | lf | 3.92 | 2.16 | 6.08 |
| red oak | 1C@.038 | lf | 4.27 | 2.16 | 6.43 |
| **All sizes and wood species of chair rail** | | | | | |
| remove | 1D@.026 | lf | — | 1.01 | 1.01 |
| remove for work, then reinstall | 6C@.065 | lf | — | 3.23 | 3.23 |

*2-1/2" chair rail*

**Drip cap.** Includes drip cap, finish nails, silicone caulking as needed, and installation labor.

| | | | | | |
|---|---|---|---|---|---|
| **Replace 1-5/8" drip cap** | | | | | |
| paint-grade pine | 1C@.038 | lf | 1.94 | 2.16 | 4.10 |
| redwood | 1C@.038 | lf | 2.25 | 2.16 | 4.41 |
| cedar | 1C@.038 | lf | 2.09 | 2.16 | 4.25 |

| | Craft@Hrs | Unit | Material | Labor | Total |
|---|---|---|---|---|---|
| **Replace 2-1/4" drip cap** | | | | | |
| paint-grade pine | 1C@.038 | lf | 2.16 | 2.16 | 4.32 |
| redwood | 1C@.038 | lf | 2.50 | 2.16 | 4.66 |
| cedar | 1C@.038 | lf | 2.35 | 2.16 | 4.51 |
| **All sizes and wood species of drip cap** | | | | | |
| remove | 1D@.032 | lf | — | 1.24 | 1.24 |
| remove for work, then reinstall | 6C@.083 | lf | — | 4.13 | 4.13 |

**Astragal.** Includes astragal, finish nails or fasteners, and installation labor. Installation productivity is based on installation of a replacement astragal in previously installed doors.

| | Craft@Hrs | Unit | Material | Labor | Total |
|---|---|---|---|---|---|
| **Replace 1-3/4" astragal** | | | | | |
| paint-grade pine | 1C@.041 | lf | 4.04 | 2.33 | 6.37 |
| stain-grade pine | 1C@.041 | lf | 4.67 | 2.33 | 7.00 |
| poplar | 1C@.041 | lf | 5.03 | 2.33 | 7.36 |
| mahogany | 1C@.041 | lf | 5.95 | 2.33 | 8.28 |
| red oak | 1C@.041 | lf | 6.46 | 2.33 | 8.79 |
| **Replace 2-1/4" astragal** | | | | | |
| paint-grade pine | 1C@.041 | lf | 4.88 | 2.33 | 7.21 |
| stain-grade pine | 1C@.041 | lf | 5.64 | 2.33 | 7.97 |
| poplar | 1C@.041 | lf | 6.10 | 2.33 | 8.43 |
| mahogany | 1C@.041 | lf | 7.21 | 2.33 | 9.54 |
| red oak | 1C@.041 | lf | 7.81 | 2.33 | 10.14 |
| **All sizes and wood species of astragal** | | | | | |
| remove | 1D@.032 | lf | — | 1.24 | 1.24 |
| remove for work, then reinstall | 6C@.083 | lf | — | 4.13 | 4.13 |

**Cove.** Includes cove, finish nails, and installation labor. Outside joints are mitered; inside joints are coped. Includes 4% waste.

| | Craft@Hrs | Unit | Material | Labor | Total |
|---|---|---|---|---|---|
| **Replace 1/2" cove** | | | | | |
| paint-grade pine | 1C@.041 | lf | .76 | 2.33 | 3.09 |
| stain-grade pine | 1C@.041 | lf | .88 | 2.33 | 3.21 |
| poplar | 1C@.041 | lf | .97 | 2.33 | 3.30 |
| mahogany | 1C@.041 | lf | 1.11 | 2.33 | 3.44 |
| red oak | 1C@.041 | lf | 1.19 | 2.33 | 3.52 |
| **Replace 3/4" cove** | | | | | |
| paint-grade pine | 1C@.041 | lf | .87 | 2.33 | 3.20 |
| stain-grade pine | 1C@.041 | lf | 1.01 | 2.33 | 3.34 |
| poplar | 1C@.041 | lf | 1.11 | 2.33 | 3.44 |
| mahogany | 1C@.041 | lf | 1.27 | 2.33 | 3.60 |
| red oak | 1C@.041 | lf | 1.35 | 2.33 | 3.68 |
| **Replace 1" cove** | | | | | |
| paint-grade pine | 1C@.041 | lf | 1.07 | 2.33 | 3.40 |
| stain-grade pine | 1C@.041 | lf | 1.24 | 2.33 | 3.57 |
| poplar cove | 1C@.041 | lf | 1.38 | 2.33 | 3.71 |
| mahogany cove | 1C@.041 | lf | 1.57 | 2.33 | 3.90 |
| red oak cove | 1C@.041 | lf | 1.70 | 2.33 | 4.03 |
| **All sizes and wood species of cove** | | | | | |
| remove | 1D@.032 | lf | — | 1.24 | 1.24 |
| remove for work, then reinstall | 6C@.065 | lf | — | 3.23 | 3.23 |

| | Craft@Hrs | Unit | Material | Labor | Total |
|---|---|---|---|---|---|

**Ceiling cove.** Includes ceiling cove (sometimes called "sprung cove"), finish nails, and installation labor. Outside joints are mitered; inside joints are coped. Includes 4% waste.

| | Craft@Hrs | Unit | Material | Labor | Total |
|---|---|---|---|---|---|
| Replace 2-1/2" ceiling cove | | | | | |
|     paint-grade pine | 1C@.046 | lf | 1.90 | 2.62 | 4.52 |
|     stain-grade pine | 1C@.046 | lf | 2.20 | 2.62 | 4.82 |
|     poplar | 1C@.046 | lf | 2.36 | 2.62 | 4.98 |
|     mahogany | 1C@.046 | lf | 2.85 | 2.62 | 5.47 |
|     red oak | 1C@.046 | lf | 3.09 | 2.62 | 5.71 |
| Replace 3-1/2" ceiling cove | | | | | |
|     paint-grade pine | 1C@.046 | lf | 2.43 | 2.62 | 5.05 |
|     stain-grade pine | 1C@.046 | lf | 2.85 | 2.62 | 5.47 |
|     poplar | 1C@.046 | lf | 3.06 | 2.62 | 5.68 |
|     mahogany | 1C@.046 | lf | 3.67 | 2.62 | 6.29 |
|     red oak | 1C@.046 | lf | 4.02 | 2.62 | 6.64 |
| All sizes and wood species of cove | | | | | |
|     remove | 1D@.032 | lf | — | 1.24 | 1.24 |
|     remove for work, then reinstall | 6C@.065 | lf | — | 3.23 | 3.23 |

*"sprung" cove*

**Half-round.** Includes half-round, finish nails, and installation labor. Outside joints are mitered; inside joints are coped. Includes 4% waste.

| | Craft@Hrs | Unit | Material | Labor | Total |
|---|---|---|---|---|---|
| Replace 1" half-round | | | | | |
|     paint-grade pine | 1C@.041 | lf | .87 | 2.33 | 3.20 |
|     stain-grade pine | 1C@.041 | lf | 1.03 | 2.33 | 3.36 |
|     poplar | 1C@.041 | lf | 1.11 | 2.33 | 3.44 |
|     mahogany | 1C@.041 | lf | 1.29 | 2.33 | 3.62 |
|     red oak | 1C@.041 | lf | 1.40 | 2.33 | 3.73 |
| Replace 2" half-round | | | | | |
|     paint-grade pine | 1C@.041 | lf | 1.23 | 2.33 | 3.56 |
|     stain-grade pine | 1C@.041 | lf | 1.43 | 2.33 | 3.76 |
|     poplar | 1C@.041 | lf | 1.56 | 2.33 | 3.89 |
|     mahogany | 1C@.041 | lf | 1.85 | 2.33 | 4.18 |
|     red oak | 1C@.041 | lf | 2.01 | 2.33 | 4.34 |

Replace 3" half-round
    add 19% to the cost of 2" half-round
Replace 4" half-round
    add 40% to the cost of 2" half-round

| | Craft@Hrs | Unit | Material | Labor | Total |
|---|---|---|---|---|---|
| All sizes and wood species of half-round | | | | | |
|     remove | 1D@.032 | lf | — | 1.24 | 1.24 |
|     remove for work, then reinstall | 6C@.083 | lf | — | 4.13 | 4.13 |

**Quarter-round.** Includes quarter-round, finish nails, and installation labor. Outside joints are mitered; inside joints are coped. Includes 4% waste.

| | Craft@Hrs | Unit | Material | Labor | Total |
|---|---|---|---|---|---|
| Replace 1/2" quarter-round | | | | | |
|     paint-grade pine | 1C@.041 | lf | .64 | 2.33 | 2.97 |
|     stain-grade pine | 1C@.041 | lf | .74 | 2.33 | 3.07 |
|     poplar | 1C@.041 | lf | .83 | 2.33 | 3.16 |
|     mahogany | 1C@.041 | lf | .98 | 2.33 | 3.31 |
|     red oak | 1C@.041 | lf | 1.09 | 2.33 | 3.42 |

| | Craft@Hrs | Unit | Material | Labor | Total |
|---|---|---|---|---|---|
| **Replace 3/4" quarter-round** | | | | | |
| paint-grade pine | 1C@.041 | lf | .76 | 2.33 | 3.09 |
| stain-grade pine | 1C@.041 | lf | .90 | 2.33 | 3.23 |
| poplar | 1C@.041 | lf | .97 | 2.33 | 3.30 |
| mahogany | 1C@.041 | lf | 1.16 | 2.33 | 3.49 |
| red oak | 1C@.041 | lf | 1.29 | 2.33 | 3.62 |
| **Replace 1" quarter-round** | | | | | |
| paint-grade pine | 1C@.041 | lf | 1.33 | 2.33 | 3.66 |
| stain-grade pine | 1C@.041 | lf | 1.58 | 2.33 | 3.91 |
| poplar | 1C@.041 | lf | 1.73 | 2.33 | 4.06 |
| mahogany | 1C@.041 | lf | 2.06 | 2.33 | 4.39 |
| red oak | 1C@.041 | lf | 2.30 | 2.33 | 4.63 |
| **All sizes and wood species of quarter-round** | | | | | |
| remove | 1D@.032 | lf | — | 1.24 | 1.24 |
| remove for work, then reinstall | 6C@.083 | lf | — | 4.13 | 4.13 |

**Corner bead.** Includes corner bead, finish nails or fasteners, and installation labor. Material costs for standard corner beads include a 4% allowance for waste. No waste included for turned corner beads with double finials.

| | Craft@Hrs | Unit | Material | Labor | Total |
|---|---|---|---|---|---|
| **Replace corner bead** | | | | | |
| paint-grade pine | 1C@.077 | lf | 1.47 | 4.38 | 5.85 |
| stain-grade pine | 1C@.077 | lf | 1.77 | 4.38 | 6.15 |
| stain-grade pine, turned with double finials | 1C@.077 | lf | 19.30 | 4.38 | 23.68 |
| mahogany | 1C@.077 | lf | 3.29 | 4.38 | 7.67 |
| mahogany, turned with double finials | 1C@.077 | lf | 23.80 | 4.38 | 28.18 |
| red oak | 1C@.077 | lf | 4.04 | 4.38 | 8.42 |
| red oak, turned with double finials | 1C@.077 | lf | 25.40 | 4.38 | 29.78 |
| clear plastic | 1C@.032 | lf | 1.36 | 1.82 | 3.18 |
| **All styles and material types of corner bead** | | | | | |
| remove | 1D@.043 | lf | — | 1.67 | 1.67 |
| remove for work, then reinstall | 6C@.113 | lf | — | 5.62 | 5.62 |

*standard*

*turned with double finials*

**Bed mold.** Includes 2-1/2" bed molding, finish nails, and installation labor. Outside joints are mitered; inside joints are coped. Includes 4% waste.

| | Craft@Hrs | Unit | Material | Labor | Total |
|---|---|---|---|---|---|
| **Replace bed mold** | | | | | |
| paint-grade pine | 1C@.038 | lf | 2.09 | 2.16 | 4.25 |
| stain-grade pine | 1C@.038 | lf | 2.44 | 2.16 | 4.60 |
| poplar | 1C@.038 | lf | 2.66 | 2.16 | 4.82 |
| mahogany | 1C@.038 | lf | 3.19 | 2.16 | 5.35 |
| red oak | 1C@.038 | lf | 3.46 | 2.16 | 5.62 |
| **All wood species of bed mold** | | | | | |
| remove | 1D@.026 | lf | — | 1.01 | 1.01 |
| remove for work, then reinstall | 6C@.065 | lf | — | 3.23 | 3.23 |

**Crown mold.** Includes crown molding, finish nails, and installation labor. Outside joints are mitered; inside joints are coped. Includes 4% waste.

| | Craft@Hrs | Unit | Material | Labor | Total |
|---|---|---|---|---|---|
| **Replace 3-1/2" bed mold** | | | | | |
| paint-grade pine | 1C@.046 | lf | 2.68 | 2.62 | 5.30 |
| stain-grade pine | 1C@.046 | lf | 3.15 | 2.62 | 5.77 |
| poplar | 1C@.046 | lf | 3.42 | 2.62 | 6.04 |
| mahogany | 1C@.046 | lf | 4.09 | 2.62 | 6.71 |
| red oak | 1C@.046 | lf | 4.42 | 2.62 | 7.04 |

| | Craft@Hrs | Unit | Material | Labor | Total |
|---|---|---|---|---|---|
| **Replace 4-1/2" crown mold** | | | | | |
| paint-grade pine | 1C@.046 | lf | 3.96 | 2.62 | 6.58 |
| stain-grade pine | 1C@.046 | lf | 4.64 | 2.62 | 7.26 |
| poplar | 1C@.046 | lf | 5.04 | 2.62 | 7.66 |
| mahogany | 1C@.046 | lf | 6.43 | 2.62 | 9.05 |
| red oak | 1C@.046 | lf | 6.95 | 2.62 | 9.57 |
| **All sizes and wood species of crown mold** | | | | | |
| remove | 1D@.026 | lf | — | 1.01 | 1.01 |
| remove for work, then reinstall | 6C@.065 | lf | — | 3.23 | 3.23 |

**Hand rail.** Includes wood hand rail, brackets with screws, and installation labor. Also includes 4% waste.

| | Craft@Hrs | Unit | Material | Labor | Total |
|---|---|---|---|---|---|
| **Replace hand rail** | | | | | |
| paint-grade pine | 1C@.098 | lf | 3.41 | 5.58 | 8.99 |
| stain-grade pine | 1C@.098 | lf | 4.65 | 5.58 | 10.23 |
| mahogany | 1C@.098 | lf | 6.62 | 5.58 | 12.20 |
| red oak | 1C@.098 | lf | 7.07 | 5.58 | 12.65 |
| **All wood species of hand rail** | | | | | |
| remove | 1D@.028 | lf | — | 1.09 | 1.09 |
| remove for work, then reinstall | 6C@.154 | lf | — | 7.65 | 7.65 |

**Specialty molding.** Includes specialty molding, finish nails, and installation labor. Outside joints are mitered; inside joints are coped. Includes 4% waste. Specialty molding is an all-purpose pricing item for all standard trimwork that has all vertical milling and is commonly available in home improvement centers throughout North America. This includes molding such as crown, chair rail, panel molds, cabinet trim and so forth.

| | Craft@Hrs | Unit | Material | Labor | Total |
|---|---|---|---|---|---|
| **Replace 3/4" specialty molding with vertical milling** | | | | | |
| paint-grade pine | 1C@.041 | lf | 3.18 | 2.33 | 5.51 |
| stain-grade pine | 1C@.041 | lf | 3.68 | 2.33 | 6.01 |
| poplar | 1C@.041 | lf | 3.97 | 2.33 | 6.30 |
| mahogany | 1C@.041 | lf | 4.96 | 2.33 | 7.29 |
| red oak | 1C@.041 | lf | 5.38 | 2.33 | 7.71 |
| polyurethane | 1C@.041 | lf | 4.72 | 2.33 | 7.05 |
| stain-grade polyurethane | 1C@.041 | lf | 5.08 | 2.33 | 7.41 |
| **Other 3/4" styles** | | | | | |
| deduct for molding with embossed patterns (pine moldings only) | — | % | -41.0 | — | — |
| add for molding with hand carvings | — | % | 64.0 | — | — |
| add for molding with heavy hand carvings | — | % | 198.0 | — | — |
| **Replace 1-1/2" specialty molding with vertical milling** | | | | | |
| paint-grade pine | 1C@.041 | lf | 3.60 | 2.33 | 5.93 |
| stain-grade pine | 1C@.041 | lf | 4.22 | 2.33 | 6.55 |
| poplar | 1C@.041 | lf | 4.54 | 2.33 | 6.87 |
| mahogany | 1C@.041 | lf | 5.63 | 2.33 | 7.96 |
| red oak | 1C@.041 | lf | 6.16 | 2.33 | 8.49 |
| polyurethane | 1C@.041 | lf | 7.45 | 2.33 | 9.78 |
| stain-grade polyurethane | 1C@.041 | lf | 7.99 | 2.33 | 10.32 |
| **Replace other 1-1/2" styles of specialty molding** | | | | | |
| deduct for molding with embossed patterns (pine moldings only) | — | % | -37.0 | — | — |
| add for molding with hand carvings | — | % | 66.0 | — | — |
| add for molding with heavy hand carvings | — | % | 205.0 | — | — |

*dentil*

*bead and reel*

*bead*

*rope*

|  | Craft@Hrs | Unit | Material | Labor | Total |
|---|---|---|---|---|---|
| **Replace 2-1/2" specialty molding with vertical milling** | | | | | |
| paint-grade pine | 1C@.041 | lf | 4.07 | 2.33 | 6.40 |
| stain-grade pine | 1C@.041 | lf | 4.71 | 2.33 | 7.04 |
| poplar | 1C@.041 | lf | 5.10 | 2.33 | 7.43 |
| mahogany | 1C@.041 | lf | 6.31 | 2.33 | 8.64 |
| red oak | 1C@.041 | lf | 6.88 | 2.33 | 9.21 |
| polyurethane | 1C@.041 | lf | 8.35 | 2.33 | 10.68 |
| stain-grade polyurethane | 1C@.041 | lf | 8.95 | 2.33 | 11.28 |
| **Replace other 2-1/2" styles of specialty molding** | | | | | |
| deduct for molding with embossed patterns (pine moldings only) | — | % | -37.0 | — | — |
| add for molding with hand carvings | — | % | 68.0 | — | — |
| add for molding with heavy hand carvings | — | % | 209.0 | — | — |
| **Replace 3-1/2" specialty molding with vertical milling** | | | | | |
| paint-grade pine | 1C@.041 | lf | 4.51 | 2.33 | 6.84 |
| stain-grade pine | 1C@.041 | lf | 5.27 | 2.33 | 7.60 |
| poplar | 1C@.041 | lf | 5.65 | 2.33 | 7.98 |
| mahogany | 1C@.041 | lf | 7.02 | 2.33 | 9.35 |
| red oak | 1C@.041 | lf | 7.64 | 2.33 | 9.97 |
| polyurethane | 1C@.041 | lf | 9.26 | 2.33 | 11.59 |
| stain-grade polyurethane | 1C@.041 | lf | 9.95 | 2.33 | 12.28 |
| **Replace other 3-1/2" styles of specialty molding** | | | | | |
| deduct for molding with embossed patterns (pine moldings only) | — | % | -38.0 | — | — |
| add for molding with hand carving | — | % | 69.0 | — | — |
| add for molding with heavy hand carving | — | % | 213.0 | — | — |
| **Replace 5" specialty molding with vertical milling** | | | | | |
| paint-grade pine | 1C@.050 | lf | 6.50 | 2.85 | 9.35 |
| stain-grade pine | 1C@.050 | lf | 7.57 | 2.85 | 10.42 |
| poplar | 1C@.050 | lf | 8.15 | 2.85 | 11.00 |
| mahogany | 1C@.050 | lf | 10.10 | 2.85 | 12.95 |
| red oak | 1C@.050 | lf | 11.00 | 2.85 | 13.85 |
| polyurethane | 1C@.050 | lf | 13.30 | 2.85 | 16.15 |
| stain-grade polyurethane | 1C@.050 | lf | 14.20 | 2.85 | 17.05 |
| **Replace other 5" styles of vertical molding** | | | | | |
| deduct for molding with embossed patterns (pine moldings only) | — | % | -39.0 | — | — |
| add for molding with hand carving | — | % | 71.0 | — | — |
| add for molding with heavy hand carving | — | % | 219.0 | — | — |
| **Replace 8" specialty molding with vertical milling** | | | | | |
| paint-grade pine | 1C@.055 | lf | 10.60 | 3.13 | 13.73 |
| stain-grade pine | 1C@.055 | lf | 12.40 | 3.13 | 15.53 |
| poplar | 1C@.055 | lf | 13.20 | 3.13 | 16.33 |
| mahogany | 1C@.055 | lf | 16.80 | 3.13 | 19.93 |
| red oak | 1C@.055 | lf | 18.20 | 3.13 | 21.33 |
| polyurethane | 1C@.055 | lf | 21.90 | 3.13 | 25.03 |
| stain-grade polyurethane | 1C@.055 | lf | 23.60 | 3.13 | 26.73 |

*reed*

*acanthus*

*leaf and tongue*

*laurel and ribbon*

*shell*

*oak leaf and ribbon*

*meander*

*fret*

*egg and dart*

| | Craft@Hrs | Unit | Material | Labor | Total |
|---|---|---|---|---|---|
| Replace other 8" styles of specialty molding | | | | | |
| deduct for molding with embossed patterns (pine moldings only) | — | % | -41.0 | — | — |
| add for molding with hand carving | — | % | 75.0 | — | — |
| add for molding with heavy hand carving | — | % | 232.0 | — | — |
| All widths and types of specialty moldings | | | | | |
| remove | 1D@.032 | lf | — | 1.24 | 1.24 |
| remove for work then reinstall | | | | | |
| wall molding | 6C@.065 | lf | — | 3.23 | 3.23 |
| window or door casing | 6C@.083 | lf | — | 4.13 | 4.13 |

*bundled reeds*

*ribbon*

*grape*

**Custom-milled moldings.** Includes custom-milled molding, fasteners, and installation labor. Includes 4% waste. Custom milled to match existing pattern or a specially designed pattern. All milling is horizontal. Custom moldings are most common when repairing a historical structure that contains moldings that are no longer manufactured. Some custom homes also have custom moldings designed by an architect or designer. A custom molder knife is cut to match the existing molding and moldings are run to match. Linear foot prices do not include pattern charges, design charges, mill charges, molder setup charges, or minimum charges for small runs.

| | Craft@Hrs | Unit | Material | Labor | Total |
|---|---|---|---|---|---|
| Setup charges, replace only | | | | | |
| molder setup charge | — | ea | 232.00 | — | 232.00 |
| molder custom knife charges | — | ea | 516.00 | — | 516.00 |
| Replace pine custom molding | | | | | |
| 1" to 2" | 1C@.041 | lf | 2.12 | 2.33 | 4.45 |
| 2" to 3" | 1C@.041 | lf | 2.38 | 2.33 | 4.71 |
| 3" to 4" | 1C@.050 | lf | 3.37 | 2.85 | 6.22 |
| 4" to 5" | 1C@.050 | lf | 5.35 | 2.85 | 8.20 |
| 6" to 7" | 1C@.055 | lf | 8.80 | 3.13 | 11.93 |
| 7" to 8" | 1C@.055 | lf | 12.50 | 3.13 | 15.63 |
| Replace other wood species of custom molding | | | | | |
| add for poplar molding | — | % | 7.0 | — | — |
| add for mahogany molding | — | % | 21.0 | — | — |
| add for red oak molding | — | % | 30.0 | — | — |
| All sizes and wood species of custom molding | | | | | |
| remove | 1D@.032 | lf | — | 1.24 | 1.24 |

**Panel molding corner radius.** Includes panel corner radius, fasteners, and installation labor. Panel corner radius pieces are manufactured and often precut to match standard straight moldings. The corner radius is installed at corners of the molding to provide a radius instead of a 90-degree angle.

| | Craft@Hrs | Unit | Material | Labor | Total |
|---|---|---|---|---|---|
| Replace | | | | | |
| standard | 1C@.149 | ea | 2.41 | 8.48 | 10.89 |
| with vertical milling | 1C@.149 | ea | 5.69 | 8.48 | 14.17 |
| with embossed pattern | 1C@.149 | ea | 4.70 | 8.48 | 13.18 |
| with hand carvings | 1C@.149 | ea | 8.69 | 8.48 | 17.17 |
| with heavy hand carvings | 1C@.149 | ea | 12.40 | 8.48 | 20.88 |
| All types | | | | | |
| remove | 1D@.034 | ea | — | 1.32 | 1.32 |

| | Craft@Hrs | Unit | Material | Labor | Total |
|---|---|---|---|---|---|

**Closet shelf brackets, shelving and rod.** Includes shelf brackets, wood closet rod cut to length or metal telescoping closet rod, and bullnose shelf up to 16" wide, screws, and installation labor.

| | Craft@Hrs | Unit | Material | Labor | Total |
|---|---|---|---|---|---|
| replace | 1C@.332 | lf | 13.90 | 18.90 | 32.80 |
| remove | 1D@.063 | lf | — | 2.45 | 2.45 |
| remove for work, then reinstall | 6C@.500 | lf | — | 24.90 | 24.90 |

**Closet organizer system.** Includes closet shelves, side supports, rods, brackets, and — depending on quality — drawers. Installation labor includes some custom fitting to match walls. Closets are typically measured and a matching prefabricated unit installed. However, higher grades may include some custom work.

| | Craft@Hrs | Unit | Material | Labor | Total |
|---|---|---|---|---|---|
| Replace | | | | | |
| standard grade | 1C@.304 | sf | 13.00 | 17.30 | 30.30 |
| high grade | 1C@.414 | sf | 15.70 | 23.60 | 39.30 |
| deluxe grade | 1C@.526 | sf | 19.90 | 29.90 | 49.80 |
| All grades | | | | | |
| remove | 1D@.047 | sf | — | 1.83 | 1.83 |
| remove for work, then reinstall | 6C@.696 | sf | — | 34.60 | 34.60 |

**Linen closet shelves.** Includes bullnose paint-grade shelves up to 16" wide built on runners attached to walls and installation labor. Runners are made of pine or paint-grade casing. Shelves are spaced from 16" to 24" apart.

| | Craft@Hrs | Unit | Material | Labor | Total |
|---|---|---|---|---|---|
| Replace | | | | | |
| standard grade | 1C@.673 | lf | 10.40 | 38.30 | 48.70 |
| high grade | 1C@.673 | lf | 11.30 | 38.30 | 49.60 |
| pull-out shelves | 1C@.695 | lf | 13.10 | 39.50 | 52.60 |
| All grades and styles | | | | | |
| remove | 1D@.034 | lf | — | 1.32 | 1.32 |
| remove for work, then reinstall | 6C@.934 | lf | — | 46.40 | 46.40 |

**Closet rod.** Includes wood closet rod cut to length or metal expanding rod with installation labor. Includes screws to attach rod but does not include rod brackets.

| | Craft@Hrs | Unit | Material | Labor | Total |
|---|---|---|---|---|---|
| Replace | | | | | |
| pine | 1C@.080 | lf | 3.97 | 4.55 | 8.52 |
| hardwood | 1C@.080 | lf | 5.01 | 4.55 | 9.56 |
| All closet rods | | | | | |
| remove | 1D@.035 | lf | — | 1.36 | 1.36 |
| remove for work, then reinstall | 6C@.120 | lf | — | 5.96 | 5.96 |

**Cedar closet lining.** Includes tongue-and-groove aromatic cedar boards, finish nails, construction glue, and installation labor. Often installed on walls and ceilings of closet.

| | Craft@Hrs | Unit | Material | Labor | Total |
|---|---|---|---|---|---|
| replace aromatic tongue-&-groove board | 1C@.051 | sf | .23 | 2.90 | 3.13 |
| remove | 1D@.028 | sf | — | 1.09 | 1.09 |
| replace aromatic 1/4" veneer plywood | 1C@.037 | sf | 3.70 | 2.11 | 5.81 |
| remove | 1D@.022 | sf | — | .86 | .86 |

|  | Craft@Hrs | Unit | Material | Labor | Total |
|---|---|---|---|---|---|

**Built-in bookcase.** Includes finish boards, finish plywood, trimwork, brackets, fasteners, finish nails, and installation labor. Does not include lighting, caulking, finishing, or painting. Shelves may be manufactured or cut to width on site. Recessed and adjustable shelf hardware is also included but all shelves may not be adjustable. Shelves spaced approximately 12" on center. Measure square feet of bookcase face.

| | Craft@Hrs | Unit | Material | Labor | Total |
|---|---|---|---|---|---|
| 8" deep, replace | | | | | |
| paint-grade pine | 1C@.269 | sf | 9.19 | 15.30 | 24.49 |
| stain-grade pine | 1C@.269 | sf | 10.70 | 15.30 | 26.00 |
| mahogany | 1C@.269 | sf | 11.60 | 15.30 | 26.90 |
| oak | 1C@.269 | sf | 13.60 | 15.30 | 28.90 |
| walnut | 1C@.269 | sf | 18.70 | 15.30 | 34.00 |
| 12" deep, replace | | | | | |
| paint-grade pine | 1C@.304 | sf | 12.10 | 17.30 | 29.40 |
| stain-grade pine | 1C@.304 | sf | 13.90 | 17.30 | 31.20 |
| mahogany | 1C@.304 | sf | 15.00 | 17.30 | 32.30 |
| oak | 1C@.304 | sf | 18.00 | 17.30 | 35.30 |
| walnut | 1C@.304 | sf | 24.30 | 17.30 | 41.60 |
| 18" deep, replace | | | | | |
| paint-grade pine | 1C@.317 | sf | 15.70 | 18.00 | 33.70 |
| stain-grade pine | 1C@.317 | sf | 18.60 | 18.00 | 36.60 |
| mahogany | 1C@.317 | sf | 19.90 | 18.00 | 37.90 |
| oak | 1C@.317 | sf | 23.50 | 18.00 | 41.50 |
| walnut | 1C@.317 | sf | 32.30 | 18.00 | 50.30 |
| 24" deep, replace | | | | | |
| paint-grade pine | 1C@.332 | sf | 20.70 | 18.90 | 39.60 |
| stain-grade pine | 1C@.332 | sf | 24.20 | 18.90 | 43.10 |
| mahogany | 1C@.332 | sf | 26.00 | 18.90 | 44.90 |
| oak | 1C@.332 | sf | 30.90 | 18.90 | 49.80 |
| walnut | 1C@.332 | sf | 42.40 | 18.90 | 61.30 |
| All bookcases, any wood species or depth | | | | | |
| remove | 1D@.051 | sf | — | 1.98 | 1.98 |

**Fireplace mantel beam.** Includes mantel beam, fasteners, and installation labor. Some custom fitting to match is included. Does not include wall framing, masonry work, caulking, sanding, or painting.

| | Craft@Hrs | Unit | Material | Labor | Total |
|---|---|---|---|---|---|
| Replace fireplace mantel beam | | | | | |
| rough sawn | 1C@.539 | lf | 12.50 | 30.70 | 43.20 |
| glue laminated | 1C@.539 | lf | 35.60 | 30.70 | 66.30 |
| All fireplace mantel beams, any type | | | | | |
| remove | 1D@.080 | lf | — | 3.11 | 3.11 |
| remove for work, then reinstall | 6C@.799 | lf | — | 39.70 | 39.70 |

economy                          high                          custom

standard                          deluxe                          custom deluxe

| | Craft@Hrs | Unit | Material | Labor | Total |
|---|---|---|---|---|---|

**Fireplace mantel.** Includes manufactured fireplace mantel to match fireplace opening, fasteners, masonry fasteners, and installation labor. Some custom fitting to match walls is included as is assembly of the mantel on site as needed. Does not include masonry work, caulking, sanding, or painting. Measure the LF of mantel width. Economy grade: paint-grade pine with simple pattern and moldings. Standard grade: paint- or stain-grade pine with dentil patterns and fluted pilasters. High grade: red oak, birch or stain-grade pine with a combination of some of the following: carved moldings, carved onlays, embossed patterns, fluted pilasters and face projections. Deluxe and higher grades: cherry or walnut, heart pine, red oak, birch or yellow pine with increasingly elaborate combinations of the elements listed for high grade, as well as the following: heavy hand carvings, carved or ornate (e.g. lion's head) corbels, circular patterns and moldings, round columns, curved pilasters, capitals (Ionic, Tuscan, Scamozzi, Corinthian, etc.), circular opening, paneling or mirror mantel.

| | Craft@Hrs | Unit | Material | Labor | Total |
|---|---|---|---|---|---|
| Replace | | | | | |
| economy grade | 1C@.653 | lf | 68.50 | 37.20 | 105.70 |
| standard grade | 1C@.653 | lf | 146.00 | 37.20 | 183.20 |
| high grade | 1C@.653 | lf | 318.00 | 37.20 | 355.20 |
| deluxe grade | 1C@.653 | lf | 712.00 | 37.20 | 749.20 |
| custom grade | 1C@.653 | lf | 1,420.00 | 37.20 | 1,457.20 |
| custom deluxe grade | 1C@.653 | lf | 2,180.00 | 37.20 | 2,217.20 |
| All grades | | | | | |
| remove | 1D@.094 | lf | — | 3.66 | 3.66 |
| remove for work, then reinstall | 6C@.828 | lf | — | 41.20 | 41.20 |

economy          high          custom

standard          deluxe          custom deluxe

| | Craft@Hrs | Unit | Material | Labor | Total |
|---|---|---|---|---|---|

**Coffered ceiling.** Includes wood underframing and fire-taped drywall for coffers that measure between 42" to 48" on center with installation labor. Depending on grade, may also include finish drywall, millwork, finish hardware, finish plywood, onlays, corbels, and labor to install them. Does not include electrical work or fixtures, prepwork, painting or staining and varnishing. All inside molding joints are coped. Economy grade: coffers are finished drywall with corner bead, inside corners trimmed with 3-1/2" crown mold or similar. Standard grade: coffers and beams finished drywall, inside corners trimmed with vertical pattern moldings. High grade: covered with wood paneling, inside corners trimmed with vertical pattern or embossed moldings and coffers contain panel moldings. Deluxe grade: covered with hardwood plywood, inside corners trimmed with hand-carved moldings. Custom grade: covered with wood paneling, inside corners trimmed with heavy hand-carved moldings, wood onlays at each corner, recessed panels on beams or in coffers, corbels at wall corners. Custom deluxe grade: covered with wood paneling, inside corners trimmed with heavy hand-carved moldings, ornate wood onlays at each corner, recessed panels on beams or in coffers, ornately carved corbels (e.g. lion's head) at wall corners.

| | Craft@Hrs | Unit | Material | Labor | Total |
|---|---|---|---|---|---|
| Replace | | | | | |
| economy grade | 1C@.248 | sf | 13.30 | 14.10 | 27.40 |
| standard grade | 1C@.276 | sf | 18.70 | 15.70 | 34.40 |
| high grade | 1C@.308 | sf | 21.90 | 17.50 | 39.40 |
| deluxe grade | 1C@.347 | sf | 32.60 | 19.70 | 52.30 |
| custom grade | 1C@.430 | sf | 46.40 | 24.50 | 70.90 |
| custom deluxe grade | 1C@.567 | sf | 69.00 | 32.30 | 101.30 |
| All grades | | | | | |
| remove | 1D@.047 | sf | — | 1.83 | 1.83 |

|  | Craft@Hrs | Unit | Material | Labor | Total |
|---|---|---|---|---|---|

**Niche with casing and shelf bracket.** Includes prefabricated niche with shelf bracket and hardware necessary to install in wall, and installation labor. Does not include wall framing. Made of high density polyurethane. Add **17%** to materials cost for niches made from fiber reinforced plaster.

**Replace**

| | | | | | |
|---|---|---|---|---|---|
| standard niche | 1C@1.31 | ea | 236.00 | 74.50 | 310.50 |
| with clamshell top | 1C@1.31 | ea | 415.00 | 74.50 | 489.50 |
| with clamshell top and clamshell shelf bracket | 1C@1.31 | ea | 536.00 | 74.50 | 610.50 |

*standard*

**All types**

| | | | | | |
|---|---|---|---|---|---|
| remove | 1D@.317 | ea | — | 12.30 | 12.30 |
| remove for work, then reinstall | 6C@2.13 | ea | — | 106.00 | 106.00 |

*clamshell top*

*fleur-sawn*         *picket-sawn*         *ball-and-dowel*         *spindle*

**Gingerbread running trim.** Includes manufactured and assembled gingerbread running trim, fasteners, glue as needed, and installation labor. Does not include paint prep, painting, or caulking. Running trim maintains a consistent width and is used in a variety of applications. Paint-grade poplar. Add **30%** to materials cost for red oak.

| | Craft@Hrs | Unit | Material | Labor | Total |
|---|---|---|---|---|---|
| Fleur-sawn, replace | 1C@.160 | lf | 36.30 | 9.10 | 45.40 |
| Picket-sawn, replace | 1C@.160 | lf | 47.00 | 9.10 | 56.10 |
| **Ball-and-dowel, replace** | | | | | |
| 2" wide | 1C@.160 | lf | 11.10 | 9.10 | 20.20 |
| 4" wide | 1C@.160 | lf | 17.00 | 9.10 | 26.10 |
| 6" wide | 1C@.160 | lf | 19.20 | 9.10 | 28.30 |
| 8" wide | 1C@.160 | lf | 22.90 | 9.10 | 32.00 |
| 10" wide | 1C@.160 | lf | 28.90 | 9.10 | 38.00 |
| 12" wide | 1C@.160 | lf | 34.30 | 9.10 | 43.40 |
| 14" wide | 1C@.160 | lf | 41.50 | 9.10 | 50.60 |
| **Spindle, replace** | | | | | |
| 2" wide | 1C@.160 | lf | 10.50 | 9.10 | 19.60 |
| 4" wide | 1C@.160 | lf | 13.10 | 9.10 | 22.20 |
| 6" wide | 1C@.160 | lf | 17.00 | 9.10 | 26.10 |
| 8" wide | 1C@.160 | lf | 20.40 | 9.10 | 29.50 |
| 10" wide | 1C@.160 | lf | 27.80 | 9.10 | 36.90 |
| 12" wide | 1C@.160 | lf | 33.40 | 9.10 | 42.50 |
| 14" wide | 1C@.160 | lf | 40.70 | 9.10 | 49.80 |
| **All styles and sizes** | | | | | |
| remove | 1D@.038 | lf | — | 1.48 | 1.48 |
| remove for work, then reinstall | 6C@.224 | lf | — | 11.10 | 11.10 |

|  | Craft@Hrs | Unit | Material | Labor | Total |
|---|---|---|---|---|---|

**Gingerbread bracket.** Includes manufactured and assembled bracket, fasteners, glue as needed, and installation labor. Does not include paint prep, painting, or caulking. All grades made from paint-grade poplar. Add **30%** to materials cost for red oak.

| Replace | | | | | |
|---|---|---|---|---|---|
| standard grade, longest leg up to 12" long | 1C@.348 | ea | 38.80 | 19.80 | 58.60 |
| high grade, longest leg up to 23" long | 1C@.348 | ea | 47.00 | 19.80 | 66.80 |
| deluxe grade, longest leg up to 30" long | 1C@.348 | ea | 51.80 | 19.80 | 71.60 |
| custom grade, longest leg up to 30" long, | | | | | |
|    with very ornate sawn pattern | 1C@.348 | ea | 58.70 | 19.80 | 78.50 |
| All grades | | | | | |
|    remove | 1D@.154 | ea | — | 5.99 | 5.99 |

**Gingerbread fan bracket.** Includes manufactured and assembled gingerbread fan bracket, fasteners, glue as needed, and installation labor. Does not include paint prep, painting, or caulking. Arched spandrels have arched end sections that typically contain either sawn woodwork or a spindle fan. The higher the grade the longer the leg against the wall and the more ornate the sawn woodwork. Highest grades may include post drops in the center section. All grades made from paint-grade poplar. Add **30%** to materials cost for red oak.

| Replace | | | | | |
|---|---|---|---|---|---|
| standard grade, longest leg up to 14" long | 1C@.348 | ea | 46.10 | 19.80 | 65.90 |
| high grade, longest leg up to 25" long | 1C@.348 | ea | 51.60 | 19.80 | 71.40 |
| deluxe grade, longest leg up to 32" long | 1C@.348 | ea | 64.00 | 19.80 | 83.80 |
| custom grade, longest leg up to 32" long, | | | | | |
|    with very ornate sawn pattern | 1C@.348 | ea | 81.80 | 19.80 | 101.60 |
| All grades | | | | | |
|    remove | 1D@.154 | ea | — | 5.99 | 5.99 |

**Gingerbread post bracket.** Includes turned or sawn elements in post bracket with fasteners, glue as needed, and installation labor. Does not include paint prep, painting, or caulking. Made from paint-grade poplar. Add **30%** to materials cost for red oak. The higher the grade the more ornate the pattern.

| Replace | | | | | |
|---|---|---|---|---|---|
| standard grade | 1C@.348 | ea | 59.40 | 19.80 | 79.20 |
| high grade | 1C@.348 | ea | 74.10 | 19.80 | 93.90 |
| deluxe grade | 1C@.348 | ea | 86.80 | 19.80 | 106.60 |
| All grades | | | | | |
|    remove | 1D@.154 | ea | — | 5.99 | 5.99 |
|    remove for work, then reinstall | 6C@.431 | ea | — | 21.40 | 21.40 |

| | Craft@Hrs | Unit | Material | Labor | Total |
|---|---|---|---|---|---|

**Gingerbread corbel.** Includes manufactured and assembled corbel, fasteners, glue as needed, and installation labor. Does not include paint prep, painting, or caulking. All grades made from paint-grade poplar. Add **30%** to materials cost for red oak. Simple sawn patterns for standard and high grades, other grades more ornate.

| | Craft@Hrs | Unit | Material | Labor | Total |
|---|---|---|---|---|---|
| Replace | | | | | |
| standard grade, longest leg up to 12" long | 1C@.359 | ea | 42.40 | 20.40 | 62.80 |
| high grade, longest leg up to 16" long | 1C@.359 | ea | 61.90 | 20.40 | 82.30 |
| deluxe grade, longest leg up to 20" long | 1C@.359 | ea | 85.60 | 20.40 | 106.00 |
| custom grade, longest leg up to 20" long, with very ornate sawn pattern | 1C@.359 | ea | 124.00 | 20.40 | 144.40 |
| All grades | | | | | |
| remove | 1D@.160 | ea | — | 6.22 | 6.22 |
| remove for work, then reinstall | 6C@.434 | ea | — | 21.60 | 21.60 |

**Gingerbread door or window header.** Includes manufactured and assembled gingerbread door or window header, fasteners, glue as needed, and installation labor. Does not include paint prep, painting, or caulking. All grades made from paint-grade poplar. Add **30%** to materials cost for red oak.

| | Craft@Hrs | Unit | Material | Labor | Total |
|---|---|---|---|---|---|
| Replace | | | | | |
| standard grade, up to 14" long | 1C@.232 | lf | 63.20 | 13.20 | 76.40 |
| high grade, up to 25" long | 1C@.232 | lf | 88.30 | 13.20 | 101.50 |
| deluxe grade, up to 36" long | 1C@.232 | lf | 119.00 | 13.20 | 132.20 |
| All grades | | | | | |
| remove | 1D@.037 | lf | — | 1.44 | 1.44 |
| remove for work, then reinstall | 6C@.333 | lf | — | 16.60 | 16.60 |

**Gingerbread post drop.** Includes turned or sawn post drop with fasteners, glue as needed, and installation labor. Does not include paint prep, painting, or caulking. Paint-grade poplar. Add **30%** to materials cost for red oak.

| | Craft@Hrs | Unit | Material | Labor | Total |
|---|---|---|---|---|---|
| Replace | | | | | |
| 10" long | 1C@.322 | ea | 9.42 | 18.30 | 27.72 |
| 12" long | 1C@.322 | ea | 11.70 | 18.30 | 30.00 |
| 18" long | 1C@.322 | ea | 14.00 | 18.30 | 32.30 |
| 24" long | 1C@.322 | ea | 16.70 | 18.30 | 35.00 |
| All sizes | | | | | |
| remove | 1D@.154 | ea | — | 5.99 | 5.99 |
| remove for work, then reinstall | 6C@.410 | ea | — | 20.40 | 20.40 |

| | Craft@Hrs | Unit | Material | Labor | Total |
|---|---|---|---|---|---|

**Gingerbread spandrel.** Includes manufactured and assembled gingerbread spandrel, fasteners, glue as needed, and installation labor. Spandrels come in typical opening sizes or can be custom-ordered to fit. Does not include paint prep, painting, or caulking. Spandrels are horizontal decorative elements for exterior and interior openings. Typically both corners and the center contain sawn elements. The remaining space is filled with either ball-and-dowel or spindle elements. All grades made from paint-grade poplar. Add **30%** to materials cost for red oak.

| | Craft@Hrs | Unit | Material | Labor | Total |
|---|---|---|---|---|---|
| Replace | | | | | |
| standard grade, up to 6" deep in center, legs up to 14" long | 1C@.237 | lf | 30.20 | 13.50 | 43.70 |
| high grade, up to 9" deep in center, legs up to 17" long | 1C@.237 | lf | 38.10 | 13.50 | 51.60 |
| custom grade, up to 13" deep in center, legs up to 21" long | 1C@.237 | lf | 49.80 | 13.50 | 63.30 |
| deluxe grade, up to 16" deep in center, legs up to 24" long | 1C@.237 | lf | 67.60 | 13.50 | 81.10 |
| custom deluxe grade, up to 22" deep in center, legs up to 31" long | 6C@.272 | lf | 84.90 | 13.50 | 98.40 |
| All grades | | | | | |
| remove | 1D@.038 | lf | — | 1.48 | 1.48 |
| remove for work, then reinstall | 6C@.341 | lf | — | 16.90 | 16.90 |

*high*

*deluxe*

**Gingerbread arch spandrel.** Includes manufactured to size and assembled arch spandrel, fasteners, glue as needed, and installation labor. Does not include paint prep, painting, or caulking. Also does not include extra work or trim that may be required when installing in out-of-plumb structures. Arched spandrels have arched end sections that typically contain either sawn woodwork or a spindle fan. The higher the grade the longer the leg against the wall and the more ornate the sawn woodwork. Highest grades may include post drops in the center section. All grades made from paint-grade poplar. Add **30%** to materials cost for red oak.

| | Craft@Hrs | Unit | Material | Labor | Total |
|---|---|---|---|---|---|
| Replace | | | | | |
| standard grade, legs up to 12" long | 1C@.237 | lf | 57.70 | 13.50 | 71.20 |
| high grade, legs up to 20" long | 1C@.237 | lf | 71.80 | 13.50 | 85.30 |
| custom grade, legs up to 22" long | 1C@.237 | lf | 82.90 | 13.50 | 96.40 |
| deluxe grade, legs up to 26" long | 1C@.237 | lf | 92.90 | 13.50 | 106.40 |
| Replace custom deluxe grade, legs up to 28" long | 1C@.237 | lf | 109.00 | 13.50 | 122.50 |
| All grades | | | | | |
| remove | 1D@.038 | lf | — | 1.48 | 1.48 |
| remove for work, then reinstall | 6C@.341 | lf | — | 16.90 | 16.90 |

*custom*

*custom deluxe*

| | Craft@Hrs | Unit | Material | Labor | Total |
|---|---|---|---|---|---|

standard    high    deluxe    custom deluxe

**Gingerbread window cornice.** Includes manufactured and assembled gingerbread window cornice, fasteners, glue as needed, and installation labor. Window cornices come in typical opening sizes or can be custom-ordered to fit. Does not include paint prep, painting, or caulking. All grades made from paint-grade poplar. Add **30%** to materials cost for red oak. Standard grade: made from finish board with bed mold on top and simple panel mold on bottom. High grade: side brackets with sawn drop, front cornice of 2" to 4" ball-and-dowel running trim. Deluxe grade: side brackets with sawn drop and spindles, front cornice of 6" to 8" spindle running trim with sawn work at center. Custom grade: side brackets with sawn drop and spindles, front cornice of 6" to 8" spindle running trim with very ornately sawn woodwork at center.

| | Craft@Hrs | Unit | Material | Labor | Total |
|---|---|---|---|---|---|
| **Replace** | | | | | |
| standard grade, 5" deep and 6" high | 1C@.242 | lf | 28.40 | 13.80 | 42.20 |
| high grade, 5-1/2" deep and 8-1/2" high | 1C@.242 | lf | 35.30 | 13.80 | 49.10 |
| deluxe grade, 8" deep and 9" high | 1C@.242 | lf | 44.60 | 13.80 | 58.40 |
| custom grade, 8" deep and 9" high | 1C@.242 | lf | 46.40 | 13.80 | 60.20 |
| custom deluxe grade, 8" deep and 9" high | 1C@.242 | lf | 54.00 | 13.80 | 67.80 |
| **All grades** | | | | | |
| remove | 1D@.041 | lf | — | 1.59 | 1.59 |
| remove for work, then reinstall | 6C@.352 | lf | — | 17.50 | 17.50 |

**Gingerbread gable ornament.** Includes manufactured and assembled gable ornament built to match the slope of the roof, fasteners, glue as needed, and installation labor. Does not include paint prep, painting, or caulking. Gable ornaments can be ordered for roofs of any slope. They are typically found on roofs with a slope of 6-in-12 or more. Ornaments are placed in the gables at the peak of the roof. All grades are made from paint-grade poplar. Add **30%** to materials cost for red oak.

| | Craft@Hrs | Unit | Material | Labor | Total |
|---|---|---|---|---|---|
| **Replace** | | | | | |
| standard grade, longest leg up to 32" | 1C@.582 | ea | 162.00 | 33.10 | 195.10 |
| high grade, longest leg up to 36" | 1C@.582 | ea | 278.00 | 33.10 | 311.10 |
| deluxe grade, longest leg up to 45" | 1C@.582 | ea | 423.00 | 33.10 | 456.10 |
| custom grade, longest leg up to 48" | 1C@.582 | ea | 748.00 | 33.10 | 781.10 |
| custom deluxe grade, longest leg up to 60" | 1C@.582 | ea | 912.00 | 33.10 | 945.10 |
| **All grades** | | | | | |
| remove | 1D@.254 | ea | — | 9.88 | 9.88 |
| remove for work, then reinstall | 6C@1.08 | ea | — | 53.70 | 53.70 |

standard

custom deluxe

**Gingerbread gable finial.** Includes turned or sawn gable finial with fasteners, glue as needed, and installation labor. Does not include paint prep, painting, or caulking. Finials are placed at the peak of the roof on each end. All grades are made from cedar.

| | Craft@Hrs | Unit | Material | Labor | Total |
|---|---|---|---|---|---|
| **Replace** | | | | | |
| standard grade, with 28" post | 1C@.560 | ea | 100.00 | 31.90 | 131.90 |
| high grade, with 34" post | 1C@.560 | ea | 135.00 | 31.90 | 166.90 |
| **All grades** | | | | | |
| remove | 1D@.239 | ea | — | 9.30 | 9.30 |
| remove for work, then reinstall | 6C@1.03 | ea | — | 51.20 | 51.20 |

| | Craft@Hrs | Unit | Material | Labor | Total |
|---|---|---|---|---|---|

**Porch post.** Includes post, hardware, and installation labor. Does not include bracing. For stain-grade pine add **16%** to material costs. Non-laminated posts made from clear, select Douglas fir or clear all-heart redwood. Standard grade posts may be made from cedar. Square posts are hollow and include a structural post inside. Standard grade: turned post, sometimes called colonist style. High grade: turned post with flutes, or square post with flutes trimmed with molding at base, 1/3 up the shaft and 12" to 16" from the top. Deluxe grade: turned post with spiral pattern or square post with flutes trimmed with panels 1/3 up the shaft, capped at base and top of panels with moldings and molding trim about 12" to 16" from top.

| | Craft@Hrs | Unit | Material | Labor | Total |
|---|---|---|---|---|---|
| **Replace 4" x 4" porch post** | | | | | |
| standard grade | 1C@.135 | lf | 11.60 | 7.68 | 19.28 |
| high grade | 1C@.135 | lf | 23.20 | 7.68 | 30.88 |
| deluxe grade | 1C@.135 | lf | 65.60 | 7.68 | 73.28 |
| **Replace 6" x 6" porch post** | | | | | |
| standard grade | 1C@.135 | lf | 17.30 | 7.68 | 24.98 |
| high grade | 1C@.135 | lf | 34.80 | 7.68 | 42.48 |
| deluxe grade | 1C@.135 | lf | 43.60 | 7.68 | 51.28 |
| **Replace 8" x 8" porch post** | | | | | |
| standard grade | 1C@.135 | lf | 19.60 | 7.68 | 27.28 |
| high grade | 1C@.135 | lf | 39.50 | 7.68 | 47.18 |
| deluxe grade | 1C@.135 | lf | 49.80 | 7.68 | 57.48 |
| **All sizes and grades of porch post** | | | | | |
| remove | 1D@.127 | lf | — | 4.94 | 4.94 |
| remove for work, then reinstall | 6C@.216 | lf | — | 10.70 | 10.70 |

*standard*   *high*   *high*   *deluxe*

*acanthus*   *ribbon*   *grape*   *shell*   *floral*

**Carved wood onlay.** Includes wood onlay, finish nails or brads, glue as needed, and installation labor. Does not include sanding, caulking, or finishing. Onlays are available in a wide variety of styles and prices. Use these listings as indicators of complexity and price range. Made from maple. Add **25%** to material costs for red oak.

| | Craft@Hrs | Unit | Material | Labor | Total |
|---|---|---|---|---|---|
| **Replace small carved wood onlay** | | | | | |
| acanthus | 1C@.519 | ea | 45.10 | 29.50 | 74.60 |
| ribbon | 1C@.519 | ea | 47.20 | 29.50 | 76.70 |
| grape | 1C@.519 | ea | 75.80 | 29.50 | 105.30 |
| shell | 1C@.519 | ea | 66.20 | 29.50 | 95.70 |
| floral | 1C@.519 | ea | 69.20 | 29.50 | 98.70 |
| **Replace medium carved wood onlay** | | | | | |
| acanthus | 1C@.519 | ea | 70.20 | 29.50 | 99.70 |
| ribbon | 1C@.519 | ea | 73.60 | 29.50 | 103.10 |
| grape | 1C@.519 | ea | 117.00 | 29.50 | 146.50 |
| shell | 1C@.519 | ea | 103.00 | 29.50 | 132.50 |
| floral | 1C@.519 | ea | 107.00 | 29.50 | 136.50 |

| | Craft@Hrs | Unit | Material | Labor | Total |
|---|---|---|---|---|---|
| **Replace large carved wood onlay** | | | | | |
| acanthus | 1C@.519 | ea | 89.30 | 29.50 | 118.80 |
| ribbon | 1C@.519 | ea | 94.70 | 29.50 | 124.20 |
| grape | 1C@.519 | ea | 146.00 | 29.50 | 175.50 |
| shell | 1C@.519 | ea | 131.00 | 29.50 | 160.50 |
| floral | 1C@.519 | ea | 135.00 | 29.50 | 164.50 |
| **All grades and styles of onlay** | | | | | |
| remove | 1D@.062 | ea | — | 2.41 | 2.41 |
| remove for work, then reinstall | 6C@.743 | ea | — | 36.90 | 36.90 |

**Finish board.** Includes finish nails and installation. S4S = Smooth four sides. Includes 4% waste.

| | Craft@Hrs | Unit | Material | Labor | Total |
|---|---|---|---|---|---|
| **Replace S4S select pine finish board** | | | | | |
| 1" x 2" | 1C@.049 | lf | .80 | 2.79 | 3.59 |
| 1" x 4" | 1C@.049 | lf | 1.56 | 2.79 | 4.35 |
| 1" x 6" | 1C@.049 | lf | 2.37 | 2.79 | 5.16 |
| 1" x 8" | 1C@.049 | lf | 3.17 | 2.79 | 5.96 |
| 1" x 10" | 1C@.049 | lf | 3.94 | 2.79 | 6.73 |
| 1" x 12" | 1C@.049 | lf | 4.72 | 2.79 | 7.51 |
| **Replace other wood species S4S finish board** | | | | | |
| add for S4S poplar | — | % | 3.0 | — | — |
| add for S4S mahogany | — | % | 13.0 | — | — |
| add for S4S red oak | — | % | 17.0 | — | — |
| **Other finish board costs, replace** | | | | | |
| add for bullnose on 1 x boards | — | lf | .73 | — | .73 |
| **All sizes and wood species of S4S finish board** | | | | | |
| remove | 1D@.026 | lf | — | 1.01 | 1.01 |
| remove for work, then reinstall | 6C@.080 | lf | — | 3.98 | 3.98 |

**1/4" finish veneer plywood.** Includes finish nails and installation.

| | Craft@Hrs | Unit | Material | Labor | Total |
|---|---|---|---|---|---|
| **Replace** | | | | | |
| aromatic cedar | 1C@.028 | sf | 3.70 | 1.59 | 5.29 |
| birch | 1C@.028 | sf | 3.58 | 1.59 | 5.17 |
| cherry | 1C@.028 | sf | 4.00 | 1.59 | 5.59 |
| chestnut | 1C@.028 | sf | 6.31 | 1.59 | 7.90 |
| knotty pine | 1C@.028 | sf | 2.81 | 1.59 | 4.40 |
| lauan mahogany | 1C@.028 | sf | 1.42 | 1.59 | 3.01 |
| mahogany | 1C@.028 | sf | 4.04 | 1.59 | 5.63 |
| pecan | 1C@.028 | sf | 4.14 | 1.59 | 5.73 |
| red oak | 1C@.028 | sf | 3.62 | 1.59 | 5.21 |
| rosewood | 1C@.028 | sf | 5.59 | 1.59 | 7.18 |
| teak | 1C@.028 | sf | 7.42 | 1.59 | 9.01 |
| walnut | 1C@.028 | sf | 5.35 | 1.59 | 6.94 |
| **All wood species of 1/4" finish veneer plywood** | | | | | |
| remove | 1D@.022 | sf | — | .86 | .86 |
| remove for work, then reinstall | 6C@.042 | sf | — | 2.09 | 2.09 |

| | Craft@Hrs | Unit | Material | Labor | Total |
|---|---|---|---|---|---|
| **Time & Material Charts** (selected items) **Finish Carpentry Materials** | | | | | |
| Clamshell base | | | | | |
| 1-1/2" stain-grade pine ($1.19 lf, 1 lf), 7% waste | — | lf | 1.27 | — | 1.27 |
| 3-1/2" stain-grade pine ($1.91 lf, 1 lf), 7% waste | — | lf | 2.04 | — | 2.04 |
| Pattern base | | | | | |
| 1-1/2" stain-grade pine ($1.42 lf, 1 lf), 7% waste | — | lf | 1.52 | — | 1.52 |
| 2-1/2" stain-grade pine ($2.31 lf, 1 lf), 7% waste | — | lf | 2.47 | — | 2.47 |
| 3-1/2" stain-grade pine ($3.05 lf, 1 lf), 7% waste | — | lf | 3.26 | — | 3.26 |
| Base shoe | | | | | |
| 3/4" stain-grade pine ($.72 lf, 1 lf), 7% waste | — | lf | .77 | — | .77 |
| Clamshell casing | | | | | |
| 1-1/2" stain-grade pine ($1.24 lf, 1 lf), 5% waste | — | lf | 1.30 | — | 1.30 |
| 2-1/2" stain-grade pine ($1.40 lf, 1 lf), 5% waste | — | lf | 1.47 | — | 1.47 |
| 3-1/2" stain-grade pine ($1.99 lf, 1 lf), 5% waste | — | lf | 2.09 | — | 2.09 |
| Pattern casing | | | | | |
| 1-1/2" stain-grade pine ($1.50 lf, 1 lf), 5% waste | — | lf | 1.58 | — | 1.58 |
| 2-1/2" stain-grade pine ($2.40 lf, 1 lf), 5% waste | — | lf | 2.52 | — | 2.52 |
| 3-1/2" stain-grade pine ($3.19 lf, 1 lf), 5% waste | — | lf | 3.35 | — | 3.35 |
| Window moldings | | | | | |
| 2-1/2" stain-grade pine stool ($2.70 lf, 1 lf), 4% waste | — | lf | 2.81 | — | 2.81 |
| 3-1/2" stain-grade pine apron ($1.77 lf, 1 lf), 4% waste | — | lf | 1.84 | — | 1.84 |
| Chair rail | | | | | |
| 2-1/2" stain-grade pine ($2.34 lf, 1 lf), 4% waste | — | lf | 2.43 | — | 2.43 |
| 3-1/2" stain-grade pine ($2.95 lf, 1 lf), 4% waste | — | lf | 3.07 | — | 3.07 |
| Drip cap | | | | | |
| 1-5/8" redwood ($2.17 lf, 1 lf), 4% waste | — | lf | 2.26 | — | 2.26 |
| 2-1/4" redwood ($2.41 lf, 1 lf), 4% waste | — | lf | 2.51 | — | 2.51 |

| | Craft@Hrs | Unit | Material | Labor | Total |
|---|---|---|---|---|---|
| **Astragal** | | | | | |
| 1-3/4" stain-grade pine | | | | | |
| ($4.47 lf, 1 lf), 4% waste | — | lf | 4.65 | — | 4.65 |
| 2-1/4" stain-grade pine | | | | | |
| ($5.43 lf, 1 lf), 4% waste | — | lf | 5.65 | — | 5.65 |
| **Cove** | | | | | |
| 1/2" stain-grade pine | | | | | |
| ($.85 lf, 1 lf), 4% waste | — | lf | .88 | — | .88 |
| 3/4" stain-grade pine | | | | | |
| ($.95 lf, 1 lf), 4% waste | — | lf | .99 | — | .99 |
| 1" stain-grade pine | | | | | |
| ($1.18 lf, 1 lf), 4% waste | — | lf | 1.23 | — | 1.23 |
| 2-1/2" stain-grade pine | | | | | |
| ($2.10 lf, 1 lf), 4% waste | — | lf | 2.18 | — | 2.18 |
| 3-1/2" stain-grade pine | | | | | |
| ($2.71 lf, 1 lf), 4% waste | — | lf | 2.82 | — | 2.82 |
| **Half-round** | | | | | |
| 1" stain-grade pine | | | | | |
| ($.99 lf, 1 lf), 4% waste | — | lf | 1.03 | — | 1.03 |
| 2" stain-grade pine | | | | | |
| ($1.38 lf, 1 lf), 4% waste | — | lf | 1.44 | — | 1.44 |
| **Quarter-round** | | | | | |
| 1/2" stain-grade pine | | | | | |
| ($.72 lf, 1 lf), 4% waste | — | lf | .75 | — | .75 |
| 3/4" stain-grade pine | | | | | |
| ($.87 lf, 1 lf), 4% waste | — | lf | .90 | — | .90 |
| 1" stain-grade pine | | | | | |
| ($1.53 lf, 1 lf), 4% waste | — | lf | 1.59 | — | 1.59 |
| **Corner bead** | | | | | |
| stain-grade pine | | | | | |
| ($1.69 lf, 1 lf), 4% waste | — | lf | 1.76 | — | 1.76 |
| turned stain-grade pine with finials | | | | | |
| ($18.60 lf, 1 lf), 4% waste | — | lf | 19.30 | — | 19.30 |
| clear plastic | | | | | |
| ($1.31 lf, 1 lf), 4% waste | — | lf | 1.36 | — | 1.36 |
| **Bed mold** | | | | | |
| 2-1/2" stain-grade pine | | | | | |
| ($2.36 lf, 1 lf), 4% waste | — | lf | 2.45 | — | 2.45 |
| **Crown** | | | | | |
| 3-1/2" stain-grade pine ($3.02 lf, 1 lf), 4% waste | — | lf | 3.14 | — | 3.14 |
| 4-1/2" stain-grade pine ($4.45 lf, 1 lf), 4% waste | — | lf | 4.63 | — | 4.63 |
| **Hand rail** | | | | | |
| stain-grade pine ($4.45 lf, 1 lf), 4% waste | — | lf | 4.63 | — | 4.63 |

| | Craft@Hrs | Unit | Material | Labor | Total |
|---|---|---|---|---|---|
| Specialty moldings, 3/4" | | | | | |
| stain-grade pine with vertical milling ($3.55 lf, 1 lf), 4% waste | — | lf | 3.69 | — | 3.69 |
| stain-grade pine embossed ($2.08 lf, 1 lf), 4% waste | — | lf | 2.16 | — | 2.16 |
| stain-grade pine with hand carving ($6.54 lf, 1 lf), 4% waste | — | lf | 6.80 | — | 6.80 |
| stain-grade pine with heavy hand carving ($12.80 lf, 1 lf), 4% waste | — | lf | 13.30 | — | 13.30 |
| Specialty moldings, 1-1/2" | | | | | |
| stain-grade pine with vertical milling ($4.04 lf, 1 lf), 4% waste | — | lf | 4.20 | — | 4.20 |
| stain-grade pine embossed ($2.39 lf, 1 lf), 4% waste | — | lf | 2.49 | — | 2.49 |
| stain-grade pine with hand carving ($7.47 lf, 1 lf), 4% waste | — | lf | 7.77 | — | 7.77 |
| stain-grade pine with heavy hand carving ($14.30 lf, 1 lf), 4% waste | — | lf | 14.90 | — | 14.90 |
| Specialty moldings, 2-1/2" | | | | | |
| stain-grade pine with vertical milling ($4.56 lf, 1 lf), 4% waste | — | lf | 4.74 | — | 4.74 |
| stain-grade pine embossed ($2.68 lf, 1 lf), 4% waste | — | lf | 2.79 | — | 2.79 |
| stain-grade pine with hand carving ($8.37 lf, 1 lf), 4% waste | — | lf | 8.70 | — | 8.70 |
| stain-grade pine with heavy hand carving ($16.20 lf, 1 lf), 4% waste | — | lf | 16.85 | — | 16.85 |
| Specialty moldings, 3-1/2" | | | | | |
| stain-grade pine with vertical milling ($5.03 lf, 1 lf), 4% waste | — | lf | 5.23 | — | 5.23 |
| stain-grade pine embossed ($2.98 lf, 1 lf), 4% waste | — | lf | 3.10 | — | 3.10 |
| stain-grade pine with hand carving ($9.31 lf, 1 lf), 4% waste | — | lf | 9.68 | — | 9.68 |
| stain-grade pine with heavy hand carving ($18.30 lf, 1 lf), 4% waste | — | lf | 19.00 | — | 19.00 |
| Specialty moldings, 5" | | | | | |
| stain-grade pine with vertical milling ($7.26 lf, 1 lf), 4% waste | — | lf | 7.55 | — | 7.55 |
| stain-grade pine embossed ($4.29 lf, 1 lf), 4% waste | — | lf | 4.46 | — | 4.46 |
| stain-grade pine with hand carving ($13.30 lf, 1 lf), 4% waste | — | lf | 13.80 | — | 13.80 |
| stain-grade pine with heavy hand carving ($26.20 lf, 1 lf), 4% waste | — | lf | 27.20 | — | 27.20 |

| | Craft@Hrs | Unit | Material | Labor | Total |
|---|---|---|---|---|---|
| **Specialty moldings, 8"** | | | | | |
| stain-grade pine with vertical milling | | | | | |
| ($11.80 lf, 1 lf), 4% waste | — | lf | 12.30 | — | 12.30 |
| stain-grade pine embossed | | | | | |
| ($7.02 lf, 1 lf), 4% waste | — | lf | 7.30 | — | 7.30 |
| stain-grade pine with hand carving | | | | | |
| ($21.90 lf, 1 lf), 4% waste | — | lf | 22.80 | — | 22.80 |
| stain-grade pine with heavy hand carving | | | | | |
| ($42.90 lf, 1 lf), 4% waste | — | lf | 44.60 | — | 44.60 |
| **Custom-milled moldings** | | | | | |
| molder setup charge, ($232.00 ea) | — | ea | 232.00 | — | 232.00 |
| molder custom knife charges, ($503.00 ea) | — | ea | 503.00 | — | 503.00 |
| 2" to 3" pine, ($2.29 lf, 1 lf), 4% waste | — | lf | 2.38 | — | 2.38 |
| 2" to 3" poplar, ($2.52 lf, 1 lf), 4% waste | — | lf | 2.62 | — | 2.62 |
| 2" to 3" mahogany, ($3.02 lf, 1 lf), 4% waste | — | lf | 3.14 | — | 3.14 |
| 2" to 3" red oak, ($3.30 lf, 1 lf), 4% waste | — | lf | 3.43 | — | 3.43 |
| **Inside corner radius for panel molding** | | | | | |
| standard | | | | | |
| ($2.30 ea, 1 ea), 4% waste | — | ea | 2.39 | — | 2.39 |
| with heavy carving | | | | | |
| ($11.80 ea, 1 ea), 4% waste | — | ea | 12.30 | — | 12.30 |
| **Closet work** | | | | | |
| shelf brackets, shelving, & rod | | | | | |
| ($13.40 lf, 1 lf), 4% waste | — | lf | 13.90 | — | 13.90 |
| organizer system, standard grade | | | | | |
| ($12.40 sf, 1 sf), 4% waste | — | sf | 12.90 | — | 12.90 |
| organizer system, deluxe grade | | | | | |
| ($19.20 sf, 1 sf), 4% waste | — | sf | 20.00 | — | 20.00 |
| linen closet shelves, standard grade | | | | | |
| ($9.97 lf, 1 lf), 4% waste | — | lf | 10.40 | — | 10.40 |
| linen closet pull-out shelves | | | | | |
| ($12.70 ea, 1 ea), 4% waste | — | ea | 13.20 | — | 13.20 |
| closet rod, pine | | | | | |
| ($3.80 lf, 1 lf), 4% waste | — | lf | 3.95 | — | 3.95 |
| **Built-in bookcase** | | | | | |
| 8" deep stain-grade pine | | | | | |
| ($10.20 sf, 1 sf), 4% waste | — | sf | 10.60 | — | 10.60 |
| 12" deep stain-grade pine | | | | | |
| ($13.40 sf, 1 sf), 4% waste | — | sf | 13.90 | — | 13.90 |
| 18" deep stain-grade pine | | | | | |
| ($17.70 sf, 1 sf), 4% waste | — | sf | 18.40 | — | 18.40 |
| 24" deep stain-grade pine | | | | | |
| ($23.20 sf, 1 sf), 4% waste | — | sf | 24.10 | — | 24.10 |
| **Fireplace mantel beam** | | | | | |
| rough sawn, ($11.90 lf, 1 lf), 4% waste | — | lf | 12.40 | — | 12.40 |
| glue laminated, ($33.90 lf, 1 lf), 4% waste | — | lf | 35.30 | — | 35.30 |
| **Fireplace mantel** | | | | | |
| economy grade ($68.50 lf, 1 lf) | — | lf | 71.20 | — | 71.20 |
| custom deluxe grade ($2,170.00 lf, 1 lf) | — | lf | 2,260.00 | — | 2,260.00 |

| | Craft@Hrs | Unit | Material | Labor | Total |
|---|---|---|---|---|---|
| Coffered ceiling | | | | | |
| economy grade, ($11.40 sf, 1 sf), 12% waste | — | sf | 12.80 | — | 12.80 |
| custom deluxe grade, ($59.80 sf, 1 sf), 12% waste | — | sf | 67.00 | — | 67.00 |
| Niche with casing and shelf bracket | | | | | |
| standard | — | ea | 236.00 | — | 236.00 |
| with clamshell top | — | ea | 415.00 | — | 415.00 |
| clamshell top and clamshell shelf | — | ea | 536.00 | — | 536.00 |
| Gingerbread running trim | | | | | |
| fleur-sawn, ($35.70 lf, 1 lf), 2% waste | — | lf | 36.40 | — | 36.40 |
| picket-sawn, ($46.10 lf, 1 lf), 2% waste | — | lf | 47.00 | — | 47.00 |
| 2" ball-and-dowel, ($10.90 lf, 1 lf), 2% waste | — | lf | 11.10 | — | 11.10 |
| 14" ball-and-dowel, ($40.40 lf, 1 lf), 2% waste | — | lf | 41.20 | — | 41.20 |
| 2" spindle, ($10.30 lf, 1 lf), 2% waste | — | lf | 10.50 | — | 10.50 |
| 14" spindle, ($39.70 lf, 1 lf), 2% waste | — | lf | 40.50 | — | 40.50 |
| Gingerbread bracket | | | | | |
| standard grade, ($38.80 ea) | — | ea | 38.80 | — | 38.80 |
| custom grade, ($58.70 ea) | — | ea | 58.70 | — | 58.70 |
| Gingerbread fan bracket | | | | | |
| standard grade, ($46.10 ea) | — | ea | 46.10 | — | 46.10 |
| custom grade, ($81.80 ea) | — | ea | 81.80 | — | 81.80 |
| Gingerbread post bracket | | | | | |
| standard grade, ($59.40 ea) | — | ea | 59.40 | — | 59.40 |
| deluxe grade, ($86.80 ea) | — | ea | 86.80 | — | 86.80 |
| Gingerbread corbel | | | | | |
| standard grade, ($42.40 ea) | — | ea | 42.40 | — | 42.40 |
| custom grade, ($124.00 ea) | — | ea | 124.00 | — | 124.00 |
| Gingerbread door or window header | | | | | |
| standard grade, ($63.20 ea) | — | ea | 63.20 | — | 63.20 |
| deluxe grade, ($119.00 ea) | — | ea | 119.00 | — | 119.00 |
| Gingerbread post drop | | | | | |
| 10", ($9.42 ea) | — | ea | 9.42 | — | 9.42 |
| 24", ($16.60 ea) | — | ea | 16.60 | — | 16.60 |
| Gingerbread spandrel | | | | | |
| standard grade, ($30.20 lf) | — | lf | 30.20 | — | 30.20 |
| custom deluxe grade, ($84.90 lf) | — | lf | 84.90 | — | 84.90 |
| Gingerbread arch spandrel | | | | | |
| standard grade, ($57.70 lf) | — | lf | 57.70 | — | 57.70 |
| custom deluxe grade, ($109.00 lf) | — | lf | 109.00 | — | 109.00 |
| Gingerbread window cornice | | | | | |
| standard grade, ($28.40 lf) | — | lf | 28.40 | — | 28.40 |
| custom deluxe grade, ($54.00 lf) | — | lf | 54.00 | — | 54.00 |
| Gingerbread gable ornament | | | | | |
| standard grade, ($162.00 ea) | — | ea | 162.00 | — | 162.00 |
| custom deluxe grade, ($912.00 ea) | — | ea | 912.00 | — | 912.00 |
| Gingerbread gable finial | | | | | |
| standard grade, ($99.70 ea) | — | ea | 99.70 | — | 99.70 |
| high grade, ($135.00 ea) | — | ea | 135.00 | — | 135.00 |

|  | Craft@Hrs | Unit | Material | Labor | Total |
|---|---|---|---|---|---|
| **Porch post** | | | | | |
| 4" x 4", standard grade | | | | | |
| ($92.90 8' post, 8 lf), 0% waste | — | lf | 11.60 | — | 11.60 |
| 4" x 4", deluxe grade | | | | | |
| ($526.00 8' post, 8 lf), 0% waste | — | lf | 65.80 | — | 65.80 |
| 6" x 6", standard grade | | | | | |
| ($136.00 8' post, 8 lf), 0% waste | — | lf | 17.00 | — | 17.00 |
| 6" x 6", deluxe grade | | | | | |
| ($349.00 8' post, 8 lf), 0% waste | — | lf | 43.60 | — | 43.60 |
| 8" x 8", standard grade | | | | | |
| ($156.00 8' post, 8 lf), 0% waste | — | lf | 19.50 | — | 19.50 |
| 8" x 8", deluxe grade | | | | | |
| ($397.00 8' post, 8 lf), 0% waste | — | lf | 49.60 | — | 49.60 |
| **Carved wood onlay** | | | | | |
| medium acanthus ($70.20 ea) | — | ea | 70.20 | — | 70.20 |
| medium ribbon ($73.60 ea) | — | ea | 73.60 | — | 73.60 |
| medium grape ($117.00 ea) | — | ea | 117.00 | — | 117.00 |
| medium shell ($103.00 ea) | — | ea | 103.00 | — | 103.00 |
| medium floral ($107.00 ea) | — | ea | 107.00 | — | 107.00 |
| **Finish board** | | | | | |
| 1" x 12" S4S select pine | | | | | |
| ($4.53 lf, 1 lf), 4% waste | — | lf | 4.71 | — | 4.71 |
| **Hardwood plywood** | | | | | |
| 1/4" aromatic cedar veneer | | | | | |
| ($113.00 sheet, 32 sf), 4% waste | — | sf | 3.67 | — | 3.67 |
| 1/4" birch veneer | | | | | |
| ($110.00 sheet, 32 sf), 4% waste | — | sf | 3.58 | — | 3.58 |
| 1/4" cherry veneer | | | | | |
| ($123.00 sheet, 32 sf), 4% waste | — | sf | 3.99 | — | 3.99 |
| 1/4" chestnut veneer | | | | | |
| ($195.00 sheet, 32 sf), 4% waste | — | sf | 6.33 | — | 6.33 |
| 1/4" knotty pine veneer | | | | | |
| ($85.90 sheet, 32 sf), 4% waste | — | sf | 2.79 | — | 2.79 |
| 1/4" lauan mahogany veneer | | | | | |
| ($44.10 sheet, 32 sf), 4% waste | — | sf | 1.44 | — | 1.44 |
| 1/4" mahogany veneer | | | | | |
| ($125.00 sheet, 32 sf), 4% waste | — | sf | 4.07 | — | 4.07 |
| 1/4" pecan veneer | | | | | |
| ($127.00 sheet, 32 sf), 4% waste | — | sf | 4.13 | — | 4.13 |
| 1/4" red oak veneer | | | | | |
| ($111.00 sheet, 32 sf), 4% waste | — | sf | 3.61 | — | 3.61 |
| 1/4" rosewood veneer | | | | | |
| ($173.00 sheet, 32 sf), 4% waste | — | sf | 5.63 | — | 5.63 |
| 1/4" teak veneer | | | | | |
| ($228.00 sheet, 32 sf), 4% waste | — | sf | 7.42 | — | 7.42 |
| 1/4" walnut veneer | | | | | |
| ($162.00 sheet, 32 sf), 4% waste | — | sf | 5.26 | — | 5.26 |

## Finish Carpentry Labor

| Laborer | base wage | paid leave | true wage | taxes & ins. | total |
|---|---|---|---|---|---|
| Carpenter | $31.10 | 2.43 | $33.53 | 23.37 | $56.90 |
| Carpenter's helper | $22.40 | 1.75 | $24.15 | 18.25 | $42.40 |
| Demolition laborer | $20.70 | 1.61 | $22.31 | 16.59 | $38.90 |

**Paid leave** is calculated based on two weeks paid vacation, one week sick leave, and seven paid holidays. Employer's matching portion of **FICA** is 7.65 percent. **FUTA** (Federal Unemployment) is .8 percent. **Worker's compensation** for the finish carpentry trade was calculated using a national average of 16.85 percent. **Unemployment insurance** was calculated using a national average of 8 percent. **Health insurance** was calculated based on a projected national average for 2015 of $1,025 per employee (and family when applicable) per month. Employer pays 80 percent for a per month cost of $820 per employee. **Retirement** is based on a 401(k) retirement program with employer matching of 50 percent. Employee contributions to the 401(k) plan are an average of 6 percent of the true wage. **Liability insurance** is based on a national average of 10.0 percent.

## Finish Carpentry Labor Productivity

| | Craft@Hrs | Unit | Material | Labor | Total |
|---|---|---|---|---|---|
| Demolition of finish carpentry | | | | | |
| remove wall molding (base, chair rail, crown) | 1D@.026 | lf | — | 1.01 | 1.01 |
| remove door and window molding | 1D@.032 | lf | — | 1.24 | 1.24 |
| remove base or corner block | 1D@.036 | ea | — | 1.40 | 1.40 |
| remove head block | 1D@.037 | ea | — | 1.44 | 1.44 |
| remove overdoor molding | 1D@.028 | lf | — | 1.09 | 1.09 |
| remove window stool | 1D@.026 | lf | — | 1.01 | 1.01 |
| remove window apron | 1D@.028 | lf | — | 1.09 | 1.09 |
| remove corner bead | 1D@.043 | lf | — | 1.67 | 1.67 |
| remove hand rail | 1D@.028 | lf | — | 1.09 | 1.09 |
| remove shelf brackets, shelving, and rod | 1D@.063 | lf | — | 2.45 | 2.45 |
| remove closet organizer system | 1D@.047 | sf | — | 1.83 | 1.83 |
| remove linen closet shelves | 1D@.034 | lf | — | 1.32 | 1.32 |
| remove closet rod | 1D@.035 | lf | — | 1.36 | 1.36 |
| remove tongue-and-groove cedar closet lining | 1D@.028 | sf | — | 1.09 | 1.09 |
| remove cedar veneer plywood closet lining | 1D@.022 | sf | — | .86 | .86 |
| remove built-in bookcase | 1D@.051 | sf | — | 1.98 | 1.98 |
| remove fireplace mantel beam | 1D@.080 | lf | — | 3.11 | 3.11 |
| remove fireplace mantel | 1D@.094 | lf | — | 3.66 | 3.66 |
| remove coffered ceiling | 1D@.047 | sf | — | 1.83 | 1.83 |
| remove niche | 1D@.317 | ea | — | 12.30 | 12.30 |
| remove gingerbread running trim | 1D@.038 | lf | — | 1.48 | 1.48 |
| remove gingerbread bracket | 1D@.154 | ea | — | 5.99 | 5.99 |
| remove gingerbread corbel | 1D@.160 | ea | — | 6.22 | 6.22 |
| remove gingerbread door or window header | 1D@.037 | lf | — | 1.44 | 1.44 |
| remove gingerbread post drop | 1D@.154 | ea | — | 5.99 | 5.99 |
| remove gingerbread spandrel | 1D@.038 | lf | — | 1.48 | 1.48 |
| remove gingerbread window cornice | 1D@.041 | lf | — | 1.59 | 1.59 |
| remove gingerbread gable ornament | 1D@.254 | ea | — | 9.88 | 9.88 |
| remove gingerbread gable finial | 1D@.239 | ea | — | 9.30 | 9.30 |
| remove porch post | 1D@.127 | lf | — | 4.94 | 4.94 |
| remove onlay | 1D@.062 | ea | — | 2.41 | 2.41 |
| remove finish trim board | 1D@.026 | lf | — | 1.01 | 1.01 |
| remove finish plywood | 1D@.022 | sf | — | .86 | .86 |

|  | Craft@Hrs | Unit | Material | Labor | Total |
|---|---|---|---|---|---|
| **Finish carpentry crew** | | | | | |
| finish carpentry　finish carpenter | $56.90 | | | | |
| finish carpentry　carpenter's helper | $42.40 | | | | |
| finish carpentry　finish crew | $49.70 | | | | |
| **Install molding** | | | | | |
| base, chair rail | 1C@.038 | lf | — | 2.16 | 2.16 |
| window or door casing or panel moldings | 1C@.041 | lf | — | 2.33 | 2.33 |
| crown | 1C@.046 | lf | — | 2.62 | 2.62 |
| **Install casing on curved window or door** | | | | | |
| half-round top window or door per lf | 1C@.144 | lf | — | 8.19 | 8.19 |
| elliptical top window or door per lf | 1C@.144 | lf | — | 8.19 | 8.19 |
| round window per lf of diameter | 1C@.294 | lf | — | 16.70 | 16.70 |
| **Install wood key in curved molding** | | | | | |
| install | 1C@.251 | ea | — | 14.30 | 14.30 |
| **Install base, corner, or head block** | | | | | |
| install | 1C@.063 | ea | — | 3.58 | 3.58 |
| **Install overdoor molding** | | | | | |
| install | 1C@.041 | lf | — | 2.33 | 2.33 |
| **Install door architrave** | | | | | |
| interior | 1C@.062 | lf | — | 3.53 | 3.53 |
| exterior | 1C@.080 | lf | — | 4.55 | 4.55 |
| **Install exterior door surround** | | | | | |
| economy grade | 1C@.234 | lf | — | 13.30 | 13.30 |
| custom deluxe grade | 1C@.431 | lf | — | 24.50 | 24.50 |
| **Install exterior window surround** | | | | | |
| economy grade | 1C@.207 | lf | — | 11.80 | 11.80 |
| custom deluxe grade | 1C@.322 | lf | — | 18.30 | 18.30 |
| **Install window trim** | | | | | |
| stool | 1C@.058 | lf | — | 3.30 | 3.30 |
| apron | 1C@.049 | lf | — | 2.79 | 2.79 |
| **Install corner bead** | | | | | |
| wood | 1C@.077 | lf | — | 4.38 | 4.38 |
| plastic | 1C@.032 | lf | — | 1.82 | 1.82 |
| **Install hand rail** | | | | | |
| install | 1C@.098 | lf | — | 5.58 | 5.58 |
| **Install panel molding inside corner radius** | | | | | |
| install | 1C@.149 | ea | — | 8.48 | 8.48 |
| **Install closet shelf brackets, shelving, & rod** | | | | | |
| install | 1C@.332 | lf | — | 18.90 | 18.90 |
| **Install closet organizer system** | | | | | |
| standard grade | 1C@.304 | sf | — | 17.30 | 17.30 |
| deluxe grade | 1C@.526 | sf | — | 29.90 | 29.90 |
| **Install linen closet shelves** | | | | | |
| typical | 1C@.673 | lf | — | 38.30 | 38.30 |
| with pull-out shelves | 1C@.695 | lf | — | 39.50 | 39.50 |
| **Install closet rod** | | | | | |
| install | 1C@.080 | lf | — | 4.55 | 4.55 |

| | Craft@Hrs | Unit | Material | Labor | Total |
|---|---|---|---|---|---|
| Install closet lining | | | | | |
| tongue-&-groove cedar board | 1C@.051 | sf | — | 2.90 | 2.90 |
| 1/4" cedar veneer plywood | 1C@.037 | sf | — | 2.11 | 2.11 |
| Install built-in bookcase | | | | | |
| 8" deep | 1C@.269 | sf | — | 15.30 | 15.30 |
| 12" deep | 1C@.304 | sf | — | 17.30 | 17.30 |
| 18" deep | 1C@.317 | sf | — | 18.00 | 18.00 |
| 24" deep | 1C@.332 | sf | — | 18.90 | 18.90 |
| Install fireplace mantel beam | | | | | |
| install | 1C@.539 | lf | — | 30.70 | 30.70 |
| Install fireplace mantel | | | | | |
| install | 1C@.653 | lf | — | 37.20 | 37.20 |
| Install coffered ceiling | | | | | |
| economy grade | 1C@.248 | sf | — | 14.10 | 14.10 |
| custom deluxe grade | 1C@.567 | sf | — | 32.30 | 32.30 |
| Install niche | | | | | |
| with casing and shelf bracket | 1C@1.31 | ea | — | 74.50 | 74.50 |
| Install gingerbread | | | | | |
| running trim | 1C@.160 | lf | — | 9.10 | 9.10 |
| post bracket | 1C@.348 | ea | — | 19.80 | 19.80 |
| corbel | 1C@.359 | ea | — | 20.40 | 20.40 |
| door or window header | 1C@.232 | lf | — | 13.20 | 13.20 |
| post drop | 1C@.322 | ea | — | 18.30 | 18.30 |
| spandrel | 1C@.237 | lf | — | 13.50 | 13.50 |
| window cornice | 1C@.242 | lf | — | 13.80 | 13.80 |
| gable ornament | 1C@.582 | ea | — | 33.10 | 33.10 |
| gable finial | 1C@.560 | ea | — | 31.90 | 31.90 |
| Install porch post | | | | | |
| install | 1C@.135 | lf | — | 7.68 | 7.68 |
| Install carved wood onlay | | | | | |
| install | 1C@.519 | ea | — | 29.50 | 29.50 |
| Install finish board trim | | | | | |
| install | 1C@.049 | lf | — | 2.79 | 2.79 |
| Install 1/4" hardwood plywood | | | | | |
| install | 1C@.028 | sf | — | 1.59 | 1.59 |

# Fireplaces

| | Craft@Hrs | Unit | Material | Labor | Total |
|---|---|---|---|---|---|

**Fireplace.** Includes concrete reinforced hearth, ash drop, fire brick, damper, throat, smoke shelf and smoke chamber. Does not include foundation, flue or chimney, face, or finish hearth.

| | Craft@Hrs | Unit | Material | Labor | Total |
|---|---|---|---|---|---|
| **Open front fireplace** | | | | | |
| 30" wide by 16" deep by 29" high | 1M@16.1 | ea | 533.00 | 956.00 | 1,489.00 |
| 36" wide by 16" deep by 29" high | 1M@16.9 | ea | 640.00 | 1,000.00 | 1,640.00 |
| 40" wide by 16" deep by 29" high | 1M@17.5 | ea | 712.00 | 1,040.00 | 1,752.00 |
| 48" wide by 18" deep by 32" high | 1M@18.5 | ea | 855.00 | 1,100.00 | 1,955.00 |
| *open front* | | | | | |
| **Open front and one side fireplace** | | | | | |
| 32" wide by 16" deep by 26" high | 1M@16.7 | ea | 501.00 | 992.00 | 1,493.00 |
| 40" wide by 16" deep by 29" high | 1M@17.5 | ea | 695.00 | 1,040.00 | 1,735.00 |
| 48" wide by 20" deep by 29" high *open front and side* | 1M@18.9 | ea | 835.00 | 1,120.00 | 1,955.00 |
| **Open two faces fireplace** | | | | | |
| 32" wide by 28" deep by 29" high | 1M@18.5 | ea | 489.00 | 1,100.00 | 1,589.00 |
| 36" wide by 28" deep by 29" high | 1M@18.9 | ea | 551.00 | 1,120.00 | 1,671.00 |
| 40" wide by 28" deep by 29" high | 1M@19.2 | ea | 613.00 | 1,140.00 | 1,753.00 |
| *"see through"* | | | | | |
| **Open two faces and one side fireplace** | | | | | |
| 36" wide by 32" deep by 27" high | 1M@19.2 | ea | 599.00 | 1,140.00 | 1,739.00 |
| 36" wide by 36" deep by 27" high | 1M@20.0 | ea | 675.00 | 1,190.00 | 1,865.00 |
| 44" wide by 40" deep by 27" high *open two faces and side* | 1M@20.4 | ea | 898.00 | 1,210.00 | 2,108.00 |
| Remove fireplace | 1D@3.85 | ea | — | 150.00 | 150.00 |

**Prefabricated fireplace.** Zero clearance box. Does not include flue. Actual sizes and style available vary from manufacturer to manufacturer. Choose the size and style that most closely matches.

| | Craft@Hrs | Unit | Material | Labor | Total |
|---|---|---|---|---|---|
| **Open front prefabricated fireplace** | | | | | |
| replace, 30" wide by 16" deep by 29" high | 1M@4.55 | ea | 603.00 | 270.00 | 873.00 |
| replace, 36" wide by 16" deep by 29" high | 1M@4.55 | ea | 731.00 | 270.00 | 1,001.00 |
| replace, 40" wide by 16" deep by 29" high | 1M@4.55 | ea | 1,220.00 | 270.00 | 1,490.00 |
| replace, 48" wide by 18" deep by 32" high *open front* | 1M@4.55 | ea | 1,480.00 | 270.00 | 1,750.00 |
| **Open front convection prefabricated fireplace** | | | | | |
| replace, 30" wide by 16" deep by 29" high | 1M@4.76 | ea | 692.00 | 283.00 | 975.00 |
| replace, 36" wide by 16" deep by 29" high | 1M@4.76 | ea | 841.00 | 283.00 | 1,124.00 |
| replace, 40" wide by 16" deep by 29" high | 1M@4.76 | ea | 936.00 | 283.00 | 1,219.00 |
| replace, 48" wide by 18" deep by 32" high | 1M@4.76 | ea | 1,120.00 | 283.00 | 1,403.00 |
| **Open front forced air prefabricated fireplace** | | | | | |
| replace, 30" wide by 16" deep by 29" high | 1M@5.26 | ea | 754.00 | 312.00 | 1,066.00 |
| replace, 36" wide by 16" deep by 29" high | 1M@5.26 | ea | 911.00 | 312.00 | 1,223.00 |
| replace, 40" wide by 16" deep by 29" high | 1M@5.26 | ea | 1,010.00 | 312.00 | 1,322.00 |
| replace, 48" wide by 18" deep by 32" high | 1M@5.26 | ea | 1,210.00 | 312.00 | 1,522.00 |
| **Open front and one side prefabricated fireplace** | | | | | |
| replace, 32" wide by 16" deep by 26" high | 1M@4.55 | ea | 1,010.00 | 270.00 | 1,280.00 |
| replace, 40" wide by 16" deep by 29" high | 1M@4.76 | ea | 1,210.00 | 283.00 | 1,493.00 |
| replace, 48" wide by 20" deep by 29" high *open front and side* | 1M@5.26 | ea | 1,460.00 | 312.00 | 1,772.00 |

| | Craft@Hrs | Unit | Material | Labor | Total |
|---|---|---|---|---|---|
| Open two faces (see through) prefabricated fireplace | | | | | |
| replace, 32" wide by 28" deep by 29" high | 1M@4.55 | ea | 1,220.00 | 270.00 | 1,490.00 |
| replace, 36" wide by 28" deep by 29" high | 1M@4.76 | ea | 1,480.00 | 283.00 | 1,763.00 |
| replace, 40" wide by 28" deep by 29" high | 1M@5.26 | ea | 1,790.00 | 312.00 | 2,102.00 |
| *"see through"* | | | | | |
| Open two faces and one side prefabricated fireplace | | | | | |
| replace, 36" wide by 32" deep by 27" high | 1M@4.55 | ea | 1,460.00 | 270.00 | 1,730.00 |
| replace, 36" wide by 36" deep by 27" high | 1M@4.76 | ea | 1,750.00 | 283.00 | 2,033.00 |
| replace, 44" wide by 40" deep by 27" high | 1M@5.26 | ea | 2,090.00 | 312.00 | 2,402.00 |
| *open two faces and side* | | | | | |
| Remove, prefabricated fireplace | 1D@2.44 | ea | — | 94.90 | 94.90 |

**Fireplace form.** Does not include face, hearth, flue or chimney. Actual sizes and style available vary from manufacturer to manufacturer. Choose the size and style that most closely matches.

| | Craft@Hrs | Unit | Material | Labor | Total |
|---|---|---|---|---|---|
| Open front fireplace form | | | | | |
| replace, 30" wide by 16" deep by 29" high | 1M@3.03 | ea | 692.00 | 180.00 | 872.00 |
| replace, 36" wide by 16" deep by 29" high | 1M@3.03 | ea | 834.00 | 180.00 | 1,014.00 |
| replace, 40" wide by 16" deep by 29" high | 1M@3.03 | ea | 926.00 | 180.00 | 1,106.00 |
| replace, 48" wide by 18" deep by 32" high | 1M@3.03 | ea | 1,130.00 | 180.00 | 1,310.00 |
| *open front* | | | | | |
| Open front and one side fireplace form | | | | | |
| replace, 32" wide by 16" deep by 26" high | 1M@3.03 | ea | 1,280.00 | 180.00 | 1,460.00 |
| replace, 40" wide by 16" deep by 29" high | 1M@3.03 | ea | 1,540.00 | 180.00 | 1,720.00 |
| replace, 48" wide by 20" deep by 29" high | 1M@3.03 | ea | 2,850.00 | 180.00 | 3,030.00 |
| *open front and side* | | | | | |
| Open two faces fireplace form | | | | | |
| replace, 32" wide by 28" deep by 29" high | 1M@3.03 | ea | 1,560.00 | 180.00 | 1,740.00 |
| replace, 36" wide by 28" deep by 29" high | 1M@3.03 | ea | 1,770.00 | 180.00 | 1,950.00 |
| replace, 40" wide by 28" deep by 29" high | 1M@3.03 | ea | 1,950.00 | 180.00 | 2,130.00 |
| *"see through"* | | | | | |
| Open two faces and one side fireplace form | | | | | |
| replace, 36" wide by 32" deep by 27" high | 1M@3.03 | ea | 1,930.00 | 180.00 | 2,110.00 |
| replace, 36" wide by 36" deep by 27" high | 1M@3.03 | ea | 2,170.00 | 180.00 | 2,350.00 |
| replace, 44" wide by 40" deep by 27" high *open two faces and side* | 1M@3.03 | ea | 2,410.00 | 180.00 | 2,590.00 |
| Remove, fireplace form | 1D@2.78 | ea | — | 108.00 | 108.00 |

**Fireplace furnace.**

| | Craft@Hrs | Unit | Material | Labor | Total |
|---|---|---|---|---|---|
| replace, typical | 1M@34.5 | ea | 6,390.00 | 2,050.00 | 8,440.00 |
| remove | 1D@3.85 | ea | — | 150.00 | 150.00 |

**Fire brick.** Installation of fire brick with fire clay only, no surrounding masonry.

| | Craft@Hrs | Unit | Material | Labor | Total |
|---|---|---|---|---|---|
| replace, complete fireplace | 1M@3.03 | ea | 169.00 | 180.00 | 349.00 |
| replace, concrete simulated firebrick (complete fireplace) | 1M@1.85 | ea | 127.00 | 110.00 | 237.00 |
| remove, fire brick | 1D@.952 | ea | — | 37.00 | 37.00 |
| remove, concrete simulated fire brick | 1D@.529 | ea | — | 20.60 | 20.60 |

| | Craft@Hrs | Unit | Material | Labor | Total |
|---|---|---|---|---|---|

**Fireplace chimney.** All brick types. Does not include foundation.

| | Craft@Hrs | Unit | Material | Labor | Total |
|---|---|---|---|---|---|
| replace, 16" by 16" with one 8" x 8" flue | 5M@2.21 | lf | 45.10 | 126.00 | 171.10 |
| replace, 16" by 24" with two 8" x 8" flues | 5M@3.09 | lf | 59.50 | 176.00 | 235.50 |
| replace, 16" by 20" with one 8" x 12" flue | 5M@2.24 | lf | 53.60 | 128.00 | 181.60 |
| replace, 20" by 24" with two 8" x 12" flues | 5M@3.15 | lf | 68.70 | 180.00 | 248.70 |
| replace, 20" by 20" with one 12" x 12" flue | 5M@2.27 | lf | 56.80 | 129.00 | 185.80 |
| replace, 20" by 32" with two 12" x 12" flues | 5M@3.24 | lf | 78.60 | 185.00 | 263.60 |
| replace, 20" by 24" with one 12" x 16" flue | 5M@2.31 | lf | 60.10 | 132.00 | 192.10 |
| replace, 20" by 40" with two 12" x 16" flues | 5M@3.30 | lf | 100.00 | 188.00 | 288.00 |
| replace, 24" by 24" with one 16" x 16" flue | 5M@2.35 | lf | 63.30 | 134.00 | 197.30 |
| replace, 24" by 40" with two 16" x 16" flues | 5M@3.36 | lf | 112.00 | 192.00 | 304.00 |
| remove, one flue | 1D@.346 | lf | — | 13.50 | 13.50 |
| remove, two flues | 1D@.472 | lf | — | 18.40 | 18.40 |
| add for bend in one flue | 5M@3.33 | ea | 29.90 | 190.00 | 219.90 |
| add for bend in two flues | 5M@4.05 | ea | 33.60 | 231.00 | 264.60 |

add 14% for stone facing on chimney

**Reline chimney using grout and inflatable tube method.** With a technique designed and licensed by Ahrens Chimney Technique. Replace only.

| | Craft@Hrs | Unit | Material | Labor | Total |
|---|---|---|---|---|---|
| reline | 1M@.604 | lf | 7.86 | 35.90 | 43.76 |
| add per bend in chimney | 1M@3.08 | ea | 23.20 | 183.00 | 206.20 |
| minimum charge | 1M@4.00 | ea | 46.70 | 238.00 | 284.70 |

**2" concrete chimney cap.** Poured in place.

| | Craft@Hrs | Unit | Material | Labor | Total |
|---|---|---|---|---|---|
| replace, single flue | 1M@1.00 | ea | 20.50 | 59.40 | 79.90 |
| replace, double flue | 1M@1.49 | ea | 32.70 | 88.50 | 121.20 |
| remove, single flue | 1D@.303 | ea | — | 11.80 | 11.80 |
| remove, double flue | 1D@.362 | ea | — | 14.10 | 14.10 |

**Cast stone chimney cap.** Manufactured cast stone cap with decorative patterns. Grades have progressively more complex molding patterns on edge.

| | Craft@Hrs | Unit | Material | Labor | Total |
|---|---|---|---|---|---|
| replace, standard grade | 1M@1.28 | ea | 196.00 | 76.00 | 272.00 |
| replace, high grade | 1M@1.28 | ea | 234.00 | 76.00 | 310.00 |
| replace, deluxe grade | 1M@1.28 | ea | 310.00 | 76.00 | 386.00 |
| remove | 1D@.362 | ea | — | 14.10 | 14.10 |

**Galvanized steel chimney cap.** For use on metal or masonry flues, with spark arrestor.

| | Craft@Hrs | Unit | Material | Labor | Total |
|---|---|---|---|---|---|
| replace, cap | 2M@.298 | ea | 156.00 | 16.20 | 172.20 |
| remove | 1D@.177 | ea | — | 6.89 | 6.89 |
| remove for work, then reinstall | 2M@.498 | ea | — | 27.10 | 27.10 |

**Chimney bird screen.** Replace only.

| | Craft@Hrs | Unit | Material | Labor | Total |
|---|---|---|---|---|---|
| for single flue | 2M@.437 | ea | 60.30 | 23.80 | 84.10 |
| for double flue | 2M@.476 | ea | 74.00 | 25.90 | 99.90 |

| | Craft@Hrs | Unit | Material | Labor | Total |
|---|---|---|---|---|---|

**Chimney pot.** Grades have progressively more ornate designs on pot. Deluxe and above grades also have patterns around top edge.

| | Craft@Hrs | Unit | Material | Labor | Total |
|---|---|---|---|---|---|
| replace, standard grade | 1M@1.18 | ea | 251.00 | 70.10 | 321.10 |
| replace, high grade | 1M@1.18 | ea | 369.00 | 70.10 | 439.10 |
| replace, deluxe grade | 1M@1.18 | ea | 462.00 | 70.10 | 532.10 |
| replace, custom grade | 1M@1.18 | ea | 570.00 | 70.10 | 640.10 |
| replace, custom deluxe grade | 1M@1.18 | ea | 727.00 | 70.10 | 797.10 |
| remove | 1D@.469 | ea | — | 18.20 | 18.20 |
| remove for work, then reinstall | 1M@2.04 | ea | — | 121.00 | 121.00 |

*standard*

*high*

*custom deluxe*

**Fireplace grate.**

| | Craft@Hrs | Unit | Material | Labor | Total |
|---|---|---|---|---|---|
| replace, 22" x 16" | 2M@.119 | ea | 61.60 | 6.49 | 68.09 |
| replace, 28" x 16" | 2M@.119 | ea | 78.60 | 6.49 | 85.09 |
| replace, 32" x 16" | 2M@.119 | ea | 89.90 | 6.49 | 96.39 |
| replace, 38" x 16" | 2M@.119 | ea | 102.00 | 6.49 | 108.49 |
| replace, 38" x 20" | 2M@.119 | ea | 107.00 | 6.49 | 113.49 |
| replace, 32" x 28" | 2M@.119 | ea | 117.00 | 6.49 | 123.49 |
| replace, 36" x 28" | 2M@.119 | ea | 124.00 | 6.49 | 130.49 |
| replace, 40" x 28" | 2M@.119 | ea | 129.00 | 6.49 | 135.49 |
| replace, 36" x 32" | 2M@.119 | ea | 136.00 | 6.49 | 142.49 |
| replace, 36" x 36" | 2M@.119 | ea | 153.00 | 6.49 | 159.49 |
| replace, 44" x 40" | 2M@.119 | ea | 208.00 | 6.49 | 214.49 |
| remove | 1D@.030 | ea | — | 1.17 | 1.17 |
| remove for work, then reinstall | 2M@.147 | ea | — | 8.01 | 8.01 |

**Fireplace screen.**

| | Craft@Hrs | Unit | Material | Labor | Total |
|---|---|---|---|---|---|
| replace, standard grade | 2M@.794 | ea | 136.00 | 43.30 | 179.30 |
| replace, high grade | 2M@.794 | ea | 209.00 | 43.30 | 252.30 |
| replace, deluxe grade | 2M@.794 | ea | 285.00 | 43.30 | 328.30 |
| remove | 1D@.185 | ea | — | 7.20 | 7.20 |
| remove for work, then reinstall | 2M@1.19 | ea | — | 64.90 | 64.90 |

| | Craft@Hrs | Unit | Material | Labor | Total |
|---|---|---|---|---|---|
| **Fireplace door.** Standard grade has black face, higher grades have brass face. | | | | | |
| replace, standard grade | 2M@1.00 | ea | 232.00 | 54.50 | 286.50 |
| replace, high grade | 2M@1.00 | ea | 353.00 | 54.50 | 407.50 |
| replace, deluxe grade | 2M@1.00 | ea | 460.00 | 54.50 | 514.50 |
| replace, custom grade | 2M@1.00 | ea | 613.00 | 54.50 | 667.50 |
| remove | 1D@.253 | ea | — | 9.84 | 9.84 |
| remove for work, then reinstall | 2M@1.56 | ea | — | 85.00 | 85.00 |
| **Fireplace clean-out.** Cast iron door and jamb. | | | | | |
| replace, 8" x 8" | 1M@.625 | ea | 25.80 | 37.10 | 62.90 |
| replace, 12" x 12" | 1M@.625 | ea | 54.00 | 37.10 | 91.10 |
| replace, 18" x 24" | 1M@.625 | ea | 160.00 | 37.10 | 197.10 |
| remove | 1D@.069 | ea | — | 2.68 | 2.68 |
| salvage, then reinstall | 1M@.971 | ea | — | 57.70 | 57.70 |
| **Damper.** Replace only. | | | | | |
| Rotary controlled damper | | | | | |
| for 30" wide fireplace | 1M@1.11 | ea | 107.00 | 65.90 | 172.90 |
| for 36" wide fireplace | 1M@1.11 | ea | 116.00 | 65.90 | 181.90 |
| for 40" wide fireplace | 1M@1.11 | ea | 145.00 | 65.90 | 210.90 |
| for 48" wide fireplace | 1M@1.11 | ea | 169.00 | 65.90 | 234.90 |
| Poker controlled damper | | | | | |
| for 30" wide fireplace | 1M@.901 | ea | 85.00 | 53.50 | 138.50 |
| for 36" wide fireplace | 1M@.901 | ea | 90.90 | 53.50 | 144.40 |
| for 40" wide fireplace | 1M@.901 | ea | 111.00 | 53.50 | 164.50 |
| for 48" wide fireplace | 1M@.901 | ea | 133.00 | 53.50 | 186.50 |
| **Chimney pipe.** Stainless steel. | | | | | |
| Double wall chimney pipe | | | | | |
| replace, 8" diameter | 2M@.578 | lf | 36.80 | 31.50 | 68.30 |
| replace, 10" diameter | 2M@.578 | lf | 53.00 | 31.50 | 84.50 |
| replace, 12" diameter | 2M@.578 | lf | 70.10 | 31.50 | 101.60 |
| replace, 14" diameter | 2M@.578 | lf | 87.30 | 31.50 | 118.80 |
| Triple wall chimney pipe | | | | | |
| replace, 8" diameter | 2M@.578 | lf | 46.70 | 31.50 | 78.20 |
| replace, 10" diameter | 2M@.578 | lf | 67.70 | 31.50 | 99.20 |
| replace, 12" diameter | 2M@.578 | lf | 89.90 | 31.50 | 121.40 |
| replace, 14" diameter | 2M@.578 | lf | 111.00 | 31.50 | 142.50 |
| Remove | 1D@.021 | lf | — | .82 | .82 |
| Additional chimney pipe costs | | | | | |
| add through interior ceiling | 2M@1.11 | ea | 64.00 | 60.50 | 124.50 |
| add through roof | 2M@2.94 | ea | 179.00 | 160.00 | 339.00 |
| remove for work, then reinstall | 2M@.884 | lf | — | 48.20 | 48.20 |

| | Craft@Hrs | Unit | Material | Labor | Total |
|---|---|---|---|---|---|

**Gas log lighter.** Log lighter, valve, key and up to 24 lf copper gas piping.

| | Craft@Hrs | Unit | Material | Labor | Total |
|---|---|---|---|---|---|
| replace, typical | 2M@1.18 | ea | 120.00 | 64.30 | 184.30 |
| remove | 1D@.227 | ea | — | 8.83 | 8.83 |
| remove for work, then reinstall | 2M@1.96 | ea | — | 107.00 | 107.00 |

**Gas fireplace kit.**

| | Craft@Hrs | Unit | Material | Labor | Total |
|---|---|---|---|---|---|
| replace, typical | 2M@1.25 | ea | 738.00 | 68.10 | 806.10 |
| remove | 1D@.251 | ea | — | 9.76 | 9.76 |
| remove for work, then reinstall | 2M@2.13 | ea | — | 116.00 | 116.00 |

**Marble fireplace face.** Economy grade: Marble tiles laid around inside of mantel. Standard grade: Single or large pieces of marble up to 5' tall and 4' wide, polished or natural finish. High grade: Same as standard grade, but with simple designs around the opening and at corner (cove or similar). Pieces may be up to 8' tall and 6' wide. Deluxe grade: Same as high grade, but with ornate designs around opening and at corner (crown or similar).

| | Craft@Hrs | Unit | Material | Labor | Total |
|---|---|---|---|---|---|
| replace, economy grade | 1M@3.57 | ea | 121.00 | 212.00 | 333.00 |
| remove, economy | 1D@1.66 | ea | — | 64.60 | 64.60 |
| replace, standard grade | 1M@7.63 | ea | 369.00 | 453.00 | 822.00 |
| replace, high grade | 1M@7.81 | ea | 603.00 | 464.00 | 1,067.00 |
| replace, deluxe grade | 1M@8.00 | ea | 899.00 | 475.00 | 1,374.00 |
| remove | 1D@3.03 | ea | — | 118.00 | 118.00 |

**Brick fireplace face.** Economy grade: Brick face in stacked or running bond, up to 5' tall and 5' wide. Standard grade: Brick face in specialty bond (see Masonry), up to 5' tall and 5' wide. May include built-in shelf brackets or small patterns in face. Or, may be same as economy, except 8' tall and 6' wide. High grade: Same as standard grade, but with arch over opening, or may be up to 11' high and 7' wide. Deluxe grade: Brick face in specialty bond, such as herringbone or basket weave mixed with other patterns (see Masonry for brick bonds), 5' tall and 5' wide. May have arched openings or curving sides. May be same as high grade except up to 8' tall and 6' wide; same as standard except up to 11' tall and 7' wide; or same as economy except up to 15' tall and 10' wide.

| | Craft@Hrs | Unit | Material | Labor | Total |
|---|---|---|---|---|---|
| replace, economy grade | 1M@16.1 | ea | 342.00 | 956.00 | 1,298.00 |
| replace, standard grade | 1M@20.4 | ea | 380.00 | 1,210.00 | 1,590.00 |
| replace, high grade | 1M@25.0 | ea | 461.00 | 1,490.00 | 1,951.00 |
| replace, deluxe grade | 1M@32.3 | ea | 560.00 | 1,920.00 | 2,480.00 |
| remove | 1D@3.23 | ea | — | 126.00 | 126.00 |

**Rubble stone fireplace face.** Economy grade: Flagstone or equivalent stone, up to 5' tall and 5' wide. Standard grade: Sandstone, limestone or similar, up to 5' tall and 5' wide. Or, same as economy, except up to 8' tall and 6' wide. High grade: Higher priced stones or stones with high-priced finishes, up to 5' tall and 5' wide. Or, same as standard, except up to 8' tall and 6' wide; or same as economy except up to 10' tall and 7' wide. Deluxe grade: Specialty stones or stones with high-priced finishes, up to 5' tall and 5' wide, with arch over opening or other specialty components. May be same as high, except up to 8' tall and 6' wide; same as standard, except 11' tall and 7' wide; or same as economy, except up to 14' tall and 8' wide.

| | Craft@Hrs | Unit | Material | Labor | Total |
|---|---|---|---|---|---|
| replace, economy grade | 1M@17.5 | ea | 582.00 | 1,040.00 | 1,622.00 |
| replace, standard grade | 1M@22.3 | ea | 648.00 | 1,320.00 | 1,968.00 |
| replace, high grade | 1M@27.1 | ea | 784.00 | 1,610.00 | 2,394.00 |
| replace, deluxe grade | 1M@34.5 | ea | 951.00 | 2,050.00 | 3,001.00 |
| remove | 1D@3.45 | ea | — | 134.00 | 134.00 |

|  | Craft@Hrs | Unit | Material | Labor | Total |
|---|---|---|---|---|---|

**Ashlar stone fireplace face.** Economy grade: Lowest priced stone in area, up to 5' tall and 5' wide. Standard grade: Sandstone, limestone or similar stone, up to 5' tall and 5' wide. Or, same as economy, except up to 8' tall and 6' wide. High grade: Specialty high-priced stones or stones with high-priced finishes, up to 5' tall and 5' wide. Or, same as standard, except up to 8' tall and 6' wide; or same as economy except, up to 10' tall and 7' wide. Deluxe grade: Specialty high-priced stones or stones with high-priced finishes, up to 5' tall and 5' wide, with arch over opening or other specialty components or designs. May be same as high, except up to 8' tall and 6' wide; same as standard, except 11' tall and 7' wide; or same as economy, except up to 14' tall and 8' wide.

| | Craft@Hrs | Unit | Material | Labor | Total |
|---|---|---|---|---|---|
| replace, economy grade | 1M@17.2 | ea | 677.00 | 1,020.00 | 1,697.00 |
| replace, standard grade | 1M@21.7 | ea | 753.00 | 1,290.00 | 2,043.00 |
| replace, high grade | 1M@26.3 | ea | 911.00 | 1,560.00 | 2,471.00 |
| replace, deluxe grade | 1M@33.3 | ea | 1,100.00 | 1,980.00 | 3,080.00 |
| remove | 1D@3.45 | ea | — | 134.00 | 134.00 |

**Tile fireplace face.** Economy grade: Standard priced tiles laid around inside of mantel. Standard grade: High priced tiles. High grade: Specialty antique tiles, including designer hand-painted designs and raised pattern designs. May include tiles in fireback. Deluxe grade: Same as high grade with specialty trim pieces and patterns that match antique Victorian styles.

| | Craft@Hrs | Unit | Material | Labor | Total |
|---|---|---|---|---|---|
| replace, economy grade | 1M@3.70 | ea | 94.80 | 220.00 | 314.80 |
| remove, economy | 1D@1.82 | ea | — | 70.80 | 70.80 |
| replace, standard grade | 1M@7.94 | ea | 195.00 | 472.00 | 667.00 |
| replace, high grade | 1M@8.06 | ea | 254.00 | 479.00 | 733.00 |
| replace, deluxe grade | 1M@8.26 | ea | 541.00 | 491.00 | 1,032.00 |
| remove | 1D@2.94 | ea | — | 114.00 | 114.00 |

**Fireplace hearth.** Economy grade is flat hearth. All other grades are raised hearths. See fireplace face items for more information about quality.

| | Craft@Hrs | Unit | Material | Labor | Total |
|---|---|---|---|---|---|
| Marble fireplace hearth | | | | | |
| replace, economy grade | 1M@2.16 | ea | 184.00 | 128.00 | 312.00 |
| remove, economy | 1D@.775 | ea | — | 30.10 | 30.10 |
| replace, standard grade | 1M@4.60 | ea | 300.00 | 273.00 | 573.00 |
| replace, high grade | 1M@4.73 | ea | 485.00 | 281.00 | 766.00 |
| replace, deluxe grade | 1M@4.83 | ea | 723.00 | 287.00 | 1,010.00 |
| remove | 1D@1.45 | ea | — | 56.40 | 56.40 |
| Brick fireplace hearth | | | | | |
| replace, economy grade | 1M@7.04 | ea | 228.00 | 418.00 | 646.00 |
| replace, standard grade | 1M@8.85 | ea | 252.00 | 526.00 | 778.00 |
| replace, high grade | 1M@9.44 | ea | 308.00 | 561.00 | 869.00 |
| replace, deluxe grade | 1M@11.1 | ea | 372.00 | 659.00 | 1,031.00 |
| remove | 1D@1.52 | ea | — | 59.10 | 59.10 |
| Rubble stone fireplace hearth | | | | | |
| replace, economy grade | 1M@7.63 | ea | 388.00 | 453.00 | 841.00 |
| replace, standard grade | 1M@9.63 | ea | 431.00 | 572.00 | 1,003.00 |
| replace, high grade | 1M@10.2 | ea | 522.00 | 606.00 | 1,128.00 |
| replace, deluxe grade | 1M@12.0 | ea | 633.00 | 713.00 | 1,346.00 |
| remove | 1D@1.56 | ea | — | 60.70 | 60.70 |
| Ashlar stone fireplace hearth | | | | | |
| replace, economy grade | 1M@7.46 | ea | 451.00 | 443.00 | 894.00 |
| replace, standard grade | 1M@9.44 | ea | 503.00 | 561.00 | 1,064.00 |
| replace, high grade | 1M@10.0 | ea | 609.00 | 594.00 | 1,203.00 |
| replace, deluxe grade | 1M@11.8 | ea | 739.00 | 701.00 | 1,440.00 |
| remove | 1D@1.56 | ea | — | 60.70 | 60.70 |

| | Craft@Hrs | Unit | Material | Labor | Total |
|---|---|---|---|---|---|
| Tile fireplace hearth | | | | | |
| replace, economy grade | 1M@2.24 | ea | 144.00 | 133.00 | 277.00 |
| remove, economy | 1D@.875 | ea | — | 34.00 | 34.00 |
| replace, standard grade | 1M@4.77 | ea | 195.00 | 283.00 | 478.00 |
| replace, high grade | 1M@4.88 | ea | 254.00 | 290.00 | 544.00 |
| replace, deluxe grade | 1M@5.00 | ea | 541.00 | 297.00 | 838.00 |
| remove | 1D@1.43 | ea | — | 55.60 | 55.60 |

## Time & Material Charts (selected items)
## Fireplace Materials (Also see material prices with the line items above.)

| | Craft@Hrs | Unit | Material | Labor | Total |
|---|---|---|---|---|---|
| Fireplace | | | | | |
| 30" wide by 16" deep by 29" high, open front | — | ea | 533.00 | — | 533.00 |
| 32" wide by 16" deep by 26" high, open front and one side | — | ea | 501.00 | — | 501.00 |
| 32" wide by 28" deep by 29" high, open two sides | — | ea | 489.00 | — | 489.00 |
| 36" wide by 32" deep by 27" high, open two faces and one side | — | ea | 599.00 | — | 599.00 |
| Prefabricated fireplace | | | | | |
| 30" wide by 16" deep by 29" high, open front | — | ea | 603.00 | — | 603.00 |
| 32" wide by 16" deep by 26" high, open front and one side | — | ea | 1,010.00 | — | 1,010.00 |
| 32" wide by 28" deep by 29" high, open two faces (see through) | — | ea | 1,220.00 | — | 1,220.00 |
| 36" wide by 32" deep by 27" high, open two faces and one side | — | ea | 1,460.00 | — | 1,460.00 |
| Fireplace form | | | | | |
| 30" wide by 16" deep by 29" high, open front | — | ea | 692.00 | — | 692.00 |
| 32" wide by 16" deep by 26" high, open front and one side | — | ea | 1,280.00 | — | 1,280.00 |
| 32" wide by 28" deep by 29" high, open two faces (see through) | — | ea | 1,560.00 | — | 1,560.00 |
| 36" wide by 32" deep by 27" high, open two faces and one side | — | ea | 1,930.00 | — | 1,930.00 |
| Fireplace chimney | | | | | |
| 16" by 16" with one 8" x 8" flue | — | lf | 45.10 | — | 45.10 |
| 16" by 24" with two 8" x 8" flues | — | lf | 59.50 | — | 59.50 |
| 20" by 32" with two 12" x 12" flues | — | lf | 78.60 | — | 78.60 |
| 20" by 40" with two 12" x 16" flues | — | lf | 100.00 | — | 100.00 |
| 24" by 40" with two 16" x 16" flues | — | lf | 112.00 | — | 112.00 |

| | Craft@Hrs | Unit | Material | Labor | Total |
|---|---|---|---|---|---|
| Marble fireplace facing | | | | | |
| economy grade | — | ea | 121.00 | — | 121.00 |
| deluxe grade | — | ea | 899.00 | — | 899.00 |
| Brick fireplace facing | | | | | |
| economy grade | — | ea | 342.00 | — | 342.00 |
| deluxe grade | — | ea | 560.00 | — | 560.00 |
| Rubble stone fireplace facing | | | | | |
| economy grade | — | ea | 582.00 | — | 582.00 |
| deluxe grade | — | ea | 951.00 | — | 951.00 |
| Ashlar stone fireplace facing | | | | | |
| economy grade | — | ea | 677.00 | — | 677.00 |
| deluxe grade | — | ea | 1,100.00 | — | 1,100.00 |
| Tile fireplace facing | | | | | |
| economy grade | — | ea | 94.80 | — | 94.80 |
| deluxe grade | — | ea | 541.00 | — | 541.00 |
| Marble fireplace hearth | | | | | |
| economy grade | — | ea | 184.00 | — | 184.00 |
| deluxe grade | — | ea | 723.00 | — | 723.00 |
| Brick fireplace hearth | | | | | |
| economy grade | — | ea | 228.00 | — | 228.00 |
| deluxe grade | — | ea | 372.00 | — | 372.00 |
| Rubble stone fireplace hearth | | | | | |
| economy grade | — | ea | 388.00 | — | 388.00 |
| deluxe grade | — | ea | 633.00 | — | 633.00 |
| Ashlar stone fireplace hearth | | | | | |
| economy grade | — | ea | 451.00 | — | 451.00 |
| deluxe grade | — | ea | 739.00 | — | 739.00 |
| Tile fireplace hearth | | | | | |
| economy grade | — | ea | 144.00 | — | 144.00 |
| deluxe grade | — | ea | 541.00 | — | 541.00 |

## Fireplace Labor

| Laborer | base wage | paid leave | true wage | taxes & ins. | total |
|---|---|---|---|---|---|
| Mason | $32.10 | 2.50 | $34.60 | 24.80 | $59.40 |
| Mason's helper | $29.20 | 2.28 | $31.48 | 23.02 | $54.50 |
| Demolition laborer | $20.70 | 1.61 | $22.31 | 16.59 | $38.90 |

**Paid leave** is calculated based on two weeks paid vacation, one week sick leave, and seven paid holidays. Employer's matching portion of **FICA** is 7.65 percent. **FUTA** (Federal Unemployment) is .8 percent. **Worker's compensation** for the masonry (fireplaces) trade was calculated using a national average of 19.00 percent. **Unemployment insurance** was calculated using a national average of 8 percent. **Health insurance** was calculated based on a projected national average for 2015 of $1,025 per employee (and family when applicable) per month. Employer pays 80 percent for a per month cost of $820 per employee. **Retirement** is based on a 401(k) retirement program with employer matching of 50 percent. Employee contributions to the 401(k) plan are an average of 6 percent of the true wage. **Liability insurance** is based on a national average of 10.0 percent.

|  | Craft@Hrs | Unit | Material | Labor | Total |
|---|---|---|---|---|---|

## Fireplace Labor Productivity

Demolition of fireplaces

|  | Craft@Hrs | Unit | Material | Labor | Total |
|---|---|---|---|---|---|
| remove fireplace | 1D@3.85 | ea | — | 150.00 | 150.00 |
| remove prefabricated fireplace | 1D@2.44 | ea | — | 94.90 | 94.90 |
| remove fire brick | 1D@.952 | ea | — | 37.00 | 37.00 |
| remove concrete simulated firebrick | 1D@.529 | ea | — | 20.60 | 20.60 |
| remove chimney with single flue | 1D@.346 | lf | — | 13.50 | 13.50 |
| remove chimney with double flue | 1D@.472 | lf | — | 18.40 | 18.40 |
| remove 2" concrete single flue cap | 1D@.303 | ea | — | 11.80 | 11.80 |
| remove 2" concrete double flue cap | 1D@.362 | ea | — | 14.10 | 14.10 |
| remove galvanized steel cap | 1D@.177 | ea | — | 6.89 | 6.89 |
| remove chimney pot | 1D@.469 | ea | — | 18.20 | 18.20 |
| remove fireplace grate | 1D@.030 | ea | — | 1.17 | 1.17 |
| remove fireplace screen | 1D@.185 | ea | — | 7.20 | 7.20 |
| remove fireplace door | 1D@.253 | ea | — | 9.84 | 9.84 |
| remove fireplace clean-out | 1D@.069 | ea | — | 2.68 | 2.68 |
| remove chimney pipe | 1D@.021 | lf | — | .82 | .82 |
| remove gas log lighter | 1D@.227 | ea | — | 8.83 | 8.83 |
| remove gas fireplace kit | 1D@.251 | ea | — | 9.76 | 9.76 |
| remove marble fireplace face | 1D@3.03 | ea | — | 118.00 | 118.00 |
| remove brick fireplace face | 1D@3.23 | ea | — | 126.00 | 126.00 |
| remove stone fireplace face | 1D@3.45 | ea | — | 134.00 | 134.00 |
| remove tile fireplace face | 1D@2.94 | ea | — | 114.00 | 114.00 |
| remove marble fireplace hearth | 1D@1.45 | ea | — | 56.40 | 56.40 |
| remove brick fireplace hearth | 1D@1.52 | ea | — | 59.10 | 59.10 |
| remove stone fireplace hearth | 1D@1.56 | ea | — | 60.70 | 60.70 |
| remove tile fireplace hearth | 1D@1.43 | ea | — | 55.60 | 55.60 |

## Fireplace crew

| build fireplace | mason | $59.40 |
|---|---|---|
| build fireplace | mason's helper | $54.50 |
| build fireplace | mason & helper | $57.00 |

Build open front fireplace

|  | Craft@Hrs | Unit | Material | Labor | Total |
|---|---|---|---|---|---|
| 30" wide by 16" by 29" | 1M@16.1 | ea | — | 956.00 | 956.00 |
| 36" wide by 16" by 29" | 1M@16.9 | ea | — | 1,000.00 | 1,000.00 |
| 40" wide by 16" by 29" | 1M@17.5 | ea | — | 1,040.00 | 1,040.00 |
| 48" wide by 18" by 32" | 1M@18.5 | ea | — | 1,100.00 | 1,100.00 |

Build open front and one side fireplace

|  | Craft@Hrs | Unit | Material | Labor | Total |
|---|---|---|---|---|---|
| 32" wide by 16" by 26" | 1M@16.7 | ea | — | 992.00 | 992.00 |
| 40" wide by 16" by 29" | 1M@17.5 | ea | — | 1,040.00 | 1,040.00 |
| 48" wide by 20" by 29" | 1M@18.9 | ea | — | 1,120.00 | 1,120.00 |

Build open two faces (see through) fireplace

|  | Craft@Hrs | Unit | Material | Labor | Total |
|---|---|---|---|---|---|
| 32" wide by 28" by 29" | 1M@18.5 | ea | — | 1,100.00 | 1,100.00 |
| 36" wide by 28" by 29" | 1M@18.9 | ea | — | 1,120.00 | 1,120.00 |
| 40" wide by 28" by 29" | 1M@19.2 | ea | — | 1,140.00 | 1,140.00 |

| | Craft@Hrs | Unit | Material | Labor | Total |
|---|---|---|---|---|---|
| **Build open two faces and one side fireplace** | | | | | |
| 36" wide by 32" by 27" | 1M@19.2 | ea | — | 1,140.00 | 1,140.00 |
| 36" wide by 36" by 27" | 1M@20.0 | ea | — | 1,190.00 | 1,190.00 |
| 44" wide by 40" by 27" | 1M@20.4 | ea | — | 1,210.00 | 1,210.00 |
| **Install prefabricated fireplace** | | | | | |
| radiation | 1M@4.55 | ea | — | 270.00 | 270.00 |
| convection | 1M@4.76 | ea | — | 283.00 | 283.00 |
| forced-air | 1M@5.26 | ea | — | 312.00 | 312.00 |
| **Install fireplace form** | | | | | |
| form | 1M@3.03 | ea | — | 180.00 | 180.00 |
| **Install fireplace furnace** | | | | | |
| typical | 1M@34.5 | ea | — | 2,050.00 | 2,050.00 |
| **Install fire brick** | | | | | |
| complete fireplace | 1M@3.03 | ea | — | 180.00 | 180.00 |
| concrete simulated firebrick (complete fireplace) | 1M@1.85 | ea | — | 110.00 | 110.00 |
| **Build brick chimney** | | | | | |
| 16" by 16" with one 8" x 8" flue | 5M@2.21 | lf | — | 126.00 | 126.00 |
| 16" by 24" with two 8" x 8" flues | 5M@3.09 | lf | — | 176.00 | 176.00 |
| 16" by 20" with one 8" x 12" flue | 5M@2.24 | lf | — | 128.00 | 128.00 |
| 20" by 24" with two 8" x 12" flues | 5M@3.15 | lf | — | 180.00 | 180.00 |
| 20" by 20" with one 12" x 12" flue | 5M@2.27 | lf | — | 129.00 | 129.00 |
| 20" by 32" with two 12" x 12" flues | 5M@3.24 | lf | — | 185.00 | 185.00 |
| 20" by 24" with one 12" x 16" flue | 5M@2.31 | lf | — | 132.00 | 132.00 |
| 20" by 40" with two 12" x 16" flues | 5M@3.30 | lf | — | 188.00 | 188.00 |
| 24" by 24" with one 16" x 16" flue | 5M@2.35 | lf | — | 134.00 | 134.00 |
| 24" by 40" with two 16" x 16" flues | 5M@3.36 | lf | — | 192.00 | 192.00 |
| add for bend in one flue | 5M@3.33 | ea | — | 190.00 | 190.00 |
| add for bend in two flues | 5M@4.05 | ea | — | 231.00 | 231.00 |
| **Pour 2" thick concrete chimney cap** | | | | | |
| single flue | 1M@1.00 | ea | — | 59.40 | 59.40 |
| double flue | 1M@1.49 | ea | — | 88.50 | 88.50 |
| **Install cast stone chimney cap** | | | | | |
| typical | 1M@1.28 | ea | — | 76.00 | 76.00 |
| **Install galvanized steel chimney cap** | | | | | |
| with spark arrestor | 2M@.298 | ea | — | 16.20 | 16.20 |
| **Install chimney pot** | | | | | |
| typical | 1M@1.18 | ea | — | 70.10 | 70.10 |
| **Install chimney bird screen** | | | | | |
| for single flue | 2M@.437 | ea | — | 23.80 | 23.80 |
| for double flue | 2M@.476 | ea | — | 25.90 | 25.90 |
| **Install fireplace grate** | | | | | |
| typical | 2M@.119 | ea | — | 6.49 | 6.49 |
| **Install fireplace screen** | | | | | |
| typical | 2M@.794 | ea | — | 43.30 | 43.30 |

| | Craft@Hrs | Unit | Material | Labor | Total |
|---|---|---|---|---|---|
| Install fireplace door | | | | | |
| typical | 2M@1.00 | ea | — | 54.50 | 54.50 |
| Install fireplace clean-out | | | | | |
| typical | 1M@.625 | ea | — | 37.10 | 37.10 |
| Install fireplace damper | | | | | |
| rotary control | 1M@1.11 | ea | — | 65.90 | 65.90 |
| poker control | 1M@.901 | ea | — | 53.50 | 53.50 |
| Install chimney pipe | | | | | |
| typical | 2M@.578 | lf | — | 31.50 | 31.50 |
| add through interior ceiling | 2M@1.11 | ea | — | 60.50 | 60.50 |
| add through roof | 2M@2.94 | ea | — | 160.00 | 160.00 |
| Install gas log lighter | | | | | |
| typical | 2M@1.18 | ea | — | 64.30 | 64.30 |
| Install gas fireplace kit | | | | | |
| typical | 2M@1.25 | ea | — | 68.10 | 68.10 |
| Install fireplace face | | | | | |
| marble economy grade | 1M@3.57 | ea | — | 212.00 | 212.00 |
| marble deluxe grade | 1M@8.00 | ea | — | 475.00 | 475.00 |
| brick economy grade | 1M@16.1 | ea | — | 956.00 | 956.00 |
| brick deluxe grade | 1M@32.3 | ea | — | 1,920.00 | 1,920.00 |
| rubble stone economy grade | 1M@17.5 | ea | — | 1,040.00 | 1,040.00 |
| rubble stone deluxe grade | 1M@34.5 | ea | — | 2,050.00 | 2,050.00 |
| ashlar stone economy grade | 1M@17.2 | ea | — | 1,020.00 | 1,020.00 |
| ashlar stone deluxe grade | 1M@33.3 | ea | — | 1,980.00 | 1,980.00 |
| ashlar stone economy grade | 1M@3.70 | ea | — | 220.00 | 220.00 |
| ashlar stone deluxe grade | 1M@8.26 | ea | — | 491.00 | 491.00 |
| Install fireplace hearth | | | | | |
| marble economy grade | 1M@2.16 | ea | — | 128.00 | 128.00 |
| marble deluxe grade | 1M@4.83 | ea | — | 287.00 | 287.00 |
| brick economy grade | 1M@7.04 | ea | — | 418.00 | 418.00 |
| brick deluxe grade | 1M@11.1 | ea | — | 659.00 | 659.00 |
| rubble stone economy grade | 1M@7.63 | ea | — | 453.00 | 453.00 |
| rubble stone deluxe grade | 1M@12.0 | ea | — | 713.00 | 713.00 |
| ashlar stone economy grade | 1M@7.46 | ea | — | 443.00 | 443.00 |
| ashlar stone deluxe grade | 1M@11.8 | ea | — | 701.00 | 701.00 |
| tile economy grade | 1M@2.24 | ea | — | 133.00 | 133.00 |
| tile deluxe grade | 1M@5.00 | ea | — | 297.00 | 297.00 |

| | Craft@Hrs | Unit | Material | Labor | Total |
|---|---|---|---|---|---|

# Flooring

**Carpet.** Includes carpet, tackless strips, seaming tape, and installation. Includes 12% waste. Does not include pad. Carpet is available in virtually every price imaginable. These prices should be considered allowances for typical grades found in residential and light commercial structures. Lower grades have thin pile that can be pulled aside to expose the backing. Top grades include wool carpets, pattern carpets, and 52-ounce cut pile carpets.

| | Craft@Hrs | Unit | Material | Labor | Total |
|---|---|---|---|---|---|
| replace, economy grade | 5I@.138 | sy | 22.20 | 6.60 | 28.80 |
| replace, standard grade | 5I@.138 | sy | 26.90 | 6.60 | 33.50 |
| replace, high grade | 5I@.138 | sy | 35.70 | 6.60 | 42.30 |
| replace, deluxe grade | 5I@.138 | sy | 42.80 | 6.60 | 49.40 |
| replace, custom grade | 5I@.138 | sy | 51.70 | 6.60 | 58.30 |
| remove | 1D@.062 | sy | — | 2.41 | 2.41 |
| remove for work, then re-lay | 5I@.211 | sy | — | 10.10 | 10.10 |

**Glue-down carpet.** Includes carpet, glue, seaming material, and installation. Includes 12% waste. Pad may be integrated into carpet. These prices should be considered allowances for typical grades found in residential and light commercial structures.

| | Craft@Hrs | Unit | Material | Labor | Total |
|---|---|---|---|---|---|
| replace, economy grade | 5I@.167 | sy | 16.80 | 7.98 | 24.78 |
| replace, standard grade | 5I@.167 | sy | 19.50 | 7.98 | 27.48 |
| replace, high grade | 5I@.167 | sy | 25.80 | 7.98 | 33.78 |
| replace, deluxe grade | 5I@.167 | sy | 31.20 | 7.98 | 39.18 |
| remove | 1D@.155 | sy | — | 6.03 | 6.03 |

**Indoor-outdoor carpet.** Includes carpet, glue, seaming material, and installation. Includes 12% waste. Pad may be integrated into carpet. These prices should be considered allowances for typical grades found in residential and light commercial structures. Higher grades are similar to commercial quality glue-down carpet, lowest grade is plastic imitation grass.

| | Craft@Hrs | Unit | Material | Labor | Total |
|---|---|---|---|---|---|
| replace, economy grade | 5I@.167 | sy | 12.30 | 7.98 | 20.28 |
| replace, standard grade | 5I@.167 | sy | 17.50 | 7.98 | 25.48 |
| replace, high grade | 5I@.167 | sy | 25.80 | 7.98 | 33.78 |
| replace, deluxe grade | 5I@.167 | sy | 39.30 | 7.98 | 47.28 |
| remove | 1D@.153 | sy | — | 5.95 | 5.95 |

**Wool carpet.** Includes carpet, tackless strips, seaming tape, and installation. Includes 12% waste. Does not include pad. These prices should be considered allowances for typical grades of wool carpet found in residential and light commercial structures. Lower grades have thin pile that can be pulled aside to expose the backing. Top grades include patterns and thick piles. Many synthetic fiber carpets mimic the look of wool and can be hard to differentiate. If on a fire job, wool carpet has a noticeable "burnt-hair" smell.

| | Craft@Hrs | Unit | Material | Labor | Total |
|---|---|---|---|---|---|
| replace, standard grade | 5I@.139 | sy | 33.20 | 6.64 | 39.84 |
| replace, high grade | 5I@.139 | sy | 41.70 | 6.64 | 48.34 |
| replace, deluxe grade | 5I@.139 | sy | 54.80 | 6.64 | 61.44 |
| replace, custom grade | 5I@.139 | sy | 69.50 | 6.64 | 76.14 |
| remove | 1D@.062 | sy | — | 2.41 | 2.41 |

**Carpet installation on stairs.** Includes extra labor, waste and tackless strips needed to install carpet on steps. Does not include the carpet or pad. Installation can be either waterfall or tuck style.

| | Craft@Hrs | Unit | Material | Labor | Total |
|---|---|---|---|---|---|
| per step | 5I@.180 | ea | 1.84 | 8.60 | 10.44 |

| | Craft@Hrs | Unit | Material | Labor | Total |
|---|---|---|---|---|---|
| **Carpet pad.** Includes carpet pad, glue, and installation. | | | | | |
| replace, urethane rebound | 5I@.017 | sy | 6.07 | .81 | 6.88 |
| replace, urethane | 5I@.017 | sy | 4.06 | .81 | 4.87 |
| replace, rubber waffle | 5I@.017 | sy | 4.63 | .81 | 5.44 |
| replace, jute | 5I@.017 | sy | 4.24 | .81 | 5.05 |
| remove | 1D@.030 | sy | — | 1.17 | 1.17 |
| **Add for carpet cove.** Carpet wrapped up the wall up to 8" high with metal cap. Grades refer to allowances for quality of carpet. | | | | | |
| replace, economy grade | 5I@.135 | lf | 2.81 | 6.45 | 9.26 |
| replace, standard grade | 5I@.135 | lf | 3.50 | 6.45 | 9.95 |
| replace, high grade | 5I@.135 | lf | 4.63 | 6.45 | 11.08 |
| replace, deluxe grade | 5I@.135 | lf | 5.60 | 6.45 | 12.05 |
| replace, custom grade | 5I@.135 | lf | 6.59 | 6.45 | 13.04 |
| remove | 1D@.022 | lf | — | .86 | .86 |
| remove for work, then re-lay | 5I@.211 | lf | — | 10.10 | 10.10 |
| **Carpet tile.** Includes carpet tile, glue when needed, and installation. Includes 12% waste. | | | | | |
| replace, economy grade | 5I@.107 | sy | 36.20 | 5.11 | 41.31 |
| replace, standard grade | 5I@.107 | sy | 43.50 | 5.11 | 48.61 |
| replace, high grade | 5I@.107 | sy | 55.50 | 5.11 | 60.61 |
| remove | 1D@.155 | sy | — | 6.03 | 6.03 |
| **Minimum charge.** | | | | | |
| for carpeting work | 5I@2.50 | ea | 80.00 | 120.00 | 200.00 |
| **Stone floor.** Grades vary by region. Standard grade includes flagstone, Chattahoochee, and some sandstone. High grade includes better sandstone and lower to medium grade limestone. Deluxe grade includes higher grade limestone, sandstone and granite. | | | | | |
| replace, standard grade | 5I@.191 | sf | 8.17 | 9.13 | 17.30 |
| replace, high grade | 5I@.191 | sf | 10.80 | 9.13 | 19.93 |
| replace, deluxe grade | 5I@.191 | sf | 13.00 | 9.13 | 22.13 |
| replace, salvage, then reinstall | 5I@.500 | sf | 1.54 | 23.90 | 25.44 |
| remove | 1D@.082 | sf | — | 3.19 | 3.19 |
| regrout | 5I@.038 | sf | .66 | 1.82 | 2.48 |
| minimum charge | 5I@3.00 | ea | — | 143.00 | 143.00 |
| **Marble floor.** Includes marble tile, grout, mortar, and installation. Allowance is for typical grades of marble used in residential and light commercial structures. | | | | | |
| replace, standard grade | 5I@.189 | sf | 13.70 | 9.03 | 22.73 |
| replace, high grade | 5I@.189 | sf | 28.60 | 9.03 | 37.63 |
| replace, deluxe grade | 5I@.189 | sf | 44.60 | 9.03 | 53.63 |
| remove | 1D@.080 | sf | — | 3.11 | 3.11 |
| regrout | 5I@.034 | sf | .51 | 1.63 | 2.14 |
| minimum charge | 5I@3.00 | ea | 98.80 | 143.00 | 241.80 |

| | Craft@Hrs | Unit | Material | Labor | Total |
|---|---|---|---|---|---|

**Slate floor.** Allowances Includes slate tile, grout, mortar, and installation. Allowances for typical grades of slate used in residential and light commercial structures.

| | Craft@Hrs | Unit | Material | Labor | Total |
|---|---|---|---|---|---|
| replace, standard grade | 5I@.189 | sf | 10.60 | 9.03 | 19.63 |
| replace, high grade | 5I@.189 | sf | 13.10 | 9.03 | 22.13 |
| replace, deluxe grade | 5I@.189 | sf | 15.70 | 9.03 | 24.73 |
| remove | 1D@.080 | sf | — | 3.11 | 3.11 |
| regrout | 5I@.034 | sf | .51 | 1.63 | 2.14 |
| salvage, then reinstall | 5I@.490 | sf | .97 | 23.40 | 24.37 |
| minimum charge | 5I@3.00 | ea | 96.20 | 143.00 | 239.20 |

**Tile floor.** Includes tile, grout, mortar, and installation. Allowances for typical grades of tile used in residential and light commercial structures. Tile quality can be hard to judge. Higher quality tile has distinct patterns. Blurry or fuzzy patterns are a sign of lower quality tile. Sharp edges and clear patterns are usually a sign of high quality tile. Higher quality tile is also free from blemishes, has consistently straight edges, is uniform in size, lies flat, and is free of glaze cracks (sometimes called alligatoring or lizard tails). Although color will vary in all tiles, even in the same dye lot, higher grade tile is more consistent in color. Some high grade tile will violate some of these indicators but in most cases they are good rules of thumb.

| | Craft@Hrs | Unit | Material | Labor | Total |
|---|---|---|---|---|---|
| replace, standard grade | 5I@.180 | sf | 6.87 | 8.60 | 15.47 |
| replace, high grade | 5I@.180 | sf | 9.12 | 8.60 | 17.72 |
| replace, deluxe grade | 5I@.180 | sf | 11.30 | 8.60 | 19.90 |
| remove | 1D@.080 | sf | — | 3.11 | 3.11 |
| regrout tile floor | 5I@.035 | sf | .82 | 1.67 | 2.49 |
| minimum charge | 5I@3.00 | ea | 80.00 | 143.00 | 223.00 |

**Quarry tile floor.** Includes quarry tile, grout, mortar, and installation. Allowances for typical grades of quarry tile used in residential and light commercial structures. Quarry tile is clay-based and unglazed and typically comes in earth tones. Quarry tile quality can be hard to judge. Higher quality tile is free from blemishes, has consistently straight edges, is uniform in size, lays flat, and is free of defects. Although color will vary in all tile even in the same dye lot, higher grade tile is more consistent in color. Some high grade tile will violate some of these indicators but in most cases they are good rules of thumb. Does not include sealer.

| | Craft@Hrs | Unit | Material | Labor | Total |
|---|---|---|---|---|---|
| replace, standard grade | 5I@.143 | sf | 9.06 | 6.84 | 15.90 |
| replace, high grade | 5I@.143 | sf | 13.30 | 6.84 | 20.14 |
| replace, deluxe grade | 5I@.143 | sf | 18.00 | 6.84 | 24.84 |
| remove | 1D@.078 | sf | — | 3.03 | 3.03 |

**Tile base.** Allowances for typical grades of tile used in residential and light commercial structures.

| | Craft@Hrs | Unit | Material | Labor | Total |
|---|---|---|---|---|---|
| replace, standard grade | 5I@.128 | lf | 5.78 | 6.12 | 11.90 |
| replace, high grade | 5I@.128 | lf | 7.72 | 6.12 | 13.84 |
| replace, deluxe grade | 5I@.128 | lf | 9.65 | 6.12 | 15.77 |
| remove | 1D@.061 | lf | — | 2.37 | 2.37 |

**Precast terrazzo floor tiles.** Includes precast 12" x 12" terrazzo tile, self-leveling compound as needed, mortar, and installation. Cast in gray cement. Add **2%** for white cement.

| | Craft@Hrs | Unit | Material | Labor | Total |
|---|---|---|---|---|---|
| replace, standard grade | 5I@.116 | sf | 17.20 | 5.54 | 22.74 |
| replace, high grade | 5I@.116 | sf | 19.20 | 5.54 | 24.74 |
| remove | 1D@.081 | sf | — | 3.15 | 3.15 |
| minimum charge | 5I@3.00 | ea | 80.00 | 143.00 | 223.00 |

**Precast terrazzo base.** Includes precast terrazzo base, mortar, and installation. Cast in gray cement.

| | Craft@Hrs | Unit | Material | Labor | Total |
|---|---|---|---|---|---|
| replace, 6" high | 5I@.256 | sf | 11.30 | 12.20 | 23.50 |
| replace, 8" high | 5I@.256 | sf | 12.30 | 12.20 | 24.50 |
| remove | 1D@.061 | sf | — | 2.37 | 2.37 |

| | Craft@Hrs | Unit | Material | Labor | Total |
|---|---|---|---|---|---|

**Cast-in-place thinset terrazzo floor.** Includes terrazzo, zinc divider strips, equipment, and installation. Cast in gray cement. Add **3%** for brass divider strips. Standard grade is 1-1/2" deep, high grade is up to 3" thick.

| | Craft@Hrs | Unit | Material | Labor | Total |
|---|---|---|---|---|---|
| replace, standard grade | 5I@.128 | sf | 3.68 | 6.12 | 9.80 |
| replace, high grade | 5I@.128 | sf | 5.51 | 6.12 | 11.63 |
| remove | 1D@.082 | sf | — | 3.19 | 3.19 |
| minimum charge | 5I@5.00 | ea | 116.00 | 239.00 | 355.00 |

**Vinyl floor.** Includes sheet vinyl in either 6' or 12' widths, vinyl glue, and installation. Allowances for typical grades of vinyl used in residential and light commercial structures. Higher quality vinyl is thicker at 25-30 mils than lower quality vinyl which can be as thin as 10 to 15 mils. Blurry or fuzzy patterns are a sign of lower quality vinyl. Sharp edges, bright colors, and clear patterns are usually a sign of high quality vinyl. Higher quality vinyl is also free from blemishes. Does not include vinyl cove. Estimate vinyl cove separately.

| | Craft@Hrs | Unit | Material | Labor | Total |
|---|---|---|---|---|---|
| replace, economy grade | 5I@.183 | sy | 20.10 | 8.75 | 28.85 |
| replace, standard grade | 5I@.183 | sy | 26.20 | 8.75 | 34.95 |
| replace, high grade | 5I@.183 | sy | 32.90 | 8.75 | 41.65 |
| replace, deluxe grade | 5I@.183 | sy | 46.20 | 8.75 | 54.95 |
| remove | 1D@.175 | sy | — | 6.81 | 6.81 |
| minimum charge | 5I@3.00 | ea | 67.80 | 143.00 | 210.80 |

**Vinyl tile floor.** Includes vinyl tile with either a "peel-and-stick" or dry back, vinyl glue as needed, and installation. Allowances for typical grades of vinyl tile used in residential and light commercial structures. Higher quality vinyl tile is thicker at 25-30 mils than lower quality vinyl tile which can be as thin as 15 mils. Blurry or fuzzy patterns are a sign of lower quality vinyl. Sharp edges and clear patterns are usually a sign of high quality vinyl tile. Higher quality vinyl tile is also free from blemishes.

| | Craft@Hrs | Unit | Material | Labor | Total |
|---|---|---|---|---|---|
| replace, economy grade | 5I@.029 | sf | 1.41 | 1.39 | 2.80 |
| replace, standard grade | 5I@.029 | sf | 2.25 | 1.39 | 3.64 |
| replace, high grade | 5I@.029 | sf | 2.51 | 1.39 | 3.90 |
| replace, deluxe grade | 5I@.029 | sf | 3.97 | 1.39 | 5.36 |
| remove | 1D@.024 | sf | — | .93 | .93 |
| minimum charge | 5I@2.00 | ea | 43.10 | 95.60 | 138.70 |

**Resilient tile floor.** Includes resilient tile with either a "peel-and-stick" or dry back, vinyl glue as needed, and installation. Allowances for typical grades of resilient tile used in residential and light commercial structures. Higher quality resilient tile is thicker at 25-30 mils than lower quality tile which can be as thin as 15 mils. Blurry or fuzzy patterns are a sign of lower quality tile. Sharp edges and clear patterns are usually a sign of high quality resilient tile. Higher quality resilient tile is also free from blemishes.

| | Craft@Hrs | Unit | Material | Labor | Total |
|---|---|---|---|---|---|
| replace, economy grade | 5I@.029 | sf | 1.55 | 1.39 | 2.94 |
| replace, standard grade | 5I@.029 | sf | 1.95 | 1.39 | 3.34 |
| replace, high grade | 5I@.029 | sf | 2.25 | 1.39 | 3.64 |
| replace, deluxe grade | 5I@.029 | sf | 3.27 | 1.39 | 4.66 |
| remove | 1D@.024 | sf | — | .93 | .93 |
| minimum charge | 5I@2.00 | ea | 43.10 | 95.60 | 138.70 |

**Antique style linoleum.** Includes linoleum flooring, linoleum glue, and installation. Not to be confused with vinyl flooring. Antique style linoleum is no longer made in the USA and must be imported from Europe. In recent years linoleum has become much more common in commercial and residential applications. Tiles are normally available in limited styles and colors.

| | Craft@Hrs | Unit | Material | Labor | Total |
|---|---|---|---|---|---|
| replace, plain and marbleized | 5I@.189 | sy | 46.10 | 9.03 | 55.13 |
| replace, inlaid & molded | 5I@.189 | sy | 59.90 | 9.03 | 68.93 |
| replace, battleship | 5I@.189 | sy | 42.20 | 9.03 | 51.23 |
| replace, tile | 5I@.032 | sf | 6.31 | 1.53 | 7.84 |
| remove | 1D@.175 | sy | — | 6.81 | 6.81 |
| minimum charge | 5I@3.50 | ea | 130.00 | 167.00 | 297.00 |

|  | Craft@Hrs | Unit | Material | Labor | Total |
|---|---|---|---|---|---|

**Vinyl cove.** Includes the additional labor and material cost to wrap vinyl up a wall with a metal cap. Add to the cost of vinyl floor covering with the same quality.

|  | Craft@Hrs | Unit | Material | Labor | Total |
|---|---|---|---|---|---|
| replace, 4" high | 5I@.091 | lf | 2.81 | 4.35 | 7.16 |
| replace, 6" high | 5I@.091 | lf | 2.96 | 4.35 | 7.31 |
| replace, 8" high | 5I@.091 | lf | 3.22 | 4.35 | 7.57 |
| remove | 1D@.036 | lf | — | 1.40 | 1.40 |
| minimum charge | 5I@1.25 | ea | 36.90 | 59.80 | 96.70 |

**Rubber base.** Includes rubber base, glue, and installation. Economy grade is black or brown 2-1/2" high. Standard grade is 4" high standard colors. High grade is 6" high. Deluxe grade is 6" high, specialty colors.

|  | Craft@Hrs | Unit | Material | Labor | Total |
|---|---|---|---|---|---|
| replace, economy grade | 5I@.020 | lf | 1.99 | .96 | 2.95 |
| replace, standard grade | 5I@.020 | lf | 2.51 | .96 | 3.47 |
| replace, high grade | 5I@.020 | lf | 3.36 | .96 | 4.32 |
| replace, deluxe grade | 5I@.020 | lf | 3.97 | .96 | 4.93 |
| remove | 1D@.011 | lf | — | .43 | .43 |
| minimum charge | 5I@.750 | ea | 24.60 | 35.90 | 60.50 |

**Maple strip flooring.** Includes maple strip flooring boards, nails, and installation. Strip flooring is up to 3/4" thick and up to 3-1/4" wide. Grading information based on rules established by the Maple Flooring Manufacturers Association (MFMA). All wood is kiln-dried, tongue-and-groove, end-matched and hollow or scratch backed. Does not include vapor barrier or sleepers.

|  | Craft@Hrs | Unit | Material | Labor | Total |
|---|---|---|---|---|---|
| replace, first grade | 5I@.088 | sf | 10.70 | 4.21 | 14.91 |
| replace, second grade | 5I@.088 | sf | 8.26 | 4.21 | 12.47 |
| replace, third grade | 5I@.088 | sf | 6.31 | 4.21 | 10.52 |
| remove | 1D@.020 | sf | — | .78 | .78 |

**Red oak strip flooring.** Strip flooring is up to 3/4" thick and up to 3-1/4" wide. Grading information based on rules established by the National Oak Flooring Manufacturers Association (NOFMA). All wood is kiln-dried, tongue-and-groove, end-matched and hollow or scratch backed.

|  | Craft@Hrs | Unit | Material | Labor | Total |
|---|---|---|---|---|---|
| replace, select & better grade | 5I@.088 | sf | 9.79 | 4.21 | 14.00 |
| replace, #1 common grade | 5I@.088 | sf | 8.15 | 4.21 | 12.36 |
| replace, #2 common grade | 5I@.088 | sf | 5.77 | 4.21 | 9.98 |
| remove | 1D@.020 | sf | — | .78 | .78 |

**Red oak strip flooring, quartersawn.**

|  | Craft@Hrs | Unit | Material | Labor | Total |
|---|---|---|---|---|---|
| replace, clear grade | 5I@.088 | sf | 23.60 | 4.21 | 27.81 |
| replace, select grade | 5I@.088 | sf | 19.50 | 4.21 | 23.71 |
| remove | 1D@.020 | sf | — | .78 | .78 |

**Prefinished red oak strip flooring.** Includes pre-finished red oak strip flooring boards, nails, and installation. Strip flooring is up to 3/4" thick and up to 3-1/4" wide. Grading information based on rules established by the National Oak Flooring Manufacturers Association (NOFMA). All wood is kiln-dried, tongue-and-groove, end-matched and hollow or scratch backed. Does not include vapor barrier or sleepers.

|  | Craft@Hrs | Unit | Material | Labor | Total |
|---|---|---|---|---|---|
| replace, prime grade | 5I@.091 | sf | 11.10 | 4.35 | 15.45 |
| replace, standard & better grade | 5I@.091 | sf | 9.44 | 4.35 | 13.79 |
| replace, standard grade | 5I@.091 | sf | 15.80 | 4.35 | 20.15 |
| replace, tavern & better grade | 5I@.091 | sf | 26.50 | 4.35 | 30.85 |
| replace, tavern grade | 5I@.091 | sf | 45.00 | 4.35 | 49.35 |
| remove | 1D@.020 | sf | — | .78 | .78 |

| | Craft@Hrs | Unit | Material | Labor | Total |
|---|---|---|---|---|---|

**Red oak plank flooring.** Includes red oak planks, nails, and installation. Plank flooring is up to 3/4" thick and over 3-1/4" wide. Floors that contain a mix of plank and strip floor widths are usually considered plank floors. Grading information based on rules established by the National Oak Flooring Manufacturers Association (NOFMA). Does not include vapor barrier or sleepers.

| | Craft@Hrs | Unit | Material | Labor | Total |
|---|---|---|---|---|---|
| replace, select & better grade | 5I@.079 | sf | 21.80 | 3.78 | 25.58 |
| replace, #1 common grade | 5I@.079 | sf | 18.00 | 3.78 | 21.78 |
| replace, #2 common grade | 5I@.079 | sf | 12.80 | 3.78 | 16.58 |
| remove | 1D@.019 | sf | — | .74 | .74 |

**Maple parquet or block flooring.** Clear grade. Includes parquet blocks, adhesive, and installation. Face pieces are practically clear, may have some small areas of bright sap. For select grade deduct **8%**. For #1 common grade deduct **15%**.

| | Craft@Hrs | Unit | Material | Labor | Total |
|---|---|---|---|---|---|
| replace, unit block | 5I@.092 | sf | 7.95 | 4.40 | 12.35 |
| replace, laminated block | 5I@.092 | sf | 9.37 | 4.40 | 13.77 |
| replace, slat block | 5I@.092 | sf | 10.20 | 4.40 | 14.60 |
| remove | 1D@.018 | sf | — | .70 | .70 |

**Prefinished maple parquet or block flooring.** Prime grade. Face pieces are almost flawless with very small character marks. (Sap and color variations are not flaws.) For standard grade deduct **10%**. For tavern grade deduct **14%**.

| | Craft@Hrs | Unit | Material | Labor | Total |
|---|---|---|---|---|---|
| replace, unit block | 5I@.094 | sf | 8.99 | 4.49 | 13.48 |
| replace, laminated block | 5I@.094 | sf | 10.40 | 4.49 | 14.89 |
| replace, slat block | 5I@.094 | sf | 11.10 | 4.49 | 15.59 |
| remove | 1D@.018 | sf | — | .70 | .70 |

**Red oak parquet or block flooring.** Clear grade. Face pieces are practically clear, may have some small areas of bright sap. For select grade deduct **8%**. For #1 common grade deduct **15%**.

| | Craft@Hrs | Unit | Material | Labor | Total |
|---|---|---|---|---|---|
| replace, unit block | 5I@.092 | sf | 9.26 | 4.40 | 13.66 |
| replace, laminated block | 5I@.092 | sf | 10.90 | 4.40 | 15.30 |
| replace, slat block | 5I@.092 | sf | 11.60 | 4.40 | 16.00 |
| remove | 1D@.018 | sf | — | .70 | .70 |

**Prefinished red oak parquet or block flooring.** Prime grade. Face pieces are almost flawless with very small character marks. (Sap and color variations are not flaws.) For standard grade deduct **10%**. For Tavern grade deduct **14%**.

| | Craft@Hrs | Unit | Material | Labor | Total |
|---|---|---|---|---|---|
| replace, unit block | 5I@.094 | sf | 10.50 | 4.49 | 14.99 |
| replace, laminated block | 5I@.094 | sf | 12.20 | 4.49 | 16.69 |
| replace, slat block | 5I@.094 | sf | 13.00 | 4.49 | 17.49 |
| remove | 1D@.018 | sf | — | .70 | .70 |

**Additional cost for parquet.** Pickets are mitered wood trim around edges of block.

| | Craft@Hrs | Unit | Material | Labor | Total |
|---|---|---|---|---|---|
| Add for pickets around unit block | — | % | 8.0 | — | — |

**Additional wood species.** Add to the costs of red oak for these wood species.

| | Craft@Hrs | Unit | Material | Labor | Total |
|---|---|---|---|---|---|
| deduct for beech flooring | — | % | -7.0 | — | — |
| deduct for birch flooring | — | % | -7.0 | — | — |
| deduct for ash flooring | — | % | -6.0 | — | — |
| add for cherry flooring | — | % | 46.0 | — | — |
| add for Brazilian cherry | — | % | 45.0 | — | — |
| deduct for hickory flooring | — | % | -5.0 | — | — |
| add for teak flooring | — | % | 182.0 | — | — |
| add for walnut flooring | — | % | 70.0 | — | — |
| deduct for white oak | — | % | -7.0 | — | — |
| add for bamboo | — | % | 37.0 | — | — |

| | Craft@Hrs | Unit | Material | Labor | Total |
|---|---|---|---|---|---|

**Southern pine strip flooring.** Strip flooring is up to 3/4" thick and up to 3-1/4" wide. Grading information based on rules established by the Southern Pine Inspection Bureau (SPIB). All wood is kiln-dried, tongue-&-groove, end-matched and hollow or scratch backed.

| | Craft@Hrs | Unit | Material | Labor | Total |
|---|---|---|---|---|---|
| replace, B&B grade | 5I@.088 | sf | 3.84 | 4.21 | 8.05 |
| replace, C & better grade | 5I@.088 | sf | 3.53 | 4.21 | 7.74 |
| replace, C grade | 5I@.088 | sf | 3.14 | 4.21 | 7.35 |
| remove | 1D@.020 | sf | — | .78 | .78 |

**Southern pine plank flooring.** Plank flooring is up to 3/4" thick and over 3-1/4" wide. Floors that contain a mix of plank and strip floor widths are usually considered plank floors. See southern pine strip flooring above for grading information.

| | Craft@Hrs | Unit | Material | Labor | Total |
|---|---|---|---|---|---|
| replace, B&B grade | 5I@.079 | sf | 4.63 | 3.78 | 8.41 |
| replace, C & better grade | 5I@.079 | sf | 4.20 | 3.78 | 7.98 |
| replace, C grade | 5I@.079 | sf | 3.81 | 3.78 | 7.59 |
| remove | 1D@.019 | sf | — | .74 | .74 |

**Douglas fir strip flooring.** Douglas fir or western hemlock, or white fir, or Sitka spruce. Strip flooring is up to 3/4" thick and up to 3-1/4" wide. Grading information based on rules established by the West Coast Lumbermen's Inspection Bureau (WCLIB). All wood is kiln-dried, tongue-&-groove, end-matched and hollow or scratch backed.

| | Craft@Hrs | Unit | Material | Labor | Total |
|---|---|---|---|---|---|
| replace, C & better grade | 5I@.088 | sf | 4.12 | 4.21 | 8.33 |
| replace, D grade | 5I@.088 | sf | 3.81 | 4.21 | 8.02 |
| replace, E grade | 5I@.088 | sf | 3.41 | 4.21 | 7.62 |
| remove | 1D@.020 | sf | — | .78 | .78 |

**Douglas fir plank flooring.** Plank flooring is up to 3/4" thick and over 3-1/4" wide. Floors that contain a mix of plank and strip floor widths are usually considered plank floors. See Douglas fir strip flooring for grading information.

| | Craft@Hrs | Unit | Material | Labor | Total |
|---|---|---|---|---|---|
| replace, C & better grade | 5I@.079 | sf | 5.02 | 3.78 | 8.80 |
| replace, D grade | 5I@.079 | sf | 4.60 | 3.78 | 8.38 |
| replace, E grade | 5I@.079 | sf | 4.06 | 3.78 | 7.84 |
| remove | 1D@.019 | sf | — | .74 | .74 |

**Reclaimed antique longleaf pine flooring.** Includes reclaimed antique longleaf pine flooring boards, nails, and installation. Strip or plank flooring. Although longleaf pine was once common in Southeastern America, new lumber is no longer available. Longleaf pine must be salvaged from existing structures. (Although Goodwin Heart Pine Company of Micanopy, Florida does salvage logs that sank to the bottom of rivers.) Grading is based on grades marketed by Mountain Lumber Company, Inc. of Ruckersville, Virginia. Does not include vapor barrier or sleepers.

| | Craft@Hrs | Unit | Material | Labor | Total |
|---|---|---|---|---|---|
| replace, crown grade | 5I@.088 | sf | 19.20 | 4.21 | 23.41 |
| replace, select prime grade | 5I@.088 | sf | 15.10 | 4.21 | 19.31 |
| replace, prime grade | 5I@.088 | sf | 14.60 | 4.21 | 18.81 |
| replace, naily grade | 5I@.088 | sf | 12.80 | 4.21 | 17.01 |
| replace, cabin grade | 5I@.088 | sf | 12.90 | 4.21 | 17.11 |
| replace, distressed grade | 5I@.088 | sf | 23.10 | 4.21 | 27.31 |
| remove | 1D@.020 | sf | — | .78 | .78 |

**Sand, edge, and fill wood floor.** Replace only.

| | Craft@Hrs | Unit | Material | Labor | Total |
|---|---|---|---|---|---|
| new | 5I@.026 | sf | .36 | 1.24 | 1.60 |
| light sand | 5I@.030 | sf | .31 | 1.43 | 1.74 |
| medium sand | 5I@.033 | sf | .43 | 1.58 | 2.01 |
| heavy sand | 5I@.041 | sf | .49 | 1.96 | 2.45 |

| | Craft@Hrs | Unit | Material | Labor | Total |
|---|---|---|---|---|---|

**Sleepers on concrete floor, 24" on center.** Glued and nailed with case-hardened nails to concrete floor.

| | Craft@Hrs | Unit | Material | Labor | Total |
|---|---|---|---|---|---|
| replace, 1" x 2" | 5I@.008 | sf | .28 | .38 | .66 |
| replace, 1" x 3" | 5I@.009 | sf | .45 | .43 | .88 |
| replace, 2" x 4" | 5I@.012 | sf | 1.09 | .57 | 1.66 |
| replace, 2" x 6" | 5I@.013 | sf | 1.63 | .62 | 2.25 |
| remove | 1D@.007 | sf | — | .27 | .27 |

**Floor underlayment.** Includes underlayment board, construction adhesive, staples or nails, and installation. When removing heavily glued and stapled underlayment, double the removal cost. Also includes 5% waste.

| | Craft@Hrs | Unit | Material | Labor | Total |
|---|---|---|---|---|---|
| Particleboard underlayment | | | | | |
| replace, 3/8" | 5I@.167 | sy | 5.46 | 7.98 | 13.44 |
| replace, 1/2" | 5I@.168 | sy | 5.66 | 8.03 | 13.69 |
| replace, 5/8" | 5I@.168 | sy | 6.28 | 8.03 | 14.31 |
| replace, 3/4" | 5I@.169 | sy | 7.26 | 8.08 | 15.34 |
| Hardboard underlayment | | | | | |
| replace, 1/4" | 5I@.174 | sy | 7.44 | 8.32 | 15.76 |
| Plywood underlayment | | | | | |
| replace, 1/2" | 5I@.168 | sy | 9.44 | 8.03 | 17.47 |
| remove | 1D@.070 | sy | — | 2.72 | 2.72 |
| Minimum charge | 5I@1.50 | ea | 49.30 | 71.70 | 121.00 |

## Time & Material Charts (selected items)
## Flooring Materials

| | Craft@Hrs | Unit | Material | Labor | Total |
|---|---|---|---|---|---|
| Carpet | | | | | |
| economy grade, ($19.40 sy, 1 sy), 12% waste | — | sy | 21.70 | — | 21.70 |
| custom grade, ($45.50 sy, 1 sy), 12% waste | — | sy | 51.00 | — | 51.00 |
| Glue-down carpet | | | | | |
| economy grade, ($14.70 sy, 1 sy), 12% waste | — | sy | 16.50 | — | 16.50 |
| deluxe grade, ($27.50 sy, 1 sy), 12% waste | — | sy | 30.80 | — | 30.80 |
| Indoor-outdoor carpet | | | | | |
| economy grade, ($10.80 sy, 1 sy), 12% waste | — | sy | 12.10 | — | 12.10 |
| deluxe grade, ($34.60 sy, 1 sy), 12% waste | — | sy | 38.80 | — | 38.80 |
| Wool carpet | | | | | |
| standard grade, ($30.00 sy, 1 sy), 12% waste | — | sy | 33.60 | — | 33.60 |
| custom grade, ($61.20 sy, 1 sy), 12% waste | — | sy | 68.50 | — | 68.50 |
| Simulated wool berber carpet | | | | | |
| standard grade, ($26.50 sy, 1 sy), 12% waste | — | sy | 29.70 | — | 29.70 |
| custom grade, ($43.00 sy, 1 sy), 12% waste | — | sy | 48.20 | — | 48.20 |
| Carpet pad | | | | | |
| urethane rebound, ($5.34 sy, 1 sy), 12% waste | — | sy | 5.98 | — | 5.98 |
| jute, ($3.73 sy, 1 sy), 12% waste | — | sy | 4.18 | — | 4.18 |
| Carpet tile | | | | | |
| standard grade, ($31.90 sy, 1 sy), 12% waste | — | sy | 35.70 | — | 35.70 |
| custom grade, ($48.70 sy, 1 sy), 12% waste | — | sy | 54.50 | — | 54.50 |
| Stone floor | | | | | |
| standard grade, ($7.83 sf, 1 sf), 4% waste | — | sf | 8.77 | — | 8.77 |
| deluxe grade, ($12.40 sf, 1 sf), 4% waste | — | sf | 13.90 | — | 13.90 |

| | Craft@Hrs | Unit | Material | Labor | Total |
|---|---|---|---|---|---|
| **Marble floor** | | | | | |
| standard grade, ($13.10 sf, 1 sf), 4% waste | — | sf | 13.60 | — | 13.60 |
| deluxe grade, ($42.70 sf, 1 sf), 4% waste | — | sf | 44.40 | — | 44.40 |
| **Slate floor** | | | | | |
| standard grade, ($10.20 sf, 1 sf), 4% waste | — | sf | 10.60 | — | 10.60 |
| deluxe grade, ($15.20 sf, 1 sf), 4% waste | — | sf | 15.80 | — | 15.80 |
| **Tile floor** | | | | | |
| standard grade, ($6.60 sf, 1 sf), 4% waste | — | sf | 6.86 | — | 6.86 |
| deluxe grade, ($10.90 sf, 1 sf), 4% waste | — | sf | 11.30 | — | 11.30 |
| **Quarry tile floor** | | | | | |
| standard grade, ($8.70 sf, 1 sf), 4% waste | — | sf | 9.05 | — | 9.05 |
| deluxe grade, ($17.40 sf, 1 sf), 4% waste | — | sf | 18.10 | — | 18.10 |
| **Precast terrazzo floor tiles** | | | | | |
| standard grade, ($16.30 sf, 1 sf), 4% waste | — | sf | 17.00 | — | 17.00 |
| high grade, ($18.40 sf, 1 sf), 4% waste | — | sf | 19.10 | — | 19.10 |
| **Cast-in-place thinset terrazzo floor** | | | | | |
| standard grade, ($3.24 sf, 1 sf), 12% waste | — | sf | 3.63 | — | 3.63 |
| high grade, ($4.85 sf, 1 sf), 12% waste | — | sf | 5.43 | — | 5.43 |
| **Vinyl floor** | | | | | |
| economy grade, ($17.70 sy, 1 sy), 12% waste | — | sy | 19.80 | — | 19.80 |
| deluxe grade, ($40.60 sy, 1 sy), 12% waste | — | sy | 45.50 | — | 45.50 |
| **Vinyl tile floor** | | | | | |
| economy grade, ($1.31 sf, 1 sf), 12% waste | — | sf | 1.47 | — | 1.47 |
| deluxe grade, ($3.48 sf, 1 sf), 12% waste | — | sf | 3.90 | — | 3.90 |
| **Resilient tile floor** | | | | | |
| economy grade, ($1.37 sf, 1 sf), 12% waste | — | sf | 1.53 | — | 1.53 |
| deluxe grade, ($2.88 sf, 1 sf), 12% waste | — | sf | 3.23 | — | 3.23 |
| **Antique style linoleum** | | | | | |
| battleship, ($37.10 sy, 1 sy), 12% waste | — | sy | 41.60 | — | 41.60 |
| **Rubber base** | | | | | |
| economy grade, ($1.75 lf, 1 lf), 12% waste | — | lf | 1.96 | — | 1.96 |
| deluxe grade, ($3.48 lf, 1 lf), 12% waste | — | lf | 3.90 | — | 3.90 |
| **Strip flooring** | | | | | |
| maple, first grade, ($10.10 sf, 1 sf), 6% waste | — | sf | 10.70 | — | 10.70 |
| red oak, select & better grade, ($9.22 sf, 1 sf), 6% waste | — | sf | 9.77 | — | 9.77 |
| red oak, quarter sawn, clear grade, ($22.20 sf, 1 sf), 6% waste | — | sf | 23.50 | — | 23.50 |
| prefinished red oak, prime grade, ($10.50 sf, 1 sf), 6% waste | — | sf | 11.10 | — | 11.10 |
| **Plank flooring** | | | | | |
| red oak, select & better grade, ($20.30 sf, 1 sf), 6% waste | — | sf | 21.50 | — | 21.50 |
| **Parquet or block flooring** | | | | | |
| maple, slat block, clear grade, ($9.83 sf, 1 sf), 4% waste | — | sf | 10.20 | — | 10.20 |
| prefinished maple, slat block, prime grade, ($8.70 sf, 1 sf), 4% waste | — | sf | 9.05 | — | 9.05 |

| | Craft@Hrs | Unit | Material | Labor | Total |
|---|---|---|---|---|---|
| red oak, slat block, clear grade, ($8.95 sf, 1 sf), 4% waste | — | sf | 9.31 | — | 9.31 |
| prefinished red oak, slat block, prime grade, ($10.20 sf, 1 sf), 4% waste | — | sf | 10.60 | — | 10.60 |
| Softwood flooring | | | | | |
| Southern pine strip, B&B grade, ($3.61 sf, 1 sf), 6% waste | — | sf | 3.83 | — | 3.83 |
| Southern pine plank, B&B grade, ($4.36 sf, 1 sf), 6% waste | — | sf | 4.62 | — | 4.62 |
| Douglas fir strip, C & better grade, ($3.87 sf, 1 sf), 6% waste | — | sf | 4.10 | — | 4.10 |
| Douglas fir plank, C & better grade, ($4.72 sf, 1 sf), 6% waste | — | sf | 5.00 | — | 5.00 |
| reclaimed antique longleaf pine, crown grade, ($18.00 sf, 1 sf), 6% waste | — | sf | 19.10 | — | 19.10 |
| Sleepers on concrete floor, 24" on center | | | | | |
| 1" x 2" | — | sf | .27 | — | .27 |
| 2" x 4" | — | sf | 1.06 | — | 1.06 |
| Floor underlayment | | | | | |
| 3/8" particleboard, ($18.30 sheet, 3.56 sy), 5% waste | — | sy | 5.40 | — | 5.40 |
| 1/2" particleboard, ($19.10 sheet, 3.56 sy), 5% waste | — | sy | 5.64 | — | 5.64 |
| 5/8" particleboard, ($21.40 sheet, 3.56 sy), 5% waste | — | sy | 6.31 | — | 6.31 |
| 3/4" particleboard, ($24.50 sheet, 3.56 sy), 5% waste | — | sy | 7.22 | — | 7.22 |
| 1/4" hardboard, ($12.70 sheet, 1.78 sy), 5% waste | — | sy | 7.49 | — | 7.49 |
| 1/2" plywood, ($31.90 sheet, 3.56 sy), 5% waste | — | sy | 9.41 | — | 9.41 |

## Flooring Labor

| Laborer | base wage | paid leave | true wage | taxes & ins. | total |
|---|---|---|---|---|---|
| Flooring installer | $30.80 | 2.40 | $33.20 | 21.50 | $54.70 |
| Flooring installer's helper | $22.20 | 1.73 | $23.93 | 16.97 | $40.90 |
| Demolition laborer | $20.70 | 1.61 | $22.31 | 16.59 | $38.90 |

**Paid leave** is calculated based on two weeks paid vacation, one week sick leave, and seven paid holidays. Employer's matching portion of **FICA** is 7.65 percent. **FUTA** (Federal Unemployment) is .8 percent. **Worker's compensation** for the flooring trade was calculated using a national average of 11.50 percent. **Unemployment insurance** was calculated using a national average of 8 percent. **Health insurance** was calculated based on a projected national average for 2015 of $1,025 per employee (and family when applicable) per month. Employer pays 80 percent for a per month cost of $820 per employee. **Retirement** is based on a 401(k) retirement program with employer matching of 50 percent. Employee contributions to the 401(k) plan are an average of 6 percent of the true wage. **Liability insurance** is based on a national average of 10.0 percent.

| | Craft@Hrs | Unit | Material | Labor | Total |
|---|---|---|---|---|---|
| **Flooring Labor Productivity** | | | | | |
| Demolition of flooring | | | | | |
| remove carpet | 1D@.062 | sy | — | 2.41 | 2.41 |
| remove glue-down carpet | 1D@.155 | sy | — | 6.03 | 6.03 |
| remove indoor-outdoor carpet | 1D@.153 | sy | — | 5.95 | 5.95 |
| remove carpet pad | 1D@.030 | sy | — | 1.17 | 1.17 |
| remove carpet cove | 1D@.022 | lf | — | .86 | .86 |
| remove carpet tile | 1D@.155 | sy | — | 6.03 | 6.03 |
| remove stone floor | 1D@.082 | sf | — | 3.19 | 3.19 |
| remove marble floor | 1D@.080 | sf | — | 3.11 | 3.11 |
| remove slate floor | 1D@.080 | sf | — | 3.11 | 3.11 |
| remove tile floor | 1D@.080 | sf | — | 3.11 | 3.11 |
| remove quarry tile floor | 1D@.078 | sf | — | 3.03 | 3.03 |
| remove tile base | 1D@.061 | lf | — | 2.37 | 2.37 |
| remove precast terrazzo floor tiles | 1D@.081 | sf | — | 3.15 | 3.15 |
| remove cast-in-place terrazzo floor | 1D@.082 | sf | — | 3.19 | 3.19 |
| remove vinyl floor | 1D@.175 | sy | — | 6.81 | 6.81 |
| remove vinyl tile floor | 1D@.024 | sf | — | .93 | .93 |
| remove resilient tile floor | 1D@.024 | sf | — | .93 | .93 |
| remove antique style linoleum floor | 1D@.175 | sy | — | 6.81 | 6.81 |
| remove vinyl cove | 1D@.036 | lf | — | 1.40 | 1.40 |
| remove rubber base | 1D@.011 | lf | — | .43 | .43 |
| remove wood strip flooring | 1D@.020 | sf | — | .78 | .78 |
| remove wood plank flooring | 1D@.019 | sf | — | .74 | .74 |
| remove wood unit block flooring | 1D@.018 | sf | — | .70 | .70 |
| remove floor sleepers | 1D@.007 | sf | — | .27 | .27 |
| remove floor underlayment | 1D@.070 | sy | — | 2.72 | 2.72 |

**Flooring crew**

| | | | | | | |
|---|---|---|---|---|---|---|
| install flooring | flooring installer | $54.70 | | | | |
| install flooring | flooring installer's helper | $40.90 | | | | |
| install flooring | flooring crew | $47.80 | | | | |

| | Craft@Hrs | Unit | Material | Labor | Total |
|---|---|---|---|---|---|
| Install carpet | | | | | |
| typical on tackless | 5I@.138 | sy | — | 6.60 | 6.60 |
| cove | 5I@.135 | lf | — | 6.45 | 6.45 |
| remove for work, then re-lay | 5I@.211 | sy | — | 10.10 | 10.10 |
| glue-down | 5I@.167 | sy | — | 7.98 | 7.98 |
| wool or simulated wool | 5I@.139 | sy | — | 6.64 | 6.64 |
| add per step for installation on stairs | 5I@.180 | ea | — | 8.60 | 8.60 |
| pad | 5I@.017 | sy | — | .81 | .81 |
| tile | 5I@.107 | sy | — | 5.11 | 5.11 |
| Install stone floor | | | | | |
| typical | 5I@.191 | sf | — | 9.13 | 9.13 |
| salvage, then reinstall | 5I@.500 | sf | — | 23.90 | 23.90 |
| regrout | 5I@.038 | sf | — | 1.82 | 1.82 |
| Install marble floor | | | | | |
| typical | 5I@.189 | sf | — | 9.03 | 9.03 |
| regrout | 5I@.034 | sf | — | 1.63 | 1.63 |

| | Craft@Hrs | Unit | Material | Labor | Total |
|---|---|---|---|---|---|
| **Install slate floor** | | | | | |
| typical | 5I@.189 | sf | — | 9.03 | 9.03 |
| regrout | 5I@.034 | sf | — | 1.63 | 1.63 |
| salvage, then reinstall | 5I@.490 | sf | — | 23.40 | 23.40 |
| **Install tile floor** | | | | | |
| typical | 5I@.180 | sf | — | 8.60 | 8.60 |
| regrout | 5I@.035 | sf | — | 1.67 | 1.67 |
| base | 5I@.128 | lf | — | 6.12 | 6.12 |
| **Install quarry tile floor** | | | | | |
| typical | 5I@.143 | sf | — | 6.84 | 6.84 |
| **Install terrazzo floor** | | | | | |
| precast tiles | 5I@.116 | sf | — | 5.54 | 5.54 |
| precast base | 5I@.256 | sf | — | 12.20 | 12.20 |
| cast-in-place thinset | 5I@.128 | sf | — | 6.12 | 6.12 |
| **Install vinyl floor** | | | | | |
| sheet goods | 5I@.183 | sy | — | 8.75 | 8.75 |
| cove | 5I@.091 | lf | — | 4.35 | 4.35 |
| tile | 5I@.029 | sf | — | 1.39 | 1.39 |
| resilient tile | 5I@.029 | sf | — | 1.39 | 1.39 |
| **Install antique-style linoleum** | | | | | |
| typical | 5I@.189 | sy | — | 9.03 | 9.03 |
| tile | 5I@.032 | sf | — | 1.53 | 1.53 |
| **Install rubber base** | | | | | |
| typical | 5I@.020 | lf | — | .96 | .96 |
| **Install wood floor** | | | | | |
| hardwood strip | 5I@.088 | sf | — | 4.21 | 4.21 |
| prefinished hardwood strip | 5I@.091 | sf | — | 4.35 | 4.35 |
| hardwood plank | 5I@.079 | sf | — | 3.78 | 3.78 |
| parquet or block | 5I@.092 | sf | — | 4.40 | 4.40 |
| prefinished hardwood block or parquet | 5I@.094 | sf | — | 4.49 | 4.49 |
| softwood strip | 5I@.088 | sf | — | 4.21 | 4.21 |
| softwood plank | 5I@.079 | sf | — | 3.78 | 3.78 |
| **Sand, edge, and fill wood floor** | | | | | |
| new | 5I@.026 | sf | — | 1.24 | 1.24 |
| light sand | 5I@.030 | sf | — | 1.43 | 1.43 |
| medium | 5I@.033 | sf | — | 1.58 | 1.58 |
| heavy sand | 5I@.041 | sf | — | 1.96 | 1.96 |
| **Install sleepers on concrete floor, 24" on center** | | | | | |
| 1" x 2" | 5I@.008 | sf | — | .38 | .38 |
| 1" x 3" | 5I@.009 | sf | — | .43 | .43 |
| 2" x 4" | 5I@.012 | sf | — | .57 | .57 |
| 2" x 6" | 5I@.013 | sf | — | .62 | .62 |
| **Install floor underlayment** | | | | | |
| 3/8" particleboard | 5I@.167 | sy | — | 7.98 | 7.98 |
| 1/2" particleboard | 5I@.168 | sy | — | 8.03 | 8.03 |
| 5/8" particleboard | 5I@.168 | sy | — | 8.03 | 8.03 |
| 3/4" particleboard | 5I@.169 | sy | — | 8.08 | 8.08 |
| 1/4" hardboard | 5I@.174 | sy | — | 8.32 | 8.32 |
| 1/2" plywood | 5I@.168 | sy | — | 8.03 | 8.03 |

| | Craft@Hrs | Unit | Material | Labor | Equip. | Total |
|---|---|---|---|---|---|---|

# Hazardous Materials

## Minimum charge.

| | Craft@Hrs | Unit | Material | Labor | Equip. | Total |
|---|---|---|---|---|---|---|
| asbestos removal | 1H@16.0 | ea | 180.00 | 782.00 | 246.00 | 1,208.00 |

## Asbestos analysis. Includes up to four hours, up to 12 analyzed samples, and a written report indicating severity of asbestos risk for a typical home or small commercial structure.

| | Craft@Hrs | Unit | Material | Labor | Equip. | Total |
|---|---|---|---|---|---|---|
| analysis | 1H@16.7 | ea | — | 817.00 | — | 817.00 |

## Seal area for asbestos work. Seal area where asbestos exists. Includes tape along all seams, caulk or foam insulation in any cracks, and negative air vent system.

| | Craft@Hrs | Unit | Material | Labor | Equip. | Total |
|---|---|---|---|---|---|---|
| plastic cover attached to ceiling | 1H@.044 | sf | 1.73 | 2.15 | — | 3.88 |
| plastic cover attached to walls | 1H@.042 | sf | 1.79 | 2.05 | — | 3.84 |
| plastic cover and plywood over floor (2 layers) | 1H@.102 | sf | 2.81 | 4.99 | — | 7.80 |
| temporary containment walls with plastic cover | 1H@.179 | sf | 3.38 | 8.75 | — | 12.13 |

## Prefabricated decontamination unit. Four day minimum. Includes decontamination equipment, shower, and clean room.

| | Craft@Hrs | Unit | Material | Labor | Equip. | Total |
|---|---|---|---|---|---|---|
| per day | — | dy | — | — | 105.00 | 105.00 |

## Encapsulate asbestos-based acoustical ceiling. Penetrating sealant sprayed on ceiling with airless sprayer.

| | Craft@Hrs | Unit | Material | Labor | Equip. | Total |
|---|---|---|---|---|---|---|
| with sealant | 1H@.014 | sf | .43 | .68 | .15 | 1.26 |

## Remove asbestos-based materials. Includes full Tyvek suits for workers changed four times per eight hour shift, respirators (add **20%** for respirators with air supply), air monitoring, supervision by qualified hygiene professionals, final seal of scraped or demo'ed walls, final seal and disposal of plastic cover materials, disposal in fiber drums and hauling to dump. Does not include dump fees (typically about $12.00 per drum).

| | Craft@Hrs | Unit | Material | Labor | Equip. | Total |
|---|---|---|---|---|---|---|
| scrape acoustical ceiling | 1H@.034 | sf | .09 | 1.66 | .23 | 1.98 |
| insulation over 1/2" to 3/4" pipe | 1H@.026 | lf | .20 | 1.27 | .12 | 1.59 |
| insulation over 1" to 3" pipe | 1H@.080 | lf | .40 | 3.91 | .26 | 4.57 |
| asbestos-based siding | 1H@.179 | sf | 1.16 | 8.75 | .27 | 10.18 |
| asbestos-based plaster | 1H@.137 | sf | .77 | 6.70 | .27 | 7.74 |

| | Craft@Hrs | Unit | Material | Labor | Total |
|---|---|---|---|---|---|

## Time & Material Charts (selected items)
## Materials for Hazardous Materials Removal

| | Craft@Hrs | Unit | Material | Labor | Total |
|---|---|---|---|---|---|
| polyethylene (plastic), ($.27 sf) | — | sf | .27 | — | .27 |
| Tyvek whole body suit, ($20.60 ea) | — | ea | 20.60 | — | 20.60 |
| respirator cartridge, ($5.85 ea) | — | ea | 5.85 | — | 5.85 |
| glove bag, 7 mil., 50" x 64", ($11.30 ea) | — | ea | 11.30 | — | 11.30 |
| glove bag, 10 mil., 44" x 60", ($12.20 ea) | — | ea | 12.20 | — | 12.20 |
| 3 cf disposable polyethylene bags, 6 mil, ($1.46 ea) | — | ea | 1.46 | — | 1.46 |
| 3 cf disposable fiber drums, ($12.30 ea) | — | ea | 12.30 | — | 12.30 |
| caution labels, ($.30 ea) | — | ea | .30 | — | .30 |
| encapsulation quality sealant, ($106.00 gal) | — | gal | 106.00 | — | 106.00 |
| vent fan filters, ($10.10 ea) | — | ea | 10.10 | — | 10.10 |
| respirator, ($30.30 ea) | — | ea | 30.30 | — | 30.30 |

|  | Craft@Hrs | Unit | Material | Labor | Equip. | Total |
|---|---|---|---|---|---|---|
| **Hazardous Materials Rental Equipment** | | | | | | |
| negative air vent system, two fans | — | day | — | — | 77.60 | 77.60 |
| HEPA vacuum cleaner, 16 gallon wet/dry | — | day | — | — | 98.80 | 98.80 |
| airless sprayer unit | — | day | — | — | 70.40 | 70.40 |
| light stand | — | day | — | — | 28.30 | 28.30 |
| prefabricated decontamination unit | — | day | — | — | 106.00 | 106.00 |

**Hazardous Materials Labor**

| Laborer | base wage | paid leave | true wage | taxes & ins. | total |
|---|---|---|---|---|---|
| Haz. mat. laborer | $24.30 | 1.90 | $26.20 | 22.70 | $48.90 |

**Paid leave** is calculated based on two weeks paid vacation, one week sick leave, and seven paid holidays. Employer's matching portion of **FICA** is 7.65 percent. **FUTA** (Federal Unemployment) is .8 percent. **Worker's compensation** for the hazardous materials trade was calculated using a national average of 28.40 percent. **Unemployment insurance** was calculated using a national average of 8 percent. **Health insurance** was calculated based on a projected national average for 2015 of $1,025 per employee (and family when applicable) per month. Employer pays 80 percent for a per month cost of $820 per employee. **Retirement** is based on a 401(k) retirement program with employer matching of 50 percent. Employee contributions to the 401(k) plan are an average of 6 percent of the true wage. **Liability insurance** is based on a national average of 10.0 percent.

|  | Craft@Hrs | Unit | Material | Labor | Total |
|---|---|---|---|---|---|
| **Hazardous Materials Labor Productivity** | | | | | |
| Minimum charge for asbestos removal | 1H@16.0 | ea | — | 782.00 | 782.00 |
| Asbestos analysis typical home | 1H@16.7 | ea | — | 817.00 | 817.00 |
| Seal area for work | | | | | |
| attach plastic cover to ceiling | 1H@.044 | sf | — | 2.15 | 2.15 |
| attach plastic cover to walls | 1H@.042 | sf | — | 2.05 | 2.05 |
| attach plastic cover & plywood to floor | 1H@.102 | sf | — | 4.99 | 4.99 |
| build walls and attach plastic cover | 1H@.179 | sf | — | 8.75 | 8.75 |
| Remove asbestos-based materials | | | | | |
| scrape acoustical ceiling | 1H@.034 | sf | — | 1.66 | 1.66 |
| encapsulate acoustical ceiling with sealant | 1H@.014 | sf | — | .68 | .68 |
| insulation over 1/2" to 3/4" pipe | 1H@.026 | lf | — | 1.27 | 1.27 |
| insulation over 1" to 3" pipe | 1H@.080 | lf | — | 3.91 | 3.91 |
| siding | 1H@.179 | sf | — | 8.75 | 8.75 |
| plaster | 1H@.137 | sf | — | 6.70 | 6.70 |

|  | Craft@Hrs | Unit | Material | Labor | Total |
|---|---|---|---|---|---|

# HVAC

**Duct work.** Replace only.

|  | Craft@Hrs | Unit | Material | Labor | Total |
|---|---|---|---|---|---|
| per duct | 2H@5.00 | ea | 201.00 | 308.00 | 509.00 |
| per sf of floor | 2H@.032 | sf | .63 | 1.97 | 2.60 |
| for home to 1,200 sf | 2H@35.7 | ea | 605.00 | 2,200.00 | 2,805.00 |
| for home 1,200 to 1,900 sf | 2H@43.8 | ea | 939.00 | 2,690.00 | 3,629.00 |
| for home 1,900 to 2,400 sf | 2H@53.7 | ea | 1,210.00 | 3,300.00 | 4,510.00 |
| for home 2,400 to 2,900 sf | 2H@70.0 | ea | 1,450.00 | 4,310.00 | 5,760.00 |
| for home 2,900 to 3,400 sf | 2H@100 | ea | 1,720.00 | 6,150.00 | 7,870.00 |
| for home 3,400 to 3,900 sf | 2H@130 | ea | 1,960.00 | 8,000.00 | 9,960.00 |
| for home 3,900 to 4,500 sf | 2H@163 | ea | 2,270.00 | 10,000.00 | 12,270.00 |

*duct work*

**Electric forced-air furnace.** Includes connection only. Does not include wiring run, plenums, ducts, or flues.

|  | Craft@Hrs | Unit | Material | Labor | Total |
|---|---|---|---|---|---|
| replace, 10,200 btu | 2H@10.8 | ea | 534.00 | 664.00 | 1,198.00 |
| replace, 17,100 btu | 2H@11.4 | ea | 564.00 | 701.00 | 1,265.00 |
| replace, 27,300 btu | 2H@12.6 | ea | 627.00 | 775.00 | 1,402.00 |
| replace, 34,100 btu | 2H@13.8 | ea | 691.00 | 849.00 | 1,540.00 |
| remove | 1D@1.89 | ea | — | 73.50 | 73.50 |
| remove for work, then reinstall | 2H@5.21 | ea | — | 320.00 | 320.00 |

**Gas forced-air furnace.** Includes connection only. Does not include wiring run, plenums, ducts, or flues.

|  | Craft@Hrs | Unit | Material | Labor | Total |
|---|---|---|---|---|---|
| replace, 45,000 btu | 2H@11.3 | ea | 564.00 | 695.00 | 1,259.00 |
| replace, 60,000 btu | 2H@12.3 | ea | 627.00 | 756.00 | 1,383.00 |
| replace, 75,000 btu | 2H@13.4 | ea | 691.00 | 824.00 | 1,515.00 |
| replace, 100,000 btu | 2H@15.0 | ea | 754.00 | 923.00 | 1,677.00 |
| replace, 125,000 btu | 2H@16.4 | ea | 878.00 | 1,010.00 | 1,888.00 |
| replace, 150,000 btu | 2H@17.3 | ea | 1,080.00 | 1,060.00 | 2,140.00 |
| remove | 1D@1.82 | ea | — | 70.80 | 70.80 |
| remove for work, then reinstall | 2H@5.08 | ea | — | 312.00 | 312.00 |

**Oil forced-air furnace.** Includes connection only. Does not include wiring run, plenums, ducts, or flues.

|  | Craft@Hrs | Unit | Material | Labor | Total |
|---|---|---|---|---|---|
| replace, 56,000 btu | 2H@12.4 | ea | 1,240.00 | 763.00 | 2,003.00 |
| replace, 84,000 btu | 2H@12.8 | ea | 1,510.00 | 787.00 | 2,297.00 |
| replace, 95,000 btu | 2H@13.2 | ea | 1,580.00 | 812.00 | 2,392.00 |
| replace, 134,000 btu | 2H@17.8 | ea | 1,880.00 | 1,090.00 | 2,970.00 |
| remove | 1D@2.04 | ea | — | 79.40 | 79.40 |
| remove for work, then reinstall | 2H@5.45 | ea | — | 335.00 | 335.00 |

**Service furnace.** Replace only.

|  | Craft@Hrs | Unit | Material | Labor | Total |
|---|---|---|---|---|---|
| typical | 2H@1.71 | ea | 12.20 | 105.00 | 117.20 |

**Heat pump with supplementary heat coil.** Includes heat pump with supplementary coil and installation. Includes some fitting and materials to connect to existing work but does not include electrical wiring runs, or interior pipe.

|  | Craft@Hrs | Unit | Material | Labor | Total |
|---|---|---|---|---|---|
| replace, 2 ton | 2H@19.5 | ea | 3,140.00 | 1,200.00 | 4,340.00 |
| replace, 4 ton | 2H@29.1 | ea | 5,640.00 | 1,790.00 | 7,430.00 |
| replace, 5 ton | 2H@34.9 | ea | 6,270.00 | 2,150.00 | 8,420.00 |
| remove | 1D@2.33 | ea | — | 90.60 | 90.60 |
| remove for work, then reinstall | 2H@21.9 | ea | — | 1,350.00 | 1,350.00 |

| | Craft@Hrs | Unit | Material | Labor | Total |
|---|---|---|---|---|---|

**Humidifier.** Includes humidifier and installation. Installed in existing ductwork. Centrifugal atomizing.

| | Craft@Hrs | Unit | Material | Labor | Total |
|---|---|---|---|---|---|
| replace, 5 pounds per hour | 2H@3.83 | ea | 1,880.00 | 236.00 | 2,116.00 |
| replace, 10 pounds per hour | 2H@4.44 | ea | 2,190.00 | 273.00 | 2,463.00 |
| remove | 1D@1.69 | ea | — | 65.70 | 65.70 |
| remove for work, then reinstall | 2H@2.98 | ea | — | 183.00 | 183.00 |

**Furnace vent pipe, double wall (all fuels).** Includes double wall flue, sheet-metal screws, metallic duct tape, and installation.

| | Craft@Hrs | Unit | Material | Labor | Total |
|---|---|---|---|---|---|
| replace, 3" diameter | 2H@.283 | lf | 5.03 | 17.40 | 22.43 |
| replace, 4" diameter | 2H@.318 | lf | 6.15 | 19.60 | 25.75 |
| replace, 5" diameter | 2H@.351 | lf | 7.29 | 21.60 | 28.89 |
| replace, 6" diameter | 2H@.390 | lf | 8.54 | 24.00 | 32.54 |
| replace, 7" diameter | 2H@.486 | lf | 12.60 | 29.90 | 42.50 |
| replace, 8" diameter | 2H@.533 | lf | 14.00 | 32.80 | 46.80 |
| remove | 1D@.040 | lf | — | 1.56 | 1.56 |
| remove for work, then reinstall | 2H@.283 | lf | — | 17.40 | 17.40 |

**Central air conditioning system.** Includes condensing unit, coil, copper lines and installation.

| | Craft@Hrs | Unit | Material | Labor | Total |
|---|---|---|---|---|---|
| replace, complete, 1 ton | 2H@6.12 | ea | 1,000.00 | 376.00 | 1,376.00 |
| replace, 1-1/2 ton | 2H@7.08 | ea | 1,130.00 | 435.00 | 1,565.00 |
| replace, 2 ton | 2H@8.52 | ea | 1,230.00 | 524.00 | 1,754.00 |
| replace, 3 ton | 2H@7.33 | ea | 2,010.00 | 451.00 | 2,461.00 |
| replace, 4 ton | 2H@16.2 | ea | 2,490.00 | 996.00 | 3,486.00 |
| replace, 5 ton | 2H@23.3 | ea | 3,080.00 | 1,430.00 | 4,510.00 |
| replace, air conditioning unit service | 1D@2.93 | ea | 56.40 | 114.00 | 170.40 |

**Recharge AC system with refrigerant.** Includes refrigerant and labor to recover, evacuate and recharge AC system.

| | Craft@Hrs | Unit | Material | Labor | Total |
|---|---|---|---|---|---|
| replace, 5 lbs | 2H@1.50 | ea | 144.00 | 92.30 | 236.30 |
| replace, 10 lbs | 2H@1.65 | ea | 290.00 | 101.00 | 391.00 |
| replace, 14 lbs | 2H@1.80 | ea | 408.00 | 111.00 | 519.00 |

**Through-wall AC unit.** Includes through-wall AC unit with built-in thermostat and installation. Does not include wall framing or electrical wiring runs.

| | Craft@Hrs | Unit | Material | Labor | Total |
|---|---|---|---|---|---|
| replace, 5,000 btu | 2H@8.83 | ea | 1,030.00 | 543.00 | 1,573.00 |
| replace, 8,000 btu | 2H@9.11 | ea | 1,070.00 | 560.00 | 1,630.00 |
| replace, 12,000 btu | 2H@10.6 | ea | 1,240.00 | 652.00 | 1,892.00 |
| replace, 18,000 btu | 2H@11.8 | ea | 1,580.00 | 726.00 | 2,306.00 |
| remove | 1D@1.49 | ea | — | 58.00 | 58.00 |
| remove for work, then reinstall | 2H@4.98 | ea | — | 306.00 | 306.00 |

**Through-wall combination AC and heat unit.**

| | Craft@Hrs | Unit | Material | Labor | Total |
|---|---|---|---|---|---|
| replace, 6,000 btu AC and 4,040 btu heat unit | 2H@10.2 | ea | 1,580.00 | 627.00 | 2,207.00 |
| replace, 9,500 btu AC and 4,040 btu heat unit | 2H@10.5 | ea | 1,800.00 | 646.00 | 2,446.00 |
| replace, 11,300 btu AC and 9,200 btu heat unit | 2H@12.2 | ea | 2,190.00 | 750.00 | 2,940.00 |
| remove | 1D@1.56 | ea | — | 60.70 | 60.70 |
| remove for work, then reinstall | 2H@5.35 | ea | — | 329.00 | 329.00 |

| | Craft@Hrs | Unit | Material | Labor | Total |
|---|---|---|---|---|---|
| **Evaporative cooler.** Roof mount. Includes up to 36 lf of copper water supply tubing and electrical hookup. | | | | | |
| replace, 2,000 cfm | 2H@7.49 | ea | 973.00 | 461.00 | 1,434.00 |
| replace, 4,300 cfm | 2H@9.55 | ea | 1,310.00 | 587.00 | 1,897.00 |
| replace, 4,700 cfm | 2H@10.1 | ea | 1,370.00 | 621.00 | 1,991.00 |
| replace, 5,600 cfm | 2H@10.9 | ea | 1,580.00 | 670.00 | 2,250.00 |
| remove | 1D@1.64 | ea | — | 63.80 | 63.80 |
| replace, grille | 2H@.680 | ea | 87.80 | 41.80 | 129.60 |
| remove, grille | 1D@.167 | ea | — | 6.50 | 6.50 |
| remove for work, then reinstall | 2H@9.42 | ea | — | 579.00 | 579.00 |
| **Cold-air grille.** | | | | | |
| replace, cold-air return | 2H@.952 | ea | 37.60 | 58.50 | 96.10 |
| remove | 1D@.167 | ea | — | 6.50 | 6.50 |
| remove cold-air return for work, then reinstall | 2H@.248 | ea | — | 15.30 | 15.30 |
| **Heat register.** | | | | | |
| replace, heat register | 2H@.630 | ea | 25.00 | 38.70 | 63.70 |
| remove | 1D@.135 | ea | — | 5.25 | 5.25 |
| remove heat register for work, then reinstall | 2H@.160 | ea | — | 9.84 | 9.84 |
| **Thermostat.** Includes thermostat and installation. Does not include thermostat wire. | | | | | |
| replace, heat only | 2H@1.53 | ea | 56.40 | 94.10 | 150.50 |
| replace, heat and air conditioning | 2H@2.38 | ea | 100.00 | 146.00 | 246.00 |
| replace, programmable | 2H@3.49 | ea | 113.00 | 215.00 | 328.00 |
| replace, programmable with zone control | 2H@4.29 | ea | 137.00 | 264.00 | 401.00 |
| remove | 1D@.233 | ea | — | 9.06 | 9.06 |
| remove for work, then reinstall | 2H@.622 | ea | — | 38.30 | 38.30 |

## Time & Material Charts (selected items)
## HVAC Materials

| | | Unit | Material | Labor | Total |
|---|---|---|---|---|---|
| Ductwork materials | | | | | |
| per sf of floor | — | sf | .63 | — | .63 |
| Electric forced-air furnace | | | | | |
| 10,200 btu | — | ea | 534.00 | — | 534.00 |
| 34,100 btu | — | ea | 691.00 | — | 691.00 |
| Gas forced-air furnace | | | | | |
| 45,000 btu | — | ea | 564.00 | — | 564.00 |
| 100,000 btu | — | ea | 1,080.00 | — | 1,080.00 |
| Oil forced-air furnace | | | | | |
| 56,000 btu | — | ea | 1,240.00 | — | 1,240.00 |
| 134,000 btu | — | ea | 1,880.00 | — | 1,880.00 |

## HVAC Labor

| Laborer | base wage | paid leave | true wage | taxes & ins. | total |
|---|---|---|---|---|---|
| HVAC installer | $35.60 | 2.78 | $38.38 | 23.12 | $61.50 |
| Demolition laborer | $20.70 | 1.61 | $22.31 | 16.59 | $38.90 |

| | Craft@Hrs | Unit | Material | Labor | Total |
|---|---|---|---|---|---|

**Paid leave** is calculated based on two weeks paid vacation, one week sick leave, and seven paid holidays. Employer's matching portion of **FICA** is 7.65 percent. **FUTA** (Federal Unemployment) is .8 percent. **Worker's compensation** for the HVAC trade was calculated using a national average of 9.37 percent. **Unemployment insurance** was calculated using a national average of 8 percent. **Health insurance** was calculated based on a projected national average for 2015 of $1,025 per employee (and family when applicable) per month. Employer pays 80 percent for a per month cost of $820 per employee. **Retirement** is based on a 401(k) retirement program with employer matching of 50 percent. Employee contributions to the 401(k) plan are an average of 6 percent of the true wage. **Liability insurance** is based on a national average of 10.0 percent.

## HVAC Labor Productivity

| | Craft@Hrs | Unit | Material | Labor | Total |
|---|---|---|---|---|---|
| Demolition of HVAC equipment | | | | | |
| remove electric forced-air furnace | 1D@1.89 | ea | — | 73.50 | 73.50 |
| remove gas forced-air furnace | 1D@1.82 | ea | — | 70.80 | 70.80 |
| remove oil forced-air furnace | 1D@2.04 | ea | — | 79.40 | 79.40 |
| remove heat pump | 1D@2.33 | ea | — | 90.60 | 90.60 |
| remove humidifier | 1D@1.69 | ea | — | 65.70 | 65.70 |
| remove through-wall AC unit | 1D@1.49 | ea | — | 58.00 | 58.00 |
| remove combination AC and heat unit | 1D@1.56 | ea | — | 60.70 | 60.70 |
| remove evaporative cooler | 1D@1.64 | ea | — | 63.80 | 63.80 |
| remove heat register | 1D@.135 | ea | — | 5.25 | 5.25 |
| remove thermostat | 1D@.233 | ea | — | 9.06 | 9.06 |
| Install electric forced-air furnace | | | | | |
| 10,200 btu | 2H@10.8 | ea | — | 664.00 | 664.00 |
| 34,100 btu | 2H@13.8 | ea | — | 849.00 | 849.00 |
| Install gas forced-air furnace | | | | | |
| 45,000 btu | 2H@11.3 | ea | — | 695.00 | 695.00 |
| 150,000 btu | 2H@17.3 | ea | — | 1,060.00 | 1,060.00 |
| Install oil forced-air furnace | | | | | |
| 56,000 btu | 2H@12.4 | ea | — | 763.00 | 763.00 |
| 134,000 btu | 2H@17.8 | ea | — | 1,090.00 | 1,090.00 |
| Install heat pump with supplementary heat coil | | | | | |
| 2 ton | 2H@19.5 | ea | — | 1,200.00 | 1,200.00 |
| Install humidifier | | | | | |
| 5 pounds per hour | 2H@3.83 | ea | — | 236.00 | 236.00 |
| Double wall furnace flue (all fuels) | | | | | |
| 4" diameter | 2H@.318 | lf | — | 19.60 | 19.60 |
| 8" diameter | 2H@.533 | lf | — | 32.80 | 32.80 |
| Through-wall AC unit | | | | | |
| 5,000 btu | 2H@8.83 | ea | — | 543.00 | 543.00 |
| 18,000 btu | 2H@11.8 | ea | — | 726.00 | 726.00 |
| Through-wall combination AC and heat unit | | | | | |
| 6,000 btu AC and 4,040 btu heat unit | 2H@10.2 | ea | — | 627.00 | 627.00 |
| 11,300 btu AC and 9,200 btu heat unit | 2H@12.2 | ea | — | 750.00 | 750.00 |
| Evaporative cooler | | | | | |
| 2,000 cfm | 2H@7.49 | ea | — | 461.00 | 461.00 |
| 5,600 cfm | 2H@10.9 | ea | — | 670.00 | 670.00 |
| Thermostat | | | | | |
| heat only | 2H@1.53 | ea | — | 94.10 | 94.10 |
| heat and air conditioning | 2H@2.38 | ea | — | 146.00 | 146.00 |
| programmable | 2H@3.49 | ea | — | 215.00 | 215.00 |
| programmable, with zone control | 2H@4.29 | ea | — | 264.00 | 264.00 |

| | Craft@Hrs | Unit | Material | Labor | Total |
|---|---|---|---|---|---|

# Insulation

## Minimum charge.

| | Craft@Hrs | Unit | Material | Labor | Total |
|---|---|---|---|---|---|
| for insulation work | 1I@3.10 | ea | 49.10 | 131.00 | 180.10 |

## Vermiculite attic insulation. Poured by hand from 3 cf bags.

| | Craft@Hrs | Unit | Material | Labor | Total |
|---|---|---|---|---|---|
| replace, 3" deep | 1I@.008 | sf | 1.36 | .34 | 1.70 |
| replace, 4" deep | 1I@.009 | sf | 1.83 | .38 | 2.21 |
| replace, 5" deep | 1I@.009 | sf | 2.29 | .38 | 2.67 |
| replace, 6" deep | 1I@.010 | sf | 2.75 | .42 | 3.17 |
| remove, 3" | 1D@.014 | sf | — | .54 | .54 |
| remove, 4" | 1D@.017 | sf | — | .66 | .66 |
| remove, 5" | 1D@.020 | sf | — | .78 | .78 |
| remove, 6" | 1D@.025 | sf | — | .97 | .97 |

## Blown mineral wool attic insulation.

| | Craft@Hrs | Unit | Material | Labor | Total |
|---|---|---|---|---|---|
| R11 (3-1/2" deep) | 1I@.010 | sf | .72 | .42 | 1.14 |
| R19 (6" deep) | 1I@.011 | sf | 1.08 | .46 | 1.54 |
| R30 (10" deep) | 1I@.013 | sf | 1.74 | .55 | 2.29 |
| R38 (12" deep) | 1I@.016 | sf | 2.37 | .67 | 3.04 |
| remove, R11 | 1D@.012 | sf | — | .47 | .47 |
| remove, R19 | 1D@.013 | sf | — | .51 | .51 |
| remove, R30 | 1D@.019 | sf | — | .74 | .74 |
| remove, R38 | 1D@.022 | sf | — | .86 | .86 |

## Blown cellulose attic insulation.

| | Craft@Hrs | Unit | Material | Labor | Total |
|---|---|---|---|---|---|
| R12 (3-1/2" deep) | 1I@.010 | sf | .70 | .42 | 1.12 |
| R21 (6" deep) | 1I@.012 | sf | 1.05 | .51 | 1.56 |
| R33 (10" deep) | 1I@.013 | sf | 1.69 | .55 | 2.24 |
| R42 (12" deep) | 1I@.016 | sf | 2.28 | .67 | 2.95 |
| remove, R12 | 1D@.014 | sf | — | .54 | .54 |
| remove, R21 | 1D@.015 | sf | — | .58 | .58 |
| remove, R33 | 1D@.023 | sf | — | .89 | .89 |
| remove, R42 | 1D@.026 | sf | — | 1.01 | 1.01 |

## Blown fiberglass attic insulation.

| | Craft@Hrs | Unit | Material | Labor | Total |
|---|---|---|---|---|---|
| R11 (5" deep) | 1I@.010 | sf | .63 | .42 | 1.05 |
| R19 (8" deep) | 1I@.011 | sf | .90 | .46 | 1.36 |
| R30 (13" deep) | 1I@.013 | sf | 1.48 | .55 | 2.03 |
| R38 (16" deep) | 1I@.016 | sf | 2.02 | .67 | 2.69 |
| remove, R11 | 1D@.012 | sf | — | .47 | .47 |
| remove, R19 | 1D@.013 | sf | — | .51 | .51 |
| remove, R30 | 1D@.019 | sf | — | .74 | .74 |
| remove, R38 | 1D@.022 | sf | — | .86 | .86 |

## Add to blow insulation into existing wall.

| | Craft@Hrs | Unit | Material | Labor | Total |
|---|---|---|---|---|---|
| add for wall with stucco | — | % | — | 285.0 | — |
| add for wall with siding | — | % | — | 233.0 | — |
| add for wall with masonry veneer | — | % | — | 318.0 | — |
| add for wall with interior drywall | — | % | — | 216.0 | — |

| | Craft@Hrs | Unit | Material | Labor | Total |
|---|---|---|---|---|---|
| **Fiberglass batt insulation,** installed in ceiling, attic, or floor. | | | | | |
| R11 (3-1/2" deep) | 1I@.009 | sf | .51 | .38 | .89 |
| R19 (6" deep) | 1I@.011 | sf | .77 | .46 | 1.23 |
| R30 (9-1/2" deep) | 1I@.012 | sf | 1.26 | .51 | 1.77 |
| R38 (12" deep) | 1I@.015 | sf | 1.69 | .63 | 2.32 |
| remove, R11 | 1D@.009 | sf | — | .35 | .35 |
| remove, R19 | 1D@.013 | sf | — | .51 | .51 |
| remove, R30 | 1D@.015 | sf | — | .58 | .58 |
| remove, R38 | 1D@.018 | sf | — | .70 | .70 |
| | | | | | |
| **Fiberglass batt insulation,** installed in wall. | | | | | |
| R6 (1-3/4" deep) (between furring strips) | 1I@.010 | sf | .29 | .42 | .71 |
| R11 (3-1/2" deep) | 1I@.011 | sf | .51 | .46 | .97 |
| R19 (6" deep) | 1I@.013 | sf | .77 | .55 | 1.32 |
| R19 (8" deep) | 1I@.015 | sf | 1.00 | .63 | 1.63 |
| remove, R6 | 1D@.007 | sf | — | .27 | .27 |
| remove, R11 | 1D@.009 | sf | — | .35 | .35 |
| remove, R19 (6" deep) | 1D@.013 | sf | — | .51 | .51 |
| remove, R19 (8" deep) | 1D@.015 | sf | — | .58 | .58 |
| | | | | | |
| **Add for batt face.** | | | | | |
| add for Kraft face | — | % | 8.0 | — | — |
| add for foil face | — | % | 10.0 | — | — |
| add for plastic vapor barrier | — | % | 14.0 | — | — |
| | | | | | |
| **Rigid foam insulation board.** Includes rigid foam board, glue and/or nails, and installation on walls or roof. | | | | | |
| 1/2" | 1I@.014 | sf | .65 | .59 | 1.24 |
| 3/4" | 1I@.014 | sf | .77 | .59 | 1.36 |
| 1" | 1I@.014 | sf | 1.00 | .59 | 1.59 |
| 2" | 1I@.014 | sf | 1.34 | .59 | 1.93 |
| remove | 1D@.007 | sf | — | .27 | .27 |

## Time & Material Charts (selected items)
## Insulation Materials

| | | Unit | Material | Labor | Total |
|---|---|---|---|---|---|
| Vermiculite attic insulation | | | | | |
| 3" deep, ($1.31 sf, 1 sf), 4% waste | — | sf | 1.36 | — | 1.36 |
| 4" deep, ($1.75 sf, 1 sf), 4% waste | — | sf | 1.82 | — | 1.82 |
| 5" deep, ($2.20 sf, 1 sf), 4% waste | — | sf | 2.29 | — | 2.29 |
| 6" deep, ($2.65 sf, 1 sf), 4% waste | — | sf | 2.76 | — | 2.76 |
| Blown mineral wool insulation | | | | | |
| R11 (3-1/2" deep), ($.70 sf, 1 sf), 4% waste | — | sf | .73 | — | .73 |
| R19 (6" deep), ($1.03 sf, 1 sf), 4% waste | — | sf | 1.07 | — | 1.07 |
| R30 (10" deep), ($1.68 sf, 1 sf), 4% waste | — | sf | 1.75 | — | 1.75 |
| R38 (12" deep), ($2.26 sf, 1 sf), 4% waste | — | sf | 2.35 | — | 2.35 |

| | Craft@Hrs | Unit | Material | Labor | Total |
|---|---|---|---|---|---|
| Blown cellulose insulation | | | | | |
| R12 blown (3-1/2" deep), ($.68 sf, 1 sf), 4% waste | — | sf | .71 | — | .71 |
| R21 blown (6" deep), ($1.00 sf, 1 sf), 4% waste | — | sf | 1.04 | — | 1.04 |
| R33 blown (10" deep), ($1.62 sf, 1 sf), 4% waste | — | sf | 1.68 | — | 1.68 |
| R42 blown (12" deep), ($2.19 sf, 1 sf), 4% waste | — | sf | 2.28 | — | 2.28 |
| Blown fiberglass insulation | | | | | |
| R11 (5" deep), ($.61 sf, 1 sf), 4% waste | — | sf | .63 | — | .63 |
| R19 (8" deep), ($.86 sf, 1 sf), 4% waste | — | sf | .89 | — | .89 |
| R30 (13" deep), ($1.42 sf, 1 sf), 4% waste | — | sf | 1.48 | — | 1.48 |
| R38 (16" deep), ($1.94 sf, 1 sf), 4% waste | — | sf | 2.02 | — | 2.02 |
| Fiberglass batt insulation in ceiling or floor | | | | | |
| R11 (3-1/2" deep), ($.48 sf, 1 sf), 4% waste | — | sf | .50 | — | .50 |
| R19 (6" deep), ($.74 sf, 1 sf), 4% waste | — | sf | .77 | — | .77 |
| R30 (9-1/2" deep), ($1.21 sf, 1 sf), 4% waste | — | sf | 1.26 | — | 1.26 |
| R38 (12" deep), ($1.62 sf, 1 sf), 4% waste | — | sf | 1.68 | — | 1.68 |
| Fiberglass batt insulation in wall | | | | | |
| R6 (1-3/4" deep) (between furring strips), ($.28 sf, 1 sf), 4% waste | — | sf | .29 | — | .29 |
| R11 (3-1/2" deep), ($.48 sf, 1 sf), 4% waste | — | sf | .50 | — | .50 |
| R19 (6" deep), ($.74 sf, 1 sf), 4% waste | — | sf | .77 | — | .77 |
| R25 (8" deep), ($.95 sf, 1 sf), 4% waste | — | sf | .99 | — | .99 |
| Rigid foam insulation board | | | | | |
| 1/2", ($.62 sf, 1 sf), 4% waste | — | sf | .64 | — | .64 |
| 3/4", ($.74 sf, 1 sf), 4% waste | — | sf | .77 | — | .77 |
| 1", ($.95 sf, 1 sf), 4% waste | — | sf | .99 | — | .99 |
| 2", ($1.29 sf, 1 sf), 4% waste | — | sf | 1.34 | — | 1.34 |

## Insulation Labor

| Laborer | base wage | paid leave | true wage | taxes & ins. | total |
|---|---|---|---|---|---|
| Insulation installer | $21.30 | 1.66 | $22.96 | 19.14 | $42.10 |
| Demolition laborer | $20.70 | 1.62 | $22.32 | 16.58 | $38.90 |

**Paid leave** is calculated based on two weeks paid vacation, one week sick leave, and seven paid holidays. Employer's matching portion of **FICA** is 7.65 percent. **FUTA** (Federal Unemployment) is .8 percent. **Worker's compensation** for the insulation trade was calculated using a national average of 22.20 percent. **Unemployment insurance** was calculated using a national average of 8 percent. **Health insurance** was calculated based on a projected national average for 2015 of $1,025 per employee (and family when applicable) per month. Employer pays 80 percent for a per month cost of $820 per employee. **Retirement** is based on a 401(k) retirement program with employer matching of 50 percent. Employee contributions to the 401(k) plan are an average of 6 percent of the true wage. **Liability insurance** is based on a national average of 10.0 percent.

| | Craft@Hrs | Unit | Material | Labor | Total |
|---|---|---|---|---|---|

## Insulation Labor Productivity

| | Craft@Hrs | Unit | Material | Labor | Total |
|---|---|---|---|---|---|
| Pour vermiculite attic insulation | | | | | |
| 3" deep | 1I@.008 | sf | — | .34 | .34 |
| 4" deep | 1I@.009 | sf | — | .38 | .38 |
| 5" deep | 1I@.009 | sf | — | .38 | .38 |
| 6" deep | 1I@.010 | sf | — | .42 | .42 |
| Blow in mineral wool insulation | | | | | |
| R11 (3-1/2" deep) | 1I@.010 | sf | — | .42 | .42 |
| R19 (6" deep) | 1I@.011 | sf | — | .46 | .46 |
| R30 (10" deep) | 1I@.013 | sf | — | .55 | .55 |
| R38 (12" deep) | 1I@.016 | sf | — | .67 | .67 |
| Blow in cellulose insulation | | | | | |
| R12 (3-1/2" deep) | 1I@.010 | sf | — | .42 | .42 |
| R21 (6" deep) | 1I@.012 | sf | — | .51 | .51 |
| R33 (10" deep) | 1I@.013 | sf | — | .55 | .55 |
| R42 (12" deep) | 1I@.016 | sf | — | .67 | .67 |
| Blow in fiberglass insulation | | | | | |
| R11 (5" deep) | 1I@.010 | sf | — | .42 | .42 |
| R19 (8" deep) | 1I@.011 | sf | — | .46 | .46 |
| R30 (13" deep) | 1I@.013 | sf | — | .55 | .55 |
| R38 (16" deep) | 1I@.016 | sf | — | .67 | .67 |
| Install fiberglass batt insulation in ceiling or floor | | | | | |
| R11 (3-1/2" deep) | 1I@.009 | sf | — | .38 | .38 |
| R19 (6" deep) | 1I@.011 | sf | — | .46 | .46 |
| R30 (9-1/2" deep) | 1I@.012 | sf | — | .51 | .51 |
| R38 (12" deep) | 1I@.015 | sf | — | .63 | .63 |
| Install fiberglass batt insulation in wall | | | | | |
| R6 (1-3/4" deep) (between furring strips) | 1I@.010 | sf | — | .42 | .42 |
| R11 (3-1/2" deep) | 1I@.011 | sf | — | .46 | .46 |
| R19 (6" deep) | 1I@.013 | sf | — | .55 | .55 |
| R25 (8" deep) | 1I@.015 | sf | — | .63 | .63 |
| Install rigid foam insulation board | | | | | |
| all thicknesses | 1I@.014 | sf | — | .59 | .59 |

| | Craft@Hrs | Unit | Material | Labor | Total |
|---|---|---|---|---|---|

# Manufactured Housing

**Mini price list.** This chapter contains some of the most common items found in manufactured housing.

## Appliances

**Clothes line.** Steel posts, umbrella-style supports with vinyl-coated rayon lines.

| | Craft@Hrs | Unit | Material | Labor | Total |
|---|---|---|---|---|---|
| replace, 30-line, exterior | 7M@1.06 | ea | 169.00 | 44.30 | 213.30 |
| remove | 1D@.264 | ea | — | 10.30 | 10.30 |
| replace, 7-line, exterior | 7M@1.02 | ea | 101.00 | 42.60 | 143.60 |
| remove | 1D@.251 | ea | — | 9.76 | 9.76 |
| remove, then reinstall | 7M@.348 | ea | — | 14.50 | 14.50 |

**Sidewall exhaust ventilator.** Louvered inside grille, insulated outside door, approximately 9" x 9".

| | Craft@Hrs | Unit | Material | Labor | Total |
|---|---|---|---|---|---|
| replace, 2" to 3" thick walls | 7M@1.96 | ea | 69.10 | 81.90 | 151.00 |
| replace, 2-3/4" to 4" thick walls | 7M@1.96 | ea | 71.80 | 81.90 | 153.70 |
| remove | 1D@.374 | ea | — | 14.50 | 14.50 |
| remove, then reinstall | 7M@3.04 | ea | 2.80 | 127.00 | 129.80 |

## Cabinets

**Mobile-home type cabinets, average grade.**

| | Craft@Hrs | Unit | Material | Labor | Total |
|---|---|---|---|---|---|
| replace, lower units | 7M@.205 | lf | 65.10 | 8.57 | 73.67 |
| replace, upper units | 7M@.169 | lf | 44.20 | 7.06 | 51.26 |
| replace, lower island units | 7M@.256 | lf | 91.20 | 10.70 | 101.90 |
| replace, upper island units | 7M@.184 | lf | 78.80 | 7.69 | 86.49 |
| remove | 1D@.116 | lf | — | 4.51 | 4.51 |
| remove, then reinstall | 7M@.236 | lf | — | 9.86 | 9.86 |

## Doors

**Access door.**

| | Craft@Hrs | Unit | Material | Labor | Total |
|---|---|---|---|---|---|
| replace, water heater or furnace | 7M@.820 | ea | 59.80 | 34.30 | 94.10 |
| remove | 1D@.554 | ea | — | 21.60 | 21.60 |
| remove, then reinstall | 7M@1.02 | ea | — | 42.60 | 42.60 |

**Mobile-home type entry door, fiberglass.**

| | Craft@Hrs | Unit | Material | Labor | Total |
|---|---|---|---|---|---|
| replace, flush | 7M@.771 | ea | 132.00 | 32.20 | 164.20 |
| replace, flush with fixed lite | 7M@.771 | ea | 151.00 | 32.20 | 183.20 |
| replace, flush with sliding window | 7M@.771 | ea | 165.00 | 32.20 | 197.20 |
| remove | 1D@.581 | ea | — | 22.60 | 22.60 |
| remove, then reinstall | 7M@1.22 | ea | — | 51.00 | 51.00 |

| | Craft@Hrs | Unit | Material | Labor | Total |
|---|---|---|---|---|---|

### Mobile-home type combination entry door (with storm door).

| | Craft@Hrs | Unit | Material | Labor | Total |
|---|---|---|---|---|---|
| replace, flush | 7M@.875 | ea | 171.00 | 36.60 | 207.60 |
| replace, flush with fixed lite | 7M@.875 | ea | 196.00 | 36.60 | 232.60 |
| replace, flush with sliding window | 7M@.875 | ea | 218.00 | 36.60 | 254.60 |
| remove | 1D@.696 | ea | — | 27.10 | 27.10 |
| remove, then reinstall | 7M@1.09 | ea | — | 45.60 | 45.60 |

## Door Hardware

### Mobile-home type lockset.

| | Craft@Hrs | Unit | Material | Labor | Total |
|---|---|---|---|---|---|
| replace, interior passage | 7M@.398 | ea | 16.80 | 16.60 | 33.40 |
| replace, interior privacy | 7M@.398 | ea | 19.40 | 16.60 | 36.00 |
| remove | 1D@.240 | ea | — | 9.34 | 9.34 |
| remove, then reinstall | 7M@.462 | ea | — | 19.30 | 19.30 |

### Mobile-home type entrance lockset.

| | Craft@Hrs | Unit | Material | Labor | Total |
|---|---|---|---|---|---|
| replace, standard | 7M@.569 | ea | 38.20 | 23.80 | 62.00 |
| remove | 1D@.297 | ea | — | 11.60 | 11.60 |
| remove, then reinstall | 7M@.755 | ea | — | 31.60 | 31.60 |

### Mobile-home type deadbolt.

| | Craft@Hrs | Unit | Material | Labor | Total |
|---|---|---|---|---|---|
| replace, standard | 7M@.651 | ea | 24.90 | 27.20 | 52.10 |
| remove | 1D@.207 | ea | — | 8.05 | 8.05 |
| remove, then reinstall | 7M@.771 | ea | — | 32.20 | 32.20 |

## Electrical

### Light fixture, mobile-home type.

| | Craft@Hrs | Unit | Material | Labor | Total |
|---|---|---|---|---|---|
| replace, average quality | 7M@.590 | ea | 16.50 | 24.70 | 41.20 |
| replace, high quality | 7M@.590 | ea | 26.60 | 24.70 | 51.30 |
| remove | 1D@.426 | ea | — | 16.60 | 16.60 |
| remove, then reinstall | 7M@.633 | ea | — | 26.50 | 26.50 |

## Finish Carpentry

### Casing (door or window).

| | Craft@Hrs | Unit | Material | Labor | Total |
|---|---|---|---|---|---|
| replace, 2-1/2" prefinished plastic | 7M@.038 | lf | .34 | 1.59 | 1.93 |
| remove | 1D@.017 | lf | — | .66 | .66 |

### Ceiling cove.

| | Craft@Hrs | Unit | Material | Labor | Total |
|---|---|---|---|---|---|
| replace, 3/4" prefinished plastic | 7M@.038 | lf | .39 | 1.59 | 1.98 |
| remove | 1D@.017 | lf | — | .66 | .66 |

### Gimp molding.

| | Craft@Hrs | Unit | Material | Labor | Total |
|---|---|---|---|---|---|
| replace, 3/4" prefinished plastic | 7M@.038 | lf | .34 | 1.59 | 1.93 |
| replace, 1" prefinished plastic | 7M@.038 | lf | .47 | 1.59 | 2.06 |
| remove | 1D@.017 | lf | — | .66 | .66 |

| | Craft@Hrs | Unit | Material | Labor | Total |
|---|---|---|---|---|---|
| **Outside corner trim.** | | | | | |
| replace, 1" prefinished plastic | 7M@.038 | lf | .34 | 1.59 | 1.93 |
| remove | 1D@.017 | lf | — | .66 | .66 |
| **Shoe molding.** | | | | | |
| replace, 3/4" prefinished plastic | 7M@.038 | lf | .34 | 1.59 | 1.93 |
| remove | 1D@.017 | lf | — | .66 | .66 |

**Foundations, Setup and Site Prep**

**Anchor.** Galvanized

| | Craft@Hrs | Unit | Material | Labor | Total |
|---|---|---|---|---|---|
| replace, 30" auger type | 7M@.410 | ea | 14.00 | 17.10 | 31.10 |
| replace, 48" auger type | 7M@.410 | ea | 17.00 | 17.10 | 34.10 |
| remove | 1D@.138 | ea | — | 5.37 | 5.37 |
| replace, slab type (includes concrete slab) | 7M@.514 | ea | 23.10 | 21.50 | 44.60 |
| remove | 1D@.209 | ea | — | 8.13 | 8.13 |

**Adjustable jack.**

| | | | | | |
|---|---|---|---|---|---|
| replace, from 1'8" to 3' | 7M@.307 | ea | 44.20 | 12.80 | 57.00 |
| replace, from 3'1" to 5' | 7M@.307 | ea | 55.40 | 12.80 | 68.20 |
| replace, from 4'6" to 7'9" | 7M@.307 | ea | 71.80 | 12.80 | 84.60 |
| remove | 1D@.116 | ea | — | 4.51 | 4.51 |
| remove, then reinstall | 7M@.462 | ea | — | 19.30 | 19.30 |

**Raise, setup, block, and level.**

| | | | | | |
|---|---|---|---|---|---|
| replace, single wide | 7M@18.4 | ea | — | 769.00 | 769.00 |
| replace, double wide | 7M@24.6 | ea | — | 1,030.00 | 1,030.00 |
| replace, triple wide | 7M@34.9 | ea | — | 1,460.00 | 1,460.00 |

**Relevel.**

| | | | | | |
|---|---|---|---|---|---|
| replace, single wide | 7M@5.14 | ea | 47.00 | 215.00 | 262.00 |
| replace, double wide | 7M@12.3 | ea | 93.90 | 514.00 | 607.90 |
| replace, triple wide | 7M@19.5 | ea | 142.00 | 815.00 | 957.00 |

**Site prep.**

| | | | | | |
|---|---|---|---|---|---|
| replace, standard conditions | 7M@54.4 | ea | — | 2,270.00 | 2,270.00 |

**Tie-down strap.** Galvanized. Frame type includes adapter and is 6' long. Roof type is 37' long.

| | | | | | |
|---|---|---|---|---|---|
| replace, frame type | 7M@.205 | ea | 12.80 | 8.57 | 21.37 |
| remove | 1D@.168 | ea | — | 6.54 | 6.54 |
| replace, roof type | 7M@.256 | ea | 30.40 | 10.70 | 41.10 |
| remove | 1D@.255 | ea | — | 9.92 | 9.92 |

**Utility hookup.**

| | | | | | |
|---|---|---|---|---|---|
| replace, sewer & water | 7M@24.0 | ea | — | 1,000.00 | 1,000.00 |
| replace, electrical | 7M@25.4 | ea | — | 1,060.00 | 1,060.00 |

| | Craft@Hrs | Unit | Material | Labor | Total |
|---|---|---|---|---|---|

## HVAC

### Baseboard heater, mobile-home type, electric.

| | Craft@Hrs | Unit | Material | Labor | Total |
|---|---|---|---|---|---|
| replace, 1,500 watt | 7M@.205 | lf | 12.60 | 8.57 | 21.17 |
| replace, 2,000 watt | 7M@.205 | lf | 17.10 | 8.57 | 25.67 |
| replace, 2,500 watt | 7M@.205 | lf | 19.40 | 8.57 | 27.97 |
| remove | 1D@.116 | lf | — | 4.51 | 4.51 |
| remove, then reinstall | 7M@.307 | lf | — | 12.80 | 12.80 |

### Furnace, mobile-home type, gas or electric.

| | Craft@Hrs | Unit | Material | Labor | Total |
|---|---|---|---|---|---|
| replace, 35,000 btu | 7M@5.14 | ea | 666.00 | 215.00 | 881.00 |
| replace, 55,000 btu | 7M@5.63 | ea | 1,020.00 | 235.00 | 1,255.00 |
| replace, 70,000 btu | 7M@6.15 | ea | 1,170.00 | 257.00 | 1,427.00 |
| replace, 80,000 btu | 7M@6.15 | ea | 1,230.00 | 257.00 | 1,487.00 |
| replace, 100,000 btu | 7M@6.15 | ea | 1,410.00 | 257.00 | 1,667.00 |
| replace, 125,000 btu | 7M@6.15 | ea | 1,530.00 | 257.00 | 1,787.00 |
| remove | 1D@1.45 | ea | — | 56.40 | 56.40 |
| remove, then reinstall | 7M@8.72 | ea | — | 364.00 | 364.00 |

## Moving & Towing

### Transport fees.

| | Craft@Hrs | Unit | Material | Labor | Total |
|---|---|---|---|---|---|
| replace, average, per section, per mile | 7M@.079 | mi | — | 3.30 | 3.30 |
| replace, average, pilot car, per mile | 7M@.024 | mi | — | 1.00 | 1.00 |

## Plumbing

### Water heater, mobile-home style, electric.

| | Craft@Hrs | Unit | Material | Labor | Total |
|---|---|---|---|---|---|
| replace, 10 gallon | 7M@1.54 | ea | 134.00 | 64.40 | 198.40 |
| replace, 20 gallon | 7M@1.54 | ea | 150.00 | 64.40 | 214.40 |
| replace, 30 gallon | 7M@1.54 | ea | 191.00 | 64.40 | 255.40 |
| replace, 40 gallon | 7M@1.54 | ea | 209.00 | 64.40 | 273.40 |
| replace, 50 gallon | 7M@1.54 | ea | 268.00 | 64.40 | 332.40 |
| remove | 1D@.869 | ea | — | 33.80 | 33.80 |
| remove, then reinstall | 7M@1.95 | ea | — | 81.50 | 81.50 |

### Water heater, mobile-home style, gas.

| | Craft@Hrs | Unit | Material | Labor | Total |
|---|---|---|---|---|---|
| replace, 20 gallon | 7M@1.90 | ea | 150.00 | 79.40 | 229.40 |
| replace, 30 gallon | 7M@1.90 | ea | 183.00 | 79.40 | 262.40 |
| replace, 40 gallon | 7M@1.90 | ea | 215.00 | 79.40 | 294.40 |
| replace, 50 gallon | 7M@1.90 | ea | 262.00 | 79.40 | 341.40 |
| remove | 1D@.869 | ea | — | 33.80 | 33.80 |
| remove, then reinstall | 7M@1.95 | ea | — | 81.50 | 81.50 |

|  | Craft@Hrs | Unit | Material | Labor | Total |
|---|---|---|---|---|---|
| **Roofing** | | | | | |
| **Drip edge.** | | | | | |
| replace, aluminum | 7M@.031 | lf | .34 | 1.30 | 1.64 |
| remove | 1D@.004 | lf | — | .16 | .16 |
| replace, galvanized | 7M@.031 | lf | .34 | 1.30 | 1.64 |
| remove | 1D@.004 | lf | — | .16 | .16 |
| **Flashing.** | | | | | |
| replace, aluminum, flexible | 7M@.031 | lf | 1.41 | 1.30 | 2.71 |
| replace, galvanized | 7M@.031 | lf | 1.28 | 1.30 | 2.58 |
| remove | 1D@.004 | lf | — | .16 | .16 |
| **J-rail.** | | | | | |
| replace, aluminum | 7M@.031 | lf | .47 | 1.30 | 1.77 |
| remove | 1D@.004 | lf | — | .16 | .16 |
| **Roof coating.** | | | | | |
| replace, complete roof (all types) | 7M@.006 | sf | .22 | .25 | .47 |
| replace, seams and edges only | 7M@.009 | lf | .22 | .38 | .60 |
| **Roof repair.** | | | | | |
| replace, patch | 7M@.771 | ea | 5.94 | 32.20 | 38.14 |
| replace, section | 7M@.102 | lf | 5.36 | 4.26 | 9.62 |
| remove | 1D@.023 | lf | — | .89 | .89 |
| **Rough Carpentry** | | | | | |
| **Belt rail.** | | | | | |
| replace, 1" x 2" | 7M@.020 | lf | .22 | .84 | 1.06 |
| replace, 1" x 4" | 7M@.026 | lf | .47 | 1.09 | 1.56 |
| remove | 1D@.011 | lf | — | .43 | .43 |
| replace, 1" x 2", including dado cut | 7M@.041 | lf | .22 | 1.71 | 1.93 |
| replace, 1" x 4", including dado cut | 7M@.046 | lf | .47 | 1.92 | 2.39 |
| remove | 1D@.017 | lf | — | .66 | .66 |
| **Exterior wall, mobile home, with belt rail.** | | | | | |
| replace, 2" x 2" | 7M@.307 | lf | 8.04 | 12.80 | 20.84 |
| replace, 2" x 4" | 7M@.361 | lf | 11.20 | 15.10 | 26.30 |
| remove | 1D@.047 | lf | — | 1.83 | 1.83 |
| replace, 2" x 6" | 7M@.410 | lf | 16.30 | 17.10 | 33.40 |
| remove | 1D@.047 | lf | — | 1.83 | 1.83 |
| **Interior wall, mobile home.** | | | | | |
| replace, 2" x 2" | 7M@.205 | lf | 7.21 | 8.57 | 15.78 |
| replace, 2" x 4" | 7M@.277 | lf | 9.89 | 11.60 | 21.49 |
| replace, 2" x 6" | 7M@.287 | lf | 14.70 | 12.00 | 26.70 |
| remove | 1D@.041 | lf | — | 1.59 | 1.59 |

| | Craft@Hrs | Unit | Material | Labor | Total |
|---|---|---|---|---|---|
| **Joist system, mobile home, per joist, 2" x 6".** | | | | | |
| replace, 10' | 7M@.216 | ea | 12.50 | 9.03 | 21.53 |
| remove | 1D@.139 | ea | — | 5.41 | 5.41 |
| replace, 12' | 7M@.259 | ea | 15.00 | 10.80 | 25.80 |
| remove | 1D@.145 | ea | — | 5.64 | 5.64 |
| replace, 14' | 7M@.302 | ea | 17.30 | 12.60 | 29.90 |
| remove | 1D@.151 | ea | — | 5.87 | 5.87 |
| replace, 16' | 7M@.346 | ea | 19.90 | 14.50 | 34.40 |
| remove | 1D@.157 | ea | — | 6.11 | 6.11 |
| **Joist system, mobile home, per joist, 2" x 8".** | | | | | |
| replace, 10' | 7M@.220 | ea | 14.00 | 9.20 | 23.20 |
| remove | 1D@.145 | ea | — | 5.64 | 5.64 |
| replace, 12' | 7M@.261 | ea | 16.50 | 10.90 | 27.40 |
| remove | 1D@.151 | ea | — | 5.87 | 5.87 |
| replace, 14' | 7M@.307 | ea | 19.40 | 12.80 | 32.20 |
| remove | 1D@.157 | ea | — | 6.11 | 6.11 |
| replace, 16' | 7M@.352 | ea | 22.30 | 14.70 | 37.00 |
| remove | 1D@.163 | ea | — | 6.34 | 6.34 |
| **Joist system, mobile home, per sf.** | | | | | |
| replace, 2" x 6", 16" on center | 7M@.021 | sf | 1.28 | .88 | 2.16 |
| replace, 2" x 8", 16" on center | 7M@.024 | sf | 1.52 | 1.00 | 2.52 |
| remove | 1D@.014 | sf | — | .54 | .54 |
| replace, 2" x 6", 24" on center | 7M@.018 | sf | .93 | .75 | 1.68 |
| replace, 2" x 8", 24" on center | 7M@.017 | sf | 1.17 | .71 | 1.88 |
| remove | 1D@.011 | sf | — | .43 | .43 |
| **Rafter, mobile home, 2" x 8".** | | | | | |
| replace, 10' | 7M@.307 | ea | 12.70 | 12.80 | 25.50 |
| replace, 12' | 7M@.327 | ea | 15.30 | 13.70 | 29.00 |
| replace, 14' | 7M@.349 | ea | 17.90 | 14.60 | 32.50 |
| replace, 16' | 7M@.391 | ea | 20.20 | 16.30 | 36.50 |
| remove | 1D@.127 | ea | — | 4.94 | 4.94 |
| **Truss, mobile home, bow roof.** | | | | | |
| replace, 10' | 7M@.361 | ea | 30.50 | 15.10 | 45.60 |
| replace, 12' | 7M@.391 | ea | 36.40 | 16.30 | 52.70 |
| replace, 14' | 7M@.422 | ea | 42.80 | 17.60 | 60.40 |
| replace, 16' | 7M@.462 | ea | 47.60 | 19.30 | 66.90 |
| remove | 1D@.151 | ea | — | 5.87 | 5.87 |
| **Truss, mobile home, gable roof.** | | | | | |
| replace, 10' | 7M@.410 | ea | 31.80 | 17.10 | 48.90 |
| replace, 12' | 7M@.431 | ea | 37.50 | 18.00 | 55.50 |
| replace, 14' | 7M@.450 | ea | 44.40 | 18.80 | 63.20 |
| replace, 16' | 7M@.462 | ea | 50.90 | 19.30 | 70.20 |
| remove | 1D@.151 | ea | — | 5.87 | 5.87 |

|  | Craft@Hrs | Unit | Material | Labor | Total |
|---|---|---|---|---|---|
| **Siding** | | | | | |
| **Horizontal lap siding, mobile home, all styles.** | | | | | |
| replace, aluminum | 7M@.014 | sf | .59 | .59 | 1.18 |
| remove | 1D@.011 | sf | — | .43 | .43 |
| replace, vinyl | 7M@.014 | sf | .47 | .59 | 1.06 |
| remove | 1D@.011 | sf | — | .43 | .43 |
| **Vertical siding, mobile home style, all patterns.** | | | | | |
| replace, aluminum | 7M@.014 | sf | .70 | .59 | 1.29 |
| remove | 1D@.011 | sf | — | .43 | .43 |
| **Shutters, mobile home style, per pair, 9" wide.** | | | | | |
| replace, 24" tall | 7M@.205 | ea | 34.60 | 8.57 | 43.17 |
| replace, 28" tall | 7M@.205 | ea | 35.90 | 8.57 | 44.47 |
| replace, 35" tall | 7M@.205 | ea | 38.10 | 8.57 | 46.67 |
| replace, 39" tall | 7M@.205 | ea | 39.50 | 8.57 | 48.07 |
| replace, 41" tall | 7M@.205 | ea | 40.90 | 8.57 | 49.47 |
| replace, 53" tall | 7M@.205 | ea | 44.20 | 8.57 | 52.77 |
| replace, 71" tall | 7M@.205 | ea | 52.40 | 8.57 | 60.97 |
| remove | 1D@.081 | ea | — | 3.15 | 3.15 |
| remove, then reinstall | 7M@.307 | ea | — | 12.80 | 12.80 |
| **Shutters, mobile home style, per pair, 12" wide.** | | | | | |
| replace, 24" tall | 7M@.256 | ea | 37.20 | 10.70 | 47.90 |
| replace, 28" tall | 7M@.256 | ea | 40.10 | 10.70 | 50.80 |
| replace, 35" tall | 7M@.256 | ea | 42.90 | 10.70 | 53.60 |
| replace, 39" tall | 7M@.256 | ea | 44.20 | 10.70 | 54.90 |
| replace, 47" tall | 7M@.256 | ea | 47.00 | 10.70 | 57.70 |
| replace, 55" tall | 7M@.256 | ea | 44.20 | 10.70 | 54.90 |
| replace, 63" tall | 7M@.256 | ea | 54.00 | 10.70 | 64.70 |
| replace, 71" tall | 7M@.256 | ea | 56.60 | 10.70 | 67.30 |
| replace, 80" tall | 7M@.256 | ea | 58.10 | 10.70 | 68.80 |
| remove | 1D@.081 | ea | — | 3.15 | 3.15 |
| remove, then reinstall | 7M@.361 | ea | — | 15.10 | 15.10 |
| **Steps** | | | | | |
| **Redwood frame, steps, and side handrails (no landing).** | | | | | |
| replace, 24" high x 48" wide, 3 steps | 7M@6.42 | ea | 121.00 | 268.00 | 389.00 |
| replace, 28" high x 48" wide, 4 steps | 7M@6.54 | ea | 140.00 | 273.00 | 413.00 |
| replace, 32" high x 48" wide, 4 steps | 7M@6.85 | ea | 163.00 | 286.00 | 449.00 |
| remove | 1D@.429 | ea | — | 16.70 | 16.70 |
| **Redwood frame, steps, and railing, 48" x 48" landing.** | | | | | |
| replace, 24" high x 48" wide, 3 steps | 7M@7.52 | ea | 155.00 | 314.00 | 469.00 |
| replace, 28" high x 48" wide, 4 steps | 7M@7.71 | ea | 173.00 | 322.00 | 495.00 |
| replace, 32" high x 48" wide, 4 steps | 7M@8.13 | ea | 201.00 | 340.00 | 541.00 |
| remove | 1D@.522 | ea | — | 20.30 | 20.30 |

| | Craft@Hrs | Unit | Material | Labor | Total |
|---|---|---|---|---|---|
| **Steel frame, steps, and side handrails (no landing).** | | | | | |
| replace, 24" high x 48" wide, 3 steps | 7M@1.02 | ea | 165.00 | 42.60 | 207.60 |
| replace, 28" high x 48" wide, 4 steps | 7M@1.02 | ea | 194.00 | 42.60 | 236.60 |
| replace, 32" high x 48" wide, 4 steps | 7M@1.02 | ea | 209.00 | 42.60 | 251.60 |
| remove | 1D@.370 | ea | — | 14.40 | 14.40 |
| **Steel frame and railing, wood steps with 27" x 36" landing.** | | | | | |
| replace, 24" high x 36" wide, 2 steps | 7M@1.23 | ea | 222.00 | 51.40 | 273.40 |
| replace, 28" high x 36" wide, 3 steps | 7M@1.23 | ea | 254.00 | 51.40 | 305.40 |
| replace, 32" high x 36" wide, 3 steps | 7M@1.23 | ea | 263.00 | 51.40 | 314.40 |
| remove | 1D@.370 | ea | — | 14.40 | 14.40 |
| **Steel frame, steps, and railing, 27" x 72" landing.** | | | | | |
| replace, 24" high x 72" wide, 3 steps | 7M@1.25 | ea | 325.00 | 52.30 | 377.30 |
| replace, 28" high x 72" wide, 4 steps | 7M@1.25 | ea | 365.00 | 52.30 | 417.30 |
| replace, 32" high x 72" wide, 4 steps | 7M@1.25 | ea | 381.00 | 52.30 | 433.30 |
| remove | 1D@.370 | ea | — | 14.40 | 14.40 |
| **Steel frame and railing, wood steps with 4' x 5-1/2' landing.** | | | | | |
| replace, 24" high x 48" wide, 2 steps | 7M@2.00 | ea | 587.00 | 83.60 | 670.60 |
| replace, 28" high x 48" wide, 3 steps | 7M@2.00 | ea | 624.00 | 83.60 | 707.60 |
| replace, 32" high x 48" wide, 3 steps | 7M@2.00 | ea | 691.00 | 83.60 | 774.60 |
| remove | 1D@.522 | ea | — | 20.30 | 20.30 |
| **Steel frame and railing, wood steps with 9' x 5' landing.** | | | | | |
| replace, 24" high x 36" wide, 2 steps | 7M@2.05 | ea | 1,070.00 | 85.70 | 1,155.70 |
| replace, 28" high x 36" wide, 3 steps | 7M@2.05 | ea | 1,140.00 | 85.70 | 1,225.70 |
| replace, 32" high x 36" wide, 3 steps | 7M@2.05 | ea | 1,180.00 | 85.70 | 1,265.70 |
| remove | 1D@.522 | ea | — | 20.30 | 20.30 |

## Skirting

| | Craft@Hrs | Unit | Material | Labor | Total |
|---|---|---|---|---|---|
| **Aluminum skirting, solid with vented panels.** | | | | | |
| replace, 24" tall | 7M@.056 | lf | 4.78 | 2.34 | 7.12 |
| replace, 28" tall | 7M@.056 | lf | 5.83 | 2.34 | 8.17 |
| replace, 30" tall | 7M@.056 | lf | 5.94 | 2.34 | 8.28 |
| replace, 36" tall | 7M@.056 | lf | 7.21 | 2.34 | 9.55 |
| replace, 42" tall | 7M@.056 | lf | 9.44 | 2.34 | 11.78 |
| remove skirting | 1D@.023 | lf | — | .89 | .89 |
| replace, add for access doors | 7M@.664 | ea | 60.80 | 27.80 | 88.60 |
| remove access doors | 1D@.116 | ea | — | 4.51 | 4.51 |
| **Vinyl skirting, simulated rock.** | | | | | |
| replace, 30" tall | 7M@.056 | lf | 11.20 | 2.34 | 13.54 |
| replace, 36" tall | 7M@.056 | lf | 14.20 | 2.34 | 16.54 |
| replace, 48" tall | 7M@.056 | lf | 19.50 | 2.34 | 21.84 |
| remove skirting | 1D@.023 | lf | — | .89 | .89 |
| replace, add for access doors | 7M@.664 | ea | 63.70 | 27.80 | 91.50 |
| remove access doors | 1D@.116 | ea | — | 4.51 | 4.51 |

| | Craft@Hrs | Unit | Material | Labor | Total |
|---|---|---|---|---|---|
| **Vinyl skirting, solid with vented panels.** | | | | | |
| replace, 24" tall | 7M@.056 | lf | 4.31 | 2.34 | 6.65 |
| replace, 28" tall | 7M@.056 | lf | 5.13 | 2.34 | 7.47 |
| replace, 30" tall | 7M@.056 | lf | 5.23 | 2.34 | 7.57 |
| replace, 36" tall | 7M@.056 | lf | 6.53 | 2.34 | 8.87 |
| replace, 42" tall | 7M@.056 | lf | 8.40 | 2.34 | 10.74 |
| remove skirting | 1D@.023 | lf | — | .89 | .89 |
| replace, add for access doors | 7M@.664 | ea | 54.70 | 27.80 | 82.50 |
| remove access doors | 1D@.116 | ea | — | 4.51 | 4.51 |
| **Wood skirting, rough-sawn plywood.** | | | | | |
| replace, 24" tall | 7M@.056 | lf | 3.03 | 2.34 | 5.37 |
| replace, 28" tall | 7M@.056 | lf | 3.61 | 2.34 | 5.95 |
| replace, 30" tall | 7M@.056 | lf | 3.72 | 2.34 | 6.06 |
| replace, 36" tall | 7M@.056 | lf | 4.54 | 2.34 | 6.88 |
| replace, 42" tall | 7M@.056 | lf | 5.94 | 2.34 | 8.28 |
| remove skirting | 1D@.023 | lf | — | .89 | .89 |
| replace, add for access doors | 7M@.664 | ea | 38.50 | 27.80 | 66.30 |
| remove access doors | 1D@.116 | ea | — | 4.51 | 4.51 |
| **Wood skirting, T1-11 or hardboard.** | | | | | |
| replace, 24" tall | 7M@.056 | lf | 2.80 | 2.34 | 5.14 |
| replace, 28" tall | 7M@.056 | lf | 3.49 | 2.34 | 5.83 |
| replace, 30" tall | 7M@.056 | lf | 3.49 | 2.34 | 5.83 |
| replace, 36" tall | 7M@.056 | lf | 4.31 | 2.34 | 6.65 |
| replace, 42" tall | 7M@.056 | lf | 5.59 | 2.34 | 7.93 |
| remove skirting | 1D@.023 | lf | — | .89 | .89 |
| replace, add for access doors | 7M@.664 | ea | 37.20 | 27.80 | 65.00 |
| remove access doors | 1D@.116 | ea | — | 4.51 | 4.51 |

## Wall and Ceiling Panels

| | Craft@Hrs | Unit | Material | Labor | Total |
|---|---|---|---|---|---|
| **Ceiling panel, drywall with textured finish.** | | | | | |
| replace, 3/8", no battens | 7M@.026 | sf | .72 | 1.09 | 1.81 |
| replace, 3/8" with battens | 7M@.029 | sf | .82 | 1.21 | 2.03 |
| remove | 1D@.007 | sf | — | .27 | .27 |
| **Wall panel, drywall.** | | | | | |
| replace, 1/2" with vinyl | 7M@.028 | sf | 1.21 | 1.17 | 2.38 |
| replace, 1/2" with wallpaper | 7M@.028 | sf | .96 | 1.17 | 2.13 |
| remove | 1D@.007 | sf | — | .27 | .27 |
| **Ceiling and wall panel attachment.** | | | | | |
| replace, batten | 7M@.017 | lf | .20 | .71 | .91 |
| replace, screw with rosette | 7M@.005 | ea | .29 | .21 | .50 |
| replace, screw with wing clip | 7M@.005 | ea | .43 | .21 | .64 |
| remove | 1D@.002 | ea | — | .08 | .08 |

| | Craft@Hrs | Unit | Material | Labor | Total |
|---|---|---|---|---|---|

## Windows

### Awning window, mobile home.

| | Craft@Hrs | Unit | Material | Labor | Total |
|---|---|---|---|---|---|
| replace, 14" x 27" with 2 lites | 7M@.801 | ea | 82.90 | 33.50 | 116.40 |
| replace, 14" x 39" with 3 lites | 7M@.801 | ea | 102.00 | 33.50 | 135.50 |
| replace, 24" x 27" with 2 lites | 7M@.801 | ea | 102.00 | 33.50 | 135.50 |
| replace, 30" x 27" with 2 lites | 7M@.801 | ea | 110.00 | 33.50 | 143.50 |
| replace, 30" x 39" with 3 lites | 7M@.801 | ea | 132.00 | 33.50 | 165.50 |
| replace, 30" x 53" with 4 lites | 7M@.801 | ea | 165.00 | 33.50 | 198.50 |
| replace, 36" x 39" with 3 lites | 7M@.801 | ea | 153.00 | 33.50 | 186.50 |
| replace, 36" x 53" with 4 lites | 7M@.801 | ea | 180.00 | 33.50 | 213.50 |
| replace, 46" x 27" with 2 lites | 7M@.801 | ea | 140.00 | 33.50 | 173.50 |
| replace, 46" x 39" with 3 lites | 7M@.801 | ea | 165.00 | 33.50 | 198.50 |
| remove | 1D@.348 | ea | — | 13.50 | 13.50 |
| remove, then reinstall | 7M@1.02 | ea | — | 42.60 | 42.60 |

### Skylight, fixed, mobile home.

| | Craft@Hrs | Unit | Material | Labor | Total |
|---|---|---|---|---|---|
| replace, 14" x 22" | 7M@1.79 | ea | 82.20 | 74.80 | 157.00 |
| replace, 14" x 46" | 7M@1.79 | ea | 144.00 | 74.80 | 218.80 |
| replace, 22" x 22" | 7M@1.79 | ea | 94.60 | 74.80 | 169.40 |
| replace, 22" x 34" | 7M@1.79 | ea | 334.00 | 74.80 | 408.80 |
| remove | 1D@.581 | ea | — | 22.60 | 22.60 |
| remove, then reinstall | 7M@2.25 | ea | — | 94.10 | 94.10 |

### Skylight, ventilating, mobile home.

| | Craft@Hrs | Unit | Material | Labor | Total |
|---|---|---|---|---|---|
| replace, 14" x 22" | 7M@2.25 | ea | 102.00 | 94.10 | 196.10 |
| replace, 14" x 46" | 7M@2.25 | ea | 164.00 | 94.10 | 258.10 |
| replace, 22" x 22" | 7M@2.25 | ea | 110.00 | 94.10 | 204.10 |
| replace, 22" x 34" | 7M@2.25 | ea | 384.00 | 94.10 | 478.10 |
| remove | 1D@.581 | ea | — | 22.60 | 22.60 |
| remove, then reinstall | 7M@2.56 | ea | — | 107.00 | 107.00 |

## Time & Material Charts (selected items)
## Manufactured Housing Materials

See Manufactured Housing material prices with the line items above.

## Manufactured Housing Labor

| Laborer | base wage | paid leave | true wage | taxes & ins. | total |
|---|---|---|---|---|---|
| MH repair specialist | $22.80 | 1.78 | $24.58 | 17.22 | $41.80 |
| MH repair specialist's helper | $11.40 | .89 | $12.29 | 11.21 | $23.50 |

**Paid leave** is calculated based on two weeks paid vacation, one week sick leave, and seven paid holidays. Employer's matching portion of **FICA** is 7.65 percent. **FUTA** (Federal Unemployment) is .8 percent. **Worker's compensation** was calculated using a national average of 11.60 percent for a manufactured housing repair professional. **Unemployment insurance** was calculated using a national average of 8 percent. **Health insurance** was calculated based on a projected national average for 2015 of $1,025 per employee (and family when applicable) per month. Employer pays 80 percent for a per month cost of $820 per employee. **Retirement** is based on a 401(k) retirement program with employer matching of 50 percent. Employee contributions to the 401(k) plan are an average of 6 percent of the true wage. **Liability insurance** is based on a national average of 10.0 percent.

|  | Craft@Hrs | Unit | Material | Labor | Total |
|---|---|---|---|---|---|

## Masking & Moving

### Minimum charge.

| | Craft@Hrs | Unit | Material | Labor | Total |
|---|---|---|---|---|---|
| for masking or moving work | 3L@2.25 | ea | 19.70 | 79.90 | 99.60 |

### Mask room.

| | Craft@Hrs | Unit | Material | Labor | Total |
|---|---|---|---|---|---|
| Small | 3L@1.11 | ea | 3.85 | 39.40 | 43.25 |
| Average size | 3L@1.28 | ea | 4.36 | 45.40 | 49.76 |
| Large | 3L@1.52 | ea | 5.11 | 54.00 | 59.11 |
| Very large | 3L@1.85 | ea | 5.39 | 65.70 | 71.09 |
| Per lf of wall | 3L@.032 | lf | .11 | 1.14 | 1.25 |

### Mask window.

| | Craft@Hrs | Unit | Material | Labor | Total |
|---|---|---|---|---|---|
| Small | 3L@.263 | ea | 1.93 | 9.34 | 11.27 |
| Average size | 3L@.308 | ea | 2.04 | 10.90 | 12.94 |
| Large | 3L@.371 | ea | 2.16 | 13.20 | 15.36 |
| Very large | 3L@.455 | ea | 2.27 | 16.20 | 18.47 |

### Mask door or opening.

| | Craft@Hrs | Unit | Material | Labor | Total |
|---|---|---|---|---|---|
| Small | 3L@.260 | ea | 2.12 | 9.23 | 11.35 |
| Average size | 3L@.303 | ea | 2.23 | 10.80 | 13.03 |
| Large | 3L@.364 | ea | 2.35 | 12.90 | 15.25 |
| Very large | 3L@.444 | ea | 2.45 | 15.80 | 18.25 |
| Per lf of opening | 3L@.030 | lf | .07 | 1.07 | 1.14 |

### Mask woodwork.

| | Craft@Hrs | Unit | Material | Labor | Total |
|---|---|---|---|---|---|
| Per lf | 3L@.029 | lf | .07 | 1.03 | 1.10 |

### Mask electrical.

| | Craft@Hrs | Unit | Material | Labor | Total |
|---|---|---|---|---|---|
| Baseboard heater | 3L@.222 | ea | 1.62 | 7.88 | 9.50 |
| Light fixture | 3L@.182 | ea | 1.24 | 6.46 | 7.70 |
| Outlet or switch (remove cover) | 3L@.114 | ea | .30 | 4.05 | 4.35 |

### Mask bathroom.

| | Craft@Hrs | Unit | Material | Labor | Total |
|---|---|---|---|---|---|
| Small | 3L@1.16 | ea | 3.88 | 41.20 | 45.08 |
| Average size | 3L@1.35 | ea | 4.41 | 47.90 | 52.31 |
| Large | 3L@1.61 | ea | 5.19 | 57.20 | 62.39 |
| Very large | 3L@2.00 | ea | 5.53 | 71.00 | 76.53 |

### Mask kitchen.

| | Craft@Hrs | Unit | Material | Labor | Total |
|---|---|---|---|---|---|
| Small | 3L@1.20 | ea | 4.58 | 42.60 | 47.18 |
| Average size | 3L@1.41 | ea | 5.01 | 50.10 | 55.11 |
| Large | 3L@1.69 | ea | 5.47 | 60.00 | 65.47 |
| Very large | 3L@2.13 | ea | 5.71 | 75.60 | 81.31 |

| | Craft@Hrs | Unit | Material | Labor | Total |
|---|---|---|---|---|---|
| **Mask tile, marble, or stone.** | | | | | |
| Per lf of edge | 3L@.031 | lf | .09 | 1.10 | 1.19 |
| | | | | | |
| **Move and cover room contents.** | | | | | |
| Small | 3L@1.25 | ea | 10.80 | 44.40 | 55.20 |
| Average | 3L@1.52 | ea | 12.10 | 54.00 | 66.10 |
| Heavy or above average | 3L@1.92 | ea | 13.90 | 68.20 | 82.10 |
| Very heavy or above average | 3L@2.70 | ea | 16.10 | 95.90 | 112.00 |

## Time & Material Charts (selected items)
## Masking & Moving Materials

See Masking & Moving material prices with the line items above.

## Masking & Moving Labor

| Laborer | base wage | paid leave | true wage | taxes & ins. | total |
|---|---|---|---|---|---|
| Laborer | $18.60 | 1.45 | $20.05 | 15.45 | $35.50 |

**Paid leave** is calculated based on two weeks paid vacation, one week sick leave, and seven paid holidays. Employer's matching portion of **FICA** is 7.65 percent. **FUTA** (Federal Unemployment) is .8 percent. **Worker's compensation** for the masking & moving trade was calculated using a national average of 13.75 percent. **Unemployment insurance** was calculated using a national average of 8 percent. **Health insurance** was calculated based on a projected national average for 2015 of $1,025 per employee (and family when applicable) per month. Employer pays 80 percent for a per month cost of $820 per employee. **Retirement** is based on a 401(k) retirement program with employer matching of 50 percent. Employee contributions to the 401(k) plan are an average of 6 percent of the true wage. **Liability insurance** is based on a national average of 10.0 percent.

| | Craft@Hrs | Unit | Material | Labor | Total |
|---|---|---|---|---|---|

# Masonry

## Minimum charge.

| | Craft@Hrs | Unit | Material | Labor | Total |
|---|---|---|---|---|---|
| for masonry work | 4M@5.25 | ea | 188.00 | 273.00 | 461.00 |

**Brick walls.** All brick walls are made from average to high quality face brick. Standard quality bricks will be up to 15% less and higher quality bricks will vary by as much as 45%. Brick sizes come in two general categories: non-modular and modular. Actual dimensions for non-modular standard bricks are 3-3/4" thick by 2-1/4" high by 8" long; non-modular oversize bricks are 3-3/4" thick by 2-3/4" high by 8" long; non-modular three-inch bricks are 3" thick by 2-3/4" high by 9-3/4" long. Three-inch bricks also come in lengths of 9-5/8" and 8-3/4" and widths vary from 2-5/8" to 3". They are normally used as veneer units. Modular bricks are designed to fit together with a minimum of cutting which saves labor and reduces waste. Nominal dimensions for modular bricks include the manufactured dimensions plus the thickness of the mortar joint for which the unit was designed (usually 1/2"). Actual brick sizes vary from manufacturer to manufacturer. The sizes in this section are typical.

## Deduct for common brick.

| | Craft@Hrs | Unit | Material | Labor | Total |
|---|---|---|---|---|---|
| instead of average to high quality face brick | — | % | -16.0 | — | — |

**4" wide brick wall.** With 3/8" wide mortar joints. Includes 4% waste for brick and 25% waste for mortar.

| | Craft@Hrs | Unit | Material | Labor | Total |
|---|---|---|---|---|---|
| replace, standard non-modular brick | 4M@.170 | sf | 7.15 | 8.84 | 15.99 |
| replace, oversize non-modular brick | 4M@.168 | sf | 5.96 | 8.74 | 14.70 |
| replace, three-inch non-modular brick | 4M@.167 | sf | 5.88 | 8.68 | 14.56 |
| replace, standard brick | 4M@.169 | sf | 5.08 | 8.79 | 13.87 |
| replace, engineer brick | 4M@.141 | sf | 5.27 | 7.33 | 12.60 |
| replace, jumbo closure brick | 4M@.120 | sf | 5.29 | 6.24 | 11.53 |
| replace, double brick | 4M@.101 | sf | 4.34 | 5.25 | 9.59 |
| replace, Roman brick | 4M@.160 | sf | 7.04 | 8.32 | 15.36 |
| replace, Norman brick | 4M@.130 | sf | 5.76 | 6.76 | 12.52 |

| | | Craft@Hrs | Unit | Material | Labor | Total |
|---|---|---|---|---|---|---|
| replace, Norwegian brick | | 4M@.111 | sf | 4.44 | 5.77 | 10.21 |
| jumbo utility brick | | 4M@.102 | sf | 5.67 | 5.30 | 10.97 |
| triple brick | | 4M@.096 | sf | 4.63 | 4.99 | 9.62 |
| remove | | 1D@.087 | sf | — | 3.38 | 3.38 |

**6" wide brick wall.** With 3/8" wide mortar joints. Includes 4% waste for brick and 25% waste for mortar.

| | | Craft@Hrs | Unit | Material | Labor | Total |
|---|---|---|---|---|---|---|
| replace, Norwegian brick wall | | 4M@.124 | sf | 6.12 | 6.45 | 12.57 |
| replace, Norman brick wall | | 4M@.148 | sf | 7.53 | 7.70 | 15.23 |
| replace, jumbo brick wall | | 4M@.113 | sf | 6.85 | 5.88 | 12.73 |
| remove | | 1D@.104 | sf | — | 4.05 | 4.05 |

**8" wide brick wall.** With 3/8" wide mortar joints. Includes 4% waste for brick and 25% waste for mortar.

| | | Craft@Hrs | Unit | Material | Labor | Total |
|---|---|---|---|---|---|---|
| replace, jumbo brick | | 4M@.127 | sf | 7.97 | 6.60 | 14.57 |
| remove | | 1D@.132 | sf | — | 5.13 | 5.13 |

**8" wide double wythe brick wall.** With 3/8" wide mortar joints. Includes 4% waste for brick and 25% waste for mortar.

| | | Craft@Hrs | Unit | Material | Labor | Total |
|---|---|---|---|---|---|---|
| replace, standard non-modular brick | | 4M@.307 | sf | 14.90 | 16.00 | 30.90 |
| replace, oversize non-modular brick | | 4M@.303 | sf | 12.30 | 15.80 | 28.10 |
| replace, three-inch non-modular brick | | 4M@.300 | sf | 12.20 | 15.60 | 27.80 |
| replace, standard brick | | 4M@.305 | sf | 10.70 | 15.90 | 26.60 |

| | | Craft@Hrs | Unit | Material | Labor | Total |
|---|---|---|---|---|---|---|
| replace, engineer brick | | 4M@.253 | sf | 11.00 | 13.20 | 24.20 |
| replace, jumbo closure brick | | 4M@.216 | sf | 11.00 | 11.20 | 22.20 |
| replace, double brick | | 4M@.181 | sf | 9.14 | 9.41 | 18.55 |
| replace, Roman brick | | 4M@.287 | sf | 14.70 | 14.90 | 29.60 |
| replace, Norman brick | | 4M@.234 | sf | 11.90 | 12.20 | 24.10 |
| replace, Norwegian brick | | 4M@.199 | sf | 9.34 | 10.30 | 19.64 |
| replace, jumbo utility brick | | 4M@.184 | sf | 11.70 | 9.57 | 21.27 |
| replace, triple brick | | 4M@.173 | sf | 9.72 | 9.00 | 18.72 |
| remove | | 1D@.132 | sf | — | 5.13 | 5.13 |

**8" wide brick & block wall.** 8" wide wall with 4" wide brick and 4" wide concrete block. With 3/8" wide mortar joints. Includes 4% waste for brick and block and 25% waste for mortar.

| | | Craft@Hrs | Unit | Material | Labor | Total |
|---|---|---|---|---|---|---|
| replace, standard non-modular brick | | 4M@.233 | sf | 10.30 | 12.10 | 22.40 |
| replace, oversize non-modular brick | | 4M@.231 | sf | 9.10 | 12.00 | 21.10 |
| replace, three-inch non-modular brick | | 4M@.230 | sf | 9.05 | 12.00 | 21.05 |
| replace, standard brick | | 4M@.233 | sf | 8.21 | 12.10 | 20.31 |

| | | Craft@Hrs | Unit | Material | Labor | Total |
|---|---|---|---|---|---|---|
| replace, engineer brick | | 4M@.206 | sf | 8.42 | 10.70 | 19.12 |
| replace, jumbo closure brick | | 4M@.188 | sf | 8.44 | 9.78 | 18.22 |
| replace, double brick | | 4M@.170 | sf | 7.50 | 8.84 | 16.34 |
| replace, Roman brick | | 4M@.224 | sf | 10.20 | 11.60 | 21.80 |
| replace, Norman brick | | 4M@.197 | sf | 8.90 | 10.20 | 19.10 |
| replace, Norwegian brick | | 4M@.180 | sf | 7.58 | 9.36 | 16.94 |
| replace, jumbo utility brick | | 4M@.172 | sf | 8.78 | 8.94 | 17.72 |
| replace, triple brick | | 4M@.166 | sf | 7.77 | 8.63 | 16.40 |
| remove | | 1D@.132 | sf | — | 5.13 | 5.13 |

**10" wide brick & block wall.** 10" wide wall with 4" wide brick and 6" wide concrete block. With 3/8" wide mortar joints. Includes 4% waste for brick and block and 25% waste for mortar.

| | | Craft@Hrs | Unit | Material | Labor | Total |
|---|---|---|---|---|---|---|
| replace, standard non-modular brick | | 4M@.236 | sf | 10.80 | 12.30 | 23.10 |
| replace, oversize non-modular brick | | 4M@.234 | sf | 9.54 | 12.20 | 21.74 |
| replace, three-inch non-modular brick | | 4M@.233 | sf | 9.50 | 12.10 | 21.60 |

| | | Craft@Hrs | Unit | Material | Labor | Total |
|---|---|---|---|---|---|---|
| replace, standard brick | | 4M@.235 | sf | 8.69 | 12.20 | 20.89 |
| replace, engineer brick | | 4M@.209 | sf | 8.88 | 10.90 | 19.78 |
| replace, jumbo closure brick | | 4M@.190 | sf | 8.90 | 9.88 | 18.78 |
| replace, double brick | | 4M@.173 | sf | 7.93 | 9.00 | 16.93 |
| replace, Roman brick | | 4M@.226 | sf | 10.70 | 11.80 | 22.50 |
| replace, Norman brick | | 4M@.200 | sf | 9.36 | 10.40 | 19.76 |
| replace, Norwegian brick | | 4M@.182 | sf | 8.07 | 9.46 | 17.53 |
| replace, jumbo utility brick | | 4M@.175 | sf | 9.24 | 9.10 | 18.34 |
| replace, triple brick | | 4M@.170 | sf | 8.23 | 8.84 | 17.07 |
| remove | | 1D@.149 | sf | — | 5.80 | 5.80 |

| | Craft@Hrs | Unit | Material | Labor | Total |
|---|---|---|---|---|---|

**12" wide brick & block wall.** 12" wide wall with 4" wide brick and 8" wide concrete block. With 3/8" wide mortar joints. Includes 4% waste for brick and block and 25% waste for mortar.

| | | Craft@Hrs | Unit | Material | Labor | Total |
|---|---|---|---|---|---|---|
| replace, standard non-modular brick | | 4M@.240 | sf | 11.50 | 12.50 | 24.00 |
| replace, oversize non-modular brick | | 4M@.239 | sf | 10.30 | 12.40 | 22.70 |
| replace, three-inch non-modular brick | | 4M@.237 | sf | 10.30 | 12.30 | 22.60 |
| replace, standard brick | | 4M@.240 | sf | 9.49 | 12.50 | 21.99 |
| replace, engineer brick | | 4M@.214 | sf | 9.70 | 11.10 | 20.80 |
| replace, jumbo closure brick | | 4M@.195 | sf | 9.71 | 10.10 | 19.81 |
| replace, double brick | | 4M@.178 | sf | 8.75 | 9.26 | 18.01 |
| replace, Roman brick | | 4M@.231 | sf | 11.40 | 12.00 | 23.40 |
| replace, Norman brick | | 4M@.204 | sf | 10.20 | 10.60 | 20.80 |
| replace, Norwegian brick | | 4M@.187 | sf | 8.86 | 9.72 | 18.58 |
| replace, jumbo utility brick | | 4M@.180 | sf | 10.10 | 9.36 | 19.46 |
| replace, triple brick | | 4M@.174 | sf | 9.05 | 9.05 | 18.10 |
| remove | | 1D@.177 | sf | — | 6.89 | 6.89 |

| | Craft@Hrs | Unit | Material | Labor | Total |
|---|---|---|---|---|---|

**12" wide triple wythe brick wall.** With 3/8" wide mortar joints.  Includes 4% waste for brick and 25% waste for mortar.

| | Craft@Hrs | Unit | Material | Labor | Total |
|---|---|---|---|---|---|
| replace, standard non-modular brick | 4M@.433 | sf | 22.00 | 22.50 | 44.50 |
| replace, oversize non-modular brick | 4M@.427 | sf | 18.00 | 22.20 | 40.20 |
| replace, three-inch non-modular brick | 4M@.424 | sf | 18.20 | 22.00 | 40.20 |
| replace, standard brick | 4M@.429 | sf | 15.70 | 22.30 | 38.00 |
| replace, engineer brick | 4M@.357 | sf | 16.20 | 18.60 | 34.80 |
| replace, jumbo closure brick | 4M@.305 | sf | 16.20 | 15.90 | 32.10 |
| replace, double brick | 4M@.255 | sf | 13.50 | 13.30 | 26.80 |
| replace, Roman brick | 4M@.407 | sf | 21.80 | 21.20 | 43.00 |
| replace, Norman brick | 4M@.330 | sf | 17.80 | 17.20 | 35.00 |
| replace, Norwegian brick | 4M@.282 | sf | 14.00 | 14.70 | 28.70 |
| replace, jumbo utility brick | 4M@.260 | sf | 17.50 | 13.50 | 31.00 |
| replace, triple brick | 4M@.244 | sf | 14.60 | 12.70 | 27.30 |
| remove | 1D@.177 | sf | — | 6.89 | 6.89 |

| | | Craft@Hrs | Unit | Material | Labor | Total |
|---|---|---|---|---|---|---|

**10" wide brick & block cavity wall.** Made from 4" wide brick and 4" wide concrete block. With 2" dead air space (see page 239 for foam insulation in air space) and 3/8" wide mortar joints. Includes 4% waste for brick and block and 25% waste for mortar.

| | | Craft@Hrs | Unit | Material | Labor | Total |
|---|---|---|---|---|---|---|
| replace, standard non-modular brick | | 4M@.244 | sf | 10.40 | 12.70 | 23.10 |
| replace, oversize non-modular brick | | 4M@.240 | sf | 9.23 | 12.50 | 21.73 |
| replace, three-inch non-modular brick | | 4M@.240 | sf | 9.18 | 12.50 | 21.68 |
| replace, standard brick | | 4M@.244 | sf | 8.38 | 12.70 | 21.08 |
| replace, engineer brick | | 4M@.216 | sf | 8.56 | 11.20 | 19.76 |
| replace, jumbo closure brick | | 4M@.196 | sf | 8.58 | 10.20 | 18.78 |
| replace, double brick | | 4M@.178 | sf | 7.62 | 9.26 | 16.88 |
| replace, Roman brick | | 4M@.234 | sf | 10.30 | 12.20 | 22.50 |
| replace, Norman brick | | 4M@.206 | sf | 9.05 | 10.70 | 19.75 |
| replace, Norwegian brick | | 4M@.188 | sf | 7.72 | 9.78 | 17.50 |
| replace, jumbo utility brick | | 4M@.180 | sf | 8.95 | 9.36 | 18.31 |
| replace, triple brick | | 4M@.174 | sf | 7.91 | 9.05 | 16.96 |
| remove | | 1D@.132 | sf | — | 5.13 | 5.13 |

| | | Craft@Hrs | Unit | Material | Labor | Total |
|---|---|---|---|---|---|---|

**10" wide brick cavity wall.** Made from 4" wide brick on both sides. With 2" dead air space (see cavity wall insulation below) and 3/8" wide mortar joints. Includes 4% waste for brick and 25% waste for mortar.

| | | Craft@Hrs | Unit | Material | Labor | Total |
|---|---|---|---|---|---|---|
| replace, standard non-modular brick | | 4M@.321 | sf | 15.00 | 16.70 | 31.70 |
| replace, oversize non-modular brick | | 4M@.317 | sf | 12.40 | 16.50 | 28.90 |
| replace, three-inch non-modular brick | | 4M@.314 | sf | 12.30 | 16.30 | 28.60 |
| replace, standard brick | | 4M@.319 | sf | 10.80 | 16.60 | 27.40 |
| replace, engineer brick | | 4M@.266 | sf | 11.10 | 13.80 | 24.90 |
| replace, jumbo closure brick | | 4M@.226 | sf | 11.10 | 11.80 | 22.90 |
| replace, double brick | | 4M@.189 | sf | 9.28 | 9.83 | 19.11 |
| replace, Roman brick | | 4M@.301 | sf | 14.80 | 15.70 | 30.50 |
| replace, Norman brick | | 4M@.245 | sf | 12.10 | 12.70 | 24.80 |
| replace, Norwegian brick | | 4M@.209 | sf | 9.49 | 10.90 | 20.39 |
| replace, jumbo utility brick | | 4M@.193 | sf | 11.90 | 10.00 | 21.90 |
| replace, triple brick | | 4M@.181 | sf | 9.88 | 9.41 | 19.29 |
| remove | | 1D@.132 | sf | — | 5.13 | 5.13 |

**Add for cavity wall insulation.**

| | | Craft@Hrs | Unit | Material | Labor | Total |
|---|---|---|---|---|---|---|
| 2" polystyrene | | 4M@.001 | sf | 1.07 | .05 | 1.12 |

| | Craft@Hrs | Unit | Material | Labor | Total |
|---|---|---|---|---|---|

**Brick veneer.** With 3/8" wide mortar joints. Includes 4% waste for brick and 25% waste for mortar.

*common bond*

| | Craft@Hrs | Unit | Material | Labor | Total |
|---|---|---|---|---|---|
| replace, standard non-modular brick | 4M@.144 | sf | 7.15 | 7.49 | 14.64 |
| replace, oversize non-modular brick | 4M@.143 | sf | 5.96 | 7.44 | 13.40 |
| replace, three-inch non-modular brick | 4M@.141 | sf | 5.88 | 7.33 | 13.21 |
| replace, used brick | 4M@.144 | sf | 10.30 | 7.49 | 17.79 |
| replace, standard brick | 4M@.144 | sf | 5.08 | 7.49 | 12.57 |
| replace, engineer brick | 4M@.119 | sf | 5.27 | 6.19 | 11.46 |
| replace, jumbo closure brick | 4M@.102 | sf | 5.29 | 5.30 | 10.59 |
| replace, double brick | 4M@.085 | sf | 4.34 | 4.42 | 8.76 |
| replace, Roman brick | 4M@.136 | sf | 7.04 | 7.07 | 14.11 |
| replace, Norman brick | 4M@.110 | sf | 5.76 | 5.72 | 11.48 |
| replace, Norwegian brick | 4M@.094 | sf | 4.44 | 4.89 | 9.33 |
| replace, jumbo utility brick | 4M@.087 | sf | 5.67 | 4.52 | 10.19 |
| replace, triple brick | 4M@.082 | sf | 4.63 | 4.26 | 8.89 |
| remove | 1D@.082 | sf | — | 3.19 | 3.19 |

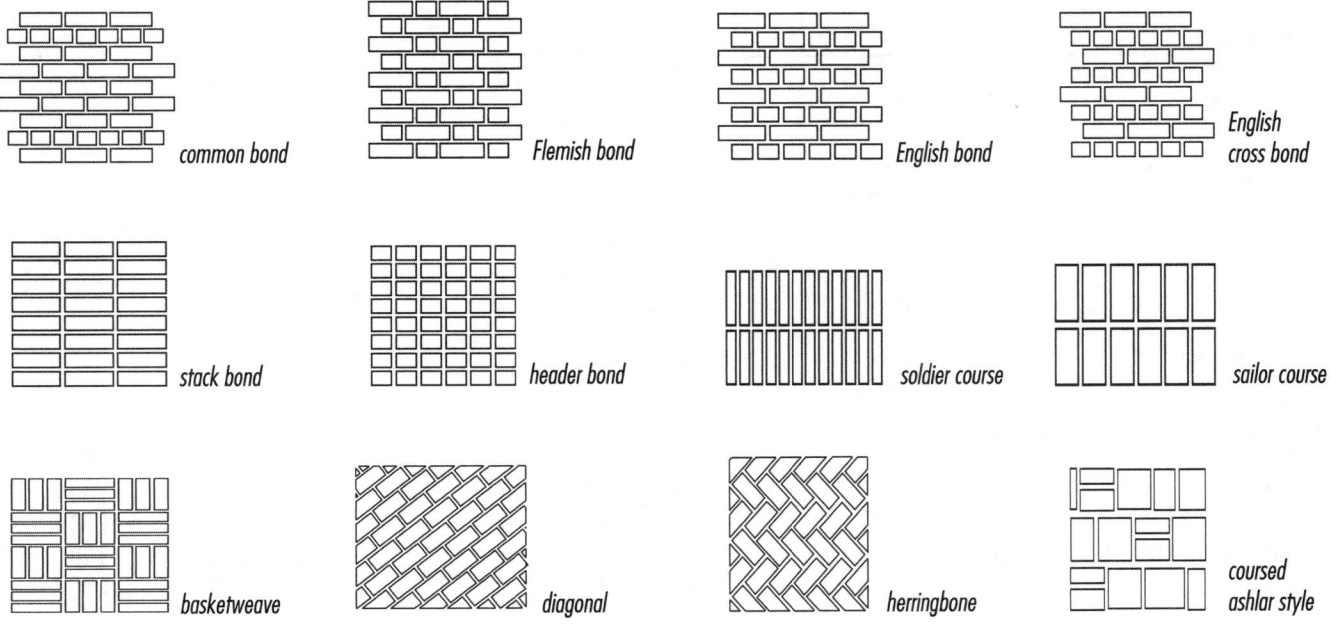

common bond  Flemish bond  English bond  English cross bond

stack bond  header bond  soldier course  sailor course

basketweave  diagonal  herringbone  coursed ashlar style

| | Craft@Hrs | Unit | Material | Labor | Total |
|---|---|---|---|---|---|

**Add for other brick bonds.** All brick prices above are for running bond. For other bonds add the percentage listed below.

| | Craft@Hrs | Unit | Material | Labor | Total |
|---|---|---|---|---|---|
| add for common bond | | | | | |
| (also called American bond) | — | % | — | 16.0 | — |
| add for Flemish bond | — | % | — | 54.0 | — |
| add for English bond | — | % | — | 65.0 | — |
| add for English cross bond | | | | | |
| (also called Dutch bond) | — | % | — | 65.0 | — |
| add for stack bond | — | % | — | 8.0 | — |
| add for false all header bond | — | % | — | 116.0 | — |
| add for all header bond | — | % | — | 115.0 | — |
| add for soldier course | — | % | — | 15.0 | — |
| add for sailor course | — | % | — | 5.0 | — |
| add for basketweave | — | % | — | 122.0 | — |
| add for herringbone weave | — | % | — | 125.0 | — |
| add for diagonal bond | — | % | — | 90.0 | — |
| add for coursed ashlar style brick bond | | | | | |
| with two sizes of bricks | — | % | — | 70.0 | — |
| add for curved brick walls | — | % | — | 27.0 | — |

**Add for openings in brick wall.** Use only if sf of opening has been deducted from sf price. Includes angle iron lintel. Replace only.

| | Craft@Hrs | Unit | Material | Labor | Total |
|---|---|---|---|---|---|
| 4" wide wall | 4M@.260 | lf | 6.00 | 13.50 | 19.50 |
| 6" wide wall | 4M@.263 | lf | 10.40 | 13.70 | 24.10 |
| 8" wide wall | 4M@.265 | lf | 10.40 | 13.80 | 24.20 |
| 10" wide wall | 4M@.270 | lf | 12.00 | 14.00 | 26.00 |
| 12" wide wall | 4M@.272 | lf | 12.00 | 14.10 | 26.10 |

| | Craft@Hrs | Unit | Material | Labor | Total |
|---|---|---|---|---|---|

## Add for raked joints.

| | Craft@Hrs | Unit | Material | Labor | Total |
|---|---|---|---|---|---|
| raked joints | 4M@.006 | sf | — | .31 | .31 |

*flat (jack arch)*      *elliptical*      *semi-circular*

## Brick arch. Per lf of opening. Replace only.

| | Craft@Hrs | Unit | Material | Labor | Total |
|---|---|---|---|---|---|
| flat (jack arch) | 4M@1.49 | lf | 18.90 | 77.50 | 96.40 |
| elliptical | 4M@1.85 | lf | 22.40 | 96.20 | 118.60 |
| semi-circular | 4M@1.96 | lf | 22.40 | 102.00 | 124.40 |
| add to brace from below for repairs | 4M@.556 | lf | 17.00 | 28.90 | 45.90 |
| minimum | 4M@10.0 | ea | 114.00 | 520.00 | 634.00 |

**Concrete block walls.** Unless otherwise noted all concrete block walls are made from 8" x 16" face block with 3/8" wide mortar joints. Cells are 36" on center and at each corner and include one length of #4 rebar in field cells and 2 lengths in corner cells for an average of 1.4 in each grouted cell. A horizontal bond beam is also calculated for every 8' of wall height and includes two lengths of #4 rebar. Ladder type horizontal wire reinforcing appears in every other course. Also includes 4% waste for block and 25% waste for mortar.

## Concrete block wall.

| | Craft@Hrs | Unit | Material | Labor | Total |
|---|---|---|---|---|---|
| replace, 4" wide | 4M@.089 | sf | 2.71 | 4.63 | 7.34 |
| replace, 6" wide | 4M@.092 | sf | 3.17 | 4.78 | 7.95 |
| replace, 8" wide | 4M@.097 | sf | 3.99 | 5.04 | 9.03 |
| replace, 10" wide | 4M@.103 | sf | 4.92 | 5.36 | 10.28 |
| replace, 12" wide | 4M@.122 | sf | 6.26 | 6.34 | 12.60 |
| remove, 4" | 1D@.087 | sf | — | 3.38 | 3.38 |
| remove, 6" | 1D@.104 | sf | — | 4.05 | 4.05 |
| remove, 8" | 1D@.132 | sf | — | 5.13 | 5.13 |
| remove, 10" | 1D@.149 | sf | — | 5.80 | 5.80 |
| remove, 12" | 1D@.177 | sf | — | 6.89 | 6.89 |

## Lightweight concrete block wall.

| | Craft@Hrs | Unit | Material | Labor | Total |
|---|---|---|---|---|---|
| replace, 4" wide | 4M@.083 | sf | 2.89 | 4.32 | 7.21 |
| replace, 6" wide | 4M@.086 | sf | 3.35 | 4.47 | 7.82 |
| replace, 8" wide | 4M@.091 | sf | 4.20 | 4.73 | 8.93 |
| replace, 10" wide | 4M@.097 | sf | 5.14 | 5.04 | 10.18 |
| replace, 12" wide | 4M@.114 | sf | 6.64 | 5.93 | 12.57 |
| remove, 4" | 1D@.087 | sf | — | 3.38 | 3.38 |
| remove, 6" | 1D@.104 | sf | — | 4.05 | 4.05 |
| remove, 8" | 1D@.132 | sf | — | 5.13 | 5.13 |
| remove, 10" | 1D@.149 | sf | — | 5.80 | 5.80 |
| remove, 12" | 1D@.177 | sf | — | 6.89 | 6.89 |

| | Craft@Hrs | Unit | Material | Labor | Total |
|---|---|---|---|---|---|

### Slump block wall.  4" x 16" face.

| | Craft@Hrs | Unit | Material | Labor | Total |
|---|---|---|---|---|---|
| replace, 4" wide | 4M@.089 | sf | 4.56 | 4.63 | 9.19 |
| replace, 6" wide | 4M@.092 | sf | 5.58 | 4.78 | 10.36 |
| replace, 8" wide | 4M@.097 | sf | 6.91 | 5.04 | 11.95 |
| replace, 10" wide | 4M@.103 | sf | 8.21 | 5.36 | 13.57 |
| replace, 12" wide | 4M@.122 | sf | 10.30 | 6.34 | 16.64 |
| remove, 4" | 1D@.087 | sf | — | 3.38 | 3.38 |
| remove, 6" | 1D@.104 | sf | — | 4.05 | 4.05 |
| remove, 8" | 1D@.132 | sf | — | 5.13 | 5.13 |
| remove, 10" | 1D@.149 | sf | — | 5.80 | 5.80 |
| remove, 12" | 1D@.177 | sf | — | 6.89 | 6.89 |

### Fluted block wall (fluted one side).

| | Craft@Hrs | Unit | Material | Labor | Total |
|---|---|---|---|---|---|
| replace, 4" wide | 4M@.089 | sf | 3.91 | 4.63 | 8.54 |
| replace, 6" wide | 4M@.092 | sf | 4.47 | 4.78 | 9.25 |
| replace, 8" wide | 4M@.097 | sf | 5.66 | 5.04 | 10.70 |
| replace, 10" wide | 4M@.103 | sf | 6.97 | 5.36 | 12.33 |
| replace, 12" wide | 4M@.122 | sf | 9.07 | 6.34 | 15.41 |
| remove, 4" | 1D@.087 | sf | — | 3.38 | 3.38 |
| remove, 6" | 1D@.104 | sf | — | 4.05 | 4.05 |
| remove, 8" | 1D@.132 | sf | — | 5.13 | 5.13 |
| remove, 10" | 1D@.149 | sf | — | 5.80 | 5.80 |
| remove, 12" | 1D@.177 | sf | — | 6.89 | 6.89 |

### Fluted block wall (fluted two sides).

| | Craft@Hrs | Unit | Material | Labor | Total |
|---|---|---|---|---|---|
| replace, 4" wide | 4M@.089 | sf | 4.43 | 4.63 | 9.06 |
| replace, 6" wide | 4M@.092 | sf | 5.09 | 4.78 | 9.87 |
| replace, 8" wide | 4M@.097 | sf | 6.40 | 5.04 | 11.44 |
| replace, 10" wide | 4M@.103 | sf | 7.90 | 5.36 | 13.26 |
| replace, 12" wide | 4M@.122 | sf | 10.30 | 6.34 | 16.64 |
| remove, 4" | 1D@.087 | sf | — | 3.38 | 3.38 |
| remove, 6" | 1D@.104 | sf | — | 4.05 | 4.05 |
| remove, 8" | 1D@.132 | sf | — | 5.13 | 5.13 |
| remove, 10" | 1D@.149 | sf | — | 5.80 | 5.80 |
| remove, 12" | 1D@.177 | sf | — | 6.89 | 6.89 |

### Glazed block wall (glazed one side).

| | Craft@Hrs | Unit | Material | Labor | Total |
|---|---|---|---|---|---|
| replace, 4" wide | 4M@.089 | sf | 15.40 | 4.63 | 20.03 |
| replace, 6" wide | 4M@.092 | sf | 15.90 | 4.78 | 20.68 |
| replace, 8" wide | 4M@.097 | sf | 16.80 | 5.04 | 21.84 |
| replace, 10" wide | 4M@.103 | sf | 17.80 | 5.36 | 23.16 |
| replace, 12" wide | 4M@.122 | sf | 18.50 | 6.34 | 24.84 |
| remove, 4" | 1D@.087 | sf | — | 3.38 | 3.38 |
| remove, 6" | 1D@.104 | sf | — | 4.05 | 4.05 |
| remove, 8" | 1D@.132 | sf | — | 5.13 | 5.13 |
| remove, 10" | 1D@.149 | sf | — | 5.80 | 5.80 |
| remove, 12" | 1D@.177 | sf | — | 6.89 | 6.89 |

| | Craft@Hrs | Unit | Material | Labor | Total |
|---|---|---|---|---|---|
| **Glazed block wall (glazed two sides).** | | | | | |
| replace, 4" wide | 4M@.089 | sf | 22.40 | 4.63 | 27.03 |
| replace, 6" wide | 4M@.092 | sf | 23.90 | 4.78 | 28.68 |
| replace, 8" wide | 4M@.097 | sf | 25.10 | 5.04 | 30.14 |
| replace, 10" wide | 4M@.103 | sf | 26.00 | 5.36 | 31.36 |
| replace, 12" wide | 4M@.122 | sf | 26.80 | 6.34 | 33.14 |
| remove, 4" | 1D@.087 | sf | — | 3.38 | 3.38 |
| remove, 6" | 1D@.104 | sf | — | 4.05 | 4.05 |
| remove, 8" | 1D@.132 | sf | — | 5.13 | 5.13 |
| remove, 10" | 1D@.149 | sf | — | 5.80 | 5.80 |
| remove, 12" | 1D@.177 | sf | — | 6.89 | 6.89 |
| **Split-face block wall.** | | | | | |
| replace, 4" wide | 4M@.089 | sf | 4.21 | 4.63 | 8.84 |
| replace, 6" wide | 4M@.092 | sf | 5.02 | 4.78 | 9.80 |
| replace, 8" wide | 4M@.097 | sf | 6.62 | 5.04 | 11.66 |
| replace, 10" wide | 4M@.103 | sf | 7.40 | 5.36 | 12.76 |
| replace, 12" wide | 4M@.122 | sf | 9.58 | 6.34 | 15.92 |
| remove, 4" | 1D@.087 | sf | — | 3.38 | 3.38 |
| remove, 6" | 1D@.104 | sf | — | 4.05 | 4.05 |
| remove, 8" | 1D@.132 | sf | — | 5.13 | 5.13 |
| remove, 10" | 1D@.149 | sf | — | 5.80 | 5.80 |
| remove, 12" | 1D@.177 | sf | — | 6.89 | 6.89 |
| **Split-rib block wall.** | | | | | |
| replace, 4" wide | 4M@.089 | sf | 3.98 | 4.63 | 8.61 |
| replace, 6" wide | 4M@.092 | sf | 4.35 | 4.78 | 9.13 |
| replace, 8" wide | 4M@.097 | sf | 6.55 | 5.04 | 11.59 |
| replace, 10" wide | 4M@.103 | sf | 7.48 | 5.36 | 12.84 |
| replace, 12" wide | 4M@.122 | sf | 8.47 | 6.34 | 14.81 |
| remove, 4" | 1D@.087 | sf | — | 3.38 | 3.38 |
| remove, 6" | 1D@.104 | sf | — | 4.05 | 4.05 |
| remove, 8" | 1D@.132 | sf | — | 5.13 | 5.13 |
| remove, 10" | 1D@.149 | sf | — | 5.80 | 5.80 |
| remove, 12" | 1D@.177 | sf | — | 6.89 | 6.89 |

**Screen block.** 12" x 12" face.

| 4" wide screen block | | | | | |
|---|---|---|---|---|---|
| replace, pattern two sides | 4M@.089 | sf | 7.76 | 4.63 | 12.39 |
| replace, pattern four sides | 4M@.089 | sf | 14.30 | 4.63 | 18.93 |
| remove | 1D@.087 | sf | — | 3.38 | 3.38 |

| | Craft@Hrs | Unit | Material | Labor | Total |
|---|---|---|---|---|---|
| **Other block colors.** | | | | | |
| add for light ochre colored concrete block | — | % | 11.0 | — | — |
| add darker ochre colored concrete block | — | % | 17.0 | — | — |
| add for dark or bright colored concrete block | — | % | 28.0 | — | — |
| **Interlocking block.** | | | | | |
| add for interlocking concrete block | — | % | 15.0 | — | — |
| **Block polystyrene insulation inserts.** Additional cost to purchase block with polystyrene inserts already installed. Replace only. | | | | | |
| 6" block | — | sf | 1.22 | — | 1.22 |
| 8" block | — | sf | 1.31 | — | 1.31 |
| 10" block | — | sf | 1.48 | — | 1.48 |
| 12" block | — | sf | 1.58 | — | 1.58 |
| **Block silicone treated perlite or vemiculite loose insulation.** Includes 3% waste. Replace only. | | | | | |
| 6" block | 4M@.004 | sf | .48 | .21 | .69 |
| 8" block | 4M@.005 | sf | .71 | .26 | .97 |
| 10" block | 4M@.005 | sf | .87 | .26 | 1.13 |
| 12" block | 4M@.005 | sf | 1.26 | .26 | 1.52 |
| **Add for pilaster in block wall.** 16" x 16" pilaster, single piece. For double piece 16" x 20" pilaster add **15%**. Replace only. | | | | | |
| per vertical lf | 4M@.294 | lf | 17.50 | 15.30 | 32.80 |

*block pilaster*

| | Craft@Hrs | Unit | Material | Labor | Total |
|---|---|---|---|---|---|
| **Other block wall additions and deductions.** Replace only. | | | | | |
| deduct for block walls used as backing | 4M@.005 | sf | — | -.26 | -.26 |
| deduct for wall with no horizontal wire reinforcement | 4M@.001 | sf | -.22 | -.05 | -.27 |
| deduct for wall with no vertical reinforcement | 4M@.006 | sf | -.78 | -.31 | -1.09 |
| deduct for wall with vertical reinforcement every 48" | 4M@.005 | sf | -.22 | -.26 | -.48 |
| add for wall with vertical reinforcement every 24" | 4M@.005 | sf | .27 | .26 | .53 |
| deduct for wall with no bond beam reinforcement | 4M@.004 | sf | -.61 | -.21 | -.82 |
| add for wall with bond beam reinforcement every 4' | 4M@.006 | sf | .40 | .31 | .71 |
| add for high strength concrete block, 3,000 psi (add to materials cost only) | — | % | 19.0 | — | — |
| add for high strength concrete block, 5,000 psi (add to materials cost only) | — | % | 21.0 | — | — |

| | Craft@Hrs | Unit | Material | Labor | Total |
|---|---|---|---|---|---|

**Bond beam.** Includes two lengths of #4 rebar. Replace only.

| | Craft@Hrs | Unit | Material | Labor | Total |
|---|---|---|---|---|---|
| 6" wide | 4M@.026 | lf | 1.82 | 1.35 | 3.17 |
| 8" wide | 4M@.029 | lf | 2.13 | 1.51 | 3.64 |
| 10" wide | 4M@.031 | lf | 2.50 | 1.61 | 4.11 |
| 12" wide | 4M@.034 | lf | 2.90 | 1.77 | 4.67 |

**Parging block walls.**

| | Craft@Hrs | Unit | Material | Labor | Total |
|---|---|---|---|---|---|
| Parge block foundation wall | 4P@.019 | sf | .47 | 1.02 | 1.49 |

**Grade beam cap on block wall.** In some states, concrete block walls are capped with a grade beam. This not only adds strength but also levels the wall top. Because the mason does not take care to maintain a level wall, deduct **25%** from the labor cost for block walls capped with a grade beam. Up to 16" tall with four lengths of #4 rebar. Rebar from grouted cells is also bent into the grade beam.

| | Craft@Hrs | Unit | Material | Labor | Total |
|---|---|---|---|---|---|
| replace, 6" wide | 4M@.106 | lf | 10.40 | 5.51 | 15.91 |
| replace, 8" wide | 4M@.110 | lf | 13.50 | 5.72 | 19.22 |
| replace, 10" wide | 4M@.115 | lf | 16.30 | 5.98 | 22.28 |
| replace, 12" wide | 4M@.120 | lf | 19.40 | 6.24 | 25.64 |
| remove | 1D@.363 | lf | — | 14.10 | 14.10 |

**Masonry fence.**

| | Craft@Hrs | Unit | Material | Labor | Total |
|---|---|---|---|---|---|
| Deduct for concrete block or brick wall installed as fence | — | % | -8.0 | — | — |

**Clay backing tile wall.** 12" x 12" face tile with 3/8" wide mortar joints. Includes 4% waste for tile and 25% waste for mortar.

| | Craft@Hrs | Unit | Material | Labor | Total |
|---|---|---|---|---|---|
| replace, 4" thick | 4M@.112 | sf | 6.45 | 5.82 | 12.27 |
| replace, 6" thick | 4M@.127 | sf | 6.46 | 6.60 | 13.06 |
| replace, 8" thick | 4M@.145 | sf | 6.46 | 7.54 | 14.00 |
| remove, 4" | 1D@.087 | sf | — | 3.38 | 3.38 |
| remove, 6" | 1D@.104 | sf | — | 4.05 | 4.05 |
| remove, 8" | 1D@.132 | sf | — | 5.13 | 5.13 |

**Structural tile wall.** 8" x 16" face tile with 3/8" wide mortar joints. Includes 4% waste for tile and 25% waste for mortar.

| | Craft@Hrs | Unit | Material | Labor | Total |
|---|---|---|---|---|---|
| replace, 4" thick, glazed one side | 4M@.204 | sf | 8.66 | 10.60 | 19.26 |
| replace, 4" thick, glazed two sides | 4M@.214 | sf | 13.10 | 11.10 | 24.20 |
| replace, 6" thick, glazed one side | 4M@.243 | sf | 11.40 | 12.60 | 24.00 |
| replace, 6" thick, glazed two sides | 4M@.253 | sf | 17.60 | 13.20 | 30.80 |
| replace, 8" thick, glazed one side | 4M@.263 | sf | 15.40 | 13.70 | 29.10 |
| remove, 4" | 1D@.087 | sf | — | 3.38 | 3.38 |
| remove, 6" | 1D@.104 | sf | — | 4.05 | 4.05 |
| remove, 8" | 1D@.132 | sf | — | 5.13 | 5.13 |

|  | Craft@Hrs | Unit | Material | Labor | Total |
|---|---|---|---|---|---|

**Gypsum partition tile wall.** 12" x 30" face tile with 3/8" wide mortar joints. Includes 4% waste for tile and 25% waste for mortar.

| | Craft@Hrs | Unit | Material | Labor | Total |
|---|---|---|---|---|---|
| replace, 4" thick | 4M@.057 | sf | 2.42 | 2.96 | 5.38 |
| replace, 6" thick | 4M@.083 | sf | 3.50 | 4.32 | 7.82 |
| remove, 4" | 1D@.087 | sf | — | 3.38 | 3.38 |
| remove, 6" | 1D@.132 | sf | — | 5.13 | 5.13 |

*gypsum partition tile*

**Glass block wall.** White mortar with 3/8" wide joints and ladder type wire reinforcing every other course. Includes 4% waste for glass blocks and 25% waste for mortar.

| | Craft@Hrs | Unit | Material | Labor | Total |
|---|---|---|---|---|---|
| Thinline smooth-face glass block wall | | | | | |
| replace, 4" x 8" | 4M@.333 | sf | 29.00 | 17.30 | 46.30 |
| replace, 6" x 6" | 4M@.310 | sf | 26.60 | 16.10 | 42.70 |
| replace, 6" x 8" | 4M@.267 | sf | 20.10 | 13.90 | 34.00 |
| Smooth-face glass block wall | | | | | |
| replace, 4" x 8" | 4M@.333 | sf | 36.10 | 17.30 | 53.40 |
| replace, 6" x 6" | 4M@.310 | sf | 32.00 | 16.10 | 48.10 |
| replace, 6" x 8" | 4M@.267 | sf | 29.00 | 13.90 | 42.90 |
| replace, 8" x 8" | 4M@.208 | sf | 22.60 | 10.80 | 33.40 |
| replace, 12" x 12" | 4M@.175 | sf | 26.30 | 9.10 | 35.40 |
| remove | 1D@.084 | sf | — | 3.27 | 3.27 |
| Add for solar UV reflective glass block | — | % | 80.0 | — | — |
| Add for patterned face on glass block | — | % | 4.0 | — | — |
| Add for tinted glass block | — | % | 12.0 | — | — |
| Deduct for natural gray mortar in glass block wall | — | % | -2.0 | — | — |
| Deduct for colored mortar in glass block wall | — | % | -1.0 | — | — |

**Pavers.** Pavers on sand base have sand embedded in joints with vibrating compactor. Mortar base pavers have grouted joints. Includes 4% waste for pavers and 25% waste for mortar when used.

| | Craft@Hrs | Unit | Material | Labor | Total |
|---|---|---|---|---|---|
| Natural concrete pavers | | | | | |
| replace, sand base | 4M@.147 | sf | 5.39 | 7.64 | 13.03 |
| replace, mortar base | 4M@.180 | sf | 5.39 | 9.36 | 14.75 |
| Adobe pavers | | | | | |
| replace, sand base | 4M@.147 | sf | 2.26 | 7.64 | 9.90 |
| replace, mortar base | 4M@.180 | sf | 2.26 | 9.36 | 11.62 |
| Brick, standard grade paving | | | | | |
| replace, sand base | 4M@.147 | sf | 2.97 | 7.64 | 10.61 |
| replace, mortar base | 4M@.180 | sf | 3.06 | 9.36 | 12.42 |
| Brick, high grade paving | | | | | |
| replace, sand base | 4M@.147 | sf | 3.94 | 7.64 | 11.58 |
| replace, mortar base | 4M@.180 | sf | 3.94 | 9.36 | 13.30 |
| Brick, deluxe grade paving | | | | | |
| replace, sand base | 4M@.147 | sf | 4.77 | 7.64 | 12.41 |
| replace, mortar base | 4M@.180 | sf | 4.88 | 9.36 | 14.24 |
| remove, sand base | 1D@.084 | sf | — | 3.27 | 3.27 |
| remove, mortar base | 1D@.120 | sf | — | 4.67 | 4.67 |
| Paving made from full-size bricks | | | | | |
| replace, laid face up | 4M@.185 | sf | 5.24 | 9.62 | 14.86 |
| replace, laid edge up | 4M@.208 | sf | 8.06 | 10.80 | 18.86 |
| remove | 1D@.090 | sf | — | 3.50 | 3.50 |

*basketweave*

| | Craft@Hrs | Unit | Material | Labor | Total |
|---|---|---|---|---|---|

**Additional paver costs.**

| | Craft@Hrs | Unit | Material | Labor | Total |
|---|---|---|---|---|---|
| add for curved edges | 4M@.078 | lf | 1.80 | 4.06 | 5.86 |
| add for steps installed over concrete | 4M@.270 | lf | .86 | 14.00 | 14.86 |
| add for steps installed over sand base | 4M@.294 | lf | .80 | 15.30 | 16.10 |
| add for separate pattern at edges | 4M@.076 | lf | 1.75 | 3.95 | 5.70 |
| add for non-square with interlocking patterns | — | % | 17.0 | — | — |
| add for diagonal pattern | — | % | 8.0 | — | — |
| add for basketweave pattern | — | % | 17.0 | — | — |
| add for herringbone pattern | — | % | 14.0 | — | — |

**Stone walls.** Stone walls are made from average to high quality stone. Prices are for stone quarried within 150 miles of the job site. Cast stone is made from a composite of crushed limestone and quartz sand. Granite is a good quality gray stone. Add **28%** for light red (pink), light purple, and light brown. Add **88%** for deep green, red, purple, blue, black, charcoal, and brown. Limestone is standard stock. Add **15%** for select stock and deduct **10%** for rustic stock. Marble is Grade A, average to high priced. Marble varies widely in price with little relationship to color and often even the quality of the stone. The more expensive grades are Italian. Sandstone is standard grade and varies from very hard rock to fairly soft. Use for brownstone work. Slate is standard grade, all colors.

Stone finishes are generally organized in this price book as natural, rough, and smooth. In practice there are many variations of each type of finish. Stone with natural finishes show the cleaving or sawing marks made in the quarry. Rough finishes are applied after the stone is quarried to achieve a specific rough look. Smooth finishes are achieved by polishing the stone. All molded work is finished smooth.

To estimate by the perch, multiply the cf price by 24.75. (A perch is 16-1/2' long, 1' high and 1-1/2' wide or 24-3/4 cubic feet.)

**Rubble stone wall.** Stone walls laid in a variety of rubble patterns, per cubic foot of stone. Includes an average of 1/3 cubic foot of mortar per cubic foot of wall.

| | Craft@Hrs | Unit | Material | Labor | Total |
|---|---|---|---|---|---|
| replace, coral stone | 4M@.518 | cf | 50.50 | 26.90 | 77.40 |
| replace, fieldstone with no mortar | 4M@.481 | cf | 37.00 | 25.00 | 62.00 |
| replace, fieldstone | 4M@.518 | cf | 60.30 | 26.90 | 87.20 |
| replace, lava stone | 4M@.518 | cf | 58.00 | 26.90 | 84.90 |
| replace, river stone | 4M@.518 | cf | 61.50 | 26.90 | 88.40 |
| remove, no mortar | 1D@.259 | cf | — | 10.10 | 10.10 |
| remove, mortar | 1D@.439 | cf | — | 17.10 | 17.10 |

*rubble lay*

**Ashlar stone wall.** Stone walls laid in a variety of ashlar patterns, per cubic foot of stone. Stone is 3-1/2" to 6" wide and various lengths and thickness. Includes mortar.

| | Craft@Hrs | Unit | Material | Labor | Total |
|---|---|---|---|---|---|
| Limestone stone wall | | | | | |
| replace, natural finish | 4M@.472 | cf | 48.70 | 24.50 | 73.20 |
| replace, rough finish | 4M@.472 | cf | 54.20 | 24.50 | 78.70 |
| replace, smooth finish | 4M@.472 | cf | 77.40 | 24.50 | 101.90 |
| Marble stone wall | | | | | |
| replace, natural finish | 4M@.472 | cf | 111.00 | 24.50 | 135.50 |
| replace, rough finish | 4M@.472 | cf | 120.00 | 24.50 | 144.50 |
| replace, smooth finish | 4M@.472 | cf | 150.00 | 24.50 | 174.50 |
| Sandstone wall | | | | | |
| replace, natural finish | 4M@.472 | cf | 46.80 | 24.50 | 71.30 |
| replace, rough finish | 4M@.472 | cf | 52.10 | 24.50 | 76.60 |
| replace, smooth finish | 4M@.472 | cf | 74.60 | 24.50 | 99.10 |
| remove | 1D@.439 | cf | — | 17.10 | 17.10 |

*ashlar lay*

| | Craft@Hrs | Unit | Material | Labor | Total |
|---|---|---|---|---|---|

*semi-circular*  *elliptical arch*  *flat arch*

## Arch in stone wall.  Replace only.

| | Craft@Hrs | Unit | Material | Labor | Total |
|---|---|---|---|---|---|
| flat arch in stone wall | 4M@2.86 | lf | 114.00 | 149.00 | 263.00 |
| elliptical arch in stone wall | 4M@3.58 | lf | 135.00 | 186.00 | 321.00 |
| semi-circular arch in stone wall | 4M@3.70 | lf | 135.00 | 192.00 | 327.00 |
| Add for curved stone wall | — | % | 27.0 | — | — |

## Stone rubble veneer.

| | Craft@Hrs | Unit | Material | Labor | Total |
|---|---|---|---|---|---|
| raplace, coral stone | 4M@.243 | sf | 16.80 | 12.60 | 29.40 |
| replace, field stone | 4M@.243 | sf | 13.70 | 12.60 | 26.30 |
| replace, flagstone | 4M@.243 | sf | 8.59 | 12.60 | 21.19 |
| replace, lava stone | 4M@.243 | sf | 13.10 | 12.60 | 25.70 |
| replace, river stone | 4M@.243 | sf | 14.00 | 12.60 | 26.60 |
| replace, sandstone | 4M@.243 | sf | 19.40 | 12.60 | 32.00 |
| remove | 1D@.106 | sf | — | 4.12 | 4.12 |

## Stone ashlar veneer.

| | Craft@Hrs | Unit | Material | Labor | Total |
|---|---|---|---|---|---|
| Flagstone veneer | | | | | |
| replace | 4M@.236 | sf | 9.98 | 12.30 | 22.28 |
| Limestone veneer | | | | | |
| replace, natural finish | 4M@.236 | sf | 11.00 | 12.30 | 23.30 |
| replace, rough finish | 4M@.236 | sf | 12.10 | 12.30 | 24.40 |
| replace, smooth finish | 4M@.236 | sf | 17.20 | 12.30 | 29.50 |
| Marble veneer | | | | | |
| replace, natural finish | 4M@.236 | sf | 24.50 | 12.30 | 36.80 |
| replace, rough finish | 4M@.236 | sf | 26.70 | 12.30 | 39.00 |
| replace, smooth finish | 4M@.236 | sf | 32.90 | 12.30 | 45.20 |
| Sandstone veneer | | | | | |
| replace, natural finish | 4M@.236 | sf | 10.50 | 12.30 | 22.80 |
| replace, rough finish | 4M@.236 | sf | 11.60 | 12.30 | 23.90 |
| replace, smooth finish | 4M@.236 | sf | 16.40 | 12.30 | 28.70 |
| Remove | 1D@.106 | sf | — | 4.12 | 4.12 |

| | Craft@Hrs | Unit | Material | Labor | Total |
|---|---|---|---|---|---|

*flat arch*          *elliptical arch*          *semi-circular arch*          *rustication*

## Arch in stone veneer. Replace only.

| | Craft@Hrs | Unit | Material | Labor | Total |
|---|---|---|---|---|---|
| flat arch | 4M@1.75 | lf | 25.00 | 91.00 | 116.00 |
| elliptical arch | 4M@2.17 | lf | 29.80 | 113.00 | 142.80 |
| semi-circular arch | 4M@2.30 | lf | 29.80 | 120.00 | 149.80 |
| add to support arch from below | 4M@.556 | lf | 17.00 | 28.90 | 45.90 |
| add for curved stone veneer | — | % | 27.0 | — | — |
| add for rusticated stone | — | % | 55.0 | — | — |

## Keystone. For use in stone or brick arches.

| | Craft@Hrs | Unit | Material | Labor | Total |
|---|---|---|---|---|---|
| replace, concrete | 4M@.606 | ea | 67.40 | 31.50 | 98.90 |
| replace, cast stone | 4M@.606 | ea | 92.20 | 31.50 | 123.70 |
| replace, natural finish | 4M@.606 | ea | 147.00 | 31.50 | 178.50 |
| replace, with straight patterns | 4M@.606 | ea | 189.00 | 31.50 | 220.50 |
| replace, with complex straight patterns (Gothic) | 4M@.606 | ea | 239.00 | 31.50 | 270.50 |
| replace, with light hand carvings | 4M@.606 | ea | 364.00 | 31.50 | 395.50 |
| replace, with medium hand carvings | 4M@.606 | ea | 467.00 | 31.50 | 498.50 |
| replace, with heavy hand carvings | 4M@.606 | ea | 655.00 | 31.50 | 686.50 |
| remove | 1D@.198 | ea | — | 7.70 | 7.70 |
| remove for work, then reinstall | 4M@1.02 | ea | — | 53.00 | 53.00 |

## Quoin. In brick, stone, or stucco walls. Made from alternate courses of headers and stretchers. Price each includes one header and one stretcher (two stones). Cast stone quoins also include both sides. Quoins are plain, beveled, chamfered, rusticated, or rough tooled.

| | Craft@Hrs | Unit | Material | Labor | Total |
|---|---|---|---|---|---|
| replace, cast stone | 4M@.164 | ea | 148.00 | 8.53 | 156.53 |
| replace, limestone | 4M@.164 | ea | 168.00 | 8.53 | 176.53 |
| replace, sandstone | 4M@.164 | ea | 158.00 | 8.53 | 166.53 |
| remove | 1D@.196 | ea | — | 7.62 | 7.62 |
| remove for work, then reinstall (per stone) | 4M@.434 | ea | — | 22.60 | 22.60 |

*stone quoin*

## Cultured stone veneer panels. 3/4" to 1-1/2" thick.

| | Craft@Hrs | Unit | Material | Labor | Total |
|---|---|---|---|---|---|
| replace, smooth finish | 4M@.263 | sf | 7.58 | 13.70 | 21.28 |
| replace, rough finish | 4M@.263 | sf | 10.20 | 13.70 | 23.90 |
| replace, terrazzo style finish | 4M@.263 | sf | 23.10 | 13.70 | 36.80 |
| remove | 1D@.074 | sf | — | 2.88 | 2.88 |

## Ceramic veneer panels.

| | Craft@Hrs | Unit | Material | Labor | Total |
|---|---|---|---|---|---|
| replace, precast | 4M@.263 | sf | 18.50 | 13.70 | 32.20 |
| remove | 1D@.074 | sf | — | 2.88 | 2.88 |

| | Craft@Hrs | Unit | Material | Labor | Total |
|---|---|---|---|---|---|

**Natural stone veneer panels.** Granite, slate, and marble panels are 3/4" to 1-1/2" thick. Limestone and sandstone panels are 2" to 3" thick. See page 248 for more information about quality and finishes.

| | Craft@Hrs | Unit | Material | Labor | Total |
|---|---|---|---|---|---|
| Granite veneer | | | | | |
| replace, natural finish | 4M@.298 | sf | 34.30 | 15.50 | 49.80 |
| replace, rough finish | 4M@.298 | sf | 36.40 | 15.50 | 51.90 |
| replace, smooth finish | 4M@.298 | sf | 42.00 | 15.50 | 57.50 |
| Limestone veneer | | | | | |
| replace, natural finish | 4M@.298 | sf | 15.70 | 15.50 | 31.20 |
| replace, rough finish | 4M@.298 | sf | 23.60 | 15.50 | 39.10 |
| replace, smooth finish | 4M@.298 | sf | 31.10 | 15.50 | 46.60 |
| Marble veneer | | | | | |
| replace, natural finish | 4M@.298 | sf | 39.40 | 15.50 | 54.90 |
| replace, rough finish | 4M@.298 | sf | 51.30 | 15.50 | 66.80 |
| replace, smooth finish | 4M@.298 | sf | 64.40 | 15.50 | 79.90 |
| Sandstone veneer | | | | | |
| replace, natural finish | 4M@.298 | sf | 28.10 | 15.50 | 43.60 |
| replace, rough finish | 4M@.298 | sf | 30.80 | 15.50 | 46.30 |
| replace, smooth finish | 4M@.298 | sf | 34.40 | 15.50 | 49.90 |
| Slate veneer | | | | | |
| replace, natural finish | 4M@.298 | sf | 29.00 | 15.50 | 44.50 |
| replace, rough finish | 4M@.298 | sf | 31.50 | 15.50 | 47.00 |
| replace, smooth finish | 4M@.298 | sf | 35.20 | 15.50 | 50.70 |
| Remove stone veneer panel | 1D@.074 | sf | — | 2.88 | 2.88 |

**Door architrave.** Standard grade: Cast stone is 6" or less wide with simple straight patterns. High grade: Cast stone is 6" or less wide with more complex (Gothic) patterns. Deluxe grade: Same as high grade, but with arched top or flat top and decorative work around corners or center of header. Or, it may have straight patterns with cast stone up to 10" wide. Custom grade: Cast stone 6" or less wide with hand carvings on header. Or, it may be up to 10" wide with complex patterns (Gothic) and an arched top; or, it may have straight patterns with cast stone up to 12" wide. Custom deluxe grade: Cast stone 6" or less wide with heavy hand carvings on header (e.g. lion's face or human face) or lighter hand carvings throughout. Or, it may be up to 12" wide with complex straight patterns (Gothic). With arched top.

| | Craft@Hrs | Unit | Material | Labor | Total |
|---|---|---|---|---|---|
| Cast stone architrave | | | | | |
| replace, standard grade | 4M@.980 | lf | 29.20 | 51.00 | 80.20 |
| replace, high grade | 4M@.980 | lf | 32.00 | 51.00 | 83.00 |
| replace, deluxe grade | 4M@.980 | lf | 43.20 | 51.00 | 94.20 |
| replace, custom grade | 4M@.980 | lf | 53.00 | 51.00 | 104.00 |
| replace, custom deluxe grade | 4M@.980 | lf | 67.80 | 51.00 | 118.80 |
| Limestone architrave | | | | | |
| replace, standard grade | 4M@.980 | lf | 56.90 | 51.00 | 107.90 |
| replace, high grade | 4M@.980 | lf | 103.00 | 51.00 | 154.00 |
| replace, deluxe grade | 4M@.980 | lf | 150.00 | 51.00 | 201.00 |
| replace, custom grade | 4M@.980 | lf | 185.00 | 51.00 | 236.00 |
| replace, custom deluxe grade | 4M@.980 | lf | 228.00 | 51.00 | 279.00 |
| Marble architrave | | | | | |
| replace, standard grade | 4M@.980 | lf | 84.80 | 51.00 | 135.80 |
| replace, high grade | 4M@.980 | lf | 132.00 | 51.00 | 183.00 |
| replace, deluxe grade | 4M@.980 | lf | 179.00 | 51.00 | 230.00 |
| replace, custom grade | 4M@.980 | lf | 214.00 | 51.00 | 265.00 |
| replace, custom deluxe grade | 4M@.980 | lf | 253.00 | 51.00 | 304.00 |

| | Craft@Hrs | Unit | Material | Labor | Total |
|---|---|---|---|---|---|
| **Sandstone architrave** | | | | | |
| replace, standard grade | 4M@.980 | lf | 51.00 | 51.00 | 102.00 |
| replace, high grade | 4M@.980 | lf | 98.20 | 51.00 | 149.20 |
| replace, deluxe grade | 4M@.980 | lf | 144.00 | 51.00 | 195.00 |
| replace, custom grade | 4M@.980 | lf | 180.00 | 51.00 | 231.00 |
| replace, custom deluxe grade | 4M@.980 | lf | 220.00 | 51.00 | 271.00 |
| Remove door architrave | 1D@.131 | lf | — | 5.10 | 5.10 |

**Window architrave.** See Door architrave for more information on grades.

| | Craft@Hrs | Unit | Material | Labor | Total |
|---|---|---|---|---|---|
| **Cast stone architrave** | | | | | |
| replace, standard grade | 4M@1.00 | lf | 28.30 | 52.00 | 80.30 |
| replace, high grade | 4M@1.00 | lf | 31.20 | 52.00 | 83.20 |
| replace, deluxe grade | 4M@1.00 | lf | 42.20 | 52.00 | 94.20 |
| replace, custom grade | 4M@1.00 | lf | 51.50 | 52.00 | 103.50 |
| replace, custom deluxe grade | 4M@1.00 | lf | 65.90 | 52.00 | 117.90 |
| **Limestone architrave** | | | | | |
| replace, standard grade | 4M@1.00 | lf | 55.20 | 52.00 | 107.20 |
| replace, high grade | 4M@1.00 | lf | 101.00 | 52.00 | 153.00 |
| replace, deluxe grade | 4M@1.00 | lf | 146.00 | 52.00 | 198.00 |
| replace, custom grade | 4M@1.00 | lf | 180.00 | 52.00 | 232.00 |
| replace, custom deluxe grade | 4M@1.00 | lf | 219.00 | 52.00 | 271.00 |
| **Marble architrave** | | | | | |
| replace, standard grade | 4M@1.00 | lf | 82.50 | 52.00 | 134.50 |
| replace, high grade | 4M@1.00 | lf | 129.00 | 52.00 | 181.00 |
| replace, deluxe grade | 4M@1.00 | lf | 174.00 | 52.00 | 226.00 |
| replace, custom grade | 4M@1.00 | lf | 206.00 | 52.00 | 258.00 |
| replace, custom deluxe grade | 4M@1.00 | lf | 245.00 | 52.00 | 297.00 |
| **Sandstone architrave** | | | | | |
| replace, standard grade | 4M@1.00 | lf | 52.50 | 52.00 | 104.50 |
| replace, high grade | 4M@1.00 | lf | 98.50 | 52.00 | 150.50 |
| replace, deluxe grade | 4M@1.00 | lf | 143.00 | 52.00 | 195.00 |
| replace, custom grade | 4M@1.00 | lf | 178.00 | 52.00 | 230.00 |
| replace, custom deluxe grade | 4M@1.00 | lf | 216.00 | 52.00 | 268.00 |
| Remove window architrave | 1D@.131 | lf | — | 5.10 | 5.10 |

**Additional stone architrave costs.**

| | Craft@Hrs | Unit | Material | Labor | Total |
|---|---|---|---|---|---|
| add for round or elliptical window | — | % | 65.0 | — | — |
| replace section cut to match | 4M@3.34 | ea | 742.00 | 174.00 | 916.00 |

| | Craft@Hrs | Unit | Material | Labor | Total |
|---|---|---|---|---|---|

**Cut trim or cornice stone.** Per 4" of width. Use for friezes, architraves, cornices, string courses, band courses, and so on. Cut Stone: All horizontal patterns are shallow. Typical depth is 3/4" or less but may be as deep as 1". Complex horizontal patterns are deep Gothic style reliefs that require two passes through the stone planer. Vertical patterns are straight vertical cuts like dentil, meander, or fretwork. Light hand carvings are usually less than 3/4" deep and do not cover the entire face of the stone with detailed work. Medium hand carvings are heavier carvings like vermiculation, Acanthus, and so forth. Heavy hand carvings are heavy and deep carvings including a lion's face, a human face etc.

| | Craft@Hrs | Unit | Material | Labor | Total |
|---|---|---|---|---|---|
| **Cut stone trim** | | | | | |
| replace, all horizontal patterns | 4M@.370 | lf | 18.00 | 19.20 | 37.20 |
| replace, complex horizontal patterns (Gothic) | 4M@.370 | lf | 25.10 | 19.20 | 44.30 |
| replace, with vertical patterns | 4M@.370 | lf | 27.90 | 19.20 | 47.10 |
| replace, with light hand carvings | 4M@.370 | lf | 39.40 | 19.20 | 58.60 |
| replace, with medium hand carvings | 4M@.370 | lf | 48.90 | 19.20 | 68.10 |
| replace, with heavy hand carvings | 4M@.370 | lf | 63.90 | 19.20 | 83.10 |
| **Limestone trim** | | | | | |
| replace, all horizontal patterns | 4M@.370 | lf | 27.40 | 19.20 | 46.60 |
| replace, complex horizontal patterns (Gothic) | 4M@.370 | lf | 52.10 | 19.20 | 71.30 |
| replace, with vertical patterns | 4M@.370 | lf | 99.40 | 19.20 | 118.60 |
| replace, with light hand carvings | 4M@.370 | lf | 146.00 | 19.20 | 165.20 |
| replace, with medium hand carvings | 4M@.370 | lf | 181.00 | 19.20 | 200.20 |
| replace, with heavy hand carvings | 4M@.370 | lf | 221.00 | 19.20 | 240.20 |
| **Marble trim** | | | | | |
| replace, all horizontal patterns | 4M@.370 | lf | 52.30 | 19.20 | 71.50 |
| replace, complex horizontal patterns (Gothic) | 4M@.370 | lf | 77.20 | 19.20 | 96.40 |
| replace, with vertical patterns | 4M@.370 | lf | 124.00 | 19.20 | 143.20 |
| replace, with light hand carvings | 4M@.370 | lf | 170.00 | 19.20 | 189.20 |
| replace, with medium hand carvings | 4M@.370 | lf | 205.00 | 19.20 | 224.20 |
| replace, with heavy hand carvings | 4M@.370 | lf | 245.00 | 19.20 | 264.20 |
| **Sandstone trim**  *horizontal patterns* | | | | | |
| replace, all horizontal patterns | 4M@.370 | lf | 21.90 | 19.20 | 41.10 |
| replace, complex horizontal patterns (Gothic) | 4M@.370 | lf | 46.50 | 19.20 | 65.70 |
| replace, with vertical patterns | 4M@.370 | lf | 93.70 | 19.20 | 112.90 |
| replace, with light hand carvings | 4M@.370 | lf | 140.00 | 19.20 | 159.20 |
| replace, with medium hand carvings | 4M@.370 | lf | 175.00 | 19.20 | 194.20 |
| replace, with heavy hand carvings | 4M@.370 | lf | 215.00 | 19.20 | 234.20 |
| Remove cut trim | 1D@.104 | lf | — | 4.05 | 4.05 |
| Replace section cut to match | 4M@2.94 | ea | 609.00 | 153.00 | 762.00 |

| | Craft@Hrs | Unit | Material | Labor | Total |
|---|---|---|---|---|---|

**Cut stone sill or stool.** Up to 10" wide.

| | Craft@Hrs | Unit | Material | Labor | Total |
|---|---|---|---|---|---|
| replace, 1-1/2" bluestone | 4M@.334 | lf | 18.30 | 17.40 | 35.70 |
| replace, 4" cast stone | 4M@.334 | lf | 12.80 | 17.40 | 30.20 |
| replace, 1-1/2" granite | 4M@.334 | lf | 20.00 | 17.40 | 37.40 |
| replace, 4" granite | 4M@.334 | lf | 36.00 | 17.40 | 53.40 |
| replace, 1-1/2" limestone | 4M@.334 | lf | 18.00 | 17.40 | 35.40 |
| replace, 4" limestone | 4M@.334 | lf | 32.30 | 17.40 | 49.70 |
| replace, 1-1/2" marble | 4M@.334 | lf | 21.30 | 17.40 | 38.70 |
| replace, 1-1/2" sandstone | 4M@.334 | lf | 13.10 | 17.40 | 30.50 |
| replace, 4" sandstone | 4M@.334 | lf | 25.90 | 17.40 | 43.30 |
| replace, 1-1/2" slate | 4M@.334 | lf | 21.40 | 17.40 | 38.80 |
| remove | 1D@.110 | lf | — | 4.28 | 4.28 |

**Terra cotta wall cap.**

| | Craft@Hrs | Unit | Material | Labor | Total |
|---|---|---|---|---|---|
| replace, 10" wide | 4M@.185 | lf | 9.68 | 9.62 | 19.30 |
| replace, 12" wide | 4M@.185 | lf | 15.80 | 9.62 | 25.42 |
| remove | 1D@.063 | lf | — | 2.45 | 2.45 |

**Aluminum wall cap.**

| | Craft@Hrs | Unit | Material | Labor | Total |
|---|---|---|---|---|---|
| replace, all wall widths | 4M@.181 | lf | 18.30 | 9.41 | 27.71 |
| remove | 1D@.019 | lf | — | .74 | .74 |

**Wall coping stones.** From 4" to 6" thick at center tapering or curved taper to edges. Widths over 8" include drip grooves on each side.

| | Craft@Hrs | Unit | Material | Labor | Total |
|---|---|---|---|---|---|
| Concrete wall coping stones | | | | | |
| replace, 10" wide | 4M@.167 | lf | 20.00 | 8.68 | 28.68 |
| replace, 12" wide | 4M@.167 | lf | 20.80 | 8.68 | 29.48 |
| replace, 14" wide | 4M@.167 | lf | 26.60 | 8.68 | 35.28 |
| Granite wall coping stones | | | | | |
| replace, 8" wide | 4M@.185 | lf | 40.10 | 9.62 | 49.72 |
| replace, 10" wide | 4M@.185 | lf | 46.40 | 9.62 | 56.02 |
| replace, 12" wide | 4M@.185 | lf | 52.50 | 9.62 | 62.12 |
| Limestone wall coping stones | | | | | |
| replace, 8" wide | 4M@.185 | lf | 23.90 | 9.62 | 33.52 |
| replace, 10" wide | 4M@.185 | lf | 24.40 | 9.62 | 34.02 |
| replace, 12" wide | 4M@.185 | lf | 28.40 | 9.62 | 38.02 |
| Marble coping stones | | | | | |
| replace, 8" wide | 4M@.185 | lf | 34.00 | 9.62 | 43.62 |
| replace, 10" wide | 4M@.185 | lf | 42.10 | 9.62 | 51.72 |
| replace, 12" wide | 4M@.185 | lf | 52.50 | 9.62 | 62.12 |
| Remove coping stones | 1D@.104 | lf | — | 4.05 | 4.05 |

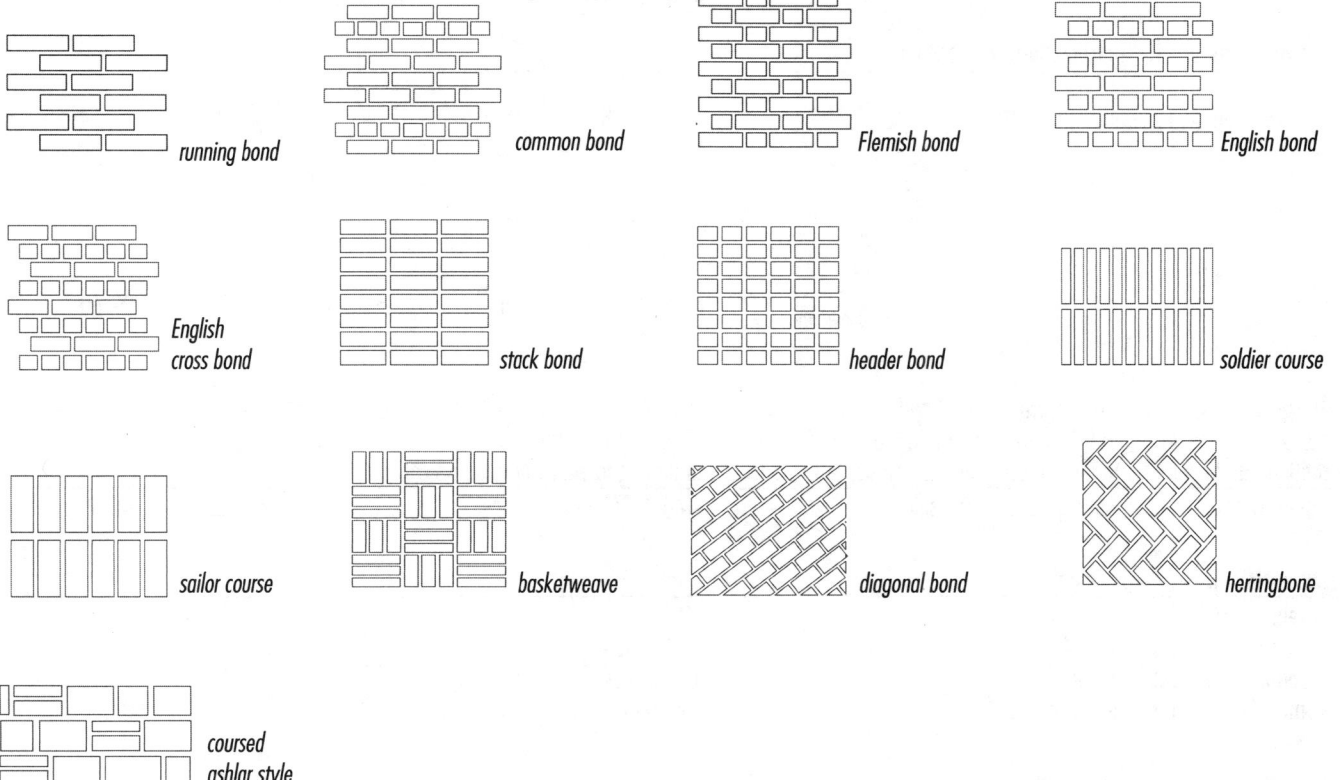

running bond    common bond    Flemish bond    English bond

English cross bond    stack bond    header bond    soldier course

sailor course    basketweave    diagonal bond    herringbone

coursed ashlar style

|  | Craft@Hrs | Unit | Material | Labor | Total |
|---|---|---|---|---|---|
| **Repoint brick wall.** Tuck pointing. To mask and grout deduct **12%**. Replace only. | | | | | |
| running bond | 4M@.108 | sf | .47 | 5.62 | 6.09 |
| common bond (also called American bond) | 4M@.111 | sf | .47 | 5.77 | 6.24 |
| Flemish bond | 4M@.121 | sf | .47 | 6.29 | 6.76 |
| English bond | 4M@.128 | sf | .47 | 6.66 | 7.13 |
| English cross bond (also called Dutch bond) | 4M@.128 | sf | .47 | 6.66 | 7.13 |
| stack bond | 4M@.082 | sf | .47 | 4.26 | 4.73 |
| all header bond | 4M@.093 | sf | .47 | 4.84 | 5.31 |
| soldier course | 4M@.106 | sf | .47 | 5.51 | 5.98 |
| sailor course | 4M@.099 | sf | .47 | 5.15 | 5.62 |
| basketweave | 4M@.164 | sf | .47 | 8.53 | 9.00 |
| herringbone weave | 4M@.167 | sf | .47 | 8.68 | 9.15 |
| diagonal bond | 4M@.144 | sf | .47 | 7.49 | 7.96 |
| coursed ashlar style bond with two sizes of bricks | 4M@.120 | sf | .47 | 6.24 | 6.71 |
| add to repoint brick wall with hard mortar | — | % | 12.0 | — | — |
| add to repoint brick wall with very hard mortar | — | % | 22.0 | — | — |
| add to repoint brick wall with butter joint mortar | — | % | 18.0 | — | — |
| minimum | 4M@5.00 | ea | 22.60 | 260.00 | 282.60 |

| | Craft@Hrs | Unit | Material | Labor | Total |
|---|---|---|---|---|---|
| **Repoint stone wall.** Tuck pointing. Replace only. | | | | | |
| repoint rubble lay wall | 4M@.278 | sf | 2.14 | 14.50 | 16.64 |
| repoint ashlar wall | 4M@.260 | sf | 1.66 | 13.50 | 15.16 |
| minimum | 4M@5.00 | ea | 22.60 | 260.00 | 282.60 |

*ashlar lay*

**Salvage bricks.** Existing bricks are removed and old mortar chipped away. An average of 75% of the bricks are salvaged. To replace the missing bricks, 25% of the salvaged bricks are sawn in half length wise and back filled with mortar to fit. Finish wall includes 50% full bricks and 50% backfilled half bricks. Normally not used for large walls, but on sections of damaged wall where bricks cannot be matched.

| | Craft@Hrs | Unit | Material | Labor | Total |
|---|---|---|---|---|---|
| remove brick veneer, salvage bricks, and relay | 4M@.877 | sf | 2.45 | 45.60 | 48.05 |

**Brick wall repair.** Replace only.

| | Craft@Hrs | Unit | Material | Labor | Total |
|---|---|---|---|---|---|
| replace single brick | 4M@.430 | sf | 2.84 | 22.40 | 25.24 |
| tooth in brick patch up to 4 sf | 4M@.504 | sf | 52.30 | 26.20 | 78.50 |
| tooth in brick patch over 4 sf | 4M@.408 | sf | 13.10 | 21.20 | 34.30 |
| minimum charge to repair brick wall | 4M@11.5 | ea | 86.00 | 598.00 | 684.00 |

**Stone wall repair.** Replace only.

| | Craft@Hrs | Unit | Material | Labor | Total |
|---|---|---|---|---|---|
| replace single stone | 4M@.451 | ea | 5.51 | 23.50 | 29.01 |
| tooth in stone patch up to 4 sf | 4M@.566 | ea | 101.00 | 29.40 | 130.40 |
| tooth in stone patch over 4 sf | 4M@.585 | ea | 25.20 | 30.40 | 55.60 |
| remove segment of rubble wall and relay | 5M@4.00 | cf | 6.08 | 228.00 | 234.08 |
| remove segment of rubble veneer and relay | 5M@1.92 | sf | 2.03 | 109.00 | 111.03 |
| remove segment of ashlar wall and relay | 5M@3.85 | cf | 4.42 | 219.00 | 223.42 |
| remove segment of ashlar veneer and relay | 5M@1.89 | sf | 1.49 | 108.00 | 109.49 |
| minimum charge to repair stone wall | 4M@12.7 | ea | 164.00 | 660.00 | 824.00 |

**Stone carving.** Work performed on site or in a shop within 150 miles of the site. Does not include clay or plaster model. Models for light carvings may run 15% less, and models for heavy carvings like faces may run 20% to 45% more. It is not unusual for models to cost as much as or more than the actual carvings. Replace only.

| | Craft@Hrs | Unit | Material | Labor | Total |
|---|---|---|---|---|---|
| with light hand carvings | 6M@.015 | si | — | 1.44 | 1.44 |
| with medium hand carvings | 6M@.022 | si | — | 2.11 | 2.11 |
| with heavy hand carvings | 6M@.031 | si | — | 2.98 | 2.98 |
| add to match existing work | — | % | — | 120.0 | — |
| clay or plaster model for stone carvings | — | si | 2.02 | — | 2.02 |
| minimum charge for model for stone carvings | — | ea | 208.00 | — | 208.00 |

*vermiculation*

**Carved stone repair.** Replace only.

| | Craft@Hrs | Unit | Material | Labor | Total |
|---|---|---|---|---|---|
| repair carved stone with epoxy | 1M@.024 | si | .31 | 1.43 | 1.74 |
| repair carved stone with stucco | 1M@.022 | si | .03 | 1.31 | 1.34 |
| minimum charge to repair carved stone | 4M@4.58 | ea | 47.40 | 238.00 | 285.40 |

| | Craft@Hrs | Unit | Material | Labor | Total |
|---|---|---|---|---|---|

**Stone repair.**  Replace only.

| | Craft@Hrs | Unit | Material | Labor | Total |
|---|---|---|---|---|---|
| epoxy repair and pin broken stone | 1M@1.33 | ea | 12.30 | 79.00 | 91.30 |
| reconstitute delaminating stone with epoxy & pins | 1M@.013 | si | .34 | .77 | 1.11 |
| reface damaged stone with grout mixed to match | 1M@.149 | si | .03 | 8.85 | 8.88 |
| minimum charge for epoxy repair work | 4M@3.17 | ea | 47.40 | 165.00 | 212.40 |

**Clean masonry.**  Replace only.

| | Craft@Hrs | Unit | Material | Labor | Total |
|---|---|---|---|---|---|
| hand clean brick wall | 3M@.042 | sf | .08 | 1.76 | 1.84 |
| hand clean stone wall | 3M@.045 | sf | .08 | 1.89 | 1.97 |
| pressure spray brick wall | 3M@.011 | sf | .11 | .46 | .57 |
| pressure spray stone wall | 3M@.011 | sf | .11 | .46 | .57 |
| steam clean brick wall | 3M@.015 | sf | — | .63 | .63 |
| steam clean stone wall | 3M@.016 | sf | — | .67 | .67 |
| wet sandblast brick wall | 3M@.046 | sf | .43 | 1.93 | 2.36 |
| wet sandblast stone wall | 3M@.048 | sf | .43 | 2.02 | 2.45 |

**Cut opening in masonry wall.**  Cut masonry wall with concrete saw.  Replace only.

| | Craft@Hrs | Unit | Material | Labor | Total |
|---|---|---|---|---|---|
| Cut opening in brick wall | | | | | |
|   to 6" thick | 5M@.179 | lf | — | 10.20 | 10.20 |
|   7" to 12" thick | 5M@.200 | lf | — | 11.40 | 11.40 |
|   veneer | 5M@.172 | lf | — | 9.80 | 9.80 |
| Cut opening in stone wall | | | | | |
|   to 6" thick | 5M@.200 | lf | — | 11.40 | 11.40 |
|   to 7" to 12" thick | 5M@.226 | lf | — | 12.90 | 12.90 |
|   stone veneer | 5M@.192 | lf | — | 10.90 | 10.90 |

**Shore masonry opening for repairs.**  Replace only.

| | Craft@Hrs | Unit | Material | Labor | Total |
|---|---|---|---|---|---|
| flat opening, per lf of header | 5M@.385 | lf | 16.00 | 21.90 | 37.90 |
| arched opening | 5M@.504 | lf | 17.00 | 28.70 | 45.70 |

**Concrete lintel.**  Replace only.

| | | Craft@Hrs | Unit | Material | Labor | Total |
|---|---|---|---|---|---|---|
| 4" wide wall | | 5M@.078 | lf | 13.00 | 4.45 | 17.45 |
| 6" wide wall | *lintel with plain key* | 5M@.100 | lf | 17.50 | 5.70 | 23.20 |
| 8" wide wall | | 5M@.112 | lf | 18.90 | 6.38 | 25.28 |
| 10" wide wall | *lintel with winged key* | 5M@.135 | lf | 32.30 | 7.70 | 40.00 |
| 12" wide wall | | 5M@.149 | lf | 42.90 | 8.49 | 51.39 |
| add for key cast into lintel | *lintel with recessed key* | — | ea | 66.10 | — | 66.10 |

| | Craft@Hrs | Unit | Material | Labor | Total |
|---|---|---|---|---|---|
| **Angle iron lintel.** Replace only. | | | | | |
| 4" wide wall | 4M@.067 | lf | 5.21 | 3.48 | 8.69 |
| 6" wide wall | 4M@.067 | lf | 10.40 | 3.48 | 13.88 |
| 8" wide wall | 4M@.073 | lf | 11.10 | 3.80 | 14.90 |
| 10" wide wall | 4M@.074 | lf | 12.40 | 3.85 | 16.25 |
| 12" wide wall | 4M@.075 | lf | 18.00 | 3.90 | 21.90 |

## Time & Material Charts (selected items)
## Masonry Materials

| | Craft@Hrs | Unit | Material | Labor | Total |
|---|---|---|---|---|---|
| Rebar | | | | | |
| #3 (3/8" .376 pound per lf), ($4.71 per 20' bar, 20 lf), 4% waste | — | lf | .25 | — | .25 |
| #4 (1/2" .668 pounds per lf), ($6.00 per 20' bar, 20 lf), 4% waste | — | lf | .31 | — | .31 |
| #5 (5/8" 1.043 pounds per lf), ($9.30 per 20' bar, 20 lf), 4% waste | — | lf | .49 | — | .49 |
| #6 (3/4" 1.502 pounds per lf), ($14.20 per 20' bar, 20 lf), 4% waste | — | lf | .74 | — | .74 |
| Mortar and grout supplies | | | | | |
| gypsum cement, ($22.40 per bag, 80 lb), 12% waste | — | lb | .31 | — | .31 |
| masonry cement, ($9.48 per bag, 70 lb), 12% waste | — | lb | .16 | — | .16 |
| white masonry cement, ($28.50 per bag, 70 lb), 12% waste | — | lb | .46 | — | .46 |
| hydrated lime, ($9.76 per bag, 50 lb), 12% waste | — | lb | .22 | — | .22 |
| double hydrated lime, ($13.20 per bag, 50 lb), 12% waste | — | lb | .29 | — | .29 |
| screened and washed sand, delivered, ($32.90 per ton, 1 ton), 0% waste | — | ton | 32.90 | — | 32.90 |
| Reinforcing wire strip | | | | | |
| 4" ladder style, ($.20 lf, 1 lf), 2% waste | — | lf | .20 | — | .20 |
| 12" ladder style, ($.26 lf, 1 lf), 2% waste | — | lf | .27 | — | .27 |
| 4" truss style, ($.25 lf, 1 lf), 2% waste | — | lf | .26 | — | .26 |
| 12" truss style, ($.31 lf, 1 lf), 2% waste | — | lf | .32 | — | .32 |
| add 30% for galvanized | | | | | |

| | Craft@Hrs | Unit | Material | Labor | Total |
|---|---|---|---|---|---|
| Masonry ties | | | | | |
| galvanized 22 gauge corrugated veneer wall tie, ($.25 ea, 1 ea), 2% waste | — | ea | .26 | — | .26 |
| galvanized 16 gauge corrugated veneer wall tie, ($.26 ea, 1 ea), 2% waste | — | ea | .27 | — | .27 |
| rectangular galvanized wall tie, ($.29 ea, 1 ea), 2% waste | — | ea | .30 | — | .30 |
| galvanized "Z" style cavity wall tie, ($.28 ea, 1 ea), 2% waste | — | ea | .29 | — | .29 |
| Grout | | | | | |
| for 6" wide bond beam, ($1.05 lf, 1 lf), 11% waste | — | lf | 1.17 | — | 1.17 |
| for 8" wide bond beam, ($1.33 lf, 1 lf), 11% waste | — | lf | 1.48 | — | 1.48 |
| for 10" wide bond beam, ($1.65 lf, 1 lf), 11% waste | — | lf | 1.83 | — | 1.83 |
| for 12" wide bond beam, ($2.02 lf, 1 lf), 11% waste | — | lf | 2.24 | — | 2.24 |
| for cells in 6" wide concrete block, ($1.28 lf, 1 lf), 11% waste | — | lf | 1.42 | — | 1.42 |
| for cells in 8" wide concrete block, ($1.88 lf, 1 lf), 11% waste | — | lf | 2.09 | — | 2.09 |
| for cells in 10" wide concrete block, ($2.38 lf, 1 lf), 11% waste | — | lf | 2.64 | — | 2.64 |
| for cells in 12" wide concrete block, ($3.03 lf, 1 lf), 11% waste | — | lf | 3.36 | — | 3.36 |
| 3/8" brick mortar | | | | | |
| for 4" wide std non-modular or 3", ($10.80 cf, 25 sf), 25% waste | — | sf | .54 | — | .54 |
| for 4" wide oversize non-modular, ($10.80 cf, 26 sf), 25% waste | — | sf | .53 | — | .53 |
| for 4" wide engineer, ($10.80 cf, 27 sf), 25% waste | — | sf | .50 | — | .50 |
| for 4" wide jumbo closure, ($10.80 cf, 31 sf), 25% waste | — | sf | .44 | — | .44 |
| for 4" wide double, ($10.80 cf, 37 sf), 25% waste | — | sf | .36 | — | .36 |
| for 4" wide Roman, ($10.80 cf, 21 sf), 25% waste | — | sf | .64 | — | .64 |
| for 4" wide Norman, ($10.80 cf, 26 sf), 25% waste | — | sf | .53 | — | .53 |
| for 4" wide Norwegian, ($10.80 cf, 30 sf), 25% waste | — | sf | .45 | — | .45 |
| for 4" wide jumbo utility, ($10.80 cf, 36 sf), 25% waste | — | sf | .38 | — | .38 |
| for 4" wide triple, ($10.80 cf, 44 sf), 25% waste | — | sf | .31 | — | .31 |

| | Craft@Hrs | Unit | Material | Labor | Total |
|---|---|---|---|---|---|
| for 6" wide Norwegian,<br>($10.80 cf, 20 sf), 25% waste | — | sf | .68 | — | .68 |
| for 6" wide Norman,<br>($10.80 cf, 16.8 sf), 25% waste | — | sf | .80 | — | .80 |
| for 6" wide jumbo,<br>($10.80 cf, 24 sf), 25% waste | — | sf | .56 | — | .56 |
| for 8" wide jumbo,<br>($10.80 cf, 18 sf), 25% waste | — | sf | .75 | — | .75 |
| **3/8" concrete block mortar (8" x 16" face)** | | | | | |
| for 4" wide, ($10.80 cf, 40 sf), 25% waste | — | sf | .34 | — | .34 |
| for 6" wide, ($10.80 cf, 30 sf), 25% waste | — | sf | .45 | — | .45 |
| for 8" wide, ($10.80 cf, 25 sf), 25% waste | — | sf | .54 | — | .54 |
| for 10" wide, ($10.80 cf, 20.5 sf), 25% waste | — | sf | .66 | — | .66 |
| for 12" wide, ($10.80 cf, 16.6 sf), 25% waste | — | sf | .81 | — | .81 |
| **3/8" concrete slump block mortar (4" x 16" face)** | | | | | |
| for 4" wide, ($10.80 cf, 34 sf), 25% waste | — | sf | .40 | — | .40 |
| for 6" wide, ($10.80 cf, 24 sf), 25% waste | — | sf | .56 | — | .56 |
| for 8" wide, ($10.80 cf, 21 sf), 25% waste | — | sf | .64 | — | .64 |
| for 10" wide, ($10.80 cf, 16.5 sf), 25% waste | — | sf | .81 | — | .81 |
| for 12" wide, ($10.80 cf, 12.6 sf), 25% waste | — | sf | 1.08 | — | 1.08 |
| **3/8" concrete screen block mortar (12" x 12" face)** | | | | | |
| for 4" wide, ($10.80 cf, 35.6 sf), 25% waste | — | sf | .38 | — | .38 |
| **3/8" backing tile mortar (12" x 12" face)** | | | | | |
| for 4" thick, ($10.80 cf, 35.6 sf), 25% waste | — | sf | .38 | — | .38 |
| for 6" thick, ($10.80 cf, 26.5 sf), 25% waste | — | sf | .51 | — | .51 |
| for 8" thick, ($10.80 cf, 22.5 sf), 25% waste | — | sf | .60 | — | .60 |
| **3/8" structural tile mortar (8" x 16" face)** | | | | | |
| for 4" thick, ($10.80 cf, 40 sf), 25% waste | — | sf | .34 | — | .34 |
| for 6" thick, ($10.80 cf, 30 sf), 25% waste | — | sf | .45 | — | .45 |
| for 8" thick, ($10.80 cf, 25 sf), 25% waste | — | sf | .54 | — | .54 |
| **3/8" gypsum partition tile mortar (12" x 30" face)** | | | | | |
| for 4" thick, ($10.80 cf, 78 sf), 25% waste | — | sf | .18 | — | .18 |
| for 6" thick, ($10.80 cf, 66 sf), 25% waste | — | sf | .20 | — | .20 |
| **3/8" white mortar for glass blocks** | | | | | |
| for block with 4" x 8" face,<br>($13.70 cf, 26 sf), 25% waste | — | sf | .66 | — | .66 |
| for block with 6" x 6" face,<br>($13.70 cf, 29 sf), 25% waste | — | sf | .59 | — | .59 |
| for block with 6" x 8" face,<br>($13.70 cf, 36 sf), 25% waste | — | sf | .48 | — | .48 |
| for block with 8" x 8" face,<br>($13.70 cf, 44 sf), 25% waste | — | sf | .39 | — | .39 |
| for block with 12" x 12" face,<br>($13.70 cf, 35.6 sf), 25% waste | — | sf | .48 | — | .48 |
| deduct for natural gray mortar in glass block wall | — | % | -22.0 | — | — |
| deduct for colored mortar in glass block wall | — | % | -8.0 | — | — |

| | Craft@Hrs | Unit | Material | Labor | Total |
|---|---|---|---|---|---|
| Mortar for stone walls | | | | | |
| mortar for rubble stone wall, ($10.80 cf, 4.41 sf), 32% waste | — | cf | 3.23 | — | 3.23 |
| mortar for ashlar stone wall, ($10.80 cf, 5.5 sf), 25% waste | — | cf | 2.45 | — | 2.45 |
| mortar for rubble stone veneer, ($10.80 cf, 13.2 sf), 32% waste | — | sf | 1.08 | — | 1.08 |
| mortar for ashlar stone veneer, ($10.80 cf, 16.5 sf), 25% waste | — | sf | .81 | — | .81 |
| Brick | | | | | |
| deduct for common brick | — | % | -16.0 | — | — |
| add $706 per thousand for glazed brick | | | | | |
| 4" wide standard non-modular, ($928.00 per thousand, 1,000 ea), 4% waste | — | ea | .97 | — | .97 |
| 4" wide oversize non-modular, ($924.00 per thousand, 1,000 ea), 4% waste | — | ea | .96 | — | .96 |
| 4" wide three-inch non-modular, ($915.00 per thousand, 1,000 ea), 4% waste | — | ea | .96 | — | .96 |
| 4" wide standard, ($739.00 per thousand, 1,000 ea), 4% waste | — | ea | .77 | — | .77 |
| 4" wide used, ($1,600.00 per thousand, 1,000 ea), 4% waste | — | ea | 1.66 | — | 1.66 |
| 4" wide engineer, ($909.00 per thousand, 1,000 ea), 4% waste | — | ea | .95 | — | .95 |
| 4" wide jumbo closure, ($1,120.00 per thousand, 1,000 ea), 4% waste | — | ea | 1.16 | — | 1.16 |
| 4" wide double, ($1,190.00 per thousand, 1,000 ea), 4% waste | — | ea | 1.24 | — | 1.24 |
| 4" wide Roman, ($1,290.00 per thousand, 1,000 ea), 4% waste | — | ea | 1.34 | — | 1.34 |
| 4" wide Norman, ($1,240.00 per thousand, 1,000 ea), 4% waste | — | ea | 1.29 | — | 1.29 |
| 4" wide Norwegian, ($1,120.00 per thousand, 1,000 ea), 4% waste | — | ea | 1.16 | — | 1.16 |
| 4" wide jumbo utility, ($1,830.00 per thousand, 1,000 ea), 4% waste | — | ea | 1.90 | — | 1.90 |
| 4" wide triple, ($1,940.00 per thousand, 1,000 ea), 4% waste | — | ea | 2.02 | — | 2.02 |
| 6" wide Norwegian, ($1,780.00 per thousand, 1,000 ea), 4% waste | — | ea | 1.85 | — | 1.85 |
| 6" wide Norman, ($2,140.00 per thousand, 1,000 ea), 4% waste | — | ea | 1.72 | — | 1.72 |
| 6" wide jumbo, ($2,070.00 per thousand, 1,000 ea), 4% waste | — | ea | 2.23 | — | 2.23 |
| 8" wide jumbo, ($2,820.00 per thousand, 1,000 ea), 4% waste | — | ea | 2.93 | — | 2.93 |

|  | Craft@Hrs | Unit | Material | Labor | Total |
|---|---|---|---|---|---|
| Concrete block | | | | | |
| 4" wide, | | | | | |
| ($1,280.00 per thousand, 1,000 ea), 4% waste | — | ea | 1.33 | — | 1.33 |
| 6" wide, | | | | | |
| ($1,440.00 per thousand, 1,000 ea), 4% waste | — | ea | 1.50 | — | 1.50 |
| 8" wide, | | | | | |
| ($1,800.00 per thousand, 1,000 ea), 4% waste | — | ea | 1.87 | — | 1.87 |
| 10" wide, | | | | | |
| ($2,260.00 per thousand, 1,000 ea), 4% waste | — | ea | 2.35 | — | 2.35 |
| 12" wide, | | | | | |
| ($3,050.00 per thousand, 1,000 ea), 4% waste | — | ea | 3.17 | — | 3.17 |
| Lightweight concrete block | | | | | |
| 4" wide, | | | | | |
| ($1,460.00 per thousand, 1,000 ea), 4% waste | — | ea | 1.52 | — | 1.52 |
| 6" wide, | | | | | |
| ($1,600.00 per thousand, 1,000 ea), 4% waste | — | ea | 1.66 | — | 1.66 |
| 8" wide, | | | | | |
| ($2,020.00 per thousand, 1,000 ea), 4% waste | — | ea | 2.10 | — | 2.10 |
| 10" wide, | | | | | |
| ($2,500.00 per thousand, 1,000 ea), 4% waste | — | ea | 2.60 | — | 2.60 |
| 12" wide, | | | | | |
| ($3,420.00 per thousand, 1,000 ea), 4% waste | — | ea | 3.56 | — | 3.56 |
| Slump block | | | | | |
| 4" wide, | | | | | |
| ($1,370.00 per thousand, 1,000 ea), 4% waste | — | ea | 1.42 | — | 1.42 |
| 6" wide, | | | | | |
| ($1,630.00 per thousand, 1,000 ea), 4% waste | — | ea | 1.70 | — | 1.70 |
| 8" wide, | | | | | |
| ($2,040.00 per thousand, 1,000 ea), 4% waste | — | ea | 2.12 | — | 2.12 |
| 10" wide, | | | | | |
| ($2,390.00 per thousand, 1,000 ea), 4% waste | — | ea | 2.49 | — | 2.49 |
| 12" wide, | | | | | |
| ($3,080.00 per thousand, 1,000 ea), 4% waste | — | ea | 3.20 | — | 3.20 |
| Fluted block (fluted one side) | | | | | |
| 4" wide, | | | | | |
| ($2,340.00 per thousand, 1,000 ea), 4% waste | — | ea | 2.43 | — | 2.43 |
| 6" wide, | | | | | |
| ($2,620.00 per thousand, 1,000 ea), 4% waste | — | ea | 2.72 | — | 2.72 |
| 8" wide, | | | | | |
| ($3,290.00 per thousand, 1,000 ea), 4% waste | — | ea | 3.42 | — | 3.42 |
| 10" wide, | | | | | |
| ($4,120.00 per thousand, 1,000 ea), 4% waste | — | ea | 4.28 | — | 4.28 |
| 12" wide, | | | | | |
| ($5,530.00 per thousand, 1,000 ea), 4% waste | — | ea | 5.78 | — | 5.78 |

| | Craft@Hrs | Unit | Material | Labor | Total |
|---|---|---|---|---|---|
| Fluted block (fluted two sides) | | | | | |
| 4" wide, | | | | | |
| ($2,810.00 per thousand, 1,000 ea), 4% waste | — | ea | 2.92 | — | 2.92 |
| 6" wide, | | | | | |
| ($3,150.00 per thousand, 1,000 ea), 4% waste | — | ea | 3.28 | — | 3.28 |
| 8" wide, | | | | | |
| ($3,970.00 per thousand, 1,000 ea), 4% waste | — | ea | 4.13 | — | 4.13 |
| 10" wide, | | | | | |
| ($4,960.00 per thousand, 1,000 ea), 4% waste | — | ea | 5.16 | — | 5.16 |
| 12" wide, | | | | | |
| ($6,720.00 per thousand, 1,000 ea), 4% waste | — | ea | 6.99 | — | 6.99 |
| Glazed block (glazed one side) | | | | | |
| 4" wide, | | | | | |
| ($12,800.00 per thousand, 1,000 ea), 4% waste | — | ea | 13.30 | — | 13.30 |
| 6" wide, | | | | | |
| ($13,000.00 per thousand, 1,000 ea), 4% waste | — | ea | 13.50 | — | 13.50 |
| 8" wide, | | | | | |
| ($13,500.00 per thousand, 1,000 ea), 4% waste | — | ea | 14.00 | — | 14.00 |
| 10" wide, | | | | | |
| ($14,000.00 per thousand, 1,000 ea), 4% waste | — | ea | 14.60 | — | 14.60 |
| 12" wide, | | | | | |
| ($14,200.00 per thousand, 1,000 ea), 4% waste | — | ea | 14.80 | — | 14.80 |
| Glazed block (glazed two sides) | | | | | |
| 4" wide, | | | | | |
| ($19,000.00 per thousand, 1,000 ea), 4% waste | — | ea | 19.80 | — | 19.80 |
| 6" wide, | | | | | |
| ($20,200.00 per thousand, 1,000 ea), 4% waste | — | ea | 21.00 | — | 21.00 |
| 8" wide, | | | | | |
| ($20,800.00 per thousand, 1,000 ea), 4% waste | — | ea | 21.60 | — | 21.60 |
| 10" wide, | | | | | |
| ($21,400.00 per thousand, 1,000 ea), 4% waste | — | ea | 22.30 | — | 22.30 |
| 12" wide, | | | | | |
| ($21,800.00 per thousand, 1,000 ea), 4% waste | — | ea | 22.70 | — | 22.70 |
| Split-face block | | | | | |
| 4" wide, | | | | | |
| ($2,650.00 per thousand, 1,000 ea), 4% waste | — | ea | 2.76 | — | 2.76 |
| 6" wide, | | | | | |
| ($3,130.00 per thousand, 1,000 ea), 4% waste | — | ea | 3.26 | — | 3.26 |
| 8" wide, | | | | | |
| ($4,220.00 per thousand, 1,000 ea), 4% waste | — | ea | 4.39 | — | 4.39 |
| 10" wide, | | | | | |
| ($4,4500.00 per thousand, 1,000 ea), 4% waste | — | ea | 4.63 | — | 4.63 |
| 12" wide, | | | | | |
| ($6,010.00 per thousand, 1,000 ea), 4% waste | — | ea | 6.25 | — | 6.25 |

| | Craft@Hrs | Unit | Material | Labor | Total |
|---|---|---|---|---|---|
| Split-rib block | | | | | |
| 4" wide, | | | | | |
| ($2,400.00 per thousand, 1,000 ea), 4% waste | — | ea | 2.50 | — | 2.50 |
| 6" wide, | | | | | |
| ($2,520.00 per thousand, 1,000 ea), 4% waste | — | ea | 2.62 | — | 2.62 |
| 8" wide, | | | | | |
| ($4,100.00 per thousand, 1,000 ea), 4% waste | — | ea | 4.26 | — | 4.26 |
| 10" wide, | | | | | |
| ($4,560.00 per thousand, 1,000 ea), 4% waste | — | ea | 4.74 | — | 4.74 |
| 12" wide, | | | | | |
| ($5,060.00 per thousand, 1,000 ea), 4% waste | — | ea | 5.26 | — | 5.26 |
| Screen block | | | | | |
| 4" wide, pattern two sides, | | | | | |
| ($6,970.00 per thousand, 1,000 ea), 4% waste | — | ea | 7.25 | — | 7.25 |
| 4" wide, pattern four sides, | | | | | |
| ($13,200.00 per thousand, 1,000 ea), 4% waste | — | ea | 13.70 | — | 13.70 |
| Silicone treated perlite or vermiculite loose fill | | | | | |
| in 6" wide block, ($9.76 4 cf bag, 21 sf), 3% waste | — | sf | .47 | — | .47 |
| in 8" wide block, ($9.76 4 cf bag, 14.5 sf), 3% waste | — | sf | .69 | — | .69 |
| in 10" wide block, ($9.76 4 cf bag, 11.5 sf), 3% waste | — | sf | .88 | — | .88 |
| in 12" wide block, ($9.76 4 cf bag, 8 sf), 3% waste | — | sf | 1.26 | — | 1.26 |
| Glass block | | | | | |
| 4" x 8" thinline smooth-face, ($27.00 sf, 1 sf), | | | | | |
| 4% waste | — | sf | 28.10 | — | 28.10 |
| 6" x 6" thinline smooth-face, ($25.20 sf, 1 sf), | | | | | |
| 4% waste | — | sf | 26.20 | — | 26.20 |
| 4" x 8" smooth-face, ($34.10 sf, 1 sf), 4% waste | — | sf | 35.50 | — | 35.50 |
| 6" x 6" smooth-face, ($30.40 sf, 1 sf), 4% waste | — | sf | 31.60 | — | 31.60 |
| 8" x 8" smooth-face, ($21.30 sf, 1 sf), 4% waste | — | sf | 22.20 | — | 22.20 |
| add for solar UV reflective | — | % | 83.0 | — | — |
| add for patterned face | — | % | 11.0 | — | — |
| add for tinted | — | % | 55.0 | — | — |
| Rubble stone | | | | | |
| coral stone rubble, ($44.80 cf, 1 cf), 4% waste | — | cf | 46.60 | — | 46.60 |
| fieldstone rubble, ($35.70 cf, 1 cf), 4% waste | — | cf | 37.10 | — | 37.10 |
| flagstone rubble, ($20.40 cf, 1 cf), 4% waste | — | cf | 21.20 | — | 21.20 |
| river stone rubble, ($36.50 cf, 1 cf), 4% waste | — | cf | 38.00 | — | 38.00 |
| lava stone rubble, ($34.30 cf, 1 cf), 4% waste | — | cf | 35.70 | — | 35.70 |
| sandstone rubble, ($52.30 cf, 1 cf), 4% waste | — | cf | 54.40 | — | 54.40 |
| Ashlar stone | | | | | |
| flagstone, ($21.40 cf, 1 cf), 4% waste | — | cf | 22.30 | — | 22.30 |
| limestone, natural finish, ($29.00 cf, 1 cf), 4% waste | — | cf | 30.20 | — | 30.20 |
| limestone, rough finish, ($32.40 cf, 1 cf), 4% waste | — | cf | 33.70 | — | 33.70 |
| limestone, smooth finish, ($47.10 cf, 1 cf), 4% waste | — | cf | 49.00 | — | 49.00 |
| marble, natural finish, ($68.70 cf, 1 cf), 4% waste | — | cf | 71.40 | — | 71.40 |
| marble, rough finish, ($74.20 cf, 1 cf), 4% waste | — | cf | 77.20 | — | 77.20 |
| marble, smooth finish, ($91.90 cf, 1 cf), 4% waste | — | cf | 95.60 | — | 95.60 |

| | Craft@Hrs | Unit | Material | Labor | Total |
|---|---|---|---|---|---|
| sandstone, natural finish, ($28.50 cf, 1 cf), 4% waste | — | cf | 29.60 | — | 29.60 |
| sandstone, rough finish, ($31.20 cf, 1 cf), 4% waste | — | cf | 32.40 | — | 32.40 |
| sandstone, smooth finish, ($45.20 cf, 1 cf), 4% waste | — | cf | 47.00 | — | 47.00 |
| Wall coping | | | | | |
| aluminum, all wall widths, ($17.60 lf, 1 lf), 4% waste | — | lf | 18.30 | — | 18.30 |
| 10" wide concrete, ($18.80 lf, 1 lf), 2% waste | — | lf | 19.20 | — | 19.20 |
| 14" wide concrete, ($25.10 lf, 1 lf), 2% waste | — | lf | 25.60 | — | 25.60 |
| 8" wide granite, ($38.60 lf, 1 lf), 2% waste | — | lf | 39.40 | — | 39.40 |
| 12" wide granite, ($50.80 lf, 1 lf), 2% waste | — | lf | 51.80 | — | 51.80 |
| 8" wide limestone, ($22.80 lf, 1 lf), 2% waste | — | lf | 23.30 | — | 23.30 |
| 12" wide limestone, ($27.10 lf, 1 lf), 2% waste | — | lf | 27.60 | — | 27.60 |
| 8" wide marble, ($33.40 lf, 1 lf), 2% waste | — | lf | 34.10 | — | 34.10 |
| 10" wide marble, ($51.60 lf, 1 lf), 2% waste | — | lf | 52.60 | — | 52.60 |

## Masonry Labor

| Laborer | base wage | paid leave | true wage | taxes & ins. | total |
|---|---|---|---|---|---|
| Mason | $32.10 | 2.50 | $34.60 | 24.80 | $59.40 |
| Mason's helper | $29.20 | 2.28 | $31.48 | 23.02 | $54.50 |
| Hod carrier | $21.80 | 1.70 | $23.50 | 18.50 | $42.00 |
| Plasterer | $29.80 | 2.32 | $32.12 | 21.38 | $53.50 |
| Stone carver | $54.00 | 4.21 | $58.21 | 37.79 | $96.00 |
| Demolition laborer | $20.70 | 1.61 | $22.31 | 16.59 | $38.90 |

**Paid leave** is calculated based on two weeks paid vacation, one week sick leave, and seven paid holidays. Employer's matching portion of **FICA** is 7.65 percent. **FUTA** (Federal Unemployment) is .8 percent. **Worker's compensation** was calculated using a national average of 19.00 percent for masonry workers and 13.00 percent for plastering workers. **Unemployment insurance** was calculated using a national average of 8 percent. **Health insurance** was calculated based on a projected national average for 2015 of $1,025 per employee (and family when applicable) per month. Employer pays 80 percent for a per month cost of $820 per employee. **Retirement** is based on a 401(k) retirement program with employer matching of 50 percent. Employee contributions to the 401(k) plan are an average of 6 percent of the true wage. **Liability insurance** is based on a national average of 10.0 percent.

| | Craft@Hrs | Unit | Material | Labor | Total |
|---|---|---|---|---|---|
| **Masonry Labor Productivity** | | | | | |
| Demolition of masonry | | | | | |
| remove 4" masonry wall | 1D@.087 | sf | — | 3.38 | 3.38 |
| remove 12" masonry wall | 1D@.177 | sf | — | 6.89 | 6.89 |
| remove brick veneer | 1D@.082 | sf | — | 3.19 | 3.19 |
| remove block wall pilaster | 1D@.121 | lf | — | 4.71 | 4.71 |
| remove block wall grade beam cap | 1D@.363 | lf | — | 14.10 | 14.10 |
| remove terra cotta wall cap | 1D@.063 | lf | — | 2.45 | 2.45 |
| remove coping stone | 1D@.104 | lf | — | 4.05 | 4.05 |
| remove glass block wall | 1D@.084 | sf | — | 3.27 | 3.27 |
| remove pavers on mortar base | 1D@.120 | sf | — | 4.67 | 4.67 |
| remove pavers on sand base | 1D@.084 | sf | — | 3.27 | 3.27 |
| remove stone rubble wall with no mortar | 1D@.259 | cf | — | 10.10 | 10.10 |
| remove stone rubble wall with mortar | 1D@.439 | cf | — | 17.10 | 17.10 |
| remove ashlar wall | 1D@.439 | cf | — | 17.10 | 17.10 |
| remove stone veneer | 1D@.106 | sf | — | 4.12 | 4.12 |
| remove keystone | 1D@.198 | ea | — | 7.70 | 7.70 |

| | Craft@Hrs | Unit | Material | Labor | Total |
|---|---|---|---|---|---|
| remove quoin | 1D@.196 | ea | — | 7.62 | 7.62 |
| remove veneer panels | 1D@.074 | sf | — | 2.88 | 2.88 |
| remove door or window architrave | 1D@.131 | lf | — | 5.10 | 5.10 |
| remove trim or cornice stones | 1D@.104 | ea | — | 4.05 | 4.05 |
| remove stone window sill | 1D@.110 | lf | — | 4.28 | 4.28 |
| remove precast concrete lintel | 1D@.120 | lf | — | 4.67 | 4.67 |

## Masonry crew

| | | |
|---|---|---|
| install masonry | mason | $59.40 |
| install masonry | mason's helper | $54.50 |
| install masonry | hod carrier / laborer | $42.00 |
| install masonry | masonry crew | $52.00 |

## Mason & helper

| | | |
|---|---|---|
| install masonry | mason | $59.40 |
| install masonry | mason's helper | $54.50 |
| install masonry | mason & helper | $57.00 |

Install brick wall

| | Craft@Hrs | Unit | Material | Labor | Total |
|---|---|---|---|---|---|
| 4" wide standard non-modular | 4M@.170 | sf | — | 8.84 | 8.84 |
| 4" wide oversize non-modular | 4M@.168 | sf | — | 8.74 | 8.74 |
| 4" wide three-inch non-modular | 4M@.167 | sf | — | 8.68 | 8.68 |
| 4" wide standard | 4M@.169 | sf | — | 8.79 | 8.79 |
| 4" wide engineer | 4M@.141 | sf | — | 7.33 | 7.33 |
| 4" wide jumbo closure | 4M@.120 | sf | — | 6.24 | 6.24 |
| 4" wide double | 4M@.101 | sf | — | 5.25 | 5.25 |
| 4" wide Roman | 4M@.160 | sf | — | 8.32 | 8.32 |
| 4" wide Norman | 4M@.130 | sf | — | 6.76 | 6.76 |
| 4" wide Norwegian | 4M@.111 | sf | — | 5.77 | 5.77 |
| 4" wide jumbo utility | 4M@.102 | sf | — | 5.30 | 5.30 |
| 4" wide triple | 4M@.096 | sf | — | 4.99 | 4.99 |
| 6" wide Norwegian | 4M@.124 | sf | — | 6.45 | 6.45 |
| 6" wide Norman | 4M@.148 | sf | — | 7.70 | 7.70 |
| 6" wide jumbo | 4M@.113 | sf | — | 5.88 | 5.88 |
| 8" wide jumbo | 4M@.127 | sf | — | 6.60 | 6.60 |

Install 8" wide double wythe brick wall

| | Craft@Hrs | Unit | Material | Labor | Total |
|---|---|---|---|---|---|
| with standard non-modular brick | 4M@.307 | sf | — | 16.00 | 16.00 |
| with oversize non-modular brick | 4M@.303 | sf | — | 15.80 | 15.80 |
| with three-inch non-modular brick | 4M@.300 | sf | — | 15.60 | 15.60 |
| with standard brick | 4M@.305 | sf | — | 15.90 | 15.90 |
| with engineer brick | 4M@.253 | sf | — | 13.20 | 13.20 |
| with jumbo closure brick | 4M@.216 | sf | — | 11.20 | 11.20 |
| with double brick | 4M@.181 | sf | — | 9.41 | 9.41 |
| with Roman brick | 4M@.287 | sf | — | 14.90 | 14.90 |
| with Norman brick | 4M@.234 | sf | — | 12.20 | 12.20 |
| with Norwegian brick | 4M@.199 | sf | — | 10.30 | 10.30 |
| with jumbo utility | 4M@.184 | sf | — | 9.57 | 9.57 |
| with triple brick | 4M@.173 | sf | — | 9.00 | 9.00 |

| | Craft@Hrs | Unit | Material | Labor | Total |
|---|---|---|---|---|---|
| **Install 8" wide wall with 4" wide brick and 4" wide concrete block** | | | | | |
| with standard non-modular brick | 4M@.233 | sf | — | 12.10 | 12.10 |
| with standard brick | 4M@.233 | sf | — | 12.10 | 12.10 |
| with engineer brick | 4M@.206 | sf | — | 10.70 | 10.70 |
| with jumbo closure brick | 4M@.188 | sf | — | 9.78 | 9.78 |
| with double brick | 4M@.170 | sf | — | 8.84 | 8.84 |
| with Roman brick | 4M@.224 | sf | — | 11.60 | 11.60 |
| with Norman brick | 4M@.197 | sf | — | 10.20 | 10.20 |
| with Norwegian brick | 4M@.180 | sf | — | 9.36 | 9.36 |
| with jumbo utility brick | 4M@.172 | sf | — | 8.94 | 8.94 |
| with triple brick | 4M@.166 | sf | — | 8.63 | 8.63 |
| **Install 10" wide wall with 4" wide brick and 6" wide concrete block** | | | | | |
| with standard non-modular brick | 4M@.236 | sf | — | 12.30 | 12.30 |
| with standard brick | 4M@.235 | sf | — | 12.20 | 12.20 |
| with engineer brick | 4M@.209 | sf | — | 10.90 | 10.90 |
| with jumbo brick | 4M@.190 | sf | — | 9.88 | 9.88 |
| with double brick | 4M@.173 | sf | — | 9.00 | 9.00 |
| with Roman brick | 4M@.226 | sf | — | 11.80 | 11.80 |
| with Norman brick | 4M@.200 | sf | — | 10.40 | 10.40 |
| with Norwegian brick | 4M@.182 | sf | — | 9.46 | 9.46 |
| with jumbo utility brick | 4M@.175 | sf | — | 9.10 | 9.10 |
| with triple brick | 4M@.170 | sf | — | 8.84 | 8.84 |
| **Install 12" wide wall with 4" wide brick and 8" wide concrete block** | | | | | |
| with standard non-modular brick | 4M@.240 | sf | — | 12.50 | 12.50 |
| with standard brick | 4M@.240 | sf | — | 12.50 | 12.50 |
| with engineer brick | 4M@.214 | sf | — | 11.10 | 11.10 |
| with jumbo closure brick | 4M@.195 | sf | — | 10.10 | 10.10 |
| with double brick | 4M@.178 | sf | — | 9.26 | 9.26 |
| with Roman brick | 4M@.231 | sf | — | 12.00 | 12.00 |
| with Norman brick | 4M@.204 | sf | — | 10.60 | 10.60 |
| with Norwegian brick | 4M@.187 | sf | — | 9.72 | 9.72 |
| with jumbo utility brick | 4M@.180 | sf | — | 9.36 | 9.36 |
| with triple brick | 4M@.174 | sf | — | 9.05 | 9.05 |
| **Install 12" wide triple wythe wall** | | | | | |
| with standard non-modular brick | 4M@.433 | sf | — | 22.50 | 22.50 |
| with oversize non-modular brick | 4M@.427 | sf | — | 22.20 | 22.20 |
| with three-inch non-modular brick | 4M@.424 | sf | — | 22.00 | 22.00 |
| with standard brick | 4M@.429 | sf | — | 22.30 | 22.30 |
| with engineer brick | 4M@.357 | sf | — | 18.60 | 18.60 |
| with jumbo closure brick | 4M@.305 | sf | — | 15.90 | 15.90 |
| with double brick | 4M@.255 | sf | — | 13.30 | 13.30 |
| with Roman brick | 4M@.407 | sf | — | 21.20 | 21.20 |
| with Norman brick | 4M@.330 | sf | — | 17.20 | 17.20 |
| with Norwegian brick | 4M@.282 | sf | — | 14.70 | 14.70 |
| with jumbo utility brick | 4M@.260 | sf | — | 13.50 | 13.50 |
| with triple brick | 4M@.244 | sf | — | 12.70 | 12.70 |

| | Craft@Hrs | Unit | Material | Labor | Total |
|---|---|---|---|---|---|
| **Install 10" wide cavity wall with 4" brick and 4" concrete block** | | | | | |
| with standard non-modular brick | 4M@.244 | sf | — | 12.70 | 12.70 |
| with standard brick | 4M@.243 | sf | — | 12.60 | 12.60 |
| with engineer brick | 4M@.216 | sf | — | 11.20 | 11.20 |
| with jumbo closure brick | 4M@.196 | sf | — | 10.20 | 10.20 |
| with double brick | 4M@.178 | sf | — | 9.26 | 9.26 |
| with Roman brick | 4M@.234 | sf | — | 12.20 | 12.20 |
| with Norman brick | 4M@.206 | sf | — | 10.70 | 10.70 |
| with Norwegian brick | 4M@.188 | sf | — | 9.78 | 9.78 |
| with jumbo utility brick | 4M@.180 | sf | — | 9.36 | 9.36 |
| with triple brick | 4M@.174 | sf | — | 9.05 | 9.05 |
| **Install 10" wide cavity wall with 4" brick on both sides** | | | | | |
| with standard non-modular brick | 4M@.321 | sf | — | 16.70 | 16.70 |
| with oversize non-modular brick | 4M@.317 | sf | — | 16.50 | 16.50 |
| with three-inch non-modular brick | 4M@.314 | sf | — | 16.30 | 16.30 |
| with standard brick | 4M@.319 | sf | — | 16.60 | 16.60 |
| with engineer brick | 4M@.266 | sf | — | 13.80 | 13.80 |
| with jumbo closure brick | 4M@.226 | sf | — | 11.80 | 11.80 |
| with double brick | 4M@.189 | sf | — | 9.83 | 9.83 |
| with Roman brick | 4M@.301 | sf | — | 15.70 | 15.70 |
| with Norman brick | 4M@.245 | sf | — | 12.70 | 12.70 |
| with Norwegian brick | 4M@.209 | sf | — | 10.90 | 10.90 |
| with jumbo utility brick | 4M@.193 | sf | — | 10.00 | 10.00 |
| with triple brick | 4M@.181 | sf | — | 9.41 | 9.41 |
| **Install brick veneer** | | | | | |
| with standard brick | 4M@.144 | sf | — | 7.49 | 7.49 |
| with oversize non-modular brick | 4M@.143 | sf | — | 7.44 | 7.44 |
| with three-inch non-modular brick | 4M@.141 | sf | — | 7.33 | 7.33 |
| with standard brick | 4M@.144 | sf | — | 7.49 | 7.49 |
| with engineer brick | 4M@.119 | sf | — | 6.19 | 6.19 |
| with jumbo closure brick | 4M@.102 | sf | — | 5.30 | 5.30 |
| with double brick | 4M@.085 | sf | — | 4.42 | 4.42 |
| with Roman brick | 4M@.136 | sf | — | 7.07 | 7.07 |
| with Norman brick | 4M@.110 | sf | — | 5.72 | 5.72 |
| with Norwegian brick | 4M@.094 | sf | — | 4.89 | 4.89 |
| with jumbo utility brick | 4M@.087 | sf | — | 4.52 | 4.52 |
| with triple brick | 4M@.082 | sf | — | 4.26 | 4.26 |
| **Install brick arch** | | | | | |
| flat brick arch | 4M@1.49 | lf | — | 77.50 | 77.50 |
| elliptical brick arch | 4M@1.85 | lf | — | 96.20 | 96.20 |
| semi-circular brick arch | 4M@1.96 | lf | — | 102.00 | 102.00 |
| **Install block wall with 8" x 16" face** | | | | | |
| 4" wide | 4M@.089 | sf | — | 4.63 | 4.63 |
| 6" wide | 4M@.092 | sf | — | 4.78 | 4.78 |
| 8" wide | 4M@.097 | sf | — | 5.04 | 5.04 |
| 10" wide | 4M@.103 | sf | — | 5.36 | 5.36 |
| 12" wide | 4M@.122 | sf | — | 6.34 | 6.34 |

| | Craft@Hrs | Unit | Material | Labor | Total |
|---|---|---|---|---|---|
| **Install block wall with 4" x 16" face** | | | | | |
| 4" wide | 4M@.102 | sf | — | 5.30 | 5.30 |
| 6" wide | 4M@.106 | sf | — | 5.51 | 5.51 |
| 8" wide | 4M@.112 | sf | — | 5.82 | 5.82 |
| 10" wide | 4M@.119 | sf | — | 6.19 | 6.19 |
| 12" wide | 4M@.140 | sf | — | 7.28 | 7.28 |
| **Install lightweight block wall with 8" x 16" face** | | | | | |
| 4" wide | 4M@.083 | sf | — | 4.32 | 4.32 |
| 6" wide | 4M@.086 | sf | — | 4.47 | 4.47 |
| 8" wide | 4M@.091 | sf | — | 4.73 | 4.73 |
| 10" wide | 4M@.097 | sf | — | 5.04 | 5.04 |
| 12" wide | 4M@.114 | sf | — | 5.93 | 5.93 |
| **Form and pour grade-beam cap on block wall** | | | | | |
| 6" wide | 4M@.106 | lf | — | 5.51 | 5.51 |
| 12" wide | 4M@.120 | lf | — | 6.24 | 6.24 |
| **Install glass block** | | | | | |
| 4" x 8" | 4M@.333 | sf | — | 17.30 | 17.30 |
| 6" x 8" | 4M@.267 | sf | — | 13.90 | 13.90 |
| 8" x 8" | 4M@.208 | sf | — | 10.80 | 10.80 |
| 12" x 12" | 4M@.175 | sf | — | 9.10 | 9.10 |
| **Install pavers** | | | | | |
| on sand base | 4M@.147 | sf | — | 7.64 | 7.64 |
| mortar base | 4M@.180 | sf | — | 9.36 | 9.36 |
| full-size bricks, laid face up | 4M@.185 | sf | — | 9.62 | 9.62 |
| full-size bricks, laid edge up | 4M@.208 | sf | — | 10.80 | 10.80 |
| add for paver steps installed over concrete | 4M@.270 | lf | — | 14.00 | 14.00 |
| add for paver steps installed over sand base | 4M@.294 | lf | — | 15.30 | 15.30 |
| add for separate pattern at edges of pavers | 4M@.076 | lf | — | 3.95 | 3.95 |
| **Lay stone wall** | | | | | |
| field stone rubble with no mortar | 4M@.481 | cf | — | 25.00 | 25.00 |
| rubble wall | 4M@.518 | cf | — | 26.90 | 26.90 |
| ashlar wall | 4M@.472 | cf | — | 24.50 | 24.50 |
| add to install flat arch | 4M@2.86 | lf | — | 149.00 | 149.00 |
| add to install elliptical arch | 4M@3.58 | lf | — | 186.00 | 186.00 |
| add to install semi-circular arch | 4M@3.70 | lf | — | 192.00 | 192.00 |
| **Lay stone veneer** | | | | | |
| rubble | 4M@.243 | sf | — | 12.60 | 12.60 |
| ashlar | 4M@.236 | sf | — | 12.30 | 12.30 |
| add to install flat arch | 4M@1.75 | lf | — | 91.00 | 91.00 |
| add to install elliptical arch | 4M@2.17 | lf | — | 113.00 | 113.00 |
| add to install semi-circular arch | 4M@2.30 | lf | — | 120.00 | 120.00 |
| **Install veneer panels** | | | | | |
| cultured stone | 4M@.263 | sf | — | 13.70 | 13.70 |
| natural stone | 4M@.298 | sf | — | 15.50 | 15.50 |
| **Install stone architrave** | | | | | |
| door | 4M@.980 | lf | — | 51.00 | 51.00 |
| window | 4M@1.00 | lf | — | 52.00 | 52.00 |
| **Install trim or cornice stones** | | | | | |
| install | 4M@.370 | lf | — | 19.20 | 19.20 |

| | Craft@Hrs | Unit | Material | Labor | Total |
|---|---|---|---|---|---|
| **Install wall cap or coping** | | | | | |
| terra cotta | 4M@.185 | lf | — | 9.62 | 9.62 |
| aluminum | 4M@.181 | lf | — | 9.41 | 9.41 |
| concrete coping | 4M@.167 | lf | — | 8.68 | 8.68 |
| stone coping | 4M@.185 | lf | — | 9.62 | 9.62 |
| **Salvage brick veneer** | | | | | |
| remove, salvage bricks, and relay | 4M@.877 | sf | — | 45.60 | 45.60 |
| **Repoint brick wall** | | | | | |
| running bond | 4M@.108 | sf | — | 5.62 | 5.62 |
| common bond (also called American bond) | 4M@.111 | sf | — | 5.77 | 5.77 |
| Flemish bond | 4M@.121 | sf | — | 6.29 | 6.29 |
| English bond | 4M@.128 | sf | — | 6.66 | 6.66 |
| English cross bond (also called Dutch bond) | 4M@.128 | sf | — | 6.66 | 6.66 |
| stack bond | 4M@.082 | sf | — | 4.26 | 4.26 |
| all header bond | 4M@.093 | sf | — | 4.84 | 4.84 |
| soldier course | 4M@.106 | sf | — | 5.51 | 5.51 |
| sailor course | 4M@.099 | sf | — | 5.15 | 5.15 |
| basketweave | 4M@.164 | sf | — | 8.53 | 8.53 |
| herringbone weave | 4M@.167 | sf | — | 8.68 | 8.68 |
| diagonal bond | 4M@.144 | sf | — | 7.49 | 7.49 |
| coursed ashlar style bond | 4M@.120 | sf | — | 6.24 | 6.24 |
| **Repoint stone wall** | | | | | |
| rubble | 4M@.278 | sf | — | 14.50 | 14.50 |
| ashlar | 4M@.260 | sf | — | 13.50 | 13.50 |
| **Stone wall repair** | | | | | |
| repair carved stone with epoxy | 1M@.024 | si | — | 1.43 | 1.43 |
| repair carved stone with stucco or grout | 1M@.022 | si | — | 1.31 | 1.31 |
| epoxy repair and pin broken stone | 1M@1.33 | ea | — | 79.00 | 79.00 |
| reconstitute delaminating stone with epoxy | 1M@.013 | si | — | .77 | .77 |
| reface stone with grout mixed to match | 1M@.149 | sf | — | 8.85 | 8.85 |
| remove segment of rubble wall and relay | 5M@4.00 | cf | — | 228.00 | 228.00 |
| remove segment of rubble veneer and relay | 5M@1.92 | sf | — | 109.00 | 109.00 |
| remove segment of ashlar wall and relay | 5M@3.85 | cf | — | 219.00 | 219.00 |
| remove segment of ashlar veneer and relay | 5M@1.89 | sf | — | 108.00 | 108.00 |
| **Carve stone** | | | | | |
| with light hand carvings | 6M@.015 | si | — | 1.44 | 1.44 |
| with medium hand carvings | 6M@.022 | si | — | 2.11 | 2.11 |
| with heavy hand carvings | 6M@.031 | si | — | 2.98 | 2.98 |

# Mold Remediation

### Dealing with Mold

Mold remediation is an important consideration when dealing with almost any type of structural damage. The prices in this chapter are primarily based on the standards developed by the city of New York (recently updated) and by applying the EPA's guidelines for mold remediation in schools and commercial buildings to residential buildings.

### Mitigation

Mold issues point out the importance of immediately removing any source of invading moisture. Mold can begin to grow immediately and can become a problem even when moisture is removed within 24 to 48 hours. Paying for after-hours mitigation work to remove the source of any moisture, dehumidifying, and aggressively drying items that sponsor mold is well worth the cost.

### Testing

Not all molds are judged to be as harmful as others. Most of the harmful types of molds have been generally classified as "black molds." Black molds include aspergillus (more than 50 species), cladosporium, fusarium, stachybotrus chartarum, trichoderma, memnoniella, and penicillium. Molds may emit both spores and gas and many are still hazardous even when they are not alive. To get a clear picture of the types of molds present and the hazards they present, testing may be necessary.

### Mold Specialists

All workers involved in mold remediation should be well trained and, when possible, certified. In many cases it is advantageous to hire an environmental consultant to help determine the best process and to oversee the work. The prices in this chapter assume that all work is done by qualified and certified staff supervised by an environmental consultant or someone on staff with similar credentials and abilities.

### Containment

Severely mold-contaminated areas must be contained in ways that are similar to procedures used when dealing with asbestos and other types of hazardous materials. Contaminated areas must be sealed off from non-contaminated areas. Negative air pressure should be maintained in the contaminated area so air-borne mold spores and gas will not escape. Ventilating fans must filter any possible mold spores and gas from the air before it is ventilated to the exterior of the contaminated areas. Entry and exit from the contaminated area must be done through a decontamination area.

### Personal Protection Equipment

All workers involved in mold remediation must wear personal protection equipment. Although the level and type of the mold involved may change some aspects of the personal protection equipment needed, in general, this chapter assumes workers wear a fit-tested half- or full-force respirator with a HEPA, organic/chemical cartridge. Although the New York standards suggest an N-95 rated mask in some circumstances, many specialists feel a better standard for their employees is to always require a respirator. If an N-95 mask is judged to be sufficient, care must be taken to ensure that the mask is actually N-95 rated. The N-95 mask looks very similar to other types of masks often worn when doing routine demolition. However, the N-95 mask is substantially more effective than standard masks.

Mold remediation specialists should also wear nitrile disposable gloves or, when working with debris that contains sharp edges, puncture-proof gloves. Workers should also wear level-B protective clothing that covers both the head and feet.

### Levels of Remediation

The New York City Department of Health & Mental Hygiene, Bureau of Environmental & Occupational Disease Epidemiology has issued a document called Guidelines on Assessment and Remediation of Fungi in Indoor Environments (http://home2.nyc.gov/html/doh/html/epi/moldrpt1.shtml). We highly recommend reading this document and using it as a guideline. A key part of this document is the section titled Remediation. This section discusses the types of remediation recommended for different levels of mold growth. The prices in this chapter are based on this document's description of Level III mold growth and above, although some items also apply to Level II.

### For More Information

A large body of information about mold remediation is now available on the Internet. Typing "Mold Remediation" in Google or a similar search engine will yield a wealth of results. We recommend viewing the New York City standards (http://home2.nyc.gov/html/doh/html/epi/moldrpt1.shtml) and visiting the EPA's web site (www.epa.gov/mold) as two excellent places to start.

| | Craft@Hrs | Unit | Material | Labor | Total |
|---|---|---|---|---|---|
| **Minimum charge.** | | | | | |
| for mold remediation work | | | | | |
| when containment is required | 9Z@6.00 | ea | 204.00 | 188.00 | 392.00 |
| for mold remediation testing | 9Z@1.25 | ea | — | 39.30 | 39.30 |
| **Testing.** | | | | | |
| Anderson N-6 bioaerosol sampler | — | ea | 120.00 | — | 120.00 |
| Spore trap | — | ea | 78.80 | — | 78.80 |
| Prolab test kit (3 sampling methods) | — | ea | 81.30 | — | 81.30 |
| Swab/tape sampler | — | ea | 86.00 | — | 86.00 |
| Surface sampling test | — | sf | 66.90 | — | 66.90 |
| Air sampling test | — | ea | 120.00 | — | 120.00 |
| **Environmental consultant.** | | | | | |
| Environmental consultant, per hour | 9Z@1.00 | hr | — | 31.40 | 31.40 |
| Minimum charge for mold remediation testing | 9Z@4.00 | ea | — | 126.00 | 126.00 |
| **Containment.** Plastic cover is two layers of plastic attached with duct tape. | | | | | |
| Plastic cover attached to ceiling | 9Z@.036 | sf | 1.53 | 1.13 | 2.66 |
| Plastic cover attached to walls | 9Z@.035 | sf | 1.44 | 1.10 | 2.54 |
| Plastic cover and plywood over floor (2 layers) | 9Z@.084 | sf | 2.83 | 2.64 | 5.47 |
| Temporary containment walls with plastic cover | 9Z@.142 | sf | 3.52 | 4.46 | 7.98 |
| Airlock for containment area | 9Z@7.41 | ea | 296.00 | 233.00 | 529.00 |

| | Craft@Hrs | Unit | Material | Labor | Equip. | Total |
|---|---|---|---|---|---|---|
| **Containment equipment.** | | | | | | |
| Prefabricated decontamination unit, rent per day | — | dy | — | — | 105.00 | 105.00 |
| Exhaust fan, HEPA filtered for containment area, rent per day | — | dy | — | — | 139.00 | 139.00 |
| Negative air machine with air scrubber, rent per day | — | dy | — | — | 126.00 | 126.00 |
| **Dumpsters.** | | | | | | |
| Dumpster, with locking doors, 5 to 6 cy | — | ea | — | — | 139.00 | 139.00 |
| Dumpster, with locking doors, 10 to 12 cy | — | ea | — | — | 224.00 | 224.00 |
| Dumpster, with locking doors, 30 cy | — | ea | — | — | 622.00 | 622.00 |

| | Craft@Hrs | Unit | Material | Labor | Total |
|---|---|---|---|---|---|

**Tear out flooring.** Removing mold-contaminated flooring includes cutting into strips or smaller pieces as needed, and bagging, or placing in a haz-mat drum for carpet tackless strip.

| | Craft@Hrs | Unit | Material | Labor | Total |
|---|---|---|---|---|---|
| Remove mold-contaminated carpet | 9Z@.006 | sf | .10 | .19 | .29 |
| Remove mold-contaminated carpet pad | 9Z@.007 | sf | .10 | .22 | .32 |
| Remove mold-contaminated carpet tackless strip | 9Z@.004 | lf | .36 | .13 | .49 |
| Remove mold-contaminated glue down carpet | 9Z@.008 | sf | .10 | .25 | .35 |
| Remove mold-contaminated vinyl floor from underlayment | 9Z@.008 | sf | .10 | .25 | .35 |
| Remove mold-contaminated vinyl floor from concrete | 9Z@.009 | sf | .10 | .28 | .38 |
| Remove mold-contaminated underlayment | 9Z@.008 | sf | .23 | .25 | .48 |
| Remove mold-contaminated wood floor | 9Z@.012 | sf | .23 | .38 | .61 |

**Tear out wall finishes.** Removing mold-contaminated wall finishes includes cutting into strips or breaking into smaller pieces as needed, and bagging, or placing in a haz-mat drum.

| | Craft@Hrs | Unit | Material | Labor | Total |
|---|---|---|---|---|---|
| Remove mold-contaminated drywall | 9Z@.006 | sf | .23 | .19 | .42 |
| Remove mold-contaminated plaster | 9Z@.007 | sf | .23 | .22 | .45 |
| Remove mold-contaminated wood paneling | 9Z@.004 | sf | .23 | .13 | .36 |
| Remove mold-contaminated trimwork | 9Z@.004 | lf | .10 | .13 | .23 |
| Remove mold-contaminated concrete backer board | 9Z@.008 | sf | .23 | .25 | .48 |
| Remove mold-contaminated wallpaper | 9Z@.001 | sf | — | .03 | .03 |

**Tear out door.** Removing mold-contaminated doors includes cutting into smaller pieces, and bagging, or placing in a haz-mat drum.

| | Craft@Hrs | Unit | Material | Labor | Total |
|---|---|---|---|---|---|
| Remove mold-contaminated hollow-core door | 9Z@.067 | ea | 4.02 | 2.10 | 6.12 |
| Remove mold-contaminated solid-core door | 9Z@.091 | ea | 6.03 | 2.86 | 8.89 |

**Tear out insulation.** Removing mold-contaminated insulation includes placing in a bag for disposal.

| | Craft@Hrs | Unit | Material | Labor | Total |
|---|---|---|---|---|---|
| Remove mold-contaminated batt insulation | 9Z@.002 | sf | .03 | .06 | .09 |
| Remove mold-contaminated loose-fill insulation | 9Z@.004 | sf | .03 | .13 | .16 |

**Tear out ceiling finishes.** Removing mold-contaminated ceiling finishes includes breaking into smaller pieces and bagging or placing in a haz-mat drum.

| | Craft@Hrs | Unit | Material | Labor | Total |
|---|---|---|---|---|---|
| Remove mold-contaminated acoustic ceiling tile | 9Z@.006 | sf | .10 | .19 | .29 |
| Remove mold-contaminated ceiling furring strips | 9Z@.009 | sf | .10 | .28 | .38 |
| Remove mold-contaminated wall furring strips | 9Z@.008 | sf | .10 | .25 | .35 |
| Remove mold-contaminated suspended ceiling tile | 9Z@.005 | sf | .10 | .16 | .26 |

**Tear out complete room.** Includes stripping the mold-contaminated room to bare walls and sub-floor. All debris is cut or broken into smaller pieces then bagged or placed in haz-mat drums.

| | Craft@Hrs | Unit | Material | Labor | Total |
|---|---|---|---|---|---|
| Strip mold-contaminated room | 9Z@.166 | sf | 1.56 | 5.21 | 6.77 |
| Strip mold-contaminated bathroom | 9Z@.214 | sf | 2.04 | 6.72 | 8.76 |
| Strip mold-contaminated kitchen | 9Z@.187 | sf | 1.67 | 5.87 | 7.54 |
| Strip mold-contaminated utility room | 9Z@.173 | sf | 1.67 | 5.43 | 7.10 |
| Strip mold-contaminated laundry room | 9Z@.189 | sf | 1.67 | 5.93 | 7.60 |

**Haz-mat drums & bags.**

| | Craft@Hrs | Unit | Material | Labor | Total |
|---|---|---|---|---|---|
| 3 cf disposable fiber drum | — | ea | 12.10 | — | 12.10 |
| 3 cf disposable bag | — | ea | 1.42 | — | 1.42 |

| | Craft@Hrs | Unit | Material | Labor | Total |
|---|---|---|---|---|---|

**Treat with antimicrobial spray.**  Includes treating the mold-contaminated surface, rinsing, wiping and drying.

| | Craft@Hrs | Unit | Material | Labor | Total |
|---|---|---|---|---|---|
| Treat floor with antimicrobial spray | 9Z@.015 | sf | .31 | .47 | .78 |
| Treat walls with antimicrobial spray | 9Z@.013 | sf | .31 | .41 | .72 |
| Treat ceiling with antimicrobial spray | 9Z@.014 | sf | .31 | .44 | .75 |
| Treat trimwork with antimicrobial spray | 9Z@.012 | lf | .25 | .38 | .63 |
| Treat door with antimicrobial spray | 9Z@.295 | ea | 5.02 | 9.26 | 14.28 |
| Treat suspended ceiling grid with antimicrobial spray | 9Z@.012 | sf | .24 | .38 | .62 |
| Treat light fixture with antimicrobial spray | 9Z@.185 | ea | 4.85 | 5.81 | 10.66 |
| Treat switch/outlet & box with antimicrobial spray | 9Z@.171 | ea | 2.91 | 5.37 | 8.28 |

**Clean HVAC.**

| | Craft@Hrs | Unit | Material | Labor | Total |
|---|---|---|---|---|---|
| Clean mold-contaminated ductwork, per diffuser or cold-air return | 9Z@.655 | ea | 19.40 | 20.60 | 40.00 |
| Clean mold-contaminated furnace | 9Z@4.49 | ea | 15.80 | 141.00 | 156.80 |

**Cleaning rule of thumb.**  A general rule of thumb for cleaning items not listed in this chapter.

| | Craft@Hrs | Unit | Material | Labor | Total |
|---|---|---|---|---|---|
| Add to cleaning prices to clean mold-contaminated items | — | % | — | 28.0 | — |

**Treat mold-contaminated framing with antimicrobial spray.**

| | Craft@Hrs | Unit | Material | Labor | Total |
|---|---|---|---|---|---|
| Treat furring strips with antimicrobial spray | 9Z@.002 | sf | .12 | .06 | .18 |
| Treat beams with antimicrobial spray | 9Z@.006 | lf | .12 | .19 | .31 |
| Treat 2" x 4" framing with antimicrobial spray | 9Z@.003 | sf | .23 | .09 | .32 |
| Treat 2" x 6" framing with antimicrobial spray | 9Z@.003 | sf | .28 | .09 | .37 |
| Treat 2" x 8" framing with antimicrobial spray | 9Z@.004 | sf | .31 | .13 | .44 |
| Treat 2" x 10" framing with antimicrobial spray | 9Z@.004 | sf | .36 | .13 | .49 |
| Treat 2" x 12" framing with antimicrobial spray | 9Z@.005 | sf | .38 | .16 | .54 |

**Treat mold-contaminated trusses with antimicrobial spray.**

| | Craft@Hrs | Unit | Material | Labor | Total |
|---|---|---|---|---|---|
| Treat floor trusses with antimicrobial spray | 9Z@.011 | sf | .54 | .35 | .89 |
| Treat 4/12 trusses with antimicrobial spray | 9Z@.049 | sf | .67 | 1.54 | 2.21 |
| Treat 6/12 trusses with antimicrobial spray | 9Z@.066 | sf | .79 | 2.07 | 2.86 |
| Treat 8/12 trusses with antimicrobial spray | 9Z@.084 | sf | .96 | 2.64 | 3.60 |
| Treat 10/12 trusses with antimicrobial spray | 9Z@.100 | sf | 1.31 | 3.14 | 4.45 |
| Treat 12/12 trusses with antimicrobial spray | 9Z@.118 | sf | 1.56 | 3.71 | 5.27 |
| Treat 17/12 trusses with antimicrobial spray | 9Z@.142 | sf | 1.73 | 4.46 | 6.19 |
| Treat sheathing with antimicrobial spray | 9Z@.002 | sf | .24 | .06 | .30 |

**Encapsulate with sealer.**  Cleaning mold-contaminated items and treating with an antimicriboial spray probably won't remove all mold spores or gas from the air.  Since there is always some level of mold in the air, the goal is to reduce the mold to normal levels.  In some cases it may be desirable to encapsulate cleaned areas to further reduce the likelihood of continuing problems from previously affected areas.

| | Craft@Hrs | Unit | Material | Labor | Total |
|---|---|---|---|---|---|
| Encapsulate cleaned floor with sealer | 9Z@.008 | sf | .36 | .25 | .61 |
| Encapsulate cleaned wall with sealer | 9Z@.007 | sf | .36 | .22 | .58 |
| Encapsulate cleaned ceiling with sealer | 9Z@.007 | sf | .36 | .22 | .58 |

| | Craft@Hrs | Unit | Material | Labor | Total |
|---|---|---|---|---|---|
| **Encapsulate framing.** | | | | | |
| Encapsulate treated furring strips with sealer | 9Z@.008 | sf | .42 | .25 | .67 |
| Encapsulate treated beams with sealer | 9Z@.008 | sf | .53 | .25 | .78 |
| Encapsulate treated 2" x 4" framing with sealer | 9Z@.006 | sf | .63 | .19 | .82 |
| Encapsulate treated 2" x 6" framing with sealer | 9Z@.007 | sf | .70 | .22 | .92 |
| Encapsulate treated 2" x 8" framing with sealer | 9Z@.008 | sf | .75 | .25 | 1.00 |
| Encapsulate treated 2" x 10" framing with sealer | 9Z@.009 | sf | .82 | .28 | 1.10 |
| Encapsulate treated 2" x 12" framing with sealer | 9Z@.010 | sf | .90 | .31 | 1.21 |
| Encapsulate treated floor trusses with sealer | 9Z@.016 | sf | .99 | .50 | 1.49 |
| Encapsulate treated 4/12 trusses with sealer | 9Z@.019 | sf | 1.56 | .60 | 2.16 |
| Encapsulate treated 6/12 trusses with sealer | 9Z@.037 | sf | 1.74 | 1.16 | 2.90 |
| Encapsulate treated 8/12 trusses with sealer | 9Z@.055 | sf | 1.89 | 1.73 | 3.62 |
| Encapsulate treated 10/12 trusses with sealer | 9Z@.074 | sf | 2.07 | 2.32 | 4.39 |
| Encapsulate treated 12/12 trusses with sealer | 9Z@.093 | sf | 2.22 | 2.92 | 5.14 |
| Encapsulate treated 17/12 trusses with sealer | 9Z@.112 | sf | 2.52 | 3.52 | 6.04 |
| Encapsulate treated sheathing with sealer | 9Z@.008 | sf | .41 | .25 | .66 |

**Encapsulation rule of thumb.** A general rule of thumb for encapsulating items not listed in this chapter.

| | Craft@Hrs | Unit | Material | Labor | Total |
|---|---|---|---|---|---|
| Add to painting cost to encapsulate | — | % | — | 34.0 | — |

**Fog treatment.**

| | Craft@Hrs | Unit | Material | Labor | Total |
|---|---|---|---|---|---|
| Treat area with antibacterial and antifungal fog | 9Z@.001 | cf | .01 | .03 | .04 |

| | Craft@Hrs | Unit | Material | Labor | Equip. | Total |
|---|---|---|---|---|---|---|
| **Dehumidifier.** Reducing the relative humidity in the room can be an important part of stopping the growth and spread of mold. Most experts want relative humidity at 60 percent or below and many shoot for around 40 percent. | | | | | | |
| Dehumidifier unit, 5 gallon daily capacity, rental per day | — | dy | — | — | 35.30 | 35.30 |
| Dehumidifier unit, 10 gallon daily capacity, rental per day | — | dy | — | — | 42.20 | 42.20 |
| Dehumidifier unit, 19 gallon daily capacity, rental per day | — | dy | — | — | 70.40 | 70.40 |
| Dehumidifier unit, 24 gallon daily capacity, rental per day | — | dy | — | — | 98.70 | 98.70 |
| Dehumidifier unit, 28 gallon daily capacity, rental per day | — | dy | — | — | 106.00 | 106.00 |
| **Drying fans.** | | | | | | |
| Drying fan, rental per day | — | dy | — | — | 36.00 | 36.00 |
| Drying fan, large, rental per day | — | dy | — | — | 42.20 | 42.20 |
| Drying fan, wall cavity, rental per day | — | dy | — | — | 49.60 | 49.60 |

## Time & Material Charts (selected items)
## Mold Remediation Materials

See Mold Remediation material prices with the line items above.

### Mold Remediation Labor

| Laborer | base wage | paid leave | true wage | taxes & ins. | total |
|---|---|---|---|---|---|
| Mildew remediation specialist | $19.50 | 1.52 | $21.02 | 17.78 | $38.80 |
| Mildew remediation assistant | $10.90 | .85 | $11.75 | 12.25 | $24.00 |

**Paid leave** is calculated based on two weeks paid vacation, one week sick leave, and seven paid holidays. Employer's matching portion of **FICA** is 7.65 percent. **FUTA** (Federal Unemployment) is .8 percent. **Worker's compensation** for the mold remediation trade was calculated using a national average of 23.04 percent. **Unemployment insurance** was calculated using a national average of 8 percent. **Health insurance** was calculated based on a projected national average for 2015 of $1,025 per employee (and family when applicable) per month. Employer pays 80 percent for a per month cost of $820 per employee. **Retirement** is based on a 401(k) retirement program with employer matching of 50 percent. Employee contributions to the 401(k) plan are an average of 6 percent of the true wage. **Liability insurance** is based on a national average of 10.0 percent.

| | Craft@Hrs | Unit | Material | Labor | Total |
|---|---|---|---|---|---|

# Outbuildings

**Metal storage shed.** Prefabricated metal storage shed with baked enamel finish and gable roof. Includes assembly. Does not include concrete slab or footings. Add **16%** for gambrel roof. Add **30%** for vinyl covered metal.

| | Craft@Hrs | Unit | Material | Labor | Total |
|---|---|---|---|---|---|
| 8' x 6' metal storage shed | | | | | |
| replace | 5C@6.51 | ea | 328.00 | 276.00 | 604.00 |
| remove | 1D@2.50 | ea | — | 97.30 | 97.30 |
| 8' x 10' metal storage shed | | | | | |
| replace | 5C@7.01 | ea | 440.00 | 297.00 | 737.00 |
| remove | 1D@2.74 | ea | — | 107.00 | 107.00 |
| 9' x 10' metal storage shed | | | | | |
| replace | 5C@7.51 | ea | 460.00 | 318.00 | 778.00 |
| remove | 1D@2.86 | ea | — | 111.00 | 111.00 |
| 10' x 12' metal storage shed | | | | | |
| replace | 5C@8.01 | ea | 718.00 | 340.00 | 1,058.00 |
| remove | 1D@3.04 | ea | — | 118.00 | 118.00 |

**Wood storage shed.** Pre-built and delivered to site. Painted with trim, truss gambrel roof, panel siding, 1/2" roof sheathing, 3/4" tongue-and-groove floor sheathing with floor skids. Does not include footings or pier blocks. Deduct **12%** for gable roof. Deduct **15%** for gambrel roof on top of walls that are 5' tall or less.

| | Craft@Hrs | Unit | Material | Labor | Total |
|---|---|---|---|---|---|
| 8' x 6' wood storage shed | | | | | |
| replace | 5C@7.01 | ea | 761.00 | 297.00 | 1,058.00 |
| remove | 1D@3.28 | ea | — | 128.00 | 128.00 |
| 8' x 10' wood storage shed | | | | | |
| replace | 5C@7.51 | ea | 1,790.00 | 318.00 | 2,108.00 |
| remove | 1D@3.84 | ea | — | 149.00 | 149.00 |
| 9' x 10' wood storage shed | | | | | |
| replace | 5C@8.01 | ea | 2,050.00 | 340.00 | 2,390.00 |
| remove | 1D@4.26 | ea | — | 166.00 | 166.00 |
| 10' x 12' wood storage shed | | | | | |
| replace | 5C@8.50 | ea | 2,390.00 | 360.00 | 2,750.00 |
| remove | 1D@4.67 | ea | — | 182.00 | 182.00 |

**Gazebo.** High quality octagonal gazebos priced by diameter. Made from D grade or better kiln-dried western red cedar surfaced four sides. Wood cedar shingles. Prefabricated parts assembled on site. Standard grade: Cupola, simple fretwork and rails with cross-grain detailing. High grade: Cupola, fretwork and raised-panel rails. Deluxe grade: Cupola, Queen Anne fretwork and rails. Add **116%** to 15' diameter for 21' diameter triple roof gazebo, add **$217** for bench in 9' and 12' diameter gazebos. Add **$244** for bench in 15', add **$606** for bow roof (all sizes). Add **$352** for steps with balustrades. Deduct **25%** for no floor deck. Deduct **17%** if made from select #1 grade western red cedar.

| | Craft@Hrs | Unit | Material | Labor | Total |
|---|---|---|---|---|---|
| 9' gazebo | | | | | |
| replace, standard grade | 1C@13.1 | ea | 8,010.00 | 745.00 | 8,755.00 |
| replace, high grade | 1C@15.0 | ea | 9,750.00 | 854.00 | 10,604.00 |
| replace, deluxe grade | 1C@17.5 | ea | 11,000.00 | 996.00 | 11,996.00 |
| remove | 1D@4.43 | ea | — | 172.00 | 172.00 |
| 12' gazebo | | | | | |
| replace, standard grade | 1C@17.5 | ea | 11,400.00 | 996.00 | 12,396.00 |
| replace, high grade | 1C@17.5 | ea | 12,900.00 | 996.00 | 13,896.00 |
| replace, deluxe grade | 1C@17.5 | ea | 15,000.00 | 996.00 | 15,996.00 |
| remove | 1D@5.57 | ea | — | 217.00 | 217.00 |

*single roof*  *double roof*

| | Craft@Hrs | Unit | Material | Labor | Total |
|---|---|---|---|---|---|
| **15' gazebo** | | | | | |
| replace, standard grade | 1C@21.0 | ea | 15,700.00 | 1,190.00 | 16,890.00 |
| replace, high grade | 1C@26.2 | ea | 19,000.00 | 1,490.00 | 20,490.00 |
| replace, deluxe grade | 1C@26.2 | ea | 21,000.00 | 1,490.00 | 22,490.00 |
| remove | 1D@7.13 | ea | — | 277.00 | 277.00 |

*triple roof*

**Free-standing greenhouse.** Residential style, aluminum frame. Automatic electric roof vent.

| | Craft@Hrs | Unit | Material | Labor | Total |
|---|---|---|---|---|---|
| **8' x 9' free-standing greenhouse** | | | | | |
| replace | 6C@15.0 | ea | 5,750.00 | 746.00 | 6,496.00 |
| remove | 1D@3.04 | ea | — | 118.00 | 118.00 |
| **8' x 11' free-standing greenhouse** | | | | | |
| replace | 6C@15.0 | ea | 6,270.00 | 746.00 | 7,016.00 |
| remove | 1D@3.44 | ea | — | 134.00 | 134.00 |
| **8' x 14' free-standing greenhouse** | | | | | |
| replace | 6C@17.5 | ea | 6,540.00 | 870.00 | 7,410.00 |
| remove | 1D@4.01 | ea | — | 156.00 | 156.00 |
| **8' x 17' free-standing greenhouse** | | | | | |
| replace | 6C@17.5 | ea | 7,810.00 | 870.00 | 8,680.00 |
| remove | 1D@4.33 | ea | — | 168.00 | 168.00 |

**Lean-to greenhouse.** Residential style, aluminum frame. Manually controlled vents.

| | Craft@Hrs | Unit | Material | Labor | Total |
|---|---|---|---|---|---|
| **4' x 8' lean-to greenhouse** | | | | | |
| replace | 6C@8.76 | ea | 2,440.00 | 435.00 | 2,875.00 |
| remove | 1D@2.86 | ea | — | 111.00 | 111.00 |
| **7' x 14' lean-to greenhouse** | | | | | |
| replace | 6C@13.1 | ea | 6,240.00 | 651.00 | 6,891.00 |
| remove | 1D@3.28 | ea | — | 128.00 | 128.00 |
| **8' x 16' lean-to greenhouse** | | | | | |
| replace | 6C@15.0 | ea | 7,630.00 | 746.00 | 8,376.00 |
| remove | 1D@3.49 | ea | — | 136.00 | 136.00 |

**Screened swimming pool enclosure.** Aluminum frame, vinyl screen.

| | Craft@Hrs | Unit | Material | Labor | Total |
|---|---|---|---|---|---|
| **Screened swimming pool enclosure** | | | | | |
| replace | 6C@.018 | sf | 7.52 | .89 | 8.41 |
| remove | 1D@.009 | sf | — | .35 | .35 |

**Chickhee hut.** Per square foot of floor. Typically found in the southern United States.

| | Craft@Hrs | Unit | Material | Labor | Total |
|---|---|---|---|---|---|
| **Chickhee hut** | | | | | |
| replace | 5C@1.23 | sf | 29.90 | 52.20 | 82.10 |
| remove | 1D@.100 | sf | — | 3.89 | 3.89 |
| **Thatched roof for hut, per square foot of roof area** | | | | | |
| replace | 5C@.754 | sf | 5.87 | 32.00 | 37.87 |
| remove | 1D@.038 | sf | — | 1.48 | 1.48 |

| | Craft@Hrs | Unit | Material | Labor | Total |
|---|---|---|---|---|---|

# Painting

**Painting coats.**  Prices for one coat, two coats and three coats do **not** include: the primer coat, sealer coat or stain.  To estimate painting, add the cost of the primer coat to the number of paint coats.  For example, to estimate the cost to prime a wall then paint with two coats, add the prime price to the two coats price.  To estimate the cost to stain an item then cover with two coats of varnish, add the stain cost to the two coats price (unless otherwise noted).

## Minimum charge.

| | Craft@Hrs | Unit | Material | Labor | Total |
|---|---|---|---|---|---|
| for painting work | 5F@3.00 | ea | 44.90 | 165.00 | 209.90 |

## Acoustic ceilings.

| | Craft@Hrs | Unit | Material | Labor | Total |
|---|---|---|---|---|---|
| Paint acoustic ceiling texture | | | | | |
| prime | 5F@.011 | sf | .35 | .61 | .96 |
| 1 coat | 5F@.011 | sf | .38 | .61 | .99 |
| 2 coats | 5F@.017 | sf | .54 | .94 | 1.48 |
| 3 coats | 5F@.023 | sf | .73 | 1.27 | 2.00 |
| Paint acoustical ceiling tile | | | | | |
| prime | 5F@.011 | sf | .35 | .61 | .96 |
| 1 coat | 5F@.011 | sf | .38 | .61 | .99 |
| 2 coats | 5F@.017 | sf | .54 | .94 | 1.48 |
| 3 coats | 5F@.023 | sf | .73 | 1.27 | 2.00 |

## Awnings and carports.

| | Craft@Hrs | Unit | Material | Labor | Total |
|---|---|---|---|---|---|
| Paint aluminum carport or awning | | | | | |
| prime | 5F@.006 | sf | .26 | .33 | .59 |
| 1 coat | 5F@.006 | sf | .29 | .33 | .62 |
| 2 coats | 5F@.010 | sf | .38 | .55 | .93 |
| 3 coats | 5F@.013 | sf | .52 | .72 | 1.24 |

## Drywall, plaster and stucco.

| | Craft@Hrs | Unit | Material | Labor | Total |
|---|---|---|---|---|---|
| Paint plaster or drywall | | | | | |
| prime | 5F@.006 | sf | .17 | .33 | .50 |
| 1 coat | 5F@.006 | sf | .18 | .33 | .51 |
| 2 coats | 5F@.010 | sf | .26 | .55 | .81 |
| 3 coats | 5F@.013 | sf | .33 | .72 | 1.05 |
| Paint stucco | | | | | |
| prime | 5F@.014 | sf | .29 | .77 | 1.06 |
| 1 coat | 5F@.015 | sf | .31 | .83 | 1.14 |
| 2 coats | 5F@.023 | sf | .42 | 1.27 | 1.69 |
| 3 coats | 5F@.030 | sf | .56 | 1.65 | 2.21 |

| | Craft@Hrs | Unit | Material | Labor | Total |
|---|---|---|---|---|---|

**Columns.** Deduct **26%** for pilasters, pilaster capitals, pilaster pedestals, and so on.

| Paint column | | | | | |
|---|---|---|---|---|---|
| prime | 5F@.017 | lf | .44 | .94 | 1.38 |
| 1 coat | 5F@.017 | lf | .50 | .94 | 1.44 |
| 2 coats | 5F@.027 | lf | .70 | 1.49 | 2.19 |
| 3 coats | 5F@.036 | lf | .92 | 1.98 | 2.90 |
| Stain & varnish column | | | | | |
| stain | 5F@.016 | lf | .47 | .88 | 1.35 |
| 1 coat | 5F@.016 | lf | .52 | .88 | 1.40 |
| 2 coats | 5F@.025 | lf | .73 | 1.38 | 2.11 |
| 3 coats | 5F@.033 | lf | .98 | 1.82 | 2.80 |
| Paint capital, simple design | | | | | |
| prime | 5F@.650 | ea | 24.60 | 35.80 | 60.40 |
| 1 coat | 5F@.670 | ea | 27.20 | 36.90 | 64.10 |
| 2 coats | 5F@1.03 | ea | 38.00 | 56.80 | 94.80 |
| 3 coats | 5F@1.40 | ea | 50.50 | 77.10 | 127.60 |
| Paint capital, complex design | | | | | |
| prime | 5F@.839 | ea | 31.90 | 46.20 | 78.10 |
| 1 coat | 5F@.863 | ea | 35.10 | 47.60 | 82.70 |
| 2 coats | 5F@1.33 | ea | 48.70 | 73.30 | 122.00 |
| 3 coats | 5F@1.80 | ea | 64.80 | 99.20 | 164.00 |
| Stain & varnish capital, simple design | | | | | |
| Stain | 5F@.670 | ea | 27.10 | 36.90 | 64.00 |
| 1 coat | 5F@.691 | ea | 30.30 | 38.10 | 68.40 |
| 2 coats | 5F@1.06 | ea | 42.10 | 58.40 | 100.50 |
| 3 coats | 5F@1.44 | ea | 55.90 | 79.30 | 135.20 |
| Stain & varnish capital, complex design | | | | | |
| stain | 5F@.930 | ea | 35.00 | 51.20 | 86.20 |
| 1 coat | 5F@.957 | ea | 38.70 | 52.70 | 91.40 |
| 2 coats | 5F@1.47 | ea | 54.10 | 81.00 | 135.10 |
| 3 coats | 5F@2.00 | ea | 71.70 | 110.00 | 181.70 |
| Paint column pedestal | | | | | |
| prime | 5F@.536 | ea | 20.40 | 29.50 | 49.90 |
| 1 coat | 5F@.552 | ea | 22.40 | 30.40 | 52.80 |
| 2 coats | 5F@.848 | ea | 31.40 | 46.70 | 78.10 |
| 3 coats | 5F@1.15 | ea | 41.40 | 63.40 | 104.80 |
| Stain & varnish column pedestal | | | | | |
| stain | 5F@.590 | ea | 22.30 | 32.50 | 54.80 |
| 1 coat | 5F@.608 | ea | 24.90 | 33.50 | 58.40 |
| 2 coats | 5F@.935 | ea | 34.50 | 51.50 | 86.00 |
| 3 coats | 5F@1.27 | ea | 45.70 | 70.00 | 115.70 |

**Concrete.**

| Paint concrete floor | | | | | |
|---|---|---|---|---|---|
| prime | 5F@.008 | sf | .23 | .44 | .67 |
| 1 coat | 5F@.008 | sf | .26 | .44 | .70 |
| 2 coats | 5F@.012 | sf | .35 | .66 | 1.01 |
| 3 coats | 5F@.016 | sf | .47 | .88 | 1.35 |

| | Craft@Hrs | Unit | Material | Labor | Total |
|---|---|---|---|---|---|
| Paint concrete wall | | | | | |
|     prime | 5F@.008 | sf | .23 | .44 | .67 |
|     1 coat | 5F@.008 | sf | .26 | .44 | .70 |
|     2 coats | 5F@.013 | sf | .35 | .72 | 1.07 |
|     3 coats | 5F@.017 | sf | .47 | .94 | 1.41 |
| Paint concrete step (per step) | | | | | |
|     prime | 5F@.023 | ea | .72 | 1.27 | 1.99 |
|     1 coat | 5F@.024 | ea | .80 | 1.32 | 2.12 |
|     2 coats | 5F@.037 | ea | 1.10 | 2.04 | 3.14 |
|     3 coats | 5F@.050 | ea | 1.46 | 2.76 | 4.22 |

**Doors.** Unless otherwise noted, does not include jamb and casing. Includes painting both sides of door. Folding and by-passing doors are for both sides of each section. Add **20%** for half-round or elliptical top door.

| | Craft@Hrs | Unit | Material | Labor | Total |
|---|---|---|---|---|---|
| Paint folding door | | | | | |
|     prime | 5F@.402 | ea | 14.10 | 22.20 | 36.30 |
|     1 coat | 5F@.413 | ea | 15.60 | 22.80 | 38.40 |
|     2 coats | 5F@.636 | ea | 21.60 | 35.00 | 56.60 |
|     3 coats | 5F@.861 | ea | 28.80 | 47.40 | 76.20 |
| Stain & varnish folding door | | | | | |
|     stain | 5F@.614 | ea | 20.90 | 33.80 | 54.70 |
|     1 coat | 5F@.632 | ea | 23.10 | 34.80 | 57.90 |
|     2 coats | 5F@.972 | ea | 32.10 | 53.60 | 85.70 |
|     3 coats | 5F@1.32 | ea | 42.40 | 72.70 | 115.10 |
| Paint half-louvered folding door | | | | | |
|     prime | 5F@.451 | ea | 15.60 | 24.90 | 40.50 |
|     1 coat | 5F@.464 | ea | 17.10 | 25.60 | 42.70 |
|     2 coats | 5F@.713 | ea | 24.30 | 39.30 | 63.60 |
|     3 coats | 5F@.966 | ea | 32.30 | 53.20 | 85.50 |
| Stain & varnish half-louvered folding door | | | | | |
|     stain | 5F@.688 | ea | 23.10 | 37.90 | 61.00 |
|     1 coat | 5F@.709 | ea | 25.30 | 39.10 | 64.40 |
|     2 coats | 5F@1.09 | ea | 35.40 | 60.10 | 95.50 |
|     3 coats | 5F@1.48 | ea | 47.30 | 81.50 | 128.80 |
| Paint full-louvered folding door | | | | | |
|     prime | 5F@.507 | ea | 17.10 | 27.90 | 45.00 |
|     1 coat | 5F@.520 | ea | 19.40 | 28.70 | 48.10 |
|     2 coats | 5F@.800 | ea | 26.80 | 44.10 | 70.90 |
|     3 coats | 5F@1.09 | ea | 35.80 | 60.10 | 95.90 |
| Stain & varnish full-louvered folding door | | | | | |
|     stain | 5F@.774 | ea | 25.30 | 42.60 | 67.90 |
|     1 coat | 5F@.796 | ea | 28.40 | 43.90 | 72.30 |
|     2 coats | 5F@1.22 | ea | 39.40 | 67.20 | 106.60 |
|     3 coats | 5F@1.66 | ea | 51.90 | 91.50 | 143.40 |
| Paint folding panel door | | | | | |
|     prime | 5F@.439 | ea | 15.40 | 24.20 | 39.60 |
|     1 coat | 5F@.453 | ea | 16.90 | 25.00 | 41.90 |
|     2 coats | 5F@.697 | ea | 23.70 | 38.40 | 62.10 |
|     3 coats | 5F@.944 | ea | 31.70 | 52.00 | 83.70 |

|  | Craft@Hrs | Unit | Material | Labor | Total |
|---|---|---|---|---|---|
| **Stain & varnish folding panel door** | | | | | |
| stain | 5F@.673 | ea | 22.40 | 37.10 | 59.50 |
| 1 coat | 5F@.693 | ea | 25.00 | 38.20 | 63.20 |
| 2 coats | 5F@1.07 | ea | 34.90 | 59.00 | 93.90 |
| 3 coats | 5F@1.44 | ea | 46.20 | 79.30 | 125.50 |
| **Paint bypassing door** | | | | | |
| prime | 5F@.830 | ea | 18.00 | 45.70 | 63.70 |
| 1 coat | 5F@.854 | ea | 19.80 | 47.10 | 66.90 |
| 2 coats | 5F@1.32 | ea | 27.30 | 72.70 | 100.00 |
| 3 coats | 5F@1.78 | ea | 36.50 | 98.10 | 134.60 |
| **Stain & varnish bypassing door** | | | | | |
| stain | 5F@1.27 | ea | 26.20 | 70.00 | 96.20 |
| 1 coat | 5F@1.31 | ea | 29.00 | 72.20 | 101.20 |
| 2 coats | 5F@2.01 | ea | 40.20 | 111.00 | 151.20 |
| 3 coats | 5F@2.72 | ea | 53.80 | 150.00 | 203.80 |
| **Paint half-louvered bypassing door** | | | | | |
| prime | 5F@.933 | ea | 19.90 | 51.40 | 71.30 |
| 1 coat | 5F@.960 | ea | 22.00 | 52.90 | 74.90 |
| 2 coats | 5F@1.48 | ea | 30.60 | 81.50 | 112.10 |
| 3 coats | 5F@2.00 | ea | 40.50 | 110.00 | 150.50 |
| **Stain & varnish half-louvered bypassing door** | | | | | |
| stain | 5F@1.43 | ea | 29.00 | 78.80 | 107.80 |
| 1 coat | 5F@1.47 | ea | 32.40 | 81.00 | 113.40 |
| 2 coats | 5F@2.26 | ea | 44.90 | 125.00 | 169.90 |
| 3 coats | 5F@3.05 | ea | 59.60 | 168.00 | 227.60 |
| **Paint full-louvered bypassing door** | | | | | |
| prime | 5F@1.05 | ea | 22.00 | 57.90 | 79.90 |
| 1 coat | 5F@1.08 | ea | 24.50 | 59.50 | 84.00 |
| 2 coats | 5F@1.66 | ea | 34.10 | 91.50 | 125.60 |
| 3 coats | 5F@2.24 | ea | 45.10 | 123.00 | 168.10 |
| **Stain & varnish full-louvered bypassing door** | | | | | |
| stain | 5F@1.60 | ea | 32.40 | 88.20 | 120.60 |
| 1 coat | 5F@1.65 | ea | 35.90 | 90.90 | 126.80 |
| 2 coats | 5F@2.53 | ea | 50.00 | 139.00 | 189.00 |
| 3 coats | 5F@3.43 | ea | 66.40 | 189.00 | 255.40 |
| **Paint bypassing panel door** | | | | | |
| prime | 5F@.899 | ea | 19.80 | 49.50 | 69.30 |
| 1 coat | 5F@.926 | ea | 21.90 | 51.00 | 72.90 |
| 2 coats | 5F@1.42 | ea | 30.40 | 78.20 | 108.60 |
| 3 coats | 5F@1.93 | ea | 40.20 | 106.00 | 146.20 |
| **Stain & varnish bypassing panel door** | | | | | |
| stain | 5F@1.38 | ea | 28.90 | 76.00 | 104.90 |
| 1 coat | 5F@1.42 | ea | 32.30 | 78.20 | 110.50 |
| 2 coats | 5F@2.18 | ea | 44.80 | 120.00 | 164.80 |
| 3 coats | 5F@2.96 | ea | 59.30 | 163.00 | 222.30 |
| **Paint interior door** | | | | | |
| prime | 5F@.340 | ea | 10.70 | 18.70 | 29.40 |
| 1 coat | 5F@.349 | ea | 11.70 | 19.20 | 30.90 |
| 2 coats | 5F@.538 | ea | 16.20 | 29.60 | 45.80 |
| 3 coats | 5F@.729 | ea | 22.20 | 40.20 | 62.40 |

| | Craft@Hrs | Unit | Material | Labor | Total |
|---|---|---|---|---|---|
| **Stain & varnish interior door** | | | | | |
| stain | 5F@.519 | ea | 15.90 | 28.60 | 44.50 |
| 1 coat | 5F@.534 | ea | 18.10 | 29.40 | 47.50 |
| 2 coats | 5F@.822 | ea | 24.90 | 45.30 | 70.20 |
| 3 coats | 5F@1.11 | ea | 32.60 | 61.20 | 93.80 |
| **Paint half-louvered door** | | | | | |
| prime | 5F@.381 | ea | 11.70 | 21.00 | 32.70 |
| 1 coat | 5F@.392 | ea | 13.20 | 21.60 | 34.80 |
| 2 coats | 5F@.603 | ea | 18.30 | 33.20 | 51.50 |
| 3 coats | 5F@.818 | ea | 24.30 | 45.10 | 69.40 |
| **Stain & varnish half-louvered door** | | | | | |
| stain | 5F@.583 | ea | 18.00 | 32.10 | 50.10 |
| 1 coat | 5F@.601 | ea | 19.80 | 33.10 | 52.90 |
| 2 coats | 5F@.924 | ea | 27.30 | 50.90 | 78.20 |
| 3 coats | 5F@1.25 | ea | 36.50 | 68.90 | 105.40 |
| **Paint full-louvered door** | | | | | |
| prime | 5F@.428 | ea | 13.20 | 23.60 | 36.80 |
| 1 coat | 5F@.439 | ea | 14.60 | 24.20 | 38.80 |
| 2 coats | 5F@.677 | ea | 20.40 | 37.30 | 57.70 |
| 3 coats | 5F@.917 | ea | 26.80 | 50.50 | 77.30 |
| **Stain & varnish full-louvered door** | | | | | |
| stain | 5F@.655 | ea | 19.90 | 36.10 | 56.00 |
| 1 coat | 5F@.673 | ea | 22.00 | 37.10 | 59.10 |
| 2 coats | 5F@1.04 | ea | 30.60 | 57.30 | 87.90 |
| 3 coats | 5F@1.40 | ea | 40.50 | 77.10 | 117.60 |
| **Paint door jamb & casing** | | | | | |
| prime | 5F@.013 | lf | .29 | .72 | 1.01 |
| 1 coat | 5F@.011 | lf | .31 | .61 | .92 |
| 2 coats | 5F@.017 | lf | .42 | .94 | 1.36 |
| 3 coats | 5F@.023 | lf | .56 | 1.27 | 1.83 |
| **Stain & varnish door jamb & casing** | | | | | |
| stain | 5F@.019 | lf | .41 | 1.05 | 1.46 |
| 1 coat | 5F@.017 | lf | .46 | .94 | 1.40 |
| 2 coats | 5F@.026 | lf | .64 | 1.43 | 2.07 |
| 3 coats | 5F@.035 | lf | .86 | 1.93 | 2.79 |
| **Paint French door** | | | | | |
| prime | 5F@.818 | ea | 18.30 | 45.10 | 63.40 |
| 1 coat | 5F@.841 | ea | 20.40 | 46.30 | 66.70 |
| 2 coats | 5F@1.30 | ea | 28.00 | 71.60 | 99.60 |
| 3 coats | 5F@1.75 | ea | 37.20 | 96.40 | 133.60 |
| **Stain & varnish French door** | | | | | |
| stain | 5F@1.25 | ea | 26.60 | 68.90 | 95.50 |
| 1 coat | 5F@1.29 | ea | 29.50 | 71.10 | 100.60 |
| 2 coats | 5F@1.98 | ea | 41.00 | 109.00 | 150.00 |
| 3 coats | 5F@2.68 | ea | 54.70 | 148.00 | 202.70 |
| **Paint full-lite door** | | | | | |
| prime | 5F@.587 | ea | 17.80 | 32.30 | 50.10 |
| 1 coat | 5F@.605 | ea | 19.70 | 33.30 | 53.00 |
| 2 coats | 5F@.930 | ea | 27.10 | 51.20 | 78.30 |
| 3 coats | 5F@1.26 | ea | 36.10 | 69.40 | 105.50 |

| | Craft@Hrs | Unit | Material | Labor | Total |
|---|---|---|---|---|---|
| **Stain & varnish full-lite door** | | | | | |
| stain | 5F@.899 | ea | 26.10 | 49.50 | 75.60 |
| 1 coat | 5F@.926 | ea | 28.90 | 51.00 | 79.90 |
| 2 coats | 5F@1.42 | ea | 40.20 | 78.20 | 118.40 |
| 3 coats | 5F@1.93 | ea | 53.60 | 106.00 | 159.60 |
| **Paint panel door** | | | | | |
| prime | 5F@.704 | ea | 19.40 | 38.80 | 58.20 |
| 1 coat | 5F@.724 | ea | 21.50 | 39.90 | 61.40 |
| 2 coats | 5F@1.11 | ea | 29.80 | 61.20 | 91.00 |
| 3 coats | 5F@1.51 | ea | 39.80 | 83.20 | 123.00 |
| **Stain & varnish panel door** | | | | | |
| stain | 5F@1.08 | ea | 28.50 | 59.50 | 88.00 |
| 1 coat | 5F@1.11 | ea | 31.90 | 61.20 | 93.10 |
| 2 coats | 5F@1.70 | ea | 44.10 | 93.70 | 137.80 |
| 3 coats | 5F@2.31 | ea | 58.70 | 127.00 | 185.70 |
| **Paint transom** | | | | | |
| prime | 5F@.370 | ea | 8.80 | 20.40 | 29.20 |
| 1 coat | 5F@.381 | ea | 9.76 | 21.00 | 30.76 |
| 2 coats | 5F@.585 | ea | 13.40 | 32.20 | 45.60 |
| 3 coats | 5F@.794 | ea | 18.20 | 43.70 | 61.90 |
| **Stain & varnish transom** | | | | | |
| stain | 5F@.565 | ea | 12.90 | 31.10 | 44.00 |
| 1 coat | 5F@.583 | ea | 14.40 | 32.10 | 46.50 |
| 2 coats | 5F@.897 | ea | 19.90 | 49.40 | 69.30 |
| 3 coats | 5F@1.21 | ea | 26.40 | 66.70 | 93.10 |
| **Paint storm door** | | | | | |
| prime | 5F@.379 | ea | 9.14 | 20.90 | 30.04 |
| 1 coat | 5F@.390 | ea | 10.10 | 21.50 | 31.60 |
| 2 coats | 5F@.601 | ea | 14.10 | 33.10 | 47.20 |
| 3 coats | 5F@.814 | ea | 18.80 | 44.90 | 63.70 |
| **Stain & varnish storm door** | | | | | |
| stain | 5F@.581 | ea | 13.40 | 32.00 | 45.40 |
| 1 coat | 5F@.599 | ea | 15.10 | 33.00 | 48.10 |
| 2 coats | 5F@.919 | ea | 21.00 | 50.60 | 71.60 |
| 3 coats | 5F@1.25 | ea | 27.40 | 68.90 | 96.30 |
| **Paint Dutch door** | | | | | |
| prime | 5F@.666 | ea | 19.20 | 36.70 | 55.90 |
| 1 coat | 5F@.686 | ea | 21.40 | 37.80 | 59.20 |
| 2 coats | 5F@1.06 | ea | 29.70 | 58.40 | 88.10 |
| 3 coats | 5F@1.43 | ea | 39.50 | 78.80 | 118.30 |
| **Stain & varnish Dutch door** | | | | | |
| stain | 5F@1.02 | ea | 28.10 | 56.20 | 84.30 |
| 1 coat | 5F@1.05 | ea | 31.40 | 57.90 | 89.30 |
| 2 coats | 5F@1.61 | ea | 43.50 | 88.70 | 132.20 |
| 3 coats | 5F@2.19 | ea | 58.10 | 121.00 | 179.10 |
| **Paint steel entry door** | | | | | |
| prime | 5F@.621 | ea | 17.00 | 34.20 | 51.20 |
| 1 coat | 5F@.639 | ea | 19.10 | 35.20 | 54.30 |
| 2 coats | 5F@.982 | ea | 26.50 | 54.10 | 80.60 |
| 3 coats | 5F@1.33 | ea | 35.20 | 73.30 | 108.50 |

|  | Craft@Hrs | Unit | Material | Labor | Total |
|---|---|---|---|---|---|
| **Paint wood entry door** | | | | | |
| prime | 5F@.742 | ea | 18.60 | 40.90 | 59.50 |
| 1 coat | 5F@.763 | ea | 19.90 | 42.00 | 61.90 |
| 2 coats | 5F@1.18 | ea | 27.00 | 65.00 | 92.00 |
| 3 coats | 5F@1.59 | ea | 37.90 | 87.60 | 125.50 |
| **Stain & varnish wood entry door** | | | | | |
| stain | 5F@1.13 | ea | 26.60 | 62.30 | 88.90 |
| 1 coat | 5F@1.17 | ea | 28.90 | 64.50 | 93.40 |
| 2 coats | 5F@1.80 | ea | 37.20 | 99.20 | 136.40 |
| 3 coats | 5F@2.43 | ea | 51.80 | 134.00 | 185.80 |
| **Paint entry door side lite** | | | | | |
| prime | 5F@.673 | ea | 14.60 | 37.10 | 51.70 |
| 1 coat | 5F@.691 | ea | 16.10 | 38.10 | 54.20 |
| 2 coats | 5F@1.06 | ea | 22.40 | 58.40 | 80.80 |
| 3 coats | 5F@1.44 | ea | 29.90 | 79.30 | 109.20 |
| **Stain & varnish entry door side lite** | | | | | |
| stain | 5F@1.03 | ea | 21.40 | 56.80 | 78.20 |
| 1 coat | 5F@1.06 | ea | 23.80 | 58.40 | 82.20 |
| 2 coats | 5F@1.63 | ea | 33.00 | 89.80 | 122.80 |
| 3 coats | 5F@2.20 | ea | 44.10 | 121.00 | 165.10 |
| **Paint entry door fan lite** | | | | | |
| prime | 5F@.635 | ea | 12.90 | 35.00 | 47.90 |
| 1 coat | 5F@.655 | ea | 14.40 | 36.10 | 50.50 |
| 2 coats | 5F@1.01 | ea | 20.00 | 55.70 | 75.70 |
| 3 coats | 5F@1.36 | ea | 26.50 | 74.90 | 101.40 |
| **Stain & varnish entry door fan lite** | | | | | |
| stain | 5F@.971 | ea | 19.00 | 53.50 | 72.50 |
| 1 coat | 5F@1.00 | ea | 21.20 | 55.10 | 76.30 |
| 2 coats | 5F@1.54 | ea | 29.10 | 84.90 | 114.00 |
| 3 coats | 5F@2.08 | ea | 38.70 | 115.00 | 153.70 |
| **Paint cafe doors** | | | | | |
| prime | 5F@.592 | ea | 14.40 | 32.60 | 47.00 |
| 1 coat | 5F@.610 | ea | 15.80 | 33.60 | 49.40 |
| 2 coats | 5F@.937 | ea | 22.00 | 51.60 | 73.60 |
| 3 coats | 5F@1.27 | ea | 29.30 | 70.00 | 99.30 |
| **Stain & varnish cafe doors** | | | | | |
| stain | 5F@.906 | ea | 21.20 | 49.90 | 71.10 |
| 1 coat | 5F@.933 | ea | 23.40 | 51.40 | 74.80 |
| 2 coats | 5F@1.43 | ea | 32.50 | 78.80 | 111.30 |
| 3 coats | 5F@1.94 | ea | 43.20 | 107.00 | 150.20 |
| **Paint wood sliding patio door** | | | | | |
| prime | 5F@.646 | ea | 6.20 | 35.60 | 41.80 |
| 1 coat | 5F@.665 | ea | 6.90 | 36.60 | 43.50 |
| 2 coats | 5F@1.02 | ea | 9.56 | 56.20 | 65.76 |
| 3 coats | 5F@1.39 | ea | 12.70 | 76.60 | 89.30 |
| **Stain & varnish wood sliding patio door** | | | | | |
| stain | 5F@.988 | ea | 9.09 | 54.40 | 63.49 |
| 1 coat | 5F@1.02 | ea | 10.10 | 56.20 | 66.30 |
| 2 coats | 5F@1.56 | ea | 14.00 | 86.00 | 100.00 |
| 3 coats | 5F@2.12 | ea | 18.60 | 117.00 | 135.60 |

| | Craft@Hrs | Unit | Material | Labor | Total |
|---|---|---|---|---|---|
| Paint garage door | | | | | |
| prime | 5F@.006 | sf | .26 | .33 | .59 |
| 1 coat | 5F@.006 | sf | .29 | .33 | .62 |
| 2 coats | 5F@.009 | sf | .38 | .50 | .88 |
| 3 coats | 5F@.013 | sf | .52 | .72 | 1.24 |
| Stain & varnish garage door | | | | | |
| stain | 5F@.009 | sf | .36 | .50 | .86 |
| 1 coat | 5F@.009 | sf | .41 | .50 | .91 |
| 2 coats | 5F@.014 | sf | .56 | .77 | 1.33 |
| 3 coats | 5F@.019 | sf | .74 | 1.05 | 1.79 |

## Medicine cabinet.

| | Craft@Hrs | Unit | Material | Labor | Total |
|---|---|---|---|---|---|
| Paint medicine cabinet | | | | | |
| prime | 5F@.404 | ea | 4.23 | 22.30 | 26.53 |
| 1 coat | 5F@.417 | ea | 4.73 | 23.00 | 27.73 |
| 2 coats | 5F@.639 | ea | 6.55 | 35.20 | 41.75 |
| 3 coats | 5F@.868 | ea | 8.67 | 47.80 | 56.47 |
| Stain & varnish medicine cabinet | | | | | |
| stain | 5F@.619 | ea | 6.21 | 34.10 | 40.31 |
| 1 coat | 5F@.637 | ea | 6.92 | 35.10 | 42.02 |
| 2 coats | 5F@.978 | ea | 9.58 | 53.90 | 63.48 |
| 3 coats | 5F@1.32 | ea | 12.80 | 72.70 | 85.50 |

## Exterior light fixture post.

| | Craft@Hrs | Unit | Material | Labor | Total |
|---|---|---|---|---|---|
| Paint exterior light-fixture post | | | | | |
| prime | 5F@.079 | ea | 5.15 | 4.35 | 9.50 |
| 1 coat | 5F@.081 | ea | 5.73 | 4.46 | 10.19 |
| 2 coats | 5F@.125 | ea | 7.96 | 6.89 | 14.85 |
| 3 coats | 5F@.170 | ea | 10.60 | 9.37 | 19.97 |

**Fences.** Wood fence prices are for one side only. Ornamental iron fence prices are for both sides.

| | Craft@Hrs | Unit | Material | Labor | Total |
|---|---|---|---|---|---|
| Paint 4' high wood fence | | | | | |
| prime | 5F@.051 | lf | 1.15 | 2.81 | 3.96 |
| 1 coat | 5F@.053 | lf | 1.28 | 2.92 | 4.20 |
| 2 coats | 5F@.081 | lf | 1.80 | 4.46 | 6.26 |
| 3 coats | 5F@.109 | lf | 2.37 | 6.01 | 8.38 |
| Seal or stain 4' high wood fence | | | | | |
| varnish | 5F@.078 | lf | 1.68 | 4.30 | 5.98 |
| 1 coat | 5F@.080 | lf | 1.89 | 4.41 | 6.30 |
| 2 coats | 5F@.123 | lf | 2.62 | 6.78 | 9.40 |
| 3 coats | 5F@.167 | lf | 3.48 | 9.20 | 12.68 |
| Paint 6' high wood fence | | | | | |
| prime | 5F@.077 | lf | 1.68 | 4.24 | 5.92 |
| 1 coat | 5F@.079 | lf | 1.89 | 4.35 | 6.24 |
| 2 coats | 5F@.122 | lf | 2.62 | 6.72 | 9.34 |
| 3 coats | 5F@.165 | lf | 3.48 | 9.09 | 12.57 |

| | Craft@Hrs | Unit | Material | Labor | Total |
|---|---|---|---|---|---|
| Seal or stain 6' high wood fence | | | | | |
| varnish | 5F@.117 | lf | 2.49 | 6.45 | 8.94 |
| 1 coat | 5F@.121 | lf | 2.75 | 6.67 | 9.42 |
| 2 coats | 5F@.186 | lf | 3.84 | 10.20 | 14.04 |
| 3 coats | 5F@.251 | lf | 5.11 | 13.80 | 18.91 |
| Paint 8' high wood fence | | | | | |
| prime | 5F@.102 | lf | 2.21 | 5.62 | 7.83 |
| 1 coat | 5F@.105 | lf | 2.46 | 5.79 | 8.25 |
| 2 coats | 5F@.162 | lf | 3.43 | 8.93 | 12.36 |
| 3 coats | 5F@.219 | lf | 4.55 | 12.10 | 16.65 |
| Seal or stain 8' high wood fence | | | | | |
| varnish | 5F@.156 | lf | 3.26 | 8.60 | 11.86 |
| 1 coat | 5F@.161 | lf | 3.61 | 8.87 | 12.48 |
| 2 coats | 5F@.247 | lf | 5.04 | 13.60 | 18.64 |
| 3 coats | 5F@.334 | lf | 6.68 | 18.40 | 25.08 |
| Paint 3' high picket fence | | | | | |
| prime | 5F@.041 | lf | .89 | 2.26 | 3.15 |
| 1 coat | 5F@.042 | lf | .99 | 2.31 | 3.30 |
| 2 coats | 5F@.064 | lf | 1.36 | 3.53 | 4.89 |
| 3 coats | 5F@.087 | lf | 1.83 | 4.79 | 6.62 |
| Paint 5' high picket fence | | | | | |
| prime | 5F@.065 | lf | 1.44 | 3.58 | 5.02 |
| 1 coat | 5F@.067 | lf | 1.58 | 3.69 | 5.27 |
| 2 coats | 5F@.103 | lf | 2.20 | 5.68 | 7.88 |
| 3 coats | 5F@.140 | lf | 2.93 | 7.71 | 10.64 |
| Paint 48" high ornamental iron fence | | | | | |
| prime | 5F@.077 | lf | 1.60 | 4.24 | 5.84 |
| 1 coat | 5F@.079 | lf | 1.81 | 4.35 | 6.16 |
| 2 coats | 5F@.121 | lf | 2.49 | 6.67 | 9.16 |
| 3 coats | 5F@.164 | lf | 3.30 | 9.04 | 12.34 |
| Paint 60" high ornamental iron fence | | | | | |
| prime | 5F@.096 | lf | 2.15 | 5.29 | 7.44 |
| 1 coat | 5F@.098 | lf | 2.40 | 5.40 | 7.80 |
| 2 coats | 5F@.151 | lf | 3.32 | 8.32 | 11.64 |
| 3 coats | 5F@.205 | lf | 4.43 | 11.30 | 15.73 |
| Paint 72" high ornamental iron fence | | | | | |
| prime | 5F@.115 | lf | 3.03 | 6.34 | 9.37 |
| 1 coat | 5F@.118 | lf | 3.35 | 6.50 | 9.85 |
| 2 coats | 5F@.182 | lf | 4.68 | 10.00 | 14.68 |
| 3 coats | 5F@.247 | lf | 6.21 | 13.60 | 19.81 |

**Finish carpentry.**

| | Craft@Hrs | Unit | Material | Labor | Total |
|---|---|---|---|---|---|
| Paint wood trim, simple design | | | | | |
| prime | 5F@.011 | lf | .17 | .61 | .78 |
| 1 coat | 5F@.011 | lf | .18 | .61 | .79 |
| 2 coats | 5F@.017 | lf | .26 | .94 | 1.20 |
| 3 coats | 5F@.023 | lf | .33 | 1.27 | 1.60 |

| | Craft@Hrs | Unit | Material | Labor | Total |
|---|---|---|---|---|---|
| Stain & varnish wood trim, simple design | | | | | |
| stain | 5F@.016 | lf | .26 | .88 | 1.14 |
| 1 coat | 5F@.017 | lf | .18 | .94 | 1.12 |
| 2 coats | 5F@.026 | lf | .26 | 1.43 | 1.69 |
| 3 coats | 5F@.035 | lf | .33 | 1.93 | 2.26 |
| Paint wood trim, ornate design | | | | | |
| prime | 5F@.013 | lf | .22 | .72 | .94 |
| 1 coat | 5F@.014 | lf | .24 | .77 | 1.01 |
| 2 coats | 5F@.021 | lf | .33 | 1.16 | 1.49 |
| 3 coats | 5F@.028 | lf | .44 | 1.54 | 1.98 |
| Stain & varnish wood trim, ornate design | | | | | |
| stain | 5F@.020 | lf | .32 | 1.10 | 1.42 |
| 1 coat | 5F@.021 | lf | .35 | 1.16 | 1.51 |
| 2 coats | 5F@.032 | lf | .50 | 1.76 | 2.26 |
| 3 coats | 5F@.044 | lf | .66 | 2.42 | 3.08 |
| Paint wood trim, very ornate design | | | | | |
| prime | 5F@.017 | lf | .26 | .94 | 1.20 |
| 1 coat | 5F@.017 | lf | .29 | .94 | 1.23 |
| 2 coats | 5F@.026 | lf | .38 | 1.43 | 1.81 |
| 3 coats | 5F@.035 | lf | .52 | 1.93 | 2.45 |
| Stain & varnish wood trim, very ornate design | | | | | |
| stain | 5F@.025 | lf | .36 | 1.38 | 1.74 |
| 1 coat | 5F@.026 | lf | .41 | 1.43 | 1.84 |
| 2 coats | 5F@.040 | lf | .56 | 2.20 | 2.76 |
| 3 coats | 5F@.054 | lf | .74 | 2.98 | 3.72 |
| Paint interior architrave, simple design | | | | | |
| prime | 5F@.015 | lf | .26 | .83 | 1.09 |
| 1 coat | 5F@.015 | lf | .29 | .83 | 1.12 |
| 2 coats | 5F@.023 | lf | .38 | 1.27 | 1.65 |
| 3 coats | 5F@.032 | lf | .52 | 1.76 | 2.28 |
| Stain & varnish interior architrave, simple design | | | | | |
| stain | 5F@.023 | lf | .36 | 1.27 | 1.63 |
| 1 coat | 5F@.023 | lf | .41 | 1.27 | 1.68 |
| 2 coats | 5F@.036 | lf | .56 | 1.98 | 2.54 |
| 3 coats | 5F@.048 | lf | .74 | 2.64 | 3.38 |
| Paint interior architrave, complex design | | | | | |
| prime | 5F@.030 | lf | .35 | 1.65 | 2.00 |
| 1 coat | 5F@.030 | lf | .38 | 1.65 | 2.03 |
| 2 coats | 5F@.047 | lf | .54 | 2.59 | 3.13 |
| 3 coats | 5F@.063 | lf | .73 | 3.47 | 4.20 |
| Stain & varnish interior architrave, complex design | | | | | |
| stain | 5F@.045 | lf | .52 | 2.48 | 3.00 |
| 1 coat | 5F@.047 | lf | .58 | 2.59 | 3.17 |
| 2 coats | 5F@.072 | lf | .84 | 3.97 | 4.81 |
| 3 coats | 5F@.097 | lf | 1.09 | 5.34 | 6.43 |
| Paint exterior architrave, simple design | | | | | |
| prime | 5F@.033 | lf | .49 | 1.82 | 2.31 |
| 1 coat | 5F@.035 | lf | .53 | 1.93 | 2.46 |
| 2 coats | 5F@.053 | lf | .74 | 2.92 | 3.66 |
| 3 coats | 5F@.072 | lf | .99 | 3.97 | 4.96 |

|  | Craft@Hrs | Unit | Material | Labor | Total |
|---|---|---|---|---|---|
| **Paint exterior architrave, complex design** | | | | | |
| prime | 5F@.067 | lf | .99 | 3.69 | 4.68 |
| 1 coat | 5F@.069 | lf | 1.10 | 3.80 | 4.90 |
| 2 coats | 5F@.106 | lf | 1.53 | 5.84 | 7.37 |
| 3 coats | 5F@.143 | lf | 2.04 | 7.88 | 9.92 |
| **Paint exterior door surround, simple design** | | | | | |
| prime | 5F@.117 | lf | 1.98 | 6.45 | 8.43 |
| 1 coat | 5F@.120 | lf | 2.19 | 6.61 | 8.80 |
| 2 coats | 5F@.185 | lf | 3.04 | 10.20 | 13.24 |
| 3 coats | 5F@.251 | lf | 4.02 | 13.80 | 17.82 |
| **Paint exterior door surround, complex design** | | | | | |
| prime | 5F@.287 | lf | 4.20 | 15.80 | 20.00 |
| 1 coat | 5F@.296 | lf | 4.65 | 16.30 | 20.95 |
| 2 coats | 5F@.455 | lf | 6.45 | 25.10 | 31.55 |
| 3 coats | 5F@.617 | lf | 8.60 | 34.00 | 42.60 |
| **Paint exterior window surround, simple design** | | | | | |
| prime | 5F@.117 | lf | 1.98 | 6.45 | 8.43 |
| 1 coat | 5F@.120 | lf | 2.19 | 6.61 | 8.80 |
| 2 coats | 5F@.185 | lf | 3.04 | 10.20 | 13.24 |
| 3 coats | 5F@.251 | lf | 4.02 | 13.80 | 17.82 |
| **Paint exterior window surround, complex design** | | | | | |
| prime | 5F@.287 | lf | 4.20 | 15.80 | 20.00 |
| 1 coat | 5F@.296 | lf | 4.65 | 16.30 | 20.95 |
| 2 coats | 5F@.455 | lf | 6.45 | 25.10 | 31.55 |
| 3 coats | 5F@.617 | lf | 8.60 | 34.00 | 42.60 |
| **Paint closet rod, shelf, and brackets** | | | | | |
| prime | 5F@.127 | lf | .31 | 7.00 | 7.31 |
| 1 coat | 5F@.131 | lf | .34 | 7.22 | 7.56 |
| 2 coats | 5F@.201 | lf | .47 | 11.10 | 11.57 |
| 3 coats | 5F@.274 | lf | .63 | 15.10 | 15.73 |
| **Paint closet organizer system** | | | | | |
| prime | 5F@.011 | sf | .34 | .61 | .95 |
| 1 coat | 5F@.011 | sf | .37 | .61 | .98 |
| 2 coats | 5F@.017 | sf | .53 | .94 | 1.47 |
| 3 coats | 5F@.023 | sf | .72 | 1.27 | 1.99 |
| **Paint bookcase** | | | | | |
| prime | 5F@.014 | sf | .78 | .77 | 1.55 |
| 1 coat | 5F@.015 | sf | .87 | .83 | 1.70 |
| 2 coats | 5F@.023 | sf | 1.18 | 1.27 | 2.45 |
| 3 coats | 5F@.030 | sf | 1.58 | 1.65 | 3.23 |
| **Stain & varnish bookcase** | | | | | |
| stain | 5F@.022 | sf | 1.13 | 1.21 | 2.34 |
| 1 coat | 5F@.023 | sf | 1.25 | 1.27 | 2.52 |
| 2 coats | 5F@.035 | sf | 1.71 | 1.93 | 3.64 |
| 3 coats | 5F@.047 | sf | 2.33 | 2.59 | 4.92 |
| **Paint fireplace mantel beam** | | | | | |
| prime | 5F@.018 | lf | .38 | .99 | 1.37 |
| 1 coat | 5F@.018 | lf | .43 | .99 | 1.42 |
| 2 coats | 5F@.028 | lf | .60 | 1.54 | 2.14 |
| 3 coats | 5F@.038 | lf | .80 | 2.09 | 2.89 |

| | Craft@Hrs | Unit | Material | Labor | Total |
|---|---|---|---|---|---|
| **Stain & varnish mantel beam** | | | | | |
| stain | 5F@.027 | lf | .58 | 1.49 | 2.07 |
| 1 coat | 5F@.028 | lf | .64 | 1.54 | 2.18 |
| 2 coats | 5F@.043 | lf | .89 | 2.37 | 3.26 |
| 3 coats | 5F@.059 | lf | 1.17 | 3.25 | 4.42 |
| **Paint fireplace mantel** | | | | | |
| prime | 5F@.025 | lf | .52 | 1.38 | 1.90 |
| 1 coat | 5F@.026 | lf | .58 | 1.43 | 2.01 |
| 2 coats | 5F@.040 | lf | .84 | 2.20 | 3.04 |
| 3 coats | 5F@.054 | lf | 1.09 | 2.98 | 4.07 |
| **Stain & varnish mantel** | | | | | |
| stain | 5F@.038 | lf | .78 | 2.09 | 2.87 |
| 1 coat | 5F@.039 | lf | .87 | 2.15 | 3.02 |
| 2 coats | 5F@.061 | lf | 1.18 | 3.36 | 4.54 |
| 3 coats | 5F@.082 | lf | 1.58 | 4.52 | 6.10 |
| **Paint coffered ceiling, simple design** | | | | | |
| prime | 5F@.017 | sf | .62 | .94 | 1.56 |
| 1 coat | 5F@.018 | sf | .69 | .99 | 1.68 |
| 2 coats | 5F@.027 | sf | .97 | 1.49 | 2.46 |
| 3 coats | 5F@.037 | sf | 1.25 | 2.04 | 3.29 |
| **Stain & varnish coffered ceiling, simple design** | | | | | |
| stain | 5F@.026 | sf | .90 | 1.43 | 2.33 |
| 1 coat | 5F@.027 | sf | 1.01 | 1.49 | 2.50 |
| 2 coats | 5F@.042 | sf | 1.38 | 2.31 | 3.69 |
| 3 coats | 5F@.056 | sf | 1.85 | 3.09 | 4.94 |
| **Paint coffered ceiling, complex design** | | | | | |
| prime | 5F@.041 | sf | 1.10 | 2.26 | 3.36 |
| 1 coat | 5F@.042 | sf | 1.23 | 2.31 | 3.54 |
| 2 coats | 5F@.065 | sf | 1.69 | 3.58 | 5.27 |
| 3 coats | 5F@.089 | sf | 2.26 | 4.90 | 7.16 |
| **Stain & varnish coffered ceiling, complex design** | | | | | |
| stain | 5F@.063 | sf | 1.60 | 3.47 | 5.07 |
| 1 coat | 5F@.065 | sf | 1.81 | 3.58 | 5.39 |
| 2 coats | 5F@.100 | sf | 2.49 | 5.51 | 8.00 |
| 3 coats | 5F@.135 | sf | 3.30 | 7.44 | 10.74 |
| **Paint niche** | | | | | |
| prime | 5F@.538 | ea | 10.10 | 29.60 | 39.70 |
| 1 coat | 5F@.554 | ea | 11.20 | 30.50 | 41.70 |
| 2 coats | 5F@.852 | ea | 15.50 | 46.90 | 62.40 |
| 3 coats | 5F@1.15 | ea | 20.90 | 63.40 | 84.30 |
| **Stain & varnish niche** | | | | | |
| stain | 5F@.823 | ea | 14.90 | 45.30 | 60.20 |
| 1 coat | 5F@.845 | ea | 16.20 | 46.60 | 62.80 |
| 2 coats | 5F@1.30 | ea | 22.80 | 71.60 | 94.40 |
| 3 coats | 5F@1.76 | ea | 30.40 | 97.00 | 127.40 |
| **Paint gingerbread running trim** | | | | | |
| prime | 5F@.045 | lf | 1.56 | 2.48 | 4.04 |
| 1 coat | 5F@.047 | lf | 1.71 | 2.59 | 4.30 |
| 2 coats | 5F@.072 | lf | 2.43 | 3.97 | 6.40 |
| 3 coats | 5F@.097 | lf | 3.23 | 5.34 | 8.57 |

| | Craft@Hrs | Unit | Material | Labor | Total |
|---|---|---|---|---|---|
| **Stain & varnish gingerbread running trim** | | | | | |
| stain | 5F@.069 | lf | 2.31 | 3.80 | 6.11 |
| 1 coat | 5F@.071 | lf | 2.53 | 3.91 | 6.44 |
| 2 coats | 5F@.110 | lf | 3.54 | 6.06 | 9.60 |
| 3 coats | 5F@.148 | lf | 4.73 | 8.15 | 12.88 |
| **Paint gingerbread bracket** | | | | | |
| prime | 5F@.336 | ea | 2.37 | 18.50 | 20.87 |
| 1 coat | 5F@.345 | ea | 2.64 | 19.00 | 21.64 |
| 2 coats | 5F@.534 | ea | 3.67 | 29.40 | 33.07 |
| 3 coats | 5F@.722 | ea | 4.86 | 39.80 | 44.66 |
| **Stain & varnish gingerbread bracket** | | | | | |
| stain | 5F@.516 | ea | 3.48 | 28.40 | 31.88 |
| 1 coat | 5F@.529 | ea | 3.85 | 29.10 | 32.95 |
| 2 coats | 5F@.814 | ea | 5.37 | 44.90 | 50.27 |
| 3 coats | 5F@1.10 | ea | 7.10 | 60.60 | 67.70 |
| **Paint gingerbread corbel** | | | | | |
| prime | 5F@.330 | ea | 2.33 | 18.20 | 20.53 |
| 1 coat | 5F@.341 | ea | 2.59 | 18.80 | 21.39 |
| 2 coats | 5F@.522 | ea | 3.58 | 28.80 | 32.38 |
| 3 coats | 5F@.709 | ea | 4.77 | 39.10 | 43.87 |
| **Stain & varnish gingerbread corbel** | | | | | |
| stain | 5F@.504 | ea | 3.42 | 27.80 | 31.22 |
| 1 coat | 5F@.520 | ea | 3.80 | 28.70 | 32.50 |
| 2 coats | 5F@.800 | ea | 5.28 | 44.10 | 49.38 |
| 3 coats | 5F@1.08 | ea | 7.01 | 59.50 | 66.51 |
| **Paint gingerbread door or window header** | | | | | |
| prime | 5F@.054 | lf | .78 | 2.98 | 3.76 |
| 1 coat | 5F@.055 | lf | .87 | 3.03 | 3.90 |
| 2 coats | 5F@.085 | lf | 1.18 | 4.68 | 5.86 |
| 3 coats | 5F@.115 | lf | 1.58 | 6.34 | 7.92 |
| **Stain & varnish gingerbread door or window header** | | | | | |
| stain | 5F@.082 | lf | 1.13 | 4.52 | 5.65 |
| 1 coat | 5F@.084 | lf | 1.25 | 4.63 | 5.88 |
| 2 coats | 5F@.130 | lf | 1.71 | 7.16 | 8.87 |
| 3 coats | 5F@.176 | lf | 2.33 | 9.70 | 12.03 |
| **Paint gingerbread spandrel** | | | | | |
| prime | 5F@.075 | lf | .82 | 4.13 | 4.95 |
| 1 coat | 5F@.077 | lf | .90 | 4.24 | 5.14 |
| 2 coats | 5F@.119 | lf | 1.24 | 6.56 | 7.80 |
| 3 coats | 5F@.161 | lf | 1.63 | 8.87 | 10.50 |
| **Stain & varnish gingerbread spandrel** | | | | | |
| stain | 5F@.115 | lf | 1.17 | 6.34 | 7.51 |
| 1 coat | 5F@.118 | lf | 1.31 | 6.50 | 7.81 |
| 2 coats | 5F@.182 | lf | 1.83 | 10.00 | 11.83 |
| 3 coats | 5F@.247 | lf | 2.43 | 13.60 | 16.03 |
| **Paint gingerbread gable ornament** | | | | | |
| prime | 5F@.747 | ea | 16.80 | 41.20 | 58.00 |
| 1 coat | 5F@.767 | ea | 18.90 | 42.30 | 61.20 |
| 2 coats | 5F@1.18 | ea | 26.20 | 65.00 | 91.20 |
| 3 coats | 5F@1.60 | ea | 34.80 | 88.20 | 123.00 |
| add 51% to stain and varnish | | | | | |

| | Craft@Hrs | Unit | Material | Labor | Total |
|---|---|---|---|---|---|
| Paint gingerbread gable finial | | | | | |
| prime | 5F@.253 | ea | 3.35 | 13.90 | 17.25 |
| 1 coat | 5F@.260 | ea | 3.72 | 14.30 | 18.02 |
| 2 coats | 5F@.401 | ea | 5.15 | 22.10 | 27.25 |
| 3 coats | 5F@.543 | ea | 6.90 | 29.90 | 36.80 |
| add 51% to stain and varnish | | | | | |
| Paint porch post | | | | | |
| prime | 5F@.118 | ea | 5.37 | 6.50 | 11.87 |
| 1 coat | 5F@.122 | ea | 5.95 | 6.72 | 12.67 |
| 2 coats | 5F@.187 | ea | 8.25 | 10.30 | 18.55 |
| 3 coats | 5F@.253 | ea | 11.00 | 13.90 | 24.90 |
| Stain & varnish porch post | | | | | |
| stain | 5F@.181 | ea | 7.85 | 9.97 | 17.82 |
| 1 coat | 5F@.186 | ea | 8.70 | 10.20 | 18.90 |
| 2 coats | 5F@.287 | ea | 12.20 | 15.80 | 28.00 |
| 3 coats | 5F@.388 | ea | 16.00 | 21.40 | 37.40 |

**Flooring.** See Flooring for costs to prep wood floors for finish.

| | Craft@Hrs | Unit | Material | Labor | Total |
|---|---|---|---|---|---|
| Seal stone floor | | | | | |
| seal | 5F@.011 | sf | .22 | .61 | .83 |
| 1 coat | 5F@.011 | sf | .24 | .61 | .85 |
| 2 coats | 5F@.017 | sf | .33 | .94 | 1.27 |
| 3 coats | 5F@.023 | sf | .44 | 1.27 | 1.71 |
| Paint wood floor | | | | | |
| prime | 5F@.012 | sf | .28 | .66 | .94 |
| 1 coat | 5F@.012 | sf | .30 | .66 | .96 |
| 2 coats | 5F@.019 | sf | .41 | 1.05 | 1.46 |
| 3 coats | 5F@.026 | sf | .54 | 1.43 | 1.97 |
| Stain & varnish wood floor | | | | | |
| stain | 5F@.018 | sf | .38 | .99 | 1.37 |
| 1 coat | 5F@.019 | sf | .43 | 1.05 | 1.48 |
| 2 coats | 5F@.029 | sf | .60 | 1.60 | 2.20 |
| 3 coats | 5F@.039 | sf | .80 | 2.15 | 2.95 |

**Paneling.**

| | Craft@Hrs | Unit | Material | Labor | Total |
|---|---|---|---|---|---|
| Paint wall paneling, simple pattern | | | | | |
| prime | 5F@.012 | sf | .41 | .66 | 1.07 |
| 1 coat | 5F@.012 | sf | .46 | .66 | 1.12 |
| 2 coats | 5F@.019 | sf | .64 | 1.05 | 1.69 |
| 3 coats | 5F@.026 | sf | .86 | 1.43 | 2.29 |
| Stain & varnish wall paneling, simple pattern | | | | | |
| stain | 5F@.018 | sf | .60 | .99 | 1.59 |
| 1 coat | 5F@.019 | sf | .66 | 1.05 | 1.71 |
| 2 coats | 5F@.029 | sf | .92 | 1.60 | 2.52 |
| 3 coats | 5F@.039 | sf | 1.23 | 2.15 | 3.38 |
| Paint wall paneling, ornate pattern | | | | | |
| prime | 5F@.017 | sf | .54 | .94 | 1.48 |
| 1 coat | 5F@.017 | sf | .62 | .94 | 1.56 |

| | Craft@Hrs | Unit | Material | Labor | Total |
|---|---|---|---|---|---|
| 2 coats | 5F@.027 | sf | .87 | 1.49 | 2.36 |
| 3 coats | 5F@.036 | sf | 1.14 | 1.98 | 3.12 |
| **Stain & varnish wall paneling, ornate pattern** | | | | | |
| stain | 5F@.026 | sf | .82 | 1.43 | 2.25 |
| 1 coat | 5F@.027 | sf | .90 | 1.49 | 2.39 |
| 2 coats | 5F@.041 | sf | 1.24 | 2.26 | 3.50 |
| 3 coats | 5F@.056 | sf | 1.63 | 3.09 | 4.72 |
| **Paint wall paneling, very ornate pattern** | | | | | |
| prime | 5F@.028 | sf | .66 | 1.54 | 2.20 |
| 1 coat | 5F@.029 | sf | .74 | 1.60 | 2.34 |
| 2 coats | 5F@.044 | sf | 1.04 | 2.42 | 3.46 |
| 3 coats | 5F@.060 | sf | 1.38 | 3.31 | 4.69 |
| **Stain & varnish wall paneling, very ornate pattern** | | | | | |
| stain | 5F@.043 | sf | .98 | 2.37 | 3.35 |
| 1 coat | 5F@.044 | sf | 1.08 | 2.42 | 3.50 |
| 2 coats | 5F@.068 | sf | 1.51 | 3.75 | 5.26 |
| 3 coats | 5F@.093 | sf | 1.99 | 5.12 | 7.11 |

## Masonry.

| | Craft@Hrs | Unit | Material | Labor | Total |
|---|---|---|---|---|---|
| **Paint concrete block (unpainted block)** | | | | | |
| prime | 5F@.014 | sf | .41 | .77 | 1.18 |
| 1 coat | 5F@.015 | sf | .46 | .83 | 1.29 |
| 2 coats | 5F@.023 | sf | .64 | 1.27 | 1.91 |
| 3 coats | 5F@.030 | sf | .86 | 1.65 | 2.51 |
| deduct 26% for previously painted block or brick | | | | | |
| **Paint brick (unpainted brick)** | | | | | |
| prime | 5F@.017 | sf | .43 | .94 | 1.37 |
| 1 coat | 5F@.017 | sf | .49 | .94 | 1.43 |
| 2 coats | 5F@.026 | sf | .69 | 1.43 | 2.12 |
| 3 coats | 5F@.035 | sf | .90 | 1.93 | 2.83 |
| **Paint stone wall** | | | | | |
| prime | 5F@.010 | sf | .32 | .55 | .87 |
| 1 coat | 5F@.010 | sf | .35 | .55 | .90 |
| 2 coats | 5F@.016 | sf | .50 | .88 | 1.38 |
| 3 coats | 5F@.021 | sf | .66 | 1.16 | 1.82 |
| **Seal stone wall** | | | | | |
| seal | 5F@.008 | sf | .43 | .44 | .87 |
| 1 coat | 5F@.009 | sf | .49 | .50 | .99 |
| 2 coats | 5F@.013 | sf | .69 | .72 | 1.41 |
| 3 coats | 5F@.018 | sf | .90 | .99 | 1.89 |

## Roofing.

| | Craft@Hrs | Unit | Material | Labor | Total |
|---|---|---|---|---|---|
| **Paint metal roofing** | | | | | |
| prime | 5F@.017 | sf | .46 | .94 | 1.40 |
| 1 coat | 5F@.018 | sf | .51 | .99 | 1.50 |
| 2 coats | 5F@.027 | sf | .72 | 1.49 | 2.21 |
| 3 coats | 5F@.037 | sf | .97 | 2.04 | 3.01 |

| | Craft@Hrs | Unit | Material | Labor | Total |
|---|---|---|---|---|---|
| Treat wood shingles or shakes with shingle oil | | | | | |
| treat | 5F@.013 | sf | .31 | .72 | 1.03 |
| 1 coat | 5F@.014 | sf | .34 | .77 | 1.11 |
| 2 coats | 5F@.021 | sf | .47 | 1.16 | 1.63 |
| 3 coats | 5F@.028 | sf | .63 | 1.54 | 2.17 |

## Rough carpentry.

| | Craft@Hrs | Unit | Material | Labor | Total |
|---|---|---|---|---|---|
| Seal wall framing, for odor control, smoke-stained framing | | | | | |
| seal | 5F@.018 | sf | .22 | .99 | 1.21 |
| 1 coat | 5F@.018 | sf | .24 | .99 | 1.23 |
| 2 coats | 5F@.028 | sf | .33 | 1.54 | 1.87 |
| 3 coats | 5F@.038 | sf | .44 | 2.09 | 2.53 |
| Seal floor framing | | | | | |
| seal | 5F@.022 | sf | .29 | 1.21 | 1.50 |
| 1 coat | 5F@.023 | sf | .31 | 1.27 | 1.58 |
| 2 coats | 5F@.035 | sf | .42 | 1.93 | 2.35 |
| 3 coats | 5F@.047 | sf | .56 | 2.59 | 3.15 |
| Seal roof framing | | | | | |
| seal | 5F@.028 | sf | .35 | 1.54 | 1.89 |
| 1 coat | 5F@.029 | sf | .38 | 1.60 | 1.98 |
| 2 coats | 5F@.044 | sf | .54 | 2.42 | 2.96 |
| 3 coats | 5F@.059 | sf | .73 | 3.25 | 3.98 |

## Siding.

| | Craft@Hrs | Unit | Material | Labor | Total |
|---|---|---|---|---|---|
| Paint exterior siding | | | | | |
| prime | 5F@.016 | sf | .32 | .88 | 1.20 |
| 1 coat | 5F@.016 | sf | .34 | .88 | 1.22 |
| 2 coats | 5F@.025 | sf | .49 | 1.38 | 1.87 |
| 3 coats | 5F@.033 | sf | .65 | 1.82 | 2.47 |
| Stain exterior siding | | | | | |
| stain | 5F@.015 | sf | .52 | .83 | 1.35 |
| 1 coat | 5F@.015 | sf | .58 | .83 | 1.41 |
| 2 coats | 5F@.023 | sf | .84 | 1.27 | 2.11 |
| 3 coats | 5F@.032 | sf | 1.09 | 1.76 | 2.85 |
| Paint window shutter (per shutter, per side) | | | | | |
| prime | 5F@.379 | ea | 7.01 | 20.90 | 27.91 |
| 1 coat | 5F@.390 | ea | 7.78 | 21.50 | 29.28 |
| 2 coats | 5F@.601 | ea | 10.80 | 33.10 | 43.90 |
| 3 coats | 5F@.814 | ea | 14.40 | 44.90 | 59.30 |
| Stain window shutter (per shutter, per side) | | | | | |
| stain | 5F@.581 | ea | 10.30 | 32.00 | 42.30 |
| 1 coat | 5F@.596 | ea | 11.40 | 32.80 | 44.20 |
| 2 coats | 5F@.917 | ea | 15.80 | 50.50 | 66.30 |
| 3 coats | 5F@1.24 | ea | 21.20 | 68.30 | 89.50 |
| Paint exterior fascia | | | | | |
| prime | 5F@.011 | lf | .11 | .61 | .72 |
| 1 coat | 5F@.011 | lf | .14 | .61 | .75 |
| 2 coats | 5F@.017 | lf | .22 | .94 | 1.16 |
| 3 coats | 5F@.023 | lf | .30 | 1.27 | 1.57 |

| | Craft@Hrs | Unit | Material | Labor | Total |
|---|---|---|---|---|---|
| **Stain exterior wood fascia** | | | | | |
| stain | 5F@.010 | lf | .20 | .55 | .75 |
| 1 coat | 5F@.010 | lf | .22 | .55 | .77 |
| 2 coats | 5F@.016 | lf | .31 | .88 | 1.19 |
| 3 coats | 5F@.021 | lf | .41 | 1.16 | 1.57 |
| **Paint exterior soffit** | | | | | |
| prime | 5F@.011 | sf | .32 | .61 | .93 |
| 1 coat | 5F@.012 | sf | .35 | .66 | 1.01 |
| 2 coats | 5F@.018 | sf | .50 | .99 | 1.49 |
| 3 coats | 5F@.024 | sf | .66 | 1.32 | 1.98 |
| **Stain exterior wood soffit** | | | | | |
| stain | 5F@.012 | sf | .41 | .66 | 1.07 |
| 1 coat | 5F@.012 | sf | .46 | .66 | 1.12 |
| 2 coats | 5F@.019 | sf | .64 | 1.05 | 1.69 |
| 3 coats | 5F@.026 | sf | .86 | 1.43 | 2.29 |
| **Paint rain gutter or downspout** | | | | | |
| prime | 5F@.018 | lf | .28 | .99 | 1.27 |
| 1 coat | 5F@.019 | lf | .30 | 1.05 | 1.35 |
| 2 coats | 5F@.029 | lf | .41 | 1.60 | 2.01 |
| 3 coats | 5F@.039 | lf | .54 | 2.15 | 2.69 |

## Stairs.

| | Craft@Hrs | Unit | Material | Labor | Total |
|---|---|---|---|---|---|
| **Paint stair balustrade** | | | | | |
| prime | 5F@.190 | lf | 3.81 | 10.50 | 14.31 |
| 1 coat | 5F@.195 | lf | 4.24 | 10.70 | 14.94 |
| 2 coats | 5F@.300 | lf | 5.93 | 16.50 | 22.43 |
| 3 coats | 5F@.407 | lf | 7.87 | 22.40 | 30.27 |
| **Stain & varnish stair balustrade** | | | | | |
| stain | 5F@.290 | lf | 5.63 | 16.00 | 21.63 |
| 1 coat | 5F@.298 | lf | 6.22 | 16.40 | 22.62 |
| 2 coats | 5F@.459 | lf | 8.67 | 25.30 | 33.97 |
| 3 coats | 5F@.621 | lf | 11.50 | 34.20 | 45.70 |
| **Paint stair riser** | | | | | |
| prime | 5F@.112 | ea | 3.22 | 6.17 | 9.39 |
| 1 coat | 5F@.115 | ea | 3.56 | 6.34 | 9.90 |
| 2 coats | 5F@.177 | ea | 4.94 | 9.75 | 14.69 |
| 3 coats | 5F@.240 | ea | 6.59 | 13.20 | 19.79 |
| **Stain & varnish stair riser** | | | | | |
| stain | 5F@.171 | ea | 4.73 | 9.42 | 14.15 |
| 1 coat | 5F@.176 | ea | 5.19 | 9.70 | 14.89 |
| 2 coats | 5F@.271 | ea | 7.26 | 14.90 | 22.16 |
| 3 coats | 5F@.368 | ea | 9.65 | 20.30 | 29.95 |
| **Paint stair tread** | | | | | |
| prime | 5F@.121 | ea | 3.56 | 6.67 | 10.23 |
| 1 coat | 5F@.125 | ea | 3.96 | 6.89 | 10.85 |
| 2 coats | 5F@.192 | ea | 5.49 | 10.60 | 16.09 |
| 3 coats | 5F@.260 | ea | 7.29 | 14.30 | 21.59 |

| | Craft@Hrs | Unit | Material | Labor | Total |
|---|---|---|---|---|---|
| Stain & varnish stair tread | | | | | |
| stain | 5F@.185 | ea | 5.19 | 10.20 | 15.39 |
| 1 coat | 5F@.191 | ea | 5.83 | 10.50 | 16.33 |
| 2 coats | 5F@.294 | ea | 8.06 | 16.20 | 24.26 |
| 3 coats | 5F@.399 | ea | 10.80 | 22.00 | 32.80 |
| Paint stair bracket | | | | | |
| prime | 5F@.092 | ea | 2.94 | 5.07 | 8.01 |
| 1 coat | 5F@.094 | ea | 3.27 | 5.18 | 8.45 |
| 2 coats | 5F@.145 | ea | 4.56 | 7.99 | 12.55 |
| 3 coats | 5F@.196 | ea | 6.04 | 10.80 | 16.84 |
| Stain & varnish stair bracket | | | | | |
| stain | 5F@.140 | ea | 4.34 | 7.71 | 12.05 |
| 1 coat | 5F@.144 | ea | 4.82 | 7.93 | 12.75 |
| 2 coats | 5F@.222 | ea | 6.69 | 12.20 | 18.89 |
| 3 coats | 5F@.300 | ea | 8.90 | 16.50 | 25.40 |

## Window.

| | Craft@Hrs | Unit | Material | Labor | Total |
|---|---|---|---|---|---|
| Paint small window (per side) | | | | | |
| prime | 5F@.295 | ea | 10.20 | 16.30 | 26.50 |
| 1 coat | 5F@.304 | ea | 11.30 | 16.80 | 28.10 |
| 2 coats | 5F@.467 | ea | 15.60 | 25.70 | 41.30 |
| 3 coats | 5F@.633 | ea | 21.00 | 34.90 | 55.90 |
| Paint average size window | | | | | |
| prime | 5F@.422 | ea | 15.50 | 23.30 | 38.80 |
| 1 coat | 5F@.433 | ea | 17.00 | 23.90 | 40.90 |
| 2 coats | 5F@.666 | ea | 23.80 | 36.70 | 60.50 |
| 3 coats | 5F@.901 | ea | 31.90 | 49.60 | 81.50 |
| Paint large window | | | | | |
| prime | 5F@.534 | ea | 19.70 | 29.40 | 49.10 |
| 1 coat | 5F@.549 | ea | 21.80 | 30.20 | 52.00 |
| 2 coats | 5F@.845 | ea | 30.30 | 46.60 | 76.90 |
| 3 coats | 5F@1.15 | ea | 40.20 | 63.40 | 103.60 |
| Paint very large window | | | | | |
| prime | 5F@.668 | ea | 28.00 | 36.80 | 64.80 |
| 1 coat | 5F@.687 | ea | 31.30 | 37.90 | 69.20 |
| 2 coats | 5F@1.06 | ea | 43.30 | 58.40 | 101.70 |
| 3 coats | 5F@1.43 | ea | 57.30 | 78.80 | 136.10 |

## Wallpaper.

| | Craft@Hrs | Unit | Material | Labor | Total |
|---|---|---|---|---|---|
| Paint wallpaper | | | | | |
| prime | 5F@.011 | sf | .26 | .61 | .87 |
| 1 coat | 5F@.011 | sf | .29 | .61 | .90 |
| 2 coats | 5F@.017 | sf | .38 | .94 | 1.32 |
| 3 coats | 5F@.023 | sf | .52 | 1.27 | 1.79 |

## Strip paint. Cost to strip paint that does not contain lead.

| | Craft@Hrs | Unit | Material | Labor | Total |
|---|---|---|---|---|---|
| Strip paint or varnish from trim, simple design | | | | | |
| strip | 5F@.081 | lf | 1.88 | 4.46 | 6.34 |
| 1 coat | 5F@.083 | lf | 2.20 | 4.57 | 6.77 |
| 2 coats | 5F@.126 | lf | 2.97 | 6.94 | 9.91 |
| 3 coats | 5F@.172 | lf | 3.88 | 9.48 | 13.36 |

|  | Craft@Hrs | Unit | Material | Labor | Total |
|---|---|---|---|---|---|
| **Strip paint or varnish from trim, complex design** | | | | | |
| strip | 5F@.153 | lf | 2.28 | 8.43 | 10.71 |
| 1 coat | 5F@.158 | lf | 2.53 | 8.71 | 11.24 |
| 2 coats | 5F@.291 | lf | 4.02 | 16.00 | 20.02 |
| 3 coats | 5F@.513 | lf | 6.11 | 28.30 | 34.41 |
| **Strip paint or varnish from door (slab only)** | | | | | |
| strip | 5F@.529 | ea | 20.40 | 29.10 | 49.50 |
| 1 coat | 5F@.545 | ea | 24.30 | 30.00 | 54.30 |
| 2 coats | 5F@.845 | ea | 34.30 | 46.60 | 80.90 |
| 3 coats | 5F@1.27 | ea | 51.00 | 70.00 | 121.00 |
| **Strip paint or varnish from door jamb and casing** | | | | | |
| strip | 5F@.092 | lf | 3.22 | 5.07 | 8.29 |
| 1 coat | 5F@.095 | lf | 3.79 | 5.23 | 9.02 |
| 2 coats | 5F@.146 | lf | 5.10 | 8.04 | 13.14 |
| 3 coats | 5F@.198 | lf | 6.69 | 10.90 | 17.59 |

## Time & Material Charts (selected items)
## Painting Materials

|  | Craft@Hrs | Unit | Material | Labor | Total |
|---|---|---|---|---|---|
| **Prime or seal** | | | | | |
| primer or sealer, plaster or drywall<br>($29.70 gallon, 178 sf) | — | sf | .17 | — | .17 |
| primer or sealer, interior door<br>($29.70 gallon, 2.8 ea) | — | ea | 10.60 | — | 10.60 |
| primer or sealer, entry door<br>($29.70 gallon, 1.6 ea) | — | ea | 18.60 | — | 18.60 |
| primer or sealer, wood trim, simple design<br>($29.70 gallon, 178 lf) | — | lf | .17 | — | .17 |
| primer or sealer, exterior siding<br>($29.70 gallon, 94 sf) | — | sf | .32 | — | .32 |
| primer or sealer, stair balustrade<br>($29.70 gallon, 7.8 lf) | — | lf | 3.81 | — | 3.81 |
| **Paint, one coat** | | | | | |
| oil or latex paint, plaster or drywall<br>($37.90 gallon, 205 sf) | — | sf | .18 | — | .18 |
| oil or latex paint, interior door<br>($37.90 gallon, 3.2 ea) | — | ea | 11.80 | — | 11.80 |
| oil or latex paint, entry door<br>($37.90 gallon, 1.9 ea) | — | ea | 19.90 | — | 19.90 |
| oil or latex paint, wood trim, simple design<br>($37.90 gallon, 205 lf) | — | lf | .18 | — | .18 |
| oil or latex paint, exterior siding<br>($37.90 gallon, 108 sf) | — | sf | .35 | — | .35 |
| oil or latex paint, stair balustrade<br>($37.90 gallon, 8.9 lf) | — | lf | 4.26 | — | 4.26 |

| | Craft@Hrs | Unit | Material | Labor | Total |
|---|---|---|---|---|---|
| **Paint, two coats** | | | | | |
| oil or latex paint, plaster or drywall ($37.90 gallon, 151 sf) | — | sf | .25 | — | .25 |
| oil or latex paint, interior door ($37.90 gallon, 2.3 ea) | — | ea | 16.50 | — | 16.50 |
| oil or latex paint, entry door ($37.90 gallon, 1.4 ea) | — | ea | 27.10 | — | 27.10 |
| oil or latex paint, wood trim, simple design ($37.90 gallon, 151 lf) | — | lf | .25 | — | .25 |
| oil or latex paint, exterior siding ($37.90 gallon, 78 sf) | — | sf | .49 | — | .49 |
| oil or latex paint, stair balustrade ($37.90 gallon, 6.4 lf) | — | lf | 5.92 | — | 5.92 |
| **Paint, three coats** | | | | | |
| oil or latex paint, plaster or drywall ($37.90 gallon, 113 sf) | — | sf | .34 | — | .34 |
| oil or latex paint, interior door ($37.90 gallon, 1.7 ea) | — | ea | 22.30 | — | 22.30 |
| oil or latex paint, entry door ($37.90 gallon, 1.0 ea) | — | ea | 37.90 | — | 37.90 |
| oil or latex paint, wood trim, simple design ($37.90 gallon, 113 lf) | — | lf | .34 | — | .34 |
| oil or latex paint, exterior siding ($37.90 gallon, 58 sf) | — | sf | .65 | — | .65 |
| oil or latex paint, stair balustrade ($37.90 gallon, 4.8 lf) | — | lf | 7.90 | — | 7.90 |
| **Stain** | | | | | |
| stain, interior door ($40.00 gallon, 2.5 ea) | — | ea | 16.00 | — | 16.00 |
| stain, entry door ($40.00 gallon, 1.5 ea) | — | ea | 26.70 | — | 26.70 |
| stain, wood trim, simple design ($40.00 gallon, 159 lf) | — | lf | .25 | — | .25 |
| stain, exterior siding, one coat ($40.00 gallon, 77 sf) | — | sf | .52 | — | .52 |
| stain, stair balustrade ($40.00 gallon, 7.1 lf) | — | lf | 5.63 | — | 5.63 |
| **Varnish, one coat** | | | | | |
| varnish, clear, interior door ($51.90 gallon, 2.9 ea) | — | ea | 17.90 | — | 17.90 |
| varnish, clear, entry door ($51.90 gallon, 1.8 ea) | — | ea | 28.80 | — | 28.80 |
| varnish, clear, wood trim, simple design ($51.90 gallon, 284 lf) | — | lf | .18 | — | .18 |
| varnish, clear, stair balustrade ($51.90 gallon, 8.4 lf) | — | lf | 6.18 | — | 6.18 |

| | Craft@Hrs | Unit | Material | Labor | Total |
|---|---|---|---|---|---|
| Varnish, two coats | | | | | |
| varnish, clear, interior door ($51.90 gallon, 2.1 ea) | — | ea | 24.70 | — | 24.70 |
| varnish, clear, entry door ($51.90 gallon, 1.4 ea) | — | ea | 37.10 | — | 37.10 |
| varnish, clear, wood trim, simple design ($51.90 gallon, 208 lf) | — | lf | .25 | — | .25 |
| varnish, clear, stair balustrade ($51.90 gallon, 6.0 lf) | — | lf | 8.65 | — | 8.65 |
| Varnish, three coats | | | | | |
| varnish, clear, interior door ($51.90 gallon, 1.6 ea) | — | ea | 32.40 | — | 32.40 |
| varnish, clear, entry door ($51.90 gallon, 1.0 ea) | — | ea | 51.90 | — | 51.90 |
| varnish, clear, wood trim, simple design ($51.90 gallon, 156 lf) | — | lf | .33 | — | .33 |
| varnish, clear, stair balustrade ($51.90 gallon, 4.5 lf) | — | lf | 11.50 | — | 11.50 |

## Painting Labor

| | base wage | paid leave | true wage | taxes & ins. | total |
|---|---|---|---|---|---|
| Laborer | | | | | |
| Painter | $30.60 | 2.39 | $32.99 | 22.21 | $55.20 |

**Paid leave** is calculated based on two weeks paid vacation, one week sick leave, and seven paid holidays. Employer's matching portion of **FICA** is 7.65 percent. **FUTA** (Federal Unemployment) is .8 percent. **Worker's compensation** for the painting trade was calculated using a national average of 14.20 percent. **Unemployment insurance** was calculated using a national average of 8 percent. **Health insurance** was calculated based on a projected national average for 2015 of $1,025 per employee (and family when applicable) per month. Employer pays 80 percent for a per month cost of $820 per employee. **Retirement** is based on a 401(k) retirement program with employer matching of 50 percent. Employee contributions to the 401(k) plan are an average of 6 percent of the true wage. **Liability insurance** is based on a national average of 10.0 percent.

| | Craft@Hrs | Unit | Material | Labor | Total |
|---|---|---|---|---|---|
| **Painting Labor Productivity** | | | | | |
| Prime or seal | | | | | |
| acoustic ceiling texture | 5F@.011 | sf | — | .61 | .61 |
| plaster or drywall | 5F@.006 | sf | — | .33 | .33 |
| masonry, block | 5F@.014 | sf | — | .77 | .77 |
| concrete floor | 5F@.008 | sf | — | .44 | .44 |
| wood floor | 5F@.012 | sf | — | .66 | .66 |
| folding door | 5F@.402 | ea | — | 22.20 | 22.20 |
| bypassing door | 5F@.830 | ea | — | 45.70 | 45.70 |
| interior door | 5F@.340 | ea | — | 18.70 | 18.70 |
| door jamb & casing | 5F@.013 | lf | — | .72 | .72 |
| wood entry door | 5F@.742 | ea | — | 40.90 | 40.90 |
| wood sliding patio door | 5F@.646 | ea | — | 35.60 | 35.60 |
| garage door | 5F@.006 | sf | — | .33 | .33 |
| 4' high wood fence (per side) | 5F@.051 | lf | — | 2.81 | 2.81 |
| 48" high ornamental iron fence (both sides) | 5F@.077 | lf | — | 4.24 | 4.24 |

| | Craft@Hrs | Unit | Material | Labor | Total |
|---|---|---|---|---|---|
| wood trim, simple design | 5F@.011 | lf | — | .61 | .61 |
| wood trim, very ornate design | 5F@.017 | lf | — | .94 | .94 |
| seal smoke-stained frame walls | 5F@.018 | sf | — | .99 | .99 |
| seal smoke-stained joists | 5F@.022 | sf | — | 1.21 | 1.21 |
| seal smoke-stained rafters or trusses | 5F@.028 | sf | — | 1.54 | 1.54 |
| siding | 5F@.016 | sf | — | .88 | .88 |
| stucco | 5F@.014 | sf | — | .77 | .77 |
| stair balustrade | 5F@.190 | lf | — | 10.50 | 10.50 |
| small window | 5F@.295 | ea | — | 16.30 | 16.30 |
| very large window | 5F@.668 | ea | — | 36.80 | 36.80 |

**Paint, one coat**

| | Craft@Hrs | Unit | Material | Labor | Total |
|---|---|---|---|---|---|
| acoustic ceiling texture | 5F@.011 | sf | — | .61 | .61 |
| plaster or drywall | 5F@.006 | sf | — | .33 | .33 |
| masonry, block | 5F@.015 | sf | — | .83 | .83 |
| concrete floor | 5F@.008 | sf | — | .44 | .44 |
| wood floor | 5F@.012 | sf | — | .66 | .66 |
| folding door | 5F@.413 | ea | — | 22.80 | 22.80 |
| bypassing door | 5F@.854 | ea | — | 47.10 | 47.10 |
| interior door | 5F@.349 | ea | — | 19.20 | 19.20 |
| door jamb & casing | 5F@.011 | lf | — | .61 | .61 |
| wood entry door | 5F@.763 | ea | — | 42.00 | 42.00 |
| wood sliding patio door | 5F@.665 | sf | — | 36.60 | 36.60 |
| garage door | 5F@.006 | sf | — | .33 | .33 |
| 4' high wood fence (per side) | 5F@.053 | lf | — | 2.92 | 2.92 |
| 48" high ornamental iron fence (both sides) | 5F@.079 | lf | — | 4.35 | 4.35 |
| wood trim, simple design | 5F@.011 | lf | — | .61 | .61 |
| wood trim, very ornate design | 5F@.017 | lf | — | .94 | .94 |
| siding | 5F@.016 | sf | — | .88 | .88 |
| stucco | 5F@.015 | sf | — | .83 | .83 |
| stair balustrade | 5F@.195 | lf | — | 10.70 | 10.70 |
| small window | 5F@.304 | ea | — | 16.80 | 16.80 |
| very large window | 5F@.687 | ea | — | 37.90 | 37.90 |

**Paint, two coats**

| | Craft@Hrs | Unit | Material | Labor | Total |
|---|---|---|---|---|---|
| acoustic ceiling texture | 5F@.017 | sf | — | .94 | .94 |
| plaster or drywall | 5F@.010 | sf | — | .55 | .55 |
| masonry, block | 5F@.023 | sf | — | 1.27 | 1.27 |
| concrete floor | 5F@.012 | sf | — | .66 | .66 |
| wood floor | 5F@.019 | sf | — | 1.05 | 1.05 |
| folding door | 5F@.636 | ea | — | 35.00 | 35.00 |
| bypassing door | 5F@1.32 | ea | — | 72.70 | 72.70 |
| interior door | 5F@.538 | ea | — | 29.60 | 29.60 |
| door jamb & casing | 5F@.017 | lf | — | .94 | .94 |
| wood entry door | 5F@1.18 | ea | — | 65.00 | 65.00 |
| wood sliding patio door | 5F@1.02 | sf | — | 56.20 | 56.20 |
| garage door | 5F@.009 | sf | — | .50 | .50 |
| 4' high wood fence (per side) | 5F@.081 | lf | — | 4.46 | 4.46 |
| 48" high ornamental iron fence (both sides) | 5F@.121 | lf | — | 6.67 | 6.67 |
| wood trim, simple design | 5F@.017 | lf | — | .94 | .94 |
| wood trim, very ornate design | 5F@.026 | lf | — | 1.43 | 1.43 |
| siding | 5F@.025 | sf | — | 1.38 | 1.38 |
| stucco | 5F@.023 | sf | — | 1.27 | 1.27 |

| | Craft@Hrs | Unit | Material | Labor | Total |
|---|---|---|---|---|---|
| stair balustrade | 5F@.300 | lf | — | 16.50 | 16.50 |
| small window | 5F@.467 | ea | — | 25.70 | 25.70 |
| very large window | 5F@1.06 | ea | — | 58.40 | 58.40 |

**Paint, three coats**

| | Craft@Hrs | Unit | Material | Labor | Total |
|---|---|---|---|---|---|
| acoustic ceiling texture | 5F@.023 | sf | — | 1.27 | 1.27 |
| plaster or drywall | 5F@.013 | sf | — | .72 | .72 |
| masonry, block | 5F@.030 | sf | — | 1.65 | 1.65 |
| concrete floor | 5F@.016 | sf | — | .88 | .88 |
| wood floor | 5F@.026 | sf | — | 1.43 | 1.43 |
| folding door | 5F@.861 | ea | — | 47.40 | 47.40 |
| bypassing door | 5F@1.78 | ea | — | 98.10 | 98.10 |
| interior door | 5F@.729 | ea | — | 40.20 | 40.20 |
| door jamb & casing | 5F@.023 | lf | — | 1.27 | 1.27 |
| wood entry door | 5F@1.59 | ea | — | 87.60 | 87.60 |
| wood sliding patio door | 5F@1.39 | sf | — | 76.60 | 76.60 |
| garage door | 5F@.013 | sf | — | .72 | .72 |
| 4' high wood fence (per side) | 5F@.109 | lf | — | 6.01 | 6.01 |
| 48" high ornamental iron fence (both sides) | 5F@.164 | lf | — | 9.04 | 9.04 |
| wood trim, simple design | 5F@.023 | lf | — | 1.27 | 1.27 |
| wood trim, very ornate design | 5F@.035 | lf | — | 1.93 | 1.93 |
| siding | 5F@.033 | sf | — | 1.82 | 1.82 |
| stucco | 5F@.030 | sf | — | 1.65 | 1.65 |
| stair balustrade | 5F@.407 | lf | — | 22.40 | 22.40 |
| small window | 5F@.633 | ea | — | 34.90 | 34.90 |
| very large window | 5F@1.43 | ea | — | 78.80 | 78.80 |

**Stain**

| | Craft@Hrs | Unit | Material | Labor | Total |
|---|---|---|---|---|---|
| wood floor | 5F@.018 | sf | — | .99 | .99 |
| folding door | 5F@.614 | ea | — | 33.80 | 33.80 |
| bypassing door | 5F@1.27 | ea | — | 70.00 | 70.00 |
| interior door | 5F@.519 | ea | — | 28.60 | 28.60 |
| French door | 5F@1.25 | ea | — | 68.90 | 68.90 |
| panel door | 5F@1.08 | ea | — | 59.50 | 59.50 |
| door jamb & casing | 5F@.019 | lf | — | 1.05 | 1.05 |
| wood entry door | 5F@1.13 | ea | — | 62.30 | 62.30 |
| wood sliding patio door | 5F@.988 | ea | — | 54.40 | 54.40 |
| garage door | 5F@.009 | sf | — | .50 | .50 |
| 4' high wood fence (per side) | 5F@.078 | lf | — | 4.30 | 4.30 |
| wood trim, simple design | 5F@.016 | lf | — | .88 | .88 |
| wood trim, very ornate design | 5F@.025 | lf | — | 1.38 | 1.38 |
| wood paneling, simple pattern | 5F@.018 | sf | — | .99 | .99 |
| wood paneling, very ornate pattern | 5F@.043 | sf | — | 2.37 | 2.37 |
| siding | 5F@.015 | sf | — | .83 | .83 |
| stair balustrade | 5F@.290 | lf | — | 16.00 | 16.00 |

**Varnish, one coat**

| | Craft@Hrs | Unit | Material | Labor | Total |
|---|---|---|---|---|---|
| wood floor | 5F@.019 | sf | — | 1.05 | 1.05 |
| folding door | 5F@.632 | ea | — | 34.80 | 34.80 |
| bypassing door | 5F@1.31 | ea | — | 72.20 | 72.20 |
| interior door | 5F@.534 | ea | — | 29.40 | 29.40 |

| | Craft@Hrs | Unit | Material | Labor | Total |
|---|---|---|---|---|---|
| French door | 5F@1.29 | ea | — | 71.10 | 71.10 |
| panel door | 5F@1.11 | ea | — | 61.20 | 61.20 |
| door jamb & casing | 5F@.017 | lf | — | .94 | .94 |
| wood entry door | 5F@1.17 | ea | — | 64.50 | 64.50 |
| wood sliding patio door | 5F@1.02 | ea | — | 56.20 | 56.20 |
| garage door | 5F@.009 | sf | — | .50 | .50 |
| 4' high wood fence (per side) | 5F@.080 | lf | — | 4.41 | 4.41 |
| wood trim, simple design | 5F@.017 | lf | — | .94 | .94 |
| wood trim, very ornate design | 5F@.026 | lf | — | 1.43 | 1.43 |
| wood paneling, simple pattern | 5F@.019 | sf | — | 1.05 | 1.05 |
| wood paneling, very ornate pattern | 5F@.044 | sf | — | 2.42 | 2.42 |
| siding | 5F@.015 | sf | — | .83 | .83 |
| stair balustrade | 5F@.298 | lf | — | 16.40 | 16.40 |
| **Varnish, two coats** | | | | | |
| wood floor | 5F@.029 | sf | — | 1.60 | 1.60 |
| folding door | 5F@.972 | ea | — | 53.60 | 53.60 |
| bypassing door | 5F@2.01 | ea | — | 111.00 | 111.00 |
| interior door | 5F@.822 | ea | — | 45.30 | 45.30 |
| French door | 5F@1.98 | ea | — | 109.00 | 109.00 |
| panel door | 5F@1.70 | ea | — | 93.70 | 93.70 |
| door jamb & casing | 5F@.026 | lf | — | 1.43 | 1.43 |
| wood entry door | 5F@1.80 | ea | — | 99.20 | 99.20 |
| wood sliding patio door | 5F@1.56 | ea | — | 86.00 | 86.00 |
| garage door | 5F@.014 | sf | — | .77 | .77 |
| 4' high wood fence (per side) | 5F@.123 | lf | — | 6.78 | 6.78 |
| wood trim, simple design | 5F@.026 | lf | — | 1.43 | 1.43 |
| wood trim, very ornate design | 5F@.040 | lf | — | 2.20 | 2.20 |
| wood paneling, simple pattern | 5F@.029 | sf | — | 1.60 | 1.60 |
| wood paneling, very ornate pattern | 5F@.068 | sf | — | 3.75 | 3.75 |
| siding | 5F@.023 | sf | — | 1.27 | 1.27 |
| stair balustrade | 5F@.459 | lf | — | 25.30 | 25.30 |
| **Varnish, three coats** | | | | | |
| wood floor | 5F@.039 | sf | — | 2.15 | 2.15 |
| folding door | 5F@1.32 | ea | — | 72.70 | 72.70 |
| bypassing door | 5F@2.72 | ea | — | 150.00 | 150.00 |
| interior door | 5F@1.11 | ea | — | 61.20 | 61.20 |
| French door | 5F@2.68 | ea | — | 148.00 | 148.00 |
| panel door | 5F@2.31 | ea | — | 127.00 | 127.00 |
| door jamb & casing | 5F@.035 | lf | — | 1.93 | 1.93 |
| wood entry door | 5F@2.43 | ea | — | 134.00 | 134.00 |
| wood sliding patio door | 5F@2.12 | ea | — | 117.00 | 117.00 |
| garage door | 5F@.019 | sf | — | 1.05 | 1.05 |
| 4' high wood fence (per side) | 5F@.167 | lf | — | 9.20 | 9.20 |
| wood trim, simple design | 5F@.035 | lf | — | 1.93 | 1.93 |
| wood trim, very ornate design | 5F@.054 | lf | — | 2.98 | 2.98 |
| wood paneling, simple pattern | 5F@.039 | sf | — | 2.15 | 2.15 |
| wood paneling, very ornate pattern | 5F@.093 | sf | — | 5.12 | 5.12 |
| siding | 5F@.032 | sf | — | 1.76 | 1.76 |
| stair balustrade | 5F@.621 | lf | — | 34.20 | 34.20 |

| | Craft@Hrs | Unit | Material | Labor | Total |
|---|---|---|---|---|---|

# Paneling

## Minimum charge.

| | Craft@Hrs | Unit | Material | Labor | Total |
|---|---|---|---|---|---|
| for paneling work | 8P@3.25 | ea | 29.00 | 162.00 | 191.00 |
| for frame-and-panel wall work | 8P@4.00 | ea | 86.40 | 199.00 | 285.40 |

## Hardboard paneling. Includes finish hardboard paneling, finish nails, construction adhesive as needed, and installation. Paneling is prefinished. Includes 5% waste.

| | Craft@Hrs | Unit | Material | Labor | Total |
|---|---|---|---|---|---|
| replace, economy grade | 8P@.033 | sf | .96 | 1.64 | 2.60 |
| replace, standard grade | 8P@.033 | sf | 1.16 | 1.64 | 2.80 |
| replace, high grade | 8P@.033 | sf | 1.78 | 1.64 | 3.42 |
| replace, with simulated brick face | 8P@.033 | sf | 1.23 | 1.64 | 2.87 |
| replace, with simulated stone face | 8P@.033 | sf | 1.29 | 1.64 | 2.93 |
| remove | 1D@.007 | sf | — | .27 | .27 |

## Pegboard. Includes tempered pegboard, fasteners, spacers, construction adhesive as needed, and installation. Includes 5% waste.

| | Craft@Hrs | Unit | Material | Labor | Total |
|---|---|---|---|---|---|
| replace | 8P@.030 | sf | .92 | 1.49 | 2.41 |
| remove | 1D@.007 | sf | — | .27 | .27 |

## Plywood paneling. Includes finish plywood, finish nails, construction adhesive as needed, and installation. Plywood is unfinished with top grade veneer. Includes 5% waste.

1/4" plywood paneling

| | Craft@Hrs | Unit | Material | Labor | Total |
|---|---|---|---|---|---|
| replace, ash | 8P@.036 | sf | 4.06 | 1.79 | 5.85 |
| replace, birch | 8P@.036 | sf | 2.02 | 1.79 | 3.81 |
| replace, cherry | 8P@.036 | sf | 4.54 | 1.79 | 6.33 |
| replace, hickory | 8P@.036 | sf | 4.28 | 1.79 | 6.07 |
| replace, knotty pine | 8P@.036 | sf | 3.42 | 1.79 | 5.21 |
| replace, mahogany | 8P@.036 | sf | 3.72 | 1.79 | 5.51 |
| replace, white maple | 8P@.036 | sf | 3.02 | 1.79 | 4.81 |
| replace, red or white oak | 8P@.036 | sf | 2.22 | 1.79 | 4.01 |
| replace, quartersawn red or white oak | 8P@.036 | sf | 3.90 | 1.79 | 5.69 |
| replace, walnut | 8P@.036 | sf | 5.91 | 1.79 | 7.70 |
| replace, rough-sawn cedar | 8P@.036 | sf | 2.82 | 1.79 | 4.61 |
| remove | 1D@.008 | sf | — | .31 | .31 |

## Add for wall molding on plywood paneling. Includes 6% waste. Add to plywood paneling prices above for moldings that form repeating squares on wall with radius corners. Add 11% for slope-matched wall molding along stairways.

| | Craft@Hrs | Unit | Material | Labor | Total |
|---|---|---|---|---|---|
| add for standard grade | — | % | 44.0 | — | — |
| add for high grade | — | % | 53.0 | — | — |
| add for deluxe grade | — | % | 70.0 | — | — |
| add for custom | — | % | 84.0 | — | — |

## Plywood paneling with grooves. Includes 5% waste. Includes prefinished plywood, finish nails, construction adhesive as needed, and installation.

1/4" plywood paneling with grooves

| | Craft@Hrs | Unit | Material | Labor | Total |
|---|---|---|---|---|---|
| replace, ash | 8P@.036 | sf | 3.95 | 1.79 | 5.74 |
| replace, birch | 8P@.036 | sf | 1.98 | 1.79 | 3.77 |
| replace, cherry | 8P@.036 | sf | 4.41 | 1.79 | 6.20 |
| replace, hickory | 8P@.036 | sf | 4.17 | 1.79 | 5.96 |
| replace, knotty pine | 8P@.036 | sf | 3.35 | 1.79 | 5.14 |

| | Craft@Hrs | Unit | Material | Labor | Total |
|---|---|---|---|---|---|
| replace, mahogany | 8P@.036 | sf | 3.62 | 1.79 | 5.41 |
| replace, white maple | 8P@.036 | sf | 2.95 | 1.79 | 4.74 |
| replace, red or white oak | 8P@.036 | sf | 2.17 | 1.79 | 3.96 |
| replace, quartersawn red or white oak | 8P@.036 | sf | 3.76 | 1.79 | 5.55 |
| replace, walnut | 8P@.036 | sf | 5.77 | 1.79 | 7.56 |
| replace, rough-sawn cedar | 8P@.036 | sf | 2.74 | 1.79 | 4.53 |
| remove | 1D@.008 | sf | — | .31 | .31 |

**Board-on-board or board-and-batten paneling.** Includes boards, battens, finish nails, and installation. Board-and-batten and board-on-board paneling is installed vertically. Includes 4% waste. Prices for paneling are slightly higher than the same materials used in siding because there are more angles indoors.

| | | Craft@Hrs | Unit | Material | Labor | Total |
|---|---|---|---|---|---|---|
| replace, pine board-on-board | board-and-batten | 8P@.038 | sf | 4.92 | 1.89 | 6.81 |
| replace, pine board-and-batten | | 8P@.042 | sf | 4.81 | 2.09 | 6.90 |
| remove | | 1D@.011 | sf | — | .43 | .43 |

*board-on-board*

**Add for angled paneling installations.**

| | Craft@Hrs | Unit | Material | Labor | Total |
|---|---|---|---|---|---|
| add for chevron | — | % | — | 10.0 | — |
| add for herringbone | — | % | — | 18.0 | — |

**Tongue-&-groove paneling.** Includes tongue-&-groove boards, finish nails, and installation. Boards are unfinished. Includes 5% waste.

| | Craft@Hrs | Unit | Material | Labor | Total |
|---|---|---|---|---|---|
| replace, pine tongue-&-groove, simple pattern | 8P@.047 | sf | 5.11 | 2.34 | 7.45 |
| replace, pine tongue-&-groove, fancy pattern | 8P@.047 | sf | 5.45 | 2.34 | 7.79 |
| replace, pine tongue-&-groove, ornate pattern | 8P@.047 | sf | 6.35 | 2.34 | 8.69 |
| replace, cedar tongue-&-groove closet lining | 8P@.047 | sf | 2.92 | 2.34 | 5.26 |
| remove | 1D@.011 | sf | — | .43 | .43 |

**Add for wainscot installations.**

| | Craft@Hrs | Unit | Material | Labor | Total |
|---|---|---|---|---|---|
| add for paneling installed as wainscoting | — | % | — | 14.0 | — |

**Pine frame-and-panel wall.** Includes framing lumber and furring strips as needed for backing, panels and/or finish plywood, moldings between panels, may include tongue-&-groove stiles and rails, crown, base, and other finish millwork such as casing dentil mold, cove, and so forth, framing nails, finish nails, glue, fasteners, and installation. Includes 5% waste.

| | Craft@Hrs | Unit | Material | Labor | Total |
|---|---|---|---|---|---|
| replace, standard grade | 8P@.725 | sf | 24.70 | 36.00 | 60.70 |
| replace, high grade | 8P@.870 | sf | 33.90 | 43.20 | 77.10 |
| replace, deluxe grade | 8P@1.05 | sf | 40.10 | 52.20 | 92.30 |
| replace, custom grade | 8P@1.25 | sf | 59.70 | 62.10 | 121.80 |
| remove | 1D@.019 | sf | — | .74 | .74 |

**Oak frame-and-panel wall.** Includes framing lumber and furring strips as needed for backing, panels and/or finish plywood, moldings between panels, may include tongue-&-groove stiles and rails, crown, base, and other finish millwork such as casing dentil mold, cove, and so forth, framing nails, finish nails, glue, fasteners, and installation. Includes 5% waste.

| | Craft@Hrs | Unit | Material | Labor | Total |
|---|---|---|---|---|---|
| replace, standard grade | 8P@.725 | sf | 33.30 | 36.00 | 69.30 |
| replace, high grade | 8P@.870 | sf | 45.70 | 43.20 | 88.90 |
| replace, deluxe grade | 8P@1.05 | sf | 53.70 | 52.20 | 105.90 |
| replace, custom grade | 8P@1.25 | sf | 80.10 | 62.10 | 142.20 |
| remove | 1D@.019 | sf | — | .74 | .74 |

|  | Craft@Hrs | Unit | Material | Labor | Total |
|---|---|---|---|---|---|

**Walnut frame-and-panel wall.** Includes framing lumber and furring strips as needed for backing, panels and/or finish plywood, moldings between panels, may include tongue-&-groove stiles and rails, crown, base, and other finish millwork such as casing dentil mold, cove, and so forth, framing nails, finish nails, glue, fasteners, and installation. Includes 5% waste.

|  | Craft@Hrs | Unit | Material | Labor | Total |
|---|---|---|---|---|---|
| replace, standard grade | 8P@.725 | sf | 55.10 | 36.00 | 91.10 |
| replace, high grade | 8P@.870 | sf | 75.20 | 43.20 | 118.40 |
| replace, deluxe grade | 8P@1.05 | sf | 88.50 | 52.20 | 140.70 |
| replace, custom grade | 8P@1.25 | sf | 131.00 | 62.10 | 193.10 |
| remove | 1D@.019 | sf | — | .74 | .74 |

**Add for other wood species in frame-and-panel walls.** For panel walls made from other woods add the percentages to the cost of oak panel walls.

|  | Craft@Hrs | Unit | Material | Labor | Total |
|---|---|---|---|---|---|
| add for quartersawn oak | — | % | 12.0 | — | — |
| add for cherry | — | % | 17.0 | — | — |
| add for teak | — | % | 65.0 | — | — |
| add for mahogany | — | % | 10.0 | — | — |
| add for hickory | — | % | 14.0 | — | — |

## Time & Material Charts (selected items)
## Paneling Materials

| Hardboard paneling | Craft@Hrs | Unit | Material | Labor | Total |
|---|---|---|---|---|---|
| economy grade ($29.20 sheet, 32 sf), 5% waste | — | sf | .96 | — | .96 |
| high grade ($50.60 sheet, 32 sf), 5% waste | — | sf | 1.76 | — | 1.76 |

| 1/4" plywood paneling | Craft@Hrs | Unit | Material | Labor | Total |
|---|---|---|---|---|---|
| rough-sawn cedar ($85.20 sheet, 32 sf), 5% waste | — | sf | 2.79 | — | 2.79 |
| ash ($124.00 sheet, 32 sf), 5% waste | — | sf | 4.07 | — | 4.07 |
| birch ($61.50 sheet, 32 sf), 5% waste | — | sf | 2.02 | — | 2.02 |
| cherry ($137.00 sheet, 32 sf), 5% waste | — | sf | 4.49 | — | 4.49 |
| hickory ($129.00 sheet, 32 sf), 5% waste | — | sf | 4.23 | — | 4.23 |
| knotty pine ($105.00 sheet, 32 sf), 5% waste | — | sf | 3.44 | — | 3.44 |
| mahogany ($112.00 sheet, 32 sf), 5% waste | — | sf | 3.68 | — | 3.68 |
| white maple ($91.50 sheet, 32 sf), 5% waste | — | sf | 3.00 | — | 3.00 |
| red or white oak ($67.40 sheet, 32 sf), 5% waste | — | sf | 2.22 | — | 2.22 |
| quartersawn red or white oak ($117.00 sheet, 32 sf), 5% waste | — | sf | 3.84 | — | 3.84 |
| walnut ($182.00 sheet, 32 sf), 5% waste | — | sf | 5.97 | — | 5.97 |

| 1/4" plywood paneling with grooves | Craft@Hrs | Unit | Material | Labor | Total |
|---|---|---|---|---|---|
| rough-sawn cedar ($83.50 sheet, 32 sf), 5% waste | — | sf | 2.74 | — | 2.74 |
| ash ($120.00 sheet, 32 sf), 5% waste | — | sf | 3.94 | — | 3.94 |
| birch ($59.90 sheet, 32 sf), 5% waste | — | sf | 1.96 | — | 1.96 |
| cherry ($133.00 sheet, 32 sf), 5% waste | — | sf | 4.37 | — | 4.37 |
| hickory ($127.00 sheet, 32 sf), 5% waste | — | sf | 4.17 | — | 4.17 |
| knotty pine ($102.00sheet, 32 sf), 5% waste | — | sf | 3.35 | — | 3.35 |
| mahogany ($110.00 sheet, 32 sf), 5% waste | — | sf | 3.61 | — | 3.61 |
| white maple ($89.50 sheet, 32 sf), 5% waste | — | sf | 2.94 | — | 2.94 |
| red or white oak ($65.90 sheet, 32 sf), 5% waste | — | sf | 2.16 | — | 2.16 |

| | Craft@Hrs | Unit | Material | Labor | Total |
|---|---|---|---|---|---|
| quartersawn red or white oak | | | | | |
| ($113.00 sheet, 32 sf), 5% waste | — | sf | 3.71 | — | 3.71 |
| walnut ($177.00 sheet, 32 sf), 5% waste | — | sf | 5.81 | — | 5.81 |
| Pine board paneling | | | | | |
| board-on-board ($4.71 sf), 4% waste | — | sf | 4.90 | — | 4.90 |
| board-and-batten ($4.61 sf), 4% waste | — | sf | 4.84 | — | 4.84 |
| tongue-&-groove, simple ($4.88 sf), 4% waste | — | sf | 5.08 | — | 5.08 |
| tongue-&-groove, ornate ($6.12 sf), 4% waste | — | sf | 6.36 | — | 6.36 |
| Frame-and-panel wall | | | | | |
| pine, standard grade ($23.40 sf), 6% waste | — | sf | 24.80 | — | 24.80 |
| pine, custom grade ($56.00 sf), 6% waste | — | sf | 59.40 | — | 59.40 |
| oak, standard grade ($31.50 sf), 6% waste | — | sf | 33.40 | — | 33.40 |
| oak, custom grade ($75.40 sf), 6% waste | — | sf | 79.90 | — | 79.90 |
| walnut, standard grade ($51.80 sf), 6% waste | — | sf | 54.90 | — | 54.90 |
| walnut, custom grade ($125.00 sf), 6% waste | — | sf | 133.00 | — | 133.00 |

## Paneling Labor

| Laborer | base wage | paid leave | true wage | taxes & ins. | total |
|---|---|---|---|---|---|
| Paneling installer | $31.10 | 2.43 | $33.53 | 23.37 | $56.90 |
| Paneling installer's helper | $22.40 | 1.75 | $24.15 | 18.25 | $42.40 |
| Demolition laborer | $20.70 | 1.61 | $22.31 | 16.59 | $38.90 |

**Paid leave** is calculated based on two weeks paid vacation, one week sick leave, and seven paid holidays. Employer's matching portion of **FICA** is 7.65 percent. **FUTA** (Federal Unemployment) is .8 percent. **Worker's compensation** for the paneling trade was calculated using a national average of 16.85 percent. **Unemployment insurance** was calculated using a national average of 8 percent. **Health insurance** was calculated based on a projected national average for 2015 of $1,025 per employee (and family when applicable) per month. Employer pays 80 percent for a per month cost of $820 per employee. **Retirement** is based on a 401(k) retirement program with employer matching of 50 percent. Employee contributions to the 401(k) plan are an average of 6 percent of the true wage. **Liability insurance** is based on a national average of 10.0 percent.

| | Craft@Hrs | Unit | Material | Labor | Total |
|---|---|---|---|---|---|
| **Paneling Labor Productivity** | | | | | |
| Demolition of paneling | | | | | |
| remove hardboard paneling | 1D@.007 | sf | — | .27 | .27 |
| remove pegboard | 1D@.007 | sf | — | .27 | .27 |
| remove plywood paneling | 1D@.008 | sf | — | .31 | .31 |
| remove board paneling | 1D@.011 | sf | — | .43 | .43 |
| remove tongue-&-groove paneling | 1D@.011 | sf | — | .43 | .43 |
| remove frame-and-panel wall | 1D@.019 | sf | — | .74 | .74 |

## Paneling installation crew

| | | | |
|---|---|---|---|
| install paneling | paneling installer | $56.90 | |
| install paneling | installer's helper | $42.40 | |
| install paneling | paneling crew | $49.70 | |

| | Craft@Hrs | Unit | Material | Labor | Total |
|---|---|---|---|---|---|
| Install paneling | | | | | |
| hardboard | 8P@.033 | sf | — | 1.64 | 1.64 |
| pegboard | 8P@.030 | sf | — | 1.49 | 1.49 |
| plywood | 8P@.036 | sf | — | 1.79 | 1.79 |
| board-on-board | 8P@.038 | sf | — | 1.89 | 1.89 |
| board-and-batten | 8P@.042 | sf | — | 2.09 | 2.09 |
| tongue-&-groove | 8P@.047 | sf | — | 2.34 | 2.34 |
| Install frame-and-panel wall | | | | | |
| standard grade | 8P@.725 | sf | — | 36.00 | 36.00 |
| high grade | 8P@.870 | sf | — | 43.20 | 43.20 |
| deluxe grade | 8P@1.05 | sf | — | 52.20 | 52.20 |
| custom grade | 8P@1.25 | sf | — | 62.10 | 62.10 |

| | Craft@Hrs | Unit | Material | Labor | Total |
|---|---|---|---|---|---|

## Plaster & Stucco

**Flexible molds.** Cracks to decorative plaster that are longer than a hairline are often repaired using flexible molds. Flexible molds are made by constructing a wood box to fit around the area where the mold will be taken. A release agent is sprayed on the box and the original plaster to help the mold release when dried. Cold-cure silicone is usually used to make the mold, although many professionals use hot-melt mold-making compounds.

### Minimum charge.

| | Craft@Hrs | Unit | Material | Labor | Total |
|---|---|---|---|---|---|
| for plaster wall or ceiling repair | 6P@4.00 | ea | 63.30 | 199.00 | 262.30 |

### Plaster repair.

| | Craft@Hrs | Unit | Material | Labor | Total |
|---|---|---|---|---|---|
| repair hair-line plaster crack | 6P@.065 | lf | .41 | 3.24 | 3.65 |
| repair plaster crack less than 1" wide | 6P@.081 | lf | .64 | 4.03 | 4.67 |
| patch small plaster hole less than 2" square | 6P@.841 | ea | 1.91 | 41.90 | 43.81 |
| patch plaster hole 2" to 10" square | 6P@1.06 | ea | 8.57 | 52.80 | 61.37 |
| patch plaster hole 10" to 20" square | 6P@1.32 | ea | 14.80 | 65.70 | 80.50 |
| patch plaster section | 6P@.156 | sf | 3.14 | 7.77 | 10.91 |
| repair plaster wall outside corner damage | 6P@.289 | lf | 4.03 | 14.40 | 18.43 |
| repair plaster wall inside corner damage | 6P@.204 | lf | 3.32 | 10.20 | 13.52 |

### Plaster pilaster or column repair.

| | Craft@Hrs | Unit | Material | Labor | Total |
|---|---|---|---|---|---|
| repair section of plaster pilaster or column | 6P@.908 | lf | 27.90 | 45.20 | 73.10 |

### Plaster molding or enrichment repair. Repair to enrichments, moldings, ceiling rose or medallion.

| | Craft@Hrs | Unit | Material | Labor | Total |
|---|---|---|---|---|---|
| repair crack less than 1/4" | 6P@.071 | lf | .41 | 3.54 | 3.95 |
| take flexible mold of plaster molding | 6P@.588 | ea | 54.30 | 29.30 | 83.60 |
| create running mold for plaster molding | 6P@4.00 | ea | 71.40 | 199.00 | 270.40 |
| repair section | 6P@1.28 | ea | 8.38 | 63.70 | 72.08 |
| minimum charge | 6P@3.50 | ea | 35.20 | 174.00 | 209.20 |

**Acoustical plaster.** Includes painted metal lath or gypsum lath, lath nails, acoustical plaster, corner bead, and installation. Installation includes placing of lath on frame walls, three coats over lath with corner bead on outside corners and a trowel finish. Includes expansion metal on large walls. *Note:* During and prior to the 1970s, acoustical plaster often contained asbestos. Acoustical plaster need not contain asbestos fibers and the contemporary mixes quoted here do not. However, acoustical plaster installations are now rare and many building owners replace acoustical plaster with other styles of like kind and quality.

| | Craft@Hrs | Unit | Material | Labor | Total |
|---|---|---|---|---|---|
| Two coats of acoustical plaster on 3/8" gypsum lath | | | | | |
| replace, on wall | 6P@.051 | sf | 1.67 | 2.54 | 4.21 |
| replace, on ceiling | 6P@.061 | sf | 1.67 | 3.04 | 4.71 |
| remove | 1D@.023 | sf | — | .89 | .89 |
| Three coats of acoustical plaster on painted metal lath | | | | | |
| replace, on wall | 6P@.057 | sf | 1.45 | 2.84 | 4.29 |
| replace, on ceiling | 6P@.068 | sf | 1.45 | 3.39 | 4.84 |
| remove | 1D@.024 | sf | — | .93 | .93 |

|  | Craft@Hrs | Unit | Material | Labor | Total |
|---|---|---|---|---|---|

**Gypsum plaster.** Includes painted metal lath or gypsum lath, lath nails, gypsum plaster, corner bead, and installation. Installation includes placing of lath on frame walls, three coats over lath with corner bead on outside corners and a trowel finish. Includes expansion metal on large walls.

| Two coats of gypsum plaster on 3/8" gypsum lath |  |  |  |  |  |
|---|---|---|---|---|---|
| replace, on wall | 6P@.052 | sf | 1.45 | 2.59 | 4.04 |
| replace, on ceiling | 6P@.062 | sf | 1.45 | 3.09 | 4.54 |
| remove | 1D@.023 | sf | — | .89 | .89 |
| Three coats of gypsum plaster on painted metal lath |  |  |  |  |  |
| replace, on wall | 6P@.058 | sf | 1.23 | 2.89 | 4.12 |
| replace, on ceiling | 6P@.069 | sf | 1.23 | 3.44 | 4.67 |
| remove | 1D@.024 | sf | — | .93 | .93 |

**Perlite or vermiculite plaster.** Includes painted metal or gypsum lath, lath nails, plaster with perlite or vermiculite, corner bead, and installation. Installation includes placing of lath on frame walls, three coats over lath with corner bead on outside corners and a trowel finish. Includes expansion metal on large walls. Plaster with perlite and vermiculite is lighter than gypsum plaster and provides higher insulation value. Often used on firewalls and as a protective coat for structural steel beams and posts.

| Two coats of perlite plaster on 3/8" gypsum lath |  |  |  |  |  |
|---|---|---|---|---|---|
| replace, on wall | 6P@.059 | sf | 1.53 | 2.94 | 4.47 |
| replace, on ceiling | 6P@.071 | sf | 1.53 | 3.54 | 5.07 |
| remove | 1D@.023 | sf | — | .89 | .89 |
| Three coats of perlite plaster on painted metal lath |  |  |  |  |  |
| replace, on wall | 6P@.069 | sf | 2.49 | 3.44 | 5.93 |
| replace, on ceiling | 6P@.083 | sf | 2.49 | 4.13 | 6.62 |
| remove | 1D@.024 | sf | — | .93 | .93 |

**Keene's cement plaster.** Includes painted metal or gypsum lath, lath nails, Keene's plaster, corner bead, and installation. Installation includes placing of lath on frame walls, three coats over lath with corner bead on outside corners and a trowel finish. Includes expansion metal on large walls. Keene's plaster was developed in the late 19th century. It's a modified gypsum plaster with its chief benefit being superior hardness. It has often been used to make imitation marble and architectural casts. Keene's plaster is rarely used in contemporary construction.

| Two coats of Keene's plaster on 3/8" gypsum lath |  |  |  |  |  |
|---|---|---|---|---|---|
| replace, on wall | 6P@.075 | sf | 1.82 | 3.74 | 5.56 |
| replace, on ceiling | 6P@.090 | sf | 1.82 | 4.48 | 6.30 |
| remove | 1D@.023 | sf | — | .89 | .89 |
| Three coats of Keene's plaster on painted metal lath |  |  |  |  |  |
| replace, on wall | 6P@.082 | sf | 1.58 | 4.08 | 5.66 |
| replace, on ceiling | 6P@.093 | sf | 1.58 | 4.63 | 6.21 |
| remove | 1D@.024 | sf | — | .93 | .93 |

**Thin-coat plaster.** Includes gypsum lath, gypsum board nails or screws, plaster, tape, corner bead, and installation. Installation includes thin-coat over gypsum lath with corner bead on outside corners and a trowel finish. Currently the most common type of plaster installation in new homes (according to the Northwest Wall and Ceiling Bureau).

| replace, on 3/8" thick gypsum lath | 6P@.044 | sf | .52 | 2.19 | 2.71 |
|---|---|---|---|---|---|
| replace, on 1/2" thick gypsum lath | 6P@.044 | sf | .37 | 2.19 | 2.56 |
| remove | 1D@.021 | sf | — | .82 | .82 |

| | Craft@Hrs | Unit | Material | Labor | Total |
|---|---|---|---|---|---|

**Additional plaster costs.**

| | | | | | |
|---|---|---|---|---|---|
| add for curved wall | — | % | 28.0 | — | — |
| add for plaster installed on old-style wood lath | — | % | 60.0 | — | — |

**Plaster pilaster or column.** Includes gypsum lath, plaster, tape, corner bead, and installation labor. Does not include framing of column. Plaster columns may also be prefabricated units designed to encase a structural post.

| | Craft@Hrs | Unit | Material | Labor | Total |
|---|---|---|---|---|---|
| Square plaster pilaster | | | | | |
| replace pilaster, plain | 6P@.189 | lf | 4.72 | 9.41 | 14.13 |
| replace pilaster, rusticated | 6P@.227 | lf | 4.73 | 11.30 | 16.03 |
| remove | 1D@.043 | lf | — | 1.67 | 1.67 |
| Square plaster column | | | | | |
| replace column, plain | 6P@.345 | lf | 9.43 | 17.20 | 26.63 |
| replace column, rusticated | 6P@.436 | lf | 9.49 | 21.70 | 31.19 |
| remove | 1D@.077 | lf | — | 3.00 | 3.00 |
| Add for round pilaster or column | — | % | 30.0 | — | — |

**Cast-in-place plaster molding.** Includes plaster and installation labor. For straight-pattern moldings cast in place on walls and/or ceilings using a running mold. Inside corners require a great deal of handwork by a skilled specialist who may be hard to find in some regions of North America. Outside corners are less complex. Does not include scaffolding or knife charges.

| | Craft@Hrs | Unit | Material | Labor | Total |
|---|---|---|---|---|---|
| to 3" wide | 6P@1.56 | lf | 8.47 | 77.70 | 86.17 |
| over 3" to 6" wide | 6P@1.69 | lf | 16.80 | 84.20 | 101.00 |
| over 6" to 14" wide | 6P@1.89 | lf | 31.50 | 94.10 | 125.60 |
| add for inside corner | 6P@3.23 | ea | 8.57 | 161.00 | 169.57 |
| add for outside corner | 6P@1.54 | ea | 2.28 | 76.70 | 78.98 |

**Production plaster molding.** Includes prefabricated plaster molding, fasteners, adhesive, caulk, and installation labor. Installation is per manufacturer's specs, usually with a combination of adhesive and fasteners. Touch-up material is provided to hide fasteners. Prefabricated plaster moldings are available from specialized suppliers in a wide variety of patterns. Be careful not to confuse plaster moldings with those made of imitation polyurethane or similar materials.

| | Craft@Hrs | Unit | Material | Labor | Total |
|---|---|---|---|---|---|
| to 3" wide | 6P@.263 | lf | 35.20 | 13.10 | 48.30 |
| over 3" to 6" wide | 6P@.270 | lf | 52.40 | 13.40 | 65.80 |
| over 6" to 14" wide | 6P@.287 | lf | 84.50 | 14.30 | 98.80 |
| add for inside corner | 6P@.333 | ea | 1.87 | 16.60 | 18.47 |
| add for outside corner | 6P@.333 | ea | 2.12 | 16.60 | 18.72 |

**Plaster enrichment.** Includes prefabricated plaster enrichment, fasteners, adhesive, and installation labor. Installation is per manufacturer's specs, usually with a combination of adhesive and fasteners. Touch-up material is provided to hide fasteners. Enrichments are placed on walls or ceilings to further accent friezes, cornices, ceiling medallions and so forth. Be careful not to confuse plaster enrichments with those made of imitation polyurethane or similar materials.

| | Craft@Hrs | Unit | Material | Labor | Total |
|---|---|---|---|---|---|
| straight patterns | 6P@.263 | lf | 32.20 | 13.10 | 45.30 |
| ornate patterns | 6P@.270 | lf | 48.40 | 13.40 | 61.80 |
| very ornate patterns | 6P@.287 | lf | 70.00 | 14.30 | 84.30 |

**Plaster frieze.** Includes prefabricated plaster frieze, fasteners, adhesive, and installation labor. Installation is per manufacturer's specs, usually with a combination of adhesive and fasteners. Touch-up material is provided to hide fasteners. Plaster friezes are usually flat with ornate patterns, and can be up to 14" wide. Be careful not to confuse plaster moldings with imitation polyurethane or similar moldings.

| | Craft@Hrs | Unit | Material | Labor | Total |
|---|---|---|---|---|---|
| straight patterns | 6P@.263 | lf | 53.60 | 13.10 | 66.70 |
| ornate patterns | 6P@.270 | lf | 80.80 | 13.40 | 94.20 |
| very ornate patterns | 6P@.287 | lf | 117.00 | 14.30 | 131.30 |

| | Craft@Hrs | Unit | Material | Labor | Total |
|---|---|---|---|---|---|

**Plaster architrave.** Includes prefabricated plaster architrave, fasteners, adhesive, and installation labor. Most complex plaster architraves are production units built by a specialty supplier.

| | Craft@Hrs | Unit | Material | Labor | Total |
|---|---|---|---|---|---|
| plain | 6P@.154 | lf | 3.78 | 7.67 | 11.45 |
| rusticated | 6P@.185 | lf | 4.03 | 9.21 | 13.24 |
| straight patterns | 6P@.477 | lf | 4.64 | 23.80 | 28.44 |
| ornate patterns | 6P@.699 | lf | 4.75 | 34.80 | 39.55 |

**Plaster ceiling medallion.** Includes prefabricated plaster ceiling medallion, fasteners, adhesive, and installation labor. Installation is per manufacturer's specs, usually with a combination of adhesive and fasteners. Touch-up material is provided to hide fasteners. Plaster ceiling medallions are usually round or oval in shape, designed for the center of the ceiling. Be careful not to confuse plaster medallions with imitation polyurethane or similar medallions.

| | Craft@Hrs | Unit | Material | Labor | Total |
|---|---|---|---|---|---|
| simple pattern | 6P@.908 | ea | 188.00 | 45.20 | 233.20 |
| ornate pattern | 6P@.952 | ea | 358.00 | 47.40 | 405.40 |
| very ornate pattern | 6P@1.00 | ea | 655.00 | 49.80 | 704.80 |

**Plaster ceiling rose.** Includes prefabricated plaster ceiling rose, fasteners, adhesive, and installation labor. Installation is per manufacturer's specs, usually with a combination of adhesive and fasteners. Touch-up material is provided to hide fasteners. Plaster ceiling roses are very ornate ceiling medallions common to Victorian homes.

| | Craft@Hrs | Unit | Material | Labor | Total |
|---|---|---|---|---|---|
| small | 6P@.908 | ea | 319.00 | 45.20 | 364.20 |
| average size | 6P@.952 | ea | 488.00 | 47.40 | 535.40 |
| large | 6P@1.00 | ea | 926.00 | 49.80 | 975.80 |

**Stucco.** Includes felt or building paper, metal lath, and control joint and corner metal.

Three coat Portland cement stucco

| | Craft@Hrs | Unit | Material | Labor | Total |
|---|---|---|---|---|---|
| replace, sand float finish | 6P@.096 | sf | 1.27 | 4.78 | 6.05 |
| replace, sand float finish, on masonry | 6P@.075 | sf | .49 | 3.74 | 4.23 |
| replace, trowel float finish | 6P@.142 | sf | 1.28 | 7.07 | 8.35 |
| replace, trowel float finish, on masonry | 6P@.121 | sf | .51 | 6.03 | 6.54 |
| remove | 1D@.027 | sf | — | 1.05 | 1.05 |

**Additional stucco costs.**

| | Craft@Hrs | Unit | Material | Labor | Total |
|---|---|---|---|---|---|
| add for application on soffits | — | % | 26.0 | — | — |
| add for colors | — | % | 10.0 | — | — |
| add for white cement | — | % | 19.0 | — | — |
| add for pebble dash (rough cast) finish | — | % | 32.0 | — | — |
| add for vermiculated stucco finish | — | % | 88.0 | — | — |
| patch single "stone" section in stucco rustication | 6P@.769 | ea | 6.62 | 38.30 | 44.92 |
| add for stucco quoin | 6P@.624 | ea | 10.30 | 31.10 | 41.40 |
| add for stucco key | 6P@1.08 | ea | 15.70 | 53.80 | 69.50 |
| add for stucco raised trim | 6P@.149 | lf | 4.01 | 7.42 | 11.43 |
| add for stucco raised curved trim | 6P@.251 | lf | 4.65 | 12.50 | 17.15 |
| add for stucco color change | 6P@.054 | ea | .27 | 2.69 | 2.96 |

**Synthetic stucco.** Includes cement board or polystyrene foam insulation board, adhesive primer, color coat stucco, and corner mesh.

| | Craft@Hrs | Unit | Material | Labor | Total |
|---|---|---|---|---|---|
| replace, over 1/2" cement board | 6P@.074 | sf | 1.21 | 3.69 | 4.90 |
| replace, over 1" insulating foam board | 6P@.074 | sf | .97 | 3.69 | 4.66 |
| replace, over 2" insulating foam board | 6P@.074 | sf | 1.06 | 3.69 | 4.75 |
| remove | 1D@.027 | sf | — | 1.05 | 1.05 |

| | Craft@Hrs | Unit | Material | Labor | Total |
|---|---|---|---|---|---|
| **Additional synthetic stucco costs.** | | | | | |
| add for synthetic stucco quoin | 6P@.935 | ea | 5.81 | 46.60 | 52.41 |
| add for synthetic stucco key | 6P@1.61 | ea | 8.94 | 80.20 | 89.14 |
| add for synthetic stucco raised trim | 6P@.223 | lf | 2.26 | 11.10 | 13.36 |
| add for synthetic stucco raised curved trim | 6P@.373 | lf | 2.62 | 18.60 | 21.22 |
| add for synthetic stucco color change | 6P@.081 | lf | .13 | 4.03 | 4.16 |
| **Minimum charge.** | | | | | |
| for stucco repair | 6P@5.25 | ea | 73.40 | 261.00 | 334.40 |
| **Stucco repair.**  For repair of standard or synthetic stucco. | | | | | |
| repair hair-line stucco crack | 6P@.066 | lf | .42 | 3.29 | 3.71 |
| repair stucco crack less than 1" wide | 6P@.083 | lf | .66 | 4.13 | 4.79 |
| patch small stucco hole less than 2" square | 6P@.855 | ea | 1.96 | 42.60 | 44.56 |
| patch stucco hole 2" to 10" square | 6P@1.09 | ea | 8.76 | 54.30 | 63.06 |
| patch stucco hole 10" to 20" square | 6P@1.33 | ea | 15.20 | 66.20 | 81.40 |
| patch stucco section | 6P@.159 | sf | 3.22 | 7.92 | 11.14 |
| repair stucco wall outside corner damage | 6P@.296 | lf | 4.13 | 14.70 | 18.83 |
| repair stucco wall inside corner damage | 6P@.208 | lf | 3.40 | 10.40 | 13.80 |

**Stucco pilaster or column.**  Includes stucco and installation labor. Use as additional costs for stucco columns when estimating standard or synthetic stucco. Does not include framing of column. Stucco columns may also be prefabricated units.

| | Craft@Hrs | Unit | Material | Labor | Total |
|---|---|---|---|---|---|
| Square stucco pilaster | | | | | |
| replace pilaster, plain | 6P@.192 | lf | 4.88 | 9.56 | 14.44 |
| replace pilaster, rusticated | 6P@.230 | lf | 4.92 | 11.50 | 16.42 |
| remove | 1D@.048 | lf | — | 1.87 | 1.87 |
| Square stucco column | | | | | |
| replace column, plain | 6P@.349 | lf | 9.81 | 17.40 | 27.21 |
| replace column, rusticated | 6P@.441 | lf | 9.86 | 22.00 | 31.86 |
| remove | 1D@.083 | lf | — | 3.23 | 3.23 |

| | Craft@Hrs | Unit | Material | Labor | Total |
|---|---|---|---|---|---|
| **Additional stucco pilaster or column costs.** | | | | | |
| add for round stucco pilaster or column | — | % | 30.0 | — | — |
| repair section of stucco pilaster or column | 6P@.925 | ea | 27.90 | 46.10 | 74.00 |
| minimum charge | 6P@1.50 | ea | 49.30 | 74.70 | 124.00 |

**Stucco architrave.**  Includes foam, stucco, fasteners, adhesive, caulk, and installation labor. Many stucco architraves are built from shaped foam covered with synthetic stucco. Some complex stucco architraves are production units built by a specialty supplier.

| | Craft@Hrs | Unit | Material | Labor | Total |
|---|---|---|---|---|---|
| plain | 6P@.156 | lf | 3.93 | 7.77 | 11.70 |
| rusticated | 6P@.188 | lf | 3.96 | 9.36 | 13.32 |
| straight patterns | 6P@.482 | lf | 4.21 | 24.00 | 28.21 |
| ornate patterns | 6P@.708 | lf | 4.80 | 35.30 | 40.10 |
| take flexible mold of existing architrave | 6P@.595 | ea | 54.30 | 29.60 | 83.90 |
| create mold for architrave | 6P@4.00 | ea | 71.40 | 199.00 | 270.40 |
| repair section | 6P@1.35 | ea | 8.76 | 67.20 | 75.96 |
| minimum charge | 6P@3.75 | ea | 35.20 | 187.00 | 222.20 |

| | Craft@Hrs | Unit | Material | Labor | Total |
|---|---|---|---|---|---|

## Time & Material Charts (selected items)
### Plaster and Stucco Materials

| | Craft@Hrs | Unit | Material | Labor | Total |
|---|---|---|---|---|---|
| Gauging plaster, ($30.30 100 lb. bag, 1 ea), 21% waste | — | ea | 36.60 | — | 36.60 |
| Gypsum plaster, ($26.60 80 lb. bag, 1 ea), 21% waste | — | ea | 32.20 | — | 32.20 |
| Thin-coat plaster, ($16.50 50 lb. bag, 1 ea), 21% waste | — | ea | 20.00 | — | 20.00 |
| Keene's cement, ($34.60 100 lb. bag, 1 ea), 21% waste | — | ea | 41.90 | — | 41.90 |
| Perlite or vermiculite plaster, ($23.00 100 lb. bag, 1 ea), 21% waste | — | ea | 27.80 | — | 27.80 |
| 3/8" perforated gypsum lath, ($22.90 sheet, 32 sf), 4% waste | — | sf | .75 | — | .75 |
| 1/2" perforated gypsum lath, ($24.40 sheet, 32 sf), 4% waste | — | sf | .79 | — | .79 |
| Painted metal lath, ($.37 sf, 1 sf), 4% waste | — | sf | .38 | — | .38 |
| Painted stucco mesh, ($.57 sf, 1 sf), 4% waste | — | sf | .59 | — | .59 |

### Plaster & Stucco Labor

| Laborer | base wage | paid leave | true wage | taxes & ins. | total |
|---|---|---|---|---|---|
| Plasterer | $29.80 | 2.32 | $32.12 | 21.38 | $53.50 |
| Plasterer's helper | $25.20 | 1.97 | $27.17 | 18.83 | $46.00 |
| Demolition laborer | $20.70 | 1.61 | $22.31 | 16.59 | $38.90 |

**Paid leave** is calculated based on two weeks paid vacation, one week sick leave, and seven paid holidays. Employer's matching portion of FICA is 7.65 percent. **FUTA** (Federal Unemployment) is .8 percent. **Worker's compensation** for the plaster and stucco trade was calculated using a national average of 13.00 percent. **Unemployment insurance** was calculated using a national average of 8 percent. **Health insurance** was calculated based on a projected national average for 2015 of $1,025 per employee (and family when applicable) per month. Employer pays 80 percent for a per month cost of $820 per employee. **Retirement** is based on a 401(k) retirement program with employer matching of 50 percent. Employee contributions to the 401(k) plan are an average of 6 percent of the true wage. **Liability insurance** is based on a national average of 10.0 percent.

| | Craft@Hrs | Unit | Material | Labor | Total |
|---|---|---|---|---|---|

### Plaster & Stucco Labor Productivity

| | Craft@Hrs | Unit | Material | Labor | Total |
|---|---|---|---|---|---|
| Demolition of plaster and stucco | | | | | |
| remove plaster on gypsum lath | 1D@.023 | sf | — | .89 | .89 |
| remove plaster on metal lath | 1D@.024 | sf | — | .93 | .93 |
| remove thin-coat plaster on gypsum | 1D@.021 | sf | — | .82 | .82 |
| remove plaster pilaster | 1D@.043 | lf | — | 1.67 | 1.67 |
| remove plaster column | 1D@.077 | lf | — | 3.00 | 3.00 |

| | Craft@Hrs | Unit | Material | Labor | Total |
|---|---|---|---|---|---|
| remove stucco | 1D@.027 | sf | — | 1.05 | 1.05 |
| remove synthetic stucco on cement board | 1D@.027 | sf | — | 1.05 | 1.05 |
| remove stucco pilaster | 1D@.048 | lf | — | 1.87 | 1.87 |
| remove stucco column | 1D@.083 | lf | — | 3.23 | 3.23 |

**Plaster installation crew**

| | | | | | |
|---|---|---|---|---|---|
| install plaster | plasterer | $53.50 | | | |
| install plaster | plasterer's helper | $46.00 | | | |
| install plaster | plastering crew | $49.80 | | | |

| | Craft@Hrs | Unit | Material | Labor | Total |
|---|---|---|---|---|---|
| **Install acoustical plaster** | | | | | |
| two coat on 3/8" gypsum lath on wall | 6P@.051 | sf | — | 2.54 | 2.54 |
| two coat on 3/8" gypsum lath on ceiling | 6P@.061 | sf | — | 3.04 | 3.04 |
| three coat on painted metal lath on wall | 6P@.057 | sf | — | 2.84 | 2.84 |
| three coat on painted metal lath on ceiling | 6P@.068 | sf | — | 3.39 | 3.39 |
| **Install gypsum plaster** | | | | | |
| two coat on 3/8" gypsum lath on wall | 6P@.052 | sf | — | 2.59 | 2.59 |
| two coat on 3/8" gypsum lath on ceiling | 6P@.062 | sf | — | 3.09 | 3.09 |
| three coat on painted metal lath on wall | 6P@.058 | sf | — | 2.89 | 2.89 |
| three coat on painted metal lath on ceiling | 6P@.069 | sf | — | 3.44 | 3.44 |
| **Install perlite or vermiculite plaster** | | | | | |
| two coat on 3/8" gypsum lath on wall | 6P@.059 | sf | — | 2.94 | 2.94 |
| two coat on 3/8" gypsum lath on ceiling | 6P@.071 | sf | — | 3.54 | 3.54 |
| three coat on painted metal lath on wall | 6P@.069 | sf | — | 3.44 | 3.44 |
| three coat on painted metal lath on ceiling | 6P@.083 | sf | — | 4.13 | 4.13 |
| **Install Keene's cement plaster** | | | | | |
| two coat on 3/8" gypsum lath on wall | 6P@.075 | sf | — | 3.74 | 3.74 |
| two coat on 3/8" gypsum lath on ceiling | 6P@.090 | sf | — | 4.48 | 4.48 |
| three coat on painted metal lath on wall | 6P@.082 | sf | — | 4.08 | 4.08 |
| three coat on painted metal lath on ceiling | 6P@.093 | sf | — | 4.63 | 4.63 |
| **Install thin-coat plaster** | | | | | |
| on 3/8" thick gypsum lath | 6P@.044 | sf | — | 2.19 | 2.19 |
| on 1/2" thick gypsum lath | 6P@.044 | sf | — | 2.19 | 2.19 |
| **Install three-coat Portland cement stucco** | | | | | |
| sand float finish | 6P@.096 | sf | — | 4.78 | 4.78 |
| sand float finish, on masonry | 6P@.075 | sf | — | 3.74 | 3.74 |
| trowel float finish | 6P@.142 | sf | — | 7.07 | 7.07 |
| trowel float finish, on masonry | 6P@.121 | sf | — | 6.03 | 6.03 |
| **Install synthetic stucco** | | | | | |
| all applications | 6P@.074 | sf | — | 3.69 | 3.69 |

| Plumbing | Craft@Hrs | Unit | Material | Labor | Total |
|---|---|---|---|---|---|

## Minimum charge.

| | Craft@Hrs | Unit | Material | Labor | Total |
|---|---|---|---|---|---|
| for plumbing work | 7P@2.75 | ea | 53.30 | 184.00 | 237.30 |

**Black steel supply pipe.** Field threaded with fitting or coupling every 8.5 lf and hanger every 10 lf.

| | Craft@Hrs | Unit | Material | Labor | Total |
|---|---|---|---|---|---|
| 1/2" pipe | 7P@.127 | lf | 3.15 | 8.48 | 11.63 |
| 3/4" pipe | 7P@.136 | lf | 3.37 | 9.08 | 12.45 |
| 1" pipe | 7P@.158 | lf | 4.48 | 10.60 | 15.08 |
| 2" pipe | 7P@.231 | lf | 8.72 | 15.40 | 24.12 |

**Replace section of black steel supply pipe.** Includes cut-out in drywall, replacement pipe section and couplings. Does not include wall repair (see Drywall).

| | Craft@Hrs | Unit | Material | Labor | Total |
|---|---|---|---|---|---|
| all sizes | 7P@1.02 | ea | 37.30 | 68.10 | 105.40 |

**Brass water supply pipe.** Field threaded with fitting or coupling every 8.5 lf and hanger every 10 lf.

| | Craft@Hrs | Unit | Material | Labor | Total |
|---|---|---|---|---|---|
| 1/2" pipe | 7P@.172 | lf | 9.32 | 11.50 | 20.82 |
| 3/4"pipe | 7P@.180 | lf | 12.40 | 12.00 | 24.40 |
| 1" pipe | 7P@.192 | lf | 16.50 | 12.80 | 29.30 |
| 2" pipe | 7P@.210 | lf | 40.90 | 14.00 | 54.90 |

**Replace section of brass water supply pipe.** Includes cut-out in drywall, replacement pipe section and couplings. Does not include wall repair (see Drywall).

| | Craft@Hrs | Unit | Material | Labor | Total |
|---|---|---|---|---|---|
| all sizes | 7P@1.39 | ea | 76.70 | 92.90 | 169.60 |

**Copper water supply pipe.** With sweated fitting or coupling every 8.5 lf and hanger every 10 lf.

| | Craft@Hrs | Unit | Material | Labor | Total |
|---|---|---|---|---|---|
| Type K copper pipe | | | | | |
| 1/2" pipe | 7P@.104 | lf | 3.22 | 6.95 | 10.17 |
| 3/4"pipe | 7P@.109 | lf | 3.30 | 7.28 | 10.58 |
| 1" pipe | 7P@.122 | lf | 6.20 | 8.15 | 14.35 |
| 2" pipe | 7P@.202 | lf | 14.40 | 13.50 | 27.90 |
| Type L copper pipe | | | | | |
| 1/2" pipe | 7P@.104 | lf | 2.81 | 6.95 | 9.76 |
| 3/4" pipe | 7P@.109 | lf | 3.03 | 7.28 | 10.31 |
| 1" pipe | 7P@.122 | lf | 5.34 | 8.15 | 13.49 |
| 2" pipe | 7P@.202 | lf | 13.20 | 13.50 | 26.70 |
| Type M copper pipe | | | | | |
| 1/2" pipe | 7P@.104 | lf | 2.32 | 6.95 | 9.27 |
| 3/4" pipe | 7P@.109 | lf | 3.03 | 7.28 | 10.31 |
| 1" pipe | 7P@.122 | lf | 4.20 | 8.15 | 12.35 |

**Replace section of copper water supply pipe.** Includes cut-out in drywall, replacement pipe section and couplings. Does not include wall repair (see Drywall).

| | Craft@Hrs | Unit | Material | Labor | Total |
|---|---|---|---|---|---|
| all types and sizes | 7P@.827 | ea | 28.20 | 55.20 | 83.40 |

**Galvanized steel water supply pipe.** Field threaded with fitting or coupling every 8.5 lf and hanger every 10 lf.

| | Craft@Hrs | Unit | Material | Labor | Total |
|---|---|---|---|---|---|
| 1/2" pipe | 7P@.129 | lf | 3.80 | 8.62 | 12.42 |
| 3/4" pipe | 7P@.136 | lf | 4.12 | 9.08 | 13.20 |
| 1" pipe | 7P@.155 | lf | 5.92 | 10.40 | 16.32 |
| 2" pipe | 7P@.231 | lf | 10.80 | 15.40 | 26.20 |

| | Craft@Hrs | Unit | Material | Labor | Total |
|---|---|---|---|---|---|

**Replace section of galvanized steel water supply pipe.** Includes cut-out in drywall, replacement pipe section and couplings. Does not include wall repair (see Drywall).

| | Craft@Hrs | Unit | Material | Labor | Total |
|---|---|---|---|---|---|
| all sizes | 7P@1.04 | ea | 45.40 | 69.50 | 114.90 |

**CPVC water supply pipe, schedule 40.** With fitting or coupling every 8.5 lf and hanger every 3.5 lf.

| | Craft@Hrs | Unit | Material | Labor | Total |
|---|---|---|---|---|---|
| 1/2" pipe | 7P@.153 | lf | 4.91 | 10.20 | 15.11 |
| 3/4" pipe | 7P@.162 | lf | 5.98 | 10.80 | 16.78 |
| 1" pipe | 7P@.189 | lf | 7.30 | 12.60 | 19.90 |

**PVC cold water supply pipe, schedule 40.** With fitting or coupling every 8.5 lf and hanger every 3.5 lf.

| | Craft@Hrs | Unit | Material | Labor | Total |
|---|---|---|---|---|---|
| 1/2" pipe | 7P@.153 | lf | 2.85 | 10.20 | 13.05 |
| 3/4" pipe | 7P@.162 | lf | 2.95 | 10.80 | 13.75 |
| 1" pipe | 7P@.189 | lf | 3.42 | 12.60 | 16.02 |

**Replace section of PVC or CPVC water supply pipe.** Includes cut-out in drywall, replacement pipe section and couplings. Does not include wall repair (see Drywall).

| | Craft@Hrs | Unit | Material | Labor | Total |
|---|---|---|---|---|---|
| all sizes | 7P@1.23 | ea | 22.40 | 82.20 | 104.60 |

**Minimum charge.**

| | Craft@Hrs | Unit | Material | Labor | Total |
|---|---|---|---|---|---|
| for water supply pipe work | 7P@1.82 | ea | 79.90 | 122.00 | 201.90 |

**Cast-iron DWV pipe.** Lead and oakum joints with fitting every 9.5 lf.

| | Craft@Hrs | Unit | Material | Labor | Total |
|---|---|---|---|---|---|
| 2" pipe | 7P@.236 | lf | 8.05 | 15.80 | 23.85 |
| 3" pipe | 7P@.248 | lf | 11.00 | 16.60 | 27.60 |
| 4" pipe | 7P@.270 | lf | 14.70 | 18.00 | 32.70 |
| 5" pipe | 7P@.304 | lf | 19.40 | 20.30 | 39.70 |
| 6" pipe | 7P@.317 | lf | 23.50 | 21.20 | 44.70 |

**Replace section of cast-iron DWV pipe.** Includes cut-out in drywall, replacement pipe section and couplings. Does not include wall repair (see Drywall).

| | Craft@Hrs | Unit | Material | Labor | Total |
|---|---|---|---|---|---|
| all sizes | 7P@1.67 | ea | 141.00 | 112.00 | 253.00 |

**Repack cast-iron pipe joint with oakum and caulk.**

| | Craft@Hrs | Unit | Material | Labor | Total |
|---|---|---|---|---|---|
| all sizes | 7P@.181 | ea | 17.00 | 12.10 | 29.10 |

**Cast-iron no-hub DWV pipe.** With fitting or coupling every 9.5 lf.

| | Craft@Hrs | Unit | Material | Labor | Total |
|---|---|---|---|---|---|
| 2" pipe | 7P@.210 | lf | 9.53 | 14.00 | 23.53 |
| 3" pipe | 7P@.223 | lf | 12.90 | 14.90 | 27.80 |
| 4" pipe | 7P@.242 | lf | 16.00 | 16.20 | 32.20 |
| 5" pipe | 7P@.272 | lf | 23.10 | 18.20 | 41.30 |
| 6" pipe | 7P@.283 | lf | 26.90 | 18.90 | 45.80 |

**Replace section of cast-iron no-hub DWV pipe.** Includes cut-out in drywall, replacement pipe section and couplings. Does not include wall repair (see Drywall).

| | Craft@Hrs | Unit | Material | Labor | Total |
|---|---|---|---|---|---|
| all sizes | 7P@1.49 | ea | 109.00 | 99.50 | 208.50 |

**Repair pin-hole leak in cast-iron no-hub DWV pipe with epoxy.**

| | Craft@Hrs | Unit | Material | Labor | Total |
|---|---|---|---|---|---|
| all sizes | 7P@.544 | ea | 12.00 | 36.30 | 48.30 |

| | Craft@Hrs | Unit | Material | Labor | Total |
|---|---|---|---|---|---|

**PVC DWV pipe.** With fitting or coupling every 8.5 lf and hanger every 10 lf.

| | Craft@Hrs | Unit | Material | Labor | Total |
|---|---|---|---|---|---|
| 1-1/4" pipe | 7P@.198 | lf | 3.78 | 13.20 | 16.98 |
| 1-1/2" pipe | 7P@.229 | lf | 4.20 | 15.30 | 19.50 |
| 2" pipe | 7P@.251 | lf | 4.47 | 16.80 | 21.27 |
| 3" pipe | 7P@.281 | lf | 6.55 | 18.80 | 25.35 |
| 4" pipe | 7P@.310 | lf | 8.40 | 20.70 | 29.10 |
| 5" pipe | 7P@.347 | lf | 11.50 | 23.20 | 34.70 |
| 6" pipe | 7P@.379 | lf | 16.40 | 25.30 | 41.70 |

**Replace section of PVC DWV pipe.** Includes cut-out in drywall, replacement pipe section and couplings. Does not include wall repair (see Drywall).

| | Craft@Hrs | Unit | Material | Labor | Total |
|---|---|---|---|---|---|
| all sizes | 7P@1.45 | ea | 53.90 | 96.90 | 150.80 |

**Minimum charge for DWV line work.**

| | Craft@Hrs | Unit | Material | Labor | Total |
|---|---|---|---|---|---|
| all types | 7P@1.54 | ea | 85.30 | 103.00 | 188.30 |

**Exterior lines.** Includes excavation up to 8' deep, backfill, laying pipe, pipe, and fittings. Does not include mobilization or shoring.

| | Craft@Hrs | Unit | Material | Labor | Total |
|---|---|---|---|---|---|
| Sewer line | | | | | |
| 4" pipe | 7P@1.64 | lf | 34.90 | 110.00 | 144.90 |
| 6" pipe | 7P@1.69 | lf | 49.30 | 113.00 | 162.30 |
| Water supply line | | | | | |
| 1" pipe | 7P@1.64 | lf | 23.50 | 110.00 | 133.50 |
| 1-1/2" pipe | 7P@1.69 | lf | 27.80 | 113.00 | 140.80 |
| Minimum charge for exterior line work | 7P@10.0 | ea | 138.00 | 668.00 | 806.00 |

**Interior water supply shut-off valve with pressure valve.**

| | Craft@Hrs | Unit | Material | Labor | Total |
|---|---|---|---|---|---|
| for 1-1/2" line | 7P@1.10 | ea | 542.00 | 73.50 | 615.50 |
| for 2" line | 7P@1.10 | ea | 697.00 | 73.50 | 770.50 |

**Repair underground line.** Includes excavation to specified depth, backfill, laying pipe, pipe, and fittings. Does not include mobilization or shoring.

| | Craft@Hrs | Unit | Material | Labor | Total |
|---|---|---|---|---|---|
| 4' deep or less | 7P@1.67 | lf | 73.10 | 112.00 | 185.10 |
| 4' to 8' deep | 7P@2.16 | lf | 73.10 | 144.00 | 217.10 |
| 8' to 12' deep | 7P@3.04 | lf | 73.10 | 203.00 | 276.10 |
| 12' to 16' deep | 7P@4.35 | lf | 73.10 | 291.00 | 364.10 |

**Break-out existing concrete slab and install pipe.** Saw concrete slab and break-out, hand excavate, lay pipe, hand backfill, and patch concrete. Includes sand bed for pipe as necessary. Does not include pipe, couplings or fittings.

| | Craft@Hrs | Unit | Material | Labor | Total |
|---|---|---|---|---|---|
| all sizes and types of pipe | 7P@2.23 | lf | 23.60 | 149.00 | 172.60 |
| minimum charge | 7P@12.5 | ea | 147.00 | 835.00 | 982.00 |

**Complete house supply lines, waste lines and finish fixtures.** Includes all rough sewer, drain, vent, and water supply lines for entire house with installation. Installation includes tie-in to sewer line, tie-in to city water meter, pressure regulator when needed, main shut off valve and successful completion of all pressure tests. Includes finish fixtures installed with all lines connected and ready to pass final inspection. Grades refer to quality of plumbing fixtures. For residential structures only.

| | Craft@Hrs | Unit | Material | Labor | Total |
|---|---|---|---|---|---|
| economy grade (PVC DWV, PVC & CPVC supply) | 7P@.081 | sf | 3.01 | 5.41 | 8.42 |
| standard grade (PVC DWV, Cu supply) | 7P@.085 | sf | 4.83 | 5.68 | 10.51 |
| high grade (PVC DWV, Cu supply) | 7P@.086 | sf | 5.25 | 5.74 | 10.99 |
| deluxe grade (cast-iron DWV, Cu supply) | 7P@.091 | sf | 6.04 | 6.08 | 12.12 |
| custom deluxe grade (cast-iron DWV, Cu supply) | 9P@.108 | sf | 6.64 | 5.76 | 12.40 |

| | Craft@Hrs | Unit | Material | Labor | Total |
|---|---|---|---|---|---|

**Complete house rough plumbing (no fixtures).** Includes all rough sewer, drain, vent, and water supply lines for entire house with installation. Installation includes tie-in to sewer line, tie-in to city water meter, pressure regulator when needed, main shut off valve and successful completion of all pressure tests. Lines are capped at locations and not connected to fixtures. Does not include fixtures.

| | Craft@Hrs | Unit | Material | Labor | Total |
|---|---|---|---|---|---|
| economy grade (PVC DWV, PVC & CPVC supply) | 7P@.038 | sf | .79 | 2.54 | 3.33 |
| standard grade (PVC DWV, Cu supply) | 7P@.042 | sf | 1.18 | 2.81 | 3.99 |
| high grade (cast-iron DWV, Cu supply) | 7P@.045 | sf | 1.68 | 3.01 | 4.69 |

**Complete house plumbing fixtures.** Includes finish fixtures installed with all lines connected and ready to pass final inspection. Grades refer to quality of plumbing fixtures. For residential structures only. Does not include rough plumbing.

| | Craft@Hrs | Unit | Material | Labor | Total |
|---|---|---|---|---|---|
| economy grade | 7P@.043 | sf | 2.23 | 2.87 | 5.10 |
| standard grade | 7P@.044 | sf | 3.66 | 2.94 | 6.60 |
| high grade | 7P@.044 | sf | 4.06 | 2.94 | 7.00 |
| deluxe grade | 7P@.045 | sf | 4.35 | 3.01 | 7.36 |
| custom deluxe grade | 9P@.054 | sf | 4.93 | 2.88 | 7.81 |

**Rough plumbing, bathroom.** Does not include fixtures.

Two fixture bathroom

(typically 1 toilet and 1 sink)

| | Craft@Hrs | Unit | Material | Labor | Total |
|---|---|---|---|---|---|
| plastic supply & plastic DWV | 7P@19.6 | ea | 452.00 | 1,310.00 | 1,762.00 |
| copper supply & plastic DWV | 7P@20.4 | ea | 548.00 | 1,360.00 | 1,908.00 |
| copper supply & cast-iron DWV | 7P@21.3 | ea | 625.00 | 1,420.00 | 2,045.00 |

Three fixture bathroom

(typically 1 toilet, 1 sink and a shower or bathtub)

| | Craft@Hrs | Unit | Material | Labor | Total |
|---|---|---|---|---|---|
| plastic supply & plastic DWV | 7P@25.1 | ea | 587.00 | 1,680.00 | 2,267.00 |
| copper supply & plastic DWV | 7P@26.3 | ea | 707.00 | 1,760.00 | 2,467.00 |
| copper supply & cast-iron DWV | 7P@28.7 | ea | 805.00 | 1,920.00 | 2,725.00 |

Four fixture bathroom

(typically 1 toilet, 1 sink, 1 shower and a bathtub)

| | Craft@Hrs | Unit | Material | Labor | Total |
|---|---|---|---|---|---|
| plastic supply & plastic DWV | 7P@33.4 | ea | 726.00 | 2,230.00 | 2,956.00 |
| copper supply & plastic DWV | 7P@35.8 | ea | 873.00 | 2,390.00 | 3,263.00 |
| copper supply & cast-iron DWV | 7P@38.5 | ea | 999.00 | 2,570.00 | 3,569.00 |

Five fixture bathroom

(typically 1 toilet, 2 sinks, 1 shower and a bathtub)

| | Craft@Hrs | Unit | Material | Labor | Total |
|---|---|---|---|---|---|
| plastic supply & plastic DWV | 7P@41.8 | ea | 873.00 | 2,790.00 | 3,663.00 |
| copper supply & plastic DWV | 7P@43.5 | ea | 1,050.00 | 2,910.00 | 3,960.00 |
| copper supply & cast-iron DWV | 7P@45.4 | ea | 1,200.00 | 3,030.00 | 4,230.00 |

**Rough plumbing by room.** Includes all rough sewer, drain, vent, and water supply lines with installation. Lines are capped at locations and not connected to fixtures. Does not include fixtures.

Laundry room plumbing

(includes supply valves and recessed wall box)

| | Craft@Hrs | Unit | Material | Labor | Total |
|---|---|---|---|---|---|
| plastic supply & plastic DWV | 7P@6.49 | ea | 194.00 | 434.00 | 628.00 |
| copper supply & plastic DWV | 7P@6.81 | ea | 233.00 | 455.00 | 688.00 |
| copper supply & cast-iron DWV | 7P@7.19 | ea | 273.00 | 480.00 | 753.00 |

Laundry room with sink plumbing

(includes above plus plumbing for 1 to 2 hole laundry sink)

| | Craft@Hrs | Unit | Material | Labor | Total |
|---|---|---|---|---|---|
| plastic supply & plastic DWV | 7P@12.7 | ea | 459.00 | 848.00 | 1,307.00 |
| copper supply & plastic DWV | 7P@13.0 | ea | 553.00 | 868.00 | 1,421.00 |
| copper supply & cast-iron DWV | 7P@13.3 | ea | 632.00 | 888.00 | 1,520.00 |

|  | Craft@Hrs | Unit | Material | Labor | Total |
|---|---|---|---|---|---|
| **Kitchen plumbing** | | | | | |
| (includes supply valves, recessed wall box and plumbing for sink) | | | | | |
| plastic supply & plastic DWV | 7P@8.20 | ea | 332.00 | 548.00 | 880.00 |
| copper supply & plastic DWV | 7P@8.54 | ea | 374.00 | 570.00 | 944.00 |
| copper supply & cast-iron DWV | 7P@8.78 | ea | 414.00 | 587.00 | 1,001.00 |
| **Kitchen with ice maker plumbing** | | | | | |
| (includes ice maker with line from sink to refrigerator) | | | | | |
| plastic supply & plastic DWV | 7P@9.81 | ea | 380.00 | 655.00 | 1,035.00 |
| copper supply & plastic DWV | 7P@10.1 | ea | 420.00 | 675.00 | 1,095.00 |
| copper supply & cast-iron DWV | 7P@10.4 | ea | 459.00 | 695.00 | 1,154.00 |

## Rough plumbing by fixture.

|  | Craft@Hrs | Unit | Material | Labor | Total |
|---|---|---|---|---|---|
| **Wet bar plumbing** | | | | | |
| plastic supply & plastic DWV | 7P@7.41 | ea | 167.00 | 495.00 | 662.00 |
| copper supply & plastic DWV | 7P@7.69 | ea | 194.00 | 514.00 | 708.00 |
| copper supply & cast-iron DWV | 7P@7.94 | ea | 233.00 | 530.00 | 763.00 |
| **Bathroom sink plumbing** | | | | | |
| plastic supply & plastic DWV | 7P@7.41 | ea | 167.00 | 495.00 | 662.00 |
| copper supply & plastic DWV | 7P@7.69 | ea | 201.00 | 514.00 | 715.00 |
| copper supply & cast-iron DWV | 7P@7.94 | ea | 240.00 | 530.00 | 770.00 |
| **Kitchen sink plumbing** | | | | | |
| plastic supply & plastic DWV | 7P@8.20 | ea | 288.00 | 548.00 | 836.00 |
| copper supply & plastic DWV | 7P@8.54 | ea | 327.00 | 570.00 | 897.00 |
| copper supply & cast-iron DWV | 7P@8.78 | ea | 366.00 | 587.00 | 953.00 |
| **Laundry room sink plumbing** | | | | | |
| plastic supply & plastic DWV | 7P@6.49 | ea | 160.00 | 434.00 | 594.00 |
| copper supply & plastic DWV | 7P@6.81 | ea | 194.00 | 455.00 | 649.00 |
| copper supply & cast-iron DWV | 7P@7.19 | ea | 233.00 | 480.00 | 713.00 |
| **Bathtub or shower plumbing** | | | | | |
| plastic supply & plastic DWV | 7P@6.90 | ea | 240.00 | 461.00 | 701.00 |
| copper supply & plastic DWV | 7P@7.26 | ea | 295.00 | 485.00 | 780.00 |
| copper supply & cast-iron DWV | 7P@7.58 | ea | 347.00 | 506.00 | 853.00 |
| **Toilet plumbing** | | | | | |
| plastic supply & plastic DWV | 7P@5.85 | ea | 206.00 | 391.00 | 597.00 |
| copper supply & plastic DWV | 7P@6.21 | ea | 253.00 | 415.00 | 668.00 |
| copper supply & cast-iron DWV | 7P@6.45 | ea | 300.00 | 431.00 | 731.00 |
| **Bidet plumbing** | | | | | |
| plastic supply & plastic DWV | 7P@6.49 | ea | 233.00 | 434.00 | 667.00 |
| copper supply & plastic DWV | 7P@6.90 | ea | 288.00 | 461.00 | 749.00 |
| copper supply & cast-iron DWV | 7P@7.13 | ea | 341.00 | 476.00 | 817.00 |
| **Clothes washer plumbing** | | | | | |
| plastic supply & plastic DWV | 7P@7.26 | ea | 167.00 | 485.00 | 652.00 |
| copper supply & plastic DWV | 7P@7.52 | ea | 201.00 | 502.00 | 703.00 |
| copper supply & cast-iron DWV | 7P@7.75 | ea | 240.00 | 518.00 | 758.00 |
| **Dishwasher plumbing** | | | | | |
| plastic supply & plastic DWV | 7P@1.39 | ea | 29.50 | 92.90 | 122.40 |
| copper supply & plastic DWV | 7P@1.49 | ea | 37.40 | 99.50 | 136.90 |
| copper supply & cast-iron DWV | 7P@1.59 | ea | 45.20 | 106.00 | 151.20 |

| | Craft@Hrs | Unit | Material | Labor | Total |
|---|---|---|---|---|---|
| **Exterior hose bibb (freeze-proof)** | | | | | |
| plastic supply | 7P@3.55 | ea | 101.00 | 237.00 | 338.00 |
| copper supply | 7P@3.51 | ea | 138.00 | 234.00 | 372.00 |
| **Evaporative cooler plumbing** | | | | | |
| copper supply line | 7P@2.68 | ea | 75.80 | 179.00 | 254.80 |
| **Refrigerator with ice maker** | | | | | |
| **and/or water dispenser plumbing** | | | | | |
| plastic supply line | 7P@2.10 | ea | 18.50 | 140.00 | 158.50 |
| copper supply line | 7P@2.21 | ea | 48.00 | 148.00 | 196.00 |
| **Floor drain** | | | | | |
| in-floor French drain | 7P@3.23 | ea | 145.00 | 216.00 | 361.00 |
| in-floor drain connected to sewer | 7P@5.27 | ea | 353.00 | 352.00 | 705.00 |

**Faucet.** Some faucet quality "rules of thumb." Economy: Light gauge metal, chrome plated. May have some plastic components. Little or no pattern. Standard: Heavier gauge metal, chrome or brass plated with little or no pattern or wood handles made of ash or oak. High: Brass, chrome over brass, or nickel over brass with minimal detail or plated hardware with ornate detail or European style curved plastic or with porcelain components. Deluxe: Brass, chrome over brass, or nickel over brass with ornate detail.

**Bathroom sink faucet.** Includes bathroom sink faucet, feeder tubes, and installation.

| | Craft@Hrs | Unit | Material | Labor | Total |
|---|---|---|---|---|---|
| replace, economy grade | 7P@.557 | ea | 134.00 | 37.20 | 171.20 |
| replace, standard grade | 7P@.557 | ea | 240.00 | 37.20 | 277.20 |
| replace, high grade | 7P@.557 | ea | 452.00 | 37.20 | 489.20 |
| replace, deluxe grade | 7P@.557 | ea | 781.00 | 37.20 | 818.20 |
| remove | 1D@.356 | ea | — | 13.80 | 13.80 |
| remove for work, then reinstall | 7P@.833 | ea | — | 55.60 | 55.60 |

**Bidet faucet.** Includes bidet faucet, feeder tubes, and installation.

| | Craft@Hrs | Unit | Material | Labor | Total |
|---|---|---|---|---|---|
| replace, standard grade | 7P@.595 | ea | 392.00 | 39.70 | 431.70 |
| replace, high grade | 7P@.595 | ea | 625.00 | 39.70 | 664.70 |
| replace, deluxe grade | 7P@.595 | ea | 1,030.00 | 39.70 | 1,069.70 |
| remove | 1D@.356 | ea | — | 13.80 | 13.80 |
| remove for work, then reinstall | 7P@.869 | ea | — | 58.00 | 58.00 |

**Kitchen sink faucet.** Includes kitchen sink faucet, feeder tubes, and installation.

| | Craft@Hrs | Unit | Material | Labor | Total |
|---|---|---|---|---|---|
| replace, economy grade | 7P@.561 | ea | 145.00 | 37.50 | 182.50 |
| replace, standard grade | 7P@.561 | ea | 265.00 | 37.50 | 302.50 |
| replace, high grade | 7P@.561 | ea | 507.00 | 37.50 | 544.50 |
| replace, deluxe grade | 7P@.561 | ea | 873.00 | 37.50 | 910.50 |
| remove | 1D@.356 | ea | — | 13.80 | 13.80 |
| remove for work, then reinstall | 7P@.869 | ea | — | 58.00 | 58.00 |

**Laundry sink faucet.** Includes laundry sink faucet, feeder tubes, and installation.

| | Craft@Hrs | Unit | Material | Labor | Total |
|---|---|---|---|---|---|
| replace, economy grade | 7P@.546 | ea | 79.90 | 36.50 | 116.40 |
| replace, standard grade | 7P@.546 | ea | 145.00 | 36.50 | 181.50 |
| replace, high grade | 7P@.546 | ea | 201.00 | 36.50 | 237.50 |
| replace, deluxe grade | 7P@.546 | ea | 353.00 | 36.50 | 389.50 |
| remove | 1D@.356 | ea | — | 13.80 | 13.80 |
| remove for work, then reinstall | 7P@.820 | ea | — | 54.80 | 54.80 |

| | Craft@Hrs | Unit | Material | Labor | Total |
|---|---|---|---|---|---|

**Shower faucet.** Includes shower faucet and installation.

| | Craft@Hrs | Unit | Material | Labor | Total |
|---|---|---|---|---|---|
| replace, economy grade | 7P@.576 | ea | 180.00 | 38.50 | 218.50 |
| replace, standard grade | 7P@.576 | ea | 320.00 | 38.50 | 358.50 |
| replace, high grade | 7P@.576 | ea | 548.00 | 38.50 | 586.50 |
| replace, deluxe grade | 7P@.576 | ea | 815.00 | 38.50 | 853.50 |
| remove | 1D@.356 | ea | — | 13.80 | 13.80 |
| remove for work, then reinstall | 7P@.884 | ea | — | 59.10 | 59.10 |

**Bathtub faucet.** Includes bathtub faucet and installation.

| | Craft@Hrs | Unit | Material | Labor | Total |
|---|---|---|---|---|---|
| replace, economy grade | 7P@.567 | ea | 201.00 | 37.90 | 238.90 |
| replace, standard grade | 7P@.567 | ea | 359.00 | 37.90 | 396.90 |
| replace, high grade | 7P@.567 | ea | 615.00 | 37.90 | 652.90 |
| replace, deluxe grade | 7P@.567 | ea | 906.00 | 37.90 | 943.90 |
| remove | 1D@.356 | ea | — | 13.80 | 13.80 |
| remove for work, then reinstall | 7P@.878 | ea | — | 58.70 | 58.70 |

**Bathtub with shower faucet.** Includes bathtub with shower faucet and installation.

| | Craft@Hrs | Unit | Material | Labor | Total |
|---|---|---|---|---|---|
| replace, economy grade | 7P@.606 | ea | 219.00 | 40.50 | 259.50 |
| replace, standard grade | 7P@.606 | ea | 392.00 | 40.50 | 432.50 |
| replace, high grade | 7P@.606 | ea | 675.00 | 40.50 | 715.50 |
| replace, deluxe grade | 7P@.606 | ea | 993.00 | 40.50 | 1,033.50 |
| remove | 1D@.401 | ea | — | 15.60 | 15.60 |
| remove for work, then reinstall | 7P@.901 | ea | — | 60.20 | 60.20 |

**Wet bar sink faucet.** Includes wet bar sink faucet, feeder tubes, and installation.

| | Craft@Hrs | Unit | Material | Labor | Total |
|---|---|---|---|---|---|
| replace, economy grade | 7P@.542 | ea | 120.00 | 36.20 | 156.20 |
| replace, standard grade | 7P@.542 | ea | 213.00 | 36.20 | 249.20 |
| replace, high grade | 7P@.542 | ea | 406.00 | 36.20 | 442.20 |
| replace, deluxe grade | 7P@.542 | ea | 693.00 | 36.20 | 729.20 |
| remove | 1D@.356 | ea | — | 13.80 | 13.80 |
| remove for work, then reinstall | 7P@.801 | ea | — | 53.50 | 53.50 |

**Refurbish and repack faucet.**

| | Craft@Hrs | Unit | Material | Labor | Total |
|---|---|---|---|---|---|
| all types | 7P@.454 | ea | 26.50 | 30.30 | 56.80 |

**Bathroom sink.** With visible plumbing, including water feeds, P-trap, escutcheons, to wall or floor. Does not include faucet.

| | Craft@Hrs | Unit | Material | Labor | Total |
|---|---|---|---|---|---|
| Wall-hung porcelain-enamel cast iron bathroom sink | | | | | |
| replace, oval | 7P@.878 | ea | 579.00 | 58.70 | 637.70 |
| replace, round | 7P@.878 | ea | 574.00 | 58.70 | 632.70 |
| replace, hexagonal | 7P@.878 | ea | 620.00 | 58.70 | 678.70 |
| Wall-hung porcelain-enamel steel bathroom sink | | | | | |
| replace, oval | 7P@.878 | ea | 487.00 | 58.70 | 545.70 |
| replace, round | 7P@.878 | ea | 480.00 | 58.70 | 538.70 |
| replace, hexagonal | 7P@.878 | ea | 521.00 | 58.70 | 579.70 |
| Wall-hung vitreous china bathroom sink | | | | | |
| replace, oval | 7P@.878 | ea | 468.00 | 58.70 | 526.70 |
| replace, oval with pattern | 7P@.878 | ea | 615.00 | 58.70 | 673.70 |
| replace, round | 7P@.878 | ea | 459.00 | 58.70 | 517.70 |

| | Craft@Hrs | Unit | Material | Labor | Total |
|---|---|---|---|---|---|
| replace, round with pattern | 7P@.878 | ea | 599.00 | 58.70 | 657.70 |
| replace, hexagonal | 7P@.878 | ea | 480.00 | 58.70 | 538.70 |
| remove | 1D@.367 | ea | — | 14.30 | 14.30 |
| **Remove wall-hung bathroom sink for work,** | | | | | |
| then reinstall, all types | 7P@1.09 | ea | — | 72.80 | 72.80 |
| **Self-rimming vitreous china bathroom sink** | | | | | |
| replace, oval | 7P@.910 | ea | 420.00 | 60.80 | 480.80 |
| replace, oval with pattern | 7P@.910 | ea | 553.00 | 60.80 | 613.80 |
| replace, round | 7P@.910 | ea | 414.00 | 60.80 | 474.80 |
| replace, round with pattern | 7P@.910 | ea | 540.00 | 60.80 | 600.80 |
| replace, hexagonal | 7P@.910 | ea | 434.00 | 60.80 | 494.80 |
| **Self-rimming stainless steel bathroom sink** | | | | | |
| replace, oval | 7P@.910 | ea | 452.00 | 60.80 | 512.80 |
| replace, oval, scalloped | 7P@.910 | ea | 521.00 | 60.80 | 581.80 |
| **Self-rimming polished brass bathroom skin** | | | | | |
| replace, oval | 7P@.910 | ea | 499.00 | 60.80 | 559.80 |
| replace, oval with hammered finish | 7P@.910 | ea | 565.00 | 60.80 | 625.80 |
| replace, oval with scalloped finish | 7P@.910 | ea | 625.00 | 60.80 | 685.80 |
| remove | 1D@.367 | ea | — | 14.30 | 14.30 |
| **Remove self-rimming bathroom sink for work,** | | | | | |
| then reinstall, all types | 7P@1.14 | ea | — | 76.20 | 76.20 |
| **Under-counter vitreous china bathroom sink** | | | | | |
| replace, oval | 7P@.953 | ea | 441.00 | 63.70 | 504.70 |
| replace, oval with pattern | 7P@.953 | ea | 579.00 | 63.70 | 642.70 |
| replace, round | 7P@.953 | ea | 434.00 | 63.70 | 497.70 |
| replace, round sink with pattern | 7P@.953 | ea | 565.00 | 63.70 | 628.70 |
| replace, hexagonal | 7P@.953 | ea | 452.00 | 63.70 | 515.70 |
| remove | 1D@.367 | ea | — | 14.30 | 14.30 |
| **Remove under-counter sink for work,** | | | | | |
| then reinstall, all types | 7P@1.18 | ea | — | 78.80 | 78.80 |

**Kitchen sink.** With visible plumbing, including water feeds, P-trap, escutcheons, to wall or floor. Does not include faucet.

| | Craft@Hrs | Unit | Material | Labor | Total |
|---|---|---|---|---|---|
| **Porcelain-enamel cast-iron kitchen sink** | | | | | |
| replace, 24" by 21" single-bowl | 7P@.925 | ea | 459.00 | 61.80 | 520.80 |
| replace, 30" by 21" single-bowl | 7P@.925 | ea | 565.00 | 61.80 | 626.80 |
| replace, 32" by 21" double-bowl | 7P@.925 | ea | 675.00 | 61.80 | 736.80 |
| replace, 42" by 21" triple-bowl | 7P@.925 | ea | 1,450.00 | 61.80 | 1,511.80 |
| **Porcelain-enamel steel kitchen sink** | | | | | |
| replace, 24" by 21" single-bowl | 7P@.925 | ea | 233.00 | 61.80 | 294.80 |
| replace, 30" by 21" single-bowl | 7P@.925 | ea | 273.00 | 61.80 | 334.80 |
| replace, 32" by 21" double-bowl | 7P@.925 | ea | 281.00 | 61.80 | 342.80 |
| replace, 42" by 21" triple-bowl | 7P@.925 | ea | 1,260.00 | 61.80 | 1,321.80 |
| **Stainless steel kitchen sink** | | | | | |
| replace, 19" by 18" single-bowl | 7P@.925 | ea | 347.00 | 61.80 | 408.80 |
| replace, 25" by 22" single-bowl | 7P@.925 | ea | 374.00 | 61.80 | 435.80 |
| replace, 33" by 22" double-bowl | 7P@.925 | ea | 499.00 | 61.80 | 560.80 |
| replace, 43" by 22" double-bowl | 7P@.925 | ea | 533.00 | 61.80 | 594.80 |
| replace, 43" by 22" triple-bowl | 7P@.925 | ea | 720.00 | 61.80 | 781.80 |
| remove | 1D@.370 | ea | — | 14.40 | 14.40 |
| **Remove kitchen sink for work, then reinstall** | | | | | |
| all types | 7P@1.11 | ea | — | 74.10 | 74.10 |

| | Craft@Hrs | Unit | Material | Labor | Total |
|---|---|---|---|---|---|

**Laundry sink.** With visible plumbing, including water feeds, P-trap, escutcheons, to wall or floor. Does not include faucet.

| | Craft@Hrs | Unit | Material | Labor | Total |
|---|---|---|---|---|---|
| Stainless steel laundry sink in countertop | | | | | |
| replace, 22" x 17" single | 7P@.901 | ea | 492.00 | 60.20 | 552.20 |
| replace, 19" x 22" single | 7P@.901 | ea | 527.00 | 60.20 | 587.20 |
| replace, 33" x 22" double | 7P@.901 | ea | 565.00 | 60.20 | 625.20 |
| Porcelain-enamel cast-iron laundry sink on black iron frame | | | | | |
| replace, 24" x 20" single | 7P@.833 | ea | 693.00 | 55.60 | 748.60 |
| replace, 24" x 23" single | 7P@.833 | ea | 753.00 | 55.60 | 808.60 |
| Plastic laundry sink with plastic legs | | | | | |
| replace, 18" x 23" single | 7P@.833 | ea | 185.00 | 55.60 | 240.60 |
| replace, 20" x 24" single | 7P@.833 | ea | 240.00 | 55.60 | 295.60 |
| replace, 36" x 23" double | 7P@.833 | ea | 288.00 | 55.60 | 343.60 |
| replace, 40" x 24" double | 7P@.833 | ea | 392.00 | 55.60 | 447.60 |
| remove | 1D@.370 | ea | — | 14.40 | 14.40 |
| Remove laundry sink for work, then reinstall | | | | | |
| all types | 7P@1.12 | ea | — | 74.80 | 74.80 |

**Wet bar sink.** With visible plumbing, including water feeds, P-trap, escutcheons, to wall or floor. Does not include faucet.

| | Craft@Hrs | Unit | Material | Labor | Total |
|---|---|---|---|---|---|
| Self-rimming wet bar sink | | | | | |
| replace, vitreous china | 7P@.910 | ea | 758.00 | 60.80 | 818.80 |
| replace, vitreous china with pattern | 7P@.910 | ea | 901.00 | 60.80 | 961.80 |
| replace, porcelain-enamel cast iron | 7P@.910 | ea | 594.00 | 60.80 | 654.80 |
| replace, porcelain-enamel steel | 7P@.910 | ea | 332.00 | 60.80 | 392.80 |
| replace, stainless steel | 7P@.910 | ea | 259.00 | 60.80 | 319.80 |
| replace, scalloped stainless steel | 7P@.910 | ea | 374.00 | 60.80 | 434.80 |
| replace, polished brass | 7P@.910 | ea | 513.00 | 60.80 | 573.80 |
| replace, hammered finish brass | 7P@.910 | ea | 587.00 | 60.80 | 647.80 |
| replace, scalloped polished brass | 7P@.910 | ea | 659.00 | 60.80 | 719.80 |
| remove | 1D@.356 | ea | — | 13.80 | 13.80 |
| remove for work, then reinstall | 7P@1.14 | ea | — | 76.20 | 76.20 |
| Under-counter wet bar sink | | | | | |
| replace, vitreous china | 7P@.953 | ea | 468.00 | 63.70 | 531.70 |
| replace, vitreous china with pattern | 7P@.953 | ea | 607.00 | 63.70 | 670.70 |
| replace, porcelain-enamel cast iron | 7P@.953 | ea | 579.00 | 63.70 | 642.70 |
| replace, porcelain-enamel steel | 7P@.953 | ea | 327.00 | 63.70 | 390.70 |
| replace, stainless steel | 7P@.953 | ea | 253.00 | 63.70 | 316.70 |
| replace, scalloped stainless steel | 7P@.953 | ea | 366.00 | 63.70 | 429.70 |
| replace, polished brass | 7P@.953 | ea | 499.00 | 63.70 | 562.70 |
| replace, hammered finish brass | 7P@.953 | ea | 574.00 | 63.70 | 637.70 |
| replace, scalloped polished brass | 7P@.953 | ea | 641.00 | 63.70 | 704.70 |
| remove | 1D@.356 | ea | — | 13.80 | 13.80 |
| remove for work, then reinstall | 7P@1.18 | ea | — | 78.80 | 78.80 |

**Additional sink costs.**

| | Craft@Hrs | Unit | Material | Labor | Total |
|---|---|---|---|---|---|
| add for brass supply and waste lines | — | ea | 182.00 | — | 182.00 |
| add for almond colored porcelain enamel | — | % | 33.0 | — | — |
| add for colored porcelain enamel | — | % | 65.0 | — | — |

| | Craft@Hrs | Unit | Material | Labor | Total |
|---|---|---|---|---|---|

**Sink finish plumbing.** With visible plumbing, including water feeds, P-trap, escutcheons, to wall or floor. Does not include faucet.

| | Craft@Hrs | Unit | Material | Labor | Total |
|---|---|---|---|---|---|
| replace, chrome | 7P@.475 | ea | 160.00 | 31.70 | 191.70 |
| replace, brass | 7P@.475 | ea | 259.00 | 31.70 | 290.70 |
| replace, chrome-plated brass | 7P@.475 | ea | 332.00 | 31.70 | 363.70 |

**Toilet finish plumbing.** Includes cold water supply, shut-off valve, wax ring, and toilet bolts.

| | Craft@Hrs | Unit | Material | Labor | Total |
|---|---|---|---|---|---|
| replace, chrome | 7P@.345 | ea | 106.00 | 23.00 | 129.00 |
| replace, brass | 7P@.345 | ea | 174.00 | 23.00 | 197.00 |

**Bidet finish plumbing.** Includes water supply lines with shut-off valves.

| | Craft@Hrs | Unit | Material | Labor | Total |
|---|---|---|---|---|---|
| replace, standard grade | 7P@1.47 | ea | 540.00 | 98.20 | 638.20 |
| replace, deluxe grade | 7P@1.47 | ea | 792.00 | 98.20 | 890.20 |
| remove | 1D@.360 | ea | — | 14.00 | 14.00 |
| remove for work, then reinstall | 7P@2.38 | ea | 2.61 | 159.00 | 161.61 |

**Toilet.** Includes toilet, wax bowl ring, fastener bolts with caps, and installation. Economy grade toilets are typically white with round bowls. Standard grade toilets are typically white with elongated bowls. High and deluxe grades are typically low-tank toilets, in a variety of colors, with elongated bowls. Deluxe grade may also be "jet" toilets which combine low-water consumption with a direct-fed jet, siphon-assisted blow out action.

| | Craft@Hrs | Unit | Material | Labor | Total |
|---|---|---|---|---|---|
| replace, economy grade | 7P@1.33 | ea | 206.00 | 88.80 | 294.80 |
| replace, standard grade | 7P@1.33 | ea | 253.00 | 88.80 | 341.80 |
| replace, high grade | 7P@1.33 | ea | 366.00 | 88.80 | 454.80 |
| replace, deluxe grade | 7P@1.33 | ea | 632.00 | 88.80 | 720.80 |
| remove | 1D@.346 | ea | — | 13.50 | 13.50 |
| remove for work, then reinstall | 7P@2.16 | ea | 2.61 | 144.00 | 146.61 |

**Toilet seat.**

| | Craft@Hrs | Unit | Material | Labor | Total |
|---|---|---|---|---|---|
| replace, plain round | 7P@.223 | ea | 33.20 | 14.90 | 48.10 |
| replace, hardwood | 7P@.223 | ea | 33.20 | 14.90 | 48.10 |
| replace, with pattern | 7P@.223 | ea | 53.30 | 14.90 | 68.20 |
| replace, elongated | 7P@.223 | ea | 73.20 | 14.90 | 88.10 |
| replace, padded | 7P@.223 | ea | 59.90 | 14.90 | 74.80 |
| remove | 1D@.139 | ea | — | 5.41 | 5.41 |
| remove for work, then reinstall | 7P@.323 | ea | — | 21.60 | 21.60 |

**Bathtub.** Includes standard chrome drain and overflow assembly. Does not include faucet.

| | Craft@Hrs | Unit | Material | Labor | Total |
|---|---|---|---|---|---|
| **48" long by 44" deep bathtub** | | | | | |
| replace, cast-iron corner | 7P@2.93 | ea | 2,400.00 | 196.00 | 2,596.00 |
| replace, acrylic fiberglass corner | 7P@1.79 | ea | 980.00 | 120.00 | 1,100.00 |
| **60" long by 32" deep bathtub** | | | | | |
| replace, acrylic fiberglass | 7P@1.79 | ea | 446.00 | 120.00 | 566.00 |
| replace, porcelain-enamel cast iron | 7P@2.93 | ea | 1,100.00 | 196.00 | 1,296.00 |
| replace, porcelain-enamel steel | 7P@2.93 | ea | 441.00 | 196.00 | 637.00 |
| **72" long by 36" deep bathtub** | | | | | |
| replace, acrylic fiberglass | 7P@1.79 | ea | 926.00 | 120.00 | 1,046.00 |
| replace, porcelain-enamel cast iron | 7P@2.93 | ea | 2,280.00 | 196.00 | 2,476.00 |
| replace, porcelain-enamel steel | 7P@2.93 | ea | 693.00 | 196.00 | 889.00 |
| **Remove bathtub** | | | | | |
| cast-iron or steel | 1D@1.61 | ea | — | 62.60 | 62.60 |
| fiberglass | 1D@1.02 | ea | — | 39.70 | 39.70 |

| | Craft@Hrs | Unit | Material | Labor | Total |
|---|---|---|---|---|---|
| Remove for work, then reinstall | | | | | |
| fiberglass | 7P@3.45 | ea | — | 230.00 | 230.00 |
| cast-iron or steel | 7P@5.27 | ea | — | 352.00 | 352.00 |

**Bathtub with whirlpool jets.** Includes standard chrome drain and overflow assembly and jets and electrical pump hookup. Does not include faucet or electrical rough wiring.

| | Craft@Hrs | Unit | Material | Labor | Total |
|---|---|---|---|---|---|
| 60" long by 32" deep whirlpool bathtub | | | | | |
| replace, acrylic fiberglass | 7P@3.45 | ea | 2,330.00 | 230.00 | 2,560.00 |
| replace, porcelain-enamel cast-iron | 7P@4.00 | ea | 5,580.00 | 267.00 | 5,847.00 |
| 72" long by 36" deep whirlpool bathtub | | | | | |
| replace, acrylic fiberglass | 7P@3.45 | ea | 4,870.00 | 230.00 | 5,100.00 |
| replace, porcelain-enamel cast-iron | 7P@4.00 | ea | 11,700.00 | 267.00 | 11,967.00 |
| Fiberglass whirlpool bathtub | | | | | |
| replace, 60" long by 30" deep | 7P@3.45 | ea | 3,200.00 | 230.00 | 3,430.00 |
| replace, 66" long by 48" deep | 7P@3.45 | ea | 4,260.00 | 230.00 | 4,490.00 |
| replace, 72" long by 36" deep | 7P@3.45 | ea | 4,060.00 | 230.00 | 4,290.00 |
| replace, 72" long by 42" deep | 7P@3.45 | ea | 5,130.00 | 230.00 | 5,360.00 |
| replace, 83" long by 65" deep | 7P@3.45 | ea | 8,790.00 | 230.00 | 9,020.00 |
| remove, cast-iron or steel | 1D@2.13 | ea | — | 82.90 | 82.90 |
| remove, fiberglass | 1D@1.45 | ea | — | 56.40 | 56.40 |
| Remove whirlpool bathtub for work, then reinstall | | | | | |
| fiberglass | 7P@6.66 | ea | — | 445.00 | 445.00 |
| cast-iron or steel for work | 7P@9.10 | ea | — | 608.00 | 608.00 |

**Bathtub and shower combination.** Includes manufactured integrated bathtub and shower unit, assembly of unit, attachment hardware and fasteners, plumbers putty, P-trap with connectors, and installation. Installation includes placement of tub, placement of drain assembly, and connection to waste line with P-trap. Does not include wall framing, tub/shower faucet, or installation of the tub/shower faucet. High and deluxe quality usually indicates thicker fiberglass with glossier finishes and more ornate soap and wash cloth compartments.

| | Craft@Hrs | Unit | Material | Labor | Total |
|---|---|---|---|---|---|
| Acrylic fiberglass bathtub and shower | | | | | |
| replace, standard grade | 7P@3.23 | ea | 620.00 | 216.00 | 836.00 |
| replace, high grade | 7P@3.23 | ea | 980.00 | 216.00 | 1,196.00 |
| replace, deluxe grade | 7P@3.23 | ea | 1,240.00 | 216.00 | 1,456.00 |
| remove | 1D@1.69 | ea | — | 65.70 | 65.70 |
| remove for work, then reinstall | 7P@5.57 | ea | — | 372.00 | 372.00 |

**Shower stall.** Includes manufactured shower stall, assembly of shower stall, attachment hardware and fasteners, plumbers putty, P-trap with connectors, and installation. Installation includes placement of stall with concrete beneath pan, placement of drain assembly, and connection to waste line with P-trap. Does not include wall framing, shower faucet, or installation of the shower faucet.

| | Craft@Hrs | Unit | Material | Labor | Total |
|---|---|---|---|---|---|
| 32" wide by 32" deep shower stall | | | | | |
| replace, acrylic fiberglass | 7P@2.70 | ea | 513.00 | 180.00 | 693.00 |
| replace, acrylic fiberglass with terrazzo base | 7P@2.70 | ea | 615.00 | 180.00 | 795.00 |
| replace, metal | 7P@2.70 | ea | 240.00 | 180.00 | 420.00 |
| 48" wide by 35" deep shower stall | | | | | |
| replace, acrylic fiberglass | 7P@2.70 | ea | 587.00 | 180.00 | 767.00 |
| 60" wide by 35" deep shower stall | | | | | |
| replace, acrylic fiberglass | 7P@2.70 | ea | 647.00 | 180.00 | 827.00 |
| remove | 1D@1.22 | ea | — | 47.50 | 47.50 |
| Remove shower stall for work, then reinstall | 7P@4.35 | ea | — | 291.00 | 291.00 |

| | Craft@Hrs | Unit | Material | Labor | Total |
|---|---|---|---|---|---|

**Shower pan.** Includes pan, waterproof membrane when needed, drain assembly, and installation. Does not include framing. Does not include installation of tile or tile mortar bed.

| | Craft@Hrs | Unit | Material | Labor | Total |
|---|---|---|---|---|---|
| typical size | 7P@1.02 | ea | 73.20 | 68.10 | 141.30 |
| large size | 7P@1.02 | ea | 113.00 | 68.10 | 181.10 |

**Shower base.** Includes prefabricated shower base, concrete mix when needed, plumbers putty, caulk, attachment hardware and fasteners, P-trap with connectors, and installation. Installation includes placement of shower base, placement of drain assembly, and connection to waste line with P-trap. Some lower-grade shower bases require concrete to support the base. Does not include framing.

| | Craft@Hrs | Unit | Material | Labor | Total |
|---|---|---|---|---|---|
| fiberglass | 7P@1.05 | ea | 167.00 | 70.10 | 237.10 |
| terrazzo style | 7P@1.05 | ea | 599.00 | 70.10 | 669.10 |
| Corner entry shower base | | | | | |
| fiberglass | 7P@1.05 | ea | 201.00 | 70.10 | 271.10 |
| terrazzo style | 7P@1.05 | ea | 659.00 | 70.10 | 729.10 |

**Bathtub surround.** Includes bathtub surround, construction adhesive and/or attachment hardware, caulk, and installation. Surround includes coverage of the three walls surrounding bathtub: two widths and one length. Does not include wall framing, doors, or shower curtain rod.

| | Craft@Hrs | Unit | Material | Labor | Total |
|---|---|---|---|---|---|
| Cultured stone bathtub surround | | | | | |
| replace, all types | 7P@2.00 | ea | 799.00 | 134.00 | 933.00 |
| Fiberglass bathtub surround | | | | | |
| replace, standard grade | 7P@1.54 | ea | 468.00 | 103.00 | 571.00 |
| replace, high grade | 7P@1.54 | ea | 732.00 | 103.00 | 835.00 |
| replace, deluxe grade | 7P@1.54 | ea | 1,040.00 | 103.00 | 1,143.00 |
| remove | 1D@.893 | ea | — | 34.70 | 34.70 |
| Remove for work, then reinstall bathtub surround | | | | | |
| all types | 7P@2.63 | ea | — | 176.00 | 176.00 |

**Glass shower.** Includes wall panels, glass panels, integrated door with hardware, shower base, concrete mix (when needed), and installation. Installation includes placement of shower base, placement of drain assembly, and connection to waste line with P-trap. Fiberglass panels are placed on two walls, glass on one wall, and a glass door on one wall. Corner entry showers have two glass walls and a corner entry door. Some lower-grade shower bases require concrete to support the base. Does not include shower faucet or installation of shower faucet.

| | Craft@Hrs | Unit | Material | Labor | Total |
|---|---|---|---|---|---|
| Glass shower with cultured slabs on walls | | | | | |
| replace, standard grade | 7P@2.33 | ea | 1,040.00 | 156.00 | 1,196.00 |
| replace, high grade | 7P@2.33 | ea | 1,180.00 | 156.00 | 1,336.00 |
| Corner entry glass shower with cultured slabs on walls | | | | | |
| replace, standard grade | 7P@2.70 | ea | 1,360.00 | 180.00 | 1,540.00 |
| replace, high grade | 7P@2.70 | ea | 1,520.00 | 180.00 | 1,700.00 |
| Glass shower with fiberglass panels on walls | | | | | |
| replace, standard grade | 7P@2.08 | ea | 952.00 | 139.00 | 1,091.00 |
| replace, high grade | 7P@2.08 | ea | 1,070.00 | 139.00 | 1,209.00 |
| Corner entry glass shower with fiberglass panels on walls | | | | | |
| replace, standard grade | 7P@2.44 | ea | 1,240.00 | 163.00 | 1,403.00 |
| replace, high grade | 7P@2.44 | ea | 1,400.00 | 163.00 | 1,563.00 |
| remove | 1D@1.22 | ea | — | 47.50 | 47.50 |
| Remove glass shower for work, then reinstall | | | | | |
| all types | 7P@3.13 | ea | — | 209.00 | 209.00 |

|  | Craft@Hrs | Unit | Material | Labor | Total |
|---|---|---|---|---|---|

**Sliding glass bathtub door.** Includes sliding bathtub doors, track, hardware, caulk, and installation. Installation includes assembly of unit per manufacturer's specs and caulking.

| Sliding glass bathtub door with mill finish trim | | | | | |
|---|---|---|---|---|---|
| replace | 7P@1.37 | ea | 300.00 | 91.50 | 391.50 |
| replace, with fancy glass | 7P@1.37 | ea | 380.00 | 91.50 | 471.50 |
| Sliding glass bathtub door with gold finish trim | | | | | |
| replace | 7P@1.37 | ea | 366.00 | 91.50 | 457.50 |
| replace, with fancy glass | 7P@1.37 | ea | 468.00 | 91.50 | 559.50 |
| Sliding glass bathtub door with brass trim | | | | | |
| replace | 7P@1.37 | ea | 693.00 | 91.50 | 784.50 |
| replace, with etched glass | 7P@1.37 | ea | 873.00 | 91.50 | 964.50 |
| remove | 1D@.516 | ea | — | 20.10 | 20.10 |
| remove for work, then reinstall | 7P@2.28 | ea | — | 152.00 | 152.00 |

**Folding plastic bathtub door.** Includes folding bathtub door, track, hardware, caulk, and installation. Installation includes assembly of unit per manufacturer's specs and caulking.

| replace, typical | 7P@1.25 | ea | 295.00 | 83.50 | 378.50 |
|---|---|---|---|---|---|
| remove | 1D@.502 | ea | — | 19.50 | 19.50 |
| remove for work, then reinstall | 7P@1.69 | ea | — | 113.00 | 113.00 |

**Shower door.** Includes door, hardware, caulk, and installation. Installation includes assembly of unit per manufacturer's specs and caulking.

| replace, solid glass | 7P@1.20 | ea | 353.00 | 80.20 | 433.20 |
|---|---|---|---|---|---|
| replace, mill finish trim with fancy glass | 7P@1.20 | ea | 400.00 | 80.20 | 480.20 |
| replace, gold finish trim | 7P@1.20 | ea | 392.00 | 80.20 | 472.20 |
| replace, gold finish trim with fancy glass | 7P@1.20 | ea | 446.00 | 80.20 | 526.20 |
| replace, brass finish trim | 7P@1.20 | ea | 667.00 | 80.20 | 747.20 |
| replace, brass trim with etched glass | 7P@1.20 | ea | 753.00 | 80.20 | 833.20 |
| remove | 1D@.484 | ea | — | 18.80 | 18.80 |
| remove door for work, then reinstall | 7P@1.64 | ea | — | 110.00 | 110.00 |

**Gas water heater.** Includes gas water heater and installation. Installation includes placement on site and connection to existing gas lines, water lines, and vent pipes. Does not include drain pan.

| Gas water heater | | | | | |
|---|---|---|---|---|---|
| replace, 10 gallon | 7P@3.34 | ea | 426.00 | 223.00 | 649.00 |
| replace, 20 gallon | 7P@3.34 | ea | 459.00 | 223.00 | 682.00 |
| replace, 30 gallon | 7P@3.34 | ea | 521.00 | 223.00 | 744.00 |
| replace, 40 gallon | 7P@3.34 | ea | 540.00 | 223.00 | 763.00 |
| replace, 50 gallon | 7P@3.34 | ea | 625.00 | 223.00 | 848.00 |
| replace, 75 gallon | 7P@3.34 | ea | 1,110.00 | 223.00 | 1,333.00 |
| remove | 1D@1.11 | ea | — | 43.20 | 43.20 |
| remove for work, then reinstall | 7P@5.01 | ea | — | 335.00 | 335.00 |

| | Craft@Hrs | Unit | Material | Labor | Total |
|---|---|---|---|---|---|

**Electric water heater.** Includes electrical water heater and installation. Installation includes placement on site and connection to existing electrical, water lines, and vent pipes. Does not include drain pan.

| Electric water heater | | | | | |
|---|---|---|---|---|---|
| replace, 10 gallon | 7P@3.13 | ea | 332.00 | 209.00 | 541.00 |
| replace, 20 gallon | 7P@3.13 | ea | 420.00 | 209.00 | 629.00 |
| replace, 30 gallon | 7P@3.13 | ea | 480.00 | 209.00 | 689.00 |
| replace, 40 gallon | 7P@3.13 | ea | 513.00 | 209.00 | 722.00 |
| replace, 50 gallon | 7P@3.13 | ea | 615.00 | 209.00 | 824.00 |
| replace, 75 gallon | 7P@3.13 | ea | 1,130.00 | 209.00 | 1,339.00 |
| remove | 1D@1.06 | ea | — | 41.20 | 41.20 |
| replace element | 7P@1.28 | ea | 128.00 | 85.50 | 213.50 |
| remove for work, then reinstall | 7P@4.75 | ea | — | 317.00 | 317.00 |

**Water softener.** Includes water softener, water softener salt, and installation. Installation includes placement on site and connection to existing water lines. Typically includes one to two bags of water softener salt.

| Automatic two tank | | | | | |
|---|---|---|---|---|---|
| replace, up to 30 grains/gallon | 7P@3.34 | ea | 753.00 | 223.00 | 976.00 |
| replace, up to 100 grains/gallon | 7P@3.34 | ea | 1,600.00 | 223.00 | 1,823.00 |
| remove | 1D@.408 | ea | — | 15.90 | 15.90 |
| remove for work, then reinstall | 7P@5.27 | ea | — | 352.00 | 352.00 |

**Septic system with leach field.** Includes mobilization, excavation, backfill, gravel, crushed stone, pipe, couplings, connectors, building paper, tank, and distribution box.

| Septic system and leach field with concrete tank | | | | | |
|---|---|---|---|---|---|
| 1,000 gallon with 1,000 sf leach field | 7P@77.7 | ea | 3,470.00 | 5,190.00 | 8,660.00 |
| 1,000 gallon with 2,000 sf leach field | 7P@112 | ea | 4,990.00 | 7,480.00 | 12,470.00 |
| 1,250 gallon with 1,000 sf leach field | 7P@79.7 | ea | 3,740.00 | 5,320.00 | 9,060.00 |
| 1,250 gallon with 2,000 sf leach field | 7P@114 | ea | 5,270.00 | 7,620.00 | 12,890.00 |
| 1,500 gallon with 1,000 sf leach field | 7P@80.7 | ea | 4,000.00 | 5,390.00 | 9,390.00 |
| 1,500 gallon with 2,000 sf leach field | 7P@115 | ea | 5,480.00 | 7,680.00 | 13,160.00 |
| Septic system and leach field with fiberglass tank | | | | | |
| 1,000 gallon with 1,000 sf leach field | 7P@77.5 | ea | 3,320.00 | 5,180.00 | 8,500.00 |
| 1,000 gallon with 2,000 sf leach field | 7P@112 | ea | 4,870.00 | 7,480.00 | 12,350.00 |
| 1,250 gallon with 1,000 sf leach field | 7P@79.2 | ea | 3,590.00 | 5,290.00 | 8,880.00 |
| 1,250 gallon with 2,000 sf leach field | 7P@114 | ea | 5,130.00 | 7,620.00 | 12,750.00 |
| 1,500 gallon with 1,000 sf leach field | 7P@80.3 | ea | 3,870.00 | 5,360.00 | 9,230.00 |
| 1,500 gallon with 2,000 sf leach field | 7P@115 | ea | 5,330.00 | 7,680.00 | 13,010.00 |
| Septic system and leach field with polyethylene tank | | | | | |
| 1,000 gallon with 1,000 sf leach field | 7P@77.5 | ea | 3,050.00 | 5,180.00 | 8,230.00 |
| 1,000 gallon with 2,000 sf leach field | 7P@112 | ea | 4,590.00 | 7,480.00 | 12,070.00 |
| 1,250 gallon with 1,000 sf leach field | 7P@79.2 | ea | 3,320.00 | 5,290.00 | 8,610.00 |
| 1,250 gallon with 2,000 sf leach field | 7P@114 | ea | 4,870.00 | 7,620.00 | 12,490.00 |
| 1,500 gallon with 1,000 sf leach field | 7P@80.3 | ea | 3,590.00 | 5,360.00 | 8,950.00 |
| 1,500 gallon with 2,000 sf leach field | 7P@115 | ea | 5,070.00 | 7,680.00 | 12,750.00 |

|  | Craft@Hrs | Unit | Material | Labor | Total |
|---|---|---|---|---|---|

**Submersible water pump.** Includes wiring and placement for well up to 100' deep.

|  | Craft@Hrs | Unit | Material | Labor | Total |
|---|---|---|---|---|---|
| replace, 1/2 hp | 7P@5.52 | ea | 732.00 | 369.00 | 1,101.00 |
| replace, 3/4 hp | 7P@5.52 | ea | 799.00 | 369.00 | 1,168.00 |
| replace, 1 hp | 7P@5.52 | ea | 815.00 | 369.00 | 1,184.00 |
| replace, 1-1/2 hp | 7P@5.52 | ea | 1,010.00 | 369.00 | 1,379.00 |
| replace, 2 hp | 7P@5.52 | ea | 1,110.00 | 369.00 | 1,479.00 |
| replace, 3 hp | 7P@5.52 | ea | 1,450.00 | 369.00 | 1,819.00 |
| replace, 5 hp | 7P@5.52 | ea | 1,670.00 | 369.00 | 2,039.00 |
| remove | 1D@1.75 | ea | — | 68.10 | 68.10 |
| remove for work then reinstall | 7P@7.69 | ea | — | 514.00 | 514.00 |

**Sump pump.** Basement style installation, includes up to 45 lf of 1-1/2" PVC pipe and wiring hookup. Does not include rough electrical.

| Plastic pipe sump pump | Craft@Hrs | Unit | Material | Labor | Total |
|---|---|---|---|---|---|
| replace, 1/4 hp | 7P@1.39 | ea | 273.00 | 92.90 | 365.90 |
| replace, 1/3 hp | 7P@1.39 | ea | 327.00 | 92.90 | 419.90 |
| replace, 1/2 hp | 7P@1.39 | ea | 434.00 | 92.90 | 526.90 |
| Cast-iron pipe sump pump |  |  |  |  |  |
| replace, 1/4 hp | 7P@1.39 | ea | 332.00 | 92.90 | 424.90 |
| replace, 1/3 hp | 7P@1.39 | ea | 374.00 | 92.90 | 466.90 |
| replace, 1/2 hp | 7P@1.39 | ea | 487.00 | 92.90 | 579.90 |
| remove | 1D@.561 | ea | — | 21.80 | 21.80 |
| remove for work, then reinstall | 7P@2.42 | ea | — | 162.00 | 162.00 |

**Antique style sink faucet.** Antique style faucets are usually brass, chrome over brass, or nickel over brass. Often used in homes that are not historical.

|  | Craft@Hrs | Unit | Material | Labor | Total |
|---|---|---|---|---|---|
| replace, standard grade | 7P@.557 | ea | 240.00 | 37.20 | 277.20 |
| replace, high grade | 7P@.557 | ea | 406.00 | 37.20 | 443.20 |
| replace, deluxe grade | 7P@.557 | ea | 548.00 | 37.20 | 585.20 |
| replace, custom grade | 7P@.557 | ea | 805.00 | 37.20 | 842.20 |
| replace, custom deluxe grade | 7P@.557 | ea | 1,150.00 | 37.20 | 1,187.20 |
| remove | 1D@.356 | ea | — | 13.80 | 13.80 |
| remove for work, then reinstall | 7P@.833 | ea | — | 55.60 | 55.60 |

**Antique style bathtub faucet.** Antique style are usually brass, chrome over brass, or nickel over brass with ornate detail. Often used in homes that are not historical.

|  | Craft@Hrs | Unit | Material | Labor | Total |
|---|---|---|---|---|---|
| replace, economy grade | 7P@.893 | ea | 305.00 | 59.70 | 364.70 |
| replace, standard grade | 7P@.893 | ea | 527.00 | 59.70 | 586.70 |
| replace, high grade | 7P@.893 | ea | 707.00 | 59.70 | 766.70 |
| replace, deluxe grade | 7P@.893 | ea | 1,040.00 | 59.70 | 1,099.70 |
| replace, custom grade | 7P@.893 | ea | 1,450.00 | 59.70 | 1,509.70 |
| remove | 1D@.360 | ea | — | 14.00 | 14.00 |
| remove for work, then reinstall | 7P@1.14 | ea | — | 76.20 | 76.20 |

**Antique style bathtub faucet with hand-held shower.** Antique styles are usually brass, chrome over brass, or nickel over brass with ornate detail. Often used in homes that are not historical.

|  | Craft@Hrs | Unit | Material | Labor | Total |
|---|---|---|---|---|---|
| replace, standard grade | 7P@.989 | ea | 480.00 | 66.10 | 546.10 |
| replace, high grade | 7P@.989 | ea | 820.00 | 66.10 | 886.10 |
| replace, deluxe grade | 7P@.989 | ea | 1,100.00 | 66.10 | 1,166.10 |
| replace, custom grade | 7P@.989 | ea | 1,600.00 | 66.10 | 1,666.10 |
| remove | 1D@.363 | ea | — | 14.10 | 14.10 |
| remove for work, then reinstall | 7P@1.19 | ea | — | 79.50 | 79.50 |

| | Craft@Hrs | Unit | Material | Labor | Total |
|---|---|---|---|---|---|

**Antique style bathtub faucet with shower conversion.** With exposed shower supply pipe and circular shower curtain rod.

| | Craft@Hrs | Unit | Material | Labor | Total |
|---|---|---|---|---|---|
| replace, standard grade | 7P@2.16 | ea | 615.00 | 144.00 | 759.00 |
| replace, high grade | 7P@2.16 | ea | 894.00 | 144.00 | 1,038.00 |
| replace, deluxe grade | 7P@2.16 | ea | 1,080.00 | 144.00 | 1,224.00 |
| replace, custom grade | 7P@2.16 | ea | 1,520.00 | 144.00 | 1,664.00 |
| remove | 1D@.505 | ea | — | 19.60 | 19.60 |
| remove for work, then reinstall | 7P@3.13 | ea | — | 209.00 | 209.00 |

**Antique style tub supply lines.** Exposed lines are used on antique style bathtubs.

| Claw-foot bathtub supply lines | | | | | |
|---|---|---|---|---|---|
| replace, chrome-plated brass | 7P@1.12 | ea | 247.00 | 74.80 | 321.80 |
| replace, brass | 7P@1.12 | ea | 213.00 | 74.80 | 287.80 |
| remove | 1D@.429 | ea | — | 16.70 | 16.70 |

**Antique style bathtub drain.**

| Claw-foot bathtub drain | | | | | |
|---|---|---|---|---|---|
| replace, chrome-plated brass | 7P@1.15 | ea | 228.00 | 76.80 | 304.80 |
| replace, brass | 7P@1.15 | ea | 180.00 | 76.80 | 256.80 |
| remove | 1D@.436 | ea | — | 17.00 | 17.00 |

**Antique style bathtub free-standing supply lines.**

| Free-standing water feeds for claw-foot or slipper bathtub | | | | | |
|---|---|---|---|---|---|
| replace, chrome-plated brass | 7P@1.22 | ea | 353.00 | 81.50 | 434.50 |
| replace, brass | 7P@1.22 | ea | 414.00 | 81.50 | 495.50 |
| remove | 1D@.484 | ea | — | 18.80 | 18.80 |

**Pedestal sink.** Antique or contemporary style.

| | Craft@Hrs | Unit | Material | Labor | Total |
|---|---|---|---|---|---|
| replace, economy grade | 7P@1.22 | ea | 540.00 | 81.50 | 621.50 |
| replace, standard grade | 7P@1.22 | ea | 632.00 | 81.50 | 713.50 |
| replace, high grade | 7P@1.22 | ea | 847.00 | 81.50 | 928.50 |
| replace, deluxe grade | 7P@1.22 | ea | 1,450.00 | 81.50 | 1,531.50 |
| replace, custom grade | 7P@1.22 | ea | 2,130.00 | 81.50 | 2,211.50 |
| replace, custom deluxe grade | 7P@1.22 | ea | 2,730.00 | 81.50 | 2,811.50 |
| remove | 1D@.484 | ea | — | 18.80 | 18.80 |
| remove for work, then reinstall | 7P@2.13 | ea | — | 142.00 | 142.00 |

|  | Craft@Hrs | Unit | Material | Labor | Total |
|---|---|---|---|---|---|

**Antique style pillbox toilet.** Round tank with beaded rim.

| Antique style pillbox toilet |  |  |  |  |  |
|---|---|---|---|---|---|
| replace | 7P@2.23 | ea | 2,650.00 | 149.00 | 2,799.00 |
| remove | 1D@.429 | ea | — | 16.70 | 16.70 |
| remove for work, then reinstall | 7P@3.45 | ea | — | 230.00 | 230.00 |

**Antique style low-tank toilet.** Identifiable by pipe (usually brass) running from tank to bowl.

| Low-tank toilet |  |  |  |  |  |
|---|---|---|---|---|---|
| replace, porcelain tank | 7P@2.23 | ea | 1,400.00 | 149.00 | 1,549.00 |
| replace, oak tank | 7P@2.22 | ea | 1,190.00 | 148.00 | 1,338.00 |
| remove | 1D@.429 | ea | — | 16.70 | 16.70 |
| remove for work, then reinstall | 7P@3.45 | ea | 2.61 | 230.00 | 232.61 |

**Antique style high-tank toilet.** Tank mounted high on wall. Includes brass pipe and connectors, pull chain, hardwood toilet seat, brass tank support brackets. Wood tanks include plastic liner.

| High-tank toilet |  |  |  |  |  |
|---|---|---|---|---|---|
| replace, porcelain tank | 7P@2.63 | ea | 1,740.00 | 176.00 | 1,916.00 |
| replace, oak tank | 7P@2.63 | ea | 1,520.00 | 176.00 | 1,696.00 |
| remove | 1D@.602 | ea | — | 23.40 | 23.40 |
| remove for work, then reinstall | 7P@3.70 | ea | 2.61 | 247.00 | 249.61 |

**Antique bathtub.** Does not include supply lines or faucet. Includes $115 for crating and $273 for shipping.

| Antique claw-foot or ball-foot cast iron (as is condition) |  |  |  |  |  |
|---|---|---|---|---|---|
| replace, 60" | 7P@5.27 | ea | 1,010.00 | 352.00 | 1,362.00 |
| replace, 66" | 7P@5.57 | ea | 1,110.00 | 372.00 | 1,482.00 |

**Refinished antique bathtub.** Interior and lip refinished exterior surfaces painted. Does not include visible supply lines or faucet. Includes $115 for crating and $273 for shipping.

| Antique claw-foot or ball-foot cast iron |  |  |  |  |  |
|---|---|---|---|---|---|
| replace, 48" | 7P@4.75 | ea | 3,050.00 | 317.00 | 3,367.00 |
| replace, 52" | 7P@5.01 | ea | 2,950.00 | 335.00 | 3,285.00 |
| replace, 60" | 7P@5.27 | ea | 2,650.00 | 352.00 | 3,002.00 |
| replace, 66" | 7P@5.57 | ea | 2,730.00 | 372.00 | 3,102.00 |

| | Craft@Hrs | Unit | Material | Labor | Total |
|---|---|---|---|---|---|

**Reproduction antique bathtub.** Claw foot or ball foot.  New tubs built in the antique style.  Does not include supply lines or faucet.  Includes $115 for crating and $273 for shipping.  ($195 shipping for fiberglass tubs.)

| | Craft@Hrs | Unit | Material | Labor | Total |
|---|---|---|---|---|---|
| Cast-iron reproduction bathtub | | | | | |
| replace, 60" | 7P@5.27 | ea | 2,130.00 | 352.00 | 2,482.00 |
| replace, 66" | 7P@5.57 | ea | 2,650.00 | 372.00 | 3,022.00 |
| remove | 1D@1.82 | ea | — | 70.80 | 70.80 |
| Fiberglass reproduction bathtub | | | | | |
| replace, 60" | 7P@3.13 | ea | 2,970.00 | 209.00 | 3,179.00 |
| replace, 66" | 7P@3.34 | ea | 4,000.00 | 223.00 | 4,223.00 |
| remove | 1D@1.45 | ea | — | 56.40 | 56.40 |
| remove for work, then reinstall | 7P@5.57 | ea | — | 372.00 | 372.00 |

*slipper bathtub*

**Reproduction slipper bathtub.** Claw foot or ball foot.  Does not include supply lines or faucet.  Includes $150 for crating and $273 for shipping.  ($195 shipping for fiberglass tubs.)

| | Craft@Hrs | Unit | Material | Labor | Total |
|---|---|---|---|---|---|
| replace, 60" cast-iron | 7P@5.27 | ea | 3,740.00 | 352.00 | 4,092.00 |
| replace, 66" fiberglass | 7P@5.57 | ea | 6,870.00 | 372.00 | 7,242.00 |
| remove, cast-iron | 1D@1.82 | ea | — | 70.80 | 70.80 |
| remove, fiberglass | 1D@1.45 | ea | — | 56.40 | 56.40 |

**Additional antique bathtub costs.**

| | Craft@Hrs | Unit | Material | Labor | Total |
|---|---|---|---|---|---|
| add for solid brass legs | — | ea | 120.00 | — | 120.00 |
| add for brass-plated legs | — | ea | 66.70 | — | 66.70 |
| add for oak trim around lip of antique bathtub | — | ea | 2,060.00 | — | 2,060.00 |

**Time & Material Charts** (selected items)
**Plumbing Materials**

| | Craft@Hrs | Unit | Material | Labor | Total |
|---|---|---|---|---|---|
| Black steel pipe | | | | | |
| 1/2" pipe | — | lf | 1.63 | — | 1.63 |
| 3/4" pipe | — | lf | 1.94 | — | 1.94 |
| 1" pipe | — | lf | 2.73 | — | 2.73 |
| 2" pipe | — | lf | 8.71 | — | 8.71 |
| Brass pipe | | | | | |
| 1/2" pipe | — | lf | 5.58 | — | 5.58 |
| 3/4" pipe | — | lf | 7.45 | — | 7.45 |
| 1" pipe | — | lf | 12.20 | — | 12.20 |
| 2" pipe | — | lf | 19.10 | — | 19.10 |
| Type K copper pipe | | | | | |
| 1/2" pipe | — | lf | 3.17 | — | 3.17 |
| 3/4" pipe | — | lf | 4.21 | — | 4.21 |
| 1" pipe | — | lf | 5.48 | — | 5.48 |
| 2" pipe | — | lf | 13.20 | — | 13.20 |
| Type L copper pipe | | | | | |
| 1/2" pipe | — | lf | 1.85 | — | 1.85 |
| 3/4" pipe | — | lf | 3.08 | — | 3.08 |
| 1" pipe | — | lf | 4.21 | — | 4.21 |
| 2" pipe | — | lf | 10.20 | — | 10.20 |

| | Craft@Hrs | Unit | Material | Labor | Total |
|---|---|---|---|---|---|
| Type M copper pipe | | | | | |
| 1/2" pipe | — | lf | 1.43 | — | 1.43 |
| 3/4" pipe | — | lf | 2.36 | — | 2.36 |
| 1" pipe | — | lf | 3.20 | — | 3.20 |
| Galvanized steel pipe | | | | | |
| 1/2" pipe | — | lf | 1.99 | — | 1.99 |
| 3/4" pipe | — | lf | 2.35 | — | 2.35 |
| 1" pipe | — | lf | 3.32 | — | 3.32 |
| 2" pipe | — | lf | 10.60 | — | 10.60 |
| CPVC pipe | | | | | |
| 1/2" pipe | — | lf | 1.15 | — | 1.15 |
| 3/4" pipe | — | lf | 1.41 | — | 1.41 |
| 1" pipe | — | lf | 1.69 | — | 1.69 |
| PVC pipe | | | | | |
| 1/2" pipe | — | lf | .71 | — | .71 |
| 3/4" pipe | — | lf | .77 | — | .77 |
| 1" pipe | — | lf | .85 | — | .85 |
| 1-1/2" pipe | — | lf | 1.15 | — | 1.15 |
| 2" pipe | — | lf | 1.39 | — | 1.39 |
| 3" pipe | — | lf | 2.01 | — | 2.01 |
| 4" pipe | — | lf | 2.60 | — | 2.60 |
| 5" pipe | — | lf | 3.77 | — | 3.77 |
| 6" pipe | — | lf | 4.48 | — | 4.48 |
| Cast-iron pipe | | | | | |
| 2" pipe | — | lf | 7.31 | — | 7.31 |
| 3" pipe | — | lf | 10.10 | — | 10.10 |
| 4" pipe | — | lf | 14.10 | — | 14.10 |
| 5" pipe | — | lf | 40.60 | — | 40.60 |
| 6" pipe | — | lf | 52.10 | — | 52.10 |
| No-hub cast-iron pipe | | | | | |
| 2" pipe | — | lf | 10.10 | — | 10.10 |
| 3" pipe | — | lf | 13.00 | — | 13.00 |
| 4" pipe | — | lf | 16.80 | — | 16.80 |
| 5" pipe | — | lf | 24.40 | — | 24.40 |

## Plumbing Labor

| Laborer | base wage | paid leave | true wage | taxes & ins. | total |
|---|---|---|---|---|---|
| Plumber | $28.30 | 2.99 | $41.29 | 25.51 | $66.80 |
| Plumber's helper | $29.90 | 2.33 | $32.23 | 21.07 | $53.30 |
| Demolition laborer | $20.70 | 1.61 | $22.31 | 16.59 | $38.90 |

**Paid leave** is calculated based on two weeks paid vacation, one week sick leave, and seven paid holidays. Employer's matching portion of **FICA** is 7.65 percent. **FUTA** (Federal Unemployment) is .8 percent. **Worker's compensation** for the plumbing trade was calculated using a national average of 11.00 percent. **Unemployment insurance** was calculated using a national average of 8 percent. **Health insurance** was calculated based on a projected national average for 2015 of $1,025 per employee (and family when applicable) per month. Employer pays 80 percent for a per month cost of $820 per employee. **Retirement** is based on a 401(k) retirement program with employer matching of 50 percent. Employee contributions to the 401(k) plan are an average of 6 percent of the true wage. **Liability insurance** is based on a national average of 10.0 percent.

| | Craft@Hrs | Unit | Material | Labor | Total |
|---|---|---|---|---|---|
| **Plumbing Labor Productivity** | | | | | |
| Demolition of plumbing | | | | | |
| remove faucet | 1D@.356 | ea | — | 13.80 | 13.80 |
| remove bathroom sink | 1D@.367 | ea | — | 14.30 | 14.30 |
| remove kitchen or laundry sink | 1D@.370 | ea | — | 14.40 | 14.40 |
| remove wet bar sink | 1D@.356 | ea | — | 13.80 | 13.80 |
| remove toilet | 1D@.346 | ea | — | 13.50 | 13.50 |
| remove fiberglass bathtub | 1D@1.02 | ea | — | 39.70 | 39.70 |
| remove cast-iron or steel bathtub | 1D@1.61 | ea | — | 62.60 | 62.60 |
| remove fiberglass bathtub with whirlpool jets | 1D@1.45 | ea | — | 56.40 | 56.40 |
| remove cast-iron or steel bathtub with whirlpool jets | 1D@2.13 | ea | — | 82.90 | 82.90 |
| remove bathtub and shower combination | 1D@1.69 | ea | — | 65.70 | 65.70 |
| remove shower stall | 1D@1.22 | ea | — | 47.50 | 47.50 |
| remove bathtub surround | 1D@.893 | ea | — | 34.70 | 34.70 |
| remove glass shower | 1D@1.22 | ea | — | 47.50 | 47.50 |
| remove sliding glass bathtub door | 1D@.516 | ea | — | 20.10 | 20.10 |
| remove shower door | 1D@.484 | ea | — | 18.80 | 18.80 |
| remove gas water heater | 1D@1.11 | ea | — | 43.20 | 43.20 |
| remove electric water heater | 1D@1.06 | ea | — | 41.20 | 41.20 |
| remove water softener | 1D@.408 | ea | — | 15.90 | 15.90 |
| remove submersible pump | 1D@1.75 | ea | — | 68.10 | 68.10 |
| remove sump pump | 1D@.561 | ea | — | 21.80 | 21.80 |
| remove antique style sink faucet | 1D@.356 | ea | — | 13.80 | 13.80 |
| remove antique style bathtub faucet | 1D@.360 | ea | — | 14.00 | 14.00 |
| remove claw-foot bathtub supply lines | 1D@.429 | ea | — | 16.70 | 16.70 |
| remove claw-foot bathtub drain | 1D@.436 | ea | — | 17.00 | 17.00 |
| remove free-standing water feeds | 1D@.484 | ea | — | 18.80 | 18.80 |
| remove pedestal sink | 1D@.484 | ea | — | 18.80 | 18.80 |
| remove antique style pillbox toilet | 1D@.429 | ea | — | 16.70 | 16.70 |
| remove antique style low-tank toilet | 1D@.429 | ea | — | 16.70 | 16.70 |
| remove antique style high-tank toilet | 1D@.602 | ea | — | 23.40 | 23.40 |
| remove cast-iron claw-foot bathtub | 1D@1.82 | ea | — | 70.80 | 70.80 |
| remove fiberglass claw-foot bathtub | 1D@1.45 | ea | — | 56.40 | 56.40 |
| Install field threaded pipe | | | | | |
| 1/2" | 7P@.127 | lf | — | 8.48 | 8.48 |
| 3/4" | 7P@.136 | lf | — | 9.08 | 9.08 |
| 1" | 7P@.158 | lf | — | 10.60 | 10.60 |
| 2" | 7P@.231 | lf | — | 15.40 | 15.40 |
| Install copper pipe | | | | | |
| 1/2" | 7P@.104 | lf | — | 6.95 | 6.95 |
| 3/4" | 7P@.109 | lf | — | 7.28 | 7.28 |
| 1" | 7P@.122 | lf | — | 8.15 | 8.15 |
| 2" | 7P@.202 | lf | — | 13.50 | 13.50 |

| | Craft@Hrs | Unit | Material | Labor | Total |
|---|---|---|---|---|---|
| **Install plastic pipe** | | | | | |
| 1/2" | 7P@.153 | lf | — | 10.20 | 10.20 |
| 3/4" | 7P@.162 | lf | — | 10.80 | 10.80 |
| 1" | 7P@.189 | lf | — | 12.60 | 12.60 |
| 2" | 7P@.251 | lf | — | 16.80 | 16.80 |
| 3" | 7P@.281 | lf | — | 18.80 | 18.80 |
| 4" | 7P@.310 | lf | — | 20.70 | 20.70 |
| 5" | 7P@.347 | lf | — | 23.20 | 23.20 |
| 6" | 7P@.379 | lf | — | 25.30 | 25.30 |
| **Install cast-iron pipe** | | | | | |
| 2" | 7P@.236 | lf | — | 15.80 | 15.80 |
| 3" | 7P@.248 | lf | — | 16.60 | 16.60 |
| 4" | 7P@.270 | lf | — | 18.00 | 18.00 |
| 5" | 7P@.304 | lf | — | 20.30 | 20.30 |
| 6" | 7P@.317 | lf | — | 21.20 | 21.20 |
| **Install no-hub cast-iron pipe** | | | | | |
| 2" | 7P@.210 | lf | — | 14.00 | 14.00 |
| 3" | 7P@.223 | lf | — | 14.90 | 14.90 |
| 4" | 7P@.242 | lf | — | 16.20 | 16.20 |
| 6" | 7P@.283 | lf | — | 18.90 | 18.90 |
| **Install faucet** | | | | | |
| bathroom sink | 7P@.557 | ea | — | 37.20 | 37.20 |
| kitchen sink | 7P@.561 | ea | — | 37.50 | 37.50 |
| laundry sink | 7P@.546 | ea | — | 36.50 | 36.50 |
| shower | 7P@.576 | ea | — | 38.50 | 38.50 |
| tub | 7P@.567 | ea | — | 37.90 | 37.90 |
| tub with shower | 7P@.606 | ea | — | 40.50 | 40.50 |
| **Install bathroom sink** | | | | | |
| wall-hung | 7P@.878 | ea | — | 58.70 | 58.70 |
| self-rimming | 7P@.910 | ea | — | 60.80 | 60.80 |
| under-counter | 7P@.953 | ea | — | 63.70 | 63.70 |
| **Install kitchen sink** | 7P@.925 | ea | — | 61.80 | 61.80 |
| **Install laundry sink** | | | | | |
| in countertop | 7P@.901 | ea | — | 60.20 | 60.20 |
| on legs or frame | 7P@.833 | ea | — | 55.60 | 55.60 |
| **Install wet bar sink** | | | | | |
| self-rimming | 7P@.910 | ea | — | 60.80 | 60.80 |
| under-counter | 7P@.953 | ea | — | 63.70 | 63.70 |
| **Install fixtures** | | | | | |
| toilet | 7P@1.33 | ea | — | 88.80 | 88.80 |
| cast-iron or steel bathtub | 7P@2.93 | ea | — | 196.00 | 196.00 |
| fiberglass bathtub | 7P@1.79 | ea | — | 120.00 | 120.00 |
| cast-iron or steel bathtub with whirlpool jets | 7P@4.00 | ea | — | 267.00 | 267.00 |
| fiberglass bathtub with whirlpool jets | 7P@3.45 | ea | — | 230.00 | 230.00 |
| fiberglass bathtub & shower combination | 7P@3.23 | ea | — | 216.00 | 216.00 |
| shower stall | 7P@2.70 | ea | — | 180.00 | 180.00 |

| | Craft@Hrs | Unit | Material | Labor | Total |
|---|---|---|---|---|---|
| Install shower or bathtub door | | | | | |
|    sliding bathtub door | 7P@1.37 | ea | — | 91.50 | 91.50 |
|    shower door | 7P@1.20 | ea | — | 80.20 | 80.20 |
| Install water heater | | | | | |
|    gas | 7P@3.34 | ea | — | 223.00 | 223.00 |
|    electric | 7P@3.13 | ea | — | 209.00 | 209.00 |
| Install water softener | 7P@3.34 | ea | — | 223.00 | 223.00 |
| Install septic system | | | | | |
|   with concrete tank | | | | | |
|    1,000 gallon with 1,000 sf leach field | 7P@77.7 | ea | 3,470.00 | 5,190.00 | 8,660.00 |
|    1,000 gallon with 2,000 sf leach field | 7P@112 | ea | 4,990.00 | 7,480.00 | 12,470.00 |
|   with fiberglass tank | | | | | |
|    1,000 gallon with 1,000 sf leach field | 7P@77.5 | ea | 3,320.00 | 5,180.00 | 8,500.00 |
|    1,000 gallon with 2,000 sf leach field | 7P@112 | ea | 4,870.00 | 7,480.00 | 12,350.00 |
|   with polyethylene tank | | | | | |
|    1,000 gallon with 1,000 sf leach field | 7P@77.5 | ea | 3,050.00 | 5,180.00 | 8,230.00 |
|    1,000 gallon with 2,000 sf leach field | 7P@112 | ea | 4,590.00 | 7,480.00 | 12,070.00 |
| Install water pump | | | | | |
|    submersible | 7P@5.52 | ea | — | 369.00 | 369.00 |
|    automatic sump | 7P@1.39 | ea | — | 92.90 | 92.90 |
| Install claw-foot bathtub faucet | | | | | |
|    faucet | 7P@.893 | ea | — | 59.70 | 59.70 |
|    faucet with shower conversion | 7P@2.16 | ea | — | 144.00 | 144.00 |
| Install pedestal sink | 7P@1.22 | ea | — | 81.50 | 81.50 |
| Install antique style toilet | | | | | |
|    pillbox or low tank | 7P@2.23 | ea | — | 149.00 | 149.00 |
|    high-tank | 7P@2.63 | ea | — | 176.00 | 176.00 |
| Install antique style bathtub | | | | | |
|    52" cast-iron | 7P@5.01 | ea | — | 335.00 | 335.00 |
|    60" cast-iron | 7P@5.27 | ea | — | 352.00 | 352.00 |
|    66" cast-iron | 7P@5.57 | ea | — | 372.00 | 372.00 |
|    60" reproduction fiberglass | 7P@3.13 | ea | — | 209.00 | 209.00 |
|    66" reproduction fiberglass | 7P@3.34 | ea | — | 223.00 | 223.00 |

| | Craft@Hrs | Unit | Material | Labor | Equip. | Total |
|---|---|---|---|---|---|---|

# Retaining Walls

**Retaining walls.** All walls include excavation and backfill. Measure the sf of surface area. Includes sand and/or gravel base and 2' to 3' of walls buried beneath exposed surface.

## Minimum charge.

| | Craft@Hrs | Unit | Material | Labor | Equip. | Total |
|---|---|---|---|---|---|---|
| for retaining wall work | 3R@3.50 | ea | 212.00 | 196.00 | 155.00 | 563.00 |

**Concrete retaining walls.** See Masonry for brick veneer, wall caps and wall coping. Includes 4" perforated pipe drain line at inside base that is set in gravel.

| | Craft@Hrs | Unit | Material | Labor | Equip. | Total |
|---|---|---|---|---|---|---|
| replace, typical | 3R@.227 | sf | 9.85 | 12.70 | 4.07 | 26.62 |
| remove | 1D@.345 | sf | — | 13.40 | — | 13.40 |

## Pile retaining walls with wood lagging.

| | Craft@Hrs | Unit | Material | Labor | Equip. | Total |
|---|---|---|---|---|---|---|
| replace, wood | 3R@.095 | sf | 7.57 | 5.33 | 2.39 | 15.29 |
| replace, steel | 3R@.104 | sf | 7.88 | 5.83 | 2.39 | 16.10 |
| remove, wood | 1D@.185 | sf | — | 7.20 | — | 7.20 |
| remove, steel | 1D@.204 | sf | — | 7.94 | — | 7.94 |

## Anchored tieback, for all retaining wall types.

Add for anchored tiebacks

| | Craft@Hrs | Unit | Material | Labor | Equip. | Total |
|---|---|---|---|---|---|---|
| replace | 3R@2.44 | ea | 150.00 | 137.00 | 47.00 | 334.00 |
| remove | 1D@1.81 | ea | — | 70.40 | — | 70.40 |

## Railroad tie retaining walls.

| | Craft@Hrs | Unit | Material | Labor | Equip. | Total |
|---|---|---|---|---|---|---|
| replace, with tie tiebacks | 3R@.244 | sf | 7.73 | 13.70 | 2.30 | 23.73 |
| replace, no tie tiebacks | 3R@.167 | sf | 6.99 | 9.37 | 2.04 | 18.40 |
| remove, with tie tiebacks | 1D@.199 | sf | — | 7.74 | — | 7.74 |
| remove, no tie tiebacks | 1D@.188 | sf | — | 7.31 | — | 7.31 |

## Cedar tie retaining walls.

| | Craft@Hrs | Unit | Material | Labor | Equip. | Total |
|---|---|---|---|---|---|---|
| replace, with tie tiebacks | 3R@.251 | sf | 9.85 | 14.10 | 2.13 | 26.08 |
| replace, no tie tiebacks | 3R@.169 | sf | 9.41 | 9.48 | 1.99 | 20.88 |
| remove, with tie tiebacks | 1D@.188 | sf | — | 7.31 | — | 7.31 |
| remove, no tie tiebacks | 1D@.178 | sf | — | 6.92 | — | 6.92 |

**Stone.** Includes 4" perforated pipe drain line at inside base set in gravel.

Random stone retaining walls

| | Craft@Hrs | Unit | Material | Labor | Equip. | Total |
|---|---|---|---|---|---|---|
| replace, dry set | 1M@.385 | sf | 22.20 | 22.90 | 2.39 | 47.49 |
| replace, mortar set | 1M@.333 | sf | 23.20 | 19.80 | 2.39 | 45.39 |

Cut stone retaining wall

| | Craft@Hrs | Unit | Material | Labor | Equip. | Total |
|---|---|---|---|---|---|---|
| replace, dry set | 1M@.327 | sf | 28.00 | 19.40 | 2.39 | 49.79 |
| replace, mortar set | 1M@.323 | sf | 28.90 | 19.20 | 2.39 | 50.49 |
| Remove stone retaining wall | 1D@.384 | sf | — | 14.90 | — | 14.90 |

| | Craft@Hrs | Unit | Material | Labor | Equip. | Total |
|---|---|---|---|---|---|---|

**Interlocking masonry block retaining walls.** Knock-out cap is same as solid cap except 3" to 4" back the cap is cut out to about half its thickness to allow soil and vegetation to overlap the top of the wall.

| | Craft@Hrs | Unit | Material | Labor | Equip. | Total |
|---|---|---|---|---|---|---|
| replace, typical | 3R@.313 | sf | 13.40 | 17.60 | 2.39 | 33.39 |
| remove | 1D@.333 | sf | — | 13.00 | — | 13.00 |
| add for solid cap, 4" x 16" x 10" | 3R@.048 | lf | 6.62 | 2.69 | — | 9.31 |
| add for knock-out cap, 4" x 16" x 10" | | | | | | |
| per lf of wall | 3R@.048 | lf | 7.64 | 2.69 | — | 10.33 |

**Add for fabric reinforcement.** One common brand name is called GeoGrid. Fabric ties retaining walls into hillside.

| | Craft@Hrs | Unit | Material | Labor | Equip. | Total |
|---|---|---|---|---|---|---|
| 4-1/2' deep every 2' of wall height | 3R@.007 | sf | 4.99 | .39 | — | 5.38 |
| 4-1/2' deep every 3' of wall height | 3R@.005 | sf | 3.31 | .28 | — | 3.59 |
| 6' deep every 2' of wall height | 3R@.007 | sf | 6.01 | .39 | — | 6.40 |
| 6' deep every 3' of wall height | 3R@.005 | sf | 4.01 | .28 | — | 4.29 |

**Shotcrete slope stabilization.**

| | Craft@Hrs | Unit | Material | Labor | Equip. | Total |
|---|---|---|---|---|---|---|
| Slope stabilization with wire mesh (per inch deep) | 3R@.104 | sf | 2.27 | 5.83 | .37 | 8.47 |

**Time & Material Charts** (selected items)
**Retaining Walls Materials**

See Retaining Walls material prices above.

**Retaining Walls Labor**

| Laborer | base wage | paid leave | true wage | taxes & ins. | total |
|---|---|---|---|---|---|
| Retaining wall installer | $30.30 | 2.36 | $32.66 | 23.44 | $56.10 |
| Mason | $32.10 | 2.50 | $34.60 | 24.80 | $59.40 |
| Equipment operator | $42.30 | 3.30 | $45.60 | 29.10 | $74.70 |
| Demolition laborer | $20.70 | 1.61 | $22.31 | 16.59 | $38.90 |

**Paid leave** is calculated based on two weeks paid vacation, one week sick leave, and seven paid holidays. Employer's matching portion of **FICA** is 7.65 percent. **FUTA** (Federal Unemployment) is .8 percent. **Worker's compensation** for the retaining walls trade was calculated using a national average of 19.00 percent for the retaining wall installer; 19.00 percent for the mason, and 15.00 percent for the equipment operator. **Unemployment insurance** was calculated using a national average of 8 percent. **Health insurance** was calculated based on a projected national average for 2015 of $1,025 per employee (and family when applicable) per month. Employer pays 80 percent for a per month cost of $820 per employee. **Retirement** is based on a 401(k) retirement program with employer matching of 50 percent. Employee contributions to the 401(k) plan are an average of 6 percent of the true wage. **Liability insurance** is based on a national average of 10.0 percent.

**Retaining Walls Labor Productivity**

| | Craft@Hrs | Unit | Material | Labor | Total |
|---|---|---|---|---|---|
| Install retaining wall | | | | | |
| concrete | 3R@.227 | sf | — | 12.70 | 12.70 |
| railroad tie with tie tiebacks | 3R@.244 | sf | — | 13.70 | 13.70 |
| railroad tie, no tie tiebacks | 3R@.167 | sf | — | 9.37 | 9.37 |
| cedar tie with tie tiebacks | 3R@.251 | sf | — | 14.10 | 14.10 |
| cedar tie, no tie tiebacks | 3R@.169 | sf | — | 9.48 | 9.48 |
| interlocking masonry block | 3R@.313 | sf | — | 17.60 | 17.60 |

|  | Craft@Hrs | Unit | Material | Labor | Total |
|---|---|---|---|---|---|

# Roofing

**Roofing.** Costs are based on a typical 2,550 sf house with a 6 in 12 slope roof or less. Roof height is less than 16' so ropes and other safety equipment are not required. Includes costs for ridges and rakes. Typical roof has an intersecting or L-shaped roof and two dormers. Also includes boots and flashing.

**Minimum charge.**

| | Craft@Hrs | Unit | Material | Labor | Total |
|---|---|---|---|---|---|
| for roofing work | 6R@5.50 | ea | 105.00 | 333.00 | 438.00 |

**Add for steep and complex roofs.** Cut-up roofs contain four to six intersecting roof lines. Very cut-up roofs contain seven or more.

| | Craft@Hrs | Unit | Material | Labor | Total |
|---|---|---|---|---|---|
| add for steep roofs 6-12 to 8-12 slope (all roof types) | — | % | — | 35.0 | — |
| add for steep roofs greater than 8-12 slope (all roof types) | — | % | — | 50.0 | — |
| add for cut-up roof | — | % | — | 30.0 | — |
| add for very cut-up roof | — | % | — | 50.0 | — |

**Aluminum shingles.** Includes natural finish aluminum shingles, pipe flashing, roofing felt, valley metal, drip edge, ridge cap, rust-resistant nails, and installation. Installation on roof 16' tall or less.

| | Craft@Hrs | Unit | Material | Labor | Total |
|---|---|---|---|---|---|
| replace, .02" thick | 6R@1.06 | sq | 355.00 | 64.10 | 419.10 |
| replace, .03" thick | 6R@1.06 | sq | 378.00 | 64.10 | 442.10 |
| remove, all thicknesses | 1D@1.04 | sq | — | 40.50 | 40.50 |
| add for colored aluminum shingles (all colors) | — | % | 20.0 | — | — |

**Galvanized steel shingles.** Includes galvanized steel shingles, pipe flashing, roofing felt, valley metal, drip edge, ridge cap, rust-resistant nails, and installation. Installation on roof 16' tall or less.

| | Craft@Hrs | Unit | Material | Labor | Total |
|---|---|---|---|---|---|
| replace, 26 gauge | 6R@1.11 | sq | 263.00 | 67.20 | 330.20 |
| replace, 24 gauge | 6R@1.11 | sq | 294.00 | 67.20 | 361.20 |
| replace, 22 gauge | 6R@1.11 | sq | 306.00 | 67.20 | 373.20 |
| remove, all gauges | 1D@1.04 | sq | — | 40.50 | 40.50 |
| add for shingles with baked enamel factory finish | — | % | 21.0 | — | — |
| add for metal shingles with 1" polystyrene insulation | — | % | 10.0 | — | — |

**Minimum charge.**

| | Craft@Hrs | Unit | Material | Labor | Total |
|---|---|---|---|---|---|
| for metal shingle roof repair | 6R@2.50 | ea | 66.10 | 151.00 | 217.10 |

**Asphalt shingles.** Includes asphalt shingles, pipe flashing, roofing felt, valley metal, drip edge, ridge cap, rust-resistant nails, and installation. Installation on roof 16' tall or less. Prices are for standard three-tab shingles. (20-year shinges are not available in all areas.) Add **14%** for 4 to 6 tab. Add **16%** for thatch style edge. Add **15%** for shingles with cut-outs. Add **10%** for textured shingles.

| | Craft@Hrs | Unit | Material | Labor | Total |
|---|---|---|---|---|---|
| replace, 20 year (210 to 230 lb) | 6R@1.24 | sq | 111.00 | 75.00 | 186.00 |
| replace, 25 year (220 to 240 lb) | 6R@1.24 | sq | 138.00 | 75.00 | 213.00 |
| replace, 30 year (240 to 260 lb) | 6R@1.27 | sq | 161.00 | 76.80 | 237.80 |
| replace, 40 year (260 to 300 lb) | 6R@1.27 | sq | 188.00 | 76.80 | 264.80 |
| remove | 1D@1.02 | sq | — | 39.70 | 39.70 |

| | Craft@Hrs | Unit | Material | Labor | Total |
|---|---|---|---|---|---|
| **Laminated asphalt shingles.** | | | | | |
| replace, standard grade (250 to 300 lb) | 6R@2.06 | sq | 160.00 | 125.00 | 285.00 |
| replace, standard grade (300 to 390 lb) | 6R@2.06 | sq | 185.00 | 125.00 | 310.00 |
| replace, high grade (260 to 300 lb) | 6R@2.45 | sq | 227.00 | 148.00 | 375.00 |
| replace, high grade (300 to 400 lb) | 6R@2.45 | sq | 260.00 | 148.00 | 408.00 |
| remove, all grades | 1D@1.02 | sq | — | 39.70 | 39.70 |
| **T-lock, diamond and hexagonal asphalt shingles. (Not available in all areas.)** | | | | | |
| replace, T-lock (210 to 230 lb) | 6R@1.27 | sq | 94.30 | 76.80 | 171.10 |
| replace, diamond (210 to 230 lb) | 6R@1.27 | sq | 94.30 | 76.80 | 171.10 |
| replace, hexagonal (210 to 230 lb) | 6R@1.27 | sq | 96.60 | 76.80 | 173.40 |
| remove, all styles | 1D@1.02 | sq | — | 39.70 | 39.70 |
| **Minimum charge.** | | | | | |
| for asphalt shingle roof repair | | | | | |
| all types and grades | 6R@2.50 | ea | 47.20 | 151.00 | 198.20 |

**Roll roofing.** Includes roll roofing, galvanized roofing nails, seaming tar, and installation. Overlap according to manufacturer's specifications —usually a few inches. Installation on roof 16' tall or less. Add **82%** for double selvage lay.

| | Craft@Hrs | Unit | Material | Labor | Total |
|---|---|---|---|---|---|
| replace, 90 lb | 6R@.645 | sq | 83.80 | 39.00 | 122.80 |
| replace, 110 lb | 6R@.645 | sq | 99.90 | 39.00 | 138.90 |
| replace, 140 lb | 6R@.645 | sq | 116.00 | 39.00 | 155.00 |
| remove, all weights | 1D@.735 | sq | — | 28.60 | 28.60 |

**Slate roofing.** Includes roofing slates, galvanized nails, boots and flashing, roofing felt, valley metal, drip edge, ridge cap, and installation. Installation on roof 16' tall or less. Does not include furring strips.

| | Craft@Hrs | Unit | Material | Labor | Total |
|---|---|---|---|---|---|
| replace, Vermont unfading green, clear | 6R@4.00 | sq | 985.00 | 242.00 | 1,227.00 |
| replace, Vermont unfading purple, clear | 6R@4.00 | sq | 1,010.00 | 242.00 | 1,252.00 |
| replace, Vermont unfading variegated purple, clear | 6R@4.00 | sq | 1,130.00 | 242.00 | 1,372.00 |
| replace, Vermont unfading dark gray or black, clear | 6R@4.00 | sq | 1,040.00 | 242.00 | 1,282.00 |
| replace, Vermont unfading red, clear | 6R@4.00 | sq | 2,500.00 | 242.00 | 2,742.00 |
| replace, Pennsylvania black weathering, clear | 6R@4.00 | sq | 963.00 | 242.00 | 1,205.00 |
| replace, Vermont weathering green, clear | 6R@4.00 | sq | 933.00 | 242.00 | 1,175.00 |
| remove, all types | 1D@3.70 | sq | — | 144.00 | 144.00 |
| deduct for slate with ribbons of foreign color | — | % | -15.0 | — | — |
| minimum charge for slate roof repair | 6R@4.00 | ea | 363.00 | 242.00 | 605.00 |
| replace single slate | 6R@.385 | ea | 26.30 | 23.30 | 49.60 |

**Wood shingles.** Includes wood shingles, boots, roofing felt, valley metal, drip edge, ridge cap, rust-resistant nails, and installation. Installation on roof 16' tall or less.

| | Craft@Hrs | Unit | Material | Labor | Total |
|---|---|---|---|---|---|
| Blue label cedar shingles | | | | | |
| replace, 16" (Royals) | 6R@2.86 | sq | 374.00 | 173.00 | 547.00 |
| replace, 18" (Perfections) | 6R@2.55 | sq | 397.00 | 154.00 | 551.00 |

| | Craft@Hrs | Unit | Material | Labor | Total |
|---|---|---|---|---|---|

thatch              serrated              Dutch weave              pyramid

| | Craft@Hrs | Unit | Material | Labor | Total |
|---|---|---|---|---|---|
| **Red label cedar shingles** | | | | | |
| replace, 16" (Royals) | 6R@2.86 | sq | 362.00 | 173.00 | 535.00 |
| replace, 18" (Perfections) | 6R@2.55 | sq | 383.00 | 154.00 | 537.00 |
| remove, all types | 1D@1.20 | sq | — | 46.70 | 46.70 |
| minimum charge for wood shingle repair | 6R@3.00 | ea | 92.60 | 182.00 | 274.60 |
| replace single wood shingle | 6R@.207 | ea | 19.70 | 12.50 | 32.20 |
| deduct for black label shingles | — | % | -6.0 | — | — |
| add for 16" wood shingles with 4" exposure | — | % | 20.0 | — | — |
| deduct for 16" shingles with 5-1/2" exposure | — | % | -17.0 | — | — |
| deduct for 16" shingles with 6" exposure | — | % | -20.0 | — | — |
| add for shingles treated with fire retardant | — | % | 18.0 | — | — |
| add for shingles treated with mildew retardant | — | % | 16.0 | — | — |
| add for shingle staggered installation | — | % | 16.0 | — | — |
| add for shingle thatch installation | — | % | 26.0 | — | — |
| add for shingle serrated installation | — | % | 24.0 | — | — |
| add for shingle Dutch weave installation | — | % | 38.0 | — | — |
| add for shingle pyramid installation | — | % | 45.0 | — | — |

**Wood shakes.** Includes shakes, boots, roofing felt, valley metal, drip edge, ridge cap, rust-resistant nails, and installation. Installation on roof 16' tall or less.

| | Craft@Hrs | Unit | Material | Labor | Total |
|---|---|---|---|---|---|
| **Handsplit and resawn shakes** | | | | | |
| replace, 18" medium | 6R@3.34 | sq | 243.00 | 202.00 | 445.00 |
| replace, 18" heavy | 6R@3.34 | sq | 268.00 | 202.00 | 470.00 |
| replace, 24" medium | 6R@2.86 | sq | 327.00 | 173.00 | 500.00 |
| replace, 24" heavy | 6R@2.86 | sq | 362.00 | 173.00 | 535.00 |
| **Taper split shakes** | | | | | |
| replace, 24" | 6R@2.86 | sq | 258.00 | 173.00 | 431.00 |
| **Straight split shakes** | | | | | |
| replace, 18" | 6R@3.34 | sq | 221.00 | 202.00 | 423.00 |
| replace, 24" | 6R@2.86 | sq | 233.00 | 173.00 | 406.00 |
| remove, all types and sizes | 1D@1.20 | sq | — | 46.70 | 46.70 |
| add for 8" shake exposure | — | % | 20.0 | — | — |
| deduct for 12" shake exposure | — | % | -20.0 | — | — |
| add for staggered shake installation | — | % | 16.0 | — | — |
| minimum charge for shake roof repair | 6R@3.00 | ea | 92.60 | 182.00 | 274.60 |
| replace single shake | 6R@.208 | ea | 26.30 | 12.60 | 38.90 |

| | Craft@Hrs | Unit | Material | Labor | Total |
|---|---|---|---|---|---|

**Fiber and cement shingles.** Includes fiber and cement shingles, galvanized nails, boots, roofing felt, valley metal, drip edge, ridge cap, and installation. Installation on roof 16' tall or less. Does not include furring strips. Older shingles of this type may contain asbestos. This is a hazardous material which requires special techniques and equipment to remove.

| | Craft@Hrs | Unit | Material | Labor | Total |
|---|---|---|---|---|---|
| replace, weathering shake type | 6R@2.38 | sq | 121.00 | 144.00 | 265.00 |
| replace, Spanish tile type | 6R@2.50 | sq | 150.00 | 151.00 | 301.00 |
| remove, all non-asbestos types | 1D@1.11 | sq | — | 43.20 | 43.20 |
| minimum charge for fiber and cement shingle roof repair | 6R@2.50 | ea | 55.30 | 151.00 | 206.30 |

**Granular coated metal tile.** Includes granular coated metal tile, boots, roofing felt, valley metal, drip edge, ridge cap, rust-resistant nails, and installation. Installation on roof 16' tall or less.

| | Craft@Hrs | Unit | Material | Labor | Total |
|---|---|---|---|---|---|
| replace, simple pattern | 6R@4.27 | sq | 401.00 | 258.00 | 659.00 |
| replace, complex pattern | 6R@4.27 | sq | 485.00 | 258.00 | 743.00 |
| remove, all types | 1D@1.04 | sq | — | 40.50 | 40.50 |

**Flat clay tile shingle roof.** Includes flat clay roofing tile, galvanized nails, boots, roofing felt, valley metal, drip edge, ridge cap, and installation. Installation on roof 16' tall or less. Does not include furring strips. Old style clay tile shingles.

| | Craft@Hrs | Unit | Material | Labor | Total |
|---|---|---|---|---|---|
| replace, terra cotta red | 6R@3.23 | sq | 136.00 | 195.00 | 331.00 |
| replace, glazed red | 6R@3.23 | sq | 287.00 | 195.00 | 482.00 |
| remove, all types | 1D@3.45 | sq | — | 134.00 | 134.00 |

**Mission tile roof.** Includes 30 lb felt underlayment, doubled felt on rakes and eaves, bird stop, booster tiles, ridge and rake tiles.

| | Craft@Hrs | Unit | Material | Labor | Total |
|---|---|---|---|---|---|
| replace, terra cotta red | 6R@5.56 | sq | 273.00 | 336.00 | 609.00 |
| replace, peach | 6R@5.56 | sq | 310.00 | 336.00 | 646.00 |
| replace, white | 6R@5.56 | sq | 363.00 | 336.00 | 699.00 |
| replace, color blends | 6R@5.56 | sq | 341.00 | 336.00 | 677.00 |
| replace, glazed white | 6R@5.56 | sq | 745.00 | 336.00 | 1,081.00 |
| replace, glazed gray | 6R@5.56 | sq | 752.00 | 336.00 | 1,088.00 |
| replace, glazed burgundy | 6R@5.56 | sq | 755.00 | 336.00 | 1,091.00 |
| replace, glazed terra cotta red | 6R@5.56 | sq | 753.00 | 336.00 | 1,089.00 |
| replace, glazed teal | 6R@5.56 | sq | 946.00 | 336.00 | 1,282.00 |
| replace, glazed blue | 6R@5.56 | sq | 966.00 | 336.00 | 1,302.00 |
| remove, all types and colors | 1D@3.45 | sq | — | 134.00 | 134.00 |
| add for vertical furring strips under all cap tiles | 6R@3.26 | sq | 144.00 | 197.00 | 341.00 |
| add for tiles attached with wire | 6R@2.22 | sq | 24.30 | 134.00 | 158.30 |
| add for tiles attached with stainless steel nails | — | sq | 33.50 | — | 33.50 |
| add for tiles attached with brass or copper nails | — | sq | 45.00 | — | 45.00 |
| add for tiles attached to braided wire runners | 6R@2.18 | sq | 43.40 | 132.00 | 175.40 |
| add for tiles attached with hurricane clips or locks | 6R@3.03 | sq | 29.60 | 183.00 | 212.60 |
| add for adhesive between tiles | 6R@.154 | sq | 23.40 | 9.32 | 32.72 |

**Spanish tile roof.** Includes 30 lb felt underlayment, doubled felt on rakes and eaves, bird stop, ridge and rake tiles.

| | Craft@Hrs | Unit | Material | Labor | Total |
|---|---|---|---|---|---|
| replace, terra cotta red | 6R@3.34 | sq | 172.00 | 202.00 | 374.00 |
| replace, peach | 6R@3.34 | sq | 211.00 | 202.00 | 413.00 |
| replace, white | 6R@3.34 | sq | 262.00 | 202.00 | 464.00 |
| replace, color blends | 6R@3.34 | sq | 240.00 | 202.00 | 442.00 |
| replace, glazed white | 6R@3.34 | sq | 675.00 | 202.00 | 877.00 |
| replace, glazed gray | 6R@3.34 | sq | 680.00 | 202.00 | 882.00 |

| | Craft@Hrs | Unit | Material | Labor | Total |
|---|---|---|---|---|---|
| replace, glazed burgundy | 6R@3.34 | sq | 853.00 | 202.00 | 1,055.00 |
| replace, glazed terra cotta red | 6R@3.34 | sq | 682.00 | 202.00 | 884.00 |
| replace, glazed teal | 6R@3.34 | sq | 860.00 | 202.00 | 1,062.00 |
| replace, glazed blue | 6R@3.34 | sq | 888.00 | 202.00 | 1,090.00 |
| remove, all types and colors | 1D@3.45 | sq | — | 134.00 | 134.00 |
| add for tiles attached with wire | 6R@1.75 | sq | 20.30 | 106.00 | 126.30 |
| add for tiles attached with stainless-steel nails | — | sq | 28.40 | — | 28.40 |
| add for tiles attached with brass or copper nails | — | sq | 37.90 | — | 37.90 |
| add for tiles attached to braided wire runners | 6R@1.47 | sq | 35.90 | 88.90 | 124.80 |
| add for tiles attached with hurricane clips or locks | 6R@1.82 | sq | 22.50 | 110.00 | 132.50 |
| add for tiles attached using mortar set method | 6R@2.63 | sq | 66.70 | 159.00 | 225.70 |
| add for adhesive between tiles | 6R@.137 | sq | 23.40 | 8.29 | 31.69 |

**Other clay tile grades.** Deduct from the cost of Spanish or mission tiles.

| Deduct | | | | | |
|---|---|---|---|---|---|
| for ASTM grade 2 moderate weathering tiles | — | % | -5.0 | — | — |
| for ASTM grade 3 negligible weathering tiles | — | % | -11.0 | — | — |
| for low profile Spanish or Mission tiles | — | % | -12.0 | — | — |

**Furring strips.** For roofing tiles.

| | | | | | |
|---|---|---|---|---|---|
| replace, vertically laid only | 6R@.606 | sq | 28.70 | 36.70 | 65.40 |
| remove | 1D@.478 | sq | — | 18.60 | 18.60 |
| replace, vertically and horizontally laid | 6R@.877 | sq | 47.30 | 53.10 | 100.40 |
| remove | 1D@.840 | sq | — | 32.70 | 32.70 |

**Corrugated concrete tile.** Includes corrugated concrete tile, edge cap as needed, boots, roofing felt, valley metal, drip edge, ridge cap, fasteners, and installation. Installation on roof 16' tall or less. Does not include furring strips.

| | | | | | |
|---|---|---|---|---|---|
| replace, natural gray | 6R@3.13 | sq | 146.00 | 189.00 | 335.00 |
| replace, black | 6R@3.13 | sq | 167.00 | 189.00 | 356.00 |
| replace, browns and terra cotta reds | 6R@3.13 | sq | 177.00 | 189.00 | 366.00 |
| replace, bright reds | 6R@3.13 | sq | 187.00 | 189.00 | 376.00 |
| replace, greens | 6R@3.13 | sq | 205.00 | 189.00 | 394.00 |
| replace, blues | 6R@3.13 | sq | 217.00 | 189.00 | 406.00 |
| remove, all colors | 1D@3.85 | sq | — | 150.00 | 150.00 |

**Flat concrete tile.** Includes flat concrete tile, boots, roofing felt, valley metal, drip edge, ridge cap, fasteners, and installation. Installation on roof 16' tall or less. Does not include furring strips.

| | | | | | |
|---|---|---|---|---|---|
| replace, natural gray | 6R@3.03 | sq | 134.00 | 183.00 | 317.00 |
| replace, black | 6R@3.03 | sq | 151.00 | 183.00 | 334.00 |
| replace, browns and terra cotta reds | 6R@3.03 | sq | 166.00 | 183.00 | 349.00 |
| replace, bright reds | 6R@3.03 | sq | 173.00 | 183.00 | 356.00 |
| replace, greens | 6R@3.03 | sq | 187.00 | 183.00 | 370.00 |
| replace, blues | 6R@3.03 | sq | 195.00 | 183.00 | 378.00 |
| remove, all colors | 1D@3.85 | sq | — | 150.00 | 150.00 |
| add for glazed tiles | — | % | 2.0 | — | — |
| add for painted tiles | — | % | 5.0 | — | — |

| | Craft@Hrs | Unit | Material | Labor | Total |
|---|---|---|---|---|---|

**Aluminum sheet corrugated.** Includes corrugated aluminum panels, rust-resistant nails, purlins with corrugated pattern, end caps when needed, boots, roofing felt, valley metal, drip edge, ridge cap, fasteners, and installation. Weights are per SF. Includes 4% waste.

| Corrugated aluminum roofing | | | | | |
|---|---|---|---|---|---|
| Natural finish corrugated aluminum roofing | | | | | |
| replace, 0.016" thick | 6R@.024 | sf | 1.27 | 1.45 | 2.72 |
| replace, 0.019" thick | 6R@.024 | sf | 1.36 | 1.45 | 2.81 |
| Colored finish corrugated aluminum roofing | | | | | |
| replace, 0.016" thick | 6R@.024 | sf | 1.57 | 1.45 | 3.02 |
| replace, 0.019" thick | 6R@.024 | sf | 1.73 | 1.45 | 3.18 |
| Remove, all types | 1D@.010 | sf | — | .39 | .39 |

**Aluminum sheet ribbed.** Includes aluminum ribbed panels, rust-resistant nails, purlins with ribbed pattern as needed, end caps when needed, boots, roofing felt, valley metal, drip edge, ridge cap, fasteners, and installation. Weights are per SF. Includes 4% waste. Installation on roof 16' tall or less.

| Ribbed aluminum roofing | | | | | |
|---|---|---|---|---|---|
| Natural finish ribbed aluminum roofing | | | | | |
| replace, 0.016" thick | 6R@.026 | sf | 1.32 | 1.57 | 2.89 |
| replace, 0.019" thick | 6R@.026 | sf | 1.79 | 1.57 | 3.36 |
| replace, 0.032" thick | 6R@.026 | sf | 2.59 | 1.57 | 4.16 |
| replace, 0.04" thick | 6R@.026 | sf | 3.36 | 1.57 | 4.93 |
| replace, 0.05" thick | 6R@.026 | sf | 3.97 | 1.57 | 5.54 |
| Colored finish ribbed aluminum roofing | | | | | |
| replace, 0.016" thick | 6R@.026 | sf | 1.57 | 1.57 | 3.14 |
| replace, 0.019" thick | 6R@.026 | sf | 1.76 | 1.57 | 3.33 |
| replace, 0.032" thick | 6R@.026 | sf | 2.63 | 1.57 | 4.20 |
| replace, 0.04" thick | 6R@.026 | sf | 4.49 | 1.57 | 6.06 |
| replace, 0.05" thick | 6R@.026 | sf | 5.13 | 1.57 | 6.70 |
| Remove, all types | 1D@.010 | sf | — | .39 | .39 |

**Fiberglass corrugated.** Includes fiberglass panels, rust-resistant nails, purlins with corrugated pattern, end caps when needed, boots, roofing felt, valley metal, drip edge, ridge cap, fasteners, and installation. Weights are per SF. Includes 4% waste.

| Corrugated fiberglass roofing | | | | | |
|---|---|---|---|---|---|
| replace, 8 ounce | 6R@.024 | sf | 3.34 | 1.45 | 4.79 |
| replace, 12 ounce | 6R@.024 | sf | 4.47 | 1.45 | 5.92 |
| remove, all types | 1D@.009 | sf | — | .35 | .35 |

**Galvanized steel corrugated roofing.** Includes corrugated galvanized steel panels, rust-resistant nails, purlins with corrugated pattern, end caps when needed, boots, roofing felt, valley metal, drip edge, ridge cap, fasteners, and installation. Weights are per SF. Includes 4% waste.

| | | | | | |
|---|---|---|---|---|---|
| replace, 30 gauge | 6R@.025 | sf | 1.26 | 1.51 | 2.77 |
| replace, 28 gauge | 6R@.025 | sf | 1.31 | 1.51 | 2.82 |
| replace, 26 gauge | 6R@.025 | sf | 1.36 | 1.51 | 2.87 |
| replace, 24 gauge | 6R@.025 | sf | 1.55 | 1.51 | 3.06 |
| remove, all gauges | 1D@.010 | sf | — | .39 | .39 |

| | Craft@Hrs | Unit | Material | Labor | Total |
|---|---|---|---|---|---|

## Galvanized steel ribbed roofing.

Natural finish galvanized steel ribbed roofing

| | Craft@Hrs | Unit | Material | Labor | Total |
|---|---|---|---|---|---|
| replace, 30 gauge | 6R@.026 | sf | 1.31 | 1.57 | 2.88 |
| replace, 28 gauge | 6R@.026 | sf | 1.34 | 1.57 | 2.91 |
| replace, 26 gauge | 6R@.026 | sf | 1.44 | 1.57 | 3.01 |
| replace, 24 gauge | 6R@.026 | sf | 1.63 | 1.57 | 3.20 |
| remove, all gauges | 1D@.010 | sf | — | .39 | .39 |

Colored finish galvanized steel ribbed roofing

| | Craft@Hrs | Unit | Material | Labor | Total |
|---|---|---|---|---|---|
| replace, 30 gauge | 6R@.026 | sf | 1.79 | 1.57 | 3.36 |
| replace, 28 gauge | 6R@.026 | sf | 1.89 | 1.57 | 3.46 |
| replace, 26 gauge | 6R@.026 | sf | 2.02 | 1.57 | 3.59 |
| replace, 24 gauge | 6R@.026 | sf | 2.24 | 1.57 | 3.81 |
| remove, all gauges | 1D@.010 | sf | — | .39 | .39 |

**Copper.** Includes cold-rolled copper sheets, boots, roofing felt, valley metal, drip edge, ridge cap, fasteners, anchoring clips, solder, welding rods, protective coatings, separators, sealants as recommended by copper sheet manufacturer, and installation. Installation on roof 16' tall or less.

Standing seam copper roofing, includes copper batten caps and copper batten end caps when needed

| | Craft@Hrs | Unit | Material | Labor | Total |
|---|---|---|---|---|---|
| replace, 16 ounce | 6R@6.67 | sq | 837.00 | 404.00 | 1,241.00 |
| replace, 18 ounce | 6R@7.14 | sq | 930.00 | 432.00 | 1,362.00 |
| replace, 20 ounce | 6R@7.69 | sq | 1,060.00 | 465.00 | 1,525.00 |

*standing seam*

Batten seam copper roofing

| | Craft@Hrs | Unit | Material | Labor | Total |
|---|---|---|---|---|---|
| replace, 16 ounce | 6R@7.69 | sq | 856.00 | 465.00 | 1,321.00 |
| replace, 18 ounce | 6R@8.33 | sq | 952.00 | 504.00 | 1,456.00 |
| replace, 20 ounce | 6R@9.09 | sq | 1,080.00 | 550.00 | 1,630.00 |

*batten seam*

Flat seam copper roofing

| | Craft@Hrs | Unit | Material | Labor | Total |
|---|---|---|---|---|---|
| replace, 16 ounce | 6R@7.14 | sq | 766.00 | 432.00 | 1,198.00 |
| replace, 18 ounce | 6R@7.69 | sq | 856.00 | 465.00 | 1,321.00 |
| replace, 20 ounce | 6R@8.33 | sq | 960.00 | 504.00 | 1,464.00 |
| Remove, all types | 1D@1.03 | sq | — | 40.10 | 40.10 |

*flat seam*

**Lead roofing.** Includes cold-rolled lead sheets, boots, roofing felt, valley metal, drip edge, ridge cap, fasteners, anchoring clips, solder, welding rods, protective coatings, separators, sealants as recommended by lead sheet manufacturer, and installation. Installation on roof 16' tall or less.

Batten seam

| | Craft@Hrs | Unit | Material | Labor | Total |
|---|---|---|---|---|---|
| replace, 3 lb | 6R@7.14 | sq | 938.00 | 432.00 | 1,370.00 |

Flat seam

| | Craft@Hrs | Unit | Material | Labor | Total |
|---|---|---|---|---|---|
| replace, 3 lb | 6R@7.69 | sq | 847.00 | 465.00 | 1,312.00 |
| Remove, all types | 1D@1.03 | sq | — | 40.10 | 40.10 |

**Stainless steel roofing.** Includes cold-rolled stainless steel sheets, boots, roofing felt, valley metal, drip edge, ridge cap, fasteners, anchoring clips, solder, protective coatings, sealants as recommended by manufacturer, and installation. Installation on roof 16' tall or less.

Standing seam stainless steel roofing

| | Craft@Hrs | Unit | Material | Labor | Total |
|---|---|---|---|---|---|
| replace, 28 gauge | 6R@7.14 | sq | 614.00 | 432.00 | 1,046.00 |
| replace, 26 gauge | 6R@6.67 | sq | 684.00 | 404.00 | 1,088.00 |

|  | Craft@Hrs | Unit | Material | Labor | Total |
|---|---|---|---|---|---|
| Batten seam stainless steel roofing | | | | | |
| replace, 28 gauge | 6R@7.69 | sq | 631.00 | 465.00 | 1,096.00 |
| replace, 26 gauge | 6R@7.14 | sq | 703.00 | 432.00 | 1,135.00 |
| Flat seam stainless steel roofing | | | | | |
| replace, 28 gauge | 6R@7.14 | sq | 583.00 | 432.00 | 1,015.00 |
| replace, 26 gauge | 6R@6.67 | sq | 652.00 | 404.00 | 1,056.00 |
| Remove all types of stainless steel roofing | 1D@1.03 | sq | — | 40.10 | 40.10 |

## Stainless steel roofing coated finish.

|  | Craft@Hrs | Unit | Material | Labor | Total |
|---|---|---|---|---|---|
| add for terne coated stainless steel | — | % | 13.0 | — | — |
| add for lead coated stainless steel | — | % | 14.0 | — | — |

**Terne roofing.** Includes cold-rolled terne sheets, boots, roofing felt, valley metal, drip edge, ridge cap, fasteners, anchoring clips, solder, protective coatings, sealants as recommended by manufacturer, and installation. Installation on roof 16' tall or less. Terne is short for Terneplate. Terneplate is sheet iron or steel that is plated with an alloy that is one part tin and three to four parts lead.

|  | Craft@Hrs | Unit | Material | Labor | Total |
|---|---|---|---|---|---|
| Standing seam | | | | | |
| replace, 40 lb | 6R@8.33 | sq | 1,360.00 | 504.00 | 1,864.00 |
| Batten seam | | | | | |
| replace, 40 lb | 6R@7.69 | sq | 1,410.00 | 465.00 | 1,875.00 |
| Flat seam | | | | | |
| replace, 40 lb | 6R@9.09 | sq | 1,320.00 | 550.00 | 1,870.00 |
| Remove, all types | 1D@1.03 | sq | — | 40.10 | 40.10 |

## Seamed metal roof repair. For repairs to standing seam, batten seam, or flat seam metal roofs.

|  | Craft@Hrs | Unit | Material | Labor | Total |
|---|---|---|---|---|---|
| solder patch into metal roof (less than 1' square) | 4R@1.00 | ea | 59.40 | 65.50 | 124.90 |
| minimum charge | 4R@4.00 | ea | 145.00 | 262.00 | 407.00 |

**Built-up roofing.** Includes base sheet, ply sheets, hot-mop tar, and installation. Does not include wrap up parapet wall, or finish coat. Unless indicated, does not include ballast.

|  | Craft@Hrs | Unit | Material | Labor | Equip. | Total |
|---|---|---|---|---|---|---|
| replace, 3 ply | 6R@3.34 | sq | 74.10 | 202.00 | 14.20 | 290.30 |
| replace, 4 ply | 6R@4.00 | sq | 104.00 | 242.00 | 15.80 | 361.80 |
| replace, 5 ply | 6R@4.76 | sq | 154.00 | 288.00 | 17.80 | 459.80 |
| remove, 3 ply | 1D@2.44 | sq | — | 94.90 | — | 94.90 |
| remove, 4 ply | 1D@3.03 | sq | — | 118.00 | — | 118.00 |
| remove, 5 ply | 1D@3.85 | sq | — | 150.00 | — | 150.00 |
| minimum charge | | | | | | |
| for hot asphalt work | 6R@5.00 | ea | 236.00 | 303.00 | — | 539.00 |
| add for gravel surface | | | | | | |
| embedded in flood coat | 6R@.400 | sq | 18.60 | 24.20 | 2.20 | 45.00 |
| add to remove built-up roof with ballast | 1D@.847 | sq | — | 32.90 | — | 32.90 |
| add for flood coat | 6R@.714 | sq | 23.30 | 43.20 | 5.88 | 72.38 |
| add to paint with aluminum UV coating | 6R@.834 | sq | 22.50 | 50.50 | — | 73.00 |
| add to paint with aluminum UV coating | | | | | | |
| with fiber | 6R@.834 | sq | 27.80 | 50.50 | — | 78.30 |
| add for mineral faced cap sheet | — | sq | 23.30 | — | — | 23.30 |

| | Craft@Hrs | Unit | Material | Labor | Equip. | Total |
|---|---|---|---|---|---|---|
| remove gravel, flood coat, then replace gravel | 6R@2.48 | sq | 49.80 | 150.00 | 23.80 | 223.60 |
| add per lf of parapet wall, includes cant strip and roofing wrap up wall | 6R@.226 | lf | 13.20 | 13.70 | 1.05 | 27.95 |

**SCPE elastomeric roofing.** Includes SCPE elastomeric roofing rolls and fasteners. Installation is according to manufacturer's specs using fasteners they provide. Chlorosulfonated polyethylene-hypalon roofing is abbreviated SCPE. Ballasted roofs contain 1/2 ton of stone per square.

45 mil

| | Craft@Hrs | Unit | Material | Labor | Equip. | Total |
|---|---|---|---|---|---|---|
| replace, loose laid and ballasted with stone | 6R@1.00 | sq | 226.00 | 60.50 | 4.23 | 290.73 |
| remove | 1D@2.04 | sq | — | 79.40 | — | 79.40 |
| replace, attached at seams with batten strips | 6R@.834 | sq | 237.00 | 50.50 | 6.74 | 294.24 |
| remove | 1D@.980 | sq | — | 38.10 | — | 38.10 |
| replace, fully attached to deck | 6R@1.04 | sq | 250.00 | 62.90 | 12.80 | 325.70 |
| remove | 1D@1.56 | sq | — | 60.70 | — | 60.70 |

**EPDM elastomeric roofing.** Includes EPDM roofing rolls and fasteners. Installation is according to manufacturer's specs using fasteners they provide. Ethylene propylene diene monomer roofing is abbreviated EPDM. Ballasted roofs contain 1/2-ton of stone per square.

45 mil

| | Craft@Hrs | Unit | Material | Labor | Equip. | Total |
|---|---|---|---|---|---|---|
| replace, loose laid and ballasted with stone | 6R@2.45 | sq | 127.00 | 148.00 | 4.23 | 279.23 |
| remove | 1D@2.04 | sq | — | 79.40 | — | 79.40 |
| replace, attached to deck at seams | 6R@2.00 | sq | 109.00 | 121.00 | 6.74 | 236.74 |
| remove | 1D@.980 | sq | — | 38.10 | — | 38.10 |
| replace, fully attached to deck | 6R@2.86 | sq | 151.00 | 173.00 | 12.80 | 336.80 |
| remove | 1D@1.56 | sq | — | 60.70 | — | 60.70 |

55 mil

| | Craft@Hrs | Unit | Material | Labor | Equip. | Total |
|---|---|---|---|---|---|---|
| replace, loose laid and ballasted with stone | 6R@2.51 | sq | 146.00 | 152.00 | 4.23 | 302.23 |
| remove | 1D@2.04 | sq | — | 79.40 | — | 79.40 |
| replace, attached to deck at seams | 6R@2.04 | sq | 129.00 | 123.00 | 6.74 | 258.74 |
| remove | 1D@.980 | sq | — | 38.10 | — | 38.10 |
| replace, fully attached to deck | 6R@2.95 | sq | 174.00 | 178.00 | 12.80 | 364.80 |
| remove | 1D@1.56 | sq | — | 60.70 | — | 60.70 |

60 mil

| | Craft@Hrs | Unit | Material | Labor | Equip. | Total |
|---|---|---|---|---|---|---|
| replace, loose laid and ballasted with stone | 6R@2.55 | sq | 156.00 | 154.00 | 4.23 | 314.23 |
| remove | 1D@2.04 | sq | — | 79.40 | — | 79.40 |
| replace, attached to deck at seams | 6R@2.08 | sq | 133.00 | 126.00 | 6.74 | 265.74 |
| remove | 1D@.980 | sq | — | 38.10 | — | 38.10 |
| replace, fully attached to deck | 6R@3.03 | sq | 176.00 | 183.00 | 12.80 | 371.80 |
| remove | 1D@1.56 | sq | — | 60.70 | — | 60.70 |

| | Craft@Hrs | Unit | Material | Labor | Equip. | Total |
|---|---|---|---|---|---|---|

**PVC roofing.** Includes PVC roofing rolls and fasteners. Installation is according to manufacturer's specs using fasteners they provide. Polyvinyl chloride roofing is abbreviated PVC. Ballasted roofs contain 1/2 ton of stone per square.

**45 mil**

| | Craft@Hrs | Unit | Material | Labor | Equip. | Total |
|---|---|---|---|---|---|---|
| replace, loose laid and ballasted with stone | 6R@.587 | sq | 151.00 | 35.50 | 4.23 | 190.73 |
| remove | 1D@2.04 | sq | — | 79.40 | — | 79.40 |
| replace, attached to deck at seams | 6R@.909 | sq | 191.00 | 55.00 | 6.74 | 252.74 |
| remove | 1D@.980 | sq | — | 38.10 | — | 38.10 |
| replace, fully attached to deck | 6R@1.33 | sq | 206.00 | 80.50 | 12.80 | 299.30 |
| remove | 1D@1.56 | sq | — | 60.70 | — | 60.70 |
| add for 45 mil reinforced PVC | — | % | 22.0 | — | — | — |

**48 mil**

| | Craft@Hrs | Unit | Material | Labor | Equip. | Total |
|---|---|---|---|---|---|---|
| replace, loose laid and ballasted with stone | 6R@.624 | sq | 167.00 | 37.80 | 4.23 | 209.03 |
| remove | 1D@2.04 | sq | — | 79.40 | — | 79.40 |
| replace, attached to deck at seams | 6R@1.00 | sq | 196.00 | 60.50 | 6.74 | 263.24 |
| remove | 1D@.980 | sq | — | 38.10 | — | 38.10 |
| replace, fully attached to deck | 6R@1.35 | sq | 217.00 | 81.70 | 12.80 | 311.50 |
| remove single ply roof fully adhered, no ballast | 1D@1.56 | sq | — | 60.70 | — | 60.70 |

**60 mil**

| | Craft@Hrs | Unit | Material | Labor | Equip. | Total |
|---|---|---|---|---|---|---|
| replace, loose laid and ballasted with stone | 6R@.666 | sq | 226.00 | 40.30 | 4.23 | 270.53 |
| remove single ply roof with ballast | 1D@2.04 | sq | — | 79.40 | — | 79.40 |
| replace, attached to deck at seams | 6R@1.02 | sq | 239.00 | 61.70 | 6.74 | 307.44 |
| remove single ply roof partially adhered, no ballast | 1D@.980 | sq | — | 38.10 | — | 38.10 |
| replace, fully attached to deck | 6R@1.39 | sq | 274.00 | 84.10 | 12.80 | 370.90 |
| remove single ply roof fully adhered, no ballast | 1D@1.56 | sq | — | 60.70 | — | 60.70 |

**Modified bitumen roofing.** Includes modified bitumen rolls, hot tar as needed, propane as needed, fasteners as needed, and installation. Installation is according to manufacturer's specs using fasteners they provide. Modified bitumen rolls come in two styles: hot-mop or torch-down. Hot mop styles are adhered with a coat of hot tar. Torch-down styles are melted in place with a torch along the seams. Unless indicated, does not include ballast or additional hot-mop coats.

**120 mil**

| | Craft@Hrs | Unit | Material | Labor | Equip. | Total |
|---|---|---|---|---|---|---|
| replace, loose laid and ballasted with stone | 6R@.990 | sq | 115.00 | 59.90 | 10.50 | 185.40 |
| remove | 1D@2.04 | sq | — | 79.40 | — | 79.40 |
| replace, attached to deck at seams | 6R@1.15 | sq | 109.00 | 69.60 | 10.50 | 189.10 |
| remove | 1D@.980 | sq | — | 38.10 | — | 38.10 |
| replace, fully attached to deck with torch | 6R@1.49 | sq | 107.00 | 90.10 | 12.70 | 209.80 |
| replace, fully attached to deck with hot asphalt | 6R@1.49 | sq | 120.00 | 90.10 | 16.80 | 226.90 |
| remove | 1D@1.56 | sq | — | 60.70 | — | 60.70 |

| | Craft@Hrs | Unit | Material | Labor | Equip. | Total |
|---|---|---|---|---|---|---|
| **150 mil** | | | | | | |
| replace, loose laid and ballasted | | | | | | |
|   with stone | 6R@1.00 | sq | 123.00 | 60.50 | 10.50 | 194.00 |
| remove | 1D@2.04 | sq | — | 79.40 | — | 79.40 |
| replace, attached to deck at seams | 6R@1.18 | sq | 115.00 | 71.40 | 10.50 | 196.90 |
| remove | 1D@.980 | sq | — | 38.10 | — | 38.10 |
| replace, fully attached to deck | | | | | | |
|   with torch | 6R@1.52 | sq | 113.00 | 92.00 | 12.70 | 217.70 |
| replace, fully attached to deck | | | | | | |
|   with hot asphalt | 6R@1.56 | sq | 125.00 | 94.40 | 16.80 | 236.20 |
| remove | 1D@1.56 | sq | — | 60.70 | — | 60.70 |
| **160 mil** | | | | | | |
| replace, loose laid and ballasted | | | | | | |
|   with stone | 6R@1.02 | sq | 125.00 | 61.70 | 10.50 | 197.20 |
| remove | 1D@2.04 | sq | — | 79.40 | — | 79.40 |
| replace, attached to deck at seams | 6R@1.20 | sq | 120.00 | 72.60 | 10.50 | 203.10 |
| remove | 1D@.980 | sq | — | 38.10 | — | 38.10 |
| replace, fully attached to deck | | | | | | |
|   with torch | 6R@1.54 | sq | 118.00 | 93.20 | 12.70 | 223.90 |
| replace, fully attached to deck | | | | | | |
|   with hot asphalt | 6R@1.59 | sq | 134.00 | 96.20 | 16.80 | 247.00 |
| remove | 1D@1.56 | sq | — | 60.70 | — | 60.70 |

| | Craft@Hrs | Unit | Material | Labor | Total |
|---|---|---|---|---|---|
| **Roofing felt.** | | | | | |
| replace, 15 pound | 6R@.085 | sq | 5.93 | 5.14 | 11.07 |
| replace, 30 pound | 6R@.085 | sq | 10.70 | 5.14 | 15.84 |
| remove | 6R@.089 | sq | — | 5.38 | 5.38 |
| **Ice and water shield** | | | | | |
| replace | 6R@.008 | sf | .70 | .48 | 1.18 |
| **Drip edge** | | | | | |
| replace | 6R@.006 | lf | .65 | .36 | 1.01 |
| remove | 6R@.003 | lf | — | .18 | .18 |
| **Gravel stop** | | | | | |
| replace | 6R@.006 | lf | 1.12 | .36 | 1.48 |
| remove | 6R@.003 | lf | — | .18 | .18 |
| **Step flashing** | | | | | |
| replace | 6R@.040 | lf | 1.84 | 2.42 | 4.26 |
| **Chimney saw-kerf flashing** | | | | | |
| replace | 6R@.158 | lf | 9.12 | 9.56 | 18.68 |
| minimum charge for replace | 6R@1.00 | ea | 54.80 | 60.50 | 115.30 |
| **Valley metal** | | | | | |
| replace, galvanized or aluminum | 6R@.017 | lf | 2.43 | 1.03 | 3.46 |
| replace, copper valley metal | 6R@.017 | lf | 9.81 | 1.03 | 10.84 |
| remove | 6R@.006 | ea | — | .36 | .36 |

| | Craft@Hrs | Unit | Material | Labor | Total |
|---|---|---|---|---|---|
| Pipe jack | | | | | |
| replace | 6R@.175 | ea | 12.00 | 10.60 | 22.60 |
| remove | 6R@.205 | ea | — | 12.40 | 12.40 |
| Roof vent | | | | | |
| replace, turbine | 6R@.295 | ea | 45.40 | 17.80 | 63.20 |
| replace, turtle | 6R@.253 | ea | 22.00 | 15.30 | 37.30 |
| replace, gable | 6R@.253 | ea | 27.70 | 15.30 | 43.00 |
| remove | 6R@.253 | ea | — | 15.30 | 15.30 |
| remove for work, then reinstall | 6R@.490 | ea | — | 29.60 | 29.60 |
| Furnace vent cap | | | | | |
| replace | 6R@.205 | ea | 15.80 | 12.40 | 28.20 |
| remove | 6R@.257 | ea | — | 15.50 | 15.50 |
| remove for work, then reinstall | 6R@.355 | ea | — | 21.50 | 21.50 |
| Repair leak with mastic | | | | | |
| replace, roof leak | 6R@.452 | ea | 4.35 | 27.30 | 31.65 |
| replace, flashing leak | 6R@.436 | ea | 4.35 | 26.40 | 30.75 |

## Time & Material Charts (selected items)
## Roofing Materials

See Roofing material prices above.

### Roofing Labor

| Laborer | base wage | paid leave | true wage | taxes & ins. | total |
|---|---|---|---|---|---|
| Roofer / slater | $32.60 | 2.54 | $35.14 | 30.36 | $65.50 |
| Roofer's helper | $27.20 | 2.12 | $29.32 | 26.18 | $55.50 |
| Demolition laborer | $20.70 | 1.61 | $22.31 | 16.59 | $38.90 |

**Paid leave** is calculated based on two weeks paid vacation, one week sick leave, and seven paid holidays. Employer's matching portion of **FICA** is 7.65 percent. **FUTA** (Federal Unemployment) is .8 percent. **Worker's compensation** for the roofing trade was calculated using a national average of 34.50 percent. **Unemployment insurance** was calculated using a national average of 8 percent. **Health insurance** was calculated based on a projected national average for 2015 of $1,025 per employee (and family when applicable) per month. Employer pays 80 percent for a per month cost of $820 per employee. **Retirement** is based on a 401(k) retirement program with employer matching of 50 percent. Employee contributions to the 401(k) plan are an average of 6 percent of the true wage. **Liability insurance** is based on a national average of 10.0 percent.

| | Craft@Hrs | Unit | Material | Labor | Total |
|---|---|---|---|---|---|

### Roofing Labor Productivity

| | Craft@Hrs | Unit | Material | Labor | Total |
|---|---|---|---|---|---|
| Demolition of roofing | | | | | |
| remove metal shingles | 1D@1.04 | sq | — | 40.50 | 40.50 |
| remove asphalt shingles | 1D@1.02 | sq | — | 39.70 | 39.70 |
| remove roll roofing | 1D@.735 | sq | — | 28.60 | 28.60 |
| remove slate shingles | 1D@3.70 | sq | — | 144.00 | 144.00 |
| remove wood shingles or shakes | 1D@1.20 | sq | — | 46.70 | 46.70 |
| remove fiber and cement shingles | 1D@1.11 | sq | — | 43.20 | 43.20 |
| remove mission or Spanish tile shingles | 1D@3.45 | sq | — | 134.00 | 134.00 |

| | Craft@Hrs | Unit | Material | Labor | Total |
|---|---|---|---|---|---|
| remove vertically laid furring strips | 1D@.478 | sq | — | 18.60 | 18.60 |
| remove vertical & horizontal laid furring strips | 1D@.840 | sq | — | 32.70 | 32.70 |
| remove concrete shingles | 1D@3.85 | sq | — | 150.00 | 150.00 |
| remove preformed metal roofing | 1D@.010 | sf | — | .39 | .39 |
| remove preformed fiberglass roofing | 1D@.009 | sf | — | .35 | .35 |
| remove seamed metal roofing | 1D@1.03 | sq | — | 40.10 | 40.10 |
| remove built-up 3 ply roofing | 1D@2.44 | sq | — | 94.90 | 94.90 |
| remove built-up 4 ply roofing | 1D@3.03 | sq | — | 118.00 | 118.00 |
| remove built-up 5 ply roofing | 1D@3.85 | sq | — | 150.00 | 150.00 |
| add to remove built-up roof with ballast | 1D@.847 | sq | — | 32.90 | 32.90 |
| remove single ply roof partially adhered | 1D@.980 | sq | — | 38.10 | 38.10 |
| remove single ply roof fully adhered | 1D@1.56 | sq | — | 60.70 | 60.70 |
| remove single ply roof with ballast | 1D@2.04 | sq | — | 79.40 | 79.40 |

## Roofing Crew

| | | |
|---|---|---|
| install roofing | roofer | $65.50 |
| install roofing | roofer's helper | $55.50 |
| install roofing | roofing crew | $60.50 |

## Install shingles

| | Craft@Hrs | Unit | Material | Labor | Total |
|---|---|---|---|---|---|
| aluminum shingles | 6R@1.06 | sq | — | 64.10 | 64.10 |
| galvanized steel shingles | 6R@1.11 | sq | — | 67.20 | 67.20 |
| 20 year to 25 year asphalt | 6R@1.24 | sq | — | 75.00 | 75.00 |
| 30 year to 40 year asphalt | 6R@1.27 | sq | — | 76.80 | 76.80 |
| standard grade laminated asphalt | 6R@2.06 | sq | — | 125.00 | 125.00 |
| high grade laminated asphalt | 6R@2.45 | sq | — | 148.00 | 148.00 |
| T-lock asphalt | 6R@1.27 | sq | — | 76.80 | 76.80 |
| hexagonal asphalt | 6R@1.27 | sq | — | 76.80 | 76.80 |
| diamond asphalt | 6R@1.27 | sq | — | 76.80 | 76.80 |
| **Install roll roofing** | | | | | |
| all weights | 6R@.645 | sq | — | 39.00 | 39.00 |
| **Install slate** | | | | | |
| typical | 6R@4.00 | sq | — | 242.00 | 242.00 |
| replace single slate shingle | 6R@.385 | ea | — | 23.30 | 23.30 |
| **Install wood shingles** | | | | | |
| 16" | 6R@2.86 | sq | — | 173.00 | 173.00 |
| 18" | 6R@2.55 | sq | — | 154.00 | 154.00 |
| replace single wood shingle | 6R@.208 | ea | — | 12.60 | 12.60 |
| **Install wood shakes** | | | | | |
| 18" | 6R@3.34 | sq | — | 202.00 | 202.00 |
| 24" | 6R@2.86 | sq | — | 173.00 | 173.00 |
| replace single shake | 6R@.208 | ea | — | 12.60 | 12.60 |
| **Install fiber and cement shingles** | | | | | |
| weathering shake style | 6R@2.38 | sq | — | 144.00 | 144.00 |
| Spanish tile style | 6R@2.50 | sq | — | 151.00 | 151.00 |

|  | Craft@Hrs | Unit | Material | Labor | Total |
|---|---|---|---|---|---|
| Install clay tile | | | | | |
|    flat | 6R@3.23 | sq | — | 195.00 | 195.00 |
|       mission tile | 6R@5.56 | sq | — | 336.00 | 336.00 |
|      Spanish tile | 6R@3.34 | sq | — | 202.00 | 202.00 |
| Install tile furring strips | | | | | |
|      vertically laid only | 6R@.606 | sq | — | 36.70 | 36.70 |
|      vertically and horizontally laid | 6R@.877 | sq | — | 53.10 | 53.10 |
| Install concrete tile | | | | | |
|      corrugated | 6R@3.13 | sq | — | 189.00 | 189.00 |
|      flat | 6R@3.03 | sq | — | 183.00 | 183.00 |
| Install pre-formed roofing | | | | | |
|      corrugated aluminum or fiberglass | 6R@.024 | sf | — | 1.45 | 1.45 |
|      corrugated galvanized steel | 6R@.025 | sf | — | 1.51 | 1.51 |
|      ribbed (all types) | 6R@.026 | sf | — | 1.57 | 1.57 |
| Install standing seam metal roofing | | | | | |
|      16 ounce copper | 6R@6.67 | sq | — | 404.00 | 404.00 |
|      20 ounce copper | 6R@7.69 | sq | — | 465.00 | 465.00 |
|      28 gauge stainless steel | 6R@7.14 | sq | — | 432.00 | 432.00 |
|      40 lb terne | 6R@8.33 | sq | — | 504.00 | 504.00 |
| Install batten seam metal roofing | | | | | |
|      16 ounce copper | 6R@7.69 | sq | — | 465.00 | 465.00 |
|      20 ounce copper | 6R@9.09 | sq | — | 550.00 | 550.00 |
|      28 gauge stainless steel | 6R@7.69 | sq | — | 465.00 | 465.00 |
|      26 gauge stainless steel | 6R@7.14 | sq | — | 432.00 | 432.00 |
|      3 lb lead | 6R@7.14 | sq | — | 432.00 | 432.00 |
|      40 lb terne | 6R@7.69 | sq | — | 465.00 | 465.00 |
| Install flat seam metal roofing | | | | | |
|      16 ounce copper | 6R@7.14 | sq | — | 432.00 | 432.00 |
|      20 ounce copper | 6R@8.33 | sq | — | 504.00 | 504.00 |
|      28 gauge stainless steel | 6R@7.14 | sq | — | 432.00 | 432.00 |
|      26 gauge stainless steel | 6R@6.67 | sq | — | 404.00 | 404.00 |
|      3 lb lead | 6R@7.69 | sq | — | 465.00 | 465.00 |
|      40 lb terne | 6R@9.09 | sq | — | 550.00 | 550.00 |
| Seamed metal roofing repair | | | | | |
|      solder patch (less than 1' square) | 4R@1.00 | ea | — | 65.50 | 65.50 |
| Install built-up roof | | | | | |
|      3 ply | 6R@3.34 | sq | — | 202.00 | 202.00 |
|      4 ply | 6R@4.00 | sq | — | 242.00 | 242.00 |
|      5 ply | 6R@4.76 | sq | — | 288.00 | 288.00 |

|  | Craft@Hrs | Unit | Material | Labor | Total |
|---|---|---|---|---|---|

# Rough Carpentry

## Minimum charge.

| | Craft@Hrs | Unit | Material | Labor | Total |
|---|---|---|---|---|---|
| minimum for rough carpentry work | 6C@3.00 | ea | 57.50 | 149.00 | 206.50 |

**Lumber prices.** Some lumber prices, such as oak timbers, vary by as much as 60% depending on the region. These prices will be 15% to 30% lower in the Northeast, South, and most Great Lake states and provinces. In many areas of the Western, Midwest and Mountain states and provinces, oak timbers are not available unless specially shipped for a particular job. For the most accurate results, compare your local prices with the prices found in the material charts for this section starting on page 379 and create a customized materials factor.

**Interior partition wall, per linear foot.** Includes 5% waste. Based on an average wall with 4 openings and 5 corners per 56 lf of wall. A net of 2.2 studs is added for each corner and opening. All walls have two top plates and a single bottom plate.

| | Craft@Hrs | Unit | Material | Labor | Total |
|---|---|---|---|---|---|
| 2" x 4" interior partition wall, per lf | | | | | |
| replace, 8' tall 16" on center | 6C@.241 | lf | 9.60 | 12.00 | 21.60 |
| replace, 8' tall 24" on center | 6C@.205 | lf | 8.00 | 10.20 | 18.20 |
| remove, 8' tall 16" or 24" on center | 1D@.045 | lf | — | 1.75 | 1.75 |
| replace, 10' tall 16" on center | 6C@.244 | lf | 11.30 | 12.10 | 23.40 |
| replace, 10' tall 24" on center | 6C@.207 | lf | 9.45 | 10.30 | 19.75 |
| remove, 10' tall 16" or 24" on center | 1D@.057 | lf | — | 2.22 | 2.22 |
| 2" x 6" interior partition wall, per lf | | | | | |
| replace, 8' tall 16" on center | 6C@.244 | lf | 13.70 | 12.10 | 25.80 |
| replace, 8' tall 24" on center | 6C@.207 | lf | 11.60 | 10.30 | 21.90 |
| remove, 8' tall 16" or 24" on center | 1D@.048 | lf | — | 1.87 | 1.87 |
| replace, 10' tall 16" on center | 6C@.247 | lf | 16.50 | 12.30 | 28.80 |
| replace, 10' tall 24" on center | 6C@.209 | lf | 13.50 | 10.40 | 23.90 |
| remove, 10' tall 16" or 24" on center | 1D@.060 | lf | — | 2.33 | 2.33 |
| 2" x 8" interior partition wall, per lf | | | | | |
| replace, 8' tall 16" on center | 6C@.247 | lf | 18.20 | 12.30 | 30.50 |
| replace, 8' tall 24" on center | 6C@.209 | lf | 15.10 | 10.40 | 25.50 |
| remove, 8' tall 16" or 24" on center | 1D@.049 | lf | — | 1.91 | 1.91 |
| replace, 10' tall 16" on center | 6C@.250 | lf | 21.50 | 12.40 | 33.90 |
| replace, 10' tall 24" on center | 6C@.211 | lf | 17.80 | 10.50 | 28.30 |
| remove, 10' tall 16" or 24" on center | 1D@.061 | lf | — | 2.37 | 2.37 |

**Interior bearing walls, per linear foot.** Includes studs, top plates, bottom plate, headers, and installation labor. Based on an average wall with 4 openings and 5 corners per 56 LF of wall. A net of 2.2 studs is added for each corner and opening. (Four openings are two 3' wide, one 4' wide, and one 5' wide for a total of 15 LF.) Headers in openings are made from sandwiched 2" x 10" boards with 1/2" CDX plywood stiffeners between. All walls have two top plates and a single bottom plate.

| | Craft@Hrs | Unit | Material | Labor | Total |
|---|---|---|---|---|---|
| 2" x 4" interior bearing wall, per lf | | | | | |
| replace, 8' tall 12" on center | 6C@.307 | lf | 13.80 | 15.30 | 29.10 |
| replace, 8' tall 16" on center | 6C@.261 | lf | 12.40 | 13.00 | 25.40 |
| remove, 8' tall 12" or 16" on center | 1D@.045 | lf | — | 1.75 | 1.75 |
| replace, 10' tall 12" on center | 6C@.312 | lf | 16.00 | 15.50 | 31.50 |
| replace, 10' tall 16" on center | 6C@.265 | lf | 14.00 | 13.20 | 27.20 |
| remove, 10' tall 12" or 16" on center | 1D@.057 | lf | — | 2.22 | 2.22 |

| | Craft@Hrs | Unit | Material | Labor | Total |
|---|---|---|---|---|---|
| **2" x 6" interior bearing wall, per lf** | | | | | |
| replace, 8' tall 12" on center | 6C@.310 | lf | 23.60 | 15.40 | 39.00 |
| replace, 8' tall 16" on center | 6C@.263 | lf | 21.50 | 13.10 | 34.60 |
| remove, 8' tall 12" or 16" on center | 1D@.048 | lf | — | 1.87 | 1.87 |
| replace, 10' tall 12" on center | 6C@.315 | lf | 26.60 | 15.70 | 42.30 |
| replace, 10' tall 16" on center | 6C@.267 | lf | 23.90 | 13.30 | 37.20 |
| remove, 10' tall 12" or 16" on center | 1D@.060 | lf | — | 2.33 | 2.33 |
| **2" x 8" interior bearing wall, per lf** | | | | | |
| replace, 8' tall 12" on center | 6C@.312 | lf | 30.90 | 15.50 | 46.40 |
| replace, 8' tall 16" on center | 6C@.266 | lf | 28.10 | 13.20 | 41.30 |
| remove, 8' tall 12" or 16" on center | 1D@.049 | lf | — | 1.91 | 1.91 |
| replace, 10' tall 12" on center | 6C@.317 | lf | 34.80 | 15.80 | 50.60 |
| replace, 10' tall 16" on center | 6C@.270 | lf | 31.20 | 13.40 | 44.60 |
| remove, 10' tall 12" or 16" on center | 1D@.061 | lf | — | 2.37 | 2.37 |

**Exterior walls, per linear foot.** Includes 5% waste. Includes studs, top plates, bottom plate, headers, metal let-in bracing, and installation labor. Based on an average wall with 4 openings and 5 corners per 56 LF of wall. A net of 2.2 studs is added for each corner and opening. (Four openings are two 3' wide, one 4' wide, and one 5' wide for a total of 15 LF.) Headers in openings are made from sandwiched 2" x 10" boards with 1/2" CDX plywood stiffeners between boards. Includes 4 metal let-in braces for every 56 LF of wall. All walls have two top plates and a single bottom plate. Does not include exterior sheathing.

| | Craft@Hrs | Unit | Material | Labor | Total |
|---|---|---|---|---|---|
| **2" x 4" exterior wall, per lf** | | | | | |
| replace, 8' tall 12" on center | 6C@.312 | lf | 14.10 | 15.50 | 29.60 |
| replace, 8' tall 16" on center | 6C@.267 | lf | 12.70 | 13.30 | 26.00 |
| replace, 8' tall 24" on center | 6C@.216 | lf | 11.00 | 10.70 | 21.70 |
| remove, 8' tall 12", 16" or 24" on center | 1D@.045 | lf | — | 1.75 | 1.75 |
| replace, 10' tall 12" on center | 6C@.317 | lf | 16.50 | 15.80 | 32.30 |
| replace, 10' tall 16" on center | 6C@.270 | lf | 14.30 | 13.40 | 27.70 |
| replace, 10' tall 24" on center | 6C@.217 | lf | 12.50 | 10.80 | 23.30 |
| remove, 10' tall 12", 16" or 24" on center | 1D@.057 | lf | — | 2.22 | 2.22 |
| **2" x 6" exterior wall, per lf** | | | | | |
| replace, 8' tall 12" on center | 6C@.315 | lf | 23.90 | 15.70 | 39.60 |
| replace, 8' tall 16" on center | 6C@.270 | lf | 21.70 | 13.40 | 35.10 |
| replace, 8' tall 24" on center | 6C@.218 | lf | 19.50 | 10.80 | 30.30 |
| remove, 8' tall 12", 16" or 24" on center | 1D@.045 | lf | — | 1.75 | 1.75 |
| replace, 10' tall 12" on center | 6C@.320 | lf | 27.00 | 15.90 | 42.90 |
| replace, 10' tall 16" on center | 6C@.272 | lf | 24.20 | 13.50 | 37.70 |
| replace, 10' tall 24" on center | 6C@.221 | lf | 21.50 | 11.00 | 32.50 |
| remove, 10' tall 12", 16" or 24" on center | 1D@.057 | lf | — | 2.22 | 2.22 |
| **2" x 8" exterior wall, per lf** | | | | | |
| replace, 8' tall 12" on center | 6C@.320 | lf | 31.20 | 15.90 | 47.10 |
| replace, 8' tall 16" on center | 6C@.272 | lf | 28.40 | 13.50 | 41.90 |
| replace, 8' tall 24" on center | 6C@.220 | lf | 25.30 | 10.90 | 36.20 |
| remove, 8' tall 12", 16" or 24" on center | 1D@.045 | lf | — | 1.75 | 1.75 |
| replace, 10' tall 12" on center | 6C@.323 | lf | 35.10 | 16.10 | 51.20 |
| replace, 10' tall 16" on center | 6C@.275 | lf | 31.60 | 13.70 | 45.30 |
| replace, 10' tall 24" on center | 6C@.223 | lf | 28.10 | 11.10 | 39.20 |
| remove, 10' tall 12", 16" or 24" on center | 1D@.057 | lf | — | 2.22 | 2.22 |

|  | Craft@Hrs | Unit | Material | Labor | Total |
|---|---|---|---|---|---|

**Interior partition walls, per square foot.** Includes 5% waste. Includes studs, top plates, bottom plate, and installation labor. Based on an average wall with 4 openings and 5 corners per 56 LF of wall. A net of 2.2 studs is added for each corner and opening. All walls have two top plates and a single bottom plate.

| 2" x 4" interior partition walls, per sf | | | | | |
|---|---|---|---|---|---|
| replace, 16" on center | 6C@.030 | sf | 1.19 | 1.49 | 2.68 |
| replace, 24" on center | 6C@.026 | sf | 1.01 | 1.29 | 2.30 |
| remove, 16" or 24" on center | 1D@.006 | sf | — | .23 | .23 |
| 2" x 6" interior partition walls, per sf | | | | | |
| replace, 16" on center | 6C@.030 | sf | 1.73 | 1.49 | 3.22 |
| replace, 24" on center | 6C@.026 | sf | 1.43 | 1.29 | 2.72 |
| remove, 16" or 24" on center | 1D@.006 | sf | — | .23 | .23 |
| 2" x 8" interior partition walls, per sf | | | | | |
| replace, 16" on center | 6C@.031 | sf | 4.35 | 1.54 | 5.89 |
| replace, 24" on center | 6C@.026 | sf | 3.92 | 1.29 | 5.21 |
| remove, 16" or 24" on center | 1D@.006 | sf | — | .23 | .23 |

**Sloping interior partition wall, per square foot.** Includes 5% waste. Based on an average wall with one 3' wide opening, two 4' 6" wide openings, and 2 corners per 24 lf of wall. A net of 2.4 studs is added per corner or opening. All walls have two top plates and a single bottom plate.

| 2" x 4" sloping interior partition wall, per sf | | | | | |
|---|---|---|---|---|---|
| replace, 16" on center | 6C@.041 | sf | .95 | 2.04 | 2.99 |
| replace, 24" on center | 6C@.035 | sf | .81 | 1.74 | 2.55 |
| remove, 16" or 24" on center | 1D@.006 | sf | — | .23 | .23 |
| 2" x 6" sloping interior partition wall, per sf | | | | | |
| replace, 16" on center | 6C@.042 | sf | 1.35 | 2.09 | 3.44 |
| replace, 24" on center | 6C@.036 | sf | 1.14 | 1.79 | 2.93 |
| remove, 16" or 24" on center | 1D@.006 | sf | — | .23 | .23 |
| 2" x 8" sloping interior partition wall, per sf | | | | | |
| replace, 16" on center | 6C@.042 | sf | 1.77 | 2.09 | 3.86 |
| replace, 24" on center | 6C@.036 | sf | 1.47 | 1.79 | 3.26 |
| remove, 16" or 24" on center | 1D@.006 | sf | — | .23 | .23 |

**Sloping interior bearing wall, per square foot.** Includes 5% waste. Based on an average wall with one 3' wide opening, two 4' 6" wide openings, and 2 corners per 24 lf of wall. A net of 2.4 studs is added per corner or opening. Headers in openings are made from sandwiched 2" x 10" boards with 1/2" CDX plywood stiffeners between boards. All walls have two top plates and a single bottom plate.

| 2" x 4" sloping interior bearing wall, per sf | | | | | |
|---|---|---|---|---|---|
| replace, 12" on center | 6C@.059 | sf | 1.37 | 2.93 | 4.30 |
| replace, 16" on center | 6C@.050 | sf | 1.23 | 2.49 | 3.72 |
| remove, 12" or 16" on center | 1D@.006 | sf | — | .23 | .23 |
| 2" x 6" sloping interior bearing wall, per sf | | | | | |
| replace, 12" on center | 6C@.059 | sf | 1.88 | 2.93 | 4.81 |
| replace, 16" on center | 6C@.050 | sf | 1.67 | 2.49 | 4.16 |
| remove, 12" or 16" on center | 1D@.006 | sf | — | .23 | .23 |
| 2" x 8" sloping interior bearing wall, per sf | | | | | |
| replace, 12" on center | 6C@.060 | sf | 2.30 | 2.98 | 5.28 |
| replace, 16" on center | 6C@.051 | sf | 2.05 | 2.53 | 4.58 |
| remove, 12" or 16" on center | 1D@.006 | sf | — | .23 | .23 |

| | Craft@Hrs | Unit | Material | Labor | Total |
|---|---|---|---|---|---|

**Interior bearing wall, per square foot.** Includes 5% waste. Based on an average wall with 4 openings and 5 corners per 56 lf. A net of 2.2 studs is added for each corner and opening. Openings are two 3' wide, one 4' wide, and one 5' wide for a total of 15 lf. Headers are made from sandwiched 2" x 10" boards with 1/2" CDX plywood stiffeners. All walls have two top plates and a single bottom plate.

| | Craft@Hrs | Unit | Material | Labor | Total |
|---|---|---|---|---|---|
| 2" x 4" interior bearing walls, per sf | | | | | |
| replace, 12" on center | 6C@.038 | sf | 1.75 | 1.89 | 3.64 |
| replace, 16" on center | 6C@.033 | sf | 1.53 | 1.64 | 3.17 |
| remove, 12" or 16" on center | 1D@.006 | sf | — | .23 | .23 |
| 2" x 6" interior bearing walls, per sf | | | | | |
| replace, 12" on center | 6C@.039 | sf | 2.96 | 1.94 | 4.90 |
| replace, 16" on center | 6C@.033 | sf | 2.65 | 1.64 | 4.29 |
| remove, 12" or 16" on center | 1D@.006 | sf | — | .23 | .23 |
| 2" x 8" interior bearing walls, per sf | | | | | |
| replace, 12" on center | 6C@.039 | sf | 3.87 | 1.94 | 5.81 |
| replace, 16" on center | 6C@.033 | sf | 3.50 | 1.64 | 5.14 |
| remove, 12" or 16" on center | 1D@.006 | sf | — | .23 | .23 |

**Exterior wall, per square foot.** Includes 5% waste. Based on an average wall with 4 openings and 5 corners per 56 lf of wall. A net of 2.2 studs is added for each corner and opening. Openings are two 3' wide, one 4' wide, and one 5' wide for a total of 15 lf. Headers in openings are made from sandwiched 2" x 10" boards with 1/2" CDX plywood stiffeners between boards. Includes 4 metal let-in braces for every 56 lf of wall. All walls have two top plates and a single bottom plate. Does not include exterior sheathing.

| | Craft@Hrs | Unit | Material | Labor | Total |
|---|---|---|---|---|---|
| 2" x 4" exterior walls, per sf | | | | | |
| replace, 12" on center | 6C@.040 | sf | 1.79 | 1.99 | 3.78 |
| replace, 16" on center | 6C@.034 | sf | 1.58 | 1.69 | 3.27 |
| replace, 24" on center | 6C@.027 | sf | 1.37 | 1.34 | 2.71 |
| remove, 12", 16" or 24" on center | 1D@.006 | sf | — | .23 | .23 |
| 2" x 6" exterior walls, per sf | | | | | |
| replace, 12" on center | 6C@.040 | sf | 3.02 | 1.99 | 5.01 |
| replace, 16" on center | 6C@.034 | sf | 2.70 | 1.69 | 4.39 |
| replace, 24" on center | 6C@.027 | sf | 2.42 | 1.34 | 3.76 |
| remove, 12", 16" or 24" on center | 1D@.006 | sf | — | .23 | .23 |
| 2" x 8" exterior walls, per sf | | | | | |
| replace, 12" on center | 6C@.040 | sf | 3.92 | 1.99 | 5.91 |
| replace, 16" on center | 6C@.034 | sf | 3.55 | 1.69 | 5.24 |
| replace, 24" on center | 6C@.028 | sf | 3.18 | 1.39 | 4.57 |
| remove, 12", 16" or 24" on center | 1D@.006 | sf | — | .23 | .23 |

**Sloping exterior wall, per square foot.** Includes 5% waste. Based on an average wall with one 3' wide opening, two 4' 6" wide openings, and 2 corners per 24 lf. A net of 2.4 studs is added per corner or opening. Headers in openings are made from sandwiched 2" x 10" boards with 1/2" CDX plywood stiffeners between boards. Includes 3 metal let-in braces for every 24 lf of wall. All walls have two top plates and a single bottom plate.

| | Craft@Hrs | Unit | Material | Labor | Total |
|---|---|---|---|---|---|
| 2" x 4" sloping exterior walls, per sf | | | | | |
| replace, 12" on center | 6C@.054 | sf | 1.60 | 2.68 | 4.28 |
| replace, 16" on center | 6C@.046 | sf | 1.43 | 2.29 | 3.72 |
| replace, 24" on center | 6C@.038 | sf | 1.28 | 1.89 | 3.17 |
| remove, 12", 16" or 24" on center | 1D@.006 | sf | — | .23 | .23 |
| 2" x 6" sloping exterior walls, per sf | | | | | |
| replace, 12" on center | 6C@.054 | sf | 2.15 | 2.68 | 4.83 |
| replace, 16" on center | 6C@.046 | sf | 1.92 | 2.29 | 4.21 |
| replace, 24" on center | 6C@.038 | sf | 1.68 | 1.89 | 3.57 |
| remove, 12", 16" or 24" on center | 1D@.006 | sf | — | .23 | .23 |

| | Craft@Hrs | Unit | Material | Labor | Total |
|---|---|---|---|---|---|
| **2" x 8" sloping exterior walls, per sf** | | | | | |
| replace, 12" on center | 6C@.055 | sf | 2.62 | 2.73 | 5.35 |
| replace, 16" on center | 6C@.047 | sf | 2.32 | 2.34 | 4.66 |
| replace, 24" on center | 6C@.038 | sf | 2.04 | 1.89 | 3.93 |
| remove, 12", 16" or 24" on center | 1D@.006 | sf | — | .23 | .23 |

## Additional wall framing costs.

| | Craft@Hrs | Unit | Material | Labor | Total |
|---|---|---|---|---|---|
| **Replace only** | | | | | |
| add for beam pocket in exterior or bearing wall | 6C@1.11 | ea | 47.50 | 55.20 | 102.70 |
| add to frame round- or elliptical-top door or window, per lf of opening | 6C@.587 | lf | 3.87 | 29.20 | 33.07 |
| add to frame round window, per lf window diameter | 6C@.638 | lf | 4.46 | 31.70 | 36.16 |
| add to frame bay window, per lf of wall | 6C@.582 | lf | 4.46 | 28.90 | 33.36 |
| add to frame bow window, per lf of wall | 6C@.648 | lf | 4.46 | 32.20 | 36.66 |

**California Earthquake Code.** Items that include "CEC" in the description are priced according to California earthquake code requirements. Although these Universal Building Code standards are also required in other areas, they are most commonly associated with efforts initiated in California to improve the construction and engineering of structures in quake zones.

## Additional costs for CEC bracing. Additional cost to nail, brace, and shear panel to California Earthquake Code standards. Per sf of wall.

| | Craft@Hrs | Unit | Material | Labor | Total |
|---|---|---|---|---|---|
| **Replace only** | | | | | |
| brace & shear panel interior bearing wall | 6C@.011 | sf | .31 | .55 | .86 |
| brace & shear panel sloping interior wall | 6C@.014 | sf | .35 | .70 | 1.05 |
| brace & shear panel exterior wall | 6C@.011 | sf | .38 | .55 | .93 |
| brace & shear panel sloping exterior wall | 6C@.015 | sf | .43 | .75 | 1.18 |

## Wall framing, per board foot. Includes 7% waste.

| | Craft@Hrs | Unit | Material | Labor | Total |
|---|---|---|---|---|---|
| replace, interior wall | 6C@.034 | bf | 1.28 | 1.69 | 2.97 |
| remove, interior wall | 1D@.007 | bf | — | .27 | .27 |
| replace, sloping interior wall | 6C@.047 | bf | 1.35 | 2.34 | 3.69 |
| remove, sloping interior wall | 1D@.007 | bf | — | .27 | .27 |
| replace, exterior wall | 6C@.037 | bf | 1.57 | 1.84 | 3.41 |
| remove, exterior wall | 1D@.007 | bf | — | .27 | .27 |
| replace, sloping exterior wall | 6C@.051 | bf | 1.68 | 2.53 | 4.21 |
| remove, sloping exterior wall | 1D@.007 | bf | — | .27 | .27 |

## Top plate. Includes 5% waste. Includes top plate and installation labor. Does not include labor to remove existing top plate or bracing.

| | Craft@Hrs | Unit | Material | Labor | Total |
|---|---|---|---|---|---|
| **Replace top plate** | | | | | |
| 2" x 4" | 6C@.017 | lf | .85 | .84 | 1.69 |
| 2" x 6" | 6C@.018 | lf | 1.19 | .89 | 2.08 |
| 2" x 8" | 6C@.018 | lf | 1.75 | .89 | 2.64 |
| Remove, all sizes | 1D@.013 | lf | — | .51 | .51 |

## Foundation sill plate. Includes foam sealer strip, hole drilling for anchor bolt, and fastening.

| | Craft@Hrs | Unit | Material | Labor | Total |
|---|---|---|---|---|---|
| **Replace 2" x 4" foundation sill plate** | | | | | |
| treated wood | 6C@.067 | lf | 1.37 | 3.33 | 4.70 |
| con common redwood | 6C@.065 | lf | 1.61 | 3.23 | 4.84 |
| **Replace 2" x 6" foundation sill plate** | | | | | |
| treated wood | 6C@.067 | lf | 2.05 | 3.33 | 5.38 |
| con common redwood | 6C@.065 | lf | 2.06 | 3.23 | 5.29 |

|  | Craft@Hrs | Unit | Material | Labor | Total |
|---|---|---|---|---|---|
| **Replace 2" x 8" foundation sill plate** | | | | | |
| treated-wood | 6C@.068 | lf | 2.72 | 3.38 | 6.10 |
| con common redwood | 6C@.066 | lf | 2.86 | 3.28 | 6.14 |
| Remove, all sizes and wood species | 1D@.045 | lf | — | 1.75 | 1.75 |

**Wall header beam.** Includes 5% waste. 2 x and 4 x sizes made from doubled 2 x dimensional lumber with 1/2" CDX plywood stiffeners. 6 x sizes made from tripled 2 x dimensional lumber with two 1/2" CDX plywood stiffeners. 8 x sizes made from quadrupled 2 x dimensional lumber with three 1/2" CDX plywood stiffeners.

|  | Craft@Hrs | Unit | Material | Labor | Total |
|---|---|---|---|---|---|
| **Header beam for 2" x 4" wall, replace** | | | | | |
| 4" x 6" | 6C@.040 | lf | 5.87 | 1.99 | 7.86 |
| 4" x 8" | 6C@.042 | lf | 6.64 | 2.09 | 8.73 |
| 4" x 10" | 6C@.043 | lf | 9.31 | 2.14 | 11.45 |
| 4" x 12" | 6C@.045 | lf | 11.20 | 2.24 | 13.44 |
| **Header beam for 2" x 6" wall, replace** | | | | | |
| 6" x 6" | 6C@.061 | lf | 10.50 | 3.03 | 13.53 |
| 6" x 8" | 6C@.065 | lf | 11.70 | 3.23 | 14.93 |
| 6" x 10" | 6C@.069 | lf | 16.10 | 3.43 | 19.53 |
| 6" x 12" | 6C@.074 | lf | 19.90 | 3.68 | 23.58 |
| **Header beam for 2" x 8" wall, replace** | | | | | |
| 8" x 6" | 6C@.073 | lf | 15.10 | 3.63 | 18.73 |
| 8" x 8" | 6C@.078 | lf | 17.00 | 3.88 | 20.88 |
| 8" x 10" | 6C@.085 | lf | 18.80 | 4.22 | 23.02 |
| 8" x 12" | 6C@.093 | lf | 28.40 | 4.62 | 33.02 |
| Remove, all sizes | 1D@.040 | lf | — | 1.56 | 1.56 |

**Posts.** Includes post and installation labor. Also includes 4% waste.

|  | Craft@Hrs | Unit | Material | Labor | Total |
|---|---|---|---|---|---|
| **4" x 4" posts, replace** | | | | | |
| pine | 6C@.042 | lf | 3.33 | 2.09 | 5.42 |
| con common redwood | 6C@.042 | lf | 4.08 | 2.09 | 6.17 |
| treated pine | 6C@.042 | lf | 4.35 | 2.09 | 6.44 |
| **4" x 6" posts, replace** | | | | | |
| pine | 6C@.043 | lf | 3.88 | 2.14 | 6.02 |
| con common redwood | 6C@.043 | lf | 4.37 | 2.14 | 6.51 |
| treated pine | 6C@.043 | lf | 5.03 | 2.14 | 7.17 |
| **4" x 8" posts, replace** | | | | | |
| pine | 6C@.043 | lf | 6.20 | 2.14 | 8.34 |
| con common redwood | 6C@.043 | lf | 6.26 | 2.14 | 8.40 |
| treated pine | 6C@.043 | lf | 8.05 | 2.14 | 10.19 |
| **6" x 6" posts, replace** | | | | | |
| pine | 6C@.044 | lf | 8.15 | 2.19 | 10.34 |
| con common redwood | 6C@.044 | lf | 7.04 | 2.19 | 9.23 |
| treated pine | 6C@.044 | lf | 10.60 | 2.19 | 12.79 |
| **6" x 8" posts, replace** | | | | | |
| pine | 6C@.045 | lf | 10.80 | 2.24 | 13.04 |
| con common redwood | 6C@.045 | lf | 9.40 | 2.24 | 11.64 |
| treated pine | 6C@.045 | lf | 13.90 | 2.24 | 16.14 |
| **6" x 10" posts, replace** | | | | | |
| pine | 6C@.047 | lf | 13.50 | 2.34 | 15.84 |
| con common redwood | 6C@.047 | lf | 11.70 | 2.34 | 14.04 |
| treated pine | 6C@.047 | lf | 17.80 | 2.34 | 20.14 |

| | Craft@Hrs | Unit | Material | Labor | Total |
|---|---|---|---|---|---|
| **8" x 8" posts, replace** | | | | | |
| pine | 6C@.048 | lf | 14.50 | 2.39 | 16.89 |
| con common redwood | 6C@.048 | lf | 12.50 | 2.39 | 14.89 |
| treated pine | 6C@.048 | lf | 19.10 | 2.39 | 21.49 |
| Remove, all sizes and wood species | 1D@.059 | lf | — | 2.30 | 2.30 |

**Precast concrete pier.** Includes precast concrete pier and installation labor. Installation includes hand excavation as needed.

| | Craft@Hrs | Unit | Material | Labor | Total |
|---|---|---|---|---|---|
| replace | 6C@.261 | ea | 23.10 | 13.00 | 36.10 |
| remove | 1D@.313 | ea | — | 12.20 | 12.20 |

**Adjustable steel jackpost.** Includes adjustable jack post, fasteners, and installation labor.

| | Craft@Hrs | Unit | Material | Labor | Total |
|---|---|---|---|---|---|
| **Replace** | | | | | |
| 51" to 90", 13,000 pound load maximum | 6C@.357 | ea | 64.10 | 17.70 | 81.80 |
| 20" to 36", 16,000 pound load maximum | 6C@.243 | ea | 42.00 | 12.10 | 54.10 |
| 48" to 100", 16,000 pound load maximum | 6C@.386 | ea | 72.50 | 19.20 | 91.70 |
| 37" to 60", 17,500 pound load maximum | 6C@.272 | ea | 52.90 | 13.50 | 66.40 |
| 56" to 96" to 25,000 pound load maximum | 6C@.352 | ea | 82.40 | 17.50 | 99.90 |
| Remove, all sizes | 1D@.313 | ea | — | 12.20 | 12.20 |

**Lally column.** Includes 3-1/2" diameter concrete-filled lally column, fasteners, and installation labor.

| | Craft@Hrs | Unit | Material | Labor | Total |
|---|---|---|---|---|---|
| **Replace** | | | | | |
| 6' to 8' high | 6C@.526 | ea | 101.00 | 26.10 | 127.10 |
| 8' to 10' high | 6C@.556 | ea | 112.00 | 27.60 | 139.60 |
| 10' to 12' high | 6C@.587 | ea | 138.00 | 29.20 | 167.20 |
| Remove, all sizes | 1D@.356 | ea | — | 13.80 | 13.80 |

| | Craft@Hrs | Unit | Material | Labor | Equip. | Total |
|---|---|---|---|---|---|---|
| **Glue-laminated beam, per board foot.** Includes glue-laminated beam, brackets and fasteners, and installation labor. Also includes costs for equipment — usually a fork lift — to place the beam. Includes 3% waste. | | | | | | |
| replace | 6C@.060 | bf | 5.49 | 2.98 | .49 | 8.96 |
| remove | 1D@.025 | bf | — | .97 | — | .97 |
| **Glue-laminated beam, per linear foot.** Includes 3% waste. | | | | | | |
| **3-1/8" wide glue-laminated beam, replace** | | | | | | |
| 3-1/8" x 7-1/2" | 6C@.145 | lf | 10.70 | 7.21 | .89 | 18.80 |
| 3-1/8" x 9" | 6C@.146 | lf | 12.80 | 7.26 | .89 | 20.95 |
| 3-1/8" x 10-1/2" | 6C@.172 | lf | 14.90 | 8.55 | .89 | 24.34 |
| 3-1/8" x 12" | 6C@.189 | lf | 17.10 | 9.39 | .89 | 27.38 |
| 3-1/8" x 13-1/2" | 6C@.211 | lf | 19.40 | 10.50 | .89 | 30.79 |
| 3-1/8" x 15" | 6C@.212 | lf | 21.60 | 10.50 | .89 | 32.99 |
| 3-1/8" x 16-1/2" | 6C@.214 | lf | 23.50 | 10.60 | .89 | 34.99 |
| 3-1/8" x 18" | 6C@.216 | lf | 25.50 | 10.70 | .89 | 37.09 |

| | Craft@Hrs | Unit | Material | Labor | Equip. | Total |
|---|---|---|---|---|---|---|
| **3-1/2" wide glue-laminated beam, replace** | | | | | | |
| 3-1/2" x 9" | 6C@.146 | lf | 14.20 | 7.26 | .89 | 22.35 |
| 3-1/2" x 12" | 6C@.174 | lf | 19.30 | 8.65 | .89 | 28.84 |
| 3-1/2" x 15" | 6C@.194 | lf | 23.90 | 9.64 | .89 | 34.43 |
| 3-1/2" x 19-1/2" | 6C@.221 | lf | 31.10 | 11.00 | .89 | 42.99 |
| 3-1/2" x 21" | 6C@.223 | lf | 33.40 | 11.10 | .89 | 45.39 |
| **5-1/8" wide glue-laminated beam, replace** | | | | | | |
| 5-1/8" x 7-1/2" | 6C@.173 | lf | 17.70 | 8.60 | .89 | 27.19 |
| 5-1/8" x 9" | 6C@.175 | lf | 20.90 | 8.70 | .89 | 30.49 |
| 5-1/8" x 10-1/2" | 6C@.194 | lf | 24.40 | 9.64 | .89 | 34.93 |
| 5-1/8" x 12" | 6C@.218 | lf | 28.60 | 10.80 | .89 | 40.29 |
| 5-1/8" x 13-1/2" | 6C@.221 | lf | 31.60 | 11.00 | .89 | 43.49 |
| 5-1/8" x 15" | 6C@.224 | lf | 35.10 | 11.10 | .89 | 47.09 |
| 5-1/8" x 16-1/2" | 6C@.227 | lf | 38.70 | 11.30 | .89 | 50.89 |
| 5-1/8" x 18" | 6C@.231 | lf | 42.10 | 11.50 | .89 | 54.49 |
| 5-1/8" x 19-1/2" | 6C@.234 | lf | 42.50 | 11.60 | .89 | 54.99 |
| 5-1/8" x 21" | 6C@.238 | lf | 48.90 | 11.80 | .89 | 61.59 |
| 5-1/8" x 22-1/2" | 6C@.242 | lf | 52.80 | 12.00 | .89 | 65.69 |
| 5-1/8" x 24" | 6C@.245 | lf | 56.10 | 12.20 | .89 | 69.19 |
| **6-3/4" wide glue-laminated beam, replace** | | | | | | |
| 6-3/4" x 18" | 6C@.244 | lf | 55.50 | 12.10 | .89 | 68.49 |
| 6-3/4" x 19-1/2" | 6C@.250 | lf | 60.10 | 12.40 | .89 | 73.39 |
| 6-3/4" x 24" | 6C@.267 | lf | 73.70 | 13.30 | .89 | 87.89 |
| Remove, all widths and sizes | 1D@.222 | lf | — | 8.64 | — | 8.64 |

| | Craft@Hrs | Unit | Material | Labor | Total |
|---|---|---|---|---|---|
| **Micro-laminated beam.** Includes micro-laminated beam, brackets, fasteners, and installation labor. Micro-laminated beams are often doubled as beams. Includes 4% waste. | | | | | |
| **1-3/4" wide micro-laminated beam, replace** | | | | | |
| 1-3/4" x 7-1/4" | 6C@.048 | lf | 6.26 | 2.39 | 8.65 |
| 1-3/4" x 9-1/2" | 6C@.050 | lf | 8.21 | 2.49 | 10.70 |
| 1-3/4" x 11-7/8" | 6C@.053 | lf | 10.30 | 2.63 | 12.93 |
| 1-3/4" x 14" | 6C@.056 | lf | 12.00 | 2.78 | 14.78 |
| 1-3/4" x 16" | 6C@.059 | lf | 13.70 | 2.93 | 16.63 |
| 1-3/4" x 18" | 6C@.063 | lf | 15.50 | 3.13 | 18.63 |
| Remove, all sizes | 1D@.106 | lf | — | 4.12 | 4.12 |

| | Craft@Hrs | Unit | Material | Labor | Equip. | Total |
|---|---|---|---|---|---|---|
| **Pine beam, select structural grade.** Includes beam, brackets, fasteners, and installation labor. Also includes costs for equipment — usually a fork lift — to place the beam. Deduct **12%** for #1 and better grade pine. Rough sawn. Installed as posts, beams, joists, and purlins. Pine species vary by region. Western coastal areas: Douglas fir, hemlock fir. Mountain states and provinces: spruce, pine, Douglas fir. South: southern yellow pine. Midwest: spruce, pine, Douglas fir, southern yellow pine. Southwest: southern yellow pine. Northeast: spruce, pine, Douglas fir, and hemlock fir. | | | | | | |
| **4" wide beam, replace** | | | | | | |
| 4" x 6" | 6C@.078 | lf | 4.53 | 3.88 | .89 | 9.30 |
| 4" x 8" | 6C@.092 | lf | 6.04 | 4.57 | .89 | 11.50 |
| 4" x 10" | 6C@.114 | lf | 7.57 | 5.67 | .89 | 14.13 |
| 4" x 12" | 6C@.149 | lf | 9.07 | 7.41 | .89 | 17.37 |
| 4" x 14" | 6C@.178 | lf | 10.60 | 8.85 | .89 | 20.34 |
| 4" x 16" | 6C@.180 | lf | 12.00 | 8.95 | .89 | 21.84 |

| | Craft@Hrs | Unit | Material | Labor | Equip. | Total |
|---|---|---|---|---|---|---|
| **6" wide, replace** | | | | | | |
| 6" x 6" | 6C@.102 | lf | 6.81 | 5.07 | .89 | 12.77 |
| 6" x 8" | 6C@.115 | lf | 9.07 | 5.72 | .89 | 15.68 |
| 6" x 10" | 6C@.132 | lf | 11.30 | 6.56 | .89 | 18.75 |
| 6" x 12" | 6C@.154 | lf | 13.50 | 7.65 | .89 | 22.04 |
| 6" x 14" | 6C@.169 | lf | 15.80 | 8.40 | .89 | 25.09 |
| 6" x 16" | 6C@.189 | lf | 18.20 | 9.39 | .89 | 28.48 |
| **8" wide beam, replace** | | | | | | |
| 8" x 8" | 6C@.139 | lf | 12.00 | 6.91 | .89 | 19.80 |
| 8" x 10" | 6C@.156 | lf | 15.00 | 7.75 | .89 | 23.64 |
| 8" x 12" | 6C@.182 | lf | 18.20 | 9.05 | .89 | 28.14 |
| 8" x 14" | 6C@.193 | lf | 21.00 | 9.59 | .89 | 31.48 |
| 8" x 16" | 6C@.199 | lf | 24.20 | 9.89 | .89 | 34.98 |
| **10" wide beam, replace** | | | | | | |
| 10" x 10" | 6C@.176 | lf | 19.10 | 8.75 | .89 | 28.74 |
| 10" x 12" | 6C@.196 | lf | 22.60 | 9.74 | .89 | 33.23 |
| 10" x 14" | 6C@.203 | lf | 26.40 | 10.10 | .89 | 37.39 |
| 10" x 16" | 6C@.210 | lf | 30.40 | 10.40 | .89 | 41.69 |
| **12" wide beam, replace** | | | | | | |
| 12" x 12" | 6C@.204 | lf | 27.10 | 10.10 | .89 | 38.09 |
| 12" x 14" | 6C@.213 | lf | 31.80 | 10.60 | .89 | 43.29 |
| 12" x 16" | 6C@.222 | lf | 36.10 | 11.00 | .89 | 47.99 |
| Remove, all widths and sizes | 1D@.222 | lf | — | 8.64 | — | 8.64 |

**Oak beam.** Includes beam, brackets, fasteners, and installation labor. Also includes costs for equipment — usually a fork lift — to place the beam. Installed as posts, beams, joists, and purlins. Includes 4% waste.

| | Craft@Hrs | Unit | Material | Labor | Equip. | Total |
|---|---|---|---|---|---|---|
| **4" wide oak beam, replace** | | | | | | |
| 4" x 6" | 6C@.078 | lf | 11.10 | 3.88 | .89 | 15.87 |
| 4" x 8" | 6C@.092 | lf | 14.60 | 4.57 | .89 | 20.06 |
| 4" x 10" | 6C@.114 | lf | 18.70 | 5.67 | .89 | 25.26 |
| 4" x 12" | 6C@.149 | lf | 22.20 | 7.41 | .89 | 30.50 |
| 4" x 14" | 6C@.178 | lf | 25.80 | 8.85 | .89 | 35.54 |
| 4" x 16" | 6C@.180 | lf | 29.70 | 8.95 | .89 | 39.54 |
| **6" wide oak beam, replace** | | | | | | |
| 6" x 6" | 6C@.102 | lf | 16.80 | 5.07 | .89 | 22.76 |
| 6" x 8" | 6C@.115 | lf | 23.00 | 5.72 | .89 | 29.61 |
| 6" x 10" | 6C@.132 | lf | 27.90 | 6.56 | .89 | 35.35 |
| 6" x 12" | 6C@.154 | lf | 33.30 | 7.65 | .89 | 41.84 |
| 6" x 14" | 6C@.169 | lf | 39.00 | 8.40 | .89 | 48.29 |
| 6" x 16" | 6C@.189 | lf | 44.40 | 9.39 | .89 | 54.68 |
| **8" wide oak beam, replace** | | | | | | |
| 8" x 8" | 6C@.139 | lf | 29.70 | 6.91 | .89 | 37.50 |
| 8" x 10" | 6C@.156 | lf | 37.00 | 7.75 | .89 | 45.64 |
| 8" x 12" | 6C@.182 | lf | 44.40 | 9.05 | .89 | 54.34 |
| 8" x 14" | 6C@.193 | lf | 51.80 | 9.59 | .89 | 62.28 |
| 8" x 16" | 6C@.199 | lf | 59.20 | 9.89 | .89 | 69.98 |
| **10" wide oak beam, replace** | | | | | | |
| 10" x 10" | 6C@.176 | lf | 46.20 | 8.75 | .89 | 55.84 |
| 10" x 12" | 6C@.196 | lf | 55.60 | 9.74 | .89 | 66.23 |
| 10" x 14" | 6C@.203 | lf | 64.80 | 10.10 | .89 | 75.79 |
| 10" x 16" | 6C@.210 | lf | 73.90 | 10.40 | .89 | 85.19 |

| | Craft@Hrs | Unit | Material | Labor | Equip. | Total |
|---|---|---|---|---|---|---|
| 12" wide oak beam, replace | | | | | | |
| 12" x 12" | 6C@.204 | lf | 66.70 | 10.10 | .89 | 77.69 |
| 12" x 14" | 6C@.213 | lf | 77.80 | 10.60 | .89 | 89.29 |
| 12" x 16" | 6C@.222 | lf | 88.90 | 11.00 | .89 | 100.79 |
| Remove, all widths and sizes | 1D@.222 | lf | — | 8.64 | — | 8.64 |

| | Craft@Hrs | Unit | Material | Labor | Total |
|---|---|---|---|---|---|
| **Additional beam costs.** | | | | | |
| for hand-hewn pine beam | — | si | .03 | — | .03 |
| for curved pine post & beam framing member | 4B@.909 | lf | — | 56.00 | 56.00 |
| for hand-hewn oak beam | — | si | .04 | — | .04 |
| for curved oak post & beam framing member | 4B@1.20 | lf | — | 73.90 | 73.90 |

*simple truss*  *king post truss*  *king post & struts truss*

*queen post truss*  *hammer beam truss*  *scissors truss*

| | Craft@Hrs | Unit | Material | Labor | Equip. | Total |
|---|---|---|---|---|---|---|

**Pine post & beam bent with truss.** Includes beams, posts, and installation labor. All connections between beams and posts are made from cut joints. Joints are held together with dowels that are often hand-cut from the beam material. Includes glue as needed. Does not include connecting members or their joinery. This price should not be used for similar systems made of beams that are joined with butt and miter joints often held together by steel brackets. With pine posts and beams, per SF of bent.

| | Craft@Hrs | Unit | Material | Labor | Equip. | Total |
|---|---|---|---|---|---|---|
| Replace single-story bent with | | | | | | |
| simple truss | 4B@.527 | sf | 3.87 | 32.50 | .54 | 36.91 |
| king post truss | 4B@.569 | sf | 4.29 | 35.10 | .54 | 39.93 |
| king post & struts truss | 4B@.618 | sf | 4.83 | 38.10 | .54 | 43.47 |
| queen post truss | 4B@.609 | sf | 4.51 | 37.50 | .54 | 42.55 |
| hammer beam truss | 4B@1.05 | sf | 4.75 | 64.70 | .54 | 69.99 |
| scissors truss | 4B@.989 | sf | 5.03 | 60.90 | .52 | 66.45 |
| Remove, single-story bent with truss, | | | | | | |
| all types | 1D@.071 | sf | — | 2.76 | — | 2.76 |

| | Craft@Hrs | Unit | Material | Labor | Equip. | Total |
|---|---|---|---|---|---|---|
| **Replace two-story bent with** | | | | | | |
| simple truss | 4B@.571 | sf | 3.56 | 35.20 | .54 | 39.30 |
| king post truss | 4B@.620 | sf | 3.84 | 38.20 | .54 | 42.58 |
| king post & struts truss | 4B@.679 | sf | 4.18 | 41.80 | .54 | 46.52 |
| queen post truss | 4B@.671 | sf | 3.97 | 41.30 | .54 | 45.81 |
| hammer beam truss | 4B@1.25 | sf | 4.15 | 77.00 | .54 | 81.69 |
| scissors truss | 4B@1.04 | sf | 4.27 | 64.10 | .54 | 68.91 |
| **Remove, two-story bent with truss,** | | | | | | |
| all types | 1D@.071 | sf | — | 2.76 | — | 2.76 |
| **Add for overhang drop** | 4B@20.0 | ea | 216.00 | 1,230.00 | .54 | 1,446.54 |

post & beam framing

**Pine connecting members between bents.** Includes floor joists, roof purlins, diagonal braces, and beams. Per sf of area beneath roof. Measure only one floor.

| | | | | | | |
|---|---|---|---|---|---|---|
| between single-story bents & trusses | 4B@1.11 | sf | 6.74 | 68.40 | — | 75.14 |
| remove | 1D@.214 | sf | — | 8.32 | — | 8.32 |
| between two-story bents & trusses | 4B@1.85 | sf | 10.10 | 114.00 | — | 124.10 |
| remove | 1D@.286 | sf | — | 11.10 | — | 11.10 |

**Oak post & beam bent with truss.** Includes beams, posts, and installation labor. All connections between beams are made from cut joints. Joints are held together with pegs that are often hand-cut from the beam material. Includes glue as needed. Does not include connecting members or their joinery. This price should not be used for similar systems made of posts and beams that are joined with butt and miter joints often held together by steel brackets. With oak posts and beams, per SF of bent.

| | | | | | | |
|---|---|---|---|---|---|---|
| **Replace single-story bent with** | | | | | | |
| simple truss | 4B@.527 | sf | 9.42 | 32.50 | .54 | 42.46 |
| king post truss | 4B@.569 | sf | 10.50 | 35.10 | .54 | 46.14 |
| king post & struts truss | 4B@.618 | sf | 11.70 | 38.10 | .54 | 50.34 |
| queen post truss | 4B@.609 | sf | 10.90 | 37.50 | .54 | 48.94 |
| hammer beam truss | 4B@1.05 | sf | 11.60 | 64.70 | .54 | 76.84 |
| scissors truss | 4B@.989 | sf | 12.10 | 60.90 | .54 | 73.54 |

| | Craft@Hrs | Unit | Material | Labor | Equip. | Total |
|---|---|---|---|---|---|---|
| Remove, single-story bent with truss, all types | 1D@.071 | sf | — | 2.76 | — | 2.76 |
| Replace two-story bent with | | | | | | |
|   simple truss | 4B@.571 | sf | 8.68 | 35.20 | .54 | 44.42 |
|   king post truss | 4B@.620 | sf | 9.34 | 38.20 | .54 | 48.08 |
|   king post & struts truss | 4B@.679 | sf | 10.10 | 41.80 | .54 | 52.44 |
|   queen post truss | 4B@.671 | sf | 9.64 | 41.30 | .54 | 51.48 |
|   hammer beam truss | 4B@1.25 | sf | 10.00 | 77.00 | .54 | 87.54 |
|   scissors truss | 4B@1.04 | sf | 10.40 | 64.10 | .54 | 75.04 |
| Remove, two-story bent with truss, all types | 1D@.071 | sf | — | 2.76 | — | 2.76 |
| Add for overhang drop in two-story bent | 4B@20.0 | ea | 471.00 | 1,230.00 | .54 | 1,701.54 |

**Oak connecting members between bents.** Includes floor joists, roof purlins, diagonal braces, and beams. Per sf of area beneath roof. Measure only one floor.

| | Craft@Hrs | Unit | Material | Labor | Equip. | Total |
|---|---|---|---|---|---|---|
|   between single-story bents & trusses | 4B@1.11 | sf | 16.50 | 68.40 | — | 84.90 |
|   remove | 1D@.214 | sf | — | 8.32 | — | 8.32 |
|   between two-story bents & trusses | 4B@1.85 | sf | 24.50 | 114.00 | — | 138.50 |
|   remove | 1D@.286 | sf | — | 11.10 | — | 11.10 |
| Minimum charge for post & beam framing work | 4B@20.0 | ea | 440.00 | 1,230.00 | 734.00 | 2,404.00 |

*sill corner half-lap*

*sill corner dovetail*

*sill corner tongue & fork*

*sill corner half-lap with through tenon*

*sill corner dovetail with through tenon*

*sill corner tongue & fork with through tenon*

| | Craft@Hrs | Unit | Material | Labor | Total |
|---|---|---|---|---|---|

**Post & beam joints.** A labor-only cost to cut the described joint. Does not include the beams, bracing of existing systems, or equipment costs to place replacement posts or beams. Includes cutting, drilling, and joining with pegs.

| | Craft@Hrs | Unit | Material | Labor | Total |
|---|---|---|---|---|---|
| Sill corner joints, replace | | | | | |
|   half-lap joint | 2B@1.10 | ea | — | 79.20 | 79.20 |
|   half-lap joint with through tenon | 2B@2.77 | ea | — | 199.00 | 199.00 |
|   dovetail joint | 2B@1.99 | ea | — | 143.00 | 143.00 |
|   dovetail joint with through tenon | 2B@3.86 | ea | — | 278.00 | 278.00 |
|   tongue and fork joint | 2B@1.79 | ea | — | 129.00 | 129.00 |
|   tongue and fork joint with through tenon | 2B@3.44 | ea | — | 248.00 | 248.00 |

lapped dovetail

housed lapped dovetail

tusk tenon

half-lap

through mortise & tenon

housed mortise & tenon

shouldered mortise & tenon joint

wedged dovetail mortise & tenon joint

mortise & tenon joint (90-degree intersection)

anchor-beam joint

|  | Craft@Hrs | Unit | Material | Labor | Total |
|---|---|---|---|---|---|
| Joints for connecting two timbers at 90-degree angles, replace | | | | | |
| lapped dovetail joint | 2B@2.05 | ea | — | 148.00 | 148.00 |
| housed lapped dovetail joint | 2B@2.55 | ea | — | 184.00 | 184.00 |
| tusk tenon joint | 2B@2.77 | ea | — | 199.00 | 199.00 |
| half-lap joint | 2B@1.08 | ea | — | 77.80 | 77.80 |
| through mortise & tenon joint with shoulders | 2B@2.26 | ea | — | 163.00 | 163.00 |
| housed mortise & tenon joint | 2B@2.37 | ea | — | 171.00 | 171.00 |
| shouldered mortise & tenon joint | 2B@2.34 | ea | — | 168.00 | 168.00 |
| wedged dovetail mortise & tenon joint | 2B@2.37 | ea | — | 171.00 | 171.00 |
| mortise & tenon joint (90-degree intersection) | 2B@1.25 | ea | — | 90.00 | 90.00 |
| anchor-beam joint | 2B@2.93 | ea | — | 211.00 | 211.00 |

framed overhang

through half-lap

mortise & tenon knee brace

collar tie lapped half dovetail

|  | Craft@Hrs | Unit | Material | Labor | Total |
|---|---|---|---|---|---|
| Other post & beam joints, replace only | | | | | |
| framed overhang joint | 2B@10.0 | ea | — | 720.00 | 720.00 |
| through half-lap joint | 2B@1.20 | ea | — | 86.40 | 86.40 |
| mortise & tenon knee brace joint | 2B@1.56 | ea | — | 112.00 | 112.00 |
| collar tie lapped half dovetail joint | 2B@1.96 | ea | — | 141.00 | 141.00 |

| | Craft@Hrs | Unit | Material | Labor | Total |
|---|---|---|---|---|---|

*stopped splayed scarf*    *stopped splayed scarf with through tenon*    *bladed scarf*    *bladed scarf with through tenon*    *rafter foot housed bird's mouth*

Joints for splicing together two level beams, replace only

| | Craft@Hrs | Unit | Material | Labor | Total |
|---|---|---|---|---|---|
| stopped splayed scarf joint | 2B@3.22 | ea | — | 232.00 | 232.00 |
| stopped splayed scarf joint with through tenon | 2B@5.00 | ea | — | 360.00 | 360.00 |
| bladed scarf joint | 2B@2.45 | ea | — | 176.00 | 176.00 |
| bladed scarf joint with through tenon | 2B@4.35 | ea | — | 313.00 | 313.00 |

*rafter foot beveled shoulder bird's mouth*    *rafter foot bird's mouth, purlin, and post*    *rafter foot bird's mouth*    *rafter foot bird's mouth with tenon*    *rafter peak tongue & fork*

Rafter joints, replace only

| | Craft@Hrs | Unit | Material | Labor | Total |
|---|---|---|---|---|---|
| rafter foot housed bird's mouth joint | 2B@1.39 | ea | — | 100.00 | 100.00 |
| rafter foot beveled shoulder bird's mouth joint | 2B@1.30 | ea | — | 93.60 | 93.60 |
| rafter foot bird's mouth, purlin, and post joint | 2B@3.13 | ea | — | 225.00 | 225.00 |
| rafter foot bird's mouth joint | 2B@1.00 | ea | — | 72.00 | 72.00 |
| rafter foot bird's mouth joint with tenon | 2B@2.86 | ea | — | 206.00 | 206.00 |
| rafter peak tongue & fork joint | 2B@1.79 | ea | — | 129.00 | 129.00 |

**Exterior deck joist system.** Includes 5% waste. Complete joist system. Does not include decking, railing, or stairs. Includes footings, excavation for footings, column stirrups and connectors, posts, and beams on outside edge of deck, connection with joist hangers against house, and joists.

| Replace exterior deck joist system | Craft@Hrs | Unit | Material | Labor | Total |
|---|---|---|---|---|---|
| 2" x 6" joists | 6C@.067 | sf | 2.63 | 3.33 | 5.96 |
| 2" x 8" joists | 6C@.071 | sf | 2.94 | 3.53 | 6.47 |
| 2" x 10" joists | 6C@.077 | sf | 3.71 | 3.83 | 7.54 |
| 2" x 12" joists | 6C@.083 | sf | 4.08 | 4.13 | 8.21 |
| Remove, all sizes | 1D@.013 | sf | — | .51 | .51 |

| | Craft@Hrs | Unit | Material | Labor | Total |
|---|---|---|---|---|---|

**Exterior decking.** Includes 2" x 4" decking lumber, rust-resistant screws or nails, and installation labor. Deduct **8%** for 5/4 treated wood decking (decking that is 1-1/4" thick instead of 1-1/2" thick). Includes 5% waste.

| | | | | | |
|---|---|---|---|---|---|
| 2" x 4" redwood exterior decking, replace | | | | | |
| construction common | 6C@.040 | sf | 5.16 | 1.99 | 7.15 |
| construction heart | 6C@.040 | sf | 5.95 | 1.99 | 7.94 |
| 2" x 6" redwood exterior deck, replace | | | | | |
| construction common | 6C@.037 | sf | 4.16 | 1.84 | 6.00 |
| construction heart | 6C@.037 | sf | 4.81 | 1.84 | 6.65 |
| 2" x 8" redwood exterior deck, replace | | | | | |
| construction common | 6C@.033 | sf | 4.43 | 1.64 | 6.07 |
| construction heart | 6C@.033 | sf | 5.14 | 1.64 | 6.78 |
| Treated exterior wood decking, replace | | | | | |
| 2" x 4" | 6C@.040 | sf | 4.43 | 1.99 | 6.42 |
| 2" x 6" | 6C@.037 | sf | 4.26 | 1.84 | 6.10 |
| 2" x 8" | 6C@.033 | sf | 4.22 | 1.64 | 5.86 |
| Remove, all sizes and types | 1D@.026 | sf | — | 1.01 | 1.01 |

**Exterior deck railing.** Includes 2" x 6" top rail, often routed with a bull-nose, 2" x 2" balusters placed approximately 4" on center, fasteners, and installation labor. Does not include posts. Also includes 5% waste.

| | | | | | |
|---|---|---|---|---|---|
| Replace exterior deck railing | | | | | |
| redwood construction common | 6C@.275 | lf | 9.29 | 13.70 | 22.99 |
| redwood construction heart | 6C@.275 | lf | 10.70 | 13.70 | 24.40 |
| treated wood | 6C@.275 | lf | 9.03 | 13.70 | 22.73 |
| Remove, all types | 1D@.034 | lf | — | 1.32 | 1.32 |

**Exterior deck stairs with railing, per step.** Includes up to three stringers made from 2" x 12" lumber. Each step has up to three 2" x 4" treads. Balusters are 2" x 2" placed approximately 4" on center. Balusters attach to side stringers on the bottom and a top rail at the top. Top rail is 2" x 6" often routed with a bullnose edge. Does not include foundation system for bottom of stairs. Includes 5% waste.

| | | | | | |
|---|---|---|---|---|---|
| 2' 6" wide deck stairs, replace | | | | | |
| construction common redwood | 6C@.540 | ea | 39.00 | 26.80 | 65.80 |
| construction heart redwood | 6C@.540 | ea | 41.90 | 26.80 | 68.70 |
| treated wood | 6C@.540 | ea | 38.60 | 26.80 | 65.40 |
| 3' wide exterior deck stairs, replace | | | | | |
| construction common redwood | 6C@.587 | ea | 41.60 | 29.20 | 70.80 |
| construction heart redwood | 6C@.587 | ea | 44.40 | 29.20 | 73.60 |
| treated wood | 6C@.587 | ea | 40.90 | 29.20 | 70.10 |
| Remove, all widths and types | 1D@.061 | ea | — | 2.37 | 2.37 |

*exterior deck stairs*

**Exterior deck landing.** Includes 2" x 10" joist system with 2" x 6" board decking, beams, posts, stirrups, footings, excavation for footings, all fasteners, and installation labor. Includes 5% waste.

| | | | | | |
|---|---|---|---|---|---|
| Replace exterior deck landing | | | | | |
| construction common decking | 6C@.074 | sf | 13.60 | 3.68 | 17.28 |
| construction heart decking | 6C@.074 | sf | 15.10 | 3.68 | 18.78 |
| treated wood | 6C@.074 | sf | 13.40 | 3.68 | 17.08 |
| Remove, all types | 1D@.015 | sf | — | .58 | .58 |

| | Craft@Hrs | Unit | Material | Labor | Total |
|---|---|---|---|---|---|

**Furring strips.** Includes 1" x 2" furring strips, construction adhesive, case hardened nails or powder-actuated fasteners, and installation labor. Furring strips placed as fireblocking at top and bottom of walls are included. Fireblocking furring strips inside the wall for taller walls are also included. Also includes 5% waste.

| | Craft@Hrs | Unit | Material | Labor | Total |
|---|---|---|---|---|---|
| Replace 1" x 2" furring strips applied to wood | | | | | |
|   12" on center | 6C@.015 | sf | .22 | .75 | .97 |
|   16" on center | 6C@.013 | sf | .18 | .65 | .83 |
|   24" on center | 6C@.011 | sf | .14 | .55 | .69 |
| Remove 1" x 2" furring strips applied to wood | 1D@.011 | sf | — | .43 | .43 |
| Replace 1" x 2" furring strips applied to masonry or concrete | | | | | |
|   12" on center | 6C@.020 | sf | .22 | .99 | 1.21 |
|   16" on center | 6C@.016 | sf | .18 | .80 | .98 |
|   24" on center | 6C@.014 | sf | .14 | .70 | .84 |
| Remove 1" x 2" furring strips applied to masonry or concrete | 1D@.012 | sf | — | .47 | .47 |
| Replace 2" x 2" furring strips applied to wood | | | | | |
|   12" on center | 6C@.015 | sf | .57 | .75 | 1.32 |
|   16" on center | 6C@.013 | sf | .43 | .65 | 1.08 |
|   24" on center | 6C@.011 | sf | .34 | .55 | .89 |
| Remove 2" x 2" furring strips applied to wood | 1D@.011 | sf | — | .43 | .43 |
| Replace 2" x 2" furring strips applied to masonry or concrete | | | | | |
|   12" on center | 6C@.020 | sf | .57 | .99 | 1.56 |
|   16" on center | 6C@.016 | sf | .43 | .80 | 1.23 |
|   24" on center | 6C@.014 | sf | .34 | .70 | 1.04 |
| Remove 2" x 2" furring strips applied to masonry or concrete | 1D@.012 | sf | — | .47 | .47 |

**Joist system, per square foot.** Includes 5% waste. All joist systems include joists, rim joists, blocking, and steel X braces at center span. (Except 2" x 4" joists which include solid blocking at center of span.)

| | Craft@Hrs | Unit | Material | Labor | Total |
|---|---|---|---|---|---|
| 2" x 4" joist system, replace | | | | | |
|   12" on center | 6C@.018 | sf | 1.04 | .89 | 1.93 |
|   16" on center | 6C@.014 | sf | .85 | .70 | 1.55 |
|   24" on center | 6C@.011 | sf | .61 | .55 | 1.16 |
| 2" x 6" joist system, replace | | | | | |
|   12" on center | 6C@.025 | sf | 1.52 | 1.24 | 2.76 |
|   16" on center | 6C@.019 | sf | 1.21 | .94 | 2.15 |
|   24" on center | 6C@.013 | sf | .89 | .65 | 1.54 |
| 2" x 8" joist system, replace | | | | | |
|   12" on center | 6C@.029 | sf | 1.88 | 1.44 | 3.32 |
|   16" on center | 6C@.024 | sf | 1.46 | 1.19 | 2.65 |
|   24" on center | 6C@.018 | sf | 1.05 | .89 | 1.94 |
| 2" x 10" joist system, replace | | | | | |
|   12" on center | 6C@.036 | sf | 2.81 | 1.79 | 4.60 |
|   replace, 16" on center | 6C@.029 | sf | 2.21 | 1.44 | 3.65 |
|   replace, 24" on center | 6C@.022 | sf | 1.52 | 1.09 | 2.61 |
| 2" x 12" joist system, replace | | | | | |
|   12" on center | 6C@.045 | sf | 3.20 | 2.24 | 5.44 |
|   16" on center | 6C@.033 | sf | 2.51 | 1.64 | 4.15 |
|   24" on center | 6C@.029 | sf | 1.75 | 1.44 | 3.19 |
| Remove joist system, all sizes | 1D@.014 | sf | — | .54 | .54 |

|  | Craft@Hrs | Unit | Material | Labor | Total |
|---|---|---|---|---|---|
| **Joist system, per board foot.** | | | | | |
| Replace, all sizes | 6C@.021 | bf | 1.49 | 1.04 | 2.53 |
| Remove, all sizes | 1D@.006 | bf | — | .23 | .23 |

**Laminated lumber I joist.** Includes 3% waste. The lf price includes I joist, rim joists, blocking, and steel X braces at center span.

|  | Craft@Hrs | Unit | Material | Labor | Total |
|---|---|---|---|---|---|
| 1-3/4" flange laminated lumber I joist | | | | | |
|   Replace | | | | | |
|     9-1/2" deep | 6C@.034 | lf | 2.84 | 1.69 | 4.53 |
|     11-7/8" deep | 6C@.036 | lf | 3.43 | 1.79 | 5.22 |
|     14" deep | 6C@.037 | lf | 4.21 | 1.84 | 6.05 |
| 2-5/16" flange laminated lumber I joist | | | | | |
|   Replace | | | | | |
|     11-7/8" deep | 6C@.036 | lf | 4.87 | 1.79 | 6.66 |
|     14" deep | 6C@.038 | lf | 5.95 | 1.89 | 7.84 |
|     16" deep | 6C@.039 | lf | 7.04 | 1.94 | 8.98 |
| Remove I joist, all flange sizes and depths | 1D@.014 | sf | — | .54 | .54 |

**Floor truss.** The lf price includes cat walks, diagonal braces, fasteners and rim materials.

|  | Craft@Hrs | Unit | Material | Labor | Total |
|---|---|---|---|---|---|
| Replace | | | | | |
|   for typical load | 6C@.091 | lf | 4.98 | 4.52 | 9.50 |
|   for heavy load | 6C@.094 | lf | 5.37 | 4.67 | 10.04 |
| Remove, all types | 1D@.014 | sf | — | .54 | .54 |

**Hand-framed gable roof.** Includes 5% waste. Measure the sf of area beneath roof. (The sf of bottom floor plus sf under overhangs.) Do not measure the sf of roof. Includes rafters, collar ties, a ridge board that is 2" wider than the rafter (except for 2" x 12" rafters, which have a ridge made from a 1-1/2" x 11-7/8" micro-laminated beam), rough fascia board, blocking, and wall fasteners. If roof has a hip or a Dutch hip, see page 371. There is no additional charge for a Dutch gable.

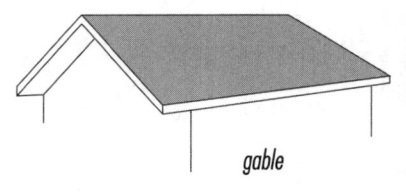
gable

|  | Craft@Hrs | Unit | Material | Labor | Total |
|---|---|---|---|---|---|
| 2" x 4" rafters for gable roof | | | | | |
|   4/12 slope, replace | 6C@.034 | sf | .74 | 1.69 | 2.43 |
|     remove | 1D@.016 | sf | — | .62 | .62 |
|   6/12 slope, replace | 6C@.036 | sf | .78 | 1.79 | 2.57 |
|     remove | 1D@.017 | sf | — | .66 | .66 |
|   8/12 slope, replace | 6C@.040 | sf | .83 | 1.99 | 2.82 |
|     remove | 1D@.019 | sf | — | .74 | .74 |
|   10/12 slope, replace | 6C@.044 | sf | .87 | 2.19 | 3.06 |
|     remove | 1D@.024 | sf | — | .93 | .93 |
|   12/12 slope, replace | 6C@.049 | sf | .93 | 2.44 | 3.37 |
|     remove | 1D@.032 | sf | — | 1.24 | 1.24 |
|   14/12 slope, replace | 6C@.054 | sf | .98 | 2.68 | 3.66 |
|     remove | 1D@.038 | sf | — | 1.48 | 1.48 |
|   16/12 slope, replace | 6C@.060 | sf | 1.05 | 2.98 | 4.03 |
|     remove | 1D@.050 | sf | — | 1.95 | 1.95 |
|   18/12 slope, replace | 6C@.067 | sf | 1.12 | 3.33 | 4.45 |
|     remove | 1D@.077 | sf | — | 3.00 | 3.00 |

| | Craft@Hrs | Unit | Material | Labor | Total |
|---|---|---|---|---|---|
| **2" x 6" rafters for gable roof** | | | | | |
| 4/12 slope, replace | 6C@.035 | sf | 1.05 | 1.74 | 2.79 |
| remove | 1D@.016 | sf | — | .62 | .62 |
| 6/12 slope, replace | 6C@.038 | sf | 1.09 | 1.89 | 2.98 |
| remove | 1D@.017 | sf | — | .66 | .66 |
| 8/12 slope, replace | 6C@.042 | sf | 1.16 | 2.09 | 3.25 |
| remove | 1D@.019 | sf | — | .74 | .74 |
| 10/12 slope, replace | 6C@.046 | sf | 1.23 | 2.29 | 3.52 |
| remove | 1D@.024 | sf | — | .93 | .93 |
| 12/12 slope, replace | 6C@.051 | sf | 1.32 | 2.53 | 3.85 |
| remove | 1D@.032 | sf | — | 1.24 | 1.24 |
| 14/12 slope, replace | 6C@.056 | sf | 1.39 | 2.78 | 4.17 |
| remove | 1D@.038 | sf | — | 1.48 | 1.48 |
| 16/12 slope, replace | 6C@.062 | sf | 1.50 | 3.08 | 4.58 |
| remove | 1D@.050 | sf | — | 1.95 | 1.95 |
| 18/12 slope, replace | 6C@.070 | sf | 1.60 | 3.48 | 5.08 |
| remove | 1D@.077 | sf | — | 3.00 | 3.00 |
| **2" x 8" rafters for gable roof** | | | | | |
| 4/12 slope, replace | 6C@.036 | sf | 1.50 | 1.79 | 3.29 |
| remove | 1D@.016 | sf | — | .62 | .62 |
| 6/12 slope, replace | 6C@.039 | sf | 1.57 | 1.94 | 3.51 |
| remove | 1D@.017 | sf | — | .66 | .66 |
| 8/12 slope, replace | 6C@.043 | sf | 1.67 | 2.14 | 3.81 |
| remove | 1D@.019 | sf | — | .74 | .74 |
| 10/12 slope, replace | 6C@.047 | sf | 1.77 | 2.34 | 4.11 |
| remove | 1D@.024 | sf | — | .93 | .93 |
| 12/12 slope, replace | 6C@.052 | sf | 1.92 | 2.58 | 4.50 |
| remove | 1D@.032 | sf | — | 1.24 | 1.24 |
| 14/12 slope, replace | 6C@.058 | sf | 2.03 | 2.88 | 4.91 |
| remove | 1D@.038 | sf | — | 1.48 | 1.48 |
| 16/12 slope, replace | 6C@.064 | sf | 2.17 | 3.18 | 5.35 |
| remove | 1D@.050 | sf | — | 1.95 | 1.95 |
| 18/12 slop, replace | 6C@.072 | sf | 2.30 | 3.58 | 5.88 |
| remove | 1D@.077 | sf | — | 3.00 | 3.00 |
| **2" x 10" rafters for gable roof** | | | | | |
| 4/12 slope, replace | 6C@.037 | sf | 1.97 | 1.84 | 3.81 |
| remove | 1D@.016 | sf | — | .62 | .62 |
| 6/12 slope, replace | 6C@.040 | sf | 2.04 | 1.99 | 4.03 |
| remove | 1D@.017 | sf | — | .66 | .66 |
| 8/12 slope, replace | 6C@.044 | sf | 2.17 | 2.19 | 4.36 |
| remove | 1D@.019 | sf | — | .74 | .74 |
| 10/12 slope, replace | 6C@.049 | sf | 2.30 | 2.44 | 4.74 |
| remove | 1D@.024 | sf | — | .93 | .93 |
| 12/12 slope, replace | 6C@.054 | sf | 2.48 | 2.68 | 5.16 |
| remove | 1D@.032 | sf | — | 1.24 | 1.24 |
| 14/12 slope, replace | 6C@.059 | sf | 2.65 | 2.93 | 5.58 |
| remove | 1D@.038 | sf | — | 1.48 | 1.48 |
| 16/12 slope, replace | 6C@.066 | sf | 2.85 | 3.28 | 6.13 |
| remove | 1D@.050 | sf | — | 1.95 | 1.95 |
| 18/12 slope, replace | 6C@.075 | sf | 3.06 | 3.73 | 6.79 |
| remove | 1D@.077 | sf | — | 3.00 | 3.00 |

2" x 12" rafters for gable roof

| | Craft@Hrs | Unit | Material | Labor | Total |
|---|---|---|---|---|---|
| 4/12 slope, replace | 6C@.038 | sf | 2.65 | 1.89 | 4.54 |
|     remove | 1D@.016 | sf | — | .62 | .62 |
| 6/12 slope, replace | 6C@.042 | sf | 2.76 | 2.09 | 4.85 |
|     remove | 1D@.017 | sf | — | .66 | .66 |
| 8/12 slope, replace | 6C@.046 | sf | 2.92 | 2.29 | 5.21 |
|     remove | 1D@.019 | sf | — | .74 | .74 |
| 10/12 slope, replace | 6C@.050 | sf | 3.08 | 2.49 | 5.57 |
|     remove | 1D@.024 | sf | — | .93 | .93 |
| 12/12 slope, replace | 6C@.056 | sf | 3.27 | 2.78 | 6.05 |
|     remove | 1D@.032 | sf | — | 1.24 | 1.24 |
| 14/12 slope, replace | 6C@.061 | sf | 3.47 | 3.03 | 6.50 |
|     remove | 1D@.038 | sf | — | 1.48 | 1.48 |
| 16/12 slope, replace | 6C@.068 | sf | 3.68 | 3.38 | 7.06 |
|     remove | 1D@.050 | sf | — | 1.95 | 1.95 |
| 18/12 slope, replace | 6C@.077 | sf | 3.94 | 3.83 | 7.77 |
|     remove | 1D@.077 | sf | — | 3.00 | 3.00 |

## Additional costs for hand-framed roofs.

| | Craft@Hrs | Unit | Material | Labor | Total |
|---|---|---|---|---|---|
| for each lf of valley | 6C@.786 | lf | 15.70 | 39.10 | 54.80 |
| for hip roof, per lf of width | 6C@.212 | lf | 2.48 | 10.50 | 12.98 |
| for Dutch-hip, per lf of width | 6C@.229 | lf | 2.73 | 11.40 | 14.13 |

*hip*

*mansard*

## Hand-framed mansard roof, per cubic foot of roof. Includes 7% waste. Roof area equals roof system width times height times length. Includes rafters, collar ties, ridge boards, hip rafters, rough fascia board, blocking, and wall fasteners.

Replace mansard roof

| | Craft@Hrs | Unit | Material | Labor | Total |
|---|---|---|---|---|---|
| 2" x 4" rafters | 6C@.005 | cf | .10 | .25 | .35 |
| 2" x 6" rafters | 6C@.005 | cf | .17 | .25 | .42 |
| 2" x 8" rafters | 6C@.005 | cf | .23 | .25 | .48 |
| 2" x 10" rafters | 6C@.005 | cf | .30 | .25 | .55 |
| 2" x 12" rafters | 6C@.006 | cf | .35 | .30 | .65 |
| Remove, all sizes | 1D@.002 | cf | — | .08 | .08 |
| Add for each lf of valley | 6C@1.08 | lf | 19.10 | 53.70 | 72.80 |

*gambrel*

## Hand-framed gambrel roof, per cubic foot of roof. Includes 7% waste. Roof area equals roof system width times height times length. Includes rafters, collar ties, ridge boards, valley rafters, rough fascia board, blocking, and wall fasteners. Does not include wall that must be built at the intersection of the top and bottom sloping roof sections.

Replace gambrel roof

| | Craft@Hrs | Unit | Material | Labor | Total |
|---|---|---|---|---|---|
| 2" x 4" rafters | 6C@.004 | cf | .15 | .20 | .35 |
| 2" x 6" rafters | 6C@.005 | cf | .22 | .25 | .47 |
| 2" x 8" rafters | 6C@.005 | cf | .31 | .25 | .56 |
| 2" x 10" rafters | 6C@.005 | cf | .40 | .25 | .65 |
| 2" x 12" rafters | 6C@.006 | cf | .45 | .30 | .75 |
| Remove, all sizes | 1D@.002 | cf | — | .08 | .08 |
| Add for each lf of valley | 6C@1.14 | lf | 19.80 | 56.70 | 76.50 |

| | Craft@Hrs | Unit | Material | Labor | Total |
|---|---|---|---|---|---|

### Hand-framed roof, per board foot. Includes 5% waste.

| Replace hand-framed roof | | | | | |
|---|---|---|---|---|---|
| gable roof | 6C@.023 | bf | 1.25 | 1.14 | 2.39 |
| hip roof | 6C@.023 | bf | 1.38 | 1.14 | 2.52 |
| Dutch-hip roof | 6C@.024 | bf | 1.39 | 1.19 | 2.58 |
| mansard roof | 6C@.026 | bf | 1.52 | 1.29 | 2.81 |
| gambrel roof | 6C@.025 | bf | 1.61 | 1.24 | 2.85 |
| Remove, all sizes | 1D@.007 | bf | — | .27 | .27 |

*Dutch hip*

### Minimum charge.

| for roof framing | 6C@3.55 | ea | 57.50 | 176.00 | 233.50 |
|---|---|---|---|---|---|

### Hand-framed shed dormer. Includes 7% waste. Complete dormer including all side walls and roof framing. Length x width of dormer.

| 4/12 slope, replace | 6C@.045 | sf | 1.23 | 2.24 | 3.47 |
|---|---|---|---|---|---|
| remove | 1D@.017 | sf | — | .66 | .66 |
| 6/12 slope, replace | 6C@.047 | sf | 1.29 | 2.34 | 3.63 |
| remove | 1D@.018 | sf | — | .70 | .70 |
| 8/12 slope, replace | 6C@.049 | sf | 1.36 | 2.44 | 3.80 |
| remove | 1D@.020 | sf | — | .78 | .78 |
| 10/12 slope, replace | 6C@.054 | sf | 1.43 | 2.68 | 4.11 |
| remove | 1D@.025 | sf | — | .97 | .97 |
| 12/12 slope, replace | 6C@.060 | sf | 1.57 | 2.98 | 4.55 |
| remove | 1D@.033 | sf | — | 1.28 | 1.28 |
| 14/12 slope, replace | 6C@.062 | sf | 1.67 | 3.08 | 4.75 |
| remove | 1D@.040 | sf | — | 1.56 | 1.56 |
| 16/12 slope, replace | 6C@.064 | sf | 1.79 | 3.18 | 4.97 |
| remove | 1D@.053 | sf | — | 2.06 | 2.06 |
| 18/12 slope, replace | 6C@.067 | sf | 1.92 | 3.33 | 5.25 |
| remove | 1D@.081 | sf | — | 3.15 | 3.15 |

### Hand-framed gable dormer. Includes framing lumber, framing nails, and installation. Installation includes all material and labor needed to place the dormer including ridge boards, rafters, jack rafters, rough fascia boards, side and front walls (when needed), roof sheathing, headers, and so on. Does not include modifications to the roof the dormer ties into, finish soffit and fascia, windows, or finish wall materials. Includes 7% waste. Measure length x width of dormer.

| 4/12 slope, replace | 6C@.047 | sf | 1.37 | 2.34 | 3.71 |
|---|---|---|---|---|---|
| remove | 1D@.017 | sf | — | .66 | .66 |
| 6/12 slope, replace | 6C@.049 | sf | 1.42 | 2.44 | 3.86 |
| remove | 1D@.018 | sf | — | .70 | .70 |
| 8/12 slope, replace | 6C@.051 | sf | 1.52 | 2.53 | 4.05 |
| remove | 1D@.020 | sf | — | .78 | .78 |
| 10/12 slope, replace | 6C@.056 | sf | 1.61 | 2.78 | 4.39 |
| remove | 1D@.025 | sf | — | .97 | .97 |
| 12/12 slope, replace | 6C@.062 | sf | 1.76 | 3.08 | 4.84 |
| remove | 1D@.033 | sf | — | 1.28 | 1.28 |
| 14/12 slope, replace | 6C@.065 | sf | 1.87 | 3.23 | 5.10 |
| remove | 1D@.040 | sf | — | 1.56 | 1.56 |
| 16/12 slope, replace | 6C@.067 | sf | 2.00 | 3.33 | 5.33 |
| remove | 1D@.053 | sf | — | 2.06 | 2.06 |
| 18/12 slope, replace | 6C@.070 | sf | 2.15 | 3.48 | 5.63 |
| remove | 1D@.081 | sf | — | 3.15 | 3.15 |

| | Craft@Hrs | Unit | Material | Labor | Total |
|---|---|---|---|---|---|

**Hand-framed hip dormer.** Includes framing lumber, framing nails, and installation. Installation includes all material and labor needed to place the dormer including ridge boards, rafters, hip rafters, jack rafters, rough fascia boards, side and front walls (when needed), roof sheathing, headers, and so on. Does not include modifications to the roof the dormer ties into, finish soffit and fascia, windows, or finish wall materials. Includes 7% waste. Measure length x width of dormer.

| | Craft@Hrs | Unit | Material | Labor | Total |
|---|---|---|---|---|---|
| 4/12 slope, replace | 6C@.049 | sf | 1.41 | 2.44 | 3.85 |
| remove | 1D@.017 | sf | — | .66 | .66 |
| 6/12 slope, replace | 6C@.051 | sf | 1.47 | 2.53 | 4.00 |
| remove | 1D@.018 | sf | — | .70 | .70 |
| 8/12 slope, replace | 6C@.053 | sf | 1.57 | 2.63 | 4.20 |
| remove | 1D@.020 | sf | — | .78 | .78 |
| 10/12 slope, replace | 6C@.058 | sf | 1.69 | 2.88 | 4.57 |
| remove | 1D@.025 | sf | — | .97 | .97 |
| 12/12 slope, replace | 6C@.065 | sf | 1.80 | 3.23 | 5.03 |
| remove | 1D@.033 | sf | — | 1.28 | 1.28 |
| 14/12 slope, replace | 6C@.067 | sf | 1.93 | 3.33 | 5.26 |
| remove | 1D@.040 | sf | — | 1.56 | 1.56 |
| 16/12 slope, replace | 6C@.070 | sf | 2.27 | 3.48 | 5.75 |
| remove | 1D@.053 | sf | — | 2.06 | 2.06 |
| 18/12 slope, replace | 6C@.073 | sf | 2.19 | 3.63 | 5.82 |
| remove | 1D@.081 | sf | — | 3.15 | 3.15 |

**Hand-framed Dutch-hip dormer.** Includes framing lumber, framing nails, and installation. Installation includes all material and labor needed to place the dormer including ridge boards, rafters, hip rafters, jack rafters, rough fascia boards, side and front walls (when needed), roof sheathing, headers, and so on. Does not include modifications to the roof the dormer ties into, finish soffit and fascia, windows, or finish wall materials. Includes 7% waste. Measure length x width of dormer.

| | Craft@Hrs | Unit | Material | Labor | Total |
|---|---|---|---|---|---|
| 4/12 slope, replace | 6C@.051 | sf | 1.45 | 2.53 | 3.98 |
| remove | 1D@.017 | sf | — | .66 | .66 |
| 6/12 slope, replace | 6C@.052 | sf | 1.52 | 2.58 | 4.10 |
| remove | 1D@.018 | sf | — | .70 | .70 |
| 8/12 slope, replace | 6C@.054 | sf | 1.61 | 2.68 | 4.29 |
| remove | 1D@.020 | sf | — | .78 | .78 |
| 10/12 slope, replace | 6C@.060 | sf | 1.73 | 2.98 | 4.71 |
| remove | 1D@.025 | sf | — | .97 | .97 |
| 12/12 slope, replace | 6C@.067 | sf | 1.87 | 3.33 | 5.20 |
| remove | 1D@.033 | sf | — | 1.28 | 1.28 |
| 14/12 slope, replace | 6C@.069 | sf | 1.98 | 3.43 | 5.41 |
| remove | 1D@.040 | sf | — | 1.56 | 1.56 |
| 16/12 slope, replace | 6C@.072 | sf | 2.11 | 3.58 | 5.69 |
| remove | 1D@.053 | sf | — | 2.06 | 2.06 |
| 18/12 slope, replace | 6C@.074 | sf | 2.25 | 3.68 | 5.93 |
| remove | 1D@.078 | sf | — | 3.03 | 3.03 |

**Hand-framed gambrel dormer.** Includes framing lumber, framing nails, and installation. Installation includes all material and labor needed to place the dormer including ridge boards, rafters, jack rafters, rough fascia boards, side and front walls (when needed), roof sheathing, headers, and so on. Does not include modifications to the roof the dormer ties into, finish soffit and fascia, windows, or finish wall materials. Includes 7% waste. Measure length x width of dormer.

| | Craft@Hrs | Unit | Material | Labor | Total |
|---|---|---|---|---|---|
| replace | 6C@.059 | sf | 1.50 | 2.93 | 4.43 |
| remove | 1D@.017 | sf | — | .66 | .66 |

|  | Craft@Hrs | Unit | Material | Labor | Total |
|---|---|---|---|---|---|

**Hand-framed roof dormer, per board foot.** Includes framing lumber, framing nails, and installation. Installation includes all material and labor needed to place the dormer including ridge boards, rafters, hip rafters, jack rafters, rough fascia boards, studs in side and front walls (when needed), headers, and so on. Does not include roof sheathing, wall sheathing, modifications to the roof the dormer ties into, finish soffit and fascia, windows, or finish wall materials. Includes 7% waste.

|  | Craft@Hrs | Unit | Material | Labor | Total |
|---|---|---|---|---|---|
| Shed dormer, replace | 6C@.034 | bf | 2.02 | 1.69 | 3.71 |
| remove shed dormer | 1D@.010 | bf | — | .39 | .39 |
| Gable dormer, replace | 6C@.035 | bf | 2.13 | 1.74 | 3.87 |
| remove gable dormer | 1D@.017 | bf | — | .66 | .66 |
| Hip dormer, replace | 6C@.036 | bf | 2.19 | 1.79 | 3.98 |
| remove hip dormer | 1D@.018 | bf | — | .70 | .70 |
| Dutch hip dormer, replace | 6C@.038 | bf | 2.24 | 1.89 | 4.13 |
| remove Dutch hip dormer | 1D@.019 | bf | — | .74 | .74 |
| Gambrel dormer, replace | 6C@.037 | bf | 2.30 | 1.84 | 4.14 |
| remove gambrel dormer | 1D@.023 | bf | — | .89 | .89 |

|  | Craft@Hrs | Unit | Material | Labor | Equip. | Total |
|---|---|---|---|---|---|---|

**Roof truss, per linear foot.** Add **10%** for treated trusses. Per lf of truss bottom chord. The lf price includes cat walks, diagonal braces, fasteners and rough fascia.

|  | Craft@Hrs | Unit | Material | Labor | Equip. | Total |
|---|---|---|---|---|---|---|
| Replace roof truss |  |  |  |  |  |  |
| flat roof | 6C@.023 | lf | 4.98 | 1.14 | .23 | 6.35 |
| 4/12 slope | 6C@.023 | lf | 5.25 | 1.14 | .23 | 6.62 |
| 6/12 slope | 6C@.023 | lf | 5.63 | 1.14 | .23 | 7.00 |
| 8/12 slope | 6C@.024 | lf | 7.61 | 1.19 | .23 | 9.03 |
| 10/12 slope | 6C@.024 | lf | 8.75 | 1.19 | .23 | 10.17 |
| 12/12 slope | 6C@.024 | lf | 10.20 | 1.19 | .23 | 11.62 |
| 14/12 slope | 6C@.025 | lf | 10.80 | 1.24 | .23 | 12.27 |
| 16/12 slope | 6C@.026 | lf | 11.60 | 1.29 | .23 | 13.12 |
| 17/12 slope | 6C@.028 | lf | 12.50 | 1.39 | .23 | 14.12 |
| Remove roof truss, all slopes | 1D@.042 | lf | — | 1.63 | — | 1.63 |

**Roof truss for heavy load, per linear foot.** For slate or tile roofing. Add **10%** for treated trusses. Per lf of truss bottom chord. The lf price includes cat walks, diagonal braces, fasteners and rough fascia.

|  | Craft@Hrs | Unit | Material | Labor | Equip. | Total |
|---|---|---|---|---|---|---|
| Replace |  |  |  |  |  |  |
| flat roof | 6C@.023 | lf | 5.28 | 1.14 | .23 | 6.65 |
| 4/12 slope | 6C@.023 | lf | 5.63 | 1.14 | .23 | 7.00 |
| 6/12 slope | 6C@.023 | lf | 5.98 | 1.14 | .23 | 7.35 |
| 8/12 slope | 6C@.024 | lf | 7.99 | 1.19 | .23 | 9.41 |
| 10/12 slope | 6C@.024 | lf | 9.15 | 1.19 | .23 | 10.57 |
| 12/12 slope | 6C@.024 | lf | 10.60 | 1.19 | .23 | 12.02 |
| 14/12 slope | 6C@.025 | lf | 11.20 | 1.24 | .23 | 12.67 |
| 16/12 slope | 6C@.026 | lf | 12.00 | 1.29 | .23 | 13.52 |
| 17/12 slope | 6C@.028 | lf | 13.00 | 1.39 | .23 | 14.62 |
| Remove roof truss, all slopes | 1D@.042 | lf | — | 1.63 | — | 1.63 |

| | Craft@Hrs | Unit | Material | Labor | Equip. | Total |
|---|---|---|---|---|---|---|

**Roof truss system, per square foot.** Add **10%** for treated trusses. Per sf of area underneath the roof. For roofs with asphalt, metal, or wood roofing. Includes cat walks, diagonal braces, fasteners and rough fascia.

| | Craft@Hrs | Unit | Material | Labor | Equip. | Total |
|---|---|---|---|---|---|---|
| 4/12 slope, replace | 6C@.012 | sf | 3.04 | .60 | .13 | 3.77 |
| remove | 1D@.017 | sf | — | .66 | — | .66 |
| 6/12 slope, replace | 6C@.012 | sf | 3.28 | .60 | .13 | 4.01 |
| remove | 1D@.018 | sf | — | .70 | — | .70 |
| 8/12 slope, replace | 6C@.012 | sf | 4.41 | .60 | .13 | 5.14 |
| remove | 1D@.021 | sf | — | .82 | — | .82 |
| 10/12 slope, replace | 6C@.013 | sf | 5.08 | .65 | .13 | 5.86 |
| remove | 1D@.025 | sf | — | .97 | — | .97 |
| 12/12 slope, replace | 6C@.013 | sf | 5.90 | .65 | .13 | 6.68 |
| remove | 1D@.034 | sf | — | 1.32 | — | 1.32 |
| 14/12 slope, replace | 6C@.013 | sf | 6.27 | .65 | .13 | 7.05 |
| remove | 1D@.040 | sf | — | 1.56 | — | 1.56 |
| 16/12 slope, replace | 6C@.013 | sf | 6.73 | .65 | .13 | 7.51 |
| remove | 1D@.053 | sf | — | 2.06 | — | 2.06 |
| 17/12 slope, replace | 6C@.013 | sf | 7.29 | .65 | .13 | 8.07 |
| remove | 1D@.082 | sf | — | 3.19 | — | 3.19 |

**Roof truss system for heavy load, per square foot.** Add **10%** for treated trusses. Per sf of area underneath the roof. For roofs with slate, tile or other heavy roofing. Includes cat walks, diagonal braces, fasteners and rough fascia.

| | Craft@Hrs | Unit | Material | Labor | Equip. | Total |
|---|---|---|---|---|---|---|
| 4/12 slope, replace | 6C@.012 | sf | 3.28 | .60 | .13 | 4.01 |
| remove | 1D@.017 | sf | — | .66 | — | .66 |
| 6/12 slope, replace | 6C@.012 | sf | 3.48 | .60 | .13 | 4.21 |
| remove | 1D@.018 | sf | — | .70 | — | .70 |
| 8/12 slope, replace | 6C@.012 | sf | 4.63 | .60 | .13 | 5.36 |
| remove | 1D@.021 | sf | — | .82 | — | .82 |
| 10/12 slope, replace | 6C@.013 | sf | 5.31 | .65 | .13 | 6.09 |
| remove | 1D@.025 | sf | — | .97 | — | .97 |
| 12/12 slope, replace | 6C@.013 | sf | 6.17 | .65 | .13 | 6.95 |
| remove | 1D@.034 | sf | — | 1.32 | — | 1.32 |
| 14/12 slope, replace | 6C@.013 | sf | 6.54 | .65 | .13 | 7.32 |
| remove | 1D@.040 | sf | — | 1.56 | — | 1.56 |
| 16/12 slope, replace | 6C@.013 | sf | 7.02 | .65 | .13 | 7.80 |
| remove | 1D@.053 | sf | — | 2.06 | — | 2.06 |
| 17/12 slope, replace | 6C@.013 | sf | 7.56 | .65 | .13 | 8.34 |
| remove | 1D@.082 | sf | — | 3.19 | — | 3.19 |

| | Craft@Hrs | Unit | Material | Labor | Total |
|---|---|---|---|---|---|

**Add for each lf of valley in truss roof, "California" fill.** Includes materials and labor for "California" fill between truss roofs with ridge board and jack rafters. Does not include sheathing.

| | Craft@Hrs | Unit | Material | Labor | Total |
|---|---|---|---|---|---|
| Replace only | 6C@.812 | lf | 31.20 | 40.40 | 71.60 |

**Add for each lf of hip or Dutch-hip in a truss roof system.** Includes additional cost for trusses designed to create a hip. Dutch-hip is stacked and hand framed.

| | Craft@Hrs | Unit | Material | Labor | Total |
|---|---|---|---|---|---|
| Replace only | | | | | |
| for hip | 6C@.360 | lf | 28.30 | 17.90 | 46.20 |
| for Dutch-hip | 6C@.407 | lf | 30.80 | 20.20 | 51.00 |

| | Craft@Hrs | Unit | Material | Labor | Total |
|---|---|---|---|---|---|

**Truss mansard roof system.** Add **10%** for treated trusses. Roof area equals the roof system width times height times length. Includes cat walks, diagonal braces, fasteners and rough fascia.

| | Craft@Hrs | Unit | Material | Labor | Total |
|---|---|---|---|---|---|
| Replace | | | | | |
|     asphalt, metal, or wood roofing | 6C@.003 | cf | .46 | .15 | .61 |
|     slate or tile roofing | 6C@.003 | cf | .57 | .15 | .72 |
| Remove, all types | 1D@.006 | sf | — | .23 | .23 |
| Add for each lf of valley in trussed mansard roof | 6C@.952 | lf | 30.90 | 47.30 | 78.20 |

**Truss gambrel roof system.** Add **10%** for treated trusses. Roof area equals the roof system width times height times length. Includes cat walks, diagonal braces, fasteners and rough fascia.

| | Craft@Hrs | Unit | Material | Labor | Total |
|---|---|---|---|---|---|
| Replace | | | | | |
|     asphalt, metal, or wood roofing | 6C@.003 | cf | .61 | .15 | .76 |
|     slate or tile roofing | 6C@.003 | cf | .68 | .15 | .83 |
| Remove, all types | 1D@.006 | sf | — | .23 | .23 |

**Add for each lf of valley in trussed gambrel roof.** Includes materials and labor to fill between truss roofs with ridge boards and jack rafters. Does not include sheathing. Replace only.

| | Craft@Hrs | Unit | Material | Labor | Total |
|---|---|---|---|---|---|
|     replace | 6C@1.16 | lf | 31.20 | 57.70 | 88.90 |

**Remove truss for work, then reinstall.**

| | Craft@Hrs | Unit | Material | Labor | Total |
|---|---|---|---|---|---|
|     replace, per lf | 6C@.091 | lf | — | 4.52 | 4.52 |

**Wall or roof sheathing.** Includes sheathing, nails, and installation. Also includes 4% waste.

| | Craft@Hrs | Unit | Material | Labor | Total |
|---|---|---|---|---|---|
| Fiberboard sheathing, replace | | | | | |
|     1/2" thick, replace | 6C@.015 | sf | .52 | .75 | 1.27 |
|     3/4" thick, replace | 6C@.015 | sf | .72 | .75 | 1.47 |
| Remove, all thicknesses | 1D@.012 | sf | — | .47 | .47 |
| Sound-deadening fiberboard sheathing | | | | | |
|     1/2", replace | 6C@.015 | sf | .51 | .75 | 1.26 |
|     remove | 1D@.012 | sf | — | .47 | .47 |
| Foil-faced foam sheathing, replace | | | | | |
|     1/2" thick | 6C@.015 | sf | .63 | .75 | 1.38 |
|     3/4" thick | 6C@.015 | sf | .84 | .75 | 1.59 |
|     1" thick | 6C@.016 | sf | 1.05 | .80 | 1.85 |
| Remove, all thicknesses | 1D@.012 | sf | — | .47 | .47 |
| CDX plywood sheathing, replace | | | | | |
|     3/8" thick | 6C@.016 | sf | .80 | .80 | 1.60 |
|     1/2" thick | 6C@.016 | sf | .73 | .80 | 1.53 |
|     5/8" thick | 6C@.016 | sf | 1.07 | .80 | 1.87 |
|     3/4" thick | 6C@.016 | sf | 1.30 | .80 | 2.10 |
| Remove, all thicknesses | 1D@.012 | sf | — | .47 | .47 |

|  | Craft@Hrs | Unit | Material | Labor | Total |
|---|---|---|---|---|---|
| Treated plywood sheathing, replace | | | | | |
| 1/2" thick | 6C@.016 | sf | .86 | .80 | 1.66 |
| 5/8" thick | 6C@.016 | sf | 1.24 | .80 | 2.04 |
| 3/4" thick | 6C@.016 | sf | 1.53 | .80 | 2.33 |
| Remove, all thicknesses | 1D@.012 | sf | — | .47 | .47 |
| Waferboard sheathing, replace | | | | | |
| 1/2" thick, replace | 6C@.016 | sf | .69 | .80 | 1.49 |
| 5/8" thick, replace | 6C@.016 | sf | 1.18 | .80 | 1.98 |
| Remove, all thicknesses | 1D@.012 | sf | — | .47 | .47 |
| Oriented strand board (OSB) sheathing, replace | | | | | |
| 1/2" thick, replace | 6C@.016 | sf | .76 | .80 | 1.56 |
| 5/8" thick, replace | 6C@.016 | sf | 1.18 | .80 | 1.98 |
| Remove, all thicknesses | 1D@.012 | sf | — | .47 | .47 |
| 3/4" tongue-&-groove sheathing, replace | | | | | |
| plywood | 6C@.016 | sf | 1.31 | .80 | 2.11 |
| waferboard | 6C@.016 | sf | 1.38 | .80 | 2.18 |
| oriented strand board (OSB) | 6C@.016 | sf | 1.39 | .80 | 2.19 |
| Remove, all types 3/4" T-&-G sheathing | 1D@.012 | sf | — | .47 | .47 |
| 1" x 6" S4S board sheathing | | | | | |
| replace | 6C@.017 | sf | 2.58 | .84 | 3.42 |
| remove | 1D@.014 | sf | — | .54 | .54 |
| 1" x 6" tongue-&-groove sheathing | | | | | |
| replace | 6C@.017 | sf | 4.04 | .84 | 4.88 |
| remove | 1D@.014 | sf | — | .54 | .54 |
| 2" x 6" tongue-&-groove sheathing | | | | | |
| replace | 6C@.017 | sf | 9.52 | .84 | 10.36 |
| remove | 1D@.016 | sf | — | .62 | .62 |
| 2" x 8" tongue-&-groove sheathing | | | | | |
| replace | 6C@.017 | sf | 6.23 | .84 | 7.07 |
| remove | 1D@.015 | sf | — | .58 | .58 |

**Add for shear-panel sheathing installation.** Includes shear paneling installed with nailing patterns and splicing according to code specifications for a shear panel.

|  | Craft@Hrs | Unit | Material | Labor | Total |
|---|---|---|---|---|---|
| replace | 6C@.003 | sf | — | .15 | .15 |

**Frame interior soffit.** Includes framing boards and nails. Interior soffits are often built around ducts, above cabinets, or for decorative purposes. Framework only. Includes fireblocking where required but does not include finish materials.

|  | Craft@Hrs | Unit | Material | Labor | Total |
|---|---|---|---|---|---|
| Frame interior soffit, two sides, replace | | | | | |
| typical | 6C@.059 | lf | 5.94 | 2.93 | 8.87 |
| with recess for indirect lighting | 6C@.100 | lf | 8.76 | 4.97 | 13.73 |
| Frame interior soffit, three sides, replace | | | | | |
| typical | 6C@.080 | lf | 7.93 | 3.98 | 11.91 |
| with recess for indirect lighting | 6C@.129 | lf | 9.59 | 6.41 | 16.00 |
| Remove interior soffit, all types | 1D@.045 | lf | — | 1.75 | 1.75 |

| | Craft@Hrs | Unit | Material | Labor | Equip. | Total |
|---|---|---|---|---|---|---|

**Factory designed and built structural panels.** Includes manufactured structural panel and installation between site-built framing members. Structural panels are often called stress-skin panels. Wall panels are installed with dimensional lumber top and bottom plates. Roof and floor panels must be installed between structural members. Does not include the cost for these structural members.

| | Craft@Hrs | Unit | Material | Labor | Equip. | Total |
|---|---|---|---|---|---|---|
| Factory-built structural wall panels, replace | | | | | | |
| 6" thick, replace | 6C@.051 | sf | 6.46 | 2.53 | .45 | 9.44 |
| 8" thick, replace | 6C@.052 | sf | 7.29 | 2.58 | .45 | 10.32 |
| 10" thick, replace | 6C@.054 | sf | 7.93 | 2.68 | .45 | 11.06 |
| 12" thick, replace | 6C@.054 | sf | 8.80 | 2.68 | .45 | 11.93 |
| Remove, all thicknesses | 1D@.007 | sf | — | .27 | — | .27 |
| Factory-built structural floor panels, replace | | | | | | |
| 6" thick, replace | 6C@.051 | sf | 6.94 | 2.53 | .45 | 9.92 |
| 8" thick, replace | 6C@.051 | sf | 7.76 | 2.53 | .45 | 10.74 |
| 10" thick, replace | 6C@.053 | sf | 8.52 | 2.63 | .45 | 11.60 |
| 12" thick, replace | 6C@.054 | sf | 9.40 | 2.68 | .43 | 12.51 |
| Remove, all thicknesses | 1D@.008 | sf | — | .31 | — | .31 |
| Factory-built structural roof panel, replace | | | | | | |
| 6" thick, replace | 6C@.061 | sf | 7.97 | 3.03 | .43 | 11.43 |
| 8" thick, replace | 6C@.062 | sf | 9.03 | 3.08 | .43 | 12.54 |
| 10" thick, replace | 6C@.063 | sf | 9.32 | 3.13 | .43 | 12.88 |
| 12" thick, replace | 6C@.066 | sf | 10.30 | 3.28 | .43 | 14.01 |
| Remove, all thicknesses | 1D@.015 | sf | — | .58 | — | .58 |

| | Craft@Hrs | Unit | Material | Labor | Total |
|---|---|---|---|---|---|

**Wood-frame chimney cricket.** Includes 5% waste.

| | Craft@Hrs | Unit | Material | Labor | Total |
|---|---|---|---|---|---|
| replace | 6C@.083 | sf | 1.75 | 4.13 | 5.88 |
| remove | 1D@.018 | sf | — | .70 | .70 |

*chimney cricket*

**Mail box.** Black, white, or grey.

| | Craft@Hrs | Unit | Material | Labor | Total |
|---|---|---|---|---|---|
| replace | 6C@.177 | ea | 13.40 | 8.80 | 22.20 |
| remove | 1D@.076 | ea | — | 2.96 | 2.96 |
| replace, mail box post | 1D@.817 | ea | 32.90 | 31.80 | 64.70 |
| remove | 1D@.429 | ea | — | 16.70 | 16.70 |
| replace, mail box with post | 1D@1.05 | ea | 46.20 | 40.80 | 87.00 |
| remove | 1D@.550 | ea | — | 21.40 | 21.40 |
| remove, then reinstall | 1D@.360 | ea | .36 | 14.00 | 14.36 |

| | Craft@Hrs | Unit | Material | Labor | Total |
|---|---|---|---|---|---|

**Time & Material Charts** (selected items)
**Rough Carpentry Materials**

| | Craft@Hrs | Unit | Material | Labor | Total |
|---|---|---|---|---|---|
| Lumber, random lengths per 1,000 bf | | | | | |
| #2 pine or better 2" wide framing lumber, ($1,190.00 per mbf, 1,000 bf), 7% waste | — | bf | 1.27 | — | 1.27 |
| #2 pine or better 1" wide framing lumber, ($1,450.00 per mbf, 1,000 bf), 7% waste | — | bf | 1.55 | — | 1.55 |
| #2 treated pine or better 2" wide framing lumber, ($1,490.00 per mbf, 1,000 bf), 7% waste | — | bf | 1.59 | — | 1.59 |
| redwood con common 2" wide framing lumber, ($2,430.00 per mbf, 1,000 bf), 7% waste | — | bf | 2.60 | — | 2.60 |
| redwood con heart 2" wide framing lumber, ($2,840.00 per mbf, 1,000 bf), 7% waste | — | bf | 3.04 | — | 3.04 |
| heavy oak timber, ($5,330.00 per mbf, 1,000 bf), 7% waste | — | bf | 5.70 | — | 5.70 |
| heavy pine timber, ($2,180.00 per mbf, 1,000 bf), 7% waste | — | bf | 2.33 | — | 2.33 |
| Fasteners and metal braces | | | | | |
| 16d gun nails, ($85.10 per box, 2,500 ea), 5% waste | — | ea | .03 | — | .03 |
| 12d gun nails, ($79.70 per box, 2,500 ea), 5% waste | — | ea | .03 | — | .03 |
| 2" gun staples, ($132.00 per box, 10,000 ea), 5% waste | — | ea | .01 | — | .01 |
| construction adhesive, per 29 ounce tube, ($8.51 per tube, 75 lf), 5% waste | — | lf | .12 | — | .12 |
| metal let-in brace with V shape for saw kerf, ($8.75 per 11.5' stick) | — | ea | 8.75 | — | 8.75 |
| metal X bracing for between joists, ($2.39 per 24" oc) | — | ea | 2.39 | — | 2.39 |
| Furring strips | | | | | |
| 1" x 2" x 8' #2 or better pine, ($1.70 ea, 8 lf), 5% waste | — | lf | .33 | — | .33 |
| 2" x 2" x 8' #2 or better pine, ($3.94 ea, 8 lf), 5% waste | — | lf | .51 | — | .51 |
| 2" x 2" x 8' con heart redwood, ($5.88 ea, 8 lf), 5% waste | — | lf | .78 | — | .78 |
| 2" x 2" x 8' con common redwood, ($5.08 ea, 8 lf), 5% waste | — | lf | .67 | — | .67 |
| #2 or better pine framing lumber | | | | | |
| 2" x 4", random lengths, ($6.31 ea, 8 lf), 5% waste | — | lf | .83 | — | .83 |
| 2" x 6", random lengths, ($9.11 ea, 8 lf), 5% waste | — | lf | 1.20 | — | 1.20 |
| 2" x 8", random lengths, 6 ($11.30 ea, 8 lf), 5% waste | — | lf | 1.48 | — | 1.48 |

| | Craft@Hrs | Unit | Material | Labor | Total |
|---|---|---|---|---|---|
| 2" x 10", random lengths, ($18.00 ea, 8 lf), 5% waste | — | lf | 2.36 | — | 2.36 |
| 2" x 12", random lengths, ($20.60 ea, 8 lf), 5% waste | — | lf | 2.71 | — | 2.71 |
| **Redwood framing lumber** | | | | | |
| 2" x 4" con heart, random lengths, ($14.10 ea, 8 lf), 5% waste | — | lf | 1.85 | — | 1.85 |
| 2" x 6" con heart, random lengths, ($16.80 ea, 8 lf), 5% waste | — | lf | 2.21 | — | 2.21 |
| 2" x 8" con heart, random lengths, ($25.00 ea, 8 lf), 5% waste | — | lf | 3.29 | — | 3.29 |
| 2" x 4" con common, random lengths, ($12.40 ea, 8 lf), 5% waste | — | lf | 1.63 | — | 1.63 |
| 2" x 6" con common, random lengths, ($14.20 ea, 8 lf), 5% waste | — | lf | 1.87 | — | 1.87 |
| 2" x 8" con common, random lengths, ($21.70 ea, 8 lf), 5% waste | — | lf | 2.85 | — | 2.85 |
| **Treated framing lumber** | | | | | |
| 2" x 4", random lengths, ($10.30 ea, 8 lf), 5% waste | — | lf | 1.35 | — | 1.35 |
| 2" x 6", random lengths, ($15.40 ea, 8 lf), 5% waste | — | lf | 2.03 | — | 2.03 |
| 2" x 8", random lengths, ($25.80 ea, 8 lf), 5% waste | — | lf | 3.39 | — | 3.39 |
| **Posts** | | | | | |
| 4" x 4" | | | | | |
| #2 or better pine, ($25.50 per 8' post), 4% waste | — | lf | 3.32 | — | 3.32 |
| construction common redwood, ($31.40 per 8' post), 4% waste | — | lf | 4.09 | — | 4.09 |
| treated pine, ($33.30 per 8' post), 4% waste | — | lf | 4.33 | — | 4.33 |
| 4" x 6" | | | | | |
| #2 or better pine, ($29.80 per 8' post), 4% waste | — | lf | 3.88 | — | 3.88 |
| construction common redwood, ($33.40 per 8' post), 4% waste | — | lf | 4.35 | — | 4.35 |
| treated pine, ($38.70 per 8' post), 4% waste | — | lf | 5.03 | — | 5.03 |
| 6" x 6" | | | | | |
| #2 or better pine, ($62.50 per 8' post), 4% waste | — | lf | 8.12 | — | 8.12 |
| construction common redwood, ($54.00 per 8' post), 4% waste | — | lf | 7.02 | — | 7.02 |
| treated pine, ($81.30 per 8' post), 4% waste | — | lf | 10.60 | — | 10.60 |
| 8" x 8" | | | | | |
| #2 or better pine, ($111.00 per 8' post), 4% waste | — | lf | 14.50 | — | 14.50 |
| con common redwood, ($96.20 per 8' post), 4% waste | — | lf | 12.50 | — | 12.50 |
| treated pine, ($143.00 per 8' post), 4% waste | — | lf | 18.60 | — | 18.60 |

| | Craft@Hrs | Unit | Material | Labor | Total |
|---|---|---|---|---|---|
| Adjustable steel jack post | | | | | |
| 51" to 90" to 13,000 pound load, ($64.10 ea) | — | ea | 64.10 | — | 64.10 |
| 20" to 36" to 16,000 pound load, ($42.00 ea) | — | ea | 42.00 | — | 42.00 |
| 37" to 60" to 17,500 pound load, ($52.90 ea) | — | ea | 52.90 | — | 52.90 |
| 56" to 96" to 25,000 pound load, ($82.40 ea) | — | ea | 82.40 | — | 82.40 |
| Lally column | | | | | |
| 3-1/2" diameter, 6' to 8', ($93.40 ea) | — | ea | 93.40 | — | 93.40 |
| 3-1/2" diameter, 8' to 10', ($105.00 ea) | — | ea | 105.00 | — | 105.00 |
| 3-1/2" diameter, 10' to 12', ($132.00 ea) | — | ea | 132.00 | — | 132.00 |
| Glue-laminated beam | | | | | |
| per bf, ($5.31 bf, 1 bf), 3% waste | — | bf | 5.47 | — | 5.47 |
| Micro-laminated beam | | | | | |
| 1-3/4" x 9-1/2", ($7.89 lf, 1 lf), 4% waste | — | lf | 8.21 | — | 8.21 |
| 1-3/4" x 11-7/8", ($9.91 lf, 1 lf), 4% waste | — | lf | 10.30 | — | 10.30 |
| 1-3/4" x 14", ($11.60 lf, 1 lf), 4% waste | — | lf | 12.10 | — | 12.10 |
| 1-3/4" x 18", ($14.90 lf, 1 lf), 4% waste | — | lf | 15.50 | — | 15.50 |
| Beams, select structural grade, per bf | | | | | |
| pine, ($2.18 bf, 1 bf), 4% waste | — | bf | 2.27 | — | 2.27 |
| oak, ($5.33 bf, 1 bf), 4% waste | — | bf | 5.54 | — | 5.54 |
| Laminated lumber I joist | | | | | |
| 1-3/4" flange, 9-1/2" deep, ($2.73 lf, 1 lf), 3% waste | — | lf | 2.81 | — | 2.81 |
| 1-3/4" flange, 11-7/8" deep, ($3.33 lf, 1 lf), 3% waste | — | lf | 3.43 | — | 3.43 |
| 1-3/4" flange, 14" deep, ($4.09 lf, 1 lf), 3% waste | — | lf | 4.21 | — | 4.21 |
| 2-5/16" flange, 11-7/8" deep, ($4.72 lf, 1 lf), 3% waste | — | lf | 4.86 | — | 4.86 |
| Floor truss | | | | | |
| typical loading, ($4.98 lf) | — | lf | 4.98 | — | 4.98 |
| heavy loading, ($5.37 lf) | — | lf | 5.37 | — | 5.37 |
| Roof truss | | | | | |
| flat, ($4.97 lf) | — | lf | 4.97 | — | 4.97 |
| 4 in 12 slope, ($5.25 lf) | — | lf | 5.25 | — | 5.25 |
| 8 in 12 slope, ($7.61 lf) | — | lf | 7.61 | — | 7.61 |
| 12 in 12 slope, ($10.20 lf) | — | lf | 10.20 | — | 10.20 |
| 17 in 12 slope, ($12.60 lf) | — | lf | 12.60 | — | 12.60 |
| Roof or wall sheathing | | | | | |
| 1/2" fiberboard, ($16.20 per 8' sheet, 32 sf), 4% waste | — | sf | .53 | — | .53 |
| 3/4" fiberboard ($22.20 per 8' sheet, 32 sf), 4% waste | — | sf | .72 | — | .72 |
| 1/2" foil-faced foam, ($19.50 per 8' sheet, 32 sf), 4% waste | — | sf | .63 | — | .63 |
| 3/4" foil-faced foam, ($24.90 per 8' sheet, 32 sf), 4% waste | — | sf | .81 | — | .81 |
| 1" foil-faced foam, ($32.40 per 8' sheet, 32 sf), 4% waste | — | sf | 1.05 | — | 1.05 |

| | Craft@Hrs | Unit | Material | Labor | Total |
|---|---|---|---|---|---|
| 1/2" CDX plywood, ($22.30 per 8' sheet, 32 sf), 4% waste | — | sf | .73 | — | .73 |
| 1/2" waferboard, ($20.70 per 8' sheet, 32 sf), 4% waste | — | sf | .68 | — | .68 |
| 1/2" oriented strand board (OSB), ($23.50 per 8' sheet, 32 sf), 4% waste | — | sf | .75 | — | .75 |
| 5/8" CDX plywood, ($32.90 per 8' sheet, 32 sf), 4% waste | — | sf | 1.07 | — | 1.07 |
| 5/8" waferboard, ($36.10 per 8' sheet, 32 sf), 4% waste | — | sf | 1.18 | — | 1.18 |
| 5/8" oriented strand board (OSB), ($36.40 per 8' sheet, 32 sf), 4% waste | — | sf | 1.19 | — | 1.19 |
| 3/4" CDX plywood, ($40.20 per 8' sheet, 32 sf), 4% waste | — | sf | 1.31 | — | 1.31 |
| 3/4" tongue-&-groove plywood, ($40.50 per 8' sheet, 32 sf), 4% waste | — | sf | 1.32 | — | 1.32 |
| 3/4" tongue-&-groove waferboard, ($42.80 per 8' sheet, 32 sf), 4% waste | — | sf | 1.39 | — | 1.39 |
| 3/4" tongue-&-groove oriented strand board (OSB), ($43.00 per 8' sheet, 32 sf), 4% waste | — | sf | 1.39 | — | 1.39 |
| 1" x 6" tongue-&-groove sheathing, ($1.95 lf, .50 sf), 4% waste | — | sf | 4.06 | — | 4.06 |
| 2" x 6" tongue-&-groove sheathing, ($4.57 lf, .50 sf), 4% waste | — | sf | 9.51 | — | 9.51 |
| Factory designed and fabricated building panel | | | | | |
| 6" thick wall panel, ($6.46 sf) | — | sf | 6.46 | — | 6.46 |
| 8" thick wall panel, ($7.29 sf) | — | sf | 7.29 | — | 7.29 |
| 10" thick floor panel, ($8.52 sf) | — | sf | 8.52 | — | 8.52 |
| 12" thick floor panel, ($9.40 sf) | — | sf | 9.40 | — | 9.40 |
| 6" thick roof panel, ($7.97 sf) | — | sf | 7.97 | — | 7.97 |
| 8" thick roof panel, ($9.03 sf) | — | sf | 9.03 | — | 9.03 |

## Rough Carpentry Labor

| Laborer | base wage | paid leave | true wage | taxes & ins. | total |
|---|---|---|---|---|---|
| Carpenter | $31.10 | 2.43 | $33.53 | 23.37 | $56.90 |
| Carpenter's helper | $22.40 | 1.75 | $24.15 | 18.25 | $42.40 |
| Post & beam carpenter | $40.20 | 3.14 | $43.34 | 28.66 | $72.00 |
| P & B carpenter's helper | $27.20 | 2.16 | $29.86 | 21.34 | $51.20 |
| Equipment operator | $42.30 | 3.30 | $45.60 | 29.10 | $74.70 |
| Demolition laborer | $20.70 | 1.61 | $22.31 | 16.59 | $38.90 |

**Paid leave** is calculated based on two weeks paid vacation, one week sick leave, and seven paid holidays. Employer's matching portion of **FICA** is 7.65 percent. **FUTA** (Federal Unemployment) is .8 percent. **Worker's compensation** for the rough carpentry trade was calculated using a national average of 16.85 percent. **Unemployment insurance** was calculated using a national average of 8 percent. **Health insurance** was calculated based on a projected national average for 2015 of $1,025 per employee (and family when applicable) per month. Employer pays 80 percent for a per month cost of $820 per employee. **Retirement** is based on a 401(k) retirement program with employer matching of 50 percent. Employee contributions to the 401(k) plan are an average of 6 percent of the true wage. **Liability insurance** is based on a national average of 10.0 percent.

|  | Craft@Hrs | Unit | Material | Labor | Total |
|---|---|---|---|---|---|
| **Rough Carpentry Labor Productivity** | | | | | |
| Demolition of rough carpentry | | | | | |
| remove 2" x 4" wall, 8' tall | 1D@.045 | lf | — | 1.75 | 1.75 |
| remove 2" x 6" wall, 8' tall | 1D@.048 | lf | — | 1.87 | 1.87 |
| remove 2" x 8" wall, 8' tall | 1D@.049 | lf | — | 1.91 | 1.91 |
| remove wood post | 1D@.059 | lf | — | 2.30 | 2.30 |
| remove glue-laminated beam | 1D@.222 | lf | — | 8.64 | 8.64 |
| remove micro-laminated beam | 1D@.106 | lf | — | 4.12 | 4.12 |
| remove sheathing | 1D@.012 | sf | — | .47 | .47 |
| remove beam | 1D@.222 | lf | — | 8.64 | 8.64 |
| remove deck planking | 1D@.026 | sf | — | 1.01 | 1.01 |
| remove deck railing | 1D@.034 | lf | — | 1.32 | 1.32 |
| remove deck stairway per step | 1D@.061 | ea | — | 2.37 | 2.37 |
| remove furring strips applied to wood | 1D@.011 | sf | — | .43 | .43 |
| remove joist system | 1D@.014 | sf | — | .54 | .54 |
| remove floor truss system | 1D@.014 | lf | — | .54 | .54 |
| remove hand-framed roof, 4 in 12 slope | 1D@.016 | sf | — | .62 | .62 |
| remove hand-framed roof, 8 in 12 slope | 1D@.019 | sf | — | .74 | .74 |
| remove hand-framed roof, 12 in 12 slope | 1D@.032 | sf | — | 1.24 | 1.24 |
| remove hand-framed roof, 16 in 12 slope | 1D@.050 | sf | — | 1.95 | 1.95 |
| remove hand-framed roof, 18 in 12 slope | 1D@.077 | sf | — | 3.00 | 3.00 |
| remove flat roof truss | 1D@.016 | sf | — | .62 | .62 |
| remove truss roof, 4 in 12 slope | 1D@.017 | sf | — | .66 | .66 |
| remove truss roof, 8 in 12 slope | 1D@.021 | sf | — | .82 | .82 |
| remove truss roof, 12 in 12 slope | 1D@.034 | sf | — | 1.32 | 1.32 |
| remove truss roof, 16 in 12 slope | 1D@.053 | sf | — | 2.06 | 2.06 |
| remove truss roof, 17 in 12 slope | 1D@.082 | sf | — | 3.19 | 3.19 |
| remove hand-framed dormer, 4 in 12 slope | 1D@.017 | sf | — | .66 | .66 |
| remove hand-framed dormer, 10 in 12 slope | 1D@.025 | sf | — | .97 | .97 |
| remove hand-framed dormer, 18 in 12 slope | 1D@.081 | sf | — | 3.15 | 3.15 |
| remove prefabricated structural wall panel | 1D@.007 | sf | — | .27 | .27 |
| remove prefabricated structural floor panel | 1D@.008 | sf | — | .31 | .31 |
| remove prefabricated structural roof panel | 1D@.015 | sf | — | .58 | .58 |

**Framing crew**

| | | | | | |
|---|---|---|---|---|---|
| rough carpentry | carpenter | $56.90 | | | |
| rough carpentry | carpenter's helper | $42.40 | | | |
| rough carpentry | framing crew | $49.70 | | | |

**Post & beam framing crew**

| | | | | | |
|---|---|---|---|---|---|
| post & beam framing | carpenter | $72.00 | | | |
| post & beam framing | carpenter's helper | $51.20 | | | |
| post & beam framing | post & beam crew | $61.20 | | | |

Build interior partition wall

| | Craft@Hrs | Unit | Material | Labor | Total |
|---|---|---|---|---|---|
| 2" x 4" 8' tall 16" on center | 6C@.241 | lf | — | 12.00 | 12.00 |
| 2" x 4" 10' tall 16" on center | 6C@.244 | lf | — | 12.10 | 12.10 |
| 2" x 6" 8' tall 16" on center | 6C@.244 | lf | — | 12.10 | 12.10 |
| 2" x 6" 10' tall 16" on center | 6C@.247 | lf | — | 12.30 | 12.30 |
| 2" x 8" 8' tall 16" on center | 6C@.247 | lf | — | 12.30 | 12.30 |
| 2" x 8" 10' tall 16" on center | 6C@.250 | lf | — | 12.40 | 12.40 |

| | Craft@Hrs | Unit | Material | Labor | Total |
|---|---|---|---|---|---|
| **Build interior bearing wall** | | | | | |
| 2" x 4" 8' tall 16" on center | 6C@.261 | lf | — | 13.00 | 13.00 |
| 2" x 4" 10' tall 16" on center | 6C@.265 | lf | — | 13.20 | 13.20 |
| 2" x 6" 8' tall 16" on center | 6C@.263 | lf | — | 13.10 | 13.10 |
| 2" x 6" 10' tall 16" on center | 6C@.267 | lf | — | 13.30 | 13.30 |
| 2" x 8" 8' tall 16" on center | 6C@.266 | lf | — | 13.20 | 13.20 |
| 2" x 8" 10' tall 16" on center | 6C@.270 | lf | — | 13.40 | 13.40 |
| **Build exterior wall** | | | | | |
| 2" x 4" 8' tall 16" on center | 6C@.267 | lf | — | 13.30 | 13.30 |
| 2" x 4" 10' tall 16" on center | 6C@.270 | lf | — | 13.40 | 13.40 |
| 2" x 6" 8' tall 16" on center | 6C@.270 | lf | — | 13.40 | 13.40 |
| 2" x 6" 10' tall 16" on center | 6C@.272 | lf | — | 13.50 | 13.50 |
| 2" x 8" 8' tall 16" on center | 6C@.272 | lf | — | 13.50 | 13.50 |
| 2" x 8" 10' tall 16" on center | 6C@.275 | lf | — | 13.70 | 13.70 |
| **Build interior partition wall per sf** | | | | | |
| 2" x 4" 16" on center | 6C@.030 | sf | — | 1.49 | 1.49 |
| 2" x 6" 16" on center | 6C@.030 | sf | — | 1.49 | 1.49 |
| 2" x 8" 16" on center | 6C@.031 | sf | — | 1.54 | 1.54 |
| **Build sloping interior partition wall per sf** | | | | | |
| 2" x 4" 16" on center | 6C@.041 | sf | — | 2.04 | 2.04 |
| 2" x 6" 16" on center | 6C@.042 | sf | — | 2.09 | 2.09 |
| 2" x 8" 16" on center | 6C@.042 | sf | — | 2.09 | 2.09 |
| **Build sloping interior bearing wall per sf** | | | | | |
| 2" x 4" 16" on center | 6C@.050 | sf | — | 2.49 | 2.49 |
| 2" x 6" 16" on center | 6C@.050 | sf | — | 2.49 | 2.49 |
| 2" x 8" 16" on center | 6C@.051 | sf | — | 2.53 | 2.53 |
| **Build interior bearing wall per sf** | | | | | |
| 2" x 4" 16" on center | 6C@.033 | sf | — | 1.64 | 1.64 |
| 2" x 6" 16" on center | 6C@.033 | sf | — | 1.64 | 1.64 |
| 2" x 8" 16" on center | 6C@.033 | sf | — | 1.64 | 1.64 |
| **Build exterior wall per sf** | | | | | |
| 2" x 4" 16" on center | 6C@.034 | sf | — | 1.69 | 1.69 |
| 2" x 6" 16" on center | 6C@.034 | sf | — | 1.69 | 1.69 |
| 2" x 8" 16" on center | 6C@.034 | sf | — | 1.69 | 1.69 |
| **Build sloping exterior wall per sf** | | | | | |
| 2" x 4" 16" on center | 6C@.046 | sf | — | 2.29 | 2.29 |
| 2" x 6" 16" on center | 6C@.046 | sf | — | 2.29 | 2.29 |
| 2" x 8" 16" on center | 6C@.047 | sf | — | 2.34 | 2.34 |
| **Build walls per bf** | | | | | |
| interior wall | 6C@.034 | bf | — | 1.69 | 1.69 |
| sloping interior wall | 6C@.047 | bf | — | 2.34 | 2.34 |
| exterior wall | 6C@.037 | bf | — | 1.84 | 1.84 |
| sloping exterior wall | 6C@.051 | bf | — | 2.53 | 2.53 |
| **Build and install wall header** | | | | | |
| (Made from 2" x dimension lumber and 1/2" cdx plywood) | | | | | |
| 4" x 10" header | 6C@.043 | lf | — | 2.14 | 2.14 |
| 4" x 12" header | 6C@.045 | lf | — | 2.24 | 2.24 |
| 6" x 10" header | 6C@.069 | lf | — | 3.43 | 3.43 |
| 6" x 12" header | 6C@.074 | lf | — | 3.68 | 3.68 |

| | Craft@Hrs | Unit | Material | Labor | Total |
|---|---|---|---|---|---|
| **Install posts** | | | | | |
| 4" x 4" post | 6C@.042 | lf | — | 2.09 | 2.09 |
| 6" x 6" post | 6C@.044 | lf | — | 2.19 | 2.19 |
| 8" x 8" post | 6C@.048 | lf | — | 2.39 | 2.39 |
| **Install adjustable steel jackpost** | | | | | |
| 20" to 36" adjustable | 6C@.243 | ea | — | 12.10 | 12.10 |
| 37" to 60" adjustable | 6C@.272 | ea | — | 13.50 | 13.50 |
| 48" to 100" adjustable | 6C@.386 | ea | — | 19.20 | 19.20 |
| 56" to 96" adjustable | 6C@.352 | ea | — | 17.50 | 17.50 |
| **Install lally column** | | | | | |
| 3-1/2" diameter, 6' to 8' | 6C@.526 | ea | — | 26.10 | 26.10 |
| 3-1/2" diameter, 8' to 10' | 6C@.556 | ea | — | 27.60 | 27.60 |
| 3-1/2" diameter, 10' to 12' | 6C@.587 | ea | — | 29.20 | 29.20 |
| **Install glue-laminated beam** | | | | | |
| per bf | 6C@.060 | bf | — | 2.98 | 2.98 |
| **Install micro-laminated beam** | | | | | |
| 1-3/4" x 7-1/4" | 6C@.048 | lf | — | 2.39 | 2.39 |
| 1-3/4" x 9-1/2" | 6C@.050 | lf | — | 2.49 | 2.49 |
| 1-3/4" x 11-7/8" | 6C@.053 | lf | — | 2.63 | 2.63 |
| 1-3/4" x 14" | 6C@.056 | lf | — | 2.78 | 2.78 |
| 1-3/4" x 18" | 6C@.063 | lf | — | 3.13 | 3.13 |
| **Install beam** | | | | | |
| 4" x 10" | 6C@.114 | lf | — | 5.67 | 5.67 |
| 4" x 12" | 6C@.149 | lf | — | 7.41 | 7.41 |
| 6" x 10" | 6C@.132 | lf | — | 6.56 | 6.56 |
| 6" x 12" | 6C@.154 | lf | — | 7.65 | 7.65 |
| 8" x 10" | 6C@.156 | lf | — | 7.75 | 7.75 |
| 8" x 12" | 6C@.182 | lf | — | 9.05 | 9.05 |
| 10" x 10" | 6C@.176 | lf | — | 8.75 | 8.75 |
| 10" x 12" | 6C@.196 | lf | — | 9.74 | 9.74 |
| 12" x 12" | 6C@.204 | lf | — | 10.10 | 10.10 |
| 12" x 16" | 6C@.222 | lf | — | 11.00 | 11.00 |

## Post & beam framing

| | Craft@Hrs | Unit | Material | Labor | Total |
|---|---|---|---|---|---|
| **Cut and assemble bent with truss** | | | | | |
| single-story with simple truss | 4B@.527 | sf | — | 32.50 | 32.50 |
| two-story with simple truss | 4B@.571 | sf | — | 35.20 | 35.20 |
| single-story with king post truss | 4B@.569 | sf | — | 35.10 | 35.10 |
| two-story with king post truss | 4B@.620 | sf | — | 38.20 | 38.20 |
| single-story with king post & struts truss | 4B@.618 | sf | — | 38.10 | 38.10 |
| two-story with king post & struts truss | 4B@.679 | sf | — | 41.80 | 41.80 |
| single-story with queen post truss | 4B@.609 | sf | — | 37.50 | 37.50 |
| two-story with queen post truss | 4B@.671 | sf | — | 41.30 | 41.30 |
| single-story with hammer beam truss | 4B@1.05 | sf | — | 64.70 | 64.70 |
| two-story with hammer beam truss | 4B@1.25 | sf | — | 77.00 | 77.00 |
| single-story with scissors truss | 4B@.989 | sf | — | 60.90 | 60.90 |
| two-story with scissors truss | 4B@1.04 | sf | — | 64.10 | 64.10 |
| add for overhang drop in two-story bent | 4B@20.0 | ea | — | 1,230.00 | 1,230.00 |

| | Craft@Hrs | Unit | Material | Labor | Total |
|---|---|---|---|---|---|
| Cut and assemble connecting members between bent (per sf of area beneath) | | | | | |
| between single-story bents | 4B@1.11 | sf | — | 68.40 | 68.40 |
| Cut post & beam framing joint and join timbers | | | | | |
| sill corner half-lap | 2B@1.10 | ea | — | 79.20 | 79.20 |
| sill corner half-lap with through tenon | 2B@2.77 | ea | — | 199.00 | 199.00 |
| sill corner dovetail | 2B@1.99 | ea | — | 143.00 | 143.00 |
| sill corner dovetail with through tenon | 2B@3.86 | ea | — | 278.00 | 278.00 |
| sill corner tongue & fork | 2B@1.79 | ea | — | 129.00 | 129.00 |
| sill corner tongue & fork with through tenon | 2B@3.44 | ea | — | 248.00 | 248.00 |
| lapped dovetail | 2B@2.05 | ea | — | 148.00 | 148.00 |
| housed lapped dovetail | 2B@2.55 | ea | — | 184.00 | 184.00 |
| tusk tenon | 2B@2.77 | ea | — | 199.00 | 199.00 |
| half-lap | 2B@1.08 | ea | — | 77.80 | 77.80 |
| through mortise & tenon with shoulders | 2B@2.26 | ea | — | 163.00 | 163.00 |
| housed mortise & tenon | 2B@2.37 | ea | — | 171.00 | 171.00 |
| shouldered mortise & tenon | 2B@2.34 | ea | — | 168.00 | 168.00 |
| wedged dovetail mortise & tenon | 2B@2.37 | ea | — | 171.00 | 171.00 |
| mortise & tenon (90 degree) | 2B@1.25 | ea | — | 90.00 | 90.00 |
| anchor-beam | 2B@2.93 | ea | — | 211.00 | 211.00 |
| framed overhang | 2B@10.0 | ea | — | 720.00 | 720.00 |
| through half-lap | 2B@1.20 | ea | — | 86.40 | 86.40 |
| mortise & tenon knee brace (45 degree) | 2B@1.56 | ea | — | 112.00 | 112.00 |
| collar tie lapped half dovetail | 2B@1.96 | ea | — | 141.00 | 141.00 |
| stopped splayed scarf | 2B@3.22 | ea | — | 232.00 | 232.00 |
| stopped splayed scarf with through tenon | 2B@5.00 | ea | — | 360.00 | 360.00 |
| bladed scarf | 2B@2.45 | ea | — | 176.00 | 176.00 |
| bladed scarf with through tenon | 2B@4.35 | ea | — | 313.00 | 313.00 |
| rafter foot housed bird's mouth | 2B@1.39 | ea | — | 100.00 | 100.00 |
| rafter foot beveled shoulder bird's mouth | 2B@1.30 | ea | — | 93.60 | 93.60 |
| rafter foot bird's mouth, purlin, & post joint | 2B@3.13 | ea | — | 225.00 | 225.00 |
| rafter foot bird's mouth joint | 2B@1.00 | ea | — | 72.00 | 72.00 |
| rafter foot bird's mouth with tenon | 2B@2.86 | ea | — | 206.00 | 206.00 |
| rafter peak tongue & fork | 2B@1.79 | ea | — | 129.00 | 129.00 |
| Build joist system for outdoor deck | | | | | |
| (with support beams, posts and concrete footing) | | | | | |
| 2" x 8" joists | 6C@.071 | sf | — | 3.53 | 3.53 |
| 2" x 10" joists | 6C@.077 | sf | — | 3.83 | 3.83 |
| 2" x 12" joists | 6C@.083 | sf | — | 4.13 | 4.13 |
| Install outdoor deck planking per sf | | | | | |
| 2" x 4" | 6C@.040 | sf | — | 1.99 | 1.99 |
| 2" x 6" | 6C@.037 | sf | — | 1.84 | 1.84 |
| 2" x 8" | 6C@.033 | sf | — | 1.64 | 1.64 |
| Install deck railing and stairs | | | | | |
| deck railing | 6C@.275 | lf | — | 13.70 | 13.70 |
| 3' wide deck stairs with balustrades | 6C@.587 | ea | — | 29.20 | 29.20 |
| deck stairway landing per sf | 6C@.074 | sf | — | 3.68 | 3.68 |

| | Craft@Hrs | Unit | Material | Labor | Total |
|---|---|---|---|---|---|
| Install furring strips | | | | | |
| on wood 16" on center | 6C@.013 | sf | — | .65 | .65 |
| on wood 24" on center | 6C@.011 | sf | — | .55 | .55 |
| on masonry or concrete 16" on center | 6C@.016 | sf | — | .80 | .80 |
| on masonry or concrete 24" on center | 6C@.014 | sf | — | .70 | .70 |
| Build joist systems with blocking and cross bracing | | | | | |
| per bf | 6C@.021 | bf | — | 1.04 | 1.04 |
| Install laminated lumber I truss | | | | | |
| 1-3/4" flange,11-7/8" deep | 6C@.036 | lf | — | 1.79 | 1.79 |
| 1-3/4" flange,14" deep | 6C@.037 | lf | — | 1.84 | 1.84 |
| 2-5/16" flange,11-7/8" deep | 6C@.036 | lf | — | 1.79 | 1.79 |
| 2-5/16" flange,14" deep | 6C@.038 | lf | — | 1.89 | 1.89 |
| 2-5/16" flange,16" deep | 6C@.039 | lf | — | 1.94 | 1.94 |
| Install floor truss | | | | | |
| typical | 6C@.091 | lf | — | 4.52 | 4.52 |
| Hand-frame roof, 24" on center | | | | | |
| Hand-frame roof with 2" x 4" rafters | | | | | |
| 4 in 12 slope | 6C@.034 | sf | — | 1.69 | 1.69 |
| 8 in 12 slope | 6C@.040 | sf | — | 1.99 | 1.99 |
| 12 in 12 slope | 6C@.049 | sf | — | 2.44 | 2.44 |
| 16 in 12 slope | 6C@.060 | sf | — | 2.98 | 2.98 |
| Hand-frame roof with 2" x 6" rafters | | | | | |
| 4 in 12 slope | 6C@.035 | sf | — | 1.74 | 1.74 |
| 8 in 12 slope | 6C@.042 | sf | — | 2.09 | 2.09 |
| 12 in 12 slope | 6C@.051 | sf | — | 2.53 | 2.53 |
| 16 in 12 slope | 6C@.062 | sf | — | 3.08 | 3.08 |
| Hand-frame roof with 2" x 8" rafters | | | | | |
| 4 in 12 slope | 6C@.036 | sf | — | 1.79 | 1.79 |
| 8 in 12 slope | 6C@.043 | sf | — | 2.14 | 2.14 |
| 12 in 12 slope | 6C@.052 | sf | — | 2.58 | 2.58 |
| 16 in 12 slope | 6C@.064 | sf | — | 3.18 | 3.18 |
| Hand-frame roof with 2" x 10" rafters | | | | | |
| 4 in 12 slope | 6C@.037 | sf | — | 1.84 | 1.84 |
| 8 in 12 slope | 6C@.044 | sf | — | 2.19 | 2.19 |
| 12 in 12 slope | 6C@.054 | sf | — | 2.68 | 2.68 |
| 16 in 12 slope | 6C@.066 | sf | — | 3.28 | 3.28 |
| Hand-frame roof with 2" x 12" rafters | | | | | |
| 4 in 12 slope | 6C@.038 | sf | — | 1.89 | 1.89 |
| 8 in 12 slope | 6C@.046 | sf | — | 2.29 | 2.29 |
| 12 in 12 slope | 6C@.056 | sf | — | 2.78 | 2.78 |
| 16 in 12 slope | 6C@.068 | sf | — | 3.38 | 3.38 |
| Additional hand-framed roof labor costs | | | | | |
| add for each lf of valley | 6C@.786 | lf | — | 39.10 | 39.10 |
| add for each lf of hip width | 6C@.212 | lf | — | 10.50 | 10.50 |
| add for each lf of Dutch hip width | 6C@.229 | lf | — | 11.40 | 11.40 |
| Hand-frame mansard roof, 24" on center  (per cf of roof) | | | | | |
| 2" x 4" rafters | 6C@.005 | cf | — | .25 | .25 |
| 2" x 8" rafters | 6C@.005 | cf | — | .25 | .25 |
| 2" x 12" rafters | 6C@.006 | cf | — | .30 | .30 |
| add for each lf of valley | 6C@1.08 | lf | — | 53.70 | 53.70 |

| | Craft@Hrs | Unit | Material | Labor | Total |
|---|---|---|---|---|---|
| **Hand-frame gambrel roof, 24" on center (per cf of roof)** | | | | | |
| 2" x 4" rafters | 6C@.004 | cf | — | .20 | .20 |
| 2" x 8" rafters | 6C@.005 | cf | — | .25 | .25 |
| 2" x 12" rafters | 6C@.006 | cf | — | .30 | .30 |
| add for each lf of valley | 6C@1.14 | lf | — | 56.70 | 56.70 |
| **Hand-frame roof per bf** | | | | | |
| gable roof | 6C@.023 | bf | — | 1.14 | 1.14 |
| hip roof | 6C@.023 | bf | — | 1.14 | 1.14 |
| Dutch hip roof | 6C@.024 | bf | — | 1.19 | 1.19 |
| mansard roof | 6C@.026 | bf | — | 1.29 | 1.29 |
| gambrel roof | 6C@.025 | bf | — | 1.24 | 1.24 |
| **Hand-frame dormer, 24" on center** | | | | | |
| shed dormer | | | | | |
| 4 in 12 slope | 6C@.045 | sf | — | 2.24 | 2.24 |
| 8 in 12 slope | 6C@.049 | sf | — | 2.44 | 2.44 |
| 12 in 12 slope | 6C@.060 | sf | — | 2.98 | 2.98 |
| 16 in 12 slope | 6C@.064 | sf | — | 3.18 | 3.18 |
| gable dormer | | | | | |
| 4 in 12 slope | 6C@.047 | sf | — | 2.34 | 2.34 |
| 8 in 12 slope | 6C@.051 | sf | — | 2.53 | 2.53 |
| 12 in 12 slope | 6C@.062 | sf | — | 3.08 | 3.08 |
| 16 in 12 slope | 6C@.067 | sf | — | 3.33 | 3.33 |
| hip dormer | | | | | |
| 4 in 12 slope | 6C@.049 | sf | — | 2.44 | 2.44 |
| 8 in 12 slope | 6C@.053 | sf | — | 2.63 | 2.63 |
| 12 in 12 slope | 6C@.065 | sf | — | 3.23 | 3.23 |
| 16 in 12 slope | 6C@.070 | sf | — | 3.48 | 3.48 |
| Dutch hip dormer | | | | | |
| 4 in 12 slope | 6C@.051 | sf | — | 2.53 | 2.53 |
| 8 in 12 slope | 6C@.054 | sf | — | 2.68 | 2.68 |
| 12 in 12 slope | 6C@.067 | sf | — | 3.33 | 3.33 |
| 16 in 12 slope | 6C@.072 | sf | — | 3.58 | 3.58 |
| gambrel dormer | | | | | |
| per length of ridge x width of dormer | 6C@.059 | sf | — | 2.93 | 2.93 |
| **Hand-frame dormer, per bf** | | | | | |
| shed dormer | 6C@.034 | bf | — | 1.69 | 1.69 |
| gable dormer | 6C@.035 | bf | — | 1.74 | 1.74 |
| hip dormer | 6C@.036 | bf | — | 1.79 | 1.79 |
| Dutch-hip dormer | 6C@.038 | bf | — | 1.89 | 1.89 |
| gambrel dormer | 6C@.037 | bf | — | 1.84 | 1.84 |
| **Install roof truss** | | | | | |
| flat roof | 6C@.023 | lf | — | 1.14 | 1.14 |
| 4 in 12 slope | 6C@.023 | lf | — | 1.14 | 1.14 |
| 8 in 12 slope | 6C@.024 | lf | — | 1.19 | 1.19 |
| 12 in 12 slope | 6C@.024 | lf | — | 1.19 | 1.19 |
| 16 in 12 slope | 6C@.026 | lf | — | 1.29 | 1.29 |

| | Craft@Hrs | Unit | Material | Labor | Total |
|---|---|---|---|---|---|
| Install truss system, 24" on center, per sf | | | | | |
| 4 in 12 slope | 6C@.012 | sf | — | .60 | .60 |
| 8 in 12 slope | 6C@.012 | sf | — | .60 | .60 |
| 12 in 12 slope | 6C@.013 | sf | — | .65 | .65 |
| 16 in 12 slope | 6C@.013 | sf | — | .65 | .65 |
| Additional truss roof costs | | | | | |
| add labor for each lf of valley | 6C@.812 | lf | — | 40.40 | 40.40 |
| add labor for each lf of width in a hip | 6C@.360 | lf | — | 17.90 | 17.90 |
| add labor for each lf of width in a Dutch hip | 6C@.407 | lf | — | 20.20 | 20.20 |
| Install mansard truss system, 24" on center, per cf | | | | | |
| per width x height x length | 6C@.003 | cf | — | .15 | .15 |
| add labor for each lf of valley | 6C@.952 | lf | — | 47.30 | 47.30 |
| Install gambrel truss system, 24" on center, per cf | | | | | |
| per width x height x length | 6C@.003 | cf | — | .15 | .15 |
| add labor for each lf of valley | 6C@1.16 | lf | — | 57.70 | 57.70 |
| Install sheathing | | | | | |
| builder board | 6C@.015 | sf | — | .75 | .75 |
| plywood, waferboard, or OSB | 6C@.016 | sf | — | .80 | .80 |
| 1" x 6" sheathing | 6C@.017 | sf | — | .84 | .84 |
| 1" x 6" tongue-&-groove | 6C@.017 | sf | — | .84 | .84 |
| 2" x 6" tongue-&-groove | 6C@.017 | sf | — | .84 | .84 |
| 2" x 8" tongue-&-groove | 6C@.017 | sf | — | .84 | .84 |
| add labor for shear-panel installation | 6C@.003 | sf | — | .15 | .15 |
| Build interior soffit | | | | | |
| two sides | 6C@.059 | lf | — | 2.93 | 2.93 |
| two sides with recess for indirect lighting | 6C@.100 | lf | — | 4.97 | 4.97 |
| three sides | 6C@.080 | lf | — | 3.98 | 3.98 |
| three sides with recess for indirect lighting | 6C@.129 | lf | — | 6.41 | 6.41 |
| Install factory designed and fabricated structural panel | | | | | |
| 6" thick wall panel | 6C@.051 | sf | — | 2.53 | 2.53 |
| 8" thick wall panel | 6C@.052 | sf | — | 2.58 | 2.58 |
| 10" thick wall panel | 6C@.054 | sf | — | 2.68 | 2.68 |
| 12" thick wall panel | 6C@.054 | sf | — | 2.68 | 2.68 |
| 6" thick floor panel | 6C@.051 | sf | — | 2.53 | 2.53 |
| 8" thick floor panel | 6C@.051 | sf | — | 2.53 | 2.53 |
| 10" thick floor panel | 6C@.053 | sf | — | 2.63 | 2.63 |
| 12" thick floor panel | 6C@.054 | sf | — | 2.68 | 2.68 |
| 6" thick roof panel | 6C@.061 | sf | — | 3.03 | 3.03 |
| 8" thick roof panel | 6C@.062 | sf | — | 3.08 | 3.08 |
| 10" thick roof panel | 6C@.063 | sf | — | 3.13 | 3.13 |
| 12" thick roof panel | 6C@.066 | sf | — | 3.28 | 3.28 |
| Wood-frame chimney cricket | | | | | |
| length of ridge x width | 6C@.083 | sf | — | 4.13 | 4.13 |

| | Craft@Hrs | Unit | Material | Labor | Total |
|---|---|---|---|---|---|

## Security Systems

### Minimum charge.

| | Craft@Hrs | Unit | Material | Labor | Total |
|---|---|---|---|---|---|
| for security system work | 7S@3.00 | ea | 31.80 | 152.00 | 183.80 |
| add for system installed in finished structure | — | % | — | 37.0 | — |

### Control panel. Includes up to 50 lf of wiring.

Replace security control panel

| | Craft@Hrs | Unit | Material | Labor | Total |
|---|---|---|---|---|---|
| standard grade | 7S@5.01 | ea | 430.00 | 255.00 | 685.00 |
| high grade | 7S@6.67 | ea | 541.00 | 339.00 | 880.00 |
| Remove, all grades | 1D@.250 | ea | — | 9.73 | 9.73 |

### Key pad. Includes up to 50 lf of wiring.

Replace security panel key pad

| | Craft@Hrs | Unit | Material | Labor | Total |
|---|---|---|---|---|---|
| typical | 7S@1.27 | ea | 221.00 | 64.50 | 285.50 |
| LED read-out | 7S@1.27 | ea | 282.00 | 64.50 | 346.50 |
| Remove security panel key pad all types | 1D@.200 | ea | — | 7.78 | 7.78 |

### Key control. Includes up to 50 lf of wiring.

| | Craft@Hrs | Unit | Material | Labor | Total |
|---|---|---|---|---|---|
| replace, outside | 7S@1.14 | ea | 130.00 | 57.90 | 187.90 |
| remove | 1D@.143 | ea | — | 5.56 | 5.56 |

### Contact. Includes up to 50 lf of wiring.

Mechanical contact, per opening

| | Craft@Hrs | Unit | Material | Labor | Total |
|---|---|---|---|---|---|
| replace | 7S@.952 | ea | 73.10 | 48.40 | 121.50 |
| remove | 1D@.143 | ea | — | 5.56 | 5.56 |

Magnetic contact, per opening

| | Craft@Hrs | Unit | Material | Labor | Total |
|---|---|---|---|---|---|
| replace | 7S@1.37 | ea | 86.10 | 69.60 | 155.70 |
| remove | 1D@.167 | ea | — | 6.50 | 6.50 |

| | Craft@Hrs | Unit | Material | Labor | Total |
|---|---|---|---|---|---|
| **Sound detector.** Includes up to 50 lf of wiring. | | | | | |
| replace | 7S@1.56 | ea | 196.00 | 79.20 | 275.20 |
| remove | 1D@.167 | ea | — | 6.50 | 6.50 |
| **Motion detector.** Includes up to 50 lf of wiring. | | | | | |
| replace | 7S@1.49 | ea | 380.00 | 75.70 | 455.70 |
| remove | 1D@.167 | ea | — | 6.50 | 6.50 |
| **Pressure mat.** Includes up to 50 lf of wiring. | | | | | |
| replace | 7S@1.52 | lf | 67.50 | 77.20 | 144.70 |
| remove | 1D@.185 | lf | — | 7.20 | 7.20 |
| **Smoke detector.** Includes up to 50 lf of wiring. | | | | | |
| replace | 7S@1.49 | ea | 240.00 | 75.70 | 315.70 |
| remove | 1D@.167 | ea | — | 6.50 | 6.50 |
| **Horn or siren.** Exterior or interior. Includes up to 50 lf of wiring. | | | | | |
| replace | 7S@1.28 | ea | 79.90 | 65.00 | 144.90 |
| remove | 1D@.143 | ea | — | 5.56 | 5.56 |
| **Panic button.** Includes up to 50 lf of wiring. | | | | | |
| replace | 7S@.644 | ea | 67.50 | 32.70 | 100.20 |
| remove | 1D@.125 | ea | — | 4.86 | 4.86 |

## Time & Material Charts (selected items)
## Security Systems Materials

See Security Systems material prices with the line items above.

## Security Systems Labor

| Laborer | base wage | paid leave | true wage | taxes & ins. | total |
|---|---|---|---|---|---|
| Security system installer | $29.40 | 2.29 | $31.69 | 19.11 | $50.80 |
| Demolition worker | $20.70 | 1.61 | $22.31 | 16.59 | $38.90 |

**Paid leave** is calculated based on two weeks paid vacation, one week sick leave, and seven paid holidays. Employer's matching portion of **FICA** is 7.65 percent. **FUTA** (Federal Unemployment) is .8 percent. **Worker's compensation** for the security systems trade was calculated using a national average of 6.75 percent. **Unemployment insurance** was calculated using a national average of 8 percent. **Health insurance** was calculated based on a projected national average for 2015 of $1,025 per employee (and family when applicable) per month. Employer pays 80 percent for a per month cost of $820 per employee. **Retirement** is based on a 401(k) retirement program with employer matching of 50 percent. Employee contributions to the 401(k) plan are an average of 6 percent of the true wage. **Liability insurance** is based on a national average of 10.0 percent.

| | Craft@Hrs | Unit | Material | Labor | Total |
|---|---|---|---|---|---|

## Security Systems Labor Productivity

Demolition of security systems

| | Craft@Hrs | Unit | Material | Labor | Total |
|---|---|---|---|---|---|
| remove control panel | 1D@.250 | ea | — | 9.73 | 9.73 |
| remove exterior key pad | 1D@.200 | ea | — | 7.78 | 7.78 |
| remove contact | 1D@.143 | ea | — | 5.56 | 5.56 |
| remove detector (all types) | 1D@.167 | ea | — | 6.50 | 6.50 |
| remove pressure mat detector | 1D@.185 | ea | — | 7.20 | 7.20 |
| remove horn or siren | 1D@.143 | ea | — | 5.56 | 5.56 |
| remove panic button | 1D@.125 | ea | — | 4.86 | 4.86 |

Install security system

| | Craft@Hrs | Unit | Material | Labor | Total |
|---|---|---|---|---|---|
| control panel, standard grade | 7S@5.01 | ea | — | 255.00 | 255.00 |
| control panel, high grade | 7S@6.67 | ea | — | 339.00 | 339.00 |
| key pad | 7S@1.27 | ea | — | 64.50 | 64.50 |
| outside key control | 7S@1.14 | ea | — | 57.90 | 57.90 |
| mechanical contact per opening | 7S@.952 | ea | — | 48.40 | 48.40 |
| magnetic contact per opening | 7S@1.37 | ea | — | 69.60 | 69.60 |
| sound detector | 7S@1.56 | ea | — | 79.20 | 79.20 |
| motion detector | 7S@1.49 | ea | — | 75.70 | 75.70 |
| pressure mat detector | 7S@1.52 | lf | — | 77.20 | 77.20 |
| smoke detector | 7S@1.49 | ea | — | 75.70 | 75.70 |
| horn or siren | 7S@1.28 | ea | — | 65.00 | 65.00 |
| panic button | 7S@.644 | ea | — | 32.70 | 32.70 |

|  | Craft@Hrs | Unit | Material | Labor | Total |
|---|---|---|---|---|---|

## Siding

### Minimum charge.

| | Craft@Hrs | Unit | Material | Labor | Total |
|---|---|---|---|---|---|
| minimum charge for siding work | 6S@3.00 | ea | 66.80 | 147.00 | 213.80 |

### Fiberglass corrugated siding. Includes fiberglass panels, rust-resistant nails, purlins with corrugated pattern, end caps when needed, boots, roofing felt, valley metal, drip edge, ridge cap, fasteners, and installation. Weights are per sf. Includes 4% waste. Greenhouse style.

| | Craft@Hrs | Unit | Material | Labor | Total |
|---|---|---|---|---|---|
| replace, 6 ounce | 6S@.028 | sf | 2.68 | 1.37 | 4.05 |
| replace, 8 ounce | 6S@.028 | sf | 2.88 | 1.37 | 4.25 |
| replace, 12 ounce | 6S@.028 | sf | 4.00 | 1.37 | 5.37 |
| remove | 1D@.007 | sf | — | .27 | .27 |

### Aluminum siding. Includes siding with trim pieces, fasteners, and installation. Also includes 4% waste.

| | Craft@Hrs | Unit | Material | Labor | Total |
|---|---|---|---|---|---|
| replace, standard grade | 6S@.034 | sf | 2.08 | 1.67 | 3.75 |
| replace, high grade | 6S@.034 | sf | 2.43 | 1.67 | 4.10 |
| replace, deluxe grade | 6S@.034 | sf | 2.88 | 1.67 | 4.55 |
| replace, custom grade | 6S@.034 | sf | 4.16 | 1.67 | 5.83 |
| remove | 1D@.008 | sf | — | .31 | .31 |
| add for insulated siding | — | sf | .58 | — | .58 |

### Cement fiber shingle siding. Includes cement fiber shingle siding, rust-resistant nails, and installation. Includes 4% waste. Also called asbestos cement. Some older styles contain dangerous asbestos which must be removed using hazardous material removal techniques.

| | Craft@Hrs | Unit | Material | Labor | Total |
|---|---|---|---|---|---|
| replace, standard grade | 6S@.045 | sf | 1.74 | 2.21 | 3.95 |
| replace, high grade | 6S@.045 | sf | 2.19 | 2.21 | 4.40 |
| remove | 1D@.013 | sf | — | .51 | .51 |
| replace single shingle | 6S@.477 | sf | 3.65 | 23.40 | 27.05 |
| minimum charge to repair cement fiber siding | 6S@3.00 | ea | 52.70 | 147.00 | 199.70 |

### Shake or wood shingle siding. Includes shake or wood shingles, rust-resistant nails, and installation. Does not include backing or furring strips. Also includes 4% waste.

| | Craft@Hrs | Unit | Material | Labor | Total |
|---|---|---|---|---|---|
| replace, standard grade | 6S@.045 | sf | 1.53 | 2.21 | 3.74 |
| replace, high grade | 6S@.045 | sf | 1.69 | 2.21 | 3.90 |
| replace, deluxe grade | 6S@.045 | sf | 2.03 | 2.21 | 4.24 |
| replace, custom grade (fancy cut) | 6S@.045 | sf | 2.75 | 2.21 | 4.96 |
| remove | 1D@.014 | sf | — | .54 | .54 |
| replace single shingle | 6S@.408 | ea | 4.40 | 20.00 | 24.40 |
| minimum charge to replace shake or wood shingle | 6S@3.25 | ea | 60.10 | 159.00 | 219.10 |

### Vinyl siding. Includes siding with trim pieces, fasteners, and installation. Includes 4% waste.

| | Craft@Hrs | Unit | Material | Labor | Total |
|---|---|---|---|---|---|
| replace, standard grade | 6S@.034 | sf | 2.42 | 1.67 | 4.09 |
| replace, high grade | 6S@.034 | sf | 2.76 | 1.67 | 4.43 |
| replace, deluxe grade | 6S@.034 | sf | 4.15 | 1.67 | 5.82 |
| remove | 1D@.007 | sf | — | .27 | .27 |
| add for insulated siding | — | sf | .66 | — | .66 |

| | Craft@Hrs | Unit | Material | Labor | Total |
|---|---|---|---|---|---|

**7/16" thick hardboard siding.** Includes hardboard lap siding, rust-resistant nails, and installation. Includes 4% waste.

| | Craft@Hrs | Unit | Material | Labor | Total |
|---|---|---|---|---|---|
| replace, standard grade | 6S@.024 | sf | .97 | 1.18 | 2.15 |
| replace, painted-board finish | 6S@.024 | sf | 1.08 | 1.18 | 2.26 |
| replace, stained-board finish | 6S@.024 | sf | 1.53 | 1.18 | 2.71 |
| replace, simulated stucco finish | 6S@.024 | sf | 1.18 | 1.18 | 2.36 |
| remove | 1D@.009 | sf | — | .35 | .35 |

**Hardboard lap siding.** Includes hardboard lap siding, rust-resistant nails, and installation. Also includes 4% waste.

| | Craft@Hrs | Unit | Material | Labor | Total |
|---|---|---|---|---|---|
| replace | 6S@.026 | sf | 1.13 | 1.27 | 2.40 |
| remove | 1D@.010 | sf | — | .39 | .39 |

**5/8" thick plywood siding, texture 1-11.** Includes texture 1-11 siding (commonly called T1-11), rust-resistant nails, and installation. Also includes 4% waste.

| | Craft@Hrs | Unit | Material | Labor | Total |
|---|---|---|---|---|---|
| replace, cedar face | 6S@.025 | sf | 2.03 | 1.23 | 3.26 |
| replace, rough-sawn cedar face | 6S@.025 | sf | 2.49 | 1.23 | 3.72 |
| replace, fir face | 6S@.025 | sf | 1.78 | 1.23 | 3.01 |
| replace, rough-sawn fir face | 6S@.025 | sf | 2.04 | 1.23 | 3.27 |
| replace, southern yellow pine face | 6S@.025 | sf | 1.49 | 1.23 | 2.72 |
| replace, redwood face | 6S@.025 | sf | 3.39 | 1.23 | 4.62 |
| remove | 1D@.010 | sf | — | .39 | .39 |
| add for factory stained siding. | — | sf | .27 | — | .27 |

**Plywood with 1" x 4" stained cedar boards.** Includes plywood siding with 1" x 4" cedar boards over joints, rust-resistant nails, and installation. Does not include finishing. Includes 4% waste.

| | Craft@Hrs | Unit | Material | Labor | Total |
|---|---|---|---|---|---|
| replace, 1/2" | 6S@.057 | sf | 5.17 | 2.79 | 7.96 |
| replace, 5/8" | 6S@.057 | sf | 5.28 | 2.79 | 8.07 |
| remove | 1D@.018 | sf | — | .70 | .70 |

**Board-and-batten siding.** Includes board-and-batten siding, rust-resistant nails, and installation. Board-and-batten siding is installed vertically. Includes 4% waste. For the wood grades shown in the price list item, deduct **9%** for next lower grade, deduct **14%** for third grade.

| | Craft@Hrs | Unit | Material | Labor | Total |
|---|---|---|---|---|---|
| replace, pine, select grade | 6S@.037 | sf | 4.89 | 1.81 | 6.70 |
| replace, cedar, A grade | 6S@.037 | sf | 5.12 | 1.81 | 6.93 |
| remove | 1D@.011 | sf | — | .43 | .43 |

*board and batten*

**Board-on-board siding.** Includes board-on-board siding, rust-resistant nails, and installation. Board-on-board siding is installed vertically. Includes 4% waste. For the wood grades shown in the price list item, deduct **9%** for next lower grade, deduct **14%** for third grade.

| | Craft@Hrs | Unit | Material | Labor | Total |
|---|---|---|---|---|---|
| replace, pine, select grade | 6S@.034 | sf | 4.99 | 1.67 | 6.66 |
| replace, cedar, A grade | 6S@.034 | sf | 5.23 | 1.67 | 6.90 |
| remove | 1D@.011 | sf | — | .43 | .43 |

*board on board*

channel rustic     shiplap     tongue-&-groove simple pattern     tongue-&-groove fancy pattern

| | Craft@Hrs | Unit | Material | Labor | Total |
|---|---|---|---|---|---|

**Channel rustic siding.** Includes channel rustic siding, rust-resistant nails, and installation. Includes **4%** waste. For the wood grades shown in the price list item, deduct **9%** for next lower grade, deduct **14%** for third grade.

| | Craft@Hrs | Unit | Material | Labor | Total |
|---|---|---|---|---|---|
| replace, pine, select grade | 6S@.039 | sf | 5.01 | 1.91 | 6.92 |
| replace, cedar, A grade | 6S@.039 | sf | 6.30 | 1.91 | 8.21 |
| replace, redwood, clear all heart grade | 6S@.039 | sf | 15.50 | 1.91 | 17.41 |
| remove | 1D@.011 | sf | — | .43 | .43 |

**Shiplap siding.** Includes shiplap siding, rust-resistant nails, and installation. Also includes **4%** waste. For the wood grades shown in the price list item, deduct **9%** for next lower grade, deduct **14%** for third grade.

| | Craft@Hrs | Unit | Material | Labor | Total |
|---|---|---|---|---|---|
| replace, pine, select grade | 6S@.039 | sf | 5.08 | 1.91 | 6.99 |
| replace, cedar, A grade | 6S@.039 | sf | 6.38 | 1.91 | 8.29 |
| replace, redwood, clear all heart grade | 6S@.039 | sf | 15.60 | 1.91 | 17.51 |
| remove | 1D@.011 | sf | — | .43 | .43 |

**Tongue-&-groove siding.** Includes tongue-and-groove siding, rust-resistant nails, and installation. Includes **4%** waste. For the wood grades shown in the price list item, deduct **9%** for next lower grade, deduct **14%** for third grade.

| | Craft@Hrs | Unit | Material | Labor | Total |
|---|---|---|---|---|---|
| replace, pine, simple pattern, select grade | 6S@.039 | sf | 5.20 | 1.91 | 7.11 |
| replace, pine, fancy pattern, select grade | 6S@.039 | sf | 5.56 | 1.91 | 7.47 |
| replace, cedar, simple pattern, A grade | 6S@.039 | sf | 6.51 | 1.91 | 8.42 |
| replace, cedar, fancy pattern, A grade | 6S@.039 | sf | 6.94 | 1.91 | 8.85 |
| replace, redwood, simple pattern, clear all heart grade | 6S@.039 | sf | 15.90 | 1.91 | 17.81 |
| replace, redwood, fancy pattern, clear all heart grade | 6S@.039 | sf | 16.80 | 1.91 | 18.71 |
| remove | 1D@.011 | sf | — | .43 | .43 |

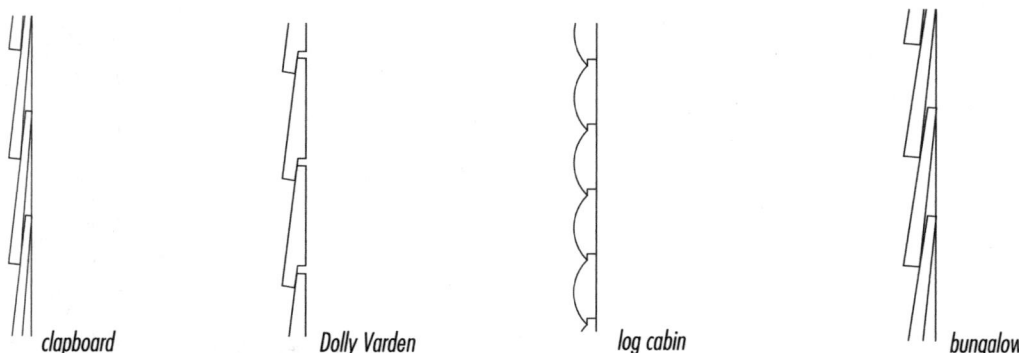

*clapboard*     *Dolly Varden*     *log cabin*     *bungalow*

| | Craft@Hrs | Unit | Material | Labor | Total |
|---|---|---|---|---|---|

**Radially sawn clapboard siding, eastern pine.** Includes radially sawn clapboard, rust-resistant nails, and installation. Includes 4% waste. True clapboard. Based on grades marketed by Donnell's Clapboard Mill of Sedgwick, Maine.

| | | | | | |
|---|---|---|---|---|---|
| replace, #1 premium clear | 6S@.055 | sf | 7.31 | 2.70 | 10.01 |
| replace, #1 New England Cape | 6S@.055 | sf | 6.37 | 2.70 | 9.07 |
| remove | 1D@.011 | sf | — | .43 | .43 |

**Resawn beveled siding.** Includes resawn, beveled clapboard, rust-resistant nails, and installation. Includes 4% waste. This siding looks like clapboard but is not radially sawn. The grain in a radially sawn board runs at a consistent 90-degree angle to the board face. In resawn boards grain orientation is inconsistent.

| | | | | | |
|---|---|---|---|---|---|
| replace, pine, select grade | 6S@.041 | sf | 2.71 | 2.01 | 4.72 |
| replace, cedar, select grade | 6S@.041 | sf | 3.39 | 2.01 | 5.40 |
| replace, redwood, clear all heart grade | 6S@.041 | sf | 8.19 | 2.01 | 10.20 |
| remove | 1D@.011 | sf | — | .43 | .43 |

**Bungalow siding.** Includes bungalow siding, rust-resistant nails, and installation. For the wood grades shown in the price list item, deduct **9%** for next lower grade, deduct **14%** for third grade. Also includes 4% waste.

| | | | | | |
|---|---|---|---|---|---|
| replace, pine, select grade | 6S@.039 | sf | 3.63 | 1.91 | 5.54 |
| replace, cedar, select grade | 6S@.039 | sf | 4.58 | 1.91 | 6.49 |
| replace, redwood, clear all heart grade | 6S@.039 | sf | 11.00 | 1.91 | 12.91 |
| remove | 1D@.011 | sf | — | .43 | .43 |

**Dolly Varden siding.** Includes Dolly Varden siding, rust-resistant nails, and installation. Includes 4% waste. For the wood grades shown in the price list item, deduct **9%** for next lower grade, deduct **14%** for third grade.

| | | | | | |
|---|---|---|---|---|---|
| replace, pine, select grade | 6S@.039 | sf | 3.92 | 1.91 | 5.83 |
| replace, cedar, select grade | 6S@.039 | sf | 4.94 | 1.91 | 6.85 |
| replace, redwood, clear all heart grade | 6S@.039 | sf | 11.80 | 1.91 | 13.71 |
| remove | 1D@.011 | sf | — | .43 | .43 |

| | Craft@Hrs | Unit | Material | Labor | Total |
|---|---|---|---|---|---|

**Log cabin siding.** Includes log cabin siding, rust-resistant nails, and installation. Includes 4% waste. For the wood grades shown in the price list item, deduct **9%** for next lower grade, deduct **14%** for third grade.

| | Craft@Hrs | Unit | Material | Labor | Total |
|---|---|---|---|---|---|
| replace, pine, select grade | 6S@.039 | sf | 3.66 | 1.91 | 5.57 |
| replace, cedar, select grade | 6S@.039 | sf | 4.62 | 1.91 | 6.53 |
| remove | 1D@.011 | sf | — | .43 | .43 |

**Add for factory stained siding.** Replace only.

| | | Unit | Material | Labor | Total |
|---|---|---|---|---|---|
| one coat | — | sf | .57 | — | .57 |
| two coat | — | sf | .82 | — | .82 |

**Wood siding repair.** Replace only.

| | Craft@Hrs | Unit | Material | Labor | Total |
|---|---|---|---|---|---|
| replace section | 6S@.827 | ea | 29.50 | 40.50 | 70.00 |
| minimum charge | 6S@3.25 | ea | 80.70 | 159.00 | 239.70 |

**Fascia.** Includes fascia material, rust-resistant fasteners, and installation. Does not include soffits or rough fascia. Includes 4% waste.

| | Craft@Hrs | Unit | Material | Labor | Total |
|---|---|---|---|---|---|
| replace, aluminum to 6" wide | 6S@.034 | lf | 2.28 | 1.67 | 3.95 |
| replace, aluminum 6" to 12" wide | 6S@.034 | lf | 3.08 | 1.67 | 4.75 |
| replace, vinyl to 6" wide | 6S@.034 | lf | 3.10 | 1.67 | 4.77 |
| replace, vinyl 6" to 12" wide | 6S@.034 | lf | 4.31 | 1.67 | 5.98 |
| replace, cedar to 6" wide | 6S@.037 | lf | 2.83 | 1.81 | 4.64 |
| replace, cedar 6" to 12" wide | 6S@.037 | lf | 3.77 | 1.81 | 5.58 |
| replace, redwood to 6" wide | 6S@.037 | lf | 6.38 | 1.81 | 8.19 |
| replace, redwood 6" to 12" wide | 6S@.037 | lf | 8.50 | 1.81 | 10.31 |
| remove, aluminum or vinyl | 1D@.006 | lf | — | .23 | .23 |
| remove, wood | 1D@.007 | lf | — | .27 | .27 |
| minimum charge | 6S@3.00 | ea | 85.90 | 147.00 | 232.90 |

**Soffit.** Includes soffit material, rust-resistant fasteners, backing as needed, and installation. Does not include finish fascia. Includes 4% waste.

| | Craft@Hrs | Unit | Material | Labor | Total |
|---|---|---|---|---|---|
| replace, aluminum | 6S@.049 | sf | 3.87 | 2.40 | 6.27 |
| replace, vinyl | 6S@.049 | sf | 5.31 | 2.40 | 7.71 |
| replace, cedar plywood | 6S@.052 | sf | 2.70 | 2.55 | 5.25 |
| replace, cedar rough-sawn plywood | 6S@.052 | sf | 2.74 | 2.55 | 5.29 |
| replace, fir plywood | 6S@.052 | sf | 2.57 | 2.55 | 5.12 |
| replace, fir rough-sawn plywood | 6S@.052 | sf | 2.66 | 2.55 | 5.21 |
| replace, redwood plywood | 6S@.052 | sf | 7.08 | 2.55 | 9.63 |
| replace, redwood rough-sawn plywood | 6S@.052 | sf | 7.19 | 2.55 | 9.74 |
| remove, aluminum or vinyl | 1D@.009 | sf | — | .35 | .35 |
| remove, wood | 1D@.010 | sf | — | .39 | .39 |

**Soffit, tongue-&-groove.** Includes 4% waste.

| | Craft@Hrs | Unit | Material | Labor | Total |
|---|---|---|---|---|---|
| replace, cedar, simple pattern | 6S@.061 | sf | 5.12 | 2.99 | 8.11 |
| replace, cedar, fancy pattern | 6S@.061 | sf | 6.16 | 2.99 | 9.15 |
| replace, fir, simple pattern | 6S@.061 | sf | 4.76 | 2.99 | 7.75 |
| replace, fir, fancy pattern | 6S@.061 | sf | 5.01 | 2.99 | 8.00 |
| replace, redwood, simple pattern | 6S@.061 | sf | 9.82 | 2.99 | 12.81 |
| replace, redwood, fancy pattern | 6S@.061 | sf | 10.70 | 2.99 | 13.69 |
| remove | 1D@.012 | sf | — | .47 | .47 |

|  | Craft@Hrs | Unit | Material | Labor | Total |
|---|---|---|---|---|---|

**Rain gutter.** Includes rain gutter with hidden rust-resistant fasteners and installation. Does not include downspouts. Includes 3% waste.

| | | | | | |
|---|---|---|---|---|---|
| replace, aluminum | 6S@.041 | lf | 5.50 | 2.01 | 7.51 |
| replace, copper built-in box | 6S@1.69 | lf | 50.70 | 82.80 | 133.50 |
| replace, copper | 6S@.041 | lf | 28.00 | 2.01 | 30.01 |
| replace, galvanized steel | 6S@.041 | lf | 13.90 | 2.01 | 15.91 |
| replace, plastic | 6S@.041 | lf | 4.43 | 2.01 | 6.44 |
| replace, redwood | 6S@.041 | lf | 62.70 | 2.01 | 64.71 |
| replace, tin built-in box | 6S@1.69 | lf | 36.20 | 82.80 | 119.00 |
| replace, tin | 6S@.041 | lf | 25.30 | 2.01 | 27.31 |
| remove | 1D@.011 | lf | — | .43 | .43 |
| remove, built-in box | 1D@.026 | lf | — | 1.01 | 1.01 |

*built-in box*

**Rain gutter downspout.** Includes manufactured downspout, fasteners, elbows, and installation. Does not include gutter. Also includes 3% waste.

| | | | | | |
|---|---|---|---|---|---|
| replace, aluminum | 6S@.038 | lf | 6.71 | 1.86 | 8.57 |
| replace, copper built-in box | 6S@.563 | lf | 32.00 | 27.60 | 59.60 |
| replace, copper | 6S@.038 | lf | 34.10 | 1.86 | 35.96 |
| replace, galvanized steel | 6S@.038 | lf | 17.30 | 1.86 | 19.16 |
| replace, plastic | 6S@.038 | lf | 5.40 | 1.86 | 7.26 |
| replace, tin built-in box | 6S@.038 | lf | 24.60 | 1.86 | 26.46 |
| replace, tin | 6S@.563 | lf | 30.70 | 27.60 | 58.30 |
| remove | 1D@.009 | lf | — | .35 | .35 |

*high grade*

*high grade*

**Rain gutter downspout conductor.** Replace only. Includes manufactured downspout conductor, fasteners, and installation. Installation includes attachment to fascia and gutters but does not include the gutters or downspouts.

| | | | | | |
|---|---|---|---|---|---|
| standard grade copper | 6S@.432 | ea | 69.20 | 21.20 | 90.40 |
| high grade copper | 6S@.432 | ea | 129.00 | 21.20 | 150.20 |
| standard grade galvanized steel | 6S@.432 | ea | 56.70 | 21.20 | 77.90 |
| high grade galvanized steel | 6S@.432 | ea | 108.00 | 21.20 | 129.20 |

| | Craft@Hrs | Unit | Material | Labor | Total |
|---|---|---|---|---|---|

**Polypropylene fixed shutter.** Per 16" wide pair. For 12" wide deduct **42%**; for 18" wide add **8%**; for 20" wide add **14%**; for 24" wide add **26%**.

| | Craft@Hrs | Unit | Material | Labor | Total |
|---|---|---|---|---|---|
| replace, 24" tall | 6S@.323 | ea | 50.40 | 15.80 | 66.20 |
| replace, 48" tall | 6S@.323 | ea | 78.60 | 15.80 | 94.40 |
| replace, 60" tall | 6S@.323 | ea | 90.80 | 15.80 | 106.60 |
| replace, 66" tall | 6S@.323 | ea | 106.00 | 15.80 | 121.80 |
| remove | 1D@.156 | ea | — | 6.07 | 6.07 |

**Wood fixed shutter.** Includes wood shutter, mounting brackets and fasteners, and installation. Does not include painting. Per 16" wide pair. For 12" wide deduct **6%**; for 18" wide add **10%**; for 20" wide add **52%**; for 24" wide add **78%**.

| | Craft@Hrs | Unit | Material | Labor | Total |
|---|---|---|---|---|---|
| replace, 36" tall | 6S@.323 | ea | 165.00 | 15.80 | 180.80 |
| replace, 48" tall | 6S@.323 | ea | 186.00 | 15.80 | 201.80 |
| replace, 60" tall | 6S@.323 | ea | 209.00 | 15.80 | 224.80 |
| replace, 72" tall | 6S@.323 | ea | 229.00 | 15.80 | 244.80 |
| remove | 1D@.156 | ea | — | 6.07 | 6.07 |

**Wood moveable shutter.** Per 16" wide pair including hardware. For 12" wide deduct **15%**; for 18" wide add **7%**; for 20" wide add **14%**; for 24" wide add **27%**. For fixed half circle top add **$146** per pair. For moveable louvers with half-circle top add **$269** per pair. For raised panel shutter with half-circle top add **$168** per pair. For Gothic peaked top (Gothic arch) add **$280** per pair.

| | Craft@Hrs | Unit | Material | Labor | Total |
|---|---|---|---|---|---|
| replace, 36" tall | 6S@.333 | ea | 262.00 | 16.30 | 278.30 |
| replace, 48" tall | 6S@.333 | ea | 301.00 | 16.30 | 317.30 |
| replace, 60" tall | 6S@.333 | ea | 353.00 | 16.30 | 369.30 |
| replace, 72" tall | 6S@.333 | ea | 436.00 | 16.30 | 452.30 |
| remove | 1D@.158 | ea | — | 6.15 | 6.15 |
| remove for work, then reinstall | 6S@.451 | ea | — | 22.10 | 22.10 |

## Time & Material Charts (selected items)
## Siding Materials

See Siding material prices with the line items above.

### Siding Labor

| Laborer | base wage | paid leave | true wage | taxes & ins. | total |
|---|---|---|---|---|---|
| Siding installer | $30.70 | 2.39 | $33.09 | 22.91 | $56.00 |
| Siding installer's helper | $22.20 | 1.73 | $23.93 | 17.97 | $41.90 |
| Demolition laborer | $20.70 | 1.61 | $22.31 | 16.59 | $38.90 |

**Paid leave** is calculated based on two weeks paid vacation, one week sick leave, and seven paid holidays. Employer's matching portion of **FICA** is 7.65 percent. **FUTA** (Federal Unemployment) is .8 percent. **Worker's compensation** for the siding trade was calculated using a national average of 16.24 percent. **Unemployment insurance** was calculated using a national average of 8 percent. **Health insurance** was calculated based on a projected national average for 2015 of $1,025 per employee (and family when applicable) per month. Employer pays 80 percent for a per month cost of $820 per employee. **Retirement** is based on a 401(k) retirement program with employer matching of 50 percent. Employee contributions to the 401(k) plan are an average of 6 percent of the true wage. **Liability insurance** is based on a national average of 10.0 percent.

| | Craft@Hrs | Unit | Material | Labor | Total |
|---|---|---|---|---|---|
| **Siding Labor Productivity** | | | | | |
| Demolition of siding | | | | | |
|     remove fiberglass corrugated siding | 1D@.007 | sf | — | .27 | .27 |
|     remove aluminum siding | 1D@.008 | sf | — | .31 | .31 |
|     remove cement fiber shingle siding | 1D@.013 | sf | — | .51 | .51 |
|     remove shake or wood shingle siding | 1D@.014 | sf | — | .54 | .54 |
|     remove vinyl siding | 1D@.007 | sf | — | .27 | .27 |
|     remove hardboard siding | 1D@.009 | sf | — | .35 | .35 |
|     remove hardboard beveled siding | 1D@.010 | sf | — | .39 | .39 |
|     remove plywood siding | 1D@.010 | sf | — | .39 | .39 |
|     remove wood siding | 1D@.011 | sf | — | .43 | .43 |
|     remove aluminum or vinyl fascia | 1D@.006 | lf | — | .23 | .23 |
|     remove wood fascia | 1D@.007 | lf | — | .27 | .27 |
|     remove aluminum or vinyl soffit | 1D@.009 | sf | — | .35 | .35 |
|     remove plywood soffit | 1D@.010 | sf | — | .39 | .39 |
|     remove tongue-&-groove soffit | 1D@.012 | sf | — | .47 | .47 |
|     remove rain gutter | 1D@.011 | lf | — | .43 | .43 |
|     remove built-in box rain gutter | 1D@.026 | lf | — | 1.01 | 1.01 |
|     remove downspout | 1D@.009 | lf | — | .35 | .35 |
|     remove fixed shutter | 1D@.156 | ea | — | 6.07 | 6.07 |
|     remove moveable shutter | 1D@.158 | ea | — | 6.15 | 6.15 |

| | Craft@Hrs | Unit | Material | Labor | Total |
|---|---|---|---|---|---|
| **Siding installation crew** | | | | | |
| install siding    siding installer | 56.00 | | | | |
| install siding    installer's helper | 41.90 | | | | |
| install siding    siding crew | 49.00 | | | | |
| | | | | | |
| **Install siding** | | | | | |
| fiberglass corrugated | 6S@.028 | sf | — | 1.37 | 1.37 |
| aluminum | 6S@.034 | sf | — | 1.67 | 1.67 |
| cement shingle | 6S@.045 | sf | — | 2.21 | 2.21 |
| shake or wood shingle | 6S@.045 | sf | — | 2.21 | 2.21 |
| vinyl | 6S@.034 | sf | — | 1.67 | 1.67 |
| 7/16" thick hardboard | 6S@.024 | sf | — | 1.18 | 1.18 |
| hardboard lap | 6S@.026 | sf | — | 1.27 | 1.27 |
| 5/8" thick plywood | 6S@.025 | sf | — | 1.23 | 1.23 |
| plywood with 1" x 4" boards | 6S@.057 | sf | — | 2.79 | 2.79 |
| board-and-batten | 6S@.037 | sf | — | 1.81 | 1.81 |
| board-on-board | 6S@.034 | sf | — | 1.67 | 1.67 |
| drop siding | 6S@.039 | sf | — | 1.91 | 1.91 |
| clapboard | 6S@.055 | sf | — | 2.70 | 2.70 |
| bevel | 6S@.041 | sf | — | 2.01 | 2.01 |
| **Install fascia** | | | | | |
| aluminum or vinyl | 6S@.034 | lf | — | 1.67 | 1.67 |
| wood fascia | 6S@.037 | lf | — | 1.81 | 1.81 |
| **Install soffit** | | | | | |
| aluminum or vinyl | 6S@.049 | sf | — | 2.40 | 2.40 |
| plywood | 6S@.052 | sf | — | 2.55 | 2.55 |
| tongue-&-groove | 6S@.061 | sf | — | 2.99 | 2.99 |
| **Install rain gutter** | | | | | |
| typical | 6S@.041 | lf | — | 2.01 | 2.01 |
| built-in box | 6S@1.69 | lf | — | 82.80 | 82.80 |
| **Install rain gutter downspout** | | | | | |
| typical half-round or "K" style | 6S@.038 | lf | — | 1.86 | 1.86 |
| built-in box | 6S@.563 | lf | — | 27.60 | 27.60 |
| **Install downspout conductor** | | | | | |
| typical | 6S@.432 | ea | — | 21.20 | 21.20 |
| **Install shutter** | | | | | |
| fixed | 6S@.323 | ea | — | 15.80 | 15.80 |
| moveable | 6S@.333 | ea | — | 16.30 | 16.30 |

| | Craft@Hrs | Unit | Material | Labor | Total |
|---|---|---|---|---|---|

## Stairs

**3' wide utility stairs.** Per step. Includes three 2" x 12" stringers and 2" dimensional lumber treads. Does not include railing.

| | | Craft@Hrs | Unit | Material | Labor | Total |
|---|---|---|---|---|---|---|
| replace stairs | | 1C@.361 | st | 22.60 | 20.50 | 43.10 |
| remove | | 1D@.101 | st | — | 3.93 | 3.93 |

*enclosed*          *one side open*          *straight stairs*

**Straight stairs.** Per step. Includes four 2" x 12" stringers reinforced with plywood or waferboard. Does not include balustrade.

| | Craft@Hrs | Unit | Material | Labor | Total |
|---|---|---|---|---|---|
| **3' wide enclosed stairs** | | | | | |
| replace covered treads and risers | 1C@.474 | st | 40.40 | 27.00 | 67.40 |
| replace with false oak tread and riser | 1C@.563 | st | 84.40 | 32.00 | 116.40 |
| replace with oak treads and paint-grade risers | 1C@.474 | st | 85.20 | 27.00 | 112.20 |
| replace with oak treads and oak risers | 1C@.474 | st | 91.10 | 27.00 | 118.10 |
| **3' wide stairs, one side open** | | | | | |
| replace covered treads and risers | 1C@.485 | st | 40.40 | 27.60 | 68.00 |
| replace with false oak tread and riser | 1C@.575 | st | 103.00 | 32.70 | 135.70 |
| replace with oak treads and paint-grade risers | 1C@.485 | st | 85.20 | 27.60 | 112.80 |
| replace with oak treads and oak risers | 1C@.485 | st | 91.10 | 27.60 | 118.70 |
| **3' wide stairs, two sides open** | | | | | |
| replace covered treads and risers | 1C@.517 | st | 40.40 | 29.40 | 69.80 |
| replace with false oak tread and riser | 1C@.607 | st | 121.00 | 34.50 | 155.50 |
| replace with oak treads and paint-grade risers | 1C@.517 | st | 85.20 | 29.40 | 114.60 |
| replace with oak treads and oak risers | 1C@.517 | st | 91.10 | 29.40 | 120.50 |
| remove | 1D@.122 | st | — | 4.75 | 4.75 |

enclosed　　　　　　　one side open　　　　　　　two sides open

|  | Craft@Hrs | Unit | Material | Labor | Total |
|---|---|---|---|---|---|

**1/4 turn stairs.** Per step. Ten step minimum. L-shaped stair system with 3' by 3' landing. Includes bearing walls, 2" x 8" joists, headers, and 3/4" tongue-&-groove sheathing. Includes four 2" x 12" stringers reinforced with plywood or waferboard. Does not include balustrade.

| | Craft@Hrs | Unit | Material | Labor | Total |
|---|---|---|---|---|---|
| **3' wide enclosed 1/4 turn stairs** | | | | | |
| replace covered treads and risers | 1C@.825 | st | 52.40 | 46.90 | 99.30 |
| replace with false oak tread and riser | 1C@1.16 | st | 101.00 | 66.00 | 167.00 |
| replace with oak treads and paint-grade risers | 1C@1.02 | st | 107.00 | 58.00 | 165.00 |
| replace with oak treads and oak risers | 1C@1.02 | st | 113.00 | 58.00 | 171.00 |
| **3' wide 1/4 turn stairs, one side open** | | | | | |
| replace covered treads and risers | 1C@.855 | st | 52.40 | 48.60 | 101.00 |
| replace with false oak tread and riser | 1C@1.20 | st | 120.00 | 68.30 | 188.30 |
| replace with oak treads and paint-grade risers | 1C@1.04 | st | 107.00 | 59.20 | 166.20 |
| replace with oak treads and oak risers | 1C@1.04 | st | 113.00 | 59.20 | 172.20 |
| **3' wide 1/4 turn stairs, two sides open** | | | | | |
| replace covered treads and risers | 1C@.885 | st | 52.40 | 50.40 | 102.80 |
| replace with false oak tread and riser | 1C@1.23 | st | 138.00 | 70.00 | 208.00 |
| replace with oak treads and paint-grade risers | 1C@1.05 | st | 107.00 | 59.70 | 166.70 |
| replace with oak treads and oak risers | 1C@1.05 | st | 113.00 | 59.70 | 172.70 |
| remove | 1D@.135 | st | — | 5.25 | 5.25 |

enclosed　　　　　　　one side open　　　　　　　two sides open

**1/2 turn stairs.** Per step. Ten step minimum. U-shaped stair system with 6' by 3' landing. Landing includes bearing walls, 2" x 8" joists, headers, and 3/4" tongue-&-groove sheathing. Each stair system includes four 2" x 12" stringers reinforced with plywood or waferboard. Does not include balustrade.

| | Craft@Hrs | Unit | Material | Labor | Total |
|---|---|---|---|---|---|
| **3' wide enclosed 1/2 turn stairs** | | | | | |
| replace covered treads and risers | 1C@.908 | st | 64.00 | 51.70 | 115.70 |
| replace with false oak tread and riser | 1C@1.26 | st | 118.00 | 71.70 | 189.70 |
| replace with oak treads and paint-grade risers | 1C@1.12 | st | 125.00 | 63.70 | 188.70 |
| replace with oak treads and oak risers | 1C@1.12 | st | 129.00 | 63.70 | 192.70 |
| **3' wide 1/2 turn stairs, one side open** | | | | | |
| replace covered treads and risers | 1C@.943 | st | 64.00 | 53.70 | 117.70 |
| replace with false oak tread and riser | 1C@1.31 | st | 156.00 | 74.50 | 230.50 |
| replace with oak treads and paint-grade risers | 1C@1.15 | st | 125.00 | 65.40 | 190.40 |
| replace with oak treads and oak risers | 1C@1.15 | st | 129.00 | 65.40 | 194.40 |
| **3' wide 1/2 turn stairs, two sides open** | | | | | |
| replace covered treads and risers | 1C@.970 | st | 64.00 | 55.20 | 119.20 |
| replace with false oak tread and riser | 1C@1.34 | st | 156.00 | 76.20 | 232.20 |
| replace with oak treads and paint-grade risers | 1C@1.16 | st | 125.00 | 66.00 | 191.00 |
| replace with oak treads and oak risers | 1C@1.16 | st | 129.00 | 66.00 | 195.00 |
| remove | 1D@.150 | st | — | 5.84 | 5.84 |

| | Craft@Hrs | Unit | Material | Labor | Total |
|---|---|---|---|---|---|

*enclosed*

*one side open*

*two sides open*

**Circular stairs.** Per step. Circular stairs usually form half of a circle or less. Based on 9' radius. Labor prices are for open or closed stringer stairs hand-framed on job site. But overall prices also apply for purchase and installation of prefabricated circular stairs. Does not include stair balustrade.

| | Craft@Hrs | Unit | Material | Labor | Total |
|---|---|---|---|---|---|
| 3' wide enclosed circular stairs | | | | | |
|     replace covered treads and risers | 1C@11.6 | st | 259.00 | 660.00 | 919.00 |
|     replace with false oak tread and riser | 1C@11.8 | st | 304.00 | 671.00 | 975.00 |
|     replace with oak treads and paint-grade risers | 1C@11.6 | st | 305.00 | 660.00 | 965.00 |
|     replace with oak treads and oak risers | 1C@11.6 | st | 310.00 | 660.00 | 970.00 |
| 3' wide circular stairs, one side open | | | | | |
|     replace covered treads and risers | 1C@11.8 | st | 259.00 | 671.00 | 930.00 |
|     replace with false oak tread and riser | 1C@12.0 | st | 323.00 | 683.00 | 1,006.00 |
|     replace with oak treads and paint-grade risers | 1C@11.8 | st | 305.00 | 671.00 | 976.00 |
|     replace with oak treads and oak risers | 1C@11.8 | st | 310.00 | 671.00 | 981.00 |
| 3' wide circular stairs, two sides open | | | | | |
|     replace covered treads and risers | 1C@11.9 | st | 259.00 | 677.00 | 936.00 |
|     replace with false oak tread and riser | 1C@12.1 | st | 340.00 | 688.00 | 1,028.00 |
|     replace with oak treads and paint-grade risers | 1C@11.9 | st | 305.00 | 677.00 | 982.00 |
|     replace with oak treads and oak risers | 1C@11.9 | st | 310.00 | 677.00 | 987.00 |
|     remove | 1D@.158 | st | — | 6.15 | 6.15 |

**Additional costs for stairs.**

| | Craft@Hrs | Unit | Material | Labor | Total |
|---|---|---|---|---|---|
|     add for 4' wide stairs | — | % | 12.0 | — | — |
|     add for 4' wide circular stairs | — | % | 16.0 | — | — |

**Add for winder on 1/4 and 1/2 turn platforms.** Winders are pie-shaped stair treads, usually placed on top of the landing. Each winder is a box made from 2" x 8" boards ripped to the height of the riser. Additional ripped 2" x 8" boards are placed 12" on center inside the box for reinforcement. (Add **3%** for risers over 7-3/8" made from ripped 2" x 10" boards.) Winders are stacked on top of each other. Replace only.

| | Craft@Hrs | Unit | Material | Labor | Total |
|---|---|---|---|---|---|
|     particleboard tread, paint-grade riser | 1C@.400 | ea | 59.60 | 22.80 | 82.40 |
|     oak tread, paint-grade riser | 1C@.400 | ea | 104.00 | 22.80 | 126.80 |
|     oak tread, oak riser | 1C@.400 | ea | 110.00 | 22.80 | 132.80 |

| | Craft@Hrs | Unit | Material | Labor | Total |
|---|---|---|---|---|---|

**Add for mitered corners.** For stairs where the bottom three steps turn at a 45-degree angle (or less) making three steps from the side and front. The three steps on the side are made from stacked boxes made from 2" x 8" boards ripped to the riser height, sheathed with 3/4" plywood then capped with the tread and riser material. Cost per side. (For example, for stairs with mitered corners on both sides, use this price twice.) Replace only.

| | Craft@Hrs | Unit | Material | Labor | Total |
|---|---|---|---|---|---|
| bottom three treads | 1C@2.32 | ea | 163.00 | 132.00 | 295.00 |

**Add for bullnose on starting step.** Red oak. Standard grade up to 4" wide. High grade up to 5" wide.

| | Craft@Hrs | Unit | Material | Labor | Total |
|---|---|---|---|---|---|
| Starting step with bullnose one side | | | | | |
| standard grade | 1C@.492 | ea | 299.00 | 28.00 | 327.00 |
| high grade | 1C@.492 | ea | 359.00 | 28.00 | 387.00 |
| Starting step with bullnose two sides | | | | | |
| standard grade | 1C@.492 | ea | 413.00 | 28.00 | 441.00 |
| high grade | 1C@.492 | ea | 499.00 | 28.00 | 527.00 |

**Prefabricated spiral stairs.** Per step. Prefabricated spiral stairs assembled and installed by carpenter on site. Treads are made from aluminum, steel, decorative cast iron (custom grade and above) or waferboard (for carpet). Includes balustrade. Add per lf for landing or balcony railing to match: Economy $69; standard $92; high $103; custom $114; deluxe $126; custom deluxe $160.

| | Craft@Hrs | Unit | Material | Labor | Total |
|---|---|---|---|---|---|
| replace, economy grade | 1C@.855 | st | 240.00 | 48.60 | 288.60 |
| replace, standard grade | 1C@.855 | st | 426.00 | 48.60 | 474.60 |
| replace, high grade | 1C@.855 | st | 468.00 | 48.60 | 516.60 |
| replace, custom grade | 1C@.855 | st | 511.00 | 48.60 | 559.60 |
| replace, deluxe grade | 1C@.855 | st | 618.00 | 48.60 | 666.60 |
| replace, custom deluxe grade | 1C@.855 | st | 674.00 | 48.60 | 722.60 |
| remove | 1D@.123 | st | — | 4.78 | 4.78 |

**Disappearing attic stairs.** Fold-up attic access stairs with side rails.

| | Craft@Hrs | Unit | Material | Labor | Total |
|---|---|---|---|---|---|
| replace, standard grade | 1C@2.39 | ea | 434.00 | 136.00 | 570.00 |
| replace, high grade | 1C@2.39 | ea | 728.00 | 136.00 | 864.00 |
| replace, deluxe grade | 1C@2.39 | ea | 1,230.00 | 136.00 | 1,366.00 |
| remove | 1D@.270 | ea | — | 10.50 | 10.50 |
| remove for work, then reinstall | 1C@3.33 | ea | — | 189.00 | 189.00 |

| | Craft@Hrs | Unit | Material | Labor | Total |
|---|---|---|---|---|---|

**Pine stair balustrade.** Balustrade built on stairs. Balusters connect directly to treads. Includes newel post. Add **9%** for red oak newel and hand rail. Add **85%** for installation on curved stairs. Deduct **10%** for balustrade installed on porch or other level application.

| | Craft@Hrs | Unit | Material | Labor | Total |
|---|---|---|---|---|---|
| 1-1/2" pine stair balusters | | | | | |
| replace, balusters | 1C@1.32 | lf | 33.70 | 75.10 | 108.80 |
| replace, fluted balusters | 1C@1.32 | lf | 40.40 | 75.10 | 115.50 |
| replace, spiral balusters | 1C@1.32 | lf | 63.00 | 75.10 | 138.10 |
| 2-1/2" pine stair balusters | | | | | |
| replace, balusters | 1C@1.33 | lf | 38.20 | 75.70 | 113.90 |
| replace, fluted balusters | 1C@1.33 | lf | 45.90 | 75.70 | 121.60 |
| replace, spiral balusters | 1C@1.33 | lf | 71.10 | 75.70 | 146.80 |
| 3-1/2" pine stair balusters | | | | | |
| replace, balusters | 1C@1.35 | lf | 46.30 | 76.80 | 123.10 |
| replace, fluted balusters | 1C@1.35 | lf | 55.70 | 76.80 | 132.50 |
| replace, spiral balusters | 1C@1.35 | lf | 86.40 | 76.80 | 163.20 |
| 5-1/2" pine stair balusters | | | | | |
| replace, balusters | 1C@1.41 | lf | 73.70 | 80.20 | 153.90 |
| replace, fluted balusters | 1C@1.41 | lf | 87.40 | 80.20 | 167.60 |
| replace, spiral balusters | 1C@1.41 | lf | 129.00 | 80.20 | 209.20 |
| Remove | 1D@.053 | lf | — | 2.06 | 2.06 |
| Remove stair balustrade for work, then reinstall | 1C@2.39 | lf | — | 136.00 | 136.00 |

**Poplar stair balustrade.** Add **9%** for red oak balustrades and newel post in poplar stair balustrade. Add **85%** for installation on curved stairs. Deduct **10%** for balustrade installed on porch or other level application.

| | Craft@Hrs | Unit | Material | Labor | Total |
|---|---|---|---|---|---|
| 1-1/2" poplar stair balusters | | | | | |
| replace, balusters | 1C@1.32 | lf | 56.00 | 75.10 | 131.10 |
| replace, fluted balusters | 1C@1.32 | lf | 67.70 | 75.10 | 142.80 |
| replace, spiral balusters | 1C@1.32 | lf | 107.00 | 75.10 | 182.10 |
| 2-1/2" poplar stair balusters | | | | | |
| replace, balusters | 1C@1.33 | lf | 63.20 | 75.70 | 138.90 |
| replace, fluted balusters | 1C@1.33 | lf | 76.40 | 75.70 | 152.10 |
| replace, spiral balusters | 1C@1.33 | lf | 121.00 | 75.70 | 196.70 |
| 3-1/2" poplar stair balusters | | | | | |
| replace, balusters | 1C@1.35 | lf | 77.10 | 76.80 | 153.90 |
| replace, fluted balusters | 1C@1.35 | lf | 93.40 | 76.80 | 170.20 |
| replace, spiral balusters | 1C@1.35 | lf | 147.00 | 76.80 | 223.80 |
| 5-1/2" poplar stair balusters | | | | | |
| replace, balusters | 1C@1.41 | lf | 120.00 | 80.20 | 200.20 |
| replace, fluted balusters | 1C@1.41 | lf | 143.00 | 80.20 | 223.20 |
| replace, spiral balusters | 1C@1.41 | lf | 221.00 | 80.20 | 301.20 |
| Remove | 1D@.053 | lf | — | 2.06 | 2.06 |
| Remove stair balustrade for work, then reinstall | 1C@2.39 | lf | — | 136.00 | 136.00 |

| | Craft@Hrs | Unit | Material | Labor | Total |
|---|---|---|---|---|---|

**Redwood stair balustrade.** Includes newel post. Add **85%** for installation on curved stairs. Deduct **10%** for balustrade installed on porch or other level application.

| | Craft@Hrs | Unit | Material | Labor | Total |
|---|---|---|---|---|---|
| 1-1/2" redwood stair balusters | | | | | |
| replace, balusters | 1C@1.32 | lf | 62.40 | 75.10 | 137.50 |
| replace, fluted balusters | 1C@1.32 | lf | 75.40 | 75.10 | 150.50 |
| replace, spiral balusters | 1C@1.32 | lf | 119.00 | 75.10 | 194.10 |
| 2-1/2" redwood stair balusters | | | | | |
| replace, balusters | 1C@1.33 | lf | 70.30 | 75.70 | 146.00 |
| replace, fluted balusters | 1C@1.33 | lf | 85.20 | 75.70 | 160.90 |
| replace, spiral balusters | 1C@1.33 | lf | 132.00 | 75.70 | 207.70 |
| 3-1/2" redwood stair balusters | | | | | |
| replace, balusters | 1C@1.35 | lf | 85.70 | 76.80 | 162.50 |
| replace, fluted balusters | 1C@1.35 | lf | 104.00 | 76.80 | 180.80 |
| replace, spiral balusters | 1C@1.35 | lf | 163.00 | 76.80 | 239.80 |
| 5-1/2" redwood stair balusters | | | | | |
| replace, balusters | 1C@1.41 | lf | 132.00 | 80.20 | 212.20 |
| replace, fluted balusters | 1C@1.41 | lf | 160.00 | 80.20 | 240.20 |
| replace, spiral balusters | 1C@1.41 | lf | 243.00 | 80.20 | 323.20 |
| Stair balustrade | | | | | |
| remove | 1D@.053 | lf | — | 2.06 | 2.06 |
| remove stair balustrade for work, then reinstall | 1C@2.39 | lf | — | 136.00 | 136.00 |

**Red oak stair balustrade.** Includes newel post. Add **85%** for installation on curved stairs. Deduct **10%** for balustrade installed on porch or other level application.

| | Craft@Hrs | Unit | Material | Labor | Total |
|---|---|---|---|---|---|
| 1-1/2" red oak stair balustrade | | | | | |
| replace, balusters | 1C@1.32 | lf | 79.00 | 75.10 | 154.10 |
| replace, fluted balusters | 1C@1.32 | lf | 95.30 | 75.10 | 170.40 |
| replace, spiral balusters | 1C@1.32 | lf | 147.00 | 75.10 | 222.10 |
| replace, hand-carved balusters | 1C@1.32 | lf | 303.00 | 75.10 | 378.10 |
| replace, heavy hand-carved balusters | 1C@1.32 | lf | 325.00 | 75.10 | 400.10 |
| 2-1/2" red oak stair balustrade | | | | | |
| replace, balusters | 1C@1.33 | lf | 88.80 | 75.70 | 164.50 |
| replace, fluted balusters | 1C@1.33 | lf | 107.00 | 75.70 | 182.70 |
| replace, spiral balusters | 1C@1.33 | lf | 168.00 | 75.70 | 243.70 |
| replace, hand-carved balusters | 1C@1.33 | lf | 307.00 | 75.70 | 382.70 |
| replace, heavy hand-carved balusters | 1C@1.33 | lf | 329.00 | 75.70 | 404.70 |
| 3-1/2" red oak stair balustrade | | | | | |
| replace, balusters | 1C@1.35 | lf | 107.00 | 76.80 | 183.80 |
| replace, fluted balusters | 1C@1.35 | lf | 129.00 | 76.80 | 205.80 |
| replace, spiral balusters | 1C@1.35 | lf | 202.00 | 76.80 | 278.80 |
| replace, hand-carved balusters | 1C@1.35 | lf | 375.00 | 76.80 | 451.80 |
| replace, heavy hand-carved balusters | 1C@1.35 | lf | 407.00 | 76.80 | 483.80 |
| 5-1/2" red oak stair balustrade | | | | | |
| replace, balusters | 1C@1.41 | lf | 172.00 | 80.20 | 252.20 |
| replace, fluted balusters | 1C@1.41 | lf | 202.00 | 80.20 | 282.20 |
| replace, spiral balusters | 1C@1.41 | lf | 307.00 | 80.20 | 387.20 |
| replace, hand-carved balusters | 1C@1.41 | lf | 365.00 | 80.20 | 445.20 |
| replace, heavy hand-carved balusters | 1C@1.41 | lf | 405.00 | 80.20 | 485.20 |
| Stair balustrade | | | | | |
| remove | 1D@.053 | lf | — | 2.06 | 2.06 |
| remove for work, then reinstall | 1C@2.39 | lf | — | 136.00 | 136.00 |

| | Craft@Hrs | Unit | Material | Labor | Total |
|---|---|---|---|---|---|

**Sawn stair balustrade.** Includes newel post.  Deduct **10%** for balustrade installed on porch or other level application.

| | Craft@Hrs | Unit | Material | Labor | Total |
|---|---|---|---|---|---|
| Pine sawn stair balustrade | | | | | |
| replace | 1C@1.32 | lf | 56.40 | 75.10 | 131.50 |
| replace, with panels | 1C@1.32 | lf | 95.50 | 75.10 | 170.60 |
| Poplar sawn stair balustrade | | | | | |
| replace | 1C@1.32 | lf | 76.80 | 75.10 | 151.90 |
| replace, with panels | 1C@1.32 | lf | 117.00 | 75.10 | 192.10 |
| Add for red oak hand rail and newel post in | | | | | |
| paint-grade sawn stair balustrade | — | lf | 16.00 | — | 16.00 |
| Redwood sawn stair balustrade | | | | | |
| replace | 1C@1.32 | lf | 129.00 | 75.10 | 204.10 |
| replace, with panels | 1C@1.32 | lf | 206.00 | 75.10 | 281.10 |
| Red oak sawn stair balustrade | | | | | |
| replace | 1C@1.32 | lf | 105.00 | 75.10 | 180.10 |
| replace, with panels | 1C@1.32 | lf | 156.00 | 75.10 | 231.10 |
| Stair balustrade | | | | | |
| remove | 1D@.053 | lf | — | 2.06 | 2.06 |
| remove for work, then reinstall | 1C@2.39 | lf | — | 136.00 | 136.00 |

*sawn balusters*

*sawn baluster panels*

*volute end*

*goose neck*

*add for 1/4 turn in stair rail*

*add for 1/2 turn in stair rail*

**Additional stair balustrade costs.** Oak, poplar, or pine. Volute post includes additional balusters and labor to install volute end with circled balusters and newel. Usually not used on stairs with balusters larger than 2-1/2".

| | Craft@Hrs | Unit | Material | Labor | Total |
|---|---|---|---|---|---|
| add for volute end | 1C@3.03 | ea | 320.00 | 172.00 | 492.00 |
| add for goose neck | 1C@2.44 | ea | 364.00 | 139.00 | 503.00 |
| add for 1/4 turn in stair rail | 1C@2.27 | ea | 112.00 | 129.00 | 241.00 |
| add for 1/2 turn in stair rail | 1C@2.44 | ea | 259.00 | 139.00 | 398.00 |

*standard*

*high grade*

*deluxe grade*

*custom grade*

**Stair bracket.** Brackets installed beneath open end of tread.

| | Craft@Hrs | Unit | Material | Labor | Total |
|---|---|---|---|---|---|
| replace, standard grade | 1C@.091 | ea | 12.60 | 5.18 | 17.78 |
| replace, high grade | 1C@.091 | ea | 14.60 | 5.18 | 19.78 |
| replace, deluxe grade | 1C@.091 | ea | 17.70 | 5.18 | 22.88 |
| replace, custom grade | 1C@.091 | ea | 19.80 | 5.18 | 24.98 |
| remove | 1D@.054 | ea | — | 2.10 | 2.10 |
| remove for work, then reinstall | 1C@.149 | ea | — | 8.48 | 8.48 |

| | Craft@Hrs | Unit | Material | Labor | Total |
|---|---|---|---|---|---|

**Molding trim beneath tread.** Up to 3/4" cove, quarter-round or similar installed beneath the open end of the tread.

| | Craft@Hrs | Unit | Material | Labor | Total |
|---|---|---|---|---|---|
| replace, pine | 1C@.108 | ea | .73 | 6.15 | 6.88 |
| replace, red oak | 1C@.108 | ea | 1.16 | 6.15 | 7.31 |
| remove | 1D@.019 | ea | — | .74 | .74 |

**Pine newel.**

Pine newel for 1-1/2" balusters
(newel is 3-1/2" to 4" wide)

| | Craft@Hrs | Unit | Material | Labor | Total |
|---|---|---|---|---|---|
| replace, newel post | 1C@.961 | ea | 57.70 | 54.70 | 112.40 |
| replace, fluted newel post | 1C@.961 | ea | 76.20 | 54.70 | 130.90 |
| replace, spiral newel post | 1C@.961 | ea | 78.40 | 54.70 | 133.10 |

Pine newel for 2-1/2" balusters
(newel is 4" to 4-1/2" wide)

| | Craft@Hrs | Unit | Material | Labor | Total |
|---|---|---|---|---|---|
| replace, newel post | 1C@.961 | ea | 69.20 | 54.70 | 123.90 |
| replace, fluted newel post | 1C@.961 | ea | 91.80 | 54.70 | 146.50 |
| replace, spiral newel post | 1C@.961 | ea | 94.20 | 54.70 | 148.90 |

Pine newel for 3-1/2" balusters
(newel is 4-1/2" to 5" wide)

| | Craft@Hrs | Unit | Material | Labor | Total |
|---|---|---|---|---|---|
| replace, newel post | 1C@.961 | ea | 83.20 | 54.70 | 137.90 |
| replace, fluted newel post | 1C@.961 | ea | 110.00 | 54.70 | 164.70 |
| replace, spiral newel post | 1C@.961 | ea | 112.00 | 54.70 | 166.70 |

Pine newel for 5-1/2" balusters
(newel is 6" to 7" wide)

| | Craft@Hrs | Unit | Material | Labor | Total |
|---|---|---|---|---|---|
| replace, newel post | 1C@.961 | ea | 130.00 | 54.70 | 184.70 |
| replace, fluted newel post | 1C@.961 | ea | 176.00 | 54.70 | 230.70 |
| replace, spiral newel post | 1C@.961 | ea | 182.00 | 54.70 | 236.70 |
| Remove | 1D@.188 | ea | — | 7.31 | 7.31 |
| Remove newel post for work, then reinstall | 1C@1.41 | ea | — | 80.20 | 80.20 |

**Poplar newel.**

Poplar newel for 1-1/2" balusters
(newel is 3-1/2" to 4" wide)

| | Craft@Hrs | Unit | Material | Labor | Total |
|---|---|---|---|---|---|
| replace, newel post | 1C@.961 | ea | 96.10 | 54.70 | 150.80 |
| replace, fluted newel post | 1C@.961 | ea | 127.00 | 54.70 | 181.70 |
| replace, spiral newel post | 1C@.961 | ea | 129.00 | 54.70 | 183.70 |

Poplar newel for 2-1/2" balusters
(newel is 4" to 4-1/2" wide)

| | Craft@Hrs | Unit | Material | Labor | Total |
|---|---|---|---|---|---|
| replace, newel post | 1C@.961 | ea | 114.00 | 54.70 | 168.70 |
| replace, fluted newel post | 1C@.961 | ea | 153.00 | 54.70 | 207.70 |
| replace, spiral newel post | 1C@.961 | ea | 157.00 | 54.70 | 211.70 |

Poplar newel for 3-1/2" balusters
(newel is 4-1/2" to 5" wide)

| | Craft@Hrs | Unit | Material | Labor | Total |
|---|---|---|---|---|---|
| replace, newel post | 1C@.961 | ea | 137.00 | 54.70 | 191.70 |
| replace, fluted newel post | 1C@.961 | ea | 186.00 | 54.70 | 240.70 |
| replace, spiral newel post | 1C@.961 | ea | 190.00 | 54.70 | 244.70 |

| | Craft@Hrs | Unit | Material | Labor | Total |
|---|---|---|---|---|---|
| Poplar newel for 5-1/2" balusters | | | | | |
| (newel is 6" to 8" wide) | | | | | |
|     replace, newel post | 1C@.961 | ea | 220.00 | 54.70 | 274.70 |
|     replace, fluted newel post | 1C@.961 | ea | 292.00 | 54.70 | 346.70 |
|     replace, spiral newel post | 1C@.961 | ea | 302.00 | 54.70 | 356.70 |
| Remove | 1D@.188 | ea | — | 7.31 | 7.31 |
| Remove newel post for work, then reinstall | 1C@1.41 | ea | — | 80.20 | 80.20 |

**Redwood newel.**

| | | | | | |
|---|---|---|---|---|---|
| Redwood newel for 1-1/2" balusters | | | | | |
| (newel is 3-1/2" to 4" wide) | | | | | |
|     replace, newel post | 1C@.961 | ea | 107.00 | 54.70 | 161.70 |
|     replace, fluted newel post | 1C@.961 | ea | 142.00 | 54.70 | 196.70 |
|     replace, spiral newel post | 1C@.961 | ea | 146.00 | 54.70 | 200.70 |
| Redwood newel for 2-1/2" balusters | | | | | |
| (newel is 4" to 4-1/2" wide) | | | | | |
|     replace, newel post | 1C@.961 | ea | 129.00 | 54.70 | 183.70 |
|     replace, fluted newel post | 1C@.961 | ea | 172.00 | 54.70 | 226.70 |
|     replace, spiral newel post | 1C@.961 | ea | 177.00 | 54.70 | 231.70 |
| Redwood newel for 3-1/2" balusters | | | | | |
| (newel is 4-1/2" to 5" wide) | | | | | |
|     replace, newel post | 1C@.961 | ea | 155.00 | 54.70 | 209.70 |
|     replace, fluted newel post | 1C@.961 | ea | 206.00 | 54.70 | 260.70 |
|     replace, spiral newel post | 1C@.961 | ea | 212.00 | 54.70 | 266.70 |
| Redwood newel for 5-1/2" balusters | | | | | |
| (newel is 6" to 8" wide) | | | | | |
|     replace, newel post | 1C@.961 | ea | 244.00 | 54.70 | 298.70 |
|     replace, fluted newel post | 1C@.961 | ea | 327.00 | 54.70 | 381.70 |
|     replace, spiral newel post | 1C@.961 | ea | 335.00 | 54.70 | 389.70 |
| Remove | 1D@.188 | ea | — | 7.31 | 7.31 |
| Remove newel post for work, then reinstall | 1C@1.41 | ea | — | 80.20 | 80.20 |

**Red oak newel.**

| | | | | | |
|---|---|---|---|---|---|
| Red oak newel for 1-1/2" balusters | | | | | |
| (newel is 3-1/2" to 4" wide) | | | | | |
|     replace, newel post | 1C@.961 | ea | 139.00 | 54.70 | 193.70 |
|     replace, fluted newel post | 1C@.961 | ea | 188.00 | 54.70 | 242.70 |
|     replace, spiral newel post | 1C@.961 | ea | 194.00 | 54.70 | 248.70 |
|     replace, hand-carved newel post | 1C@.961 | ea | 259.00 | 54.70 | 313.70 |
|     replace, heavy hand-carved newel post | 1C@.961 | ea | 281.00 | 54.70 | 335.70 |
| Red oak newel for 2-1/2" balusters | | | | | |
| (newel is 4" to 4-1/2" wide) | | | | | |
|     replace, newel post | 1C@.961 | ea | 160.00 | 54.70 | 214.70 |
|     replace, fluted newel post | 1C@.961 | ea | 213.00 | 54.70 | 267.70 |
|     replace, spiral newel post | 1C@.961 | ea | 219.00 | 54.70 | 273.70 |
|     replace, hand-carved newel post | 1C@.961 | ea | 294.00 | 54.70 | 348.70 |
|     replace, heavy hand-carved newel post | 1C@.961 | ea | 317.00 | 54.70 | 371.70 |

| | Craft@Hrs | Unit | Material | Labor | Total |
|---|---|---|---|---|---|
| Red oak newel for 3-1/2" balusters | | | | | |
| (newel is 4-1/2" to 5" wide) | | | | | |
|     replace, newel post | 1C@.961 | ea | 194.00 | 54.70 | 248.70 |
|     replace, fluted newel post | 1C@.961 | ea | 254.00 | 54.70 | 308.70 |
|     replace, spiral newel post | 1C@.961 | ea | 262.00 | 54.70 | 316.70 |
|     replace, hand-carved newel post | 1C@.961 | ea | 320.00 | 54.70 | 374.70 |
|     replace, heavy hand-carved newel post | 1C@.961 | ea | 341.00 | 54.70 | 395.70 |
| Red oak newel for 5-1/2" balusters | | | | | |
| (newel is 6" to 8" wide) | | | | | |
|     replace, newel post | 1C@.961 | ea | 307.00 | 54.70 | 361.70 |
|     replace, fluted newel post | 1C@.961 | ea | 406.00 | 54.70 | 460.70 |
|     replace, spiral newel post | 1C@.961 | ea | 418.00 | 54.70 | 472.70 |
|     replace, hand-carved newel post | 1C@.961 | ea | 569.00 | 54.70 | 623.70 |
|     replace, heavy hand-carved newel post | 1C@.961 | ea | 615.00 | 54.70 | 669.70 |
| Remove | 1D@.188 | ea | — | 7.31 | 7.31 |
| Remove newel post for work, then reinstall | 1C@1.41 | ea | — | 80.20 | 80.20 |

**Additional wood species.** Add to the cost of poplar stair components.

| | | Unit | Material | Labor | Total |
|---|---|---|---|---|---|
|     add for mahogany | — | % | 24.0 | — | — |
|     add for cherry | — | % | 43.0 | — | — |
|     add for maple | — | % | 11.0 | — | — |
|     add for birch | — | % | 2.0 | — | — |

## Time & Material Charts (selected items)
## Stairs Materials

See Stairs material prices with the line items above.

### Stairs Labor

| Laborer | base wage | paid leave | true wage | taxes & ins. | total |
|---|---|---|---|---|---|
| Carpenter | $31.10 | 2.43 | $33.53 | 23.37 | $56.90 |
| Demolition laborer | $20.70 | 1.61 | $22.31 | 16.59 | $38.90 |

**Paid leave** is calculated based on two weeks paid vacation, one week sick leave, and seven paid holidays. Employer's matching portion of **FICA** is 7.65 percent. **FUTA** (Federal Unemployment) is .8 percent. **Worker's compensation** for the stairs trade was calculated using a national average of 16.85 percent. **Unemployment insurance** was calculated using a national average of 8 percent. **Health insurance** was calculated based on a projected national average for 2015 of $1,025 per employee (and family when applicable) per month. Employer pays 80 percent for a per month cost of $820 per employee. **Retirement** is based on a 401(k) retirement program with employer matching of 50 percent. Employee contributions to the 401(k) plan are an average of 6 percent of the true wage. **Liability insurance** is based on a national average of 10.0 percent.

| | Craft@Hrs | Unit | Material | Labor | Total |
|---|---|---|---|---|---|
| **Stairs Labor Productivity** | | | | | |
| Demolition of stairs | | | | | |
|     remove utility stairs | 1D@.101 | st | — | 3.93 | 3.93 |
|     remove stairs | 1D@.122 | st | — | 4.75 | 4.75 |
|     remove 1/4 turn stairs | 1D@.135 | st | — | 5.25 | 5.25 |
|     remove 1/2 turn stairs | 1D@.150 | st | — | 5.84 | 5.84 |
|     remove circular stairs | 1D@.158 | st | — | 6.15 | 6.15 |

| | Craft@Hrs | Unit | Material | Labor | Total |
|---|---|---|---|---|---|
| remove spiral stairs | 1D@.123 | st | — | 4.78 | 4.78 |
| remove disappearing attic stairs | 1D@.270 | ea | — | 10.50 | 10.50 |
| remove stair balustrade | 1D@.053 | lf | — | 2.06 | 2.06 |
| remove stair bracket | 1D@.054 | ea | — | 2.10 | 2.10 |
| remove newel post | 1D@.188 | ea | — | 7.31 | 7.31 |
| **Build 3' wide stairs with three stringers** | | | | | |
| utility stairs | 1C@.361 | st | — | 20.50 | 20.50 |
| **Build 3' wide stairs with four stringers** | | | | | |
| 3' wide enclosed | 1C@.474 | st | — | 27.00 | 27.00 |
| 3' wide, one side open | 1C@.485 | st | — | 27.60 | 27.60 |
| 3' wide , two sides open | 1C@.517 | st | — | 29.40 | 29.40 |
| **Build 3' wide 1/4 turn stairs with four stringers,** | | | | | |
| **and a 3' x 3' landing** | | | | | |
| 3' wide enclosed | 1C@.825 | st | — | 46.90 | 46.90 |
| 3' wide enclosed & oak plank on landing | 1C@1.02 | st | — | 58.00 | 58.00 |
| 3' wide, one side open | 1C@.855 | st | — | 48.60 | 48.60 |
| 3' wide, one side open & oak plank on landing | 1C@1.04 | st | — | 59.20 | 59.20 |
| 3' wide, two sides open | 1C@.885 | st | — | 50.40 | 50.40 |
| 3' wide, two sides open & oak plank on landing | 1C@1.05 | st | — | 59.70 | 59.70 |
| **Build 3' wide 1/2 turn stairs with four stringers,** | | | | | |
| **and a 6' x 3' landing** | | | | | |
| 3' wide enclosed | 1C@.908 | st | — | 51.70 | 51.70 |
| 3' wide enclosed with oak plank on landing | 1C@1.12 | st | — | 63.70 | 63.70 |
| 3' wide, one side open | 1C@.943 | st | — | 53.70 | 53.70 |
| 3' wide, one side open & oak plank on landing | 1C@1.15 | st | — | 65.40 | 65.40 |
| 3' wide, two sides open | 1C@.970 | st | — | 55.20 | 55.20 |
| 3' wide, two sides open & oak plank on landing | 1C@1.16 | st | — | 66.00 | 66.00 |
| **Additional stair costs** | | | | | |
| add to build platform winders | 1C@.400 | ea | — | 22.80 | 22.80 |
| add to build mitered corner on bottom step | 1C@2.32 | ea | — | 132.00 | 132.00 |
| add to install bullnose starting step | 1C@.492 | ea | — | 28.00 | 28.00 |
| **Install false treads and risers** | | | | | |
| closed end | 1C@.070 | ea | — | 3.98 | 3.98 |
| open end | 1C@.090 | ea | — | 5.12 | 5.12 |
| **Build 3' wide circular stairs** | | | | | |
| enclosed | 1C@11.6 | st | — | 660.00 | 660.00 |
| one side open | 1C@11.8 | st | — | 671.00 | 671.00 |
| two sides open | 1C@11.9 | st | — | 677.00 | 677.00 |
| **Install prefabricated spiral stairs** | | | | | |
| all grades | 1C@.855 | st | — | 48.60 | 48.60 |
| **Install disappearing attic stairs** | | | | | |
| all grades | 1C@2.39 | ea | — | 136.00 | 136.00 |
| remove for work, then reinstall | 1C@3.33 | ea | — | 189.00 | 189.00 |
| **Install wood stair balustrade** | | | | | |
| with 1-1/2" balusters | 1C@1.32 | lf | — | 75.10 | 75.10 |
| with 2-1/2" balusters | 1C@1.33 | lf | — | 75.70 | 75.70 |
| with 3-1/2" balusters | 1C@1.35 | lf | — | 76.80 | 76.80 |
| with 5-1/2" balusters | 1C@1.41 | lf | — | 80.20 | 80.20 |
| remove for work, then reinstall | 1C@2.39 | lf | — | 136.00 | 136.00 |
| **Install newel post** | | | | | |
| install | 1C@.961 | ea | — | 54.70 | 54.70 |
| remove for work, then reinstall | 1C@1.41 | ea | — | 80.20 | 80.20 |

| | Craft@Hrs | Unit | Material | Labor | Total |
|---|---|---|---|---|---|

## Suspended Ceilings

**12" x 12" concealed grid suspended ceiling tile.** Includes 12" x 12" suspended ceiling tiles, and installation. Tiles are designed to be installed in a concealed grid. Does not include the concealed grid system.

| | Craft@Hrs | Unit | Material | Labor | Total |
|---|---|---|---|---|---|
| smooth face | 1S@.019 | sf | 1.47 | .88 | 2.35 |
| fissured face | 1S@.019 | sf | 1.76 | .88 | 2.64 |
| textured face | 1S@.019 | sf | 2.00 | .88 | 2.88 |
| patterned face | 1S@.019 | sf | 2.16 | .88 | 3.04 |
| remove | 1D@.006 | sf | — | .23 | .23 |

**Concealed grid for ceiling tile.** Includes main runners, cross tees, wires, and eyelet screws. Does not include tiles.

| | Craft@Hrs | Unit | Material | Labor | Total |
|---|---|---|---|---|---|
| 12" x 12" grid system | 1S@.020 | sf | 1.62 | .93 | 2.55 |
| remove | 1D@.006 | sf | — | .23 | .23 |

**Additional costs for 12" x 12" concealed grid system.**

| | Craft@Hrs | Unit | Material | Labor | Total |
|---|---|---|---|---|---|
| access panel | 1S@.725 | ea | 78.20 | 33.60 | 111.80 |
| remove | 1D@.097 | ea | — | 3.77 | 3.77 |
| relevel sagging grid | 1S@.020 | sf | — | .93 | .93 |

**2' x 4' suspended ceiling tile.** Includes 2' x 4' suspended ceiling tiles, and installation. Tiles are designed to be installed in a suspended grid. Does not include the suspended grid system.

| | Craft@Hrs | Unit | Material | Labor | Total |
|---|---|---|---|---|---|
| smooth face | 1S@.011 | sf | .65 | .51 | 1.16 |
| fissured face | 1S@.011 | sf | .87 | .51 | 1.38 |
| textured face | 1S@.011 | sf | 1.11 | .51 | 1.62 |
| patterned face | 1S@.011 | sf | 1.44 | .51 | 1.95 |
| remove | 1D@.005 | sf | — | .19 | .19 |
| add for fire-rated tile installed with clips | 1S@.008 | sf | .48 | .37 | .85 |

**2' x 4' luminous panels.** Includes luminous panels and installation. Does not include grid.

| | Craft@Hrs | Unit | Material | Labor | Total |
|---|---|---|---|---|---|
| polystyrene cracked-ice or mist white | 1S@.010 | sf | 1.56 | .46 | 2.02 |
| acrylic cracked-ice or mist white | 1S@.010 | sf | 3.02 | .46 | 3.48 |
| polystyrene egg crate | 1S@.010 | sf | 1.51 | .46 | 1.97 |
| acrylic egg crate | 1S@.010 | sf | 5.62 | .46 | 6.08 |
| acrylic egg crate with stainless steel finish | 1S@.010 | sf | 6.14 | .46 | 6.60 |
| acrylic egg crate with brass finish | 1S@.010 | sf | 6.23 | .46 | 6.69 |
| square crate polystyrene | 1S@.010 | sf | 1.48 | .46 | 1.94 |
| square crate acrylic | 1S@.010 | sf | 5.30 | .46 | 5.76 |
| square crate acrylic with stainless steel finish | 1S@.010 | sf | 5.98 | .46 | 6.44 |
| square crate acrylic with brass finish | 1S@.010 | sf | 6.05 | .46 | 6.51 |
| remove | 1D@.005 | ea | — | .19 | .19 |

**2' x 4' suspended grid for ceiling tile.** Includes main runners 4' on center, cross tees, wire, and eyelet screws. Does not include tiles or luminous panels.

| | Craft@Hrs | Unit | Material | Labor | Total |
|---|---|---|---|---|---|
| baked enamel | 1S@.013 | sf | .60 | .60 | 1.20 |
| colored baked enamel | 1S@.013 | sf | .69 | .60 | 1.29 |
| brass finish | 1S@.013 | sf | .94 | .60 | 1.54 |
| stainless steel finish | 1S@.013 | sf | 1.14 | .60 | 1.74 |
| remove | 1D@.004 | sf | — | .16 | .16 |
| add for fire-rated suspended grid | — | sf | .39 | — | .39 |

| | Craft@Hrs | Unit | Material | Labor | Total |
|---|---|---|---|---|---|

**2' x 4' narrow suspended grid.** Includes main runners 4' on center, cross tees, wire, and eyelet screws. Does not include tiles or luminous panels.

| | Craft@Hrs | Unit | Material | Labor | Total |
|---|---|---|---|---|---|
| baked enamel | 1S@.013 | sf | .64 | .60 | 1.24 |
| colored baked enamel | 1S@.013 | sf | .64 | .60 | 1.24 |
| brass finish | 1S@.013 | sf | 1.13 | .60 | 1.73 |
| stainless steel finish | 1S@.013 | sf | 1.14 | .60 | 1.74 |
| remove | 1D@.004 | sf | — | .16 | .16 |
| add for fire-rated narrow suspended grid | 1S@.013 | sf | .43 | .60 | 1.03 |

**Additional 2' x 4' suspended ceiling system costs.**

| | Craft@Hrs | Unit | Material | Labor | Total |
|---|---|---|---|---|---|
| relevel sagging suspended grid | 1S@.014 | sf | — | .65 | .65 |
| remove tiles for work, then reinstall | 1S@.011 | sf | — | .51 | .51 |
| remove tiles & blanket or insulation for work, then reinstall | 1S@.013 | sf | — | .60 | .60 |

**2' x 2' suspended ceiling tile.** Includes 2' x 2' suspended ceiling tiles, and installation. Tiles are designed to be installed in a suspended grid. Does not include the suspended grid system.

| | Craft@Hrs | Unit | Material | Labor | Total |
|---|---|---|---|---|---|
| smooth face | 1S@.009 | sf | .79 | .42 | 1.21 |
| fissured face | 1S@.009 | sf | 1.42 | .42 | 1.84 |
| textured face | 1S@.009 | sf | 1.34 | .42 | 1.76 |
| patterned face | 1S@.009 | sf | 1.75 | .42 | 2.17 |
| remove | 1D@.004 | sf | — | .16 | .16 |
| add for fire-rated tile installed with clips | 1S@.009 | sf | .58 | .42 | 1.00 |

**2' x 2' recessed edge suspended ceiling tile.** Tile only, no grid.

| | Craft@Hrs | Unit | Material | Labor | Total |
|---|---|---|---|---|---|
| smooth face | 1S@.009 | sf | .90 | .42 | 1.32 |
| fissured face | 1S@.009 | sf | 1.16 | .42 | 1.58 |
| textured face | 1S@.009 | sf | 1.55 | .42 | 1.97 |
| patterned face | 1S@.009 | sf | 2.00 | .42 | 2.42 |
| remove | 1D@.004 | sf | — | .16 | .16 |
| add for fire-rated tile installed with clips | 1S@.009 | sf | .03 | .42 | .45 |

**2' x 2' luminous panels.** Includes 2' x 2' luminous panels and installation. Does not include grid.

| | Craft@Hrs | Unit | Material | Labor | Total |
|---|---|---|---|---|---|
| polystyrene cracked-ice or mist white | 1S@.005 | sf | 1.88 | .23 | 2.11 |
| acrylic cracked-ice or mist white | 1S@.005 | sf | 3.63 | .23 | 3.86 |
| polystyrene egg crate | 1S@.005 | sf | 1.86 | .23 | 2.09 |
| acrylic egg crate | 1S@.005 | sf | 6.74 | .23 | 6.97 |
| acrylic egg crate with stainless steel finish | 1S@.005 | sf | 7.36 | .23 | 7.59 |
| acrylic egg crate with brass finish | 1S@.005 | sf | 7.47 | .23 | 7.70 |
| square crate polystyrene | 1S@.005 | sf | 1.80 | .23 | 2.03 |
| square crate acrylic | 1S@.005 | sf | 6.38 | .23 | 6.61 |
| square crate acrylic with stainless steel finish | 1S@.005 | sf | 7.19 | .23 | 7.42 |
| square crate acrylic with brass finish | 1S@.005 | sf | 7.28 | .23 | 7.51 |
| remove | 1D@.004 | sf | — | .16 | .16 |

**2' x 2' suspended grid.** Includes main runners 4' on center, cross tees, wire, and eyelet screws. Does not include tiles or luminous panels.

| | Craft@Hrs | Unit | Material | Labor | Total |
|---|---|---|---|---|---|
| baked enamel | 1S@.013 | sf | .95 | .60 | 1.55 |
| colored baked enamel | 1S@.013 | sf | 1.08 | .60 | 1.68 |
| brass finish | 1S@.013 | sf | 1.39 | .60 | 1.99 |
| stainless steel finish | 1S@.013 | sf | 1.42 | .60 | 2.02 |
| remove | 1D@.004 | sf | — | .16 | .16 |
| add for fire-rated grid | — | sf | .82 | — | .82 |

| | Craft@Hrs | Unit | Material | Labor | Total |
|---|---|---|---|---|---|

**2' x 2' narrow suspended grid.** Includes main runners 4' on center, cross tees, wire, and eyelet screws. Does not include tiles or luminous panels.

| | | | | | |
|---|---|---|---|---|---|
| baked enamel | 1S@.013 | sf | .99 | .60 | 1.59 |
| colored baked enamel | 1S@.013 | sf | 1.02 | .60 | 1.62 |
| brass finish | 1S@.013 | sf | 1.39 | .60 | 1.99 |
| stainless-steel finish | 1S@.013 | sf | 1.81 | .60 | 2.41 |
| remove | 1D@.004 | sf | — | .16 | .16 |
| add for fire-rated narrow grid | — | sf | .82 | — | .82 |

**Additional 2' x 2' suspended ceiling system costs.**

| | | | | | |
|---|---|---|---|---|---|
| relevel sagging suspended grid | 1S@.016 | sf | — | .74 | .74 |
| remove tiles for work, then reinstall | 1S@.011 | sf | — | .51 | .51 |
| remove tiles & blanket for work, then reinstall | 1S@.014 | sf | — | .65 | .65 |

**Minimum charge.**

| | | | | | |
|---|---|---|---|---|---|
| minimum for suspended ceiling work | 1S@3.00 | ea | 68.50 | 139.00 | 207.50 |

**Drop-in HVAC panels for suspended ceiling systems.** Includes manufactured HVAC panel and installation in suspended grid system. Does not include the suspended-grid system or the ductwork.

| | | | | | |
|---|---|---|---|---|---|
| cold-air return panel | 1S@.609 | ea | 66.20 | 28.30 | 94.50 |
| air diffuser panel | 1S@.609 | ea | 66.20 | 28.30 | 94.50 |
| remove | 1D@.135 | ea | — | 5.25 | 5.25 |

**Sound blanket.** Includes sound-absorbing blanket installed above suspended ceiling grid. Does not include the grid system or panels.

| | | | | | |
|---|---|---|---|---|---|
| 2" blanket above suspended grid | 1S@.009 | sf | .55 | .42 | .97 |
| remove | 1D@.008 | sf | — | .31 | .31 |
| 3" blanket above suspended grid | 1S@.009 | sf | .84 | .42 | 1.26 |
| remove | 1D@.009 | sf | — | .35 | .35 |

## Time & Material Charts (selected items)
## Suspended Ceilings Materials

Suspended ceiling with concealed grid

| | | | | | |
|---|---|---|---|---|---|
| wall angle,<br>($7.58 per 12' stick, 83 sf), 4% waste | — | sf | .09 | — | .09 |
| main tee,<br>($9.64 per 12' stick, 15.00 sf), 4% waste | — | sf | .67 | — | .67 |
| cross tee (12" x 12" installation),<br>($.92 per 1' stick, 1.14 sf), 4% waste | — | sf | .84 | — | .84 |

Suspended ceiling grid baked enamel finish

| | | | | | |
|---|---|---|---|---|---|
| wall angle,<br>($5.90 per 12' stick, 43.20 sf), 4% waste | — | sf | .15 | — | .15 |
| main tee,<br>($9.64 per 12' stick, 27.48 sf), 4% waste | — | sf | .36 | — | .36 |
| cross tee in 2' x 4' installation,<br>($3.24 per 4' stick, 41.60 sf), 4% waste | — | sf | .08 | — | .08 |

| | Craft@Hrs | Unit | Material | Labor | Total |
|---|---|---|---|---|---|
| cross tee in 2' x 2' installation, ($1.93 per 2' stick, 4.58 sf), 4% waste | — | sf | .44 | — | .44 |
| 12" x 12" suspended tile for concealed grid system | | | | | |
| smooth face, ($1.40 per tile, 1 sf), 5% waste | — | sf | 1.47 | — | 1.47 |
| patterned face, ($2.06 per tile, 1 sf), 5% waste | — | sf | 2.16 | — | 2.16 |
| add for fire rating, ($.50 per tile, 1 sf), 5% waste | — | sf | .53 | — | .53 |
| 2' x 4' suspended tile | | | | | |
| smooth face, ($4.89 per tile, 8 sf), 5% waste | — | sf | .64 | — | .64 |
| patterned face, ($10.90 per tile, 8 sf), 5% waste | — | sf | 1.43 | — | 1.43 |
| add for 2' x 4' tile with fire rating, ($3.18 per tile, 8 sf), 5% waste | — | sf | .42 | — | .42 |
| 2' x 4' luminous panel | | | | | |
| polystyrene cracked-ice or mist white, ($11.90 per panel, 8 sf), 4% waste | — | sf | 1.55 | — | 1.55 |
| acrylic mist white, ($23.30 per panel, 8 sf), 4% waste | — | sf | 3.03 | — | 3.03 |
| polystyrene egg crate, ($11.70 per panel, 8 sf), 4% waste | — | sf | 1.52 | — | 1.52 |
| acrylic egg crate, ($43.40 per panel, 8 sf), 4% waste | — | sf | 5.65 | — | 5.65 |
| acrylic egg crate with stainless steel finish, ($47.10 per panel, 8 sf), 4% waste | — | sf | 6.13 | — | 6.13 |
| acrylic egg crate with brass finish, ($47.70 per panel, 8 sf), 4% waste | — | sf | 6.20 | — | 6.20 |

## Suspended Ceilings Labor

| Laborer | base wage | paid leave | true wage | taxes & ins. | total |
|---|---|---|---|---|---|
| Installer | $29.70 | 2.32 | $32.02 | 20.98 | $53.00 |
| Installer's helper | $21.50 | 1.68 | $23.18 | 16.62 | $39.80 |
| Electrician | $36.10 | 2.82 | $38.92 | 22.38 | $61.30 |
| Demolition laborer | $20.70 | 1.61 | $22.31 | 16.59 | $38.90 |

**Paid leave** is calculated based on two weeks paid vacation, one week sick leave, and seven paid holidays. Employer's matching portion of **FICA** is 7.65 percent. **FUTA** (Federal Unemployment) is .8 percent. **Worker's compensation** for the suspended trades was calculated using a national average of 11.70 percent . **Unemployment insurance** was calculated using a national average of 8 percent. **Health insurance** was calculated based on a projected national average for 2015 of $1,025 per employee (and family when applicable) per month. Employer pays 80 percent for a per month cost of $820 per employee. **Retirement** is based on a 401(k) retirement program with employer matching of 50 percent. Employee contributions to the 401(k) plan are an average of 6 percent of the true wage. **Liability insurance** is based on a national average of 10.0 percent.

| | Craft@Hrs | Unit | Material | Labor | Total |
|---|---|---|---|---|---|
| **Suspended Ceilings Labor Productivity** | | | | | |
| Demolition of suspended ceiling systems | | | | | |
| remove 2' x 4' ceiling tiles | 1D@.005 | sf | — | .19 | .19 |
| remove 2' x 4' suspended grid only | 1D@.004 | sf | — | .16 | .16 |
| remove 2' x 4' suspended tiles & grid | 1D@.009 | sf | — | .35 | .35 |
| remove 2' x 2' suspended tiles only | 1D@.004 | sf | — | .16 | .16 |
| remove 2' x 2' grid only | 1D@.004 | sf | — | .16 | .16 |
| remove 2' x 2' tiles & grid | 1D@.008 | sf | — | .31 | .31 |
| remove 12" x 12" ceiling tiles only | 1D@.006 | sf | — | .23 | .23 |
| remove 12" x 12" grid only | 1D@.006 | sf | — | .23 | .23 |
| remove 12" x 12" tiles & grid | 1D@.012 | sf | — | .47 | .47 |
| **Suspended ceiling installation crew** | | | | | |
| install suspended ceiling      installer | $53.00 | | | | |
| install suspended ceiling      installer's helper | $39.80 | | | | |
| install suspended ceiling      installation crew | $46.40 | | | | |
| Install 2' x 4' suspended ceiling | | | | | |
| grid only | 1S@.013 | sf | — | .60 | .60 |
| grid and tiles | 1S@.024 | sf | — | 1.11 | 1.11 |
| ceiling tiles only | 3S@.011 | sf | — | .44 | .44 |
| luminous panels | 3S@.010 | sf | — | .40 | .40 |
| Install 12" x 12" concealed suspended ceiling | | | | | |
| grid only | 1S@.020 | sf | — | .93 | .93 |
| grid and tiles | 1S@.039 | sf | — | 1.81 | 1.81 |
| tiles only | 1S@.019 | sf | — | .88 | .88 |

| | Craft@Hrs | Unit | Material | Labor | Total |
|---|---|---|---|---|---|

# Swimming Pools

## Minimum charge.

| | Craft@Hrs | Unit | Material | Labor | Total |
|---|---|---|---|---|---|
| for swimming pool work | 8S@5.00 | ea | 53.10 | 324.00 | 377.10 |

## Swimming pools.
Per square feet of walls and bottom of pool. Includes all equipment (average to high quality) and 6" x 6" tile border. Does not include coping or deck.

| | Craft@Hrs | Unit | Material | Labor | Total |
|---|---|---|---|---|---|
| Gunite with plaster | | | | | |
| replace | 8S@.203 | sf | 39.40 | 13.10 | 52.50 |
| remove | 1D@.245 | sf | — | 9.53 | 9.53 |
| Concrete with vinyl liner | | | | | |
| replace | 8S@.166 | sf | 27.40 | 10.70 | 38.10 |
| remove | 1D@.212 | sf | — | 8.25 | 8.25 |
| Galvanized steel with vinyl liner | | | | | |
| replace | 8S@.135 | sf | 23.50 | 8.73 | 32.23 |
| remove | 1D@.142 | sf | — | 5.52 | 5.52 |
| Aluminum with vinyl liner | | | | | |
| replace | 8S@.141 | sf | 23.70 | 9.12 | 32.82 |
| remove | 1D@.142 | sf | — | 5.52 | 5.52 |
| Fiberglass | | | | | |
| replace | 8S@.174 | sf | 36.60 | 11.30 | 47.90 |
| remove | 1D@.121 | sf | — | 4.71 | 4.71 |

## Coping.

| | Craft@Hrs | Unit | Material | Labor | Total |
|---|---|---|---|---|---|
| replace, brick | 8S@.228 | lf | 21.20 | 14.80 | 36.00 |
| replace, precast concrete | 8S@.198 | lf | 19.00 | 12.80 | 31.80 |
| replace, flagstone | 8S@.254 | lf | 22.90 | 16.40 | 39.30 |
| remove | 1D@.050 | lf | — | 1.95 | 1.95 |
| remove, then reinstall | 8S@.311 | lf | 1.07 | 20.10 | 21.17 |

## Swimming pool decks.

| | Craft@Hrs | Unit | Material | Labor | Total |
|---|---|---|---|---|---|
| Concrete with epoxy aggregate surface | | | | | |
| replace | 8S@.045 | sf | 3.40 | 2.91 | 6.31 |
| remove | 1D@.049 | sf | — | 1.91 | 1.91 |
| Stamped and dyed concrete | | | | | |
| replace | 8S@.040 | sf | 3.09 | 2.59 | 5.68 |
| remove | 1D@.049 | sf | — | 1.91 | 1.91 |

## Bond beam repair.

| | Craft@Hrs | Unit | Material | Labor | Total |
|---|---|---|---|---|---|
| replace | 8S@1.07 | lf | 12.70 | 69.20 | 81.90 |

## Regrout tile swimming pool.

| | Craft@Hrs | Unit | Material | Labor | Total |
|---|---|---|---|---|---|
| replace | 8S@.024 | sf | .20 | 1.55 | 1.75 |

## Leak detection.

| | Craft@Hrs | Unit | Material | Labor | Total |
|---|---|---|---|---|---|
| replace | 8S@4.11 | ea | 3.99 | 266.00 | 269.99 |

|  | Craft@Hrs | Unit | Material | Labor | Total |
|---|---|---|---|---|---|
| **Repair leak underwater.** | | | | | |
| in vinyl lining | 8S@3.62 | ea | 16.70 | 234.00 | 250.70 |
| with hydraulic cement | 8S@4.48 | ea | 27.40 | 290.00 | 317.40 |
| rusted rebar & stain, patch with plaster | 8S@7.01 | ea | 48.40 | 454.00 | 502.40 |
| plaster popoff | 8S@4.22 | ea | 21.20 | 273.00 | 294.20 |
| **Replaster swimming pool.** | | | | | |
| replace | 8S@.038 | sf | 2.10 | 2.46 | 4.56 |
| **Paint pool.** | | | | | |
| replace, rubber base paint | 8S@.027 | sf | 1.01 | 1.75 | 2.76 |
| replace, epoxy paint | 8S@.035 | sf | 1.13 | 2.26 | 3.39 |
| **Vinyl liner.** | | | | | |
| replace | 8S@.022 | sf | 3.42 | 1.42 | 4.84 |
| **Tile border.** | | | | | |
| replace, 6" x 6" | 8S@.232 | lf | 10.30 | 15.00 | 25.30 |
| replace, 12" x 12" | 8S@.316 | lf | 13.40 | 20.40 | 33.80 |
| remove | 1D@.062 | lf | — | 2.41 | 2.41 |
| remove, then reinstall | 8S@.631 | lf | 1.13 | 40.80 | 41.93 |
| **Acid wash.** | | | | | |
| wash | 8S@.004 | sf | .18 | .26 | .44 |
| minimum charge to acid wash | 8S@3.99 | ea | 26.50 | 258.00 | 284.50 |
| **Drain pool.** | | | | | |
| drain | 8S@4.20 | ea | — | 272.00 | 272.00 |
| drain and clean | 8S@9.40 | ea | 22.50 | 608.00 | 630.50 |
| **Shock treatment.** | | | | | |
| chemical shock | 8S@1.25 | ea | 45.50 | 80.90 | 126.40 |
| **Open pool.** | | | | | |
| open for summer | 8S@3.26 | ea | 68.00 | 211.00 | 279.00 |
| **Close pool.** | | | | | |
| close for winter | 8S@5.01 | ea | 90.80 | 324.00 | 414.80 |
| **Caulk expansion joint.** | | | | | |
| replace | 8S@.029 | lf | 3.02 | 1.88 | 4.90 |

| | Craft@Hrs | Unit | Material | Labor | Total |
|---|---|---|---|---|---|

## Temporary

**Emergency board up.** Prices are for work done between 7:00 a.m. and 6:00 p.m. Monday through Friday. Add **25%** for emergency work between 6:00 p.m. and 10:00 p.m. Monday through Friday. Add **65%** for emergency work between 10:00 p.m. and 7:00 a.m. Monday through Friday, on weekends, or on holidays.

### Cover opening.

| | Craft@Hrs | Unit | Material | Labor | Total |
|---|---|---|---|---|---|
| with single sheet of plywood | 1C@.715 | ea | 25.70 | 40.70 | 66.40 |
| with two sheets of plywood | 1C@.908 | ea | 51.50 | 51.70 | 103.20 |
| install temporary framing and cover opening | 1C@.022 | sf | 1.15 | 1.25 | 2.40 |

### Cover roof or wall.

| | Craft@Hrs | Unit | Material | Labor | Total |
|---|---|---|---|---|---|
| with tarp | 1C@.009 | sf | .75 | .51 | 1.26 |
| with plastic | 1C@.009 | sf | .37 | .51 | .88 |

### Minimum charge.

| | Craft@Hrs | Unit | Material | Labor | Total |
|---|---|---|---|---|---|
| minimum for emergency board up | 1C@4.00 | ea | 143.00 | 228.00 | 371.00 |

### Temporary electric power.

| | Craft@Hrs | Unit | Material | Labor | Total |
|---|---|---|---|---|---|
| electrical hookup | 1C@1.38 | ea | 132.00 | 78.50 | 210.50 |
| power, per week | — | wk | 112.00 | — | 112.00 |

### Temporary heating.

| | Craft@Hrs | Unit | Material | Labor | Total |
|---|---|---|---|---|---|
| per week | — | wk | 221.00 | — | 221.00 |

| | Craft@Hrs | Unit | Material | Labor | Equip. | Total |
|---|---|---|---|---|---|---|

**Scaffolding.** Per week. Per sf of wall that scaffolding covers. 60" wide scaffolding attached with scissor braces.

| | Craft@Hrs | Unit | Material | Labor | Equip. | Total |
|---|---|---|---|---|---|---|
| per sf of wall covered by scaffold | — | sf | — | — | .27 | .27 |
| add for hook-end cat walk | — | ea | — | — | 1.49 | 1.49 |
| add for tented scaffolding | 1C@.005 | sf | — | .28 | .34 | .62 |
| delivery, set-up, and take down | 1C@.005 | sf | — | .28 | — | .28 |
| minimum charge for scaffolding | 1C@1.00 | ea | — | 56.90 | 69.70 | 126.60 |

### Temporary chain-link fence. Per job, up to 12 months.

| | Craft@Hrs | Unit | Material | Labor | Equip. | Total |
|---|---|---|---|---|---|---|
| 5' tall | 1C@.118 | lf | — | 6.71 | 3.78 | 10.49 |
| 6' tall | 1C@.123 | lf | — | 7.00 | 3.91 | 10.91 |
| minimum charge for chain-link fence | 1C@3.00 | ea | — | 171.00 | 196.00 | 367.00 |

### Office trailer.

| | Craft@Hrs | Unit | Material | Labor | Equip. | Total |
|---|---|---|---|---|---|---|
| 8' x 32', per week | — | ea | — | — | 77.50 | 77.50 |

### Storage trailer.

| | Craft@Hrs | Unit | Material | Labor | Equip. | Total |
|---|---|---|---|---|---|---|
| per week | — | ea | — | — | 46.00 | 46.00 |

| | Craft@Hrs | Unit | Material | Labor | Equip. | Total |
|---|---|---|---|---|---|---|

**Portable toilet.**

| | | | | | | |
|---|---|---|---|---|---|---|
| chemical, per week | — | ea | — | — | 39.10 | 39.10 |

**Reflective barricades.**

| | | | | | | |
|---|---|---|---|---|---|---|
| folding, per week | — | ea | — | — | 6.41 | 6.41 |
| folding with flashing light, per week | — | ea | — | — | 8.10 | 8.10 |

**Traffic cone.**

| | | | | | | |
|---|---|---|---|---|---|---|
| 28" high, per week | — | ea | — | — | .69 | .69 |

| | Craft@Hrs | Unit | Material | Labor | Total |
|---|---|---|---|---|---|

**Job site security.** Per hour.

| | | | | | |
|---|---|---|---|---|---|
| security guard | 1C@.346 | hr | — | 19.70 | 19.70 |
| security guard with dog | 1C@.477 | hr | — | 27.10 | 27.10 |
| minimum charge for security guard | 1C@7.00 | ea | — | 398.00 | 398.00 |

**Orange plastic safety fence.**

| | | | | | |
|---|---|---|---|---|---|
| 4' tall | 1C@.004 | lf | .57 | .23 | .80 |
| 5' tall | 1C@.004 | lf | .86 | .23 | 1.09 |

**Safety tape.**

| | | | | | |
|---|---|---|---|---|---|
| plastic, "do not cross" barricade tape | 1C@.002 | lf | .03 | .11 | .14 |

**Time & Material Charts** (selected items)
**Temporary Items Materials**

See Temporary material prices with the line items above.

**Temporary Items Labor**

| Laborer | base wage | paid leave | true wage | taxes & ins. | total |
|---|---|---|---|---|---|
| Carpenter | $31.10 | 2.43 | $33.53 | 23.37 | $56.90 |

**Paid leave** is calculated based on two weeks paid vacation, one week sick leave, and seven paid holidays. Employer's matching portion of **FICA** is 7.65 percent. **FUTA** (Federal Unemployment) is .8 percent. **Worker's compensation** for carpentry work in the temporary trade was calculated using a national average of 16.85 percent. **Unemployment insurance** was calculated using a national average of 8 percent. **Health insurance** was calculated based on a projected national average for 2015 of $1,025 per employee (and family when applicable) per month. Employer pays 80 percent for a per month cost of $820 per employee. **Retirement** is based on a 401(k) retirement program with employer matching of 50 percent. Employee contributions to the 401(k) plan are an average of 6 percent of the true wage. **Liability insurance** is based on a national average of 10.0 percent.

| | Craft@Hrs | Unit | Material | Labor | Total |
|---|---|---|---|---|---|
| **Temporary Items Labor Productivity** | | | | | |

| Temporary board up and fencing | | | | | |
|---|---|---|---|---|---|
| cover opening with single sheet of plywood | 1C@.715 | ea | — | 40.70 | 40.70 |
| cover opening with two sheets of plywood | 1C@.908 | ea | — | 51.70 | 51.70 |
| install temporary framing and cover opening | 1C@.022 | sf | — | 1.25 | 1.25 |
| cover roof or wall with tarp | 1C@.009 | sf | — | .51 | .51 |
| cover roof or wall with plastic | 1C@.009 | sf | — | .51 | .51 |
| install temporary 5' tall chain link fence | 1C@.118 | lf | — | 6.71 | 6.71 |
| install temporary 6' tall chain link fence | 1C@.123 | lf | — | 7.00 | 7.00 |

| | Craft@Hrs | Unit | Material | Labor | Total |
|---|---|---|---|---|---|

## Tile
with Cultured Marble

### Minimum charge.

| | Craft@Hrs | Unit | Material | Labor | Total |
|---|---|---|---|---|---|
| minimum for tile work | 1T@4.00 | ea | 62.90 | 216.00 | 278.90 |

### Tile bathtub surround.
Includes tile, mortar, grout, caulk, specialty tile pieces (such as corner pieces, soap dish, and so on), and installation. Surround includes coverage of the three walls surrounding bathtub: two widths and one length. Includes one soap dish. Does not include doors, or shower curtain rod.

| | Craft@Hrs | Unit | Material | Labor | Total |
|---|---|---|---|---|---|
| **6' tall tile bathtub surround** | | | | | |
| replace, adhesive set on moisture-resistant drywall | 1T@5.26 | ea | 370.00 | 284.00 | 654.00 |
| replace, adhesive set on tile backer board | 1T@5.26 | ea | 409.00 | 284.00 | 693.00 |
| remove | 1D@2.86 | ea | — | 111.00 | 111.00 |
| replace, mortar set | 1T@7.69 | ea | 434.00 | 415.00 | 849.00 |
| remove | 1D@3.56 | ea | — | 138.00 | 138.00 |
| **7' tall tile bathtub surround** | | | | | |
| replace, adhesive set on moisture-resistant drywall | 1T@6.24 | ea | 428.00 | 337.00 | 765.00 |
| replace, adhesive set on tile backer board | 1T@6.24 | ea | 479.00 | 337.00 | 816.00 |
| remove | 1D@2.94 | ea | — | 114.00 | 114.00 |
| replace, mortar set | 1T@8.33 | ea | 509.00 | 450.00 | 959.00 |
| remove | 1D@3.70 | ea | — | 144.00 | 144.00 |
| **8' tall tile bathtub surround** | | | | | |
| replace, adhesive set on moisture-resistant drywall | 1T@7.15 | ea | 490.00 | 386.00 | 876.00 |
| replace, adhesive set on tile backer board | 1T@7.15 | ea | 546.00 | 386.00 | 932.00 |
| remove | 1D@3.03 | ea | — | 118.00 | 118.00 |
| replace, mortar set | 1T@9.09 | ea | 577.00 | 491.00 | 1,068.00 |
| remove | 1D@3.84 | ea | — | 149.00 | 149.00 |

### Tile shower.
Includes walls, floor, all trim pieces, and one tile soap dish. Does not include shower pan, fixtures, door or any plumbing.

| | Craft@Hrs | Unit | Material | Labor | Total |
|---|---|---|---|---|---|
| **36" x 36" tile shower** | | | | | |
| replace, adhesive set on tile backer board | 1T@7.69 | ea | 609.00 | 415.00 | 1,024.00 |
| remove | 1D@3.33 | ea | — | 130.00 | 130.00 |
| replace, mortar set | 1T@9.09 | ea | 641.00 | 491.00 | 1,132.00 |
| remove | 1D@3.70 | ea | — | 144.00 | 144.00 |
| add for tile ceiling | 1T@.870 | ea | 94.30 | 47.00 | 141.30 |
| **36" x 48" tile shower** | | | | | |
| replace, adhesive set on tile backer board | 1T@9.09 | ea | 680.00 | 491.00 | 1,171.00 |
| remove | 1D@3.45 | ea | — | 134.00 | 134.00 |
| replace, mortar set | 1T@10.0 | ea | 710.00 | 540.00 | 1,250.00 |
| remove | 1D@3.45 | ea | — | 134.00 | 134.00 |
| add for tile ceiling | 1T@1.14 | ea | 113.00 | 61.60 | 174.60 |

### Tile accessory.
In shower or bathtub surround.

| | Craft@Hrs | Unit | Material | Labor | Total |
|---|---|---|---|---|---|
| add for soap holder or other accessory | 1T@.418 | ea | 41.50 | 22.60 | 64.10 |

| | Craft@Hrs | Unit | Material | Labor | Total |
|---|---|---|---|---|---|

**Cultured marble bathtub surround.** Includes cultured marble bathtub surround, construction adhesive and/or attachment hardware, caulk, and installation. Surround includes coverage of the three walls surrounding bathtub: two widths and one length. Typically each wall is covered with one solid piece. Does not include wall framing, doors, or shower curtain rod.

| | Craft@Hrs | Unit | Material | Labor | Total |
|---|---|---|---|---|---|
| replace, typical | 1T@3.86 | ea | 451.00 | 208.00 | 659.00 |
| remove | 1D@1.28 | ea | — | 49.80 | 49.80 |

**Tile window sill.** Includes tile, mortar, grout, caulk, and installation.

| | Craft@Hrs | Unit | Material | Labor | Total |
|---|---|---|---|---|---|
| replace, 4" wall | 1T@.063 | lf | 7.45 | 3.40 | 10.85 |
| replace, 6" wall | 1T@.063 | lf | 7.96 | 3.40 | 11.36 |
| replace, 8" wall | 1T@.065 | lf | 8.67 | 3.51 | 12.18 |
| remove | 1D@.059 | lf | — | 2.30 | 2.30 |

**Cultured marble window sill.** Includes cultured marble sill, construction adhesive, caulk, and installation.

| | Craft@Hrs | Unit | Material | Labor | Total |
|---|---|---|---|---|---|
| replace, 4" wall | 1T@.053 | lf | 7.70 | 2.86 | 10.56 |
| replace, 6" wall | 1T@.053 | lf | 9.80 | 2.86 | 12.66 |
| replace, 8" wall | 1T@.054 | lf | 13.20 | 2.92 | 16.12 |
| remove | 1D@.018 | lf | — | .70 | .70 |

**Tile repair.**

| | Craft@Hrs | Unit | Material | Labor | Total |
|---|---|---|---|---|---|
| regrout | 1T@.040 | sf | .36 | 2.16 | 2.52 |
| replace, single tile | 1T@.926 | ea | — | 50.00 | 50.00 |

## Time & Material Charts (selected items)
## Tile Materials

See Tile material prices with the line items above.

## Tile Labor

| Laborer | base wage | paid leave | true wage | taxes & ins. | total |
|---|---|---|---|---|---|
| Tile layer | $29.00 | 2.26 | $31.26 | 22.74 | $54.00 |
| Demolition worker | $20.70 | 1.61 | $22.31 | 16.59 | $38.90 |

**Paid leave** is calculated based on two weeks paid vacation, one week sick leave, and seven paid holidays. Employer's matching portion of **FICA** is 7.65 percent. **FUTA** (Federal Unemployment) is .8 percent. **Worker's compensation** for the tile trade was calculated using a national average of 19.00 percent. **Unemployment insurance** was calculated using a national average of 8 percent. **Health insurance** was calculated based on a projected national average for 2015 of $1,025 per employee (and family when applicable) per month. Employer pays 80 percent for a per month cost of $820 per employee. **Retirement** is based on a 401(k) retirement program with employer matching of 50 percent. Employee contributions to the 401(k) plan are an average of 6 percent of the true wage. **Liability insurance** is based on a national average of 10.0 percent.

| | Craft@Hrs | Unit | Material | Labor | Total |
|---|---|---|---|---|---|

## Wall Coverings

**Strip wallpaper.** Add **25%** for two layers, **36%** for three layers and **42%** for four layers. Remove only.

| | Craft@Hrs | Unit | Material | Labor | Total |
|---|---|---|---|---|---|
| strippable | 3H@.013 | sf | — | .58 | .58 |
| nonstrippable | 3H@.021 | sf | — | .94 | .94 |

**Minimum charge.**

| | Craft@Hrs | Unit | Material | Labor | Total |
|---|---|---|---|---|---|
| for wall covering work | 3H@3.00 | ea | 41.70 | 135.00 | 176.70 |

**Wallpaper underliner.** Includes sizing, blank stock underliner, wallpaper paste, and installation. Used to cover flaws in walls before wallpaper is installed. Sometimes used to cover paneling.

| | Craft@Hrs | Unit | Material | Labor | Total |
|---|---|---|---|---|---|
| replace blank stock | 3H@.013 | sf | .68 | .58 | 1.26 |
| remove | 1D@.017 | sf | — | .66 | .66 |

**Grass cloth wallpaper.** Includes wall sizing and 21% waste. Add **$.39** per sf to patch small holes, gouges, and cracks.

| | Craft@Hrs | Unit | Material | Labor | Total |
|---|---|---|---|---|---|
| replace standard grade | 3H@.034 | sf | 2.07 | 1.53 | 3.60 |
| replace high grade | 3H@.034 | sf | 3.34 | 1.53 | 4.87 |
| remove | 1D@.017 | sf | — | .66 | .66 |

**Paper wallpaper.** From flat to high gloss papers. Includes wall sizing and 21% waste. Add **$.39** per sf to patch small holes, gouges, and cracks.

| | Craft@Hrs | Unit | Material | Labor | Total |
|---|---|---|---|---|---|
| replace standard grade | 3H@.026 | sf | 1.10 | 1.17 | 2.27 |
| replace high grade | 3H@.026 | sf | 1.50 | 1.17 | 2.67 |
| remove | 1D@.017 | sf | — | .66 | .66 |

**Vinyl-coated wallpaper.** Vinyl with paper back. Includes wall sizing and 21% waste. Add **$.39** per sf to patch small holes, gouges, and cracks.

| | Craft@Hrs | Unit | Material | Labor | Total |
|---|---|---|---|---|---|
| replace standard grade | 3H@.028 | sf | 1.40 | 1.26 | 2.66 |
| replace high grade | 3H@.028 | sf | 1.87 | 1.26 | 3.13 |
| remove | 1D@.017 | sf | — | .66 | .66 |

**Vinyl wallpaper.** Seams overlapped, then cut. Includes wall sizing and 21% waste. Add **$.39** per sf to patch small holes, gouges, and cracks.

| | Craft@Hrs | Unit | Material | Labor | Total |
|---|---|---|---|---|---|
| replace standard grade | 3H@.028 | sf | 1.48 | 1.26 | 2.74 |
| replace high grade | 3H@.028 | sf | 1.97 | 1.26 | 3.23 |
| remove | 1D@.017 | sf | — | .66 | .66 |

**Foil wallpaper.** Includes wall sizing and 21% waste. Add **$.39** per sf to patch small holes, gouges, and cracks.

| | Craft@Hrs | Unit | Material | Labor | Total |
|---|---|---|---|---|---|
| replace standard grade | 3H@.027 | sf | 1.79 | 1.21 | 3.00 |
| replace high grade | 3H@.027 | sf | 2.28 | 1.21 | 3.49 |
| remove | 1D@.017 | sf | — | .66 | .66 |

**Wallpaper border.** Includes sizing, wallpaper border, wallpaper paste, and installation. All styles. Use remove price when removing only the border and no adjoining wallpaper on the same wall.

| | Craft@Hrs | Unit | Material | Labor | Total |
|---|---|---|---|---|---|
| replace standard grade | 3H@.023 | lf | 1.97 | 1.03 | 3.00 |
| replace high grade | 3H@.023 | lf | 2.75 | 1.03 | 3.78 |
| remove | 1D@.013 | lf | — | .51 | .51 |

| | Craft@Hrs | Unit | Material | Labor | Total |
|---|---|---|---|---|---|

**Anaglypta embossed wall or ceiling covering.** Includes Anaglypta style embossed wall or ceiling covering, adhesive, and installation. Does not include painting. Wall or ceiling coverings are heavy, highly embossed panels made from material similar to linoleum. Must be painted. Higher grades contain cotton fibers for extra strength and durability. Anaglypta is a registered trademark. Includes 21% waste.

| | Craft@Hrs | Unit | Material | Labor | Total |
|---|---|---|---|---|---|
| replace standard grade | 3H@.045 | sf | 1.60 | 2.02 | 3.62 |
| replace high grade | 3H@.045 | sf | 2.27 | 2.02 | 4.29 |
| replace deluxe grade | 3H@.045 | sf | 2.52 | 2.02 | 4.54 |
| remove | 1D@.023 | sf | — | .89 | .89 |

**Lincrusta embossed wall or ceiling covering.** Lincrusta style, deeply embossed wall or ceiling covering, adhesive, and installation. Lincrusta wall coverings are made from material similar to linoleum. Must be painted. Higher grades contain cotton fibers for extra strength and durability. Does not include painting. Lincrusta is a registered trademark. Lincrusta is typically much heavier than Anaglypta. Includes 21% waste.

| | Craft@Hrs | Unit | Material | Labor | Total |
|---|---|---|---|---|---|
| replace standard grade | 3H@.056 | sf | 4.60 | 2.51 | 7.11 |
| replace high grade | 3H@.056 | sf | 6.21 | 2.51 | 8.72 |
| replace deluxe grade | 3H@.056 | sf | 7.70 | 2.51 | 10.21 |
| remove | 1D@.033 | sf | — | 1.28 | 1.28 |

**Anaglypta embossed frieze.** Includes Anaglypta style, deeply embossed frieze, adhesive, and installation. Friezes are heavy, highly embossed trim pieces that are 12" to 21" wide. Friezes are made from material similar to linoleum. Must be painted. Higher grades contain cotton fibers for extra strength and durability. Does not include painting. Anaglypta is a registered trademark.

| | Craft@Hrs | Unit | Material | Labor | Total |
|---|---|---|---|---|---|
| replace standard grade | 3H@.043 | lf | 4.94 | 1.93 | 6.87 |
| replace high grade | 3H@.043 | lf | 5.59 | 1.93 | 7.52 |
| remove | 1D@.019 | lf | — | .74 | .74 |

**Lincrusta embossed frieze.** Includes Lincrusta style, deeply embossed frieze, adhesive, and installation. Friezes are heavy, highly embossed trim pieces that are approximately 21" wide. Friezes are made from material similar to linoleum. Must be painted. Higher grades contain cotton fibers for extra strength and durability. Does not include painting. Lincrusta is a registered trademark.

| | Craft@Hrs | Unit | Material | Labor | Total |
|---|---|---|---|---|---|
| replace standard grade | 3H@.053 | lf | 5.75 | 2.38 | 8.13 |
| replace high grade | 3H@.053 | lf | 7.16 | 2.38 | 9.54 |
| remove | 1D@.027 | lf | — | 1.05 | 1.05 |

**Anaglypta embossed pelmet.** Includes Anaglypta style embossed pelmet, adhesive, and installation. Pelmets are narrower and often less ornate than friezes and are from 4" to 7" wide. Pelmets are made from material similar to linoleum. Must be painted. Higher grades contain cotton fibers for extra strength and durability. Does not include painting. Anaglypta is a registered trademark.

| | Craft@Hrs | Unit | Material | Labor | Total |
|---|---|---|---|---|---|
| replace standard grade | 3H@.040 | lf | 3.09 | 1.80 | 4.89 |
| replace high grade | 3H@.040 | lf | 4.39 | 1.80 | 6.19 |
| remove | 1D@.019 | lf | — | .74 | .74 |

**Anaglypta embossed dado.** Includes Anaglypta style embossed dado wall covering, adhesive, and installation. Dados are heavy, highly embossed wall panels made from material similar to linoleum. Must be painted. Higher grades contain cotton fibers for extra strength and durability. Does not include painting. Anaglypta is a registered trademark.

| | Craft@Hrs | Unit | Material | Labor | Total |
|---|---|---|---|---|---|
| replace standard grade | 3H@.111 | lf | 23.80 | 4.98 | 28.78 |
| replace high grade | 3H@.111 | lf | 29.50 | 4.98 | 34.48 |
| remove | 1D@.128 | lf | — | 4.98 | 4.98 |

| | Craft@Hrs | Unit | Material | Labor | Total |
|---|---|---|---|---|---|

## Time & Material Charts (selected items)
## Wall Coverings Materials

Wallpaper materials were calculated based on double European size rolls with approximately 28 sf per single roll and 56 sf in a double roll. (Most manufacturers no longer make American size rolls which contained approximately 36 sf per single roll and 72 sf in a double roll.) Prices include sizing and glue application, even on pre-pasted rolls.

| | Craft@Hrs | Unit | Material | Labor | Total |
|---|---|---|---|---|---|
| Wallpaper underliner | | | | | |
| blank stock, | | | | | |
| ($29.50 double roll, 56 sf), 21% waste | — | sf | .64 | — | .64 |
| Grass cloth wallpaper | | | | | |
| standard grade grass cloth wallpaper, | | | | | |
| ($91.80 double roll, 56 sf), 21% waste | — | sf | 1.98 | — | 1.98 |
| high grade grass cloth wallpaper, | | | | | |
| ($147.00 double roll, 56 sf), 21% waste | — | sf | 3.18 | — | 3.18 |
| Paper wallpaper | | | | | |
| standard grade, | | | | | |
| ($48.60 double roll, 56 sf), 21% waste | — | sf | 1.05 | — | 1.05 |
| high grade, | | | | | |
| ($67.00 double roll, 56 sf), 21% waste | — | sf | 1.45 | — | 1.45 |
| Vinyl-coated wallpaper | | | | | |
| standard grade, | | | | | |
| ($61.90 double roll, 56 sf), 21% waste | — | sf | 1.34 | — | 1.34 |
| high grade, | | | | | |
| ($82.00 double roll, 56 sf), 21% waste | — | sf | 1.77 | — | 1.77 |
| Vinyl wallpaper | | | | | |
| standard grade, | | | | | |
| ($65.70 double roll, 56 sf), 21% waste | — | sf | 1.42 | — | 1.42 |
| high grade, | | | | | |
| ($86.60 double roll, 56 sf), 21% waste | — | sf | 1.88 | — | 1.88 |
| Foil wallpaper | | | | | |
| standard grade, | | | | | |
| ($79.80 double roll, 56 sf), 21% waste | — | sf | 1.73 | — | 1.73 |
| high grade, | | | | | |
| ($100.00 double roll, 56 sf), 21% waste | — | sf | 2.17 | — | 2.17 |
| Wallpaper border | | | | | |
| standard grade, | | | | | |
| ($46.20 bolt, 30 lf), 21% waste | — | lf | 1.86 | — | 1.86 |
| high grade, | | | | | |
| ($65.20 bolt, 30 lf), 21% waste | — | lf | 2.63 | — | 2.63 |

| | Craft@Hrs | Unit | Material | Labor | Total |
|---|---|---|---|---|---|
| Anaglypta embossed wall or ceiling covering | | | | | |
| standard grade, | | | | | |
| ($70.70 double roll, 56 sf), 21% waste | — | sf | 1.52 | — | 1.52 |
| high grade, | | | | | |
| ($100.00 double roll, 56 sf), 21% waste | — | sf | 2.17 | — | 2.17 |
| deluxe grade, | | | | | |
| ($113.00 double roll, 56 sf), 21% waste | — | sf | 2.44 | — | 2.44 |
| Lincrusta embossed wall or ceiling covering | | | | | |
| standard grade, | | | | | |
| ($204.00 double roll, 56 sf), 21% waste | — | sf | 4.40 | — | 4.40 |
| high grade, | | | | | |
| ($275.00 double roll, 56 sf), 21% waste | — | sf | 5.94 | — | 5.94 |
| deluxe grade, | | | | | |
| ($341.00 double roll, 56 sf), 21% waste | — | sf | 7.37 | — | 7.37 |
| Anaglypta embossed frieze | | | | | |
| standard grade, | | | | | |
| ($141.00 bolt, 33 lf), 13% waste | — | lf | 4.83 | — | 4.83 |
| high grade, | | | | | |
| ($160.00 bolt, 33 lf), 13% waste | — | lf | 5.48 | — | 5.48 |
| Lincrusta embossed frieze | | | | | |
| standard grade, | | | | | |
| ($166.00 bolt, 33 lf), 12% waste | — | lf | 5.63 | — | 5.63 |
| high grade, | | | | | |
| ($207.00 bolt, 33 lf), 12% waste | — | lf | 7.02 | — | 7.02 |
| Anaglypta embossed pelmet | | | | | |
| standard grade, | | | | | |
| ($88.60 bolt, 33 lf), 13% waste | — | lf | 3.03 | — | 3.03 |
| high grade, | | | | | |
| ($126.00 bolt, 33 lf), 13% waste | — | lf | 4.32 | — | 4.32 |
| Anaglypta embossed dado (five panels per box) | | | | | |
| standard grade, | | | | | |
| ($341.00 box, 16 lf), 10% waste | — | lf | 23.40 | — | 23.40 |
| high grade, | | | | | |
| ($424.00 box, 16 lf), 10% waste | — | lf | 29.20 | — | 29.20 |

## Wall Coverings Labor

| Laborer | base wage | paid leave | true wage | taxes & ins. | total |
|---|---|---|---|---|---|
| Wallpaper hanger | $25.30 | 1.97 | $27.27 | 17.63 | $44.90 |

**Paid leave** is calculated based on two weeks paid vacation, one week sick leave, and seven paid holidays. Employer's matching portion of **FICA** is 7.65 percent. **FUTA** (Federal Unemployment) is .8 percent. **Worker's compensation** for the wall coverings trade was calculated using a national average of 8.40 percent. **Unemployment insurance** was calculated using a national average of 8 percent. **Health insurance** was calculated based on a projected national average for 2015 of $1,025 per employee (and family when applicable) per month. Employer pays 80 percent for a per month cost of $820 per employee. **Retirement** is based on a 401(k) retirement program with employer matching of 50 percent. Employee contributions to the 401(k) plan are an average of 6 percent of the true wage. **Liability insurance** is based on a national average of 10.0 percent.

| | Craft@Hrs | Unit | Material | Labor | Total |
|---|---|---|---|---|---|
| **Wall Coverings Labor Productivity** | | | | | |
| Remove wallpaper | | | | | |
|    strippable | 3H@.013 | sf | — | .58 | .58 |
|    nonstrippable | 3H@.021 | sf | — | .94 | .94 |
| Install wallpaper | | | | | |
|    underliner | 3H@.013 | sf | — | .58 | .58 |
|    grass cloth wallpaper | 3H@.034 | sf | — | 1.53 | 1.53 |
|    paper wallpaper | 3H@.026 | sf | — | 1.17 | 1.17 |
|    vinyl coated | 3H@.028 | sf | — | 1.26 | 1.26 |
|    vinyl | 3H@.028 | sf | — | 1.26 | 1.26 |
|    foil | 3H@.027 | sf | — | 1.21 | 1.21 |
| Install wallpaper border | | | | | |
|    all styles | 3H@.023 | lf | — | 1.03 | 1.03 |
| Install Anaglypta embossed wall or ceiling covering | | | | | |
|    wall or ceiling | 3H@.045 | sf | — | 2.02 | 2.02 |
| Install Lincrusta embossed wall or ceiling covering | | | | | |
|    wall or ceiling | 3H@.056 | sf | — | 2.51 | 2.51 |
| Install embossed frieze | | | | | |
|    Anaglypta | 3H@.043 | lf | — | 1.93 | 1.93 |
|    Lincrusta | 3H@.053 | lf | — | 2.38 | 2.38 |
| Install Anaglypta embossed pelmet | | | | | |
|    all grades | 3H@.040 | lf | — | 1.80 | 1.80 |
| Install Anaglypta embossed dado | | | | | |
|    all grades | 3H@.111 | lf | — | 4.98 | 4.98 |

| | Craft@Hrs | Unit | Material | Labor | Equip. | Total |
|---|---|---|---|---|---|---|

## Water Extraction

**Emergency Service.** All prices are for work done between 7:00 a.m. and 6:00 p.m. Monday through Friday. Add **25%** for emergency work between 6:00 p.m. and 10:00 p.m. Monday through Friday. Add **65%** for emergency work between 10 p.m. and 7:00 a.m. Monday through Friday, on weekends, or on holidays.

**Minimum charge.**

| | Craft@Hrs | Unit | Material | Labor | Equip. | Total |
|---|---|---|---|---|---|---|
| for water extraction work | 9S@3.50 | ea | — | 170.00 | 139.00 | 309.00 |

**Equipment delivery, setup, and take-home charge.** Per loss charge to deliver water extraction equipment, set the equipment up, and take the equipment home once the water is extracted and drying is complete.

| | Craft@Hrs | Unit | Material | Labor | Equip. | Total |
|---|---|---|---|---|---|---|
| minimum | — | ea | — | — | 43.40 | 43.40 |

**Extract water from carpet.** Lightly soaked: carpet and pad are wet but water does not rise around feet as carpet is stepped on. Typically wet: water in carpet and pad rises around feet as carpet is stepped on. Heavily soaked: water is visible over the surface of the carpet mat. Very heavily soaked: standing water over the surface of the carpet.

| | Craft@Hrs | Unit | Material | Labor | Equip. | Total |
|---|---|---|---|---|---|---|
| lightly soaked | 9S@.005 | sf | — | .24 | .09 | .33 |
| typically wet | 9S@.007 | sf | — | .34 | .10 | .44 |
| heavily soaked | 9S@.010 | sf | — | .49 | .12 | .61 |
| very heavily soaked | 9S@.014 | sf | — | .68 | .16 | .84 |

**Dehumidifiers.** Does not include delivery, setup and take-home (see above). Does include daily monitoring and adjustment.

| | Craft@Hrs | Unit | Material | Labor | Equip. | Total |
|---|---|---|---|---|---|---|
| 10 gallon daily capacity | 9S@.410 | day | — | 20.00 | 43.40 | 63.40 |
| 19 gallon daily capacity | 9S@.410 | day | — | 20.00 | 72.50 | 92.50 |
| 24 gallon daily capacity | 9S@.410 | day | — | 20.00 | 100.00 | 120.00 |

**Drying fan.** Does not include delivery, setup and take-home (see above). Does not include daily monitoring and adjustment.

| | Craft@Hrs | Unit | Material | Labor | Equip. | Total |
|---|---|---|---|---|---|---|
| typical | 9S@.104 | day | — | 5.06 | 36.10 | 41.16 |

**Hang & dry carpet in plant.** Square foot price to haul carpet to plant, hang, and dry. Includes transport to and from plant. Does not include carpet removal or reinstallation.

| | Craft@Hrs | Unit | Material | Labor | Equip. | Total |
|---|---|---|---|---|---|---|
| carpet | 9S@.005 | sf | — | .24 | .13 | .37 |
| oriental rug | 9S@.008 | sf | — | .39 | .22 | .61 |

**Minimum charge.**

| | Craft@Hrs | Unit | Material | Labor | Equip. | Total |
|---|---|---|---|---|---|---|
| to hang and dry carpet in plant | 9S@2.03 | sf | — | 98.90 | 69.70 | 168.60 |

| | Craft@Hrs | Unit | Material | Labor | Total |
|---|---|---|---|---|---|

**Germicide and mildewcide treatment.** Treatments to kill germs and mildew in wet carpet.

| | Craft@Hrs | Unit | Material | Labor | Total |
|---|---|---|---|---|---|
| germicide | 9S@.003 | sf | .03 | .15 | .18 |
| mildewcide | 9S@.003 | sf | .03 | .15 | .18 |

**Detach, lift & block carpet for drying.**

| | Craft@Hrs | Unit | Material | Labor | Total |
|---|---|---|---|---|---|
| remove | 9S@.004 | sf | — | .19 | .19 |

| | Craft@Hrs | Unit | Material | Labor | Total |
|---|---|---|---|---|---|

**Remove wet carpet and pad.** See Flooring chapter for prices to tear-out dry carpet and pad.

| | Craft@Hrs | Unit | Material | Labor | Total |
|---|---|---|---|---|---|
| remove wet carpet | 9S@.080 | sy | — | 3.90 | 3.90 |
| remove wet carpet pad | 9S@.005 | sf | — | .24 | .24 |

**Pad and block furniture.**

| | Craft@Hrs | Unit | Material | Labor | Total |
|---|---|---|---|---|---|
| small room | 9S@.399 | ea | — | 19.40 | 19.40 |
| average room | 9S@.558 | ea | — | 27.20 | 27.20 |
| large room | 9S@.720 | ea | — | 35.10 | 35.10 |
| very large room | 9S@.997 | ea | — | 48.60 | 48.60 |

## Time & Material Charts (selected items)
## Water Extraction Materials

See Water Extraction material prices above.

| | Craft@Hrs | Unit | Material | Labor | Equip. | Total |
|---|---|---|---|---|---|---|

### Water Extraction Rental Equipment

| | Craft@Hrs | Unit | Material | Labor | Equip. | Total |
|---|---|---|---|---|---|---|
| Dehumidifiers rental | | | | | | |
| 10 gallon daily capacity | — | day | — | — | 43.40 | 43.40 |
| 19 gallon daily capacity | — | day | — | — | 72.50 | 72.50 |
| 24 gallon daily capacity | — | day | — | — | 100.00 | 100.00 |
| Drying fan rental | | | | | | |
| typical | — | day | — | — | 36.10 | 36.10 |

### Water Extraction Labor

| Laborer | base wage | paid leave | true wage | taxes & ins. | total |
|---|---|---|---|---|---|
| Water extractor | $27.00 | 2.11 | $29.11 | 19.59 | $48.70 |

**Paid Leave** is calculated based on two weeks paid vacation, one week sick leave, and seven paid holidays. Employer's matching portion of **FICA** is 7.65 percent. **FUTA** (Federal Unemployment) is .8 percent. **Worker's compensation** for the water extraction trade was calculated using a national average of 12.09 percent. **Unemployment insurance** was calculated using a national average of 8 percent. **Health insurance** was calculated based on a projected national average for 2015 of $1,025 per employee (and family when applicable) per month. Employer pays 80 percent for a per month cost of $820 per employee. **Retirement** is based on a 401(k) retirement program with employer matching of 50 percent. Employee contributions to the 401(k) plan are an average of 6 percent of the true wage. **Liability insurance** is based on a national average of 10.0 percent.

| | Craft@Hrs | Unit | Material | Labor | Total |
|---|---|---|---|---|---|

### Water Extraction Labor Productivity

| | Craft@Hrs | Unit | Material | Labor | Total |
|---|---|---|---|---|---|
| Extract water from carpet | | | | | |
| from lightly soaked carpet | 9S@.005 | sf | — | .24 | .24 |
| from very heavily soaked carpet | 9S@.014 | sf | — | .68 | .68 |
| Pad and block furniture for water extraction | | | | | |
| small room | 9S@.399 | ea | — | 19.40 | 19.40 |
| very large room | 9S@.997 | ea | — | 48.60 | 48.60 |

| | Craft@Hrs | Unit | Material | Labor | Total |
|---|---|---|---|---|---|

# Windows

**Remove window.** Tear-out and debris removal to a truck or dumpster on site. Does not include hauling, dumpster, or dump fees. No salvage value is assumed.

| | Craft@Hrs | Unit | Material | Labor | Total |
|---|---|---|---|---|---|
| small (4 to 10 sf) | 1D@.397 | ea | 1.83 | 15.40 | 17.23 |
| average (11 to 16 sf) | 1D@.407 | ea | 1.83 | 15.80 | 17.63 |
| large (17 to 29 sf) | 1D@.424 | ea | 1.83 | 16.50 | 18.33 |
| very large (30 sf and larger) | 1D@.433 | ea | 1.83 | 16.80 | 18.63 |

**Remove window for work then reinstall.**

| | Craft@Hrs | Unit | Material | Labor | Total |
|---|---|---|---|---|---|
| small (4 to 10 sf) | 1C@1.23 | ea | 1.83 | 70.00 | 71.83 |
| average (11 to 16 sf) | 1C@1.72 | ea | 1.83 | 97.90 | 99.73 |
| large (17 to 29 sf) | 1C@2.51 | ea | 1.83 | 143.00 | 144.83 |
| very large (30 sf and larger) | 1C@3.70 | ea | 1.83 | 211.00 | 212.83 |

**Other window options.** All windows in this chapter are double-glazed (insulated) units with clear glass. Use for all window types except skylights and roof windows. Higher quality windows may have Low-E or argon gas or both. Low-E: A coating that increases heat retention in winter and reduces the sun's ultraviolet rays that fade carpet and upholstery. Also called high-performance glass or other brand names. Argon gas: An odorless gas that improves the window's energy efficiency when injected between panes of glass. Argon is usually not available for windows with true divided lights. The windows in this chapter do not include Low-E or argon. To add, see table below; for skylights and roof windows, see page 442. Thermal Break: Aluminum is an excellent conductor, which means heat and cold easily flow through it, reducing efficiency. To cure this, a plastic or rubber spacer is introduced into the jamb to break the flow of hot or cold.

| | Craft@Hrs | Unit | Material | Labor | Total |
|---|---|---|---|---|---|
| deduct for single-glazed window (all types) | — | sf | - 5.86 | — | - 5.86 |
| add for gray or bronze tinted glass (all window types) | — | sf | 3.77 | — | 3.77 |
| add 8% for Low-E between panes (all window types) | | | | | |
| add 5% for argon fill between panes (all window types) | | | | | |
| add 11% for thermal break (aluminum windows only) | | | | | |

**Add for alternative glazing (all window types)**

| | Craft@Hrs | Unit | Material | Labor | Total |
|---|---|---|---|---|---|
| tempered | — | sf | 10.00 | — | 10.00 |
| laminated | — | sf | 6.58 | — | 6.58 |
| obscure | — | sf | 1.31 | — | 1.31 |
| polished wire | — | sf | 30.80 | — | 30.80 |

**Aluminum.** All aluminum windows are double-glazed, clear glass with white or bronze finish frames. For mill-finish windows deduct **13%**. All costs are for standard windows. Manufacturers' window sizes vary. For standard units round to the nearest size. For custom sizes add **80%**. **Grilles and Grid.** For aluminum grid between panes of glass or removable grilles outside of window add (per window): half-round **$24**, half-elliptical **$40**, round **$24**, elliptical **$32**, quarter-round **$24**, casement **$31**, awning **$31**, single-hung **$24**, sliding **$27**, fixed (picture) **$29**.

| | | Craft@Hrs | Unit | Material | Labor | Total |
|---|---|---|---|---|---|---|
| Half-round aluminum window top | | | | | | |
| 24" x 12" | | 1C@.991 | ea | 389.00 | 56.40 | 445.40 |
| 36" x 18" | | 1C@.991 | ea | 485.00 | 56.40 | 541.40 |
| 48" x 24" | | 1C@1.39 | ea | 575.00 | 79.10 | 654.10 |
| 72" x 36" | *half-round* | 1C@2.00 | ea | 854.00 | 114.00 | 968.00 |
| Half-elliptical aluminum window top | | | | | | |
| 36" x 15" | | 1C@.991 | ea | 743.00 | 56.40 | 799.40 |
| 48" x 16" | | 1C@.991 | ea | 824.00 | 56.40 | 880.40 |
| 60" x 19" | | 1C@1.39 | ea | 905.00 | 79.10 | 984.10 |
| 90" x 20" | *half-elliptical* | 1C@2.00 | ea | 1,330.00 | 114.00 | 1,444.00 |

| | Craft@Hrs | Unit | Material | Labor | Total |
|---|---|---|---|---|---|
| **Round aluminum window** | | | | | |
| 20" x 20" | 1C@.991 | ea | 788.00 | 56.40 | 844.40 |
| 30" x 30" | 1C@.991 | ea | 963.00 | 56.40 | 1,019.40 |
| 40" x 40" | 1C@1.39 | ea | 1,110.00 | 79.10 | 1,189.10 |
| 48" x 48" | 1C@2.00 | ea | 1,220.00 | 114.00 | 1,334.00 |
| **Elliptical aluminum window** | | | | | |
| 15" x 24" | 1C@.991 | ea | 1,470.00 | 56.40 | 1,526.40 |
| 24" x 36" | 1C@.991 | ea | 1,630.00 | 56.40 | 1,686.40 |
| 25" x 40" | 1C@1.39 | ea | 1,740.00 | 79.10 | 1,819.10 |
| 30" x 48" | 1C@2.00 | ea | 1,890.00 | 114.00 | 2,004.00 |
| **Quarter-round aluminum window** | | | | | |
| 24" x 24" | 1C@.991 | ea | 641.00 | 56.40 | 697.40 |
| 36" x 36" | 1C@.991 | ea | 919.00 | 56.40 | 975.40 |
| **18" wide aluminum casement window** | | | | | |
| 36" tall | 1C@.991 | ea | 465.00 | 56.40 | 521.40 |
| 48" tall | 1C@.991 | ea | 503.00 | 56.40 | 559.40 |
| 60" tall | 1C@.991 | ea | 577.00 | 56.40 | 633.40 |
| **24" wide aluminum casement window** | | | | | |
| 36" tall | 1C@.991 | ea | 502.00 | 56.40 | 558.40 |
| 48" tall | 1C@.991 | ea | 543.00 | 56.40 | 599.40 |
| 60" tall | 1C@1.39 | ea | 614.00 | 79.10 | 693.10 |
| **30" wide aluminum casement window** | | | | | |
| 48" tall | 1C@1.39 | ea | 588.00 | 79.10 | 667.10 |
| 60" tall | 1C@1.39 | ea | 656.00 | 79.10 | 735.10 |
| **36" wide aluminum casement window** | | | | | |
| 48" tall | 1C@1.39 | ea | 697.00 | 79.10 | 776.10 |
| 60" tall | 1C@1.39 | ea | 799.00 | 79.10 | 878.10 |
| **24" wide aluminum awning windows** | | | | | |
| 20" tall | 1C@.991 | ea | 430.00 | 56.40 | 486.40 |
| 24" tall | 1C@.991 | ea | 484.00 | 56.40 | 540.40 |
| 30" tall | 1C@.991 | ea | 527.00 | 56.40 | 583.40 |
| **30" wide aluminum awning window** | | | | | |
| 20" tall | 1C@.991 | ea | 500.00 | 56.40 | 556.40 |
| 24" tall | 1C@.991 | ea | 546.00 | 56.40 | 602.40 |
| 30" tall | 1C@.991 | ea | 595.00 | 56.40 | 651.40 |
| **36" wide aluminum awning window** | | | | | |
| 24" tall | 1C@.991 | ea | 591.00 | 56.40 | 647.40 |
| 30" tall | 1C@.991 | ea | 663.00 | 56.40 | 719.40 |
| **40" wide aluminum awning window** | | | | | |
| 24" tall | 1C@.991 | ea | 653.00 | 56.40 | 709.40 |
| 30" tall | 1C@.991 | ea | 738.00 | 56.40 | 794.40 |

*round*

*elliptical*

*quarter-round*

*casement*

| | Craft@Hrs | Unit | Material | Labor | Total |
|---|---|---|---|---|---|
| **24" wide aluminum double-hung window** | | | | | |
| 36" tall | 1C@.991 | ea | 252.00 | 56.40 | 308.40 |
| 48" tall | 1C@.991 | ea | 281.00 | 56.40 | 337.40 |
| 60" tall | 1C@.991 | ea | 317.00 | 56.40 | 373.40 |
| 72" tall | 1C@.991 | ea | 355.00 | 56.40 | 411.40 |
| **36" wide aluminum double-hung window** | | | | | |
| 36" tall | 1C@.991 | ea | 310.00 | 56.40 | 366.40 |
| 48" tall | 1C@.991 | ea | 344.00 | 56.40 | 400.40 |
| 60" tall | 1C@.991 | ea | 371.00 | 56.40 | 427.40 |
| 72" tall | 1C@1.39 | ea | 407.00 | 79.10 | 486.10 |
| **42" wide aluminum double-hung window** | | | | | |
| 36" tall | 1C@.991 | ea | 340.00 | 56.40 | 396.40 |
| 48" tall | 1C@.991 | ea | 372.00 | 56.40 | 428.40 |
| 60" tall | 1C@1.39 | ea | 407.00 | 79.10 | 486.10 |
| 72" tall | 1C@1.39 | ea | 442.00 | 79.10 | 521.10 |
| **24" wide aluminum single-hung window** | | | | | |
| 36" tall | 1C@.991 | ea | 208.00 | 56.40 | 264.40 |
| 48" tall | 1C@.991 | ea | 238.00 | 56.40 | 294.40 |
| 60" tall | 1C@.991 | ea | 274.00 | 56.40 | 330.40 |
| 72" tall | 1C@.991 | ea | 313.00 | 56.40 | 369.40 |
| **36" wide aluminum single-hung window** | | | | | |
| 36" tall | 1C@.991 | ea | 267.00 | 56.40 | 323.40 |
| 48" tall | 1C@.991 | ea | 304.00 | 56.40 | 360.40 |
| 60" tall | 1C@.991 | ea | 329.00 | 56.40 | 385.40 |
| 72" tall | 1C@1.39 | ea | 364.00 | 79.10 | 443.10 |
| **42" wide aluminum single-hung window** | | | | | |
| 36" tall | 1C@.991 | ea | 300.00 | 56.40 | 356.40 |
| 48" tall | 1C@.991 | ea | 330.00 | 56.40 | 386.40 |
| 60" tall | 1C@1.39 | ea | 364.00 | 79.10 | 443.10 |
| 72" tall | 1C@1.39 | ea | 399.00 | 79.10 | 478.10 |
| **36" wide aluminum sliding window** | | | | | |
| 24" tall | 1C@.991 | ea | 90.60 | 56.40 | 147.00 |
| 36" tall | 1C@.991 | ea | 100.00 | 56.40 | 156.40 |
| 48" tall | 1C@.991 | ea | 140.00 | 56.40 | 196.40 |
| 60" tall | 1C@.991 | ea | 185.00 | 56.40 | 241.40 |
| **48" wide aluminum sliding window** | | | | | |
| 24" tall | 1C@.991 | ea | 101.00 | 56.40 | 157.40 |
| 36" tall | 1C@.991 | ea | 112.00 | 56.40 | 168.40 |
| 48" tall | 1C@.991 | ea | 156.00 | 56.40 | 212.40 |
| 60" tall | 1C@1.39 | ea | 206.00 | 79.10 | 285.10 |
| **60" wide aluminum sliding window** | | | | | |
| 24" tall | 1C@.991 | ea | 111.00 | 56.40 | 167.40 |
| 36" tall | 1C@.991 | ea | 123.00 | 56.40 | 179.40 |
| 48" tall | 1C@1.39 | ea | 170.00 | 79.10 | 249.10 |
| 60" tall | 1C@1.39 | ea | 226.00 | 79.10 | 305.10 |
| **72" wide aluminum sliding window** | | | | | |
| 24" tall | 1C@.991 | ea | 132.00 | 56.40 | 188.40 |
| 36" tall | 1C@1.39 | ea | 145.00 | 79.10 | 224.10 |
| 48" tall | 1C@1.39 | ea | 202.00 | 79.10 | 281.10 |
| 60" tall | 1C@2.00 | ea | 267.00 | 114.00 | 381.00 |

*double-hung*

| | Craft@Hrs | Unit | Material | Labor | Total |
|---|---|---|---|---|---|
| **24" wide aluminum fixed (picture) window** | | | | | |
| 36" tall | 1C@.991 | ea | 130.00 | 56.40 | 186.40 |
| 48" tall | 1C@.991 | ea | 186.00 | 56.40 | 242.40 |
| 60" tall | 1C@.991 | ea | 220.00 | 56.40 | 276.40 |
| 72" tall | 1C@.991 | ea | 238.00 | 56.40 | 294.40 |
| **30" wide aluminum fixed (picture) window** | | | | | |
| 36" tall | 1C@.991 | ea | 154.00 | 56.40 | 210.40 |
| 48" tall | 1C@.991 | ea | 196.00 | 56.40 | 252.40 |
| 60" tall | 1C@.991 | ea | 213.00 | 56.40 | 269.40 |
| 72" tall | 1C@.991 | ea | 274.00 | 56.40 | 330.40 |
| **36" wide aluminum fixed (picture) window** | | | | | |
| 36" tall | 1C@.991 | ea | 167.00 | 56.40 | 223.40 |
| 48" tall | 1C@.991 | ea | 223.00 | 56.40 | 279.40 |
| 60" tall | 1C@.991 | ea | 226.00 | 56.40 | 282.40 |
| 72" tall | 1C@1.39 | ea | 319.00 | 79.10 | 398.10 |
| **42" wide aluminum fixed (picture) window** | | | | | |
| 36" tall | 1C@.991 | ea | 186.00 | 56.40 | 242.40 |
| 48" tall | 1C@.991 | ea | 266.00 | 56.40 | 322.40 |
| 60" tall | 1C@1.39 | ea | 321.00 | 79.10 | 400.10 |
| 72" tall | 1C@1.39 | ea | 369.00 | 79.10 | 448.10 |
| **48" wide aluminum fixed (picture) window** | | | | | |
| 36" tall | 1C@.991 | ea | 223.00 | 56.40 | 279.40 |
| 48" tall | 1C@.991 | ea | 274.00 | 56.40 | 330.40 |
| 60" tall | 1C@1.39 | ea | 351.00 | 79.10 | 430.10 |
| 72" tall | 1C@1.39 | ea | 401.00 | 79.10 | 480.10 |
| **60" wide aluminum fixed (picture) window** | | | | | |
| 36" tall | 1C@.991 | ea | 226.00 | 56.40 | 282.40 |
| 48" tall | 1C@1.39 | ea | 284.00 | 79.10 | 363.10 |
| 60" tall | 1C@1.39 | ea | 330.00 | 79.10 | 409.10 |
| 72" tall | 1C@2.00 | ea | 440.00 | 114.00 | 554.00 |
| **72" wide aluminum fixed (picture) window** | | | | | |
| 36" tall | 1C@2.00 | ea | 319.00 | 114.00 | 433.00 |
| 48" tall | 1C@2.00 | ea | 404.00 | 114.00 | 518.00 |
| 60" tall | 1C@2.94 | ea | 440.00 | 167.00 | 607.00 |
| 72" tall | 1C@2.94 | ea | 524.00 | 167.00 | 691.00 |

**Vinyl.** All vinyl windows are double-glazed with clear glass. All costs are for standard windows. Manufacturers' window sizes vary. For standard units round measurements to the nearest size. Add approximately **80%** for custom sizes. Some manufacturers provide a less rigid, lower grade of windows for **15%** less. For aluminum grid between panes of glass or removable grilles outside of window add: half-round **$24**, half-elliptical **$40**, round **$24**, elliptical **$32**, quarter-round **$24**, casement **$31**, awning **$31**, single-hung **$24**, sliding **$27**, fixed (picture) **$29**.

| | Craft@Hrs | Unit | Material | Labor | Total |
|---|---|---|---|---|---|
| **Half-round vinyl window top** | | | | | |
| 24" x 12" | 1C@.991 | ea | 276.00 | 56.40 | 332.40 |
| 36" x 18" | 1C@.991 | ea | 335.00 | 56.40 | 391.40 |
| 48" x 24" | 1C@1.39 | ea | 487.00 | 79.10 | 566.10 |
| 72" x 36" | 1C@2.00 | ea | 721.00 | 114.00 | 835.00 |
| **Half-elliptical vinyl window top** | | | | | |
| 36" x 15" | 1C@.991 | ea | 625.00 | 56.40 | 681.40 |
| 48" x 16" | 1C@.991 | ea | 568.00 | 56.40 | 624.40 |
| 60" x 19" | 1C@1.39 | ea | 521.00 | 79.10 | 600.10 |
| 90" x 20" | 1C@2.00 | ea | 1,110.00 | 114.00 | 1,224.00 |

*half-round*

*half-elliptical*

| | | Craft@Hrs | Unit | Material | Labor | Total |
|---|---|---|---|---|---|---|
| **Round vinyl window** | | | | | | |
| 20" x 20" | | 1C@.991 | ea | 664.00 | 56.40 | 720.40 |
| 30" x 30" | | 1C@.991 | ea | 660.00 | 56.40 | 716.40 |
| 40" x 40" | | 1C@1.39 | ea | 936.00 | 79.10 | 1,015.10 |
| 48" x 48" | *round* | 1C@2.00 | ea | 1,020.00 | 114.00 | 1,134.00 |
| **Elliptical vinyl window** | | | | | | |
| 15" x 24" | | 1C@.991 | ea | 1,250.00 | 56.40 | 1,306.40 |
| 24" x 36" | | 1C@.991 | ea | 1,120.00 | 56.40 | 1,176.40 |
| 25" x 40" | | 1C@1.39 | ea | 1,460.00 | 79.10 | 1,539.10 |
| 30" x 48" | *elliptical* | 1C@2.00 | ea | 1,580.00 | 114.00 | 1,694.00 |
| **Quarter-round vinyl window** | | | | | | |
| 24" x 24" | | 1C@.991 | ea | 540.00 | 56.40 | 596.40 |
| 36" x 36" | | 1C@.991 | ea | 634.00 | 56.40 | 690.40 |
| **18" wide vinyl casement window** | *quarter-round* | | | | | |
| 36" tall | | 1C@.991 | ea | 392.00 | 56.40 | 448.40 |
| 48" tall | | 1C@.991 | ea | 423.00 | 56.40 | 479.40 |
| 60" tall | | 1C@.991 | ea | 488.00 | 56.40 | 544.40 |
| **24" wide vinyl casement window** | | | | | | |
| 36" tall | | 1C@.991 | ea | 421.00 | 56.40 | 477.40 |
| 48" tall | *casement* | 1C@.991 | ea | 457.00 | 56.40 | 513.40 |
| 60" tall | | 1C@1.39 | ea | 518.00 | 79.10 | 597.10 |
| **30" wide vinyl casement window** | | | | | | |
| 48" tall | | 1C@1.39 | ea | 497.00 | 79.10 | 576.10 |
| 60" tall | | 1C@1.39 | ea | 553.00 | 79.10 | 632.10 |
| **36" wide vinyl casement window (double)** | | | | | | |
| 48" tall | | 1C@1.39 | ea | 589.00 | 79.10 | 668.10 |
| 60" tall | | 1C@1.39 | ea | 677.00 | 79.10 | 756.10 |
| **24" wide vinyl awning window** | | | | | | |
| 20" tall | | 1C@.991 | ea | 363.00 | 56.40 | 419.40 |
| 24" tall | | 1C@.991 | ea | 407.00 | 56.40 | 463.40 |
| 30" tall | | 1C@.991 | ea | 446.00 | 56.40 | 502.40 |
| **30" wide vinyl awning window** | *awning* | | | | | |
| 20" tall | | 1C@.991 | ea | 419.00 | 56.40 | 475.40 |
| 24" tall | | 1C@.991 | ea | 458.00 | 56.40 | 514.40 |
| 30" tall | | 1C@.991 | ea | 503.00 | 56.40 | 559.40 |
| **36" wide vinyl awning window** | | | | | | |
| 24" tall | | 1C@.991 | ea | 501.00 | 56.40 | 557.40 |
| 30" tall | | 1C@.991 | ea | 559.00 | 56.40 | 615.40 |

| | Craft@Hrs | Unit | Material | Labor | Total |
|---|---|---|---|---|---|
| **40" wide vinyl awning window** | | | | | |
| 24" tall | 1C@.991 | ea | 432.00 | 56.40 | 488.40 |
| 30" tall | 1C@.991 | ea | 623.00 | 56.40 | 679.40 |
| **24" wide vinyl single-hung window** | | | | | |
| 36" tall | 1C@.991 | ea | 176.00 | 56.40 | 232.40 |
| 48" tall | 1C@.991 | ea | 202.00 | 56.40 | 258.40 |
| 60" tall | 1C@.991 | ea | 231.00 | 56.40 | 287.40 |
| 72" tall | 1C@.991 | ea | 266.00 | 56.40 | 322.40 |

*single-hung*

| | Craft@Hrs | Unit | Material | Labor | Total |
|---|---|---|---|---|---|
| **36" wide vinyl single-hung window** | | | | | |
| 36" tall | 1C@.991 | ea | 226.00 | 56.40 | 282.40 |
| 48" tall | 1C@.991 | ea | 257.00 | 56.40 | 313.40 |
| 60" tall | 1C@.991 | ea | 278.00 | 56.40 | 334.40 |
| 72" tall | 1C@1.39 | ea | 307.00 | 79.10 | 386.10 |
| **42" wide vinyl single-hung window** | | | | | |
| 36" tall | 1C@.991 | ea | 252.00 | 56.40 | 308.40 |
| 48" tall | 1C@.991 | ea | 279.00 | 56.40 | 335.40 |
| 60" tall | 1C@1.39 | ea | 331.00 | 79.10 | 410.10 |
| 72" tall | 1C@1.39 | ea | 337.00 | 79.10 | 416.10 |
| **48" wide vinyl sliding window** | | | | | |
| 24" tall | 1C@.991 | ea | 186.00 | 56.40 | 242.40 |
| 36" tall | 1C@.991 | ea | 226.00 | 56.40 | 282.40 |
| 48" tall | 1C@.991 | ea | 259.00 | 56.40 | 315.40 |
| 60" tall | 1C@.991 | ea | 307.00 | 56.40 | 363.40 |

*sliding*

| | Craft@Hrs | Unit | Material | Labor | Total |
|---|---|---|---|---|---|
| **60" wide vinyl sliding window** | | | | | |
| 36" tall | 1C@.991 | ea | 257.00 | 56.40 | 313.40 |
| 48" tall | 1C@.991 | ea | 300.00 | 56.40 | 356.40 |
| 60" tall | 1C@1.39 | ea | 366.00 | 79.10 | 445.10 |
| **72" wide vinyl sliding window** | | | | | |
| 48" tall | 1C@1.39 | ea | 339.00 | 79.10 | 418.10 |
| 60" tall | 1C@1.39 | ea | 396.00 | 79.10 | 475.10 |
| **24" wide vinyl fixed (picture) window** | | | | | |
| 36" tall | 1C@.991 | ea | 110.00 | 56.40 | 166.40 |
| 48" tall | 1C@.991 | ea | 154.00 | 56.40 | 210.40 |
| 60" tall | 1C@.991 | ea | 186.00 | 56.40 | 242.40 |
| 72" tall | 1C@.991 | ea | 202.00 | 56.40 | 258.40 |

*fixed (picture)*

| | Craft@Hrs | Unit | Material | Labor | Total |
|---|---|---|---|---|---|
| **30" wide vinyl fixed (picture) window** | | | | | |
| 36" tall | 1C@.991 | ea | 133.00 | 56.40 | 189.40 |
| 48" tall | 1C@.991 | ea | 163.00 | 56.40 | 219.40 |
| 60" tall | 1C@.991 | ea | 182.00 | 56.40 | 238.40 |
| 72" tall | 1C@.991 | ea | 231.00 | 56.40 | 287.40 |

|  | Craft@Hrs | Unit | Material | Labor | Total |
|---|---|---|---|---|---|
| **36" wide vinyl fixed (picture) window** | | | | | |
| 36" tall | 1C@.991 | ea | 181.00 | 56.40 | 237.40 |
| 48" tall | 1C@.991 | ea | 189.00 | 56.40 | 245.40 |
| 60" tall | 1C@.991 | ea | 192.00 | 56.40 | 248.40 |
| 72" tall | 1C@1.39 | ea | 269.00 | 79.10 | 348.10 |
| **42" wide vinyl fixed (picture) window** | | | | | |
| 36" tall | 1C@.991 | ea | 180.00 | 56.40 | 236.40 |
| 48" tall | 1C@.991 | ea | 257.00 | 56.40 | 313.40 |
| 60" tall | 1C@1.39 | ea | 313.00 | 79.10 | 392.10 |
| 72" tall | 1C@1.39 | ea | 359.00 | 79.10 | 438.10 |
| **48" wide vinyl fixed (picture) window** | | | | | |
| 36" tall | 1C@.991 | ea | 189.00 | 56.40 | 245.40 |
| 48" tall | 1C@.991 | ea | 231.00 | 56.40 | 287.40 |
| 60" tall | 1C@1.39 | ea | 300.00 | 79.10 | 379.10 |
| 72" tall | 1C@1.39 | ea | 339.00 | 79.10 | 418.10 |
| **60" wide vinyl fixed (picture) window** | | | | | |
| 36" tall | 1C@.991 | ea | 192.00 | 56.40 | 248.40 |
| 48" tall | 1C@1.39 | ea | 240.00 | 79.10 | 319.10 |
| 60" tall | 1C@1.39 | ea | 279.00 | 79.10 | 358.10 |
| 72" tall | 1C@2.00 | ea | 370.00 | 114.00 | 484.00 |
| **72" wide vinyl fixed (picture) window** | | | | | |
| 36" tall | 1C@2.00 | ea | 269.00 | 114.00 | 383.00 |
| 48" tall | 1C@2.00 | ea | 339.00 | 114.00 | 453.00 |
| 60" tall | 1C@2.94 | ea | 370.00 | 167.00 | 537.00 |
| 72" tall | 1C@2.94 | ea | 442.00 | 167.00 | 609.00 |

**Wood.** All wood windows are double-glazed with clear glass. Interiors are natural wood and exteriors are primed wood or aluminum clad or vinyl clad. Hardware on wood windows is bright brass, brushed brass, antique brass or white. All costs are for standard windows. Manufacturers' window sizes vary. For standard units, round measurements to the nearest size. Add approximately **80%** for custom sizes.

| | | Craft@Hrs | Unit | Material | Labor | Total |
|---|---|---|---|---|---|---|
| **Half-round wood window top** | | | | | | |
| 24" x 12" | | 1C@.991 | ea | 808.00 | 56.40 | 864.40 |
| 36" x 18" | | 1C@.991 | ea | 1,040.00 | 56.40 | 1,096.40 |
| 48" x 24" | | 1C@1.39 | ea | 1,020.00 | 79.10 | 1,099.10 |
| 60" x 30" | *half-round* | 1C@2.00 | ea | 1,420.00 | 114.00 | 1,534.00 |
| **Half-elliptical wood window top** | | | | | | |
| 36" x 15" | | 1C@.991 | ea | 1,280.00 | 56.40 | 1,336.40 |
| 48" x16" | | 1C@.991 | ea | 1,400.00 | 56.40 | 1,456.40 |
| 60" x 17" | *half-elliptical* | 1C@1.39 | ea | 1,480.00 | 79.10 | 1,559.10 |
| 72" x 19" | | 1C@2.00 | ea | 1,800.00 | 114.00 | 1,914.00 |

Additional costs for half-round and
half-elliptical wood windows
   add 114% for true divided light, spoke pattern
   (half-round or half-elliptical)

| | | Craft@Hrs | Unit | Material | Labor | Total |
|---|---|---|---|---|---|---|
| add for 3 spoke hub grille (half-round window) | | | | | | |
| all sizes | | — | ea | 24.50 | — | 24.50 |

| | Craft@Hrs | Unit | Material | Labor | Total |
|---|---|---|---|---|---|
| **Round wood window** | | | | | |
| 30" x 30" | 1C@.991 | ea | 1,760.00 | 56.40 | 1,816.40 |
| 48" x 48" | 1C@.991 | ea | 2,040.00 | 56.40 | 2,096.40 |
| **Elliptical (oval) wood window** | | | | | |
| 25" x 30" | 1C@.991 | ea | 2,050.00 | 56.40 | 2,106.40 |
| 30" x 36" | 1C@.991 | ea | 2,300.00 | 56.40 | 2,356.40 |
| **Additional round and elliptical wood window costs** | | | | | |
| add for 4-lite grille in round or elliptical window | | | | | |
| all sizes | — | ea | 21.80 | — | 21.80 |
| add for 9-lite grille in round or elliptical window | | | | | |
| all sizes | — | ea | 28.00 | — | 28.00 |
| add for sunburst grille in round or elliptical window | | | | | |
| all sizes | — | ea | 34.10 | — | 34.10 |
| **Quarter-round wood window** | | | | | |
| 24" x 24" | 1C@.991 | ea | 994.00 | 56.40 | 1,050.40 |
| 36" x 36" | 1C@.991 | ea | 1,170.00 | 56.40 | 1,226.40 |

*single spoke grille*    *double spoke grille*    *radial bar grille*    *double radial grille*

| **Additional quarter-round wood window costs** | | | | | |
|---|---|---|---|---|---|
| add for single spoke grille | | | | | |
| all sizes | — | ea | 30.60 | — | 30.60 |
| add for double spoke grille | | | | | |
| all sizes | — | ea | 35.40 | — | 35.40 |
| add for single radial bar grille | | | | | |
| all sizes | — | ea | 41.50 | — | 41.50 |
| add for double radial bar grille | | | | | |
| all sizes | — | ea | 46.40 | — | 46.40 |

| | Craft@Hrs | Unit | Material | Labor | Total |
|---|---|---|---|---|---|
| **18" wide wood casement window** | | | | | |
| 36" tall | 1C@.991 | ea | 267.00 | 56.40 | 323.40 |
| 48" tall | 1C@.991 | ea | 358.00 | 56.40 | 414.40 |
| 60" tall | 1C@.991 | ea | 427.00 | 56.40 | 483.40 |
| 72" tall | 1C@.991 | ea | 502.00 | 56.40 | 558.40 |
| **24" wide wood casement window** | | | | | |
| 36" tall | 1C@.991 | ea | 339.00 | 56.40 | 395.40 |
| 48" tall | 1C@.991 | ea | 385.00 | 56.40 | 441.40 |
| 60" tall | 1C@1.39 | ea | 450.00 | 79.10 | 529.10 |
| 72" tall | 1C@.991 | ea | 524.00 | 56.40 | 580.40 |
| **30" wide wood casement window** | | | | | |
| 48" tall | 1C@1.39 | ea | 434.00 | 79.10 | 513.10 |
| 60" tall | 1C@1.39 | ea | 510.00 | 79.10 | 589.10 |
| 72" tall | 1C@.991 | ea | 553.00 | 56.40 | 609.40 |
| **36" wide wood casement window** | | | | | |
| 48" tall | 1C@1.39 | ea | 489.00 | 79.10 | 568.10 |
| 60" tall | 1C@1.39 | ea | 575.00 | 79.10 | 654.10 |
| 72" tall | 1C@1.39 | ea | 627.00 | 79.10 | 706.10 |
| **Additional casement window costs** | | | | | |
| add 87% for authentic divided lites | | | | | |
| add for removable wood grille | | | | | |
| all sizes | — | ea | 15.10 | — | 15.10 |
| add for aluminum grille between panes | | | | | |
| all sizes | — | ea | 14.00 | — | 14.00 |
| **24" wide wood awning window** | | | | | |
| 20" tall | 1C@.991 | ea | 284.00 | 56.40 | 340.40 |
| 24" tall | 1C@.991 | ea | 309.00 | 56.40 | 365.40 |
| 30" tall | 1C@.991 | ea | 331.00 | 56.40 | 387.40 |
| **30" wide wood awning window** | | | | | |
| 20" tall | 1C@.991 | ea | 302.00 | 56.40 | 358.40 |
| 24" tall | 1C@.991 | ea | 321.00 | 56.40 | 377.40 |
| 30" tall | 1C@1.39 | ea | 342.00 | 79.10 | 421.10 |
| **36" wide wood awning window** | | | | | |
| 20" tall | 1C@.991 | ea | 319.00 | 56.40 | 375.40 |
| 24" tall | 1C@1.39 | ea | 342.00 | 79.10 | 421.10 |
| 30" tall | 1C@1.39 | ea | 363.00 | 79.10 | 442.10 |
| **48" wide wood awning window** | | | | | |
| 20" tall | 1C@.991 | ea | 383.00 | 56.40 | 439.40 |
| 24" tall | 1C@1.39 | ea | 393.00 | 79.10 | 472.10 |
| 30" tall | 1C@1.39 | ea | 438.00 | 79.10 | 517.10 |
| **Additional awning window costs** | | | | | |
| add 80% for authentic divided lites | | | | | |
| add for removable wood grille | | | | | |
| all sizes | — | ea | 17.00 | — | 17.00 |
| add for aluminum grille between panes | | | | | |
| all sizes | — | ea | 15.80 | — | 15.80 |

*awning*

| | Craft@Hrs | Unit | Material | Labor | Total |
|---|---|---|---|---|---|
| **24" wide wood double-hung window** | | | | | |
| 36" tall | 1C@.991 | ea | 288.00 | 56.40 | 344.40 |
| 48" tall | 1C@.991 | ea | 336.00 | 56.40 | 392.40 |
| 60" tall | 1C@.991 | ea | 377.00 | 56.40 | 433.40 |
| 72" tall | 1C@.991 | ea | 426.00 | 56.40 | 482.40 |
| **36" wide wood double-hung window** | | | | | |
| 36" tall | 1C@.991 | ea | 351.00 | 56.40 | 407.40 |
| 48" tall | 1C@.991 | ea | 405.00 | 56.40 | 461.40 |
| 60" tall | 1C@.991 | ea | 458.00 | 56.40 | 514.40 |
| 72" tall | 1C@1.39 | ea | 519.00 | 79.10 | 598.10 |
| **48" wide wood double-hung window** | | | | | |
| 36" tall | 1C@.991 | ea | 447.00 | 56.40 | 503.40 |
| 48" tall | 1C@.991 | ea | 447.00 | 56.40 | 503.40 |
| 60" tall | 1C@1.39 | ea | 516.00 | 79.10 | 595.10 |
| 72" tall | 1C@1.39 | ea | 597.00 | 79.10 | 676.10 |

*double-hung window*

**Additional double-hung window costs**

add 105% for authentic divided lites

add for removable wood grille

| | | Unit | Material | Labor | Total |
|---|---|---|---|---|---|
| all sizes | — | ea | 17.00 | — | 17.00 |

add for aluminum grille between panes

| | | Unit | Material | Labor | Total |
|---|---|---|---|---|---|
| all sizes | — | ea | 15.80 | — | 15.80 |

| | Craft@Hrs | Unit | Material | Labor | Total |
|---|---|---|---|---|---|
| **24" wide wood single-hung window** | | | | | |
| 36" tall | 1C@.991 | ea | 214.00 | 56.40 | 270.40 |
| 48" tall | 1C@.991 | ea | 262.00 | 56.40 | 318.40 |
| 60" tall | 1C@.991 | ea | 305.00 | 56.40 | 361.40 |
| 72" tall | 1C@.991 | ea | 352.00 | 56.40 | 408.40 |
| **36" wide wood single-hung window** | | | | | |
| 36" tall | 1C@.991 | ea | 276.00 | 56.40 | 332.40 |
| 48" tall | 1C@.991 | ea | 330.00 | 56.40 | 386.40 |
| 60" tall | 1C@.991 | ea | 384.00 | 56.40 | 440.40 |
| 72" tall | 1C@1.39 | ea | 445.00 | 79.10 | 524.10 |
| **40" wide wood single-hung window** | | | | | |
| 36" tall | 1C@.991 | ea | 373.00 | 56.40 | 429.40 |
| 48" tall | 1C@.991 | ea | 373.00 | 56.40 | 429.40 |
| 60" tall | 1C@1.39 | ea | 443.00 | 79.10 | 522.10 |
| 72" tall | 1C@1.39 | ea | 523.00 | 79.10 | 602.10 |

*single-hung window*

**Additional single-hung window costs**

add 105% for authentic divided lites

add for removable wood grille

| | | Unit | Material | Labor | Total |
|---|---|---|---|---|---|
| all sizes | — | ea | 17.00 | — | 17.00 |

add for aluminum grille between panes

| | | Unit | Material | Labor | Total |
|---|---|---|---|---|---|
| all sizes | — | ea | 15.80 | — | 15.80 |

add 97% for segmented top

| | Craft@Hrs | Unit | Material | Labor | Total |
|---|---|---|---|---|---|
| 48" wide wood sliding window | | | | | |
| 24" tall | 1C@.991 | ea | 420.00 | 56.40 | 476.40 |
| 36" tall | 1C@.991 | ea | 453.00 | 56.40 | 509.40 |
| 48" tall | 1C@.991 | ea | 535.00 | 56.40 | 591.40 |
| 60" tall | 1C@.991 | ea | 611.00 | 56.40 | 667.40 |
| 60" wide wood sliding window | | | | | |
| 36" tall | 1C@.991 | ea | 542.00 | 56.40 | 598.40 |
| 48" tall | 1C@.991 | ea | 613.00 | 56.40 | 669.40 |
| 60" tall | 1C@1.39 | ea | 702.00 | 79.10 | 781.10 |
| 72" wide wood sliding window | | | | | |
| 48" tall | 1C@1.39 | ea | 690.00 | 79.10 | 769.10 |
| 60" tall | 1C@1.39 | ea | 780.00 | 79.10 | 859.10 |

*sliding*

Additional sliding window costs
 add 90% for authentic divided lites
 add for removable wood grille

| | | | | | |
|---|---|---|---|---|---|
| all sizes | — | ea | 17.00 | — | 17.00 |
| add for aluminum grille between panes | | | | | |
| all sizes | — | ea | 15.80 | — | 15.80 |

| | Craft@Hrs | Unit | Material | Labor | Total |
|---|---|---|---|---|---|
| 24" wide wood fixed (picture) window | | | | | |
| 36" tall | 1C@.991 | ea | 245.00 | 56.40 | 301.40 |
| 48" tall | 1C@.991 | ea | 289.00 | 56.40 | 345.40 |
| 60" tall | 1C@.991 | ea | 334.00 | 56.40 | 390.40 |
| 72" tall | 1C@.991 | ea | 383.00 | 56.40 | 439.40 |

*fixed (picture)*

| | Craft@Hrs | Unit | Material | Labor | Total |
|---|---|---|---|---|---|
| 36" wide wood fixed (picture) window | | | | | |
| 36" tall | 1C@.991 | ea | 307.00 | 56.40 | 363.40 |
| 48" tall | 1C@.991 | ea | 359.00 | 56.40 | 415.40 |
| 60" tall | 1C@.991 | ea | 414.00 | 56.40 | 470.40 |
| 72" tall | 1C@1.39 | ea | 475.00 | 79.10 | 554.10 |
| 48" wide wood fixed (picture) window | | | | | |
| 36" tall | 1C@.991 | ea | 404.00 | 56.40 | 460.40 |
| 48" tall | 1C@.991 | ea | 404.00 | 56.40 | 460.40 |
| 60" tall | 1C@1.39 | ea | 473.00 | 79.10 | 552.10 |
| 72" tall | 1C@1.39 | ea | 553.00 | 79.10 | 632.10 |
| 60" wide wood fixed (picture) window | | | | | |
| 48" tall | 1C@1.39 | ea | 478.00 | 79.10 | 557.10 |
| 60" tall | 1C@1.39 | ea | 550.00 | 79.10 | 629.10 |
| 72" tall | 1C@2.00 | ea | 641.00 | 114.00 | 755.00 |
| 72" wide wood fixed (picture) window | | | | | |
| 60" tall | 1C@2.00 | ea | 627.00 | 114.00 | 741.00 |
| 72" tall | 1C@2.00 | ea | 716.00 | 114.00 | 830.00 |

Additional fixed window costs.
 add 80% for authentic divided lites
 add for removable wood grille

| | | | | | |
|---|---|---|---|---|---|
| all sizes | — | ea | 18.30 | — | 18.30 |
| add for aluminum grille between panes | | | | | |
| all sizes | — | ea | 17.00 | — | 17.00 |

 add 97% for segmented top

|  | Craft@Hrs | Unit | Material | Labor | Total |
|---|---|---|---|---|---|

**Skylight.** Includes skylight, frame, nails, flashing, peel-and-stick moisture barrier, framed curb (when required by manufacturer), and installation. Flashing is for a roof with low-profile roofing such as asphalt shingles. For tile shingles or ribbed metal roofing, use the price list item that adds an additional cost for a high-profile roof. Curbs are usually required on low-slope roofs. A special sloped curb is usually required on flat roofs. Does not include roof framing, shingles, or interior finishes.

| | Craft@Hrs | Unit | Material | Labor | Total |
|---|---|---|---|---|---|
| **Additional skylight costs** | | | | | |
| add for laminated glass over tempered glass in skylight or roof window, all types | — | ea | 44.10 | — | 44.10 |
| add for Low-E in skylight or roof window all types | — | ea | 11.00 | — | 11.00 |
| add for argon gas filled skylight or roof window all types | — | ea | 9.75 | — | 9.75 |
| add for bronze or gray tint (all sizes) all types | — | ea | 18.30 | — | 18.30 |
| add for skylight or roof window installed on high-profile roof, all types | — | ea | 28.00 | — | 28.00 |
| add for skylight or roof window installed on low-slope roof, all types | — | ea | 369.00 | — | 369.00 |
| add for skylight or roof window installed on flat roof, all types | — | ea | 383.00 | — | 383.00 |
| **Single dome skylight** | | | | | |
| 24" x 24" | 1C@2.62 | ea | 79.40 | 149.00 | 228.40 |
| 24" x 48" | 1C@2.62 | ea | 157.00 | 149.00 | 306.00 |
| 30" x 30" | 1C@2.62 | ea | 125.00 | 149.00 | 274.00 |
| 48" x 48" | 1C@2.62 | ea | 399.00 | 149.00 | 548.00 |
| **Double dome skylight** | | | | | |
| 24" x 24" | 1C@2.62 | ea | 106.00 | 149.00 | 255.00 |
| 24" x 48" | 1C@2.62 | ea | 218.00 | 149.00 | 367.00 |
| 30" x 30" | 1C@2.62 | ea | 204.00 | 149.00 | 353.00 |
| 48" x 48" | 1C@2.62 | ea | 470.00 | 149.00 | 619.00 |
| **Triple dome skylight** | | | | | |
| 24" x 24" | 1C@2.62 | ea | 138.00 | 149.00 | 287.00 |
| 24" x 48" | 1C@2.62 | ea | 316.00 | 149.00 | 465.00 |
| 30" x 30" | 1C@2.62 | ea | 251.00 | 149.00 | 400.00 |
| 48" x 48" | 1C@2.62 | ea | 602.00 | 149.00 | 751.00 |
| **Single dome ventilating skylight** | | | | | |
| 24" x 24" | 1C@2.78 | ea | 167.00 | 158.00 | 325.00 |
| 24" x 48" | 1C@2.78 | ea | 329.00 | 158.00 | 487.00 |
| 30" x 30" | 1C@2.78 | ea | 263.00 | 158.00 | 421.00 |
| 48" x 48" | 1C@2.78 | ea | 830.00 | 158.00 | 988.00 |
| **Double dome ventilating skylight** | | | | | |
| 24" x 24" | 1C@2.78 | ea | 221.00 | 158.00 | 379.00 |
| 24" x 48" | 1C@2.78 | ea | 457.00 | 158.00 | 615.00 |
| 30" x 30" | 1C@2.78 | ea | 424.00 | 158.00 | 582.00 |
| 48" x 48" | 1C@2.78 | ea | 975.00 | 158.00 | 1,133.00 |
| **Triple dome ventilating skylight** | | | | | |
| 24" x 24" | 1C@2.78 | ea | 283.00 | 158.00 | 441.00 |
| 24" x 48" | 1C@2.78 | ea | 656.00 | 158.00 | 814.00 |
| 30" x 30" | 1C@2.78 | ea | 521.00 | 158.00 | 679.00 |
| 48" x 48" | 1C@2.78 | ea | 1,250.00 | 158.00 | 1,408.00 |

|  | Craft@Hrs | Unit | Material | Labor | Total |
|---|---|---|---|---|---|
| **22" wide fixed skylight** | | | | | |
| 28" long | 1C@2.69 | ea | 288.00 | 153.00 | 441.00 |
| 38" long | 1C@2.69 | ea | 337.00 | 153.00 | 490.00 |
| 48" long | 1C@2.69 | ea | 375.00 | 153.00 | 528.00 |
| 55" long | 1C@2.69 | ea | 411.00 | 153.00 | 564.00 |
| **30" wide fixed skylight** | | | | | |
| 38" long | 1C@2.69 | ea | 389.00 | 153.00 | 542.00 |
| 55" long | 1C@2.69 | ea | 476.00 | 153.00 | 629.00 |
| **44" wide fixed skylight** | | | | | |
| 28" long | 1C@2.69 | ea | 423.00 | 153.00 | 576.00 |
| 48" long | 1C@2.69 | ea | 540.00 | 153.00 | 693.00 |
| **22" wide fixed skylight with ventilation flap** | | | | | |
| 28" long | 1C@2.69 | ea | 327.00 | 153.00 | 480.00 |
| 38" long | 1C@2.69 | ea | 375.00 | 153.00 | 528.00 |
| 48" long | 1C@2.69 | ea | 417.00 | 153.00 | 570.00 |
| 55" long | 1C@2.69 | ea | 442.00 | 153.00 | 595.00 |
| **30" wide fixed skylight with ventilation flap** | | | | | |
| 38" long | 1C@2.69 | ea | 440.00 | 153.00 | 593.00 |
| 55" long | 1C@2.69 | ea | 514.00 | 153.00 | 667.00 |
| **44" wide fixed skylight with ventilation flap** | | | | | |
| 28" long | 1C@2.69 | ea | 492.00 | 153.00 | 645.00 |
| 48" long | 1C@2.69 | ea | 591.00 | 153.00 | 744.00 |
| **22" wide ventilating skylight** | | | | | |
| 28" long | 1C@2.94 | ea | 544.00 | 167.00 | 711.00 |
| 38" long | 1C@2.94 | ea | 591.00 | 167.00 | 758.00 |
| 48" long | 1C@2.94 | ea | 646.00 | 167.00 | 813.00 |
| 55" long | 1C@2.94 | ea | 673.00 | 167.00 | 840.00 |
| **30" wide ventilating skylight** | | | | | |
| 38" long | 1C@2.94 | ea | 656.00 | 167.00 | 823.00 |
| 55" long | 1C@2.94 | ea | 758.00 | 167.00 | 925.00 |
| **44" wide ventilating skylight** | | | | | |
| 28" long | 1C@2.94 | ea | 691.00 | 167.00 | 858.00 |
| 48" long | 1C@2.94 | ea | 845.00 | 167.00 | 1,012.00 |
| **22" wide roof window** | | | | | |
| 28" long | 1C@2.94 | ea | 742.00 | 167.00 | 909.00 |
| 48" long | 1C@2.94 | ea | 820.00 | 167.00 | 987.00 |
| **30" wide roof window** | | | | | |
| 38" long | 1C@2.94 | ea | 824.00 | 167.00 | 991.00 |
| 55" long | 1C@2.94 | ea | 941.00 | 167.00 | 1,108.00 |
| **44" wide roof window** | | | | | |
| 55" long | 1C@2.94 | ea | 1,020.00 | 167.00 | 1,187.00 |
| **Add for cord-operated roller shades** | | | | | |
| 28" long | 1C@.832 | ea | 78.20 | 47.30 | 125.50 |
| 38" long | 1C@.832 | ea | 78.20 | 47.30 | 125.50 |
| 48" long | 1C@.832 | ea | 78.20 | 47.30 | 125.50 |
| 55" long | 1C@.832 | ea | 78.20 | 47.30 | 125.50 |

| | Craft@Hrs | Unit | Material | Labor | Total |
|---|---|---|---|---|---|
| Add for motorized rod cord control for roller shades | | | | | |
| all sizes | — | ea | 244.00 | — | 244.00 |
| Add for manually controlled Venetian blinds | | | | | |
| 28" long | — | ea | 110.00 | — | 110.00 |
| 38" long | — | ea | 131.00 | — | 131.00 |
| 48" long | — | ea | 138.00 | — | 138.00 |
| 55" long | — | ea | 174.00 | — | 174.00 |
| Add for electrically controlled skylight system | | | | | |
| 28" long | 1C@2.00 | ea | 180.00 | 114.00 | 294.00 |
| 38" long | 1C@2.00 | ea | 180.00 | 114.00 | 294.00 |
| 48" long | 1C@2.00 | ea | 180.00 | 114.00 | 294.00 |
| 55" long | 1C@2.00 | ea | 180.00 | 114.00 | 294.00 |
| Add for electrically controlled window or skylight opener | | | | | |
| 28" long | 1C@1.39 | ea | 180.00 | 79.10 | 259.10 |
| 38" long | 1C@1.39 | ea | 180.00 | 79.10 | 259.10 |
| 48" long | 1C@1.39 | ea | 180.00 | 79.10 | 259.10 |
| 55" long | 1C@1.39 | ea | 180.00 | 79.10 | 259.10 |
| Add for infrared remote control system for opener | | | | | |
| 28" long | 1C@1.11 | ea | 396.00 | 63.20 | 459.20 |
| 38" long | 1C@1.11 | ea | 396.00 | 63.20 | 459.20 |
| 48" long | 1C@1.11 | ea | 396.00 | 63.20 | 459.20 |
| 55" long | 1C@1.11 | ea | 396.00 | 63.20 | 459.20 |

### Storm window.

| | Craft@Hrs | Unit | Material | Labor | Total |
|---|---|---|---|---|---|
| 24" wide aluminum storm window | | | | | |
| 24" tall | 1C@1.00 | ea | 85.50 | 56.90 | 142.40 |
| 36" tall | 1C@1.00 | ea | 124.00 | 56.90 | 180.90 |
| 48" tall | 1C@1.00 | ea | 154.00 | 56.90 | 210.90 |
| 60" tall | 1C@1.00 | ea | 174.00 | 56.90 | 230.90 |
| 36" wide aluminum storm window | | | | | |
| 24" tall | 1C@1.00 | ea | 124.00 | 56.90 | 180.90 |
| 36" tall | 1C@1.00 | ea | 163.00 | 56.90 | 219.90 |
| 48" tall | 1C@1.00 | ea | 192.00 | 56.90 | 248.90 |
| 60" tall | 1C@1.08 | ea | 218.00 | 61.50 | 279.50 |
| 48" wide aluminum storm window | | | | | |
| 24" tall | 1C@1.00 | ea | 154.00 | 56.90 | 210.90 |
| 36" tall | 1C@1.00 | ea | 192.00 | 56.90 | 248.90 |
| 48" tall | 1C@1.08 | ea | 228.00 | 61.50 | 289.50 |
| 60" tall | 1C@1.08 | ea | 266.00 | 61.50 | 327.50 |
| 60" wide aluminum storm window | | | | | |
| 24" tall | 1C@1.00 | ea | 174.00 | 56.90 | 230.90 |
| 36" tall | 1C@1.08 | ea | 218.00 | 61.50 | 279.50 |
| 48" tall | 1C@1.08 | ea | 266.00 | 61.50 | 327.50 |
| 60" tall | 1C@1.08 | ea | 310.00 | 61.50 | 371.50 |
| 72" wide aluminum storm window | | | | | |
| 24" tall | 1C@1.00 | ea | 192.00 | 56.90 | 248.90 |
| 36" tall | 1C@1.08 | ea | 247.00 | 61.50 | 308.50 |
| 48" tall | 1C@1.08 | ea | 303.00 | 61.50 | 364.50 |
| 60" tall | 1C@1.22 | ea | 356.00 | 69.40 | 425.40 |

|  | Craft@Hrs | Unit | Material | Labor | Total |
|---|---|---|---|---|---|
| **24" wide wood storm window** | | | | | |
| 24" tall | 1C@1.00 | ea | 102.00 | 56.90 | 158.90 |
| 36" tall | 1C@1.00 | ea | 145.00 | 56.90 | 201.90 |
| 48" tall | 1C@1.00 | ea | 167.00 | 56.90 | 223.90 |
| 60" tall | 1C@1.00 | ea | 191.00 | 56.90 | 247.90 |
| **36" wide wood storm window** | | | | | |
| 24" tall | 1C@1.00 | ea | 145.00 | 56.90 | 201.90 |
| 36" tall | 1C@1.00 | ea | 176.00 | 56.90 | 232.90 |
| 48" tall | 1C@1.00 | ea | 206.00 | 56.90 | 262.90 |
| 60" tall | 1C@1.08 | ea | 237.00 | 61.50 | 298.50 |
| **48" wide wood storm window** | | | | | |
| 24" tall | 1C@1.00 | ea | 167.00 | 56.90 | 223.90 |
| 36" tall | 1C@1.00 | ea | 206.00 | 56.90 | 262.90 |
| 48" tall | 1C@1.08 | ea | 247.00 | 61.50 | 308.50 |
| 60" tall | 1C@1.08 | ea | 285.00 | 61.50 | 346.50 |
| **60" wide wood storm window** | | | | | |
| 24" tall | 1C@1.00 | ea | 191.00 | 56.90 | 247.90 |
| 36" tall | 1C@1.08 | ea | 237.00 | 61.50 | 298.50 |
| 48" tall | 1C@1.08 | ea | 285.00 | 61.50 | 346.50 |
| 60" tall | 1C@1.08 | ea | 336.00 | 61.50 | 397.50 |
| **72" wide wood storm window** | | | | | |
| 24" tall | 1C@1.00 | ea | 206.00 | 56.90 | 262.90 |
| 36" tall | 1C@1.08 | ea | 267.00 | 61.50 | 328.50 |
| 48" tall | 1C@1.08 | ea | 327.00 | 61.50 | 388.50 |
| 60" tall | 1C@1.22 | ea | 385.00 | 69.40 | 454.40 |

**Window screen.** Includes prefabricated window screen with aluminum frame and installation. Screens are made to match existing windows and include a tinted or mill-finish frame with fiberglass mesh.

|  | Craft@Hrs | Unit | Material | Labor | Total |
|---|---|---|---|---|---|
| **24" wide window screen** | | | | | |
| 24" tall | 1C@.125 | ea | 14.00 | 7.11 | 21.11 |
| 36" tall | 1C@.125 | ea | 16.90 | 7.11 | 24.01 |
| 48" tall | 1C@.125 | ea | 19.30 | 7.11 | 26.41 |
| 60" tall | 1C@.125 | ea | 23.10 | 7.11 | 30.21 |
| **36" wide window screen** | | | | | |
| 24" tall | 1C@.125 | ea | 16.40 | 7.11 | 23.51 |
| 36" tall | 1C@.125 | ea | 17.70 | 7.11 | 24.81 |
| 48" tall | 1C@.125 | ea | 24.50 | 7.11 | 31.61 |
| 60" tall | 1C@.125 | ea | 26.90 | 7.11 | 34.01 |

**Reglaze window.** Includes removal of damaged glass, replacement of gaskets or glazing compound, and glass piece to fit. Does not include replacement parts in window or door frame.

|  | Craft@Hrs | Unit | Material | Labor | Total |
|---|---|---|---|---|---|
| **Reglaze windows with clear glass** | | | | | |
| 1/8" thick | 1C@.063 | sf | 5.12 | 3.58 | 8.70 |
| 3/16" thick | 1C@.063 | sf | 6.84 | 3.58 | 10.42 |
| 1/4" thick | 1C@.063 | sf | 5.59 | 3.58 | 9.17 |
| 3/8" thick | 1C@.063 | sf | 18.10 | 3.58 | 21.68 |
| **Reglaze window with tempered glass** | | | | | |
| 1/8" thick | 1C@.063 | sf | 8.55 | 3.58 | 12.13 |
| 3/16" thick | 1C@.063 | sf | 10.00 | 3.58 | 13.58 |
| 1/4" thick | 1C@.063 | sf | 10.60 | 3.58 | 14.18 |

| | Craft@Hrs | Unit | Material | Labor | Total |
|---|---|---|---|---|---|
| Reglaze window with laminated glass | | | | | |
|    1/4" thick | 1C@.063 | sf | 12.80 | 3.58 | 16.38 |
|    3/8" thick | 1C@.063 | sf | 17.50 | 3.58 | 21.08 |
| Reglaze window with polished wire glass | | | | | |
|    1/4" thick | 1C@.063 | sf | 33.60 | 3.58 | 37.18 |
| Minimum charge for reglazing | | | | | |
|    all types of glass | 1C@2.50 | ea | 42.60 | 142.00 | 184.60 |
| **Repair antique double-hung window.** | | | | | |
|    rehang sash weight | 1C@2.27 | ea | 21.80 | 129.00 | 150.80 |
|    refurbish | 1C@3.13 | ea | 38.90 | 178.00 | 216.90 |
|    recondition | 1C@2.08 | ea | 19.70 | 118.00 | 137.70 |

## Time & Material Charts (selected items)
## Windows Materials

See Windows material prices with the line items above.

## Windows Labor

| Laborer | base wage | paid leave | true wage | taxes & ins. | total |
|---|---|---|---|---|---|
| Carpenter | $31.10 | 2.43 | $33.53 | 23.37 | $56.90 |
| Demolition laborer | $20.70 | 1.61 | $22.31 | 16.59 | $38.90 |

**Paid leave** is calculated based on two weeks paid vacation, one week sick leave, and seven paid holidays. Employer's matching portion of **FICA** is 7.65 percent. **FUTA** (Federal Unemployment) is .8 percent. **Worker's compensation** for the windows trade was calculated using a national average of 16.85 percent. **Unemployment insurance** was calculated using a national average of 8 percent. **Health insurance** was calculated based on a projected national average for 2015 of $1,025 per employee (and family when applicable) per month. Employer pays 80 percent for a per month cost of $820 per employee. **Retirement** is based on a 401(k) retirement program with employer matching of 50 percent. Employee contributions to the 401(k) plan are an average of 6 percent of the true wage. **Liability insurance** is based on a national average of 10.0 percent.

| | Craft@Hrs | Unit | Material | Labor | Total |
|---|---|---|---|---|---|
| **Windows Labor Productivity** | | | | | |
| Remove window | | | | | |
|    small (4 to 10 sf) | 1D@.397 | ea | — | 15.40 | 15.40 |
|    average size (11 to 16 sf) | 1D@.407 | ea | — | 15.80 | 15.80 |
|    large (17 to 29 sf) | 1D@.424 | ea | — | 16.50 | 16.50 |
|    very large (30 sf and larger) | 1D@.433 | ea | — | 16.80 | 16.80 |
| Remove window for work & reinstall | | | | | |
|    small (4 to 10 sf) | 1C@1.23 | ea | — | 70.00 | 70.00 |
|    average size (11 to 16 sf) | 1C@1.72 | ea | — | 97.90 | 97.90 |
|    large (17 to 28 sf) | 1C@2.51 | ea | — | 143.00 | 143.00 |
|    very large (30 sf and larger) | 1C@3.70 | ea | — | 211.00 | 211.00 |

| | Craft@Hrs | Unit | Material | Labor | Total |
|---|---|---|---|---|---|
| **Install window** | | | | | |
| small (4 to 10 sf) | 1C@.991 | ea | — | 56.40 | 56.40 |
| average size (11 to 16 sf) | 1C@1.39 | ea | — | 79.10 | 79.10 |
| large (17 to 28 sf) | 1C@2.00 | ea | — | 114.00 | 114.00 |
| very large (30 sf and larger) | 1C@2.94 | ea | — | 167.00 | 167.00 |
| **Install skylight or roof window** | | | | | |
| dome ventilating | 1C@2.78 | ea | — | 158.00 | 158.00 |
| fixed | 1C@2.69 | ea | — | 153.00 | 153.00 |
| ventilating | 1C@2.94 | ea | — | 167.00 | 167.00 |
| cord-operated roller shades | 1C@.832 | ea | — | 47.30 | 47.30 |
| electrically controlled system | 1C@2.00 | ea | — | 114.00 | 114.00 |
| electrically controlled opener | 1C@1.39 | ea | — | 79.10 | 79.10 |
| infrared remote control system for opener | 1C@1.11 | ea | — | 63.20 | 63.20 |
| **Install storm window** | | | | | |
| small (4 to 14 sf) | 1C@1.00 | ea | — | 56.90 | 56.90 |
| average size (15 to 25 sf) | 1C@1.08 | ea | — | 61.50 | 61.50 |
| large storm (26 sf and larger) | 1C@1.22 | ea | — | 69.40 | 69.40 |
| **Reglaze window** | | | | | |
| remove and replace glass | 1C@.063 | sf | — | 3.58 | 3.58 |
| **Repair antique double-hung window** | | | | | |
| rehang sash weight | 1C@2.27 | ea | — | 129.00 | 129.00 |
| refurbish | 1C@3.13 | ea | — | 178.00 | 178.00 |
| recondition | 1C@2.08 | ea | — | 118.00 | 118.00 |

# QuickCalculators

*QuickCalculators* are designed to help you quickly calculate quantities and the surface areas of some basic room shapes. Pages 450-463 contain *QuickCalculators* that are designed to calculate quantities, and pages 464-469 contain *QuickCalculators* that are designed to calculate the surface area of rooms.

Instruction for each *QuickCalculator* sheet are contained above the page.

The person who purchased this book or the person for whom this book was purchased may photocopy or otherwise reproduce the *QuickCalculator* pages so long as:

❶ the Craftsman Book Company copyright notice clearly appears on all reproduced copies.

❷ the sheets are reproduced for that person's use only.

❸ the sheets are not reproduced for resale or as part of a package that is produced for resale.

❹ the sheets are not used in any promotional or advertising materials.

# QuickCalculator mathematics

## CIRCLE

### Area

❶ = Pi x radius²
❷ = .7854 x diameter²
❸ = .0796 x perimeter²

### Perimeter

❶ = Pi x diameter

## PARALLELOGRAM

### Area

❶ = base x height

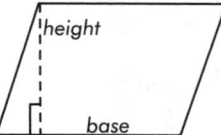

## PRISM

### Area

❶ = sum of sides ÷ 2 x radius

## RECTANGLE

### Area

❶ = length x width

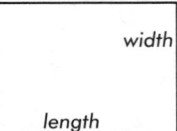

## TRAPEZOID

### Area

❶ = base + top ÷ 2 x height

## TRIANGLE

### Area

❶ = base x height ÷ 2

## PYTHAGOREAN THEOREM

### Rafter length

❶ rafter length² = rise² + run²

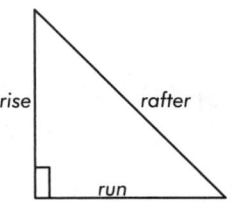

## CONVERSION FACTORS

| DIVIDE | BY | TO CONVERT TO |
|---|---|---|
| square inches | 144 | square feet |
| square inches | 144 | board feet |
| cubic inches | 1,728 | cubic feet |
| cubic inches | 46,656 | cubic yards |
| square feet | 9 | square yards |
| square feet | 100 | squares |
| cubic feet | 27 | cubic yards |
| feet | 16.5 | rods |
| rods | 40 | furlongs |
| feet | 5,280 | miles |
| meters | 1,609 | miles |
| yards | 1,760 | miles |

| MULTIPLY | BY | TO CONVERT TO |
|---|---|---|
| inches | 2.54 | centimeters |
| square inches | 6.4516 | square centimeters |
| square inches | .0069 | square feet |
| square feet | 9.29 | square centimeters |
| square feet | .0929 | square meters |
| square yards | .8361 | square meters |
| square meters | 1.1959 | square yards |
| centimeters | .3937 | inches |
| feet | .3048 | meters |
| meters | 3.281 | feet |
| yards | 91.44 | centimeters |
| yards | .9144 | meters |
| cubic feet | .0283 | cubic meters |
| cubic meters | 35.3145 | cubic feet |
| cubic meters | 1.3079 | cubic yards |
| cubic yards | .7646 | cubic meters |
| cubic inches | 16.3872 | cubic centimeters |
| cubic centimeters | .0610 | cubic inches |
| cubic meters | 1,000 | cubic liters |

# USING THE BEARING WALL
## QuickCalculator

**A** Calculates the lineal feet of studs in a wall *before* adding for openings and corners. The length of the wall (Answer 1) is converted into inches by multiplying it by 12. The number of studs is calculated by dividing the wall length in inches by the stud centers (Answer 8), then adding 1 for the first stud. The calculation should now be rounded *up*, then multiplied by the wall height (Answer 4).

**B** Calculates the lineal feet of studs typically added for openings and corners. The number of openings (Answer 6) is multiplied by 2.4 (the *average* additional studs typically needed for an opening). The number of corners (Answer 7) is multiplied by 2.6 (the *average* additional studs typically needed at corners). The studs for openings and corners are added together, then should be rounded *up*. The total additional studs is then multiplied by the wall height (Answer 4).

**C** Calculates the total lineal feet of lumber in the wall. The length of the wall (Answer 1) is multiplied by the number of plates (Answer 3). The lineal feet of plates is added to the lineal feet of studs (Sum A) and additional studs (Sum B).

QUICK CALCULATOR

# Bearing Wall

Use this sheet and a calculator to determine the board feet in a bearing wall.
Calculate each line from left to right. Do math in parentheses first.

1. The wall(s) are **33.5** lineal feet long.
2. The studs are **2** inches thick.
3. There are **3** plates.
5. The studs are **6** inches wide.
4. The wall(s) are **8** feet tall.
6. There are **5** door and window openings.
8. The studs are **16** inches on center.
7. There are **4** corners.
10. There are **17.5** lineal feet of header.
9. The headers are **10** inches wide.

**A** Lf of studs (before openings)

$$\boxed{33.5}_{\text{ANSWER 1}} \times 12 \div \left( \boxed{16}_{\text{ANSWER 8}} + 1 \right)^* \times \boxed{8}_{\text{ANSWER 4}} = \boxed{216}_{\text{SUM A}}$$

**B** Lf of studs in openings

$$\left( \boxed{5}_{\text{ANSWER 6}} \times 2.4 \right) + \left( \boxed{4}_{\text{ANSWER 7}} \times 2.6 \right)^* \times \boxed{8}_{\text{ANSWER 4}} = \boxed{184}_{\text{SUM B}}$$

**C** Lineal feet of board in wall

$$\boxed{33.5}_{\text{ANSWER 1}} \times \boxed{3}_{\text{ANSWER 3}} + \boxed{216}_{\text{SUM A}} + \boxed{184}_{\text{SUM B}} = \boxed{501}_{\text{SUM C}}$$

**D** Board feet in headers

$$\boxed{17.5}_{\text{ANSWER 10}} \times \boxed{10}_{\text{ANSWER 9}} \times \boxed{6}_{\text{ANSWER 5}} \div 12 = \boxed{88}_{\text{SUM D}}$$

**E** Total board feet

$$\boxed{501}_{\text{SUM C}} \times \boxed{6}_{\text{ANSWER 5}} \times \boxed{2}_{\text{ANSWER 2}} \div 12 + \boxed{88}_{\text{SUM D}} = \boxed{589}_{\text{SUM E}}$$

*Round up answer to next whole number here before continuing with calculation.

Converting Inches to Decimal Feet

1" = .084 • 2" = .167 • 3" = .25 • 4" = .334 • 5" = .417 • 6" = .5 • 7" = .584 • 8" = .667 • 9" = .75 • 10" = .834 • 11" = .917

**D** Calculates the board feet in the headers. The lineal feet of headers (Answer 10) is multiplied by the header width (Answer 9), then multiplied by the wall thickness (Answer 5). This total is divided by 12 to convert to board feet.

**E** Calculates the total board feet in the wall. The lineal feet of board in the wall (Sum C) is multiplied by the wall width (Answer 5) then by the stud thickness (Answer 2). The total is divided by 12 to convert to board feet then added to the board feet in the headers (Sum D).

## QUICK FACTS

☞ See page 449 for more information about the geometric formulas used in this *QuickCalculator*. See page 357 for wall framing priced per board foot.

## QUICK CALCULATOR

# Bearing Wall

*Use this sheet and a calculator to determine the board feet in a bearing wall.*
*Calculate each line from left to right. Do math in parentheses first.*

❶ The wall(s) are _____ lineal feet long.

❷ The studs are _____ inches thick.

❸ There are _____ plates.

❹ The wall(s) are _____ feet tall.

❺ The studs are _____ inches wide.

❻ There are _____ door and window openings.

❼ There are _____ corners.

❽ The studs are _____ inches on center.

❾ The headers are _____ inches wide.

❿ There are _____ lineal feet of header.

Ⓐ Lf of studs (before openings) ········▶ ( [ANSWER 1] × 12 ÷ [ANSWER 8] +1 )* × [ANSWER 4] = [SUM A]

Ⓑ Lf of studs in openings ······▶ (( [ANSWER 6] × 2.4 ) + ( [ANSWER 7] × 2.6 ))* × [ANSWER 4] = [SUM B]

Ⓒ Lineal feet of board in wall ·······▶ [ANSWER 1] × [ANSWER 3] + [SUM A] + [SUM B] = [SUM C]

Ⓓ Board feet in headers ·················▶ [ANSWER 10] × [ANSWER 9] × [ANSWER 5] ÷ 12 = [SUM D]

Ⓔ Total board feet ·········▶ [SUM C] × [ANSWER 5] × [ANSWER 2] ÷ 12 + [SUM D] = [SUM E]

*Round up answer to next whole number here before continuing with calculation.*

**Converting Inches to Decimal Feet** | 1" = .084 • 2" = .167 • 3" = .25 • 4" = .334 • 5" = .417 • 6" = .5 • 7" = .584 • 8" = .667 • 9" = .75 • 10" = .834 • 11" = .917

# USING THE CONCRETE WALL & FOOTING
## QUICKCALCULATOR

**A** Calculates the cubic yards of footing by multiplying Answer 2 by 12 to convert the length of the footing to inches. The length in inches is then multiplied by the thickness (Answer 4) and by the width (Answer 5) to determine the cubic inches in the footing. The cubic inches are converted to cubic feet by dividing by 1,728. The cubic feet are then converted to cubic yards by dividing by 27.

**B** Calculates the cubic yards of foundation wall by multiplying Answer 2 by 12 to convert the length of the wall to inches. The length in inches is then multiplied by the thickness (Answer 1) and by the height (Answer 3) to determine the cubic inches in the wall. The cubic inches are converted to cubic feet by dividing by 1,728. The cubic feet are then converted to cubic yards by dividing by 27.

**C** Calculates the total cubic yards of concrete in the wall & footing by adding the cubic yards of footing (Sum A) to the cubic yards of foundation wall (Sum B).

## QUICK FACTS

☞ The sample *QuickCalculator* sheet shown above (in the printed book) contains quantities that have been rounded. We suggest rounding to two decimal places. We also suggest rounding the final total (Sum C) up to the next 1/4 yards since this is how concrete must usually be ordered. (In the example the Sum C total of 4.45 should be rounded up to 4.5 cubic yards.) See pages 56-59 for concrete walls and footings per cubic yard.

☞ See page 449 for more information about the geometric formulas used in this *QuickCalculator*.

# Concrete Wall & Footing

*Use this sheet and a calculator to determine the cubic yards of concrete in a foundation wall and footing.*
*Calculate each line from left to right.*

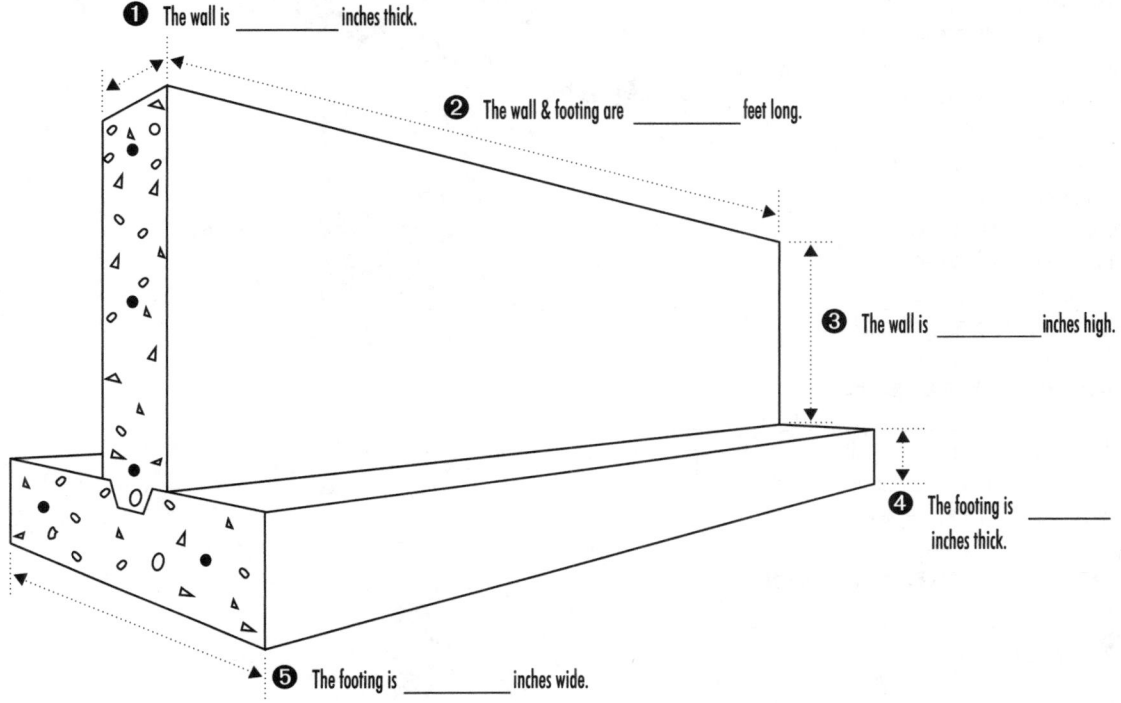

❶ The wall is _____ inches thick.

❷ The wall & footing are _____ feet long.

❸ The wall is _____ inches high.

❹ The footing is _____ inches thick.

❺ The footing is _____ inches wide.

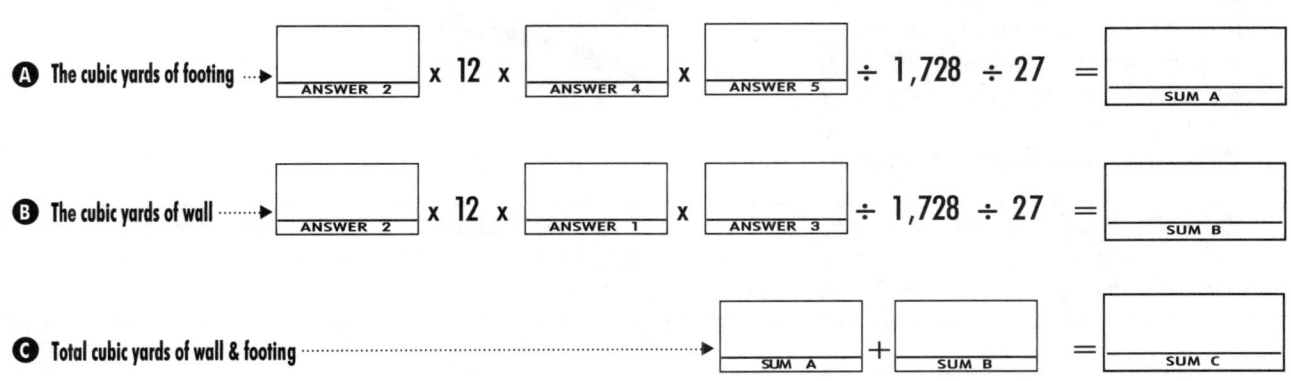

**A** The cubic yards of footing ···➤ [ ANSWER 2 ] x 12 x [ ANSWER 4 ] x [ ANSWER 5 ] ÷ 1,728 ÷ 27 = [ SUM A ]

**B** The cubic yards of wall ······➤ [ ANSWER 2 ] x 12 x [ ANSWER 1 ] x [ ANSWER 3 ] ÷ 1,728 ÷ 27 = [ SUM B ]

**C** Total cubic yards of wall & footing ·············➤ [ SUM A ] + [ SUM B ] = [ SUM C ]

**Converting Inches to Decimal Feet**   **1"** = .084 • **2"** = .167 • **3"** = .25 • **4"** = .334 • **5"** = .417 • **6"** = .5 • **7"** = .584 • **8"** = .667 • **9"** = .75 • **10"** = .834 • **11"** = .917

# USING GABLE ROOF RAFTERS
## QuickCalculator

**Ⓐ** Calculates the total number of rafters in the roof. The length of the roof (Answer 1) is converted into inches by multiplying it by 12. The number of rafters in the roof is calculated by taking the length in inches and dividing by the rafter centers (Answer 4) then adding 1 for the first rafter. Because you can never have a fraction of a rafter, the final answer should always be rounded *up* to the next *even* number. This calculates the total for one side of the roof only so the total is multiplied by 2.

**Ⓑ** Calculates the lineal feet of rafters in the roof by multiplying the number of rafters (Sum A) by the rafter length (Answer 2).

**Ⓒ** Calculates the board feet in the ridge and sub-fascia. The roof length (Answer 1) is multiplied by 3 (2 sub-fascia boards and 1 ridge) to get the total lineal feet of sub-fascia and ridge. This total is multiplied by the rafter thickness (Answer 5), then by the rafter width (Answer 3) plus 2" (e.g. a roof with 2" x 8" rafters will have 10" wide ridge and sub-fascia boards). This total is divided by 12 to get the total board feet in the ridge and sub-fascia boards.

**Ⓓ** Calculates the total board feet in the roof system. The total lineal feet of rafters (Sum B) is *multiplied* by the rafter thickness (Answer 5) then by the rafter width (Answer 3). This total is *divided* by 12 to get the total board feet in the rafters. The total board feet of rafters is then added to the total board feet in the ridge and sub-fascia boards (Sum C) for the total board feet in the entire roof system.

## QUICK FACTS

☞ The sample *QuickCalculator* sheet shown above contains quantities that have been rounded. The total number of rafters should always be rounded up to the next even number. We also suggest rounding lineal feet and board feet to the nearest whole number.

☞ See page 449 for more information about the geometric formulas used in this *QuickCalculator*. See page 372 for rafter systems priced per board foot.

**QUICK CALCULATOR**

# Gable Roof Rafters

*Use this sheet and a calculator to determine the board feet of rafters in a gable roof.*
*Calculate each line from left to right. Do math in parentheses first.*

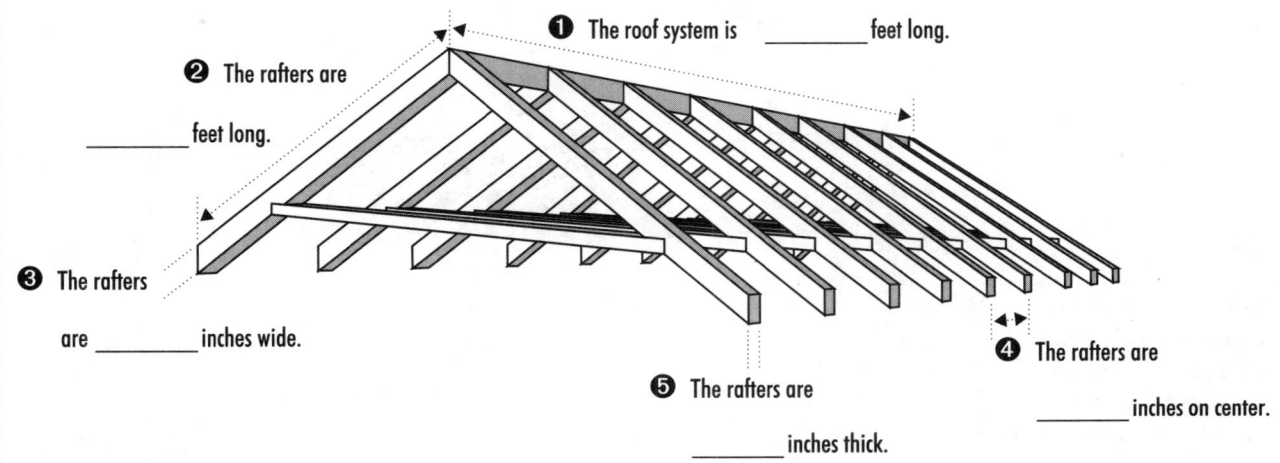

❶ The roof system is _____ feet long.

❷ The rafters are _____ feet long.

❸ The rafters are _____ inches wide.

❹ The rafters are _____ inches on center.

❺ The rafters are _____ inches thick.

Round up to next <u>even</u> number

**Ⓐ** The number of rafters ·········➤ ( [____ANSWER 1____] × 12 ÷ [____ANSWER 4____] + 1 ) × 2 = [____SUM A____]

**Ⓑ** Lineal feet of rafters ·········➤ [____SUM A____] × [____ANSWER 2____] = [____SUM B____]

**Ⓒ** Bf in ridge & sub-fascia* ··➤ [____ANSWER 1____] × 3 × [____ANSWER 5____] × ( [____ANSWER 3____] + 2 ) ÷ 12 = [____SUM C____]

**Ⓓ** Total board feet in roof** ·➤ [____SUM B____] × [____ANSWER 5____] × [____ANSWER 3____] ÷ 12 + [____SUM C____] = [____SUM D____]

*\*The ridge and sub-fascia boards are calculated to be 2 inches wider than the rafters.* *\*\*Does not include ceiling joists for the room below (as illustrated) or collar ties.*

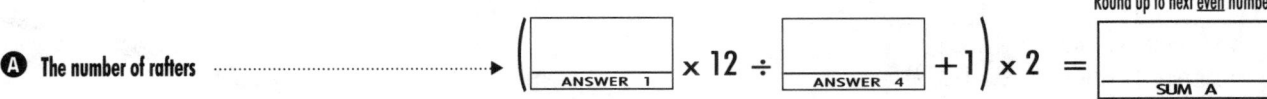

**Converting Inches to Decimal Feet** | **1**″ = .084 • **2**″ = .167 • **3**″ = .25 • **4**″ = .334 • **5**″ = .417 • **6**″ = .5 • **7**″ = .584 • **8**″ = .667 • **9**″ = .75 • **10**″ = .834 • **11**″ = .917

# USING THE GABLE ROOF TRUSSES
## QuickCalculator

**QUICK CALCULATOR**

# Gable Roof Trusses

Use this sheet and a calculator to determine the number and lineal feet of trusses in a gable roof.
Calculate each line from left to right.

❶ The roof system is  32.5  feet long.

❸ The trusses are
24  inches on center.

❷ The trust bottom chord is  20  feet wide.

**Ⓐ** Calculates the number of trusses in the roof by converting the length of the roof (Answer 1) into inches by multiplying it by 12. The number of trusses is then calculated by taking this length in inches, dividing it by the truss centers (Answer 3), then adding 1 for the first truss.

Round up to next whole number

| 32.5 | × 12 ÷ | 24 | + 1 = | 18 |
| ANSWER 1 | | ANSWER 3 | | SUM A |

Ⓐ Number of trusses

| 18 | × | 20 | = | 360 |
| SUM A | | ANSWER 2 | | SUM B |

**Ⓑ** Calculates the lineal feet of trusses by multiplying the number of trusses (Sum A) by the length of the truss bottom chord (Answer 2).

Ⓑ Lineal feet of trusses

1" = .084 • 2" = .167 • 3" = .25 • 4" = .334 • 5" = .417 • 6" = .5 • 7" = .584 • 8" = .667 • 9" = .75 • 10" = .834 • 11" = .917

Converting Inches to Decimal Feet

## QUICK FACTS

☞ The sample *QuickCalculator* sheet shown above contains quantities that have been rounded. The total number of trusses should always be rounded up to the next whole number. We also suggest rounding lineal feet lineal feet to the nearest whole number.

☞ See page 449 for more information about the geometric formulas used in this *QuickCalculator*. See page 374 for truss systems priced per lineal foot.

# Gable Roof Trusses

*Use this sheet and a calculator to determine the number and lineal feet of trusses in a gable roof.*
*Calculate each line from left to right.*

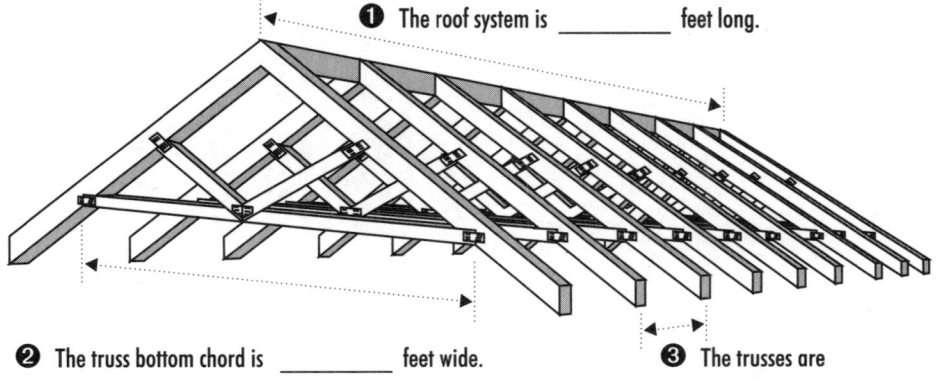

**❶** The roof system is _____ feet long.

**❷** The truss bottom chord is _____ feet wide.

**❸** The trusses are

_____ inches on center.

Round up to next whole number

**Ⓐ** Number of trusses ⟶ | ANSWER 1 | x 12 ÷ | ANSWER 3 | + 1 = | SUM A |

**Ⓑ** Lineal feet of trusses ⟶ | SUM A | x | ANSWER 2 | = | SUM B |

| Converting Inches to Decimal Feet | **1″** = .084 • **2″** = .167 • **3″** = .25 • **4″** = .334 • **5″** = .417 • **6″** = .5 • **7″** = .584 • **8″** = .667 • **9″** = .75 • **10″** = .834 • **11″** = .917 |

# USING THE GABLE ROOFING
## QuickCalculator

**A** Calculates the square feet of sheathing on the roof by multiplying the roof length (Answer 1) by the rafter length (Answer 2), then multiplying this total by 2 to calculate both sides of the roof.

**B** Calculates the squares of roofing by dividing the square feet of roof (Sum A) by 100.

---

## QUICK FACTS

☞ The sample *QuickCalculator* sheet shown above contains quantities that have been rounded. We suggest rounding sheathing to the nearest square foot and rounding squares *up* to the next 1/5 square for shakes, the next 1/4 square for wood shingles and clay tile, and the next 1/3 square for asphalt shingles.

☞ See page 449 for more information about the geometric formulas used in this *QuickCalculator*. Also see Roofing beginning on page 339.

## QUICK CALCULATOR

# Gable Roofing

*Use this sheet and a calculator to determine the square feet of sheathing and squares of roofing on a gable roof. Calculate each line from left to right.*

**❶** The roof is _____ feet long.

**❷** The rafters are

_____ feet long.

**Ⓐ** Square feet of sheathing ⋯⋯⋯⋯⋯⋯⋯⋯⋯⋯⋯⋯⋯⋯⋯⋯→ [ANSWER 1] ✕ [ANSWER 2] ✕ 2 = [SUM A]

**Ⓑ** Squares of roofing ⋯⋯⋯⋯⋯⋯⋯⋯⋯⋯⋯⋯⋯⋯⋯⋯⋯⋯⋯⋯→ [SUM A] ÷ 100 = [SUM B]

**Converting Inches to Decimal Feet** | $1'' = .084$ • $2'' = .167$ • $3'' = .25$ • $4'' = .334$ • $5'' = .417$ • $6'' = .5$ • $7'' = .584$ • $8'' = .667$ • $9'' = .75$ • $10'' = .834$ • $11'' = .917$

# USING THE JOIST SYSTEM
## QuickCalculator

**A** Calculates the total number of joists. The length of the joist system (Answer 1) is converted into inches by multiplying it by 12. The number of joists is calculated by taking the joist system length in inches and dividing it by the joist centers (Answer 4) then adding 1 for the first joist.

**B** Calculates the lineal feet of joists by multiplying the number of joists (Sum A) by the joist length (Answer 2).

**C** Calculates the lineal feet in rim joists and in solid blocking. The length of the rim joist (Answer 1) is multiplied by 2 for rim joists on both sides of the joist system. The total lineal feet of rim joists are then added to the lineal feet of solid blocking (Answer 6).

**QUICK CALCULATOR**

# Joist System

Use this sheet and a calculator to determine the lineal feet and board feet in a joist system.
Calculate each line from left to right.

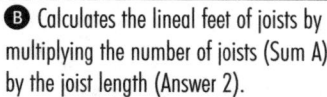

① The joist system is __25__ feet long. ② The joists are __15__ feet long. ③ The joists are __10__ inches wide.

④ The joists are __24__ inches on center.

⑤ The joists are __2__ inches thick.

⑥ There are __25__ lineal feet of solid blocking in the joist system.

Round up to next whole number

| $\boxed{25}_{\text{ANSWER 1}}$ × 12 ÷ $\boxed{24}_{\text{ANSWER 4}}$ + 1 | $\boxed{14}_{\text{SUM A}}$ |

**Ⓐ The number of joists** → $\boxed{15}_{\text{ANSWER 2}}$ × $\boxed{14}_{\text{SUM A}}$ = $\boxed{210}_{\text{SUM B}}$

**Ⓑ The lineal feet of joists** → $\boxed{25}_{\text{ANSWER 1}}$ × 2 + $\boxed{25}_{\text{ANSWER 6}}$ = $\boxed{75}_{\text{SUM C}}$

**Ⓒ The lineal feet of rim joists and blocking** → $\boxed{210}_{\text{SUM B}}$ + $\boxed{75}_{\text{SUM C}}$ = $\boxed{285}_{\text{SUM D}}$

**Ⓓ The total lineal feet of all joists and blocking** → $\boxed{285}_{\text{SUM D}}$ × $\boxed{2}_{\text{ANSWER 5}}$ × $\boxed{10}_{\text{ANSWER 3}}$ ÷ 12 = $\boxed{475}_{\text{SUM E}}$

**Ⓔ The total board feet in the joist system**

1" = .084 • 2" = .167 • 3" = .25 • 4" = .334 • 5" = .417 • 6" = .5 • 7" = .584 • 8" = .667 • 9" = .75 • 10" = .834 • 11" = .917

Converting Inches to Decimal Feet

**D** Calculates total lineal feet of lumber in the joist system by adding the lineal feet of joists (Sum B) to the lineal feet of rim joists and solid blocking (Sum C).

**E** Calculates the board feet in the joist system by multiplying the total lineal feet of joists (Sum D) by the joist thickness (Answer 5), then by the joist width (Answer 3). This total is then divided by 12.

---

### QUICK FACTS

☞ The sample *QuickCalculator* sheet shown above contains quantities that have been rounded. The total number of joists should always be rounded up to the next whole number. We also suggest rounding lineal feet and board feet to the nearest whole number.

☞ page 449 for more information about the geometric formulas used in this *QuickCalculator*. See page 369 for joist systems priced per board foot.

# Joist System

*Use this sheet and a calculator to determine the lineal feet and board feet in a joist system.*
*Calculate each line from left to right.*

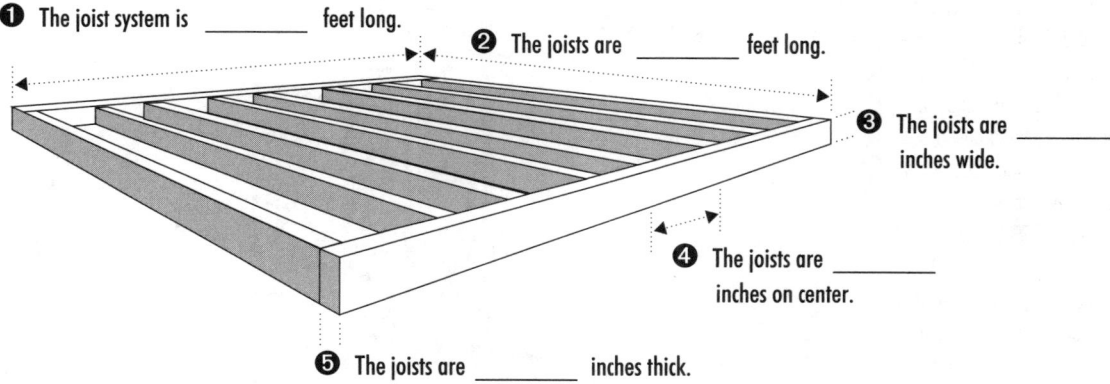

❶ The joist system is _____ feet long.

❷ The joists are _____ feet long.

❸ The joists are _____ inches wide.

❹ The joists are _____ inches on center.

❺ The joists are _____ inches thick.

❻ There are _____ lineal feet of solid blocking in the joist system.

Round up to next whole number

**Ⓐ** The number of joists ·········►  [ ANSWER 1 ]  × 12 ÷  [ ANSWER 4 ]  + 1 =  [ SUM A ]

**Ⓑ** The lineal feet of joists ·········►  [ ANSWER 2 ]  ×  [ SUM A ]  =  [ SUM B ]

**Ⓒ** The lineal feet of rim joists and blocking ·········►  [ ANSWER 1 ]  × 2 +  [ ANSWER 6 ]  =  [ SUM C ]

**Ⓓ** The total lineal feet of all joists and blocking ·········►  [ SUM B ]  +  [ SUM C ]  =  [ SUM D ]

**Ⓔ** The total board feet in the joist system ·········►  [ SUM D ]  ×  [ ANSWER 5 ]  ×  [ ANSWER 3 ]  ÷ 12 =  [ SUM E ]

| Converting Inches to Decimal Feet | 1″ = .084 • 2″ = .167 • 3″ = .25 • 4″ = .334 • 5″ = .417 • 6″ = .5 • 7″ = .584 • 8″ = .667 • 9″ = .75 • 10″ = .834 • 11″ = .917 |

# USING THE NON-BEARING WALL
## QuickCalculator

**Ⓐ** Calculates the lineal feet of studs in a wall *before* adding for openings and corners. The length of the wall (Answer 1) is converted into inches by multiplying it by 12. The number of studs is calculated by dividing the wall length in inches by the stud centers (Answer 8), then adding 1 for the first stud. The calculation should now be rounded *up*, then multiplied by the wall height (Answer 4).

**Ⓑ** Calculates the lineal feet of studs typically added for openings and corners. The number of openings (Answer 6) is multiplied by 2.4 (the *average* additional studs typically needed for an opening). The number of corners (Answer 7) is multiplied by 2.6 (the *average* additional studs typically needed at corners). The studs for openings and corners are added together, then should be rounded *up*. The total additional studs is then multiplied by the wall height (Answer 4).

**Ⓒ** Calculates the total lineal feet of lumber in the wall. The length of the wall (Answer 1) is multiplied by the number of plates (Answer 3). The lineal feet of plates is added to the lineal feet of studs (Sum A) and additional studs (Sum B).

**Ⓓ** Calculates the total board feet in the wall. The lineal feet of board in the wall (Sum C) is multiplied by the wall width (Answer 5) then by the stud thickness (Answer 2). The total is divided by 12 to convert to board feet.

## QUICK FACTS

☞ The sample *QuickCalculator* sheet shown above contains quantities that have been rounded. When calculating Sum A and Sum B we suggest rounding the calculation up to the next whole number at the asterisk. Board feet and lineal feet should be rounded.

☞ See page 449 for more information about the geometric formulas used in this *QuickCalculator*. See page 357 for walls priced per board foot.

## QUICK CALCULATOR

# Non-Bearing Wall

*Use this sheet and a calculator to determine the board feet in an interior wall.*
*Calculate each line from left to right.  Do math in parentheses first.*

❶ The wall(s) are _____ lineal feet long

❷ The studs are _____ inches thick.

❸ There are _____ plates.

❹ The wall(s) are _____ feet tall.

❺ The studs are _____ inches wide.

❻ There are _____ door and window openings.

❼ There are _____ corners.

❽ The studs are _____ inches on center.

**Ⓐ** Lf of studs (before openings) ⟶ ( [ ANSWER 1 ] × 12 ÷ [ ANSWER 8 ] + 1 )* × [ ANSWER 4 ] = [ SUM A ]

**Ⓑ** Lf of studs in openings ⟶ (( [ ANSWER 6 ] × 2.4 ) + ( [ ANSWER 7 ] × 2.6 ))* × [ ANSWER 4 ] = [ SUM B ]

**Ⓒ** Lineal feet of board in wall ⟶ [ ANSWER 1 ] × [ ANSWER 3 ] + [ SUM A ] + [ SUM B ] = [ SUM C ]

**Ⓓ** Total board feet in wall ⟶ [ SUM C ] × [ ANSWER 5 ] × [ ANSWER 2 ] ÷ 12 = [ SUM D ]

*Round up answer to next whole number here before continuing with calculation.*

| Converting Inches to Decimal Feet | 1" = .084 • 2" = .167 • 3" = .25 • 4" = .334 • 5" = .417 • 6" = .5 • 7" = .584 • 8" = .667 • 9" = .75 • 10" = .834 • 11" = .917 |

# USING THE PRISMATIC ROOM
## QuickCalculator

**Ⓐ** Calculates the perimeter of the prism by multiplying the number of prism walls (Answer 4) by the length of the prism walls (Answer 3).

**Ⓑ** Calculates the square feet of walls by multiplying the perimeter of the room (Sum A) by the room height (Answer 2).

**Ⓒ** Calculates the square feet of ceiling / floor by taking the longest dimension between walls (Answer 1) and dividing by 2 to determine the radius. The radius is multiplied by the length of each prism wall (Answer 3), divided by 2 and multiplied by the height of the walls (Answer 2).

**Ⓓ** Calculates the square yards of flooring by dividing the square feet of floor (Sum C) by 9.

## QUICK FACTS

☞ The sample *QuickCalculator* sheet shown above contains quantities that have been rounded. We suggest rounding lineal feet to two decimal places then to the nearest inch when converting to inches. Square feet should probably be rounded to the nearest square foot and square yards should be rounded up to the nearest 1/3 or 1/4 yard.

☞ See page 449 for more information about the geometric formulas used in this *QuickCalculator*.

**QUICK CALCULATOR**

# Prismatic Room

*Use this sheet and a calculator to determine the area of a prismatic room where all walls are of equal length.*
*Use for pentagonal rooms, heptagonal rooms, octagonal rooms, and so forth.*
*Calculate each line from left to right.*

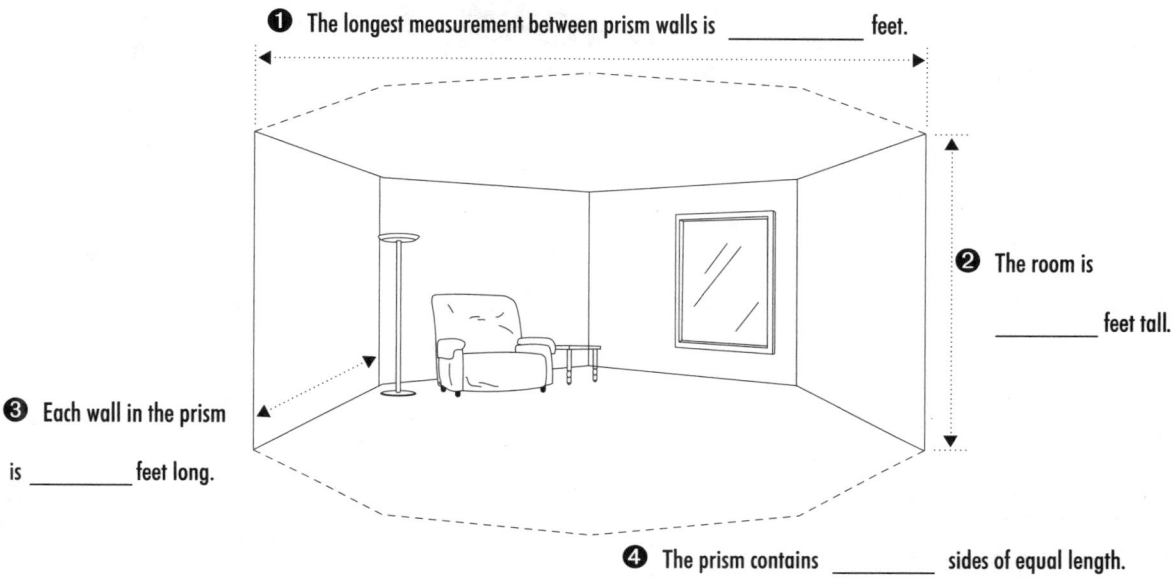

❶ The longest measurement between prism walls is _____ feet.

❷ The room is

_____ feet tall.

❸ Each wall in the prism

is _____ feet long.

❹ The prism contains _____ sides of equal length.

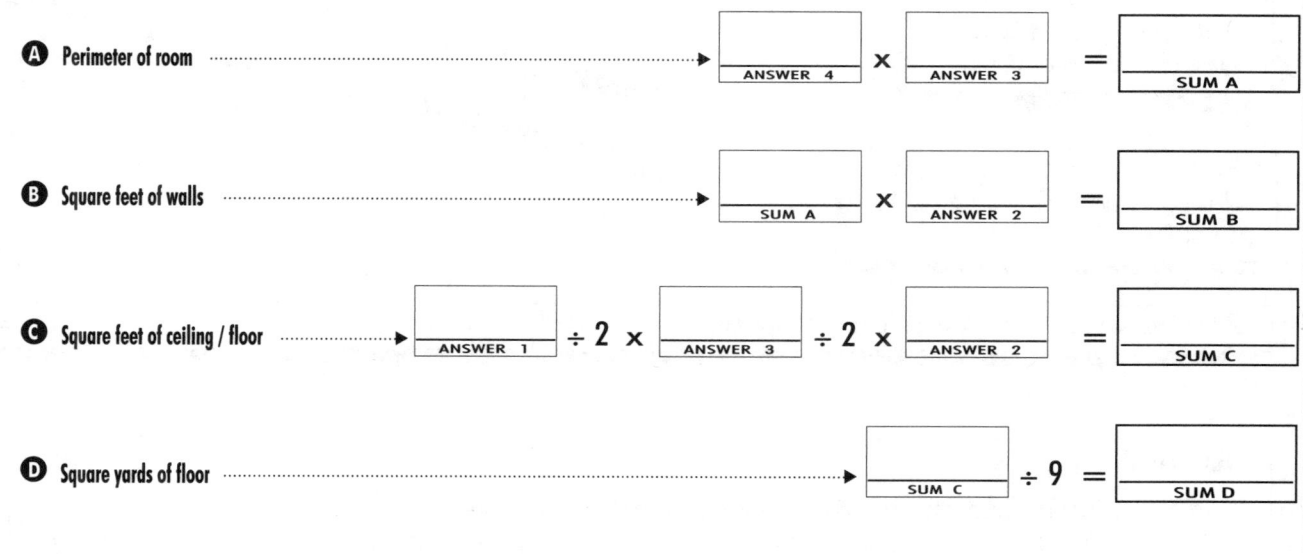

Ⓐ **Perimeter of room** ················································▶ | ANSWER 4 | ✕ | ANSWER 3 | = | SUM A |

Ⓑ **Square feet of walls** ··········································▶ | SUM A | ✕ | ANSWER 2 | = | SUM B |

Ⓒ **Square feet of ceiling / floor** ················▶ | ANSWER 1 | ÷ 2 ✕ | ANSWER 3 | ÷ 2 ✕ | ANSWER 2 | = | SUM C |

Ⓓ **Square yards of floor** ········································▶ | SUM C | ÷ 9 = | SUM D |

**Converting Inches to Decimal Feet** | **1″** = .084 • **2″** = .167 • **3″** = .25 • **4″** = .334 • **5″** = .417 • **6″** = .5 • **7″** = .584 • **8″** = .667 • **9″** = .75 • **10″** = .834 • **11″** = .917

# USING THE RECTANGULAR ROOM
## QuickCalculator

**A** Calculates the perimeter of the room by adding the length (Answer 1) to the width (Answer 3) and multiplying by 2.

**B** Calculates the square feet of walls by multiplying the perimeter of the room (Sum A) by the room height (Answer 2).

**C** Calculates the square feet of ceiling / floor by multiplying the length of the room (Answer 1) by the width (Answer 3).

**D** Calculates the square yards of flooring by dividing the square feet of floor (Sum C) by 9.

---

### QUICK FACTS

☞ The sample *QuickCalculator* sheet shown above contains quantities that have been rounded. We suggest rounding lineal feet to two decimal places then to the nearest inch when converting to inches. Square feet should probably be rounded to the nearest square foot and square yards should be rounded to the nearest 1/3 or 1/4 yard.

☞ See page 449 for more information about the geometric formulas used in this *QuickCalculator*.

## QUICK CALCULATOR

# Rectangular Room

*Use this sheet and a calculator to determine the area of a rectangular room.*
*Calculate each line from left to right. Do math in parentheses first.*

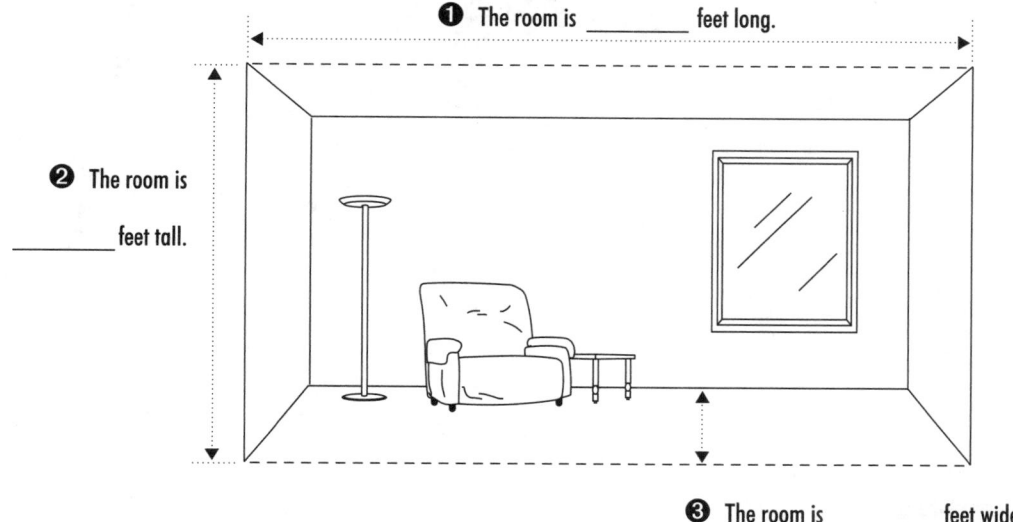

**❶** The room is _____ feet long.

**❷** The room is _____ feet tall.

**❸** The room is _____ feet wide.

**Ⓐ** Perimeter of room ············································▶ ( [ANSWER 1] + [ANSWER 3] ) × 2 = [SUM A]

**Ⓑ** Square feet of walls ············································▶ [SUM A] × [ANSWER 2] = [SUM B]

**Ⓒ** Square feet of ceiling / floor ·····················▶ [ANSWER 1] × [ANSWER 3] = [SUM C]

**Ⓓ** Square yards of floor ·····································▶ [SUM C] ÷ 9 = [SUM D]

| Converting Inches to Decimal Feet | 1″ = .084 • 2″ = .167 • 3″ = .25 • 4″ = .334 • 5″ = .417 • 6″ = .5 • 7″ = .584 • 8″ = .667 • 9″ = .75 • 10″ = .834 • 11″ = .917 |
|---|---|

# USING THE ROUND ROOM
## QuickCalculator

**A** Calculates the perimeter of the circle by multiplying the diameter (Answer 1) by Pi (3.1416).

**B** Calculates the square feet of walls by multiplying the perimeter of the room (Sum A) by the room height (Answer 2).

**C** Calculates the square feet of ceiling / floor by squaring the diameter (Answer 1 times Answer 1) and multiplying by .7854.

**D** Calculates the square yards of flooring by dividing the square feet of floor (Sum C) by 9.

---

### QUICK FACTS

☞ The sample *QuickCalculator* sheet shown above contains quantities that have been rounded. We suggest rounding lineal feet to two decimal places then to the nearest inch when converting to inches. Square feet should probably be rounded to the nearest square foot and square yards should be rounded to the nearest 1/3 or 1/4 yard.

☞ See page 449 for more information about the geometric formulas used in this *QuickCalculator*.

## QUICK CALCULATOR

# Round Room

*Use this sheet and a calculator to determine the area of a round room.*
*Calculate each line from left to right.*

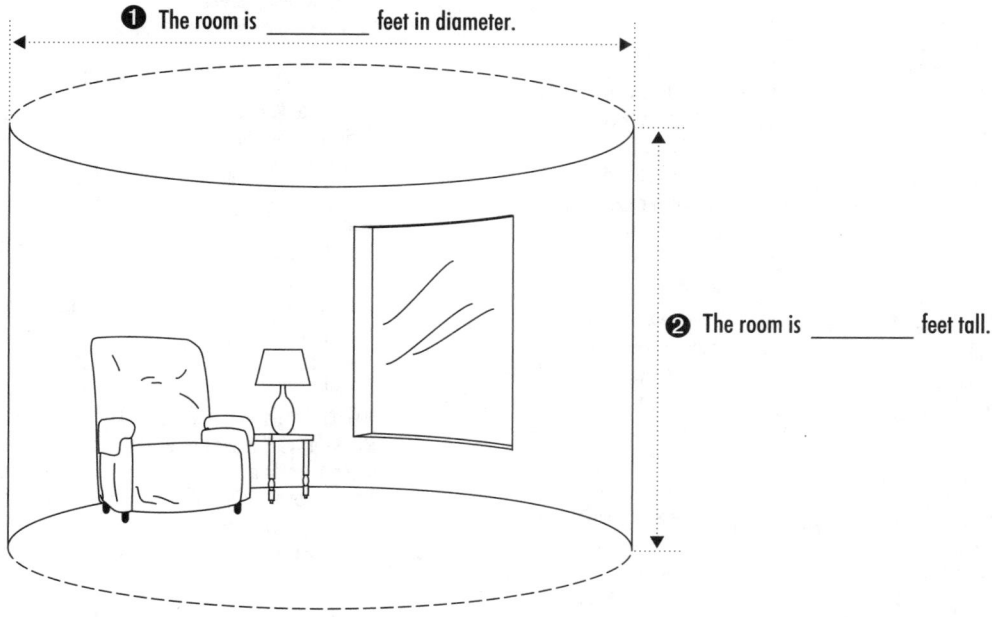

❶ The room is _____ feet in diameter.

❷ The room is _____ feet tall.

**A** Perimeter of room ·······················································▶ | ANSWER 1 | × 3.1416 = | SUM A |

**B** Square feet of walls ·······················································▶ | SUM A | × | ANSWER 2 | | SUM B |

**C** Square feet of ceiling / floor ·······································▶ | ANSWER 1 | × | ANSWER 1 | × .7854 = | SUM C |

**D** Square yards of floor ···················································▶ | SUM C | ÷ 9 = | SUM D |

| Converting Inches to Decimal Feet | **1″** = .084 • **2″** = .167 • **3″** = .25 • **4″** = .334 • **5″** = .417 • **6″** = .5 • **7″** = .584 • **8″** = .667 • **9″** = .75 • **10″** = .834 • **11″** = .917 |

# *Index*

# Practical References for Builders

## Construction Forms for Contractors

This practical guide contains 78 practical forms, letters and checklists, guaranteed to help you streamline your office, organize your jobsites, gather and organize records and documents, keep a handle on your subs, reduce estimating errors, administer change orders and lien issues, monitor crew productivity, track your equipment use, and more. Includes accounting forms, change order forms, forms for customers, estimating forms, field work forms, HR forms, lien forms, office forms, bids and proposals, subcontracts, and more. All are also on the CD-ROM included, in *Excel* spreadsheets, as formatted Rich Text that you can fill out on your computer, and as PDFs. **360 pages, 8½ x 11, $48.50**

*eBook (PDF) also available; $24.25 at* www.craftsman-book.com

## CD Estimator

CD Estimator puts at your fingertips over 150,000 construction costs for new construction, remodeling, renovation & insurance repair, home improvement, framing & finish carpentry, electrical, concrete & masonry, painting, earthwork & heavy equipment and plumbing & HVAC. Quarterly cost updates are available at no charge on the Internet. You'll also have the *National Estimator* program — a stand-alone estimating program for *Windows™* that *Remodeling* magazine called a "computer wiz," and *Job Cost Wizard*, a program that lets you export your estimates to QuickBooks Pro for actual job costing. A 60-minute interactive video teaches you how to use this CD-ROM to estimate construction costs. And to top it off, to help you create professional-looking estimates, the disk includes over 40 construction estimating and bidding forms in a format that's perfect for nearly any *Windows™* word processing or spreadsheet program.
**CD Estimator is $133.50**

## Construction Contract Writer

Relying on a "one-size-fits-all" boilerplate construction contract to fit your jobs can be dangerous — almost as dangerous as a handshake agreement. *Construction Contract Writer* lets you draft a contract in minutes that precisely fits your needs and the particular job, and meets both state and federal requirements. You just answer a series of questions — like an interview — to construct a legal contract for each project you take on.  Anticipate where disputes could arise and settle them in the contract before they happen. Include the warranty protection you intend, the payment schedule, and create subcontracts from the prime contract by just clicking a box. Includes a feedback button to an attorney on the Craftsman staff to help should you get stumped — *No extra charge.* **$149.95.**
Download the *Construction Contract Writer* at:
http://www.constructioncontractwriter.com

## National Home Improvement Estimator

Current labor and material prices for home improvement projects. Provides manhours for each job, recommended crew size, and the labor cost for removal and installation work. Material prices are current, with location adjustment factors and free monthly updates on the Web. Gives step-by-step instructions for the work, with helpful diagrams, and home improvement shortcuts and tips from experts. Includes a free download of an electronic version of the book, and *National Estimator*, a stand-alone *Windows™* estimating program. An interactive multimedia tutorial that shows how to use the software to compile home improvement cost estimates is free at www.costbook.com. **568 pages, 8½ x 11, $88.75. Revised annually**

*eBook (PDF) also available; $44.38 at* www.craftsman-book.com

## Paper Contracting: The How-To of Construction Management Contracting

Risk, and the headaches that go with it, have always been a major part of any construction project — risk of loss, negative cash flow, construction claims, regulations, excessive changes, disputes, slow pay — sometimes you'll make money, and often you won't. But many contractors today are avoiding almost all of that risk by working under a construction management contract, where they are simply a paid consultant to the owner, running the job, but leaving him the risk. This manual is the how-to of construction management contracting. You'll learn how the process works, how to get started as a CM contractor, what the job entails, how to deal with the issues that come up, when to step back, and how to get the job completed on time and on budget. Includes a link to free downloads of CM contracts legal in each state. **272 pages, 8½ x 11, $55.50**

*eBook (PDF) also available; $27.75 at* www.craftsman-book.com

## National Repair & Remodeling Estimator

The complete pricing guide for dwelling reconstruction costs. Reliable, specific data you can apply on every repair and remodeling job. Up-to-date material costs and labor figures based on thousands of jobs across the country. Provides recommended crew sizes; average production rates; exact material, equipment, and labor costs; a total unit cost and a total price including overhead and profit. Separate listings for high- and low-volume builders, so prices shown are specific for any size business. Estimating tips specific to repair and remodeling work to make your bids complete, realistic, and profitable. Includes a free download of an electronic version of the book with *National Estimator*, a stand-alone An interactive multimedia video that shows how to use the software to compile repair and remodeling cost estimates is free at www.costbook.com.
**512 pages, 8½ x 11, $88.50. Revised annually**

*eBook (PDF) also available; $44.25 at* www.craftsman-book.com

## National Building Cost Manual

Square-foot costs for residential, commercial, industrial, military, schools, greenhouses, churches and farm buildings. Includes important variables that can make any building unique from a cost standpoint. Quickly work up a reliable budget estimate based on actual materials and design features, area, shape, wall height, number of floors, and support requirements. Now includes free download of Craftsman's easy-to-use software that calculates total in-place cost estimates or appraisals. Use the regional cost adjustment factors provided to tailor the estimate to any jobsite in the U.S. Then view, print, email or save the detailed PDF report as needed.
**280 pages, 8½ x 11, $78.00. Revised annually**

*eBook (PDF) also available; $39.00 at* www.craftsman-book.com

## National Painting Cost Estimator

A complete guide to estimating painting costs for just about any type of residential, commercial, or industrial painting, whether by brush, spray, or roller. Shows typical costs and bid prices for fast, medium, and slow work, including material costs per gallon, square feet covered per gallon, square feet covered per manhour, labor, material, overhead, and taxes per 100 square feet, and how much to add for profit. Includes a free download of an electronic version of the book, with *National Estimator*, a stand-alone *Windows™* estimating program. An interactive multimedia video that shows how to use the software to compile painting cost estimates is free at www.costbook.com.
**448 pages, 8½ x 11, $88.00. Revised annually**

*eBook (PDF) also available; $44.00 at* www.craftsman-book.com

## Insurance Restoration Contracting: Startup to Success

Insurance restoration — the repair of buildings damaged by water, fire, smoke, storms, vandalism and other disasters — is an exciting field of construction that provides lucrative work that's immune to economic downturns. And, with insurance companies funding the repairs, your payment is virtually guaranteed. But this type of work requires special knowledge and equipment, and that's what you'll learn about in this book. It covers fire repairs and smoke damage, water losses and specialized drying methods, mold remediation, content restoration, even damage to mobile and manufactured homes. You'll also find information on equipment needs, training classes, estimating books and software, and how restoration leads to lucrative remodeling jobs. It covers all you need to know to start and succeed as the restoration contractor that both homeowners and insurance companies call on first for the best jobs.
**640 pages, 8½ x 11, $69.00**

*eBook (PDF) also available; $34.50 at* www.craftsman-book.com

## National Electrical Estimator

This year's prices for installation of all common electrical work: conduit, wire, boxes, fixtures, switches, outlets, loadcenters, panelboards, raceway, duct, signal systems, and more. Provides material costs, manhours per unit, and total installed cost. Explains what you should know to estimate each part of an electrical system. Includes a free download of an electronic version of the book with *National Estimator*, a stand-alone *Windows™* estimating program. An interactive multimedia video that shows how to use the software to compile electrical cost estimates is free at www.costbook.com. **552 pages, 8½ x 11, $87.75. Revised annually**

*eBook (PDF) also available; $43.88 at* www.craftsman-book.com

## Estimating Home Building Costs, Revised ~~DISCARD~~

Estimate every phase of residential construction from site costs to the profit margin you include in your bid. Shows how to keep track of manhours and make accurate labor cost estimates for site clearing and excavation, footings, foundations, framing and sheathing finishes, electrical, plumbing, and more. Provides and explains sample cost estimate worksheets with complete instructions for each job phase. This practical guide to estimating home construction costs has been updated with digital *Excel* estimating forms and worksheets that ensure accurate and complete estimates for your residential projects. Enter your project information on the worksheets and *Excel* automatically totals each material and labor cost from every stage of construction to a final cost estimate worksheet. Load the enclosed CD-ROM into your computer and create your own estimate as you follow along with the step-by-step techniques in this book. **336 pages, 8½ x 11, $38.00**

*eBook (PDF) also available; $19.00 at www.craftsman-book.com*

## Home Building Mistakes & Fixes

This is an encyclopedia of practical fixes for real-world home building and repair problems. There's never an end to "surprises" when you're in the business of building and fixing homes, yet there's little published on how to deal with construction that went wrong - where out-of-square or non-standard or jerry-rigged turns what should be a simple job into a nightmare. This manual describes jaw-dropping building mistakes that actually occurred, from disastrous misunderstandings over property lines, through basement floors leveled with an out-of-level instrument, to a house collapse when a siding crew removed the old siding. You'll learn the pitfalls the painless way, and real-world working solutions for the problems every contractor finds in a home building or repair jobsite. Includes dozens of those "surprises" and the author's step-by-step, clearly illustrated tips, tricks and workarounds for dealing with them. **384 pages, 8½ x 11, $52.50**

*eBook (PDF) also available, $26.25 at www.craftsman-book.com*

## National Construction Estimator

Current building costs for residential, commercial, and industrial construction. Estimated prices for every common building material. Provides manhours, recommended crew, and gives the labor cost for installation. Includes a free download of an electronic version of the book with *National Estimator*, a stand-alone *Windows*™ estimating program. An interactive multimedia video that shows how to use the software to compile construction cost estimates. **672 pages, 8½ x 11, $87.50. Revised annually**

*eBook (PDF) also available; $43.75 at www.craftsman-book.com*

## Building Code Compliance for Contractors & Inspectors

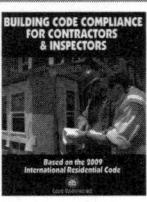

An answer book for both contractors and building inspectors, this manual explains what it takes to pass inspections under the 2009 *International Residential Code*. It includes a code checklist for every trade, covering some of the most common reasons why inspectors reject residential work — footings, foundations, slabs, framing, sheathing, plumbing, electrical, HVAC, energy conservation and final inspection. The requirement for each item on the checklist is explained, and the code section cited so you can look it up or show it to the inspector. Knowing in advance what the inspector wants to see gives you an (almost unfair) advantage. To pass inspection, do your own pre-inspection before the inspector arrives. If your work requires getting permits and passing inspections, put this manual to work on your next job. If you're considering a career in code enforcement, this can be your guidebook. **8½ x 11, 232 pages, $32.50**

*eBook (PDF) also available; $16.25 at www.craftsman-book.com*

## Markup & Profit: A Contractor's Guide, Revisited

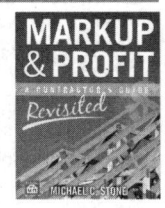

In order to succeed in a construction business, you have to be able to price your jobs to cover all labor, material and overhead expenses, and make a decent profit. But calculating markup is only part of the picture. If you're going to beat the odds and stay in business — profitably, you also need to know how to write good contracts, manage your crews, work with subcontractors and collect on your work. This book covers the business basics of running a construction company, whether you're a general or specialty contractor working in remodeling, new construction or commercial work. The principles outlined here apply to all construction-related businesses. You'll find tried and tested formulas to guarantee profits, with step-by-step instructions and easy-to-follow examples to help you learn how to operate your business successfully. Includes a link to free downloads of blank forms and checklists used in this book. **336 pages, 8½ x 11, $47.50**

*Also available as an eBook (ePub, mobi for Kindle), $39.95 at www.craftsman-book.com*

Download all of Craftsman's most popular costbooks for one low price with the Craftsman Site License. **www.craftsmansitelicense.com**